Research, Innovation, and Industry Impacts of the Metaverse

Jeetesh Kumar
Taylor's University, Malaysia

Manpreet Arora
Central University of Himachal Pradesh, India

Gul Erkol Bayram
Sinop University, Turkey

A volume in the Advances in Social Networking
and Online Communities (ASNOC) Book Series

Published in the United States of America by
IGI Global
Information Science Reference (an imprint of IGI Global)
701 E. Chocolate Avenue
Hershey PA, USA 17033
Tel: 717-533-8845
Fax: 717-533-8661
E-mail: cust@igi-global.com
Web site: http://www.igi-global.com

Library of Congress Cataloging-in-Publication Data

CIP DATA PROCESSING

Research, Innovation, and Industry Impacts of the Metaverse
 Jeetesh Kumar, Manpreet Arora, Gul Erkol Bayram
 2024 Information Science Reference

ISBN: 9798369326077(hc) I ISBN: 9798369351994(sc) I eISBN: 9798369326084

This book is published in the IGI Global book series Advances in Social Networking and Online Communities (ASNOC) (ISSN: 2328-1405; eISSN: 2328-1413)

British Cataloguing in Publication Data
A Cataloguing in Publication record for this book is available from the British Library.

For electronic access to this publication, please contact: eresources@igi-global.com.

Advances in Social Networking and Online Communities (ASNOC) Book Series

Hakikur Rahman

Ansted University Sustainability Research Institute, Malaysia

ISSN:2328-1405
EISSN:2328-1413

MISSION

The advancements of internet technologies and the creation of various social networks provide a new channel of knowledge development processes that's dependent on social networking and online communities. This emerging concept of social innovation is comprised of ideas and strategies designed to improve society.

The **Advances in Social Networking and Online Communities** book series serves as a forum for scholars and practitioners to present comprehensive research on the social, cultural, organizational, and human issues related to the use of virtual communities and social networking. This series will provide an analytical approach to the holistic and newly emerging concepts of online knowledge communities and social networks.

COVERAGE

- Networks as Institutionalized Intermediaries of KC
- Performance Evaluation and Benchmarking of Deployed Systems
- Epistemology of Knowledge Society
- E-capacity Building Programmes to Ensure Digital Cohesion and Improved E-Government Performance at Local Level
- Strategic Management and Business Process Analysis
- Leveraging Knowledge Communication in Social Networks
- General Importance and Role of Knowledge Communities
- Local E-Government Interoperability and Security
- Leveraging Knowledge Communication Networks – Approaches to Interpretations and Interventions
- Methodologies to Analyze, Design and Deploy Distributed Knowledge Management Solutions

IGI Global is currently accepting manuscripts for publication within this series. To submit a proposal for a volume in this series, please contact our Acquisition Editors at Acquisitions@igi-global.com or visit: http://www.igi-global.com/publish/.

Titles in this Series

For a list of additional titles in this series, please visit: http://www.igi-global.com/book-series/advances-social-networking-online-communities/37168

Exploring the Use of Metaverse in Business and Education
Jeetesh Kumar (Taylor's University, Malaysia) Manpreet Arora (Central University of Himachal Pradesh, India)
and Gül Erkol Bayram (Sinop University, Turkey)
Information Science Reference • copyright 2024 • 332pp • H/C (ISBN: 9798369358689) • US $245.00 (our price)

Creator's Economy in Metaverse Platforms Empowering Stakeholders Through Omnichannel Approach
Babita Singla (Chitkara Business School, Chitkara University, India) Kumar Shalender (Chitkara Business School,
Chitkara University, India) and Nripendra Singh (Pennsylvania Western University, USA)
Engineering Science Reference • copyright 2024 • 287pp • H/C (ISBN: 9798369333587) • US $315.00 (our price)

Critical Roles of Digital Citizenship and Digital Ethics
Jason D. DeHart (University of Tennessee, Knoxville, USA)
Information Science Reference • copyright 2023 • 296pp • H/C (ISBN: 9781668489345) • US $235.00 (our price)

Global Perspectives on Social Media Usage Within Governments
Chandan Chavadi (Presidency Business School, Presidency College, Bengaluru, India) and Dhanabalan Thangam
(Presidency Business School, Presidency College, Bengaluru, India)
Information Science Reference • copyright 2023 • 353pp • H/C (ISBN: 9781668474501) • US $215.00 (our price)

Social Capital in the Age of Online Networking Genesis, Manifestations, and Implications
Najmul Hoda (Umm Al-Qura University) and Arshi Naim (King Kalid University, Saudi Arabia)
Information Science Reference • copyright 2023 • 301pp • H/C (ISBN: 9781668489536) • US $215.00 (our price)

Advanced Applications of NLP and Deep Learning in Social Media Data
Ahmed A. Abd El-Latif (Menoufia University, Egypt & Prince Sultan University, Saudi Arabia) Mudasir Ahmad
Wani (Prince Sultan University, Saudi Arabia) and Mohammed A. El-Affendi (Prince Sultan University, Saudi Arabia)
Engineering Science Reference • copyright 2023 • 303pp • H/C (ISBN: 9781668469095) • US $270.00 (our price)

Community Engagement in the Online Space
Michelle Dennis (Adler University, USA) and James Halbert (Adler University, USA)
Information Science Reference • copyright 2023 • 364pp • H/C (ISBN: 9781668451908) • US $215.00 (our price)

Handbook of Research on Bullying in Media and Beyond
Gülşah Sarı (Aksaray University, Turkey)

701 East Chocolate Avenue, Hershey, PA 17033, USA
Tel: 717-533-8845 x100 • Fax: 717-533-8661
E-Mail: cust@igi-global.com • www.igi-global.com

Editorial Advisory Board

MD Tariqul, *Taylor's University, Kuala Selangor, Malaysia*
Rajesh Verma, *Mittal School of Business, India*
Chia Kei Wei, *School of Hospitality, Tourism and Events, Faculty of Social Sciences and Leisure Management, Taylor's University, Malaysia*

Table of Contents

Detailed Table of Contents

Chapter 1
Dive Into Metaverse: Concept, Evolution, Framework, Technologies, Opportunities, and Trends 1

Joana Raquel Neves, CEOS.PP, Polytechnic Institute of Coimbra, Coimbra, Portugal
Lara Mendes Bacalhau, CEOS.PP, Polytechnic Institute of Coimbra, Coimbra, Portugal

The ever-changing environment of the Metaverse claim for a study that leads to a captivating journey for readers of this chapter in which the current condition of this digital space is explained, its historical roots and evolution up to the present day, the novel prospects it offers and the revolutionary forces advancing its virtual worlds that leads to the transformative potential of this digital frontier. Through an interdisciplinary lens, this research clarifies the Metaverse by examining its fundamental elements and supporting technologies and highlighting important challenges that deserve further research. It thoroughly examines and investigates several aspects of this new paradigm in detail, providing a spotlight on everything from the functioning of virtual markets to the nuances of digital identities. The purpose of this chapter is to serve scholars, business professionals, and enthusiasts alike, a set of guidelines for a deep understanding of the current Metaverse environment and predicting its bright future highlighting its boundless opportunities.

Chapter 2
Historical Context and Evolution of Metaverse 27

Meenu Sharma, The Assam Royal Global University, India
Arpee Saikia, The Assam Royal Global University, India

The use of the metaverse in various periods is explained, including its use in novels and movies, video games, social media, industries, businesses, and headsets. This chapter is divided in to five sections: section one provides the introduction, literature review and ancient concept of metaverse; section two explains the use of term metaverse and historical context and evolution of metaverse; section three is related with use of metaverse in different sectors/fields: movies, novels, gaming, education, industry, retail, architecture, medical care and social media; section four provides a insight into prolific ways in which the metaverse was used during the Covid-19 pandemic times with special reference to the financial sector; section five describe managerial or practical applications and future research directions for the use of metaverse.

    Mohammad Imtiaz Hossain, Multimedia University, Malaysia
    Yasmin Jamadar, BRAC University, Bangladesh
    Md. Kausar Alam, BRAC University, Bangladesh
    Tanima Pal, BRAC University, Bangladesh
    Md. Tariqul Islam, Taylor's University, Malaysia
    Nusrut Sharmin, University of Chittagong, Bangladesh

This study accordingly explores the factors impacting the adoption of a metaverse in the manufacturing industry and develops a new model based on the Unified Theory of Acceptance (UTAT). Gender, age, and education were control variables. 235 questionnaire responses from employees of Malaysian manufacturing firms were collected through convenience sampling techniques and analyzed by Smart-PLS software. The findings reveal effort expectancy, perceived risk, and perceived technology accuracy have a significant relationship with intention to use a metaverse. Moreover, attitude to use evidenced mediating with perceived risk, perceived technology accuracy and intention to use a metaverse. The control variables did not evidence any impact on the intention to use a metaverse. This study provides insights to metaverse technology developers and manufacturing practitioners to explore and focus on the factors impacting the adoption of a metaverse in the manufacturing industry, as well as theoretical contributions for academia to progress further.

    Monika Chandel, Central University of Himachal Pradesh, India
    Manpreet Arora, Central University of Himachal Pradesh, India

The metaverse, a virtual realm, has drawn considerable attention from academicians as well as policymakers in recent years. In this chapter, we explored the metaverse's social, economic, and environmental effects, which align with various UN Sustainable Development Goals (SDGs), using an interdisciplinary perspective to show how it might transcend geographical borders and promote sustainability. This study adds to the ethical and sustainable development of digital technologies by analysing the opinions about the metaverse's influence on the SDGs. It will help administrations, corporations, and communities use the metaverse to make the world more inclusive, equitable, and sustainable. We are still learning how the metaverse fits into sustainable development, and scholars are examining the positive and negative aspects. This area must balance technical innovation and global sustainability as it progresses towards a more sustainable future.

    Sahil Sharma, Central University of Himachal Pradesh, India
    Anu Sohal, Central University of Himachal Pradesh, India

The advent of the metaverse offers human resource management both new opportunities and challenges as digital technologies continue to progress. To examine the state of HRM research in the metaverse era and pinpoint significant themes and gaps in the body of literature, this study conducts a bibliometric analysis. The authors examine the distribution of articles, authors, journals, and keywords associated with HRM in the context of the metaverse through a methodical examination of scholarly publications from the Scopus database. This research indicates an increasing amount of interest in this field, with studies concentrating on digital leadership, people management, remote work, and virtual collaboration. The authors offer a research agenda for the future to fill in these knowledge gaps and improve comprehension of HRM in the metaverse era. This study adds to the expanding corpus of research on HRM in digital contexts and offers insightful guidance on how to navigate the potential and difficulties presented by the metaverse for scholars, practitioners, and policymakers.

This study conducts a comprehensive bibliometric analysis using the preferred reporting items for systematic reviews and meta-analyses (PRISMA) model to explore the convergence of e-commerce, customer experience, and virtual environments in the evolving metaverse. Utilizing Scopus database data from 2010 to 2023, this research aims to map the trends, patterns, and emerging themes surrounding augmented reality (AR), virtual reality (VR), and immersive technologies, shaping consumer behaviour within virtual realms. Initial screening resulted in a substantial corpus of scholarly articles, conference papers, and reviews. Moreover, utilizing visualization tools like VOSviewer, this study provides insightful graphical representations, revealing clusters and connections among keywords, and offering a deeper understanding of the interdisciplinary nature of Metaverse in e-commerce. The analysis focuses on quantifying publication trends, identifying influential authors, institutions, and countries, and mapping key themes and connections within the domain. The analysis encompasses a range of bibliometric indicators, including publication trends, prolific authors, influential journals, and co-occurrence networks of keywords It investigates how virtual environments affect purchasing decisions, brand interactions, and loyalty-building strategies, emphasizing personalized experiences, social interactions, and gamification. The analysis also uncovers emerging research trends and gaps, suggesting avenues for further exploration, including the integration of artificial intelligence, blockchain technology, and spatial computing in enhancing e-commerce in virtual spaces. This research contributes to understanding the impact of the metaverse on e-commerce, customer experience, and engagement, providing valuable insights for academics, practitioners, and policymakers navigating this dynamic field.

Chapter 7

The concept of the metaverse is not new, as it dates back to 1992, but it is an interesting area that is receiving increased attention from researchers and marketers. This chapter provides insight into how the emerging virtual world of the metaverse is significantly enhancing the user experience in the gaming and entertainment industries by leveraging the latest technologies such as augmented reality (AR), virtual reality (VR), artificial intelligence (AI), blockchain technology, NFT, and others. This chapter aims to provide insight into the current developments in metaverse entertainment and gaming applications and how they will affect our user experience in the future. The approach used in this study is based on a comprehensive literature review on the subject of metaverse applications and their potential future in the gaming and entertainment industries. This chapter also discusses the various opportunities for the metaverse in the near future, as well as the challenges involved with it, such as privacy, security, and inclusivity.

Chapter 8

This chapter explores the connection of the metaverse and healthcare, investigating whether this integration signifies a significant shift or is just a passing trend. The chapter begins by explaining the notion of the metaverse and its ramifications in the healthcare environment, setting the stage for the next discussion. The chapter examines the possible catalyst impact by exploring several options. This text discusses the potential of the metaverse to transform medical teaching, enhance telemedicine, enable therapeutic interventions, and promote worldwide collaborative networks in healthcare. This investigation aims to ascertain whether the metaverse has the capacity to revolutionize healthcare methodologies, improve patient treatment, and overcome geographical obstacles. However, there are significant obstacles that need to be addressed in order to successfully integrate the metaverse, as outlined in the next section. The chapter examines the long-term viability of the metaverse's influence on healthcare by analyzing technological complexities, ethical considerations, and barriers to adoption. The chapter showcases real-world case studies that illustrate how metaverse technologies have shown to be valuable and enduring in the healthcare industry, in contrast to the fleeting nature of fads. This supports the premise that the metaverse has the potential to go beyond being a temporary fad and establish a significant presence in healthcare procedures. By analyzing historical similarities, this chapter investigates whether the metaverse has the characteristics of long-lasting change or whether it is prone to being quickly outdated. As the chapter approaches its end, it presents a prospective view on the development of the metaverse in the healthcare sector. The text compiles the acquired insights from the investigation and provides a detailed assessment of whether the metaverse has the potential to be a powerful catalyst or a temporary trend in the field of healthcare. This chapter examines the possible impact of integrating the metaverse into healthcare, examining whether it will be a driving force for long-term change or a passing trend.

Chapter 9

Delving into the dynamic intersections of augmented reality, artificial intelligence, blockchain, and spatial computing, this chapter offers strategic insights for brands seeking to establish a meaningful presence. From the evolution of brands in virtual environments to future trends, technological predictions and challenges, this chapter acts as a strategic roadmap. It addresses the needs of academic researchers, students, executives, and practitioners by synthesizing current research, offering practical applications, and proposing solutions. The chapter bridges the gap between theory and application, fostering a deeper understanding of the metaverse's impact on marketing, branding, and innovation. Aiming to be a valuable resource, the chapter equips a diverse audience with insights into the evolving metaverse landscape, providing a foundation for academic exploration and practical application.

Chapter 10

The term metaverse originated from the "Snow Crash" novel by Neal Stephenson in 1992. The term underwent massive evolution from a speculative concept into an immersive digital ecosystem. Technological advancement unveils the metaverse's potential in shaping the digital future more transformative and promising. The rapid growth of the metaverse extends beyond social interaction and entertainment. Metaverse has started contributing to education, commerce, and professional collaboration. The scope of this chapter is to provide a secondary analysis of the influence of metaverse in individual's lives and societal structures, using the embodied social presence theory and relying on key thematic areas (access and adoption; wellbeing; diversity and inclusion; sustainability; and empowerment) discussed by the World Economic Forum.

Chapter 11

Trade and consumer interactions with goods and services could be drastically changed by the convergence of the metaverse and commerce. Blockchain technology is used in the metaverse to facilitate the production, ownership, and exchange of virtual products and digital assets. This opens up new business opportunities and includes digital stuff such as in-game items, digital art, virtual real estate, and other digital goods. The idea of " Metaverse" and the role played by Metaverse in business and commerce are intended to be explained in this chapter. The chapter aims to address the genesis, requirements, advantages, opportunities and challenges in the area of Metaverse . It also intends to highlight the ethical considerations and the actions necessary to make the associated practices robust, viable, and effective.

Chapter 12

Metaverse has emerged as an immersive digital environment, capturing widespread attention owing to its significant impact on industrial growth. This study aims to explain the evolution of research focused on the metatarsal shift in industries. This study offers a bibliometric analysis of industrial transformation research from 2007 to 2024. The finding shows a tremendous rise in publication over time. The objective of this analysis is to extract valuable insights and trends and to shed light on the key challenges and opportunities associated with digital transformation in the industrial sector. This study provides thorough coverage of existing literature on the implications of metaverse-enabled digital transformation for the industrial revolution and explores the interplay of various factors such as technology adoption, organizational culture, and strategic planning. The study contributes to understanding the ongoing discourse on digital transformation and its impact on the industrial landscape.

The hospitality industry is one of the largest manpower-driven industries and hence generates huge employment. Strategies evolved and applied till 2019 transformed greatly facing the crisis in 2020 to cope with the prevailing circumstances for sustenance. The use of technology came greatly into effect on the Metaverse. Hence a drastic change has taken place in hospitality marketing strategy using the Tourism Marketing Union Model (TMUM). People are becoming more and more technophiles, and desire to have as much data as possible before starting the tour hoping for a hindrance-free, comfortable, and enjoyable expedition. Therefore, a complete transformation occurred in every phase of the industry, especially in the marketing sector. Cost reduction and Time-saving became the aims of new strategies and for that, Metaverse Marketing Technology (MMT), influencer marketing, and targeting the right audience through Metaverse Visual Marketing are extensively used by marketers.

This research investigates the potentials and constraints of metaverse technology within Malaysian manufacturing companies underpinned by the technology-organization-environment (TOE) theory. Firm size, firm age, annual revenue, and ownership structure were control variables. 240 questionnaire responses from Malaysian firms collected through convenience sampling techniques and analyzed by Smart-PLS software. The findings reveal technological limitations, poor diffusion through the network, lack of collaboration, and low perception of value by customers are significant constraints for the failure of metaverse technology implementation. The control variables did not evidence any impact on implementation. This study provides insights to metaverse technology developers and manufacturing practitioners besides theoretical contributions.

The notion of the metaverse has garnered substantial attention in recent years, captivating the imagination and piquing the interest of researchers, inventors, and industry executives alike. This chapter, "Unleashing the Power of Research, Innovation, and Industry Impacts: Exploring the Transformative Role of the Metaverse in Business and Commerce," seeks to investigate the potential of the metaverse and its impact on several facets of business and commerce. This proposal aims to examine the present patterns in metaverse research, which are influenced by applications that exploit the merging of interdisciplinary technologies. The advancement of developing technologies presents diverse prospects for the use of the metaverse in the realms of industry and commerce.

    Himani Gupta, Jagannath International Management School, India
    Rupinder Katoch, Lovely Professional University, India
    Manisha Gupta, Sharda University, India

This chapter examines the transfer of daily volatility returns from one block-chain asset to another and hedging alternatives. The technique is based on adequately modelling of the dynamic conditional correlation of generalised autoregressive conditional heteroscedasticity (DCC GARCH) and the hedging ratio. The results reveal that the volatility spillover impact from Etherium to other block-chain assets exists both in the short and long run. There are also hedging possibilities available between the selected block-chain assets. This implies that, prior to investing, policymakers, regulators, and investors should be aware of volatility, spillover effects, and hedging alternatives in the constituent variables.

    Manpreet Arora, School of Commerce and Management Studies, Central University of
        Himachal Pradesh, India

The incorporation of the metaverse into the world of business has brought about a significant and fundamental change, altering conventional frameworks and methods while presenting unparalleled prospects for expansion and creativity. This chapter examines the significant influence of the transformation of the metaverse on the worldwide economy, emphasising its ability to generate fresh prospects for work, labour, and employment. In addition, an attempt has been made to explore the economic consequences of the metaverse, encompassing the emergence of fresh sectors, markets, and sources of income, as well as the promotion of economic expansion and employment generation. This chapter examines the impact of the metaverse on economic development, innovation, and quality of life globally, highlighting its revolutionary capabilities. Furthermore, the author explores the significance of closing the divide between research discoveries and industrial implementations, highlighting the necessity of cooperation and information sharing to convert academic discoveries into tangible advancements that have a tangible effect on the real world. This chapter examines the impact of the metaverse on economic development, innovation, and quality of life globally.

Foreword

In an era defined by rapid technological advancement and digital transformation, the concept of the metaverse stands as a testament to humanity's boundless creativity and innovation.

The metaverse, a term first popularized by Neal Stephenson's science fiction novel "Snow Crash" and further conceptualized by subsequent thinkers and technologists, represents a convergence of virtual and physical realities. It encapsulates a vast digital dominion where users can interact, create and transact in immersive and interconnected virtual environments. From virtual reality simulations to augmented reality overlays, from blockchain-based economies to AI-driven interactions, the metaverse promises to revolutionize how we perceive, interact with, and shape our world.

This edited collection, crafted by esteemed scholars and practitioners at the forefront of their respective fields, serves as a comprehensive exploration of the multifaceted dimensions of the metaverse. Through a series of insightful chapters, readers are taken on a journey that traverses the theoretical foundations, technological innovations and practical applications of the metaverse across a spectrum of industries. One of the remarkable aspects of this edited volume is the spectra of contributors who have lent their expertise and insights to its pages. Hailing from Malaysia, Pakistan, Sri Lanka, Mexico and various states across India, the contributors represent a rich tapestry of cultural, geographical and academic backgrounds. This diversity not only enriches the scholarly discourse within the volume but also reflects the global significance and appeal of the metaverse phenomenon. By bringing together voices from different corners of the world, the volume offers a truly comprehensive and inclusive examination of the research, innovation, and industry impacts of the metaverse. Such a global perspective not only enhances the breadth and depth of the discussions but also underpins the universal relevance and applicability of the insights shared within this collection. One of the most compelling aspects of this volume is its emphasis on the intersectionality of disciplines and perspectives. By bringing together contributions from diverse fields such as; management, tourism, hospitality, sociology, psychology, economics, and beyond, the editors have created a treasure of insights that reflect the interdisciplinary nature of the metaverse phenomenon. This interdisciplinary approach not only enhances our understanding of the metaverse but also underscores the importance of collaboration and knowledge exchange in driving meaningful innovation across academia and industry. From entertainment and gaming to education and healthcare, the potential applications of the metaverse are as vast as they are transformative. By providing an in-depth analysis, the contributors have offered valuable perspectives on how the metaverse is reshaping consumer experiences, business models and societal dynamics.

At the helm of this groundbreaking volume are three distinguished editors, each bringing their unique expertise and perspectives to the fore. Dr. Jeetesh Kumar, from Taylor's University, Malaysia, is a visionary scholar whose research spans the intersections of tourism, technology, society and culture.

With a keen understanding of the global digital landscape, Kumar brings invaluable insights into the multifaceted dimensions of the metaverse phenomenon. Dr. Manpreet Arora, representing the Central University of Himachal Pradesh, India embodies a commitment to interdisciplinary scholarship and practical applications. Her intensive and extensive background in research and education uniquely positions her to navigate the complexities of the metaverse and its implications for various industries. Dr. Gül Erkol Bayram, hailing from Sinop University in Turkey, brings an international perspective to the editorial team. Her expertise in tourism, hospitality, emerging technologies and digital innovation adds depth and breadth to the discussions within the volume, ensuring a truly global perspective on the research, innovation and industry impacts of the metaverse. Together, these editors have curated a collection that not only reflects the cutting edge of scholarship but also sets the stage for meaningful dialogue and collaboration in this rapidly evolving field.

As we stand on the precipice of this new digital frontier, it is incumbent upon us to embrace the opportunities and challenges that the metaverse presents. As Vice Chancellor of the esteemed Central University of Himachal Pradesh in Dharamshala, India, it is my distinct pleasure to introduce the edited volume *Research, Innovation, and Industry Impacts of the Metaverse* published by IGI International, USA which will act as a roadmap and a call for action for the researchers, innovators, policymakers, academicians and industry leaders to collectively navigate and shape the future of the metaverse. I commend the editors and contributors for their dedication, scholarship and foresight in producing this seminal work, and I am confident that it will serve as a beacon of inspiration for generations to come.

Sat Prakash Bansal
Central University of Himachal Pradesh, Dharamshala, India

Preface

In the dynamic landscape of modern technology, few concepts have captured the imagination and attention of scholars and innovators quite like the metaverse. Its emergence marks a significant inflection point, signaling the convergence of virtual and physical realities, and offering tantalizing prospects for societal transformation. As editors of *Research, Innovation, and Industry Impacts of the Metaverse*, we are delighted to present this comprehensive volume exploring the multifaceted dimensions of the metaverse phenomenon.

The metaverse, with its roots extending into science fiction lore, has now become a tangible realm of exploration and innovation. Its relevance spans diverse domains, from the realms of academia to the corridors of industry and commerce. What sets this book apart is its endeavor to dissect the metaverse from various angles, shedding light on its technological underpinnings, academic research frontiers, real-world applications, and attendant challenges.

In the opening chapters, readers are introduced to the foundational concepts of the metaverse, tracing its historical trajectory and envisioning its future potential. Through meticulous examination, the book elucidates the intricate tapestry of metaverse technologies and frameworks, unraveling the threads that weave together virtual environments and immersive experiences.

A central focus of this volume is the exploration of academic research in the metaverse. Scholars from diverse disciplines converge to probe the boundaries of virtuality, offering insights into metaverse development, human-computer interaction, security, privacy, and ethical considerations. Their contributions not only enrich our understanding of the metaverse but also pave the way for responsible innovation and development.

Beyond academia, the book delves into the practical applications and societal impacts of the metaverse. From its role in reshaping business models and commerce to its implications for education, society, and the economy, each chapter offers invaluable perspectives on how the metaverse is reshaping our world.

Looking ahead, the book ventures into future directions and challenges, charting the course for continued exploration and growth in the metaverse. As we navigate the ethical, regulatory, and technological frontiers of this nascent domain, the insights contained within these pages will serve as beacons guiding our path forward.

In assembling this volume, our aim has been to provide a comprehensive resource that not only captures the current state of the metaverse but also stimulates further inquiry and innovation. We extend our gratitude to all the contributors whose expertise and dedication have made this endeavor possible.

It is our sincere hope that this book will serve as a catalyst for dialogue, collaboration, and discovery, inspiring readers to embark on their own journeys of exploration within the boundless realms of the metaverse.

Chapter 1: Dive Into Metaverse: Concept, Evolution, Framework, Technologies, Opportunities, and Trends

Neves and Bacalhau lead readers on an immersive journey through the current landscape of the Metaverse, tracing its historical roots, and illuminating its transformative potential. Through an interdisciplinary lens, this chapter clarifies the Metaverse's fundamental elements, technological frameworks, and emerging trends, offering insights into its functioning, virtual markets, and digital identities. Scholars, business professionals, and enthusiasts will find a comprehensive guide to understanding the Metaverse's current environment and its boundless opportunities.

Chapter 2: Historical Context and Evolution of Metaverse

Sharma and Saikia delve into the historical origins and evolution of the Metaverse, from its conceptualization in science fiction to its realization in digital realms. Exploring pivotal moments and milestones, this chapter examines the cultural, literary, and technological influences that have shaped the Metaverse's development, including its depiction in novels, movies, video games, and social media platforms.

Chapter 3: Exploring the Factors Impacting the Intention to Use Metaverse in the Manufacturing Industry Through the Lens of Unified Technology Acceptance Theory

Hossain et al. investigate the factors influencing the adoption of the Metaverse in the manufacturing industry, utilizing the Unified Theory of Acceptance. Through empirical research, they uncover significant relationships between factors such as effort expectancy, perceived risk, and technology accuracy, offering insights for developers and practitioners to enhance Metaverse adoption in manufacturing contexts.

Chapter 4: Metaverse Perspectives: Unpacking its Role in Shaping Sustainable Development Goals: A Qualitative Inquiry

Chandel and Arora explore the Metaverse's potential to advance sustainable development goals, examining its social, economic, and environmental impacts. Through qualitative inquiry, they demonstrate how the Metaverse can transcend geographical boundaries and promote sustainability, offering insights for policymakers, corporations, and communities to leverage digital technologies for inclusive, equitable, and sustainable development.

Chapter 5: Human Resource Management in the Metaverse Era: A Bibliometric Analysis and Future Research Agenda

Sharma and Sohal conduct a bibliometric analysis of human resource management in the Metaverse era, identifying key themes and gaps in the literature. Their research offers valuable insights for scholars, practitioners, and policymakers seeking to navigate the opportunities and challenges presented by the integration of digital technologies in HRM practices.

Chapter 6: From Clicks to Virtual Realms - Exploring Metaverse-driven E-commerce and Consumer Shifts: Metaverse in E-commerce and Consumer Behavior

A comprehensive bibliometric analysis by Sharma, Sharma, and Verma explores the intersection of e-commerce, consumer behavior, and the Metaverse. Mapping trends and emerging themes, their research sheds light on how immersive technologies are shaping consumer behavior within virtual environments, offering actionable insights for academics, practitioners, and policymakers in the evolving digital landscape.

Chapter 7: Metaverse: Transforming the User Experience in the Gaming and Entertainment Industry

Swami investigates how the Metaverse is revolutionizing user experiences in the gaming and entertainment sectors. By leveraging technologies such as AR, VR, AI, and blockchain, this chapter explores current developments and future opportunities, highlighting challenges such as privacy and security while envisioning a more immersive digital future.

Chapter 8: Integration of the Metaverse in the Healthcare Industry: A Catalyst for Profound Change

Pramanik explores the integration of the Metaverse in healthcare, examining its potential to transform medical education, telemedicine, and therapeutic interventions. By navigating opportunities and challenges, this chapter offers insights into leveraging digital technologies to overcome geographical barriers and enhance patient care in a globalized world.

Chapter 9: Navigating the Metaverse: A Comprehensive Guide to Marketing, Branding, and Innovation

Pabla and Soch provide strategic insights into leveraging the Metaverse for marketing, branding, and innovation. From understanding evolving consumer behaviors to predicting future trends, this chapter equips readers with practical strategies for establishing a meaningful presence in virtual environments and driving business growth.

Chapter 10: The 'Metaverse Society': Transformative Effects of Metaverse on Society

Nawaz et al. analyze the transformative effects of the Metaverse on society, drawing on theories of social presence and thematic areas outlined by the World Economic Forum. By exploring access, wellbeing, diversity, sustainability, and empowerment, this chapter offers a comprehensive understanding of how digital technologies are reshaping individual lives and societal structures.

Chapter 11: Navigating the Metaverse in Business and Commerce: Opportunities, Challenges, and Ethical Considerations in Virtual Worlds

Shukla and Taneja examine the role of the Metaverse in business and commerce, addressing its genesis, requirements, advantages, challenges, and ethical considerations. By exploring opportunities for virtual commerce and navigating ethical dilemmas, this chapter offers a roadmap for businesses to thrive in virtual environments while upholding responsible practices.

Chapter 12: The Metaversal Shift: A Bibliometric Analysis of Industry Transformation

Kaushal and Duhoon conduct a bibliometric analysis of the Metaverse's impact on industrial transformation, exploring trends, insights, and challenges. By synthesizing existing literature, their research provides valuable insights into the implications of digital transformation in various industries, guiding stakeholders in navigating the evolving landscape of technological innovation.

Chapter 13: Transformation of Marketing Strategy by Metaverse in Hospitality Industry Facing Crisis

Jamader et al. analyze the transformation of marketing strategy in the hospitality industry, leveraging the Metaverse to navigate crises and embrace technological innovations. By exploring new strategies such as Metaverse Marketing Technology and influencer marketing, this chapter offers insights for marketers seeking to adapt to changing consumer behaviors and preferences.

Chapter 14: Unlocking the Potentials and Constraints of Metaverse Implementation in Manufacturing Firms

Hossain et al. investigate the potentials and constraints of Metaverse implementation in Malaysian manufacturing firms, utilizing the Technology-Organization-Environment theory. By identifying technological limitations and organizational challenges, this research offers insights for developers and practitioners to enhance Metaverse adoption and implementation in manufacturing contexts.

Chapter 15: Unleashing the Power of Research, Innovation, and Industry Impacts: Exploring the Transformative Role of the Metaverse in Business and Commerce

Kumar explores the transformative role of the Metaverse in business and commerce, examining current research patterns and technological applications. By synthesizing interdisciplinary technologies and exploring emerging trends, this chapter offers insights into harnessing the potential of the Metaverse to drive innovation and industry impacts in a rapidly evolving digital landscape.

Chapter 16: Exploring Safe Hedging Options for Blockchain Assets in the Face of Covid-19-Induced Volatility

Gupta et al. examine safe hedging options for blockchain assets amidst Covid-19-induced volatility, utilizing dynamic conditional correlation modeling. By analyzing volatility spillover effects and hedging alternatives, this research offers insights for policymakers, regulators, and investors navigating blockchain markets in uncertain times.

Chapter 17: Metaverse Metamorphosis: Bridging the Gap Between Research Insights and Industry Applications

Arora delves into the transformative impacts of the Metaverse on research advancements and industry landscapes, examining technological, sociological, and psychological dimensions. By exploring research insights and translating them into tangible impacts, this chapter offers a comprehensive understanding of the Metaverse's implications for various industries, guiding stakeholders in navigating ethical, regulatory, and technological challenges.

In concluding this comprehensive exploration of the metaverse, we are reminded of the profound impact that digital technologies continue to have on our lives, societies, and industries. The journey through the diverse chapters of this book has illuminated the multifaceted dimensions of the metaverse, from its historical roots to its present-day applications and future potential.

As we reflect on the insights shared by esteemed contributors from around the globe, it becomes clear that the metaverse is more than just a technological phenomenon—it is a catalyst for societal transformation, innovation, and collaboration. From its role in reshaping industries such as healthcare, manufacturing, and hospitality to its implications for marketing, branding, and human resource management, the metaverse presents boundless opportunities for exploration and growth.

However, amidst the excitement and promise of the metaverse, we must also confront the challenges and ethical considerations that accompany its development and adoption. Issues such as privacy, security, inclusivity, and digital equity demand our attention as we navigate this rapidly evolving digital landscape. By addressing these challenges with foresight and responsibility, we can ensure that the metaverse serves as a force for positive change and empowerment.

As editors, we extend our deepest gratitude to all the contributors whose expertise, dedication, and passion have made this volume possible. Their scholarly contributions have enriched our understanding of the metaverse and inspired us to continue exploring its potential for research, innovation, and industry impacts.

It is our sincere hope that this book will serve as a valuable resource for scholars, practitioners, policymakers, and enthusiasts alike, sparking dialogue, collaboration, and discovery in the dynamic realm of the metaverse. As we embark on this journey of exploration and innovation, let us remain mindful of the transformative power of the metaverse and its capacity to shape the future of our digital world.

Editors:

Jeetesh Kumar
Taylor's University, Malaysia

Manpreet Arora
Central University of Himachal Pradesh, Dharamshala, India

Gül Erkol Bayram
Sinop University, Turkey

Acknowledgement

As editors of the edited volume *Research, Innovation, and Industry Impacts of the Metaverse*, we extend our heartfelt gratitude to the individuals who have supported us throughout this endeavor.

First and foremost, we express our deepest appreciation to our parents and family members for their unwavering love, encouragement, and understanding. Their steadfast support has been the cornerstone of our academic pursuits and professional endeavors, and we are profoundly grateful for their endless sacrifices and guidance.

Additionally, we would like to extend special thanks to specific individuals whose contributions have been instrumental in shaping this volume. Dr. Manpreet Arora extends her sincere gratitude to **Professor Sat Prakash Bansal**, the Honorable Vice Chancellor of Central University of Himachal Pradesh and **Dr Sunita Bansal**, (Mrs. HVC) for their unwavering support and mentorship. She also expresses heartfelt appreciation to her father, **S. Surinder Singh Arora**, for his boundless love, wisdom, and encouragement throughout her academic journey, she remembers fondly her mother Late Arvind Arora who acted as a pillar and guiding star in her life and career at this moment where this academic venture adds up to her career.

Dr. Gül Erkol Bayram extends her gratitude to Professor Marco Valeri from Niccolò Cusano University, Italy, and Associate Researcher at Magellan Research Center, Iaelyon Business, for his invaluable guidance and collaboration. She also extends her thanks to Mohammad Nawaz Tunio from the University of Sufism and Modern Sciences, Bhitshah, Pakistan, for his insightful contributions and support.

We are truly grateful to all the contributors, reviewers, colleagues, and friends who have generously shared their expertise, feedback, and encouragement throughout the development of this book. Your collective efforts have enriched the scholarly discourse and made this volume possible.

Finally, we express our appreciation to the publishers, editors, and staff involved in the publication process for their professionalism, dedication, and support.

Thank you all for your invaluable contributions and unwavering support.

Sincerely,

Jeetesh Kumar
Taylor's University, Malaysia

Manpreet Arora
Central University of Himachal Pradesh, Dharamshala, India

Gül Erkol Bayram
Sinop University, Turkey

Chapter 1
Dive Into Metaverse:
Concept, Evolution, Framework, Technologies, Opportunities, and Trends

Joana Raquel Neves
CEOS.PP, Polytechnic Institute of Coimbra, Coimbra, Portugal

Lara Mendes Bacalhau
ⓘD https://orcid.org/0000-0001-9674-4167
CEOS.PP, Polytechnic Institute of Coimbra, Coimbra, Portugal

ABSTRACT

The ever-changing environment of the Metaverse claim for a study that leads to a captivating journey for readers of this chapter in which the current condition of this digital space is explained, its historical roots and evolution up to the present day, the novel prospects it offers and the revolutionary forces advancing its virtual worlds that leads to the transformative potential of this digital frontier. Through an interdisciplinary lens, this research clarifies the Metaverse by examining its fundamental elements and supporting technologies and highlighting important challenges that deserve further research. It thoroughly examines and investigates several aspects of this new paradigm in detail, providing a spotlight on everything from the functioning of virtual markets to the nuances of digital identities. The purpose of this chapter is to serve scholars, business professionals, and enthusiasts alike, a set of guidelines for a deep understanding of the current Metaverse environment and predicting its bright future highlighting its boundless opportunities.

INTRODUCTION

The dawn of the Metaverse heralds a paradigm shift in our conception of digital spaces, presenting a transformative vision of interconnected virtual environments that transcend the boundaries of traditional media and communication platforms. Rooted in Virtual Reality (VR), Augmented Reality (AR), and Spatial Computing, the Metaverse represents a convergence of technological innovation, social interaction, and cultural expression, offering boundless opportunities for exploration, creativity, and collaboration.

DOI: 10.4018/979-8-3693-2607-7.ch001

The authors of this chapter sought to carry out academic research on the Metaverse to unravel its complexities, understand its implications, and contribute to the academic discourse around this emerging digital phenomenon. To write this chapter, the authors have drawn on a diverse range of scholarly works, including those by Burlington (2021), Bhattacharya et al. (2023), Sullivan & Tyson (2023), and Lv et al. (2022), among others, which provide an interdisciplinary perspective and valuable insights into the technological, socio-economic, and ethical considerations of data governance in the Metaverse. The study sought to cover the breadth and depth of this emergent digital phenomenon.

At its core, the Metaverse represents a fusion of virtual and physical realities, blurring the boundaries between the digital and the physical. It offers users a gateway to immersive and interactive experiences, where they can traverse virtual landscapes, engage with digital artifacts, and interact with other users in real time. From virtual marketplaces and entertainment venues to educational platforms and social networks, the Metaverse offers a kaleidoscope of possibilities of virtual environments that cater to its inhabitants' diverse interests and preferences. The Metaverse can be applied in numerous fields such as videogame industry, art, event industry, manufacturing, retail, financial services, fashion, media and communication, hospitality, tourism, healthcare, workspace, education, among others (Athar et al., 2023; Bruni et al., 2023; Cali et al., 2022; Chen, 2023; Fazio et al., 2023; Gao & Braud, 2023; Jung et al., 2024; Kaddoura & Al Husseiny, 2023; Mogaji, 2023; Mogaji et al., 2024; Mohamed & Naqishbandi, 2023; Nuñez et al., 2024; Profumo et al., 2024; Wong et al., 2023; Yang & Wang, 2023; Yaqoob et al., 2023; Zainurin et al., 2023).

Technologically, the Metaverse is underpinned by a sophisticated infrastructure of computational systems, networking protocols, and immersive interfaces. Scholars such as Bhattacharya et al. (2023) have delved into the intricacies of VR technology, exploring its capabilities, limitations, and potential applications in the context of the Metaverse. By understanding the technological foundations of the Metaverse, we can better appreciate its evolution and anticipate future developments in this dynamic digital landscape.

Moreover, the Metaverse holds profound socio-economic implications, shaping the way we work, play, and interact with one another. As Sullivan & Tyson (2023) have highlighted, privacy, security, and digital rights loom large in the Metaverse, raising important ethical questions about data governance, identity management, and algorithmic bias. By critically examining these ethical considerations, we can foster a more inclusive and equitable Metaverse that prioritizes the well-being and autonomy of its users.

With these considerations in mind, this chapter aims to contribute to a deeper understanding of the Metaverse, informed by interdisciplinary inquiry and scholarly rigor. By drawing on insights from diverse fields such as computer science, sociology, economics, and ethics, it seeks to highlight the multifaceted nature of the Metaverse and offer insights into its potential impact on individuals, communities, and society.

In short, the authors of this study invite readers to embark on a voyage of exploration and discovery into the Metaverse. Through rigorous analysis, critical reflection, and interdisciplinary dialogue, the research has endeavored to deepen the understanding of this transformative digital landscape and chart a course toward a more informed and inclusive future.

In the following chapters, a comprehensive exploration of the Metaverse will be attempted, delving into its conceptual underpinnings, historical evolution, and the technological frameworks that enable its immersive experiences. The dynamics of metamarkets will be analyzed, opportunities in various sectors will be identified and the emerging trends shaping the Metaverse landscape will be examined. Additionally, it will examine the complexities of digital identities and propose future research directions. This structured investigation aims to offer readers a deeper understanding of the Metaverse and its potential implications for individuals and society.

CONCEPT OF METAVERSE

The term 'Metaverse' was coined by Neal Stephenson in his science fiction novel, 'Snow Crash' (1992), where he envisioned a computer-generated universe accessed through goggles and earphones, describing it as 'the Metaverse.' This term combines the prefix 'meta,' meaning 'beyond,' with 'verse,' evoking the concept of the universe (Bale et al., 2022; Cheng et al., 2022; Hackl, 2020; Ng, 2022; Park & Kim, 2022).

The Metaverse has roots in video game infrastructures developed over decades (Faraboschi et al., 2022), with pioneering platforms like There (1998), RuneScape (2001), and Second Life (2003) laying the groundwork for online virtual worlds where users socialize as avatars (Clement, 2023). Second Life is often regarded as the first iteration of the Metaverse, facilitating interactions between consumers and businesses (Dwivedi et al., 2022). Recent advancements in AR and VR technologies have further enhanced the immersive nature of these platforms (Cipresso et al., 2018; Trevor, 2022).

The Cambridge Dictionary defines the Metaverse as a virtual world where humans, as avatars, interact with each other in a three-dimensional space that mimics reality' (*Metaverse*). In essence, the Metaverse can be conceptualized as a social structure (Novak, 2022) that embodies the principles of Web 3.0 (Xu et al., 2022) and integrates blockchain and computer interfaces (Ahn et al., 2022), allowing users to establish virtual identities and socialize in digital environments (Zyda, 2022), blurring the boundaries between the virtual and real worlds (Al-Ghaili et al., 2022).

According to Trevor (2022), the Metaverse is an open, collective virtual space that bridges the gap between physical and virtual realities, offering immersive experiences and hosting diverse activities within isolated environments. Table 1 presents alternative definitions of the Metaverse.

EVOLUTION OF METAVERSE

The evolution of the Metaverse is intricately linked to technological advancements and shifts in online paradigms. The emergence of decentralized networks, the introduction of cryptocurrencies, and the rise of digital collectibles like Non-Fungible Tokens (NFTs) have spurred a renewed focus on the concept of the Metaverse (Golf-Papez et al., 2022). Major technology companies, game publishers, and brands have converged to create immersive digital spaces, exemplified by Meta's Horizon platform and Microsoft's Mesh platform announced in 2021 (Bonetti et al., 2018; Zyda, 2022).

Significant milestones have propelled the evolution of the Metaverse. The widespread adoption of virtual worlds since the turn of the millennium laid the groundwork for the Metaverse's emergence, while advancements in VR and AR technologies have enhanced user immersion and interaction (Neves et al., 2024). Blockchain technology, particularly through the utilization of NFTs, has enabled the creation and ownership of unique digital assets within the Metaverse, while generative agents have facilitated the development of virtual societies.

Understanding the evolution of the Metaverse necessitates a historical perspective on internet technologies, particularly the evolution of the web. The transition from Web 1.0 to Web 2.0 marked a shift towards user-generated content and social connectivity, facilitated by advancements in mobile internet

Table 1. Metaverse concepts

Authors	Concept of Metaverse
Acevedo Nieto (2022)	A Metaverse is an online universe in permanent mutation, change, and development. Similarly, a Metaverse is a virtual, online world in which different avatars interact, but which, unlike massively multiplayer online role-playing games (MMORPGs), does not have a single competitive purpose: it is a virtual world in which avatars interact with each other, with the objective-based exclusively on a system of levels.
Afrashtehfar and Abu-Fanas (2022)	The Metaverse is a virtual environment that simulates the natural world through multisensory interactions with 3D objects. In other words, the Metaverse ecosystem is a simulation of the 3D world or twin world.
Bibri et al. (2022)	The Metaverse is an idea of a hypothetical set of "parallel virtual worlds" that embody ways of living in virtual credible cities as an alternative to data-driven smart cities in the future.
Golf-Papez et al. (2022)	The Metaverse is an ecosystem of interconnected, shared digital and physical environments that can be experienced synchronously, persistently, and interoperably, in which physical and technological realities are harmoniously enhanced.
Kim et al. (2022)	With the development of immersive experience technology, the Metaverse is a cyberspace, which will establish itself as an expanding reality of the physical world.
Lv et al. (2022)	The spread of digital twins to other domains, such as people and society, is what the Metaverse is all about.
Kim (2021)	[The Metaverse] is an interoperable network of shared virtual environments where people can interact synchronously through their avatars with other agents and/or objects.

Source: Self Elaboration

access and the proliferation of social media platforms (Hester et al., 2016; Oliveira, 2023). This era witnessed the dominance of platforms like Facebook, Instagram, and Twitter, driving significant economic growth and reshaping online business models (Nath, 2022).

Web 3.0 represents the latest phase in the evolution of the web, characterized by decentralization and personalized content delivery. Cryptoeconomic networks like Bitcoin underpin Web 3.0, offering users greater control over their data and privacy (Ashmore & Venz, 2023). Artificial intelligence (AI) and natural language processing (NLP) technologies enable intelligent content distribution tailored to individual preferences, revolutionizing advertising strategies and communication (Goel et al., 2022).

Table 2 provides a comparative overview of the key phases in the evolution of the web, highlighting the progression from static web pages to decentralized, AI-driven platforms in Web 3.0.

The evolution of the web has revolutionized online interactions, shifting from simple messaging to encompassing e-commerce and immersive virtual experiences that transcend physical boundaries. Games within the Metaverse have surged in popularity, paralleling the evolution of the web, and enabling the creation of virtual worlds that mirror physical reality (Novak, 2022).

Web 3.0 represents a significant leap forward, characterized by immersive realities such as VR, AR, mixed reality (MR), and extended reality (XR). These technological advancements, coupled with the development of AI, have empowered brands to deliver unique, personalized, and interactive virtual experiences, capturing consumers' attention and fostering engagement (Goel et al., 2022).

As technology continues to advance, the evolution of the web is propelling us toward Web 4.0, heralded as the era of AI (Oliveira, 2023). In this new phase, complete decentralization of processes is anticipated, facilitated by blockchain technology, to create a secure and transparent online environment where users can interact and transact without intermediaries (Chaves, 2023). This transition holds the promise of reshaping digital interactions and further blurring the boundaries between physical and virtual realms, with technologies that have been improved shown in the next section.

Table 2. Evolution of the web

	Web 1.0	Web 2.0	Web 3.0
Timeline	1990-2004	2004-2016	2016 - now
Interaction	Read	Read and write	Read, write, and own
Support	Static text	Interactive content	Virtual economies
Organization	On-prem servers	Cloud	Blockchain
Infrastructure	Centralized	Centralized	Decentralized
Virtual Worlds	Second Life	Minecraft	Decentraland
Browers		Google Chrome	Brave
Payment Platforms		Paypal	Metamask
Operating Systems		Windows, Mac OS, Android	Ethereum, EOS
Social Networks		Facebook, Youtube	Steem

Source: Adaptation of Kujur and Chhetri (2015); Sandal et al. (2023)

TECHNOLOGIES POWERING THE METAVERSE

In the dynamic environment of the Metaverse, the confluence of immersive technologies, virtual economies, and interactive games represents a transformative paradigm in digital spatial computing. In this way, the dimensions of the technologies that underpin the Metaverse are Immersive Realities, Markets in the Metaverse, and Gamification in the Metaverse. Immersive realities represent an integration of VR, AR, and MR technologies, facilitating deep levels of immersion and presence in virtual environments, as is possible to seen in Figure 1.

Markets in the Metaverse outline complex virtual economies where digital goods, assets, and services are traded, signifying a fundamental evolution in digital commerce and interaction paradigms. On

Figure 1. Metaverse technologies
Source: Self Elaboration

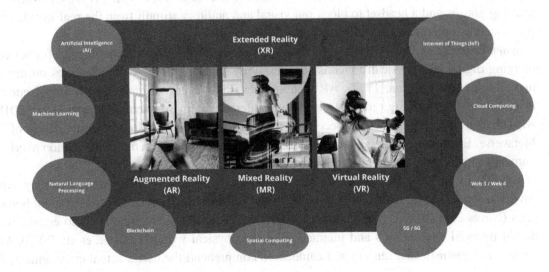

the other hand, gamification in the Metaverse takes advantage of gamified mechanics and incentives to optimize user engagement and interactivity, promoting nuanced and rewarding experiences in virtual realms. Collectively, these technological foundations form the fundamental structure of the expansive and multifaceted Metaverse, heralding new modes of expression, commerce, and socio-cultural interaction in the digital realm.

To understand the technological dimensions of Metaverse, we should see in detail the components of Immersive Realities, Markets in the Metaverse, and Gamification in the Metaverse, that are explained in the next subsections.

1. Immersive Realities

Immersive realities are gaining prominence as they enable brands to offer interactive products and services, facilitating immersive experiences in shopping, gaming, and social environments (Cheng et al., 2022; Kumawat et al., 2020). Various definitions of immersive virtual realities exist, with Taçgın and Dalgarno (2021) describing it as a 3D environment generated by a computer that affects users' perception of reality. Srikanth Vemula (2020) defines immersive VR as the perception of being physically present in a non-physical world created through images, sounds, or other stimuli. In essence, immersive VR aims to fully immerse users in a generated world, providing the sensation of presence in a synthetic environment ("Immersive Virtual Reality," 2008). Immersive realities include virtual reality, augmented reality, and mixed reality that can be joined under the extended reality "umbrella". Which of these realities can be briefly defined as follows:

- *Virtual Reality (VR):* VR is characterized as modeling and simulation that allows interaction with a three-dimensional, artificial visual environment (Harley, 2022). It enables users to immerse themselves in a simulation of reality using interactive devices. VR applications provide an illusion of telepresence, allowing users to have real-time experiences such as picking up and manipulating objects and visiting virtual environments (Lowood, 2022). VR technologies have evolved over the years, categorized into three main types: non-immersive, immersive, and semi-immersive. Non-immersive systems, known as desktop VR systems, enable interaction with the virtual environment from a computer, while semi-immersive systems extend immersion by providing a visual experience without physical sensations. Immersive systems offer a realistic virtual experience that requires additional devices for implementation (Bamodu & Ye, 2013). VR typically involves wearing glasses and a headset to block out visual and auditory stimuli from the real world, complemented by other technologies for enhanced experiences.
- *Augmented Reality (AR):* AR is a core component of the Metaverse's technological framework, merging digital and physical domains seamlessly by superimposing virtual features on the actual environment (Azuma, 1997). AR technologies allow users to interact with digital content in real-time, transforming ordinary places into interactive environments (Bonetti et al., 2018). AR enhances the ordinary world, becoming a crucial component of the immersive fabric of the Metaverse. Examples of AR implementation include interactive marketing, information overlays, immersive navigation, and contextualized data.
- *Mixed Reality (MR):* MR coordinates virtual and real worlds within the Metaverse's dynamic environment, providing users with an immersive experience that transcends conventional boundaries (Neves et al., 2024). MR combines aspects of VR and AR, enabling users to engage with digital material that coexists and interacts with the physical world (Calzone et al., 2023). MR devices use sophisticated sensors and cameras to comprehend the user's actual environment, fa-

cilitating a dynamic and context-aware digital overlay. Users can interact with digital elements in real-world contexts more naturally and intuitively, enhancing immersion and participation in the digital world (Guan et al., 2023). Spatial computation plays a crucial role in MR within the Metaverse, enabling the provision of dynamic and context-aware digital overlays.

The Extended Reality (XR) serves as an umbrella term for all immersive technologies within the Metaverse, including VR, AR, and MR, extending the limits of human perception and interaction in digital contexts (Abrash, 2021). By integrating various immersive technologies, XR offers users a wide range of experiences, from fully virtual to augmented and everything in between (Berglund et al., 2018). XR blurs the boundaries between real and virtual worlds within the Metaverse, providing users with a seamless and flexible digital environment (Koohang et al., 2023). Users can interact with digital information in ways that mimic and enhance interactions in the real world, redefining their perception and interaction with digital environments within the Metaverse (Bhattacharya et al., 2023).

2. Markets in Metaverse

The intricate web of technologies within the Metaverse orchestrates the functionality and dynamism of digital markets, reshaping traditional commerce and value exchange (Bhattacharya et al., 2023). The Metaverse, characterized by a fusion of AR, VR, blockchain, and decentralized technologies, emerges as a multifaceted marketplace, transforming economic paradigms. Lets see these technologies:

- *Decentralized Ledger Technologies (DLT) and Blockchain:* At the core of the Metaverse's economic environment lies the revolutionary impact of decentralized ledger technology, led by blockchain. Blockchain technology ensures transparency and immutability, addressing concerns about the ownership and legitimacy of digital assets (Massaro, 2023). In the Metaverse, blockchain creates decentralized markets where users can securely exchange virtual products, digital assets, and NFTs, with provenance guaranteed by cryptography (Huynh-The et al., 2023).

- *Smart Contracts:* Smart contracts play a pivotal role in the dynamics of the Metaverse's markets by enabling self-executing agreements. These programmable contracts automate and uphold transaction rules, ensuring transparency and reducing the need for intermediaries (Wu & Liu, 2023). Smart contracts facilitate smooth digital asset exchange in the decentralized markets of the Metaverse, minimizing counterparty risks and enabling efficient and trustless transactions (Koohang et al., 2023).

- *Tokenization of Assets:* Tokenization, enabled by blockchain technology, converts intangible digital assets into marketable tokens, including virtual real estate, collectible digital items, and representations of real-world assets (Vidal-Tomás, 2023). In Metaverse marketplaces, tokenization enhances accessibility, liquidity, and divisibility, fostering fractional ownership and democratizing participation in the digital economy (Lee et al., 2023).

- *Non-fungible tokens (NFTs) and the Digitalization of Value:* NFTs serve as the foundation of individualized value in the Metaverse, reflecting ownership of distinct digital goods. NFTs redefine ownership, scarcity, and value attribution in a transparent, decentralized framework, encompassing art, virtual real estate, and technological objects as prominent digital assets (Wu & Liu, 2023). By redefining concepts of value, NFTs drive a paradigm shift in the Metaverse's markets, empowering creators and collectors alike (Sung et al., 2023).

- *Virtual Economies and Digital Exchange Platforms:* Dynamic virtual economies thrive within the Metaverse, supported by digital currencies exclusive to virtual environments. Digital exchange platforms serve as market intermediaries, facilitating the seamless conversion of various digital assets and currencies (Vidal-Tomás, 2023). These platforms integrate liquidity pools, advanced trading methods, and decentralized finance (DeFi) components, enhancing the liquidity and efficacy of Metaverse markets (Koohang et al., 2023).

The Metaverse's marketplaces evolve as complex ecosystems in the fusion of decentralized technology, revolutionizing digital commerce. The Metaverse heralds a new era of economic interactions, where traditional boundaries dissolve, and the digitization of value becomes integral to this emerging digital frontier.

3. Gamification in Metaverse

Gamification within the expansive Metaverse transcends mere amusement to become a ubiquitous force that modifies user engagement, behavior, and interaction. This section explores the technologies supporting gamification in the Metaverse, shedding light on the interplay between immersive technologies, AI, and game mechanics that redefine digital experiences. These technologies can be defined as:

- *Game Mechanics:* The core of Metaverse gamification comprises a complex set of game mechanics designed to elicit user behaviors (Thomas et al., 2023). Elements such as points, badges, leaderboards, and quests act as behavioral catalysts, encouraging active engagement, cooperation, and exploration within the Metaverse. A robust technology foundation is essential to coordinate various gameplay elements seamlessly (Arya et al., 2023).
- *AI and Dynamic Gameplay:* AI advancements drive gamified experiences in the Metaverse, enabling automatic adjustment and customization of games based on user data and behavior. AI systems enhance Metaverse environments by facilitating interactions between non-player characters (NPCs) and generating procedural content (Pérez et al., 2023). These environments adapt in real-time to user actions and preferences, enriching immersion, and personalization (Proelss et al., 2023).
- *Social Dynamics and Collaborative Gamification:* Gamification fosters communication and teamwork within the Metaverse, a social and cooperative environment. Gamified social dynamics promote alliances, group challenges, and collaborative content creation. Technological frameworks such as shared virtual spaces, AI-driven matchmaking systems, and communication tools facilitate collaborative gamification, enhancing engagement and interaction (Park & Kim, 2022; Wanick & Stallwood, 2022).

In summary, a symbiotic integration of game mechanics, AI, immersive technologies, blockchain, and cooperative frameworks drives gamification in the Metaverse. Together, these elements create a vibrant online environment where users actively shape the Metaverse's narrative, fostering engagement and community participation, from the same frameworks, as seen next section.

FRAMEWORK OF METAVERSE

1. Immersive Realities

Immersive realities, bridging the digital and physical realms, form the cornerstone of the Metaverse's architecture. AR and VR seamlessly intertwine within the Metaverse, offering interactive experiences that redefine digital engagement (Al-Ghaili et al., 2022).

In the Metaverse, users seamlessly transition between AR and VR experiences, crafting a continuous digital narrative. AR enhances real-world interactions, seamlessly integrating with fully immersive VR environments. This versatility enables a wide array of activities within the Metaverse, ranging from social interactions to entertainment and collaborative workspaces (Bale et al., 2022).

Immersive realities in the Metaverse extend beyond mere entertainment. Organizations leverage AR to create interactive product showcases, while VR revolutionizes remote work and learning through virtual conferences and training environments. As immersive technologies converge within the Metaverse, distinctions between the real and virtual blur, usher in a new era of creative exploration (Hackl, 2020), leading to new engagement and entertainment experiences, like gamification.

2. Gamification as a strategy in Metaverse

Gamification emerges as a pivotal element within the Metaverse, driving consumer engagement and brand differentiation (Park & Kim, 2022). It permeates the consumer experience, fostering brand collaboration and elevating exclusivity through mechanisms like NFTs (Faraboschi et al., 2022).

Game development companies wield significant influence beyond traditional gaming domains, impacting various social and economic facets, including AI and entertainment media (Carew, 2022). The gamification trend extends beyond gaming, with emerging technologies incorporating gaming mechanisms to enhance user interactions (Smith & Shakeri, 2022).

Incorporating gaming elements within the Metaverse fosters user enjoyment, creativity, and loyalty, driving sustained engagement (Jungherr & Schlarb, 2022). Advergaming, where brands integrate into gaming environments, blurs the lines between advertising and entertainment, presenting both advantages and challenges (Daimiel et al., 2022).

Global brands such as Nike, Gucci, and Hyundai are actively embracing gamification within the Metaverse, leveraging immersive virtual worlds to engage consumers (Daimiel et al., 2022). These initiatives underscore the Metaverse's evolution into a decentralized marketing ecosystem, where brands navigate immersive realities to enhance consumer experiences and foster brand loyalty (Joy et al., 2022) in the metamarkets as can be seen in the next section.

METAMARKETS

Consumer perceptions of brands transcend traditional mediums, encompassing all experiences across physical and digital realms (Keller, 2001). Understanding these experiences is crucial in the Metaverse, where 85% to 95% of consumer actions are driven by subconscious, emotional impulses (Lindstrom, 2009). In this expansive digital landscape, influencing positive consumer experiences and fostering brand interaction and retention is paramount (Kim, 2021).

Customizable experiences reign supreme in the Metaverse, with consumers seeking immersive, multi-dimensional encounters (Panda, 2022). Virtually replicating real-world activities—from sports to commerce—underscores the Metaverse's versatility and appeal (Jeon, 2022).

Luxury brands capitalize on consumer desires for exclusivity and personalization within the Metaverse, with limited-edition products driving avatar differentiation. For example, Balenciaga has partnered with

Fortnite, personifying avatars with their clothing and establishing a dedicated department for virtual realities (Dobre et al., 2021; Jeon, 2022; Rauschnabel et al., 2022).

Immersive technologies, particularly AI, enhance consumer interactions with products and services, bolstering online commerce retention (Trevor, 2022). Experiential immersion is paramount in guiding consumers through the purchasing journey, heightening brand engagement and perceived value (Schnack et al., 2021; Solomon, 2018).

Younger generations, steeped in technology and novelty, are predisposed to immersive experiences, with Millennials and Generation Z driving Metaverse engagement. For instance, Samsung, Gucci, and Louis Vuitton are actively establishing a Metaverse presence, leveraging partnerships and immersive experiences to engage consumers (Joy et al., 2022). While Generation X exhibits less enthusiasm, younger cohorts embrace immersive social networks and gaming platforms, positioning them as key players in Metaverse interactions (Jackson, 2023).

Brands across various sectors, notably fashion, and technology, are actively establishing Metaverse presence, leveraging partnerships and immersive experiences to engage consumers. For example, Volvo virtual showrooms and training platforms, reshaping production, and consumer engagement paradigms (Bidar, 2022; Volvo, 2022). Table 3 shows more brands incorporated in the Metaverse world.

Investments in Metaverse branding underscore its significance, with companies prioritizing immersive experiences to capture consumer attention. In the first quarter of 2022, notable brands like Nike and Atari invested significantly in branding and positioning within the Metaverse (Clement, 2022). As Metaverse adoption surges, marketing strategies emphasize emotional connections and gamification to foster brand engagement across diverse consumer experiences (Arya et al., 2023; Berlo et al., 2021; Nevelsteen, 2018). Another example is the Coca-Cola company strategy in the metaverse, which sells NFTs in platforms like Decentraland, which is exploring opportunities to engage with consumers and provide a decentralized cycle economy (Kim, 2021).

While gamification trends show promise, particularly in enhancing brand engagement, further research is needed to understand its impact on the Metaverse and its influence on consumer-brand relationships (Thomas et al., 2023). In other words, gamification is an opportunity in the Metaverse, which some brands are already implementing, but is possible to see other opportunities.

Table 3. Sample of brands on metaverse

Categories	Brands
Experience	Fortnite, Minecraft, EA, Nintendo, Netflix, Second Life, Zoom, Youtube, Twitch, Twitter, Gather (…)
Discovery	Unity, Discord, Google, Steam, Epic Games, (…)
Economic developers	Roblox, Adobe, Microsoft, Sandbox, Decentraland, Shopify, Rokoko (…)
Computing	Unity, Autodesk, Matterport, Google AI, Open AI, Descartes Labs (…)
Decentralization	Ethereum, Microsoft, ubuntu, IBM, OpenSea, Polygon (…)
Human Interfaces	Apple, Oculus, Xbox, PlayStation, Samsung, Huawei, Neurolink, Razer, Magic Leap, Amazon Alexa (…)
Infrastructure	Aws, Azure, NVidia, Dfinity, AMD, Intel, Sony, At&T, Akamai, Qualcom (…)

Source: Adaptation of Zyda (2022)

OPPORTUNITIES IN THE METAVERSE

The Metaverse, as an evolving virtual realm, presents boundless opportunities for creativity across diverse domains. From economic innovation to educational transformation, the following opportunities are poised to reshape various industries within the Metaverse:

- *Economic aspects:* The Metaverse serves as an expanding economic frontier, offering novel avenues for entrepreneurship, innovation, and value generation. Virtual marketplaces, decentralized finance (DeFi) infrastructures, and asset tokenization present uncharted economic landscapes ripe for exploration. Organizations can delve into digital entrepreneurship, virtual real estate development, and the creation of virtual goods and services, fostering a dynamic Metaverse economy (Vidal-Tomás, 2023). For example, the Nike brand has created virtual sneakers and clothing that users can purchase and wear in their virtual worlds, like Roblox and Fortnite, as well as played events and experiences on these platforms.

- *Skill Development:* With the Metaverse's growth comes a demand for diverse skill sets, ranging from blockchain engineering to virtual experience design. This surge in demand translates into increased job opportunities and avenues for skill enhancement, enabling individuals to contribute to the Metaverse ecosystem while gaining valuable expertise in cutting-edge industries (Al-Ghaili et al., 2022). For example, the company Mango Excellent Media Co. is exploring exquisite VR content, digital identities, and NFT trading platforms to build the Mango Planet Metaverse. Another example is the investment of Meta group in VR/AR technologies and the aim to cover around 1 billion of people in the metaverse, with the assistance of VR gaming (Qi, 2022).

- *Virtual Marketing and Commerce:* Businesses can engage with customers in novel ways through virtual commerce in the Metaverse. By establishing virtual storefronts, hosting virtual events, and leveraging immersive advertising, brands can reach a global audience. The Metaverse presents opportunities for innovative storytelling, brand experiences, and consumer engagement in dynamic virtual environments as digital marketing strategies evolve (Lee et al., 2023). For example, the Samsung brand has been exploring the Metaverse reality through the creation of virtual showrooms for their products and hosting events, allowing the leveraging of this virtual reality technology to enhance consumer engagement and allow the presentation of their products in innovative ways.

- *Educational Transformation:* The Metaverse revolutionizes education by offering immersive and interactive learning experiences. Virtual classrooms, collaborative educational platforms, and simulations enhance the educational landscape, providing educators, content providers, and edtech developers with opportunities to advance digital education (Al-Adwan et al., 2023; Vemula, 2020; Wu & Liu, 2023). For example, related to virtual classrooms, platforms like EngageVR enable educators to create immersive virtual classrooms where students can attend lectures, collaborate on projects, and participate in interactive learning experiences from anywhere in the world (Engage, 2024). Another example is the company edX which partnered with Meta to launch a learning ecosystem, that includes immersive learning materials and training sessions (Podmurnyi, 2022).

- *Entertainment and Cultural Experiences:* The Metaverse offers a platform for entertainment beyond conventional boundaries, allowing creators to reimagine gaming, storytelling, and cultural events. Artists, musicians, and storytellers can leverage virtual platforms to reach global audiences, while virtual events and performances serve as innovative venues for artistic expression and collaboration (Wanick & Stallwood, 2022). For example, the pop star and songwriter Ariana Grande performed in the Metaverse inside the hit video game Fortnite, where millions of gamers assisted her (BBC, 2021).

- *Healthcare Improvements:* Virtual simulations, telemedicine, and digital therapies redefine healthcare experiences within the Metaverse. Opportunities abound for healthcare professionals, developers, and innovators to contribute to virtual health services, patient care simulations, and therapeutic interventions within immersive digital environments (Koohang et al., 2023). For example, the telemedicine platform such as XRHealth leverages virtual reality to facilitate remote consultations, allowing healthcare professionals to diagnose and treat patients in immersive virtual environments (Orr, 2022).
- *Social Impact:* The Metaverse provides avenues to address social challenges and promote inclusivity. Virtual spaces can foster community building, support social activism, and create accessible environments for individuals with diverse abilities. Initiatives focused on social impact, cultural exchange, and global collaboration find new avenues for realization within the Metaverse (Davis et al., 2009; Sowmya et al., 2023).

Based on these opportunities, some trends are now beginning to emerge in the Metaverse, which we'll look at in the next section of this chapter.

TRENDS SHAPING THE METAVERSE

The Metaverse is rapidly evolving, shaped by key trends that merge technological, social, and ethical dimensions. These trends include the rise of DAOs and NFT integration, convergence with real-world applications, AI-driven personalization, sustainability considerations, and the push for Metaverse interoperability. In other words, decentralized technologies promote interoperability between different platforms and virtual worlds inside the Metaverse, allowing for seamless integration of advertising campaigns, data sharing, and cross-platform interactions from brands to users, as presented by Kim (2021).

- *DAOs:* Decentralized Autonomous Organizations (DAOs) are reshaping the Metaverse by facilitating group decision-making and resource distribution through smart contracts, challenging traditional governance models (Calzada, 2023).
- *Integration of NFTs:* NFTs represent ownership and individuality in the Metaverse, impacting virtual economies by reinventing concepts of scarcity and provenance across various digital assets (Bhattacharya et al., 2023).
- *Convergence with physical world applications:* The Metaverse is increasingly integrated with practical applications in industries like healthcare, education, and remote work, transforming how we interact and learn (Bhattacharya et al., 2023).
- *AI-driven personalization and user experience:* AI plays a key role in personalizing user experiences in the Metaverse by analyzing behavior and interactions to customize virtual environments, enhancing immersion and user-centricity (Fu et al., 2023). As referred by Kim (2021) AI technologies can enhance personalization and improve targeting in virtual environments and with NLP

can facilitate natural interactions between users and brands, leading to more engaging and effective communication in Metaverse, providing, for example, through virtual assistants.

- *Emergence of Metaverse Interoperability:* Interoperability efforts aim to enable seamless communication and engagement across multiple Metaverse platforms, allowing users to move between virtual worlds effortlessly (Naderi & Shojaei, 2023; Park et al., 2023).
- *Sustainable Environmental Practices and Ethical Issues:* Rising awareness of ethical issues and environmental impacts prompts the development of sustainable practices and ethical frameworks to mitigate the negative effects of Metaverse expansion (Bale et al., 2022). Given the relevance of ethical issues in Metaverse, an exclusive section has been included in this chapter to highlight dimensions such as privacy concerns, data governance, and algorithmic biases.

Understanding these trends is crucial for predicting the Metaverse's trajectory and adapting to its evolving landscape and the new user identity – data identity.

DIGITAL IDENTITIES

The transition of human existence into the digital realm is epitomized by the emergence of the Metaverse, highlighting the evolving nature of identities over time (Burlington, 2021). Within this expansive digital frontier, the concept of self takes on a new dimension, transcending the physical constraints of our tangible world. At the heart of this transformative journey lies the development of digital identities, where avatars serve as conduits for self-expression within the infinite expanse of VR.

Avatars, as representations of users in the Metaverse, liberate individuals from the constraints of physical appearance. Through the creation of these virtual personas, individuals enter a realm of customization and personalization that extends beyond the boundaries of the physical realm. Digital identities are molded to reflect cultural influences, aspirational narratives, and personal preferences, fostering a journey of self-expression and discovery (Han et al., 2023). Kim (2021) states that digital identities play a crucial role in the metaverse, for brands and companies to understand how the users communicate, establish relationships, present themselves, and purchase behavior within virtual spaces to advertisers and marketers operating in this reality, with authentic strategies.

The concept of digital twins - virtual counterparts intricately linked to identity verification—underscores the critical importance of security and trust within this digital landscape. Operating in conjunction with authentication technologies such as voice recognition and biometrics, digital twins safeguard the integrity of digital identities, providing users with confidence and assurance as they navigate the Metaverse (Lv et al., 2022).

The consistency of identities across platforms in the Metaverse defines this online environment as distinctive. Users seamlessly traverse a variety of virtual environments while maintaining consistency in their presence. This continuity fosters a connected experience that enables collaboration across platforms and the establishment of a unified digital identity spanning different virtual worlds (Rad & Far, 2023).

However, privacy and security concerns loom large in this expansive canvas of digital identities. Robust frameworks safeguard personal data, empower users with control over data access, and ensure ethical handling of consent within the dynamic ecosystem of the Metaverse (Sullivan & Tyson, 2023). Striking a balance between the imperatives of security and privacy becomes a complex endeavor in this evolving landscape.

As digital identities evolve, they transcend mere representations to acquire social capital and reputations. A user's contributions, interactions, and behavior within online communities coalesce to shape their digital reputation, measuring their authority and reliability. Redefining social interactions in the Metaverse, these reputational dynamics introduce a novel dimension of digital sociality that both echoes and diverges from its physical counterpart (Kim et al., 2023).

Conventional notions of selfhood are challenged by the Metaverse in this exploration of digital identities. It offers individuals a blank canvas for exploration, reinvention, and expression of their digital selves beyond the confines of the real world. The interconnectedness and interoperability of these digital identities paint a complex yet captivating portrait of the evolving human experience within the dynamically evolving Metaverse. There are countless opportunities and advantages within the Metaverse, however, it also carries risks and ethical considerations to be considered, as with digital identities and as will be explained below.

ETHICAL CONSIDERATIONS AND RISKS IN THE METAVERSE

In any technological scenario, there is a greater concern with matters relating to virtual security, transparency of models, clarity in the provision of data, and security in the often-personal data provided. As it is a virtual world, made up of decentralized processes, it is essential to check the ethical considerations and risks that this reality can entail for companies and users. This study will be focused on three dimensions: privacy concerns, data governance, and algorithmic biases.

- *Privacy concerns:* Data privacy is the right of users to have control over how the information is collected, used, and shared about them. In practical scenarios, the law generally protects Personal Identifiable Information (PII), which implicates non-public information and can be tied back to an "identified" or "identifiable" person, on a sub-set of personal information is sensitive information, which may have additional stricter privacy rules (such as social security numbers, financial information, and others).

As users immerse themselves in virtual worlds, the metaverse poses so far unseen concerns to individual privacy rights. The massive gathering and use of personal data by virtual world providers and metaverse platforms is one of the most urgent issues. The ubiquitous monitoring present in these settings, which includes user behavior tracking and preference profiling, presents serious concerns regarding data security and privacy. Users may have trust breaches and worries about data misuse if they are uneasy about how much their interactions and behaviors are being watched and evaluated (Han et al., 2022).

Users' privacy worries are further compounded by the lack of openness surrounding data-gathering procedures, which leaves them unsure of how their information is shared and used (Han et al., 2022; Munn & Weijers, 2023). People can be used and manipulated in the metaverse environment if there aren't any explicit rules and accountability systems in place. To defend user rights and rebuild confidence in virtual environments, it is imperative to provide strong privacy measures and encourage greater transparency in data management procedures. This is because there is still a lack of regulation in the metaverse as, for example, a commercial enterprise, due to the lack of adequate legal protections or resources in cases of privacy breaches, and disputes, among other events (Munn & Weijers, 2023). This vulnerability leads to other security breaches, such as data leaks and privacy violations, putting users' information at risk.

Another situation that can raise privacy considerations is the lack of recognition of virtual goods as private property, ownership of assets, and the security of end users in virtual spaces that need standardized legal protection (Munn & Weijers, 2023).

- *Data governance:* Ensuring the responsible governance and utilization of user data in the metaverse requires effective data governance (Han et al., 2022). Regulating and safeguarding data across many platforms and experiences is a huge difficulty, though, because many virtual environments are decentralized (Munn & Weijers, 2023). These difficulties are made worse by the lack of established procedures and control frameworks, which leaves openings for potential data breaches and abuse.

Stakeholders must work together to create thorough data governance frameworks that give user consent, data protection, and accountability the highest priority to address these problems. To reduce the possibility of unauthorized access or data infringements is necessary the implement strong security measures in addition to procedures for transparent data collection and processing (Munn & Weijers, 2023). Furthermore, encouraging data independence and giving users more control over their data can support the development of trust and confidence in metaverse platforms, which will increase user involvement and engagement.

- *Algorithmic biases:* The metaverse's user experiences and interactions are greatly shaped by algorithms, which have an impact on everything from social interactions to content recommendations. These algorithms are not impervious to prejudices, though, and prejudice can still exist in virtual environments where it is tolerated (Ariel Gendler, 2023). Inadvertent reinforcement of societal biases and exclusionary behaviors via algorithmic decision-making processes, for instance, may result in unequal representation and access inside the metaverse. In other words, the term "algorithmic bias" describes the unfair or discriminating results that algorithms generate because of faulty programming or biased input. This may result in decision-making processes that reinforce past biases, stereotypes, and injustices (Carter & Egliston, 2023).

A multimodal strategy that includes locating, reducing, and fixing discriminating algorithms is needed to address algorithmic biases. In addition to encouraging diversity and inclusion in data collecting and algorithm training procedures, this calls for continual research and development efforts to identify and address biases in algorithmic systems (Carter & Egliston, 2023). All users can benefit from a more inclusive and equitable metaverse by reducing the influence of biases and implementing principles of justice, transparency, and accountability in algorithm design and implementation (Han et al., 2022; Munn & Weijers, 2023).

IMPLICATIONS AND FUTURE RESEARCH

As the Metaverse continues its expansion, the exploration of future research avenues becomes imperative to unravel its intricacies and anticipate emerging challenges. Several promising directions beckon academic inquiry, each offering a unique lens through which the Metaverse's evolution can be comprehensively understood.

First, investigations into the ethical considerations surrounding digital identities within the Metaverse stand as a crucial avenue. Examining the subtleties of security, privacy, and data utilization might help to clarify the moral dilemmas raised by the gathering and handling of user data, offering important new perspectives on ethical Metaverse activities.

Second, the evolving landscape of human-computer interaction within the Metaverse warrants investigation. An analysis of how people engage with avatars, immersive technology, and virtual environments provides ways to improve user experiences, ensure accessibility, and promote diversity in the digital world.

Third, research into the cultural and social impacts of the Metaverse offers a wealth of opportunities. Determining how the Metaverse affects distinct cultures on a cultural and socioeconomic level provides insights into broader societal ramifications. Understanding how digital identities impact cultural expression, representation, and standards within virtual environments is crucial, particularly in educational contexts.

The transformative potential of the Metaverse in education opens a promising frontier for research. Investigating the effectiveness of virtual classrooms, collaborative learning environments, and the influence of digital identities on learning outcomes contributes to ongoing discussions about the future of education.

Additionally, exploring the relationship between extended Metaverse activity and mental health and well-being is insightful. Studies in this field can shed light on the effects on individuals and offer tactics to ensure a healthy and fulfilling virtual experience.

Fourth, analyzing the impact of decentralized technologies, such as blockchain, on the virtual economy and digital identities is essential. This includes examining governance structures, decentralized identity solutions, and the effects of blockchain on security and vulnerability in the Metaverse.

Moreover, studying the impact of AI-driven customization on user engagement, social dynamics, and ethical considerations contributes to a nuanced understanding of evolving virtual interactions.

Finally, directing future research toward Metaverse interoperability and cross-cultural perspectives is crucial. Understanding how smooth transitions between virtual environments affect user experiences and exploring the technological, social, and economic elements of building a more integrated Metaverse provides valuable insights. Additionally, studying digital identities in the Metaverse from a cross-cultural perspective offers important insights into how different cultures view and interact with virtual representations.

By delving into these subjects, researchers can enhance the understanding of the Metaverse's multiple elements and ensure that academic research remains aligned with this constantly evolving digital frontier.

CONCLUSION

In reviewing the Metaverse comprehensively, this piece has delved into its foundational elements, explored virtual worlds, examined technological underpinnings, and delineated new directions and trends. Rather than offering prescriptive directives, the suggested future research directions serve as scholarly guideposts, grounded in ethical considerations, human-computer interaction, and societal impacts.

As elucidated in this chapter, the Metaverse is not a static entity but a multifaceted and dynamic subject deserving of ongoing scientific inquiry. The proposed research avenues represent ripe areas for exploration, guided by a commitment to rigorous research methodologies, ethical scrutiny, and a steadfast dedication to advancing academic discourse.

This chapter invites the academic community to discuss the future evolution of Metaverse. The outlined future research trajectories do not signify uncertainty but rather reflect an evolving scholarly dedication to unraveling the complexities of this digital realm. As scholars, it is incumbent upon us to uphold rigorous research standards and contribute substantively to the unfolding narrative of the Metaverse.

In summary, this chapter serves as both a culmination and a prologue - a culmination of collective endeavors to shed light on various facets of the Metaverse and a prologue to the next phase of scholarly inquiry. As we navigate the scholarly landscape of the Metaverse, the trajectory is one of continuous exploration, with the shared pursuit of understanding and discovery propelling scholarly pursuits forward. The Metaverse, with its expansive terrain, awaits further scholarly scrutiny, and it is through collaborative efforts that the narrative of this digital frontier will unfold.

ACKNOWLEDGMENT

The authors are grateful for the support to this research given by the Polytechnic Institute of Coimbra, Coimbra Business School, Quinta Agrícola - Bencanta, 3045-231 Coimbra, Portugal, and the CEOS. PP, ISCAP, Polytechnic of Porto, Portugal.

REFERENCES

Abrash, M. (2021, Dec 11-16). Creating the Future: Augmented Reality, the next Human-Machine Interface. *IEEE International Electron Devices Meeting*. IEEE International Electron Devices Meeting (IEDM), San Francisco, CA. 10.1109/IEDM19574.2021.9720526

Acevedo Nieto, J. (2022). Una introducción al metaverso: conceptualización y alcance de un nuevo universe. *adComunica*, (24), 41-56. doi:10.6035/adcomunica.6544

Afrashtehfar, K. I., & Abu-Fanas, A. S. H. (2022). Metaverse, Crypto, and NFTs in Dentistry. *Education Sciences*, *12*(8), 538. https://www.mdpi.com/2227-7102/12/8/538. doi:10.3390/educsci12080538

Ahn, S. J., Kim, J., & Kim, J. (2022). The future of advertising research in virtual, augmented, and extended realities. *International Journal of Advertising*, 1–9. doi:10.1080/02650487.2022.2137316

Al-Adwan, A. S., Li, N., Al-Adwan, A., Abbasi, G. A., Albelbis, N. A., & Habibi, A. (2023). Extending the Technology Acceptance Model (TAM) to Predict University Students' Intentions to Use Metaverse-Based Learning Platforms. *Education and Information Technologies*, *28*(11), 15381–15413. doi:10.1007/s10639-023-11816-3 PMID:37361794

Al-Ghaili, A. M., Kasim, H., Al-Hada, N. M., Hassan, Z. B., Othman, M., Tharik, J. H., Kasmani, R. M., & Shayea, I. (2022). A review of Metaverse's definitions, architecture, applications, challenges, issues, solutions, and future trends. *IEEE Access : Practical Innovations, Open Solutions*, *10*, 125835–125866. doi:10.1109/ACCESS.2022.3225638

Ariel Gendler, M. (2023). De la cibernética al metaverso: Una genealogía de características, transparencias y opacidades algorítmicas. *Disparidades. Revista de Antropologia*, *78*(1), e001b. doi:10.3989/dra.2023.001b

Arya, V., Sambyal, R., Sharma, A., & Dwivedi, Y. K. (2023). Brands are calling your AVATAR in Metaverse-A study to explore XR-based gamification marketing activities & consumer-based brand equity in virtual world. *Journal of Consumer Behaviour*. doi:10.1002/cb.2214

Ashmore, D., & Venz, S. (2023). *A brief history of Web 3.0*. Forbes Advisor. Retrieved May 20th, 2023 from https://www.forbes.com/advisor/au/investing/cryptocurrency/what-is-web-3-0/

Azuma, R. T. (1997). A Survey of Augmented Reality. *Presence (Cambridge, Mass.)*, *6*(4), 355–385. doi:10.1162/pres.1997.6.4.355

Bale, A. S., Ghorpade, N., Hashim, M. F., Vaishnav, J., Almaspoor, Z., & Agostini, A. (2022). A comprehensive study on Metaverse and its impacts on humans. *Advances in Human-Computer Interaction*, *2022*, 1-11. *Article, 3247060*. Advance online publication. doi:10.1155/2022/3247060

Bamodu, O., & Ye, X. (2013). Virtual Reality and Virtual Reality System Components. *Advanced Materials Research*, *765-767*, 1169–1172. doi:10.4028/www.scientific.net/AMR.765-767.1169

BBC. (2021). *Ariana Grande sings in Fortnite's metaverse*. BBC. https://www.bbc.com/news/av/technology-58146042

Berglund, Å. F., Gong, L., & Li, D. (2018). Testing and validating Extended Reality (xR) technologies in manufacturing. *Procedia Manufacturing*, *25*, 31–38. doi:10.1016/j.promfg.2018.06.054

Berlo, Z. M. C., Reijmersdal, E. A., & Eisend, M. (2021). The Gamification of Branded Content: A Meta-Analysis of Advergame Effects. *Journal of Advertising*, *50*(2), 179–196. doi:10.1080/00913367.2020.1858462

Bhattacharya, P., Saraswat, D., Savaliya, D., Sanghavi, S., Verma, A., Sakariya, V., Tanwar, S., Sharma, R., Raboaca, M. S., & Manea, D. L. (2023). Towards Future Internet: The Metaverse Perspective for Diverse Industrial Applications. *Mathematics*, *11*(4), 941. doi:10.3390/math11040941

Bibri, S. E., Allam, Z., & Krogstie, J. (2022). The Metaverse as a virtual form of data-driven smart urbanism: Platformization and its underlying processes, institutional dimensions, and disruptive impacts. *Computational Urban Science*, *2*(1), 24. doi:10.1007/s43762-022-00051-0 PMID:35974838

Bidar, M. (2022). *Companies race to build "digital twins" in the metaverse*. CBS News. https://www.cbsnews.com/news/metaverse-amazon-bmw-lockheed-martin-adobe-digital-twin/

Bonetti, F., Warnaby, G., & Quinn, L. (2018). Augmented Reality and Virtual Reality in Physical and Online Retailing: A Review, Synthesis and Research Agenda. In T. Jung & M. C. tom Dieck (Eds.), *Augmented Reality and Virtual Reality: Empowering Human, Place and Business* (pp. 119–132). Springer International Publishing., doi:10.1007/978-3-319-64027-3_9

Bruni, R., Piccarozzi, M., & Caboni, F. (2023). Defining the Metaverse with challenges and opportunities in the business environment. *Journal of Marketing Theory and Practice*, 1–18. Advance online publication. doi:10.1080/10696679.2023.2273555

Burlington. (2021). *Searching for utopia: from dinosaurs to the metaverse*. Burlington. https://www.burlington.org.uk/archive/editorial/searching-for-utopia-from-dinosaurs-to-the-metaverse

Cali, U., Kuzlu, M., Karaarslan, E., & Jovanovic, V. (2022). *Opportunities and Challenges in Metaverse for Industry 4.0 and Beyond Applications.* IEEE 1st Global Emerging Technology Blockchain Forum - Blockchain and Beyond, (IGETblockchain), Irvine, CA. https://doi.org/ doi:10.1109/iGETblockchain56591.2022.10087104

Calzada, I. (2023). Disruptive Technologies for e-Diasporas: Blockchain, DAOs, Data Cooperatives, Metaverse, and ChatGPT. *Futures, 154,* 103258. doi:10.1016/j.futures.2023.103258

Calzone, N., Sileo, M., Mozzillo, R., Pierri, F., & Caccavale, F. (2023). Mixed Reality Platform Supporting Human-Robot Interaction. Advances on Mechanics, Design Engineering and Manufacturing IV, Cham. doi:10.1007/978-3-031-15928-2_102

Carew, A. (2022). A whole new world: Metaverse as fairytale in Belle. *Metro*(212), 92-97. https://search.informit.org/doi/abs/10.3316/informit.938183067792285

Carter, M., & Egliston, B. (2023). What are the risks of Virtual Reality data? Learning Analytics, Algorithmic Bias and a Fantasy of Perfect Data. *New Media & Society, 25*(3), 485–504. doi:10.1177/14614448211012794

Chaves, A. (2023). *O que é Web 5.0 e qual a diferença da web3?* Be(in)Crypto. https://br.beincrypto.com/aprender/o-que-e-web-5-0/

Chen, Z. S. (2023). Beyond Reality: Examining the Opportunities and Challenges of Cross-Border Integration between Metaverse and Hospitality Industries. *Journal of Hospitality Marketing & Management, 32*(7), 967–980. doi:10.1080/19368623.2023.2222029

Cheng, R. Z., Wu, N., Chen, S. Q., & Han, B. (2022, Mar 12-16). Reality check of metaverse: A first look at commercial social virtual reality platforms. *2022 IEEE Conference on Virtual Reality and 3D User Interfaces Abstracts and Workshops.* IEEE. 10.1109/VRW55335.2022.00040

Cipresso, P., Giglioli, I. A. C., Raya, M. A., & Riva, G. (2018). The Past, Present, and Future of Virtual and Augmented Reality Research: A Network and Cluster Analysis of the Literature. *Frontiers in Psychology, 9,* 2086. doi:10.3389/fpsyg.2018.02086 PMID:30459681

Clement, J. (2022). *In what type of projects does your company invest in the metaverse?* Statista. https://www.statista.com/statistics/1302200/metaverse-project-investment-businesses/

Clement, J. (2023). *Video game industry - statistics & facts.* Statista. https://www.statista.com/topics/868/video-games/#topicOverview

Daimiel, G. B., Estrella, E. C. M., & Ormaechea, S. L. (2022). Analysis of the use of advergaming and metaverse in Spain and Mexico. *Revista Latina De Comunicacion Social, 80*(80), 155–178. doi:10.4185/RLCS-2022-1802

Davis, A., Khazanchi, D., Murphy, J., Zigurs, I., & Owens, D. (2009). Avatars, People, and Virtual Worlds: Foundations for Research in Metaverses. *Journal of the Association for Information Systems, 10*(2), 90–117. doi:10.17705/1jais.00183

Dobre, C., Milovan, A. M., Dutu, C., Preda, G., & Agapie, A. (2021). The Common Values of Social Media Marketing and Luxury Brands. The Millennials and Generation Z Perspective. *Journal of Theoretical and Applied Electronic Commerce Research, 16*(7), 2532–2553. doi:10.3390/jtaer16070139

Dwivedi, Y. K., Hughes, L., Baabdullah, A. M., Ribeiro-Navarrete, S., Giannakis, M., Al-Debei, M. M., Dennehy, D., Metri, B., Buhalis, D., Cheung, C. M. K., Conboy, K., Doyle, R., Dubey, R., Dutot, V., Felix, R., Goyal, D. P., Gustafsson, A., Hinsch, C., Jebabli, I., & Wamba, S. F. (2022). Metaverse beyond the hype: Multidisciplinary perspectives on emerging challenges, opportunities, and agenda for research, practice and policy. *International Journal of Information Management, 66*, 102542. doi:10.1016/j.ijinfomgt.2022.102542

Engage. (2024). *Engage Studio*. EngageVR. https://engagevr.io/engage-studio/

Faraboschi, P., Frachtenberg, E., Laplante, P., Milojicic, D., & Saracco, R. (2022). Virtual worlds (Metaverse): From skepticism, to fear, to immersive opportunities. *Computer, 55*(10), 100–106. doi:10.1109/MC.2022.3192702

Fazio, G., Fricano, S., Iannolino, S., & Pirrone, C. (2023). Metaverse and tourism development: Issues and opportunities in stakeholders' perception. *Information Technology & Tourism, 25*(4), 507–528. doi:10.1007/s40558-023-00268-7

Fu, Y. C., Li, C. L., Yu, F. R., Luan, T. H., Zhao, P. C., & Liu, S. (2023). A Survey of Blockchain and Intelligent Networking for the Metaverse. *IEEE Internet of Things Journal, 10*(4), 3587–3610. doi:10.1109/JIOT.2022.3222521

Gao, Z., & Braud, T. (2023). VR-driven museum opportunities: Digitized archives in the age of the metaverse. *Artnodes, 0*(32). Advance online publication. doi:10.7238/artnodes.v0i32.402462

Goel, A. K., Bakshi, R., & Agrawal, K. K. (2022). Web 3.0 and Decentralized Applications. *Materials Proceedings, 10*(1), 8. https://www.mdpi.com/2673-4605/10/1/8

Golf-Papez, M., Heller, J., Hilken, T., Chylinski, M., de Ruyter, K., Keeling, D. I., & Mahr, D. (2022). Embracing falsity through the metaverse: The case of synthetic customer experiences. *Business Horizons, 65*(6), 739–749. doi:10.1016/j.bushor.2022.07.007

Guan, J., Morris, A., & Irizawa, J. (2023). *Extending the Metaverse: Hyper-Connected Smart Environments with Mixed Reality and the Internet of Things*. 30th IEEE Conference Virtual Reality and 3D User Interfaces (IEEE VR), Shanghai. 10.1109/VRW58643.2023.00251

Hackl, C. (2020). The Metaverse is coming and it's a very big deal. *Forbes*. https://www.forbes.com/sites/cathyhackl/2020/07/05/the-metaverse-is-coming--its-a-very-big-deal/

Han, D.-I. D., Bergs, Y., & Moorhouse, N. (2022). Virtual reality consumer experience escapes: Preparing for the metaverse. *Virtual Reality (Waltham Cross), 26*(4), 1443–1458. doi:10.1007/s10055-022-00641-7

Han, E., Miller, M. R., DeVeaux, C., Jun, H., Nowak, K. L., Hancock, J. T., Ram, N., & Bailenson, J. N. (2023). People, places, and time: A large-scale, longitudinal study of transformed avatars and environmental context in group interaction in the metaverse. *Journal of Computer-Mediated Communication, 28*(2), zmac031. doi:10.1093/jcmc/zmac031

Harley, D. (2022). "This would be sweet in VR": On the discursive newness of virtual reality. *New Media & Society, 17*, 1461444821084655. doi:10.1177/14614448221084655

Hester, A. J., Hutchins, H. M., & Burke-Smalley, L. A. (2016). Web 2.0 and Transfer: Trainers' Use of Technology to Support Employees' Learning Transfer on the Job. *Performance Improvement Quarterly*, *29*(3), 231–255. doi:10.1002/piq.21225

Huynh-The, T., Gadekallu, T. R., Wang, W. Z., Yenduri, G., Ranaweera, P., Pham, Q. V., da Costa, D. B., & Liyanage, M. (2023). Blockchain for the metaverse: A Review. *Future Generation Computer Systems*, *143*, 401–419. doi:10.1016/j.future.2023.02.008

Immersive Virtual Reality. (2008). In B. Furht (Ed.), *Encyclopedia of Multimedia* (pp. 345–346). Springer US., doi:10.1007/978-0-387-78414-4_85

Jackson, R. (2023). *Young users favor immersive media over social media. Why it matters?* TipRanks. https://www.nasdaq.com/articles/young-users-favor-immersive-media-over-social-media.-why-it-matters

Jeon, Y. A. (2022). Reading Social Media Marketing Messages as Simulated Self Within a Metaverse: An Analysis of Gaze and Social Media Engagement Behaviors within a Metaverse Platform. *Proceedings - 2022 IEEE Conference on Virtual Reality and 3D User Interfaces Abstracts and Workshops, VRW 2022*. IEEE. 10.1109/VRW55335.2022.00068

Joy, A., Zhu, Y., Pena, C., & Brouard, M. (2022). Digital future of luxury brands: Metaverse, digital fashion, and non-fungible tokens. *Strategic Change*, *31*(3), 337–343. doi:10.1002/jsc.2502

Jung, T. M., Cho, J. S., Han, D. I. D., Ahn, S. J., Gupta, M., Das, G., Heo, C. Y., Loureiro, S. M. C., Sigala, M., Trunfio, M., Taylor, A., & Dieck, M. C. T. (2024). Metaverse for service industries: Future applications, opportunities, challenges and research directions. *Computers in Human Behavior*, *151*, 108039. Advance online publication. doi:10.1016/j.chb.2023.108039

Jungherr, A., & Schlarb, D. B. (2022). The extended reach of game engine companies: how companies like epic games and unity technologies provide platforms for extended reality applications and the Metaverse. *Social Media + Society*, *8*(2), 12. doi:10.1177/20563051221107641

Kaddoura, S., & Al Husseiny, F. (2023). The rising trend of Metaverse in education: Challenges, opportunities, and ethical considerations. *PeerJ. Computer Science*, *9*, e1252. doi:10.7717/peerj-cs.1252 PMID:37346578

Keller, K. L. (2001). *Building Customer-Based Brand Equity: A Blueprint for Creating Strong Brands* (01-107). (Working Paper). M. S. Institute. http://anandahussein.lecture.ub.ac.id/files/2015/09/article-4.pdf

Kim, D., Lee, H. K., & Chung, K. (2023). Avatar-mediated experience in the metaverse: The impact of avatar realism on user-avatar relationship. *Journal of Retailing and Consumer Services*, *73*, 103382. doi:10.1016/j.jretconser.2023.103382

Kim, J. (2021). Advertising in the Metaverse: Research Agenda. *Journal of Interactive Advertising*, *21*(3), 141–144. doi:10.1080/15252019.2021.2001273

Kim, J., Hwang, L., Kwon, S., & Lee, S. (2022). Change in Blink Rate in the Metaverse VR HMD and AR Glasses Environment. *International Journal of Environmental Research and Public Health*, *19*(14), 8551. https://www.mdpi.com/1660-4601/19/14/8551. doi:10.3390/ijerph19148551 PMID:35886402

Koohang, A., Nord, J. H., Ooi, K. B., Tan, G. W. H., Al-Emran, M., Aw, E. C. X., Baabdullah, A. M., Buhalis, D., Cham, T. H., Dennis, C., Dutot, V., Dwivedi, Y. K., Hughes, L., Mogaji, E., Pandey, N., Phau, I., Raman, R., Sharma, A., Sigala, M., & Wong, L. W. (2023). Shaping the Metaverse into Reality: A Holistic Multidisciplinary Understanding of Opportunities, Challenges, and Avenues for Future Investigation. *Journal of Computer Information Systems, 63*(3), 735–765. doi:10.1080/08874417.2023.2165197

Kumawat, V., Dhaked, R., Sharma, L., & Jain, S. (2020). Evolution of Immersive Technology. *Journey of Computational Reality.*

Lee, C. T., Ho, T. Y., & Xie, H. H. (2023). Building brand engagement in metaverse commerce: The role of branded non-fungible toekns (BNFTs). *Electronic Commerce Research and Applications, 58*, 101248. Advance online publication. doi:10.1016/j.elerap.2023.101248

Lindstrom, M. (2009). *Buy.ology: A ciência do Neuromarketing.* Gestão Plus.

Lowood, H. E. (2022). *virtual reality.* Encyclopedia Britannica. https://www.britannica.com/technology/virtual-reality

Lv, Z., Qiao, L., Li, Y., Yuan, Y., & Wang, F. Y. (2022). BlockNet: Beyond reliable spatial Digital Twins to Parallel Metaverse. *Patterns (New York, N.Y.), 3*(5), 100468. doi:10.1016/j.patter.2022.100468 PMID:35607617

Massaro, M. (2023). Digital transformation in the healthcare sector through blockchain technology. Insights from academic research and business developments. *Technovation, 120*, 102386. doi:10.1016/j.technovation.2021.102386

Mogaji, E. (2023). Metaverse influence on transportation: A mission impossible? *Transportation Research Interdisciplinary Perspectives, 22*, 100954. doi:10.1016/j.trip.2023.100954

Mogaji, E., Dwivedi, Y. K., & Raman, R. (2024). Fashion marketing in the metaverse. *Journal of Global Fashion Marketing, 15*(1), 115–130. doi:10.1080/20932685.2023.2249483

Mohamed, E. S., & Naqishbandi, T. A. (2023). Metaverse! Possible Potential Opportunities and Trends in E-Healthcare and Education. *International Journal of E-Adoption, 15*(2), 1–21. doi:10.4018/IJEA.316537

Munn, N., & Weijers, D. (2023). The real ethical problem with metaverses. *Frontiers in Human Dynamics, 5*, 1226848. doi:10.3389/fhumd.2023.1226848

Naderi, H., & Shojaei, A. (2023). Digital twinning of civil infrastructures: Current state of model architectures, interoperability solutions, and future prospects. *Automation in Construction, 149*, 104785. doi:10.1016/j.autcon.2023.104785

NathK. (2022). Evolution of the Internet from Web 1.0 to Metaverse: The Good, The Bad and The Ugly. TechRxiv. doi:10.36227/techrxiv.19743676

Nevelsteen, K. J. L. (2018). Virtual world, defined from a technological perspective and applied to video games, mixed reality, and the Metaverse. *Computer Animation and Virtual Worlds, 29*(1), 22, Article e1752. doi:10.1002/cav.1752

Neves, J., Bacalhau, L. M., & Santos, V. (2024). *A Systematic Review on the Customer Journey Between Two Worlds: Reality and Immersive World*. Marketing and Smart Technologies.

Ng, D. T. K. (2022). What is the metaverse? Definitions, technologies and the community of inquiry. *Australasian Journal of Educational Technology, 38*(4), 190–205. doi:10.14742/ajet.7945

Novak, K. (2022). Introducing the Metaverse, Again! *TechTrends, 66*(5), 737–739. doi:10.1007/s11528-022-00767-0

Nuñez, J., Krynski, L., & Otero, P. (2024). The metaverse in the world of health: The present future. Challenges and opportunities. *Archivos Argentinos de Pediatria, 122*(1). doi:10.5546/aap.2022-02942. eng PMID:37171469

Oliveira, C. M. (2023). *Humantech Marketing: o marketing molecular e humano*. Conjuntura Actual Editora.

Orr, E. (2022). The Metaverse Can Create A Boundless Healthcare Experience. *Forbes*. https://www.forbes.com/sites/forbestechcouncil/2022/01/26/the-metaverse-can-create-a-boundless-healthcare-experience/?sh=1b21c0ab2340

Panda, T. K. (2022). In the world of Metaverse. *NMIMS Management Review, 30*(03), 03-05. doi:10.53908/NMMR.300210

Park, A., Wilson, M., Robson, K., Demetis, D., & Kietzmann, J. (2023). Interoperability: Our exciting and terrifying Web3 future. *Business Horizons, 66*(4), 529–541. doi:10.1016/j.bushor.2022.10.005

Park, S., & Kim, S. (2022). Identifying world types to deliver gameful experiences for sustainable learning in the Metaverse. *Sustainability, 14*(3), 14. doi:10.3390/su14031361

Pérez, J., Castro, M., & López, G. (2023). Serious Games and AI: Challenges and Opportunities for Computational Social Science. *IEEE Access : Practical Innovations, Open Solutions, 11*, 62051–62061. doi:10.1109/ACCESS.2023.3286695

Podmurnyi, S. (2022). Business Insights On The Opportunity For The Educational Metaverse. *Forbes*. https://www.forbes.com/sites/forbestechcouncil/2022/08/05/business-insights-on-the-opportunity-for-the-educational-metaverse/?sh=240d59874a3f

Proelss, J., Sévigny, S., & Schweizer, D. (2023). GameFi: The perfect symbiosis of blockchain, tokens, DeFi, and NFTs? *International Review of Financial Analysis, 90*, 102916. doi:10.1016/j.irfa.2023.102916

Profumo, G., Testa, G., Viassone, M., & Ben Youssef, K. (2024). Metaverse and the fashion industry: A systematic literature review. *Journal of Global Fashion Marketing, 15*(1), 131–154. doi:10.1080/20932685.2023.2270587

Qi, W. (2022). The Investment Value of Metaverse in the Media and Entertainment Industry. *BCP Business &amp. Management, 34*, 279–283. doi:10.54691/bcpbm.v34i.3026

Rad, A. I., & Far, S. B. (2023). SocialFi transforms social media: An overview of key technologies, challenges, and opportunities of the future generation of social media. *Social Network Analysis and Mining, 13*(1), 42. doi:10.1007/s13278-023-01050-7

Rauschnabel, P. A., Babin, B. J., tom Dieck, M. C., Krey, N., & Jung, T. (2022). What is augmented reality marketing? Its definition, complexity, and future. *Journal of Business Research*, *142*, 1140–1150. doi:10.1016/j.jbusres.2021.12.084

Sandal, M. M., Taner, T., Firat, B. B., Ünal, H. T., Ulucan, S., & Mendı, A. F. Ö, Ö., & Nacar, M. A. (2023, 8-10 June 2023). *WEB 3.0 Applications and Projections. 2023 5th International Congress on Human-Computer Interaction, Optimization and Robotic Applications (HORA)*. IEEE. 10.1109/HORA58378.2023.10156728

Schnack, A., Wright, M. J., & Elms, J. (2021). Investigating the impact of shopper personality on behaviour in immersive Virtual Reality store environments. *Journal of Retailing and Consumer Services*, *61*, 102581. doi:10.1016/j.jretconser.2021.102581

Smith, A. H., & Shakeri, M. (2022). The future's not what It used to be: Urban wormholes, simulation, participation, and planning in the Metaverse. *Urban Planning*, *7*(2), 214–217. doi:10.17645/up.v7i2.5893

Solomon, P. R. (2018). Neuromarketing: Applications, Challenges and Promises. *Biomedical Journal of Scientific & Technical Research*, *12*(2). doi:10.26717/BJSTR.2018.12.002230

Sowmya, G., Chakraborty, D., Polisetty, A., Khorana, S., & Buhalis, D. (2023). Use of metaverse in socializing: Application of the big five personality traits framework. *Psychology and Marketing*, *40*(10), 2132–2150. doi:10.1002/mar.21863

Stephenson, N. (1992). Snow Crash (Spectra, Ed.). Bantam Books.

Sullivan, C., & Tyson, S. (2023). A global digital identity for all: The next evolution. *Policy Design and Practice*, *6*(4), 433–445. doi:10.1080/25741292.2023.2267867

Sung, E., Kwon, O., & Sohn, K. (2023). NFT luxury brand marketing in the metaverse: Leveraging blockchain-certified NFTs to drive consumer behavior. *Psychology and Marketing*, *40*(11), 2306–2325. doi:10.1002/mar.21854

Taçgın, Z., & Dalgarno, B. (2021). Building an Instructional Design Model for Immersive Virtual Reality Learning Environments. In *Designing* (pp. 20–47). Deploying, and Evaluating Virtual and Augmented Reality in Education. doi:10.4018/978-1-7998-5043-4.ch002

Thomas, N. J., Baral, R., Crocco, O. S., & Mohanan, S. (2023). A framework for gamification in the metaverse era: How designers envision gameful experience. *Technological Forecasting and Social Change*, *193*, 122544. Advance online publication. doi:10.1016/j.techfore.2023.122544

Trevor, A. (2022). *Metaverso 360 - La guida più completa su Metaverse e investimenti, web 3.0, NFT, DeFi, augemented reality (AR), cryptoassets, digital real estate e future networking*. Independently published.

Vemula, S. (2020). Leveraging VR/AR/MR and AI as Innovative Educational Practices for "iGeneration" Students. In Handbook of Research on Equity in Computer Science in P-16 Education (pp. 265-277). doi:10.4018/978-1-7998-4739-7.ch015

Vidal-Tomás, D. (2023). The illusion of the metaverse and meta-economy. *International Review of Financial Analysis*, *86*, 102560. doi:10.1016/j.irfa.2023.102560

Volvo. (2022). *The Volvoverse: Volvo Cars launches first car in the metaverse.* Volvo. https://www.volvocars.com/au/news/technology/The-Volvoverse/

Wanick, V., & Stallwood, J. (2022). *Brand storytelling, gamification, and social media marketing in the "Metaverse": a case study of The Ralph Lauren winter escape.*

Wong, L. W., Tan, G. W. H., Ooi, K. B., & Dwivedi, Y. K. (2023). Metaverse in hospitality and tourism: A critical reflection. *International Journal of Contemporary Hospitality Management.* doi:10.1108/IJCHM-05-2023-0586

Wu, C. H., & Liu, C. Y. (2023). Educational Applications of Non-Fungible Token (NFT). *Sustainability (Basel), 15*(1), 7. Advance online publication. doi:10.3390/su15010007

Xu, M., Ng, W. C., Lim, W. Y. B., Kang, J., Xiong, Z., Niyato, D., Yang, Q., Shen, X. S., & Miao, C. (2022). A Full Dive into Realizing the Edge-enabled Metaverse: Visions, Enabling Technologies, and Challenges. *IEEE Communications Surveys and Tutorials, 1.* doi:10.1109/COMST.2022.3221119

Yang, F. X., & Wang, Y. (2023). Rethinking Metaverse Tourism: A Taxonomy and an Agenda for Future Research. *Journal of Hospitality & Tourism Research (Washington, D.C.).* doi:10.1177/10963480231163509

Yaqoob, I., Salah, K., Jayaraman, R., & Omar, M. (2023). Metaverse applications in smart cities: Enabling technologies, opportunities, challenges, and future directions. *Internet of Things : Engineering Cyber Physical Human Systems, 23,* 100884. doi:10.1016/j.iot.2023.100884

Zainurin, M. Z. L., Masri, M. H., Besar, M. H. A., & Anshari, M. (2023). Towards an understanding of metaverse banking: A conceptual paper. *Journal of Financial Reporting and Accounting, 21*(1), 178–190. doi:10.1108/JFRA-12-2021-0487

Zyda, M. (2022). Let's rename everything "the Metaverse!". *Computer, 55*(3), 124–129. doi:10.1109/MC.2021.3130480

KEY TERMS AND DEFINITIONS

Augmented Reality (AR): Technology that covers digital content into the physical world, enhancing the user's perception of reality by adding virtual elements to their surroundings.

Decentralized Autonomous Organizations (DAOs): Operate without centralized control, governed by smart contracts and member decision-making for resource distribution.

Digital Identity: Representation of an individual or entity in the digital realm through avatars or online profiles, reflecting personal characteristics, preferences, and interactions.

Ethical Considerations: Reflecting on the societal impact of technological advancements ensures that digital innovations respect privacy, security, and human rights while considering moral implications.

Gamification: The process of adding game elements such as points, rewards, and challenges to non-game contexts to increase engagement and motivation.

Human-Computer Interaction (HCI): Studies the interaction between people and digital technologies, focusing on user interface design, usability, and user experience.

Interoperability: Ability of different systems or platforms to communicate, exchange data, and operate seamlessly together enabling users to move between virtual environments with ease.

Metaverse: A digital space where users can interact and engage with others through immersive technologies, such as virtual reality and augmented reality, overreaching physical boundaries.

Non-fungible tokens (NFTs): Unique digital assets stored on a blockchain representing ownership of digital or physical items and enabling secure verification of authenticity and ownership.

Virtual reality (VR): Immerses users in a simulated environment allowing them to interact with a computer-generated world as if it were real.

Chapter 2
Historical Context and Evolution of Metaverse

Meenu Sharma

https://orcid.org/0000-0003-0493-556X

The Assam Royal Global University, India

Arpee Saikia

The Assam Royal Global University, India

ABSTRACT

The use of the metaverse in various periods is explained, including its use in novels and movies, video games, social media, industries, businesses, and headsets. This chapter is divided in to five sections: section one provides the introduction, literature review and ancient concept of metaverse; section two explains the use of term metaverse and historical context and evolution of metaverse; section three is related with use of metaverse in different sectors/fields: movies, novels, gaming, education, industry, retail, architecture, medical care and social media; section four provides a insight into prolific ways in which the metaverse was used during the Covid-19 pandemic times with special reference to the financial sector; section five describe managerial or practical applications and future research directions for the use of metaverse.

METAVERSE: LITERATURE REVIEW AND ANCIENT CONCEPT OF METAVERSE

Introduction

The current technological world is going through monumental changes over the past few years. The year 2015 marked the beginning of the Industry 3.0 phase. This phase saw the advent of a massive proportion of data conversion into bytes being uploaded into the cloud servers around the world. Following this transformative stage was Industry 4.0 which witnessed the exponential rise of artificial intelligence or AI. The world was connected even better due to the billions of devices being added to the deluge of data. It was virtually impossible to handle such huge amount of data manually and therefore machine-

DOI: 10.4018/979-8-3693-2607-7.ch002

intervention was the need of the hour. The colossal amount of data needed to be handled to meet the demands of the big-tech world. The metaverse's enabling technologies have been developed over many years. Enterprise-focused metaverses has figure out how to accommodate digital twins that are more intricate and modular, enhancing design, testing, and expert collaboration. In the interim, the design, construction, and operation of buildings, transit networks, and smart cities are already being optimized with the use of digital twins and digital threads (Ritterbusch & Teichmann, 2023). Virginie Maillard, head of Siemens U.S. technology, has explained that these technologies will soon have a significant impact on how businesses operate in the simulation and digital twin spaces. There is still more room for advancement in other groundbreaking metaverse technologies like 5G connectivity, AI, machine learning, 3D engines, cloud, edge computing, and extended reality (Ball, 2022). The future is here, in many senses, according to PwC vice chair Emmanuelle Rivet "The metaverse is an evolution and convergence of technologies that businesses are currently using and experimenting with today."

Literature Review

Children with attention deficit hyperactivity disorder can benefit from using 3D virtual worlds to improve their language communication skills (LCS) (Lan, 2024). According to the study, children with ADHD significantly improved their LCS and learning behavior.

To reap the benefits of diversification, investors and portfolio managers ought to think about including NFTs into their S&P 500 or Bitcoin portfolios (BenMabrouk, 2024).

"Digital health" is described by the World Health Organization as using information and communication technology to enhance one's health. The use of these digital tools has increased significantly in recent years, which has significantly altered conventional healthcare paradigms (Joia Nuñeza, 2024).

The financial management pre-alarm model of neural network's random parameter selection and local extremum phenomena cause the forecast results to be highly erratic. In the standard BPNN, a genetic algorithm (GA) with ergodic properties is added. When it comes to forecasting the financial status of virtual currency in the online game Metaverse, the financial management model performs better (Li, 2024). This gives each particle ergodic properties, regulates the degree of particle aggregation, prevents the occurrence of local extremum, finds the global optimal value, and guarantees the model's pre-alarm outcomes.

The predominant pattern of media development in the modern era has long been the integration of media due to the ongoing advancements in science and technology. The metaverse is a new area for video game development from the standpoint of media integration (Chen, 2024). For the decentralized dynamic database of security cloud storage, it performs security certification using the blockchain's Myrtle tree optimization method. to guarantee the security of video game play within the meta-universe.

With Facebook's formal name change to Meta in October 2021, social networks and three-dimensional (3D) virtual worlds have adopted the metaverse as the new standard. Through the application of numerous relevant technologies, the metaverse seeks to provide consumers with 3D immersive and individualized experiences. How to secure users' digital material and data in the metaverse is a natural question, notwithstanding its popularity and advantages (Huynh-The T. T., 2024). The study demonstrated how blockchain affects major metaverse-enabling technologies such as digital twins, big data, artificial intelligence, multi-sensory and immersive applications, and the Internet of Things.

The idea that there is no difference between one's online and offline identities is the foundation of Generation Z society and the metaverse. Owing to advances in technology in deep learning-based high-precision recognition models and natural generation models, the Metaverse is being upgraded in several ways, including mobile-based always-on access and connectivity with reality through virtual money (Park S. M., 2022). The application of fundamental techniques is necessary for the realization of the Metaverse into three components: user interaction, implementation, and application. These components are hardware, software and contents.

Considering the opportunities that today's post-digital techno-cultures bring, Virtual Museum (VM) considers the processes and semantic models that it uses to realize its Metaverse (Maurizio Unali, 2024). Since the 1980s, when the multidisciplinary concept of virtual reality (VM) first emerged in response to the era's technical advances, it has experimented with a range of online and offline interaction modes as well as many conformative dimensions of digital space.

As an emerging platform for improving customer satisfaction experiences almost identical to those in physical businesses, marketing practitioners and academics are still interested in technological metaverse and NFTs (Olaleye, 2023). Through the lens of bibliometric analysis using R Bibliometrix, the effects of combining the metaverse and NFTs in marketing are investigated.

In the sphere of education, virtual reality techniques are employed because they have the potential to make learning more interesting, immersive, and enjoyable. Virtual reality has the potential to be a useful tool for raising student motivation for learning and has a good impact on the educational process. The learning process can be accelerated by combining standard teaching and learning methods with augmented reality and virtual reality (Kumar, 2024). The usage of virtual reality (VR) can improve student engagement and learning. In our highly digitalized world, virtual reality-based education has the power to totally change the manner that educational content is presented.

This qualitative study used systematic Literature review to lay down it's arguments and theories.

Ancient Concept of Metaverse

The concepts of Multiverse and metaverse have existed in several stories, tales and folklores which discusses about the idea of an alternate world. The concept of an alternate universe has found its presence in Hindu mythology, which depicts infinite universes. The whole idea and premises of parallel universes is a question to modern scientists but is quite natural to Indian traditions. During the epic battle of Kurukshetra between paternal cousins Pandavas and Kauravas, Lord Krishna had agreed to be an ally of the Pandavas.In one episode when the famous warrior Arjuna was contemplating his decisions and choices pertaining to war,Lord Krishna took his "Viswaroop" and showed Arjuna a scene of multiple cosmic creations and destructions.In his narration which is compiled in the form of Bhagwad Gita,he explains to Arjuna thatthere lies different universes in different parts of the former's body. He explains to his friend Arjuna that there aremany powerful creators or Brahmas and many more enormous universes than this universe, the existence of a hypothetical self-contained plane of existence, co-existing with each other thereby establishing the concept of parallel universes in the psyche of his friend (Jana, 2023).

In Hindu philosophy and texts, "Maya" refers to the illusion, temporary and destructible nature of the material world that humans live in. It can be considered as an earlier manifestation of the digital metaverse, where reality may be far from what human minds can imagine it to be. The ancient Indian texts talk about various "lokas" or realms.These realms were characterized by different features and residents. The residents reflected the essence of the realms namely Swarglog or heaven where the gods, demi gods and celestial beings resided,Naraklok where the demons, or rakshases existed and finally the Earthly realm i.e the dhartilok where the mortals resided.The mythology also mentions about a prominent figure,Naradmuni who had the power of travelling to all the loks or realms was a "Realm traveller". The fact that there are realms beyond what the human eyes can see was established way before modern scientific brains proposed the same.In Hinduism, the Vedas are regarded as the oldest sacred texts.These texts provide insight into different areas including rituals, medicine, science music to name only a few areas. References to a concept resembling the modern day metaverse is found in both the Vedas and the Puranas.In the Vedas, Akasha is depicted as a realm where the human mind connects with universal consciousness, providing a glimpse into infinite dimensions of existence. Akashais often translated as "ether," "space," or "sky.". Akasha is described as a space where consciousness surpasses the limitations of time and matter. The mind is limitless and goes beyond any boundary. This concept reflects the idea of an alternative, virtual space where individuals can interact, coexist, and explore without physical constraints. 'Maya' is another prominent word which features in the ancient Hindu texts.The idea of "yugas"or cycles of time or epochs, each with a reincarnation of Lord Vishnu could be metaphorical or an indication for the evolution of digital realities. Like how the world transitions through different yugas, the digital realm has evolved through various stages or timelines. Rooted in ancient philosophy spanning across nations and modern technology, the metaverse is an amalgamation of ancient wisdom and modern-day innovation. Metaverse blurs the lines between the past and future and provides unimaginable opportunities for the human minds to imagine and explore.

The year 1956 witnessed the infamous rivalry between the United States of America and the Union of Soviet Socialist Republics. The year saw an American scientist Morton Heilig transforming his Brooklyn motorcycle ride into a shared experience through the Sensorama, the first Virtual Reality machine which helped the audience to feel what he felt while riding. This lead to an immersive experience characterized by a 3D video with surrounding sounds, scents, and a vibrating chair recreating the real life bike riding experience.

METAVERSE: HISTORICAL CONTEXT AND EVOLUTION

Use of Term Metaverse

The term metaverse was phrased by Neal Stephenson in the year 1992 in his seminal work *Snow Crash*. In his book he describes a 3D virtual collective shared space created by converging virtually enhanced digital and physical reality. Another literary work that has inspired the creation of the metaverse is Ernest Cline's Ready Player One which was published in 2011 and was so successful that renowned director Steven Spielberg adapted it into a blockbuster Hollywood film in 2018. In 2017, a digital space Decentraland enabled anyone to own an estate on the blockchain and, as such, to start a new virtual business and earn continuously. The Metaverse is an evolution of the internet into an immersive augmented reality experience that integrates all societal activities, from work to sleep to entertainment, into a unified virtual world. The blockchain technology brings Web 3.0 and Metaverse on to a similar platform. People can experience the large virtual space in an organic way because of advancements made in virtual and augmented reality technology.AI is widely used in the metaverse. AI tracking systems have the capability of following and copying human motions and expressions, they can enhance the naturalness and realism of our avatars. Since all works are protected by copyright and are difficult to tamper with, blockchain offers a safe platform for artists in the metaverse. The gaming world is not new to the world of Metaverse, Numiverse, the first anime metaverse on the Venom blockchain has come into existence which provides an "Utopian Escape" to its users (Robertson, 2021).

Historical Context and Evolution of Metaverse

During the nineteenth century in 1838, Sir Charles Wheatstone, a physicist, presented the idea of "binocular vision," which required producing a single three-dimensional view. This was the first instance of virtual reality. The results of this early study led to the creation of stereoscopes, which employ the same technology as modern virtual reality headsets: the illusion of depth to produce an image.

American science fiction author Stanley Weinbaum introduced readers to the idea of virtual reality with Pygmalion's Spectacles, which was first published in 1935. The protagonist of the novel totally immerses himself in a made-up world, creating the illusion that it is real, by donning goggles that mimic every sense experienced by a human. The term "virtual reality," also known as "la réalité virtuelle," was used in 1938. Antoine Artaud, a French writer and poet, is frequently cited as its creator. In his collection of writings, The Theater and its Double, he talked about how theaters might stage people, things, and images to create other worlds.

In 1962, American director Morton Heilig created a device that gave users the impression that they were riding a motorcycle in a different place. The Sensorama was a gadget that combined effects including a moving seat, fragrances, and 3D screens to immerse its users in a virtual environment. Despite never making it past the prototype stage, the machine showed that it was possible to make it harder to distinguish between truth and illusion. Director Morton Heilig of the United States created the Sensorama system, which uses a 3D video, a vibrating chair, a fan, and fragrances to replicate the feeling of riding a motorcycle throughout Midtown Manhattan. John Licata, chief innovation foresight strategist and vice president of SAP New Venture Technologies Future Hub, stated that "the Sensorama was by far the ultimate advancement that laid the groundwork for what the immersive virtual environment could become."

The Aspen Movie Map, created in the 1970s by the Massachusetts Institute of Technology, lets visitors explore Aspen, Colorado, through computer-generated imagery. This was the first time they had used virtual reality to transport clients to a different area. Multi-User Dungeon1, released in 1978, was the first multiplayer virtual environment to be played in real time. Jaron Lanier and Thomas G. Zimmerman, pioneers in virtual reality, founded VPL Research, Inc. in 1984. They were among the first to build and market virtual reality headsets and data gloves, also known as wired gloves. It provides situations of how virtual reality can be applied in business and creative settings."While there's a host of prior thinking and experiments (including a great 1965 paper by Ivan Sutherland imagining an 'Ultimate Display' that recognizably describes this sci-fi staple), Jaron Lanier's VPL Research started to commercialize goggles and gloves to facilitate augmented reality and virtual reality interactions," as stated by Alex Weishaupl, managing director of Protiviti Digital

The first draft of the World Wide Web was written in 1989 by British computer scientist Tim Berners-Lee when he was working at CERN. Information could be transferred globally between universities and other institutions back when the web was initially invented. This was a major improvement over earlier text-based sharing platforms like Gopher and proprietary bulletin board systems. The public was able to access a client and server for a network of linked web pages with text, images, and audio.

SEGA debuted popular virtual reality arcade devices in the early 1990s, such as the SEGA Virtual Reality-1 motion simulator, which was put in many arcades. The term "metaverse" was initially used in

1992 in Neal Stephenson's fantasy novel Snow Crash. The American science fiction author imagined a dystopian future society in which people may utilize computer avatars to travel to a better reality. The author used the phrase to describe a virtual environment where each person has an avatar, or a digital representation of their real identity. The name was derived from combining the words "meta" and "universe".

As people purchase, construct, and refurbish virtual real estate, the alternate reality grows from its initial 65,536 km road around a man-made planet. In this perspective, all people are connected to a single world. Avatars are controlled by the individual and can range from highly customized beautiful works of art to generic Walmart products referred to as "Clints" and "Brandys."

If the term has been around for many years, why did it suddenly gain popularity in 2021, primary causes are: a few metaverse-related technologies, like HTC's VR headsets, have developed over time, a growing number of individuals are starting to understand the idea of blockchain and Blockchain creates and stores enormous amounts of difficult-to-tamper-with transaction data using cryptography and other technology. The growth of the metaverse is propelled by blockchain due to "unhackability" and "immutability."

Platform security is essential in virtual environments since hacker assaults and data leaks happen often. The metaverse's evolution has accelerated due to the COVID-19 pandemic. The epidemic has drastically altered people's lives, requiring most of them to work remotely. This has led to a huge rise in the need for virtual world connection. The proof-of-work (PoW) concept was developed in 1993 by computer scientists Moni Naor and Cynthia Dwork to stop service abuses such as network spam and denial-of-service assaults. To use the software, users must complete a difficult but easily verifiable cryptography task. Afterward, the fundamental ideas are codified and serve as the foundation for Bitcoin.

Renowned video game developer Richard Garriott originally used the term in 1997 while working on Ultima Online, an online role-playing game that was released a year later and is widely regarded as the first Massively Multiplayer Online game.

The practice of superimposing graphics on top of real-world views was quickly copied by other sports broadcasters after Sportsvision showed the first National Football League game live in 1998, complete with a yellow yard marker.

Five years before Apple released its first iPhone, in 2002, HTC created the first smartphone in history using the Microsoft operating system. But in the last few years, it has transformed into a metaverse business, launching the first virtual reality glasses, HTC VIVE, in 2016.

Second Life is a multimedia platform that Linden Lab launched in 2003 and marked the beginning of the twenty-first century. Users can connect to shared virtual spaces with their computers and explore, interact, and create there—even if it's not immersive because there are no goggles or gloves required. More than just a game, Second Life is an online community where everyone may create a new online persona. Introduced by Linden Lab, Second Life is a shared 3D virtual world where users may build things, explore, interact with others, and exchange virtual goods. Almost 70 million Second Life accounts are active at the moment. What a shared virtual world should seem like was established by the virtual space.

The year 2006 saw the launch of the Roblox gaming platform by Roblox Corporation, which lets users play a variety of multiplayer games. Users can also create their own games to play and share with others. In addition to offering free gameplay, Roblox has an in-game store where users can purchase virtual cash called Robux. Google introduced Street View in 2007 as an extension to its Maps product. Users can turn a map into a realistic image of the real world with the aid of Street View. A street can be viewed by anyone in real time on a computer or mobile device.

The first widely used decentralized blockchain and cryptocurrency, Bitcoin, was originally made public by Satoshi Nakamoto in 2008. He subsequently mined the first Bitcoin in 2009. Under the pseudonym Satoshi Nakamoto, the first public blockchain and Bitcoin were established via a proof-of-work technique. It eventually ascended to the top of the bitcoin value list, demonstrating that decentralized ledgers can secure volume transactions. Excessive speculation fuels interest in a range of alternative cryptocurrencies and in novel approaches to establishing decentralized markets that are not dominated by one party. The Oculus Rift virtual reality headset prototype was developed in 2010 by 18-year-old inventor and entrepreneur Palmer Luckey. The cutting-edge headset offers a 90-degree field of vision and leverages computer processing power to entice people to experience virtual reality (Rosenblum & Cross, 1997).

The Gacha model for video games is presented. By using a combination of skill and luck, players can earn currency and in-game rewards by playing toy vending machines or gachas.

Ready Player One, written by Ernest Cline, was published in 2011. It offered us yet another look at a fully realized world where we may escape from reality. Following the novel's immediate popularity, director Steven Spielberg turned it into a movie in 2018. The shared virtual environment idea became well-known after Steven Spielberg's 2018 film adaption.

In 2012, entrepreneur Palmer Luckey launched Oculus on Kickstarter, the first low-cost VR headgear with hardware that lets users interact with a 3D virtual environment for work, play, and leisure. Facebook purchased Oculus in 2014, two years later, in an effort to make the technology available to more people. Israeli entrepreneur Yoni Assia introduced Colored Coins in 2012 with a blog post titled "Bitcoin 2. X (aka Colored Bitcoin) - initial specs." This creates the framework for a brand-new method of creating, purchasing, selling, and owning assets on top of a public blockchain.

In 2014, Kevin McCoy and Anil Dash created Quantum, the first non-fungible token (NFT) ever created. It included a picture of an octagon with pixels on it. It was minted on the Namecoin blockchain and was referred to as "monetized graphics" rather than an NFT. Facebook paid $2 billion to acquire Oculus Virtual Reality in 2014. The first Cardboard gadget and Google's augmented reality glasses were released in 2014, making it a significant year for XR. In the same year, Samsung and Sony each released their own virtual reality headsets. Cardboard is a low-cost cardboard virtual reality viewer designed by Google for cellphones. The first non-fungible token was created by American internet entrepreneur Anil Dash and artist Kevin McCoy. It is a unique virtual asset that is protected by encryption. This offers chances for virtual creative experiments, concert tickets, and novel play-to-earn experiences. Digital engineering company Virtusa's executive vice-president and head of technology, Frank Palermo, said, "The fast growth and general acceptance of the paradigm was a critical milestone for the metaverse."

The idea of Ethereum was first proposed by Vitalik Buterin in a blog post titled Ethereum: The Ultimate Smart Contract and Decentralized Application Platform, which was published in 2013.

Then in 2015, Ethereum, a decentralized computer platform, was introduced. With Ethereum, developers can use smart contracts to experiment with their own code to construct DApps. Ethereum is introduced by English computer scientist Gavin Wood and Canadian programmer Vitalik Buterin. It has characteristics that allow users to create decentralized applications on a blockchain. "Ethereum introduced a practical take on smart contracts, which is the foundation for offerings like NFTs and the ability to 'own' assets in a distributed environment," Weishaupt stated.

Back in 2015, during the height of the social media boom on the internet and as the world began to become aware of decentralized technology, the idea for the first metaverse was conceived.

Decentralized autonomous organizations and Pokémon GO both made their debuts in 2016. The concept behind the Ethereum launch of the first Decentralized autonomous organizations, was that any member could be a part of the organization's governing body. Pokémon GO, an augmented reality game that links to a 3D map of the real world, is one of the most played smartphone games ever. It was one of the most widely used and lucrative smartphone apps globally by the end of the year, having been downloaded over 500 million times (Needleman, 2021).

With the advent of Microsoft's HoloLens headsets in 2016, mixed reality which combines virtual and augmented reality became widely accessible. via HoloLens, we can create a holographic picture in front of us that we can then place in the real world and control via augmented reality. In 2016, players of Pokémon GO, an augmented reality game, raced into their neighborhoods all over the world in an attempt to catch Pokémon. The world is first introduced to augmented reality games through Pokémon GO. Players locate, seize, and engage in combat with virtual animals linked to real-world locales using their phones.

In 2016, Based on the Ethereum blockchain, the DAO became the first decentralized autonomous organization to solicit venture capital money. Within one month of its launch, hackers embezzle a third of company funds. This destroys the business, but the concept generates new ways to jointly acquire assets and manage businesses.

IKEA made a metaverse debut in 2017 with their Place App, which lets people choose furniture and visualize how it might look in the home or place of business.

In 2018 A video game that can be played for money Axie Infinity, developed by the Vietnamese company Sky Mavis, expands the application of NFTs linked to the Ethereum network. It peaked in 2021 with over 2.7 million users, having the highest cumulative value of any play-to-earn game. Hackers had pilfered about $600 million in 2022.

In 2019, with over 250 million active players, Epic Games' Fortnite surpassed all previous records for popularity as a shared virtual environment. In order to accommodate additional virtual games and experiences, the company improves the platform. In 2020, rapper Travis Scott emceed a webcast event that attracted more than 12 million people. Subsequently, Epic integrates the platform with popular enterprise tools like geographic information systems, design, and infrastructure. In 2020, Lidar (Light Detection and Ranging) was added to the iPhone and iPad lineup, opening the door for future mixed-reality headsets and facilitating enhanced depth sensing for better images and augmented reality (Boletsis, 2017).

The year 2021 saw Facebook change its name to Meta, which solidified the metaverse's reputation as a real place rather than just a sci-fi idea. Since then, the business has spent billions of dollars creating and acquiring resources linked to the metaverse, including software, headsets for augmented and virtual reality, and metaverse content. Businesses are being courted by Microsoft "Mesh" and Facebook (Meta) Worlds to employ virtual reality (VR) and meetings for workshops, conferences, and other purposes (Brown, 2021).

Two other companies have released highly portable virtual reality headsets (HTC's Vive Flow) and smart glasses (Ray-Ban Stories).

A joint partnership between NVIDIA and Siemens to create the Industrial Metaverse was announced in 2022. The collaboration leverages Siemens' well-known proficiency in industrial automation and software, infrastructure, building technology, and transportation, along with NVIDIA's leadership in accelerated graphics and Artificial Intelligence. Video games played online already have access to metaverse technologies. Though historical claims of metaverse development started soon after the term was coined, Second Life, a virtual world platform that launched in 2003 and integrated many elements of social media into a persistent three-dimensional world with the user represented as an avatar, is frequently referred to as the first metaverse. Among the first conceptions were Active Worlds and The Palace. Among the well-known games included in the metaverse include Roblox, the game creation platform, Fortnite, World of Warcraft, Minecraft, Habbo Hotel, and Virtual Reality Chat. Since then, Roblox has heavily utilized the term in its marketing. In a January 2022 interview with Wired, Second Life developer Philip Rosedale defined metaverses as a three-dimensional Internet populated by real people.

The evolution of the metaverse and the possibilities for virtual and augmented reality events are demonstrated by the upcoming "Grand Slamming" of the Australian Open tennis tournament in the metaverse, which took place in June 2022 and was hosted by Decentraland.

USE OF METAVERSE IN DIFFERENT SECTORS/FIELDS

Metaverse in Movies and Novels

The idea of the Metaverse has gained a lot of traction in literature, video games, and film. We witness a fully developed metaverse where people can explore new realms and live out their fantasies in movies like Tron Legacy and Ready Player One. Novelists such as Neal Stephenson and Ernest Cline have written a great deal about the Metaverse. Novels: "Neuromancer" (1984) by William Gibson; "Snow Crash" (1992) by Neal Stephenson; "Altered Carbon" (2002) by Richard K. Morgan; "Ready Player One" (2011) by Ernest Cline; and "A Frayed New World" (2021) by Damini Rana. Films include The Wachowski Brothers' 1999 film "The Matrix," Steven Lisberger's 1982 film "Tron," David Cronenberg's 1999 film "eXistenZ," Josef Rusnak's 1999 film "The Thirteenth Floor," Steven Spielberg's 2018 film "Ready Player One," and Shawn Levy's 2021 film "Free Guy."

In addition to having the ability to personalize our avatar and digital assets, we may imagine ourselves to be "in" a virtual world and sense the presence of others. The 2009 film "Avatar" features a representation of the metaverse. Jake, the main character in the film, is paralyzed, but upon arriving in Pandora, he transforms into a Na'vi and gains the ability to walk and run. But he still has his awareness, which is a hybrid of reality (his consciousness) and virtuality (Na'vi's body).

Metaverse in Gaming

For many years, games have made substantial use of Augmented Reality/Virtual Reality and metaverse elements. With the development of this technology, game developers will be able to produce visually stunning games that enhance player interaction with their surroundings. To give customers the impression that they are in a real-world setting, the images and visuals will only get better. It is impossible to overlook this market's anticipated expansion. The global market for metaverse gaming is predicted to grow to a value of over $660 billion. The comparison between the metaverse and a video game has been made by some. That might be the case (Rajan, et al., 2018).

We see the metaverse in gaming as a collection of social and personal identities. A single game or platform is now frequently referred to by businesses as a "Metaverse." By this concept, everything can be considered a metaverse, including internet games and VR music concerts. In summary, although metaverses are not merely games, games can be thought of as part of them.

A gaming firm called Roblox was founded on the idea of the metaverse. Users of the platform can play other people's games in addition to creating their own using the Roblox Studio engine. Additionally, trading on the platform is possible using the virtual currency Robux. In March 2021, Roblox effectively went public in the US.

Metaverse technology has the potential to increase the diversity and intrigue of sports. In addition, Meta's "Virtual Gym" opened, enabling customers to work out at home and maintain their fitness levels without having to purchase flywheels or treadmills. Additionally, Mark Zuckerberg posted a video of him fencing in the metaverse alongside Olympic gold medalist Lee Kiefer.

Metaverse in Education

The education system has been utilizing the aid of the metaverse and Augmented Reality/Virtual Reality. Additionally, it would improve their learning outcomes by maintaining students' focus on the material they are studying. Virtual reality and augmented reality are already being used in education because of resources like Google Arts & Cultures.

The application of metaverse in education is one of the key areas. Creating a 3D interactive learning environment, the gaming business Roblox has also entered the education sector, hoping to serve over 100 million students by 2030. Education has become more engaging and dynamic with the use of the metaverse. For instance, students studying ancient Egyptian civilization used to be limited to viewing the picture of the pyramids in their history textbooks (Pellas, Mystakidis, & Kazanidis, 2021).

Students can discover the culture of ancient Egypt by going straight into the pyramid and even getting a virtual reality look at the mummy because of the metaverse. Furthermore, with the Metaverse platform, students can collaborate to build rockets and tour space stations and experiences that are not possible with books.

Students' involvement with a variety of courses can be improved by creating immersive educational experiences with the help of the metaverse. Making concepts tangible in the virtual world is especially helpful for subjects like anatomy and physics, which are difficult to visualize. It also offers a perfect setting for role-playing, which improves the efficacy of training activities. As stated by Aji Abraham of Armia Systems Inc. The metaverse is an immersive environment designed for one-to-one or one-to-many instruction using interactive 3D models, remote video conferencing, and other technologies. According to Sean Barker, cloud EQ Academic simulations in colleges are one real-world use for the metaverse. This is an option for students, particularly in hybrid or virtual learning environments, to obtain "hands-on experience" without having to leave the classroom. Before ever working on their first deal, novice analysts may, for instance, go through an M&A process and comprehend all the key processes according to Deal Room's Kison Patel

Metaverse in Industry

Using the industrial metaverse, digital twins of actual physical infrastructure and products are created. Workers can use these digital twins to fuel risk-free trial and error experiments, identify issues before they arise. Metaverse facilitate early-level Product Development. It enables the design team to quickly change course and make pertinent and appropriate design decisions. For industries, using the metaverse to develop products at an early stage would be a profitable "low-hanging fruit" use case, according to Bosch Global Software Technologies Pvt Ltd., Srinivasulu Nasam.

Metaverse and Property: The real estate market is quite profitable, and this also applies to the virtual world. This refers to the selling of digital land in a virtual environment. As an illustration, the primary asset of the decentralized Ethereum blockchain network is Decentraland Island. Plots of land are exchangeable for NFTs. 34,356 lots of land, with a combined market value of over $30 million at the time, were up for bid at Decentraland's inaugural auction held in late 2017. Microsoft concentrates on its core competencies—services associated with "work." For remote work and virtual meetings, it offer a more engaging and customized experiece (Park, 2022).

In addition to participating in online meetings, exchanging data and documents, and holding lengthy lectures, we may host huge seminars on the Mesh for Microsoft Teams space. Its most notable feature is the ability to build customized avatars—a digital representation of yourself that can even imitate your motions and facial expressions. Instruction and Upkeep for Industrial Systems Within the industrial sector, the metaverse presents opportunities to increase efficiency. The display and monitoring of vital indicators, as well as practical instruction, are made simpler by the visual depiction of complicated systems.

Metaverse in Retail

Brands might be promoted through the metaverse in ways that have never been seen before. Customers will be able to interact with potential customers more deeply and receive a higher response rate thanks to these technologies. Virtual reality experience booths are another tool that shops may employ. This is essential to raise customer response rates, which can lead to increased revenue.

Ikea is one of the many outstanding examples. The Ikea Place App allows users to virtually "position" furniture in their own spaces. The item is automatically resized by the software to fit the customer's room's proportions. Metaverse provides Virtual Marketplace. Virtual Reality Chat is a massively multiplayer virtual reality game in which users can engage and converse with one another via virtual characters.

Nike and other brands from all areas of life might decide to join the Virtual Reality and Non-Fungible Token industry. Maybe in the future, Nike's virtual world will show us sparks flying between these two ideas. Online Shops Virtual business, or "v-commerce," is one real-world use for the metaverse. Companies may design dynamic, three-dimensional virtual storefronts that provide customers with a distinctive and captivating shopping experience. Before making a purchase, customers can engage with goods or services in a lifelike digital setting, giving merchants useful data and possibly increasing consumer happiness, according to Hello Data AI's Marc Rutzen. It facilitate in linking Brands and Consumers. There is a brand issue with the metaverse. When people hear the term "metaverse," many immediately think of virtual reality or the virtual world. However, the theories underlying the metaverse are far more expansive, opening up new avenues for connecting not just people but also brands and consumers. Metaverse promotes Customized Internet Purchasing means prefer to study things before buy them, whether it's a couch or an item of apparel. The metaverse facilitates the customization of the customer's experience, making it both realistic and virtual. Retailers can save money and time by using it to manage a physical shop and process returns. Working remotely is one scenario where the metaverse is put to use. This combines the freedom of working remotely with in-person office companionship, according to EZ Cloud's Andrew Blackman

Metaverse in Architecture

Architects can visualize their work in a 3D environment by using AR/VR and the metaverse. This would entail making a virtual environment and populating it with structures, vegetation, and other natural features. Using this technology, they can build objects and interact with the real environment. It would also make it easier to show clients what they have made or will build. Virtual reality is used by New York-based Ennead Architects to help clients visualize data and space in three dimensions.

Metaverse in Medical Care

Physicians can develop 3D clinical devices using Augmented Reality/Virtual Reality and the metaverse. They can enhance a patient's experience by engagingly using this technology. After that, they can keep an eye on a patient's vital signs virtually. They can also give patients apps to track their blood pressure, weight, and other parameters and make tests more user-friendly. The metaverse can bring about several significant changes in the field of medicine. Here are a few illustrations. Remote health care: When people were unwell in the past, they visited the hospital or clinic to see a doctor.

Phone conversations or video chats might be utilized to finish the consultation for certain straight-forward illnesses. Patient can wear virtual reality equipment and attend the doctor's office, for instance, if patients are in other place but the finest specialist for patients' ailment is in the other place. Local medical institutions offer scans and examinations, real-time data transmission to the doctor allows the other doctor to provide patient with remote consultation assistance. Managing personal health information and medical records is a particularly safe usage for this capability. Creating a "virtual twin" of any item, procedure, or system is referred to as a digital twin (Huynh-The, 2023). When used in the context of metaverse medicine, it entails creating a virtual patient duplicate in order to assess the patient's reaction to various drugs following surgery, recuperation, etc. Safer for the actual patient is the Media and the Social media sector can benefit from the creation of virtual worlds through the metaverse.

Metaverse in Social Media

Instant Messaging Virtual Universe, an online social network game that was developed in 2004 and allows users to create 3D avatars and communicate with one another, has become more and more well-known in the social media space. Additionally, one of the largest social media companies globally, Facebook, changed its name to Meta in 2021, a sign of the direction social networks are taking. Meta is the tech company most committed to building the metaverse. The fundamental idea of Facebook is "connections between people." These days, people communicate with family and friends on Facebook through posting and like content, messaging via Messenger, participating in live broadcasts, and other primarily text-based, passive activities. "Connections between people" is still at the center of Facebook's metaverse, but the environment is now three dimensions, allowing for more varied and realistic interaction.

Anyone can play cards, have conversations, and have coffee in this area as if the others were actually at their side. Anyone can use their phone to make video calls to their family.

USE OF METAVERSE IN COVID-19 PERIOD AND IN FINANCIAL SECTOR

Metaverse and COVID-19

COVID-19 pandemic's effects on remote work can be lessened more effectively in the metaverse. Colleagues who work remotely communicate with each other via conference calls, messaging apps, or emails. While it reduces commute time, there is less social interaction and the employer cannot monitor the status of the workers. Because of this, several managers requested that staff members come back to work following the pandemic.

Facebook launched a service dubbed "Workrooms" in August 2021, which enables remote work using virtual reality technologies. Colleagues can meet, communicate, by creating virtual offices using Facebook Workrooms anywhere, even on beaches and in the mountains. Businesses will benefit from lower office rental costs and reduced commute times as a result, which will boost productivity.

Metaverse and Non-Fungible Token

The term "fungible tokens" describes tokens with a fixed value that are divisible. All digital crypto-currencies are fungible tokens, including Ether (ETH) and Bitcoin (BTC). Digital crypto-currencies also come in the form of "non-fungible tokens," which are distinct, non-divisible, and irreplaceable tokens. Any digital artwork, including images, audio files, videos, etc., can serve as examples. In the past, it was simple to copy these digital data, but now NFTs allow ownership. It is also extremely hard to duplicate. It can therefore be auctioned off like actual artwork, regardless of whether it is a short film, meme, or article. The digital artist Beeple sold his artwork for $69 million in a Non-Fungible Token auction in 2021. The same year, an Iranian cryptocurrency entrepreneur purchased Jack Dorsey's first-ever tweet, which was turned into an Non-Fungible Token and sold for $2.9 million. This Non-Fungible Token was to be sold by the business owner in April 2022. His first bid was $48 million, but he only placed a winning bid of $280 in the end. Non-Fungible Tokens are blockchain-based ownership certificates that hold the key to the virtual world's economy. An unchanging, duplicable, and unbreakable encryption key safeguards each Non-Fungible Token, enabling it to validate a person's digital assets and virtual identity, a crucial function for the metaverse.

MANAGERIAL OR PRACTICAL APPLICATIONS OF METAVERSE AND FUTURE RESEARCH DIRECTIONS

Managerial or Practical Applications of Metaverse

The metaverse can be used practically for online instruction and training. Many companies are searching for ways to provide remote training to their staff as remote work becomes more common. Training can be given in a novel method that is immersive, interactive, and engaging thanks to the metaverse. Virtual conferences and gatherings are among the most useful uses for the metaverse. The pandemic has made many events virtual, but the metaverse provides a special means of bringing people together virtually. Product demonstrations and virtual showrooms can also be made with the metaverse. A vehicle manufacturer might, for instance, design a virtual showroom where clients can view and test drive their newest models in a lifelike three-dimensional setting.

Many companies are looking for ways to train their staff remotely as remote work becomes more common. A novel approach to providing immersive, interactive, and interesting instruction is through the metaverse. Creating virtual homes that may be rented or sold to anyone worldwide is made possible by the metaverse in a distinctive fashion. Virtual marketing and advertising includes the metaverse. Virtual advertising can be a fresh approach to get customers' attention in light of the rise of ad blockers and the growing difficulties of reaching audiences through traditional media. Businesses can design immersive, interactive ads in the metaverse that let customers interact with their brand in a special way. The metaverse presents a novel approach to providing healthcare services in a virtual setting, especially with the advent of telemedicine.

Future Research Directions

The Metaverse may eventually offer incredibly lifelike virtual worlds that appeal to all of our senses, including sight, sound, touch, taste, and smell. Virtual tourism and training simulations, in addition to gaming and entertainment, would be revolutionized by this immersive experience. The Metaverse is expected to rely even more heavily on blockchain technology. Decentralized ledgers are perfect for handling digital assets, virtual property, and in-game money because they provide unmatched security and transparency. Anticipate a growing convergence of blockchain technology and the Metaverse, allowing users to transact in and really own digital assets within virtual environments, ranging from virtual real estate to uncommon rarities.

The future Metaverse will be significantly shaped by artificial intelligence. Virtual experiences will be customized to each user's preferences and requirements thanks to AI-driven customisation. AI is going to transform the Metaverse into a highly personalized environment, whether it be through content curation, learning material adaptation, or the creation of innovative gaming challenges. The impact of the Metaverse will go beyond work and entertainment to include additional real-world uses. The Metaverse will be a vital tool for teaching, testing, and experiencing real-world events in a secure and regulated digital environment. Applications ranging from urban planning and design to healthcare simulations and disaster preparedness drills will rely on it. The Metaverse will unavoidably run across moral and legal issues as it develops.

The protection of virtual identities, digital ownership rights, and data privacy will all become more important issues. Ensuring the responsible and ethical development of the Metaverse will need policymakers, corporations, and users to adeptly manage these intricate concerns.

CONCLUSION

Corporate world has been experiencing a huge rise in the use of AR/VR and the metaverse. The metaverse will give businesses a means of customer communication that will significantly improve workers' productivity and management process. A concept rooted in ancient texts and books of religion spanning across various nations and centuries, metaverse has transformed into an indispensable part of modern day's technological advancements. With the potential to completely change how we interact with technology and the virtual world, metaverse is positioned at a turning point in our digital history. It is the result of years of technical progress, combining social connectivity, blockchain, artificial intelligence, and augmented and virtual reality into a seamless digital fabric. It is impossible to overestimate the importance of the Metaverse since it signifies a radical change in how we view, engage with, and use the digital world. Services in the metaverse provide an immersive, networked, and interactive environment where the lines between the real and virtual worlds are blurred. People can go across a variety of virtual environments there, mingle, work, learn, and amuse themselves in ways that were previously only possible in science fiction. There is no denying the advantages, which range from better digital experiences to fresh business prospects and better healthcare. It is very important to tread very carefully while navigating the world of technology consumption. Integrating metaverse into the very fabric and essence of how humans function, one must be conscious while using Artificial Intelligence (AI) in any form. It becomes very easy to depend on modern technology like metaverse, however, we need to make a conscious decision as to what extent the lines between the virtual and real world can be blurred. Hence, it is important to go cautiously, addressing privacy, ethical, and legal issues as one moves ahead.

Funding

This research received no external funding.

Conflicts of Interest

The author declares no conflict of interest.

REFERENCES

Ball, M. (2022). *The Metaverse: And How it Will Revolutionize Everything*. Liveright Publishing. doi:10.15358/9783800669400

BenMabrouk, H. S., Sassi, S., Soltane, F., & Abid, I. (2024). Connectedness and portfolio hedging between NFTs segments, American stocks and cryptocurrencies Nexus. *International Review of Financial Analysis*, *91*, 102959. doi:10.1016/j.irfa.2023.102959

Boletsis, C. (2017). The New Era of Virtual Reality Locomotion: A Systematic Literature Review of Techniques and a Proposed Typology. *Multimodal Technologies and Interaction*, *1*(4), 24. doi:10.3390/mti1040024

Brown, D. (2021). "What is the 'metaverse'? Facebook says it's the future of the Internet. *The Washington Post*.

Chen, N. C. (2024). Analysis on the Development of the Meta Universe to the Generation of Electronic Games from the Perspective of Media Convergence. *Computer-Aided Design and Applications*.

Huynh-The, T. G., Gadekallu, T. R., Wang, W., Yenduri, G., Ranaweera, P., Pham, Q.-V., da Costa, D. B., & Liyanage, M. (2023). Blockchain for the metaverse: A Review. *Future Generation Computer Systems*, *143*, 401–419. doi:10.1016/j.future.2023.02.008

Huynh-The, T. T. (2024). Blockchain for the metaverse: A Review. *Future Generation Computer Systems*.

Jana, K. (2023, June 17). Metatext and metaverse. *The Telegraph Online*.

Joia Nuñeza, L. K. (2024). The metaverse in the world of health: The present future. Challenges and opportunities. *Archivos Argentinos de Pediatria*. PMID:37171469

Kumar, M. (2024). Virtual Reality in Education: Analyzing the Literature and Bibliometric State of Knowledge. In Transforming Education with Virtual Reality (pp. 379-402). Wiley Online Library.

Lan, Y. J. (2024). 3D immersive scaffolding game for enhancing Mandarin learning in children with ADHD. *Journal of Educational Technology & Society*.

Li, J. J. (2024). Virtual Currency and Smart Financial Management in Immersive Online Games in the Metaverse Environment. *Computer-Aided Design and Applications*.

Maurizio Unali, G. C. (2024). Towards a Virtual Museum of Ephemeral Architecture: Methods, Techniques and Semantic Models for a Post-digital Metaverse. In M. R. Andrea Giordano, Beyond Digital Representation. Springer Nature Switzerland.

Needleman, S. E. (2021). The Amazing Things You'll Do in the 'Metaverse' and What It Will Take to Get There. *The Wall Street Journal*.

Olaleye, S. (2023). The Bibliometric Commingling of Metaverse and Non-fungible Tokens in Marketing. In J. R. Reis, Marketing and Smart Technologies. Springer Nature Singapore.

Park, S. M., & Kim, Y.-G. (2022). A Metaverse: Taxonomy, Components, Applications, and Open Challenges. *IEEE Access : Practical Innovations, Open Solutions*, *10*, 4209–4251. doi:10.1109/ACCESS.2021.3140175

Park, S. M., & Kim, Y.-G. (2022). A Metaverse: Taxonomy, Components, Applications, and Open Challenges. *IEEE Access : Practical Innovations, Open Solutions*, *10*, 4209–4251. doi:10.1109/ACCESS.2021.3140175

Pellas, N., Mystakidis, S., & Kazanidis, I. (2021). Immersive Virtual Reality in K-12 and Higher Education: A systematic review of the last decade scientific literature. *Virtual Reality (Waltham Cross)*, *25*(3), 835–861. doi:10.1007/s10055-020-00489-9

Rajan, A., Nassiri, N., Akre, V., Ravikumar, R., Nabeel, A., Buti, M., et al. (2018). *Virtual Reality Gaming Addiction*. Fifth HCT Information Technology Trends (ITT).

Rosenblum, L., & Cross, R. (1997). Challenges in Virtual Reality. In *In Visualization and Modelling*. Academic Press.

Chapter 3

Exploring the Factors Impacting the Intention to Use Metaverse in the Manufacturing Industry Through the Lens of Unified Technology Acceptance Theory

Mohammad Imtiaz Hossain
iD https://orcid.org/0000-0002-9637-3201
Multimedia University, Malaysia

Tanima Pal
BRAC University, Bangladesh

Yasmin Jamadar
BRAC University, Bangladesh

Md. Tariqul Islam
iD https://orcid.org/0000-0002-7367-2989
Taylor's University, Malaysia

Md. Kausar Alam
iD https://orcid.org/0000-0002-9748-5862
BRAC University, Bangladesh

Nusrut Sharmin
University of Chittagong, Bangladesh

ABSTRACT

This study accordingly explores the factors impacting the adoption of a metaverse in the manufacturing industry and develops a new model based on the Unified Theory of Acceptance (UTAT). Gender, age, and education were control variables. 235 questionnaire responses from employees of Malaysian manufacturing firms were collected through convenience sampling techniques and analyzed by Smart-PLS software. The findings reveal effort expectancy, perceived risk, and perceived technology accuracy have a significant relationship with intention to use a metaverse. Moreover, attitude to use evidenced mediating with perceived risk, perceived technology accuracy and intention to use a metaverse. The control variables did not evidence any impact on the intention to use a metaverse. This study provides insights to metaverse technology developers and manufacturing practitioners to explore and focus on the factors impacting the adoption of a metaverse in the manufacturing industry, as well as theoretical contributions for academia to progress further.

DOI: 10.4018/979-8-3693-2607-7.ch003

INTRODUCTION

The metaverse, a fully immersive virtual environment where users engage with each other and digital entities, has attracted considerable attention due to its potential to reshape industries (e.g., Smith & Jones, 2023). Manufacturing, a sector poised for significant transformation, has received limited attention in previous research regarding metaverse adoption, particularly in understanding user perceptions. This study addresses this gap by investigating factors influencing metaverse adoption in manufacturing, aiming to contribute to the field by developing a new model based on the Unified Technology Acceptance Theory (UTAT) (Davis et al., 1989).

The metaverse, a term coined by Neal Stephenson in his 1992 science fiction novel "Snow Crash," has evolved from conceptual origins to a sophisticated virtual environment (Stephenson, 1992). Types of metaverses include social, gaming, and enterprise-oriented, each catering to diverse user needs (Villalonga-Gómez et al., 2023). This evolution is marked by a rich tapestry of activities and applications, spanning entertainment, education, and business (Huang et al., 2021).

Within business, the metaverse facilitates virtual meetings, collaborative product development, and immersive training simulations (Huang et al., 2021). In manufacturing, its potential lies in streamlining processes, enhancing collaboration, and optimizing supply chain management. These applications underscore the transformative potential of the metaverse in redefining traditional business operations.

Despite its potential, implementing the metaverse in manufacturing poses challenges including technical hurdles, security concerns, and the need for an organizational cultural shift (Yao et al., 2024). Overcoming these challenges requires a nuanced understanding of the factors influencing the intention to use the metaverse in the manufacturing sector. The research domain of metaverse is new and there is a dearth of research on influencing factors on intention to use the metaverse in manufacturing industry and how do these factors drive or affect metaverse adoption attitude.

The implementation of the metaverse in manufacturing faces several technical hurdles that could impact its widespread adoption. One significant challenge is the current limitations in hardware and software for Virtual Reality (VR) and Augmented Reality (AR) technologies (Smith & Jones, 2023). These technologies may lack the necessary power and affordability to enable immersive experiences and smooth interaction in factory settings (Smith & Jones, 2023).

Additionally, the reliance on reliable and high-speed internet connectivity is crucial for real-time data transmission and low latency within the metaverse. However, deficiencies in existing network infrastructure, particularly in remote areas, pose a potential hindrance to seamless metaverse operation (Gupta & Singh, 2022). The integration of metaverse technologies with existing manufacturing systems and data platforms is vital for efficient workflows. However, complexities in integrating diverse data formats and protocols can create obstacles, leading to information silos (Li & Zhang, 2021). Furthermore, interoperability issues between different metaverse platforms could hinder collaboration between partners and suppliers, especially when using incompatible systems. The lack of standardized protocols may limit the full potential of the metaverse ecosystem (Huang et al., 2021).

Security concerns represent another critical challenge in metaverse implementation within manufacturing. Protecting sensitive manufacturing data and intellectual property is paramount, as data breaches and unauthorized access can have severe consequences (Chen et al., 2022). The susceptibility of virtual environments to cyberattacks, such as malware injection and data manipulation, underscores the need for robust cybersecurity protocols and user authentication systems (Yu & Fang, 2020). Ensuring the physical safety of workers interacting with virtual elements within the manufacturing environment is also crucial, considering potential hazards like collisions with physical objects or virtual reality sickness (Lee et al., 2023).

Apart from technical challenges, an organizational cultural shift to adopt new technologies is necessary for successful metaverse adoption in manufacturing industry. Change management becomes crucial, requiring organizations to adapt and train employees to embrace new workflows and technologies in manufacturing industry. Resistance to change, stemming from concerns about job displacement, privacy, or the unknown, can hinder adoption and necessitate effective communication and addressing of concerns (Smith & Jones, 2023). Moreover, addressing the skills gap is essential, as upskilling and reskilling the workforce may be necessary to meet the demands of working in a metaverse manufacturing environment. New skills, including virtual collaboration, data analysis, and digital problem-solving, may become imperative for employees (Lin & Huang, 2022) in manufacturing firms.

A comprehensive literature review reveals studies employing various methodologies exploring factors such as user experience, perceived usefulness, and perceived ease of use (Davis, 1989). However, a gap exists in understanding the unique challenges faced by manufacturing companies. Previous studies serve as a foundation but underscore the necessity of tailoring insights to the manufacturing context. Previous studies highlight the multifaceted nature of metaverse adoption, revealing both positive and negative aspects (Lin, 2019). However, gaps emerge when considering the industry-specific nuances of manufacturing. These gaps prompt the need for a dedicated exploration of factors influencing metaverse adoption within Malaysian manufacturing companies. Thus the objective of this study is to examine the impact of performance expectancy, effort expectancy, perceived risk, resistance to accept, and perceived technology accuracy on intention to use a metaverse and the mediating role of attitude to use metaverse on these associations in Malaysian manufacturing industry.

This research aims to contribute to the growing body of knowledge on metaverse adoption by providing a comprehensive understanding of factors influencing intention to use in the manufacturing industry. The development of a new model based on the Unified Technology Acceptance Theory (Davis et al., 1989) will offer practical insights for manufacturing companies navigating the intricate landscape of metaverse adoption.

LITERATURE REVIEW

Unified Technology Acceptance Theory

The metaverse, a fully immersive virtual environment, has garnered significant attention across industries due to its potential transformative impact (Smith & Jones, 2023). In the manufacturing sector, where processes, collaboration, and supply chain management are crucial, understanding the factors influencing the intention to use the metaverse is essential for successful integration (Huang et al., 2021). This literature review delves into the Unified Technology Acceptance Theory (UTAT) as a framework for comprehending the variables influencing metaverse adoption in manufacturing (Davis et al., 1989).

UTAT, proposed by Davis et al. in 1989, is an extension of the original Technology Acceptance Model (TAM) (Davis et al., 1989) and TAM posits that perceived ease of use and perceived usefulness are crucial determinants of users' acceptance of technology (Lin, 2019). UTAT builds upon this foundation by incorporating additional factors that influence technology acceptance. It emphasizes the role of external variables such as social influence, facilitating conditions, and cognitive instrumental processes (Lin, 2019).

UTAT emerged in response to the limitations of TAM, aiming to enhance the model's explanatory power and predictive capability (Yao et al., 2024). TAM primarily focused on individual perceptions, overlooking the broader contextual factors influencing technology adoption. UTAT addressed this limitation by incorporating external variables, providing a more comprehensive understanding of the complex nature of technology acceptance and exploring the variables in UTAT and how these are relevant to adopt Metaverse (Chen et al., 2022).

Performance Expectancy (PE)

PE refers to users' perceived ability of the technology to achieve desired tasks (e.g., Davis et al., 1989). In the context of manufacturing metaverse adoption, PE assesses how users perceive the metaverse's capability to enhance collaboration, streamline processes, and optimize supply chain management. Positive perceptions of these benefits contribute to a higher intention to use (Davis et al., 1989).

Effort Expectancy (EE)

EE represents the perceived ease of using a technology (e.g., Venkatesh et al., 2003). Manufacturing professionals are more likely to adopt the metaverse if they perceive it as user-friendly and easily integrated into their workflows. Low effort expectancy can be a barrier to adoption (Venkatesh et al., 2003).

Resistance to Accept (RA)

RA gauges the degree of resistance to adopting a new technology (e.g., Tornatzky & Fleischer, 1990). Manufacturing employees might resist the metaverse due to concerns about work routine changes, job displacement, or uncertainties. Understanding and mitigating resistance is crucial for successful implementation (Tornatzky & Fleischer, 1990).

Perceived Risk (PR)

PR assesses users' perception of potential negative consequences associated with technology adoption (e.g., Taylor & Todd, 1995). Manufacturing professionals might perceive risks related to data security, privacy issues, and metaverse reliability. Addressing and minimizing perceived risks is vital for fostering positive adoption intentions (Taylor & Todd, 1995).

Perceived Technology Accuracy (PTA)

PTA reflects users' perception of technology accuracy and reliability (e.g., Lee et al., 2023). In manufacturing, accurate and reliable data within the metaverse is crucial for decision-making. High PTA contributes positively to the intention to use the metaverse (Lee et al., 2023).

HYPOTHESIS DEVELOPMENT

Performance Expectancy and Attitude and Intention to Use Metaverse

In general, users are more likely to embrace a new system if they perceive it as useful, efficient, and capable of enhancing their performance (Venkatesh et al., 2003). High-performance expectancy often fosters positive attitudes towards technology adoption, as users tend to assess potential benefits and advantages before committing to using technology.

Within the context of the metaverse, performance expectancy becomes a key determinant of user attitudes and intentions (Venkatesh et al., 2003; Li et al., 2021). A positive attitude towards the metaverse is more likely when users perceive it as a platform that can fulfill their expectations and enrich their overall virtual experience. The immersive and interactive nature of the metaverse makes performance expectancy critical in shaping user perceptions.

The relationship between performance expectancy and technology adoption has been explored in several studies. For instance, Davis (1989) introduced the Technology Acceptance Model (TAM), emphasizing the significance of perceived usefulness and ease of use. Venkatesh et al. (2003) extended TAM with the Unified Theory of Acceptance and Use of Technology (UTAUT), highlighting performance expectancy as a critical factor. In the context of the metaverse, recent studies by Li et al. (2021) and Kim et al. (2022) provide valuable insights into the complex dynamics of metaverse adoption through their exploration of performance expectancy's role in shaping user attitudes and intentions.

H1: Performance Expectancy has significant impact on Intention to Use Metaverse

H2: Attitude to use mediates between Performance Expectancy and Intention to Use Metaverse

Effort Expectancy and Attitude and Intention to Use Metaverse

Beyond perceived benefits (performance expectancy), users also consider the perceived effort required to utilize a technology, known as effort expectancy. This factor, along with attitude, plays a crucial role in shaping their intention to use new technologies. Studies like Venkatesh et al. (2003) have shown that low effort expectancy, alongside high perceived usefulness, often leads to positive attitudes and increased technology adoption.

In the context of the metaverse, effort expectancy becomes another critical lens through which users judge it's potential. A complex virtual environment can be daunting if navigating it requires significant effort or mastering intricate interfaces. Conversely, intuitive controls, seamless interactions, and user-friendly interfaces can drastically reduce perceived effort, fostering a more positive attitude toward adoption.

The connection between effort expectancy and attitude towards technology adoption has been explored in various studies. For instance, Agarwal and Prasad (2000) found that low effort expectancy significantly diminished users' willingness to adopt e-commerce platforms. More recently, Kim et al. (2022) investigated the metaverse specifically, highlighting the importance of user-friendly interfaces and intuitive controls in shaping positive attitudes and intentions. Their findings suggest that minimizing perceived effort within the metaverse is crucial for attracting and retaining users.

Understanding the interplay between effort expectancy, attitude, and intention to use the metaverse is critical for developers and designers aiming to foster its widespread adoption. By prioritizing user-friendliness, intuitiveness, and seamless interaction, they can reduce perceived effort, cultivate positive attitudes, and ultimately encourage users to explore the vast potential of the metaverse.

H3: Effort Expectancy has significant impact on Intention to Use Metaverse

H4: Attitude to use mediates between Effort Expectancy and Intention to Use Metaverse

Resistance to Accept and Attitude and Intention to Use Metaverse

Resistance to accept the metaverse, characterized by individuals' reluctance or hesitation towards embracing virtual environments, is a significant factor influencing their intention to use this emerging technology. Users may harbor concerns, skepticism, or preconceived notions that hinder their willingness to fully engage with the metaverse (Rogers, 2003; Venkatesh and Davis, 2000).

Within the metaverse, users may exhibit resistance stemming from various factors, including unfamiliarity with virtual interactions, concerns about the impact on real-world relationships, or apprehensions regarding the value proposition of virtual experiences. Overcoming this resistance is crucial for fostering widespread adoption and encouraging users to explore the diverse possibilities within the metaverse.

Barriers to overcoming resistance may include a lack of understanding about the metaverse's potential, misconceptions about its purpose, or concerns about the societal impact of virtual interactions. Developers and advocates of the metaverse can address these barriers through informative campaigns, educational initiatives, and highlighting the positive aspects of virtual engagement. Clear communication about the benefits and addressing misconceptions can help alleviate resistance (Rogers, 2003; Venkatesh and Davis, 2000).

Building trust in the metaverse involves addressing users' concerns and establishing credibility in the technology's capability to enhance rather than diminish real-world experiences. Transparent communication, user testimonials, and success stories within the metaverse can contribute to building trust and mitigating resistance to acceptance.

Research in the field of technology adoption has explored the concept of resistance to new technologies. Studies by Rogers (2003) in the Diffusion of Innovations theory and Venkatesh and Davis (2000) in the context of the Technology Acceptance Model provide insights into overcoming resistance through effective communication and demonstrating the value of innovations. While specific studies on metaverse resistance may be limited, lessons from technology adoption research remain relevant.

Addressing and mitigating resistance to accept the metaverse is essential for its successful integration into mainstream culture. Developers, educators, and influencers should collaborate to provide accurate information, showcase positive experiences, and emphasize the metaverse's potential benefits. By navigating skepticism and fostering a positive narrative, stakeholders can encourage users to overcome resistance and embrace the metaverse for its diverse and transformative offerings (Rogers, 2003; Venkatesh and Davis, 2000).

H5: Resistance to accept has significant impact on Intention to Use Metaverse

H6: Attitude to use mediates between Resistance to accept and Intention to Use Metaverse

Perceived Risk and Intention to Use Metaverse

Perceived risk, the apprehension individuals feel regarding potential negative consequences associated with technology, is a critical factor influencing their intention to use the metaverse (Dinev and Hart,

2006). Users assess risks related to privacy, security, and unforeseen challenges, which can significantly impact their willingness to adopt and engage with the metaverse.

In the metaverse, users grapple with concerns related to the security of personal information, potential identity theft, or unauthorized access to virtual spaces: the fear of experiencing adverse consequences, both within the virtual realm and in connection with real-world implications, can create hesitancy and resistance to metaverse adoption (Dinev and Hart, 2006).

Barriers to addressing perceived risk may include a lack of transparent privacy policies, instances of cyber threats within the metaverse, or the potential for misinformation (Dinev and Hart, 2006). Developers and platform providers can mitigate these concerns by implementing robust security measures, transparent data handling practices, and fostering a culture of trust within the metaverse community.

Factors such as reputation, reliability, and transparent communication about security measures play a crucial role in building trust and reducing perceived risk (Dinev and Hart, 2006; Siponen and Vance, 2010). Collaborative efforts within the metaverse community to address and rectify security concerns contribute to a more positive environment, encouraging users to embrace the metaverse with greater confidence.

Research by Dinev and Hart (2006) has explored the connection between perceived risk and online technologies, emphasizing the importance of trust-building mechanisms. Additionally, studies in the context of virtual worlds, like the work of Siponen and Vance (2010), underscore the significance of mitigating perceived risks for user adoption.

Effectively managing perceived risks is essential for the sustained growth and adoption of the metaverse. Developers and stakeholders must prioritize transparent communication, robust security measures, and community collaboration to address and alleviate concerns related to perceived risk (Dinev and Hart, 2006; Siponen and Vance, 2010). By fostering a secure and trustworthy metaverse environment, users are more likely to feel confident in their intention to explore and engage with the diverse possibilities offered by virtual spaces.

H7: perceived risks has significant impact on Intention to Use Metaverse

H8: Attitude to use mediates between perceived risks and Intention to Use Metaverse

Perceived Technology Accuracy and Attitude and Intention to Use Metaverse

Perceived technology accuracy, reflecting users' confidence in the reliability and precision of metaverse technologies, is a fundamental factor shaping their intention to use the metaverse. Users' assessments of the technology's effectiveness and accuracy significantly influence their attitudes and willingness to invest time and effort in virtual experiences (Lee et al., 2012; Li et al., 2021).

In the metaverse, users seek assurance that the technology accurately represents their actions, interactions with others, and the immersive environment itself. Concerns about glitches, inaccuracies, or technological limitations may deter individuals from fully embracing the metaverse experience.

Barriers to perceived technology accuracy may include frequent technical glitches, limitations in graphical representation, or inconsistencies in user experiences. Developers can enhance accuracy by continuously refining algorithms, addressing technical challenges promptly, and ensuring a seamless and consistent metaverse environment.

User confidence in the metaverse's technological accuracy directly impacts their engagement and intention to use the platform. A reliable and accurate representation of the virtual world fosters trust and encourages users to explore, create, and interact within the metaverse with a sense of confidence and satisfaction.

Research by Lee et al. (2012) has delved into the relationship between perceived technology accuracy and user satisfaction in virtual environments. Similarly, studies by Li et al. (2021) emphasize the importance of continuous technological advancements and accuracy in shaping positive attitudes toward metaverse adoption.

Ensuring and communicating the accuracy of metaverse technologies is paramount for sustained user trust and adoption. Developers should prioritize technological advancements, address glitches promptly, and provide users with a consistently reliable virtual experience. By establishing a foundation of trust through accurate representation, the metaverse can attract and retain users, driving positive attitudes and intentions toward immersive virtual engagement (Lee et al., 2012; Li et al., 2021).

H9: Perceived technology accuracy has significant impact on Intention to Use Metaverse

H10: Attitude to use mediates between perceived technology accuracy and Intention to Use Metaverse

METHODOLOGY

The study applies positivism philosophy, quantitative survey method, cross-sectional time horizon and deductive approach. Data was collected through structured questionnaire to get more data in a quick time frame. The items were adapted from the previous studies and applied a five-point likert scale. Measurement items are provided in Table 1. Three (3) academicians and three (3) industry players checked the item's relevancy and quality. The sentence structures of the items were revised in accordance with the

Figure 1. Conceptual model

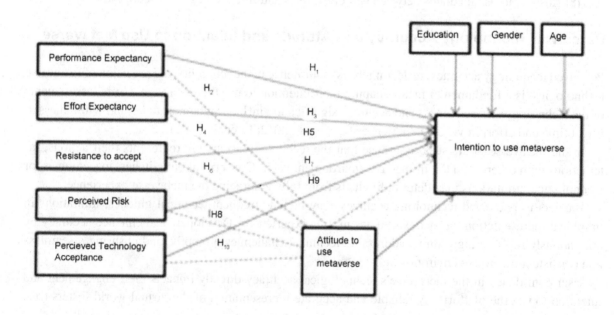

feedback provided by experts and respondents. The researchers considered dropping few questions to ensure relevancy of the items with the context.

The study is of a cross-sectional nature as data was obtained at a singular point in time. A pilot study was performed consists 30 respondents. The respondents were employees of manufacturing firms. The non- probability sampling method and convenience sampling technique were employed as the sample frame was not available. By using the G-power software, based on the six (6) predictors in this study's framework, 146 sample sizes are suggested (Figure 2). However, 240 responses were received after distributing questionnaire through a Google form link in various sources such as social media groups of manufacturer and email sending personally. 235 questionnaires were found usable for final analysis.

FINDINGS AND DISCUSSION

Non-Response Bias (NRB) and Common Method Bias (CMB)

This study employs the Wallace & Cooke (1990) approach to examine NRB. NRB guarantees that the survey accurately reflects the desired study population. The researchers analysed the mean and standard

Table 1. Measurement scales of constructs

Constructs	Items	Sources
Performance Expectancy	PE1 I think metaverse is helpful for manufacturing industry. PE2 I think metaverse could solve manufacturing related problems. PE3 I think metaverse can manage manufacturing related issues quickly. PE4 I think metaverse can increase the capability of manufacturing -management.	Venkatesh et al. (2003), Venkatesh et al. (2012)
Effort expectancy	EP1 I think I can easily learn to use metaverse. EP2 I can understand the service information on metaverse. EP3 I can easily use metaverse. EP4 I can get the skill of using metaverse.	Venkatesh et al. (2003), Venkatesh et al. (2012)
Resistance to accept	RA1 I have a negative opinion about metaverse RA2 I will refuse even if someone recommends using metaverse RA3 I feel reluctant to us metaverse RA4 I have something to criticize about using metaverse	Ju & Lee (2021)
Perceived Risk	PR1 I am concerned about cheating of metaverse information. PR2 I worry about problems of metaverse information PR3 I worry that my consumption will not provide value for my money.	Efendioğlu (2023).
Perceived Technology Accuracy	PTA1 I can rely on the services provided by metaverse. PTA2 My metaverse services offer consistent results over time. PTA3 I think metaverse have good working standards continuously. PTA4 I think the metaverse services are reliable. PTA5 I feel confident that metaverse services are offering error-free results.	Yang et al. (2022)
Attitude to use metaverse	AU1 I am interested in using metaverse AU2 I am likely to use metaverse because of its attractiveness AU3 I feel my work overall will be better with metaverse	Albayati (2024).
Intention to Use metaverse	IUES1 I intend to use metaverse to manage my business in the future. IUES2 I will always try to use metaverse to manage my day to day business operation in the future. IUES3 I plan to use metaverse frequently to manage my business in the future. IUES4 I would be willing to develop a habit of using metaverse soon. IUES5 I predict I will use metaverse to manage my health information.	Yang et al. (2022)

Figure 2. Sample size determinations using G-power software

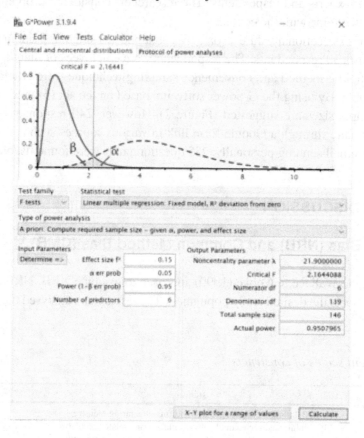

Table 2. Demographic data (n = 235)

Sample characteristics	Categories	Frequency
Gender	Male	165
	Female	64
	Prefer not to say	6
Age	20- 25 years	37
	26 - 31 years	60
	32 - 37 years	47
	38-43 years	49
	More than 43 Years	42
Education	No formal education	12
	Vocational	7
	Foundation	1
	SPM	10
	STPM	3
	Diploma	42
	Bachelor	83
	Masters	63
	PhD	14

deviation for the first 30 and final 30 respondents. They found no significant differences between the two groups, confirming the absence of NRB in the study.

Based on (Kock, 2015), if all VIFs in the inner model resulting from a full collinearity test are equal to or lower than 5.0, the model can consider free of CMB. The model is free from CMB because the VIFs are lower than 5.0 (Table 5).

Demographics Data

Table 2 showed that majority of the responses were male (165). Most of the respondents are 26-31 years old (60), and bachelor degree holder (83).

Measurement Model

Figure 3. The measurement model

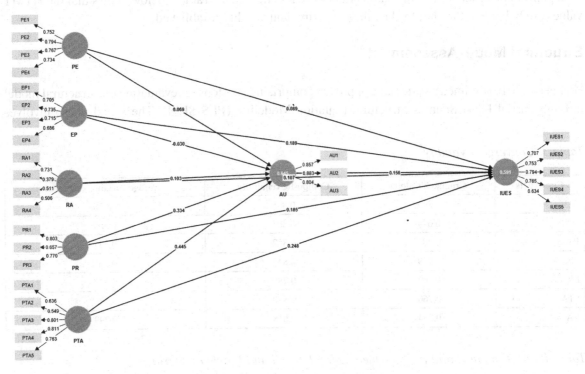

Convergent Validity

Convergent validity, as defined by Bagozzi et al. (1981), pertains to the degree of correlation among multiple indicators or measures of the same construct. The calculation of the Average Variance Extracted (AVE) involves squaring the loading of each indicator on a construct and computing the mean value, following the approach outlined by Hair et al. (2019). Internal consistency, or reliability, is assessed using Cronbach's alpha coefficient, a measure introduced by Cronbach (1951) to evaluate the reliability of a set of survey items. Composite reliability, akin to Cronbach's alpha, serves as a gauge of internal consistency in scale items, as proposed by Netemeyer et al. (2003).

The outcomes presented in Table 3 demonstrate that all the items' except RA's Average Variance Extracted (AVE) values surpass the 0.5 thresholds recommended by Hair et al. (2019). Additionally, constructs except RA's Cronbach's alpha and composite reliability exceed the 0.6 threshold, as suggested by Shi et al. (2012). These findings indicate that the measures exhibit acceptable reliability and high internal consistency, supporting the convergent validity of the study.

Discriminant Validity

Fornell & Larcker (1981) criteria and Heterotrait-Monotrait (HTMT) ratio were applied to confirm discriminant validity. Table 4 demonstrates that the square root of AVE is higher than its correlation with other variables, confirming discriminant validity.

Henseler et al. (2015) proposed the HTMT method, which confirms discriminant validity between each pair of constructs if the correlation values are less than 0.90. Table 5 below shows that the HTMT values are below the threshold value, thus, discriminant validity established.

Structural Model Assessment

Hair et al. (2019) outlined a systematic approach comprising six steps for evaluating the structural model through Partial Least Squares Structural Equation Modeling (PLS-SEM). The initial phase involves

Table 3. Convergent Validity

Constructs	Cronbach's alpha	Composite reliability	Average variance extracted
AU	0.805	0.885	0.720
EP	0.674	0.803	0.505
IUES	0.782	0.852	0.537
PE	0.759	0.847	0.580
PR	0.602	0.789	0.557
PTA	0.760	0.840	0.517
RA	0.234	0.618	0.299

Table 4. Discriminant validity assessment using Fornell and Larcker criteria

Constructs	AU	EP	IUES	PE	PR	PTA	RA
AU	0.849						
EP	0.410	0.710					
IUES	0.650	0.530	0.733				
PE	0.512	0.256	0.487	0.762			
PR	0.709	0.451	0.647	0.490	0.746		
PTA	0.747	0.518	0.691	0.553	0.679	0.719	
RA	0.514	0.400	0.517	0.392	0.506	0.509	0.547

Table 5. Discriminant validity assessment using Heterotrait-Monotrait (HTMT)

Constructs	AU	EP	IUES	PE	PR	PTA	RA
AU							
EP	0.557						
IUES	0.815	0.723					
PE	0.652	0.362	0.626				
PR	0.898	0.706	0.836	0.718			
PTA	0.846	0.735	0.893	0.728	0.800		
RA	0.822	0.898	0.843	0.852	0.796	0.850	

addressing latent collinearity issues. Subsequently, the examination of the significance and relevance of relationships within the structural model is undertaken. This is followed by the assessment of the variance explained by the dependent variable (R^2), the effect size (f^2), and the predictive relevance (Q^2predict). Finally, an evaluation of the corresponding t-values of the path coefficients is conducted through bootstrapping, employing 5,000 resamples with a two-tailed test at a significance level of 0.05. The results encompassing R^2, f^2, inner and outer model's Variance Inflation Factor (VIF), and Q^2predict are presented in Table 6 below.

The coefficient R^2 signifies the proportion of variance in the endogenous variable attributed to all exogenous variables. Ranging from 0 to 1, a higher R^2 indicates enhanced predictive accuracy. The conventional benchmarks for R^2 values categorize them as weak (0.25), moderate (0.50), and substantial (0.75) levels of predictive accuracy (Hair et al., 2019). In this study, the model prediction exhibited strong, as evidenced by R^2 value of 0.637 and 0.580.

Assessing the effect size of predictor constructs using Cohen's f^2 (Cohen, 2013) provides insight into their relative impact on an endogenous construct. Cohen defines effect sizes as high (0.35), medium (0.15), and small (0.02) based on f^2 values. The current study's results, presented in Table 6, indicate small effect sizes for the exogenous variables.

The examination of collinearity in Table 6 reveals no multicollinearity concerns in the current study. Both inner model's Variance Inflation Factor (VIF) and outer model's VIF values fall below the threshold of 5.

In PLS version 4, Q^2-Predicts systematically remove and predict each data point of indicators within the reflective measurement model of the endogenous construct. This test evaluates the predictive ca-

Table 6. Quality of the structural model

Endogenous Variables	R^2	Q^2predict	Exogenous Variables	f^2	VIF
AU	0.637	0.620	AU	0.021	2.818
IUES	0.580	0.547	EP	0.060	1.449
			PE	0.013	1.539
			PR	0.035	2.380
			PTA	0.051	2.971
			RA	0.018	1.530

pabilities of items related to endogenous variables in the structural model. As indicated in Table 6, a Q^2-Predict value exceeding 0 signifies the model's predictive capacity (Hair et al., 2019), establishing a higher level of predictive relevance in the study.

The researchers evaluated the association between constructs in the structural model based on the p-value and t-statistics value. The hypothesized relationship was perceived as significantly accepted when p values were less than 0.05 and T statistics were above 1.96 (Hair *et al.*, 2019). Table 7 indicates

Table 7. Path coefficient result for hypotheses

Paths	Original sample	T values	P values	Result
PE -> IUES	0.089	1.350	0.17	Not supported
EP -> IUES	0.189	3.060	0.00	Supported
RA -> IUES	0.107	1.856	0.06	Not supported
PR -> IUES	0.185	2.464	0.01	Supported
PTA -> IUES	0.248	2.869	0.00	Supported
PE -> AU -> IUES	0.011	1.065	0.28	Not supported
EP -> AU -> IUES	-0.005	0.581	0.56	Not supported
RA -> AU -> IUES	0.016	1.283	0.19	Not supported
PR -> AU -> IUES	0.052	1.924	0.05	Supported
PTA -> AU -> IUES	0.069	2.081	0.03	Supported

Figure 4. The structural model

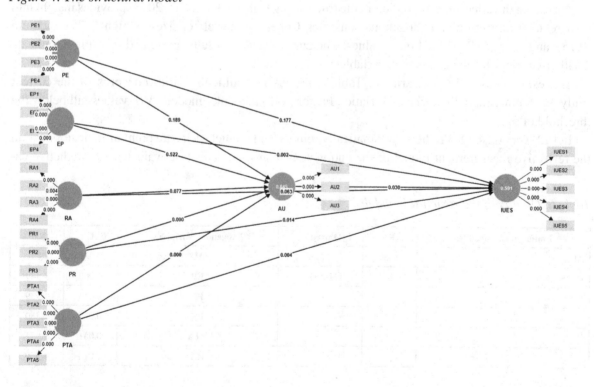

that EP, PR, PTA have a significant relationship with IUES. Moreover, AU evidenced mediating with PR-IUES and PTA-IUES. Control variables did not show any influence in intention to use metaverse.

Performance expectancy is not significant in predicting intention to use metaverse technology in the manufacturing industry in Malaysia due to factors such as limited awareness and understanding, lack of relevance or fit, resource constraints, technological complexity and risk, cultural and organizational factors, and external pressures and market dynamics.

Effort expectancy is significant in predicting intention to use metaverse technology in the manufacturing industry in Malaysia due to factors such as user-friendly interfaces, availability of training and support resources, compatibility with existing systems, perceived usefulness and relevance, peer influence and social norms, and perceptions of complexity and technical skills.

Resistance to accept new technology often stems from a lack of awareness or understanding of its potential benefits and implications. However, if professionals in the manufacturing industry in Malaysia are adequately informed about the capabilities and applications of metaverse technology, they may be less resistant to adopting it. Education and awareness-building efforts can help mitigate resistance by addressing misconceptions and highlighting the value proposition of metaverse technology.

Metaverse technology encompasses a wide range of advanced and cutting-edge technologies, including virtual reality (VR), augmented reality (AR), artificial intelligence (AI), and blockchain. Professionals in the manufacturing industry in Malaysia may perceive metaverse technology as complex and unfamiliar, leading to concerns about their ability to understand, implement, and use it effectively. The perceived technological complexity can increase perceived risk and hesitation towards adopting metaverse technology.

Perceived technology accuracy is significant in predicting intention to use metaverse technology in the manufacturing industry in Malaysia due to its potential impact on operational efficiency, quality control, safety, risk management, product design, decision support, strategic planning, and customer satisfaction. Addressing concerns about technology accuracy requires ensuring that metaverse technology platforms deliver reliable, precise, and trustworthy information and experiences that meet the needs and expectations of professionals in the manufacturing industry.

Moreover, AU evidenced no mediating influence with PE-IUES, EP-IUES and RA-IUES. In manufacturing firms, individuals may primarily focus on how metaverse technology helps them perform specific tasks or achieve organizational goals rather than forming attitudes towards the technology itself. Their intention to use the technology may be driven more by practical considerations such as perceived usefulness and ease of use rather than subjective evaluations or attitudes towards the technology.

Individuals in Malaysian manufacturing firms may have neutral or ambivalent attitudes towards metaverse technology, meaning they neither strongly favor nor strongly oppose its use. In such cases, attitudes may not play a significant mediating role in influencing intention to use the technology, as individuals may base their decisions more on objective assessments of the technology's utility and feasibility.

Contributions

Explaining the impact of performance expectancy, effort expectancy, resistance to accept, perceived risk, and perceived technology accuracy on intention to use a metaverse extends the Unified Theory of Acceptance (UTAT) by incorporating additional factors and contextual considerations relevant to the adoption of emerging technologies like the metaverse. This enhanced model allows researchers and practitioners to better identify, measure, and address the multifaceted determinants of technology adoption, thereby contributing to more effective strategies for promoting the adoption and use of the metaverse in various domains.

Understanding the intricate relationship between performance expectancy, attitude, and intention to use the metaverse is essential for designers, developers, and policymakers aiming to enhance the adoption and acceptance of this evolving technology. Understanding those factors can help manufacturing companies tailor their adoption strategies. For instance, if perceived risk is identified as a significant barrier, strategies to mitigate these risks can be developed, such as offering training programs or providing guarantees on the performance of the metaverse technology. Insights gained from the study can aid in the allocation of resources towards areas that are identified as crucial influencers of intention to use a metaverse. This could involve investing in technologies that enhance performance expectancy or efforts to minimize perceived risks associated with metaverse adoption. Companies can prioritize technologies with a proven track record of accuracy and reliability, thereby increasing confidence among users and enhancing their intention to use. Insights from the study can also inform the development of organizational policies related to metaverse adoption. This might include policies addressing data security and privacy concerns, as well as guidelines for acceptable use of metaverse technologies within the manufacturing context. Early adoption of metaverse technologies can provide manufacturing companies with a competitive advantage in the market.

Limitations and Future Research Directions

Despite significant theoretical and empirical contributions, this study acknowledges a few limitations. First, a single survey method can cause CMB issues. However, statistical post-hoc procedures were taken into account to eradicate this issue. Secondly, this study examines a single country (Malaysia) and single industry (Manufacturing). Service firms from other regions can be explored. Thirdly, this study used single method and cross-sectional quantitative survey. Other researchers can use comparative, qualitative, mixed or longitudinal studies to enhance generability. Other moderating or mediating variables, such as social influence, facilitating conditions etc., can be considered with this model.

REFERENCES

Agarwal, R., & Prasad, J. (2000). The role of e-commerce success factors in customer satisfaction. *Journal of the Academy of Marketing Science*, 28(1), 18–25. doi:10.1177/0092070300281002

Albayati, H. (2024). Investigating undergraduate students' perceptions and awareness of using ChatGPT as a regular assistance tool: A user acceptance perspective study. *Computers and Education: Artificial Intelligence*, 6, 100203. doi:10.1016/j.caeai.2024.100203

Bagozzi, R. P., Yi, Y., & Phillips, L. W. (1991). Assessing construct validity in organizational research. *Administrative Science Quarterly*, 36(3), 421–458. doi:10.2307/2393203

Chen, X., Li, H., Zhao, J., & Li, H. (2022). Security and privacy issues in the metaverse: A survey. *ACM Computing Surveys*, 55(2), 1–41.

Cohen, J., Cohen, P., West, S. G., & Aiken, L. S. (2013). *Applied multiple regression/correlation analysis for the behavioral sciences*. Routledge. doi:10.4324/9780203774441

Cronbach, L. J. (1951). Coefficient alpha and the internal structure of tests. *psychometrika, 16*(3), 297-334.

Davis, F. D. (1989). Perceived usefulness, perceived ease of use, and user acceptance of information technology. *Management Information Systems Quarterly, 13*(3), 319–340. doi:10.2307/249008

Davis, F. D., Bagozzi, R. P., & Warshaw, P. R. (1989). User acceptance of computer technology: A comparison of two theoretical models. *Management Science, 35*(8), 982–1003. doi:10.1287/mnsc.35.8.982

Dinev, T., & Hart, P. J. (2006). An empirical examination of the deLone and McLean model of information systems success. *Management Information Systems Quarterly, 30*(3), 691–721.

Efendioğlu, İ. H. (2023). The Effect Of Information About Metaverse On The Consumer's Purchase Intention. *Journal of Global Business and Technology, 19*(1), 63–77.

Fornell, C., & Larcker, D. F. (1981). Evaluating structural equation models with unobservable variables and measurement error. *JMR, Journal of Marketing Research, 18*(1), 39–50. doi:10.1177/002224378101800104

Gupta, R., & Singh, S. (2022). Network infrastructure for the metaverse: Requirements and challenges. *IEEE Internet of Things Journal, 9*(12), 13298–13310.

Hair, J. F., Risher, J. J., Sarstedt, M., & Ringle, C. M. (2019). When to use and how to report the results of PLS-SEM. *European Business Review, 31*(1), 2–24. doi:10.1108/EBR-11-2018-0203

Henseler, J., Ringle, C. M., & Sarstedt, M. (2015). A new criterion for assessing discriminant validity in variance-based structural equation modeling. *Journal of the Academy of Marketing Science, 43*(1), 115–135. doi:10.1007/s11747-014-0403-8

Huang, Y., Wu, S., & Zhao, X. (2021). The metaverse for business: Opportunities and challenges. *Journal of Management Information Systems, 38*(3), 1089–1111.

Ju, N., & Lee, K. H. (2021). Perceptions and resistance to accept smart clothing: Moderating effect of consumer innovativeness. *Applied Sciences (Basel, Switzerland), 11*(7), 3211. doi:10.3390/app11073211

Kim, Y., Park, J., & Sohn, D. (2022). Understanding user acceptance of the metaverse: Integrating the technology acceptance model and the flow theory. *Journal of Information Technology Management, 13*(2), 357–377.

Kock, N. (2015). Common method bias in PLS-SEM: A full collinearity assessment approach. [ijec]. *International Journal of e-Collaboration, 11*(4), 1–10. doi:10.4018/ijec.2015100101

Lee, J., Park, H., & Song, J. (2023). Safety assessment of augmented reality and virtual reality in the metaverse: A review. *International Journal of Occupational Safety and Health*, •••, 1–10.

Lee, Y., Kim, J., & Lee, Y. (2012). The role of perceived realism and trust in the continued usage of virtual worlds. *Computers in Human Behavior, 28*(2), 346–352.

Li, H., Li, Z., & Zhang, X. (2021). Understanding users' acceptance of the metaverse: An extended UTAUT model and empirical test. *International Journal of Information Management, 59*, 102495.

Li, H., & Zhang, Y. (2021). Data integration challenges and technologies in the metaverse. *IEEE Access : Practical Innovations, Open Solutions, 9*, 149696–149709.

Lin, C. C., & Huang, Y. (2022). The impact of metaverse technology on human resource development: A review of the literature. *Journal of Human Resources Development, 41*(4), 599–618.

Lin, H. (2019). The acceptance of virtual worlds: A meta-analysis. *Computers in Human Behavior, 93*, 113–122.

Netemeyer, R. G., Bearden, W. O., & Sharma, S. (2003). *Scaling procedures: Issues and applications.* Sage publications.

Rogers, E. M. (2003). *Diffusion of innovations.* Simon and Schuster.

Shi, J., Mo, X., & Sun, Z. (2012). Content validity index in scale development. *Zhong nan da xue xue bao. Yi xue ban= Journal of Central South University. Medical Science, 37*(2), 152–155.

Siponen, M., & Vance, A. (2010). User trust in information systems: A critical review of the literature. *Management Information Systems Quarterly, 34*(2), 339–368.

Smith, J., & Jones, A. (2023). The metaverse: A potential game-changer for industries. *Journal of Emerging Technologies, 12*(3), 45–62.

Stephenson, N. (1992). *Snow Crash.* Bantam Books.

Taylor, S. E., & Todd, P. A. (1995). Understanding information technology use as a process: A conceptual model of user acceptance and use. *Management Information Systems Quarterly, 19*(4), 197–217.

Tornatzky, L. G., & Fleischer, M. (1990). *The process of technological innovation.* Lexington Books.

Venkatesh, V., Brown, S. A., & Bala, H. (2013). Bridging the qualitative-quantitative divide: Guidelines for conducting mixed methods research in information systems. *Management Information Systems Quarterly, 37*(1), 21–54. doi:10.25300/MISQ/2013/37.1.02

Venkatesh, V., & Davis, F. D. (2000). A theoretical extension of the technology acceptance model: Four longitudinal field studies. *Management Science, 46*(2), 186–204. doi:10.1287/mnsc.46.2.186.11926

Venkatesh, V., Morris, M. G., Davis, G. B., & Davis, F. D. (2003). User acceptance of information technology: Toward a unified view. *Management Information Systems Quarterly, 27*(3), 425–478. doi:10.2307/30036540

Villalonga-Gómez, C., Ortega-Fernández, E., & Borau-Boira, E. (2023). Fifteen years of metaverse in Higher Education: A systematic literature review. *IEEE Transactions on Learning Technologies, 16*(6), 1057–1070. doi:10.1109/TLT.2023.3302382

Wallace, R. S. O., & Cooke, T. E. (1990). The diagnosis and resolution of emerging issues in corporate disclosure practices. *Accounting and Business Research, 20*(78), 143–151. doi:10.1080/00014788.1990.9728872

Yang, Q., Al Mamun, A., Hayat, N., Salleh, M. F. M., Jingzu, G., & Zainol, N. R. (2022). Modelling the mass adoption potential of wearable medical devices. *PLoS One, 17*(6), e0269256. doi:10.1371/journal.pone.0269256 PMID:35675373

Yao, X., Ma, N., Zhang, J., Wang, K., Yang, E., & Faccio, M. (2024). Enhancing wisdom manufacturing as industrial metaverse for industry and society 5.0. *Journal of Intelligent Manufacturing*, *35*(1), 235–255. doi:10.1007/s10845-022-02027-7

Yu, X., & Fang, B. (2020). *Cybersecurity challenges and opportunities in the metaverse.* Research Gate.

Chapter 4
Metaverse Perspectives:
Unpacking Its Role in Shaping Sustainable Development Goals – A Qualitative Inquiry

Monika Chandel

https://orcid.org/0000-0001-8179-6175

Central University of Himachal Pradesh, India

Manpreet Arora

https://orcid.org/0000-0002-4939-1992

Central University of Himachal Pradesh, India

ABSTRACT

The metaverse, a virtual realm, has drawn considerable attention from academicians as well as policymakers in recent years. In this chapter, we explored the metaverse's social, economic, and environmental effects, which align with various UN Sustainable Development Goals (SDGs), using an interdisciplinary perspective to show how it might transcend geographical borders and promote sustainability. This study adds to the ethical and sustainable development of digital technologies by analysing the opinions about the metaverse's influence on the SDGs. It will help administrations, corporations, and communities use the metaverse to make the world more inclusive, equitable, and sustainable. We are still learning how the metaverse fits into sustainable development, and scholars are examining the positive and negative aspects. This area must balance technical innovation and global sustainability as it progresses towards a more sustainable future.

INTRODUCTION

The term "metaverse" has attracted attention as a possible accelerator for global sustainability as the world becomes more digitally linked. The metaverse, a virtual shared area that merges physical and digital worlds, may help fulfil Sustainable Development Goals in many ways. The metaverse, a virtual realm has drawn considerable attention from academicians as well as policymakers in recent years. This is due to the integration of platforms like Facebook, Instagram, and WhatsApp under the term "Meta",

DOI: 10.4018/979-8-3693-2607-7.ch004

to encompass all types of digital communication and virtual environments. The COVID-19 epidemic has further added to this phenomenon since the need for online social engagement has increased because of the cancellation of face-to-face gatherings (Maden & Yücenur, 2024). It is not just about online gaming and browsing anymore; people are envisioning it as a potential new dimension of the internet that can contribute to creating a more inclusive society.

The concept of sustainable development has been subject to several interpretations, with the most often cited definition being from "Our Common Future", commonly referred to as the Brundtland Report (WCED, 1987): *"Sustainable development is the development that meets the needs of the present without compromising the ability of future generations to meet their own needs."* The 2030 Agenda for Sustainable Development and its Sustainable Development Goals (SDGs) are the primary global framework for international cooperation, with sustainability as its core principle. Modern technologies are crucial in attaining the three fundamental aspects of sustainable development: the environment, the economy, and society. These technologies might potentially have both beneficial and detrimental effects on sustainable development (Al-Emran, 2023). Sustainable entrepreneurial and environmental activities prioritise overall well-being, which extends beyond financial considerations, by emphasising wellness and spirituality. Integrating such sustainable initiatives can enhance spirituality, and wellness which can foster and bolster entrepreneurship as well as the economy. The cultivation of an inventive and creative mindset can be fostered through the prioritisation of values, awareness, and connectivity (Arora et al., 2023).

The metaverse is an integral component of the fourth industrial revolution, sometimes known as "Industry 4.0." The Industry 4.0 enabling technologies encompass a range of distinct advancements, such as the Internet of Things (IoT), Cloud Computing, Edge Computing/Fog Computing, Big Data Analytics, Artificial Intelligence (AI), Machine Learning (ML), Blockchain, Augmented Reality (AR), Virtual Reality (VR), Mixed Reality (MR), Digital Twin, Metaverse, and Robotics (Pachouri et al., 2024). These technologies are being implemented across various industries, including finance, retail, logistics, manufacturing, education, healthcare, business and management, telecommunication, tourism and hospitality, agriculture, smart cities etc. The implementation of these technologies differs throughout industries, and several sectors are actively investigating how to use these advances to enhance efficiency, production, and creativity, while also prioritizing the creation of a more sustainable environment which aligns with the UN Sustainable Development Goals. VR has the potential to augment student learning and involvement. Virtual reality-based education has the potential to revolutionise the delivery of educational content in our highly digitalized society. Virtual reality is based on the idea of generating a virtual environment, whether it is actual or imagined, and enabling people to not only observe it but also engage with it (Arora, 2024). There is a growing demand for skilled people in this field due to a range of global developments, including the excessive use of technology, demographic transitions, changes in labour requirements, a strong reliance on digitalization, and the adoption of disruptive technologies. Investing in technical skill-building activities can enhance the economic prospects of a country. In a more competitive economic landscape, the optimal investment strategy entails the cultivation of a diverse set of abilities aimed at enhancing the overall skill set of the general populace (Arora & Chandel, 2023).

Currently, there is little research that specifically examines the connection between the Sustainable Development Goals (SDGs) outlined in the United Nations 2030 Agenda and the subject of the metaverse. We explored the metaverse's social, economic, and environmental effects using an interdisciplinary perspective to show how it might transcend geographical borders and promote sustainability. This study adds to the ethical and sustainable development of digital technologies by analysing the opinions about the metaverse's influence on the SDGs. It helps administrations, corporations, and communities use the metaverse to make the world more inclusive, equitable, and sustainable. We must comprehend the metaverse's effects on sustainable development to create a future where technology drives good global change.

Research Questions

1. How do individuals perceive the metaverse's impact on the Sustainable Development Goals (SDGs) and what connections do they make between metaverse activities and SDG achievement?
2. In what ways do participants see the metaverse influencing social inclusion, economic development, and environmental sustainability, and how do these perceptions align with established SDG principles?
3. What recommendations do participants provide for positive contributions to SDGs within the metaverse, and how can these insights inform ethical guidelines and best practices in the metaverse ecosystem?

Metaverse Across Various Industries

The Metaverse is a conceptual notion of a theoretical "parallel virtual world" that embodies different methods of living and working in the virtual world as an alternative to the future's smart cities. Emerging new technologies, like Artificial Intelligence, Big Data, the Internet of Things (IoT), and Digital Twins, provide extensive datasets and powerful computational insights into human behaviour (Allam et al., 2022). The Metaverse is expected to provide an array of possibilities across various sectors (Arpacı et al., 2022). Despite being in its initial phases of research and application, the metaverse holds the potential to significantly change how companies engage with consumers across both the virtual and physical worlds. Service businesses are actively investigating the potential of the metaverse to enhance client experiences by offering more immersive, interactive, and captivating interactions (Jung et al., 2024). Technological breakthroughs have significantly disrupted the banking industry. The metaverse's influence on the financial industry has become very significant (Ooi et al., 2023). Understanding the evolving banking industry and the influence of technological progress is essential for banks to effectively handle the difficulties and possibilities brought out by digital transformation.

Digital travellers may experience space travel and other unthinkable things in the metaverse, creating an astounding future. After the pandemic, COVID-19 travel anxiety has increased interest in virtual settings like metaverse travel. The 'new normal' has revived travellers' cost-conscious and tech-savvy behaviour, influencing their choices for innovative, engaging, and rewarding travel experiences (Zaman et al., 2022). Go and Kang (2022) performed research to provide a clear definition of metaverse tourism and to offer insights and future directions for studying the potential of metaverse tourism in the context of sustainable tourism. The study examined the capacity of the metaverse to support sustainable tourism, drawing on reports from the United Nations World Tourism Organization (UNWTO), data from Google Trends, and prior research in the fields of human-computer interactions, virtual reality, and cognitive studies. This study discovered that metaverse goods and experiences have the potential to enhance the variety of tourism resources and promote sustainable tourism by offering alternative and viable options. Developing licensed and viable metaverse tourism goods and experiences has the potential to enhance profitability for tourist destinations and should be aligned with the Sustainable Development Goals (SDGs) set by the United Nations World Tourism Organization (UNWTO). Utilizing metaverse tourism goods and experiences is a novel strategy for achieving the overall Sustainable Development Goals (SDGs).

The COVID-19 epidemic has caused significant disruptions to the education system, prompting a strong emphasis on the urgent need to speed up digitalizing education. The impact of AI and big data on contemporary enterprises is significant. Due to the vast amount of different information included in big data, modern businesses rely on AI-assisted technologies, tools, and gadgets to process it efficiently and meaningfully. Hence, business leaders and entrepreneurs must prioritise many viewpoints to effectively address a wide array of challenges and issues, especially considering the recent crises triggered by the COVID-19 epidemic (Arora & Sharma, 2022). The Metaverse offers a potential option for social engagement and further development of educational activities (Arpacı & Bahari, 2023). The metaverse has the potential to bring the imagination to life by incorporating diverse technologies, serving as a platform for sustainable education that transcends the limitations of space and time. This can ensure that all learners have the same educational opportunities by establishing inventive educational atmospheres. Thus, enabling the achievement of SDG 4 (quality education) (Park & Kim, 2022). Non-fungible tokens (NFTs) which is a blockchain technology have enabled educational institutions to incentivize students by using NFTs as rewards. This is achieved via the automated processing of transaction information and the execution of buying and selling activities employing smart contract technology. The system facilitates the creation of recognition tiers and motivates students to earn NFT recognition awards (Wu & Liu, 2022). The educational applications of NFTs comprise, "textbooks", "micro-certificates", "transcripts and records", "scholarships and rights", "master classes and content creation", "learning experiences", "registration and data collecting", "patents", "innovation", and "research, art, payment, and deposit" (Wu & Liu, 2022).

The global fashion sector is valued at approximately US $1 trillion, making it one of the most environmentally unfriendly industries worldwide. The emergence of digital fashion offers the possibility to separate some essential elements of the fashion business from their physical dependencies. Given the surging interest in the metaverse, nonfungible tokens, the swift advancement of augmented reality (AR) and virtual reality (VR) technology, and the increasing involvement of prominent fashion brands in gaming, comprehending the commercial viability of digital fashion is becoming gradually essential (Schauman et al., 2023). Fashion brands use the metaverse to create brand credibility and attract new customers by generating and/or extending product ideas in virtual reality. Brand interest in the metaverse as an alternative channel rises with paid digital marketing prices. The metaverse offers the fashion industry a limitless online format for product and brand concept development, reaching new customer groups, a new multi-channel approach, more space for testing new products, developing the customer experience, holding their attention, etc (Alexandrova & Poddubnaya, 2023). This can significantly help in achieving SDG 12 (responsible production and consumption) and SDG 9 (industry, innovation, and infrastructure)

Metaverse implementations are beginning to appear in several sectors, offering improved industrial services and contributing to the development of a more sustainable society (Society 5.0). Simultaneously, there are numerous obstacles to the use of the metaverse (Tlili et al., 2023). Although the Metaverse encourages social engagement among users, there is a lack of understanding of the factors that impact its social viability (Arpacı et al., 2022). Nevertheless, there are still ethical, human, social, and cultural concerns about the impact of the Metaverse on the quality of human social relationships and its potential to transform the overall quality of life (Allam et al., 2022). The use of the metaverse in industries is still at an early stage, with most of the research being implemented in the education and health sectors.

Furthermore, there is an uneven spatial dispersion of research on the metaverse across many sectors, necessitating further international cooperation to promote the global adoption of the metaverse (Tlili et al., 2023).

METHODOLOGY

This study utilizes a qualitative research approach with an exploratory design to examine people's opinions of the metaverse and its possible influence on Sustainable Development Goals (SDGs). The research used a convenience sample method, specifically targeting about 10 to 15 people from various backgrounds, including academia, industry, and the public. The questionnaire aims to evaluate participants' comprehension of the metaverse, their knowledge of SDGs, and their perspectives on the potential impact of the metaverse on sustainable development.

A primary investigation was conducted, which was intentionally sent to students, researchers, academics, and professionals from several disciplines. The questionnaire aimed to examine participants' perspectives and viewpoints about the following topics: Metaverse awareness by formulating inquiries to evaluate participants' understanding of the metaverse. along with, presenting inquiries aimed at eliciting participants' viewpoints on how the metaverse impacts sustainable development, either by supporting it or hindering it. The process of data analysis will include content and narrative analysis, with a specific emphasis on discerning repetitive patterns, themes, and insights within the qualitative replies. The responses were not hampered and presented as it is. The findings are put together at the end of the discussion section. The study recognizes some limitations, such as the presence of sample bias and the inherent subjectivity of qualitative research.

RESULTS

Metaverse Understanding

In this section, the opinions of the participants about their understanding of the term metaverse and its applicability in various sectors are stated. The participants are asked to describe what they think when they hear the term "Metaverse" and what is its applicability in various sectors.

P1. "Metaverse is hypothetical reality stimulated with the help of the internet. It has its potential in the sectors like hospitality industry, marketing sector, and most significantly manufacturing firms."

P2. "Virtual 3D space"

P3. "The metaverse is a hypothetical, immersive 3D environment where we can experience life in ways, we would not be able to in the physical world. It is believed to be the next iteration of the internet, and it is taking AR/VR to the next level."

P4. "A communal virtual shared area that blends elements of social networking, online gaming, augmented reality, and virtual reality is referred to as the "metaverse". It is envisioned as an immersive, networked virtual world where users can communicate in real-time with virtual settings and one another."

P5. "Metaverse is a virtual world created using virtual and augmented reality. application in various sectors such as education, entertainment, real estate, shopping etc"

P6. "Metaverse is helpful in the achievement of 3D virtual space where humans experience life in ways they could not in the physical world."

P7. "My own digital world where I can interact with various people and can create our own virtual space. this can help in faster transmission of sensitive information as well as provide a secure space."

P8. "Metaverse is the virtual reality where you can create your virtual avatar and execute activities. Metaverse is the upcoming future and its application can be seen in various sections such as banking, gaming, real estate, healthcare sector etc."

P9. "Access points for the metaverse include general-purpose computers and smartphones, augmented reality, mixed reality, and virtual reality. Dependence on VR technology has limited metaverse development and wide-scale adoption."

P10. "The metaverse is like a big, shared digital space where you can play games, learn, work, and hang out with others using virtual reality. It could change how we do things online, making it more immersive and interactive in areas like gaming, education, work, and socializing."

Many of the respondents described the metaverse as a digital world where they can create their virtual world with the help of augmented reality and various other technologies. It was seen that the metaverse can be useful in almost all industries today be it technology-oriented or human-oriented like sports and healthcare.

SDG and Metaverse Linkage

This section highlights the linkages between the SDGs and metaverse technologies and the participants apprehension as specifically what SDGs can be achieved with the help of metaverse technologies

P1. "Yes, the metaverse will positively relate to SDG-9,11,12. Like usage metaverse will lead to industry, innovation, and infrastructure growth in terms of as creation of stimulations and will have less wastage in terms of actual concrete materials. Likewise, the metaverse will inculcate sustainability in terms of longer use of tools. Lastly, SDG-12 will benefit by creation of the products which are environmentally friendly and easy to use."

P2. "It will create a revolution in the education process by giving a real-life experience via online platforms."

P3. "Digital technologies have the potential to revolutionize education by making it more accessible, interactive, and personalized. The metaverse has the potential to contribute to the achievement of quality education in SDG 4."

P4. "There are various Sustainable Development Goals (SDGs) that the metaverse may help achieve. For example, it could improve accessibility to education through immersive learning, support environmental sustainability by eliminating the need for physical travel through virtual meetings, and promote international cooperation in the face of obstacles."

P5. "Quality education, life on land, affordable and clean energy"

P6. "Metaverse is helpful in achieving all SDGs"

P7. "Almost all the SDGs can be benefitted from the adoption of metaverse technologies. specifically, it can help in achieving the SDG 4, SDG 5, SDG 7, SDG 8, SDG 9, SDG11, SDG 12 and SDG 17 the most."

P8. "By providing virtual education, it can lead to quality education. By reducing a little of carbon footprint, it may also contribute to climate action."

P9. "Metaverse technology can accelerate the transmission of information. This accelerated speed can be directed towards the field of environmental research in general and towards research for carbon-neutral fuels in specific. This would create a sustainable world."

P10. "SDG 9".

From the opinions gathered it is quite clear that almost all the SDGs can be achieved with the help of metaverse technologies. Such as using metaverse in education for SDG 4, in the healthcare sector for SDG 3, and in industries such as manufacturing, hospitality, banking and commerce for SDG 8, SDG 9 and SDG 12.

Social, Environmental, and Economic Aspects

Further to highlight the three pillars of sustainability i.e., Social, economic and environmental participants were asked to provide their insights on how the metaverse influences social inclusivity, impacts the environment and promotes economic growth.

SOCIAL INCLUSIVITY THROUGH METAVERSE

P1. "Metaverse will adhere to inclusivity by managing the solving the conflicts among the diversity of the people. Moreover, through the metaverse, people can relate to the common problem and can empathize by helping others."

P2. "I don't think it can be of that much help to fill the gap. As people require proper training to utilize any kind of platform effectively and without any personal willpower, it's very difficult to get people of different sociocultural backgrounds on the same page."

P3. "The metaverse has the potential to play a significant role in promoting social justice and creating a more inclusive world. Through virtual experiences, people can interact with others from different backgrounds and cultures, learn about social issues, and participate in advocacy and activism."

P4. "The metaverse presents an opportunity to promote social inclusion and diversity by providing a virtual space where people from different socioeconomic origins and cultural backgrounds can interact and work together without being physically bound. It might present chances for international cooperation, language acquisition, and cross-cultural exchange."

P5. "The Metaverse could revolutionize social interactions, offering a novel platform for meaningful connections and reshaping the way people engage with each other."

P6. "The metaverse has the potential to enhance social inclusion by providing a platform for diverse cultural"

P7. "Metaverse can help in reducing the gaps among people which are the result of their cultural backgrounds and various socioeconomic factors by providing an equitable platform to all."

P8. "In my opinion, the metaverse will influence social inclusion and diversity making individuals interact with people with different cultural backgrounds and socio-economic factors in virtual reality by creating their avatars. It may be positive or negative."

P9. "Metaverse technology or any other technology for that matter, technology by nature is not inclusive. This is the truth because technology is never inclusively distributed. Rich people always have better technology at their disposal. Therefore, metaverse technology like any other technology would not create social inclusion and would not increase the acceptance of diversity in the society."

P10. "Metaverse provides a platform for different backgrounds and different cultures to interact with each other that is not possible in physical conditions."

Influence on the Environment

P1. "Metaverse will be like two sides of a coin having both negative and positive impacts on the environment. The overuse of it will lead to radiation and harm the environment. On the flip side, virtual designing likewise will help in decreasing the waste."

P2. "No, it will help the environment by reducing offline storage and reducing document work."

P3. "Metaverse could lead to an influx of greenhouse gas emissions. Virtual reality technology and data centres use AI and cloud services, which require quite large amounts of energy."

P4. "The development and broad application of the metaverse may give rise to environmental issues, especially when it comes to the higher energy requirements of data centres that host virtual worlds. The SDGs about environmental sustainability may be challenged by this increased demand for computer resources. To achieve these objectives, initiatives such as increasing awareness about reducing the carbon footprint connected to digital activities, investigating sustainable technologies, and optimizing energy efficiency in metaverse infrastructure should be undertaken."

P5. "Environmental impact of the Metaverse raises concerns, particularly in terms of increased energy consumption for server infrastructure and hardware production."

P6. "The metaverse could pose environmental concerns, particularly if the infrastructure supporting it relies heavily on energy-intensive technologies."

P7. "It can reduce paper waste, carbon emissions and industrial waste to some extent as people can meet and share in a virtual world thus helping in achieving environmental sustainability."

P8. "The potential environmental impact of the metaverse raises concerns about increased energy consumption, electronic waste, and resource usage. Balancing the development of the metaverse with sustainability goals outlined in the SDGs requires careful consideration of energy-efficient technologies, responsible resource management, and eco-friendly practices to minimize negative environmental effects. Achieving alignment involves prioritizing sustainable development practices, renewable energy sources, and circular economy principles within the metaverse infrastructure."

P9. "Symbolic one-rupee amounts have been allocated by the politicians towards environmental research. They do not give a fuck about the environment. But they should. The answer to your question is that as long as metaverse technology or any other technology runs on hydrocarbon fuels and not carbon-neutral fuels, the environment of our earth will not improve."

P10. "It will increase the emission of greenhouse gas that will challenge to achieve SDG goal 13."

CONTRIBUTION TO ECONOMIC DEVELOPMENT, JOB CREATION, AND ENTREPRENEURSHIP

P1. "It will have a increase the employability of people."

P2. "It will take away job of millions of people who have manual work like data entries, enquiries, front office jobs etc."

P3. "Economic empowerment is addressed through discussions on virtual economies within the Metaverse, highlighting opportunities for entrepreneurship, job creation, and financial inclusion. This exploration corresponds to SDG 1 (No Poverty), SDG 8 (Decent Work and Economic Growth), and SDG 10 (Reduced Inequality)."

P4. "The metaverse has the ability to boost the economy by opening up new doors for entrepreneurship and the creation of jobs. Jobs in virtual economies such as content creation, tech assistance, and virtual real estate development can be created within the metaverse. It might also make remote work and teamwork easier, advancing SDG 8 (Decent Work and Economic Growth). In line with SDG 9 (Industry, Innovation, and Infrastructure), metaverse platforms can help foster entrepreneurship and innovation in the ICT sector."

P5. "Metaverse has the potential to boost economic development by creating jobs, fostering entrepreneurship, and promoting innovation. This aligns with Sustainable Development Goals 8 and 9, focusing on decent work, economic growth, and industry, innovation, and infrastructure."

P6. "This can lead to the growth of a digital economy, creating jobs and supporting entrepreneurial ventures."

P7. "Metaverse require certain IT skills and innovation which can lead to job creation requiring such skills in various industries. as innovation often creates entrepreneurship which further leads to more jobs hence overall economic development will benefit from it."

P8. "The metaverse has the potential to contribute significantly to economic development, job creation, and entrepreneurship in alignment with Sustainable Development Goals (SDGs) 8 and 9. It can facilitate remote work, enabling a global talent pool, fostering inclusivity, and reducing geographical constraints. Virtual economies within the metaverse can stimulate entrepreneurship through innovative business models, creating diverse employment opportunities. Developments in virtual infrastructure can support sustainable urban planning and reduce environmental impact, aligning with SDGs focused on industry, innovation, and sustainable cities."

P9. "Metaverse technology like any other technology is being built by the big private companies. The leader is Microsoft. But not counting the IIT and IIM class companies, the normal private companies would continue to run the status quo. The answer to your question about SDG 8 and the phrase decent work would remain an ideal only achieved after death. The normal sons and daughters would still not find decent work. I do not consider Rs. 30,000 jobs with 24-hour by seven days disrespect towards the employee as jobs. You have a job on paper. The dark truth is that you are a contract labour."

P10. "The distorting of actual and virtual boundaries will lead to increased purchases and language in the metaverse, which will accelerate global economic development. The experiences that society has with virtual professions that offer significant value will be preserved by a virtual economy."

The participants provided some positive and some negative perspectives on the influence of metaverse technologies in creating a more inclusive society which is environmentally sustainable and promotes economic growth which are discussed in the findings section of this chapter in detail.

What Can Be Done for the Future

When the participants were asked what could be done in the future they thought of some specific actions or initiatives within the metaverse that they believe individuals and organizations should undertake to contribute positively to the SDGs following were their answers.

P1. "All the educational certificates and libraries can be in one single place for easy access all around the world."

P2. "The public sector, the private sector, and the academicians must work together to raise awareness in this area. It is clear that when all of these activities come together, they create a more substantial impact."

P3. "No, the Sustainable Development Goals (SDGs) can be favourably impacted by encouraging digital inclusivity, virtual space education, and sustainable metaverse activities."

P4. "Metaverse promotes diversity and creates virtual spaces aligned with social and environmental goals. This involves supporting ethical virtual businesses, developing educational platforms, and fostering global collaborations within the virtual realm. Integrating sustainability principles into the Metaverse design and operation is key for a meaningful impact on SDG achievement."

P5. "To provide more security guidelines and regulations so that by wrong persons these technologies should not be misused. Another thing that requires attention from various relevant authorities and organizations is to act regarding the awareness among people about metaverse and different usage and application of metaverse."

P6. "1. Inclusivity: Ensure equitable access to the metaverse, addressing digital divides and making virtual spaces accessible to diverse populations.

2. Educational Initiatives: Promote digital literacy and skills development programs within the metaverse to empower individuals and communities, aligning with SDG 4 (Quality Education).

3. Sustainable Practices: Implement environmentally conscious measures in the development and maintenance of virtual worlds, supporting SDG 13 (Climate Action).

4. Diversity and Inclusion: Foster diverse representation in virtual environments, promoting inclusivity and combating discrimination, contributing to SDG 5 (Gender Equality) and SDG 10 (Reduced Inequality).

5. Social Impact Ventures: Support or create virtual projects and businesses that address social and environmental challenges, contributing to SDGs such as SDG 1 (No Poverty) and SDG 3 (Good Health and Well-being).

6. Data Ethics: Prioritize user privacy and data ethics in metaverse development, aligning with SDG 16 (Peace, Justice, and Strong Institutions)."

P7. "Organisations have never, do not and would never give a damn about environment, sustainability and such other ideals."

P8. "No Idea."

P9. "Metaverse will contribute to increasing the global economy which will help to reduce poverty, increase jobs, and increase technological infrastructure."

P10. "Metaverse can help in building more resilient societies and can promote peace and prosperity."

The respondents urged to focus on ethical issues and data privacy which are big concerns regarding the use of AI technologies such as metaverse itself. Furthermore, the environmental impact of these machinery should also be looked at. Strict laws and regulations adhering to the production and usage of these technologies should be implemented.

INTEGRATION OF FINDINGS

The "metaverse" is a shared virtual world created by combining physical and virtual reality, which includes Virtual meetings, gaming, education, social interactions, business, and other digital activities. Metaverse has the potential to achieve almost all the 17 sustainable development goals. The goals which can benefit the most from the emergence of metaverse technologies are SDG 3 (good health and wellbeing) by incorporating metaverse in healthcare, SDG 4 (quality education) by bringing virtual reality to the classrooms, SDG 7 (Affordable and green energy) through technological advancements focused on enhancing energy efficiency in server facilities and overall infrastructure that supports virtual experiences. Further, it can also help in achieving SDG 8 (Decent Work and Economic Growth) and SDG 9 (Industry, Innovation, and Infrastructure) by fostering more job opportunities and innovations in almost every industry be it finance, retail, manufacturing, commerce, healthcare, agriculture, and business etc. lastly, metaverse can help in achieving SDG 10 (Reduced Inequality) by providing equitable access to digital experiences and SDG 17 (partnership for goals) as collaboration between public and private organizations is often necessary for the advancement of the metaverse. Collaboration among governments, technology corporations, and other stakeholders in developing the metaverse could support both the inclusivity and sustainability of virtual worlds.

When we talk about the three pillars of sustainability that is social inclusion, environmental sustainability, and economic growth all three of them can be achieved through metaverse technologies. Metaverse provides a safe and sound platform which is free from any discrimination and cultural barriers and hence can support social inclusivity. As we are approaching a world where more environmentally conscious practices are appreciated and needed in almost every industry and even in day-to-day life metaverse can be very helpful. However, teaching people these technologies and getting them to use them in real life is still a challenge that requires attention from policymakers and practitioners in the field of metaverse.

Metaverse plays a very crucial role in the environmental aspect of sustainable development. On the positive side where using these technologies such as virtual meetings and interactions has the potential to decrease the need for actual travel, which results in decreased carbon emissions linked with travel and transportation. Metaverse can also provide remote work opportunities which can lower the need for huge office buildings and associated environmental expenses. On the negative side, the creation and maintenance of virtual worlds, notably those that need detailed visualizations and computational aspects, may lead to high consumption of energy. Additionally, the manufacturing of hardware components for virtual reality equipment and other technologies used in the metaverse may include the extraction and utilization of materials that have environmental consequences and can create electronic waste if not handled appropriately. to overcome these developers should prioritize the use of renewable energy sources and the integration of energy-efficient technology while building and managing metaverse infrastructure. The focus should be on promoting virtual collaboration and interactions to minimize the need for physical travel. The authorities should Implement and make sure that everyone is following strict environmental regulations in the creation and operation of metaverse technologies which could help in reducing negative impacts. The contribution of the metaverse to economic development, job creation, and entrepreneurship is multifaceted. Metaverse enables economic development by facilitating the emergence of new industries and markets. These can include virtual properties, virtual goods and services, digital artwork, and many more. The metaverse necessitates ongoing technological advancement, resulting in increased demand for research and development projects. Consequently, this attracts investments and develops a culture of technical progress, which is crucial for economic growth. Metaverse can create more tech-savvy job opportunities as it requires software developers, graphic designers, UX designers, and others to build and maintain the metaverse. Metaverse virtual currencies, markets, and assets may provide finance, economics, and analytics professionals with new job opportunities as well. Virtual experiences, gaming, art, and events fuel the metaverse. Creative professionals like content creators, 3D modellers, animators, and authors get employment opportunities which overall helps in economic development. Metaverse is primarily dependent on technology, which offers the potential for businesses to innovate and create new apps, platforms, and tools to improve the virtual experience. Entrepreneurs can create and operate businesses within the metaverse by producing virtual goods, services, and experiences.

It is crucial to acknowledge the obstacles such as digital inequality, data privacy concerns, and regulatory issues which need attention so that equitable distribution of the positive aspects of the metaverse can be guaranteed. Furthermore, the long-term effects of the metaverse on employment and business creation are going to depend on how societies adapt and handle these new technologies. Like any other research, ours is also not free from any limitations. First, the sampling technique chosen for the following research is convenience sampling to get the results which can lead to sample bias. Another, limitation of the research is purely qualitative hence it adheres to the limitation of qualitative research as well. Additionally, the limitation of qualitative research can impact the output of this research, as it is based on people's opinions which can vary from place to place and time to time.

Future Directions and Policy Implications

The metaverse has the potential to improve social inclusion by offering a platform for people from different backgrounds to engage with one another, regardless of their geographical location. Nevertheless, there may be difficulties in guaranteeing accessibility, tackling cultural complexes, and minimizing the possibility of excluding certain groups of people. Efforts must be taken to actively encourage inclusion, diversity, and cultural sensitivity in the planning and management of metaverse environments. The environmental implications of the metaverse revolve around heightened energy usage in data centres, device production, and electronic trash accumulation. Green data centres and sustainable technology practices are going to be crucial to mitigate negative impacts. The metaverse can enhance economic growth by establishing fresh markets, generating employment opportunities, and assisting in entrepreneurial endeavours. Nevertheless, it is essential to thoroughly analyse and tackle the possibility of job loss and skill deficiency, while also guaranteeing equitable economic participation, particularly for vulnerable communities. Virtual volunteering, educational courses, and responsible digital citizenship initiatives may bolster the metaverse's contribution to accomplishing the Sustainable Development Goals (SDGs). To summarize, the development and acceptance of the metaverse provide a multitude of possibilities and difficulties in many aspects, necessitating a deliberate and all-encompassing strategy to assure compatibility with the Sustainable Development Goals.

CONCLUSION

As discussed above metaverse can be proved a very useful tool in attaining so many SDGs such as SDG 4 (quality education), SDG 5(women's empowerment), SDG 8 (decent work and economic growth), SDG 12 (responsible production and consumption) and SDG 17 (partnership for achieving all goals) etc. metaverse can not only provide a platform for people from all around the world to gather at one platform but also share their experiences, knowledge and create a community from which everyone can benefit. It was also found in the study that most of the participants just limited the term metaverse to virtual reality. But it is an umbrella term which encompasses much more. The respective organizations and authorities should focus more on educating the people about the uses of metaverse technologies in various sectors so that their full potential can be harnessed to create a sustainable environment. We are still learning how the metaverse fits into sustainable development, and scholars are examining the positive and negative aspects. This area must balance technical innovation and global sustainability as it progresses for a more sustainable future.

REFERENCES

Al-Emran, M. (2023). Beyond technology acceptance: Development and evaluation of technology-environmental, economic, and social sustainability theory. *Technology in Society*, *75*, 102383. doi:10.1016/j.techsoc.2023.102383

Alexandrova, E., & Poddubnaya, M. (2023). Metaverse in fashion industry development: applications and challenges. *E3S Web of Conferences, 420*, 06019. doi:10.1051/e3sconf/202342006019

Allam, Z., Sharifi, A., Bibri, S. E., Jones, D. S., & Krogstie, J. (2022). The Metaverse as a virtual form of smart Cities: Opportunities and challenges for environmental, economic, and social sustainability in urban futures. *Smart Cities*, *5*(3), 771–801. doi:10.3390/smartcities5030040

Arora, M. (2024). Virtual Reality in Education Analyzing the literature and bibliometric state of knowledge. In *Transforming Education with Virtual Reality* (pp. 379–402). Wiley. doi:10.1002/9781394200498.ch22

Arora, M., & Chandel, M. (2023). SDGs and Skill Development: Perspectivizing future insights for the tourism industry. In Springer international handbooks of education (pp. 1–20). Springer. doi:10.1007/978-981-99-3895-7_26-1

Arora, M., Dhiman, V., & Sharma, R. L. (2023). Exploring the Dimensions of Spirituality, Wellness and Value Creation amidst Himalayan Regions Promoting Entrepreneurship and Sustainability. *Journal of Tourismology*. doi:10.26650/jot.2023.9.2.1327877

Arora, M., & Sharma, R. L. (2022). Artificial intelligence and big data: Ontological and communicative perspectives in multi-sectoral scenarios of modern businesses. *Foresight*, *25*(1), 126–143. doi:10.1108/FS-10-2021-0216

Arpacı, İ., & Bahari, M. (2023). Investigating the role of psychological needs in predicting the educational sustainability of Metaverse using a deep learning-based hybrid SEM-ANN technique. *Interactive Learning Environments*, 1–13. doi:10.1080/10494820.2022.2164313

Go, H., & Kang, M. (2022). Metaverse tourism for sustainable tourism development: Tourism Agenda 2030. *Tourism Review*, *78*(2), 381–394. doi:10.1108/TR-02-2022-0102

Jung, T., Cho, J., Han, D. D., Ahn, S. J., Gupta, M., Das, G. D., Heo, C. Y., Loureiro, S. M. C., Σιγάλα, M., Trunfio, M., Taylor, A., & Dieck, M. C. T. (2024). Metaverse for service industries: Future applications, opportunities, challenges and research directions. *Computers in Human Behavior*, *151*, 108039. doi:10.1016/j.chb.2023.108039

Maden, A., & Yücenur, G. N. (2024). Evaluation of sustainable metaverse characteristics using scenario-based fuzzy cognitive map. *Computers in Human Behavior*, *152*, 108090. doi:10.1016/j.chb.2023.108090

Ooi, K., Tan, G. W., Aw, E. C., Cham, T., Dwivedi, Y. K., Dwivedi, R., Hughes, L., Kar, A. K., Loh, X., Mogaji, E., Phau, I., & Sharma, A. (2023). Banking in the metaverse: A new frontier for financial institutions. *International Journal of Bank Marketing*, *41*(7), 1829–1846. doi:10.1108/IJBM-03-2023-0168

Pachouri, V., Singh, R., Gehlot, A., Pandey, S., Akram, S. V., & Abbas, M. I. (2024). Empowering sustainability in the built environment: A technological Lens on industry 4.0 Enablers. *Technology in Society*, *76*, 102427. doi:10.1016/j.techsoc.2023.102427

Park, S., & Kim, S. (2022). Identifying world types to deliver gameful experiences for sustainable learning in the metaverse. *Sustainability (Basel)*, *14*(3), 1361. doi:10.3390/su14031361

Schauman, S., Greene, S. K., & Korkman, O. (2023). Sufficiency and the dematerialization of fashion: How digital substitutes are creating new market opportunities. *Business Horizons*, *66*(6), 741–751. doi:10.1016/j.bushor.2023.03.003

Tlili, A., Huang, R., & Kinshuk, K. (2023). Metaverse for climbing the ladder toward 'Industry 5.0' and 'Society 5.0'? *Service Industries Journal*, *43*(3–4), 260–287. doi:10.1080/02642069.2023.2178644

World Commission on Environment and Development (WCED). (1987). *Our Common Future (Brundtland Report)*. United Nations. https://sustainabledevelopment.un.org

Wu, C., & Liu, C. (2022). Educational Applications of Non-Fungible Token (NFT). *Sustainability (Basel)*, *15*(1), 7. doi:10.3390/su15010007

Zaman, U., Koo, I., Abbasi, S., Raza, S. H., & Qureshi, M. G. (2022). Meet your digital twin in space? Profiling international expat's readiness for metaverse space travel, Tech-Savviness, COVID-19 travel anxiety, and travel fear of missing out. *Sustainability (Basel)*, *14*(11), 6441. doi:10.3390/su14116441

Chapter 5
Human Resource Management in the Metaverse Era:
A Bibliometric Analysis and Future Research Agenda

Sahil Sharma

iD https://orcid.org/0000-0002-0139-254X
Central University of Himachal Pradesh, India

Anu Sohal

iD https://orcid.org/0000-0003-4737-0992
Central University of Himachal Pradesh, India

ABSTRACT

The advent of the metaverse offers human resource management both new opportunities and challenges as digital technologies continue to progress. To examine the state of HRM research in the metaverse era and pinpoint significant themes and gaps in the body of literature, this study conducts a bibliometric analysis. The authors examine the distribution of articles, authors, journals, and keywords associated with HRM in the context of the metaverse through a methodical examination of scholarly publications from the Scopus database. This research indicates an increasing amount of interest in this field, with studies concentrating on digital leadership, people management, remote work, and virtual collaboration. The authors offer a research agenda for the future to fill in these knowledge gaps and improve comprehension of HRM in the metaverse era. This study adds to the expanding corpus of research on HRM in digital contexts and offers insightful guidance on how to navigate the potential and difficulties presented by the metaverse for scholars, practitioners, and policymakers.

INTRODUCTION

Recent years have seen remarkable growth in technology, which has completely changed many aspects of human life, including how we communicate and work together. The rise of the Metaverse, a virtual

DOI: 10.4018/979-8-3693-2607-7.ch005

environment where users may communicate in real-time with digital items and each other, is one of the most exciting advances in this field. As it presents previously unheard-of chances for cooperation, invention, and creativity, this virtual environment is becoming a more interesting subject for interdisciplinary study (Bennet & McWhorter, 2022). Given the increasing attention being paid to the metaverse, its implications must be investigated for several fields, one of which is human resource management (HRM). Managing an organization's most precious asset, its people, is the responsibility of HRM. HRM procedures must adapt as technology continues to change the workplace (Arora, 2020).

Technological advancements have increased learning capacity and performance, which has changed how workers interact with one another and their jobs (Chaudhary et al., 2023). Within this framework, the metaverse offers HRM new and exciting opportunities for hiring, development, teamwork, and employee engagement. However, to fully utilise the metaverse in HRM, it is imperative to comprehend the existing state of study in this field, identify important themes and trends, and suggest possible directions for further investigation.

The metaverse is set to transform many elements of management and the workplace, including human resource management. It will profoundly transform how people interact and operate in virtual settings, affecting the recruitment, training, and performance review processes. The metaverse will demand new methods of staff training and assistance, supplied through fresh channels. This transition will also transform workplace productivity and engagement tactics. Onboarding and training in the metaverse will take place in remote, risk-free environments, giving managers hands-on experience and allowing them to resolve concerns more efficiently. Overall, Bloomberg Intelligence predicts that the metaverse will generate a major business opportunity, with revenues reaching USD 800 billion by the end of 2024 (Koohang et al., 2023).

As research into human resource management and the metaverse evolves, advanced research approaches will be required to meet the expectations of both industry and academia. Currently in its early phases, research in the area is projected to progress, resulting in a better understanding of the metaverse's impact on HR management. The ability for users to enter virtual office settings while interacting with digital avatars of employees constitutes a major change in HR management, providing a more personalized experience and insight into organizational culture. The metaverse's ability to recreate real-world surroundings makes it useful for a variety of HR services such as recruitment, training, employee relations, and regulatory compliance, big corporate firms will benefit from this optimal utilisation of human resources (Arora & Sharma, 2023). This innovative approach to working in the metaverse has the potential to alter hybrid work patterns by allowing for remote collaboration and true participation.

Metaverse

Metaverse, a term first coined by Neal Stephenson in 1992, is the 3D iteration of the internet which is facilitated by VR (Virtual Reality) and AR (Augmented Reality) technologies. The metaverse architecture is composed of different technologies like machine learning, blockchain, and 3-D graphics and is usually used via VR-enabled headsets like *Apple Vision Pro* and *Meta Oculus*. Initially developed as a concept for playing interactive video games, the metaverse has split into many contours (Yilmaz et al., 2023). Started with interactive meetings, the metaverse technology has now applications in productivity, learning environments, e-commerce, healthcare, and but not limited to, real estate. The COVID-19 situation triggered the need for exponential development of virtual technologies. Though already in existence, the companies' view towards virtual technologies tilted positively, after the pandemic. *Meta* is pioneering the haptics technology as well which will enable users to feel texture, pressure, and movement as well.

The concept of the metaverse has roots dating back to Stephenson's novel "Snow Crash" (1992), where the term was first introduced almost 30 years ago. Over time, various scholars have attempted to define the metaverse, with definitions shaped by the technological landscape of their era. Dickey (1999) defines the metaverse as "The ultimate 3D interactive world in which users interact (by way of realistic-looking avatars) in a fully immersive virtual world" (p. 40). This definition emphasizes the immersive and interactive qualities of the metaverse, wherein users navigate and engage with virtual environments using avatars. Schlemmer & Backes (2015) provide a definition stating that "The word metaverse is a compound word with "meta", meaning "beyond", and "verse" as an abbreviation for "universe", thus constituting a virtual reality universe" (p. 49). This definition highlights the metaverse's vast and comprehensive nature, suggesting it as a realm beyond traditional conceptions of reality. The latest definition is given by Kevin (2022) explaining the metaverse as "a network of interconnected experiences and applications, devices and products, tools and infrastructure".

Some individuals perceive the metaverse as simply a rebranding of VR or AR. However, it encompasses far more than these technologies alone (Park & Kim, 2022). The framework for a metaverse (see Figure 1), explaining that the metaverse varies from traditional VR or AR systems in three important ways: "shared," "persistent," and "de-centralized." Sharedness refers to user interactions in a virtual environment, whereas persistence refers to the ability to live, work, study, and create in the virtual world continuously. Decentralization, as enabled by technology such as blockchains, assures the security and integrity of economic activity and personal property. These capabilities need the use of artificial intelligence (AI) to enforce creator-defined rules and provide immersive experiences. Systems that lack these traits, such as single-user VR training systems, are not considered part of the metaverse, which stresses multi-user interactions and persistent virtual life (Hwang & Chien, 2022).

Figure 1. The framework of a metaverse
Source: *Hwang & Chien (2022)*

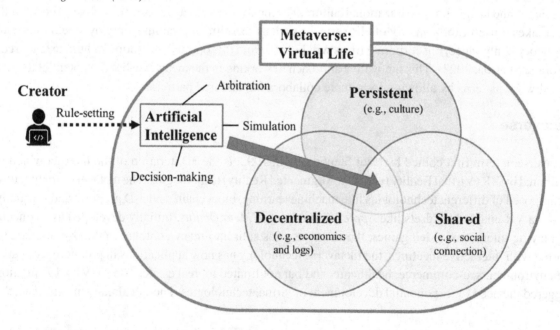

Metaverse and Human Resources

Metaverse seems to be a boon to employee productivity with enhanced teamwork and collaboration. *Accenture* uses the metaverse for onboarding and convening remote work, *BMW* for creative collaboration, *Hyundai* for training the workers, etc. The concept of 'digital human' is being researched for better collaboration between human resources (Yu et al., 2022). The training component of human resource management is witnessing a revolution through the metaverse, especially in the medical field among other domains. The use of metaverse in training increases the efficacy of the training programs to a greater extent (Hajjami & Park, 2023). Immersive reality platforms have gained attraction due to a lack of engagement on 2D interactive platforms like *Google Meet*. By creating a digital avatar for employees, companies can simulate real-life scenarios, thus creating more engagement. Metaverse also solves the loss of informal and spontaneous conversations in 2D virtual platforms.

In any organization, human capital is an important factor for adopting new technologies. As the metaverse continues to grow, conventional professions like real estate companies, professionals in event management, designers, content creators, and architects are transitioning into virtual realms by adapting and acquiring new skills relevant to operating in the metaverse (Vig, 2023). The metaverse also offers a dynamic learning environment where employees can engage in immersive training programs, simulations, and virtual classrooms (Arora, 2024; Dutta et al., 2023). Moreover, with the help of the metaverse, teams can come together in virtual environments to brainstorm ideas, work on projects, and solve problems in real-time, regardless of geographic boundaries. Virtual meeting places can be customized to replicate various work settings, from boardrooms to casual coffee shops, allowing for natural and spontaneous interactions that boost team cohesion and innovation. The metaverse also improves employees' well-being by providing a virtual office environment that aids in time management and work-life balance, fostering a sense of community among employees, and providing positive experiences through virtual spaces for relaxation and socialization, thereby reducing feelings of isolation (Arora & Rathore, 2023; Park et al., 2023).

The principal aim of this study is to present a comprehensive summary of the existing body of research on the relationship between the metaverse and human resources. The purpose of this study is to investigate the scope and depth of this topic by addressing the following questions:

RQ1. In what ways has scholarly inquiry assessed the connection between human resource management and the metaverse?

RQ2. Which studies are important and what research themes are most prevalent in this field?

RQ3. Which conceptual frameworks or structures serve as the foundation for the research done in this area?

By answering these questions, we hope to shed light on the status of the metaverse and HRM research at the moment, point out areas that still need to be investigated and suggest a path forward for future studies in this emerging subject. In the end, this research aims to further knowledge about how the metaverse might transform HRM procedures and result in more creative and successful methods of managing human resources in the digital era.

RESEARCH METHODOLOGY

Search Strategy and Data Retrieval Process

Figure 2 illustrates the data retrieval process extracted from the Scopus database, highlighting the systematic approach used to retrieve relevant literature for analysis. The data extracted from the Scopus database were analyzed using the R 4.03 package programme "Biblioshiny", which is an R-based package and web application designed specifically for bibliometric analysis (Nazma et al., 2023). Unlike other traditional literature reviews, bibliometric reviews emphasize the visualization and analysis of substantial amounts of literature-specific data, providing deeper thoughts into research trends and patterns (Donthu et al., 2021).

Analysis Method

A bibliometric analysis was performed to analyse the dynamics of human resources in the metaverse world. The bibliometric analysis is a useful technique for academics to systematically investigate and analyse large volumes of literature, as it provides insights into the dynamics and trajectory of scholarly discourse within a given area (Dhiman & Arora, 2024). The final search was realized in February 2024 on the Scopus database using the keywords "metaverse" AND "human resource management" OR "HRM" OR "human resource". To achieve the objectives outlined in the study, the science mapping method was used, which is the combination of "classification and visualization" (Boyack & Klavans, 2014) using the RStudio software (Aria & Cuccurullo, 2017). Classification methods are used to categorize and organize information (such as publications, documents, countries, and journals), whereas visualization tools are used to represent the classified data in a graphical format (Zupic & Cater, 2015).

Figure 2. Data retrieval process
Source: *Created by the authors*

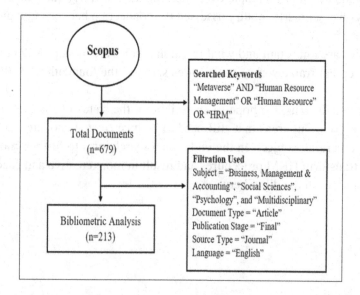

In the present study, the objectives will be addressed through the application of performance analysis techniques using bibliometric methods.

RESULTS

Figure 3 provides a brief overview of the bibliometric analysis conducted on a dataset comprising 213 selected documents spanning from 2009 to 2024. The analysis reveals that research on the intersection of the metaverse and human resources has garnered considerable attention, with 131 distinct journals showing receptivity to this area of study. There has been an annual growth rate of 26.75% in publications on this topic, highlighting its increasing significance over time. These journals collectively feature a total of 706 authors, 898 authors' keywords, and 16,987 references. Out of 213 documents, 36 documents are solo-authored, depicting a prevalent trend of collaboration among researchers in the field. Moreover, this overview represents that there is 43.66% international co-authorship, highlighting the collaborative efforts among researchers across different geographical locations. As of February 2024, the average number of citations per document stands at 6.023, indicating the impact and influence of research in this burgeoning field.

Performance Analysis

3.1.1. Publication Trends

Figure 4 illustrates the annual distribution of publications spanning from 2009-2023. It was found that the first article related to this topic was published back in 2009, followed by a significant gap until 2012. Figure 4 represents that up to 2020, there was a dearth of publications in this domain. However, in 2022, there was a substantial increase in the number of published articles (34). The reason could be the increase in the trend of application of metaverse in human-computer interaction (Hwang & Chien,

Figure 3. Descriptive summary of 213 documents for bibliometric analysis
Source: *Extracted from RStudio*

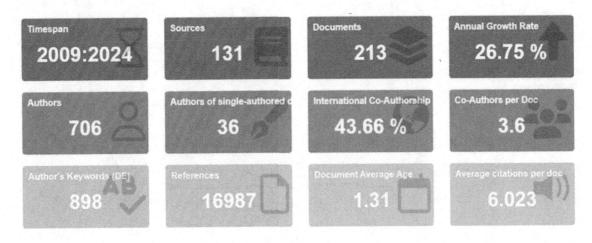

2022). The year 2023 was the most productive in terms of total production count (134). As for 2024, the published articles were not depicted due to non-completion of the year, but it is worth noting that around 35 research articles were published in January-February 2024.

3.1.2. Publication Outlets

Table 1 provides an overview of the top 10 leading journals publishing articles related to metaverse and human resources. The most prominent journal in this field is the *Contemporary Readings in Law and Social Justice,* which is a US-based journal having the highest number of published articles (29) on the subject of social sciences. It was followed by the Switzerland journal *Sustainability*, with a total number of 10 publications, and the US-based *Technological Forecasting and Social Change,* with 6 publications.

Figure 4. Annual publication trend between period 2009-2023. Data for 2024 (January-February) is not depicted for the publication trend due to the non-completion of the year.
Source: *Authors' compilation (Data retrieved from Scopus on February 2024)*

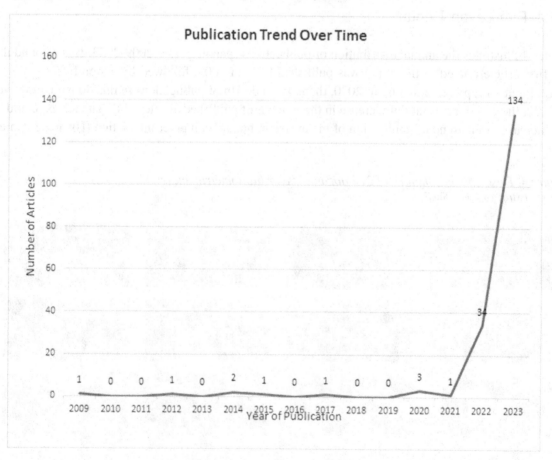

Table 1. The top ten leading journals

Source Title	Country	h-index	NP	Subject Area
Contemporary Readings in Law and Social Justice	United States	16	29	Social Sciences
Sustainability (Switzerland)	Switzerland	136	10	Computer Science, Energy, Environment Science, Social Sciences
Technological Forecasting and Social Change	United States	155	6	Psychology and Business, Management, and Accounting
Computers in Human Behavior	United Kingdom	226	5	Psychology, Arts and Humanities, and Computer Science
Journal of Cleaner Production	United Kingdom	268	4	Business, Management, and Accounting, Energy, Engineering, Environmental Science
Journal of Open Innovation: Technology, Market, and Complexity	Switzerland	38	4	Social Sciences, Economics, Econometrics and Finance
Journal of Business Research	United States	236	3	Business, Management, and Accounting
Psychology and Marketing	United States	133	3	Psychology and Business, Management, and Accounting
International Journal of Contemporary Hospitality Management	United Kingdom	113	2	Business, Management, and Accounting
Organizational Psychology Review	United States	36	2	Psychology and Business, Management, and Accounting

Note: NP = Number of publications (among a pool of 213 articles)
Source: Authors' compilation from SCOPUS database

3.1.3. Most Cited Articles

Table 2 presents the top 10 highly cited articles in the field of metaverse and human resources based on global citations. "Global Citation" is the total number of Scopus citations for a publication, whereas "Local Citation" is the number of times a manuscript has been cited by other papers within the 213 documents network (Fahimnia et al., 2015). As per global citations, article by Dwivedi et al. (2023) titled "*"So what if ChatGPT wrote it?" Multidisciplinary perspectives on opportunities, challenges and implications of generative conversational AI for research, practice and policy*" is the most cited article, with a total number of 474 citations. It is followed by Buhalis et al. (2023) titled "*Smart hospitality: from smart cities and smart tourism towards agile business ecosystems in networked destinations*" and Lăzăroiu et al. (2022), titled "*Artificial intelligence-based decision-making algorithms, Internet of Things sensing networks, and sustainable cyber-physical management systems in big data-driven cognitive manufacturing*", with a total global citation of 54 and 50 respectively.

3.1.4. Most Cited Countries

Table 3 presents the leading countries in the realms of metaverse and human resources. According to total citations, the United Kingdom emerges as the most cited country, boasting the highest count of 595 citations, with an average annual citation of 22.0 and 76 published articles. It was followed by Romania with the second-highest citation count of 115, with an average annual citation of 7.20 and 32 published articles. According to the number of published articles, China, India, the UK, and the USA, stand out as the leading countries. China has dominated the research field with the highest production, contributing 87 research articles, followed closely by India with 80 articles, the UK with 76 articles, and the USA with 71 articles.

Table 2. The top ten most cited articles

Author(s)	Article Title	Local Citations*	Global Citations**
Dwivedi et al. (2023)	"So what if ChatGPT wrote it?" Multidisciplinary perspectives on opportunities, challenges and implications of generative conversational AI for research, practice and policy	15	474
Buhalis et al. (2023)	Smart hospitality: from smart cities and smart tourism towards agile business ecosystems in networked destinations	0	54
Lăzăroiu et al. (2022)	Artificial intelligence-based decision-making algorithms, Internet of Things sensing networks, and sustainable cyber-physical management systems in big data-driven cognitive manufacturing	0	50
Pellas & Kazanidis (2015)	On the value of Second Life for students' engagement in blended and online courses: A comparative study from the Higher Education in Greece	0	45
Polas et al. (2022)	Artificial Intelligence, Blockchain Technology, and Risk-Taking Behavior in the 4.0IR Metaverse Era: Evidence from Bangladesh-Based SMEs	3	33
McKenzie et al. (2012)	User-generated online content 1: Overview, current state and context	0	32
Kraus et al. (2023)	From moon landing to metaverse: Tracing the evolution of Technological Forecasting and Social Change	0	26
Tlili et al. (2023)	Metaverse for climbing the ladder toward 'Industry 5.0' and 'Society 5.0'?	1	25
Novak et al. (2022)	Big Data-driven Governance of Smart Sustainable Intelligent Transportation Systems: Autonomous Driving Behaviors, Predictive Modeling Techniques, and Sensing and Computing Technologies	3	23
Sharifi et al. (2023)	Progress and prospects in planning: A bibliometric review of literature in Urban Studies and Regional and Urban Planning	0	20

*Local Citation: citation within the 213 documents
**Global Citation: actual citation of SCOPUS
Source: Authors' compilation from the SCOPUS database

Table 3. The top ten highly cited countries

Country	TC	AAC	TP
United Kingdom	595	22.00	76
Romania	115	7.20	32
China	73	3.60	87
Canada	64	8.00	20
Italy	60	12.00	17
USA	59	3.30	71
Bangladesh	36	12.00	8
India	28	1.90	80
Australia	27	5.40	17
Japan	20	20.00	1

Note: TC = Total Citation; AAC = Average Annual Citation; TP = Total Publication
Source: Extracted from RStudio

Conceptual Structure Through Science Mapping

3.2.1. Co-Occurrence Network Analysis

Figure 5 presents the network analysis of authors' keywords, which are selected and created by the authors of the research articles to reflect the important content provided in the publication. Co-occurrence analysis finds a discipline's overarching themes by creating thematic connections with other keywords (Dhiman & Arora, 2023). This analysis provided a dataset of 36 keywords which were divided into six clusters, each representing different thematic areas within the research domain:

Cluster 1 (purple) – The first cluster has a total of 11 keywords such as artificial intelligence (AI), human, article, learning, humans, human experiment, adult, education, female, male, and controlled study. The most frequent keywords that appeared within the cluster are "human", "articles", and "learning" which suggests a focus on exploring how AI and human-centric learning methodologies intersect within the context of the metaverse.

Cluster 2 (green) – The second cluster has a total of 7 keywords such as virtual reality (VR), human computer interaction, behavioural research, design, marketing, business research, and communication. The most frequent keywords that appeared within the cluster are "virtual reality" and "human computer interaction". This cluster indicates a focus on understanding user experiences, behaviour, and interactions within virtual environments.

Cluster 3 (red) – The third cluster has a total of 6 keywords such as sustainable development, innovation, sustainability, literature review, commerce, and knowledge management. The most frequent keywords observed within the cluster are "sustainable development" and "innovation". This cluster suggests an interest in exploring how the metaverse can contribute to sustainable innovations and knowledge-sharing practices.

Cluster 4 (blue) – The fourth cluster has a total of 7 keywords that include metaverses, augmented reality (AR), computation theory, decision making, consumer behaviour, and decisions making. The most frequent keyword observed within the cluster is "metaverses". This cluster indicates a focus on the technological aspects of the metaverse, particularly how AR and decision-making algorithms impact human interactions and experiences.

The other two clusters are comparatively small in size. The fifth cluster (yellow) has a total of only 3 keywords that include block-chain, blockchain, and digital storage. The last and smallest cluster has only 2 keywords, supply chain management and efficiency. Despite limited keywords, these two clusters point towards a focused inquiry into the role of blockchain and supply chain management within the field of metaverse.

Moreover, the various keywords in all the clusters, the keywords such as "human", "articles", "learning", "virtual reality", metaverses", "innovation", and "sustainable development" exhibit high frequencies of occurrence. This suggests that these keywords serve as a research hotspot within the realm of the nexus of metaverse and human resources. Further, they demonstrate strong connections with other keywords, as indicated by their large circle size, underscoring their high relevance in the field.

3.2.2. Thematic Map and Future Scope

The authors conducted an additional analysis to strengthen the findings and provide guidance for future research. The "bibliometrix" package in RStudio software provides an evolution of themes and thematic

Figure 5. Co-occurrence network
Source: *Extracted from RStudio*

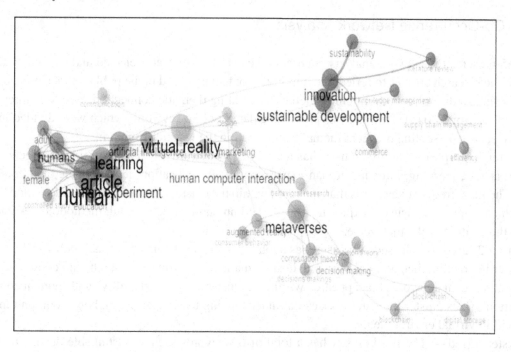

maps (Dhiman & Arora, 2023). The themes in the map are divided into four quadrants based on their centrality and density (see Figure 6). According to Cobo et al. (2011), the bottom right and left quadrants show emerging or underlying and crucial themes, whereas the top right and left quadrants are categorized as specialized and developed themes.

The upper left quadrant of the analysis represents the niche themes that have been developed but remain somewhat isolated within the research landscape. The themes covered in the first quadrant are human resource management practice, resource management, least squares approximations, and organizational, and theoretical framework. While these themes have been explored to some extent, there is room for improvement by incorporating new and insightful content that expands upon these existing themes. On the other hand, the upper right quadrant of the analysis represents motor themes that have grown substantially and are considered fundamental pillars shaping the research area. The topics covered in the second quadrant are sustainable development, metaverses, virtual reality, augmented reality, commerce, big data, blockchain, computation theory, decision-making, human resource management, knowledge management, technology adoption, innovation, resource management, human-computer interaction, human experiment, artificial neural network, personnel training, behaviour management, supply chain management, efficiency etc. These topics are not only foundational but also serve as base studies for further research and are considered important topics for research in the field of metaverse and human resources.

The lower left quadrant of the analysis represents the emerging or declining themes within the research landscape. The topics covered in the third quadrant are performance, structural equation models, climate change, and software. While these themes have received some attention, their importance and relevance in the field of metaverse and human resources are less pronounced than those in the upper right quadrant. Researchers may explore these themes with different constructs to identify their potential. Conversely, the lower right quadrant represents basic themes that are underexplored and have a very high level of relevance in the research. The topics covered in the fourth quadrant are economic and social effects, consumption behaviour, and social media. Despite their high relevance, these themes have received less attention. Therefore, the researchers are encouraged to focus on these particular themes to enhance the existing studies related to metaverse and human resources. By delving into these underexplored areas, researchers have the opportunity to uncover new insights and address gaps in the literature.

DISCUSSIONS

The metaverse and human resource management (HRM) intersection bibliometric analysis has yielded important insights into the present and future orientations of this developing field of study. The identification of significant themes, trends, and patterns in scholarly publications has provided a thorough overview of the body of literature. The bibliometric analysis reveals that there has been a notable surge in research on the subject, especially in the last several years. This is indicative of the growing understanding of the possible influence of the Metaverse on HRM procedures and organisational dynamics. The examination of the domain covered a wide range of subjects, such as talent manage-

Figure 6. Thematic evolution map
Source: *Extracted from RStudio*

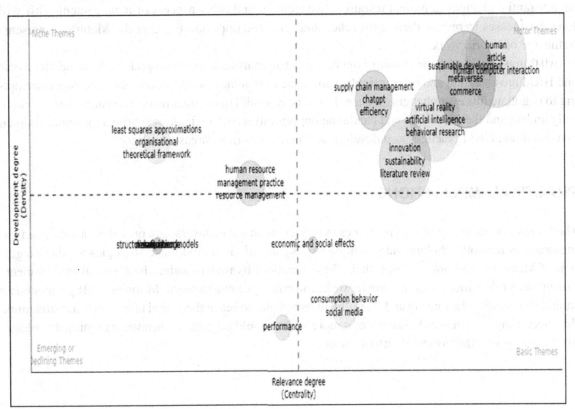

ment, employee engagement, virtual teams, and remote work, demonstrating the complex interplay between HRM and the Metaverse.

The analysis also emphasised how multidisciplinary this field of study is, with contributions from management, computer science, psychology, and sociology. This multidisciplinary method emphasises how difficult it is to research how technology and human behaviour interact in the workplace. The analysis also revealed important research gaps and areas that warrant further study. For example, despite a wealth of study on the potential advantages of the Metaverse for HRM, such as increased flexibility and collaboration, additional practical studies are required to support these assertions and examine any potential disadvantages or difficulties. Furthermore, the analysis identified patterns in research output related to geography and institutions, pointing to possible areas of collaboration and regions of focus for researchers and institutions. Future research projects and collaboration between various academic institutions and geographical areas may benefit from this.

The Metaverse can have AI-powered human-like bots for assistance. The separation of work and home life provides clarity to the employees. With the growing reliance of industries on technology, the metaverse will make its presence felt in almost all industries. For example, the concept of "Metaversity" has traction among academics, but the national boundaries will be blurred in terms of talent. The research on metaverse has accelerated after the COVID-19 pandemic. With industries looking for alternatives at similar times, the research trend on the topic is expected to remain positive. As Metaverse is still in its nascent stage, there are to be many research iterations till we get a product viable enough to replace the traditional scheme of things. Human resource management as well as other facets of management will be affected by this change in business but as hybrid work is the new reality, it's time for the companies to contemplate their future in the metaverse. As a result, there will be substantial changes in human resource management and other aspects of management. This will force businesses to review their approaches and seize the opportunities that the Metaverse presents in the age of hybrid work.

All things considered, the results of our bibliometric analysis help us comprehend how the Metaverse and HRM are changing and offer insightful guidance to scholars, practitioners, and legislators attempting to negotiate this ever-changing terrain. It will be essential to conduct further research in this field to fully understand the Metaverse and tackle the opportunities and difficulties it brings for organizational behaviour and HRM practices as it develops and permeates more areas of society.

PRACTICAL IMPLICATIONS

The review conducted on human resources management in the metaverse era provides various practical implications for both scholars and practitioners. Organizations should make strategies for the integration of Metaverse technologies into their HRM practices by understanding how virtual environments can enhance talent management, remote work, and employee engagement. Moreover, HR professionals should also modify their hiring and recruitment techniques to reach the global talent pool and streamline the onboarding experience. Managers of remote teams should upgrade to metaverse to mitigate engagement issues with other forms of virtual teams.

LIMITATIONS

While our study on bibliometric analysis of the metaverse and human resource management makes a unique and valuable contribution to the current literature, certain limitations need to be addressed in future research. Firstly, our data was sourced solely from a single database, Scopus, which may limit the generalizability of the results, suggesting the need to explore additional databases like Web of Science, EBSCOhost, ProQuest, Lens, Dimensions etc. to enhance the breadth of future studies. Moreover, since the concept of the metaverse is relatively dynamic and continually evolving, bibliometric analyses may struggle to capture the diversified source and lack relevant findings. Lastly, this review exclusively focused on published articles, perhaps ignoring valuable insights from other document types such as websites, white papers, newspaper articles, book chapters, and discussion notes. Future studies can explore these document types to enrich the studies. Despite these limitations, this literature review provides a comprehensive overview of the continue practices of human resources in the metaverse era.

CONCLUSION

The bibliometric analysis based on the HRM practices in the metaverse era offers both opportunities and challenges. This study highlights the multidisciplinary nature of this field and key trends. As the metaverse evolves, organizations must adapt their HRM practices to fully leverage its potential. By understanding the practical implications, organizations can effectively integrate metaverse technologies into their strategies, focusing on global talent acquisition, immersive training programs, virtual collaboration, and employee well-being. Addressing limitations and gaps in research is crucial for a comprehensive understanding of this rapidly evolving landscape. By leveraging insights from this study, organizations can capitalize on the metaverse's opportunities while managing its challenges, leading to more innovative and inclusive HRM practices in the digital age.

REFERENCES

Aria, M., & Cuccurullo, C. (2017). Bibliometrix: An R-tool for comprehensive science mapping analysis. *Journal of Informetrics*, *11*(4), 959–975. doi:10.1016/j.joi.2017.08.007

Arora, M. (2020). Post-truth and marketing communication in technological age. In *Handbook of research on innovations in technology and marketing for the connected consumer* (pp. 94–108). IGI Global., doi:10.4018/978-1-7998-0131-3.ch005

Arora, M. (2024). Virtual Reality in Education: Analyzing the Literature and Bibliometric State of Knowledge. *Transforming Education with Virtual Reality*, 379-402. doi:10.1002/9781394200498.ch22

Arora, M., & Rathore, S. (2023). Sustainability Reporting and Research and Development in Tourism Industry: A Qualitative Inquiry of Present Trends and Avenues. In International Handbook of Skill, Education, Learning, and Research Development in Tourism and Hospitality (pp. 1-17). Singapore: Springer Nature Singapore. doi:10.1007/978-981-99-3895-7_33-1

Arora, M., & Sharma, R. L. (2023). Artificial intelligence and big data: ontological and communicative perspectives in multi-sectoral scenarios of modern businesses. *Foresight, 25*(1), 126-143. doi:10.1108/FS-10-2021-0216

Bennett, E. E., & McWhorter, R. R. (2022). Dancing in the paradox: Virtual human resource development, online teaching, and learning. *Advances in Developing Human Resources*, 24(2), 99–116. doi:10.1177/15234223221079440

Boyack, K. W., & Klavans, R. (2014). Including cited non-source items in a large-scale map of science: What difference does it make? *Journal of Informetrics, 8*(3), 569–580. doi:10.1016/j.joi.2014.04.001

Buhalis, D., O'Connor, P., & Leung, R. (2023). Smart hospitality: From smart cities and smart tourism towards agile business ecosystems in networked destinations. *International Journal of Contemporary Hospitality Management*, 35(1), 369–393. doi:10.1108/IJCHM-04-2022-0497

Chaudhary, M., Jaswal, N., & Sohal, A. (2023). Demystifying the Relationship Between Emotional Intelligence and Leadership Effectiveness: Focusing on Mental Health and Happiness. In AI and Emotional Intelligence for Modern Business Management (pp. 113-133). IGI Global. doi:10.4018/979-8-3693-0418-1.ch008

Cobo, M. J., López-Herrera, A. G., Herrera-Viedma, E., & Herrera, F. (2011). Science mapping software tools: Review, analysis, and cooperative study among tools. *Journal of the American Society for Information Science and Technology*, 62(7), 1382–1402. doi:10.1002/asi.21525

Dhiman, V., & Arora, M. (2023). How foresight has evolved since 1999? Understanding its themes, scope and focus. *foresight*. doi:10.1108/FS-01-2023-0001

Dhiman, V., & Arora, M. (2024). *Exploring the linkage between business incubation and entrepreneurship: understanding trends, themes and future research agenda*. LBS Journal of Management & Research., doi:10.1108/LBSJMR-06-2023-0021

Dickey, M. D. (1999). *3D virtual worlds and learning: an analysis of the impact of design affordances and limitations in active worlds, blaxxun interactive, and onlive! Traveler; and a study of the implementation of active worlds for formal and informal education*. [Doctoral dissertation, The Ohio State University].

Donthu, N., Kumar, S., Mukherjee, D., Pandey, N., & Lim, W. M. (2021). How to conduct a bibliometric analysis: An overview and guidelines. *Journal of Business Research, 133*, 285–296. doi:10.1016/j.jbusres.2021.04.070

Dutta, D., Srivastava, Y., & Singh, E. (2023). Metaverse in the tourism sector for talent management: A technology in practice lens. *Information Technology & Tourism*, 25(3), 331–365. doi:10.1007/s40558-023-00258-9

Dwivedi, Y. K., Kshetri, N., Hughes, L., Slade, E. L., Jeyaraj, A., Kar, A. K., Baabdullah, A. M., Koohang, A., Raghavan, V., Ahuja, M., Albanna, H., Albashrawi, M. A., Al-Busaidi, A. S., Balakrishnan, J., Barlette, Y., Basu, S., Bose, I., Brooks, L., Buhalis, D., ... Wright, R. (2023). "So what if ChatGPT wrote it?" Multidisciplinary perspectives on opportunities, challenges and implications of generative conversational AI for research, practice and policy. *International Journal of Information Management*, *71*, 102642. doi:10.1016/j.ijinfomgt.2023.102642

Fahimnia, B., Sarkis, J., & Davarzani, H. (2015). Green supply chain management: A review and bibliometric analysis. *International Journal of Production Economics*, *162*, 101–114. doi:10.1016/j.ijpe.2015.01.003

Hajjami, O., & Park, S. (2023). Using the metaverse in training: Lessons from real cases. *European Journal of Training and Development*. Advance online publication. doi:10.1108/EJTD-12-2022-0144

Hwang, G. J., & Chien, S. Y. (2022). Definition, roles, and potential research issues of the metaverse in education: An artificial intelligence perspective. *Computers and Education: Artificial Intelligence*, *3*, 100082. doi:10.1016/j.caeai.2022.100082

KevinsJ. (2022) Metaverse as a New Emerging Technology: An Interrogation of Opportunities and Legal Issues: Some Introspection (SSRN paper 4050898). doi:10.2139/ssrn.4050898

Koohang, A., Nord, J. H., Ooi, K. B., Tan, G. W. H., Al-Emran, M., Aw, E. C. X., Baabdullah, A. M., Buhalis, D., Cham, T.-H., Dennis, C., Dutot, V., Dwivedi, Y. K., Hughes, L., Mogaji, E., Pandey, N., Phau, I., Raman, R., Sharma, A., Sigala, M., & Wong, L. W. (2023). Shaping the metaverse into reality: A holistic multidisciplinary understanding of opportunities, challenges, and avenues for future investigation. *Journal of Computer Information Systems*, *63*(3), 735–765. doi:10.1080/08874417.2023.2165197

Lazaroiu, G., Androniceanu, A., Grecu, I., Grecu, G., & Neguriţă, O. (2022). Artificial intelligence-based decision-making algorithms, Internet of Things sensing networks, and sustainable cyber-physical management systems in big data-driven cognitive manufacturing. *Oeconomia Copernicana*, *13*(4), https://doi.org/. doi:1047-1080

Nazma, R. B., & Devi, R. (2023). Sustainable Development Using Green Finance and Triple Bottom Line: A Bibliometric Review. *Management*, *1*, 22. doi:10.1177/ijim.231184138

Park, H., Ahn, D., & Lee, J. (2023). Towards a Metaverse Workspace: Opportunities, Challenges, and Design Implications. In *Proceedings of the 2023 CHI Conference on Human Factors in Computing Systems* (pp. 1-20). ACM. 10.1145/3544548.3581306

Park, S. M., & Kim, Y. G. (2022). A metaverse: Taxonomy, components, applications, and open challenges. *IEEE Access: Practical Innovations, Open Solutions*, *10*, 4209–4251. doi:10.1109/ACCESS.2021.3140175

Schlemmer, E., & Backes, L. (2015). The metaverse: 3D digital virtual worlds. In *Learning in Metaverses: Co-Existing in Real Virtuality* (pp. 48–81). IGI Global., doi:10.4018/978-1-4666-6351-0.ch003

Stephenson, N. (1992). *Snow Crash: A Novel*. Bantam Books.

Vig, S. (2023). Preparing for the New Paradigm of Business: The Metaverse. *Foresight and STI Governance (Foresight-Russia till No. 3/2015), 17*(3), 6-18. doi:10.17323/2500-2597.2023.3.6.18

Yilmaz, M., O'Farrell, E. & Clarke, P. (2023). Examining the training and education potential of the metaverse: results from an empirical study of next generation SAFe training. *Journal of Software: Evolution and Process*. doi:10.1002/smr.2531

Yu, F., Jian, S., Shen, C., Xue, W., & Fu, Y. (2022). On the Issue of "Digital Human" in the context of digital transformation. In *2022 International Conference on Culture-Oriented Science and Technology (CoST)* (pp. 258-262). IEEE. 10.1109/CoST57098.2022.00060

Zupic, I., & Čater, T. (2015). Bibliometric methods in management and organization. *Organizational Research Methods*, *18*(3), 429–472. doi:10.1177/1094428114562629

Chapter 6
From Clicks to Virtual Realms:
Exploring Metaverse–Driven E–Commerce and Consumer Shifts

Animesh Kumar Sharma
https://orcid.org/0000-0002-6673-319X
Lovely Professional University, India

Rahul Sharma
https://orcid.org/0000-0001-8880-7527
Lovely Professional University, India

Rajesh Verma
Lovely Professional University, India

ABSTRACT

This study conducts a comprehensive bibliometric analysis using the preferred reporting items for systematic reviews and meta-analyses (PRISMA) model to explore the convergence of e-commerce, customer experience, and virtual environments in the evolving metaverse. Utilizing Scopus database data from 2010 to 2023, this research aims to map the trends, patterns, and emerging themes surrounding augmented reality (AR), virtual reality (VR), and immersive technologies, shaping consumer behaviour within virtual realms. Initial screening resulted in a substantial corpus of scholarly articles, conference papers, and reviews. Moreover, utilizing visualization tools like VOSviewer, this study provides insightful graphical representations, revealing clusters and connections among keywords, and offering a deeper understanding of the interdisciplinary nature of Metaverse in e-commerce. The analysis focuses on quantifying publication trends, identifying influential authors, institutions, and countries, and mapping key themes and connections within the domain. The analysis encompasses a range of bibliometric indicators, including publication trends, prolific authors, influential journals, and co-occurrence networks of keywords It investigates how virtual environments affect purchasing decisions, brand interactions, and loyalty-building strategies, emphasizing personalized experiences, social interactions, and gamification. The analysis also uncovers emerging research trends and gaps, suggesting avenues for further exploration, including the integration of artificial intelligence, blockchain technology, and spatial computing

DOI: 10.4018/979-8-3693-2607-7.ch006

in enhancing e-commerce in virtual spaces. This research contributes to understanding the impact of the metaverse on e-commerce, customer experience, and engagement, providing valuable insights for academics, practitioners, and policymakers navigating this dynamic field.

INTRODUCTION

Digital technology development has had a profound impact on how businesses interact with their customers, constantly changing the face of commerce (Silitonga et al., 2024). A new age is about to begin, driven by developments in immersive technologies such as augmented reality (AR), virtual reality (VR), and others (Gasmi and Benlamri, 2022). In this new era, e-commerce is going to be significantly impacted by the idea of the Metaverse (Toraman and Geçit, 2023). In his 1992 novel "Snow Crash," science fiction writer Neal Stephenson first introduced the term "Metaverse," which describes a communal virtual area made up of linked virtual worlds, augmented reality settings, and the internet (Zakarneh et al., 2024). Here, users can engage, create, transact, and explore in fully virtual surroundings, symbolising the confluence of the physical and digital worlds. The Metaverse has gained traction in recent years as both startups and industry titans in technology have made significant investments in creating immersive digital experiences (Jeong et al., 2022). These encounters go beyond the confines of conventional e-commerce, giving customers a new way to interact and engage with goods and services. Metaverse has the power to completely transform e-commerce in several ways, including by improving customer interaction, changing the way people shop, and creating new avenues for companies to thrive in a society where everything is connected by technology (Periyasami and Periyasamy, 2022). Comparing the Metaverse to conventional e-commerce platforms, one can have a more engaging and dynamic buying experience. Thanks to augmented reality (AR) and virtual reality (VR) technology, users can browse products in 3D, explore virtual storefronts, and even try them on. Customers' levels of engagement and happiness can rise when they have an immersive experience that mimics what it feels like to be in a physical store (Baskaran, 2023). Massive volumes of user data are gathered and analysed by the Metaverse to provide highly customised product recommendations and customisation possibilities based on unique needs and preferences. Businesses may improve their conversion rates and the shopping experience considerably by implementing this degree of personalisation.

Through virtual surroundings, users can shop with friends, relatives, or other like-minded persons in the Metaverse, which promotes social connections and community participation (Oh et al., 2023). To foster a feeling of community and belonging around brands and products, social shopping experiences can incorporate live streaming, virtual events, and interactive discussions. By employing storytelling tactics, businesses may utilise the Metaverse to create virtual brand experiences and narratives that captivate people closer (Sutherland and Barker, 2023). A company can stand out in a competitive market by using interactive storytelling, virtual brand activations, and immersive product launches to strengthen emotional connections with its target audience. Branded virtual items, in-game advertising, virtual events, and virtual real estate sales are just a few of the new revenue streams and monetization opportunities that the Metaverse offers start-ups (Mancuso et al., 2023). Enterprises can expand their sources of income and reach untapped markets and consumer groups by capitalising on these prospects. Huge volumes of data about user behaviour, interactions, and preferences are produced by the Metaverse; this data provides businesses with important insights to improve their customer experiences, product offers, and marketing campaigns. To help organisations make data-driven decisions and remain ahead of market trends, advanced analytics tools and machine learning algorithms can analyse this data in real time.

The metaverse overcomes geographic boundaries, giving companies access to a worldwide customer base without being constrained by physical locations or distribution routes (Allam et al., 2022). Access to markets and possibilities is made more democratic by this worldwide accessibility, which puts independent producers and small enterprises on an even playing field with larger organisations. Exciting opportunities for e-commerce are presented by Metaverse, which redefines the shopping experience, boosts customer engagement, and creates new opportunities for companies to prosper in a linked digital environment (Dwivedi et al., 2022). Businesses may stay ahead of the curve and provide their clients with unique, immersive, and personalised experiences by embracing Metaverse and utilising its potential (Yemenici, 2022). In this chapter, we conduct a bibliometric study using the Preferred Reporting Items for Systematic Reviews and Meta-Analyses (PRISMA) methodology to investigate previous studies and the relationship between virtual reality, e-commerce, and the growing metaverse. This chapter provides an understanding of how the Metaverse might affect e-commerce, examining how it might change the way people buy, improve customer interaction, and open up new business prospects in a digital world where everything is connected. Additionally, this chapter attempts to explain future directions regarding the incorporation of the metaverse into online shopping procedures.

REVIEW OF LITERATURE

In recent years, the idea of the metaverse, a virtual reality environment where users can communicate with other users and a computer-generated world has drawn a lot of interest. Furthermore, because of modifications in consumer behaviour and technological improvements, the e-commerce landscape has changed. The idea of the metaverse a shared virtual environment for all—was born out of the convergence of augmented reality (AR), virtual reality (VR), and other digital platforms in recent years (Cappannari and Vitillo, 2021). In addition to changing the entertainment and gaming industries, this virtual world is also having a big impact on e-commerce and consumer behaviour. The concept of metaverse, a virtual realm where users interact with digital things in real-time, has emerged from the confluence of virtual reality (VR), augmented reality (AR), and numerous immersive technologies (Bibri and Jagatheesaperumal, 2022).

Metaverse and Virtual Reality (VR) Technologies

The metaverse's evolution has been made possible by the rise of virtual reality technologies. Slater and Sanchez-Vives (2016) emphasise immersive virtual reality (VR) and how compelling virtual environments can be made with it. Furthermore, Dincelli and Yayla (2022) talk about how technology is advancing to create connected virtual worlds, which are the foundation of the metaverse. Online shopping experiences can take on additional dimensions thanks to the metaverse's connection with e-commerce systems. To improve sensory experiences and boost purchase intentions, Liberatore and Wagner (2021) contend that immersive technologies like virtual reality (VR) and augmented reality (AR) allow users to interact with items in virtual settings. The immersive quality of the metaverse encourages a sense of presence and interaction, which lowers the anxiety that comes with making purchases online and increases customer confidence (Han et al., 2022). Furthermore, metaverse-powered e-commerce sites enable customised and engaging buying experiences. Rana et al. (2022) claim that AI-powered assistants installed in virtual shops may adjust to user preferences and make customised product recommendations, simulating the kind of individualised customer care found in physical retail establishments. Likewise, Allam et al. (2022) underscore the significance of social interactions in the metaverse, stressing how peer recommendations and social validation impact buying choices in virtual spaces.

Evolution of E-Commerce in the Metaverse

With the increasing accessibility of virtual reality technologies, e-commerce companies are investigating prospects in the metaverse. Companies are using virtual environments to provide realistic shopping experiences that let customers browse products in a simulated context (Xi and Hamari, 2021). Furthermore, Billewar et al. (2022) talk about how e-commerce platforms can include augmented reality (AR) and virtual reality (VR) technologies to improve the entire purchasing experience for customers. Thanks to developments in virtual reality (VR), augmented reality (AR), and mixed reality (MR) technologies, Kraus et al. (2022) describe how the metaverse has transformed from a theoretical idea to an actual platform. With immersive and engaging experiences that go beyond standard web interfaces, e-commerce within the metaverse offers a fresh take on online buying. The potential of virtual reality commerce (VRC) is that customers visually browse products and make purchases in a simulated setting (Dong et al., 2021). Businesses now face both new opportunities and challenges as e-commerce becomes more metaverse-driven. Some of these challenges include developing compelling virtual shops and incorporating seamless payment systems (Koohang et al., 2023).

Consumer Behaviour in the Metaverse

The changing preferences and behaviour of consumers are impacted by the metaverse. Consumers may be more influenced to make purchases by the immersive experiences provided by virtual environments (Lombart et al., 2020). Furthermore, as shoppers try to interact with people in virtual places as they shop, the study highlights the significance of social interactions within the metaverse (Hennig-Thurau et al., 2023).

Challenges and Opportunities

The metaverse offers chances for innovative e-commerce but also has drawbacks for both customers and companies. In their discussion of privacy and security concerns in virtual environments, Kim et al. (2023) emphasise the importance of taking strong precautions to safeguard user data. Furthermore, Yaqoob et al. (2023) emphasise how critical it is to remove technological obstacles to guarantee the smooth integration of e-commerce platforms with the metaverse. Notwithstanding its possible advantages, metaverse-driven e-commerce presents some difficulties. Widespread adoption may be hampered by technical issues including bandwidth and hardware requirements (Zawish et al., 2024). Furthermore, protecting data security and privacy in virtual environments continues to be a worry for both companies and customers. These difficulties do, yet also offer chances for development and innovation. Businesses that can successfully negotiate the metaverse's intricacies stand to benefit from a competitive advantage by providing distinctive and customised purchasing experiences.

Technical constraints, privacy problems, and regulatory obstacles are some of the challenges that metaverse-driven e-commerce faces, despite its potential benefits. Torous et al. (2021), found the complicated issues with data security and trust when real-world data is integrated with virtual environments. It is anticipated that to overcome these obstacles and realise the complete potential of the metaverse for e-commerce, experts stress the significance of interdisciplinary partnerships (Bibri and Jagatheesaperumal, 2023). Retailers and marketers face difficulties with metaverse-driven e-commerce, despite the great prospects it offers. In the metaverse, for example, users traverse virtual worlds with real-world ramifications, raising privacy and security problems (Ali et al., 2023). Furthermore, concerns regarding brand legitimacy and intellectual property rights are brought up by the growth of virtual markets (Hamza and Pradana, 2022). To increase engagement and loyalty, astute brands are utilising gamification and immersive storytelling to take advantage of the metaverse's ability to create closer ties with customers (Mittal and Bansal, 2023).

Exploring the possibilities of metaverse-driven e-commerce and its influence on customer behaviour is becoming more and more popular in the future. Wedel et al. (2020) predict that virtual environments will see a growing number of personalised shopping experiences and immersive product demos. Shen et al. (2021) also suggest doing further research on the psychological components of consumer behaviour in the metaverse, including how virtual interactions affect buying decisions.

Metaverse and E-Commerce Integration

The term "metaverse" refers to a network of virtual environments where people can communicate in real-time with one another and digital items. E-commerce sites are progressively connecting with the metaverse to produce immersive buying experiences as a result of technological advancements. For example, customers can browse and buy things using virtual avatars in virtual reality stores (Alzayat and Lee, 2021). In addition to improving the purchasing experience, this integration gives companies new opportunities to interact creatively with their customers. The metaverse is a virtual environment where people can communicate in real-time with one another and digital items. Using this immersive environment, e-commerce in the metaverse creates virtual shops where customers may browse, buy, and engage in new ways with goods and services (Enache, 2022). Businesses may now create virtual identities and interact with customers in incredibly immersive settings thanks to platforms like Roblox and Decentraland, which are leading the way in metaverse-driven e-commerce (Dwivedi et al., 2022).

Consumer Engagement and Immersion

The emphasis on consumer participation and immersion is one of the fundamental features of e-commerce powered by the metaverse. According to research, customers may be more engaged and satisfied when they have immersive experiences provided by the metaverse (Bousba and Arya 2022). Customers can see products in a virtual environment thanks to VR and AR technologies, which help them make better-educated purchases. Additionally, the metaverse's social component promotes a sense of community and belonging by enabling users to communicate with one another, ask for advice, and discuss their buying experiences. Social relationships, sensory experiences, and digital identities are some of the variables that influence consumer behaviour in the metaverse. Purchase intentions and brand perceptions are influenced by consumers' feelings of presence and immersion in virtual environments (Huang et al., 2024). Furthermore, Horng and Wu (2020) found that virtual communities and social networks have a big impact on how consumers choose to behave. In the metaverse, companies can improve customer engagement and loyalty by employing gamification and personalised experiences (Arya et al., 2023).

Consumer Shifts and Behavior

There have been significant changes in customer behaviour because of the metaverse's integration with e-commerce platforms. Bag et al. (2022) found in the study that traditional metrics used to measure online buying, like website traffic and conversion rates, may not be an effective indicator of customer engagement today. Instead, key indications of consumer behaviour are measurements like the amount of time spent in virtual environments and social interactions within the metaverse. Furthermore, the blending of real and virtual worlds has given rise to new ways for consumers to express themselves and define their identities, which has an impact on their purchasing behaviour and brand loyalty (Wongkitrungrueng and Suprawan, 2023). A fundamental shift in how customers interact with online buying is brought about by the convergence of e-commerce and the metaverse. Businesses must adjust as virtual reality technologies develop to satisfy the changing demands and tastes of customers in virtual settings. Businesses can take advantage of new chances to improve online purchasing and propel growth in the digital marketplace by comprehending the junction of consumer movements and metaverse-driven e-commerce.

The emergence of the metaverse has led to significant changes in consumer behaviour, which has prompted scholars to explore novel consumption patterns and reasons. Barrera and Shah (2023) studied that virtual world immersion promotes a feeling of escape by enabling users to explore alternative identities and satisfy aspirational desires through the customisation of their avatars and virtual belongings. Cheng et al. (2023) provide additional evidence in support of this escapism, arguing that people can experiment with self-expression and fantasy consumption without fear of repercussions in the actual world because of the anonymity provided by the metaverse. Consumer behaviour has undergone significant changes because of the metaverse's development. Customers are interacting with products in three dimensions and exploring virtual places, which leads to higher degrees of personalisation and engagement (Hollebeek et al., 2020). Customers can see how things fit and seem in real-time via virtual try-on experiences, for instance, which decreases purchase reluctance and improves the whole shopping experience (Hwangbo et al., 2020). Furthermore, community-driven commerce is encouraged by the metaverse's social aspect, allowing users to recommend, evaluate, and transact with other users (Chen et al., 2023). Moreover, e-commerce powered by the metaverse blurs the lines between online and offline experiences, resulting in the emergence of "phygital" consumption. Romano et al. (2021) studied that buyers are looking for smooth transitions between digital and physical worlds, and they are using augmented reality to see things in real life before deciding to buy them. The increasing significance of omnichannel strategies in metaverse-driven retailing is highlighted by this merging of digital and physical channels.

RESEARCH METHODOLOGY

This research adopts a systematic approach to explore and analyze the existing literature on consumer engagement in the metaverse from 2010 to 2023. The methodology involves several sequential steps, including data collection, bibliometric analysis, and data interpretation (Dhiman and Arora, 2024).

Research Design

The study employed a bibliometric analysis approach to examine the trends, patterns, and themes in the literature related to consumer engagement in the metaverse. Bibliometric analysis allows for a quantitative assessment of scholarly publications, facilitating the identification of key authors, journals, and research themes (Dhiman and Arora, 2024).

Data Collection

The selection of keywords is crucial for retrieving relevant literature from the Scopus database. Selecting appropriate keywords is paramount for effectively retrieving relevant literature from the vast repository of the Scopus database, which encompasses a diverse array of scholarly works. Considering this, a meticulous approach was undertaken to pinpoint keywords that directly correlate with the research topic. The chosen keywords were meticulously curated to encapsulate various facets of the subject matter. These keywords include "metaverse," representing the evolving virtual space where digital interactions occur; "e-commerce," denoting the electronic trading of goods and services; "customer experience," emphasizing the quality of interactions between consumers and businesses; "customer engagement," highlighting the active involvement of consumers with brands or products; "virtual realms," delineating the immersive digital environments within the metaverse; "consumer shift," elucidating the changing preferences and behaviours of consumers; and "metaverse in e-commerce," underscoring the intersection between virtual reality and online commerce. By strategically incorporating these keywords, the search process aims to yield comprehensive insights into the dynamics of the metaverse within the realm of e-commerce, facilitating a deeper understanding of consumer behaviour, market trends, and technological advancements in this burgeoning domain. These keywords were selected to ensure comprehensive coverage of the literature related to consumer engagement in the metaverse and its intersection with e-commerce.

The primary data source for this study is the Scopus database, which is a comprehensive repository of scholarly publications across various disciplines. Scopus provides access to a vast collection of peer-reviewed journals, conference proceedings, and other scholarly documents, making it an ideal resource for bibliometric analysis. A comprehensive study has been conducted with meticulous attention to inclusion and exclusion criteria. In the process of selecting relevant studies, certain parameters were established to ensure the quality and relevance of the data. The inclusion criteria comprised publications written exclusively in English, articles published within the timeframe spanning from 2010 to 2023, articles explicitly centring on consumer engagement within the metaverse, and those available in full-text format. Conversely, publications in languages other than English, articles published before 2010 or after 2023, articles not directly addressing consumer engagement in the metaverse, and inaccessible or incomplete publications were excluded from the study. This rigorous selection process aimed to gather a focused and comprehensive dataset for analysis, thereby enhancing the validity and reliability of the study's findings.

Bibliometric Analysis

Scopus is utilized as the primary database for retrieving relevant literature on consumer engagement in the metaverse. Scopus offers advanced search functionalities and citation analysis tools, enabling a comprehensive bibliometric analysis of the research output in this domain. This analysis is focused on articles published between 2010 and 2023 to capture the recent developments and trends in consumer engagement in the metaverse. The selected keywords are used to construct search queries tailored to the research topic. Boolean operators (AND, OR, NOT) are employed to refine the search queries and enhance the relevance of the retrieved results. The Preferred Reporting Items for Systematic Reviews and Meta-Analyses (PRISMA) framework will be employed to ensure transparency and rigour in the data extraction and analysis process. PRISMA provides a structured approach for conducting systematic literature reviews, thereby minimizing bias, and enhancing the reproducibility of this study. VOSViewer, a widely used software tool for bibliometric analysis, will be utilized to analyze and visualize the bibliographic data obtained from Scopus. VOSViewer enables the generation of bibliometric maps, co-authorship networks, and keyword co-occurrence networks, facilitating a comprehensive understanding of the research landscape. The retrieved publications are screened based on the inclusion and exclusion criteria outlined earlier. Duplicate records were removed, and the remaining articles underwent a thorough review to identify relevant studies focusing on consumer engagement in the metaverse. Key metrics such as publication year, authorship patterns, citation counts, journal impact factors, and keyword frequencies are extracted from the selected articles using Scopus and VOSViewer. The extracted data is synthesized to identify trends, patterns, and gaps in the literature on consumer engagement in the metaverse. The findings will be interpreted considering the research objectives and theoretical frameworks, providing insights into the evolving nature of consumer behaviour in virtual environments.

Research Questions

RQ1: What are the publication trends in the intersection of metaverse and e-commerce over the past decade, and how have they evolved?

RQ2: Who are the most influential authors, which institutions are leading in research output on virtual realms and consumer shifts and which key themes and connections are identified through co-occurrence networks of keywords in publications discussing customer engagement and metaverse in e-commerce?

RQ3: How do publication trends differ across countries concerning the integration of metaverse technologies into e-commerce platforms, and which countries are emerging as key contributors in this domain?

RESULTS AND DISCUSSIONS

The results of the study are summed up here. One other method for examining the intellectual structure of a study topic is bibliometric mapping, which appeared recently. Investigating this structure involves looking at the co-occurrence of author keywords and the bibliographic coupling of nations. With the help of the VOSviewer programme (University of Leiden, Netherlands), two-dimensional (2D) bibliometric networks that are easy to use and analyse in any study area may be created, explored, and visualised. Many different scientific domains have made use of this program. Below are the sections where the findings are shown. Analysis was conducted on 132 documents, of which 72 (54.54%) were categorised as journal publications (articles), and 60 (45.46%) as conference papers. The results are summarised in Fig 1 showing the PRISMA technique used in this study.

Figure 1. PRISMA

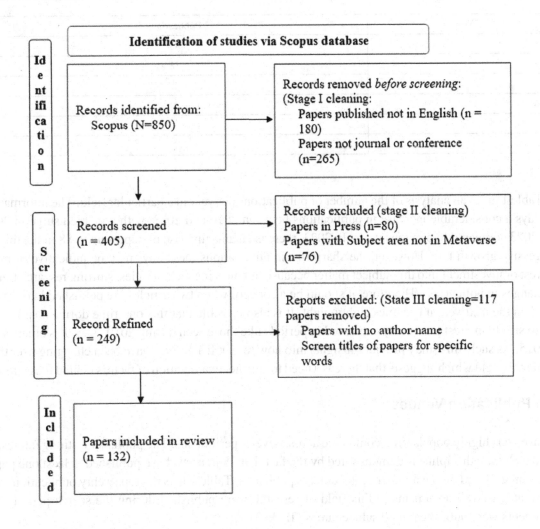

Trends in Publications

We found that the most often occurring keywords in technology for research on sustainable healthcare include metaverse, e-commerce, customer engagement, customer experience, consumer shifts, virtual realms and metaverse in e-commerce. The prevalence of "metaverse in e-commerce" indicates a rise in interest in the application of algorithms for data analysis and prediction in patient monitoring, treatment planning, and illness diagnosis. The terms "consumer shift" and "virtual realms" highlight the emphasis on leveraging modern technology in e-commerce.

Table 1 displays the year of publication and the most referenced publications (titles). This is quite useful for figuring out the themes that scholars in a field concentrate on. Examining superior articles could aid future scholars in developing their writing skills. These were the most often produced pieces in the region.

Table 1. Year wise publication

Year	Publications
2023	88
2022	38
2021	2
2016	1
2015	1
2010	2

Table 1 gives an analysis of the number of publications per year in a particular field. The information displays a considerable increase in publications between 2010 and 2023, with a marked surge in 2022 and 2023 compared to previous years. In 2023, there is an amazing rise of papers up to 88 indicating an impressive growth rate. However, the sharp rise in publications these days may be indicative of more interest or investment into this subject matter because of emerging technologies, shifting research trends or changes in policy(ies). Therefore, it should be a concern when two articles are published in one year and then the next year it becomes eighty-eight. It is also possible that this one-time dormant spike was due to steady interest previously expressed in periods like those seen during 2010 as well as others such as 2015. As such, this study provides insights into how research activities have been changing over time within this field which suggests that there is a need for further examination of factors behind these trends.

Top Publication Venues

Metaverse is highly popular in e-commerce across several periodicals. The publishers' strong interest in this developing discipline is demonstrated by the fact that 95 journals have published at least one paper in this area. Based on the number of documents published, Table 2 lists the top twenty publication sites where at least 180 documents in this field of research were published during the search period. 267 documents were published in 20 subject areas (Table 3).

In table 2, an analysis of publications across different venues is presented to provide an understanding of research output distribution. Significantly, "Linguistic and Philosophical Investigations" has the highest number of publications, which suggests its focus on linguistic and philosophical issues. After this, four articles were published in "Review of Contemporary Philosophy," "ACM International Conference Proceeding Series," "Influencer Marketing Applications within the Metaverse" as well as "Lecture Notes in Computer Science," thus indicating different interests from current philosophy to computer science and metaverse related subjects. Besides, the table often reveals several publication locations such as academic journals and conference proceedings that highlight the interdisciplinary nature of research space. The way that publications are distributed across different outlets gives insight into what scholarly communities value most among other things in linguistics, philosophy, computer sciences and emerging areas like metaverse studies.

Table 3 presents the analysis of publications across various subject areas. It shows that Computer Science has the highest number of publications with 68 articles while Business, Management, and Accounting have 45 publications. Engineering and Social Sciences are tied for third position with 27 publications each. Besides, other subject areas such as Economics, Arts and Humanities, Decision Sciences, Mathematics,

Table 2. Publication venue and number of publications

Publication Venue	No. of Publications
Linguistic And Philosophical Investigations	7
Review Of Contemporary Philosophy	5
ACM International Conference Proceeding Series	4
Influencer Marketing Applications Within the Metaverse	4
Lecture Notes in Computer Science Including Subseries Lecture Notes in Artificial Intelligence and Lecture Notes in Bioinformatics	4
Analysis And Metaphysics	3
Studies In Computational Intelligence	3
2023 International Seminar on Application for Technology of Information and Communication Smart Technology Based on Industry 4 0 A New Way Of Recovery From Global Pandemic And Global Economic Crisis Isemantic 2023	2
Business Horizons	2
Cyberpsychology Behavior and Social Networking	2
Developments In Marketing Science Proceedings of The Academy of Marketing Science	2
Electronic Commerce Research	2
Frontiers In Artificial Intelligence and Applications	2
Handbook Of Research on Consumer Behavioral Analytics in Metaverse and The Adoption of a Virtual World	2
Journal Of Cosmetic Dermatology	2

Energy etc., exhibit a reducing trend in publication volume over the years as indicated by this analysis. From this data, one can deduce that some fields such as medicine have relatively low publishing levels compared to other fields like computer science or business which have many researchers working on them. In turn, this could be crucial for informing scientists about where research is happening most and thereby, they would be able to make informed decisions regarding their studies in addition to providing information on where academic resources should be allocated.

The Most Prolific Nations and Institutions

A total of 182 countries have contributed to the journal and conference publications of works on health-care technology. The dispersion of papers among various countries is indicative of the diversity and international scope of research on the metaverse and e-commerce. It suggests that scholars are actively working on this topic and bringing their diverse viewpoints and methods to the table. Finding the most inventive and active locations in a research field can have an impact on future international partnerships among researchers. Table 4 shows the top fifteen (15) countries with the largest research output in metaverse, regions, and institutions. In terms of metaverse technology, the India and US have the most documents (20), followed by the United Kingdom (15 documents), South Korea (13), China (9), Italy (9), Slovakia (8), Romania (7), Australia (6), Malaysia (6), Canada (4), and other countries that also contribute. It is crucial to remember that this does not always imply the highest degree of network participation or worldwide impact in Metaverse technology. The findings show that the US is actively contributing significantly to developments and breakthroughs in e-commerce technology. Furthermore,

Table 3. Subject area and number of publications

Subject Area	No. of Publications
Computer Science	68
Business, Management and Accounting	45
Engineering	27
Social Sciences	27
Economics, Econometrics and Finance	20
Arts and Humanities	18
Decision Sciences	14
Mathematics	13
Energy	7
Materials Science	6
Psychology	6
Physics and Astronomy	5
Chemical Engineering	2
Environmental Science	2
Medicine	2
Agricultural and Biological Sciences	1
Biochemistry, Genetics and Molecular Biology	1
Earth and Planetary Sciences	1
Multidisciplinary	1
Nursing	1

the fact that the UK, Canada, India, Australia, and China are among the top contributors shows that there is interest worldwide and that efforts are being made to work together to use technology to overcome the difficulties associated with metaverse e-commerce. The findings once more highlight how important international cooperation and knowledge sharing are to e-commerce technology research. Finally, the presence of several nations contributing to the corpus of knowledge suggests the possibility of global collaborations, the exchange of effective strategies, and joint efforts to progress the area.

Co-Authorship Analysis

The co-authorship analysis of the reviewed manuscript using VOSviewer is displayed in Fig. 2. The plot was limited to writers who had at least 500 citations across five co-authored works. The arrows show the co-authorship connections between them. The size of each node in the dataset corresponds to the number of publications a researcher has co-authored. We saw a high dynamic of information exchange, cross-disciplinary teamwork, and idea flow in the field of technology for sustainable research. The result confirms the preliminary findings (see Table 5). In the field of metaverse in e-commerce technology, we have noted that Kwon, K.H. has several works. One more time, the clones between authors suggest that authors in this discipline collaborate more frequently.

Table 4. Countries and respective publications

Country	No. of Publications
India	20
United States	20
United Kingdom	15
South Korea	13
China	9
Italy	9
Slovakia	8
Romania	7
Australia	6
Malaysia	6
Canada	4
Germany	4
Morocco	4
Taiwan	4
United Arab Emirates	4

Table 5. Authors and number of publications

Author Name	No. of Publications
Kwon, K.H.	3
Lee, J.	3
Grupac, M.	2
Horak, J.	2
Korbel, J.J.	2
Lee, C.C.	2
Popescu, G.H.	2
Riva, G.	2
Valaskova, K.	2
Zarnekow, R.	2
Ahmed, E.	1
Ahn, S.J.	1
Al-Adaileh, A.	1
Al-Kfairy, M.	1

Table 5 presents the analysis of authors and their number of publications. Kwon, K.H. and Lee, J. have the highest number of publications, with three each. Following closely are Grupac, M., Horak, J., Korbel, J.J., Lee, C.C., Popescu, G.H., Riva, G., Valaskova, K., and Zarnekow, R., each with two publications. Other authors such as Ahmed E., Ahn S.J., Al Adaileh A. and Al-Kfairy M. have one publication each. Such distribution propounds that Kwon's inclusion in the list shows him as a highly productive author within this dataset where his input may be for instance significant than others or he was focused on it extensively in this field leading to multiple articles published under his name over time while some others whom we do not know well were only able to bring out one title per person thus trying to explain many things but this is hard since they can also produce highly valuable research output just like anybody else who could perhaps think that they are still new in this area compared to him or her at least until further research is done about them through which case any conclusions might come out later than expected should any findings be found by researchers concerning their work; however, no enough information has been given regarding these issues yet, therefore, our point remains valid enough before considering all aspects together again?. Additionally? a few more names appear alongside several authors who underlie series works and put together really many texts. Further on – there's another issue: other investigators' names have similar counting. This table provides a snapshot of author productivity within the field of study, highlighting both individual contributions and collaborative efforts. Deeper insights into the research landscape as well as potential avenues for future investigation can be gained from an examination of these publications themselves through further analysis of them would yield insightful knowledge about what is happening academically and how such work could be taken on in the future.

Co-Occurrence of Keywords

The current study investigated how knowledge is distributed in this field using keyword analysis. In addition, we were able to find new research directions because the links among the different themes were clear. Keyword co-occurrence in the documents this study examined is displayed in Table 6 and Fig. 2. The 182 documents examined in this paper contained a total of 557 keywords. The density-based spatial clustering was utilised in conjunction with the full counting strategy during the network development. The circles for the terms "metaverse," "virtual reality," "augmented reality," "customer experience," "electronic commerce," "immersive" "e-commerce," and other terms linked to making decisions are noticeably larger than the circles for the other categories.

Table 6 analyses the frequency of each keyword within the group of keywords extracted from the publication. As it can be seen, "Metaverse" exists the most, 60 times, and its derivative "Metaverses" exists 34 times. This signals high interest in the research related to the Metaverse concept. The terms directly connected with virtual and augmented reality, like "Virtual Reality" or "Augmented Reality," are also strong, which proves that these technologies are becoming relevant. Other important keywords were "Customer Experience," "Electronic Commerce," and "Sales," thereby assuming an important thematic focus to be around the area of overlap of immersive technologies with consumer behaviour and commerce applications. Interestingly, there are variances within the isolation of terms like "E- Commerces" and "E-commerce," meaning probably some form of mismatch of keywords within the literature. All in all, this table of information shows valuable results within the thematic landscape of the research and reflects what has been outlined and the possible avenues for further investigation. That demonstrates a huge focus with immense research having been put into vast fields of research interests, ranging from immersive technologies to economics, virtual environments to e-commerce, and other technological advancements that are involved in this, such as blockchain and digital twin technologies. "The big new rise of 'Metaverse' and 'Virtual Reality' suggests that interest associated with digital experiences and virtual environments was growing.

Table 6. Keywords and number of publications

Keywords	No. of Publications
Metaverse	60
Metaverses	34
Virtual Reality	25
Augmented Reality	19
Customer Experience	12
Electronic Commerce	11
Immersive	11
Sales	10
E- Commerces	9
E-commerce	9
Block-chain	8
Blockchain	8
Digital Twin	7
Consumer Behavior	6
Human	6
Internet Of Things	6
Marketing	6
Retail	6
Virtual Worlds	6
Avatar	5

Future Trends of Metaverse in E-Commerce

The future trends of the metaverse in e-commerce are likely to revolutionize the way we shop, interact, and experience online retail. Here are some potential trends to watch out for:

Virtual Stores and Marketplaces: E-commerce systems will build online shops and marketplaces in the metaverse where customers can peruse merchandise in fully immersive three-dimensional spaces. Compared to conventional e-commerce websites, these virtual storefronts will provide a more dynamic and interesting shopping experience.

Virtual Try-On and Product Visualization: Customers will be able to virtually try on clothing, see furniture in their homes, and test out products before making a purchase thanks to advances in virtual reality (VR) and augmented reality (AR) technologies. This will make physical storefronts less necessary and improve the online shopping experience.

Social Shopping Experiences: Users will be able to shop in virtual locations with friends, family, or online communities thanks to the integration of social aspects within the metaverse. This social element will strengthen the feeling of community and create a more joyful and cooperative shopping environment.

Personalized Recommendations and AI Assistants: Virtual assistants with AI capabilities will offer tailored product recommendations based on users' tastes, past web surfing activity, and metaverse

Figure 2. Co-occurrences of keywords

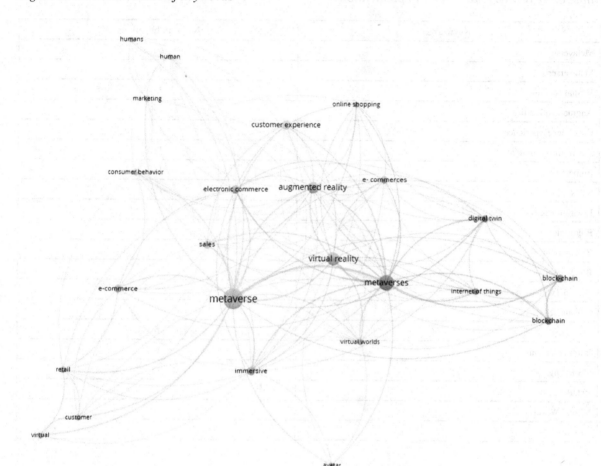

behaviour. When a user needs help or support, these AI assistants will help them along the way through their purchasing experience.

Virtual Events and Experiences: Stores and brands will use the metaverse to hold virtual events like interactive shopping, fashion shows, and product releases. A worldwide audience will be drawn to these events, which will also open new avenues for interaction and brand promotion.

Digital Assets and NFTs: In the metaverse economy, which enables users to purchase, sell, and exchange virtual products, collectables, and limited-edition items, NFTs and digital assets will be important components. Platforms for e-commerce will incorporate NFT markets and let users make money off their digital works.

Decentralized and Blockchain-based Commerce: With the use of blockchain technology, decentralised e-commerce platforms will be possible in the metaverse, providing an increased level of security, transparency, and confidence for online transactions. To ensure equitable and effective trade, smart contracts, and decentralised finance (DeFi) solutions will simplify payments.

Virtual Real Estate and Retail Spaces: Brands and merchants will make investments in virtual real estate within the metaverse to develop distinctive retail spaces and establish their presence. Customers from all around the world will be drawn to these virtual retail venues, which will act as pop-up shops, flagship stores, and experience marketing hubs.

Ultimately, by offering immersive, interactive, and customised buying experiences that surpass the constraints of conventional online retail, the metaverse will transform the future of e-commerce. We anticipate that as technology develops further, many more creative opportunities and solutions will present themselves in this quickly expanding digital environment.

IMPLICATIONS

Managerial and theoretical implications of the current research study are discussed below.

Managerial Implications

The emergence and exploration of the metaverse in e-commerce present several significant managerial implications for both retailers and marketers. Retailers and marketers need to invest in understanding how consumers interact within the metaverse environment. This includes studying user preferences, browsing patterns, purchase behaviour, and engagement metrics specific to virtual environments. Retailers should focus on creating immersive and engaging shopping experiences within the metaverse. Marketers should focus on maintaining brand consistency across virtual and physical channels while also adapting messaging and content to suit the unique characteristics of the metaverse environment. This research study of the metaverse in e-commerce underscores the transformative potential of virtual environments for retailers and marketers.

Theoretical Implications

The emergence of the Metaverse as a significant platform for various activities, including e-commerce, has sparked interest in understanding its implications for consumer behaviour. This research explores the theoretical underpinnings and implications of Metaverse-driven e-commerce on consumer shifts. By applying these theoretical frameworks, researchers can gain insights into the complex dynamics of Metaverse-driven e-commerce and its impact on consumer behaviour. Understanding these implications is essential for businesses, marketers, and policymakers seeking to navigate the evolving landscape of digital commerce in virtual worlds.

CONCLUSION

Our research sheds light on the transformative potential of the metaverse in shaping the landscape of e-commerce and consumer behaviour. Through an in-depth analysis of emerging trends, technological advancements, and consumer preferences, we have elucidated the profound impact of virtual environments on the way individuals interact, transact, and perceive products and services. The metaverse presents unprecedented opportunities for businesses to create immersive and personalized shopping experiences, fostering deeper engagement and loyalty among consumers. Moreover, it has the potential to democratize access to markets, particularly for small and medium-sized enterprises, by reducing barriers to entry and enabling innovative business models. However, amidst the promises of the metaverse, challenges such as privacy concerns, digital inequality, and regulatory uncertainties must be addressed to ensure its equitable and sustainable development. As we navigate this evolving landscape, businesses, policy-makers, and stakeholders must collaborate proactively in harnessing the full potential of the metaverse while mitigating its risks. By embracing innovation responsibly and prioritizing user-centric design principles, we can unlock new frontiers in e-commerce and consumer engagement, ushering in a future where virtual and physical worlds seamlessly converge for the benefit of all.

LIMITATIONS AND SCOPE OF FUTURE RESEARCH

The study's temporal scope is confined to the years 2010-2023, utilizing only the Scopus database. This limitation may overlook earlier seminal works or recent developments in Metaverse-driven e-commerce and consumer behaviour, potentially constraining the comprehensiveness of the analysis. Future research should extend beyond the confines of the Scopus database and encompass a broader range of scholarly repositories such as Web of Science, JSTOR, ERIC, ScienceDirect, IEEE Xplore, and others. This broader search strategy would enhance the inclusivity and diversity of the literature reviewed, providing a more comprehensive understanding of Metaverse-driven e-commerce and consumer shifts. Future research should adopt a cross-cultural perspective to investigate how cultural differences influence consumer be-haviours and preferences within the Metaverse. By examining diverse cultural contexts, researchers can uncover nuanced insights into the adoption, usage patterns, and impact of Metaverse-driven e-commerce on consumer behaviour worldwide. Complementing quantitative studies with qualitative approaches such as interviews, focus groups, or ethnographic research would provide deeper insights into the subjective experiences, motivations, and perceptions of consumers engaging with Metaverse-based platforms and virtual environments.

REFERENCES

Ali, M., Naeem, F., Kaddoum, G., & Hossain, E. (2023). Metaverse communications, networking, security, and applications: Research issues, state-of-the-art, and future directions. *IEEE Communications Surveys and Tutorials*, 1. doi:10.1109/COMST.2023.3347172

Allam, Z., Sharifi, A., Bibri, S. E., Jones, D. S., & Krogstie, J. (2022). The metaverse as a virtual form of smart cities: Opportunities and challenges for environmental, economic, and social sustainability in urban futures. *Smart Cities*, 5(3), 771–801. doi:10.3390/smartcities5030040

Alzayat, A., & Lee, S. H. M. (2021). Virtual products as an extension of my body: Exploring hedonic and utilitarian shopping value in a virtual reality retail environment. *Journal of Business Research*, 130, 348–363. doi:10.1016/j.jbusres.2021.03.017

Arya, V., Sambyal, R., Sharma, A., & Dwivedi, Y. K. (2023). Brands are calling your AVATAR in Metaverse–A study to explore XR-based gamification marketing activities & consumer-based brand equity in virtual world. *Journal of Consumer Behaviour*. doi:10.1002/cb.2214

Bag, S., Srivastava, G., Bashir, M. M. A., Kumari, S., Giannakis, M., & Chowdhury, A. H. (2022). Journey of customers in this digital era: Understanding the role of artificial intelligence technologies in user engagement and conversion. *Benchmarking, 29*(7), 2074–2098. doi:10.1108/BIJ-07-2021-0415

Barrera, K. G., & Shah, D. (2023). Marketing in the Metaverse: Conceptual understanding, framework, and research agenda. *Journal of Business Research, 155*, 113420. doi:10.1016/j.jbusres.2022.113420

Baskaran, K. (2023). Customer Experience in the E-Commerce Market Through the Virtual World of Metaverse. In *Handbook of Research on Consumer Behavioral Analytics in Metaverse and the Adoption of a Virtual World* (pp. 153–170). IGI Global. doi:10.4018/978-1-6684-7029-9.ch008

Bibri, S. E., & Jagatheesaperumal, S. K. (2023). Harnessing the potential of the metaverse and artificial intelligence for the internet of city things: Cost-effective XReality and synergistic AIoT technologies. *Smart Cities, 6*(5), 2397–2429. doi:10.3390/smartcities6050109

Billewar, S. R., Jadhav, K., Sriram, V. P., Arun, D. A., Mohd Abdul, S., Gulati, K., & Bhasin, D. N. K. K. (2022). The rise of 3D E-Commerce: The online shopping gets real with virtual reality and augmented reality during COVID-19. *World Journal of Engineering, 19*(2), 244–253. doi:10.1108/WJE-06-2021-0338

Bousba, Y., & Arya, V. (2022). Let's connect in metaverse. Brand's new destination to increase consumers' affective brand engagement & their satisfaction and advocacy. *Journal of Content. Community & Communication, 15*(8), 276–293. doi:10.31620/JCCC.06.22/19

Cappannari, L., & Vitillo, A. (2022). XR and Metaverse Software Platforms. *Roadmapping Extended Reality: Fundamentals and Applications*, 135-156. doi:10.1002/9781119865810.ch6

Chen, H., Duan, H., Abdallah, M., Zhu, Y., Wen, Y., Saddik, A. E., & Cai, W. (2023). Web3 Metaverse: State-of-the-art and vision. *ACM Transactions on Multimedia Computing Communications and Applications, 20*(4), 1–42. doi:10.1145/3630258

Cheng, X. U. (2023). From Fiction to Reality: Harnessing the Power of Imaginative Narratives to Shape the Future of the Metaverse. *Journal of Metaverse, 3*(2), 108–120. doi:10.57019/jmv.1277525

Dhiman, V. & Arora, M. (2024). Exploring the linkage between business incubation and entrepreneurship: understanding trends, themes and future research agenda. *LBS Journal of Management & Research.* doi:10.1108/LBSJMR-06-2023-0021

Dhiman, V., & Arora, M. (2024). How foresight has evolved since 1999? Understanding its themes, scope and focus. *Foresight, 26*(2), 253–271. doi:10.1108/FS-01-2023-0001

Dincelli, E., & Yayla, A. (2022). Immersive virtual reality in the age of the Metaverse: A hybrid-narrative review based on the technology affordance perspective. *The Journal of Strategic Information Systems, 31*(2), 101717. doi:10.1016/j.jsis.2022.101717

Dong, Y., Sharma, C., Mehta, A., & Torrico, D. D. (2021). Application of augmented reality in the sensory evaluation of yogurts. *Fermentation (Basel, Switzerland), 7*(3), 147. doi:10.3390/fermentation7030147

Dwivedi, Y. K., Hughes, L., Baabdullah, A. M., Ribeiro-Navarrete, S., Giannakis, M., Al-Debei, M. M., Dennehy, D., Metri, B., Buhalis, D., Cheung, C. M. K., Conboy, K., Doyle, R., Dubey, R., Dutot, V., Felix, R., Goyal, D. P., Gustafsson, A., Hinsch, C., Jebabli, I., & Wamba, S. F. (2022). Metaverse beyond the hype: Multidisciplinary perspectives on emerging challenges, opportunities, and agenda for research, practice and policy. *International Journal of Information Management*, *66*, 102542. doi:10.1016/j.ijinfomgt.2022.102542

Enache, M. C. (2022). Metaverse Opportunities for Businesses. *Annals of the University Dunarea de Jos of Galati: Fascicle: I. Economics & Applied Informatics*, *28*(1), 67–71. Advance online publication. doi:10.35219/eai15840409246

Gasmi, A., & Benlamri, R. (2022). Augmented reality, virtual reality and new age technologies demand escalates amid COVID-19. In *Novel AI and Data Science Advancements for Sustainability in the Era of COVID-19* (pp. 89–111). Academic Press. doi:10.1016/B978-0-323-90054-6.00005-2

Hamza, R., & Pradana, H. (2022). A survey of intellectual property rights protection in big data applications. *Algorithms*, *15*(11), 418. doi:10.3390/a15110418

Han, D. I. D., Bergs, Y., & Moorhouse, N. (2022). Virtual reality consumer experience escapes: Preparing for the metaverse. *Virtual Reality (Waltham Cross)*, *26*(4), 1443–1458. doi:10.1007/s10055-022-00641-7

Hennig-Thurau, T., Aliman, D. N., Herting, A. M., Cziehso, G. P., Linder, M., & Kübler, R. V. (2023). Social interactions in the metaverse: Framework, initial evidence, and research roadmap. *Journal of the Academy of Marketing Science*, *51*(4), 889–913. doi:10.1007/s11747-022-00908-0

Hollebeek, L. D., Clark, M. K., Andreassen, T. W., Sigurdsson, V., & Smith, D. (2020). Virtual reality through the customer journey: Framework and propositions. *Journal of Retailing and Consumer Services*, *55*, 102056. doi:10.1016/j.jretconser.2020.102056

Horng, S. M., & Wu, C. L. (2020). How behaviors on social network sites and online social capital influence social commerce intentions. *Information & Management*, *57*(2), 103176. doi:10.1016/j.im.2019.103176

Huang, W., Leong, Y. C., & Ismail, N. A. (2024). The influence of communication language on purchase intention in consumer contexts: The mediating effects of presence and arousal. *Current Psychology (New Brunswick, N.J.)*, *43*(1), 658–668. doi:10.1007/s12144-023-04314-9

Hwangbo, H., Kim, E. H., Lee, S. H., & Jang, Y. J. (2020). Effects of 3D virtual "try-on" on online sales and customers' purchasing experiences. *IEEE Access : Practical Innovations, Open Solutions*, *8*, 189479–189489. doi:10.1109/ACCESS.2020.3023040

Jeong, H., Yi, Y., & Kim, D. (2022). An innovative e-commerce platform incorporating metaverse to live commerce. *International Journal of Innovative Computing, Information, & Control*, *18*(1), 221–229. doi:10.24507/ijicic.18.01.221

Kim, M., Oh, J., Son, S., Park, Y., Kim, J., & Park, Y. (2023). Secure and Privacy-Preserving Authentication Scheme Using Decentralized Identifier in Metaverse Environment. *Electronics (Basel)*, *12*(19), 4073. doi:10.3390/electronics12194073

Koohang, A., Nord, J., Ooi, K., Tan, G., Al-Emran, M., Aw, E., & Wong, L. (2023). Shaping the metaverse into reality: Multidisciplinary perspectives on opportunities, challenges, and future research. *Journal of Computer Information Systems*. doi:10.1080/08874417.2023.2165197

Kraus, S., Kanbach, D. K., Krysta, P. M., Steinhoff, M. M., & Tomini, N. (2022). Facebook and the creation of the metaverse: Radical business model innovation or incremental transformation? *International Journal of Entrepreneurial Behaviour & Research, 28*(9), 52–77. doi:10.1108/IJEBR-12-2021-0984

Liberatore, M. J., & Wagner, W. P. (2021). Virtual, mixed, and augmented reality: A systematic review for immersive systems research. *Virtual Reality (Waltham Cross), 25*(3), 773–799. doi:10.1007/s10055-020-00492-0

Lombart, C., Millan, E., Normand, J. M., Verhulst, A., Labbé-Pinlon, B., & Moreau, G. (2020). Effects of physical, non-immersive virtual, and immersive virtual store environments on consumers' perceptions and purchase behavior. *Computers in Human Behavior, 110*, 106374. doi:10.1016/j.chb.2020.106374

Mancuso, I., Petruzzelli, A. M., & Panniello, U. (2023). Digital business model innovation in metaverse: How to approach virtual economy opportunities. *Information Processing & Management, 60*(5), 103457. doi:10.1016/j.ipm.2023.103457

Mittal, G., & Bansal, R. (2023). Driving Force Behind Consumer Brand Engagement: The Metaverse. In Cultural Marketing and Metaverse for Consumer Engagement (pp. 164-181). IGI Global. doi:10.4018/978-1-6684-8312-1.ch012

Oh, H. J., Kim, J., Chang, J. J., Park, N., & Lee, S. (2023). Social benefits of living in the metaverse: The relationships among social presence, supportive interaction, social self-efficacy, and feelings of loneliness. *Computers in Human Behavior, 139*, 107498. doi:10.1016/j.chb.2022.107498

Papagiannidis, S., Pantano, E., See-To, E. W., Dennis, C., & Bourlakis, M. (2017). To immerse or not? Experimenting with two virtual retail environments. *Information Technology & People, 30*(1), 163–188. doi:10.1108/ITP-03-2015-0069

Periyasami, S., & Periyasamy, A. P. (2022). Metaverse as future promising platform business model: Case study on fashion value chain. *Businesses, 2*(4), 527–545. doi:10.3390/businesses2040033

Pizzi, G., Scarpi, D., Pichierri, M., & Vannucci, V. (2019). Virtual reality, real reactions?: Comparing consumers' perceptions and shopping orientation across physical and virtual-reality retail stores. *Computers in Human Behavior, 96*, 1–12. doi:10.1016/j.chb.2019.02.008

Rana, J., Gaur, L., Singh, G., Awan, U., & Rasheed, M. I. (2022). Reinforcing customer journey through artificial intelligence: A review and research agenda. *International Journal of Emerging Markets, 17*(7), 1738–1758. doi:10.1108/IJOEM-08-2021-1214

Romano, B., Sands, S., & Pallant, J. I. (2021). Augmented reality and the customer journey: An exploratory study. *Australasian Marketing Journal, 29*(4), 354–363. doi:10.1016/j.ausmj.2020.06.010

Shen, B., Tan, W., Guo, J., Zhao, L., & Qin, P. (2021). How to promote user purchase in metaverse? A systematic literature review on consumer behavior research and virtual commerce application design. *Applied Sciences (Basel, Switzerland), 11*(23), 11087. doi:10.3390/app112311087

Silitonga, D., Rohmayanti, S. A. A., Aripin, Z., Kuswandi, D., Sulistyo, A. B., & Juhari. (2024). Edge Computing in E-commerce Business: Economic Impacts and Advantages of Scalable Information Systems. *EAI Endorsed Transactions on Scalable Information Systems*, *11*(1). Advance online publication. doi:10.4108/eetsis.4375

Slater, M., & Sanchez-Vives, M. V. (2016). Enhancing our lives with immersive virtual reality. *Frontiers in Robotics and AI*, *3*, 74. doi:10.3389/frobt.2016.00074

Sutherland, K. E., & Barker, R. (2023). The Future of Transmedia Brand Storytelling and a Model for Practice. In Transmedia Brand Storytelling: Immersive Experiences from Theory to Practice (pp. 247-271). Singapore: Springer Nature Singapore. doi:10.1007/978-981-99-4001-1_12

Toraman, Y., & Geçit, B. B. (2023). User acceptance of metaverse: An analysis for e-commerce in the framework of technology acceptance model (TAM). *Sosyoekonomi*, *31*(55), 85–104. doi:10.17233/sosyoekonomi.2023.01.05

Torous, J., Bucci, S., Bell, I. H., Kessing, L. V., Faurholt-Jepsen, M., Whelan, P., Carvalho, A. F., Keshavan, M., Linardon, J., & Firth, J. (2021). The growing field of digital psychiatry: Current evidence and the future of apps, social media, chatbots, and virtual reality. *World Psychiatry; Official Journal of the World Psychiatric Association (WPA)*, *20*(3), 318–335. doi:10.1002/wps.20883 PMID:34505369

Wedel, M., Bigné, E., & Zhang, J. (2020). Virtual and augmented reality: Advancing research in consumer marketing. *International Journal of Research in Marketing*, *37*(3), 443–465. doi:10.1016/j.ijresmar.2020.04.004

Wongkitrungrueng, A., & Suprawan, L. (2023). Metaverse meets branding: Examining consumer responses to immersive brand experiences. *International Journal of Human-Computer Interaction*, 1–20. doi:10.1080/10447318.2023.2175162

Xi, N., & Hamari, J. (2021). Shopping in virtual reality: A literature review and future agenda. *Journal of Business Research*, *134*, 37–58. doi:10.1016/j.jbusres.2021.04.075

Yaqoob, I., Salah, K., Jayaraman, R., & Omar, M. (2023). Metaverse applications in smart cities: Enabling technologies, opportunities, challenges, and future directions. *Internet of Things : Engineering Cyber Physical Human Systems*, *100884*, 100884. Advance online publication. doi:10.1016/j.iot.2023.100884

Yemenici, A. D. (2022). Entrepreneurship in the world of metaverse: Virtual or real? *Journal of Metaverse*, *2*(2), 71–82. doi:10.57019/jmv.1126135

Zakarneh, B., Annamalai, N., Alquqa, E. K., Mohamed, K. M., & Al Salhi, N. R. (2024). Virtual Reality and Alternate Realities in Neal Stephenson's—Snow Crash‖. *World Journal of English Language*, *14*(2), 244. doi:10.5430/wjel.v14n2p244

Zawish, M., Dharejo, F. A., Khowaja, S. A., Raza, S., Davy, S., Dev, K., & Bellavista, P. (2024). AI and 6G into the metaverse: Fundamentals, challenges and future research trends. *IEEE Open Journal of the Communications Society*, *5*, 730–778. doi:10.1109/OJCOMS.2024.3349465

Chapter 7
Metaverse:
Transforming the User Experience in the Gaming and Entertainment Industry

Pooja Swami
Chaudhary Devi Lal University, India

ABSTRACT

The concept of the metaverse is not new, as it dates back to 1992, but it is an interesting area that is receiving increased attention from researchers and marketers. This chapter provides insight into how the emerging virtual world of the metaverse is significantly enhancing the user experience in the gaming and entertainment industries by leveraging the latest technologies such as augmented reality (AR), virtual reality (VR), artificial intelligence (AI), blockchain technology, NFT, and others. This chapter aims to provide insight into the current developments in metaverse entertainment and gaming applications and how they will affect our user experience in the future. The approach used in this study is based on a comprehensive literature review on the subject of metaverse applications and their potential future in the gaming and entertainment industries. This chapter also discusses the various opportunities for the metaverse in the near future, as well as the challenges involved with it, such as privacy, security, and inclusivity.

INTRODUCTION

The next revolution in internet technology is "Metaverse". The metaverse can be defined as a network of interconnected virtual worlds, enabling real-time interaction between users and the digital environment. The term "metaverse" is derived from the fusion of the ancient Greek words "Meta" and "Verse." The word "verse" originates from the English term "universe," which signifies the whole universe and the word "meta" which comes from ancient Greek means both "after" and "beyond." So, this is a combination of terms meta and verse that make up the term "Metaverse," which emphasizes the fact that the virtual world is a post-real universe (Ergen, 2022). The metaverse originally is a concept from a science fiction novel Snow Crash written by an American writer Neal Stephenson which was published in 1992 and

DOI: 10.4018/979-8-3693-2607-7.ch007

today this concept has come into extensive usage in different spheres of various industries in the world via the development of technologies like virtual reality (VR), augmented reality (AR), extended reality, blockchain, and non-fungible tokens (NFTs) and its widespread application can be seen especially in the gaming and entertainment industry. These technologies facilitate in creating immersive, interactive, and innovative virtual environments, where users can engage in gaming, adventure, social interaction, and fun experiences. The metaverse is predominantly being leaded by the gaming and entertainment industries because it improves storytelling, encourages world-building by letting users customize their virtual environments, and encourages fan creativity by providing users with more control over the experiences and content they consume. As per a report from Exactitude Consultancy, the global metaverse gaming market is projected to grow from USD 90.58 Billion in 2023 to USD 874.36 Billion by 2030, with a compound annual growth rate (CAGR) of 38.25% during the projection period (Exactitude consultancy, n.d.). In the entertainment and media industry, the metaverse globally is expected to reach $221.7 billion by 2031, rising at a (CAGR) of 32.3%, as per a report published by Allied Market Research (Alliedmarketresearch., n.d.). With Metaverse's 3D capabilities, users can immerse themselves in a variety of media and entertainment activities. The literature appears to have presented an implications-based approach on a variety of aspects of the metaverse, with studies analyzing the transformational influence from institutional and societal perspectives, noting both challenges and unwanted impacts on users (Lee et al., 2021). The metaverse is an emerging subject for academics to research about, and this study provides a narrative about how the metaverse is a revolution in the gaming and entertainment industry. This chapter aims to bring insight into the applications of metaverse technologies in the gaming and entertainment industries, as well as how the metaverse is transforming the user experience in these industries and what implications it has for the future in terms of opportunities and challenges for the users and industries.

METAVERSE IN GAMING INDUSTRY

The term "metaverse" is used in the gaming industry to describe a collective virtual shared area that is created as a result of the interplay between the actual world and the virtual world. Inside the metaverse games, players have the opportunity to participate in a wide variety of activities, such as playing games, socializing with other players, creating and trading virtual assets and taking part in various types of engaging interactions (Oliveira & Cruz, 2023). Meta-gaming surpasses conventional gaming by providing a smooth and seamlessly integrated virtual world that extends across various games and experiences. The key elements of metaverse in gaming includes virtual economies with blockchain-based assets like non-fungible tokens (NFTs), content created by players, cross-platform interoperability and customized avatars for permanent identity. Gaming is becoming increasingly immersive, networked, and dynamic through the metaverse, which extends across games and platforms (Bhattacharya et al., 2023).

METAVERSE IN ENTERTAINMENT AND MEDIA INDUSTRY

In the context of the entertainment and media industry, the metaverse can be defined as the integration of advanced technologies such as virtual reality (VR), augmented reality (AR), blockchain, and artificial intelligence (AI) to provide users an immersive and stimulating environment that redefines the conventional definitions of entertainment. The introduction of virtual events and performances allows users to experience concerts and other events in a digital setting with actual artists (Baía Reis & Ashmore, 2022). Also, the immersive storytelling takes center stage with interactive stories that allow viewers to actively assess the story's progression. In virtual spaces, people can watch movies, TV shows, or live events together, making shared watching experiences possible. Virtual cinemas and theaters recreate the familiar experience of watching movies in traditional theatres while virtual museums and exhibitions provide a chance to explore the world of art, history, and culture through digital eyes (Baía Reis & Ashmore, 2022). Overall, the media and entertainment industry's metaverse represents a revolutionary change toward digital experiences that are more participatory, immersive, and linked which is influencing the content creation and its consumption.

META-GAMES ECOSYSTEM: UNDERSTANDING THE INTERCONNECTED VIRTUAL SPACE

Meta-games ecosystem is based on the fundamental structure that governs the metaverse's interconnected virtual spaces. In this context, a "meta-game" is core framework that includes different games, experiences, and interactions in the virtual environment. This ecosystem is created to allow seamless communication and interoperability between several virtual worlds, allowing players to move between them and engage with diverse content. As shown in figure 1 the metaverse gaming ecosystem consists of following components:

Avatar

A significant element that makes a virtual experience in the metaverse different from other digital platforms is the appearance of an avatar. An avatar is a visual representation of someone in a game or virtual world, serving as an alternative to the commonly known profile image. The avatar is a very authentic 360-degree representation that can convert the profile photograph into three-dimensional visuals, accompanied by remarkably human like expressions and gestures, so enhancing the whole experience (Kim et al., 2023). The avatar serves several purposes like as working, communicating, playing, designing clothes, trying them on, and shopping through different applications. It can even transfer virtual purchases made within the game into real-life products.

Presence

One of the first things a player feels is presence since the metaverse makes it possible to see the body parts, its movements, its facial expressions, and how it moves between psychological emotions as though the scene actually exists. "Presence" means a feeling of being physically present in a virtual environment. It refers to a player's sense of immersion and how connected and engaged they feel in the digital world (Voinea et al., 2022).

Homespace

Within the broader metaverse, a player's "Homespace" is their own unique, customized virtual environment or space where their avatar is located and where they can relax and rejuvenate. This space is

Figure 1. Metaverse gaming ecosystem

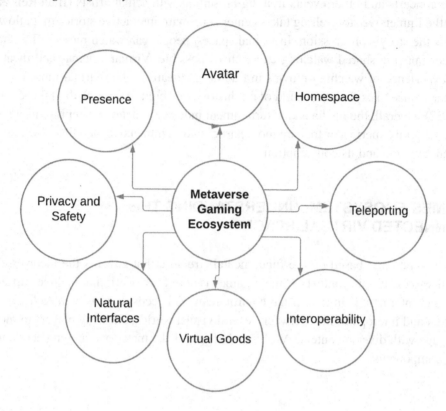

usually created according to the player's tastes and personality, giving them a spot to unwind, socialize, and engage in other activities (Macedo et al., 2022).

Teleporting

Teleporting means an avatar's ability to easily move between locations and places on a single click. The ability to teleport enables players to shop for goods and services across multiple stores and locations by simply clicking a particular button that transports them to a different space, enabling them to engage in the intended activities (Shahbaz Badr & De Amicis, 2023). This feature gives the avatar the power to jump from one exciting place to another making the whole experience fast, convenient and joyful.

Interoperability

In the context of metaverse games, interoperability means that players can move between and connect with different virtual worlds, platforms, and even across different metaverses keeping their digital presence intact throughout. It is designed to ensure that players can easily move between games and virtual universes by taking their digital items, avatars, and awards with them. This interoperability enables players to enter the metaverse from a variety of devices, including virtual reality setups, PCs, and gaming consoles, thereby ensuring a smooth experience (Li et al., 2023).

Virtual Goods

Virtual goods represent digital products or assets purchased, earned and used by players in metaverse games. Virtual goods include everything from virtual real estate and in-game currencies to fully customizable avatars, outfits, weapons and other accessories. Virtual goods are a key element of the gaming experience because they allow players to customize their avatars, express themselves, and engage in economic activities (Shen et al., 2021). Notably, these virtual products are purchased, sold, and traded in the metaverse with the use of blockchain technology.

Natural Interfaces

In metaverse games, natural interfaces are means of user interaction that imitate or match natural human movements, gestures, facial expressions or behaviors. The goal of these interfaces is to make the virtual gaming environment more immersive and intuitive. One of its example is tracking the eye movements of player that allows the game to respond to where the player is looking like aiming and selecting objects (Gao & Yu, 2023).

Privacy and Safety

Today, all electronic games are based on security and privacy features. This means that players can pick and choose who they play with and block others as required. Because these platforms are built on strong safety and security rules, players are always in a safe place. Besides these safety measures, many gaming platforms also have parental settings that allow parents limit their children's access to certain game content based on their age.

META-GAMES: THE APPLICATION OF METAVERSE IN GAMING INDUSTRY

The emergence of the metaverse signifies a revolutionary change in the digital interactions landscape, especially in the gaming industry. Beyond traditional gaming, the metaverse is an immersive, interconnected digital place for gamers where they can effortlessly travel from one virtual world to another. The following are the ways in which the integration of the metaverse into games is enhancing the gaming experience for players:

Immersive Gameplay

The metaverse fosters immersive gameplay through the integration of innovative technologies such as augmented reality, virtual reality, spatial computing, interlinked virtual environments, user-generated content and social interactions.

Enhanced Virtual Environments. Metaverse environments can provide near-realistic physics, allowing for natural and intuitive interactions with objects and their surroundings. The players can climb rocks with grips that feel like real ones and use weapons that have the same weight and momentum (Shin, 2022). For example, A famous action role-playing game developer, CD Projekt is known for creating

"Cyberpunk 2077," an open-world game set in the future. The game's rich urban landscapes, dynamic weather, and day-night cycles all contribute to the game's realistic and immersive virtual environment.

Real time Interaction. Real-time interaction enables players to interact and have conversations with one another in a virtual environment. It is implemented by a variety of techniques, including voice chat, text messaging, and, in some cases, gestures or body language, depending on the amount of immersion offered by the game. Multiplayer games primarily rely on it as it enable players to coordinate strategies, share experiences, and communicate with one another in a virtual world, fostering a sense of connection and presence (Zhao et al., 2022).

Virtual Economies and In-Game Assets

In metaverse games, "virtual economies" and "in-game assets" mean the creation of monetary systems within virtual worlds, wherein the game's resources and virtual goods have monetary value and can be purchased, sold, and traded. It enables the players to engage in economic activities that resemble real-world market dynamics which is crucial for enhancing playing experience.

Tokenization of In-Game Items. To tokenize in-game items, metaverse games commonly make use of blockchain technology. Each item is transformed into a unique, marketable asset that is represented by a non-fungible token (NFT) ensuring ownership and exclusivity (Scheiding, 2023). For example, in the game "Cryptokitties," virtual cats are converted into NFTs that can be tokenized on the Ethereum blockchain. Each Cryptokitty is a separate digital asset with its traits and qualities. The blockchain safely records who owns the cats and their traits so players can buy, sell, and breed them on outside markets.

Economic Opportunities for Players. Many metaverse platforms allow players to create and trade content of their own which can involve virtual art and designs, personalized avatars, and in-game experiences. Players can earn money from their creativity by catering to the needs and wants of their virtual community. These virtual economies are designed to mimic real-world economic systems such as farming, crafting, and resource gathering are a few examples of activities that players may take part in to generate in-game wealth (Vidal-Tomás, 2022). In the case of "Decentraland," a blockchain-based virtual world, players can buy, sell, and develop their virtual land as well as make cryptocurrency by monetizing virtual experiences.

Cross-Platform Integration

Cross-platform integration in metaverse games enables players to access their gaming experiences across a variety of devices and platforms, including desktops, smartphones, tablets, and virtual setups.

Seamless Gaming Across Devices. Simply said, "seamless gaming across devices" means that players can move freely and continue playing on other devices as well. This feature ensures a seamless and continuous gaming experience by enabling users to play the same game on many platforms, access their in-game progress, and interact with the virtual world consistently (Rane et al., 2023). For example, Epic Games' "Fortnite" allows users to use the same account across multiple devices, including desktops, gaming consoles, and smartphones. The availability of this cross-platform functionality ensures a more consistent gaming experience.

Social Interaction and Community Building. The metaverse hosts virtual events, meetings, and in-game celebrations that players can join. These events offer opportunities to socialize, make new friends, and participate in community-driven activities in the virtual games. To facilitate player-to-player interaction in the metaverse, games have integrated real-time communication capabilities which includes voice chat, text messaging, and gestures which help build community. For example, Players in "VRChat" can create their avatars, discover user-generated worlds, and communicate with others in real time. Social hubs inside the game serve as gathering areas where people gather for events, conversations, or just to socialize.

METAVERTAINMENT: THE NEW ERA OF ENTERTAINMENT INDUSTRY

When we refer to "metavertainment" it is really just a combination of the words "metaverse" and "entertainment," and it defines an act of consuming entertainment within the metaverse itself. It includes a wide variety of entertainment activities that bring people together in a shared digital space by using augmented reality and virtual reality (VR) technologies. The rising urge for work-from-home and remote working technological advancements has played an important role in the sprawling of the metaverse in the entertainment industry (Ghryani et al., 2023). Furthermore, the metaverse's ability to connect people to a community also drives its rise in the entertainment sector. The following are some of the ways in which the users are enjoying immersive experiences from the application of metaverse into entertainment:

Immersive Cinematic Experiences

With the metaverse's ability to create immersive and interactive storylines, it has changed the whole experience of watching movies. In contrast to the 2D cinematic experience, where viewers would simply recline and watch a story being unfolding on screen, the metaverse brings a new dimension—an immersive one where viewers can even interact with characters and shape the storyline.

Virtual Movie Theatres and Interactive Films. When virtual movie theaters and interactive movies come together, they create a new kind of movie theater experience in the metaverse. In these new theatres, people put on virtual reality headsets and become immersed in a shared virtual movie theater, like "Bigscreen" (Vosmeer & Schouten, 2014). Here, they can not only watch movies on a big virtual screen, but they can also use avatars to talk to friends or other watchers in real time. For example, "Number One Player" and "Out of Control Player" are the quintessential "Metaverse" films of recent times. "Number One Player" generated a remarkable revenue of 1.4 billion US dollars at the box office during its release in March 2018. Also, "Out of Control Players" earned 150 million in its first week, creating significant buzz on various social media platforms (Chaintechsource, n.d.).

Virtual Concerts and Shows. The academic literature defines virtual concerts in different ways; some definitions include holographic concerts, livestream concerts and concerts that need VR technology. Here a virtual concert is defined as any kind of musical performance where the audience is immersed in a digital environment via the use of avatars. Most of these virtual concerts are found on blockchain technology, as in The Sandbox or Decentraland or on games such as in Fortnite, Second Life, Roblox or Minecraft (Yakura & Goto, 2020). Virtual shows in the metaverse have raised the bar for entertainment, giving fans exciting and thrilling experiences. An example worth mentioning is Travis Scott's virtual music concert in Fortnite which is one of the most popular video games in the world. The concert attracted more than 12 million live viewers worldwide and featured magnificent visuals and interactive sections making it a grand success (Stefanic, 2023).

Virtual Theme Parks and Attractions

Virtual theme parks are advanced digital recreations of traditional amusement parks into fictional or fantasy-like environments built in the metaverse. These parks are built on digital technologies to provide visitors with immersive and sensory-rich experiences. Users can experience a vast variety of rides, attractions, and themed locations in these virtual places all from the comfort of their homes (Marr, 2023).

Simulated Theme Park Experiences. Simulated theme parks attempt to replicate and provide the same adventurous experience as physical amusement parks in the real world. The goal is to recreate the feel of a physical theme park, filled with thrilling roller coaster rides, interactive elements, entertainment shows, and themed zones (Marr,2023). For example, Walt Disney Co. acquired a patent in 2021 for setting up virtual world simulator projecting three-dimensional pictures onto actual objects to engage with theme park tourists, making it easier to provide personalized interactive attractions for visitors across its theme parks. The company has 12 theme parks in several countries, including the United States, Paris, Japan, Hong-Kong and China (Blockchain Council, n.d.).

Virtual Reality Rides and Adventures. VR Adventures offers 4D simulators that enable players to engage in activities such as walking, climbing, exploring, and flying within virtual environments. Virtual rides provide thrilling stimulations that virtually imitate the sensations that are experienced while riding a roller coaster, driving a racing car or participating in other thrilling activities (Spence, 2021). Virtual reality (VR) or motion simulation allows users to experience the turns, twists and speeds that are related with the adventure that they have chosen to experience. When it comes to virtual rides and experiences, Triotech is the go-to creator. As a fully interactive motion simulator, their XD Dark Ride mixes motion seats, 3D graphics, and other interactive features to create an exciting ride(Triotech, n.d.).

Sports and Live Events in the Metaverse

The sporting world is a great place to test out the cutting-edge technologies and the metaverse has emerged as the latest frontier and a great number of businesses are competing to occupy that space. In a virtual sports space, players and fans can dress as virtual avatars, shop for and wear team gear, meet other supporters, have virtual celebrations, and obviously watch all the games and activities. With the use of multi-view camera technology, fans can actually access the field itself and stroll along the athletes or cheer for the team from various locations while watching the action.

Virtual Stadiums and Arenas. "Virtual stadiums" are simulated versions of real-life stadiums used for sporting events or other forms of entertainment in online games and other virtual worlds. These virtual stadiums imitate the look and feel of actual stadiums so that users can enjoy live entertainment like musical performances, sporting events, cheering up for their favorite players and more without leaving the comfort of their place (Capasa et al., 2022). The Manchester City soccer team created history by announcing the first-ever virtual recreation of Etihad Stadium in the Metaverse. It was out of world good news for soccer fans across the world because it made it possible for soccer supporters to watch live matches from their homes without going to the stadium (Duge, 2022).

Virtual Sports Tournaments and Competitions. Tournaments and competitions in virtual sports constitute sporting events in which players battle against one another in a variety of online games or e-sports titles inside a virtual environment where players often use digital avatars to compete against one another. Websites such as Twitch, YouTube Gaming, and others provide live coverage of several virtual sports competitions (Capasa et al., 2022). As a benefit of it, viewers are able to catch every moment of the matches as they happen, while analysts and experts enrich the coverage with their live commentary on the action. The FIFAe World Cup is an e-sports competition organized by FIFA and formerly in collaboration with EA Sports. Every tournament involves participants participating in matches in the most recent version of the FIFA association football video game series. With its open qualification style, millions of people may participate in the first online stages of the FIWC, making it the biggest online esports game according to Guinness World Records (Wikipedia, 2024).

OPPORTUNITIES AND FUTURE TRENDS OF METAVERSE IN GAMING AND ENTERTAINMENT INDUSTRY

In the gaming and entertainment industries, the metaverse offers a plethora of opportunities that promise to transform user experiences and market dynamics. The metaverse is changing the gaming and entertainment industry in many ways, including the way users interact with content, the prospects for economic growth, the rate of technology advancement, and the cultural and social dynamics at play.

- Metaverse gaming has a bright future. As technology advances, we can probably expect virtual worlds to become more complex, with better visuals and greater interactions powered by AI. These advancements will make virtual and real worlds even more identical, allowing for more immersive interactions. According to Gartner, metaverse technology will lead to a 25% increase in the serious gaming industry by 2025 (Gartner, 2022).
- NFTs, along with other digital assets, will play a crucial role in shaping the economic foundation of the gaming metaverse. To make it clear, the worldwide market for blockchain gaming is projected to see a significant surge, increasing from $4.6 billion in 2022 to $65.7 billion by 2027 (Meichler, 2023). Looking at these numbers, it is not tricky to predict that the upcoming era of gaming may be linked with non-fungible tokens (NFTs).
- The metaverse provides an important chance for gaming firms to broaden their monetization techniques beyond conventional sale of games and in-game transactions. If the metaverse development functions as an independent platform, games might be transformed into apps integrated inside that platform, rather than existing as independent products. Publishers might potentially create regular income by using subscription models and micropayments inside their metaverse games (A3Logics, 2023). As an example, gamers have the option to pay recurring monthly fees for deeply engaging MMO games or engage in frequent transactions to get virtual items.
- Customer spending on virtual concerts, events, and other forms of virtual entertainment is fueling the expansion of the metaverse economy. The fact that the metaverse can satisfy people's desire to feel connected to a community will continue to contribute to its popularity in the entertainment industry in the near future. It is more evident from the Statista's findings that from 2024 to 2030, the global market for Metaverse Live Entertainment will expand at a CAGR of 10.37%, reaching a value of 221.7 billion dollars by 2030 (Statista, 2024).
- Both the Metaverse and the entertainment industries will grow in the future to unprecedented heights which will be beyond human imagination in both their own right and in tandem. Meta Hollywood in 2023, stated that it will form a partnership with the Planet Hollywood group and Meta Hollywood organization to establish a revolutionary virtual studio in the metaverse patterned like the Hollywood backlot (Metavertainment, n.d.). This foundation of the Metaverse that

it satisfies people's desire to belong to a community, communicate with others, and share one's experiences will be a game-changer in the entertainment industry.

- Mega immersive live events are expected to grow in size and level of interaction in the years to come, becoming a significant source of revenue for artists and owners of virtual worlds while also providing fans with experiences that are one of its kind. Fans will be able to interact with their favorite artists in entirely new ways and the use of (NFTs) and cryptocurrency will minimize the need on the intermediaries. Not only this, artists will be able to communicate with fans directly and sell their music to them.

According to its forecast report, Gartner ranked the metaverse as one of the five most promising new technologies and trends for the future. According to Gartner, by 2026, nearly 25% of the population will spend at least an hour each day in the metaverse, and 30% of businesses will provide services or goods dedicated to the metaverse (Gartner, 2022). Although it is still in its beginning stages, the metaverse has great potential to play a pivotal role in the Internet's future.

CHALLENGES AND CONSIDERATIONS OF METAVERSE IN GAMING AND ENTERTAINMENT INDUSTRY

In a relatively short amount of time, Metaverse has established itself as a big cannon in the gaming and entertainment industries. While the metaverse promises boundless possibilities in these industries, it also comes with a set of unique challenges that need to be brought into light and addressed to harness the full potential of the metaverse. Table No.1 shows some multifaceted challenges faced by these industries while adapting to the metaverse.

In the upcoming years, the metaverse could totally transform how we meet, socialize, and do business in the digital age and to reach this stage, however, developers have to address these complicated set of challenges. These challenges can be resolved through collaboration, using new technologies like blockchain and opting for a user-friendly approach.

IMPLICATIONS OF THE STUDY

This study has significant implications for both metaverse users like players and content consumers as well as the content creators in these industries. For the users, the metaverse has the capability to provide interconnected virtual worlds at their fingertips which users can leverage to delve into diverse activities ranging from gaming adventures to virtual social gatherings, from attending live concerts in digital venues to participating in interactive storytelling experiences. The active users as well as the potential users should quickly adapt to this shift towards a more participatory and interconnected digital environment which can enhances their engagement and satisfaction. However, users should remain vigilant of challenges that comes with these virtual environments such as inclusivity and accessibility, privacy and data security which are crucial for maintaining trust and confidence among them. As active engagement of the users in this universe is of paramount importance, therefore it is suggested to the content creators to explore innovative storytelling techniques, leveraging the immersive capabilities of virtual reality (VR), augmented reality (AR), and other advanced technologies to captivate audiences in entirely new ways.

Table 1. Challenges and considerations in meta- gaming and entertainment industries

Challenges	Gaming Industry	Entertainment Industry
Technical Infrastructure	The metaverse demands robust technical infrastructure to support its immersive experiences that includes ensuring stable platforms, overcoming device accessibility issues, and optimizing for various devices which becomes the key hurdles in delivering seamless interactions.	Adapting existing entertainment content, such as movies and shows, to virtual and augmented reality (VR/AR) formats while maintaining high-quality visuals and storytelling poses a significant challenge.
Privacy and Security Concerns	Metaverse games frequently require players to create profiles and share personal information. Protecting sensitive data from unauthorized access, breaches, and cyberattacks is of grave concern.	Hosting virtual events within the metaverse such as concerts and shows raises concerns about security and unauthorized access. Ensuring that only authorized users can attend events and preventing potential disruptions, like virtual "gate-crashing," requires robust security measures.
Regulatory Landscape	Adapting to evolving regulations related to virtual economies, user safety, and digital transactions is crucial. Accordingly, game developers need to stay informed about legal requirements and compliance standards to operate within the regulatory framework.	The global metaverse presents jurisdictional law and regulation issues. The biggest challenge for metaverse entertainment platforms is to comply to different rules in different countries, making international law navigation effective.
Interoperability and Standards	Different gaming platforms use different technologies and frameworks in their ecosystems due to which achieving interoperability in meta-games becomes a challenge as game developers, platform operators, and technology vendors have to work alongside one another	Users often engage with a mix of VR and AR within the metaverse entertainment. Interoperability here means letting users switch between multiple entertainment forms while maintaining a consistent storyline and interface. It requires the complex task of standardizing approaches to content integration and presentation.
Ethical and Social Considerations	The game business faces the problem of handling concerns about potential addiction and excessive screen time. Game designers need to teach players how to play in a healthy way and include elements that encourage responsible gaming.	In virtual world, users engage in a wide range of behaviors, from socializing and collaborating to potentially engaging in inappropriate conduct. To prevent such unethical behavior such as harassment, bullying, or offensive interactions require robust moderation tools, reporting mechanisms, and community guidelines.

For this, the content creators should focus on creativity and individuality through providing customizable avatars, user-generated content, and virtual economies which provides users with greater control over their virtual experiences which helps in enriching their overall experience. As traditional boundaries between content consumption and creation have blurred, creators need to adapt themselves quickly at the forefront of a paradigm shift in content production and distribution. At last, it can be said that implications of the metaverse in the gaming and entertainment industry requires collaboration between both users and content creators to enhance the user experience while addressing challenges at the same time.

LIMITATIONS OF THE STUDY

This chapter have some limitations which can be addressed in further studies. First, it only considers two industries which are gaming and entertainment industries, so future studies involving more industries to study the impact of metaverse such as education, retail and e-commerce, tourism etc. will help in understanding the transformational change brought by this phenomenon in more depth. Second, this study is solely based on the existing literature available in context of metaverse which is secondary in nature completely based on the review of scholarly works, consultancy firm reports, trade publications, websites, books etc so it is suggested that future research should focus on developing more empirical studies that take into account the real opinions of users in terms of the extent to which metaverse has transformed their experience of content consumption and gaming in these industries. Also, this chapter studies this phenomenon from the lens of users or content consumers so the further studies can be studied from the point of view of the impact on other stakeholders as well such platform operators, service providers, content production and distribution house, influencers etc.

CONCLUSION

The recent development of the metaverse has sparked an increasing amount of academic discussion over its pros and cons and potential for redefining many industries. Even when the metaverse is still mostly at the conceptual stage, there are vast number of potential changes it might bring about for the gaming and entertainment industries. From immersive gaming environments to interactive storytelling and virtual events, the metaverse has opened up new possibilities for both players and users alike. Furthermore, the inception of the metaverse has brought about a significant transformation in the gaming industry, enabling players to become engrossed in richly developed virtual worlds and engage in novel collaborative interactions. Similarly, the entertainment sector has also used the metaverse to create immersive content and interactive experiences that respond to users' growing interests. As technology advances, we can expect to see even more imaginative uses of the metaverse specifically in these industries. The metaverse in near future can fundamentally alter how we play, consume, and interact with gaming and entertainment content, providing endless opportunities for innovation and exploration. This chapter highlights the need for interdisciplinary research that bridges the fields of gaming, entertainment, technology, and user experience design. By fostering collaboration between experts from different disciplines, we can better understand the complex dynamics of the metaverse and develop innovative solutions to address emerging challenges. By embracing the potential of the metaverse and addressing its challenges, we can unlock new possibilities for immersive and engaging user experiences that will shape the future of entertainment for years to come.

REFERENCES

A3Logics. (2023, May 18). How Metaverse Gaming Bought Revolution in Gaming Industry. *A3logics Blog*. https://www.a3logics.com/blog/metaverse-gaming-a-revolution-in-the-gaming-industry

Baía Reis, A., & Ashmore, M. (2022). From video streaming to virtual reality worlds: An academic, reflective, and creative study on live theatre and performance in the metaverse. *International Journal of Performance Arts and Digital Media*, *18*(1), 7–28. doi:10.1080/14794713.2021.2024398

Builders of Amusement Park Rides & Media-Based Attractions. (n.d.). Triotech. https://www.trio-tech.com/

Capasa, L., Zulauf, K., & Wagner, R. (2022). Virtual Reality Experience of Mega Sports Events: A Technology Acceptance Study. *Journal of Theoretical and Applied Electronic Commerce Research*, *17*(2), 2. doi:10.3390/jtaer17020036

Disney patents technology to focus on theme park in Metaverse—Blockchain Council. (n.d.). Blockchain. https://www.blockchain-council.org/news/disney-patents-technology-to-focus-on-theme-park-in-metaverse/

Ergen, I. (2022). *Design in Metaverse: Artificial Intelligence, Game Design, Style-Gan2 and More....* Allied Publishers.

FIFAe World Cup. (2024). Wikipedia. https://en.wikipedia.org/w/index.php?title=FIFAe_World_Cup&oldid=1195690321

Gao, X., & Yu, W. (2023). Innovative Thinking About Human-Computer Interaction in Interactive Narrative Games. In X. Fang (Ed.), *HCI in Games* (pp. 89–99). Springer Nature Switzerland. doi:10.1007/978-3-031-35930-9_7

Gartner Outlines Six Trends Driving Near-Term Adoption of Metaverse Technologies. (n.d.). Gartner. Retrieved February 6, 2024, from https://www.gartner.com/en/newsroom/press-releases/2022-09-13-gartner-outlines-six-trends-driving-near-term-adoptio

Gartner Predicts 25% of People Will Spend At Least One Hour Per Day in the Metaverse by 2026. (n.d.). Gartner. https://www.gartner.com/en/newsroom/press-releases/2022-02-07-gartner-predicts-25-percent-of-people-will-spend-at-least-one-hour-per-day-in-the-metaverse-by-2026

Ghryani, L., Sidiya, A. M., Almahdi, R., & Alzaher, H. (2023). The Future Metavertainment Application development. *2023 20th Learning and Technology Conference (L&T)*, 151–156. 10.1109/LT58159.2023.10092341

Kim, D. Y., Lee, H. K., & Chung, K. (2023). Avatar-mediated experience in the metaverse: The impact of avatar realism on user-avatar relationship. *Journal of Retailing and Consumer Services*, 73, 103382. doi:10.1016/j.jretconser.2023.103382

Li, T., Yang, C., Yang, Q., Lan, S., Zhou, S., Luo, X., Huang, H., & Zheng, Z. (2023). Metaopera: A Cross-Metaverse Interoperability Protocol. *IEEE Wireless Communications*, 30(5), 136–143. doi:10.1109/MWC.011.2300042

Macedo, C. R., Miro, D. A., & Hart, T. (2022). *The Metaverse: From Science Fiction to Commercial Reality—Protecting Intellectual Property in the Virtual Landscape.* 31(1).

Meichler, M. (2023, June 19). *The Future of NFTs: Is Gaming the Solution?* NFT Evening. https://nftevening.com/the-future-of-nfts-is-gaming-the-solution/

Metaverse Live Entertainment—Global | Market Forecast. (n.d.). Statista. https://www.statista.com/outlook/amo/metaverse/metaverse-live-entertainment/worldwide

Metaverse: The Revolution of the Sports World & Entire Life. (n.d.). ISPO. https://www.ispo.com/en/news-trends/metaverse-revolution-sports-world

Metavertainment: A Vision Into The World of The Metaverse and Entertainment. (n.d.). HackerNoon. https://hackernoon.com/metavertainment-a-vision-into-the-world-of-the-metaverse-and-entertainment

Oliveira, A., & Cruz, M. (2023). Virtually Connected in a Multiverse of Madness?—Perceptions of Gaming, Animation, and Metaverse. *Applied Sciences (Basel, Switzerland)*, 13(15), 15. doi:10.3390/app13158573

Rane, N., Choudhary, S., & Rane, J. (2023). *Metaverse for Enhancing Customer Loyalty: Effective Strategies to Improve Customer Relationship, Service, Engagement, Satisfaction, and Experience* (SSRN Scholarly Paper 4624197). doi:10.2139/ssrn.4624197

Scheiding, R. (2023). Designing the Future? The Metaverse, NFTs, & the Future as Defined by Unity Users. *Games and Culture, 18*(6), 804–820. doi:10.1177/15554120221139218

Shahbaz Badr, A., & De Amicis, R. (2023). An empirical evaluation of enhanced teleportation for navigating large urban immersive virtual environments. *Frontiers in Virtual Reality, 3*, 1075811. https://www.frontiersin.org/articles/10.3389/frvir.2022.1075811. doi:10.3389/frvir.2022.1075811

Shen, B., Tan, W., Guo, J., Zhao, L., & Qin, P. (2021). How to Promote User Purchase in Metaverse? A Systematic Literature Review on Consumer Behavior Research and Virtual Commerce Application Design. *Applied Sciences (Basel, Switzerland), 11*(23), 23. doi:10.3390/app112311087

Shin, D. (2022). The actualization of meta affordances: Conceptualizing affordance actualization in the metaverse games. *Computers in Human Behavior, 133*, 107292. doi:10.1016/j.chb.2022.107292

Spence, C. (2021). Scenting Entertainment: Virtual Reality Storytelling, Theme Park Rides, Gambling, and Video-Gaming. *IPerception, 12*(4), 20416695211034538. doi:10.1177/20416695211034538 PMID:34457231

Stefanic, D. (2023, December 7). Hosting Concerts and Shows in the Metaverse. *Hyperspace^mv - the Metaverse for Business Platform.* https://hyperspace.mv/metaverse-concerts-and-shows/

Vidal-Tomás, D. (2022). The new crypto niche: NFTs, play-to-earn, and metaverse tokens. *Finance Research Letters, 47*, 102742. doi:10.1016/j.frl.2022.102742

Voinea, G. D., Gîrbacia, F., Postelnicu, C. C., Duguleana, M., Antonya, C., Soica, A., & Stănescu, R.-C. (2022). Study of Social Presence While Interacting in Metaverse with an Augmented Avatar during Autonomous Driving. *Applied Sciences (Basel, Switzerland), 12*(22), 22. Advance online publication. doi:10.3390/app122211804

Vosmeer, M., & Schouten, B. (2014). Interactive Cinema: Engagement and Interaction. In A. Mitchell, C. Fernández-Vara, & D. Thue (Eds.), *Interactive Storytelling* (Vol. 8832, pp. 140–147). Springer International Publishing., doi:10.1007/978-3-319-12337-0_14

Yakura, H., & Goto, M. (2020). Enhancing Participation Experience in VR Live Concerts by Improving Motions of Virtual Audience Avatars. *2020 IEEE International Symposium on Mixed and Augmented Reality (ISMAR)*, (pp. 555–565). IEEE. 10.1109/ISMAR50242.2020.00083

Zhao, Y., Jiang, J., Chen, Y., Liu, R., Yang, Y., Xue, X., & Chen, S. (2022). Metaverse: Perspectives from graphics, interactions and visualization. *Visual Informatics, 6*(1), 56–67. doi:10.1016/j.visinf.2022.03.002

Chapter 8
Integration of the Metaverse in the Healthcare Industry:
A Catalyst for Profound Change

Sabyasachi Pramanik

https://orcid.org/0000-0002-9431-8751

Haldia Institute of Technology, India

ABSTRACT

This chapter explores the connection of the metaverse and healthcare, investigating whether this integration signifies a significant shift or is just a passing trend. The chapter begins by explaining the notion of the metaverse and its ramifications in the healthcare environment, setting the stage for the next discussion. The chapter examines the possible catalyst impact by exploring several options. This text discusses the potential of the metaverse to transform medical teaching, enhance telemedicine, enable therapeutic interventions, and promote worldwide collaborative networks in healthcare. This investigation aims to ascertain whether the metaverse has the capacity to revolutionize healthcare methodologies, improve patient treatment, and overcome geographical obstacles. However, there are significant obstacles that need to be addressed in order to successfully integrate the metaverse, as outlined in the next section. The chapter examines the long-term viability of the metaverse's influence on healthcare by analyzing technological complexities, ethical considerations, and barriers to adoption. The chapter showcases real-world case studies that illustrate how metaverse technologies have shown to be valuable and enduring in the healthcare industry, in contrast to the fleeting nature of fads. This supports the premise that the metaverse has the potential to go beyond being a temporary fad and establish a significant presence in healthcare procedures. By analyzing historical similarities, this chapter investigates whether the metaverse has the characteristics of long-lasting change or whether it is prone to being quickly outdated. As the chapter approaches its end, it presents a prospective view on the development of the metaverse in the healthcare sector. The text compiles the acquired insights from the investigation and provides a detailed assessment of whether the metaverse has the potential to be a powerful catalyst or a temporary trend in the field of healthcare. This chapter examines the possible impact of integrating the metaverse into healthcare, examining whether it will be a driving force for long-term change or a passing trend.

DOI: 10.4018/979-8-3693-2607-7.ch008

INTRODUCTION

Ensuring healthcare is crucial for promoting the holistic well-being of individuals globally, including their physical, social, and mental health. The primary objective of every healthcare system is to allocate its resources towards endeavors that promote, sustain, restore, and improve healthcare services. Furthermore, it plays a crucial role in promoting manufacturing and economic development inside a country, as well as advancing the evolution of interactive experiences. Due to extensive exposure to technology advancements aimed at enhancing communication between caregivers, patients, and relevant stakeholders, this sector has seen significant growth and transformation. The digital healthcare revolution has brought about substantial changes in the healthcare business (Chengoden, 2023).The use of internet and digital tools in healthcare have greatly influenced the dynamic between patients and physicians. This shift may be attributed to the utilization of technologies such as blockchain, augmented reality (AR), and virtual reality (VR). The healthcare sector has made rapid progress; however it continues to face some persistent challenges, such as the overwhelming weight of chronic diseases over extended periods, escalating costs, a growing elderly population, a scarcity of healthcare professionals, and limited availability of resources (Thomason, 2021). As a result of these significant issues, individuals increasingly need access to healthcare treatments inside the confines of their own residences. The COVID-19 pandemic has significantly burdened the worldwide healthcare sector, as well as the workforce, infrastructure, and supply chain management linked to it (Benrimoh, 2022). The COVID-19 pandemic has significantly accelerated transformation in the healthcare ecosystem, compelling players to consider the use of technological advancements in this business (Bansal, 2022).The post-pandemic period has resulted in significant transformative shifts in the healthcare sector. For example, the present cohort of consumers has started to actively engage in healthcare decision-making, leading to a keen embrace of virtual healthcare systems and associated digital innovations (Wiederhold, 2022).Furthermore, there has been a significant emphasis on the use of interoperable data and data analytics, along with unprecedented therapeutic partnerships. These collaborations have compelled governments, healthcare organizations, and other stakeholders to adjust and develop new approaches (Wiederhold, 2023).Nevertheless, there exist notable challenges that must be addressed in order to shape the future trajectory of the healthcare industry. The continually evolving requirements and aims of consumers (patients) serve as the primary catalyst for improvements in this discipline. Their main objectives are establishing digitally facilitated, readily available, and smooth patient-clinician contacts, ensuring the delivery of patient-centered treatments regardless of geographical barriers and socioeconomic divisions. Each patient's health journey is unique, and it is essential to acknowledge this, provide the appropriate services, and elevate each interaction to the standard of a personalized healthcare experience. To ensure maximum customer satisfaction, facilitate monitoring, monitor health status, and encourage adherence to prescriptions, it is essential to use cutting-edge digital tools and services. The need for organizations to provide interoperability across entities and uphold customers' confidence by the demonstration of reliability, openness, and empathy in their operations has intensified due to the rising willingness of healthcare consumers to disclose their sensitive data. Assumptions are guiding the transformation of service offerings and delivery channels, with the expectation that the emphasis will transition from healthcare to encompassing both health and well-being (Thomason, 2021).Therefore, the organizations advocate for the use of self-service apps for social assistance and education, along with virtual care, remote monitoring, digital diagnostics, decision support systems, and at-home prescription delivery systems. The integration of artificial intelligence, cloud computing, augmented reality, and virtual reality technologies has significantly transformed the healthcare ecosystem. This transformation has resulted in enhanced operational capacities, improved accessibility to services, and an enhanced experience for patients and clinicians (Chengoden, 2023). The merging of the metaverse, a complex digital dimension, with the healthcare domain is an intriguing intersection where advanced technology meets crucial healthcare requirements. This chapter explores the potential and uncertainties associated with incorporating the metaverse into healthcare. It considers whether the metaverse has the potential to significantly transform medical practices, education, and patient experiences, or if it is merely a passing technological trend without lasting influence (Tan, 2022). Through an examination of the metaverse's capacity to overcome geographical barriers, transform patient-provider relationships, and revolutionize medical education, our goal is to determine whether this emerging paradigm offers a solution for sustainable advancements in healthcare or simply aligns with passing technological fads (Bansal, 2022).

Global figures from the Metaverse indicate that the healthcare services industry is projected to increase from its present value of 5.06 billion dollars in 2021 to 71.97 billion dollars by 2030. This growth is estimated to occur at a compound annual growth rate (CAGR) of 34.8 percent throughout the forecast period of 2022 to 2030.North America is expected to surpass other countries in the Metaverse industry due to its high concentration of enterprises in this sector (Mohamed, 2023). In addition, their healthcare industry has a strong infrastructure that incorporates AR-VR technology, which has led to increased investment in AR-based software updates and high-quality hardware foundation (Bhattacharya, 2022).

THEORETICAL FRAMEWORK

The Theoretical Landscape of the Metaverse in Healthcare: Visualizing the Digital Transformation

The Metaverse is a digital realm that integrates features of social networking, online gaming, augmented reality, virtual reality, and crypto-currencies. The Metaverse is a network of interconnected virtual worlds that enables users to engage in social interactions, create and participate in gaming experiences, engage in professional activities, and engage in online shopping (Chengoden, 2023).A theoretical or developing interconnected online world with digitally enduring surroundings that users may enter using AR, VR, gaming consoles, mobile devices, or regular computers to engage in real-time interactions and experiences. The healthcare system in the Metaverse provides customized healthcare experiences that are interactive, immersive, and pleasant. Utilizing these technologies allows individuals to access innovative and more cost-effective means of delivering treatment, leading to enhanced patient results (Petrigna, 2022). The Metaverse leverages the Internet to provide an immersive virtual reality environment that replicates human emotions and movements. It encompasses the whole social and economic systems of both the real and virtual worlds. The technologies of the metaverse may assist medical staff in the precise planning and diagnosis of illnesses (Wang, 2022).In 2020, the neurosurgeons at Johns Hopkins Hospital used an Augmedics AR headgear during a surgical operation. The therapy included fusing six vertebrae in the patient's spine to alleviate persistent back pain using a transparent ocular display that displayed patients' anatomical views similar to X-ray vision (Sebastian, 2022).By using headsets and the Metaverse environment, the conversion of CT scans into 3D reconstructions enables enhanced preoperative surgical planning. Furthermore, this allows surgeons to meticulously examine, separate, and alter anatomical components in order to perform essential procedures. In addition, the metaverse devices amplify the effects of prescription drugs (Lee, 2022). For example, EaseVR is a medically prescribed device that utilizes virtual reality (VR) headgear and controllers to provide cognitive behavioral therapy to people suffering from back pain. These strategies facilitate the development of interoceptive awareness, induce profound relaxation, and enable adjustments in attention that specifically target the physiological components of pain. The intricate and challenging discipline of plastic surgery involves the rebuilding of many anatomical structures in the human body. Utilizing virtual reality (VR) in the Metaverse for plastic surgery is of utmost importance as it enables patients to see the potential impact of a genuine treatment on virtual avatars, hence enhancing their comprehension of the surgeon's proficiency (Sebastian, 2022).

Proficiency in human anatomy and the ability to use versatile, individually customizable gadgets with enhanced grasping skills are essential for operating in the Metaverse (Lee, 2022). The wide range of applications for this technology includes simple treatments and complex spinal surgery, as well as tumor removal. The radiology division of the metaverse has the capacity to unlock enhanced image visualization capabilities, enabling radiologists to see dynamic pictures with greater precision. The radiology division of the Metaverse has the capacity to unlock novel image visualization capabilities, enabling radiologists to examine dynamic images in a more comprehensive way, resulting in enhanced diagnosis and accurate decision-making (Koohang, 2023). Moreover, it would provide the opportunity for enhanced radiography education and the ability to collaborate as a group on three-dimensional medical images, even when located in different geographic regions. By utilizing superior immersive content and incorporating gamification elements, the healthcare metaverse has the potential to enhance patient involvement. It can assist clinicians in elucidating intricate concepts to patients, offer step-by-step demonstrations of medical procedures, and ensure patients adhere to their prescribed medication regimen. By incorporating the patient's vital signs, CT scans, medical records, and genetic test outcomes into a digital model that replicates the patient's anatomy and physiology, the use of digital twin solutions in the Metaverse will ensure that patients are well-informed and actively involved in their treatment. Patients have the ability to access their health information via a virtual dashboard. This allows them to interact with physicians, researchers, nutritionists, and other relevant parties in order to obtain personalized care and treatment (Petrigna, 2022).The current pandemic has spurred the need for remote healthcare services, and the Metaverse has the capacity to provide a superior experience compared to conventional telemedicine systems based on videoconferencing (Mejia, 2022).Patients have the ability to use augmented reality (AR) glasses to establish immediate voice and video connections with clinicians inside the Metaverse. AR technology enables responders to directly engage and transmit real-time emergency situations to distant physicians; facilitating prompt on-site treatment (Letafati, 2023).The metaverse has the potential to revolutionize the training and education of medical professionals. AR facilitates the demonstration of practical procedures rather than the dissemination of academic information. Esteemed universities are progressively using VR, AR, mixed reality (MR), and AI-based technologies to educate medical practitioners by simulating complex real-time procedures and imparting information about the cellular composition of the human body (Rahaman, 2022).

The Metaverse comprises state-of-the-art technology advancements such as blockchain, telepresence, augmented reality, and artificial intelligence (AI), which have a substantial influence on healthcare (Letafati, 2023).

Table 1. Technological paradigms reshaping healthcare: Applications and benefits

Technology	Description and Role in Healthcare	Applications and Benefits
Electronic Health Records (EHR)	Digitalized patient records and medical history. Centralized access for healthcare professionals.	Seamless sharing of patient data among healthcare providers.
Telemedicine	Remote medical consultations via digital platforms. Video and audio communication for diagnosis.	Improved access to medical care in remote areas, reduced travel for patients.
Mobile Health (mHealth)	Health-related services and information delivered via mobile devices.	Health monitoring, medication reminders and lifestyle tracking through apps.
Wearable Devices	Devices worn by individuals to track health and fitness data.	Real-time monitoring of vital signs, physical activity, and sleep patterns.
Internet of Things (IoT)	Interconnected devices for data exchange and automation	Remote monitoring of medical equipment, predictive maintenance, and real-time patient tracking.
Health Information Exchange (HIE)	Secure sharing of patient information among healthcare providers and organizations.	Coordinated care among different health care entities, reduced duplication of tests.
Artificial Intelligence (AI)	Machine learning algorithms for data analysis, prediction, and decision support.	Personalized treatment plans, medical image analysis, drug discovery.
Big Data Analytics	Processing and analyzing large volumes of healthcare data for insights.	Identifying health trends, population health management, disease prediction.
Remote Patient Monitoring	Continuous monitoring of patients outside of traditional healthcare settings.	Chronic disease management, early detection of health deterioration.
Blockchain	Secure and transparent data storage and transactions.	Secure sharing of patient records, maintaining data integrity.
Health Apps	Mobile applications for various health-related purposes.	Health tracking, medication reminders, mental health support.
Virtual Reality (VR) and Augmented Reality (AR)	Immersive experiences for medical training, therapy, and visualization.	Surgical simulations, medical education, pain management therapies.
Genomics and Personalized Medicine	Study of individual genetic makeup for personalized treatment.	Tailored treatment plans, targeted drug therapies, disease risk assessment.

A Comprehensive Investigation of Digital and smart Enabling Technologies That Are Transforming Healthcare

The combination of these technologies forms a complex and engaging metaverse in the healthcare field, providing inventive ways to enhance patient care, medical education, and overall healthcare experiences (Letafati, 2023).

The current digital and smart healthcare technologies play a crucial role in revolutionizing the healthcare industry. They enhance patient care, improve access to medical services, increase diagnostic accuracy, and promote tailored and efficient healthcare solutions (Lee, 2022).

Exploring the Potential Benefits and Opportunities of the Metaverse in the Healthcare Industry

The use of the Metaverse in healthcare offers a multitude of advantages and prospects that have the potential to completely transform the industry:

The Metaverse provides medical professionals with enhanced training by offering realistic and immersive surroundings. These environments enable professionals to practice operations, surgeries, and patient interactions in a risk-free digital setting. As a result, there is an enhancement in the acquisition of skills and preparedness (Chengoden, 2023).

Remote Consultations: Healthcare practitioners may provide virtual patient consultations and follow-ups, allowing access to medical competence irrespective of geographic location. This improves the quality of healthcare provided to patients, particularly those residing in distant or underprivileged regions (v, 2023).

Therapeutic Interventions: Virtual reality may be used for several therapeutic objectives, including pain mitigation, stress alleviation, and exposure treatment. These therapies possess the capacity to supplement conventional treatments and enhance patient outcomes (Song, 2022).

Patient Engagement: The Metaverse has the ability to include patients in their treatment programs by providing interactive instructional material, gamified exercises, and immersive experiences. This may result in improved patient compliance and enhanced health outcomes (Athar, 2023).

Rehabilitation and Physical Therapy: Customized virtual worlds may be designed for rehabilitation activities, encouraging patients to actively engage in their recuperation. This may expedite the process of healing and enhance the overall functioning results.

Collaborative Research: Researchers and medical experts may engage in virtual environments to examine intricate data, do simulations, and enhance medical research with more efficiency (Mozumder, 2022).

The Metaverse has the potential to democratize medical education via the provision of online courses, virtual workshops, and simulations. These resources provide flexible and easily accessible learning possibilities for students and professionals worldwide (Petrigna, 2022).

Support Communities: Online support groups and communities in the virtual world may bring together persons who are dealing with similar health issues, helping to alleviate feelings of loneliness and promoting emotional wellness.

Real-time Data Visualization: Augmented reality overlays may provide medical personnel immediate access to patient data, diagnostics, and treatment plans during operations, hence improving decision-making and accuracy.

The Metaverse has the potential to decrease healthcare expenditures by eliminating the need for in-person visits and hospital stays via remote consultations, virtual follow-ups, and preventative treatments (Ali, 2023).

Personalized Medicine: The Metaverse has the potential to streamline the incorporation of patient data, allowing for tailored treatment strategies that take into account unique medical backgrounds, genetic profiles, and reactions to various medications.

Innovative Treatment Approaches: The Metaverse's capacity for creativity enables the exploration of new treatment methods, such as using virtual environments for cognitive therapy and interventions in mental health (Ganapathy, 2022).

Health Data Tracking: Wearable devices and augmented reality (AR) interfaces have the capability to provide consumers immediate health data, encouraging self-awareness and proactive management of one's health.

Continuity of Care: Patients have the ability to retrieve medical information, data, and treatment plans in a durable virtual setting, guaranteeing uninterrupted care even during the switch between healthcare providers (Song, 2022).

The Metaverse fundamentally provides a means for revolutionizing healthcare by facilitating customized, immersive, and cooperative methods that may result in enhanced patient results, optimized processes, and a healthcare system that is more accessible and efficient (Bansal, 2022).

Analysis of the Metaverse's Impact on Healthcare: Is it a Transformative Force or Just a Passing Trend?

To determine whether the metaverse signifies a significant change or a temporary trend, it requires a thorough examination of many crucial factors (Bansal, 2022). The long-term sustainability of the system depends on its capacity to adapt to technological progress and meet the evolving demands of users in many sectors (Situmorang, 2023). Furthermore, it is of utmost importance to prioritize the resolution of ethical and privacy problems, particularly in highly sensitive industries like as healthcare (Marzaleh, 2022). The legitimacy of data use for enhanced treatment and protection of patient privacy relies on achieving a balance. Furthermore, the successful integration of the metaverse into current healthcare systems requires overcoming integration problems and technological constraints. Central to its continuous success are the key factors of ensuring compatibility, data security, and accessibility (Wang, 2022). Finally, by comparing it to other healthcare trends like EHRs and telemedicine, we may get an understanding of how lasting changes occur when they clearly improve patient care, simplify procedures, and adjust efficiently. Finally, the destiny of the metaverse hinges on its capacity to negotiate these intricacies, showcasing concrete worth and flexibility, finally establishing its position as either a passing trend or a groundbreaking metamorphosis in healthcare and other fields. Examining the notion of transformation vs fad within the metaverse framework, with specific emphasis on long-term sustainability, ethical and privacy issues, integration complexities, and similarities to past healthcare fads, unveils a nuanced viewpoint on the subject (Gupta, 2023).

Evaluating the long-term sustainability: The metaverse, a digital environment formed by the merging of physical and virtual reality, has gained considerable interest due to progress in augmented reality (AR), virtual reality (VR), and other immersive technologies. The long-term sustainability of the system relies on several aspects such as technical progress, user acceptance, and economic viability (Chengoden, 2023). The metaverse has the potential to revolutionize several sectors, such as healthcare, but its success relies on effectively addressing the practical requirements and desires of its users. Should the metaverse demonstrate significant use and maintain flexibility in response to changing requirements, it has the potential to become a revolutionary influence rather than a passing trend (Moztarzadeh, 2023).

Regarding Ethical and Privacy problems: Similar to every revolutionary technology, there are substantial ethical and privacy problems. Within the healthcare industry, these concerns are magnified as a result of the delicate nature of patient data and the possibility of security breaches (Petrigna, 2022). It is crucial to guarantee data security, get user permission, and implement adequate anonymization. Moreover, concerns emerge about the possibility of depersonalization in patient care and the ethical ramifications of integrating real and virtual medical procedures. Effectively addressing these issues will be essential for the metaverse to establish confidence and demonstrate its enduring worth (Moztarzadeh, 2023).

Overcoming technological obstacles is necessary to integrate the metaverse into healthcare (Bhugaonkar, 2022). It is crucial to have smooth compatibility across different virtual platforms, electronic health records (EHR) systems, medical equipment, and real-time patient data. It is crucial to have standardized protocols and APIs to ensure safe data flow. Furthermore, overcoming the challenge of providing accessibility to patients with diverse abilities and demographics is a major obstacle. Failure to adequately tackle these integration obstacles may result in the metaverse retaining its status as a specialized tool rather than a revolutionary trend in healthcare (Garavand, 2022).

Analyzing the Integration of Metaverse in Comparison to Previous Healthcare Trends: In order to determine if the metaverse signifies a substantial change or a passing trend, it is advantageous to draw comparisons with prior advancements in healthcare technology. Electronic health records (EHRs), telemedicine, and wearable health gadgets, first met with doubt, have now become essential components of healthcare provision (Zhang, 2023). The success of these trends was propelled by their capacity to improve patient care, optimize processes, and adjust to changing demands. For the metaverse to be successful, it must show distinct benefits compared to current approaches and adapt as healthcare progresses (Song, 2022).

To ascertain whether the metaverse is a transformative force or a passing trend, a thorough assessment of its enduring sustainability, ethical implications, technological obstacles, and similarities to past healthcare patterns is necessary (Kim, 2023). The metaverse has the capacity to greatly influence healthcare by facilitating remote consultations, medical education, and treatment, among other uses (Yang, 2022). Nevertheless, the achievement of its goals relies on surmounting technological obstacles, tackling ethical considerations, and demonstrating its practical worth in the long run. It is of utmost importance to approach the integration of the metaverse into healthcare with a combination of hope and careful evaluation (Situmorang, 2023).

Exploring the Intersection of the Metaverse and Healthcare: Exemplary Cases and Optimal Approaches

The table presents a succinct summary of case studies, success stories, lessons learned, best practices, and case examples that demonstrate the beneficial impact of incorporating the Metaverse into healthcare. The "Case Studies" section features instances such as the use of virtual reality (VR) for pain treatment at Cedars-Sinai Medical Center and VR-based surgical training conducted by Osso VR. The "Success

Table 2. The use of metaverse in the healthcare industry has yielded notable achievements and exemplary approaches

Case Studies	Success Stories and Best Practices	Case Examples: Positive Impact on Patient Outcomes
Cedars-Sinai Medical Center - VR Pain Management: Utilized virtual reality (VR) to reduce anxiety and pain perception during medical procedures.	**User-Centric Design:** Design virtual experiences with user-friendliness in mind.	**Virtual Physical Therapy for Seniors:** Improved mobility and quality of life through engaging VR-based physical therapy.
Osso VR - Surgical Training: Developed VR-based surgical training platform resulting in increased procedural accuracy and safety.	**Ethical Considerations:** Prioritize patient privacy and consent while exploring new applications.	**Pain Distraction for Pediatric Procedures:** Lowered anxiety and pain levels during procedures for pediatric patients using immersive virtual experiences.
Mayo Clinic - Virtual Patient Consultations: Implemented virtual consultations for remote patients, leading to better chronic condition management.	**Collaboration:** Engage multidisciplinary teams for comprehensive Metaverse solutions.	
Stanford Children's Health - Pediatric Rehabilitation: Enhanced pediatric rehabilitation with engaging virtual activities, resulting in improved motor skills.		

Stories and Best Practices" section highlights the importance of user-centric design, ethical concerns, and cooperation as crucial elements for achieving effective implementation. The column titled "Case Examples: Positive Impact on Patient Outcomes" showcases the positive effects of virtual physical therapy for elderly individuals and pain distraction strategies for pediatric operations. These interventions have resulted in increased patient mobility, decreased anxiety, and higher overall quality of life (Huang, 2023). Collectively, these observations demonstrate the revolutionary capacity of the Metaverse in the field of healthcare, emphasizing the significance of meticulous strategizing, ethical deliberations, and inventive methodologies. The case studies, success stories, lessons learned, and best practices exemplify the potential of integrating Metaverse technology in healthcare. They highlight the beneficial effects on patient outcomes, medical training, and overall patient care (Dogum, 2023).

Investigating the Future of Healthcare: Utilizing the Metaverse to Achieve Significant Real-World Effects

Based on the specific technologies used, such as augmented reality (AR), life logging, virtual reality (VR), and mirror world, the prospective uses of the Metaverse in healthcare may be categorized into four distinct groups (Usmani, 2022). Using an augmented reality (AR) T-shirt in an anatomy lab would allow students to vividly see the human body. Mirror world implementation involves the use of virtual mapping and modeling techniques to create an exact reproduction of the actual world, while also including essential environmental data. The present pandemic emergency has further enhanced the use of the Metaverse. People from distant locations participate and play in games inside a virtual reality platform known as the mirror world (Petrigna, 2022).Consequently, these state-of-the-art technologies provide more precise visualizations, understanding, and application of innovative techniques. Consequently, these state-of-the-art technologies provide more precise visualizations, understanding, and application of innovative techniques. The Metaverse provides a comprehensive visual representation of physical ailments and serves as an exceptionally effective tool for surgical training, promoting optimal collaboration and immersive experiences. Despite being in the experimental phase, the use of this technology has the potential to significantly benefit healthcare education and training. In contrast to the "handicraft workshop model," characterized by inconsistent diagnostic and treatment approaches among doctors and hospitals, the Metaverse significantly enhances the delivery of comprehensive healthcare (Wiederhold, 2022). Decisions in a scenario requiring comprehensive healthcare will rely on the guidance of the specialist and the results of the many Metaverse enabling technologies. The Metaverse has a wide range of medical applications, such as research, physical assessment, diagnosis, and insurance purposes (Curtis, 2023). Potential uses of the Metaverse that may gain popularity in the near future include virtual physiotherapy, virtual biopsy, virtual psychotherapy, and virtual alarm response. The act of obtaining and analyzing an image to characterize tissues is referred to as a virtual biopsy. Virtual physiotherapy may be used to provide guidance and instruction to patients undergoing rehabilitation, aiding them in their mobility and exercise routines (Nica, 2022).

Medical Diagnosis refers to the process of identifying a disease or condition in a patient based on their symptoms, medical history, and diagnostic tests.

Medical diagnosis is the systematic determination of a patient's medical state based on an analysis of their symptoms. The integration of the Metaverse in healthcare significantly enhances the precise identification of a patient's medical conditions via the use of advanced technologies such as augmented reality (AR), virtual reality (VR), extended digital twins, blockchain, 5G, and other similar innovations

(Turab, 2023). A research paper titled "Expert Consensus on the Metaverse in Medicine" was presented, elucidating the methods and rationale for implementing the Metaverse across many healthcare domains to provide comprehensive and superior healthcare services. The metaverse has the potential to enhance the current medical Internet of Things (IoT) by addressing its limitations in terms of human-computer interaction, connection, and integration with both the physical and virtual realms (Wiederhold, 2022).

Monitoring of Patients

The healthcare sector stands to gain significant advantages from the Metaverse due to the integration of telepresence, digital twinning, and blockchain technologies, namely in the realm of patient monitoring. Telemedicine, sometimes referred to as telepresence in medicine, is the practice of providing medical treatments remotely. During emergency situations, the use of patient simulators may be employed to assess the potential impact of therapies on real patients well in advance. Utilizing blockchain technology ensures the secure storage and sharing of medical data, safeguarding its integrity and minimizing potential risks (Petrigna, 2022).Efficient patient monitoring may be achieved when these three parts are carefully constructed to work together. The Metaverse provides a solution by integrating various technologies into a unified system. COVID-19 has prompted medical experts to explore the possibility of delivering high-quality healthcare remotely, using the combination of medical advice, phone calls, or video consultations with patients (Prasetyo, 2022).Advancements in the Metaverse have enabled the healthcare sector to generate virtual environments as needed and provide medical care to impoverished individuals, regardless of their distance from healthcare facilities (Bashir, 2023).

Medical Education

The Metaverse signifies a momentous shift in medical education. The forefront innovators in the field of medical education are using IoT, blockchain, AI, AR, and VR technologies to develop the Metaverse. The discussion revolved on the impact of AI, blockchain, and the Metaverse on healthcare. The blockchain's unique identifier tags facilitate the recognition of data throughout the blockchain-powered Metaverse (Sestino, 2023).The Metaverse is an AI and blockchain-powered digital virtual universe that surpasses the limitations of the physical world (Kahambing, 2023). These technologies facilitate medical students' ability to focus on the session, actively participate in the discussion, converse in depth, and engage with more pleasure, especially in the busy clinical environment. In the conventional method of teaching, the teacher would require the medical students to personally visit a patient, followed by presenting and discussing the relevant medical facts with the group of students. The advent of digital integration and 3D technology has brought about a substantial transformation in clinical training. Currently, a cohort of medical students is being introduced to a patient in a virtual reality setting. The authors proposed a hybrid approach that combines structural equation modeling and machine learning to predict users' intends to use the Metaverse for healthcare education (Han, 2023).

Medical Procedures

The metaverse is an essential medical technology, especially in the field of surgery. Presently, doctors use tools such as VR headsets and haptic gloves to replicate real surgical operations, hence enhancing preparedness and effectiveness in the operating room. Augmented reality (AR) may enhance the convenience of surgical operations by providing physicians easy access to data. Augmented reality (AR) enables surgeons to efficiently retrieve patient information by projecting 3D virtual representations onto the patient's body, without the need for physical interaction and with ease and speed (Chen, 2022). Within the Metaverse, educators and speakers have the capability to showcase intricate processes using three-dimensional representations. In addition, patients who have had surgery might obtain counseling services via the Metaverse, as suggested by Curtis (2023).

Medical Therapeutics and Theranostics

The branch of medicine that specifically focuses on the management and treatment of illnesses is often known as medical therapy. DTx, or digital therapeutics, refer to evidence-based therapeutic approaches within the field of digital medicine. According to the Digital Therapies Alliance, digital therapies are products that use high-quality software programs to provide evidence-based therapeutic interventions for the prevention, management, or treatment of medical disorders or diseases (Thomason, 2021).The use of the underlying technology has the potential to greatly transform the field of medicine via Metaverse participation in treatments and theranostics. A digital therapy, a kind of treatment that does not need the use of pharmaceutical drugs, is gaining importance in the healthcare sector (Situmorang, 2022).

Computer vision is a technology that can analyze, inspect, visualize, and comprehend pictures and movies (Mozumder, 2023).

The Convergence of the Metaverse With Healthcare Presents Several Challenges and Dynamic Trajectories

The table presents the obstacles and prospective paths for integrating the Metaverse into the healthcare sector. Regarding challenges, it tackles issues such as safeguarding patient data privacy and security, ethical considerations, ensuring fair access to services, training healthcare professionals, meeting technical infrastructure requirements, standardizing practices, obtaining regulatory approvals, implementing realistic simulation, integrating into existing workflows, and designing user experience. The future directions section proposes various strategies to bolster security measures, establish ethical guidelines, foster accessibility initiatives, offer professional training, enhance technical connectivity, establish interoperability frameworks, engage with regulatory bodies, invest in advanced simulation technologies, develop workflow integration solutions, and prioritize user-centric design principles (Thomason, 2021). The problems and directions highlight the intricate nature and possible advantages of incorporating the Metaverse into healthcare, while underlining the need of meticulous preparation, cooperation, and creativity to navigate this dynamic environment. The difficulties and future directions emphasize the potential advantages of integrating the Metaverse in healthcare. They also emphasize the need of thoughtful analysis, cooperation, and creativity in tackling the many problems that occur in this developing field (Curtis, 2023).

CONCLUSION

This chapter provides a comprehensive examination of the applications of the Metaverse in the field of healthcare. The current situation of digital healthcare and the need to embrace the Metaverse for healthcare

Table 3. Challenges and future directions in the synergy between metaverse and healthcare

Challenge	Description	Future Directions
Privacy and Security	Ensuring the protection of sensitive patient data and maintaining a secure environment in the virtual space.	Enhanced Security Measures: Developing robust encryption and authentication methods to safeguard patient information and maintain HIPAA compliance.
Ethical Concerns	Addressing potential ethical issues related to patient consent, data ownership, and the blurring of boundaries between virtual and real experiences.	Ethical Guidelines: Establishing clear ethical guidelines and standards for the use of the Metaverse in healthcare, addressing consent, data privacy, and virtual interactions.
Access and Equity	Ensuring equal access to Metaverse-based healthcare services for all individuals, regardless of their socioeconomic status or geographical location.	Accessibility Initiatives: Implementing initiatives to provide affordable VR/AR equipment and reliable internet access to underserved populations.
Training and Familiarity	Training healthcare professionals to effectively navigate and utilize Metaverse technologies for patient care and medical education.	Professional Training Programs: Developing specialized training programs and resources for healthcare professionals to proficiently use Metaverse tools and applications.
Technical Infrastructure	Establishing the necessary technical infrastructure to support seamless integration and real-time interactions within the Metaverse.	Improved Connectivity: Investing in high-speed internet connectivity and robust VR/AR hardware to ensure smooth experiences and minimize latency.
Standardization	Establishing industry-wide standards for interoperability, data exchange, and content creation within the healthcare Metaverse.	Interoperability Frameworks: Collaborating with technology companies to develop standardized protocols and APIs that enable seamless data sharing and collaboration across platforms.
Regulatory Approval	Navigating regulatory frameworks to ensure that Metaverse-based medical applications comply with existing healthcare regulations.	Regulatory Partnerships: Collaborating with regulatory agencies to develop guidelines that balance innovation with patient safety and privacy.
Realistic Simulation	Ensuring that virtual simulations accurately replicate real-world medical scenarios for effective training and treatment planning.	Advanced Simulation Technologies: Investing in AI-driven simulations and haptic feedback systems that replicate realistic physiological responses and patient interactions.
Integration Challenges	Integrating Metaverse tools seamlessly into existing healthcare workflows and electronic health record systems.	Workflow Integration Solutions: Collaborating with health IT companies to develop interfaces and integrations that allow for efficient data exchange between the Metaverse and existing systems.
User Experience	Designing user-friendly interfaces and intuitive interactions to ensure that healthcare professionals and patients can effectively navigate the Metaverse.	User-Centric Design: Employing human-centered design principles to create Metaverse applications that prioritize user experience, making them intuitive and easy to use.

are first outlined. Subsequently, an examination of the cutting-edge technologies now used in digital and smart healthcare frameworks is conducted, following the exploration of the enabling technologies of the Metaverse. Subsequently, the potential applications of the Metaverse in the healthcare industry became evident. Specifically, the focus is on the possible use of the Metaverse in medical diagnostics, patient monitoring, healthcare education, operations, medical treatments, and theranostics. Furthermore, current and future developments in the Metaverse for healthcare are emphasizing the use of blockchain, digital twins, and telemedicine. This analysis critically evaluates the obstacles that hinder the complete realization of the Metaverse's promise in the field of healthcare, while also considering its future prospects.

Enhancing the Healthcare Industry via the Metaverse: Key Recommendations

Several recommendations have been proposed to facilitate the secure implementation of the Metaverse in healthcare. Healthcare institutions and providers should have a proactive stance towards integrating the metaverse by devising strategies to seamlessly include it into their operations. First and foremost, it is essential to form interdisciplinary teams consisting of medical specialists, technologists, and user experience experts in order to develop efficient metaverse solutions. Furthermore, it is crucial to prioritize patient-centered care inside the metaverse. This entails guaranteeing that the virtual experience improves patient outcomes and engagement, while also protecting their privacy. Moreover, it will be crucial to provide comprehensive training to healthcare personnel in order to proficiently navigate and apply metaverse technologies. Implementing strong data security protocols and clear patient consent processes are essential for establishing confidence. Moreover, it will be crucial to engage in partnerships with technological allies in order to create compatible systems that can seamlessly connect with current electronic health records and medical equipment. Regarding study fields, exploring the influence of the metaverse on the relationships between patients and doctors, the effectiveness of therapeutic treatments, and the efficiency of medical training will provide useful insights for improving and optimizing its use in healthcare settings.

REFERENCES

Ali, S., Abdullah, Armand, T. P. T., Athar, A., Hussain, A., Ali, M., Yaseen, M., Joo, M.-I., & Kim, H.-C. (2023). Metaverse in healthcare integrated with explainable ai and blockchain: Enabling immersiveness, ensuring trust, and providing patient data security. *Sensors (Basel)*, *23*(2), 565. doi:10.3390/s23020565 PMID:36679361

Athar, A., Ali, S. M., Mozumder, M. A. I., Ali, S., & Kim, H. C. (2023, February). Applications and Possible Challenges of Healthcare Metaverse. In *2023 25th International Conference on Advanced Communication Technology (ICACT)* (pp. 328-332). IEEE. 10.23919/ICACT56868.2023.10079314

Bansal, G., Rajgopal, K., Chamola, V., Xiong, Z., & Niyato, D. (2022). Healthcare in metaverse: A survey on current metaverse applications in healthcare. *IEEE Access : Practical Innovations, Open Solutions*, *10*, 119914–119946. doi:10.1109/ACCESS.2022.3219845

Bashir, A. K., Victor, N., Bhattacharya, S., Huynh-The, T., Chengoden, R., Yenduri, G., Maddikunta, P. K. R., Pham, Q.-V., Gadekallu, T. R., & Liyanage, M. (2023). Federated Learning for the Healthcare Metaverse: Concepts, Applications, Challenges, and Future Directions. *IEEE Internet of Things Journal*, *10*(24), 21873–21891. doi:10.1109/JIOT.2023.3304790

Benrimoh, D., Chheda, F. D., & Margolese, H. C. (2022). The Best Predictor of the Future—The Metaverse, Mental Health, and Lessons Learned From Current Technologies. *JMIR Mental Health*, *9*(10), e40410. doi:10.2196/40410 PMID:36306155

Bhattacharya, P., Obaidat, M. S., Savaliya, D., Sanghavi, S., Tanwar, S., & Sadaun, B. (2022, July). Metaverse assisted telesurgery in healthcare 5.0: An interplay of blockchain and explainable AI. In *2022 International Conference on Computer, Information and Telecommunication Systems (CITS)* (pp. 1-5). IEEE. 10.1109/CITS55221.2022.9832978

Bhugaonkar, K., Bhugaonkar, R., & Masne, N. (2022). The trend of metaverse and augmented & virtual reality extending to the healthcare system. *Cureus*, *14*(9). doi:10.7759/cureus.29071 PMID:36258985

Chen Y. Lin W. Zheng Y. Xue T. Chen C. Cheng G. (2022). Application of active learning strategies in metaverse to improve student engagement: An immersive blended pedagogy bridging patient care and scientific inquiry in pandemic. *Available at* SSRN 4098179. doi:10.2139/ssrn.4098179

Chengoden, R., Victor, N., Huynh-The, T., Yenduri, G., Jhaveri, R. H., Alazab, M., Bhattacharya, S., Hegde, P., Maddikunta, P. K. R., & Gadekallu, T. R. (2023). Metaverse for healthcare: A survey on potential applications, challenges and future directions. *IEEE Access : Practical Innovations, Open Solutions*, *11*, 12765–12795. doi:10.1109/ACCESS.2023.3241628

Curtis, C., & Brolan, C. E. (2023). Health care in the metaverse. *The Medical Journal of Australia*, *218*(1), 46. doi:10.5694/mja2.51793 PMID:36437589

Dogum, R., & Uribe, D. (2023). NFTs and Metaverse in Healthcare: What's the Big Opportunity? *Blockchain in Healthcare Today*, *6*(1). doi:10.30953/bhty.v6.266

Ganapathy, K. (2022). Metaverse and healthcare: A clinician's perspective. *Apollo Medicine*, *19*(4), 256–261.

Garavand, A., & Aslani, N. (2022). Metaverse phenomenon and its impact on health: A scoping review. *Informatics in Medicine Unlocked*, *32*, 101029. doi:10.1016/j.imu.2022.101029

Gupta, O. J., Yadav, S., Srivastava, M. K., Darda, P., & Mishra, V. (2023). Understanding the intention to use metaverse in healthcare utilizing a mix method approach. *International Journal of Healthcare Management*, 1–12. doi:10.1080/20479700.2023.2183579

Han, B., Wang, H., Qiao, D., Xu, J., & Yan, T. (2023). Application of Zero-Watermarking Scheme Based on Swin Transformer for Securing the Metaverse Healthcare Data. *IEEE Journal of Biomedical and Health Informatics*. Advance online publication. doi:10.1109/JBHI.2021.3123936 PMID:37028374

Huang, H., Zhang, C., Zhao, L., Ding, S., Wang, H., & Wu, H. (2023). Self-Supervised Medical Image Denoising Based on WISTA-Net for Human Healthcare in Metaverse. *IEEE Journal of Biomedical and Health Informatics*. PMID:37216248

Kahambing, J. G. (2023). Metaverse, mental health and museums in post-COVID-19. *Journal of Public Health (Oxford, England)*, *45*(2), e382–e383. doi:10.1093/pubmed/fdad002 PMID:36680432

Kim, E. J., & Kim, J. Y. (2023). The metaverse for healthcare: Trends, applications, and future directions of digital therapeutics for urology. *International Neurourology Journal*, *27*(Suppl 1), S3–S12. doi:10.5213/inj.2346108.054 PMID:37280754

Koohang, A., Nord, J. H., Ooi, K. B., Tan, G. W. H., Al-Emran, M., Aw, E. C. X., Baabdullah, A. M., Buhalis, D., Cham, T.-H., Dennis, C., Dutot, V., Dwivedi, Y. K., Hughes, L., Mogaji, E., Pandey, N., Phau, I., Raman, R., Sharma, A., Sigala, M., & Wong, L. W. (2023). Shaping the metaverse into reality: A holistic multidisciplinary understanding of opportunities, challenges, and avenues for future investigation. *Journal of Computer Information Systems*, *63*(3), 735–765. doi:10.1080/08874417.2023.2165197

Lee, C. W. (2022). Application of metaverse service to healthcare industry: A strategic perspective. *International Journal of Environmental Research and Public Health*, *19*(20), 13038. doi:10.3390/ijerph192013038 PMID:36293609

Lee, J., & Kwon, K. H. (2022). The significant transformation of life into health and beauty in metaverse era. *Journal of Cosmetic Dermatology*, *21*(12), 6575–6583. doi:10.1111/jocd.15151 PMID:35686389

Letafati, M., & Otoum, S. (2023). Digital Healthcare in The Metaverse: Insights into Privacy and Security. *arXiv preprint arXiv:2308.04438*.

Li, J. (2022). Impact of Metaverse cultural communication on the mental health of international students in China: Highlighting effects of healthcare anxiety and cyberchondria. *American Journal of Health Behavior*, *46*(6), 809–820. doi:10.5993/AJHB.46.6.21 PMID:36721290

Marzaleh, M. A., Peyravi, M., & Shaygani, F. (2022). A revolution in health: Opportunities and challenges of the Metaverse. *EXCLI Journal*, *21*, 791. PMID:35949490

Mejia, J. M. R., & Rawat, D. B. (2022, July). recent advances in a medical domain metaverse: Status, challenges, and perspective. In *2022 Thirteenth International Conference on Ubiquitous and Future Networks (ICUFN)* (pp. 357-362). IEEE. 10.1109/ICUFN55119.2022.9829645

Mohamed, E. S., Naqishbandi, T. A., & Veronese, G. (2023). Metaverse!: Possible Potential Opportunities and Trends in E-Healthcare and Education. [IJEA]. *International Journal of E-Adoption*, *15*(2), 1–21. doi:10.4018/IJEA.316537

Moztarzadeh, O., Jamshidi, M., Sargolzaei, S., Jamshidi, A., Baghalipour, N., Malekzadeh Moghani, M., & Hauer, L. (2023). Metaverse and Healthcare: Machine Learning-Enabled Digital Twins of Cancer. *Bioengineering (Basel, Switzerland)*, *10*(4), 455. doi:10.3390/bioengineering10040455 PMID:37106642

Mozumder, M. A. I., Armand, T. P. T., Imtiyaj Uddin, S. M., Athar, A., Sumon, R. I., Hussain, A., & Kim, H. C. (2023). Metaverse for Digital Anti-Aging Healthcare: An Overview of Potential Use Cases Based on Artificial Intelligence, Blockchain, IoT Technologies, Its Challenges, and Future Directions. *Applied Sciences (Basel, Switzerland)*, *13*(8), 5127. doi:10.3390/app13085127

Mozumder, M. A. I., Sheeraz, M. M., Athar, A., Aich, S., & Kim, H. C. (2022, February). Overview: Technology roadmap of the future trend of metaverse based on IoT, blockchain, AI technique, and medical domain metaverse activity. In *2022 24th International Conference on Advanced Communication Technology (ICACT)* (pp. 256-261). IEEE.

Nica, E. (2022). Virtual healthcare technologies and consultation systems, smart operating rooms, and remote sensing data fusion algorithms in the medical metaverse. *American Journal of Medical Research (New York, N.Y.)*, *9*(2), 105–120. doi:10.22381/ajmr9220227

Petrigna, L., & Musumeci, G. (2022). The metaverse: A new challenge for the healthcare system: A scoping review. *Journal of Functional Morphology and Kinesiology*, *7*(3), 63. doi:10.3390/jfmk7030063 PMID:36135421

Prasetyo, J. (2022). The Future of Post-Covid-19 Health Services using Metaverse Technology. *The Journal for Nurse Practitioners*, *6*(1), 93–99. doi:10.30994/jnp.v6i1.295

Qiu, C. S., Majeed, A., Khan, S., & Watson, M. (2022). Transforming health through the metaverse. *Journal of the Royal Society of Medicine*, *115*(12), 484–486. doi:10.1177/01410768221144763 PMID:36480946

Rahaman, T. (2022). Into the metaverse–perspectives on a new reality. *Medical Reference Services Quarterly*, *41*(3), 330–337. doi:10.1080/02763869.2022.2096341 PMID:35980623

Sebastian, S. R., & Babu, B. P. (2022). Impact of metaverse in health care: A study from the care giver's perspective. *International Journal of Community Medicine and Public Health*, *9*(12), 4613. doi:10.18203/2394-6040.ijcmph20223221

Sestino, A., & D'Angelo, A. (2023). My doctor is an avatar! The effect of anthropomorphism and emotional receptivity on individuals' intention to use digital-based healthcare services. *Technological Forecasting and Social Change*, *191*, 122505. doi:10.1016/j.techfore.2023.122505

Situmorang, D. D. B. (2022). "Rapid tele-psychotherapy" with single-session music therapy in the metaverse: An alternative solution for mental health services in the future. *Palliative & Supportive Care*, 1–2. PMID:36218066

Situmorang, D. D. B. (2023). Metaverse as a new place for online mental health services in the post-COVID-19 era: Is it a challenge or an opportunity? *Journal of Public Health (Oxford, England)*, *45*(2), e379–e380. doi:10.1093/pubmed/fdac159 PMID:36542106

Song, Y. T., & Qin, J. (2022). Metaverse and personal healthcare. *Procedia Computer Science*, *210*, 189–197. doi:10.1016/j.procs.2022.10.136

Suh, I., McKinney, T., & Siu, K. C. (2023, April). Current Perspective of Metaverse Application in Medical Education, Research and Patient Care. In Virtual Worlds, 2(2). MDPI.

Tan, T. F., Li, Y., Lim, J. S., Gunasekeran, D. V., Teo, Z. L., Ng, W. Y., & Ting, D. S. (2022). Metaverse and virtual health care in ophthalmology: Opportunities and challenges. *Asia-Pacific Journal of Ophthalmology*, *11*(3), 237–246. doi:10.1097/APO.0000000000000537 PMID:35772084

Thomason, J. (2021). Metahealth-how will the metaverse change health care? *Journal of Metaverse*, *1*(1), 13–16.

Turab, M., & Jamil, S. (2023). A Comprehensive Survey of Digital Twins in Healthcare in the Era of Metaverse. *BioMedInformatics*, *3*(3), 563–584. doi:10.3390/biomedinformatics3030039

Ullah, H., Manickam, S., Obaidat, M., Laghari, S. U. A., & Uddin, M. (2023). Exploring the Potential of Metaverse Technology in Healthcare: Applications, Challenges, and Future Directions. *IEEE Access : Practical Innovations, Open Solutions*, *11*, 69686–69707. doi:10.1109/ACCESS.2023.3286696

Usmani, S. S., Sharath, M., & Mehendale, M. (2022). Future of mental health in the metaverse. *General Psychiatry*, *35*(4), e100825. doi:10.1136/gpsych-2022-100825 PMID:36189180

Wang, G., Badal, A., Jia, X., Maltz, J. S., Mueller, K., Myers, K. J., Niu, C., Vannier, M., Yan, P., Yu, Z., & Zeng, R. (2022). Development of metaverse for intelligent healthcare. *Nature Machine Intelligence*, *4*(11), 922–929. doi:10.1038/s42256-022-00549-6 PMID:36935774

Wiederhold, B. K. (2022). Metaverse games: Game changer for healthcare? *Cyberpsychology, Behavior, and Social Networking*, *25*(5), 267–269. doi:10.1089/cyber.2022.29246.editorial PMID:35549346

Wiederhold, B. K. (2023). (Mental) Healthcare Consumerism in the Metaverse: Is There a Benefit? *Cyberpsychology, Behavior, and Social Networking, 26*(3), 145–146. doi:10.1089/cyber.2023.29269. editorial PMID:36880891

Wiederhold, B. K., & Riva, G. (2022). Metaverse creates new opportunities in healthcare. *Ann. Rev. Cyber. Telemed, 20,* 3–7.

Yang, Y., Siau, K., Xie, W., & Sun, Y. (2022). Smart health: Intelligent healthcare systems in the metaverse, artificial intelligence, and data science era. [JOEUC]. *Journal of Organizational and End User Computing, 34*(1), 1–14. doi:10.4018/JOEUC.308814

Zhang, T., Shen, J., Lai, C. F., Ji, S., & Ren, Y. (2023). Multi-server assisted data sharing supporting secure deduplication for metaverse healthcare systems. *Future Generation Computer Systems, 140,* 299–310. doi:10.1016/j.future.2022.10.031

Chapter 9
Navigating the Metaverse:
A Comprehensive Guide to Marketing, Branding, and Innovation

Harleen Pabla

ⓘ https://orcid.org/0000-0001-5038-176X

I.K. Gujral Punjab Technical University, India

Harmeen Soch

ⓘ https://orcid.org/0009-0008-4724-7314

I.K. Gujral Punjab Technical University, India

ABSTRACT

Delving into the dynamic intersections of augmented reality, artificial intelligence, blockchain, and spatial computing, this chapter offers strategic insights for brands seeking to establish a meaningful presence. From the evolution of brands in virtual environments to future trends, technological predictions and challenges, this chapter acts as a strategic roadmap. It addresses the needs of academic researchers, students, executives, and practitioners by synthesizing current research, offering practical applications, and proposing solutions. The chapter bridges the gap between theory and application, fostering a deeper understanding of the metaverse's impact on marketing, branding, and innovation. Aiming to be a valuable resource, the chapter equips a diverse audience with insights into the evolving metaverse landscape, providing a foundation for academic exploration and practical application.

INTRODUCTION

The late 1990s saw a significant disruption and radical transformation of strategic and operational practices due to the advent of the internet (Buhalis, 2003). Additionally, social media has reshaped how conventional marketing mix components are employed to engage with customers (Upadhyay et al., 2022). Nowadays, the metaverse combines advanced tech, changing consumer behavior and industry impacts. This chapter seeks to illuminate the intricate tapestry of these elements, offering a strategic compass for professionals, scholars and enthusiasts navigating the expansive landscape of the meta-

DOI: 10.4018/979-8-3693-2607-7.ch009

verse. According to Dwivedi et al., (2022), the metaverse holds the capability to expand the physical world by leveraging augmented and virtual reality technologies, enabling users to interact seamlessly in both real and simulated environments through the use of avatars and holograms. Virtual environments and immersive games like Second Life, Fortnite, Roblox and VRChat are considered precursors to the metaverse, providing valuable insights into the potential socio-economic impact of a fully operational, persistent and cross-platform metaverse.

As the metaverse transitions from a conceptual abstraction to a tangible reality, brands emerge as central players in an extraordinary transformation. The metaverse, with its immersive and interconnected attributes, disrupts traditional boundaries, opening unparalleled opportunities while simultaneously introducing unprecedented challenges. In this dynamic context, gaining a profound understanding of the metaverse's evolution becomes crucial for entities eager to leverage its transformative potential.

The metaverse, as a concept, has evolved from a speculative idea into a tangible and dynamic digital environment (Alessandrini & Rognoli, 2023). It is marked by its immersive nature, where individuals engage with a seamless blend of physical and virtual realities. This evolution dismantles the conventional constraints of space and time, offering brands a unique platform to redefine how they interact with consumers, present their products or services, and create brand experiences.

Brands now find themselves at the epicentre of this evolution, facing a landscape that demands adaptability, innovation, and a deep comprehension of the metaverse's intricacies (Wang, 2022). The immersive and interconnected nature of the metaverse opens new dimensions for brand-consumer interactions, challenging traditional marketing paradigms. Simultaneously, this transformative space introduces complexities and uncertainties that necessitate a strategic approach and a nuanced understanding of the evolving metaverse dynamics.

For those aiming to thrive in this new digital realm, recognizing the metaverse's evolution is not just a strategic choice but a fundamental necessity. It involves tracking the technological advancements, user behaviors and emerging trends within the metaverse ecosystem. Brands that stay attuned to these shifts position themselves to capitalize on the metaverse's transformative potential, forging meaningful connections with consumers and staying ahead in the ever-evolving landscape of digital innovation.

The central mission of this chapter is to provide a nuanced understanding of how marketing and branding adapt and thrive within the metaverse's immersive digital environment (Hollensen et al., 2022). By synthesizing a wealth of current research, industry best practices and emerging trends, this comprehensive guide aspires to equip a diverse readership with the insights necessary to navigate the complexities of the evolving metaverse landscape successfully.

Structured as a comprehensive guide, the subsequent sections of the chapter will unfold a narrative that commences with an exploration of the evolution of brands within the metaverse. Through the lens of case studies, early pioneers' strategies will be dissected, shedding light on creative approaches and innovative campaigns that have defined successful transitions into virtual spaces. The narrative will then transition to a consideration of the transformative benefits that marketing in the metaverse brings to both consumers and businesses, emphasizing the immersive and interconnected nature of these digital spaces.

EVOLUTION OF BRANDS IN THE METAVERSE

As the metaverse emerges as an innovative platform for brands to connect with consumers, businesses must reassess customer personas and journeys (Shen et al., 2021). In the burgeoning landscape of the metaverse, the evolution of brands stands as a testament to the transformative power of digital environments. As we delve into the metaverse's dynamic tapestry, it becomes evident that brands, once confined to traditional physical spaces and marketing paradigms, are undergoing a profound metamorphosis. In the evolution of brands within the metaverse, one crucial aspect is community building. Brands are leveraging the metaverse to foster and strengthen communities around their products or services in innovative ways (Dwivedi et al., 2022). This section serves as a comprehensive exploration into the journey of brands as they are building communities by navigating and redefining their identities within these immersive digital realms.

The metaverse represents a departure from conventional marketing avenues, compelling brands to adapt to a virtual ecosystem where consumer engagement transcends the limitations of physical spaces. In virtual worlds such as Second Life, Fortnite and Roblox, marketers are developing specialized locations where consumers can connect with one another and with the brand itself. These areas act as community engagement centres, allowing users to share their experiences, cooperate on initiatives, and connect with others who are interested in the brand. Fundamentally, the metaverse represents a transcendent domain that merges physical reality with digital virtuality, with the goal of enabling a robust and persistent multiuser experience (Mystakidis, 2022).

These early adopters navigated the uncharted territories of the metaverse, experimenting with novel approaches to brand representation. A critical aspect of this evolution lies in the strategic alignment of brand identity with the immersive nature of virtual environments (Messinger et al., 2009). Brands have not merely replicated their physical presence but have sought to establish a distinctive digital persona that resonates with the metaverse's unique dynamics.

Case studies illuminate the strategies employed by these early pioneers, offering insights into how established brands have successfully transitioned into virtual spaces. One notable trend is the cultivation of immersive brand experiences that go beyond traditional advertising. Virtual storefronts, interactive exhibits and experiential campaigns have become instrumental in shaping a brand's metaverse identity, fostering deeper connections with the digitally immersed consumer.

In the metaverse, brand evolution extends beyond visual representation to incorporate a sensory and interactive dimension. Brands are incorporating social aspects into their virtual experiences, enabling consumers to interact with one another in real time. Brands are leveraging augmented reality (AR) and virtual reality (VR) technologies to transcend the limitations of traditional mediums (Koohang et al., 2023). Through these technologies, consumers can not only witness but actively participate in brand narratives, creating a level of engagement that transcends the passive consumer experience of the physical world.

Furthermore, the metaverse facilitates a departure from linear storytelling, allowing brands to craft nonlinear and dynamic narratives that respond to user interactions (Durukal, 2022). This evolution in storytelling redefines the relationship between brands and consumers, as narratives become co-created in real-time within the virtual space (Davenport et al., 2020). Brands have become architects of experiences, constructing immersive narratives that invite consumers to explore, engage and contribute to the evolving brand story.

Crucially, the evolution of brands in the metaverse is marked by a paradigm shift in consumer-brand interactions. Traditional notions of one-way communication are replaced by a multidirectional dialogue, where consumers actively shape the brand's identity. The metaverse, with its social and interconnected nature, amplifies the significance of community engagement. Brands are cultivating communities within virtual spaces, where consumers not only consume but actively participate, share experiences, and contribute to the brand's evolving narrative (Mclean et al., 2018).

Amid this evolution, creativity has become the linchpin for brands seeking resonance in the metaverse. The ability to think beyond conventional boundaries, to innovate and experiment, has become a defining trait for brands thriving in these virtual landscapes. From gamified experiences to virtual events, brands are exploring avenues that extend beyond traditional marketing, pushing the boundaries of creativity to captivate and retain the attention of the digitally savvy consumer.

As brands evolve within the metaverse, a critical aspect of their transformation lies in the integration of authenticity. In the virtual realm, authenticity is not merely a buzzword but a cornerstone for building trust with consumers. Brands that successfully navigate this evolution strike a delicate balance between technological innovation and an authentic, human connection. This is not a departure from brand values but an elevation of these values within a digital context.

The evolution of brands in the metaverse is a dynamic and ongoing process. It is characterized by a departure from traditional marketing approaches, an embrace of immersive technologies and a redefinition of consumer-brand interactions. Early pioneers have paved the way, demonstrating that success in the metaverse requires a strategic alignment of brand identity with the unique dynamics of virtual environments. As brands continue to evolve, they are not merely adapting to the metaverse but actively shaping its contours, contributing to the ongoing narrative of this digital frontier. Few examples of brands that are building digital community are listed below:

1. Nike:
   - Nike has ventured into the metaverse by creating virtual spaces within platforms like Roblox. In these spaces, users can explore Nike-branded environments, engage in virtual activities, and even purchase virtual Nike products for their avatars.
2. Decentraland and Atari:
   - Decentraland is a virtual world built on blockchain technology, and Atari has collaborated with them to create a virtual casino within the metaverse. Users can visit this virtual casino, play games, and interact with the Atari brand in a digital space.
3. Gucci:
   - Gucci has entered the metaverse by partnering with Arianee, a blockchain protocol, to create non-fungible tokens (NFTs) for its fashion items. This allows consumers to own digital representations of Gucci products in the virtual space.
4. Samsung:
   - Samsung has explored the metaverse through partnerships with virtual reality platforms. The company has created VR experiences, allowing users to explore products and innovations in a virtual environment.
5. The Sandbox:
   - The Sandbox is a virtual world and gaming platform that allows brands to create their virtual spaces. Several brands, including Atari, Binance, and The Smurfs, have acquired virtual land and engaged with users within The Sandbox.
6. Meta (formerly Facebook):
   - Meta, the parent company of Facebook, has been actively investing in the development of the metaverse. Meta's CEO, Mark Zuckerberg, envisions a future where the company's plat-

forms are integral parts of the metaverse, facilitating social interactions, commerce, and virtual experiences.

7. Adidas:
    - Adidas has explored the metaverse through partnerships and collaborations in virtual environments. In certain metaverse platforms, users can engage with Adidas-branded content and experiences.
8. Uniqlo:
    - Uniqlo has used the Roblox platform to create a virtual store where users can explore and purchase digital versions of their clothing items for their avatars.
9. Luxury Fashion Houses:
    - Several luxury fashion brands, such as Prada and Burberry, have explored the metaverse by incorporating virtual fashion shows and creating digital versions of their products for consumers to experience in virtual environments.
10. Lenskart:
    - Lenskart, an Indian eyewear retailer, has experimented with augmented reality (AR) in its online shopping experience. While not strictly in the metaverse, AR is a technology often associated with virtual and augmented reality, providing users with interactive and engaging experiences.
11. Godrej Properties:
    - Real estate developers in India, including Godrej Properties, have explored virtual reality (VR) to provide potential buyers with immersive virtual tours of properties. While not directly in the metaverse, these applications hint at the potential for real estate engagement within virtual environments.

BENEFITS FOR CONSUMERS AND BUSINESSES

For Consumers

In the metaverse, consumers find themselves immersed in an unprecedented era of experiential engagement. The benefits for consumers are manifold, fundamentally altering the way they interact with brands and consume products and services.

Immersive Shopping Experiences: Within the metaverse, consumers are no longer confined to the limitations of traditional online shopping. Immersive virtual environments allow users to explore digital storefronts, try on virtual representations of products, and engage with brands in ways that transcend the conventional boundaries of e-commerce. This immersive shopping experience brings an element of entertainment and interactivity, enhancing the overall enjoyment of the consumer journey.

In India, certain companies have adopted immersive shopping experiences in the metaverse. Titan, a well-known watch and jewellery manufacturer, has built a virtual showroom where customers can browse their newest collections and virtually try on various watches and jewellery items before making a purchase. This immersive experience not only improves the customer journey but also creates a feeling of elegance and exclusivity.

Similarly, Fabindia, a well-known Indian lifestyle brand, has entered the metaverse by building virtual places where users can explore their collection of ethnic fashion, home décor, and personal care goods.

These virtual surroundings allow visitors to see how Fabindia's items might fit into their homes or lives, improving their purchasing experience and developing a stronger relationship with the brand.

Personalization and Customization: Metaverse marketing enables a level of personalization and customization that surpasses traditional approaches. Brands can leverage data analytics and AI-driven technologies to understand individual preferences, offering tailored recommendations and content. This personalized approach creates a more intimate and meaningful connection between consumers and brands, fostering brand loyalty and a sense of exclusivity.

Netflix India leverages personalization algorithms to recommend personalized movie and TV show suggestions to its subscribers based on their viewing history and preferences. This customized approach not only enhances the user experience but also strengthens the bond between the consumer and the brand, fostering loyalty and retention.

Another example is Lenskart, an Indian eyewear brand, which offers virtual try-on services through its website and mobile app. By leveraging augmented reality (AR) technology, Lenskart allows users to virtually try on different frames and see how they look before making a purchase. This personalized experience not only helps users find the perfect pair of glasses but also enhances their overall shopping experience, leading to increased brand satisfaction and loyalty.

Community and Social Interaction: The metaverse is inherently social, providing consumers with opportunities to connect with like-minded individuals in virtual spaces. Virtual communities centered around specific interests or brands allow consumers to share experiences, recommendations, and feedback. This social dimension enhances the sense of belonging and community, making the consumer experience more dynamic and engaging (Rathore, 2017).

Indian brand leveraging the social dimension of the metaverse is BookMyShow, a leading online ticketing platform for movies, events, and live performances. BookMyShow has introduced virtual event spaces where users can connect with fellow movie buffs, discuss upcoming releases, and participate in virtual movie screenings and discussions. This virtual community enhances the overall movie-watching experience and strengthens the bond between users and the brand.

Access to Exclusive Content and Events: Consumers in the metaverse often gain access to exclusive virtual events and content that go beyond traditional marketing strategies. Brands can host virtual product launches, immersive storytelling experiences, and exclusive events that are accessible only within the metaverse. This exclusivity enhances brand desirability and incentivizes consumer participation.

OnePlus, a popular smartphone brand, hosted a virtual product launch event within the metaverse to unveil its latest smartphone model. This virtual event allowed consumers to experience the unveiling in a dynamic and immersive environment, complete with interactive elements and exclusive behind-the-scenes content. By offering this exclusive experience only within the metaverse, OnePlus generated excitement and anticipation among its fan base, enhancing the desirability of its new product.

Similarly, Red Bull, an energy drink brand known for its extreme sports and music events, hosted a virtual music festival within the metaverse. The festival featured performances by renowned artists, interactive gaming experiences, and exclusive meet-and-greet sessions with musicians—all accessible only to attendees within the virtual environment.

Enhanced Accessibility: One of the notable advantages for consumers in the metaverse is the breaking down of geographical barriers. Virtual environments enable consumers from around the globe to engage with brands and products seamlessly, transcending the limitations of physical location. This enhanced accessibility broadens market reach, allowing consumers to participate in a globalized marketplace.

Byju's, an Indian edtech company offering online learning solutions, has expanded its reach through virtual classrooms and educational experiences within the metaverse. By providing interactive learning environments accessible to students across different regions and time zones, Byju's ensures that education remains inclusive and accessible to all, regardless of geographical constraints. This approach not only broadens Byju's market reach but also democratizes access to quality education, empowering learners from diverse backgrounds.

For Businesses

The metaverse presents businesses with a myriad of opportunities to innovate their marketing strategies and connect with consumers in unprecedented ways. The benefits for businesses extend from global reach to data-driven insights and a redefined approach to brand innovation.

Global Reach and Market Expansion: Businesses operating in the metaverse enjoy the advantage of global reach, as virtual environments are accessible to a diverse and international audience. This globalized reach opens up new markets and opportunities for expansion, allowing businesses to tap into diverse consumer demographics and cultural contexts.

Paytm, India's leading digital payments platform, has ventured into the metaverse to offer virtual banking services and financial solutions to users worldwide. By providing virtual banking experiences accessible across borders, Paytm facilitates international transactions and financial management for its global user base. This global reach not only strengthens Paytm's position as a trusted financial services provider but also fosters financial inclusion and accessibility on a global scale.

Data-Driven Insights: Marketing in the metaverse generates a wealth of data on consumer behavior, preferences, and interactions. Businesses can leverage advanced analytics to gain data-driven insights that inform decision-making processes. This granular understanding of consumer behavior enables businesses to refine their marketing strategies, optimize product offerings, and deliver more targeted and effective campaigns.

Tata Consultancy Services (TCS), one of the largest IT services firms in India, harnesses data-driven insights from virtual interactions within the metaverse to drive digital transformation initiatives for its clients. By leveraging advanced analytics and machine learning algorithms, TCS helps businesses extract actionable insights from virtual data sources to optimize operations, improve customer experiences, and drive innovation.

Reliance Jio, a leading telecommunications company in India. Reliance Jio has utilized data analytics and insights from virtual interactions within its digital platforms to gain a deep understanding of consumer preferences and behaviors.

Cost-Effective Marketing: Virtual marketing campaigns within the metaverse often offer cost-effective alternatives to traditional advertising methods. Hosting virtual events, product launches, and interactive experiences can be more economical than organizing physical events, eliminating logistical constraints and reducing associated costs. This cost-effectiveness allows businesses to allocate resources more efficiently while reaching a wider audience.

Zomato, India's largest food delivery platform. Zomato has capitalized on the cost-effectiveness of virtual marketing campaigns by hosting virtual food festivals and culinary events within the metaverse. These virtual events provide a platform for restaurants and food vendors to showcase their offerings to a global audience without the need for physical infrastructure or logistical arrangements. By leveraging virtual experiences, Zomato effectively reduces marketing costs while amplifying its brand presence and engaging customers in innovative ways.

Brand Innovation and Differentiation: The metaverse serves as a playground for brand innovation and differentiation. Businesses that creatively leverage immersive technologies, augmented reality, and virtual reality can set themselves apart from competitors. The ability to create unique and memorable experiences within the metaverse contributes to building a distinct brand identity, fostering consumer engagement and loyalty.

Tanishq is India's largest jewellery brand. Tanishq has pioneered virtual try-on experiences in the metaverse, allowing clients to virtually try on jewellery pieces via its website and mobile application. Tanishq uses AR technology to let buyers to see how jewellery pieces would appear on them before making a purchase, improving the online buying experience and distinguishing itself from traditional jewellery merchants. Tanishq's unique strategy not only distinguishes it from competitors, but also strengthens its position as a forward-thinking and customer-centric brand in the Indian jewellery industry.

Adaptability to Changing Consumer Behavior: In the fast-paced landscape of the metaverse, businesses benefit from enhanced adaptability to changing consumer behaviors and preferences. The dynamic nature of virtual environments allows for rapid experimentation with marketing strategies, enabling businesses to stay agile and responsive to evolving consumer trends. This adaptability is crucial in a digital landscape characterized by continuous innovation.

Ola is a major transportation service provider in India. Ola has embraced the metaverse to develop its service offerings and adapt to shifting consumer patterns in the transportation industry. Ola improves the customer experience by using virtual and augmented reality technology into its smartphone app, resulting in tailored transportation options. Furthermore, Hindustan Unilever Limited (HUL), one of India's leading consumer products corporations, has shown agility in adapting to changing consumer preferences in the metaverse. HUL uses virtual worlds and immersive technology to engage customers in new ways and provide individualized brand experiences.

In essence, the metaverse serves as a transformative arena where the synergy between consumers and businesses is redefined. For consumers, the metaverse offers a playground of immersive experiences, personalization, and social interaction. Businesses, on the other hand, gain access to a globalized market, data-driven insights, and opportunities for creative brand innovation. As the metaverse continues to evolve, the reciprocal relationship between consumers and businesses within this digital frontier promises to reshape the landscape of commerce and consumer engagement in profound and exciting ways.

FUTURE TRENDS IN MARKETING IN THE METAVERSE

As we gaze into the crystal ball of the metaverse's future, one prominent trend that emerges is the rise of personalized and immersive advertising experiences. Personalization, a hallmark of modern marketing, is set to reach new heights within virtual environments. The metaverse's ability to capture and process vast amounts of user data creates an unprecedented opportunity for brands to deliver hyper-personalized content and interactions. From personalized virtual storefronts to tailored product recommendations based on real-time user behavior, marketing in the metaverse will transcend one-size-fits-all approaches, ensuring that each consumer's journey is a unique and tailored experience.

Another compelling trend on the horizon is the integration of artificial intelligence (AI) within metaverse marketing strategies. AI, coupled with machine learning algorithms, will play a pivotal role in understanding and predicting consumer preferences, behaviors, and trends. This intelligence will power chatbots, virtual assistants, and AI-driven content recommendations, enhancing user engagement and providing a seamless and responsive virtual experience. The metaverse, fuelled by AI, will not only adapt to user interactions but also proactively anticipate and fulfill consumer needs, blurring the lines between the physical and virtual realms.

The emergence of virtual influencers stands as a noteworthy trend that promises to redefine the influencer marketing landscape within the metaverse. These digital avatars, created and controlled by computer algorithms or human creators, have the potential to become powerful brand ambassadors within virtual spaces (Miao et al., 2022). Virtual influencers offer a unique advantage—they are not bound by the constraints of reality, enabling brands to craft personas that align perfectly with their metaverse presence. The rise of virtual influencers signals a shift towards a new era of brand partnerships, where the authenticity and relatability of virtual entities resonate with digitally native audiences.

The metaverse is also poised to usher in a new era of experiential marketing, leveraging the immersive capabilities of virtual reality (VR) and augmented reality (AR) technologies. Brands will increasingly invest in creating virtual events, immersive product launches, and interactive experiences that transcend traditional marketing formats. Virtual reality holds the potential to transport users to entirely new worlds, providing brands with a canvas to weave compelling narratives and create memorable experiences that linger long after the virtual encounter has ended. The metaverse, with its immersive technologies, will reshape the narrative from passive consumption to active participation, turning marketing into a dynamic and participatory venture.

Blockchain technology is set to play a pivotal role in shaping the future of metaverse marketing, particularly in the realm of virtual assets and non-fungible tokens (NFTs). NFTs, which represent ownership of unique digital assets, have already gained traction in the art and gaming sectors. In the metaverse, brands can leverage blockchain to create scarcity and authenticity, turning virtual goods and experiences into valuable commodities. Virtual real estate, limited edition digital products, and exclusive virtual events represented by NFTs offer a novel way for brands to engage with consumers and create a sense of digital ownership and exclusivity.

Moreover, the metaverse is poised to become a testing ground for the convergence of the digital and physical worlds through the Internet of Things (IoT). Smart devices and wearables will bridge the gap between the virtual and physical, enabling seamless integration of consumer experiences. From virtual try-on experiences that leverage augmented reality to smart products that communicate with their virtual counterparts, the metaverse will be a playground for brands to explore innovative ways of connecting the digital and physical aspects of consumer lifestyles.

As metaverse marketing evolves, the concept of the virtual showroom will gain prominence. Brands will increasingly leverage virtual spaces to showcase products, allowing consumers to explore and interact with items before making purchasing decisions. Virtual showrooms offer a dynamic and customizable environment where brands can experiment with visual aesthetics, product placements and storytelling, creating a captivating and immersive shopping experience that goes beyond the limitations of physical retail spaces.

Furthermore, the metaverse will foster new forms of social commerce, where the lines between social interaction and commerce blur seamlessly. Virtual social spaces will become marketplaces, enabling users to discover, discuss, and purchase products within the same digital environment. The metaverse's social fabric will give rise to shared shopping experiences, where friends and communities can collectively explore virtual storefronts, share recommendations, and make group purchases, mimicking the communal aspects of traditional retail experiences.

In conclusion, the future trends in metaverse marketing herald a new era of personalized, immersive, and technologically driven consumer interactions. From the rise of virtual influencers to the integration of AI, blockchain, and IoT, the metaverse is set to redefine how brands engage with their audiences. As these trends unfold, marketers and businesses must remain agile, continuously adapting their strategies to harness the full potential of the evolving metaverse landscape. The intersection of technology, consumer behavior, and innovation within the metaverse creates a canvas where the future of marketing is not just written but dynamically shaped by the collective experiences of users in these immersive digital realms.

PREDICTIONS FOR METAVERSE TECHNOLOGIES IN THE CONTEXT OF MARKETING

In forecasting the future trajectory of the metaverse and its integration with marketing, it becomes imperative to delve into the predictions surrounding emerging technologies that will shape this dynamic landscape. This section aims to illuminate the technological horizons that marketers should anticipate and strategically navigate for successful engagement within these immersive digital realms.

Augmented Reality (AR) and Virtual Reality (VR) Integration

A pivotal prediction for metaverse technologies lies in the continued integration and advancement of augmented reality (AR) and virtual reality (VR). These technologies will play a central role in reshaping consumer experiences within the metaverse. AR, with its ability to overlay digital information onto the physical world, will enhance real-time interactions, allowing users to seamlessly blend virtual and physical elements. VR, on the other hand, will continue to create immersive and alternate realities, transforming how users engage with brands and products.

VR technology generates immersive as well as alternate realities, transporting users to virtual surroundings (Rubio-Tamayo et al., 2017). In the context of marketing, the convergence of AR and VR is expected to revolutionize product visualization and virtual try-on experiences. Consumers will be able to interact with virtual representations of products in their physical spaces, enabling a more informed and personalized purchasing process. For example, AR could facilitate virtual "try before you buy" scenarios, allowing users to visualize how furniture, clothing, or cosmetics will appear in their own living environments. In marketing, VR enables businesses to develop immersive brand experiences such as virtual showrooms, product demos and interactive narrative campaigns (Zhang & Wen, 2023). Automotive businesses, for example, may employ VR to allow customers to virtually test drive automobiles or learn about new car features in a simulated setting. Similarly, travel companies may provide virtual tours of places or hotels, allowing prospective consumers to preview their experiences before booking.

Integration of Artificial Intelligence (AI) and Machine Learning (ML)

Artificial Intelligence pertains to technologies that empower machines to acquire knowledge, reason, and exhibit behavior akin to that of humans (De Bruyn et al., 2020). The predictive capabilities of artificial intelligence (AI) and machine learning (ML) are anticipated to be pivotal in enhancing user interactions and personalization within the metaverse. AI algorithms will analyze vast datasets generated by user behavior, preferences, and interactions, enabling marketers to deliver highly targeted and contextually relevant content. This predictive intelligence will extend beyond personalized recommendations to dynamically adapting virtual environments based on individual user preferences and behavior.

In marketing, AI-driven chatbots and virtual assistants will become integral components of user engagement within the metaverse. These intelligent entities will not only assist users in navigating virtual spaces but will also offer personalized product recommendations, answer queries, and provide a tailored and responsive brand experience. The predictive power of AI will elevate consumer interactions, creating a more immersive and user-centric metaverse.

Blockchain Technology and Non-Fungible Tokens (NFTs)

Blockchains can be defined as decentralized peer-to-peer databases or ledgers where information is stored in blocks, collectively shared among all network nodes (users), overseen by everyone, and without singular ownership or control (Shah & Shay, 2019). Blockchain technology, particularly through the use of non-fungible tokens (NFTs), is poised to redefine ownership, scarcity, and authenticity within the metaverse. NFTs represent unique digital assets, and their application extends from digital art to virtual real estate and branded collectibles. In the realm of marketing, NFTs will facilitate the creation of limited edition virtual products, exclusive experiences, and even ownership of virtual spaces within the metaverse.

Predictions suggest that NFTs will become a prominent mechanism for brands to establish digital ownership and rarity, fostering a sense of exclusivity and value for consumers (Seong et al., 2021). Virtual assets represented by NFTs will be tradable, collectible, and verifiable, offering a new dimension to consumer-brand interactions. Marketers will strategically leverage blockchain technology to enhance transparency, combat counterfeiting, and create unique opportunities for consumer engagement.

Extended Reality (XR)

The concept of Extended Reality (XR), encompassing AR, VR, and mixed reality (MR), is predicted to become a holistic and interconnected technological framework within the metaverse. XR will provide users with a continuum of experiences, seamlessly transitioning between virtual, augmented, and physical realities. This integration of XR technologies will amplify the depth and richness of consumer engagements within the metaverse, enabling a spectrum of immersive experiences.

In the marketing landscape, XR will be harnessed to create multi-dimensional campaigns that transcend traditional boundaries. For instance, XR technologies could enable users to interact with virtual brand ambassadors in augmented spaces, attend virtual events in mixed reality environments, or experience products in immersive virtual showrooms. The versatility of XR will redefine the storytelling potential for brands, allowing them to craft narratives that unfold across multiple layers of reality.

Internet of Things (IoT) Integration

The seamless integration of the Internet of Things (IoT) with the metaverse is a prediction that holds substantial potential for bridging the gap between the digital and physical worlds. IoT devices, ranging from smart wearables to connected home devices, will contribute to a more interconnected and responsive metaverse. Marketers will leverage data from these devices to gain insights into user behavior, preferences, and real-world interactions, enhancing the overall personalization of marketing strategies.

In the marketing context, IoT integration will enable dynamic and context-aware advertising. For example, smart home devices could trigger personalized virtual experiences based on user preferences, creating a highly tailored and responsive brand interaction. Marketers may acquire important insights into their customers' real-world actions and settings by using data from IoT devices such as smart wearables, linked home appliances and environmental sensors (Ferreira et al., 2021). This information may be utilized to provide highly targeted and relevant adverts or brand interactions based on consumers' individual requirements and interests.

Spatial Computing and 3D Experiences

Spatial computing, which involves the use of computer algorithms to interpret and respond to the spatial context of a user's environment, is predicted to play a pivotal role in shaping 3D experiences within the metaverse. This technology will enable a more intuitive and interactive engagement, allowing users to navigate virtual spaces with natural movements and gestures. As a result, marketing within the metaverse will transcend traditional 2D interactions, embracing a three-dimensional and spatially aware approach.

In marketing, spatial computing will enhance the creation of immersive and interactive 3D advertisements and environments (Scholz & Smith, 2016). Brands will design campaigns that respond to users' physical spaces, creating a sense of depth and presence within virtual landscapes. This shift towards spatial computing will redefine how brands conceptualize and deliver marketing content, fostering a more engaging and interactive metaverse experience.

CHALLENGES FOR BRANDS

Identity and Authenticity Concerns

One of the foremost challenges that brands face in the metaverse revolves around the preservation of identity and authenticity. Establishing and maintaining a consistent brand identity is inherently challenging in virtual environments where the boundaries between the real and digital worlds blur. Brands must navigate the risk of losing their authentic voice amidst the diverse and dynamic nature of the metaverse. The challenge lies in ensuring that the virtual representation aligns seamlessly with the brand's core values and resonates authentically with the diverse user base within these digital spaces.

One potential consequence of identity and authenticity concerns in the metaverse is the risk of damaging brand reputation and trust among consumers. If a brand's virtual representation deviates significantly from its real-world identity or fails to resonate authentically with users, it can lead to confusion and even backlash from customers.

Misinformation and Brand Dilution

The metaverse, like any digital realm, is susceptible to misinformation and brand dilution. In virtual environments where user-generated content flourishes, brands may find themselves contending with inaccurate representations, rumours or malicious activities that can tarnish their reputation. Maintaining control over the narrative and addressing misinformation becomes a critical challenge. Brands must develop robust strategies to monitor and respond swiftly to any false information circulating within the metaverse to safeguard their digital presence and reputation.

To address misinformation and brand dilution in the metaverse, brands can implement proactive measures such as establishing clear guidelines and policies for user-generated content within virtual platforms. Like, WhatsApp's recent advertisements emphasize the importance of not spreading and responding to fake news (Arora, 2020). By providing users with clear instructions on acceptable behavior and content standards, brands can minimize the risk of misinformation and maintain greater control over the narrative surrounding their brand.

Regulatory and Ethical Considerations

Navigating the metaverse entails grappling with a complex web of regulatory and ethical considerations. As virtual spaces become increasingly integrated with real-world economic activities, brands must navigate jurisdictional challenges, data protection regulations, and ethical dilemmas. Ensuring compliance with diverse regulatory frameworks across different regions poses a significant challenge, particularly as the metaverse operates on a global scale. Brands must proactively address these considerations to avoid legal complications and ethical controversies that could arise in the metaverse.

Failure to adhere to regulatory frameworks across different regions can result in costly legal battles, damage to brand reputation, and loss of consumer trust. Brands can implement robust compliance programs and governance structures to ensure adherence to relevant laws and ethical standards. This may involve appointing dedicated legal and compliance teams to oversee regulatory compliance and monitor changes in legislation and best practices within virtual environments.

User Privacy and Data Security

The metaverse's immersive experiences often require extensive user data collection to personalize interactions and enhance engagement. However, this pursuit of personalization raises significant concerns regarding user privacy and data security. Brands must grapple with the challenge of striking a delicate balance between providing tailored experiences and safeguarding user privacy. Implementing robust data protection measures, transparent data usage policies, and secure storage practices are imperative to mitigate the risks associated with potential data breaches or privacy infringements.

In the event of a data breach or privacy infringement, brands may face legal consequences, regulatory fines, and reputational damage, further exacerbating the fallout from inadequate data security practices. Brands can implement comprehensive privacy-by-design principles and security protocols throughout the development and deployment of virtual experiences.

Interoperability and Standardization

The metaverse is a diverse ecosystem comprising various platforms, virtual worlds, and technologies. The lack of interoperability and standardization across these diverse elements poses a formidable challenge for brands. Implementing cohesive and seamless marketing strategies requires navigating the fragmented nature of the metaverse, where each platform may have distinct technical specifications and user interfaces.

Without interoperable systems and standards, brands may struggle to maintain consistency in their messaging, branding, and user experiences, leading to disjointed interactions with consumers. Brands must invest in adaptable technologies and strategies that can traverse these varied virtual landscapes to ensure consistent and effective engagement.

User Experience and Accessibility

Ensuring a positive and inclusive user experience is a perennial challenge for brands venturing into the metaverse. Virtual environments must be designed with accessibility in mind, considering diverse user needs and capabilities. Brands must grapple with creating immersive experiences that are inclusive for users with disabilities, accommodating various interaction methods, and ensuring compatibility with a range of devices. Striking a balance between cutting-edge innovation and accessibility is crucial to prevent alienating segments of the audience and hindering the metaverse's potential for widespread adoption.

To address user experience and accessibility challenges in the metaverse, brands can prioritize inclusive design principles and accessibility standards throughout the development and deployment of virtual experiences. This may involve conducting user testing with individuals from diverse backgrounds and abilities to identify barriers and iterate on design improvements that enhance accessibility for all users.

Monetization and Revenue Models

While the metaverse presents expansive opportunities for brand engagement, determining effective monetization and revenue models remains a complex challenge. Brands must navigate the delicate balance between providing value to users and extracting value from virtual engagements. The metaverse's economic landscape is still evolving, and brands must experiment with innovative monetization strategies, such as virtual goods, experiences, or subscription models, while ensuring that users perceive these transactions as fair and beneficial.

By investing in unique virtual goods, exclusive experiences, and premium content, brands can create value propositions that resonate with users and justify monetization efforts. Additionally, brands should prioritize building long-term relationships with users based on trust and mutual benefit, rather than pursuing short-term revenue gains at the expense of user experience.

Talent and Skill Gaps

The dynamic and technologically sophisticated nature of the metaverse introduces a talent and skill gap challenge for brands. Crafting immersive and innovative virtual experiences requires expertise in emerging technologies, such as augmented reality, virtual reality, and blockchain. Recruiting and retaining professionals with the requisite skills to navigate this evolving landscape can be a significant hurdle. Brands must invest in talent development, training, and collaboration with skilled professionals to harness the full potential of the metaverse for marketing.

This limitation can hinder brands' ability to differentiate themselves in the competitive metaverse landscape and capitalize on the unique opportunities presented by virtual engagement. So, brands can leverage external expertise and collaboration with specialized agencies, freelancers, and consultants to fill talent gaps and access specialized skills and knowledge required for successful metaverse initiatives.

Integration With Traditional Marketing Channels

Harmonizing metaverse strategies with traditional marketing channels poses a challenge for brands seeking to maintain a cohesive and omnichannel presence. While the metaverse offers novel avenues for engagement, brands must integrate these efforts seamlessly with their existing marketing initiatives. Striking the right balance between virtual and physical marketing strategies, ensuring consistent messaging across platforms, and facilitating a unified brand experience are challenges that demand strategic alignment and coordination.

To address integration challenges between the metaverse and traditional marketing channels, brands can adopt a holistic approach that prioritizes strategic alignment and coordination across all touchpoints. Understanding how customers interact with a brand in both virtual and real contexts allow companies to improve their marketing efforts and increase engagement and conversion across all touchpoints.

User Adoption and Behavior Predictability

Predicting and influencing user adoption and behavior within the metaverse is inherently challenging. The metaverse is an evolving space where user preferences, trends, and platform popularity can shift rapidly. Brands must grapple with the challenge of staying ahead of evolving user behaviors, understanding emerging trends and adapting their strategies accordingly. Predicting how users will navigate and interact within virtual environments is a complex task that demands continuous monitoring, adaptability, and responsiveness.

If brands are unable to appropriately predict and adapt to changing user preferences and trends, they risk missing out on opportunities to successfully interact with people and achieve their marketing goals. This can lead to wasted costs, reduced brand awareness, and a loss of competitive edge in the continually changing metaverse market. To address the problems of user acceptance and predictability in the metaverse, marketers may employ data-driven strategies and analytics to acquire insights into user behavior patterns and trends. In addition, companies may interact with virtual communities and influencers in the metaverse to gather insights regarding user adoption and behavior.

POTENTIAL HURDLES

Consumers and businesses alike may face challenges while engaging in the metaverse. Consumers have a learning curve while traversing virtual environments and adopting immersive technology (Ipsita et al., 2022). For example, while virtual try-on technology provided by companies like as Lenskart allows customers to virtually put on glasses, certain users may struggle to adjust to the interface or encounter technological issues, resulting in disengagement.

Another challenge for customers is the question of privacy and data security in the metaverse. As virtual environments capture massive volumes of user data, questions arise about personal information security and potential data misuse (Pearce et al., 2013). For example, customers participating in virtual events offered by firms like Swiggy may be hesitant about revealing important information in the virtual realm.

In a similar way, companies encounter difficulties in adopting efficient marketing methods in the metaverse. One issue is the fight for customer attention in tangled virtual settings. For example, while staging virtual events might be cost-effective for businesses such as Zomato, recruiting and maintaining attendees in the face of several competing experiences can be difficult, affecting the event's performance and the brand's marketing initiatives.

Another challenge for corporations is assuring inclusion and accessibility in the metaverse. Because virtual experiences rely largely on technology, there is a danger of alienating sectors of the public that do not have access to the requisite gadgets or internet connectivity. Brands like as Tanishq, who provide virtual try-on experiences, may accidentally reject consumers who do not have access to appropriate devices, restricting their reach and potential customer base.

FUTURE RESEARCH DIRECTIONS

Consumer behaviors are undergoing fundamental shifts, progressively moving towards digital consumption (Shah & Murthi, 2021). In venturing into the metaverse for marketing endeavors, brands encounter a spectrum of challenges that demand nuanced strategies and careful navigation. One of the foremost hurdles lies in preserving the authenticity and identity of the brand within the dynamic and immersive nature of virtual environments. Striking a balance between the real and digital representations of a brand poses a formidable challenge, requiring a cohesive strategy that resonates authentically with the diverse audience populating the metaverse.

A significant concern arises in the form of misinformation and brand dilution within the user-generated content prevalent in virtual spaces. Brands must grapple with the risk of inaccurate representations, rumors or malicious activities that can swiftly tarnish their reputation. Vigilant monitoring and swift responses are imperative to address misinformation promptly, safeguarding the brand's integrity and maintaining a positive virtual presence.

Regulatory and ethical considerations add a layer of complexity to metaverse marketing. The global nature of virtual interactions necessitates careful adherence to diverse regulatory frameworks, data protection laws, and ethical standards. Navigating jurisdictional challenges while ensuring ethical practices becomes an ongoing challenge for brands operating within the metaverse, demanding a proactive approach to compliance and responsible digital conduct.

User privacy and data security present perennial challenges as brands strive to deliver personalized experiences. While the metaverse relies on extensive data collection to enhance user interactions, brands must delicately balance personalization with privacy concerns. Robust data protection measures and transparent policies are essential to mitigate risks associated with potential data breaches and to instill trust among users navigating virtual environments.

Interoperability and standardization pose technical challenges for brands seeking a cohesive metaverse presence. The fragmented nature of platforms, virtual worlds, and technologies within the metaverse demands adaptable strategies and technologies. Ensuring a seamless experience across diverse virtual landscapes requires brands to invest in flexible solutions capable of traversing the varied technical specifications of different platforms (Zaman et al., 2022).

Creating an inclusive and positive user experience is a multifaceted challenge. Metaverse platforms are employed to capture live events and broadcast them within the digital environment on the host networks (Khatri, 2022). So, brands must design virtual environments that are accessible to diverse user needs and capabilities, considering factors such as disabilities and varied interaction methods. Achieving a delicate balance between cutting-edge innovation and inclusivity is essential to prevent alienating segments of the audience and hindering widespread adoption of metaverse experiences.

Monetization and revenue models within the metaverse present a complex challenge for brands. Striking the right balance between providing value to users and extracting value from virtual engagements demands innovative approaches. The evolving economic landscape of the metaverse requires brands to experiment with novel monetization strategies while ensuring perceived fairness and mutual benefit.

Talent and skill gaps emerge as brands navigate the sophisticated technological requirements of the metaverse. Recruiting and retaining professionals proficient in emerging technologies, such as augmented reality and virtual reality, becomes a strategic imperative. Brands must invest in talent development and collaborations with skilled professionals to leverage the metaverse effectively for marketing.

Integrating metaverse strategies with traditional marketing channels is a coordination challenge for brands seeking a unified brand presence. Balancing virtual and physical marketing efforts, ensuring consistent messaging, and facilitating an omnichannel brand experience require strategic alignment and seamless integration.

Predicting and influencing user adoption and behavior within the metaverse presents an ongoing challenge. Rapid shifts in user preferences and emerging trends necessitate continuous monitoring, adaptability, and responsiveness from brands navigating the dynamic landscape of virtual interactions. Brands must stay ahead of evolving user behaviors to shape effective marketing strategies within the metaverse.

Future study might look at the ethical implications of data collecting tactics in the metaverse, as well as measures for protecting user privacy and data. Future study might look at concerns of diversity, inclusion, and representation in the metaverse, particularly in marketing and branding contexts. This involves investigating how virtual environments may be structured to promote diversity and inclusion, authentically reflect underrepresented cultures, and reduce the likelihood of repeating stereotypes or prejudices. Furthermore, researchers might investigate ways for building a sense of belonging and community among various user groups in virtual environments.

As the metaverse develops, there is a need for study on regulatory frameworks and governance systems to address ethical and social problems. This involves investigating the impact of government legislation, industry standards, and self-regulatory activities in encouraging ethical behavior and responsible practices in the metaverse.

CONCLUSION

Numerous major technology companies, including Meta (formerly Facebook), Microsoft and Nvidia Corporation, are allocating substantial financial investments to construct a digital universe aligned with the concept of the metaverse (Barrera & Shah, 2023). From healthcare and education to manufacturing and finance, digital technologies are transforming company models, processes and consumer experiences, resulting in increased agility, efficiency and competitiveness in a quickly changing global economy (Berkhout & Hertin, 2004). The delicate balance between personalization and user privacy underscores the ethical considerations inherent in metaverse marketing.

The metaverse has the potential to revolutionize many parts of our life, including as entertainment, education, social interaction and business (Damar, 2021). As virtual worlds grow more immersive and linked, they will open new possibilities for collaboration, creativity, and exploration, profoundly altering how we interact with digital information and one another. Interoperability challenges necessitate adaptable strategies to traverse diverse virtual landscapes seamlessly. Achieving inclusivity in user experience remains a constant pursuit, demanding brands to craft virtual environments that cater to diverse needs.

Monetization models, talent acquisition, and the integration of metaverse strategies with traditional channels require strategic foresight and flexibility.

In the current metaverse paradigm, a transformative fusion of augmented reality, artificial intelligence, blockchain and spatial computing is redefining the landscape, presenting a future where the interactions between consumers and digital spaces surpass the limitations of both physical and virtual realms. This convergence forms the foundation for a novel era of immersive and interconnected experiences. Bridging the digital gap and providing fair access to digital technologies are critical for achieving social inclusion, economic empowerment and sustainable development (Sharma, et al., 2016). Efforts to overcome the digital literacy, infrastructural, and affordability gaps will be critical in ensuring that all individuals and communities can fully engage in the digital economy and capitalize on the possibilities provided by technology breakthroughs.

REFERENCES

Alessandrini, L., & Rognoli, V. (2023). Introducing the material experience concept in the metaverse and in virtual environments. In *Connectivity and Creativity in times of Conflict*. Academia Press. doi:10.26530/9789401496476-057

Arora, M. (2020). Post-truth and marketing communication in technological age. In *Handbook of research on innovations in technology and marketing for the connected consumer*. IGI Global. doi:10.4018/978-1-7998-0131-3.ch005

Barrera, K. G., & Shah, D. (2023). Marketing in the Metaverse: Conceptual understanding, framework, and research agenda. *Journal of Business Research*, *155*, 113420. doi:10.1016/j.jbusres.2022.113420

Berkhout, F., & Hertin, J. (2004). De-materialising and re-materialising: Digital technologies and the environment. *Futures*, *36*(8), 903–920. doi:10.1016/j.futures.2004.01.003

Buhalis, D. (2003). eTourism: Information technology for strategic tourism management. Pearson education. Pearson Education Limited.

Damar, M. (2021). Metaverse shape of your life for future: A bibliometric snapshot. *Journal of Metaverse*, *1*(1), 1–8.

Davenport, T., Guha, A., Grewal, D., & Bressgott, T. (2020). How artificial intelligence will change the future of marketing. *Journal of the Academy of Marketing Science*, *48*(1), 24–42. doi:10.1007/s11747-019-00696-0

De Bruyn, A., Viswanathan, V., Beh, Y. S., Brock, J.-K.-U., & Von Wangenheim, F. (2020). Artificial Intelligence and Marketing: Pitfalls and Opportunities. *Journal of Interactive Marketing*, *51*, 91–105. doi:10.1016/j.intmar.2020.04.007

Durukal, E. (2022). Customer online shopping experience. *Handbook of Research on Interdisciplinary Reflections of Contemporary Experiential Marketing Practices*.

Dwivedi, Y. K., Hughes, L., Baabdullah, A. M., Ribeiro-Navarrete, S., Giannakis, M., Al-Debei, M. M., Dennehy, D., Metri, B., Buhalis, D., Cheung, C. M. K., Conboy, K., Doyle, R., Dubey, R., Dutot, V., Felix, R., Goyal, D. P., Gustafsson, A., Hinsch, C., Jebabli, I., & Wamba, S. F. (2022). Metaverse beyond the hype: Multidisciplinary perspectives on emerging challenges, opportunities, and agenda for research, practice and policy. *International Journal of Information Management*, *66*, 102542. doi:10.1016/j.ijinfomgt.2022.102542

Ferreira, J. J., Fernandes, C. I., Rammal, H. G., & Veiga, P. M. (2021). Wearable technology and consumer interaction: A systematic review and research agenda. *Computers in Human Behavior*, *118*, 106710. doi:10.1016/j.chb.2021.106710

Hollensen, S., Kotler, P., & Opresnik, M. O. (2022). Metaverse – the new marketing universe. *Journal of Business Strategy*.

Ipsita, A., Erickson, L., Dong, Y., Huang, J., Bushinski, A. K., Saradhi, S., & Ramani, K. (n.d.). Towards modeling of virtual reality welding simulators to promote accessible and scalable training. *2022 CHI Conference on Human Factors in Computing Systems*, (pp. 1–21). ACM. 10.1145/3491102.3517696

Khatri, M. (2022). Revamping the marketing world with metaverse–The future of marketing. *International Journal of Computer Applications*, *975*(5), 8887. doi:10.5120/ijca2022922361

Koohang, A., Nord, J., Ooi, K., Tan, G., Al-Emran, M., Aw, E., Baabdullah, A., Buhalis, D., Cham, T., Dennis, C., Dutot, V., Dwivedi, Y., Hughes, L., Mogaji, E., Pandey, N., Phau, I., Raman, R., Sharma, A., Sigala, M., & Wong, L. (2023). Shaping the metaverse into reality: A holistic multidisciplinary understanding of opportunities, challenges, and avenues for future investigation. *Journal of Computer Information Systems*, *63*(3), 735–765. doi:10.1080/08874417.2023.2165197

Mclean, G., Al-Nabhani, K., & Wilson, A. (2018). Developing a mobile applications customer experience model (MACE)- implications for retailers. *Journal of Business Research*, *85*, 325–336. doi:10.1016/j.jbusres.2018.01.018

Messinger, P. R., Stroulia, E., Lyons, K., Bone, M., Niu, R. H., Smirnov, K., & Perelgut, S. (2009). Virtual worlds—past, present, and future: New directions in social computing. *Decision Support Systems*, *47*(3), 204–228. doi:10.1016/j.dss.2009.02.014

Miao, F., Kozlenkova, I. V., Wang, H., Xie, T., & Palmatier, R. W. (2022). An emerging theory of avatar marketing. *Journal of Marketing*, *86*(1), 67–90. doi:10.1177/0022242921996646

Mystakidis, S. (2022). *Metaverse. Encyclopedia*, *2*(1).

Pearce, M., Zeadally, S., & Hunt, R. (2013). Virtualization: Issues, security threats, and solutions. *ACM Computing Surveys*, *45*(2), 1–39. doi:10.1145/2431211.2431216

Rathore, B. (2017). Virtual consumerism: An exploration of e-commerce in the metaverse. *International Journal of New Media Studies*, *4*(2), 61–69. doi:10.58972/eiprmj.v4i2y17.109

Rubio-Tamayo, J. L., Gertrudix Barrio, M., & García García, F. (2017). Immersive environments and virtual reality: Systematic review and advances in communication, interaction and simulation. *Multimodal Technologies and Interaction*, *1*(4), 21. doi:10.3390/mti1040021

Scholz, J., & Smith, A. N. (2016). Augmented reality: Designing immersive experiences that maximize consumer engagement. *Business Horizons*, *59*(2), 149–161. doi:10.1016/j.bushor.2015.10.003

Seong, S., Hoefer, R., & McLaughlin, S. (2021). NFT revolution [in Korean]. *The Quest*.

Shah, D., & Murthi, B. P. S. (2021). Marketing in a data-driven digital world: Implications for the role and scope of marketing. *Journal of Business Research*, *125*, 772–779. doi:10.1016/j.jbusres.2020.06.062

Shah, D., & Shay, E. (2019). How and why artificial intelligence, mixed reality and blockchain technologies will change marketing we know today. Handbook of advances in marketing in an era of disruptions: Essays in honour of Jagdish N. Sheth. Sage. doi:10.4135/9789353287733.n32

Sharma, R., Fantin, A. R., Prabhu, N., Guan, C., & Dattakumar, A. (2016). Digital literacy and knowledge societies: A grounded theory investigation of sustainable development. *Telecommunications Policy*, *40*(7), 628–643. doi:10.1016/j.telpol.2016.05.003

Shen, X., Zhang, Y., Tang, Y., Qin, Y., Liu, N., & Yi, Z. (2021). A study on the impact of digital tobacco logistics on tobacco supply chain performance: Taking the tobacco industry in Guangxi as an example. *Industrial Management & Data Systems*, *122*(6), 1416–1452. doi:10.1108/IMDS-05-2021-0270

Upadhyay, Y., Paul, J., & Baber, R. (2022). Effect of online social media marketing efforts on customer response. *Journal of Consumer Behaviour*, *21*(3), 554–571. doi:10.1002/cb.2031

Wang, I. (2022). *The Digital Mind of Tomorrow: Rethink, transform, and thrive in today's fast-changing and brutal digital world*. Digital Thinker.

Zaman, U., Koo, I., Abbasi, S., Raza, S. H., & Qureshi, M. G. (2022). Meet Your Digital Twin in Space? Profiling International Expat's Readiness for Metaverse Space Travel, Tech-Savviness, COVID-19 Travel Anxiety, and Travel Fear of Missing Out. *Sustainability (Basel)*, *14*(11), 6441. doi:10.3390/su14116441

Zhang, Z., & Wen, X. (2023). Physical or virtual showroom? The decision for omni-channel retailers in the context of cross-channel free-riding. *Electronic Commerce Research*, 1–27. doi:10.1007/s10660-022-09616-x

ADDITIONAL READINGS

Ball, M. (2020). *The Metaverse: What It Is. Where to Find It, Who Will Build It*. MatthewBall.

Buhalis, D., Lin, M. S., & Leung, D. (2022). Metaverse as a driver for customer experience and value co-creation: Implications for hospitality and tourism management and marketing. *International Journal of Contemporary Hospitality Management*, *35*(2), 701–716. doi:10.1108/IJCHM-05-2022-0631

Hazan, E., Kelly, G., Khan, H., Spillecke, D., & Yee, L. (2022). Marketing in the metaverse: An opportunity for innovation and experimentation. *The McKinsey Quarterly*.

Hennig-Thurau, T., Aliman, N., Herting, A., Cziehso, G., Kübler, R., & Linder, M. (2022). *The value of real-time multisensory social interactions in the virtual-reality metaverse: Framework, empirical probes, and research roadmap*. Empirical Probes, and Research Roadmap.

Koohang, A., Nord, J., Ooi, K., Tan, G., & Al-Emran, M., & Wong, L. (2023). Shaping the metaverse into reality: Multidisciplinary perspectives on opportunities, challenges, and future research. *Journal of Computer Information Systems*. Advance online publication. doi:10.1080/08874417.2023.2165197

KEY TERMS AND DEFINITIONS

Artificial Intelligence (AI): Artificial intelligence refers to computer systems that can perform tasks that typically require human intelligence, such as problem-solving, learning, and decision-making.

Augmented Reality (AR): Augmented reality overlays digital information, such as images or data, onto the real-world environment, enhancing the user's perception of the physical world.

Extended Reality (XR): Extended reality is an umbrella term encompassing virtual reality (VR), augmented reality (AR), and mixed reality (MR), creating a spectrum of digital experiences that merge the virtual and physical worlds.

Internet of Things (IoT): The internet of things refers to the network of interconnected physical devices, such as household appliances or wearable gadgets, that can communicate and share data with each other over the internet.

Machine Learning (ML): Machine learning is a subset of artificial intelligence that involves algorithms and statistical models allowing computer systems to improve their performance on a specific task over time without explicit programming.

Non-Fungible Tokens (NFTs): Non-Fungible tokens are unique digital assets stored on a blockchain, certifying ownership and authenticity of a specific item, often used for digital art, collectibles, or virtual real estate.

Spatial Computing: Spatial computing refers to the use of computer algorithms to interpret and respond to the spatial context of a user's environment, enabling more intuitive and interactive digital experiences.

Virtual Reality (VR): Virtual reality creates a simulated digital environment that immerses users in a computer-generated reality, typically accessed through special equipment like VR headsets.

Chapter 10
The "Metaverse Society":
Transformative Effects of Metaverse on Society

Irfan Nawaz

https://orcid.org/0000-0002-3817-2858
Ministry of Human Rights, Pakistan

Nazirullah
Universiti Sultan Zainal Abidin, Malaysia

Sabeeha Rahman
Alama Iqbal Open University, Islamabad, Pakistan

Alia Shaheen
Social Welfare and Baitul Mall, Pakistan

ABSTRACT

The term metaverse originated from the "Snow Crash" novel by Neal Stephenson in 1992. The term underwent massive evolution from a speculative concept into an immersive digital ecosystem. Technological advancement unveils the metaverse's potential in shaping the digital future more transformative and promising. The rapid growth of the metaverse extends beyond social interaction and entertainment. Metaverse has started contributing to education, commerce, and professional collaboration. The scope of this chapter is to provide a secondary analysis of the influence of metaverse in individual's lives and societal structures, using the embodied social presence theory and relying on key thematic areas (access and adoption; wellbeing; diversity and inclusion; sustainability; and empowerment) discussed by the World Economic Forum.

EMBODIED SOCIAL PRESENCE THEORY

The metaverse is a virtual environment where people may engage with one another in real-time via digital avatars. This area has been shown to be versatile, accommodating many activities such as gaming, com-

DOI: 10.4018/979-8-3693-2607-7.ch010

munication, marketing, education, and commerce (Garcia et al., 2023). These metaverse efforts emphasize that the success of this technology depends on its capacity to promote and allow social interaction inside the virtual realm efficiently. Therefore, it is crucial to have a thorough understanding of human behaviour and interaction in virtual environments. The chapter used theoretical framework and grounded the Embodied Social Presence Theory (Benosman, 2023). According to this theoretical paradigm, people's views of the virtual world they engage with are significantly impacted by their embodiment inside that space. Embodiment, in this sense, refers to the depiction of a user's tangible form inside a virtual setting.

Regarding telepresence, the physical body may be compared to the technology we use since both work as mediators between the mind and the outside world, facilitating communication and engagement. According to the notion, the way a person sees themselves as part of their surroundings may significantly affect how they think and interact with their environment. This, in turn, affects their degree of focus and involvement in shared activities and communication. There is empirical research that shows how virtual embodiment affects emotional reactivity to virtual stimuli. Enhancing emotional reactions is vital in several human-computer interaction applications. This need is ascribed to the substantial impact of emotions on cognitive processes and learning results. The virtual embodiment may enhance emotional involvement, leading to more profound and efficient learning experiences. This, in turn, can positively impact the acquisition and retention of information (Ghimire, 2023).

The Embodied Social Presence Theory emphasizes the significance of purposeful shared activities in fostering social engagement in virtual settings. Participating in community activities entails collaborating towards a shared objective, which cultivates a feeling of collective purpose and cooperation and aids in the development of a sense of interconnectedness, trust, and mutual comprehension among people. The collective encounter may provide the groundwork for more robust social connections (Bektas, 2023). These digital connections are essential in virtual worlds since they allow users to establish relationships with others and form communities in online surroundings. The virtual realm provides an exceptional medium for people from diverse geographical places, cultural backgrounds, and social circumstances to engage and build connections without being limited by physical distance. The presence of a feeling of inclusion and assistance from others might be especially crucial for persons who experience a sense of social isolation or detachment in their offline existence (Oh et al., 2023). However, users do not deliberately seek out human ties in a virtual environment; instead, these connections naturally develop. In addition to participating in shared activities, it is crucial for people to also participate in ordinary tasks and events that they would normally do with others in their offline daily lives (Zamanifard & Freeman, 2023). These activities foster a feeling of normality and familiarity among those who do not have any pre-existing offline connection.

To summarise, the Embodied Social Presence Theory had a dual impact on the creation of our metaverse: it affected the incorporation of avatar embodiment and facilitated the building of social relationships. Avatar embodiment enables users of the virtual realm to create and manipulate their digital identities, which function as a depiction of their selves inside the parallel setting. This implementation allows users to have a strong sense of possession and control over their avatars, hence enhancing their sensation of being fully present in the virtual environment. Simultaneously, cultivating social connections via ordinary activities provides metaverse users with chances to participate in cooperative endeavours together. The metaverse may foster social connections among individuals by offering shared activities and promoting a feeling of community and belonging inside the virtual realm.

Defining the Metaverse and its Core Features

This section elaborates the summarized concept of metaverse and its main components. Metaverse is a contemporary concept – intersecting virtual and physical realities – representing a collaborated virtual shared space with unique characteristics. Its key components include persistence, immersion, and interoperability. Persistence delineates that it maintains an enduring existence, enabling regular interaction and content production. Immersion offers user experience within digital environments. Interoperability emphasizes seamless connectivity between diverse virtual spaces and platforms. Overall, the metaverse boasts a dynamic digital economy, mirroring real-world economic principles involving the creation, exchange, and consumption of virtual goods and services.

A term metaverse originated from the "Snow Crash" novel by Neal Stephenson in 1992. The term underwent massive evolution from speculative concept into an immersive digital ecosystem. This digital concept further shaped by a multitude of technological growth that redefined the user interaction with virtual and augmented realities. Its key components include persistence, immersion, and interoperability (Stephenson, 2003). Persistence metaverse delineates that it maintains an enduring existence, enabling regular interaction and content production. The main example of persistence metaverse is Second Life and Decentraland that allows users to create and shape their virtual environments – using user-generated content persisting over time. It encourages users to leave lasting impact, promoting the sense of continuity and evolution. In addition, the Decentraland, based on blockchain, allows users to purchase, develop and trade virtual real estate, contributing to the metaverse's landscape in a way that endures over time (Weinberger, 2022).

The immersive part of the metaverse is vividly depicted through virtual reality (VR) technologies. For instance, Oculus Rift and HTC Vive offer multisensory experiences that shifts users into fully realized virtual realms. The immersion further advanced through games like Half-Life, Alyx, in which elements like visuals, spatial audio and interactive elements used to create an environment where users experience high sense of presence. This immersive quality is at the heart of the metaverse, creating a space where the boundaries between the physical and digital worlds are blurred (Wu et al., 2023).

The third key component of metaverse is the interoperability that traverse users into diverse virtual spaces. Cryptovoxels, a virtual world on the Ethereum blockchain, is the product of interoperability by encouraging users to shift their digital assets and identity across metaverse environments. This interconnectedness empowers users to explore a variety of experiences without being confined to a single platform, fostering a more expansive and connected metaverse (Damar, 2022).

Hardware component of metaverse is equally important. The examples of this are VR headsets (Meta Quest 2), Augmented Reality (AR) googles (Microsoft's HoloLens), increase the immersive experience of users' real world surrounded with virtual components. Thus, it blurs the links between physical and virtual world (Park & Kim, 2022). On the other hand, advanced algorithms and artificial intelligence (AI) is vital part of the software side of the metaverse. SpatialOS, a platform developed by Improbable, leverages cloud-based computing and AI to create expansive and persistent virtual worlds. These digital landscapes evolve through user interactions, regularly engaging and getting dynamic experience within the metaverse. This dynamic nature is essential for keeping the metaverse fresh, responsive, and adaptable to the ever-changing preferences and needs of its users (Gill et al., 2022).

Blockchain technology is an epitome of the metaverse. It offers digital ownership, secure transactions, and virtual economies. As discussed above, Decentraland, allows users to buy, sell and trade virtual real estate and other assets. It is a glare example of persistence, interoperability of blockchain within metaverse landscape. Rsoblox, a user-generated content platform, shows participatory aspect of the metaverse (Dziatkovskii et al., 2022). It encourages users to create games, virtual items, experiences, contributing to a dynamic environment. The participatory nature of the metaverse is further evident by Fortnite owned by Epic Games. This platform offers more advanced way of hosting events like virtual concerts, and film screenings, depicting the interoperability of experiences – attracting millions of users across metaverse (Ali et al., 2023).

The rapid growth of metaverse extends beyond social interaction and entertainment. It has started contributing to the education, commerce, and professional collaboration. The persistence nature of metaverse allows access to educational content, offers evolving learning experience. The digital platforms within metaverse opens new avenues for commerce, enables users to do cross-selling of products and services in entirely new way (Allam et al., 2022).

In a nutshell, the metaverse's key components—persistence, immersion, and interoperability—manifest in various forms across platforms. The metaverse is a multifaceted digital landscape continues to grow and redefine user-interaction with virtual world. The advancement of technology unveils the potential of metaverse in shaping digital future more transformative and promising.

Access and Adoption

In this section, scholarly analysis of the metaverse underpins the factors that influence its accessibility and adoption. A fundamental measuring scale is the level of digital literacy of the potential users to navigate the virtual environment in a meaningful way (Buana, 2023). Nevertheless, the presence of digital infrastructure and its robustness are critical in the geographical accessibility of the metaverse (Hu & Liu, 2022). In addition, affordability is another parameter in the accessibility of the metaverse because the economic position is associated with the user's purchasing power in specific geographical cohorts. Besides the regulatory framework, monitoring the metaverse affects the contours of its accessibility, considering the ethical and legal considerations. The notion of metaverse rapidly evolve as a digital ecosystem, offers novelty for human interactions and experiences. The impact of metaverse on social fabric and behaviours demanded through analysis of access and adoption within this digital landscape (Bacher, 2022).

Accessing to the metaverse is influenced by various factors. First of all, technological infrastructure is the foundation stone that ensures provision of high-speed internet connections, low-latency networks, and powerful computing devices. regions where internet infrastructure is advanced, embraced the metaverse seamlessly. On the other hand, regions where this infrastructure is not the level of adopting metaverse is lagging behind. This advantage creates a potential for digital divide between developed and less-developed countries. Secondly, access to metaverse also depends on economic conditions due to high-cost equipment involved in it. VR headsets, AR glasses, and advanced computing devices might be expensive, thus, limiting access to those who cannot afford. The economic disparity in specific socio-economic groups varies in access to the metaverse. Thirdly, digital literacy in navigating the technology stands another crucial factor in access to metaverse. A person equipped with operating complex digital environments can ensure meaningful engagement in the metaverse. Its reliance on advanced technologies and interfaces is likely to handle by a person with higher level of digital literacy (Kaufman et al., 2023).

In addition to access barriers, the adoption of metaverse is contingent to various factors including user experience, content development, and social interaction, the adoption shapes people experience in their social lives and daily activities (Henz, 2022). Metaverse has variety of platforms, offering diverse and unique user experiences such as virtual concerts, social events, etc (Morales-Fernández, 2024). What a user experiences in the virtual world contribute to the overall appeal of the metaverse. Then, number of platforms within metaverse offers users to create content. As seen in Roblox, users are empowered to create and share content – promoting sense of ownership and creativity (Ryu, 2024). This sense of ownness encourages users to adopt the platform but also establishes a virtual community to offer an environment where users shape their digital experiences. Additionally, people are interacting with each other and enjoys the sense of ownership contributes towards building digital communities. This uniqueness promotes the adoption of metaverse for its novel experience. So, the communities whether they are related to education, business, gaming, IT, or real estate, are catalyst in adoption of metaverse through development of sense of belonging and shared experience. After that, adoption rate of metaverse also depends on its comp ability with existing business models, workspaces and meetings (Upadhyay et al., 2024). For instance, metaverse potentially integrates into business applications to offer seamless virtual meetings, virtual storefronts, and team building. The adoption of these technologies in a professional context is influenced by their efficacy in facilitating remote work, enhancing collaboration, and providing new avenues for business growth. Furthermore, socio-cultural acceptance of metaverse affects its adoption rate. Social attitude towards immersive technology particularly concerning privacy, ethics and physical-virtual world differentiation. As metaverse technologies become more deeply integrated into daily life, cultural acceptance and understanding will likely influence the pace and extent of adoption (Ball, 2022). Lastly, metaverse can pace its adoption through integration in education sector. This integration can offer virtual classrooms, interactive learning experiences, and customized learning environment. As educational institutions explore these possibilities, the metaverse becomes a valuable tool for learning and skill development (Garlinska et al., 2023). Such as, Garcia et al. (2022) suggested that virtual dietitian application still requires additional improvements, while metaverse applications have the potential to support dietitian applications in the modern society health sector.

The implications of metaverse access and adoption extend beyond individual experiences to shape the broader societal landscape. One of the most significant ramifications is the potential for a digital divide, wherein disparities in access to technology lead to digital exclusion. Bridging this gap requires targeted efforts to provide affordable hardware, internet connectivity, and comprehensive digital literacy programs. By addressing these factors, society can ensure a more inclusive metaverse that benefits a diverse range of individuals.

Well-Being

The modern digital landscape is dominated by a metaverse that offers an immersive user experience beyond the physical realm. This section will dissect the psycho-physical dimensions of metaverse users in the overarching concept of well-being. The metaverse allows users to transcend the limits of the physical world and get the immersive experience of digital environments. The notion of emersion potentially influences the cognitive process of humans and captivates their minds (Ud Din & Almogren, 2023). Furthermore, the experience of the metaverse is central to the more profound sense of presence, developing the incapability of distinction between the real and virtual world (Rahi et al., 2023). This phenomenon generates the debate about how users construct and shape identities within the metaverse. The metaverse users embodied themselves in digital incarnation (self-awareness, self-concept and self-philosophy) to envelop up their virtual experiences with a layer of physicality. In this context, it is crucial to examine self-perception, self-realization and interactions within the digital enclaves.

Metaverse is a virtual universe in which digital environments through customized avatars or digital representations of themselves. This nexus of virtual and physical world fades the differences in both worlds. Metaverse is a complicated aspect of metaverse engagement. For example, South Korea offers an example of how metaverse influences self-perception of users. The adoption of "Lost Ark", a virtual reality-based game, in 2018 took immersive experience to the different level. Just after its popularity, concerns raised about its addiction, compelled the South Korean Government to implement the "Shut-down Law" for tackling the potential negative effects of metaverse particularly on mental health. The law prohibits the children below the age of 16 years to play games in late-night hours. Such incidents trigger the delicate balancee between the allure of immersive virtual experiences and the need to safe-guard mental wellbeing, particularly among younger users (Lee et al., 2024).

The discourse of self-realization in metaverse goes beyond mere visual representation. The virtual experience often grapples the users with blurred identity, authenticity, and complex intersection of virtual and physical enclaves. The nexus between self-perception and metaverse takes central place in understanding broader impact of metaverse on wellbeing (Zhou, 2023). This introspection has led to a profound re-evaluation of societal norms and expectations, challenging established notions of selfhood (Özkurt, 2023). Taking Japan as a case study, where "VRChat" platform offer users to create personalized avatars and engage in real-time conversations in digital landscape. Although VRChat promotes self-expression and creativity, yet it can trigger identity crisis in complex social dynamics. The dynamic canvas of metaverse is reflection of self-realization through provision of opportunities to individuals to explore various dimensions of their identities (Mantelli, 2021). This path of self-discovery intrigued with social expectations and explore alternative expressions of self. The mediation between self-realization and social exclusion is crucial and demands for careful examination of the self-realization through metaverse. This discovery of self-realization and potential negative affects generated scholarly debate within societal constructs and norms. The power for self-expressions of identity without cultural, gender and social limits can challenge self-realization of users. This reimagining of selfhood contributes to ongoing dialogues about inclusivity, acceptance, and the fluidity of identity in the digital age (Ambika et al., 2023).

Metaverse is mainly a platform offers social interaction in virtual world. Users interact, collaborate and form connections there. This interaction reflects the convergence of local cultural into global where individuals form connections and communities by transcending geographical boundaries. The collaborative nature of virtual environments fosters a sense of shared experience and collective creation, shaping digital societies that echo and sometimes challenge real-world structures (Nunes, 2023). In 2021, Chinese Government released "The White Paper on the Development of Virtual Economy" delineating detailed set of strategies to encourage growth of virtual economies within metaverse. This step positioned China at the forefront of the metaverse revolution. It also navigates the China's proactive approach towards embracing metaverse as a catalyst for economic growth within virtual spaces. On the other hand, it raised questions on balancing the economic growth and societal wellbeing within metaverse. The real challenge would be distribution of benefits equitably. The potential disparities may challenge the metaverse engagement and questions the inclusive growth through it (Zhang et al., 2021).

The hardest path in technological revolution is maintaining balance between technological innovation and ethical limits. Interaction opportunities inside metaverse raises concerns over privacy and ethical limits. When users embody themselves in digital avatars, the virtual space tied to one's virtual identity. Germany is a country with stringent data protection mechanism provides a contrasting example in the metaverse arena. In 2022, German government introduced "Digital Ethics Charter" to set guidelines for fostering ethical behaviour in digital landscape including metaverse. Emphasizing user privacy, consent, and the responsible use of emerging technologies, this initiative underscores Germany's commitment to ethical metaverse engagement. As users embody themselves in digital avatars, Germany's approach serves as a model for creating an ethical metaverse environment that aligns with societal expectations and respects individual autonomy. The ethical considerations and privacy beyond data protection encompasses broader questions about role of metaverse in wellbeing. While users scroll inside digital space, ethical norms are likely to compromise. Thus, digital citizenship framework can be the option to tackle the ethical crisis in virtual landscape (Becker et al., 2022).

As society navigates the evolving landscape of the metaverse, it is essential to consider the implications of self-embodiment on mental health, social dynamics, and privacy. By examining the experiences of different countries, policymakers, researchers, and communities can collaboratively develop frameworks that harness the potential benefits of the metaverse while mitigating risks and fostering a digital environment that enhances overall wellbeing. The exploration of self-perception, self-realization, and ethical considerations within the metaverse underscores the need for a holistic approach that prioritizes individual agency, societal values, and the collective wellbeing of users in this digital frontier.

Diversity and Inclusion

This section navigates cultural, moral, and ethical implications in the evolution of the metaverse. The deeper analysis will discuss the potential challenges and benefits concerning users' diversity and inclusion based on respect, tolerance, equity, and justice. Examples will be presented to illuminate how metaverse can catalyze the promotion or erosion of diversity and inclusion, manifesting through customization, collaboration, communication, and instances of discrimination. The moral and ethical debate of metaverse is central to the diverse identities, cultures, and communities. Metaverse navigates the perceptions that reinforce stereotypes and foster cultural understanding among societies (De Moor et al., 2023). It is a general misconception that the metaverse is devoid of cultural norms and values that challenge existing social constructions. The values and norms contextualize the ethical dimensions of the metaverse (Zallio & Clarkson, 2022). The users' protection rights and recognitions within virtual spaces, particularly privacy, consent, and digital citizenship, contour the ethical dimension of the metaverse. Potentially, the metaverse fosters an environment of respect and tolerance, emphasizing the diverse perspectives of a rich and tolerant metaverse ecosystem (Makarigakis et al., 2023). Equity, equality, and social justice are core values of the socially conscious from the perspective of the metaverse. However, it is crucial to underpin the power dynamics within this digital realm (Saka, 2023). It allows users to express individual identity. Regardless, the potential ambushes of reinforcing stereotypes arise from the metaverse, which is the question of modern literature, and this gap will be filled.

The vast digital realm of metaverse is an immersive experience for users that reshapes inclusivity and diversity. A thin line draws between inclusion and exclusion within metaverse (Gaurav, 2022). Metaverse is being used to ensure inclusion of the excluded groups. For instance, "VR for everyone" and "Accessible Metaverse Project" are few such initiatives, striving for enhancing accessibility for persons with disabilities in South Korea (Lee, 2023; Lee et al., 2023). Using advanced technologies, it provides users adaptive experiences, through accommodating them with various sensory needs, fostering the digital inclusion. Furthermore, virtual spaces have become the places where people can exchange cultural values, tradition beyond their geographical boundaries. Japan has taken initiative titled "Global Metaverse Cultural Festivals" to offer cross-cultural interactions within metaverse. It is a platform where users from the globe can share and celebrate their cultural heritage. Such initiatives are important pillars in promotion of tolerance, diversity and encourage sense of global community within metaverse (Bardhan, 2023).

Digital inclusion takes central place in inclusivity discourse. Digital Inclusion Initiative in Germany aims to address the economic disparities within metaverse. The program focuses on establishment of inclusive platforms through provision of accessibility to users from various socio-economic backgrounds. It encourages digital literacy and reducing financial barriers and building metaverse a place accessible to larger audience. The realization towards pivotal role of metaverse, tech companies is taking initiatives to make metaverse a place of human diversity (Bibri, 2022). In the United States, "Inclusive Metaverse Task Force" is an initiative to create digital environments that resonate with users from various cultural, ethnic, and gender backgrounds (Flannery, 2022).

On the other hand, the prevalence of metaverse is potentially exacerbating digital exclusion and disparities. The special programs, and premium features are only limited to those who can afford or living in developed countries, widening the existing digital divide between developed and non-developed countries. Such steps may inadvertently contribute to the metaverse where participation is stratified based on geographical location, financial position and social status (Calzada, 2023). Nevertheless, number of cases reported digital harassment and hate speech online. The anonymity offered by metaverse somehow leverage the users for discriminatory behaviour, hate speech and online harassment. However, efforts are being made to implement moderating tools, but the arduous nature of virtual spaces make it difficult to curb digital harassment and hate speech (Dwivedi et al., 2023).

As we navigate the evolving landscape of the metaverse, it is imperative to recognize that its impact on inclusion and diversity is nuanced. Positive initiatives in South Korea, Japan, hold the promise of creating a metaverse that embraces individuals of varied backgrounds, abilities, and perspectives. However, addressing negative consequences, particularly economic disparities and digital harassment, requires proactive measures globally to mitigate potential harms and ensure that the metaverse becomes a beacon of diversity rather than a platform that perpetuates existing inequalities.

Sustainability

In this portion of the chapter, debate of metaverse revolves around the consumption of resources and waste generation. The substantial energy footprint of metaverse activities becomes a focal point, raising pertinent concerns about ecological sustainability. The nature of the metaverse compels scientists to believe that it is a crucible for innovation – a catalyst to economic growth and the digital economy. It has the potential to optimize efficiency, bolster productivity, and accelerate the overall quality of user experience (Vlăduțescu & Stănescu, 2023). On the other hand, these prospects issued a clarion call for responsible consumption of energy to ensure a sustainable trajectory. It has potential for conservation through immersive virtual experiences, ensuring that digital processes are environmentally friendly, and managing digital consumption responsibly (Jauhiainen et al., 2022). The section will draw attention to the integration of the metaverse into our digital future through resource management, water consumption, and ensuring an ecologically conscious digital landscape.

As the metaverse becomes an increasingly integral part of our digital future, the need to integrate it responsibly into our global ecosystem takes center stage. This article explores the crucial intersection of the metaverse with resource management, with a focus on water consumption and the imperative to foster an ecologically conscious digital landscape. By examining specific initiatives taken by countries, we delve into the evolving narrative of sustainability in the metaverse.

The adaptability of metaverse also facilitates resource management particularly water management, and ecology conscious digital environment. The evolving landscape of metaverse offers efficient resource management. Let's take the example of Sweden's "Green Server Project" launched in 2021, which strives for optimizing server farms to reduce energy consumption and extending ecological footprints of metaverse. By embracing energy-efficient technologies and renewable energy sources, Sweden's initiative sets a precedent for responsible resource management in the digital realm (Pareliussen & Purwin, 2023). This is one such innovative stance affirming that the growth of metaverse can be possible without resource depletion. The world should understand the sustainable approach in adoption of metaverse particularly in advancement of technologies by reflecting interconnectedness between progress and climate stewardship (Mishra & Singh, 2023).

Besides, metaverse is contingent to water consumption with special reference to cooling systems of data centres (Lloyd Owen, 2021). Learning from the experience of Singapore "WaterSmart Guidelines" in 2022, which sets parameters for water efficiency in data centre through adoption of advanced cooling technologies and responsible water usage practices. Singapore's proactive stance underscores the importance of addressing water consumption as an integral component of ecologically conscious metaverse development (Laura, 2023) (Makarigakis et al., 2023).

This forward-thinking approach of Singapore's reiterates the importance of water as a precious resource and to lay the foundation of sustainable digital practices. In quest of ecologically conscious digital landscape, world should learn from exemplary initiatives taken by few of the countries and spearhead the agenda of sustainable digital practices. The world should foster sustainable metaverse development, focusing on responsible data management, recycling of electronic waster and adherence to circular economy principles. Germany's Green Pact Initiative set a precedent for nations who are struggling to balance technological advancements with climate stewardship (Dutu-Buzura, 2021).

The integration of the metaverse into our digital future is inseparable from responsible resource management and the cultivation of an ecologically conscious landscape. Initiatives from Sweden, Singapore, and Germany showcase diverse approaches to sustainability, highlighting the global commitment to mitigating the ecological impact of the metaverse. As we navigate the digital frontier, it is imperative to view the metaverse not only as a realm of technological innovation but also as a space where ecological responsibility and digital progress converge.

By learning from these initiatives, we can forge a path toward a metaverse that not only enriches our digital experiences but also nurtures the well-being of our planet. The lessons from Sweden, Singapore, and Germany collectively contribute to a narrative of sustainability, signaling that the metaverse's growth can be synonymous with environmental consciousness. As more countries embrace responsible practices, we move closer to a digital future where ecological considerations are not an afterthought but an integral part of the metaverse's evolution.

Empowerment

In this section, an analysis of empowerment in the context of the socio-political metaverse with a special focus on governance, ownership, agency, activism, and education will be presented. Further, how the metaverse brings empowerment in gender related to education (male and female) (Brahma et al., 2023). However, the governance structures within the metaverse, dissecting the questions of authority and control, will be examined in this section. The analysis will further elaborate on the concept of ownership considering digital property rights (virtual assets and spaces). The argument will be based on the capacity of the agency of metaverse users to exert influence to make autonomous choices (choice, voice, and influence) in digital realms. The available literature provided that the socio-political landscape of the metaverse encompasses user participation in virtual governance, creative expression, and mobilization of social causes. Grounded on this, this section contributes towards a greater understanding of the socio-political facets of the metaverse and how it contributes towards empowerment.

The rise of metaverse opens new avenues of governance structures. The adaptability of metaverse compel governments to shape the governance structure through metaverse. The prominent models, inspired by metaverse are Decentralized Governance Models, such as Blockchain systems. These models are key mechanism for empowering metaverse citizens through autonomy, inclusivity, and active participation in decision-making processes (Bibri et al., 2022). Such models allow users to decide on metaverse policies, assets and experiences. This decentralization also challenges the traditional authority structures, placing governance at the core of the community. For example, Estonian's has started its e-Residency Program which leverage blockchain for secure digital identities. This initiative shows Estonia's commitment to empowering citizens in the digital space. With this digital citizenship, decentralized finance (DeFi) models within metaverse such as Aave, and Compound, challenge the traditional narrative of need of conservative intermediaries for financial operations. In these platforms, users actively participate in shaping these decentralized protocols, impacting the governance of financial interactions within the metaverse (Lemos et al., 2022). Thus, decentralized governance models redefine the power dynamic within the metaverse, illustrating a departure from traditional hierarchical structures toward community-driven decision-making (Tan, 2021).

Virtual spaces allow users to shape their environment through customizable rules and regulations. This concept of user-generated governance within metaverse changed the notion of rule-setting and enforcement (Marinescu & Iordache, 2023). Metaverse has made the users architects of virtual spaces, setting up the norms that govern their interactions. This user-focused governance models promotes the sense of ownership and empowerment. The glare example of user-generated governance is Second Life (United States) where users shape their experience, establish property rights, and can create their own economic mechanisms. The success of such platforms showcases the viability and potential of user-generated governance structures in fostering empowerment (Hobson, 2024).

The growing authority of metaverse also raises questions about implications of corporate governance on digital citizenship. The real challenge is to create balance between corporate authority and user empowerment through his meaningful voice in decision-making processes within metaverse. China's exploration of the metaverse, exemplified by companies like Tencent and its virtual world initiatives, showcases the intertwining of corporate governance and digital citizenship. Understanding how this balance is navigated in a country with a strong corporate presence informs global conversations on metaverse governance. Corporate governance structures necessitate careful consideration to prevent the concentration of authority within a few entities, emphasizing the importance of equitable power distribution (Malerba, 2023).

The governance structure dominantly aimed for empowerment of users adds a layer of complexity for traditional governments. The expanding digital realms grabble countries with questions about limitation of governments and implementation of regulatory frameworks. Striking the right balance between preserving individual freedoms, empowerment and maintaining societal order requires innovative approaches to governance that acknowledge the unique challenges posed by the metaverse (Ud Din et al., 2023).

Germany took lead in data protection regulations and adopted holistic approach to balance innovation with privacy through systematic initiatives discussed above. In contrast, European Union has initiated deliberations on adopting stringent legal frameworks for regulating metaverse. However, it is important to understand that interplay between governmental authority and metaverse governance require adaptive regulatory frameworks that respect digital citizenship.

SUMMARY OF THE CHAPTER

The novelty of the chapter lies in the embedding aspects of metaverse in the society and its transformative effects on modern society, however, most of the literature focuses on the technological aspects of metaverse. The academic discussion surrounding the metaverse spans broad and fundamental topics. Every theme discussed in the chapter revealed a unique aspect of the metaverse's influence on society. This chapter focused on the issue of Access and Adoption, examining the various elements that influence the adoption of the metaverse. Specifically, it explored the impact of technological hurdles and concerns related to inclusivity. The concept of Wellbeing in context of metaverses opened up new avenues of research. Then, Diversity and Inclusion was examined through the lens of metaverse by considering aspects of representation, prejudice, and inclusion within virtual communities. Moreover, the concept of Sustainability revealed the environmental challenges associated with the metaverse, such as carbon footprints and energy usage. At the end of the chapter, the concept of Empowerment within the metaverse and its potential to empower individuals and communities was discussed in detail. The examination extended to digital citizenship, involvement in decision-making, and the democratization of virtual spaces. This thorough examination, grounded in the aforementioned principles and embodied social presence theory, this chapter provides a holistic comprehension of the potential societal ramifications of the metaverse. It will assist study scientists in having well-informed conversations about how to fairly incorporate the metaverse into people's life. In future, cultural dynamics within virtual communities (Abdulayeva et al., 2023), economic models (Abdulayeva et al., 2023), education (Darban, 2023), health (Garcia et al., 2022), security challenges (Mughal, 2018), environmental sustainability (Sudhakar, 2023), and human-robot interaction in virtual spaces (Sudhakar, 2023) represent additional promising areas for future research exploration, contributing to a comprehensive understanding of the evolving landscape of the Metaverse.

REFERENCES

Ali, M., Naeem, F., Kaddoum, G., & Hossain, E. (2023). Metaverse communications, networking, security, and applications: Research issues, state-of-the-art, and future directions. *IEEE Communications Surveys & Tutorials*. 10.1051/shsconf/202316400001

Allam, Z., Sharifi, A., Bibri, S. E., Jones, D. S., & Krogstie, J. (2022). The metaverse as a virtual form of smart cities: Opportunities and challenges for environmental, economic, and social sustainability in urban futures. *Smart Cities*, *5*(3), 771–801. doi:10.3390/smartcities5030040

Ambika, A., Belk, R., Jain, V., & Krishna, R. (2023). The road to learning "who am I" is digitized: A study on consumer self-discovery through augmented reality tools. *Journal of Consumer Behaviour*, *22*(5), 1112–1127. doi:10.1002/cb.2185

Bacher, N. (2022). *Metaverse Retailing* University of Pavia. https://www.researchgate.net/profile/Natalie-Bacher/publication/366441739_Metaverse_Retailing

Ball, M. (2022). *The Metaverse: And How it will Revolutionize Everything.* Liveright Publishing. doi:10.15358/9783800669400

Bardhan, A. (2023). Expansion of Space in Metaverse Communication and its Probable Impact. *Society Language and Culture: A Multidisciplinary Peer-Reviewed Journal,* (4), 30-36. https://www.society-languageculture.org

Becker, S. J., Nemat, A. T., Lucas, S., Heinitz, R. M., Klevesath, M., & Charton, J. E. (2022). A Code of Digital Ethics: Laying the foundation for digital ethics in a science and technology company. *AI & Society, 38*(6), 2629–2639. doi:10.1007/s00146-021-01376-w

Bektas, H. (2023). *Revealing relevant factors impacting the viability of the metaverse by replacing online collaboration tools for business meetings* (Publication Number 60644) University of Twente]. https://essay.utwente.nl/96243/

Benosman, M. (2023). *Social Psychology in the Era of the Metaverse: An overview of recent studies*

Bibri, S. E. (2022). The social shaping of the metaverse as an alternative to the imaginaries of data-driven smart Cities: A study in science, technology, and society. *Smart Cities, 5*(3), 832–874. doi:10.3390/smartcities5030043

Bibri, S. E., Allam, Z., & Krogstie, J. (2022). The Metaverse as a virtual form of data-driven smart urbanism: Platformization and its underlying processes, institutional dimensions, and disruptive impacts. *Computational Urban Science, 2*(1), 2–22. doi:10.1007/s43762-022-00051-0 PMID:35974838

Brahma, M., Rejula, M. A., Srinivasan, B., Kumar, S., Banu, W. A., Malarvizhi, K., Priya, S. S., & Kumar, A. (2023). Learning impact of recent ICT advances based on virtual reality IoT sensors in a metaverse environment. *Measurement. Sensors, 27,* 100754. doi:10.1016/j.measen.2023.100754

Buana, I. M. W. (2023). Metaverse: Threat or Opportunity for Our Social World? In understanding Metaverse on sociological context. *Journal of Metaverse, 3*(1), 28–33. doi:10.57019/jmv.1144470

Calzada, I. (2023). Disruptive technologies for e-Diasporas: Blockchain, DAOs, data cooperatives, metaverse, and ChatGPT. *Futures, 154,* 103258. doi:10.1016/j.futures.2023.103258

Damar, M. (2022). What the literature on medicine, nursing, public health, midwifery, and dentistry reveals: An overview of the rapidly approaching metaverse. *Journal of Metaverse, 2*(2), 62–70. doi:10.57019/jmv.1132962

Darban, M. (2023). The future of virtual team learning: Navigating the intersection of AI and education. *Journal of Research on Technology in Education,* 1–17. doi:10.1080/15391523.2023.2288912

De Moor, K., Farias, M., Vinayagamoorthy, V., Daly, M., & Collingwoode-William, T. (2023). Diversity and Inclusion in Focus at ACM IMX'22 and MMSys' 22. *ACM SIGMultimedia Records, 14*(3), 1–1. doi:10.1145/3630658.3630660

Dutu-Buzura, M. (2021). European Climate Pact–Framework for Information and Participation of the Public to the Climate Change Challenge. *Romanian Journal of Public Affairs*(3), 29-40. http://www.rjpa.ro/sites/

Dwivedi, Y. K., Kshetri, N., Hughes, L., Rana, N. P., Baabdullah, A. M., Kar, A. K., Koohang, A., Ribeiro-Navarrete, S., Belei, N., Balakrishnan, J., Basu, S., Behl, A., Davies, G. H., Dutot, V., Dwivedi, R., Evans, L., Felix, R., Foster-Fletcher, R., Giannakis, M., ... Yan, M. (2023). Exploring the Darkverse: A Multi-Perspective Analysis of the Negative Societal Impacts of the Metaverse. *Information Systems Frontiers*, *25*(5), 2071–2114. doi:10.1007/s10796-023-10400-x PMID:37361890

Dziatkovskii, A., Hryneuski, U., Krylova, A., & Loy, A. C. M. (2022). Chronological Progress of Blockchain in Science, Technology, Engineering and Math (STEM): A Systematic Analysis for Emerging Future Directions. *Sustainability (Basel)*, *14*(19), 12074. doi:10.3390/su141912074

Flannery, C. B. (2022). Philosophical and Practical Privacy in the Metaverse: A Case for Data Privacy Protection under the United States Constitution. *Cornell Journal of Law and Public Policy*, *32*, 134–153. https://heinonline.org/

Gaurav, A. (2022). Metaverse and Globalization: Cultural Exchange and Digital Diplomacy. *Data Science Insights Magazine, 5*. https://insights2techinfo.com/

Ghimire, A. (2023). *AvatARoid: using a motion-mapped AR overlay to bridge the embodiment gap between robot and teleoperator in robot-mediated telepresence*. University of British Columbia.

Gill, S. S., Xu, M., Ottaviani, C., Patros, P., Bahsoon, R., Shaghaghi, A., Golec, M., Stankovski, V., Wu, H., Abraham, A., Singh, M., Mehta, H., Ghosh, S. K., Baker, T., Parlikad, A. K., Lutfiyya, H., Kanhere, S. S., Sakellariou, R., Dustdar, S., & Uhlig, S. (2022). AI for next generation computing: Emerging trends and future directions. *Internet of Things : Engineering Cyber Physical Human Systems*, *19*, 100514. doi:10.1016/j.iot.2022.100514

Henz, P. (2022). The societal impact of the Metaverse. *Discover Artificial Intelligence*, *2*(1), 19. doi:10.1007/s44163-022-00032-6

Hobson, A. (2024). Emergent Governance From Polycentric Order in Virtual Reality Social Spaces. In Law, Video Games, Virtual Realities (pp. 74-95). Routledge. https://doi.org/ doi:10.4324/9781003197805-5

Hu, Y., & Liu, C. (2022). The 'metaverse society': Beyond the discourse intrinsic potential and transformative impact. *Metaverse*, *3*(2), 14. doi:10.54517/m.v3i2.2128

Jauhiainen, J. S., Krohn, C., & Junnila, J. (2022). Metaverse and Sustainability: Systematic Review of Scientific Publications until 2022 and Beyond. *Sustainability (Basel)*, *15*(1), 346. doi:10.3390/su15010346

Kaufman, I., Horton, C., & Soltanifar, M. (2023). *Digital Marketing: Integrating Strategy, Sustainability, and Purpose*. Taylor & Francis. doi:10.4324/9781351019187

Laura, P. (2023). *A water smart city: Learning from Singapore*. https://www.beesmart.city/en/solutions/a-water-smart-city-learning-from-singapore

Lee, J.-W. (2023). The Future of Online Barrier-Free Open Space Cultural Experiences for People with Disabilities in the Post-COVID-19 Era. *Land (Basel), 13*(1), 33. doi:10.3390/land13010033

Lee, M., Min, K. Z. L., & Kim, S.-H. (2024). Does the Experience of Using Metaverse Affect the Relationship between Social Identity, Psychological Ownership, and Engagement? *Proceedings of the 57th Hawaii International Conference on System Sciences.* University of Hawai.

Lee, S., Lee, Y., & Park, E. (2023). Sustainable Vocational Preparation for Adults with Disabilities: A Metaverse-Based Approach. *Sustainability (Basel), 15*(15), 12000. doi:10.3390/su151512000

Lemos, L., Ainse, D., & Faras, A. (2022). DAO meets the Estonian e-residency program: a stance from Synergy's blockchain-based open-source toolkit. Conference Proceedings of the STS Conference Graz 2022, Lloyd Owen, D. (2021). *Defining 'Smart Water'.* Wily Online Library. https://doi.org/10.1002/9781119531241.ch4

Makarigakis, A., Partey, S., Nagabhatla, N., De Lombaerde, P., Libert, B., Trombitcaia, I., Zerrath, E., Guerrier, D., Faloutsos, D., & Krol, D. (2023). *Regional Perspectives.* https://cris.unu.edu/sites/cris.unu.edu

Malerba, S. (2023). *Exploring the Potential of the Metaverse for Value Creation: An Analysis of Opportunities, Challenges, and Societal Impact, with a Focus on the Chinese Context* Ca' Foscari University of Venice. http://dspace.unive.it/bitstream/handle/10579/24277/890613-1281454

Mantelli, A. (2021). Learning Japanese through VR technology. The case of altspace VR. *Annali di Ca'Foscari. Serie Orientale, 57,* 663–684. 10278/3742133/1/art-10.30687

Marinescu, I. A., & Iordache, D.-D. (2023). Exploring relevant technologies for simulating user interaction in Metaverse virtual spaces. *Romanian Journal of Information Technology & Automatic Control, 33*(3), 129–142. doi:10.33436/v33i3y202310

Mishra, P., & Singh, G. (2023). Energy management systems in sustainable smart cities based on the internet of energy: A technical review. *Energies, 16*(19), 6903. doi:10.3390/en16196903

Morales-Fernández, B. (2024). New Linguistic Spaces in Cyberculture: The Influence of the Metaverse on the Minification of Social Networks. In The Future of Digital Communication (pp. 27-38). CRC Press.

Mughal, A. A. (2018). Artificial Intelligence in Information Security: Exploring the Advantages, Challenges, and Future Directions. *Journal of Artificial Intelligence and Machine Learning in Management, 2*(1), 22–34.

Nunes, C. C. (2023). *The Importance on Self-Expression Through Clothing and Fashion: A view on Digital Identity and Digital Fashion* Universidade Da Beira Interior. https://ubibliorum.ubi.pt/handle/10400.6/13583

Oh, H. J., Kim, J., Chang, J. J., Park, N., & Lee, S. (2023). Social benefits of living in the metaverse: The relationships among social presence, supportive interaction, social self-efficacy, and feelings of loneliness. *Computers in Human Behavior, 139,* 107498. doi:10.1016/j.chb.2022.107498

Özkurt, M. (2023). *A Jungian Archetypal analysis of Earnest Cline's Ready Player One: quest for the Axis mMundi* Pamukkale University]. https://hdl.handle.net/11499/56004

Pareliussen, J., & Purwin, A. (2023). Climate policies and Sweden's green industrial revolution. *OECD Economics Department Working Papers*(1778), 1-48. https://doi.org/ doi:10.1787/18151973

Park, S.-M., & Kim, Y.-G. (2022). A metaverse: Taxonomy, components, applications, and open challenges. *IEEE Access: Practical Innovations, Open Solutions*, *10*, 4209–4251. doi:10.1109/ACCESS.2021.3140175

Rahi, P., Sood, S. P., Dandotiya, M., Kalhotra, S. K., & Khan, I. R. (2023). Artificial Intelligence of Things (AIoT) and Metaverse Technology for Brain Health, Mental Health, and Wellbeing. In Contemporary Applications of Data Fusion for Advanced Healthcare Informatics (pp. 429-445). IGI Global. https://doi.org/ doi:10.4018/978-1-6684-8913-0.ch019

Ryu, S. (2024). Zepeto: Developing a Business Model for the Metaverse World.

Saka, E. (2023). Metaverse and Diversity. In *The Future of Digital Communication* (pp. 73–89). CRC Press., doi:10.1201/9781003379119-6

Stephenson, N. (2003). *Snow Crash: A Novel*. Spectra.

Sudhakar, M. (2023). Artificial Intelligence Applications in Water Treatment and Water Resource Assessment: Challenges, Innovations, and Future Directions. In Intelligent Engineering Applications and Applied Sciences for Sustainability (pp. 248-269). IGI Global.

Tan A. (2021). Metaverse Realities: A Journey Through Governance, Legal Complexities, and the Promise of Virtual Worlds. SSRN. https://doi.org/ doi:10.2139/ssrn.4393422

Ud Din, I., & Almogren, A. (2023). Exploring the psychological effects of Metaverse on mental health and well-being. *Information Technology & Tourism*, *25*(3), 367–389. doi:10.1007/s40558-023-00259-8

Ud Din, I., Awan, K. A., Almogren, A., & Rodrigues, J. J. (2023). Integration of IoT and blockchain for decentralized management and ownership in the metaverse. *International Journal of Communication Systems*, *36*(18), e5612. doi:10.1002/dac.5612

Upadhyay, U., Kumar, A., Sharma, G., Saini, A. K., Arya, V., Gaurav, A., & Chui, K. T. (2024). Mitigating Risks in the Cloud-Based Metaverse Access Control Strategies and Techniques. [IJCAC]. *International Journal of Cloud Applications and Computing*, *14*(1), 1–30. doi:10.4018/IJCAC.334364

Vlăduțescu, Ș., & Stănescu, G. C. (2023). Environmental Sustainability of Metaverse: Perspectives from Romanian Developers. *Sustainability (Basel)*, *15*(15), 11704. doi:10.3390/su151511704

Weinberger, M. (2022). What Is Metaverse?—A Definition Based on Qualitative Meta-Synthesis. *Future Internet*, *14*(11), 310. doi:10.3390/fi14110310

Wu, D., Yang, Z., Zhang, P., Wang, R., Yang, B., & Ma, X. (2023). Virtual-Reality Inter-Promotion Technology for Metaverse: A Survey. *IEEE Internet of Things Journal*, *10*(18), 1–15. doi:10.1109/JIOT.2023.3265848

Zallio, M., & Clarkson, P. J. (2022). Designing the metaverse: A study on inclusion, diversity, equity, accessibility and safety for digital immersive environments. *Telematics and Informatics*, *75*, 101909. doi:10.1016/j.tele.2022.101909

Zamanifard, S., & Freeman, G. (2023). A Surprise Birthday Party in VR: Leveraging Social Virtual Reality to Maintain Existing Close Ties over Distance. International Conference on Information, Zhang, W., Zhao, S., Wan, X., & Yao, Y. (2021). Study on the effect of digital economy on high-quality economic development in China. *PLoS One*, *16*(9), e0257365. doi:10.1371/journal.pone.0257365

Zhou, Z. (2023). Will the Metaverse Revolutionize the Narrative? *Critical Arts*, 1–15. doi:10.1080/02 560046.2023.2282489

Chapter 11
Navigating the Metaverse in Business and Commerce:
Opportunities, Challenges, and Ethical Consideration in the Virtual World

Pooja Shukla
Amity University, Ranchi, India

Bhavna Taneja
iD https://orcid.org/0000-0002-5447-7758
Amity University, Ranchi, India

ABSTRACT

Trade and consumer interactions with goods and services could be drastically changed by the convergence of the metaverse and commerce. Blockchain technology is used in the metaverse to facilitate the production, ownership, and exchange of virtual products and digital assets. This opens up new business opportunities and includes digital stuff such as in-game items, digital art, virtual real estate, and other digital goods. The idea of " Metaverse" and the role played by Metaverse in business and commerce are intended to be explained in this chapter. The chapter aims to address the genesis, requirements, advantages, opportunities and challenges in the area of Metaverse . It also intends to highlight the ethical considerations and the actions necessary to make the associated practices robust, viable, and effective.

INTRODUCTION

A collaborative virtual shared space created by merging physical and virtual reality is called the "metaverse." The metaverse is a spatial computing platform built on blockchain technology that provides virtual experiences that either replace or replicate the real world and all its essential elements, including social interactions, currency, commerce, economy, and property (Gartner, 2022). The metaverse is a collection of three-dimensional virtual environments accessible via a headset, smartphone app, or the internet. The

DOI: 10.4018/979-8-3693-2607-7.ch011

metaverse's almost limitless possibilities and goals are currently making it the talk of the digital world. Due to its groundbreaking status in digital and technological discoveries, the metaverse is attracting a lot of investment. The digital and real worlds can coexist in this environment and have a major impact on key aspects of daily life. Essentially, it is a world of infinitely connected virtual communities where users can interact, create, and have fun using smartphone apps, augmented reality glasses, virtual reality headsets, and other technologies. It also covers other facets of the internet lifestyle, such as social networking and shopping.

Though the idea of the metaverse has existed for many years, the rebranding of "Meta" has brought it to the attention of the general public. By unveiling this rebranding, Meta—the "Big Tech" business that presently holds the largest interest in the Metaverse marketplace—signaled a major shift in its focus towards the creation of mixed, virtual, and augmented realities. It is reasonable to anticipate that when similar digital businesses pool their resources, future technology will influence how people live, work, and amuse themselves in urban life both locally and globally. Novelist Neal Stephenson is credited with popularizing the phrase "metaverse." His novel "Snow Crash" is widely regarded as the first to introduce the idea of the metaverse. The novel says that the metaverse consists of a virtual environment where users can communicate with one another in a common online space. It also states that the metaverse is a virtual environment that can be accessed with a virtual reality headset and used for social media, business, and entertainment purposes. The novel delves into the potential of virtual world and its potential societal implications, making it one of the first works of literature (Stephenson, 1992).

The idea of the metaverse has come to light as a revolutionary frontier in an era of unparalleled technical development, with the potential to drastically alter the business and commerce landscape. The Metaverse, which is described as a virtual shared space created by the fusion of permanent virtual world with digitally augmented physical reality, signifies a fundamental change in the way people interact, transact, and engage. People move between virtual worlds in the Metaverse with ease, taking part in activities that range from trade and education to social interactions and entertainment. Beyond the confines of actual life, this virtual environment presents countless options for creativity and discovery. The metaverse offers businesses the alluring possibility of breaking into new markets, establishing fresh connections with customers, and reinventing conventional business structures.

The metaverse opens a new floodgate of opportunities in the area of business and commerce (Swan, 2023). Developments in the field of information technology have added sophistication, leading to the development of innovative business models, products, and services. These business models, products, and services not only have the potential to upgrade the existing business paradigms but also to add new revenue streams. Using the metaverse, entrepreneurs and business houses can offer their goods and services to consumers across the globe. But despite the attraction of seemingly endless options, companies have to negotiate in a challenging and morally complex environment. Businesses that want to participate in the metaverse have to consider concerns about data security, privacy, and the morality of virtual interactions. The Metaverse will evolve into an extraordinarily comprehensive, extraordinarily transparent, and dynamically optimized system as the application scenarios mature. To make sure that the metaverse is an environment that promotes justice and fairness for all users, significant thought must be given to issues of accessibility, inclusion, and the digital divide.

REVIEW OF LITERATURE

Metaverse is a term that has acquired popularity, suggesting a revolutionary future where virtual worlds live in harmony with our daily lives Ball (2022). Metaverse aims to build a virtual world says Kim (2021), that is immersive, networked, and persistent. Social and economic connections, peer-to-peer communication, and even the ownership of virtual goods is made possible by this virtual reality (VR) and augmented reality (AR) environments.

Immersive 3D Environments

The metaverse is not one isolated, standalone platform. Popp & Cuţitoi, (2022) envisions an interconnected network of virtual spaces. It can be thought of as a collection of smoothly linked virtual worlds. Users can move freely between them with their avatars and possibly even their digital possessions. This persistence is important because the metaverse continues to exist and evolve even when certain users are not online.

Interconnectivity and Persistence

The metaverse does not exists in isolation. It is made up of network of interconnected virtual spaces. According to Moro-Visconti (2022), it is a collection of virtual worlds, seamlessly connected together. Users can without any hassle travel between them, carrying their avatars and potentially even their digital assets.

Social and Economic Interactions

The metaverse promotes social interaction and economic activity in addition to entertainment. Allam, et al., 2022, say that users can have meaningful conversations, build communities, work together on projects, and even take part in virtual economies. According to Kim et al., 2023, this can entail blending the boundaries between the real and virtual worlds by going to virtual conferences, concerts, or buying digital goods and services.

User-Generated Content and Ownership

Users are enabled to be creators rather than merely consumers by the metaverse. Chen, & Cheng (2022) say that a major part is played by user-generated content (UGC) -which enables people to create and modify their virtual environments and may even influence the metaverse's structure. Furthermore, Lee et al., 2022, reiterate that the establishment of safe and transparent digital ownership might be facilitated by ideas like blockchain technology, allowing people to trade and possess unique products or virtual land inside the metaverse.

Evolving and Unifying

The metaverse is an ever-evolving concept rather than a static one. Bolger (2021) says that it is always developing and improving its unique features and functionalities. Richter & Richter (2023) says that its flexible character makes it possible to incorporate new technologies and innovate continuously. In its perfect state, the metaverse also seeks to bring all the existing virtual experiences together into a single, coherent virtual environment.

Building Blocks of the Metaverse

The metaverse, an immersive virtual world, isn't just a futuristic concept anymore. It's actively being constructed with the help of various existing and emerging technologies. These technologies act as the foundation, laying the groundwork for the metaverse's functionalities and user experience. Let's delve into the key elements that hold this virtual space together.

Immersive Technologies - Virtual Reality (VR)

Han et al., 2022; Wu et al., 2023 say that by using headsets, virtual reality technology takes users into the center of the metaverse and creates fully replicated surroundings. These surroundings can be exact recreations of actual places or fanciful ones reveals.

Augmented Reality (AR)

Gattullo, et al., 2022 says that AR modifies the real world by superimposing digital components on top of it, unlike VR. This could provide a more integrated metaverse experience by enabling users to engage with the actual world and the virtual world at the same time states Popescu et al., 2022.

RESEARCH METHODOLOGY

The Study is basically exploratory in nature. The idea of " Metaverse" and the role played by Metaverse in business and commerce are intended to be explained in this study. The study aims to address the genesis, requirements, advantages, opportunities, and challenges in the area of Metaverse. It also intends to highlight the ethical considerations and the actions necessary to make the associated practices robust, viable, and effective. This study is based on data collected from the secondary sources. Relevant books, journals, periodicals, research papers, clippings and excerpts of newspapers, have been referred.

RESEARCH OBJECTIVES

- To study the technological foundation of the metaverse with reference to business and commerce
- To study the opportunities in the metaverse in the context of business and commerce.
- To explore challenges in applying the metaverse to business and commerce.
- To study ethical considerations in the metaverse concerning business and commerce.

TECHNOLOGICAL FOUNDATION OF METAVERSE

The metaverse, an immersive virtual world, is not just a futuristic concept anymore. It is actively being constructed with the help of various existing and emerging technologies. These technologies act as the foundation, laying the groundwork for the metaverse's functionalities and user experience. Let's delve into the key elements that hold this virtual space together:

Immersive Technologies

- **Virtual Reality (VR)**: Han et al., 2022; Wu et al., 2023 say that by using headsets, virtual reality technology takes users into the center of the metaverse and creates fully replicated surroundings. These surroundings can be exact recreations of actual places or fanciful ones reveals.
- **Augmented Reality (AR)**: Gattullo, et al., 2022 says that AR modifies the real world by superimposing digital components on top of it, unlike VR. This could provide a more integrated metaverse experience by enabling users to engage with the actual world and the virtual world at the same time states Popescu et al., 2022.

Connectivity and Infrastructure

- **Low-latency Networks:** The metaverse depends on smooth, instantaneous interactions. Low-latency, high-bandwidth networks are necessary to do this says Duong et al., 2023. Huynh et al., 2022 have expressed that to guarantee lag-free data flow and prevent interruptions, technologies like 5G and beyond will be required.
- **Cloud Computing:** Cloud computing will provide the massive volume of data and processing power needed for the metaverse says Xiang et al., 2023 . This makes it possible for data to be processed, stored, and delivered efficiently, which supports the seamless operation of the metaverse says Jiang et al., 2022.

Enabling Technologies

- **Artificial Intelligence (AI):** According to Huynh et al., 2023 artificial intelligence has a variety of functions in the metaverse,. Realistic avatars, virtual assistants, and even whole virtual worlds can be powered by it says Hwang, & Chien (2022). AI also can customize user interfaces, adjust to user preferences, and enhance the metaverse's general dynamic.
- **Blockchain Technology:** With this Blockchain Technology, digital ownership can be managed transparently and safely in the metaverse says Gadekallu et al., 2022. Users may trade and possess virtual commodities, land, and avatars via blockchain, which could lead to the creation of a virtual economy in the metaverse according to Jeon, et al., 2022.

User Interface and Interaction

- **Haptic Technologies:** Majerová, & Pera (2022) say that with the help of tactile feedback offered by these technologies, users can engage more realistically with the metaverse and feel virtual items . This has the potential to increase immersion and obfuscate the distinction between the real and virtual worlds.

- **Brain-computer interfaces (BCIs):** Though they are still in their infancy, BCIs have the power to completely change how people interact in the metaverse says Zhu, et al., 2023. In the future, these interfaces might make it possible to manage virtual environments more naturally and intuitively by using brain impulses rather than conventional controllers or keyboards.

Simply said, the metaverse is being shaped by several fundamental technologies. More breakthroughs and the incorporation of even more creative solutions are to be expected as development continues reiterates Abdelghafar et al., 2023. Beyond just being an incredible technological advancement, the metaverse can completely change the way people communicate, work, and even view the world. To appreciate both its present status and enormous promise for the future, one must have a solid understanding of its technological underpinnings.

OPPORTUNITIES IN THE METAVERSE FOR BUSINESS

The metaverse, an interconnected network of immersive virtual experiences, is rapidly gaining traction, stirring curiosity and excitement across industries. While its full potential remains under exploration, businesses in the realm of commerce stand to gain significant advantages from embracing this innovative frontier. Here are some key benefits of utilizing the metaverse for trade and business:

Redefining Customer Experiences

- **Immersion is King**: Businesses can offer fully immersive experiences on web platforms that are dynamic due to the metaverse says Erazo & Sulbarán (2022). Clients can experience product features in a virtual showroom, try on clothing in a 3D fitting room, or participate in interactive product presentations. This foster increased brand loyalty and confidence in the product. Zhou (2024) says that the metaverse enables the development and marketing of entirely new product categories. Companies can offer virtual apparel, accessories, or exclusive digital experiences for customers' avatars, creating a profitable source of income. especially for the expanding digital fashion and entertainment sectors.
- **Interactive Storytelling**: Yang (2023) says that this could include interactive product games, virtual tours of manufacturing plants, or behind-the-scenes looks at corporate culture. These interactions help businesses stand out by creating emotional connections with their customers says Deniz (2024).

Boosting Customer Engagement

- **Virtually Connecting People**: Companies can host interactive concerts, seminars, and product debuts virtually, expanding their global audience and enhancing community engagement with customers, regardless of geographical constraints says Hamilton (2022).

- Öztürk & Hersono (2023) reveals that Companies can monetize virtual events by selling tickets, offering sponsorships, or introducing in-event advertising, allowing them to generate revenue while providing valuable experiences to their target audience.
- **Market Research Insights: According to** Barrera & Shah (2023) the metaverse provides valuable data on user behavior and preferences within the virtual world, allowing businesses to gain deeper customer insights and refine their marketing strategies accordingly.
- **Enhanced Customer Support**: Businesses can offer interactive and personalized customer support through virtual assistants says Rane, et al., 2023 or customer service representatives in the metaverse, providing a more efficient and satisfying experience for customers.
- **Gamification Power:** By incorporating gamification, companies can enhance the shopping experience, such as earning points for completing tasks, receiving virtual rewards, or participating in entertaining contests says Thomas et al., 2023. This increases customer retention and sales by making shopping more enjoyable and engaging.

Transforming Collaboration and Training

- **Virtual Workspaces:** Employees can collaborate in real-time on collaborative virtual workstations created through the metaverse, regardless of their geographical location, promoting enhanced teamwork, communication, and overall productivity says Popescu (2022).
- **Interactive Training Simulations:** Companies can create interactive training simulations using the metaverse, such as safety training, operating complex machinery, and rehearsing customer service scenarios, says Ljungholm (2022) offering a more effective and engaging learning environment compared to traditional methods.
- **Streamlined Financial Transactions:** The metaverse can facilitate secure and efficient financial transactions using digital currencies says Far et al., 2023. A person can seamlessly pay for virtual goods or services within the metaverse, simplifying transactions and potentially expanding financial inclusion.
- **Financial Literacy and Education:** The metaverse can offer innovative ways to promote financial literacy and education says Bremers (2023). Interactive simulations and immersive experiences can help individuals understand complex financial concepts in a more engaging and accessible manner.

While the metaverse is still evolving, and these advantages are yet to fully materialize, the potential for innovation and transformation is undeniable. Businesses that embrace the metaverse and strategically adapt their approaches stand to gain a significant competitive advantage in the future of commerce.

The metaverse presents a transformative opportunity for commerce and finance, offering exciting possibilities and requiring careful navigation. Collaboration, responsible development, and a focus on inclusivity are essential to realizing its full potential. By charting a course that prioritizes user needs, fosters trust, and adheres to ethical principles, businesses and stakeholders can help shape a future metaverse that benefits everyone and propels commerce and finance into a new era. **The below mentioned chart provides concise overview of opportunities the metaverse offers for businesses in terms of customer experiences, engagement, collaboration and financial transactions.**

Table 1. Opportunities and their descriptions

Sl No.	Opportunities	Description
1.	Redefining Customer Experiences	1. Offer fully immersive experiences on web platforms. 2. Develop and market new product categories.
2.	Interactive Storytelling	1. Create interactive product games. 2. Offer virtual tours and behind-the-scenes looks at corporate culture.
3.	Boosting Customer Engagement	1. Host interactive concerts, seminars, and product debuts virtually. 2. Monetize virtual events.
4.	Market Research Insights	1. Gain valuable data on user behaviour and preferences. 2. Refine marketing strategies accordingly.
5.	Enhanced Customer Support	1. Offer interactive and personalized customer support through virtual assistants.
6.	Gamification Power	1. Enhance the shopping experience with gamified elements.
7.	Transforming Collaboration	1. Enable real-time collaboration regardless of geographical location. 2. Create interactive training simulations.
8.	Streamlined Financial Transactions	1. Facilitate secure and efficient financial transactions using digital currencies.
9.	Financial Literacy and Education	1. Promote financial literacy and education through interactive simulations and immersive experiences.

Source: Original

NAVIGATING CHALLENGES IN APPLYING THE METAVERSE TO BUSINESS

The metaverse, an immersive virtual environment, promises to revolutionize interaction, communication, and business. While there are clear advantages for businesses, several significant obstacles hinder its broad use, such as accessibility limitations due to technology costs, privacy and security concerns, and potential ethical considerations. Navigating these challenges responsibly while embracing its potential will be key to unlocking the true advantages the metaverse offers for businesses and commerce.

Accessibility and Cost

- **Technological Hurdle:** Bag, et al., 2023 say that costly virtual reality equipment and fast internet connections are currently required to enter the metaverse, rendering a sizable percentage of the population less accessible This unfairly disadvantages businesses and may exclude a significant portion of their potential clientele.
- **Digital Divide:** The accessibility problem is exacerbated by the digital gap between those who have access to the required technology and those who do not says Gaurav (2023). Companies must explore ways to connect with more people who may not be able to fully engage with the metaverse yet.

Privacy and Security Concerns

- **Data Security Risks:** Utilizing the metaverse requires gathering and storing user data. To avoid security lapses and safeguard user privacy, Jaber (2022) says that businesses must establish strong data security protocols, including encryption and regular audits, and foster transparency and trust with clients around data usage.

- **Monetization and Ethical Dilemmas:** The metaverse opens opportunities for new schemes and exploitative practices says McCall, et al., 2022. Companies must create explicit policies and ethical monetization methods to protect consumers against online fraud and deceptive advertising.

Interoperability and Standardization

- **Fragmented Landscape**: The metaverse is currently not a single, cohesive platform. With multiple metaverse systems and inconsistent levels of interoperability, businesses might find it challenging to navigate this fragmented ecosystem says Earhart (2012) and Goldfield (2023), presenting issues with data portability, compatibility, and reaching cliens on various platforms.
- **Lack of Standardization:** The absence of standardized protocols and regulations creates uncertainty for businesses operating within the metaverse, hindering development and making it difficult to establish consistency across different virtual spaces says Hyun (2023).

While these challenges are significant, they are not insurmountable. By focusing on inclusivity, prioritizing security, and ethical practices, advocating for standardization, and upholding ethical principles and social responsibility, businesses can navigate the metaverse's challenges and unlock its potential for innovation and transformation in commerce.

ETHICAL CONSIDERATIONS

- **Addiction and Mental Health:** The immersive nature of the metaverse raises concerns about potential addiction and detrimental effects on mental health say Usmani et al., 2022. Companies should consider these concerns and prioritize user well-being in their design.
- **Social Responsibility:** The metaverse has significant implications for social responsibility. To provide all users with a positive and inclusive experience, businesses must address the possibility of discrimination, biased algorithms, and negative social interactions in the virtual world says Jones (2023)
- **Collaboration and Standardization:** According to Hyun (2023) Businesses, technology companies, and policymakers need to collaborate to establish standardized protocols and regulations for the metaverse. This ensures interoperability between platforms, fosters trust, and facilitates secure and ethical development.
- **Addressing Accessibility and Inclusivity:** Othman, et al., 2024 say that the metaverse risks can exacerbate existing inequalities if not developed with inclusivity in mind. Addressing accessibility limitations through affordable technology and alternative access points is crucial for ensuring participation of masses.
- **Prioritizing Ethical Considerations:** R Imamguluyev et al., 2023 say that businesses need to uphold ethical principles within the metaverse, focusing on data privacy, responsible advertising, and preventing harmful behaviours. This requires transparent data practices, user control over information, and robust safeguards against potential risks.

CONCLUSION

The metaverse represents a significant evolution in how we interact with digital environments, offering profound implications for business and commerce. As a spatial computing platform built on blockchain technology, the metaverse provides immersive virtual experiences that redefine customer interactions, boost engagement, and transform collaboration and training. By leveraging the metaverse, businesses can create innovative customer experiences, access valuable market insights, and streamline financial transactions, among other benefits.

To fully realize the metaverse's potential, it is vital to comprehend these essential features. It depicts an exciting future where work, pleasure, and communication are all made possible by the increased vagueness of borders between the physical and digital worlds. Although the metaverse is still in its infancy, its development has the potential to greatly influence the course of a new era in human experience and interaction. However, the adoption of the metaverse also presents challenges, including accessibility limitations, privacy and security concerns, and ethical considerations. Addressing these challenges requires collaboration, responsible development, and a focus on inclusivity to ensure that the metaverse benefits everyone and propels commerce and finance into a new era. To sum up, the metaverse experience in business and commerce is a symphony of possibilities, where opportunity and difficulty coexist together amidst the vastness of the digital universe. Here, in the exquisite interplay of creativity and engagement, companies stand on the brink of infinite possibilities, charged with the grave responsibility of negotiating the turbulent waters of ethical consideration. By means of cooperation, investigation, and a resolute dedication to equity and inclusivity, companies have the potential to unleash the metaverse's revolutionary potential and shape a future that glows brightly with digital potential.

Future Research Scope

Future research can further explore the role of the metaverse in achieving specific business sustainability goals and investigate regulatory landscapes and best practices for promoting its sustainable use in trade and commerce. By continuing to study and adapt to the evolving landscape of the metaverse, businesses can unlock its full potential and drive innovation in the digital economy.

REFERENCES

Abdelghafar, S., Ezzat, D., Darwish, A., & Hassanien, A. E. (2023). Metaverse for Brain Computer Interface: Towards New and Improved Applications. In *The Future of Metaverse in the Virtual Era and Physical World* (pp. 43–58). Springer International Publishing. doi:10.1007/978-3-031-29132-6_3

Allam, Z., Sharifi, A., Bibri, S. E., Jones, D. S., & Krogstie, J. (2022). The metaverse as a virtual form of smart cities: Opportunities and challenges for environmental, economic, and social sustainability in urban futures. *Smart Cities*, 5(3), 771–801. doi:10.3390/smartcities5030040

Bag, S., Rahman, M. S., Srivastava, G., & Shrivastav, S. K. (2023). Unveiling metaverse potential in supply chain management and overcoming implementation challenges: An empirical study. *Benchmarking*. Advance online publication. doi:10.1108/BIJ-05-2023-0314

Ball, M. (2022). *The metaverse: and how it will revolutionize everything*. Liveright Publishing. doi:10.15358/9783800669400

Barrera, K. G., & Shah, D. (2023). Marketing in the Metaverse: Conceptual understanding, framework, and research agenda. *Journal of Business Research, 155*, 113420. doi:10.1016/j.jbusres.2022.113420

Bolger, R. K. (2021). Finding holes in the metaverse: Posthuman mystics as agents of evolutionary contextualization. *Religions, 12*(9), 768. doi:10.3390/rel12090768

Bremers, L. P. Y. (2023). *Financial Inclusion in the Metaverse: Exploring the Relationship between Education and Attitude towards Cryptocurrencies* [Bachelor's thesis, University of Twente].

Chen, Y., & Cheng, H. (2022). The economics of the metaverse: A comparison with the real economy. *Metaverse, 3*(1), 19. doi:10.54517/met.v3i1.1802

Deniz, K. (2024). Metaverse and New Narrative: Storyliving in the Age of Metaverse. In The Future of Digital Communication (pp. 39-55). CRC Press.

Duong, T. Q., Van Huynh, D., Khosravirad, S. R., Sharma, V., Dobre, O. A., & Shin, H. (2023). From digital twin to metaverse: The role of 6G ultra-reliable and low-latency communications with multi-tier computing. *IEEE Wireless Communications, 30*(3), 140–146. doi:10.1109/MWC.014.2200371

Earhart, B. (2012). Reclaiming meaning across platforms: Fragmentation and expansion of the self. *Metaverse Creativity, 2*(2), 125–138. doi:10.1386/mvcr.2.2.125_1

Erazo, J., & Sulbarán, P. (2022). Metaverse: Above an immersion in reality. *Metaverse, 3*(2), 8. doi:10.54517/m.v3i2.2155

Far, S. B., Rad, A. I., & Asaar, M. R. (2023). Blockchain and its derived technologies shape the future generation of digital businesses: A focus on decentralized finance and the Metaverse. *Data Science and Management, 6*(3), 183–197. doi:10.1016/j.dsm.2023.06.002

Gadekallu, T. R., Huynh-The, T., Wang, W., Yenduri, G., Ranaweera, P., Pham, Q. V., & Liyanage, M. (2022). Blockchain for the metaverse: A review. *arXiv preprint arXiv:2203.09738*.

Gartner. (2022). Gartner Glossary: Metaverse. https://www.gartner.com/en/information-technology/glossary/metaverse

Gattullo, M., Laviola, E., Evangelista, A., Fiorentino, M., & Uva, A. E. (2022). Towards the evaluation of augmented reality in the metaverse: Information presentation modes. *Applied Sciences (Basel, Switzerland), 12*(24), 12600. doi:10.3390/app122412600

Gaurav, A. (2023). Metaverse and Globalization: Cultural Exchange and Digital Diplomacy, Data *Science Insights Magazine, Insights2Techinfo*.

Goldfield, C. C. (2023). THE NATIONAL SECURITY LANDSCAPE ISSUES OF THE METAUERSE. *Scitech Lawyer, 19*(2), 20–25.

Hamilton, S. (2022). Deep Learning Computer Vision Algorithms, Customer Engagement Tools, and Virtual Marketplace Dynamics Data in the Metaverse Economy. *Journal of Self-Governance and Management Economics, 10*(2), 37–51.

Han, D. I. D., Bergs, Y., & Moorhouse, N. (2022). Virtual reality consumer experience escapes: Preparing for the metaverse. *Virtual Reality (Waltham Cross)*, *26*(4), 1443–1458. doi:10.1007/s10055-022-00641-7

Huynh-The, T., Pham, Q. V., Pham, X. Q., Nguyen, T. T., Han, Z., & Kim, D. S. (2023). Artificial intelligence for the metaverse: A survey. *Engineering Applications of Artificial Intelligence*, *117*, 105581. doi:10.1016/j.engappai.2022.105581

Hwang, G. J., & Chien, S. Y. (2022). Definition, roles, and potential research issues of the metaverse in education: An artificial intelligence perspective. *Computers and Education: Artificial Intelligence*, *3*, 100082. doi:10.1016/j.caeai.2022.100082

Hyun, W. (2023, February). Study on standardization for interoperable metaverse. In *2023 25th International Conference on Advanced Communication Technology (ICACT)* (pp. 319-322). IEEE. 10.23919/ICACT56868.2023.10079642

Hyun, W. (2023, February). Study on standardization for interoperable metaverse. In *2023 25th International Conference on Advanced Communication Technology (ICACT)* (pp. 319-322). IEEE. 10.23919/ICACT56868.2023.10079642

Imamguluyev, R., Umarova, N., & Mikayilova, R. (2023, August). Navigating the Ethics of the Metaverse: A Fuzzy Logic Approach to Decision-Making. In *International Conference on Intelligent and Fuzzy Systems* (pp. 53-60). Cham: Springer Nature Switzerland. 10.1007/978-3-031-39777-6_7

Jaber, T. A. (2022). Security Risks of the Metaverse World. *International Journal of Interactive Mobile Technologies*, *16*(13).

Jeon, H. J., Youn, H. C., Ko, S. M., & Kim, T. H. (2022). Blockchain and AI Meet in the Metaverse. *Advances in the Convergence of Blockchain and Artificial Intelligence*, *73*(10.5772).

Jiang, Y., Kang, J., Niyato, D., Ge, X., Xiong, Z., Miao, C., & Shen, X. (2022). Reliable distributed computing for metaverse: A hierarchical game-theoretic approach. *IEEE Transactions on Vehicular Technology*, *72*(1), 1084–1100. doi:10.1109/TVT.2022.3204839

Kim, J. (2021). Advertising in the metaverse: Research agenda. *Journal of Interactive Advertising*, *21*(3), 141–144. doi:10.1080/15252019.2021.2001273

Lee, C. T., Li, Z., & Shen, Y. C. (2024). Building bonds: An examination of relational bonding in continuous content contribution behaviors on metaverse-based non-fungible token platforms. *Internet Research*. Advance online publication. doi:10.1108/INTR-11-2022-0883

Ljungholm, D. P. (2022). Metaverse-based 3D visual modeling, virtual reality training experiences, and wearable biological measuring devices in immersive workplaces. *Psychosociological Issues in Human Resource Management*, *10*(1), 64–77. doi:10.22381/pihrm10120225

Majerová, J., & Pera, A. (2022). Haptic and biometric sensor technologies, spatio-temporal fusion algorithms, and virtual navigation tools in the decentralized and interconnected metaverse. *Review of Contemporary Philosophy*, *21*(0), 105–121. doi:10.22381/RCP2120227

McCall, R., Shell, J., Kacperski, C., Greenstein, S., Whitton, N., & Summers, J. (2022, October). Workshop on Social and Ethical Issues in Entertainment Computing. In *International Conference on Entertainment Computing* (pp. 429-435). Cham: Springer International Publishing.

Moro-Visconti, R. (2022). Metaverse: A Digital Network Valuation. In *The Valuation of Digital Intangibles: Technology, Marketing, and the Metaverse* (pp. 515–559). Springer International Publishing. doi:10.1007/978-3-031-09237-4_18

Mystakidis, S. (2022). Metaverse. [Key Characteristics of the metaverse]. *Encyclopedia, 2*(1), 486–497. doi:10.3390/encyclopedia2010031

Oh, H. J., Kim, J., Chang, J. J., Park, N., & Lee, S. (2023). Social benefits of living in the metaverse: The relationships among social presence, supportive interaction, social self-efficacy, and feelings of loneliness. *Computers in Human Behavior, 139*, 107498. doi:10.1016/j.chb.2022.107498

Othman, A., Chemnad, K., Hassanien, A. E., Tlili, A., Zhang, C. Y., Al-Thani, D., ... Altınay, Z. (2024). Accessible Metaverse: A Theoretical Framework for Accessibility and Inclusion in the Metaverse. *Multimodal Technologies and Interaction, 8*(3), 21. doi:10.3390/mti8030021

Öztürk, B., & Hersono, R. (2023). *Playing to Win: How Gamification Can Boost Customer Engagement and Turn Non-Fans into Brand Advocates.*

Popescu, G. H., Ciurlău, C. F., Stan, C. I., Băcănoiu, C., & Tănase, A. (2022). Virtual workplaces in the metaverse: Immersive remote collaboration tools, behavioral predictive analytics, and extended reality technologies. *Psychosociological Issues in Human Resource Management, 10*(1), 21–34. doi:10.22381/pihrm10120222

Popescu, G. H., Valaskova, K., & Horak, J. (2022). Augmented reality shopping experiences, retail business analytics, and machine vision algorithms in the virtual economy of the metaverse. *Journal of Self-Governance and Management Economics, 10*(2), 67–81.

Popp, J., & Cuțitoi, A. C. (2022). Immersive Visualization Systems, Spatial Simulation and Environment Mapping Algorithms, and Decision Intelligence and Modeling Tools in the Web3-powered Metaverse World. *Journal of Self-Governance and Management Economics, 10*(3), 56–72.

Rane, N., Choudhary, S., & Rane, J. (2023). Metaverse for Enhancing Customer Loyalty: Effective Strategies to Improve Customer Relationship, Service, Engagement, Satisfaction, and Experience. *Service, Engagement, Satisfaction, and Experience.*

Richter, S., & Richter, A. (2023). What is novel about the Metaverse? *International Journal of Information Management, 73*, 102684. doi:10.1016/j.ijinfomgt.2023.102684

Stephenson, N. (1992). Snow crash. *Futures, 26*(7), 798–800. doi:10.1016/0016-3287(94)90052-3

Swan, M. (2023). Metaverse Marketing: A Review and Research Agenda. *Journal of Marketing Management, 39*(3-4), 291–318.

Thomas, N. J., Baral, R., Crocco, O. S., & Mohanan, S. (2023). A framework for gamification in the metaverse era: How designers envision gameful experience. *Technological Forecasting and Social Change, 193*, 122544. doi:10.1016/j.techfore.2023.122544

Usmani, S. S., Sharath, M., & Mehendale, M. (2022). Future of mental health in the metaverse. *General Psychiatry*, *35*(4), e100825. doi:10.1136/gpsych-2022-100825 PMID:36189180

Van Huynh, D., Khosravirad, S. R., Masaracchia, A., Dobre, O. A., & Duong, T. Q. (2022). Edge intelligence-based ultra-reliable and low-latency communications for digital twin-enabled metaverse. *IEEE Wireless Communications Letters*, *11*(8), 1733–1737. doi:10.1109/LWC.2022.3179207

Wu, D., Yang, Z., Zhang, P., Wang, R., Yang, B., & Ma, X. (2023). Virtual-Reality Inter-Promotion Technology for Metaverse: A Survey. *IEEE Internet of Things Journal*, *10*(18), 15788–15809. doi:10.1109/JIOT.2023.3265848

Wynn, M., & Jones, P. (2023). New technology deployment and corporate responsibilities in the metaverse. *Knowledge (Beverly Hills, Calif.)*, *3*(4), 543–556.

Xiang, H., Zhang, X., & Bilal, M. (2023). A cloud-edge service offloading method for the metaverse in smart manufacturing. *Software, Practice & Experience*, spe.3301. doi:10.1002/spe.3301

Yang, S. (2023, April). Storytelling and user experience in the cultural metaverse. *Heliyon*, *9*(4), e14759. doi:10.1016/j.heliyon.2023.e14759 PMID:37035365

Zhou, Z. (2024). Will the Metaverse Revolutionize the Narrative? *Critical Arts*, 1–15.

Zhu, H. Y., Hieu, N. Q., Hoang, D. T., Nguyen, D. N., & Lin, C. T. (2023). A human-centric metaverse enabled by brain-computer interface: A survey. *arXiv preprint arXiv:2309.01848*.

Chapter 12
The Metaversal Shift:
A Bibliometric Analysis of Industry Transformation

Navneet Kaushal
Central University of Himachal Pradesh, India

Anshu Duhoon
Central University of Himachal Pradesh, India

ABSTRACT

Metaverse has emerged as an immersive digital environment, capturing widespread attention owing to its significant impact on industrial growth. This study aims to explain the evolution of research focused on the metatarsal shift in industries. This study offers a bibliometric analysis of industrial transformation research from 2007 to 2024. The finding shows a tremendous rise in publication over time. The objective of this analysis is to extract valuable insights and trends and to shed light on the key challenges and opportunities associated with digital transformation in the industrial sector. This study provides thorough coverage of existing literature on the implications of metaverse-enabled digital transformation for the industrial revolution and explores the interplay of various factors such as technology adoption, organizational culture, and strategic planning. The study contributes to understanding the ongoing discourse on digital transformation and its impact on the industrial landscape.

INTRODUCTION

The metaverse is emerging as a transformative trend across industries, promising to revolutionize how we interact, work, and play in digital environments. This virtual universe transcends traditional boundaries, offering immersive experiences where users can seamlessly navigate between virtual worlds, socialize with others, and engage in various activities (Dixon,2023). From gaming and entertainment to education and business, the metaverse presents boundless opportunities for innovation and collaboration. Companies are increasingly investing in metaverse technologies to create immersive virtual experiences and tap into new markets. As virtual reality (VR), augmented reality (AR), and other immersive technologies

DOI: 10.4018/979-8-3693-2607-7.ch012

advance, the metaverse is poised to become even more immersive and interconnected, blurring the lines between the physical and digital realms (Dwivedi et al.,2022).

The application of the metaverse spans across all industries, promising to revolutionize traditional business models and reshape the way to interact with digital environments. In entertainment, the metaverse offers immersive gaming experiences, interactive storytelling, and virtual events, enhancing engagement and expanding audience reach (Qi,2022). In education, it provides innovative learning environments, enabling interactive lessons, simulations, and virtual field trips that enhance student engagement and accessibility (Zonaphan et al.,2022). Within healthcare, the metaverse facilitates telemedicine, remote patient monitoring, and medical training simulations, improving access to care and enhancing medical education (Hancock,2022; Ali et al.,2023). In retail, it enables virtual stores, personalized shopping experiences, and social commerce, transforming the way consumers discover and purchase products (Abumalloh et al.,2023). In the tourism sector, it provides an avenue for cultural exchange, fostering connections between tourists and communities through shared culinary experiences with travelers and locals through common gastronomic interests (Gursoy et al., 2022). Religious tourism has always been an important aspect of the tourism industry (Kaushal et al., 2022a) and significantly contributes to the economic growth of the country (Kaushal et al., 2022b; Budovich, 2023). However, with the emergence of the metaverse, religious tourism has taken on a new dimension. It offers immersive virtual experiences that go beyond physical barriers, providing access to sacred sites and spiritual practices from all corners of the world (Ahmad et al., 2024).

The metaverse also has significant implications for communication and collaboration, enabling remote work, virtual meetings, and team collaboration in immersive digital environments (Bennett, 2022). Across industries, the metaverse fosters innovation, collaboration, and creativity, unlocking new opportunities for growth and advancement in the digital age (Mourtzis, 2023; Nabukalu & Wanjohi, 2023).

The metaverse catalyzes environmental stewardship by diminishing the necessity for extensive travel through remote work and virtual gatherings (Allam et al.,2022; Al-Emran,2023). Real-time data analytics within this digital domain empower industries with actionable insights, enabling agile decision-making and performance optimization. Small enterprises flourish in the accessible virtual marketplaces, expanding their global reach and catalyzing economic growth. Furthermore, collaborative research initiatives thrive as experts converge virtually to tackle complex challenges, propelling innovation forward (Bryda & Costa,2023). Ultimately, the symbiotic relationship between the metaverse and industry engenders a dynamic ecosystem characterized by creativity, progress, and shared prosperity.

Understanding the metaverse entails grasping a concept that transcends conventional virtual environments, constituting a collective digital universe interconnected through various digital spaces, experiences, and assets (Yang et al.,2024). At its essence, the metaverse is a persistent, shared, and immersive digital realm enabling real-time interaction for its users. Unlike disjointed online platforms, the metaverse aims for cohesion, allowing seamless navigation across diverse virtual worlds and experiences (Kadry,2022; Devlin,2023). A hallmark of the metaverse lies in its emphasis on user-generated content and creativity, empowering individuals to create, customize, and share digital assets, fostering a landscape of democratized content creation (Iden & Methlie,2012). Furthermore, the metaverse thrives on its social aspect, acting as a platform for socialization, collaboration, and community-building, mirroring real-world social dynamics. Additionally, it presents economic opportunities through virtual commerce, where users engage in buying, selling, and trading digital goods and services, propelling the emergence of a virtual economy. While the metaverse promises to revolutionize various aspects of human interaction, entertainment, and commerce, it also raises concerns regarding privacy, security, and digital rights in navigating this intricate digital realm (Bibri & Jagatheesaperumal,2023). In summary, comprehending the metaverse involves recognizing it as a dynamic and multifaceted concept poised to reshape human engagement with digital technology, albeit with challenges requiring careful consideration to ensure its inclusivity, equity, and safety for all participants.

The literature on metaverse holds significance in all domains. Even though researchers and academics are paying attention to this topic, it still requires more development (Iqbal et al., 2023; Wider et al., 2023). The existing literature on metaverse has provided inconsistent findings, making it necessary to conduct a study that comprehends, examines, and identifies the central themes in this area. To tackle this issue, the current study employs a bibliometric review approach to address the following research questions:

(a)   The publication trend over the period.
(b)   Which countries made significant contributions to this field?
(c)   What are the future avenues of this study?

The other sections of the paper are formulated as follows: The second section briefly discusses the literature review and the objectives of the study. The third section explains the research methodology. The fourth section is related to the analysis and interpretation of the data, and the last section discusses the conclusion and directions for future research.

REVIEW OF LITERATURE

The concept of Metaverse Shift, which explores the synergy between industry and the evolution of the metaverse, is a topic of growing interest and importance. Van Beers et al. (2007) provided insights into industrial symbiosis in heavy industrial regions such as Kwinana and Gladstone, highlighting the drivers, barriers, and trigger events for regional synergy initiatives. Corning (2013) discussed the role of functional synergy in evolution, suggesting a paradigm shift in understanding interdependent causal influences. Heracleous et al. (2019) examined NASA's capability evolution toward commercial space, showcasing the transition from a government-dominated to a commercially driven industry model. Shen et al. (2021) focused on promoting user purchases in the metaverse through a systematic literature review on consumer behavior research and virtual commerce application design. Li et al. (2021) analyzed the evolution of China's marine economic policy and the labor productivity growth momentum of its marine economy industries, emphasizing the structural shift effect caused by institutional changes. Hollensen et al. (2022) predicted the revolutionary impact of the Metaverse on various industries, including marketing, as the 3D version of the internet. Furthermore, Zhai et al. (2022) explored the educational metaverse as an innovative approach to high-quality education development and reshaping educational relationships. Buhalis et al. (2022) delved into the implications of the Metaverse for hospitality and tourism management and marketing, emphasizing customer experience and value co-creation. Mirza-Babaei et al. (2022) highlighted the relevance of games in the metaverse, proposing discussions on the future evolution of game research in this area. Continuing with these findings, Wang et al. (2022) presented a framework for constructing an Edu-metaverse ecosystem, leveraging new technologies like extended reality and artificial intelligence for learning environments. Garousi (2015) conducted a bibliometric analysis of the Turkish software engineering community. Muhuri et al. (2019) provided a detailed overview of Industry 4.0 through bibliometric analysis, and Furstenau et al. (2020) explored the link between sustainability and Industry 4.0. Goh et al. (2020) reviewed water utility benchmarking using bibliometric analysis. Sharma et al. (2021) discussed sustainable manufacturing and Industry 4.0, highlighting gaps in current knowledge. Chen et al. (2022) delved into the integration of Construction 4.0, Industry 4.0, and Building Information Modeling for sustainable building development within smart cities. Abbate et al. (2022) conducted a bibliometric literature review on the Metaverse, focusing on its implications for industry and society. Feng et al. (2022) analyzed the current status of Metaverse research through bibliometrics, while Rejeb et al. (2023) mapped out future research areas in the Metaverse field. Overall, these studies demonstrate the increasing interest in utilizing bibliometric analysis to understand trends, challenges, and opportunities in various industries, including software engineering, pharmaceuticals, sustainability, and the Metaverse. The integration of Industry 4.0 concepts with other disciplines, such as sustainable manufacturing and smart cities, is also a growing area of research (Yao et al.,2024). The Metaverse, in particular, is gaining attention for its potential impacts on industry and society, prompting further exploration and collaboration in this emerging field.

So, a literature-based study focusing on the synergy between industries and the evolution of the metaverse is imperative for advancing understanding in this emerging field and for contributing towards the development of robust theoretical frameworks, methodological approaches, and practical recommendations for navigating the evolving landscape of the metaverse and its intersection with industries.

RESEARCH METHODOLOGY

Prisma methodology, derived from the PRISMA (Preferred Reporting Items for Systematic Reviews and Meta-Analyses) framework commonly used in medical and health sciences, has been adapted for bibliometric analysis to ensure transparency, rigor, and reproducibility in research synthesis. In bibliometric analysis, PRISMA provides a structured approach to systematically identify, select, and synthesize relevant literature to answer specific research questions related to scholarly publications and citations (Moher et al., 2019). In the first step, a targeted search was conducted in the Scopus database by using two keywords: "Industry" AND "Metaverse". This database was selected because it is an extensive database and ensures that only the highest quality data are indexed through careful content selection and re-evaluation by an independent Content Selection and Advisory Board (Baas et al., 2020). This search resulted in 748 research articles. Then, only articles, conference papers, conference reviews, book chapters, and review papers were retained, which limits the number to 716. Thereafter, 31 research studies published in other than the English language were also excluded, and finally, 685 research articles were considered for further research (Figure 1). This review was limited only to the research articles because peer-reviewed articles are considered to have better quality than other forms such as book chapters, conference proceedings, etc. (Maier et al., 2020).

VOSviewer (Van Eck & Waltman, 2010) software has been used to create the visualization network. It presents bibliometric analysis in a way that is simple to understand (Van Eck & Waltman, 2011; Agbo et al., 2021; Duhoon & Singh, 2023).

Credibility of the Study

This study used bibliometric analysis to understand the synergy between the industry and metaverse. Bibliometric analysis is a quantitative method used to assess the impact and productivity of scholarly

Figure 1. PRISMA methodology
Source: Developed by Authors

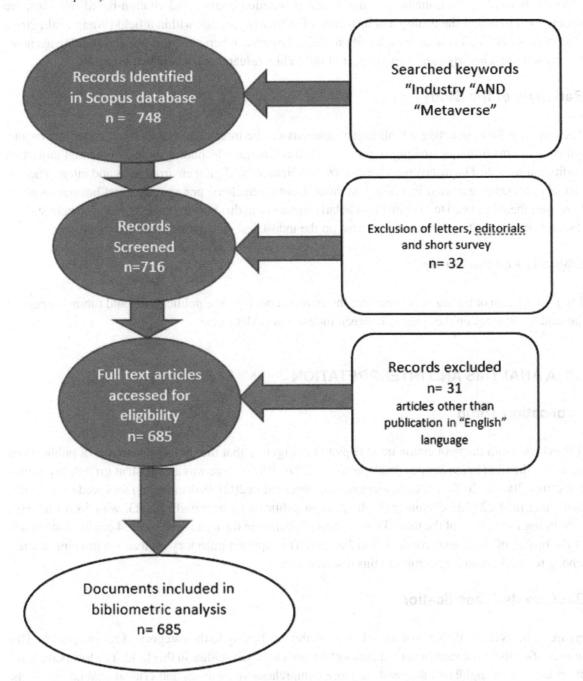

publications within a specific field or discipline (Ellegaard & Wallin,2015). It involves the systematic analysis of bibliographic data, such as citations, publication counts, authorship patterns, and journal impact factors, to gain insights into research trends, collaboration networks, and the influence of individuals, publications, or researchers.

Furthermore, bibliometric analysis can be applied to evaluate the productivity and impact of academic journals. Journal metrics, including impact factors, citation counts, and citation-based rankings, are widely used to assess the quality and influence of scholarly journals within a field (Wang et al., 2010; Cucari et al., 2023). These metrics are often utilized by researchers, institutions, and funding agencies to evaluate the scholarly output and impact of individual researchers or research groups.

Rationale of the Study

The rationale for conducting a bibliometric analysis on the intersection of the metaverse and various industries stems from the growing significance of this emerging technology and its potential impact on traditional sectors. The metaverse, characterized by immersive digital environments and interconnected virtual spaces, has garnered increasing attention from researchers, practitioners, and businesses alike. However, there is a need to explore the scholarly literature in this area to understand the current state of research, trends, and collaborations focused on the industries' engagement with the metaverse.

Objective of the Study

The primary aim of the study is to explore the growth, country-wise publications, and future avenues of the studies centered on the synergy between Industry and Metaverse.

DATA ANALYSIS AND INTERPRETATION

Publication Trend

It is evident from the publication trend depicted in Figure 2 that the initial appearance of publications related to the field in the Scopus database was in 2007. While there was a consistent growth in publications from 2007 to 2020, a notable increase was observed in 2021 (8 documents) followed by a significant surge in 2022 (133 documents). The peak in publications occurred in 2023, with 58 documents, accounting for 62.92% of the total. The subsequent decline in the trend seen in 2024 could be attributed to the timing of the search conducted in January. This upward trajectory indicates a growing interest among researchers and academics in this research area.

Documents Classification

Figure 3 shows that only 9.5% of the selected documents belong to the category of review papers. This suggests that there is a significant requirement for review-based studies in this field. The low percentage of review papers highlights the need for more comprehensive analyses and critical evaluations of the existing literature to gain a deeper understanding of the subject matter.

Figure 2. Publications growth
Source: Authors' compilation

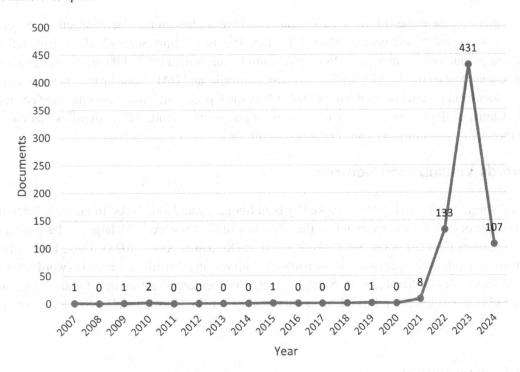

Figure 3. Documents by type
Source: Authors' compilation

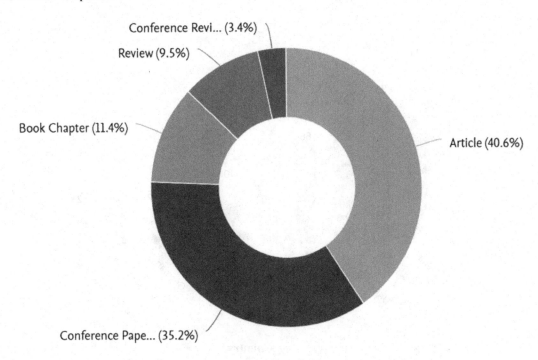

Country-wise publications

Figure 4 presents the names of the top 10 countries where studies on the interconnection between the metaverse and industry have been conducted. Leading the list is China, with 124 documents reflecting the highest productivity. Followed by India and South Korea, with a total of 99 and 91 publications.

Subsequent to the UK, Italy, Malaysia, Germany, Australia, and UAE round up the top ten countries in terms of document production. Notably, around 30% of the top ten contributors are emerging economies, namely China, Malaysia, and India. This indicates a noteworthy trend, which signifies that emerging economies are contributing to paper production in this field.

Keywords Visualization Network

Table 1 displays the top 10 keywords ranked by both frequency and total links. In the visualization network, the size of each node corresponds to the frequency of the keyword, with larger nodes representing higher frequency (Viana-Lora & Nel-lo-Andreu, 2022; Dhiman & Arora, 2024). These keywords form clusters based on their co-occurrence in the network, with varying densities for each keyword (Dharmani et al., 2021; Duhoon & Singh,2023). Notably, "metaverse" emerges as the most frequently occurring keyword (391 occurrences), followed by "virtual reality" (102), "blockchain" (68), "augmented real-

Figure 4. Top ten countries
Source: Authors' compilation

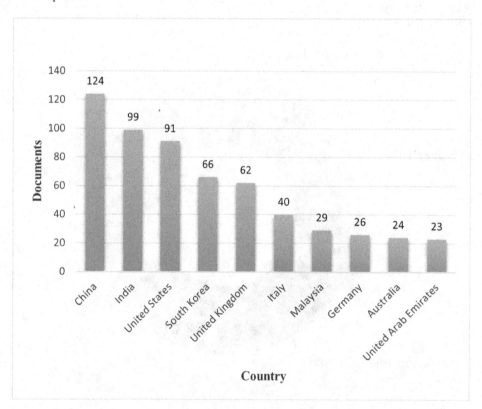

ity" (53), "artificial intelligence" (44), "extended reality" (32), "digital twin" (32), "healthcare" (23), "sustainability" (16), and "NFT"(16).

The authors' keywords are organized into six clusters (see Figure 5). The orange cluster is centered by metaverse and shows the correlation with other nodes "blockchain"," cryptocurrency"," NFT", "virtual worlds" and "Web 3". The red cluster highlights the proximity between "industry " and "sustainability," indicating a strong relationship compared to other keywords in the cluster, such as "5 G," "artificial intelligence", "building information modeling", "education", "IOT", "technology" and "tourism." The blue cluster is centered around "virtual reality" and "augmented reality" with other nodes like "avatars", "user experience" and "virtual world". In the green cluster, connections are observed among "digital twin", "federated learning", "internet of things", "security", and "training". Exploring the concept of "artificial intelligence", " the violet cluster encompasses research on "deep learning", "machine learning", "healthcare", and "IOT". Lastly, the light blue cluster elucidates the interconnections between "avatar", "gaming "and "virtual reality". The thickness of the links indicates the co-occurrence of keywords, reflecting similar research endeavors and highlighting areas that remain underexplored (Donthu et al., 2021a, b).

Figure 5. Keywords cluster map
Source: Authors' compilation

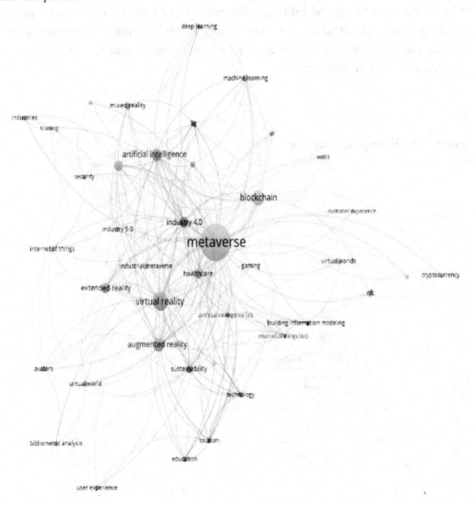

Table 1. Keyword clusters

Clusters	Total Links	Occurrences
Orange cluster	253	391
Blue cluster	32	102
Green cluster	20	32
Red cluster	19	31
Violet cluster	13	13
Light blue cluster	8	8

Source: Authors' compilation

Bibliographic Coupling

Bibliographic coupling serves as a method for science mapping, predicated on the idea that publications sharing references also share content similarities (Weinberg, 1974). Donthu et al. (2021a) and Zupic and Čater (2015) underscored the significance of bibliographic coupling, noting that it enables the grouping of publications into thematic clusters based on shared references. The graphical representation in Figure 6 illustrates the bibliographic network of authors, categorized into 12 clusters according to the intellectual connections in their work. The bibliographic coupling approach posits that papers citing the same sources are closely interconnected and should be grouped together in the visual representation's cluster solution.

Figure 6. Authors' bibliographic coupling
Source: Authors' compilation

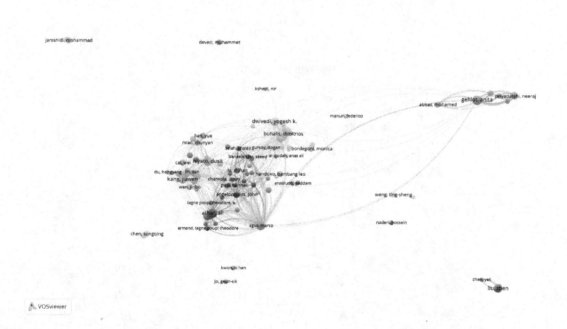

CONCLUSION

The bibliometric study on the synergy between industry and the evolution of the metaverse unveils a dynamic landscape characterized by rapid evolution and transformative shifts. Through year-wise analysis, it becomes evident how industries have progressed, marked by significant milestones and technological advancement. Keywords such as virtual reality, augmented reality, blockchain, and NFTs emerge as central themes, showcasing the key areas of industry engagement with the metaverse. These keyword clusters also show that the field of metaverse studies is predominantly focused on the healthcare industry in comparison to all other industries.

These findings hold implications for businesses, policymakers, investors, and consumers alike. Businesses can leverage insights for innovation and strategic positioning within the metaverse ecosystem, while policymakers may need to craft regulatory frameworks to support responsible development. Investors can identify promising investment opportunities, while consumers can make informed decisions about adoption and digital engagement.

However, despite these findings, bibliometric review-based study also has some limitations. Firstly, bibliometric analysis relies heavily on the availability and quality of data sources, which may not always capture the full breadth of industry-metaverse interactions (Wallin,2005). Additionally, while keywords provide valuable insights, they may not fully capture the complexity and nuances of emerging trends within the metaverse ecosystem. Furthermore, the study's focus on quantitative analysis may overlook qualitative aspects such as user experiences and cultural shifts, which are equally important in understanding industry-metaverse dynamics. Moreover, the rapidly evolving nature of both industries and the metaverse means that findings may quickly become outdated, requiring frequent updates to maintain relevance. This study's scope is limited to the Scopus database; the inclusion of other databases, such as EBSCO and Web of Science, can be used to enhance the importance of this field. However, despite these shortcomings, the study will be helpful to the researchers in acknowledging the earlier work and future directions in the field of metaverse.

While the metaverse presents innovative opportunities for industry research, challenges such as technological infrastructure constraints, accessibility and inclusivity issues, privacy and security concerns, ethical and societal implications, lack of standardization and regulation, digital divide disparities, and content quality and integrity issues need to be addressed. These limitations underscore the importance of a thoughtful and responsible approach to the development and deployment of the metaverse in industry, focusing on fostering inclusivity, safeguarding privacy and security, establishing standards and regulations, bridging digital divides, and ensuring the quality and integrity of virtual content (Raad & Rashid,2023). By addressing these limitations, researchers can maximize the potential of the metaverse while minimizing its risks and drawbacks in industry research. So, in the future, challenges related to their application can be explored to have a better understanding of metaverse applications.

REFERENCES

Abbate, S., Centobelli, P., Cerchione, R., Oropallo, E., & Riccio, E. (2022, April). *A first bibliometric literature review on Metaverse. In 2022 IEEE Technology and Engineering Management Conference.* TEMSCON EUROPE.

Abumalloh, R. A., Nilashi, M., Ooi, K. B., Wei-Han, G., Cham, T. H., Dwivedi, Y. K., & Hughes, L. (2023). The adoption of a metaverse in the retail industry and its impact on sustainable competitive advantage: The moderating impact of sustainability commitment. *Annals of Operations Research*, 1–42. doi:10.1007/s10479-023-05608-8

Agbo, F. J., Oyelere, S. S., Suhonen, J., & Tukiainen, M. (2021). Scientific production and thematic breakthroughs in smart learning environments: A bibliometric analysis. *Smart Learning Environments*, 8(1), 1–25. doi:10.1186/s40561-020-00145-4

Ahmad, M., Akram, M., & Ureeb, S. (2024). Exploring the Role of Metaverse in Promoting Religious Tourism. In *Service Innovations in Tourism: Metaverse, Immersive Technologies, and Digital Twin* (pp. 39–63). IGI Global. doi:10.4018/979-8-3693-1103-5.ch003

Al-Emran, M. (2023). Beyond technology acceptance: Development and evaluation of technology-environmental, economic, and social sustainability theory. *Technology in Society*, 75, 102383. doi:10.1016/j.techsoc.2023.102383

Ali, S., Abdullah, Armand, T. P. T., Athar, A., Hussain, A., Ali, M., Yaseen, M., Joo, M.-I., & Kim, H.-C. (2023). Metaverse in healthcare integrated with explainable ai and blockchain: Enabling immersiveness, ensuring trust, and providing patient data security. *Sensors (Basel)*, 23(2), 565. doi:10.3390/s23020565 PMID:36679361

Allam, Z., Sharifi, A., Bibri, S. E., Jones, D. S., & Krogstie, J. (2022). The metaverse as a virtual form of smart cities: Opportunities and challenges for environmental, economic, and social sustainability in urban futures. *Smart Cities*, 5(3), 771–801. doi:10.3390/smartcities5030040

Baas, J., Schotten, M., Plume, A., Côté, G., & Karimi, R. (2020). Scopus as a curated, high-quality bibliometric data source for academic research in quantitative science studies. *Quantitative Science Studies*, 1(1), 377–386. doi:10.1162/qss_a_00019

Bennett, D. (2022). Remote workforce, virtual team tasks, and employee engagement tools in a real-time interoperable decentralized metaverse. *Psychosociological Issues in Human Resource Management*, 10(1), 78–91. doi:10.22381/pihrm10120226

Bibri, S. E., & Jagatheesaperumal, S. K. (2023). Harnessing the potential of the metaverse and artificial intelligence for the internet of city things: Cost-effective XReality and synergistic AIoT technologies. *Smart Cities*, 6(5), 2397–2429. doi:10.3390/smartcities6050109

Bryda, G., & Costa, A. P. (2023). Qualitative research in digital era: Innovations, methodologies and collaborations. *Social Sciences (Basel, Switzerland)*, 12(10), 570. doi:10.3390/socsci12100570

Budovich, L. S. (2023). The impact of religious tourism on the economy and tourism industry. *Hervormde Teologiese Studies*, 79(1), 8607. doi:10.4102/hts.v79i1.8607

Buhalis, D., Lin, M. S., & Leung, D. (2022). Metaverse as a driver for customer experience and value co-creation: Implications for hospitality and tourism management and marketing. *International Journal of Contemporary Hospitality Management*, 35(2), 701–716. doi:10.1108/IJCHM-05-2022-0631

Chen, Y., Huang, D., Liu, Z., Osmani, M., & Demian, P. (2022). Construction 4.0, Industry 4.0, and Building Information Modeling (BIM) for sustainable building development within the smart city. *Sustainability (Basel)*, *14*(16), 10028. doi:10.3390/su141610028

Corning, P. A. (2013). Rotating the Necker cube: A bioeconomic approach to cooperation and the causal role of synergy in evolution. *Journal of Bioeconomics*, *15*(2), 171–193. doi:10.1007/s10818-012-9142-4

Cucari, N., Tutore, I., Montera, R., & Profita, S. (2023). A bibliometric performance analysis of publication productivity in the corporate social responsibility field: Outcomes of SciVal analytics. *Corporate Social Responsibility and Environmental Management*, *30*(1), 1–16. doi:10.1002/csr.2346

Devlin, M. (2023). *2035 AND BEYOND. A GUIDE TO THRIVING IN THE FUTURE WORKPLACE.: Unleash Your Potential in a Futuristic Career Landscape. Virtual Worlds, Skills Mastery, and Success.* Little Fish Big Impact.

Dharmani, P., Das, S., & Prashar, S. (2021). A bibliometric analysis of creative industries: Current trends and future directions. *Journal of Business Research*, *135*, 252–267. doi:10.1016/j.jbusres.2021.06.037

Dhiman, V., & Arora, M. (2024). How foresight has evolved since 1999? Understanding its themes, scope and focus. *Foresight*, *26*(2), 253–271. doi:10.1108/FS-01-2023-0001

Dixon, H. H. B. Jr. (2023). The Metaverse. *The Judges' Journal*, *62*(1), 36–38.

Donthu, N., Kumar, S., Mukherjee, D., Pandey, N., & Lim, W. M. (2021a). How to conduct a bibliometric analysis: An overview and guidelines. *Journal of Business Research*, *133*, 285–296. doi:10.1016/j.jbusres.2021.04.070

Donthu, N., Kumar, S., & Pandey, N. (2021). A retrospective evaluation of Marketing Intelligence and Planning: 1983–2019. *Marketing Intelligence & Planning*, *39*(1), 48–73. doi:10.1108/MIP-02-2020-0066

Duhoon, A., & Singh, M. (2023). Corporate Governance in Family Firms: A Bibliometric Analysis. *Management*, *1*, 22.

Duhoon, A., & Singh, M. (2023). Corporate tax avoidance: A systematic literature review and future research directions. *LBS Journal of Management & Research*, *21*(2), 197–217. doi:10.1108/LBSJMR-12-2022-0082

Dwivedi, Y. K., Hughes, L., Baabdullah, A. M., Ribeiro-Navarrete, S., Giannakis, M., Al-Debei, M. M., Dennehy, D., Metri, B., Buhalis, D., Cheung, C. M. K., Conboy, K., Doyle, R., Dubey, R., Dutot, V., Felix, R., Goyal, D. P., Gustafsson, A., Hinsch, C., Jebabli, I., ... Wamba, S. F. (2022). Metaverse beyond the hype: Multidisciplinary perspectives on emerging challenges, opportunities, and agenda for research, practice, and policy. *International Journal of Information Management*, *66*, 102542. doi:10.1016/j.ijinfomgt.2022.102542

Ellegaard, O., & Wallin, J. A. (2015). The bibliometric analysis of scholarly production: How great is the impact? *Scientometrics*, *105*(3), 1809–1831. doi:10.1007/s11192-015-1645-z PMID:26594073

Feng, X., Wang, X., & Su, Y. (2024). An analysis of the current status of metaverse research based on bibliometrics. *Library Hi Tech*, *42*(1), 284–308. doi:10.1108/LHT-10-2022-0467

Furstenau, L. B., Sott, M. K., Kipper, L. M., Machado, E. L., Lopez-Robles, J. R., Dohan, M. S., Cobo, M. J., Zahid, A., Abbasi, Q. H., & Imran, M. A. (2020). Link between sustainability and industry 4.0: Trends, challenges, and new perspectives. *IEEE Access : Practical Innovations, Open Solutions*, *8*, 140079–140096. doi:10.1109/ACCESS.2020.3012812

Garousi, V. (2015). A bibliometric analysis of the Turkish software engineering research community. *Scientometrics*, *105*(1), 23–49. doi:10.1007/s11192-015-1663-x

Goh, K. H., & See, K. F. (2021). Twenty years of water utility benchmarking: A bibliometric analysis of emerging interest in water research and collaboration. *Journal of Cleaner Production*, *284*, 124711. doi:10.1016/j.jclepro.2020.124711

Gursoy, D., Malodia, S., & Dhir, A. (2022). The metaverse in the hospitality and tourism industry: An overview of current trends and future research directions. *Journal of Hospitality Marketing & Management*, *31*(5), 527–534. doi:10.1080/19368623.2022.2072504

Hancock, K. (2022). Virtual Team Performance, Collaborative Remote Work, and Employee Engagement and Multimodal Behavioral Analytics in the Metaverse Economy. *Psychosociological Issues in Human Resource Management*, *10*(2), 55–70. doi:10.22381/pihrm10220224

Heracleous, L., Terrier, D., & Gonzalez, S. (2019). NASA's capability evolution toward commercial space. *Space Policy*, *50*, 101330. doi:10.1016/j.spacepol.2019.07.004

Hollensen, S., Kotler, P., & Opresnik, M. O. (2022). Metaverse–the new marketing universe. *The Journal of Business Strategy*, *44*(3), 119–125. doi:10.1108/JBS-01-2022-0014

Iden, J., & Methlie, L. B. (2012). The drivers of services on next-generation networks. *Telematics and Informatics*, *29*(2), 137–155. doi:10.1016/j.tele.2011.05.004

Iqbal, M. Z., & Campbell, A. G. (2023, October). Metaverse as tech for good: Current progress and emerging opportunities. In Virtual Worlds, 2(4), 326-342.

Kadry, A. (2022). The metaverse revolution and its impact on the future of advertising industry. *Journal of Design Sciences and Applied Arts*, *3*(2), 131–139. doi:10.21608/jdsaa.2022.129876.1171

Kaushal, N., Sharma, S., & Katoch, A. (2022a). The Satisfaction of Religious Tourists Visiting Shiva Circuit of Himachal Pradesh. *International Research Journal of Management Sociology & Humanities*, *13*(8), 11–19.

Kaushal, N., Sharma, S., & Katoch, A. (2022b). Problems and Challenges faced by Religious Tourists: A study of Religious Destinations of Himachal Pradesh. *International Journal of Commerce. Arts & Science*, *13*(8), 27–35.

Li, F., Xing, W., Su, M., & Xu, J. (2021). The evolution of China's marine economic policy and the labor productivity growth momentum of the marine economy and its three economic industries. *Marine Policy*, *134*, 104777. doi:10.1016/j.marpol.2021.104777

Maier, D., Maier, A., Aşchilean, I., Anastasiu, L., & Gavriş, O. (2020). The relationship between innovation and sustainability: A bibliometric review of the literature. *Sustainability (Basel)*, *12*(10), 4083. doi:10.3390/su12104083

Mirza-Babaei, P., Robinson, R., Mandryk, R., Pirker, J., Kang, C., & Fletcher, A. (2022, November). Games and the Metaverse. In *Extended abstracts of the 2022 annual symposium on computer-human interaction in play*. ACM. 10.1145/3505270.3558355

Moher, D., Liberati, A., Tetzlaff, J., & Altman, D. G. (2009). Preferred reporting items for systematic reviews and meta-analyses: The PRISMA statement. *Annals of Internal Medicine, 151*(4), 264–269. doi:10.7326/0003-4819-151-4-200908180-00135 PMID:19622511

Mourtzis, D. (2023). The Metaverse in Industry 5.0: A Human-Centric Approach towards Personalized Value Creation. *Encyclopedia, 3*(3), 1105–1120. doi:10.3390/encyclopedia3030080

Muhuri, P. K., Shukla, A. K., & Abraham, A. (2019). Industry 4.0: A bibliometric analysis and detailed overview. *Engineering Applications of Artificial Intelligence, 78*, 218–235. doi:10.1016/j.engappai.2018.11.007

Nabukalu, R., & Wanjohi, A. (2023). *Impact of Metaverse on Marketing Communication: A case study of the fashion industry*. Lulea University of Technology.

Qi, W. (2022). The Investment Value of Metaverse in the Media and Entertainment Industry. *BCP Business and Management, 34*, 279–283. doi:10.54691/bcpbm.v34i.3026

Raad, H., & Rashid, F. K. M. (2023). The Metaverse: Applications, Concerns, Technical Challenges, Future Directions and Recommendations. *IEEE Access : Practical Innovations, Open Solutions, 11*, 110850–110861. doi:10.1109/ACCESS.2023.3321650

Rejeb, A., Rejeb, K., & Treiblmaier, H. (2023). Mapping metaverse research: Identifying future research areas based on bibliometric and topic modeling techniques. *Information (Basel), 14*(7), 356. doi:10.3390/info14070356

Sharma, R., Jabbour, C. J. C., & Lopes de Sousa Jabbour, A. B. (2021). Sustainable manufacturing and industry 4.0: What we know and what we don't. *Journal of Enterprise Information Management, 34*(1), 230–266. doi:10.1108/JEIM-01-2020-0024

Shen, B., Tan, W., Guo, J., Zhao, L., & Qin, P. (2021). How to promote user purchase in metaverse? A systematic literature review on consumer behavior research and virtual commerce application design. *Applied Sciences (Basel, Switzerland), 11*(23), 11087. doi:10.3390/app112311087

Van Beers, D., Bossilkov, A., Corder, G., & Van Berkel, R. (2007). Industrial symbiosis in the Australian minerals industry: the cases of Kwinana and Gladstone.

Van Eck, N., & Waltman, L. (2010). Software survey: VOSviewer, a computer program for bibliometric mapping. *Scientometrics, 84*(2), 523–538. doi:10.1007/s11192-009-0146-3 PMID:20585380

Van Eck, N. J., & Waltman, L. (2011). Text mining and visualization using VOSviewer. arXiv preprint arXiv:1109.2058.

Viana-Lora, A., & Nel-lo-Andreu, M. G. (2022). Bibliometric analysis of trends in COVID- 19 and tourism. *Humanities & Social Sciences Communications, 9*(1), 173. doi:10.1057/s41599-022-01194-5

Wallin, J. A. (2005). Bibliometric methods: Pitfalls and possibilities. *Basic & Clinical Pharmacology & Toxicology*, *97*(5), 261–275. doi:10.1111/j.1742-7843.2005.pto_139.x PMID:16236137

Wang, M., Yu, H., Bell, Z., & Chu, X. (2022). Constructing an edu-metaverse ecosystem: A new and innovative framework. *IEEE Transactions on Learning Technologies*, *15*(6), 685–696. doi:10.1109/TLT.2022.3210828

Wang, M. H., Yu, T. C., & Ho, Y. S. (2010). A bibliometric analysis of the performance of Water Research. *Scientometrics*, *84*(3), 813–820. doi:10.1007/s11192-009-0112-0

Weinberg, B. H. (1974). Bibliographic coupling: A review. *Information Storage and Retrieval*, *10*(5–6), 189–196. doi:10.1016/0020-0271(74)90058-8

Wider, W., Jiang, L., Lin, J., Fauzi, M. A., Li, J., & Chan, C. K. (2023). Metaverse chronicles: A bibliometric analysis of its evolving landscape. *International Journal of Human-Computer Interaction*, 1–14. doi:10.1080/10447318.2023.2227825

Yang, L., Ni, S. T., Wang, Y., Yu, A., Lee, J. A., & Hui, P. (2024). Interoperability of the Metaverse: A Digital Ecosystem Perspective Review. *arXiv preprint arXiv:2403.05205*.

Yao, X., Ma, N., Zhang, J., Wang, K., Yang, E., & Faccio, M. (2024). Enhancing wisdom manufacturing as industrial metaverse for industry and society 5.0. *Journal of Intelligent Manufacturing*, *35*(1), 235–255. doi:10.1007/s10845-022-02027-7

Zhai, X., Chu, X., Wang, M., Zhang, Z., & Dong, Y. (2022). Education metaverse: Innovations and challenges of the new generation of Internet education formats. *Metaverse*, *3*(1), 13. doi:10.54517/met.v3i1.1804

Zonaphan, L., Northus, K., Wijaya, J., Achmad, S., & Sutoyo, R. (2022, November). Metaverse as a future of education: A systematic review. In *2022 8th International HCI and UX Conference in Indonesia (CHIuXiD)*, 1, 77-81). 10.1109/CHIuXiD57244.2022.10009854

Zupic, I., & Čater, T. (2015). Bibliometric methods in management and organization. *Organizational Research Methods*, *18*(3), 429–472. doi:10.1177/1094428114562629

ENDNOTES

[1]   Research Associate, School of Commerce & Management Studies, Central University of Himachal Pradesh.

[2]   Research Scholar, School of Commerce & Management Studies, Central University of Himachal Pradesh

Chapter 13
Transformation of Marketing Strategy by Metaverse in the Hospitality Industry Facing Crisis

Asik Rahaman Jamader

(iD) https://orcid.org/0000-0002-6938-5901

Pailan College of Management and Technology, India

Santanu Dasgupta

(iD) https://orcid.org/0000-0002-3060-4759

Pailan College of Management and Technology, India

Mushtaq Ahmad

The Neotia University, India

ABSTRACT

The hospitality industry is one of the largest manpower-driven industries and hence generates huge employment. Strategies evolved and applied till 2019 transformed greatly facing the crisis in 2020 to cope with the prevailing circumstances for sustenance. The use of technology came greatly into effect on the Metaverse. Hence a drastic change has taken place in hospitality marketing strategy using the Tourism Marketing Union Model (TMUM). People are becoming more and more technophiles, and desire to have as much data as possible before starting the tour hoping for a hindrance-free, comfortable, and enjoyable expedition. Therefore, a complete transformation occurred in every phase of the industry, especially in the marketing sector. Cost reduction and Time-saving became the aims of new strategies and for that, Metaverse Marketing Technology (MMT), influencer marketing, and targeting the right audience through Metaverse Visual Marketing are extensively used by marketers.

DOI: 10.4018/979-8-3693-2607-7.ch013

INTRODUCTION

Marketing is an important and inseparable part of every industry and there is no confusion in that. It supports the backbone of each and every sector by maximizing profit through well-planned and structured strategies (Ip et al., 2011). The hospitality industry is also no exception from it. It is the second-largest manpower-driven industry where marketing strategies play an important role. Marketing strategies that were applied till 2019 in the hospitality industry suddenly faced a crisis period due to COVID 19 pandemic and henceforth all the processes need to be restructured as the whole world started to live in the phase of 'new normal'. Till 2019 marketers used online and offline strategies to maximize the number of guests in the hospitality sector. But with the advent of a new normal phase, a 360-degree transformation took place in marketing strategies, instead of both online and offline, marketers focused totally on online-based strategies to target the customers. Different initiatives are taken into action to get the faith and loyalty of guests like – search engine optimization (SEO) and search engine marketing (SEM), boosting digital marketing (DM) platforms, and trying to increase customer satisfaction (CS) by posting more visual contents of hotels, content marketing (CM), etc (Law, et al., 2014). New generations and the Millennial found this online marketing process absolutely hassle-free, time-saving, and worthwhile for them, instead of other processes. Thus there is always a point of discussion whether only this new transformative strategy will be continued or alike before the crisis period, both online and offline strategies will be needed for the hospitality industry to survive in the future (Yoo, et al., 2011).

The travel and tourism sector offers an appropriate backdrop for examining the impact of advanced technology on relationship marketing since it is one of the businesses that have adopted information and communication technologies (ICT) most quickly. Buhalis claims that these innovations bring created additional growth plans for creating, developing, and commercialising client connections through a better comprehension of consumer needs as well as the fulfilment of their demands. Moreover, developments in integrated multimedia broadcasting, ICT, browser innovations, plus their confluence might effectively help to streamlining the procedure for obtaining and analyzing information related to consumers' particular requirements (Williams, A. 2006). In more detail, integrated multimedia television (iMTV) describes the growth of new communication networks that may deliver a variety of multimedia as well as World Wide Web applications. In contrast, Internet Protocol Multimedia Subsystem (IMS) is a promising technology that may be implemented in next smart phones & digitized broadcast networks to offer cutting-edge characteristics as well as additional communication services. To allow effective collection and analysis in tourism relationship marketing, this article offers a technological interaction model that elaborates on the convergence of IMS and iDTV systems (Wang, Y., & Qualls, W., 2007). The suggested system makes it easier for tourist businesses to follow individuals' choices but instead give clients greater economic benefit through personalised services since dynamic marketing strategy depends on clients' data. Because they would have a thorough understanding of the behaviour and preferences of their current or future clients, marketers will be able to base their judgments on marketing activities that are considerably greater expense. Statistical techniques, such as predicting visualization tools, are suggested in order to enable effective information analysis and processing and to best forecast future purchase trends (Pirnar, et al., 2010)

Changing Scenarios of Hospitality Marketing

The hospitality industry needs rigorous promotion and marketing to sustain itself in the ongoing competitive market. Current marketing scenarios possess a direct impact on marketing strategies. Till the year 2019, companies were following mixed strategies based on online and offline platforms like arranging and hosting various events (like exhibitions, and cultural programs) to promote the location and property, maximum discounts offered in off-seasons to attract guests, and happy hours announced in different outlets to provide guests the opportunity to taste and enjoy food and simultaneously hotels' also going to enjoy word of mouth through such events (DiPietro, et al., 2010). Except that online strategies also followed. But in the year 2020, India started facing a crisis due to the pandemic and people forcefully bound themselves at home to maintain the protocols required to sustain from Covid19 (Tuomi, et al., 2021). Therefore, a complete transformation took place in every phase of the industry, especially in the marketing sector. Cost reduction and Time-saving became the aims of new strategies and for that Mobile Marketing Technology, Influencers Marketing, and targeting the right audience through Visual Marketing are extensively used by marketers. Newer channels for interacting with target markets have emerged with the development of information technology (Inanc–Demir, M., & Kozak, M., 2019). Regardless of the type of organisation, digital marketing is now an essential component. The overwhelming importance of digital marketing has changed how businesses sell their products to current and future customers. In the hotel and tourist sectors, where clients have fast access to a wide range of information on the newest deals and greatest pricing, the need for content marketing is greater than ever (Damnjanović, et al., 2020). Nowadays, internet advertising is crucial to the success of any company in the hotel and tourist sector. Several of the earliest businesses to use digital marketing techniques were the hotel and tourist industry. Due in large part to the fact that the business largely offers experiences, this early adoption has also helped the sector to keep up with the most recent developments in digital promotion. In the past, the majority of customers in the hospitality and tourist industries used workstation as well as laptops to research locations and make reservations online. However, the business has recently seen a shift from PCs to mobile a device that has happened gradually but quickly (Leonidou, et al., 2013). This change has affected not just the aforementioned business but also digital use as a whole. Today's social media usage is shockingly different from what it was sometimes just few decades previously (Kuo, et al., 2017).

The said industry includes all the people, activities, and organizations involved in providing services for people on holiday, for example hotels, restaurants, and tour guides. Before the launch of digital marketing, the role of people who rendered these services was indispensable to the success of the business. The increasing number of mobile users, lowering prices of digital marketing services and rising effectiveness of social media strategies are a few of the multitude of reasons which has led to the widespread adoption of digital marketing strategies by the industry (Pappas, N., 2015). As such, there are modern-world start-ups coming up in the already highly saturated hospitality and tourism sector which are mobile-only. The entire industry is going mobile, quite literally. Since the invention of the internet, novel strategies for reaching target consumers with diverse services have emerged (Sigala, M. 2003). The fast growth of the internet has particularly impacted the travel and tourism sector as a whole. With the stroke of a mouse, users may compare prices for travel-related services from companies all around the world (Buhalis, D., & Sinarta, Y., 2019). The most important digital tasks to maintain are having a good website, having a presence on social media, using email marketing, being search engine optimised, and having a mobile-friendly website. Currently, internet advertising is upending sectors and altering how companies interact with their customers. The capacity of digital marketing to collect data regarding user activity as well as sustain a successful in real-time is the primary distinction between traditional and digital marketing. The upheaval in the tourist sector happened a few years ago and changed how services are delivered to customers. Market research is used in traditional marketing to gather data, which is then analysed to better understand the target consumers. The electronic nature of Internet technology offers a thorough and in-depth understanding of customer traits and behaviour in the electronic environment. The manner that company choices are made has changed as a result of this knowledge (Cline, R. S., 1999).

THE ARRIVAL OF THE INTERNET AND DIGITAL TRANSFORMATION FOR MARKETING GROW

The most significant development in marketing over the past three decades has been the widespread acceptance of the internet into daily life. When World Wide Web and Netscape Navigator were introduced, the number of individuals accessing the internet increased. Email gave way to search engines like Yahoo! and Google, as well as e-commerce websites like Amazon, as the number of users grew (Jamader, et al., 2019). This represented a gold mine for marketing. In addition to the conventional armoury of print, radio, and television commercials, email has emerged as a new outbound marketing weapon. While people could get the data, goods, plus services they wanted from the comfort of their homes thanks to search engines, new websites were being developed.

Big Data

Digital data was and is still being retained for all of this internet activity. The majority of text-based information that was "born digital" and is now known as big data was determined to be the sort of unique information that was created with the fastest rate of growth. Big data has made it feasible to follow behavioural patterns and trends, and its use in marketing is only going to grow. A number of businesses that specialise in utilising this technology have developed as advanced analytics branding has gained considerable traction (Das, et al., 2019).

Mobile Phones

Without mobile phones and tablets, wherever would we be? Advertising agencies are still catching up with the rapid growth of these new gadgets during the past ten years. Mobile phones are becoming the most popular digital device for browsing the internet, surpassing personal computers (Nayak, et al., 2022). Following the revolutionary launching of the iPhone, mobile phones did not reach the mainstream market until 2021. When we go at the present, we see that the UK alone has a smart phone ownership rate of more than 80%, with substantial rises in the percentage of 4G users and a quarter of subscribers not completing any conventional voice communication. Online and in our pockets, the world has changed. Where do we proceed from here, a combination of personalisation, accountability, as well as nimble advertising (Jamader, et al., 2021).

ACCESS TO INFORMATION THROUGH TELECOMMUNICATIONS IN DEVELOPMENT FOR MARKETING

With the help of control and, in certain circumstances, the opportunity to make purchases, interactive media in digital television systems transforms the viewer from a passive to an active participant. Interactive media, according to marketers, increases viewer engagement with the media and hence the content. It also makes it possible to display information in more visually appealing and engaging ways, and it is simple to update. In this regard, advancements in technology have already had an impact on one of the most often debated and used channels of interaction: marketing as well as its potential place on tv. Digital interactive television (iDTV), which invites users to enter a more specific tv environment as well as browse WebPages as well as other Internet-based applications, is one example of an evolutionary scientific progress (Sagayam, et al., 2022).

Based on a general interaction model, DTT networking architectures have been developed, allowing for the deployment of asymmetrical transmission of data between the service supplier as well as tele viewers. In these scenarios, upstream information transmitted is provided through a DVB-T channel, while reverse data traffic is transmitted by a variety of associated with positive (including such cell phone, cordless, or permanent connections). Such setups allow a phone company to offer digital television services that are both interactive and one-way. Another internet streaming services are TV programmes that use digital transmission standards. Interactive multimedia services also include video and audio on demand, Internet services including WWW access and e-mail, as well as videoconferencing on supply. But at the other extreme, modern machines and new services demand stringent quality and interactivity, since the previous generation of the Internet was primarily focused on the transportation of data to non-real demand service. Furthermore, in the upcoming years, it is anticipated that the demands for the supply of multimedia services would rise. There seems to be a significant tendency toward a common Internet architecture for services and applications. Customers in this situation appear to want open coverage to individualised immersive offerings on any platform (Jamader, 2022). New specifications for a future network infrastructure are brought about by this tendency. The Internet Protocol Part of the system, which was first developed to enable operators in offering cutting-edge services that will draw new customers, helps to meet this demand by bridging the gap between current traditional telecommunications and Internet applications. Using open standards that facilitate Internet-based network interfaces and fixed-mobile convergence, IMS is a fundamental network architecture that enables communication between servers and clients. IMS has a layered, functional improvement that controls how the information is handled as it travels across the infrastructure. It offers the system implementation necessary to deliver any video streaming to any mix of fixed and mobile end consumers. The creation of the IMS architecture established how applications connected with the fundamental broadband network as well as exchanged data.

By combining many telecommunications concepts into a comprehensive multimedia user experience, IMS-enabled TV systems support combination services and interaction. IMS was created in this environment to offer a private communication infrastructure with group communication, converting TV viewing from a social, participatory experience to a private, personal one. New customised TV experiences will be built specifically on presence and profile management (Jamader et al., 2023). The most accurate user profile, including their habits and wants, may be created by operators and their marketing teams. It can be quite useful for marketing purposes to have a single, uniform database that is based on the cellular world model with enhancements to fulfil iDTV unique demands.

THE TOURISM MARKETING UNION MODEL

Customer engagement relies on participatory contact to better understand the demands of Figure 1 shows a television broadcast interaction model that has been upgraded with IMS features. The suggested convergence paradigm makes it possible to gather data in real time from client sites. The IMS Module/ Database in Figure 1 houses this data, making it possible to properly serve clients and users. Modern technological developments may be the norm, allowing for an essential active interaction between the company and clients (Jamader, Chowdhary & Jha, 2023).

Throughout sequence for these two parties to work together and connect more effectively, integrating business systems through a unified platform is the first step in any corporate IT strategy. This allows customers to communicate and inform the authority's actual demands. Database analysis is the second element of this method (Das et al., 2022). The findings might serve as the foundation for algorithms designed to comprehend the wants of actual clients. Advances in iDTV, ICT, web applications, and their integration in this context should add greatly to automating and streamlining of collecting and analyzing the needed data that is essential in tourist Management (Jamader et al., 2023). Implementing the suggested strategy, Portfolio allows corporations to employ sarcastic retort marketing that cultivate relationships with consumers while also enabling user engagement via electronic content. To send used whenever to the network operator and enable the delivery of actual interactive services through iDTV systems, the use of an interaction channel is required, according to the generic interactivity model. to develop focused and effective advertising tactics, the marketing analysis step is necessary. In order to anticipate future probabilities and trends based on observed occurrences, marketers can undertake data analysis by utilising data mining techniques, such as predictive visual analytics. The suggested strategy incorporates a multi-perspective approach that integrates algorithms, predictive modelling, and reasoning based on domain expertise (Jamader, Das, & Acharya, 2022).

Figure 1. Tourism marketing union model (TMUM)

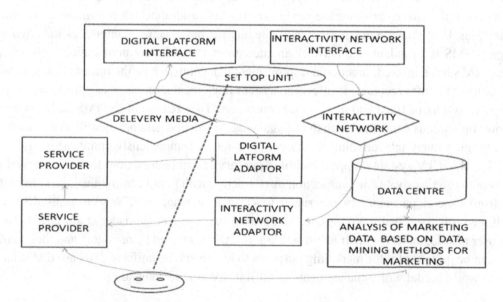

And as per the suggested strategy, collection of information will be analysed in an effort to improve consumer behaviour understanding and future purchase trends prediction. The suggested data mining approaches are utilised to determine channel strategy, product type, buying preferences, and regional market share. Then, to determine, for instance, whether novel merchandise should just be brought into the tourism industry, demographics, lifestyle factors, and purchasing behaviour are employed. Last but not least, behavioural metrics created using predictive analytics models may graphically display chosen marketing data and generate what-if scenarios to establish and confirm the proper pairings of new eco-tourism marketing. Prospective advanced analytic study often aims to make the overabundance of data inside an advantage. To make wise choices in circumstances where time is of the essence, decision-makers should be able to assess vast streams of information that are multidimensional, multi-source, and moment. People must be related to information data analysis in order to fully utilise the tremendous memory space as well as processing power of digital hardware while also bringing adaptability, imagination, as well as context to the procedure. A vitally essential of information visualization is that it enables judgement in the tourist industry to utilise sophisticated computer skills to speed up the discovery process while focusing all of their visuospatial resources on the data analysis.

Predictive visual analytics has replaced data warehousing and mining as the primary area of study for cutting-edge technology and innovation in our fast-paced world in order to handle all these challenges.

It would be simple to get the explanation by glancing at the individual in the seat next to you on the bus, by gazing up in the middle of the street, or by simply glancing about. If you do, you'll see that the individual sitting next to you is carrying a device, LED advertisements can be seen in the sky, and people are becoming more immersed in technology on a daily basis as you can see when you glance about. The majority of companies in the tourism sector are performing far better than those that aren't, according to actual data from numerous data. According to a latest studies, 3.2 billion people, or almost 50% of the world's population, are already smart phone subscribers.

CONCLUSION

This article goes into further detail on the research of IMS as a potential alternative that might be used in digitization and then the next systems, offering slightly up and additional benefit offerings. This work suggests a technological convergence model that might lead to a fresh research methodology usable in tourist Management, taking into consideration advancements in both scientific fields. Implementing the RM concept with a focus on creating high-quality relationships with customers and stakeholders is essential for competitiveness in the dynamic and uncertain economic environment of the hotel industry, which is characterised by tough competition and advanced requirement. Making sure visitors are happy is a certain method to keep loyal consumers and draw in new ones. The overarching goal of RM is to make it possible for marketers to keep track of the preferences of both current and future consumers in order to provide them with services that are more valuable overall. The suggested idea would make it possible for a more effective method of gathering and evaluating audience data information, which is essential for the best possible marketing outcomes. It might be the solution to one of the top goals on the wish lists of marketers: to advance toward one-to-one marketing contact with the target audience, capture their attention and interest, arouse their desire, and ultimately result in the compulsive or deliberate action of purchasing. Furthermore, the suggested machine learning techniques as well as internet applications improve the suggested research strategy by enabling, correspondingly, an appropriate way to analyse marketing data and an efficient way to automatically modify services for specific clients or market groups. Furthermore, the suggested machine learning techniques as well as internet applications improve the suggested research strategy by enabling, correspondingly, an appropriate way to analyse marketing data and an efficient way to automatically modify services for specific clients or market groups.

ACKNOWLEDGEMENTS

Funding: The Author declare that they do not have any funding or grant for the manuscript.

Conflict of Interest: The authors declare that they do not have any conflict of interests that influence the work reported in this paper

REFERENCES

Buhalis, D., & Sinarta, Y. (2019). Real-time co-creation and nowness service: Lessons from tourism and hospitality. *Journal of Travel & Tourism Marketing*, *36*(5), 563–582. doi:10.1080/10548408.2019.1592059

Cline, R. S. (1999). Hospitality 2000—the technology: Building customer relationships. *Journal of Vacation Marketing*, *5*(4), 376–386. doi:10.1177/135676679900500407

Damnjanović, V., Lončarić, D., & Dlačić, J. (2020). TEACHING CASE STUDY: Digital marketing strategy of Accor Hotels: shaping the future of hospitality. *Tourism and Hospitality Management*, *26*(1), 233–244.

Das, P., Jamader, A. R., Acharya, B. R., & Das, H. (2019, May). HMF Based QoS aware Recommended Resource Allocation System in Mobile Edge Computing for IoT. In *2019 International Conference on Intelligent Computing and Control Systems (ICCS)* (pp. 444-449). IEEE. 10.1109/ICCS45141.2019.9065775

DiPietro, R. B., & Wang, Y. R. (2010). Key issues for ICT applications: Impacts and implications for hospitality operations. *Worldwide Hospitality and Tourism Themes*, *2*(1), 49–67. doi:10.1108/17554211011012595

Inanc–Demir, M., & Kozak, M. (2019). Big data and its supporting elements: Implications for tourism and hospitality marketing. In *Big Data and Innovation in Tourism, Travel, and Hospitality* (pp. 213–223). Springer. doi:10.1007/978-981-13-6339-9_13

Ip, C., Leung, R., & Law, R. (2011). Progress and development of information and communication technologies in hospitality. *International Journal of Contemporary Hospitality Management*, *23*(4), 533–551. doi:10.1108/09596111111130029

Jamader, A. R. (2022). A Brief Report Of The Upcoming & Present Economic Impact To Hospitality Industry In COVID19 Situations. *Journal of Pharmaceutical Negative Results*, 2289–2302.

Jamader, A. R., Chowdhary, S., Jha, S. S., & Roy, B. (2023). Application of Economic Models to Green Circumstance for Management of Littoral Area: A Sustainable Tourism Arrangement. *SMART Journal of Business Management Studies*, *19*(1), 70–84. doi:10.5958/2321-2012.2023.00008.8

Jamader, A. R., Chowdhary, S., & Shankar Jha, S. (2023). A Road Map for Two Decades of Sustainable Tourism Development Framework. In Resilient and Sustainable Destinations After Disaster: Challenges and Strategies (pp. 9-18). Emerald Publishing Limited. doi:10.1108/978-1-80382-021-720231002

Jamader, A. R., Das, P., & Acharya, B. (2022). An Analysis of Consumers Acceptance towards Usage of Digital Payment System, Fintech and CBDC. *Fintech and CBDC (January 1, 2022)*.

Jamader, A. R., Das, P., Acharya, B., & Hu, Y. C. (2021). Overview of Security and Protection Techniques for Microgrids. In *Microgrids* (pp. 231–253). CRC Press. doi:10.1201/9781003121626-11

Jamader, A. R., Das, P., & Acharya, B. R. (2019, May). BcIoT: blockchain based DDoS prevention architecture for IoT. In *2019 International Conference on Intelligent Computing and Control Systems (ICCS)* (pp. 377-382). IEEE. 10.1109/ICCS45141.2019.9065692

Jamader, A. R., Immanuel, J. S., Ebenezer, V., Rakhi, R. A., Sagayam, K. M., & Das, P. (2023). Virtual Education, Training And Internships In Hospitality And Tourism During Covid-19 Situation. *Journal of Pharmaceutical Negative Results*, 286–290.

Kuo, C. M., Chen, L. C., & Tseng, C. Y. (2017). Investigating an innovative service with hospitality robots. *International Journal of Contemporary Hospitality Management, 29*(5), 1305–1321. doi:10.1108/IJCHM-08-2015-0414

Law, R., Buhalis, D., & Cobanoglu, C. (2014). Progress on information and communication technologies in hospitality and tourism. *International Journal of Contemporary Hospitality Management, 26*(5), 727–750. doi:10.1108/IJCHM-08-2013-0367

Leonidou, L. C., Leonidou, C. N., Fotiadis, T. A., & Zeriti, A. (2013). Resources and capabilities as drivers of hotel environmental marketing strategy: Implications for competitive advantage and performance. *Tourism Management, 35*, 94–110. doi:10.1016/j.tourman.2012.06.003

Nayak, D. K., Mishra, P., Das, P., Jamader, A. R., & Acharya, B. (2022). Application of Deep Learning in Biomedical Informatics and Healthcare. In *Smart Healthcare Analytics: State of the Art* (pp. 113–132). Springer. doi:10.1007/978-981-16-5304-9_9

Pappas, N. (2015). Marketing hospitality industry in an era of crisis. *Tourism Planning & Development, 12*(3), 333–349. doi:10.1080/21568316.2014.979226

Pirnar, I., Icoz, O., & Icoz, O. (2010). The new tourist: Impacts on the hospitality marketing strategies. *EuroCHRIE Amsterdam*, 25-28.

Das, P., Martin Sagayam, K., Rahaman Jamader, A., & Acharya, B. (2022). Remote Sensing in Public Health Environment: A Review. *Internet of Things Based Smart Healthcare: Intelligent and Secure Solutions Applying Machine Learning Techniques*, 379-397.

Sagayam, K. M., Das, P., Jamader, A. R., Acharya, B. R., Bonyah, E., & Elngar, A. A. (2022). DeepCOVIDNet [Detection of Chest Image Using Deep Learning Model.]. *COVID*, 19.

Sigala, M. (2003). Developing and benchmarking internet marketing strategies in the hotel sector in Greece. *Journal of Hospitality & Tourism Research (Washington, D.C.), 27*(4), 375–401. doi:10.1177/10963480030274001

Tuomi, A., Tussyadiah, I. P., & Stienmetz, J. (2021). Applications and implications of service robots in hospitality. *Cornell Hospitality Quarterly, 62*(2), 232–247. doi:10.1177/1938965520923961

Wang, Y., & Qualls, W. (2007). Towards a theoretical model of technology adoption in hospitality organizations. *International Journal of Hospitality Management, 26*(3), 560–573. doi:10.1016/j.ijhm.2006.03.008

Williams, A. (2006). Tourism and hospitality marketing: Fantasy, feeling and fun. *International Journal of Contemporary Hospitality Management, 18*(6), 482–495. doi:10.1108/09596110610681520

Yoo, M., Lee, S., & Bai, B. (2011). Hospitality marketing research from 2000 to 2009: topics, methods, and trends. *International Journal of Contemporary Hospitality Management.*

Chapter 14
Unlocking the Potentials and Constraints of Metaverse Implementation in Manufacturing Firms

Mohammad Imtiaz Hossain
 https://orcid.org/0000-0002-9637-3201
Multimedia University, Malaysia

Yasmin Jamadar
BRAC University, Bangladesh

Nurunnesa Begum Momo
BRAC University, Bangladesh

Nusrat Hafiz
BRAC University, Bangladesh

Rufaida Nurain Saiba
BRAC University, Bangladesh

ABSTRACT

This research investigates the potentials and constraints of metaverse technology within Malaysian manufacturing companies underpinned by the technology-organization-environment (TOE) theory. Firm size, firm age, annual revenue, and ownership structure were control variables. 240 questionnaire responses from Malaysian firms collected through convenience sampling techniques and analyzed by Smart-PLS software. The findings reveal technological limitations, poor diffusion through the network, lack of collaboration, and low perception of value by customers are significant constraints for the failure of metaverse technology implementation. The control variables did not evidence any impact on implementation. This study provides insights to metaverse technology developers and manufacturing practitioners besides theoretical contributions.

DOI: 10.4018/979-8-3693-2607-7.ch014

INTRODUCTION

Metaverse is a virtual world, which will compile virtual reality (VR) with augmented reality (AR), and will stabilize a link between the real world and a parallel virtual world for humans. The metaverse is poised to revolutionize various sectors by enhancing efficiency and reducing risks, especially in scientific experiments. For instance, businesses can leverage the metaverse to streamline tedious and hazardous tasks. A case in point is inventory management, which can be virtually automated, reducing the manual effort (Dwivedi et al., 2022). The metaverse also enables virtual property transactions.

In the realm of education, the metaverse offers immersive learning experiences, which experts argue are more effective than traditional audio-visual learning. This technology allows students to engage in realistic, risk-free learning and experimentation. Unlike the less interactive online education under Web 2.0, metaverse-based learning is highly interactive, facilitated by three-dimensional avatars. It also offers the flexibility of personalized learning schedules (Zhang, 2023).

Beyond business and education, the metaverse has significant implications for healthcare, tourism, and entertainment. It enables virtual travel to far-off places and enhances the realism of games, contributing to mental well-being. Therefore, the metaverse holds immense potential across sectors, promising risk reduction and economic growth.

Metaverse will have significance in both developed and developing countries, if they implement it after overcoming all challenges. It will be a new opportunity for businesses, they can earn more profit by showing their creativity in the virtual world. It will have virtual currency, assets, and the marketplace. Thus, it will be a new opportunity for the stakeholders to have benefits from businesses. Subsequently, manufacturing firms can do their work more smoothly with the help of it. For example: they can give training to their workers virtually and more interactively with the help of avatars. Moreover, multinational companies can run their business more effectively because it will mitigate the limitation of physical distance. Also, service industries like psychology and tourism can give their services more effectively by making the virtual experience more realistic through metaverse (Mourtzis, 2023). Besides, through it a diverse digital culture can be established, which will bring a collaborative new culture. In other words, it will bring more global connectivity through cross-cultural interactions.

While the metaverse offers numerous benefits, it also faces several implementation challenges. First, to create a realistic virtual experience, enhanced sensations are required. However, certain sensations, such as slipperiness, distinct aromas, and daylight, are more authentically experienced in the physical world. Therefore, these sensations need to be more naturally replicated in the metaverse, considering the multiple personas of human beings (Park & Kim, 2024). Nevertheless, the increased demand for high-powered technologies could negatively impact the environment, thereby undermining sustainability efforts.

Second, security and privacy are fundamental aspects of human life, and the potential for stored data and internet history to compromise these elements cannot be overlooked (Park & Kim, 2024). For example, Google Glass, despite being an innovative product, was discontinued due to privacy concerns. Moreover, legal regulations in the virtual world may differ from those in various countries, leading to potential conflicts. Cultural clashes may also arise in the metaverse. Finally, the global promotion and adoption of the metaverse present significant challenges. For instance, Google Glass was primarily used by financially stable individuals in developed countries. Consequently, individuals in developing and underdeveloped countries may require additional effort and training to adapt to this groundbreaking technology.

A collaborative digital environment that spans multiple dimensions, powered by a blend of Virtual Reality (VR), Augmented Reality (AR), and Mixed Reality (MR), holds the potential to deeply integrate the automotive and manufacturing sectors into the Metaverse. This industrial Metaverse could materialize through seamless integration of cyber-physical systems, digital twins, 5G-enabled AR, VR, and AI-driven computer vision, as well as low-latency remote control capabilities, among other technologies (Fernández-Caramés & Fraga-Lamas, 2024).

Within this industrial Metaverse, future factories would not only utilize AR/VR for on-site assistance and skills training but would also facilitate a virtual environment where individuals can work together, guided by AI algorithms to validate outcomes and rectify errors in real-time, eliminating the need for physical presence (Yao et al., 2024).

Moreover, various aspects of company operations including product design, development, trial production testing, operational management, and marketing, can be simulated and validated within this virtual ecosystem before implementation in the physical world.

Furthermore, blockchain technology could be leveraged to record decision-making processes and results, serving as a transparent basis for assessment and auditing across both virtual and physical realms (Zheng et al., 2022).

Being a developing country Malaysia began the journey with metaverse in various sectors, especially initiated with the gaming industry. As mentioned above Metaverse has a crucial role in the gaming industry. Furthermore, metaverse has not been implemented in the educational institutions but they are taking steps to start their journey with it. For instance- there are many articles where the authors proposed metaverse based education. Rahman et al. (2023) emphasized the importance of metaverse in education along with proposing a detailed figure of virtual classrooms to implement in the education sector of Malaysia. For instance, in Malaysia, the Arabic Learning Principles (ALP) were integrated with a 3D Metaverse platform to teach Arabic language skills to Muslim students (Basha, Khaleel, Mnaathr, & Rozinah, 2013). This platform included elements of traditional Arabic architecture found in mosques, allowing for congregational prayer, Quran recitation, supplication, and even the use of a compass to orient towards the Kaaba, among other features. Moreover, in the 4th industry revaluation (4IR) Malaysia already used some advanced technologies but they are not updated compared to other countries (Uddin, 2024). The reasons behind this are low education rate, lack of training, inadequate initiative and so on. Technology might cause unemployment in a short run but will create more job opportunities in the long run (Uddin, 2024). Therefore, Malaysia should adopt metaverse to boost its economy. Therefore, the journey of metaverse is not completely visible yet apart from the gaming industry and there are some prominent obstacles behind it.

Firstly, lack of knowledge, education and infrastructure are the barriers in the implementation of metaverse (Creed et al., 2024). Secondly, VR and AR and other accessories are very expensive (Mammadova, 2023), and these will be difficult for lot of firms specially SMEs to afford. Thirdly, cultural sensitivity will be another issue because metaverse is a global concept (Li, 2022), and alignment with other cultures will be a problem. Lastly, poor regulatory framework compared to other countries will hamper the privacy and security of its people, which will be a barrier. According to Ghobakhloo and Ching (2019), the utilization of high technology is observed in merely 37% of manufacturing enterprises, in contrast to a 20% prevalence within the service sector. These statistics underscore a deficiency in coordination and a proactive stance among stakeholders within the context of this nation. Creed et al. (2024) explored interaction barriers identifed across a spectrum of impairments including physical, cognitive, visual, and auditory disabilities, but no empirical quantitative study was conducted. Julian et al. (2023) mentioned the most common reason of concerns is data security and privacy. This response may reveal a lack of understanding rather than genuine concern (Seo et al., 2018). However, they also did not conduct any empirical study.

According to a tech trend survey conducted by Oppotus, it was found that 58% of respondents in Malaysia were aware of Augmented Reality (AR) (Statista, 2023). However, despite this awareness, the adoption rate of augmented reality and virtual reality (VR) among users in Malaysia is reported to be relatively low, standing at a penetration rate of only 38.2% (Statista, 2023). This discrepancy between awareness and adoption rates may suggest either a low level of acceptance of the technology or potentially subpar business performance in promoting and implementing AR and VR solutions in Malaysia. Numerous research studies have been conducted on subjects related to purchase intent, the interplay of cognition, affect, and conation, the roles of consumer control, and augmented reality, each employing various conceptual theories (Teo & Wong, 2023). However, there are limited studies to discuss the implementation challenges in Malaysian manufacturing industry.

The above discussion elaborates the crucial importance of metaverse in different sectors along with the challenges of its worldwide implication. However, this study focus on the challenges of implementing metaverse in manufacturing firms perspective. Wide and vast implication of metaverse is expected in the near future, and this study will help to predict the challenges in advance, which will help to overcome the challenges. This paper examines the influence of implementation challenges on failure to implement metaverse in manufacturing firms in Malaysia.

LITERATURE REVIEW AND HYPOTHESES DEVELOPMENT

Technology, Organization, and Environment (TOE) Framework

The Technology, Organization, and Environment (TOE) framework is a theoretical model that explains technology adoption in organizations. It describes how the process of adopting and implementing technological innovations are influenced by the technological context, organizational context, and environmental context (Wiangkham, & Vongvit, 2023). In the context of metaverse technologies, the TOE framework can be applied as follows:

Technological Context refers to the internal and external technologies relevant to the firm. In the case of metaverse technologies, it includes the existing infrastructure, the state of metaverse technology, and the firm's technological capabilities. For instance, a firm's technological limitations are among the most significant barriers to implementing metaverse technology.

Organizational Context pertains to the characteristics and resources of the organization. It includes aspects like the size of the organization, the amount of slack resources available, the level of centralization or formalization, managerial structure, and employee attitudes towards change. Factors such as traditional organizational culture, lack of stakeholder commitment, and low perception of value by customers can pose challenges to the adoption of metaverse technologies.

Environmental Context refers to the business environment in which the firm operates. It includes the industry setting, market size, competition, and the regulatory environment. Issues like lack of governance and standardization, and integration challenges can impact the implementation of metaverse technologies.

Therefore, the TOE framework provides a holistic perspective on the adoption and implementation of metaverse technologies in organizations, recognizing that both internal and external factors are important in shaping technology adoption and use. It helps in identifying potential barriers and developing suitable strategies for successful implementation.

Technological Limitations and the Failure to Implement Metaverse

Technological limitations are the challenges that are faced while using technological methods, tools, or systems. Modern people rely on technology but because of its limitations they face some obstacles (e.g., low quality, cost, time waste, risk, barriers in communication).There are different kinds of limitations, some are technical and some are human generated. For example: hacking, low-quality of bandwidth, lag etc. are the limitations. Some limitations can be eliminated through development but perception of the users is difficult to grasp. In the case of the metaverse, the boundaries between real life and virtual life will no longer exist through avatars. However, it will require vast amounts of energy and resources (Allam et al., 2022). For instance: short battery coverage of below 60 minutes was one of the limitations of revolutionary google glass (Millana et al., 2016). Besides, high powered internet is needed for implementing metaverse but in Malaysia many remote areas are lacking internet, where other countries are using 5G. However, according to the United States, the 5G network will hamper national security because the network is provided by the Chinese suppliers Huawei (Friis & Lysne, 2021). On the other hand, European countries have positive experience with 3G and 4G networks provided by Huawei, and they are preparing to adopt 5G (Friis & Lysne, 2021). Thus, the security of the 5G network is very contradictory among countries, and a high powered internet is required to implement metaverse. Thus, low speed internet and electricity issues will be a barrier in the implementation of metaverse. Therefore, the revolutionary metaverse has positive contributions along with some constraints, which will result in a failure to its implementation.

H1: Technological limitations have significant impact on the failure to implement metaverse

Lack of Governance and Standardization and the Failure to Implement

Revolutionary innovations developed, performed and implemented through some standardized framework and governance (Yang, 2023). Lack of governance and standardization causes corruption, discrimination and unfair policies. Also, it makes an impact on the sustainability and efficiency of the innovations. Equivalently, an adequate governance and standardization in the virtual world will bring equality, democracy, transparency and accountability (Allam et al., 2022). Many revolutionary innovations failed because they lacked governance and standardization. For example- one of the reasons behind the failure of the google glass was privacy and security concerns because through it users can record (Martinez-Millana et al., 2016). Likewise, metaverse will have privacy and security issues. Also, it will be challenging to make a standardized virtual law for all the countries because of different cultures, norms and laws (Allam et al., 2022). Thus, there will be cultural shock, and underdeveloped and developing countries might face pressure to adopt cultures and laws of the developing countries. Moreover, technical standards are needed to establish metaverse, and the compatible standards ensure adequate governance (Yang, 2023). In the introduction phase of metaverse, standardized frameworks are limited, and stakeholders are hoping to have appropriate standards for having security and compatibility in the virtual world (Yang, 2023). Therefore, lack of governance and standardization will be one of the reasons of the failure in metaverse implementation, and compatible, formulated and secure standards is needed to govern the virtual world successfully.

H2: Lack of governance and standardization has significant impact on the failure to implement metaverse

Integration Challenges and the Failure to Implement Metaverse

In the modern competitive era technology integration is more important and challenging than ever, and it is considered as a company's competitive advantage (Akpan et al., 2021). After intensive effort of the research & development (R&D) department, companies launch a technology but if they fail to integrate properly, they will not be able to fulfill the targeted goals. Furthermore, the product's life cycle is reduced compared to past decades because of the numerous technological developments, and cherish in the market companies need to bear challenges while integrating technologies. For instance: for seamless user experience Microsoft generated the windows 95 operating system, and while establishing it went through a lot of challenges (Akpan et al., 2021). Technological integration is complex compared to leadership, project management, and maintaining organizational structure. First reason behind it is technological integration is new and people are not familiar with it, and secondly companies select the wrong technology which causes them to face integration challenges. Subsequently, Metaverse is a revolutionary technology but companies need to choose wisely while using it and a wrong decision will cause them to face immense loss. From the above discussion we can conclude that individual companies face challenges while adopting technology but the metaverse will be adopted vastly by different companies. Therefore, the integration will be more challenging because of high power technology, cost, lack of training & awareness, cultural differences, and differences in laws, which might be the cause of the failure to implement metaverse.

H3: Integration challenges has significant impact on the failure to implement metaverse

Poor Diffusion Through the Network and the Failure to Implement Metaverse

The information, data, and innovation expand worldwide via the network diffusion (Al-Taie & Kadry, 2017). The diffusion process conducts through 3 steps, which are sender, receiver, and medium. Furthermore, through diffusion innovations spread so rapidly. For example, telephones took a few decades to become renowned in the USA, whereas people became aware of facebook in a few years because of good network structure. Similarly, in the modern era one of the revolutionary innovations of Google Company was its google glass but one of the reasons behind its failure was poor diffusion (Nunes & Filho, 2018). Moreover, the diffusion process of a network can be terminated, if the information is defective. This intervention can be a barrier for information spreading of a new product, and customers may lose their trust from the innovation (Al-Taie & Kadry, 2017). Subsequently, under metaverse all things will be virtual, and it will be a big change. Thus, strong network diffusion is mandatory to spread the innovation. For instance, as stated above, in 1992, Neal Stephenson first invented this word of metaverse in his science fiction but after around 3 and half decades people still are not familiar with the word. Therefore, poor diffusion is one of the limitations behind the lag of implementing a new innovation, and this will be a limitation of the implementation of the metaverse as well.

H4: Poor diffusion through the network has significant impact on the failure to implement metaverse

Traditional Organization Culture and the Failure to Implement Metaverse

Under traditional organizational culture the power goes to the upper management, and the organization maintains a chain of command like a pyramid. Here the main decisions come from the upper level (e.g., CEO), and then mid-level managers give instructions to meet the goals that were made by the upper level. It creates a stable work environment for the employees, and low risk associated with this type of culture. Whereas, modern organization culture has flexibility according to the need. Furthermore, generally in technological innovations the developing countries adopt lately, and the developed countries adopt fast because of their modern organizational culture (Dwivedi et al., 2022). Most organizations follow hierarchical or traditional culture in the developing and underdeveloped countries, and for this reason they are lacking behind adopting new changes (Dwivedi et al., 2022). For example: one of the reasons behind the collapse of the brand Nokia was traditional organizational culture, and this was an obstacle in its technological adoption (Peltonen, 2019). Therefore, Metaverse is a revolutionary technology which needs a lot of flexibility to adopt, and will be difficult to operate under the traditional organizational culture. In the modern era of technology organizations need to discard traditional culture, and should endorse modern culture to adopt innovative technology like metaverse.

H5: Traditional organization culture has significant impact on the failure to implement metaverse

Lack of Stakeholder Commitment and the Failure to Implement Metaverse

Stakeholders are directly or indirectly affected by the company's performance, and the stakeholders' commitment refers to the amount of involvement, support and dedication the stakeholders have for the company's success (Hossain et al., 2022). For the company's success, stakeholders' commitment plays an important role because it verifies whether the stakeholders are giving their time, effort, resources or not. Furthermore, according to some studies, lack of stakeholders' commitment leads to failure of the company's project (Hossain et al., 2022). Moreover, because of it, the organization faces many challenges, for example: dilemma in decision making, less support, misleading & misunderstanding, inflexibility, low motivation and so on. According to Bag et al. (2023), metaverse will play a vital role in the supply chain management but lack of stakeholders' commitment will be a big barrier in adopting it like any other new technology. In other words, a company's flexibility relies on how supportive the stakeholders are, and low support indicates low commitment which causes failure in the organization's project. Also, to implement metaverse a huge amount of expense needs to be borne by the stakeholders along with time, dedication and other resources (Bag et al., 2023). Moreover, an organization with low stakeholder commitment will not be able to run for a longer period because they will lose their guidance (Sheth, 2020). Therefore, stakeholders' commitment is crucial for adopting the metaverse.

H6: Lack of stakeholder commitment has significant impact on the failure to implement metaverse

Lack of Collaboration and the Failure to Implement Metaverse

Collaboration means when multiple stakeholders work together by sharing resources, knowledge, information, and other things to achieve a common goal (Hossain et al., 2022). Furthermore, collaborative works with good conflict or effective discussion between the team members will give a more optimal outcome, compared to individual work. However, maintaining collaboration is a most difficult task because people are different and their perceptions are different as well (Han, 2022). In consequence, teammates face the lack of collaboration, and to adopt any new changes a lot of collaboration is required in an organization. Subsequently, because of this issue the organizations face problems while implementing any new technology. Firstly, top management support is crucial for adopting a new technology (Hossain et al., 2024). Secondly, before collaborative technology adoption the companies need to ensure collaborative work practices in their organization. Similarly, the revolutionary metaverse needs stakeholders' collaboration to implement it worldwide because of its complexity, expensiveness, cultural differences, and lack of awareness. Thus, lack of collaboration while implementing metaverse will be one of the reasons behind its collapse.

H7: Lack of collaboration has significant impact on the failure to implement metaverse

Low Perceived Value by Customers and the Failure to Implement Metaverse

Perceived value refers to the monetary value that customers are willing to pay for a good or service (Sweeney & Soutar, 2001). Customer perceived value comes from two factors: the benefits that they get from the product, and the amount they pay for it. Higher perceived value means greater satisfaction compared to expectation, and the customers feel delighted during those scenarios. Furthermore, a perfect balance between expectation and actual benefit makes the customers satisfied. On the other hand, low perceived value indicates lower satisfaction compared to expectation, and during those situations the customer feels unsatisfied (Mainardes & Freitas, 2023). Subsequently, no product can be established for the long run without satisfying customers' perceived value. As stated above, metaverse has many limitations (e.g., security, high expense, technical issues, lack of awareness), and because of these limitations the customer might not feel the importance of metaverse. If the customers do not feel the worth of it, then there is no potential reason to establish it. For instance: Google glass was not nice-looking for some customers, and it was one of the reasons behind its failure (Martinez-Millana et al., 2016). Therefore, lack of awareness about metaverse or these above-mentioned limitations might cause low perceived value by the customers, which will make them dissatisfied. Eventually, dissatisfaction by the customers will be a cause of its failure.

H8 Low perceived value by customers has significant impact on the failure to implement metaverse

METHODOLOGY

The study applies positivism philosophy, quantitative survey method, cross-sectional time horizon and deductive approach. Data was collected through structured questionnaire to get more data in a quick time frame. The items were adapted from the previous studies and applied a five-point likert scale. Technological limitations (TL) four items, lack of governance and standardization (LGS) four items, integration challenges (IC) four items, poor diffusion through the network (PN) five items, traditional organization culture (TOC) three items, lack of stakeholder commitment (LSC) three items, lack of collaboration (LC) four items, low perception of value by customers (LVC) three items, and failure to metaverse technology implementation (FMTI) five items were adapted from Dwivedi et al. (2022), Mozumder et al. (2022), Queiroz et al. (2023).

Three (3) academicians and three (3) industry players checked the item's relevancy and quality. The sentence structures of the items were revised in accordance with the feedback provided by experts and

Figure 1. Conceptual framework

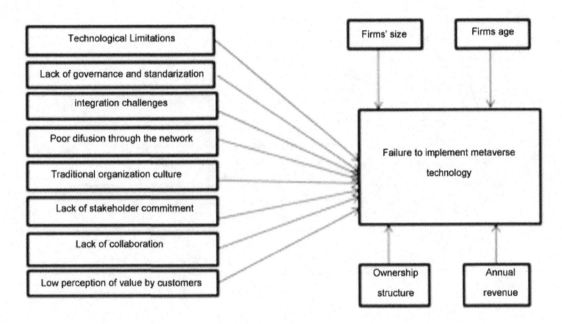

respondents. The researchers considered dropping few questions to ensure relevancy of the items with the context.

The study is of a cross-sectional nature as data was obtained at a singular point in time. A pilot study was performed consists 30 respondents. The unit of analysis was individuals consisting top and middle management officers including supervisors who have supreme knowledge about new technology implementation of the firms.

The non- probability sampling method and convenience sampling technique were employed as the sample frame was not available. By using the G-power software, based on the eight (8) predictors in this study's framework, 160 sample sizes are suggested (Figure 2). 245 responses were received after distributing questionnaire through a Google form link in various sources such as social media groups of manufacturer and email sending personally. 240 questionnaires were found usable for final analysis.

RESEARCH FINDINGS

Non-Response Bias (NRB) and Common Method Bias (CMB)

This study employs the Wallace & Cooke (1990) approach to examine NRB. NRB guarantees that the survey accurately reflects the desired study population. The researchers analysed the mean and standard deviation for the first 30 and final 30 respondents. They found no significant differences between the two groups, confirming the absence of NRB in the study.

Based on (Kock, 2015), if all VIFs in the inner model resulting from a full collinearity test are equal to or lower than 5.0, the model can consider free of CMB. The model is free from CMB because the VIFs are lower than 5.0 (Table 5).

Figure 2. Sample size determinations using G-power software

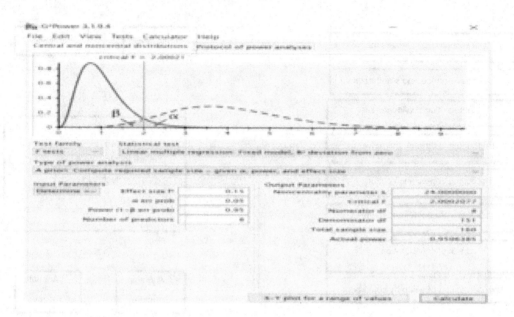

Demographics Data

Table 1 showed that majority of the responses received from Food, Beverage and Tobacco firms (75). Most of the companies are 1-10 years old (142), less than 50 employees (145) are working, annual revenue Not exceeding 10 million BDT (141) and Private-owned firms (179). Moreover, majority respondents are male (165), 26-31 years old (60), and Bachelor degree completed (83).

Measurement Model

Convergent Validity

Convergent validity, as defined by Bagozzi et al. (1981), pertains to the degree of correlation among multiple indicators or measures of the same construct. The calculation of the Average Variance Extracted (AVE) involves squaring the loading of each indicator on a construct and computing the mean value, following the approach outlined by Hair et al. (2019). Internal consistency, or reliability, is assessed using Cronbach's alpha coefficient, a measure introduced by Cronbach (1951) to evaluate the reliability of a set of survey items. Composite reliability, akin to Cronbach's alpha, serves as a gauge of internal consistency in scale items, as proposed by Netemeyer et al. (2003).

The outcomes presented in Table 2 demonstrate that all the items' except LGS and PN's Average Variance Extracted (AVE) values surpass the 0.5 thresholds recommended by Hair et al. (2019). Additionally, constructs except LGS's Cronbach's alpha and composite reliability exceed the 0.7 threshold, as suggested by Hair et al. (2019). These findings indicate that the measures exhibit acceptable reliability and high internal consistency, supporting the convergent validity of the study.

Table 1. Demographic data (n = 240)

Firms characteristics	Categories	Frequency
Type of firm	Food, Beverage and Tobacco	75
	Chemicals	14
	Fabricated metals	1
	Plastic	5
	Electrical & Electronics	29
	Machinery and Equipment	8
	Non-Metallic Mineral	6
	Transport, vehicle & equipment	8
	Rubber	3
	Basic metals	1
	Paper, printing and publishing	6
	Medical, precision and optical instruments, watches & clocks	6
	Textile, wearing apparel and leather	16
	Wood and wood products, excluding furniture	4
	Recycling	5
	Office, accounting and computing machinery	8
	Furniture	9
	Others	36
	Total	240
Firm age	Less than 1 year	17
	1 – 10 years	142
	11 - 20 years	41
	21-30 years	18
	Above 30 years	22
	Total	240
Firm size	Less than 50	145
	50–99	36
	100–299	17
	300–999	10
	1,000–1,999	11
	2,000–4,999	9
	5,000 or more	12
	Total	240
Annual revenue	Not exceeding 10 million BDT	141
	Between 11 -20 million BDT	49
	Between 21 - 30 million BDT	23
	Between 31 -40 million BDT	8
	More than 40 million BDT	19
	Total	240

continued on following page

Table 1. Continued

Firms characteristics	Categories	Frequency
Ownership structure	State-owned firms	25
	Private-owned firms	179
	Foreign-invested firms	36
	Total	240
Respondents characteristics	Categories	Frequency
Gender	Male	165
	Female	64
	Prefer not to say	11
Age	20- 25 years	42
	26 - 31 years	60
	32 - 37 years	47
	38-43 years	49
	More than 43 Years	42
Education	No formal education	12
	Vocational	7
	Foundation	6
	SPM	10
	STPM	3
	Diploma	42
	Bachelor	83
	Masters	63
	PhD	14

Discriminant validity

Fornell & Larcker (1981) criteria and Heterotrait-Monotrait (HTMT) ratio were applied to confirm discriminant validity. Table 3 demonstrates that the square root of AVE is higher than its correlation with other variables, confirming discriminant validity.

Henseler et al. (2015) proposed the HTMT method, which confirms discriminant validity between each pair of constructs if the correlation values are less than 0.90. Table 4 below shows that the HTMT values are below the threshold value, thus, discriminant validity established.

Structural Model Assessment

Hair et al. (2019) outlined a systematic approach comprising six steps for evaluating the structural model through Partial Least Squares Structural Equation Modeling (PLS-SEM). The initial phase involves addressing latent collinearity issues. Subsequently, the examination of the significance and relevance of relationships within the structural model is undertaken. This is followed by the assessment of the variance explained by the dependent variable (R^2), the effect size (f^2), and the predictive relevance (Q^2predict). Finally, an evaluation of the corresponding t-values of the path coefficients is conducted

Figure 3. The measurement model

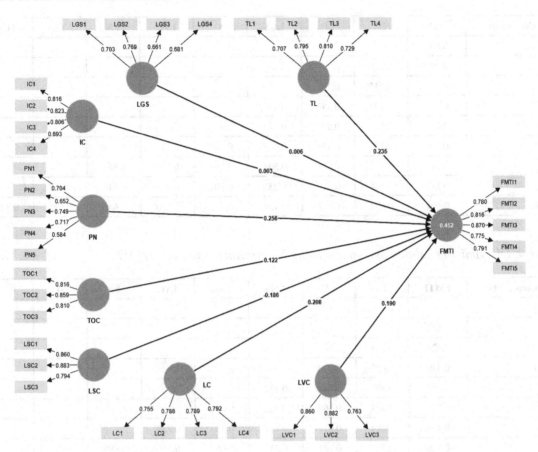

Table 2. Convergent validity

Constructs	Cronbach's alpha	Composite reliability	Average variance extracted
FMTI	0.866	0.903	0.651
IC	0.792	0.866	0.618
LC	0.788	0.862	0.610
LGS	0.668	0.797	0.496
LSC	0.802	0.883	0.717
LVC	0.784	0.875	0.700
PN	0.713	0.813	0.467
TL	0.758	0.846	0.580
TOC	0.773	0.868	0.687

through bootstrapping, employing 5,000 resamples with a two-tailed test at a significance level of 0.05. The results encompassing R^2, f^2, inner and outer model's Variance Inflation Factor (VIF), and Q^2predict are presented in Table 5 below.

Table 3. Discriminant validity assessment using Fornell and Larcker criteria

Constructs	FMTI	IC	LC	LGS	LSC	LVC	PN	TL	TOC
FMTI	0.807								
IC	0.483	0.786							
LC	0.525	0.545	0.781						
LGS	0.353	0.497	0.493	0.704					
LSC	0.434	0.659	0.598	0.403	0.847				
LVC	0.491	0.507	0.453	0.408	0.540	0.837			
PN	0.562	0.674	0.611	0.508	0.708	0.553	0.684		
TL	0.514	0.566	0.449	0.232	0.502	0.421	0.513	0.761	
TOC	0.505	0.689	0.611	0.453	0.721	0.510	0.643	0.522	0.829

Table 4. Discriminant validity assessment using Heterotrait-Monotrait (HTMT)

Constructs	FMTI	IC	LC	LGS	LSC	LVC	PN	TL	TOC
FMTI									
IC	0.577								
LC	0.626	0.688							
LGS	0.440	0.697	0.670						
LSC	0.513	0.828	0.749	0.552					
LVC	0.593	0.634	0.569	0.562	0.679				
PN	0.706	0.894	0.812	0.740	0.832	0.737			
TL	0.626	0.737	0.581	0.355	0.653	0.556	0.699		
TOC	0.608	0.879	0.783	0.637	0.814	0.649	0.862	0.686	

Table 5. Quality of the structural model

Endogenous Variables	R^2	Q^2predict	Exogenous Variables	f^2	VIF
FMTI	0.433	0.379	IC	0.000	2.639
			LC	0.040	2.001
			LGS	0.000	1.598
			LSC	0.022	2.846
			LVC	0.040	1.636
			PN	0.044	2.742
			TL	0.060	1.673
			TOC	0.010	2.736

The coefficient R^2 signifies the proportion of variance in the endogenous variable attributed to all exogenous variables. Ranging from 0 to 1, a higher R^2 indicates enhanced predictive accuracy. The conventional benchmarks for R^2 values categorize them as weak (0.25), moderate (0.50), and substantial

(0.75) levels of predictive accuracy (Hair et al., 2019). In this study, the model prediction exhibited close to moderate, as evidenced by an R^2 value of 0.433.

Assessing the effect size of predictor constructs using Cohen's f^2 (Cohen, 2013) provides insight into their relative impact on an endogenous construct. Cohen defines effect sizes as high (0.35), medium (0.15), and small (0.02) based on f^2 values. The current study's results, presented in Table 5, indicate small effect sizes for the exogenous variables.

The examination of collinearity in Table 5 reveals no multicollinearity concerns in the current study. Both inner model's Variance Inflation Factor (VIF) and outer model's VIF values fall below the threshold of 5.

In PLS version 4, Q^2-Predicts systematically remove and predict each data point of indicators within the reflective measurement model of the endogenous construct. This test evaluates the predictive capabilities of items related to endogenous variables in the structural model. As indicated in Table 5, a Q^2-Predict value exceeding 0 signifies the model's predictive capacity (Hair et al., 2019), establishing a higher level of predictive relevance in the study.

The researchers evaluated the association between constructs in the structural model based on the p-value and t-statistics value. The hypothesized relationship was perceived as significantly accepted when p values were less than 0.05 and T statistics were above 1.96 (Hair et al., 2019). Table 6 indicates that LC, LVC, PN, TL have a significant relationship with FMTI and IC, LGS, LSC, TOC have an insignificant relationship with FMTI.

Control Variables

Table 7 showed that firm age, firm size, annual revenue, ownership structure evidenced no influence in failure to metaverse technology implementation. Firm age, size, revenue, and ownership structure may not directly correlate with readiness to adopt emerging technologies like the metaverse. Malaysian manufacturing firms of varying ages, sizes, and revenue levels may demonstrate similar levels of readiness or resistance to adopting metaverse technology based on factors such as organizational culture, leadership vision, and technological capabilities.

While larger, more established firms have greater financial resources and organizational capacity, this does not necessarily translate into a greater willingness or ability to invest in metaverse technology implementation. Smaller or newer firms demonstrate agility and flexibility in adopting new technolo-

Table 6. Path coefficient result for hypotheses

Paths	Beta	T values	P values	Results
TL -> FMTI	0.235	2.995	0.003	Significant
LGS -> FMTI	0.006	0.091	0.927	Insignificant
IC -> FMTI	0.003	0.036	0.971	Insignificant
PN -> FMTI	0.256	2.840	0.005	Significant
TOC -> FMTI	0.122	1.262	0.207	Insignificant
LSC -> FMTI	-0.186	1.770	0.077	Insignificant
LC -> FMTI	0.208	2.716	0.007	Significant
LVC -> FMTI	0.190	2.121	0.034	Significant

Figure 4. The structural model

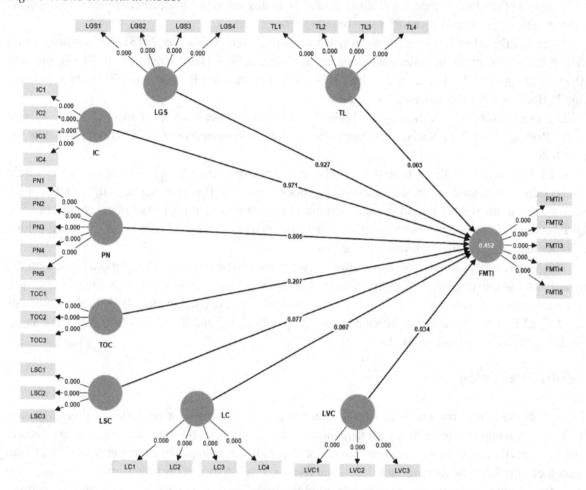

gies, while larger firms face internal barriers such as bureaucracy, inertia, or resistance to change (Polas et al., 2022).

The failure to implement metaverse technology in Malaysian manufacturing firms influenced more by external market dynamics and competitive pressures than internal firm characteristics. Factors such as market demand, industry trends, regulatory environment, and competitive landscape may play a more significant role in shaping technology adoption decisions and implementation outcomes (Hossain et al., 2023).

Table 7. Path coefficient result for control variables

Paths	Beta	T values	P values	Result
Firm age -> FMTI	-0.003	0.055	0.956	No influence
Firm size -> FMTI	-0.020	0.340	0.734	No influence
Annual revenue -> FMTI	0.065	1.060	0.289	No influence
Ownership structure -> FMTI	0.035	0.655	0.512	No influence

DISCUSSION

Result for hypothesis 1 evidenced that technological limitations have significant relationship with failure to metaverse technology implementation. The successful implementation of metaverse technology requires robust infrastructure, including high-speed internet connectivity, powerful hardware, and reliable servers. Technological limitations such as inadequate internet access, outdated hardware, or insufficient server capacity can hinder the performance and scalability of metaverse platforms, leading to user dissatisfaction and limited adoption (Wan et al., 2023). Metaverse technology often relies on interoperability across various devices, operating systems, and software applications. Technological limitations related to compatibility, such as platform-specific restrictions or lack of standardized protocols, can create barriers to seamless integration and interaction within the metaverse environment, undermining user experience and adoption. Technological limitations in implementing robust security measures, such as encryption, authentication, and data protection protocols, can compromise user trust and confidence in the safety and privacy of the metaverse environment, hindering adoption and usage (Dincelli & Yayla, 2022).

Result for hypothesis 2 evidenced that lack of governance and standardization has insignificant relationship with failure to metaverse technology implementation. Malaysian manufacturing firms may not be at the forefront of adopting advanced digital technologies like the metaverse due to various factors such as limited awareness, resource constraints, and focus on traditional manufacturing processes (Hossain et al., 2023). As a result, the absence of governance and standardization specific to metaverse technology may not directly contribute to implementation failures since these firms may not be actively pursuing such initiatives. Malaysian manufacturing firms prioritize investments in other areas of technology that are more directly related to their immediate business needs and objectives (Lada et al., 2023). For example, they may focus on upgrading production machinery, improving supply chain management systems, or implementing enterprise resource planning (ERP) software. In this context, the absence of governance and standardization for metaverse technology not be perceived as a critical factor affecting implementation success. Malaysia need to develop specific regulations or policies governing metaverse technology implementation in manufacturing firms (Ooi et al., 2023). While the absence of governance and standardization could potentially lead to challenges such as interoperability issues or data privacy concerns, the impact may be minimal if there are no explicit regulatory requirements or industry standards mandating compliance with metaverse technology.

Result for hypothesis 3 evidenced that integration challenges has insignificant relationship with failure to metaverse technology implementation. The current level of interconnectedness and digitalization in Malaysian manufacturing firms relatively low compared to firms in more advanced economies (Hossain et al., 2023). Consequently, the need for integrating metaverse technology with existing systems and processes may not be as pressing, and integration challenges may not be perceived as significant obstacles to implementation failure. The organizational readiness for digital transformation and innovation in Malaysia manufacturing firms vary. Some firms lack the internal capabilities and change management processes required to effectively integrate metaverse solutions into their operations (Lee et al., 2024). However, the impact of integration challenges on implementation failure can be limited if firms are not actively pursuing metaverse initiatives or if they are focusing on other technology priorities.

Result for hypothesis 4 evidenced that poor diffusion through the network has significant relationship with failure to metaverse technology implementation. Poor diffusion through the network implies that information about metaverse technology and its potential benefits may not reach key stakeholders within Malaysia manufacturing firms (Yao et al., 2024). If decision-makers, employees, and other relevant parties are unaware or do not fully understand the concept and value proposition of metaverse technology, they may be hesitant to invest resources or support its implementation. Inefficient diffusion through the network may result in a lack of knowledge sharing and collaboration among different departments or units within manufacturing firms. Without effective communication channels and mechanisms for sharing information about metaverse technology, opportunities for learning, experimentation, and innovation may be missed, leading to implementation failures.

Result for hypothesis 5 evidenced that traditional organization culture has insignificant relationship with failure to metaverse technology implementation. Malaysia manufacturing firms have a traditional organizational culture that prioritizes stability, hierarchy, and adherence to established practices (Adinew, 2023). However, if these firms have not yet embraced digital transformation or advanced technological solutions, the influence of traditional culture on metaverse technology implementation may be minimal. In such cases, failure to adopt metaverse technology may stem from factors unrelated to organizational culture, such as resource constraints or lack of awareness. While traditional organizational cultures value stability and continuity, they can also foster openness to innovation and adaptation. Malaysian manufacturing firms with a progressive mindset actively seek opportunities to leverage emerging technologies like the metaverse to enhance their operations and gain a competitive edge. In such organizations, traditional culture not impedes metaverse technology implementation but rather encourage exploration and experimentation. Organizations with a traditional culture can still demonstrate adaptability and flexibility in embracing new technologies. Malaysia manufacturing firms recognize the need to evolve and modernize their operations in response to changing market conditions, even if they maintain traditional cultural values. In such cases, organizational culture may not be a significant barrier to metaverse technology implementation.

Result for hypothesis 6 evidenced that lack of stakeholder commitment has insignificant relationship with failure to metaverse technology implementation. Stakeholders within Malaysian manufacturing firms may have limited awareness and understanding of metaverse technology and its potential applications. As a result, their lack of commitment may stem from a lack of familiarity with the technology rather than a deliberate resistance to its implementation. In such cases, failure to implement metaverse technology may be more closely linked to knowledge gaps or educational needs rather than stakeholder commitment. Malaysian manufacturing firms face resource constraints in terms of finances, technical expertise, and infrastructure (Lee et al., 2023). The lack of stakeholder commitment to metaverse technology implementation can be a reflection of these resource limitations rather than a fundamental opposition to the technology (Hossain et al., 2023). Stakeholders may be willing to support technology initiatives in principle but lack the resources to allocate towards implementation efforts. Stakeholder commitment to technology implementation can be influenced by competing organizational priorities and strategic objectives. Malaysian manufacturing firms may have limited capacity to invest in metaverse technology due to other pressing business needs or market challenges. In such cases, the lack of stakeholder commitment can be driven by strategic considerations rather than inherent resistance to the technology itself. Stakeholders may perceive metaverse technology as risky or uncertain, particularly if they are unfamiliar with its potential benefits and drawbacks.

Result for hypothesis 7 evidenced that the implementation of metaverse technology, a virtual world where users can communicate with each other in a computer-generated environment, can be significantly influenced by a lack of collaboration. A lack of collaboration can lead to technological limitations within an organization. Without effective collaboration, it can be challenging to overcome these limitations, which are among the most significant barriers to implementing metaverse technology (Bag et al., 2023).

Successful implementation of any new technology requires commitment from all stakeholders. This includes employees, management, and customers. If there is a lack of collaboration, it can be challenging to secure this commitment, which can lead to a failure in the implementation process.

Result for hypothesis 8 evidenced that low perception of value by customers has a significant relationship with failure to metaverse technology implementation. The success of any technology depends on its adoption by users. If customers perceive low value in the metaverse, they are less likely to use it, leading to low user adoption rates (Hadi et al., 2024). Businesses invest in new technologies like the metaverse expecting a return on their investment. If customers perceive low value, they are less likely to engage with the metaverse, affecting the ROI. Customer perception can influence the direction of innovation and development. If customers perceive low value, it may discourage further innovation and development in metaverse technology. If a company's metaverse implementation is perceived as low value by customers, it can negatively impact the company's brand reputation. Metaverse technology can provide a competitive advantage to businesses (Gauttier et al., 2024). However, if customers perceive low value, this advantage is diminished

Theoretical Implications

The current study extends Technology-Organization-Environment (TOE) theory. Investigating the constraints of implementing the metaverse allows for a deeper understanding of the technological characteristics specific to this innovative domain. The implementation of metaverse technology requires organizations to develop new capabilities, processes, and structures to leverage its potential effectively. Investigating the constraints of metaverse implementation within organizations sheds light on organizational readiness factors such as leadership support, change management practices, employee skills, and cultural alignment. Understanding how these organizational factors interact with the unique characteristics of the metaverse can provide valuable insights into the adoption process and implementation challenges. The metaverse operates within a dynamic and multifaceted environmental context that includes regulatory frameworks, industry standards, market dynamics, and societal trends. Investigating the constraints of metaverse implementation extends the TOE framework by exploring how external environmental factors influence adoption decisions and implementation strategies. This includes considerations such as legal and regulatory barriers, market competition, ecosystem partnerships, and user preferences, which shape the adoption trajectory of metaverse technologies within organizations.

Practical Implications

This study contributes in practice by highlighting the importance and significance of metaverse in different sectors (e.g., education, industry, entertainment) and identifying eight main barriers that can be faced while implementing metaverse. Although all the identified constraints are crucial, the findings provide some suggestions to focus on more on technological limitations, poor diffusion through the network, and lack of collaboration and low perception of value by customers.

Understanding the constraints can help managers develop more effective strategic plans for Metaverse implementation. By identifying barriers early on, managers can adjust their plans to mitigate risks and allocate resources more efficiently. Managers can allocate resources more effectively by understanding which constraints are most significant. This might involve investing in employee training, upgrading infrastructure, or partnering with external experts to overcome specific challenges. Identifying constraints allows managers to assess potential risks associated with Metaverse implementation and develop risk management strategies accordingly. This might involve creating contingency plans, securing insurance coverage, or implementing robust cybersecurity measures. Managers can use insights from examining constraints to inform their decisions about which Metaverse technologies to adopt. For example, if connectivity issues are identified as a significant constraint, managers might prioritize technologies that are less reliant on stable internet connections.

Implementing the Metaverse often requires significant changes in organizational culture, processes, and workflows. By understanding the constraints, managers can develop change management strategies to minimize resistance and facilitate smooth transitions. Organizations need to maintain flexible culture, rather than traditional culture. Subsequently, the stakeholders (e.g., customers, employees, suppliers) need to work together to adopt metaverse.

Furthermore, the IT facilities need to be more developed to mitigate technical problems, and network diffusion. Thus, the barriers of metaverse implementation can be diminished with a collaborative approach between stakeholders from different sectors, and it will make their work more efficient.

Limitations and Future Research Directions

Despite significant theoretical and empirical contributions, this study acknowledges a few limitations. First, a single survey method can cause CMB issues. However, statistical post-hoc procedures were taken into account to eradicate this issue. Secondly, this study examines a single counry (Malaysia) and single industry (Manufacturing). Service firms from other regions can be explored. Thirdly, this study used single method and cross-sectional quantitative survey. Other researchers can use comparative, qualitative, mixed or longitudinal studies to enhance generability. Other moderating or mediating variables, such as resource commitment, innovating behaviour of firms etc., can be considered with this model.

REFERENCES

Adinew, Y. (2023). A comparative study on motivational strategies, organizational culture, and climate in public and private institutions. *Current Psychology (New Brunswick, N.J.)*, 1–23.

Akpan, I. J., Soopramanien, D., & Kwak, D. H. (2021). Cutting-edge technologies for small business and innovation in the era of COVID-19 global health pandemic. *Journal of Small Business and Entrepreneurship*, *33*(6), 607–617. doi:10.1080/08276331.2020.1799294

Al-Taie, M. Z., & Kadry, S. (2017). Information Diffusion in Social Networks. In *Python for Graph and Network Analysis. Advanced Information and Knowledge Processing*. Springer. doi:10.1007/978-3-319-53004-8_8

Allam, Z., Sharifi, A., Bibri, S. E., Jones, D. S., & Krogstie, J. (2022). The metaverse as a virtual form of smart cities: Opportunities and challenges for environmental, economic, and social sustainability in urban futures. *Smart Cities*, *5*(3), 771–801. doi:10.3390/smartcities5030040

Bagozzi, R. P., Yi, Y., & Phillips, L. W. (1991). Assessing construct validity in organizational research. *Administrative Science Quarterly*, *36*(3), 421–458. doi:10.2307/2393203

Cohen, J., Cohen, P., West, S. G., & Aiken, L. S. (2013). *Applied multiple regression/correlation analysis for the behavioral sciences*. Routledge. doi:10.4324/9780203774441

Creed, C., Al-Kalbani, M., Theil, A., Sarcar, S., & Williams, I. (2024). Inclusive AR/VR: Accessibility barriers for immersive technologies. *Universal Access in the Information Society, 23*(1), 59–73. doi:10.1007/s10209-023-00969-0

Cronbach, L. J. (1951). Coefficient alpha and the internal structure of tests. *psychometrika, 16*(3), 297-334.

Dincelli, E., & Yayla, A. (2022). Immersive virtual reality in the age of the Metaverse: A hybrid-narrative review based on the technology affordance perspective. *The Journal of Strategic Information Systems, 31*(2), 101717. doi:10.1016/j.jsis.2022.101717

Dwivedi, Y. K., Hughes, L., Baabdullah, A. M., Ribeiro-Navarrete, S., Giannakis, M., Al-Debei, M. M., Dennehy, D., Metri, B., Buhalis, D., Cheung, C. M. K., Conboy, K., Doyle, R., Dubey, R., Dutot, V., Felix, R., Goyal, D. P., Gustafsson, A., Hinsch, C., Jebabli, I., & Wamba, S. F. (2022). Metaverse beyond the hype: Multidisciplinary perspectives on emerging challenges, opportunities, and agenda for research, practice and policy. *International Journal of Information Management, 66*, 102542. doi:10.1016/j.ijinfomgt.2022.102542

Fernández-Caramés, T. M., & Fraga-Lamas, P. (2024). Forging the Industrial Metaverse-Where Industry 5.0, Augmented and Mixed Reality, IIoT, Opportunistic Edge Computing and Digital Twins Meet. *arXiv preprint arXiv:2403.11312*.

Fornell, C., & Larcker, D. F. (1981). Evaluating structural equation models with unobservable variables and measurement error. *JMR, Journal of Marketing Research, 18*(1), 39–50. doi:10.1177/002224378101800104

Friis, K., & Lysne, O. (2021). Huawei, 5G and security: Technological limitations and political responses. *Development and Change, 52*(5), 1174–1195. doi:10.1111/dech.12680

Gauttier, S., Simouri, W., & Milliat, A. (2024). When to enter the metaverse: Business leaders offer perspectives. *The Journal of Business Strategy, 45*(1), 2–9. doi:10.1108/JBS-08-2022-0149

Ghobakhloo, M., & Ching, N. T. (2019). Adoption of digital technologies of smart manufacturing in SMEs. *Journal of Industrial Information Integration, 16*, 100107. doi:10.1016/j.jii.2019.100107

Hadi, R., Melumad, S., & Park, E. S. (2024). The Metaverse: A new digital frontier for consumer behavior. *Journal of Consumer Psychology, 34*(1), 142–166. doi:10.1002/jcpy.1356

Hair, J. F., Risher, J. J., Sarstedt, M., & Ringle, C. M. (2019). When to use and how to report the results of PLS-SEM. *European Business Review, 31*(1), 2–24. doi:10.1108/EBR-11-2018-0203

Han, E., Miller, M. R., Ram, N., Nowak, K. L., & Bailenson, J. N. (2022, May). Understanding group behavior in virtual reality: A large-scale, longitudinal study in the metaverse. In *72nd Annual International Communication Association Conference*, Paris, France.

Henseler, J., Ringle, C. M., & Sarstedt, M. (2015). A new criterion for assessing discriminant validity in variance-based structural equation modeling. *Journal of the Academy of Marketing Science, 43*(1), 115–135. doi:10.1007/s11747-014-0403-8

Hossain, M. I., Kumar, J., Islam, M. T., & Valeri, M. (2023). The interplay among paradoxical leadership, industry 4.0 technologies, organisational ambidexterity, strategic flexibility and corporate sustainable performance in manufacturing SMEs of Malaysia. *European Business Review*. doi:10.1108/EBR-04-2023-0109

Hossain, M. I., Ong, T. S., Tabash, M. I., & Teh, B. H. (2024). The panorama of corporate environmental sustainability and green values: Evidence of Bangladesh. *Environment, Development and Sustainability*, *26*(1), 1033–1059. doi:10.1007/s10668-022-02748-y

Hossain, M. I., San Ong, T., Teh, B. H., Said, R. M., & Siow, M. L. (2022). Nexus of Stakeholder Integration, Green Investment, Green Technology Adoption and Environmental Sustainability Practices: Evidence from Bangladesh Textile SMEs. *Pertanika Journal of Social Science & Humanities*, *30*(1). doi:10.47836/pjssh.30.1.14

Hossain, M. I., Teh, B. H., Dorasamy, M., Tabash, M. I., & Ong, T. S. (2023, May). Ethical Leadership, Green HRM Practices and Environmental Performance of Manufacturing SMEs at Selangor, Malaysia: Moderating Role of Green Technology Adoption. In *International Scientific Conference on Business and Economics* (pp. 85-104). Cham: Springer Nature Switzerland. 10.1007/978-3-031-42511-0_6

Julian, H. L. C., Chung, T., & Wang, Y. (2023). Adoption of Metaverse in South East Asia: Vietnam, Indonesia, Malaysia. In *Strategies and Opportunities for Technology in the Metaverse World* (pp. 196–234). IGI Global. doi:10.4018/978-1-6684-5732-0.ch012

Kock, N. (2015). Common method bias in PLS-SEM: A full collinearity assessment approach. [ijec]. *International Journal of e-Collaboration*, *11*(4), 1–10. doi:10.4018/ijec.2015100101

Lada, S., Chekima, B., Karim, M. R. A., Fabeil, N. F., Ayub, M. S., Amirul, S. M., Ansar, R., Bouteraa, M., Fook, L. M., & Zaki, H. O. (2023). Determining factors related to artificial intelligence (AI) adoption among Malaysia's small and medium-sized businesses. *Journal of Open Innovation*, *9*(4), 100144. doi:10.1016/j.joitmc.2023.100144

Lee, K. L., Teong, C. X., Alzoubi, H. M., Alshurideh, M. T., Khatib, M. E., & Al-Gharaibeh, S. M. (2024). Digital supply chain transformation: The role of smart technologies on operational performance in manufacturing industry. *International Journal of Engineering Business Management*, *16*, 18479790241234986. doi:10.1177/18479790241234986

Lee, K. L., Wong, S. Y., Alzoubi, H. M., Al Kurdi, B., Alshurideh, M. T., & El Khatib, M. (2023). Adopting smart supply chain and smart technologies to improve operational performance in manufacturing industry. *International Journal of Engineering Business Management*, *15*, 18479790231200614. doi:10.1177/18479790231200614

Li, J. (2022). Impact of Metaverse cultural communication on the mental health of international students in China: Highlighting effects of healthcare anxiety and cyberchondria. *American Journal of Health Behavior*, *46*(6), 809–820. doi:10.5993/AJHB.46.6.21 PMID:36721290

Mainardes, E. W., & Freitas, N. P. D. (2023). The effects of perceived value dimensions on customer satisfaction and loyalty: A comparison between traditional banks and fintechs. *International Journal of Bank Marketing*, *41*(3), 641–662. doi:10.1108/IJBM-10-2022-0437

Mammadova, A. (2023). *Digital big-bang Metaverse: opportunities and threats* [Master's thesis, Università Ca' Foscari Venezia]. http://dspace.unive.it/handle/10579/25766

Martinez-Millana, A., Bayo-Monton, J. L., Lizondo, A., Fernandez-Llatas, C., & Traver, V. (2016). Evaluation of Google Glass technical limitations on their integration in medical systems. *Sensors (Basel)*, *16*(12), 2142. doi:10.3390/s16122142 PMID:27983691

Mourtzis, D. (2023). The Metaverse in Industry 5.0: A Human-Centric Approach towards Personalized Value Creation. *Encyclopedia*, *3*(3), 1105–1120. doi:10.3390/encyclopedia3030080

Mozumder, M. A. I., Sheeraz, M. M., Athar, A., Aich, S., & Kim, H. C. (2022, February). Overview: Technology roadmap of the future trend of metaverse based on IoT, blockchain, AI technique, and medical domain metaverse activity. In *2022 24th International Conference on Advanced Communication Technology (ICACT)* (pp. 256-261). IEEE.

Netemeyer, R. G., Bearden, W. O., & Sharma, S. (2003). *Scaling procedures: Issues and applications.* sage publications.

Nunes, G. S., & Filho, E. J. M. A. (2018b). Consumer behavior regarding wearable technologies: Google Glass. *Innovation & Management Review*, *15*(3), 230–246. doi:10.1108/INMR-06-2018-0034

Ooi, K. B., Tan, G. W. H., Al-Emran, M., Al-Sharafi, M. A., Arpaci, I., Zaidan, A. A., ... Iranmanesh, M. (2023). The metaverse in engineering management: Overview, opportunities, challenges, and future research agenda. *IEEE Transactions on Engineering Management*.

Park, J., & Kim, N. (2024). Examining self-congruence between user and avatar in purchasing behavior from the metaverse to the real world. *Journal of Global Fashion Marketing*, *15*(1), 23–38. doi:10.1080/20932685.2023.2180768

Peltonen, T. (2019). Case Study 4: The Collapse of Nokia's Mobile Phone Business, Springer Books. In *Towards Wise Management* (pp. 163–188). Springer. doi:10.1007/978-3-319-91719-1_6

Polas, M. R. H., Jahanshahi, A. A., Kabir, A. I., Sohel-Uz-Zaman, A. S. M., Osman, A. R., & Karim, R. (2022). Artificial intelligence, blockchain technology, and risk-taking behavior in the 4.0 IR Metaverse Era: Evidence from Bangladesh-based SMEs. *Journal of Open Innovation*, *8*(3), 168. doi:10.3390/joitmc8030168

Queiroz, M. M., Wamba, S. F., Pereira, S. C. F., & Jabbour, C. J. C. (2023). The metaverse as a breakthrough for operations and supply chain management: Implications and call for action. *International Journal of Operations & Production Management*, *43*(10), 1539–1553. doi:10.1108/IJOPM-01-2023-0006

Rahman, K. R., Shitol, S. K., Islam, M. S., Iftekhar, K. T., & Pranto, S. A. H. A. (2023). Use of Metaverse Technology in Education Domain. *Journal of Metaverse*, *3*(1), 79–86. doi:10.57019/jmv.1223704

Seo, J., Kim, K., Park, M., Park, M., & Lee, K. (2018). An Analysis of Economic Impact on IOT Industry under GDPR. *Mobile Information Systems*, *2018*, 1–6. doi:10.1155/2018/6792028

Sheth, J. (2020). Business of business is more than business: Managing during the Covid crisis. *Industrial Marketing Management*, *88*, 261–264. doi:10.1016/j.indmarman.2020.05.028

Sweeney, J. C., & Soutar, G. N. (2001). Consumer perceived value: The development of a multiple item scale. *Journal of Retailing*, 77(2), 203–220. doi:10.1016/S0022-4359(01)00041-0

Teo, K. S., & Wong, Y. W. (2023). *The determinants of Augmented Reality (AR) marketing affect purchase intention in the beauty and makeup industry among gen z in Malaysia* [Doctoral dissertation, UTAR].

Uddin, M. R. (2024). The role of the digital economy in Bangladesh's economic development. *Sustainable Technology and Entrepreneurship*, 3(1), 100054. doi:10.1016/j.stae.2023.100054

Wallace, R. S. O., & Cooke, T. E. (1990). The diagnosis and resolution of emerging issues in corporate disclosure practices. *Accounting and Business Research*, 20(78), 143–151. doi:10.1080/00014788.1990.9728872

Wan, X., Zhang, G., Yuan, Y., & Chai, S. (2023). How to drive the participation willingness of supply chain members in metaverse technology adoption? *Applied Soft Computing*, 145, 110611. doi:10.1016/j.asoc.2023.110611

Wiangkham, A., & Vongvit, R. (2023). Exploring the Drivers for the Adoption of Metaverse Technology in Engineering Education using PLS-SEM and ANFIS. *Education and Information Technologies*, 1–28.

Yang, L. (2023). Recommendations for metaverse governance based on technical standards. *Humanities & Social Sciences Communications*, 10(1), 1–10. doi:10.1057/s41599-023-01750-7

Yao, X., Ma, N., Zhang, J., Wang, K., Yang, E., & Faccio, M. (2024). Enhancing wisdom manufacturing as industrial metaverse for industry and society 5.0. *Journal of Intelligent Manufacturing*, 35(1), 235–255. doi:10.1007/s10845-022-02027-7

Zhang, Q. (2023). Secure Preschool Education Using Machine Learning and Metaverse Technologies. *Applied Artificial Intelligence*, 37(1), 2222496. doi:10.1080/08839514.2023.2222496

Zheng, Z., Li, T., Li, B., Chai, X., Song, W., Chen, N., & Li, R. (2022, December). Industrial metaverse: connotation, features, technologies, applications and challenges. In *Asian Simulation Conference* (pp. 239-263). Singapore: Springer Nature Singapore. 10.1007/978-981-19-9198-1_19

Chapter 15

Unleashing the Power of Research, Innovation, and Industry Impacts:
Exploring the Transformative Role of the Metaverse in Business and Commerce

Paramjeet Kumar
iD https://orcid.org/0000-0002-3824-2289
North Eastern Hill University, India

ABSTRACT

The notion of the metaverse has garnered substantial attention in recent years, captivating the imagination and piquing the interest of researchers, inventors, and industry executives alike. This chapter, "Unleashing the Power of Research, Innovation, and Industry Impacts: Exploring the Transformative Role of the Metaverse in Business and Commerce," seeks to investigate the potential of the metaverse and its impact on several facets of business and commerce. This proposal aims to examine the present patterns in metaverse research, which are influenced by applications that exploit the merging of interdisciplinary technologies. The advancement of developing technologies presents diverse prospects for the use of the metaverse in the realms of industry and commerce.

INTRODUCTION

The metaverse has garnered considerable interest in recent years, especially due to improvements in digital technology and the emergence of immersive virtual experiences. Although there have been limited surveys conducted on the metaverse, extant research may be classified into three primary domains: defining the metaverse, identifying the necessary conditions for its implementation and utilisation, and exploring the enabling technologies, applications, and problems associated with the metaverse (Ismail & Buyya, 2023). Within the initial category, scholars have concentrated their efforts

DOI: 10.4018/979-8-3693-2607-7.ch015

on precisely delineating the nature and characteristics of the metaverse. The metaverse, as determined in a comprehensive analysis of existing literature, is a virtual world that is immersive, synchronous, and persistent. It enables users, who are represented by avatars, to engage in interactions with both the environment and other users (source) (Ismail & Buyya, 2023). Conducting research in the metaverse is essential for fully realising its potential and comprehending its influential position in the realms of business and commerce.

UNDERSTANDING THE ROLE OF INNOVATION IN BUSINESS TRANSFORMATION

In the realm of business transformation, innovation assumes a pivotal role, and its importance is further magnified within the metaverse. The information systems literature has placed significant focus on the technical advancements of digital technologies and their influence on the value generated by businesses (Verhoef et al., 2021). Yet, to truly utilise the potential of the metaverse, it is crucial to investigate how innovation may propel change within this immersive digital realm. Research on innovation in the metaverse has concentrated on diverse facets, such as the advancement of fresh digital tools and technology, the establishment of unique business models, the investigation of untapped market prospects, and the improvement of user experiences. An area of innovation in the metaverse is the rise of Non-Fungible Tokens (NFTs) and virtual currency. NFTs have emerged as a favoured avenue for online businesses to delve into the metaverse, enabling the creation of distinctive digital assets and virtual advertising campaigns (Cui & Du, 2023). This novel methodology of asset ownership and digital transactions has the capacity to transform industries like as art, gaming, fashion, and others. Another domain of advancement inside the metaverse involves the progress of wearable devices. With the increasing prevalence of the metaverse, there is an anticipated surge in the sales of wearable devices. These devices, such as virtual reality headsets and augmented reality glasses, enhance users' experience in the metaverse by offering a more immersive and participatory environment. Moreover, the incorporation of artificial intelligence and machine learning technologies into the metaverse is also fueling innovation. These technologies has the capacity to improve personalisation, optimise user experiences, and offer vital insights for enterprises operating in the metaverse.

Exploring Industry Impacts Within the Metaverse

The metaverse possesses the capacity to profoundly influence several industries, revolutionising their operational methods and client interactions. The entertainment and media business is poised to undergo significant transformation due to the metaverse. The metaverse's immersive and interactive characteristics offer novel opportunities for storytelling, gaming, and content creation. By utilising the metaverse, entertainment and media organisations have the ability to craft distinctive and captivating encounters for their viewers, effectively erasing the boundaries between virtual and physical realms. As an illustration, virtual reality technology enables the streaming of live concerts and events, enabling individuals from different parts of the globe to engage in a collective experience. This not only broadens the scope of these events but also creates new sources of income through virtual ticket sales and virtual merchandising. Commerce is another industry that can derive advantages from the metaverse.

The Transformative Role of the Metaverse in Business and Commerce

The metaverse possesses the capacity to fundamentally transform the way businesses function and interact with their clientele. Smartphone firms aim to provide a competitive metaverse experience and take the lead in its development, in collaboration with Microsoft and Facebook. The competition in the smartphone market underscores the increasing acknowledgment of the metaverse as a powerful catalyst for change in the realms of business and commerce. As cutting-edge technologies like blockchain, augmented reality, virtual reality, artificial intelligence, 3D reconstruction, and the Internet of Things persistently fuel investment prospects in the metaverse, businesses in various sectors are increasingly adopting and supporting its growth. These industry participants acknowledge that the metaverse possesses the potential to generate fresh sources of income, improve client experiences, and stimulate innovation. For instance, in the realm of commerce, enterprises have the ability to establish virtual stores within the metaverse, enabling customers to navigate and buy things in a digital setting that replicates the actual shopping encounter. This not only creates more avenues for generating revenue but also offers organisations valuable data and insights regarding customer behaviour, preferences, and trends. In addition, the metaverse has the capability to enable virtual meetings and conferences, so eliminating the necessity for physical travel and decreasing expenses for organisations. The COVID-19 epidemic has greatly expedited the transition to virtual meetings and conferences, as organisations globally have had to adjust to distant work arrangements. The metaverse presents prospects for corporations to engage in collaborative efforts and foster innovation. Companies can utilise the collaborative virtual environment offered by consumer devices to enhance teamwork, foster innovation, and facilitate problem-solving.

Collaborative virtual environments in the metaverse facilitate the convergence of employees from various locations, utilising the immersive encounter to augment communication and production. In addition, the metaverse has the potential to stimulate innovation by offering a platform for conducting experiments and developing prototypes. Enterprises have the ability to experiment with novel ideas and concepts within a simulated setting, enabling faster and more economical iterations prior to applying modifications in the tangible realm. The metaverse plays a significant role in business and commerce, and this function is reinforced by advancements in artificial intelligence technologies. By incorporating AI computing into the metaverse, businesses may utilise virtual agents and clever algorithms to improve user experiences and increase immersion. These virtual agents have the capability to offer tailored suggestions, aid, and help to users within the metaverse, resulting in a more captivating and dynamic setting. They possess the ability to adjust to users' tastes and behaviours, predict their requirements, and offer immediate support. The degree of customisation and adaptability not only improves the user's experience but also creates opportunities for precise marketing and tailored advertising within the metaverse.

The Metaverse: A New Frontier for Business Innovation

The metaverse presents a novel opportunity for corporate innovation, enabling organisations to explore and use virtual environments to engage with customers, cooperate with partners, and enhance growth and competitiveness. The metaverse disrupts conventional business paradigms and creates novel prospects for research, innovation, and industry influence by erasing the distinctions between the physical and virtual realms. Businesses may optimise their utilisation of research, innovation, and industry impacts by effectively exploiting the possibilities of the metaverse. The metaverse empowers businesses to create immersive and interactive experiences that surpass the constraints of conventional online platforms by incorporating cutting-edge technologies like blockchain, augmented reality, virtual reality, artificial intelligence, 3D reconstruction, and the Internet of Things. Furthermore, the metaverse not only enhances customer experiences but also fundamentally changes the internal operations of enterprises. Through the establishment of virtual workspaces and collaboration platforms within the metaverse, enterprises may facilitate distant collaborations, enhance productivity, cultivate creativity and innovation, and overcome geographical limitations.

Driving Commercial Success Through Metaverse Integration

Incorporating the metaverse into business structures holds the capacity to propel economic triumph throughout diverse industries. Through the use of the metaverse, businesses can tap into untapped markets, expand their customer reach, and augment their brand's prominence. They have the ability to generate virtual showrooms and storefronts, enabling customers to engage with and buy products in immersive and engaging settings. This not only improves the overall customer purchasing experience but also yields vital data and insights for targeted marketing and product development. Through the examination of user behaviour and preferences within the metaverse, firms can customise their marketing campaigns to target certain client categories, providing individualised adverts and promotions. Moreover, the metaverse offers a medium for virtual events and conferences, allowing enterprises to engage with worldwide audiences without being limited by physical boundaries. This presents possibilities for enterprises to broaden their scope, allure international partners and customers, and cultivate collaboration on a worldwide level.

Metaverse: Shaping Future Commerce and Trade

The metaverse possesses the capacity to fundamentally transform the trajectory of commerce and trade in the future. The metaverse allows businesses to create distinctive and captivating experiences for their customers, thanks to its immersive and interactive characteristics. These experiences not only allure and maintain clients but also offer opportunity for businesses to distinguish themselves in a saturated market. Furthermore, the metaverse enables effortless amalgamation of physical and digital realms, hence fostering the development of groundbreaking business frameworks. As an illustration, the metaverse has the potential to facilitate businesses in providing virtual try-on experiences for products like apparel and cosmetics, enabling buyers to preview the appearance and fit of items before to making a purchase. This not only mitigates the likelihood of product returns and enhances consumer contentment, but also diminishes expenses linked to tangible inventory and retail premises. Moreover, the metaverse holds the capacity to completely transform supply chain management. Through the creation of a virtual depiction of the complete supply chain process, firms can enhance operational efficiency, minimise inefficiencies, and enhance transparency. This can result in expedited and more efficient procedures, hence decreasing expenses and enhancing overall efficiency.

Exploring the Metaverse's Potential in the Corporate World

The metaverse presents significant promise within the corporate realm, including prospects for research, innovation, and industry ramifications. The metaverse enhances user experience by digitising real-life encounters, resulting in improved efficiency and intuitiveness in professional tasks, as well as enhancing social interactions and leisure options (Dong & Liu, 2023). Moreover, the metaverse offers a cooperative digital setting that is crucial for creating immersive experiences of superior quality. Consumer devices are essential in facilitating this environment, as they play a pivotal role in enabling people to actively participate in the metaverse. The efficacy of research in the metaverse resides in its capacity to collect and scrutinise data derived from virtual encounters. These observations can be utilised to guide strategic choices, discern client patterns, and stimulate creativity. Furthermore, the metaverse provides a distinct platform for conducting experiments and creating prototypes. Businesses have the ability to experiment with novel concepts, goods, and services in a simulated setting prior to committing resources to actual execution. This not only decreases expenses but also mitigates risks linked to failure. The metaverse offers limitless opportunities for developing innovative business models.

Revolutionizing Industries Through Research and Innovation in the Metaverse

All industries have the opportunity to gain advantages from the revolutionary capabilities of the metaverse. The media and entertainment business is highly susceptible to upheaval. The metaverse enables media and entertainment organisations to develop captivating virtual experiences for their audiences. These experiences encompass a wide variety of activities, such as virtual concerts, live events, and interactive games, providing a heightened level of involvement and entertainment. The metaverse has the potential to bring significant advantages to the manufacturing industry. Manufacturers can enhance their manufacturing processes by utilising the metaverse to generate virtual simulations, enabling improved planning and optimisation with greater efficiency and effectiveness. The metaverse has the potential to revolutionise the medical and healthcare industries. Virtual reality simulations in the metaverse offer medical professionals the opportunity to engage in lifelike training scenarios, enabling them to refine their abilities and enhance their expertise inside a secure and regulated setting. Moreover, the metaverse holds the capacity to completely transform commerce. Within the metaverse, conventional physical stores can be converted into virtual storefronts, enabling customers to peruse and acquire things from the convenience of their residences. The metaverse enables e-commerce companies to provide customised shopping experiences by incorporating virtual reality technology, allowing users to virtually try on clothing and test products prior to making a purchase.

The Future of Business: Embracing the Metaverse for Sustainable Growth

Adopting the metaverse has the potential to foster sustainable expansion for enterprises through various means. To begin with, the metaverse enables enhanced efficiency and production. Through the utilisation of virtual simulations and immersive experiences, organisations have the ability to optimise operations, decrease expenses, and enhance overall efficiency. Manufacturers can utilise virtual simulations within the metaverse to evaluate and enhance their production processes, leading to increased operational efficiency. This can result in reduced expenses and enhanced productivity, hence fostering sustainable expansion. Furthermore, the metaverse presents novel avenues for generating income and exploring entrepreneurial prospects. By using the metaverse, firms can access untapped markets and develop cutting-edge offerings. Companies have the ability to generate virtual experiences and events that appeal to a worldwide audience, so extending their influence beyond the constraints of physical boundaries. This creates other sources of income and broadens the company's operations, decreasing dependence on conventional channels. Moreover, the metaverse promotes cooperation and originality. The metaverse fosters cross-disciplinary collaborations and idea exchange by providing a virtual platform for individuals and corporations to engage and collaborate. This fosters ingenuity and originality, resulting in the creation of novel products, services, and solutions capable of tackling intricate problems and satisfying ever-changing client demands. Through the utilisation of research, innovation, and industrial impacts, the metaverse have the capability to initiate profound transformations in business and commerce. Through harnessing the potential of research, organisations can discover significant insights and patterns that can guide their strategies and decision-making in the metaverse. Moreover, cultivating a culture of innovation within the organisation can stimulate experimentation and the creation of pioneering technologies and solutions in the metaverse. These innovations can have profound and extensive effects, not just within the organisation but also across many industries and sectors. Effectively utilising the capabilities of the metaverse necessitates adopting a conscientious stance towards technology. It is crucial for businesses to give utmost importance to ethical issues, data privacy, and security in the metaverse in order to safeguard user information and uphold confidence. Furthermore, it is crucial to prioritise inclusion and accessibility in order to guarantee that all individuals, irrespective of their background or skills, may fully access and benefit from the metaverse. The metaverse has significant potential to revolutionise industry and trade, but it also poses issues and considerations that need to be tackled. An essential obstacle in the metaverse revolves on the matter of social inclusion and justice. With the increasing prevalence of the metaverse, it is imperative to prioritise the protection and equitable access to opportunities and resources for vulnerable populations in this virtual realm. Another obstacle that arises is the requirement for interoperability and standardisation. As the metaverse progresses and grows, several platforms and technologies may arise, resulting in a fragmented environment. This can impede the smooth collaboration and communication between users and businesses functioning within the metaverse. In order to surmount these obstacles, it is imperative to engage in industrial collaboration and establish partnerships. Enterprises can collaborate to build shared standards and protocols that facilitate interoperability and guarantee a unified user experience across diverse platforms. The metaverse optimises work processes by digitising real-world experiences and providing a collaborative virtual environment that improves efficiency and intuitiveness, resulting in an immersive user experience. Additionally, it offers prospects for social engagement, amusement, and the investigation of virtual realms. The metaverse amalgamates technology, innovation, and industrial effects in a revolutionary manner. By doing research and fostering innovation, businesses have the ability to harness the full potential of the metaverse in order to fundamentally transform many facets of commerce. The metaverse provides organisations with fresh opportunities for customer involvement, product development, and marketing techniques. Through the utilisation of the metaverse, businesses can generate captivating and engaging encounters for their clientele, enabling them to navigate and examine items or services within a virtual environment prior to completing a transaction. This can result in heightened consumer satisfaction and loyalty. Moreover, the metaverse possesses the capacity to profoundly alter conventional supply chains and distribution models. Through the integration of virtual reality, augmented reality, and blockchain technology, businesses may optimise operations, minimise expenses, and expand their reach to a worldwide audience more effortlessly. In order to effectively harness the potential of research, innovation, and industrial effects in the metaverse, it is crucial to examine its revolutionary influence on business and commerce using a multidimensional strategy. This entails analysing the technological, social, and economic aspects of the metaverse and examining how they interconnect. Through an analysis of how industry leaders like Meta, Microsoft, Decentraland, and Nvidia implement metaverses, we may obtain vital knowledge about the practical uses and prospective advantages of the metaverse in the business sector.

REFERENCES

Cui, H., & Du, B. (2023, February 6). *The Theoretical Basis and Landing Strategy of the Metaverse Business Model*. IEEE. doi:10.3233/FAIA230010

Dong, H., & Liu, Y. (2023, May 1). *Metaverse Meets Consumer Electronics*. IEEE. doi:10.1109/MCE.2022.3229180

IsmailL.BuyyaR. (2023, August 21). Metaverse: A Vision, Architectural Elements, and Future Directions for Scalable and Realtime Virtual Worlds. https://arxiv.org/abs/2308.10559

Verhoef, P C., Broekhuizen, T., Bart, Y., Bhattacharya, A., Dong, J Q., Fabian, N E., & Haenlein, M. (2021, January 1). Digital transformation: A multidisciplinary reflection and research agenda. doi:10.1016/j.jbusres.2019.09.022

Chapter 16
Exploring Safe Hedging Options for Blockchain Assets in the Face of COVID-19-Induced Volatility

Himani Gupta
Jagannath International Management School, India

Rupinder Katoch
ⓘD https://orcid.org/0000-0003-3191-7930
Lovely Professional University, India

Manisha Gupta
Sharda University, India

ABSTRACT

This chapter examines the transfer of daily volatility returns from one block-chain asset to another and hedging alternatives. The technique is based on adequately modelling of the dynamic conditional correlation of generalised autoregressive conditional heteroscedasticity (DCC GARCH) and the hedging ratio. The results reveal that the volatility spillover impact from Etherium to other block-chain assets exists both in the short and long run. There are also hedging possibilities available between the selected block-chain assets. This implies that, prior to investing, policymakers, regulators, and investors should be aware of volatility, spillover effects, and hedging alternatives in the constituent variables.

INTRODUCTION

Money systems have evolved greatly over the centuries. From barter to plastic money, there are a variety of different types of money. Throughout each era, technical developments, financial needs, and the equivalent efficiency of performing a transaction acted as the determinants of one money form's continuing

DOI: 10.4018/979-8-3693-2607-7.ch016

existence over another. Of today's world, there has been an increasing increase in international hostility toward the present monetary system, notably in the aftermath of the financial instability that enveloped financial markets from 2007 to 2009, resulting in catastrophic economic effects throughout the world. Bitcoin (the first cryptocurrency) was launched in 2009. As per its white paper, it sought to alter the world financial system fundamentally. Recently, the concept of bitcoin gained substantial public support as crowds began to use it for a variety of reasons, including the desire for a different monetary system that is less dependent on the present traditional one. Numerous other cryptocurrencies have benefited from this public interest, resulting in a considerable evolution of the cryptocurrency sector. The main point of contention in this issue is that virtual currency markets have no inherent worth and do not pay dividends, yet investors continue to invest and profit (Ozdemer, 2022).

Recent concerns and disagreement that has dogged the cryptocurrency market since creation, has evolved into one of the most important alternative investment venues in the financial market (Huynh et al., 2020). A keen interest in study on these themes has grown as a result of the recent quick rise in the price of cryptocurrencies such as Bitcoin, Ethereum, and Litecoin (Ozdemir, 2022). (Nakamoto, 2008) He first proposed the theories of Bitcoin, since then many investors have become interested in digital money, causing digital currency transactions to become more prominent in the business world and investing scene. Investors typically select hedging assets such as cryptocurrency to mitigate financial risk and lock in profits when financial markets become more volatile and risky.

According to Markarov & Schoar, 2020, the cryptocurrency market, which is regarded as a new class of assets, has attracted significant interest from academics, speculators, lawmakers, and authorities (Nasir et al., 2019; Kou et al., 2014). The intricacy of the cryptocurrency market may be explored from multiple angles, and the goal of our research is to build a network centered on crypto-currency information to track possible linkages, impacts, and hedging choices between different types of crypto-currencies. The World Health Organization reported corona virus, a pandemic in 2020. COVID-19 has a significant impact on practically all areas of the economy. This was the start of our research.

Throughout this COVID-19 problem, it is vital to know the cryptocurrency market dynamics, particularly the links between different cryptocurrencies. Financial advisors must adapt their asset mix to diversify risk if volatility is conveyed from one cryptocurrency to another during a crisis, and financial policymakers must adjust their rules to prevent the risk of contagion. (Caporin & Malik, 2020).

Numerous studies have concentrated on the impact of diversity, and have examined the best asset mix that may maximise returns while minimising volatility (Baur et al., 2018; Kajtazi & Moro, 2019; Urquhart & Zhang, 2019). Nonetheless, this study expands on past research in two areas. To begin, this study began with the top twenty cryptocurrencies, but owing to a lack of data availability and other precondition criteria, it has been condensed to only seven. During COVID 19, it compared the spillover effects of one crypto currency on another. Second, this study focused at the time variability in cryptocurrency diversification evaluations.

The study's uniqueness arises from the fact that, to the best of the author's knowledge, these cryptocurrencies have never been thoroughly examined for the purpose of analysing the spillover impact and hedging alternatives. These cryptocurrencies were chosen for the study because they are among the top twenty-five most widely traded cryptocurrencies, accounting for more than 90% of the total industry value.

The following is the outline of our paper. In part II, a literature review is given, and in section III, data and methods are presented. The empirical findings are reviewed in the next part, followed by the primary conclusion and policy proposal in the last section.

LITERATURE REVIEW

Our research is mostly connected to the previous studies, which seeks to comprehend the spillover impacts of multiple financial products on portfolio diversification (Ozdemir & Ozdemir, 2021; Gupta, 2023; Gupta,2024). Analyzing volatility and volatility spillover amongst stock prices, cryptocurrency, bonds etc. is a significant matter that has gained prominence in recent decades. Kuen & Hoong (1992) contrast three approaches. Specifically, the naïve technique, the exponentially weighted moving average, and the generalised autoregressive conditional heteroscedasticity (GARCH) model of volatility forecasting. Fowowe & Shaibu (2016) along with Zhang et al. (2019) concentrated on equities markets. Mensi et al. (2014), on the other hand, focused on the commodities market, Hoesli & Reka (2013) examined the real estate market, and Louzis (2015) examined the spillover effects in the money market. Numerous research has been carried during the last decade on the correlation between Bitcoin and financial markets, with the majority of findings indicating that Bitcoin is distinct from traditional investments such as stocks, monetary systems, commodity markets, debt securities, precious metals, crude oil, and other cryptocurrencies (Zhang et al., 2021)

Cryptocurrency is built on block chain technology, which allows for the safe movement of assets using cutting-edge cryptographic techniques; in certain circles, this technology has surpassed it as a financial instrument. According to Glaser et al. (2014), though cryptocurrencies are predominantly used as a capital invested, but now it can be utilised as a global currency as a result of huge corporations and other businesses deciding to use them for their payments. Additionally, it can be used as a tool for organizations to obtain funds through initial coin offerings. (Momtaz, 2021). Analyzing the market dynamics or effectiveness is a delicate investment outcome; the theory presupposes that financial markets reflect, whereas behavior finance theory contends that psychological factors significantly impact market prices. (Fama,1970; Madhavan, 2000: Barber & Odean,2008;Almansour, 2015; Almansour & Arabyat, 2017; Dyhrberg, 2016) assert that a market's informational efficiency, as well as its information structure, play a significant impact in the creation of pricing. Alvarez-Ramirez et al. (2018) and Jiang et al. (2018) stated that the bitcoin market's pricing and information systems are ineffective, which is considered inefficient. Because ineffective markets are extremely volatile, researchers focused on the bitcoin market's volatility. (Kim, 2017) Due to the high volatility, academics have focussed their efforts on the returns. Ardia et al. (2019) used time series data from 2011 to 2018 to examine the fluctuations in Bitcoin. Researcher discovered robust evidence that the GARCH model effectively estimates Bitcoin volatility. Katsiampa et al. (2019) looked at how three major cryptocurrencies (Bitcoin, Ethereum, and Litecoin) convey shock and volatility using the BEKKMGARCH model and discover bidirectional shock propagation among Bitcoin–Litecoin and Bitcoin–Ethereum pairs. Additionally, bidirectional volatility transmissions among Ethereum and Litecoin was also seen by Canh et al. (2019). By applying the DCC-MGARCH model, researcher examined the volatility dynamics of the seven largest cryptocurrencies and discover strong propagation of volatility between them. The GARCH in mean model is used by Liu & Tsyvinski (2021) to assess the degree of shock and volatility transmission across Bitcoin, Ethereum, and Litecoin. Beneki et al. (2019) explore the volatility transmission between Bitcoin and Ethereum using the BEKK-GARCH approach. They discover a one-way spillover of volatility from Ethereum to Bitcoin. Chu et al. (2017) analysed that there are seven cryptocurrencies with varying degrees of volatility.

Almansour & Inairat (2020) discovered the connection between exchange rates and Bitcoin returns, conducted a time-series study utilizing ARMA analysis, and discovered that exchange rates have a negligible effect. According to Qarni & Gulzar (2021), Bitcoin offers considerable portfolio diversification benefits for huge foreign currency holdings.

Previous research on several cryptocurrencies was already conducted. For example, Bariviera et al. (2018) analyze the 5-minute data of 12 cryptocurrencies with the help of complexity-entropy causality plane. It exhibit the same dynamics as ethereum, bitcoin and classic exhibit more determined stochastic dynamic forces.

In contrast, Jiang et al. (2018) exhibit more random walk-like behaviour. Notably, the efficacy of bitcoin futures as a hedge against other cryptocurrencies is contingent upon their correlation to bitcoin. According to Corbet et al. (2018b), litecoin, bitcoin, and ripple are all significantly related at varying intervals and so these linkages are momentary. Aslanidis et al. (2019) When applied to bitcoin and ripple, a generalized DCC class model yields similar conclusions, meaning that relationships between cryptocurrencies are favourable but changing over time. Cahn et al. (2019) demonstrate that shifts occur from more minor to more significant cryptocurrencies in terms of market capitalization and that the results from DCC-MGARCH model are suggestively significant.

As stated previously, our objective is to investigate the efficiency of hedging on bitcoin and other cryptocurrencies. Thus, it is worth noting that, while the price dynamics of bitcoin and other cryptocurrencies may appear to be relatively similar at first look, they may also exhibit distinct characteristics, particularly in a high-frequency context. As a result, bitcoin results cannot be directly transferred to further cryptocurrencies. In several ways, this work gives a perspective on the bitcoin nexus. First, we explore the cryptocurrency market association among the top seven cryptocurrencies using a time-varying dynamic conditional correlation test, which has the benefit of targeting causal periods throughout time. Second, unlike earlier research that focused on the causation between these two or three cryptocurrencies, our study examines the hedging alternatives available for investors especially portfolio managers in order to enhance returns.

RESEARCH METHODOLOGY

Data Collection

This study employed a total of twenty cryptocurrencies, however owing to the lack of a comprehensive data set, we are only able to study twelve of them i.e. BITCOIN, ETHEREUM, BNB, XRP, CARDANO, TERRA, BINANCE, DOGECOIN, POLYGONMATIC, CORONS, WRAPPED BITCOIN AND COSMOS. The sample spans January 1, 2020, to February 28, 2022, and includes 788 observations based on cryptocurrency data availability. Furthermore, because bitcoin trading is not limited to work days, the sample includes weekends. Because the cryptocurrencies were originally issued in domestic currencies, they were first transformed into return series (Gupta & Gupta,2023) using the formula: ln(Pt/Pt-1).

Econometrics Model

To evaluate our time series, we utilised R Studio, and we used ARCH and GARCH models to anticipate the cryptocurrency's volatility. The hedging ratio is estimated using a multivariate GARCH model. In financial data science, the modelling of conditional variance and conditional covariance matrices is crucial. As said by Bauwens et al. (2006), multivariate GARCH models may be divided into three types based on how the conditional covariance matrix is constructed. The Baba, Engle, Kraft, and Kroner (BEKK) GARCH model (Baba et al., 1991; Engle and Kroner,1995), Constant Conditional Correlation (CCC) GARCH model (Bollerslev, 1990), and Dynamic Conditional Correlation (DCC) GARCH model (Engle, 2002) are the three types of models. The general order of GARCH (p, q) is set to (1,1) to simplify the models. We used the DCC GARCH model in this research.

Multivariate DCC GARCH Model

In many empirical results, particularly in prior investigations, the assumption that conditional correlations are constant may appear implausible (for example: Manera et al.,2006). Engle (2002) and Tse & Tsui (2002) introduced a dynamic conditional correlation (DCC) model in order to make the conditional correlation matrix time dependent. Conditional mean and conditional variance are two elements of the DCC GARCH model.

Conditional Mean

The model's conditional mean equation is written as follows:

$$R_t = u + \gamma R_{t-1} + \varepsilon_t$$

with $\varepsilon_t = H_t^{1/2} \eta_t$

where $R_t = (R_t^s, R_{t-1}^0)'$ s the vector of cryptocurrency returns at time t, respectively.

γ = The impact of own lag and cross mean transmissions between various cryptocurrencies is measured using a 2×2 matrix of parameters.

ε_t = vector of error terms for the two series at time t,

η_t = a series of randomly distributed random errors that are spread separately and identically.

$H_t^{1/2}$ = the conditional variations of returns for several cryptocurrencies

Conditional Variance

The following are the features of the DCC-GARCH model:

$$H_t = D_t R_t D_t = p_{ijt} \sqrt{h_{iit} h_{jjt}}$$

Where, H_t is expressed as conditional variance co-variance matrix, R_t is a conditional correlation matrix in form of n x n matrix and D_t can be denoted as

$$D_t = diag(h_1 t_{1/2},..., h_1 /2nt).$$

Where D_t is a conditional standard deviation and h_{iit} is extracted to be univariate GARCH (1,1) model

$$R_t = (diagQ_t)^{-1/2} Q_t (diagQ_t)^{-1/2}$$

Where $Q_t = (1-\alpha-\beta) Q + \alpha\, u_{t-1}u_{t-1} + \beta\, Q_{t-1}$ and it refers to a n x n symmetric positive definite matrix with $u_{it} = \varepsilon_{it}/\sqrt{h_{iit}}$, $\overline{Q}$ is the n x n unconditional variance matrix of u_t.

$\alpha + \beta$ are positive and their sum is less than one. Therefore, $\alpha \geq 0$, $\beta \geq 0$ and $\alpha + \beta < 1$.

The conditional correlation coefficient p_{ij} between two markets i and j is then calculated as follows:

$$p_{ij} = \frac{\left(1-\alpha-\beta\right)\overline{q}_{ij} + \alpha u_{i,t-1}u_{j,t-1} + \beta q_{ij,t-1}}{\left(\left(1-\alpha-\beta\right)\overline{q}_{ii} + \alpha u_{i,t-1}^2 + \beta q_{ii,t-1}\right)^{1/2}\left(\left(1-\alpha-\beta\right)\overline{q}_{jj} + a u_{j,t-1}^2 + \beta q_{jj,t-1}\right)^{1/2}}$$

Where p_{ij} refers to the element located in the ith row and j^{th} column of the symmetric positive definite matrix Q_t

Joint dccα measures the short span volatility between markets and joint dccβ measures the long span volatility impact of one market over another.

Hedge Ratio and Portfolio Weights

Hedging using DCC models that allow for time-dependent conditional correlations has been done in previous studies by Lai & Sheu (2011) and Lin & Yang (2006). Because the best hedge ratio is immediately estimated based on the variance and covariance projections, estimating multivariate volatility models with flexible dynamics is critical for cryptocurrencies hedging. We estimate optimum portfolio weights for chosen cryptocurrency-based portfolios as described by Kroner & Ng (1998).

$$W_{ij,t} = \frac{h_{jj,t-h_{ij,t}}}{h_{ii,t} - 2h_{ij,t} + h_{jj,t}}$$

Where if $W_{ij,t} < 0$, then consider it to be 0

If $W_{ij,t} > 1$, then consider it to be 1

The portfolio weights between two assets are denoted by $W_{ij,t}$. It represents the weight of first asset in a one dollar portfolio of two assets and weight of another asset is deoned by 1 - $W_{ij,t}$. $h_{ij,t}$ stands for conditional covariance between two assets and $h_{ii,t}$ represents conditional variance of the particular asset.

We also compute the hedge ratio for various cryptocurrency portfolios since these ratios give investors with important information for hedging their portfolio risk (Toyoshima et al.,2013).

According to Kroner & Sultan (1993) hedge ratio can be represented as:

$$B_{ij,t} = \frac{h_{ij,t}}{h_{jj,t}}$$

Where $h_{ij,t}$ is covariance between asset i and asset j, where as $h_{jj,t}$ is variance of asset j.

EMPIRICAL RESULTS

Descriptive Statistics

The descriptive analysis of return series of selected crypto currency from 1st January 2020 to 27th February 2022 is depicted in table 1. The daily price return of 788 observations is taken. Figure 1 shows the change in closing price of selected crypto currency. Figure 2 depicts the returns of daily closing prices which is also known as volatility clustering. The lowest mean is of XRP i.e. 0.001676, whereas highest is of TERRA i.e. 0.007298. Over the time the maximum return is of BNB with 0.529243 and the minimum return is POLYGONMATIC with -0.714147. The reason can be that after every three months, the BNB repurchases its tokens with 20% of its earnings. The question now is why BNB purchased it again. BNB distributes its tokens to exchanges like Binance, where they are burnt and are no longer accessible. As a result of the token burning, the price rises. As an outcome, it will help BNB create a supply and demand gap, enhancing its value. Polygonmatic's negative returns are mostly attributable to the fact that, unlike BNB tokens, these tokens are only burnt once a year and in extremely small quantities. Polygonmatic deflation evolves over time, separating it from endless supply crypto. Standard deviation shows the volatility in the series. DOGECOIN demonstrates the greatest volatility of 0.097517 and BITCOIN demonstrates the least volatility of 0.04050 among all the variables which possess large variations. Dogecoin is a very volatile crypto market due to its meme currency qualities and ongoing backing from the Doge father, Elon Musk. The degree of volatility the crypto market is particularly high, with regular swings in cryptocurrency values that can result in profit or loss in crypto wallets. Elon Musk is the ultimate crypto influencer, with the ability to effectively regulate and mitigate the Dogecoin price in the crypto market volatility environment. DOGE tokens can frequently assist crypto investors that are interested in the meme cryptocurrency with real-world applications. On the other hand, Bitcoin is one of the market's few "physical assets" with no major revenue flow. This makes valuing it tough. Any analyst may compute any stock's "fair value," that could be deducted from cash flow and yield a specified return at the end of its life. Variance is the square of standard deviation. TERRA, DOGECOIN and POLYGONMATIC shows the positive skewness and all other variable shows the negative skewness. Negative skewness implies that there are chances of negative earnings to the investors. Kurtosis of DOGECOIN being the highest of 79.986163 and CARDANO being the lowest of 7.224901 among all variables. It shows that the values are too high. It also depicts that each variable under study is not normally distributed. It is further cross validated with the help of Jarque Berra Test. Thus, it strongly does not accept the null hypothesis with a significance threshold of 5%.

In time series analysis, stationarity of variables is more important than the normality of variables. Almost no time series data is normal but to do the analysis every time series data should be stationary. Furthermore, Phillip Perron (PP) Test and the Augmented Dicky Fuller (ADF) Test have been carried out to actually take a look at the stationarity of all twelve selected crypto currencies. The original price of the variables shows the stochastic trend which is shown if figure 1. ADF Test and PP Test also confirms that the original data has a unit root. So, the data is converted into return series. Return series is calculated as $r_t = \ln(p_t/p_{t-1})$, where p_t is a closing price at current time period and p_{t-1} is a closing price at previous day. Table 2 shows the result of stationarity of return series. ADF Test and PP Test confirms that the cryptocurrency return of selected variables are stationary at level i.e. I (0) at 1% level of significance. Thus, it strongly rejects the null hypothesis (series has unit root). It is also shown in figure 2.

Table 1. Descriptive statistics of daily returns of crypto currency

Variable	BITCOIN	ETHERIUM	BNB	XRP	CARDANO	TERRA	BINANCE	DOGECOIN	POLYGON MATIC	CORONS	WRAPPED BITCOIN	COSMOS
Mean	0.0021	0.0038	0.0041	0.0016	0.0041	0.0072	0.0022	0.0052	0.0058	0.0031	0.0020	0.0022
Median	0.0023	0.0049	0.0034	0.0013	0.0014	0.0017	0.0016	-0.0001	0.0028	0.0046	0.0022	0.0016
Maximum	0.1718	0.2307	0.5292	0.4446	0.2794	0.6409	0.2800	1.5162	0.4561	0.4490	0.1769	0.2801
Minimum	-0.4647	-0.5507	-0.5428	-0.5504	-0.5037	-0.4877	-0.5911	-0.5149	-0.7141	-0.4903	-0.4804	-0.5911
variance	0.0016	0.0028	0.0038	0.0047	0.0038	0.0068	0.0054	0.0095	0.0069	0.0036	0.0016	0.0054
Std dev	0.0405	0.05360	0.0617	0.0685	0.0622	0.0829	0.0741	0.0975	0.0834	0.0607	0.0408	0.0741
Skewness	-1.6193	-1.8758	-0.2396	-0.1691	-0.3468	0.8093	-0.8224	5.5171	0.0627	-0.2935	-2.0301	-0.8224
Kurtosis	16.7404	23.1315	18.0947	13.3076	7.2249	9.6998	8.5847	79.9861	11.0467	11.5103	25.1999	8.5847
Jarque-Bera	18133 (0.000)	9602.3 (0.00)	10822 (0.000)	5854.6 (0.000)	1742.1 (0.000)	3196.1 (0.000)	2525.6 (0.000)	215183 (0.00)	4033.1 (0.00)	4389.3 (0.000)	21513 (0.000)	2525.6 (0.000)
ADF Test	-8.3755 (0.01)	-8.2911 (0.01)	-7.1531 (0.01)	-8.1084 (0.01)	-7.8448 (0.01)	-7.762 (0.01)	-8.3585 (0.01)	-8.2535 (0.01)	-8.9606 (0.01)	-7.6223 (0.01)	-8.3856 (0.01)	-8.3585 (0.01)
PP test	-897.39 (0.01)	-898.17 (0.01)	-928.69 (0.01)	-826.65 (0.01)	-888.6 (0.01)	-888.11 (0.01)	-845.46 (0.01)	-778.7 (0.01)	-861.12 (0.01)	-937 (0.01)	-901.32 (0.01)	-845.46 (0.01)
ARCH-LM Test	15.862 (0.1976)	22.859 (0.0289)	62.733 (0.000)	36.034 (0.0003)	31.574 (0.0016)	55.659 (0.000)	17.861 (0.12)	16.812 (0.1568)	30.337 (0.002)	37.293 (0.002)	11.863 (0.4567)	17.861 (0.12)
Observations	788	788	788	788	788	788	788	788	788	788	788	788

Source: The Author

261

Figure 1. Original price series of variables
Source: The Author

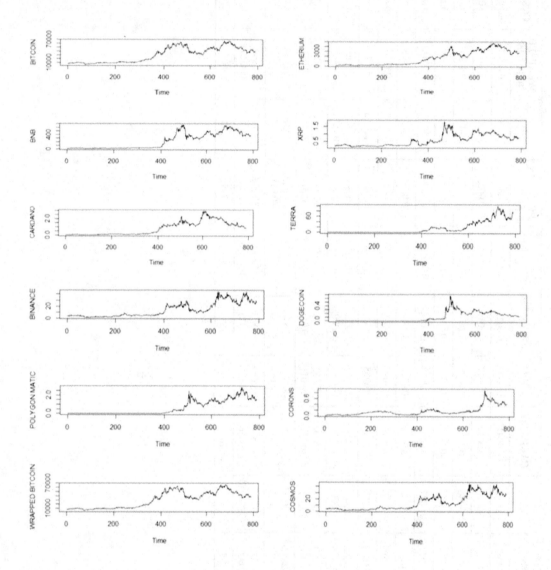

From Figure 2, it has been noticed that returns of almost all the cryptocurrency fell in first few days of COVID -19 news and there after all the returns realized negative as well as positive returns in cryptocurrency.The graphical representation gives us an idea about the behaviour of the series. It can be clearly observed that in every series huge fluctuations are accompanied by huge fluctuations, and minor are accompanied by minor, as shown in the figure 2.

ARCH Effect

Next step is to check the ARCH Effect in selected variables. GARCH model can only be applied if the three pre-requisite conditions are validated. The first and second condition is that the series should be

Figure 2. Return series of variables
Source: The Author

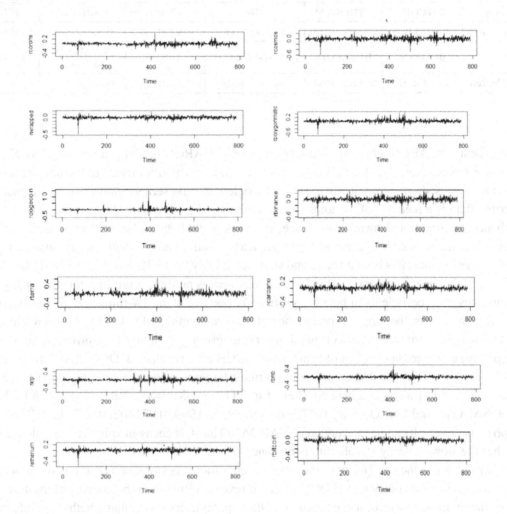

stationary and there should be volatility clustering. These two conditions are satisfied and shown in figure 2. The third condition is that there should be ARCH Effect in the series. To check the ARCH Effect we checked via LM Test. The outcomes of LM Test is shown in table 2. It shows that ETHERIUM, BNB, XRP, CARDANO, TERRA, POLYGONMATIC and CORONS have ARCH effect where as BITCOIN, NINANCE, GODECOIN, WRAPPEDBITCOIN and COSMOS does not have ARCH effect. So, our futher study will be with only those variables which have ARCH effect.

Results of Dynamic Conditional Correlation (DCC)

In this window spillover effect of ETHERIUM to BNB, XRP, CARDANO, TERRA, POLYGONMATIC and CORONS is discussed using Dynamic Conditional Correlation (DCC) model.It should be noted that the pattern of volatility clustering and ARCH effect is shown in figure 2 and table 2 for each selected crypto currency variable. The analysis is shown in table 3.Refering to the analysis mu,omega, alpha1 and

Table 2. ARCH effect

Variable	BITCOIN	ETHERIUM	BNB	XRP	CARDANO	TERRA
ARCH-LM Test	15.862 (0.1976)	22.859 (0.0289)	62.733 (0.000)	36.034 (0.0003)	31.574 (0.0016)	55.659 (0.000)
Variable	BINANCE	DOGECOIN	POLYGON MATIC	CORONS	WRAPPED BITCOIN	COSMOS
ARCH-LM Test	17.861 (0.12)	16.812 (0.1568)	30.337 (0.002)	37.293 (0.002)	11.863 (0.4567)	17.861 (0.12)

Source: The Author

beta1 represents the ARCH term and GARCH term. DCC GARCH model is a variance model. In this omega is a variance intercept, alpha gives the information how volatility reacts to the new information. It tells us if there is short-term volatility. This is modeled on time series numbers from the past of the error terms. Beta is a measure of the long-term persistence of price swings that evaluates the effect of a disturbance on conditional correlation.Hence, we can say that beta explains the conditional volatility on its own lag. If, we see the alpha and beta coefficients individually for all the cryptocurrency, at a 5% level of significance, it is both positive and significant.Only for ETHERIUM,XRP and POLYGON-MATIC, the alpha term is insignificant indicating that there is no impact on short term volatility. In all of the variables, the coefficients of beta is significantly positive at the 1% threshold of significance . It suggests that there exist the long run persistance of its own conditional volatility. As shown in table 3 coefficient of alpha term (ARCH effect) in all the cryptocurrency variables is positive and smaller than their respective estimated coefficient of beta term(GARCH effect) values in DCC Model. It depicts that the variable own volatility persistance in the long- run is larger than its own volatility persistence in the short run . The sum of alpha and beta coefficient in ETHERIUM, BNB, XRP, CARDANO, TERRA, POLYGONMATIC and CORONS are 0.972799, 0.998935, 0.999, 0.921402, 0.967435, 0.961413 and 0.983866 respectively. It can be interpreted as CARDANO has fast decay in volatility persistence where as XRP has the slowest decay in volatility persistence.

Let's have a look at the coefficient of the dynamic conditional correlation (DCC) model now. Dcca1 and dccb1 represents the coefficient of DCC model. It reveals, if there is a short-term or long-term information spillover. In other words, it can be said that these parameters shows that whether the information of one variable is having the effect on another variable or not. And if, effect is there then that effect is for shorter period of time or for longer period. From table 3, it can be seen that dcca1 and dccb1 are significantly positive at 1% level of significance.It deduces that there can be a short-term and long-term effect of news of Ehereum on other variables.Hence ETHERIUM has a spillover effect on BNB,XRP,C ARDANO,TERRA,POLYGONMATIC and CORONS. Dcca1 is 0.037236 which is positive and significant, indicates that information is spilling over or being transmitted in the short run from ETHERIUM to returns of other variables. Dccb1 is 0.937669 which is also positive and significant, indicates that the information is spilling over or being transmitted in the long run from ETHERIUM to returns of other variables. Because the sum of dcca1 and dccb1 is smaller than one, it is presumed that dynamic conditional correlation is mean reverting. Hence,cryptocurrencies are now causing quite a stir in the market. As is obvious, they have their own highs and lows depending on market conditions. However, there are variables that influence the value of cryptocurrencies. Cryptocurrencies, like any other money, derive their value through community participation. This might include coin demand, usefulness, and scarcity. In reality, the majority of cryptocurrencies emerge from private blockchain enterprises. As a result, the value of such cryptos will be determined by the company's perceived worth and project feasibility. The

Table 3. Results of DCC model

	Estimate	Std. Error	t value	Pr(>|t|)
[retherium].mu	0.0050	0.0017	3.0030	0.0027
[retherium].omega	0.0001	0.0001	1.6389	0.1012
[retherium].alpha1	0.1075	0.0636	1.6917	0.0907
[retherium].beta1	0.8653	0.0427	20.2730	0.0000
[rbnb].mu	0.0031	0.0015	2.0265	0.0427
[rbnb].omega	0.0001	0.0001	1.3451	0.1786
[rbnb].alpha1	0.1745	0.0723	2.4130	0.0158
[rbnb].beta1	0.8244	0.0583	14.1381	0.0000
[rxrp].mu	-0.0001	0.0020	-0.0391	0.9688
[rxrp].omega	0.0001	0.0001	0.6572	0.5110
[rxrp].alpha1	0.1005	0.0769	1.3065	0.1914
[rxrp].beta1	0.8985	0.0831	10.8073	0.0000
[rcardano].mu	0.0037	0.0020	1.8373	0.0662
[rcardano].omega	0.0004	0.0001	2.8687	0.0041
[rcardano].alpha1	0.1453	0.0555	2.6169	0.0089
[rcardano].beta1	0.7761	0.0496	15.6340	0.0000
[rterra].mu	0.0037	0.0027	1.3924	0.1638
[rterra].omega	0.0004	0.0003	1.2676	0.2050
[rterra].alpha1	0.1652	0.0643	2.5693	0.0102
[rterra].beta1	0.8022	0.0359	22.3204	0.0000
[rpolygonmatic].mu	0.0039	0.0023	1.6763	0.0937
[rpolygonmatic].omega	0.0004	0.0003	1.1632	0.2447
[rpolygonmatic].alpha1	0.1695	0.1055	1.6065	0.1082
[rpolygonmatic].beta1	0.7919	0.1180	6.7102	0.0000
[rcorons].mu	0.0041	0.0024	1.7327	0.0832
[rcorons].omega	0.0002	0.0001	1.9474	0.0515
[rcorons].alpha1	0.1850	0.0776	2.3847	0.0171
[rcorons].beta1	0.7989	0.0398	20.0849	0.0000
[Joint]dcca1	0.0372	0.0050	7.4659	0.0000
[Joint]dccb1	0.9377	0.0097	97.1501	0.0000

Source: The Author

effect of one cryptocurrency on another is a regular occurrence. This is what happened as a result of a major Bitcoin price fall in early 2018, which was followed by a reduction in the capitalization of all other cryptocurrencies at the same time. After Bitcoin, Ethereum is the most powerful cryptocurrency. Cryptocurrency exchange charts show that a reduction in Ethereum's price has an unavoidable influence on the exchange rates of BNB,XRP,CARDANO,TERRA,POLYGONMATIC, and CORONS. As a result, we may conclude that it may have an impact on the other cryptocurrencies under consideration.

The researcher next used the Sign Bias test to see if there was any asymmetry in the volatily. The p- value is found to be insignificant which confirms that asymmetry is not there.Therefore, asymmetry GARCH model were not applied.

The time varying conditional correlation calculated from DCC multivariate model between Etherium and BNB, Etherium and XRP, Etherium and Cardano, Etherium and Terra, Etherium and Polygonmatic & Etherium and Corons is depicted in figure 3. It is to be observed that the dynamic conditional correlation (DCC) among Etherium and BNB is all positive and more than 0.5. This suggests that portfolio can be diversified across these two cryptocurrencies data set. Similarly, the DCCs among Etherium and all sampled variables is also positive and more than 0.1 in all the cases.The DCC between each pair of cryptocurrency reach its lowest values around middle of the period i.e around January 2021. Thus,cross hedging is possible since all of the pairs have a positively correlated return movement.

Hedge Ratio and Portfolio Weight

We employ the estimates calculated from DCC GARCH model for portfolio creation and hedging methods in this section.

Hedge Ratios

To calculate the hedge ratio conditional volatility estimates generated from multivariate GARCH model are used.(Kroner & Sultan, 1993). In hedge ratio we have made the pair of two assets (one asset i and other asset j). In hedge ratio taking a long stake in a single asset might be risky so it can be offset by the short position of other asset. The hedge ratio between asset i and asset j can be calculated by:

Figure 3. Time varying conditional correlation from DCC model
Source: The Author

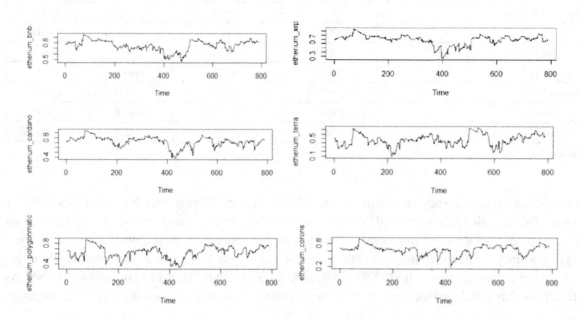

Figure 4. Graphs of hedge ratios
Source: The Author

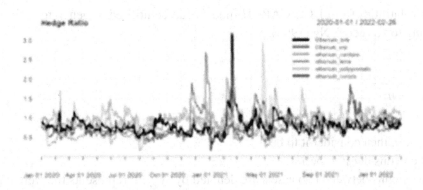

$$B_{ij,t} = \frac{h_{ij,t}}{h_{jj,t}}$$

Where $h_{ij,t}$ is covariance between asset i and asset j, where as $h_{jj,t}$ is variance of asset j. The hedge ratio of Etherium with all other variables is shown in figure 4. From figure 4, it can also be observed that there is lots of variation in all the hedge ratios. In Etherium/BNB, Etherium/XNP, Etherium/Terra and Etherium/Polygonmatic the maximum hedge ratio is observed at middle of the sample period i.e. in January 2021. Where as in the case of Etherium/Cardano the maximum hedge ratio is observed in the beginning of the sample period i.e. March 2020 and in case of Etherium/Corons the maximum hedge ratio is observed in the end of the sample period i.e. Januauary 2022.

Table 4 depicts the descriptive statistics of different pair of hedge ratio.The average hedge ratio of Etherium/BNB is 0.794,Etherium/XRP is 0.815, Etherium/Cardano is 0.8501, Etherium/Terra is 0.7088, Etherium/Polygonmatic is 0.9526 and Etherium/Corons is 0.7237. These are the important findings as it indicates that $1 long position of Etherium can be hedged for 79% with short position of BNB. Similarly, $1 long position of Etherium can be hedged for 81.5 percent with short position of XRP. The cheapest hedge is long Etherium and short Terra with 70.8 percent. The most expensive hedge is long Etherium and short Polygonmatic with the hedge ratio of 95.26 percent.From table 4 it is observed that all the hedge ratios are less than unity i.e.1.

Table 4. Hedge ratio (long/short) summary statistics

Variable	Mean ± SD	Min.	Max.
Etherium/BNB	0.794 ± 0.240	0.388	3.196
Etherium/XRP	0.815 ± 0.270	0.427	2.705
Etherium/Cardano	0.8501 ± 0.1673	0.369	1.500
Etherium/Terra	0.7088 ± 0.2625	0.1582	2.0446
Etherium/Polygonmatic	0.9526 ± 0.2358	0.3603	2.9503
Etherium/Corons	0.7237 ± 0.2123	0.1487	1.8552

Source: The Author

Portfolio Weights

The conditional volatilities from DCC GARCH models can be utilised to generate optimum portfolio weights, according to Kroner & Ng (1998).

$$W_{ij,t} = \frac{h_{jj,t-h_{ij,t}}}{h_{ii,t} - 2h_{ij,t} + h_{jj,t}}$$

Where if $W_{ij,t} < 0$, then consider it to be 0

If $W_{ij,t} > 1$, then consider it to be 1

The portfolio weights between two assets are denoted by $W_{ij,t}$. It represents the weight of first asset in a one dollar portfolio of two assets and weight of another asset is deoned by $1 - W_{ij,t}$. $h_{ij,t}$ stands for conditional covariance between two assets and $h_{ii,t}$ represents conditional variance of the particular asset.

Table 5 shows the descriptive summary of portfolio weights calculated with the help of DCC GARCH model. The average weights of Etherium/BNB is 0.51. This means that if you have a $1 portfolio, you should invest 51 percent in Etherium and 49 percent in BNB.Similarly, the average weight of Etherium/XRP indicates that 43 percent should be invested in Etherium and remaining 57 percent in XRP. The third weight of Etherium/Cardano gives us indication that only 29 percent should be invested in Etherium and 71 percent should be invested in Cardano. In the next pair of Etherium/Terra only 20 percent should be invested in Etherium and 80 percent in Terro. In addition, the average weight of Etherium/Polygonmatic portfolio shows that only 6 percent should be invested in Etherium and 94 percent in Polygonmatic. The last portfolio of Etherium/Corons shows that 43 percent should be invested in Etherium and 57 percent in Corons.

CONCLUSION AND POLICY IMPLICATIONS

As the level of investment in the cryptocurrency industry expands, it's critical to have a deeper grasp of how cryptocurrency values fluctuate. This research looks at the most popular aspects of volatility spillover and hedging options between seven popular cryptocurrencies. It investigates correlations, volatility spillovers, and hedging options between cryptocurrency returns using multivariate GARCH models. The

Table 5. Summary statistics of portfolio weights

Variable	Mean ± SD	Min.	Max.
Etherium/BNB	0.51 ± 0.337	0	1
Etherium/XRP	0.43 ± 0.389	0	1
Etherium/Cardano	0.29 ± 0.336	0	1
Etherium/Terra	0.20 ± 0.213	0	1
Etherium/Polygonmatic	0.06 ± 0.159	0	1
Etherium/Corons	0.43 ± 0.289	0	1

Source: The Author

Dynamic Conditional Correlation (DCC) model was applied to daily returns of twelve common crypto-currencies from January 2020 to February 2022, validating the pre-condition for seven cryptocurrencies. Therefore, the study is continued with seven cryptocurrencies return. The researcher tried to find out the spillover effect from Ethereum to BNB,ERP, Cordano,Terra, Polygonmatic and Corons. The result indicates that there is spillover effect both in the short and the long run from Etherium to remaining six variables. This will aid portfolio managers and investors in recognising arbitrage possibilities in both markets owing to mispricing of cryptocurrency or extreme volatility at different times. Further, it is also observed that each of the six combinations has a positive correlation. It validates that the cross hedging is possible in all the pairs.

In the next step,hedge ratios propounded by Kroner & Sultan(1993) are calculated using the DCC-MGARCH model's conditional volatilities. With a short position in BNB, a $1 long position in Etherium may be hedged for 79 percent.Similarly, $1 long position of Etherium can be hedged for 81.5 percent with short position of XRP. The most cost-effective hedge is long Etherium and short Terra. The most pricey hedge is long Etherium and short Polygonmatic. This will support future academics in examining the volatility and optimum hedging strategy of various assets in more depth.For example, the constructed hedge ratio from DCC model recommend that $1 long investment in crude oil spot may be hedged with short in crude oil futures.(Tansuchat et al., 2010) This will also aid in identifying the different hedging and trading methods that these precius metal can employ (Lau et al., 2017). This will also assist banks and investors in hedging their exposure to these markets by utilising Bitcoin as a tool for diversity. (Brière et al.,2015)

Finally, the DCC model's conditional variances and covariances may be utilised to create optimum portfolio among returns of two cryptocurrency. In the first portfolio 51% should be invested in Etherium and 49% in BNB. The second portfolio can be with 43% of investment in Etherium and 57% in XRP. In the third portfolio 29% should be invested in Etherium and 71% in Cardano. The fourth portfolio average weights shows that 20% should be invested in Etherium and 80% in Terra. Fifth portfolio should be constructed with only 6% in Etherium and 94% in Polygomatic. The last portfolio of Etherium/Corons shows that 43 percent should be invested in Etherium and 57 percent in Corons.

The similar findings show that bitcoin could be utilised to hedge against the Financial Times Stock Exchange Index. In the near run, bitcoin may also be used as a hedge against the US currency(Dyhrberg, 2016). Klein et al. (2018) compare the gold and Bitcoin, discovering that the latter is positively correlated with negative swings in developed markets. Thus, there is a hedging options between gold and Bitcoin.Conlon et.al (2020)studied Bitcoin, Ethereum and Tether. According to their findings, Bitcoin and Ethereum are inappropriate for investment. Tether, on the other hand, is a secure investment. Such negative risk hedging characteristics, on the other hand, are not always present throughout time.

Our findings shows that there is hedging options among Ethereum and other variables. Furthermore, evaluating the interconnectedness of multiple markets, particularly cryptocurrencies, is critical for investors since it allows them to analyse and make appropriate judgments about portfolio diversification options. As a result, our research will be extremely useful for investors, speculators, and portfolio managers looking to diversify their risk.But before investing policy makers, regulators, in addition to investors must be aware of volatility and spillover effect in the constituent variables.

Our study, like many studies, has shortcomings. We could only analyse the initial and relatively brief effects of this pandemic on the dynamic connectivity between the key impacted cryptocurrencies due to the brief event time and the virus's shifting nature. Future studies should look at the long-term implications of the epidemic on cryptocurrency connectivity and compare it to other financial markets and commodities.

Declaration of Conflicting Interests

The authors declared no potential conflicts of interest with respect to the research, authorship and/or publication of this article.

Funding

The authors received no financial support for the research, authorship and/or publication of this article.

Data Availability

The datasets generated during and/or analysed during the current study are available from the corresponding author on reasonable request.

REFERENCES

Almansour, B. (2015). The impact of market sentiment index on stock returns: An empirical investigation on Kuala Lumpur Stock Exchange. *Journal of Arts, Science & Commerce, 6*(3).

Almansour, B. Y., & Arabyat, Y. A. (2017). Investment decision making among Gulf investors: Behavioural finance perspective. *International Journal of Management Studies*, 24(1), 41–71. doi:10.32890/ijms.24.1.2017.10476

Almansour, B. Y., & Inairat, M. (2020). The impact of exchange rates on bitcoin returns: Further evidence from a time series framework. *International Journal of Scientific & Technology Research*, 9(02), 4577–4581.

Ardia, D., Bluteau, K., & Rüede, M. (2019). Regime changes in Bitcoin GARCH volatility dynamics. *Finance Research Letters*, 29, 266–271. doi:10.1016/j.frl.2018.08.009

Aslanidis, N., Bariviera, A. F., & Martínez-Ibañez, O. (2019). An analysis of cryptocurrencies conditional cross correlations. *Finance Research Letters*, 31, 130–137. doi:10.1016/j.frl.2019.04.019

Baba, Y., Engle, R. F., Kraft, D. F., & Kroner, K. F. (1990). *Multivariate simultaneous generalized ARCH. Manuscript, University of California*. Department of Economics.

Balcilar, M., Bouri, E., Gupta, R., & Roubaud, D. (2017). Can volume predict Bitcoin returns and volatility? A quantiles-based approach. *Economic Modelling*, 64, 74–81. doi:10.1016/j.econmod.2017.03.019

Barber, B. M., & Odean, T. (2008). All that glitters: The effect of attention and news on the buying behavior of individual and institutional investors. *Review of Financial Studies*, 21(2), 785–818. doi:10.1093/rfs/hhm079

Bariviera, A. F., Zunino, L., & Rosso, O. A. (2018). An analysis of high-frequency cryptocurrencies prices dynamics using permutation-information-theory quantifiers. *Chaos (Woodbury, N.Y.)*, *28*(7), 075511. doi:10.1063/1.5027153 PMID:30070500

Baur, D. G., Dimpfl, T., & Kuck, K. (2018). Bitcoin, gold and the US dollar–A replication and extension. *Finance Research Letters*, *25*, 103–110. doi:10.1016/j.frl.2017.10.012

Bauwens, L., Laurent, S., & Rombouts, J. V. (2006). Multivariate GARCH models: A survey. *Journal of Applied Econometrics*, *21*(1), 79–109. doi:10.1002/jae.842

Bedoui, R., Braiek, S., Guesmi, K., & Chevallier, J. (2019). RETRACTED: On the conditional dependence structure between oil, gold and USD exchange rates: Nested copula based GJR-GARCH model. *Energy Economics*, *80*, 876–889. doi:10.1016/j.eneco.2019.02.002

Beneki, C., Koulis, A., Kyriazis, N. A., & Papadamou, S. (2019). Investigating volatility transmission and hedging properties between Bitcoin and Ethereum. *Research in International Business and Finance*, *48*, 219–227. doi:10.1016/j.ribaf.2019.01.001

Bollerslev, T. (1986). Generalized autoregressive conditional heteroskedasticity. *Journal of Econometrics*, *31*(3), 307–327. doi:10.1016/0304-4076(86)90063-1

Briere, M., Oosterlinck, K., & Szafarz, A. (2015). Virtual currency, tangible return: Portfolio diversification with bitcoin. *Journal of Asset Management*, *16*(6), 365–373. doi:10.1057/jam.2015.5

Chowdhury, A. (2016). Is Bitcoin the "Paris Hilton" of the currency world? Or are the early investors onto something that will make them rich? *Journal of Investing*, *25*(1), 64–72. doi:10.3905/joi.2016.25.1.064

Chowdhury, A., & Mendelson, B. K. (2013). Virtual currency and the financial system: the case of Bitcoin (No. 2013-09). Marquette University, Center for Global and Economic Studies and Department of Economics.

Chu, J., Zhang, Y., & Chan, S. (2019). The adaptive market hypothesis in the high frequency cryptocurrency market. *International Review of Financial Analysis*, *64*, 221–231. doi:10.1016/j.irfa.2019.05.008

Conlon, T., Corbet, S., & McGee, R. J. (2020). Are cryptocurrencies a safe haven for equity markets? An international perspective from the COVID-19 pandemic. *Research in International Business and Finance*, *54*, 101248. doi:10.1016/j.ribaf.2020.101248 PMID:34170988

Corbet, S., Hou, Y. G., Hu, Y., Oxley, L., & Xu, D. (2021). Pandemic-related financial market volatility spillovers: Evidence from the Chinese COVID-19 epicentre. *International Review of Economics & Finance*, *71*, 55–81. doi:10.1016/j.iref.2020.06.022

Dyhrberg, A. H. (2016). Bitcoin, gold and the dollar–A GARCH volatility analysis. *Finance Research Letters*, *16*, 85–92. doi:10.1016/j.frl.2015.10.008

Dyhrberg, A. H. (2016). Hedging capabilities of bitcoin. Is it the virtual gold? *Finance Research Letters*, *16*, 139–144. doi:10.1016/j.frl.2015.10.025

Engle, R. F. (1982). Autoregressive conditional heteroscedasticity with estimates of the variance of United Kingdom inflation. *Econometrica*, *50*(4), 987–1007. doi:10.2307/1912773

Engle, R. F., & Kroner, K. F. (1995). Multivariate simultaneous generalized ARCH. *Econometric Theory*, *11*(1), 122–150. doi:10.1017/S0266466600009063

Erdoğdu, A. (2017). The most significant factors influencing the price of gold: An empirical analysis of the US market. *Economics*, *5*(5), 399–406.

Fama, E. F. (1970). Efficient capital markets: A review of theory and empirical work. *The Journal of Finance*, *25*(2), 383–417. doi:10.2307/2325486

Fowowe, B., & Shuaibu, M. (2016). Dynamic spillovers between Nigerian, South African and international equity markets. *Inter Economics*, *148*, 59–80. doi:10.1016/j.inteco.2016.06.003

Glaser, F., Zimmermann, K., Haferkorn, M., Weber, M. C., & Siering, M. (2014). *Bitcoin-asset or currency? revealing users' hidden intentions. Revealing Users' Hidden Intentions (April 15, 2014)*. ECIS.

Gupta, H. (2023). Analysing volatility patterns in emerging markets: symmetric or asymmetric models? *Journal of Economic and Administrative Sciences*. doi:10.1108/JEAS-07-2023-0186

Gupta, H. (2024). Asymmetric Volatility in Stock Market: Evidence from Selected Export-based Countries. *The Indian Economic Journal*, *0*(0), 00194662241238598. doi:10.1177/00194662241238598

Gupta, H., & Gupta, A. (2023). Investor's behaviour to COVID-19 vaccine: An event study on health and pharmaceutical sector in India. *International Journal of Pharmaceutical and Healthcare Marketing*, *17*(4), 429–449. doi:10.1108/IJPHM-05-2022-0053

Hashim, S. L., Ramlan, H., Razali, N. H., & Nordin, N. Z. (2017). Macroeconomic variables affecting the volatility of gold price. [GBSE]. *Journal of Global Business and Social Entrepreneurship*, *3*(5), 97–106.

Hoesli, M., & Reka, K. (2013). Volatility spillovers, comovements and contagion in securitized real estate markets. *The Journal of Real Estate Finance and Economics*, *47*(1), 1–35. doi:10.1007/s11146-011-9346-8

Huynh, T. L. D., Nasir, M. A., Vo, X. V., & Nguyen, T. T. (2020). "Small things matter most": The spillover effects in the cryptocurrency market and gold as a silver bullet. *The North American Journal of Economics and Finance*, *54*, 101277. doi:10.1016/j.najef.2020.101277

Jiang, Y., Nie, H., & Ruan, W. (2018). Time-varying long-term memory in Bitcoin market. *Finance Research Letters*, *25*, 280–284. doi:10.1016/j.frl.2017.12.009

Kajtazi, A., & Moro, A. (2019). The role of bitcoin in well diversified portfolios: A comparative global study. *International Review of Financial Analysis*, *61*, 143–157. doi:10.1016/j.irfa.2018.10.003

Katsiampa, P., Corbet, S., & Lucey, B. (2019). High frequency volatility co-movements in cryptocurrency markets. *Journal of International Financial Markets, Institutions and Money*, *62*, 35–52. doi:10.1016/j.intfin.2019.05.003

Kim, Y. B., Lee, J., Park, N., Choo, J., Kim, J. H., & Kim, C. H. (2017). When Bitcoin encounters information in an online forum: Using text mining to analyse user opinions and predict value fluctuation. *PLoS One*, *12*(5), e0177630. doi:10.1371/journal.pone.0177630 PMID:28498843

Klein, T., Thu, H. P., & Walther, T. (2018). Bitcoin is not the New Gold–A comparison of volatility, correlation, and portfolio performance. *International Review of Financial Analysis, 59*, 105–116. doi:10.1016/j.irfa.2018.07.010

Kroner, K. F., & Sultan, J. (1993). Time-varying distributions and dynamic hedging with foreign currency futures. *Journal of Financial and Quantitative Analysis, 28*(4), 535–551. doi:10.2307/2331164

Kuen, T. Y., & Hoong, T. S. (1992). Forecasting volatility in the Singapore stock market. *Asia Pacific Journal of Management, 9*(1), 1–13. doi:10.1007/BF01732034

Lai, Y. S., & Sheu, H. J. (2011). On the importance of asymmetries for dynamic hedging during the subprime crisis. *Applied Financial Economics, 21*(11), 801–813. doi:10.1080/09603107.2010.539535

Lau, M. C. K., Vigne, S. A., Wang, S., & Yarovaya, L. (2017). Return spillovers between white precious metal ETFs: The role of oil, gold, and global equity. *International Review of Financial Analysis, 52*, 316–332. doi:10.1016/j.irfa.2017.04.001

Lien, D., & Yang, L. (2006). Spot-futures spread, time-varying correlation, and hedging with currency futures. *Journal of Futures Markets, 26*(10), 1019–1038. doi:10.1002/fut.20225

Liu, Y., & Tsyvinski, A. (2021). Risks and returns of cryptocurrency. *Review of Financial Studies, 34*(6), 2689–2727. doi:10.1093/rfs/hhaa113

Lodha, S. (2017). A Cointegration and Causation Study of Gold Prices, Crude Oil Prices and Exchange Rates. *IUP Journal of Financial Risk Management, 14*(3), 55–66.

Louzis, D. P. (2015). Measuring spillover effects in Euro area financial markets: A disaggregate approach. *Empirical Economics, 49*(4), 1367–1400. doi:10.1007/s00181-014-0911-x

Madhavan, A. (2000). Market microstructure: A survey. *Journal of Financial Markets, 3*(3), 205–258. doi:10.1016/S1386-4181(00)00007-0

Manera, M., McAleer, M., & Grasso, M. (2006). Modelling time-varying conditional correlations in the volatility of Tapis oil spot and forward returns. *Applied Financial Economics, 16*(07), 525–533. doi:10.1080/09603100500426465

Mensi, W., Hammoudeh, S., Nguyen, D. K., & Yoon, S. M. (2014). Dynamic spillovers among major energy and cereal commodity prices. *Energy Economics, 43*, 225–243. doi:10.1016/j.eneco.2014.03.004

Momtaz, P. P. (2021). The pricing and performance of cryptocurrency. *European Journal of Finance, 27*(4-5), 367–380. doi:10.1080/1351847X.2019.1647259

Nakamoto, S. (2008). Bitcoin: A peer-to-peer electronic cash system. *Decentralized business review*, 21260.

Ozdemir, H., & Ozdemir, Z. A. (2021). *A Survey of Hedge and Safe Havens Assets against G-7 Stock Markets before and during the COVID-19 Pandemic* (No. 14888). IZA Discussion Papers.

Özdemir, O. (2022). Cue the volatility spillover in the cryptocurrency markets during the COVID-19 pandemic: Evidence from DCC-GARCH and wavelet analysis. *Financial Innovation, 8*(1), 1–38. doi:10.1186/s40854-021-00319-0 PMID:35132369

Qarni, M. O., & Gulzar, S. (2021). Portfolio diversification benefits of alternative currency investment in Bitcoin and foreign exchange markets. *Financial Innovation, 7*(1), 1–37. doi:10.1186/s40854-021-00233-5

Šimáková, J. (2011). Analysis of the relationship between oil and gold prices. *The Journal of Finance, 51*(1), 651–662.

Stoklasová, R. (2018). Short-term and Long-term relationships between Gold Prices and Oil Prices. *Scientific papers of the University of Pardubice. Series D. Faculty of Economics and Administration., 43*, 221–231.

TansuchatR.ChangC. L.McAleerM. (2010). Crude oil hedging strategies using dynamic multivariate GARCH. *Available at* SSRN 1531187. doi:10.2139/ssrn.1531187

Toraman, C., Basarir, C., & Bayramoglu, M. F. (2011). Effects of crude oil price changes on sector indices of Istanbul stock exchange. *European Journal of Economic and Political Studies, 4*(2), 109–124.

Toyoshima, Y., Nakajima, T., & Hamori, S. (2013). Crude oil hedging strategy: New evidence from the data of the financial crisis. *Applied Financial Economics, 23*(12), 1033–1041. doi:10.1080/09603107.2013.788779

Tse, Y. K., & Tsui, A. K. C. (2002). A multivariate generalized autoregressive conditional heteroscedasticity model with time-varying correlations. *Journal of Business & Economic Statistics, 20*(3), 351–362. doi:10.1198/073500102288618496

Urquhart, A., & Zhang, H. (2019). Is Bitcoin a hedge or safe haven for currencies? An intraday analysis. *International Review of Financial Analysis, 63*, 49–57. doi:10.1016/j.irfa.2019.02.009

Zhang, C., & Tu, X. (2016). The effect of global oil price shocks on China's metal markets. *Energy Policy, 90*, 131–139. doi:10.1016/j.enpol.2015.12.012

Zhang, D., Lei, L., Ji, Q., & Kutan, A. M. (2019). Economic policy uncertainty in the US and China and their impact on the global markets. *Economic Modelling, 79*, 47–56. doi:10.1016/j.econmod.2018.09.028

Zhang, X., Yu, L., Wang, S., & Lai, K. K. (2009). Estimating the impact of extreme events on crude oil price: An EMD-based event analysis method. *Energy Economics, 31*(5), 768–778. doi:10.1016/j.eneco.2009.04.003

Zhang, Y. J., Bouri, E., Gupta, R., & Ma, S. J. (2021). Risk spillover between Bitcoin and conventional financial markets: An expectile-based approach. *The North American Journal of Economics and Finance, 55*, 101296. doi:10.1016/j.najef.2020.101296

Chapter 17
Metaverse Metamorphosis:
Bridging the Gap Between Research Insights and Industry Applications

Manpreet Arora

https://orcid.org/0000-0002-4939-1992

School of Commerce and Management Studies, Central University of Himachal Pradesh, India

ABSTRACT

The incorporation of the metaverse into the world of business has brought about a significant and fundamental change, altering conventional frameworks and methods while presenting unparalleled prospects for expansion and creativity. This chapter examines the significant influence of the transformation of the metaverse on the worldwide economy, emphasising its ability to generate fresh prospects for work, labour, and employment. In addition, an attempt has been made to explore the economic consequences of the metaverse, encompassing the emergence of fresh sectors, markets, and sources of income, as well as the promotion of economic expansion and employment generation. This chapter examines the impact of the metaverse on economic development, innovation, and quality of life globally, highlighting its revolutionary capabilities. Furthermore, the author explores the significance of closing the divide between research discoveries and industrial implementations, highlighting the necessity of cooperation and information sharing to convert academic discoveries into tangible advancements that have a tangible effect on the real world. This chapter examines the impact of the metaverse on economic development, innovation, and quality of life globally.

INTRODUCTION

Artificial intelligence (AI) is crucial in multi-business contexts since it offers sophisticated analytics, automation, and decision-making abilities across diverse industries (Arora and Sharma; 2022). Whereas the metaverse has arisen as a powerful and game-changing force in the field of technology, with the potential to revolutionise our interactions with digital environments and each other. The metaverse fundamentally embodies the merging of virtual and physical realities, erasing the distinctions between the

DOI: 10.4018/979-8-3693-2607-7.ch017

digital and the tangible (Rathore & Arora, 2024). The metaverse differs from conventional virtual reality experiences by including a wide and linked network of virtual environments, allowing users to interact, create, and transact in real time (Narula, 2022; Bojic, 2022). The metaverse is characterised by its immersive quality, which allows users to feel fully present and have control within virtual surroundings. The metaverse allows users to utilise cutting-edge technologies like virtual reality, augmented reality, artificial intelligence, and blockchain to assume digital avatars, navigate virtual environments, and participate in various activities, including socialising, gaming, shopping, and education. This immersive experience has the capacity to transform the way we engage in work, leisure, and social interactions, surpassing the constraints of physical boundaries and temporal limits. Furthermore, the metaverse is not merely a static digital recreational area, but rather a vibrant and developing system propelled by user-created material and interactions. It encompasses the ideals of decentralisation and democratisation, giving individuals and communities the opportunity to build their own virtual experiences and economies. The metaverse provides a wide range of options for creativity, entrepreneurship, and innovation (Dhiman & Arora, 2024). It also includes virtual real estate, digital assets, virtual events, and entertainment. Nevertheless, the advent of the metaverse also gives rise to a multitude of intricate ethical, social, and economic inquiries that require meticulous examination. Concerns surrounding digital privacy, virtual identity, intellectual property rights, and algorithmic bias are becoming more relevant as the metaverse brings together virtual experiences and their real-world impacts. Moreover, the possibility of virtual addiction, social seclusion, and digital disparity emphasises the necessity for conscientious design and control to guarantee that the advantages of the metaverse are fairly distributed and available to everyone. The academia plays a crucial role in filling the knowledge gaps related to the metaverse and in advancing research, innovation, and policy formulation in this emergent domain. Academia can contribute to the responsible, equitable, and sustainable development of the metaverse by creating theoretical frameworks, analysing ethical and societal consequences, connecting academia with industry, promoting accessibility and inclusivity, and studying economic dynamics.

The incorporation of the metaverse into many industries, sectors, domains, and disciplines has the capacity to completely transform conventional processes, workflows, and experiences, while also resolving long-standing deficiencies. The benefits of utilising the metaverse are becoming more evident in several domains.

Within the field of education, the metaverse provides immersive and interactive learning environments that beyond the constraints of conventional classrooms. Students can actively participate in intricate ideas through practical simulations, computer-generated laboratories, and interactive instructional materials, promoting a more profound comprehension and long-term retention of knowledge. In addition, the metaverse promotes worldwide collaboration and provides access to educational resources, allowing learners from various backgrounds to connect and acquire knowledge from one another. The democratisation of education facilitates the elimination of geographical obstacles and socioeconomic inequities, thereby guaranteeing everyone access to high-quality education.

The metaverse has the potential to enhance patient care, medical training, and research in the field of healthcare. Virtual reality simulations enable medical students and professionals to engage in realistic settings to practise surgical operations and diagnostic skills, thereby minimising the requirement for expensive and time-consuming physical simulations. Telemedicine platforms that utilise augmented reality allow for remote consultations and diagnostics, hence increasing the availability of healthcare services in locations that lack sufficient access. In addition, the metaverse enables the exchange of data and cooperation among researchers, expediting the progress of novel treatments and therapies for diverse medical ailments. Looking further, the entertainment and gaming sectors have promptly adopted the metaverse, utilising its immersive features to develop fascinating experiences for users. Virtual reality gaming allows players to immerse themselves in imaginative realms, where they can actively engage with virtual characters, explore diverse settings, and partake in exhilarating quests. In addition, the metaverse erases the boundaries between gaming, socialising, and entertainment, offering possibilities for real-time events, virtual concerts, and interactive narrative encounters. The integration of entertainment and technology in this context improves user involvement and promotes a feeling of camaraderie among players, thus addressing the typical sense of seclusion found in conventional gaming encounters. Within the domain of business and commerce, the metaverse presents novel prospects for marketing, sales, and client interaction. Virtual showrooms and storefronts enable businesses to exhibit their products and services in immersive surroundings, offering customers a more captivating and interactive purchasing experience (Lee & Leonas, (2018); Violante, Vezzetti & Piazzolla, (2019); Hagtvedt & Chandukala, (2023); Erensoy et.al., (2022, December)). Virtual events and conferences allow companies to connect with a worldwide audience without the requirement of physical locations, resulting in cost savings and a reduced environmental footprint. In addition, the metaverse enables virtual collaboration and remote work, allowing teams to communicate across different physical locations and time zones, thus circumventing the limitations of typical office settings.

The metaverse provides architects, real estate developers, and urban planners with a potent instrument for visualising and modelling building designs and urban environments (Schumacher, 2022). Virtual reality walkthroughs enable clients to immerse themselves in architectural plans with intricate detail prior to the commencement of construction, thereby minimising expensive modifications and improving stakeholder involvement. In addition, virtual property tours allow potential buyers and renters to remotely examine real estate listings, thereby increasing market coverage and simplifying well-informed decision-making. The metaverse has the capacity to revolutionise the travel and tourism sector by providing virtual travel experiences that accurately replicate real-world destinations (Buhalis, Leung, & Lin, (2023); Um et.al., (2022, January); Gursoy, Malodia & Dhir, (2022); Volchek & Brysch, (2023, January); Go & Kang, (2023)). Virtual tourism platforms enable users to virtually see famous monuments, breathtaking natural wonders, and captivating cultural attractions without leaving their homes. These platforms offer a glimpse of other places and serve as a source of inspiration for future travel arrangements. Moreover, virtual travel experiences can accommodate persons with limited mobility or financial restrictions, hence enhancing travel accessibility and inclusivity. In the manufacturing sector, the metaverse offers opportunities for virtual prototyping, product design, and process optimization (Yao, et.al., 2024). Virtual reality simulations enable manufacturers to test product designs, manufacturing processes, and assembly lines in virtual environments, identifying potential issues and optimizing efficiency before physical production begins. Additionally, virtual collaboration platforms facilitate communication and collaboration among global teams, streamlining product development and reducing time-to-market. The metaverse offers novel opportunities for artistic and expressive endeavours across diverse creative sectors, including as art, music, film, and design (Baía Reis & Ashmore, (2022); Dionisio, et.al., (2013); Armitage, (2023); FREYERMUTH, (2022)). Virtual reality art galleries and immersive installations enable artists to exhibit their work in novel ways, reaching worldwide audiences and cultivating fresh modes of artistic expression. Virtual reality concerts and music festivals allow musicians to engage with listeners in immersive and interactive settings, surpassing the constraints of conventional live shows. Governments and public institutions have the ability to utilise the metaverse in order to enhance civic participation, public services, and governance (Allam, et.al., 2022). Virtual town halls and community forums facilitate global citizen participation in decision-making processes, hence enhancing transparency and accountability. In addition, virtual training simulations can enhance the preparedness and response capacities of government organisations and emergency responders by allowing them to practise and train for a range of scenarios, including natural disasters and public health emergencies.

The metaverse has the capacity to address enduring limitations in several businesses and sectors by offering immersive, interactive, and easily accessible solutions. The metaverse provides new solutions to solve the issues of the digital age, such as reducing geographical barriers in education and healthcare, enhancing user engagement in entertainment and gaming, and improving collaboration and productivity in business and commerce. As organisations and individuals further investigate the potential of the metaverse, the beneficial impacts are expected to increase, leading to a new era of interconnectedness, ingenuity, and advancement.

THE OPPORTUNITIES

The incorporation of the metaverse into the commercial world has fundamentally transformed the economic framework, providing many prospects for advancement, creativity, and success. The metaverse has revolutionised various industries and sectors by introducing a new era of connectivity, cooperation, and commerce. This transformation has had a significant impact on old business models and practices.

The metaverse has a profound influence on the corporate landscape by generating fresh prospects for work, labour, and employment. With the growing prevalence of virtual environments, various areas are witnessing the emergence of new jobs and job prospects; the prospects in gig economy are very bright (Arora & Singh, 2023). These include virtual reality creation, digital marketing, virtual event organising, and virtual commerce. The expansion of job options not only facilitates economic progress but also cultivates a climate of creativity and business initiative, stimulating general economic expansion and well-being. Furthermore, the metaverse presents unparalleled prospects for firms to access worldwide markets and enhance their clientele. E-commerce platforms, online marketplaces, and interactive shopping interfaces facilitate global business-customer interactions, surpassing limitations of distance and time. The extensive global presence not only enhances sales and revenue channels, but also facilitates cultural interchange and diversity, enhancing the commercial environment and promoting international collaboration and comprehension.

Moreover, the metaverse improves the efficiency and convenience of everyday activities for both companies and customers. Virtual collaboration solutions facilitate efficient cooperation among remote teams, allowing them to overcome geographical limitations and time restrictions. Virtual reality meetings, conferences, and training sessions provide immersive and interactive experiences that replicate real-world interactions, hence increasing productivity and engagement (Arora, 2024). Moreover, virtual assistants and AI-powered chatbots enhance the efficiency of customer care and support procedures by offering tailored guidance and promptly addressing inquiries.

The expansion of the metaverse also fosters economic development by generating new sectors, markets, and sources of income. The metaverse economy is primarily supported by virtual real estate, digital assets, and virtual currencies, which present many prospects for investment, speculation, and entrepreneurship. Entrepreneurial ventures contribute to a great deal towards economic development where digitalization is playing a pivotal role (Dhiman & Arora, 2024). Virtual events, entertainment experiences, and digital collectibles provide more opportunities for making money and generating revenue, stimulating economic activity and promoting job growth in many industries (Arora, Kumar & Valeri, 2023). The convergence of the metaverse and artificial intelligence (AI) offers unparalleled prospects for fostering sustainability and accelerating the attainment of the United Nations Sustainable Development Goals (SDGs). The metaverse can enhance resource management, minimise environmental impact, and expedite progress towards sustainable development goals by utilising virtual simulations, AI-powered analytics, and data-driven decision-making. Virtual reality training programmes can instruct individuals and organisations on sustainable practices, including the use of renewable energy, waste reduction, and conservation initiatives. Artificial intelligence algorithms have the capability to analyse extensive quantities of data obtained from virtual environments in order to enhance energy efficiency, transportation systems, and urban planning, resulting in the development of more sustainable and resilient cities. Furthermore, the metaverse facilitates telecommuting and virtual cooperation, so decreasing the necessity for physical transportation and travel, ultimately resulting in reduced carbon emissions and the alleviation of climate change. In addition, the widespread use of the metaverse and AI-powered technology presents novel employment prospects for achievement of SDGS in many sectors (Arora & Chandel, 2023). In various areas like AI coding, sustainability advisory, and digital advertising, it can promote fostering economic expansion and societal integration. By utilising the revolutionary capabilities of the metaverse and AI to advance sustainability and generate significant employment prospects, we can expedite the achievement of the Sustainable Development Goals (SDGs) and establish a more prosperous and fair future for everyone.

Ultimately, the transformation caused by the metaverse has fundamentally altered the entire landscape of business, opening up abundant possibilities for expansion, creativity, and success. The metaverse has the ability to greatly contribute to economic development and improve the quality of life for individuals and communities worldwide. It achieves this by introducing new job opportunities, increasing global markets, making living easier, and promoting economic growth. As businesses increasingly adopt the metaverse, we can anticipate a surge in invention, collaboration, and economic growth in the future.

ADDRESSING THE GAPS

The academic community plays a crucial role in influencing the discussion about the metaverse and in furthering our comprehension of its possible uses, consequences, and difficulties. Nevertheless, despite the growing interest and enthusiasm around this developing topic, there are certain deficiencies that academia must address in order to fully achieve the potential of the metaverse.

A notable deficiency exists in the theoretical underpinnings of the metaverse. Although there is a considerable amount of study on the technical elements of virtual reality, augmented reality, and related technologies, there is still a requirement for comprehensive theoretical frameworks that can assist us in understanding the metaverse as a complex socio-technical phenomenon. Academia can contribute by creating interdisciplinary methodologies that incorporate knowledge from disciplines such as sociology, psychology, anthropology, and communication studies to investigate the cultural, psychological, and social aspects of the metaverse. Another shortcoming lies in comprehending the ethical and societal ramifications of the metaverse. As virtual environments grow more integrated into our daily lives, it is essential to carefully analyse the ethical quandaries and societal repercussions that emerge. Topics such as digital privacy, virtual identity, digital inequality, and algorithmic prejudice necessitate meticulous examination and study. The academic community may have a significant impact by conducting empirical research, ethical investigations, and policy analysis to provide valuable insights for the responsible development and management of the metaverse.

Moreover, there exists a significant disparity in connecting the gap between academia and industry inside the dominion of the metaverse. Although academia frequently pioneers' advancements in knowledge and innovation, there can be a gap between academic research and industry practices. Academia may enhance collaboration and knowledge sharing with industry partners by implementing initiatives including collaborative research projects, industry-academic alliances, and technology transfer programmes. By closing this divide, academics can guarantee that research discoveries are converted into tangible implementations that yield societal benefits and stimulate economic expansion. Furthermore, there is a deficiency in effectively addressing the issues of accessibility and diversity inside the metaverse. With the increasing prevalence of virtual environments, it is crucial to guarantee their accessibility to individuals of diverse abilities and backgrounds. This encompasses the creation of user interfaces that are accessible to all users, the creation of technologies that aid individuals with disabilities, and the promotion of digital literacy and the enhancement of skills. Academia can take the lead in developing accessibility guidelines, conducting usability research, and advocating for inclusive design principles in the development of metaverse platforms and applications.

Ultimately, there exists a lack of comprehension of the economic workings of the metaverse. With the rise of virtual economies and digital marketplaces, it is crucial to create strong economic models and frameworks to effectively analyse and comprehend these phenomena. This encompasses the examination of virtual currencies, digital assets, virtual property rights, and the rise of novel business models and sources of income. Academia may make valuable contributions to the metaverse economy by doing empirical research, performing economic analysis, and evaluating policies. These efforts can provide valuable information for decision-making and regulation in this emerging field.

Academicians have multiple obstacles when it comes to bridging the divide between research discoveries and industry applications.

Differing Objectives and Timelines

Academia and industry can have divergent objectives and deadlines. Academia places importance on meticulous research and extensive examination of theoretical ideas, whereas industry prioritises practical resolutions and immediate results. The misalignment between academia and industry partners might pose challenges for researchers in adapting their results to meet the specific needs and limitations of the sector.

Access to Resources and Infrastructure

Scholars may encounter constraints when it comes to getting the resources and infrastructure required to transform their research into concrete applications. Industries frequently have access to specialised equipment, technology, and money that may not be easily accessible in university environments. The scarcity of resources might impede the progress and execution of research-based solutions in practical situations.

Intellectual Property and Commercialization

The presence of intellectual property rights and the need to consider commercialization might pose substantial obstacles in connecting academia and industry. Scholars may encounter difficulties in navigating the intricate realm of patents, licencing agreements, and commercialization channels, particularly when working along with corporate partners. Successfully managing the simultaneous goals of achieving high academic standards and turning research findings into profitable products necessitates skillful negotiating and meticulous strategic planning.

Communication and Collaboration

Efficient communication and collaboration between academia and industry are crucial for closing the divide between research findings and practical implementations in the business world. Nevertheless, disparities in communication methods, anticipated outcomes, and corporate cultures might impede cooperation. Academics should actively interact with industry stakeholders, establish connections, and effectively communicate their research findings in a manner that aligns with industry requirements and priorities.

Risk Aversion and Institutional Barriers

The existing institutional frameworks and motivators inside academia could unintentionally impede the willingness to take risks and engage in innovative practices. The prioritisation of publishing metrics, tenure criteria, and academic reputation may discourage academics from engaging in practical research and collaborating with industries. To overcome these institutional impediments, it is necessary to obtain support from academic institutions and to change towards acknowledging and incentivizing interdisciplinary collaboration and tangible real-world outcomes.

Interdisciplinary Collaboration and Knowledge Integration

Facilitating the connection between research findings and practical implementation in many industries often necessitates the collaboration of experts from different disciplines and the integration of their knowledge. Nevertheless, multidisciplinary research poses difficulties as a result of disciplinary silos, communication impediments, and divergent techniques. Academics should proactively pursue chances for interdisciplinary collaboration, utilise a range of views, and incorporate insights from other fields to effectively tackle difficult real-world issues.

Insufficient Practical Experience

Academicians may have a limited understanding of the real-world issues and limitations encountered by industry professionals due to their lack of firsthand experience in industry settings. Lacking practical experience, academics may face difficulties in formulating research answers that are genuinely relevant and applicable to real-life situations.

Cultural Differences

Cultural disparities exist between academia and industry, characterised by contrasting cultural environments, encompassing divergent values, conventions, and expectations. The presence of cultural disparities can impede cooperation and effective communication, resulting in misinterpretations and disputes.

Academics should be aware of these cultural distinctions and strive to establish trust and rapport with industry collaborators.

Technology Transfer and Commercialization Processes

The technology transfer and commercialization processes involve the transfer of technology from academic institutions to the industry and the conversion of research outputs into commercial products. These processes can be intricate and need a significant amount of time. Academics may have insufficient knowledge and skills to efficiently traverse these processes, resulting in delays and inefficiencies. Engaging with technology transfer offices and industry specialists can assist academics in overcoming these obstacles and optimising the influence of their research.

Resistance to Change

Resistance to change, whether it occurs in academia or industry, can hinder attempts to connect research findings with practical applications in the business world. Academics may face opposition from colleagues or administrators who are doubtful of multidisciplinary collaboration or commercialization endeavours. Likewise, individuals involved in the sector may be hesitant to embrace novel technologies or methods that question established norms. To overcome this resistance, it is necessary to have robust leadership, efficient communication, and a dedication to innovation and advancement.

Sustainability and Scalability

Academicians have the difficulty of ensuring the long-term viability and ability to expand research-driven solutions. Although academic research may produce encouraging outcomes in controlled environments, implementing these ideas on a larger scale to address the requirements of industry and society as a whole can be difficult. When developing research-driven solutions for industry applications, academicians must take into account variables such as cost-effectiveness, scalability, and long-term viability.

Ethical and Social Considerations

Academicians must confront ethical and societal considerations when applying research results to industry. Research-based solutions can potentially lead to unforeseen repercussions or ethical issues that require thorough examination and resolution. Scholars must carefully and honestly address these ethical and social factors, ensuring that their research has a beneficial impact on society as a whole.

In order to connect research findings with practical applications in industry, academics must cross a multifaceted terrain of institutional, cultural, and practical obstacles. Through promoting collaboration, communication, and interdisciplinary involvement, academics can surmount these obstacles and make valuable contributions to the creation and execution of research-based solutions that have significant effects on both industry and society.

CONCLUSION

To summarise, the metaverse signifies a fundamental change in our understanding and engagement with digital technology, presenting extraordinary possibilities as well as difficulties. As we begin this process of transforming the metaverse, it is crucial to approach it with a discerning and reflective mindset, ensuring that we balance creativity with ethical considerations and uphold the ideals of inclusivity, diversity, and sustainability. The complete use of the metaverse's potential to establish a more linked, immersive, and fair digital future can only be achieved through cooperative endeavours and careful management. Ultimately, the rise of the metaverse signifies a fundamental change in how we engage with digital technology, presenting unparalleled opportunities as well as notable obstacles. As we begin this transforming journey, it is crucial to approach the metaverse with a thoughtful and introspective perspective, acknowledging both its possibilities and its drawbacks. The metaverse has the potential to profoundly transform multiple facets of human existence, encompassing domains such as education, healthcare, entertainment, and business. The immersive and linked nature of this technology provides unprecedented prospects for creativity, collaboration, and invention. However, fully harnessing the capabilities of the metaverse necessitates thoughtful examination of the ethical, societal, and economic consequences. It is imperative to give priority to inclusivity, diversity, and sustainability while creating and implementing metaverse technologies, with the aim of ensuring that they have a positive impact on individuals and communities worldwide. Through promoting collaboration, communication, and cooperation among academia, industry, and government, we may effectively navigate the intricacies of the metaverse and utilise its revolutionary potential for the betterment of society.

Moreover, as we explore into the potentialities of the metaverse, it is imperative that we maintain a watchful eye on its potential hazards and difficulties. Topics such as digital privacy, virtual identity, economic injustice, and cultural homogenization necessitate careful examination and aggressive measures to address them. To overcome these obstacles and ensure the growth of the metaverse is proactive and ethical, we may construct a digital future that is interconnected, immersive, and equitable for everyone. In order for the metaverse to reach its maximum capabilities, it is essential for there to be a collaborative endeavour and responsible management. By engaging in cooperative efforts, fostering cross-disciplinary discussions, and exhibiting principled guidance, we have the ability to mould the metaverse into a catalyst for beneficial transformation, propelling advancements, financial expansion, and societal advancement in the future. Furthermore, as we explore the intricacies of the metaverse, it is crucial to sustain a harmonious equilibrium between groundbreaking advancements and ethical deliberations. Although the metaverse presents enticing prospects for innovation and progress, it is crucial to be aware of the potential repercussions that may arise from uncontrolled growth. Concerns like as the protection of data privacy, the presence of algorithmic bias, and the problem of digital addiction necessitate careful monitoring and regulation to protect the rights and welfare of users. By giving precedence to ethical values and adopting a human-centered design approach, we can guarantee that the metaverse will augment rather than diminish our quality of life.

Furthermore, prioritising inclusivity and accessibility is crucial in fully harnessing the capabilities of the metaverse. In our pursuit of the new digital era, it is crucial that we work towards closing the gap between those who have access to digital resources and those who do not. By giving priority to inclusivity and accessibility, we may construct a metaverse that accurately mirrors the wide range and depth of human experience.

Moreover, cultivating a culture of sustainability is crucial in constructing a metaverse that is both groundbreaking and conscientious towards the environment and society. The creation and functioning of virtual environments necessitate substantial energy and resources, and unregulated expansion could have adverse effects on the environment and worsen pre-existing inequities. Through the adoption of sustainable design methods, the reduction of carbon footprints, and the promotion of responsible consumption and production, we can lessen the negative environmental effects of the metaverse and guarantee its contribution to a more sustainable future for future generations.

To summarise, the metaverse offers a significant chance to redefine our engagement with digital technology and create our digital destiny. By adopting a thoughtful and introspective approach to the metaverse, emphasising moral issues, advocating for inclusivity and accessibility, and cultivating a sustainable culture, we may utilise its revolutionary potential to establish a more interconnected, immersive, and fair digital era. By engaging in cooperative endeavours and practicing accountable governance, we can unleash the complete capabilities of the metaverse and establish a path towards a more promising future for everyone.

REFERENCES

Allam, Z., Sharifi, A., Bibri, S. E., Jones, D. S., & Krogstie, J. (2022). The metaverse as a virtual form of smart cities: Opportunities and challenges for environmental, economic, and social sustainability in urban futures. *Smart Cities*, *5*(3), 771–801. doi:10.3390/smartcities5030040

Armitage, J. (2023). Rethinking haute couture: Julien Fournié in the virtual worlds of the metaverse. *French Cultural Studies*, *34*(2), 129–146. doi:10.1177/09571558221109708

Arora, M. (2024). Virtual Reality in Education: Analyzing the Literature and Bibliometric State of Knowledge. *Transforming Education with Virtual Reality*, 379-402.

Arora, M., & Chandel, M. (2023). SDGs and Skill Development: Perspectivizing future insights for the tourism industry. In Springer international handbooks of education (pp. 1–20). Springer. doi:10.1007/978-981-99-3895-7_26-1

Arora, M., Kumar, J., & Valeri, M. (2023). Crises and Resilience in the Age of Digitalization: Perspectivations of Past, Present and Future for tourism industry. In Emerald Publishing Limited eBooks. doi:10.1108/978-1-83797-166-420231004

Arora, M., & Sharma, R. L. (2022). Artificial intelligence and big data: Ontological and communicative perspectives in multi-sectoral scenarios of modern businesses. *Foresight*, *25*(1), 126–143. doi:10.1108/FS-10-2021-0216

Arora, M., & Singh, S. (2023). Women's empowerment through entrepreneurship in emerging economies. In Advances in logistics, operations, and management science book series (pp. 205–223). IGI Global. doi:10.4018/979-8-3693-0111-1.ch011

Baía Reis, A., & Ashmore, M. (2022). From video streaming to virtual reality worlds: An academic, reflective, and creative study on live theatre and performance in the metaverse. *International Journal of Performance Arts and Digital Media*, *18*(1), 7–28. doi:10.1080/14794713.2021.2024398

Bojic, L. (2022). Metaverse through the prism of power and addiction: What will happen when the virtual world becomes more attractive than reality? *European Journal of Futures Research*, *10*(1), 22. doi:10.1186/s40309-022-00208-4

Buhalis, D., Leung, D., & Lin, M. (2023). Metaverse as a disruptive technology revolutionising tourism management and marketing. *Tourism Management*, *97*, 104724. doi:10.1016/j.tourman.2023.104724

Dhiman, V., & Arora, M. (2024). Current State of Metaverse in Entrepreneurial Ecosystem: A Retrospective Analysis of Its Evolving Landscape. In Exploring the Use of Metaverse in Business and Education (pp. 73-87). IGI Global. doi:10.4018/979-8-3693-5868-9.ch005

Dhiman, V., & Arora, M. (2024). Exploring the linkage between business incubation and entrepreneurship: Understanding trends, themes and future research agenda. LBS Journal of Management & Research/ LBS. *Journal of Management Research*. doi:10.1108/LBSJMR-06-2023-0021

Dionisio, J. D. N., Iii, W. G. B., & Gilbert, R. (2013). 3D virtual worlds and the metaverse: Current status and future possibilities. *ACM Computing Surveys*, *45*(3), 1–38. doi:10.1145/2480741.2480751

Erensoy, A., Mathrani, A., Schnack, A., Zhao, Y., Chitale, V. S., & Baghaei, N. (2022, December). Comparing Customer Behaviours: Immersive Virtual Reality Store Experiences versus Web and Physical Store Experiences. In *2022 IEEE Asia-Pacific Conference on Computer Science and Data Engineering (CSDE)* (pp. 1-7). IEEE. 10.1109/CSDE56538.2022.10089288

Freyermuth, G. S. (2022). Vegas, Disney, and the Metaverse. *Studies of Digital Media Culture*, *14*, 17.

Go, H., & Kang, M. (2023). Metaverse tourism for sustainable tourism development: Tourism agenda 2030. *Tourism Review*, *78*(2), 381–394. doi:10.1108/TR-02-2022-0102

Gursoy, D., Malodia, S., & Dhir, A. (2022). The metaverse in the hospitality and tourism industry: An overview of current trends and future research directions. *Journal of Hospitality Marketing & Management*, *31*(5), 527–534. doi:10.1080/19368623.2022.2072504

Hagtvedt, H., & Chandukala, S. R. (2023). Immersive retailing: The in-store experience. *Journal of Retailing*, *99*(4), 505–517. doi:10.1016/j.jretai.2023.10.003

Lee, H., & Leonas, K. (2018). Consumer experiences, the key to survive in an omni-channel environment: Use of virtual technology. *Journal of Textile and Apparel, Technology and Management, 10*(3).

Narula, H. (2022). *Virtual Society: The Metaverse and the New Frontiers of Human Experience*. Crown Currency.

Rathore, S., & Arora, M. (2024). Sustainability Reporting in the Metaverse: A Multi-Sectoral Analysis. In Exploring the Use of Metaverse in Business and Education (pp. 147-165). IGI Global. doi:10.4018/979-8-3693-5868-9.ch009

Schumacher, P. (2022). The metaverse as opportunity for architecture and society: Design drivers, core competencies. *Architectural Intelligence*, *1*(1), 11. doi:10.1007/s44223-022-00010-z PMID:35993030

Um, T., Kim, H., Kim, H., Lee, J., Koo, C., & Chung, N. (2022, January). Travel Incheon as a metaverse: smart tourism cities development case in Korea. In *ENTER22 e-Tourism Conference* (pp. 226–231). Springer International Publishing. doi:10.1007/978-3-030-94751-4_20

Violante, M. G., Vezzetti, E., & Piazzolla, P. (2019). How to design a virtual reality experience that impacts the consumer engagement: The case of the virtual supermarket. [IJIDeM]. *International Journal on Interactive Design and Manufacturing, 13*(1), 243–262. doi:10.1007/s12008-018-00528-5

Volchek, K., & Brysch, A. (2023, January). Metaverse and tourism: From a new niche to a transformation. In *ENTER22 e-Tourism Conference* (pp. 300–311). Springer Nature Switzerland. doi:10.1007/978-3-031-25752-0_32

Yao, X., Ma, N., Zhang, J., Wang, K., Yang, E., & Faccio, M. (2024). Enhancing wisdom manufacturing as industrial metaverse for industry and society 5.0. *Journal of Intelligent Manufacturing, 35*(1), 235–255. doi:10.1007/s10845-022-02027-7

Compilation of References

A3Logics. (2023, May 18). How Metaverse Gaming Bought Revolution in Gaming Industry. *A3logics Blog.* https://www. a3logics.com/blog/metaverse-gaming-a-revolution-in-the-gaming-industry

Abbate, S., Centobelli, P., Cerchione, R., Oropallo, E., & Riccio, E. (2022, April). *A first bibliometric literature review on Metaverse. In 2022 IEEE Technology and Engineering Management Conference.* TEMSCON EUROPE.

Abdelghafar, S., Ezzat, D., Darwish, A., & Hassanien, A. E. (2023). Metaverse for Brain Computer Interface: Towards New and Improved Applications. In *The Future of Metaverse in the Virtual Era and Physical World* (pp. 43–58). Springer International Publishing. doi:10.1007/978-3-031-29132-6_3

Abrash, M. (2021, Dec 11-16). Creating the Future: Augmented Reality, the next Human-Machine Interface. *IEEE International Electron Devices Meeting.* IEEE International Electron Devices Meeting (IEDM), San Francisco, CA. 10.1109/IEDM19574.2021.9720526

Abumalloh, R. A., Nilashi, M., Ooi, K. B., Wei-Han, G., Cham, T. H., Dwivedi, Y. K., & Hughes, L. (2023). The adoption of a metaverse in the retail industry and its impact on sustainable competitive advantage: The moderating impact of sustainability commitment. *Annals of Operations Research*, 1–42. doi:10.1007/s10479-023-05608-8

Acevedo Nieto, J. (2022). Una introducción al metaverso: conceptualización y alcance de un nuevo universe. *adComunica,* (24), 41-56. doi:10.6035/adcomunica.6544

Adinew, Y. (2023). A comparative study on motivational strategies, organizational culture, and climate in public and private institutions. *Current Psychology (New Brunswick, N.J.)*, 1–23.

Afrashtehfar, K. I., & Abu-Fanas, A. S. H. (2022). Metaverse, Crypto, and NFTs in Dentistry. *Education Sciences, 12*(8), 538. https://www.mdpi.com/2227-7102/12/8/538. doi:10.3390/educsci12080538

Agarwal, R., & Prasad, J. (2000). The role of e-commerce success factors in customer satisfaction. *Journal of the Academy of Marketing Science, 28*(1), 18–25. doi:10.1177/0092070300281002

Agbo, F. J., Oyelere, S. S., Suhonen, J., & Tukiainen, M. (2021). Scientific production and thematic breakthroughs in smart learning environments: A bibliometric analysis. *Smart Learning Environments, 8*(1), 1–25. doi:10.1186/s40561-020-00145-4

Ahmad, M., Akram, M., & Ureeb, S. (2024). Exploring the Role of Metaverse in Promoting Religious Tourism. In *Service Innovations in Tourism: Metaverse, Immersive Technologies, and Digital Twin* (pp. 39–63). IGI Global. doi:10.4018/979-8-3693-1103-5.ch003

Ahn, S. J., Kim, J., & Kim, J. (2022). The future of advertising research in virtual, augmented, and extended realities. *International Journal of Advertising*, 1–9. doi:10.1080/02650487.2022.2137316

Akpan, I. J., Soopramanien, D., & Kwak, D. H. (2021). Cutting-edge technologies for small business and innovation in the era of COVID-19 global health pandemic. *Journal of Small Business and Entrepreneurship, 33*(6), 607–617. doi:10.1080/08276331.2020.1799294

Al-Adwan, A. S., Li, N., Al-Adwan, A., Abbasi, G. A., Albelbis, N. A., & Habibi, A. (2023). Extending the Technology Acceptance Model (TAM) to Predict University Students' Intentions to Use Metaverse-Based Learning Platforms. *Education and Information Technologies, 28*(11), 15381–15413. doi:10.1007/s10639-023-11816-3 PMID:37361794

Albayati, H. (2024). Investigating undergraduate students' perceptions and awareness of using ChatGPT as a regular assistance tool: A user acceptance perspective study. *Computers and Education: Artificial Intelligence, 6*, 100203. doi:10.1016/j.caeai.2024.100203

Al-Emran, M. (2023). Beyond technology acceptance: Development and evaluation of technology-environmental, economic, and social sustainability theory. *Technology in Society, 75*, 102383. doi:10.1016/j.techsoc.2023.102383

Alessandrini, L., & Rognoli, V. (2023). Introducing the material experience concept in the metaverse and in virtual environments. In *Connectivity and Creativity in times of Conflict*. Academia Press. doi:10.26530/9789401496476-057

Alexandrova, E., & Poddubnaya, M. (2023). Metaverse in fashion industry development: applications and challenges. *E3S Web of Conferences, 420*, 06019. doi:10.1051/e3sconf/202342006019

Al-Ghaili, A. M., Kasim, H., Al-Hada, N. M., Hassan, Z. B., Othman, M., Tharik, J. H., Kasmani, R. M., & Shayea, I. (2022). A review of Metaverse's definitions, architecture, applications, challenges, issues, solutions, and future trends. *IEEE Access : Practical Innovations, Open Solutions, 10*, 125835–125866. doi:10.1109/ACCESS.2022.3225638

Ali, M., Naeem, F., Kaddoum, G., & Hossain, E. (2023). Metaverse communications, networking, security, and applications: Research issues, state-of-the-art, and future directions. *IEEE Communications Surveys & Tutorials*. 10.1051/shsconf/202316400001

Ali, M., Naeem, F., Kaddoum, G., & Hossain, E. (2023). Metaverse communications, networking, security, and applications: Research issues, state-of-the-art, and future directions. *IEEE Communications Surveys and Tutorials, 1*. doi:10.1109/COMST.2023.3347172

Ali, S., Abdullah, Armand, T. P. T., Athar, A., Hussain, A., Ali, M., Yaseen, M., Joo, M.-I., & Kim, H.-C. (2023). Metaverse in healthcare integrated with explainable ai and blockchain: Enabling immersiveness, ensuring trust, and providing patient data security. *Sensors (Basel), 23*(2), 565. doi:10.3390/s23020565 PMID:36679361

Allam, Z., Sharifi, A., Bibri, S. E., Jones, D. S., & Krogstie, J. (2022). The Metaverse as a virtual form of smart Cities: Opportunities and challenges for environmental, economic, and social sustainability in urban futures. *Smart Cities, 5*(3), 771–801. doi:10.3390/smartcities5030040

Almansour, B. (2015). The impact of market sentiment index on stock returns: An empirical investigation on Kuala Lumpur Stock Exchange. *Journal of Arts, Science & Commerce, 6*(3).

Almansour, B. Y., & Arabyat, Y. A. (2017). Investment decision making among Gulf investors: Behavioural finance perspective. *International Journal of Management Studies, 24*(1), 41–71. doi:10.32890/ijms.24.1.2017.10476

Almansour, B. Y., & Inairat, M. (2020). The impact of exchange rates on bitcoin returns: Further evidence from a time series framework. *International Journal of Scientific & Technology Research, 9*(02), 4577–4581.

Al-Taie, M. Z., & Kadry, S. (2017). Information Diffusion in Social Networks. In *Python for Graph and Network Analysis. Advanced Information and Knowledge Processing*. Springer. doi:10.1007/978-3-319-53004-8_8

Alzayat, A., & Lee, S. H. M. (2021). Virtual products as an extension of my body: Exploring hedonic and utilitarian shopping value in a virtual reality retail environment. *Journal of Business Research*, *130*, 348–363. doi:10.1016/j.jbusres.2021.03.017

Ambika, A., Belk, R., Jain, V., & Krishna, R. (2023). The road to learning "who am I" is digitized: A study on consumer self-discovery through augmented reality tools. *Journal of Consumer Behaviour*, *22*(5), 1112–1127. doi:10.1002/cb.2185

Ardia, D., Bluteau, K., & Rüede, M. (2019). Regime changes in Bitcoin GARCH volatility dynamics. *Finance Research Letters*, *29*, 266–271. doi:10.1016/j.frl.2018.08.009

Aria, M., & Cuccurullo, C. (2017). Bibliometrix: An R-tool for comprehensive science mapping analysis. *Journal of Informetrics*, *11*(4), 959–975. doi:10.1016/j.joi.2017.08.007

Ariel Gendler, M. (2023). De la cibernética al metaverso: Una genealogía de características, transparencias y opacidades algorítmicas. *Disparidades. Revista de Antropologia*, *78*(1), e001b. doi:10.3989/dra.2023.001b

Armitage, J. (2023). Rethinking haute couture: Julien Fournié in the virtual worlds of the metaverse. *French Cultural Studies*, *34*(2), 129–146. doi:10.1177/09571558221109708

Arora, M. (2024). Virtual Reality in Education: Analyzing the Literature and Bibliometric State of Knowledge. *Transforming Education with Virtual Reality*, 379-402.

Arora, M., & Chandel, M. (2023). SDGs and Skill Development: Perspectivizing future insights for the tourism industry. In Springer international handbooks of education (pp. 1–20). Springer. doi:10.1007/978-981-99-3895-7_26-1

Arora, M., & Rathore, S. (2023). Sustainability Reporting and Research and Development in Tourism Industry: A Qualitative Inquiry of Present Trends and Avenues. In International Handbook of Skill, Education, Learning, and Research Development in Tourism and Hospitality (pp. 1-17). Singapore: Springer Nature Singapore. doi:10.1007/978-981-99-3895-7_33-1

Arora, M., & Singh, S. (2023). Women's empowerment through entrepreneurship in emerging economies. In Advances in logistics, operations, and management science book series (pp. 205–223). IGI Global. doi:10.4018/979-8-3693-0111-1.ch011

Arora, M., Dhiman, V., & Sharma, R. L. (2023). Exploring the Dimensions of Spirituality, Wellness and Value Creation amidst Himalayan Regions Promoting Entrepreneurship and Sustainability. *Journal of Tourismology*. doi:10.26650/jot.2023.9.2.1327877

Arora, M., Kumar, J., & Valeri, M. (2023). Crises and Resilience in the Age of Digitalization: Perspectivions of Past, Present and Future for tourism industry. In Emerald Publishing Limited eBooks. doi:10.1108/978-1-83797-166-420231004

Arora, M. (2020). Post-truth and marketing communication in technological age. In *Handbook of research on innovations in technology and marketing for the connected consumer* (pp. 94–108). IGI Global., doi:10.4018/978-1-7998-0131-3.ch005

Arora, M. (2024). Virtual Reality in Education Analyzing the literature and bibliometric state of knowledge. In *Transforming Education with Virtual Reality* (pp. 379–402). Wiley. doi:10.1002/9781394200498.ch22

Arora, M., & Sharma, R. L. (2022). Artificial intelligence and big data: Ontological and communicative perspectives in multi-sectoral scenarios of modern businesses. *Foresight*, *25*(1), 126–143. doi:10.1108/FS-10-2021-0216

Arpacı, İ., & Bahari, M. (2023). Investigating the role of psychological needs in predicting the educational sustainability of Metaverse using a deep learning-based hybrid SEM-ANN technique. *Interactive Learning Environments*, 1–13. doi:10.1080/10494820.2022.2164313

Arya, V., Sambyal, R., Sharma, A., & Dwivedi, Y. K. (2023). Brands are calling your AVATAR in Metaverse-A study to explore XR-based gamification marketing activities & consumer-based brand equity in virtual world. *Journal of Consumer Behaviour*. doi:10.1002/cb.2214

Ashmore, D., & Venz, S. (2023). *A brief history of Web 3.0*. Forbes Advisor. Retrieved May 20th, 2023 from https://www.forbes.com/advisor/au/investing/cryptocurrency/what-is-web-3-0/

Aslanidis, N., Bariviera, A. F., & Martínez-Ibañez, O. (2019). An analysis of cryptocurrencies conditional cross correlations. *Finance Research Letters*, *31*, 130–137. doi:10.1016/j.frl.2019.04.019

Athar, A., Ali, S. M., Mozumder, M. A. I., Ali, S., & Kim, H. C. (2023, February). Applications and Possible Challenges of Healthcare Metaverse. In *2023 25th International Conference on Advanced Communication Technology (ICACT)* (pp. 328-332). IEEE. 10.23919/ICACT56868.2023.10079314

Azuma, R. T. (1997). A Survey of Augmented Reality. *Presence (Cambridge, Mass.)*, *6*(4), 355–385. doi:10.1162/pres.1997.6.4.355

Baas, J., Schotten, M., Plume, A., Côté, G., & Karimi, R. (2020). Scopus as a curated, high-quality bibliometric data source for academic research in quantitative science studies. *Quantitative Science Studies*, *1*(1), 377–386. doi:10.1162/qss_a_00019

Baba, Y., Engle, R. F., Kraft, D. F., & Kroner, K. F. (1990). *Multivariate simultaneous generalized ARCH. Manuscript, University of California*. Department of Economics.

Bacher, N. (2022). *Metaverse Retailing* University of Pavia. https://www.researchgate.net/profile/Natalie-Bacher/publication/366441739_Metaverse_Retailing

Bagozzi, R. P., Yi, Y., & Phillips, L. W. (1991). Assessing construct validity in organizational research. *Administrative Science Quarterly*, *36*(3), 421–458. doi:10.2307/2393203

Bag, S., Rahman, M. S., Srivastava, G., & Shrivastav, S. K. (2023). Unveiling metaverse potential in supply chain management and overcoming implementation challenges: An empirical study. *Benchmarking*. Advance online publication. doi:10.1108/BIJ-05-2023-0314

Bag, S., Srivastava, G., Bashir, M. M. A., Kumari, S., Giannakis, M., & Chowdhury, A. H. (2022). Journey of customers in this digital era: Understanding the role of artificial intelligence technologies in user engagement and conversion. *Benchmarking*, *29*(7), 2074–2098. doi:10.1108/BIJ-07-2021-0415

Baía Reis, A., & Ashmore, M. (2022). From video streaming to virtual reality worlds: An academic, reflective, and creative study on live theatre and performance in the metaverse. *International Journal of Performance Arts and Digital Media*, *18*(1), 7–28. doi:10.1080/14794713.2021.2024398

Balcilar, M., Bouri, E., Gupta, R., & Roubaud, D. (2017). Can volume predict Bitcoin returns and volatility? A quantiles-based approach. *Economic Modelling*, *64*, 74–81. doi:10.1016/j.econmod.2017.03.019

Bale, A. S., Ghorpade, N., Hashim, M. F., Vaishnav, J., Almaspoor, Z., & Agostini, A. (2022). A comprehensive study on Metaverse and its impacts on humans. *Advances in Human-Computer Interaction*, *2022*, 1-11. *Article*, *3247060*. Advance online publication. doi:10.1155/2022/3247060

Ball, M. (2022). *The Metaverse: And How it Will Revolutionize Everything*. Liveright Publishing. doi:10.15358/9783800669400

Bamodu, O., & Ye, X. (2013). Virtual Reality and Virtual Reality System Components. *Advanced Materials Research*, *765-767*, 1169–1172. doi:10.4028/www.scientific.net/AMR.765-767.1169

Bansal, G., Rajgopal, K., Chamola, V., Xiong, Z., & Niyato, D. (2022). Healthcare in metaverse: A survey on current metaverse applications in healthcare. *IEEE Access : Practical Innovations, Open Solutions*, *10*, 119914–119946. doi:10.1109/ACCESS.2022.3219845

Barber, B. M., & Odean, T. (2008). All that glitters: The effect of attention and news on the buying behavior of individual and institutional investors. *Review of Financial Studies*, *21*(2), 785–818. doi:10.1093/rfs/hhm079

Bardhan, A. (2023). Expansion of Space in Metaverse Communication and its Probable Impact. *Society Language and Culture: A Multidisciplinary Peer-Reviewed Journal*, (4), 30-36. https://www.societylanguageculture.org

Bariviera, A. F., Zunino, L., & Rosso, O. A. (2018). An analysis of high-frequency cryptocurrencies prices dynamics using permutation-information-theory quantifiers. *Chaos (Woodbury, N.Y.)*, *28*(7), 075511. doi:10.1063/1.5027153 PMID:30070500

Barrera, K. G., & Shah, D. (2023). Marketing in the Metaverse: Conceptual understanding, framework, and research agenda. *Journal of Business Research*, *155*, 113420. doi:10.1016/j.jbusres.2022.113420

Bashir, A. K., Victor, N., Bhattacharya, S., Huynh-The, T., Chengoden, R., Yenduri, G., Maddikunta, P. K. R., Pham, Q.-V., Gadekallu, T. R., & Liyanage, M. (2023). Federated Learning for the Healthcare Metaverse: Concepts, Applications, Challenges, and Future Directions. *IEEE Internet of Things Journal*, *10*(24), 21873–21891. doi:10.1109/JIOT.2023.3304790

Baskaran, K. (2023). Customer Experience in the E-Commerce Market Through the Virtual World of Metaverse. In *Handbook of Research on Consumer Behavioral Analytics in Metaverse and the Adoption of a Virtual World* (pp. 153–170). IGI Global. doi:10.4018/978-1-6684-7029-9.ch008

Baur, D. G., Dimpfl, T., & Kuck, K. (2018). Bitcoin, gold and the US dollar–A replication and extension. *Finance Research Letters*, *25*, 103–110. doi:10.1016/j.frl.2017.10.012

Bauwens, L., Laurent, S., & Rombouts, J. V. (2006). Multivariate GARCH models: A survey. *Journal of Applied Econometrics*, *21*(1), 79–109. doi:10.1002/jae.842

BBC. (2021). *Ariana Grande sings in Fortnite's metaverse*. BBC. https://www.bbc.com/news/av/technology-58146042

Becker, S. J., Nemat, A. T., Lucas, S., Heinitz, R. M., Klevesath, M., & Charton, J. E. (2022). A Code of Digital Ethics: Laying the foundation for digital ethics in a science and technology company. *AI & Society*, *38*(6), 2629–2639. doi:10.1007/s00146-021-01376-w

Bedoui, R., Braiek, S., Guesmi, K., & Chevallier, J. (2019). RETRACTED: On the conditional dependence structure between oil, gold and USD exchange rates: Nested copula based GJR-GARCH model. *Energy Economics*, *80*, 876–889. doi:10.1016/j.eneco.2019.02.002

Bektas, H. (2023). *Revealing relevant factors impacting the viability of the metaverse by replacing online collaboration tools for business meetings* (Publication Number 60644) University of Twente]. https://essay.utwente.nl/96243/

Beneki, C., Koulis, A., Kyriazis, N. A., & Papadamou, S. (2019). Investigating volatility transmission and hedging properties between Bitcoin and Ethereum. *Research in International Business and Finance*, *48*, 219–227. doi:10.1016/j.ribaf.2019.01.001

BenMabrouk, H. S., Sassi, S., Soltane, F., & Abid, I. (2024). Connectedness and portfolio hedging between NFTs segments, American stocks and cryptocurrencies Nexus. *International Review of Financial Analysis*, *91*, 102959. doi:10.1016/j.irfa.2023.102959

Bennett, D. (2022). Remote workforce, virtual team tasks, and employee engagement tools in a real-time interoperable decentralized metaverse. *Psychosociological Issues in Human Resource Management*, *10*(1), 78–91. doi:10.22381/pihrm10120226

Bennett, E. E., & McWhorter, R. R. (2022). Dancing in the paradox: Virtual human resource development, online teaching, and learning. *Advances in Developing Human Resources*, *24*(2), 99–116. doi:10.1177/15234223221079440

Benosman, M. (2023). *Social Psychology in the Era of the Metaverse: An overview of recent studies*

Benrimoh, D., Chheda, F. D., & Margolese, H. C. (2022). The Best Predictor of the Future—The Metaverse, Mental Health, and Lessons Learned From Current Technologies. *JMIR Mental Health*, *9*(10), e40410. doi:10.2196/40410 PMID:36306155

Berglund, Å. F., Gong, L., & Li, D. (2018). Testing and validating Extended Reality (xR) technologies in manufacturing. *Procedia Manufacturing*, *25*, 31–38. doi:10.1016/j.promfg.2018.06.054

Berkhout, F., & Hertin, J. (2004). De-materialising and re-materialising: Digital technologies and the environment. *Futures*, *36*(8), 903–920. doi:10.1016/j.futures.2004.01.003

Berlo, Z. M. C., Reijmersdal, E. A., & Eisend, M. (2021). The Gamification of Branded Content: A Meta-Analysis of Advergame Effects. *Journal of Advertising*, *50*(2), 179–196. doi:10.1080/00913367.2020.1858462

Bhattacharya, P., Obaidat, M. S., Savaliya, D., Sanghavi, S., Tanwar, S., & Sadaun, B. (2022, July). Metaverse assisted telesurgery in healthcare 5.0: An interplay of blockchain and explainable AI. In *2022 International Conference on Computer, Information and Telecommunication Systems (CITS)* (pp. 1-5). IEEE. 10.1109/CITS55221.2022.9832978

Bhattacharya, P., Saraswat, D., Savaliya, D., Sanghavi, S., Verma, A., Sakariya, V., Tanwar, S., Sharma, R., Raboaca, M. S., & Manea, D. L. (2023). Towards Future Internet: The Metaverse Perspective for Diverse Industrial Applications. *Mathematics*, *11*(4), 941. doi:10.3390/math11040941

Bhugaonkar, K., Bhugaonkar, R., & Masne, N. (2022). The trend of metaverse and augmented & virtual reality extending to the healthcare system. *Cureus*, *14*(9). doi:10.7759/cureus.29071 PMID:36258985

Bibri, S. E. (2022). The social shaping of the metaverse as an alternative to the imaginaries of data-driven smart Cities: A study in science, technology, and society. *Smart Cities*, *5*(3), 832–874. doi:10.3390/smartcities5030043

Bibri, S. E., Allam, Z., & Krogstie, J. (2022). The Metaverse as a virtual form of data-driven smart urbanism: Platformization and its underlying processes, institutional dimensions, and disruptive impacts. *Computational Urban Science*, *2*(1), 24. doi:10.1007/s43762-022-00051-0 PMID:35974838

Bibri, S. E., & Jagatheesaperumal, S. K. (2023). Harnessing the potential of the metaverse and artificial intelligence for the internet of city things: Cost-effective XReality and synergistic AIoT technologies. *Smart Cities*, *6*(5), 2397–2429. doi:10.3390/smartcities6050109

Bidar, M. (2022). *Companies race to build "digital twins" in the metaverse*. CBS News. https://www.cbsnews.com/news/metaverse-amazon-bmw-lockheed-martin-adobe-digital-twin/

Billewar, S. R., Jadhav, K., Sriram, V. P., Arun, D. A., Mohd Abdul, S., Gulati, K., & Bhasin, D. N. K. K. (2022). The rise of 3D E-Commerce: The online shopping gets real with virtual reality and augmented reality during COVID-19. *World Journal of Engineering*, *19*(2), 244–253. doi:10.1108/WJE-06-2021-0338

Bojic, L. (2022). Metaverse through the prism of power and addiction: What will happen when the virtual world becomes more attractive than reality? *European Journal of Futures Research*, *10*(1), 22. doi:10.1186/s40309-022-00208-4

Boletsis, C. (2017). The New Era of Virtual Reality Locomotion: A Systematic Literature Review of Techniques and a Proposed Typology. *Multimodal Technologies and Interaction*, *1*(4), 24. doi:10.3390/mti1040024

Bolger, R. K. (2021). Finding holes in the metaverse: Posthuman mystics as agents of evolutionary contextualization. *Religions*, *12*(9), 768. doi:10.3390/rel12090768

Bollerslev, T. (1986). Generalized autoregressive conditional heteroskedasticity. *Journal of Econometrics*, *31*(3), 307–327. doi:10.1016/0304-4076(86)90063-1

Bonetti, F., Warnaby, G., & Quinn, L. (2018). Augmented Reality and Virtual Reality in Physical and Online Retailing: A Review, Synthesis and Research Agenda. In T. Jung & M. C. tom Dieck (Eds.), *Augmented Reality and Virtual Reality: Empowering Human, Place and Business* (pp. 119–132). Springer International Publishing., doi:10.1007/978-3-319-64027-3_9

Bousba, Y., & Arya, V. (2022). Let's connect in metaverse. Brand's new destination to increase consumers' affective brand engagement & their satisfaction and advocacy. *Journal of Content. Community & Communication*, *15*(8), 276–293. doi:10.31620/JCCC.06.22/19

Boyack, K. W., & Klavans, R. (2014). Including cited non-source items in a large-scale map of science: What difference does it make? *Journal of Informetrics*, *8*(3), 569–580. doi:10.1016/j.joi.2014.04.001

Brahma, M., Rejula, M. A., Srinivasan, B., Kumar, S., Banu, W. A., Malarvizhi, K., Priya, S. S., & Kumar, A. (2023). Learning impact of recent ICT advances based on virtual reality IoT sensors in a metaverse environment. *Measurement. Sensors*, *27*, 100754. doi:10.1016/j.measen.2023.100754

Bremers, L. P. Y. (2023). *Financial Inclusion in the Metaverse: Exploring the Relationship between Education and Attitude towards Cryptocurrencies* [Bachelor's thesis, University of Twente].

Briere, M., Oosterlinck, K., & Szafarz, A. (2015). Virtual currency, tangible return: Portfolio diversification with bitcoin. *Journal of Asset Management*, *16*(6), 365–373. doi:10.1057/jam.2015.5

Brown, D. (2021). "What is the 'metaverse'? Facebook says it's the future of the Internet. *The Washington Post*.

Bruni, R., Piccarozzi, M., & Caboni, F. (2023). Defining the Metaverse with challenges and opportunities in the business environment. *Journal of Marketing Theory and Practice*, 1–18. Advance online publication. doi:10.1080/10696679.2023.2273555

Bryda, G., & Costa, A. P. (2023). Qualitative research in digital era: Innovations, methodologies and collaborations. *Social Sciences (Basel, Switzerland)*, *12*(10), 570. doi:10.3390/socsci12100570

Buana, I. M. W. (2023). Metaverse: Threat or Opportunity for Our Social World? In understanding Metaverse on sociological context. *Journal of Metaverse*, *3*(1), 28–33. doi:10.57019/jmv.1144470

Budovich, L. S. (2023). The impact of religious tourism on the economy and tourism industry. *Hervormde Teologiese Studies*, *79*(1), 8607. doi:10.4102/hts.v79i1.8607

Buhalis, D. (2003). eTourism: Information technology for strategic tourism management. Pearson education. Pearson Education Limited.

Buhalis, D., Leung, D., & Lin, M. (2023). Metaverse as a disruptive technology revolutionising tourism management and marketing. *Tourism Management*, *97*, 104724. doi:10.1016/j.tourman.2023.104724

Buhalis, D., Lin, M. S., & Leung, D. (2022). Metaverse as a driver for customer experience and value co-creation: Implications for hospitality and tourism management and marketing. *International Journal of Contemporary Hospitality Management*, *35*(2), 701–716. doi:10.1108/IJCHM-05-2022-0631

Buhalis, D., O'Connor, P., & Leung, R. (2023). Smart hospitality: From smart cities and smart tourism towards agile business ecosystems in networked destinations. *International Journal of Contemporary Hospitality Management*, *35*(1), 369–393. doi:10.1108/IJCHM-04-2022-0497

Buhalis, D., & Sinarta, Y. (2019). Real-time co-creation and nowness service: Lessons from tourism and hospitality. *Journal of Travel & Tourism Marketing*, *36*(5), 563–582. doi:10.1080/10548408.2019.1592059

Builders of Amusement Park Rides & Media-Based Attractions. (n.d.). Triotech. https://www.trio-tech.com/

Burlington. (2021). *Searching for utopia: from dinosaurs to the metaverse*. Burlington. https://www.burlington.org.uk/archive/editorial/searching-for-utopia-from-dinosaurs-to-the-metaverse

Cali, U., Kuzlu, M., Karaarslan, E., & Jovanovic, V. (2022). *Opportunities and Challenges in Metaverse for Industry 4.0 and Beyond Applications*. IEEE 1st Global Emerging Technology Blockchain Forum - Blockchain and Beyond, (IGETblockchain), Irvine, CA. https://doi.org/ doi:10.1109/iGETblockchain56591.2022.10087104

Calzada, I. (2023). Disruptive Technologies for e-Diasporas: Blockchain, DAOs, Data Cooperatives, Metaverse, and ChatGPT. *Futures*, *154*, 103258. doi:10.1016/j.futures.2023.103258

Calzone, N., Sileo, M., Mozzillo, R., Pierri, F., & Caccavale, F. (2023). Mixed Reality Platform Supporting Human-Robot Interaction. Advances on Mechanics, Design Engineering and Manufacturing IV, Cham. doi:10.1007/978-3-031-15928-2_102

Capasa, L., Zulauf, K., & Wagner, R. (2022). Virtual Reality Experience of Mega Sports Events: A Technology Acceptance Study. *Journal of Theoretical and Applied Electronic Commerce Research*, *17*(2), 2. doi:10.3390/jtaer17020036

Cappannari, L., & Vitillo, A. (2022). XR and Metaverse Software Platforms. *Roadmapping Extended Reality: Fundamentals and Applications*, 135-156. doi:10.1002/9781119865810.ch6

Carew, A. (2022). A whole new world: Metaverse as fairytale in Belle. *Metro*(212), 92-97. https://search.informit.org/doi/abs/10.3316/informit.938183067792285

Carter, M., & Egliston, B. (2023). What are the risks of Virtual Reality data? Learning Analytics, Algorithmic Bias and a Fantasy of Perfect Data. *New Media & Society*, *25*(3), 485–504. doi:10.1177/14614448211012794

Chaudhary, M., Jaswal, N., & Sohal, A. (2023). Demystifying the Relationship Between Emotional Intelligence and Leadership Effectiveness: Focusing on Mental Health and Happiness. In AI and Emotional Intelligence for Modern Business Management (pp. 113-133). IGI Global. doi:10.4018/979-8-3693-0418-1.ch008

Chaves, A. (2023). *O que é Web 5.0 e qual a diferença da web3?* Be(in)Crypto. https://br.beincrypto.com/aprender/o-que-e-web-5-0/

Cheng, R. Z., Wu, N., Chen, S. Q., & Han, B. (2022, Mar 12-16). Reality check of metaverse: A first look at commercial social virtual reality platforms. *2022 IEEE Conference on Virtual Reality and 3D User Interfaces Abstracts and Workshops*. IEEE. 10.1109/VRW55335.2022.00040

Chengoden, R., Victor, N., Huynh-The, T., Yenduri, G., Jhaveri, R. H., Alazab, M., Bhattacharya, S., Hegde, P., Maddikunta, P. K. R., & Gadekallu, T. R. (2023). Metaverse for healthcare: A survey on potential applications, challenges and future directions. *IEEE Access : Practical Innovations, Open Solutions*, *11*, 12765–12795. doi:10.1109/ACCESS.2023.3241628

Cheng, X. U. (2023). From Fiction to Reality: Harnessing the Power of Imaginative Narratives to Shape the Future of the Metaverse. *Journal of Metaverse*, *3*(2), 108–120. doi:10.57019/jmv.1277525

Chen, H., Duan, H., Abdallah, M., Zhu, Y., Wen, Y., Saddik, A. E., & Cai, W. (2023). Web3 Metaverse: State-of-the-art and vision. *ACM Transactions on Multimedia Computing Communications and Applications*, *20*(4), 1–42. doi:10.1145/3630258

Chen, N. C. (2024). Analysis on the Development of the Meta Universe to the Generation of Electronic Games from the Perspective of Media Convergence. *Computer-Aided Design and Applications*.

Chen, X., Li, H., Zhao, J., & Li, H. (2022). Security and privacy issues in the metaverse: A survey. *ACM Computing Surveys*, *55*(2), 1–41.

Chen, Y., & Cheng, H. (2022). The economics of the metaverse: A comparison with the real economy. *Metaverse*, *3*(1), 19. doi:10.54517/met.v3i1.1802

Chen, Y., Huang, D., Liu, Z., Osmani, M., & Demian, P. (2022). Construction 4.0, Industry 4.0, and Building Information Modeling (BIM) for sustainable building development within the smart city. *Sustainability (Basel)*, *14*(16), 10028. doi:10.3390/su141610028

ChenY.LinW.ZhengY.XueT.ChenC.ChenG. (2022). Application of active learning strategies in metaverse to improve student engagement: An immersive blended pedagogy bridging patient care and scientific inquiry in pandemic. *Available at* SSRN 4098179. doi:10.2139/ssrn.4098179

Chen, Z. S. (2023). Beyond Reality: Examining the Opportunities and Challenges of Cross-Border Integration between Metaverse and Hospitality Industries. *Journal of Hospitality Marketing & Management*, *32*(7), 967–980. doi:10.1080/19368623.2023.2222029

Chowdhury, A., & Mendelson, B. K. (2013). Virtual currency and the financial system: the case of Bitcoin (No. 2013-09). Marquette University, Center for Global and Economic Studies and Department of Economics.

Chowdhury, A. (2016). Is Bitcoin the "Paris Hilton" of the currency world? Or are the early investors onto something that will make them rich? *Journal of Investing*, *25*(1), 64–72. doi:10.3905/joi.2016.25.1.064

Chu, J., Zhang, Y., & Chan, S. (2019). The adaptive market hypothesis in the high frequency cryptocurrency market. *International Review of Financial Analysis*, *64*, 221–231. doi:10.1016/j.irfa.2019.05.008

Cipresso, P., Giglioli, I. A. C., Raya, M. A., & Riva, G. (2018). The Past, Present, and Future of Virtual and Augmented Reality Research: A Network and Cluster Analysis of the Literature. *Frontiers in Psychology*, *9*, 2086. doi:10.3389/fpsyg.2018.02086 PMID:30459681

Clement, J. (2022). *In what type of projects does your company invest in the metaverse?* Statista. https://www.statista.com/statistics/1302200/metaverse-project-investment-businesses/

Clement, J. (2023). *Video game industry - statistics & facts*. Statista. https://www.statista.com/topics/868/video-games/#topicOverview

Cline, R. S. (1999). Hospitality 2000—the technology: Building customer relationships. *Journal of Vacation Marketing*, *5*(4), 376–386. doi:10.1177/135676679900500407

Cobo, M. J., López-Herrera, A. G., Herrera-Viedma, E., & Herrera, F. (2011). Science mapping software tools: Review, analysis, and cooperative study among tools. *Journal of the American Society for Information Science and Technology*, *62*(7), 1382–1402. doi:10.1002/asi.21525

Cohen, J., Cohen, P., West, S. G., & Aiken, L. S. (2013). *Applied multiple regression/correlation analysis for the behavioral sciences*. Routledge. doi:10.4324/9780203774441

Conlon, T., Corbet, S., & McGee, R. J. (2020). Are cryptocurrencies a safe haven for equity markets? An international perspective from the COVID-19 pandemic. *Research in International Business and Finance*, *54*, 101248. doi:10.1016/j.ribaf.2020.101248 PMID:34170988

Corbet, S., Hou, Y. G., Hu, Y., Oxley, L., & Xu, D. (2021). Pandemic-related financial market volatility spillovers: Evidence from the Chinese COVID-19 epicentre. *International Review of Economics & Finance*, *71*, 55–81. doi:10.1016/j.iref.2020.06.022

Corning, P. A. (2013). Rotating the Necker cube: A bioeconomic approach to cooperation and the causal role of synergy in evolution. *Journal of Bioeconomics*, *15*(2), 171–193. doi:10.1007/s10818-012-9142-4

Creed, C., Al-Kalbani, M., Theil, A., Sarcar, S., & Williams, I. (2024). Inclusive AR/VR: Accessibility barriers for immersive technologies. *Universal Access in the Information Society*, *23*(1), 59–73. doi:10.1007/s10209-023-00969-0

Cronbach, L. J. (1951). Coefficient alpha and the internal structure of tests. *psychometrika, 16*(3), 297-334.

Cucari, N., Tutore, I., Montera, R., & Profita, S. (2023). A bibliometric performance analysis of publication productivity in the corporate social responsibility field: Outcomes of SciVal analytics. *Corporate Social Responsibility and Environmental Management*, *30*(1), 1–16. doi:10.1002/csr.2346

Cui, H., & Du, B. (2023, February 6). *The Theoretical Basis and Landing Strategy of the Metaverse Business Model*. IEEE. doi:10.3233/FAIA230010

Curtis, C., & Brolan, C. E. (2023). Health care in the metaverse. *The Medical Journal of Australia*, *218*(1), 46. doi:10.5694/mja2.51793 PMID:36437589

Daimiel, G. B., Estrella, E. C. M., & Ormaechea, S. L. (2022). Analysis of the use of advergaming and metaverse in Spain and Mexico. *Revista Latina De Comunicacion Social*, *80*(80), 155–178. doi:10.4185/RLCS-2022-1802

Damar, M. (2021). Metaverse shape of your life for future: A bibliometric snapshot. *Journal of Metaverse*, *1*(1), 1–8.

Damar, M. (2022). What the literature on medicine, nursing, public health, midwifery, and dentistry reveals: An overview of the rapidly approaching metaverse. *Journal of Metaverse*, *2*(2), 62–70. doi:10.57019/jmv.1132962

Damnjanović, V., Lončarić, D., & Dlačić, J. (2020). TEACHING CASE STUDY: Digital marketing strategy of Accor Hotels: shaping the future of hospitality. *Tourism and Hospitality Management*, *26*(1), 233–244.

Darban, M. (2023). The future of virtual team learning: Navigating the intersection of AI and education. *Journal of Research on Technology in Education*, 1–17. doi:10.1080/15391523.2023.2288912

Das, P., Martin Sagayam, K., Rahaman Jamader, A., & Acharya, B. (2022). Remote Sensing in Public Health Environment: A Review. *Internet of Things Based Smart Healthcare: Intelligent and Secure Solutions Applying Machine Learning Techniques*, 379-397.

Das, P., Jamader, A. R., Acharya, B. R., & Das, H. (2019, May). HMF Based QoS aware Recommended Resource Allocation System in Mobile Edge Computing for IoT. In *2019 International Conference on Intelligent Computing and Control Systems (ICCS)* (pp. 444-449). IEEE. 10.1109/ICCS45141.2019.9065775

Davenport, T., Guha, A., Grewal, D., & Bressgott, T. (2020). How artificial intelligence will change the future of marketing. *Journal of the Academy of Marketing Science*, *48*(1), 24–42. doi:10.1007/s11747-019-00696-0

Davis, A., Khazanchi, D., Murphy, J., Zigurs, I., & Owens, D. (2009). Avatars, People, and Virtual Worlds: Foundations for Research in Metaverses. *Journal of the Association for Information Systems, 10*(2), 90–117. doi:10.17705/1jais.00183

Davis, F. D. (1989). Perceived usefulness, perceived ease of use, and user acceptance of information technology. *Management Information Systems Quarterly, 13*(3), 319–340. doi:10.2307/249008

Davis, F. D., Bagozzi, R. P., & Warshaw, P. R. (1989). User acceptance of computer technology: A comparison of two theoretical models. *Management Science, 35*(8), 982–1003. doi:10.1287/mnsc.35.8.982

De Bruyn, A., Viswanathan, V., Beh, Y. S., Brock, J.-K.-U., & Von Wangenheim, F. (2020). Artificial Intelligence and Marketing: Pitfalls and Opportunities. *Journal of Interactive Marketing, 51*, 91–105. doi:10.1016/j.intmar.2020.04.007

De Moor, K., Farias, M., Vinayagamoorthy, V., Daly, M., & Collingwoode-William, T. (2023). Diversity and Inclusion in Focus at ACM IMX'22 and MMSys' 22. *ACM SIGMultimedia Records, 14*(3), 1–1. doi:10.1145/3630658.3630660

Deniz, K. (2024). Metaverse and New Narrative: Storyliving in the Age of Metaverse. In The Future of Digital Communication (pp. 39-55). CRC Press.

Devlin, M. (2023). *2035 AND BEYOND. A GUIDE TO THRIVING IN THE FUTURE WORKPLACE.: Unleash Your Potential in a Futuristic Career Landscape. Virtual Worlds, Skills Mastery, and Success.* Little Fish Big Impact.

Dharmani, P., Das, S., & Prashar, S. (2021). A bibliometric analysis of creative industries: Current trends and future directions. *Journal of Business Research, 135*, 252–267. doi:10.1016/j.jbusres.2021.06.037

Dhiman, V., & Arora, M. (2023). How foresight has evolved since 1999? Understanding its themes, scope and focus. *foresight.* doi:10.1108/FS-01-2023-0001

Dhiman, V., & Arora, M. (2024). Current State of Metaverse in Entrepreneurial Ecosystem: A Retrospective Analysis of Its Evolving Landscape. In Exploring the Use of Metaverse in Business and Education (pp. 73-87). IGI Global. doi:10.4018/979-8-3693-5868-9.ch005

Dhiman, V., & Arora, M. (2024). *Exploring the linkage between business incubation and entrepreneurship: understanding trends, themes and future research agenda.* LBS Journal of Management & Research., doi:10.1108/LBSJMR-06-2023-0021

Dickey, M. D. (1999). *3D virtual worlds and learning: an analysis of the impact of design affordances and limitations in active worlds, blaxxun interactive, and onlive! Traveler; and a study of the implementation of active worlds for formal and informal education.* [Doctoral dissertation, The Ohio State University].

Dincelli, E., & Yayla, A. (2022). Immersive virtual reality in the age of the Metaverse: A hybrid-narrative review based on the technology affordance perspective. *The Journal of Strategic Information Systems, 31*(2), 101717. doi:10.1016/j.jsis.2022.101717

Dinev, T., & Hart, P. J. (2006). An empirical examination of the deLone and McLean model of information systems success. *Management Information Systems Quarterly, 30*(3), 691–721.

Dionisio, J. D. N., Iii, W. G. B., & Gilbert, R. (2013). 3D virtual worlds and the metaverse: Current status and future possibilities. *ACM Computing Surveys, 45*(3), 1–38. doi:10.1145/2480741.2480751

DiPietro, R. B., & Wang, Y. R. (2010). Key issues for ICT applications: Impacts and implications for hospitality operations. *Worldwide Hospitality and Tourism Themes, 2*(1), 49–67. doi:10.1108/17554211011012595

Disney patents technology to focus on theme park in Metaverse—Blockchain Council. (n.d.). Blockchain. https://www.blockchain-council.org/news/disney-patents-technology-to-focus-on-theme-park-in-metaverse/

Dixon, H. H. B. Jr. (2023). The Metaverse. *The Judges' Journal, 62*(1), 36 38.

Dobre, C., Milovan, A. M., Dutu, C., Preda, G., & Agapie, A. (2021). The Common Values of Social Media Marketing and Luxury Brands. The Millennials and Generation Z Perspective. *Journal of Theoretical and Applied Electronic Commerce Research*, *16*(7), 2532–2553. doi:10.3390/jtaer16070139

Dogum, R., & Uribe, D. (2023). NFTs and Metaverse in Healthcare: What's the Big Opportunity? *Blockchain in Healthcare Today*, *6*(1). doi:10.30953/bhty.v6.266

Dong, H., & Liu, Y. (2023, May 1). *Metaverse Meets Consumer Electronics*. IEEE. doi:10.1109/MCE.2022.3229180

Dong, Y., Sharma, C., Mehta, A., & Torrico, D. D. (2021). Application of augmented reality in the sensory evaluation of yogurts. *Fermentation (Basel, Switzerland)*, *7*(3), 147. doi:10.3390/fermentation7030147

Donthu, N., Kumar, S., Mukherjee, D., Pandey, N., & Lim, W. M. (2021). How to conduct a bibliometric analysis: An overview and guidelines. *Journal of Business Research*, *133*, 285–296. doi:10.1016/j.jbusres.2021.04.070

Donthu, N., Kumar, S., & Pandey, N. (2021). A retrospective evaluation of Marketing Intelligence and Planning: 1983–2019. *Marketing Intelligence & Planning*, *39*(1), 48–73. doi:10.1108/MIP-02-2020-0066

Duhoon, A., & Singh, M. (2023). Corporate Governance in Family Firms: A Bibliometric Analysis. *Management*, *1*, 22.

Duhoon, A., & Singh, M. (2023). Corporate tax avoidance: A systematic literature review and future research directions. *LBS Journal of Management & Research*, *21*(2), 197–217. doi:10.1108/LBSJMR-12-2022-0082

Duong, T. Q., Van Huynh, D., Khosravirad, S. R., Sharma, V., Dobre, O. A., & Shin, H. (2023). From digital twin to metaverse: The role of 6G ultra-reliable and low-latency communications with multi-tier computing. *IEEE Wireless Communications*, *30*(3), 140–146. doi:10.1109/MWC.014.2200371

Durukal, E. (2022). Customer online shopping experience. *Handbook of Research on Interdisciplinary Reflections of Contemporary Experiential Marketing Practices*.

Dutta, D., Srivastava, Y., & Singh, E. (2023). Metaverse in the tourism sector for talent management: A technology in practice lens. *Information Technology & Tourism*, *25*(3), 331–365. doi:10.1007/s40558-023-00258-9

Dutu-Buzura, M. (2021). European Climate Pact–Framework for Information and Participation of the Public to the Climate Change Challenge. *Romanian Journal of Public Affairs*(3), 29-40. http://www.rjpa.ro/sites/

Dwivedi, Y. K., Hughes, L., Baabdullah, A. M., Ribeiro-Navarrete, S., Giannakis, M., Al-Debei, M. M., Dennehy, D., Metri, B., Buhalis, D., Cheung, C. M. K., Conboy, K., Doyle, R., Dubey, R., Dutot, V., Felix, R., Goyal, D. P., Gustafsson, A., Hinsch, C., Jebabli, I., & Wamba, S. F. (2022). Metaverse beyond the hype: Multidisciplinary perspectives on emerging challenges, opportunities, and agenda for research, practice and policy. *International Journal of Information Management*, *66*, 102542. doi:10.1016/j.ijinfomgt.2022.102542

Dwivedi, Y. K., Kshetri, N., Hughes, L., Rana, N. P., Baabdullah, A. M., Kar, A. K., Koohang, A., Ribeiro-Navarrete, S., Belei, N., Balakrishnan, J., Basu, S., Behl, A., Davies, G. H., Dutot, V., Dwivedi, R., Evans, L., Felix, R., Foster-Fletcher, R., Giannakis, M., ... Yan, M. (2023). Exploring the Darkverse: A Multi-Perspective Analysis of the Negative Societal Impacts of the Metaverse. *Information Systems Frontiers*, *25*(5), 2071–2114. doi:10.1007/s10796-023-10400-x PMID:37361890

Dwivedi, Y. K., Kshetri, N., Hughes, L., Slade, E. L., Jeyaraj, A., Kar, A. K., Baabdullah, A. M., Koohang, A., Raghavan, V., Ahuja, M., Albanna, H., Albashrawi, M. A., Al-Busaidi, A. S., Balakrishnan, J., Barlette, Y., Basu, S., Bose, I., Brooks, L., Buhalis, D., ... Wright, R. (2023). "So what if ChatGPT wrote it?" Multidisciplinary perspectives on opportunities, challenges and implications of generative conversational AI for research, practice and policy. *International Journal of Information Management*, *71*, 102642. doi:10.1016/j.ijinfomgt.2023.102642

Dyhrberg, A. H. (2016). Bitcoin, gold and the dollar–A GARCH volatility analysis. *Finance Research Letters*, *16*, 85–92. doi:10.1016/j.frl.2015.10.008

Dyhrberg, A. H. (2016). Hedging capabilities of bitcoin. Is it the virtual gold? *Finance Research Letters*, *16*, 139–144. doi:10.1016/j.frl.2015.10.025

Dziatkovskii, A., Hryneuski, U., Krylova, A., & Loy, A. C. M. (2022). Chronological Progress of Blockchain in Science, Technology, Engineering and Math (STEM): A Systematic Analysis for Emerging Future Directions. *Sustainability (Basel)*, *14*(19), 12074. doi:10.3390/su141912074

Earhart, B. (2012). Reclaiming meaning across platforms: Fragmentation and expansion of the self. *Metaverse Creativity*, *2*(2), 125–138. doi:10.1386/mvcr.2.2.125_1

Efendioğlu, İ. H. (2023). The Effect Of Information About Metaverse On The Consumer's Purchase Intention. *Journal of Global Business and Technology*, *19*(1), 63–77.

Ellegaard, O., & Wallin, J. A. (2015). The bibliometric analysis of scholarly production: How great is the impact? *Scientometrics*, *105*(3), 1809–1831. doi:10.1007/s11192-015-1645-z PMID:26594073

Enache, M. C. (2022). Metaverse Opportunities for Businesses. *Annals of the University Dunarea de Jos of Galati: Fascicle: I. Economics & Applied Informatics*, *28*(1), 67–71. Advance online publication. doi:10.35219/eai15840409246

Engage. (2024). *Engage Studio*. EngageVR. https://engagevr.io/engage-studio/

Engle, R. F. (1982). Autoregressive conditional heteroscedasticity with estimates of the variance of United Kingdom inflation. *Econometrica*, *50*(4), 987–1007. doi:10.2307/1912773

Engle, R. F., & Kroner, K. F. (1995). Multivariate simultaneous generalized ARCH. *Econometric Theory*, *11*(1), 122–150. doi:10.1017/S0266466600009063

Erazo, J., & Sulbarán, P. (2022). Metaverse: Above an immersion in reality. *Metaverse*, *3*(2), 8. doi:10.54517/m.v3i2.2155

Erdoğdu, A. (2017). The most significant factors influencing the price of gold: An empirical analysis of the US market. *Economics*, *5*(5), 399–406.

Erensoy, A., Mathrani, A., Schnack, A., Zhao, Y., Chitale, V. S., & Baghaei, N. (2022, December). Comparing Customer Behaviours: Immersive Virtual Reality Store Experiences versus Web and Physical Store Experiences. In *2022 IEEE Asia-Pacific Conference on Computer Science and Data Engineering (CSDE)* (pp. 1-7). IEEE. 10.1109/CSDE56538.2022.10089288

Ergen, I. (2022). *Design in Metaverse: Artificial Intelligence, Game Design, Style-Gan2 and More....* Allied Publishers.

Fahimnia, B., Sarkis, J., & Davarzani, H. (2015). Green supply chain management: A review and bibliometric analysis. *International Journal of Production Economics*, *162*, 101–114. doi:10.1016/j.ijpe.2015.01.003

Fama, E. F. (1970). Efficient capital markets: A review of theory and empirical work. *The Journal of Finance*, *25*(2), 383–417. doi:10.2307/2325486

Faraboschi, P., Frachtenberg, E., Laplante, P., Milojicic, D., & Saracco, R. (2022). Virtual worlds (Metaverse): From skepticism, to fear, to immersive opportunities. *Computer*, *55*(10), 100–106. doi:10.1109/MC.2022.3192702

Far, S. B., Rad, A. I., & Asaar, M. R. (2023). Blockchain and its derived technologies shape the future generation of digital businesses: A focus on decentralized finance and the Metaverse. *Data Science and Management*, *6*(3), 183–197. doi:10.1016/j.dsm.2023.06.002

Fazio, G., Fricano, S., Iannolino, S., & Pirrone, C. (2023). Metaverse and tourism development: Issues and opportunities in stakeholders' perception. *Information Technology & Tourism*, *25*(4), 507–528. doi:10.1007/s40558-023-00268-7

Feng, X., Wang, X., & Su, Y. (2024). An analysis of the current status of metaverse research based on bibliometrics. *Library Hi Tech*, *42*(1), 284–308. doi:10.1108/LHT-10-2022-0467

Fernández-Caramés, T. M., & Fraga-Lamas, P. (2024). Forging the Industrial Metaverse-Where Industry 5.0, Augmented and Mixed Reality, IIoT, Opportunistic Edge Computing and Digital Twins Meet. *arXiv preprint arXiv:2403.11312*.

Ferreira, J. J., Fernandes, C. I., Rammal, H. G., & Veiga, P. M. (2021). Wearable technology and consumer interaction: A systematic review and research agenda. *Computers in Human Behavior*, *118*, 106710. doi:10.1016/j.chb.2021.106710

FIFAe World Cup. (2024). Wikipedia. https://en.wikipedia.org/w/index.php?title=FIFAe_World_Cup&oldid=1195690321

Flannery, C. B. (2022). Philosophical and Practical Privacy in the Metaverse: A Case for Data Privacy Protection under the United States Constitution. *Cornell Journal of Law and Public Policy*, *32*, 134–153. https://heinonline.org/

Fornell, C., & Larcker, D. F. (1981). Evaluating structural equation models with unobservable variables and measurement error. *JMR, Journal of Marketing Research*, *18*(1), 39–50. doi:10.1177/002224378101800104

Fowowe, B., & Shuaibu, M. (2016). Dynamic spillovers between Nigerian, South African and international equity markets. *Inter Economics*, *148*, 59–80. doi:10.1016/j.inteco.2016.06.003

Freyermuth, G. S. (2022). Vegas, Disney, and the Metaverse. *Studies of Digital Media Culture*, *14*, 17.

Friis, K., & Lysne, O. (2021). Huawei, 5G and security: Technological limitations and political responses. *Development and Change*, *52*(5), 1174–1195. doi:10.1111/dech.12680

Furstenau, L. B., Sott, M. K., Kipper, L. M., Machado, E. L., Lopez-Robles, J. R., Dohan, M. S., Cobo, M. J., Zahid, A., Abbasi, Q. H., & Imran, M. A. (2020). Link between sustainability and industry 4.0: Trends, challenges, and new perspectives. *IEEE Access : Practical Innovations, Open Solutions*, *8*, 140079–140096. doi:10.1109/ACCESS.2020.3012812

Fu, Y. C., Li, C. L., Yu, F. R., Luan, T. H., Zhao, P. C., & Liu, S. (2023). A Survey of Blockchain and Intelligent Networking for the Metaverse. *IEEE Internet of Things Journal*, *10*(4), 3587–3610. doi:10.1109/JIOT.2022.3222521

Gadekallu, T. R., Huynh-The, T., Wang, W., Yenduri, G., Ranaweera, P., Pham, Q. V., & Liyanage, M. (2022). Blockchain for the metaverse: A review. *arXiv preprint arXiv:2203.09738*.

Ganapathy, K. (2022). Metaverse and healthcare: A clinician's perspective. *Apollo Medicine*, *19*(4), 256–261.

Gao, X., & Yu, W. (2023). Innovative Thinking About Human-Computer Interaction in Interactive Narrative Games. In X. Fang (Ed.), *HCI in Games* (pp. 89–99). Springer Nature Switzerland. doi:10.1007/978-3-031-35930-9_7

Gao, Z., & Braud, T. (2023). VR-driven museum opportunities: Digitized archives in the age of the metaverse. *Artnodes*, *0*(32). Advance online publication. doi:10.7238/artnodes.v0i32.402462

Garavand, A., & Aslani, N. (2022). Metaverse phenomenon and its impact on health: A scoping review. *Informatics in Medicine Unlocked*, *32*, 101029. doi:10.1016/j.imu.2022.101029

Garousi, V. (2015). A bibliometric analysis of the Turkish software engineering research community. *Scientometrics*, *105*(1), 23–49. doi:10.1007/s11192-015-1663-x

Gartner Outlines Six Trends Driving Near-Term Adoption of Metaverse Technologies. (n.d.). Gartner. Retrieved February 6, 2024, from https://www.gartner.com/en/newsroom/press-releases/2022-09-13-gartner-outlines-six-trends-driving-near-term-adoptio

Gartner Predicts 25% of People Will Spend At Least One Hour Per Day in the Metaverse by 2026. (n.d.). Gartner. https://www.gartner.com/en/newsroom/press-releases/2022-02-07-gartner-predicts-25-percent-of-people-will-spend-at-least-one-hour-per-day-in-the-metaverse-by-2026

Gartner. (2022). Gartner Glossary: Metaverse. https://www.gartner.com/en/information-technology/glossary/metaverse

Gasmi, A., & Benlamri, R. (2022). Augmented reality, virtual reality and new age technologies demand escalates amid COVID-19. In *Novel AI and Data Science Advancements for Sustainability in the Era of COVID-19* (pp. 89–111). Academic Press. doi:10.1016/B978-0-323-90054-6.00005-2

Gattullo, M., Laviola, E., Evangelista, A., Fiorentino, M., & Uva, A. E. (2022). Towards the evaluation of augmented reality in the metaverse: Information presentation modes. *Applied Sciences (Basel, Switzerland)*, *12*(24), 12600. doi:10.3390/app122412600

Gaurav, A. (2022). Metaverse and Globalization: Cultural Exchange and Digital Diplomacy. *Data Science Insights Magazine, 5.* https://insights2techinfo.com/

Gaurav, A. (2023). Metaverse and Globalization: Cultural Exchange and Digital Diplomacy, Data *Science Insights Magazine, Insights2Techinfo.*

Gauttier, S., Simouri, W., & Milliat, A. (2024). When to enter the metaverse: Business leaders offer perspectives. *The Journal of Business Strategy*, *45*(1), 2–9. doi:10.1108/JBS-08-2022-0149

Ghimire, A. (2023). *AvatARoid: using a motion-mapped AR overlay to bridge the embodiment gap between robot and teleoperator in robot-mediated telepresence.* University of British Columbia.

Ghobakhloo, M., & Ching, N. T. (2019). Adoption of digital technologies of smart manufacturing in SMEs. *Journal of Industrial Information Integration*, *16*, 100107. doi:10.1016/j.jii.2019.100107

Ghryani, L., Sidiya, A. M., Almahdi, R., & Alzaher, H. (2023). The Future Metavertainment Application development. *2023 20th Learning and Technology Conference (L&T)*, 151–156. 10.1109/LT58159.2023.10092341

Gill, S. S., Xu, M., Ottaviani, C., Patros, P., Bahsoon, R., Shaghaghi, A., Golec, M., Stankovski, V., Wu, H., Abraham, A., Singh, M., Mehta, H., Ghosh, S. K., Baker, T., Parlikad, A. K., Lutfiyya, H., Kanhere, S. S., Sakellariou, R., Dustdar, S., & Uhlig, S. (2022). AI for next generation computing: Emerging trends and future directions. *Internet of Things : Engineering Cyber Physical Human Systems*, *19*, 100514. doi:10.1016/j.iot.2022.100514

Glaser, F., Zimmermann, K., Haferkorn, M., Weber, M. C., & Siering, M. (2014). *Bitcoin-asset or currency? revealing users' hidden intentions. Revealing Users' Hidden Intentions (April 15, 2014).* ECIS.

Goel, A. K., Bakshi, R., & Agrawal, K. K. (2022). Web 3.0 and Decentralized Applications. *Materials Proceedings*, *10*(1), 8. https://www.mdpi.com/2673-4605/10/1/8

Go, H., & Kang, M. (2022). Metaverse tourism for sustainable tourism development: Tourism Agenda 2030. *Tourism Review*, *78*(2), 381–394. doi:10.1108/TR-02-2022-0102

Goh, K. H., & See, K. F. (2021). Twenty years of water utility benchmarking: A bibliometric analysis of emerging interest in water research and collaboration. *Journal of Cleaner Production*, *284*, 124711. doi:10.1016/j.jclepro.2020.124711

Goldfield, C. C. (2023). THE NATIONAL SECURITY LANDSCAPE ISSUES OF THE METAUERSE. *Scitech Lawyer*, *19*(2), 20–25.

Golf-Papez, M., Heller, J., Hilken, T., Chylinski, M., de Ruyter, K., Keeling, D. I., & Mahr, D. (2022). Embracing falsity through the metaverse: The case of synthetic customer experiences. *Business Horizons*, *65*(6), 739–749. doi:10.1016/j. bushor.2022.07.007

Guan, J., Morris, A., & Irizawa, J. (2023). *Extending the Metaverse: Hyper-Connected Smart Environments with Mixed Reality and the Internet of Things*. 30th IEEE Conference Virtual Reality and 3D User Interfaces (IEEE VR), Shanghai. 10.1109/VRW58643.2023.00251

Gupta, H. (2023). Analysing volatility patterns in emerging markets: symmetric or asymmetric models? *Journal of Economic and Administrative Sciences*. doi:10.1108/JEAS-07-2023-0186

Gupta, H. (2024). Asymmetric Volatility in Stock Market: Evidence from Selected Export-based Countries. *The Indian Economic Journal*, *0*(0), 00194662241238598. doi:10.1177/00194662241238598

Gupta, H., & Gupta, A. (2023). Investor's behaviour to COVID-19 vaccine: An event study on health and pharmaceutical sector in India. *International Journal of Pharmaceutical and Healthcare Marketing*, *17*(4), 429–449. doi:10.1108/ IJPHM-05-2022-0053

Gupta, O. J., Yadav, S., Srivastava, M. K., Darda, P., & Mishra, V. (2023). Understanding the intention to use metaverse in healthcare utilizing a mix method approach. *International Journal of Healthcare Management*, 1–12. doi:10.1080/2 0479700.2023.2183579

Gupta, R., & Singh, S. (2022). Network infrastructure for the metaverse: Requirements and challenges. *IEEE Internet of Things Journal*, *9*(12), 13298–13310.

Gursoy, D., Malodia, S., & Dhir, A. (2022). The metaverse in the hospitality and tourism industry: An overview of current trends and future research directions. *Journal of Hospitality Marketing & Management*, *31*(5), 527–534. doi:10.1 080/19368623.2022.2072504

Hackl, C. (2020). The Metaverse is coming and it's a very big deal. *Forbes*. https://www.forbes.com/sites/cathy-hackl/2020/07/05/the-metaverse-is-coming--its-a-very-big-deal/

Hadi, R., Melumad, S., & Park, E. S. (2024). The Metaverse: A new digital frontier for consumer behavior. *Journal of Consumer Psychology*, *34*(1), 142–166. doi:10.1002/jcpy.1356

Hagtvedt, H., & Chandukala, S. R. (2023). Immersive retailing: The in-store experience. *Journal of Retailing*, *99*(4), 505–517. doi:10.1016/j.jretai.2023.10.003

Hair, J. F., Risher, J. J., Sarstedt, M., & Ringle, C. M. (2019). When to use and how to report the results of PLS-SEM. *European Business Review*, *31*(1), 2–24. doi:10.1108/EBR-11-2018-0203

Hajjami, O., & Park, S. (2023). Using the metaverse in training: Lessons from real cases. *European Journal of Training and Development*. Advance online publication. doi:10.1108/EJTD-12-2022-0144

Hamilton, S. (2022). Deep Learning Computer Vision Algorithms, Customer Engagement Tools, and Virtual Marketplace Dynamics Data in the Metaverse Economy. *Journal of Self-Governance and Management Economics*, *10*(2), 37–51.

Hamza, R., & Pradana, H. (2022). A survey of intellectual property rights protection in big data applications. *Algorithms*, *15*(11), 418. doi:10.3390/a15110418

Han, B., Wang, H., Qiao, D., Xu, J., & Yan, T. (2023). Application of Zero-Watermarking Scheme Based on Swin Transformer for Securing the Metaverse Healthcare Data. *IEEE Journal of Biomedical and Health Informatics*. Advance online publication. doi:10.1109/JBHI.2021.3123936 PMID:37028374

Hancock, K. (2022). Virtual Team Performance, Collaborative Remote Work, and Employee Engagement and Multimodal Behavioral Analytics in the Metaverse Economy. *Psychosociological Issues in Human Resource Management*, *10*(2), 55–70. doi:10.22381/pihrm10220224

Han, D.-I. D., Bergs, Y., & Moorhouse, N. (2022). Virtual reality consumer experience escapes: Preparing for the metaverse. *Virtual Reality (Waltham Cross)*, *26*(4), 1443–1458. doi:10.1007/s10055-022-00641-7

Han, E., Miller, M. R., DeVeaux, C., Jun, H., Nowak, K. L., Hancock, J. T., Ram, N., & Bailenson, J. N. (2023). People, places, and time: A large-scale, longitudinal study of transformed avatars and environmental context in group interaction in the metaverse. *Journal of Computer-Mediated Communication*, *28*(2), zmac031. doi:10.1093/jcmc/zmac031

Han, E., Miller, M. R., Ram, N., Nowak, K. L., & Bailenson, J. N. (2022, May). Understanding group behavior in virtual reality: A large-scale, longitudinal study in the metaverse. In *72nd Annual International Communication Association Conference*, Paris, France.

Harley, D. (2022). "This would be sweet in VR": On the discursive newness of virtual reality. *New Media & Society*, *17*, 14614448221084655. doi:10.1177/14614448221084655

Hashim, S. L., Ramlan, H., Razali, N. H., & Nordin, N. Z. (2017). Macroeconomic variables affecting the volatility of gold price. [GBSE]. *Journal of Global Business and Social Entrepreneurship*, *3*(5), 97–106.

Hennig-Thurau, T., Aliman, D. N., Herting, A. M., Cziehso, G. P., Linder, M., & Kübler, R. V. (2023). Social interactions in the metaverse: Framework, initial evidence, and research roadmap. *Journal of the Academy of Marketing Science*, *51*(4), 889–913. doi:10.1007/s11747-022-00908-0

Henseler, J., Ringle, C. M., & Sarstedt, M. (2015). A new criterion for assessing discriminant validity in variance-based structural equation modeling. *Journal of the Academy of Marketing Science*, *43*(1), 115–135. doi:10.1007/s11747-014-0403-8

Henz, P. (2022). The societal impact of the Metaverse. *Discover Artificial Intelligence*, *2*(1), 19. doi:10.1007/s44163-022-00032-6

Heracleous, L., Terrier, D., & Gonzalez, S. (2019). NASA's capability evolution toward commercial space. *Space Policy*, *50*, 101330. doi:10.1016/j.spacepol.2019.07.004

Hester, A. J., Hutchins, H. M., & Burke-Smalley, L. A. (2016). Web 2.0 and Transfer: Trainers' Use of Technology to Support Employees' Learning Transfer on the Job. *Performance Improvement Quarterly*, *29*(3), 231–255. doi:10.1002/piq.21225

Hobson, A. (2024). Emergent Governance From Polycentric Order in Virtual Reality Social Spaces. In Law, Video Games, Virtual Realities (pp. 74-95). Routledge. https://doi.org/ doi:10.4324/9781003197805-5

Hoesli, M., & Reka, K. (2013). Volatility spillovers, comovements and contagion in securitized real estate markets. *The Journal of Real Estate Finance and Economics*, *47*(1), 1–35. doi:10.1007/s11146-011-9346-8

Hollebeek, L. D., Clark, M. K., Andreassen, T. W., Sigurdsson, V., & Smith, D. (2020). Virtual reality through the customer journey: Framework and propositions. *Journal of Retailing and Consumer Services*, *55*, 102056. doi:10.1016/j.jretconser.2020.102056

Hollensen, S., Kotler, P., & Opresnik, M. O. (2022). Metaverse – the new marketing universe. *Journal of Business Strategy*.

Hollensen, S., Kotler, P., & Opresnik, M. O. (2022). Metaverse–the new marketing universe. *The Journal of Business Strategy*, *44*(3), 119–125. doi:10.1108/JBS-01-2022-0014

Horng, S. M., & Wu, C. L. (2020). How behaviors on social network sites and online social capital influence social commerce intentions. *Information & Management, 57*(2), 103176. doi:10.1016/j.im.2019.103176

Hossain, M. I., Teh, B. H., Dorasamy, M., Tabash, M. I., & Ong, T. S. (2023, May). Ethical Leadership, Green HRM Practices and Environmental Performance of Manufacturing SMEs at Selangor, Malaysia: Moderating Role of Green Technology Adoption. In *International Scientific Conference on Business and Economics* (pp. 85-104). Cham: Springer Nature Switzerland. 10.1007/978-3-031-42511-0_6

Hossain, M. I., Kumar, J., Islam, M. T., & Valeri, M. (2023). The interplay among paradoxical leadership, industry 4.0 technologies, organisational ambidexterity, strategic flexibility and corporate sustainable performance in manufacturing SMEs of Malaysia. *European Business Review*. doi:10.1108/EBR-04-2023-0109

Hossain, M. I., Ong, T. S., Tabash, M. I., & Teh, B. H. (2024). The panorama of corporate environmental sustainability and green values: Evidence of Bangladesh. *Environment, Development and Sustainability, 26*(1), 1033–1059. doi:10.1007/s10668-022-02748-y

Hossain, M. I., San Ong, T., Teh, B. H., Said, R. M., & Siow, M. L. (2022). Nexus of Stakeholder Integration, Green Investment, Green Technology Adoption and Environmental Sustainability Practices: Evidence from Bangladesh Textile SMEs. *Pertanika Journal of Social Science & Humanities, 30*(1). doi:10.47836/pjssh.30.1.14

Huang, H., Zhang, C., Zhao, L., Ding, S., Wang, H., & Wu, H. (2023). Self-Supervised Medical Image Denoising Based on WISTA-Net for Human Healthcare in Metaverse. *IEEE Journal of Biomedical and Health Informatics*. PMID:37216248

Huang, W., Leong, Y. C., & Ismail, N. A. (2024). The influence of communication language on purchase intention in consumer contexts: The mediating effects of presence and arousal. *Current Psychology (New Brunswick, N.J.), 43*(1), 658–668. doi:10.1007/s12144-023-04314-9

Huang, Y., Wu, S., & Zhao, X. (2021). The metaverse for business: Opportunities and challenges. *Journal of Management Information Systems, 38*(3), 1089–1111.

Hu, Y., & Liu, C. (2022). The 'metaverse society': Beyond the discourse intrinsic potential and transformative impact. *Metaverse, 3*(2), 14. doi:10.54517/m.v3i2.2128

Huynh, T. L. D., Nasir, M. A., Vo, X. V., & Nguyen, T. T. (2020). "Small things matter most": The spillover effects in the cryptocurrency market and gold as a silver bullet. *The North American Journal of Economics and Finance, 54*, 101277. doi:10.1016/j.najef.2020.101277

Huynh-The, T., Gadekallu, T. R., Wang, W. Z., Yenduri, G., Ranaweera, P., Pham, Q. V., da Costa, D. B., & Liyanage, M. (2023). Blockchain for the metaverse: A Review. *Future Generation Computer Systems, 143*, 401–419. doi:10.1016/j.future.2023.02.008

Huynh-The, T., Pham, Q. V., Pham, X. Q., Nguyen, T. T., Han, Z., & Kim, D. S. (2023). Artificial intelligence for the metaverse: A survey. *Engineering Applications of Artificial Intelligence, 117*, 105581. doi:10.1016/j.engappai.2022.105581

Hwangbo, H., Kim, E. H., Lee, S. H., & Jang, Y. J. (2020). Effects of 3D virtual "try-on" on online sales and customers' purchasing experiences. *IEEE Access : Practical Innovations, Open Solutions, 8*, 189479–189489. doi:10.1109/ACCESS.2020.3023040

Hwang, G. J., & Chien, S. Y. (2022). Definition, roles, and potential research issues of the metaverse in education: An artificial intelligence perspective. *Computers and Education: Artificial Intelligence, 3*, 100082. doi:10.1016/j.caeai.2022.100082

Hyun, W. (2023, February). Study on standardization for interoperable metaverse. In *2023 25th International Conference on Advanced Communication Technology (ICACT)* (pp. 319-322). IEEE. 10.23919/ICACT56868.2023.10079642

Iden, J., & Methlie, L. B. (2012). The drivers of services on next-generation networks. *Telematics and Informatics*, *29*(2), 137–155. doi:10.1016/j.tele.2011.05.004

Imamguluyev, R., Umarova, N., & Mikayilova, R. (2023, August). Navigating the Ethics of the Metaverse: A Fuzzy Logic Approach to Decision-Making. In *International Conference on Intelligent and Fuzzy Systems* (pp. 53-60). Cham: Springer Nature Switzerland. 10.1007/978-3-031-39777-6_7

Immersive Virtual Reality. (2008). In B. Furht (Ed.), *Encyclopedia of Multimedia* (pp. 345–346). Springer US., doi:10.1007/978-0-387-78414-4_85

Inanc–Demir, M., & Kozak, M. (2019). Big data and its supporting elements: Implications for tourism and hospitality marketing. In *Big Data and Innovation in Tourism, Travel, and Hospitality* (pp. 213–223). Springer. doi:10.1007/978-981-13-6339-9_13

Ip, C., Leung, R., & Law, R. (2011). Progress and development of information and communication technologies in hospitality. *International Journal of Contemporary Hospitality Management*, *23*(4), 533–551. doi:10.1108/09596111111130029

Ipsita, A., Erickson, L., Dong, Y., Huang, J., Bushinski, A. K., Saradhi, S., & Ramani, K. (n.d.). Towards modeling of virtual reality welding simulators to promote accessible and scalable training. *2022 CHI Conference on Human Factors in Computing Systems*, (pp. 1–21). ACM. 10.1145/3491102.3517696

Iqbal, M. Z., & Campbell, A. G. (2023, October). Metaverse as tech for good: Current progress and emerging opportunities. In Virtual Worlds, 2(4), 326-342.

IsmailL.BuyyaR. (2023, August 21). Metaverse: A Vision, Architectural Elements, and Future Directions for Scalable and Realtime Virtual Worlds. https://arxiv.org/abs/2308.10559

Jaber, T. A. (2022). Security Risks of the Metaverse World. *International Journal of Interactive Mobile Technologies*, *16*(13).

Jackson, R. (2023). *Young users favor immersive media over social media. Why it matters?* TipRanks. https://www.nasdaq.com/articles/young-users-favor-immersive-media-over-social-media.-why-it-matters

Jamader, A. R., Chowdhary, S., & Shankar Jha, S. (2023). A Road Map for Two Decades of Sustainable Tourism Development Framework. In Resilient and Sustainable Destinations After Disaster: Challenges and Strategies (pp. 9-18). Emerald Publishing Limited. doi:10.1108/978-1-80382-021-720231002

Jamader, A. R., Das, P., & Acharya, B. (2022). An Analysis of Consumers Acceptance towards Usage of Digital Payment System, Fintech and CBDC. *Fintech and CBDC (January 1, 2022)*.

Jamader, A. R. (2022). A Brief Report Of The Upcoming & Present Economic Impact To Hospitality Industry In COVID19 Situations. *Journal of Pharmaceutical Negative Results*, 2289–2302.

Jamader, A. R., Chowdhary, S., Jha, S. S., & Roy, B. (2023). Application of Economic Models to Green Circumstance for Management of Littoral Area: A Sustainable Tourism Arrangement. *SMART Journal of Business Management Studies*, *19*(1), 70–84. doi:10.5958/2321-2012.2023.00008.8

Jamader, A. R., Das, P., & Acharya, B. R. (2019, May). BcIoT: blockchain based DDoS prevention architecture for IoT. In *2019 International Conference on Intelligent Computing and Control Systems (ICCS)* (pp. 377-382). IEEE. 10.1109/ICCS45141.2019.9065692

Jamader, A. R., Das, P., Acharya, B., & Hu, Y. C. (2021). Overview of Security and Protection Techniques for Microgrids. In *Microgrids* (pp. 231–253). CRC Press. doi:10.1201/9781003121626-11

Jamader, A. R., Immanuel, J. S., Ebenezer, V., Rakhi, R. A., Sagayam, K. M., & Das, P. (2023). Virtual Education, Training And Internships In Hospitality And Tourism During Covid-19 Situation. *Journal of Pharmaceutical Negative Results*, 286–290.

Jana, K. (2023, June 17). Metatext and metaverse. *The Telegraph Online.*

Jauhiainen, J. S., Krohn, C., & Junnila, J. (2022). Metaverse and Sustainability: Systematic Review of Scientific Publications until 2022 and Beyond. *Sustainability (Basel)*, *15*(1), 346. doi:10.3390/su15010346

Jeon, H. J., Youn, H. C., Ko, S. M., & Kim, T. H. (2022). Blockchain and AI Meet in the Metaverse. *Advances in the Convergence of Blockchain and Artificial Intelligence, 73*(10.5772).

Jeon, Y. A. (2022). Reading Social Media Marketing Messages as Simulated Self Within a Metaverse: An Analysis of Gaze and Social Media Engagement Behaviors within a Metaverse Platform. *Proceedings - 2022 IEEE Conference on Virtual Reality and 3D User Interfaces Abstracts and Workshops, VRW 2022.* IEEE. 10.1109/VRW55335.2022.00068

Jeong, H., Yi, Y., & Kim, D. (2022). An innovative e-commerce platform incorporating metaverse to live commerce. *International Journal of Innovative Computing, Information, & Control*, *18*(1), 221–229. doi:10.24507/ijicic.18.01.221

Jiang, Y., Kang, J., Niyato, D., Ge, X., Xiong, Z., Miao, C., & Shen, X. (2022). Reliable distributed computing for metaverse: A hierarchical game-theoretic approach. *IEEE Transactions on Vehicular Technology*, *72*(1), 1084–1100. doi:10.1109/TVT.2022.3204839

Jiang, Y., Nie, H., & Ruan, W. (2018). Time-varying long-term memory in Bitcoin market. *Finance Research Letters*, *25*, 280–284. doi:10.1016/j.frl.2017.12.009

Joy, A., Zhu, Y., Pena, C., & Brouard, M. (2022). Digital future of luxury brands: Metaverse, digital fashion, and non-fungible tokens. *Strategic Change*, *31*(3), 337–343. doi:10.1002/jsc.2502

Julian, H. L. C., Chung, T., & Wang, Y. (2023). Adoption of Metaverse in South East Asia: Vietnam, Indonesia, Malaysia. In *Strategies and Opportunities for Technology in the Metaverse World* (pp. 196–234). IGI Global. doi:10.4018/978-1-6684-5732-0.ch012

Ju, N., & Lee, K. H. (2021). Perceptions and resistance to accept smart clothing: Moderating effect of consumer innovativeness. *Applied Sciences (Basel, Switzerland)*, *11*(7), 3211. doi:10.3390/app11073211

Jungherr, A., & Schlarb, D. B. (2022). The extended reach of game engine companies: how companies like epic games and unity technologies provide platforms for extended reality applications and the Metaverse. *Social Media + Society*, *8*(2), 12. doi:10.1177/20563051221107641

Jung, T. M., Cho, J. S., Han, D. I. D., Ahn, S. J., Gupta, M., Das, G., Heo, C. Y., Loureiro, S. M. C., Sigala, M., Trunfio, M., Taylor, A., & Dieck, M. C. T. (2024). Metaverse for service industries: Future applications, opportunities, challenges and research directions. *Computers in Human Behavior*, *151*, 108039. Advance online publication. doi:10.1016/j.chb.2023.108039

Kaddoura, S., & Al Husseiny, F. (2023). The rising trend of Metaverse in education: Challenges, opportunities, and ethical considerations. *PeerJ. Computer Science*, *9*, e1252. doi:10.7717/peerj-cs.1252 PMID:37346578

Kadry, A. (2022). The metaverse revolution and its impact on the future of advertising industry. *Journal of Design Sciences and Applied Arts*, *3*(2), 131–139. doi:10.21608/jdsaa.2022.129876.1171

Kahambing, J. G. (2023). Metaverse, mental health and museums in post-COVID-19. *Journal of Public Health (Oxford, England)*, *45*(2), e382–e383. doi:10.1093/pubmed/fdad002 PMID:36680432

Kajtazi, A., & Moro, A. (2019). The role of bitcoin in well diversified portfolios: A comparative global study. *International Review of Financial Analysis*, *61*, 143–157. doi:10.1016/j.irfa.2018.10.003

Katsiampa, P., Corbet, S., & Lucey, B. (2019). High frequency volatility co-movements in cryptocurrency markets. *Journal of International Financial Markets, Institutions and Money*, *62*, 35–52. doi:10.1016/j.intfin.2019.05.003

Kaufman, I., Horton, C., & Soltanifar, M. (2023). *Digital Marketing: Integrating Strategy, Sustainability, and Purpose.* Taylor & Francis. doi:10.4324/9781351019187

Kaushal, N., Sharma, S., & Katoch, A. (2022a). The Satisfaction of Religious Tourists Visiting Shiva Circuit of Himachal Pradesh. *International Research Journal of Management Sociology & Humanities*, *13*(8), 11–19.

Kaushal, N., Sharma, S., & Katoch, A. (2022b). Problems and Challenges faced by Religious Tourists: A study of Religious Destinations of Himachal Pradesh. *International Journal of Commerce. Arts & Science*, *13*(8), 27–35.

Keller, K. L. (2001). *Building Customer-Based Brand Equity: A Blueprint for Creating Strong Brands* (01-107). (Working Paper). M. S. Institute. http://anandahussein.lecture.ub.ac.id/files/2015/09/article-4.pdf

KevinsJ. (2022) Metaverse as a New Emerging Technology: An Interrogation of Opportunities and Legal Issues: Some Introspection (SSRN paper 4050898). doi:10.2139/ssrn.4050898

Khatri, M. (2022). Revamping the marketing world with metaverse–The future of marketing. *International Journal of Computer Applications*, *975*(5), 8887. doi:10.5120/ijca2022922361

Kim, D., Lee, H. K., & Chung, K. (2023). Avatar-mediated experience in the metaverse: The impact of avatar realism on user-avatar relationship. *Journal of Retailing and Consumer Services*, *73*, 103382. doi:10.1016/j.jretconser.2023.103382

Kim, E. J., & Kim, J. Y. (2023). The metaverse for healthcare: Trends, applications, and future directions of digital therapeutics for urology. *International Neurourology Journal*, *27*(Suppl 1), S3–S12. doi:10.5213/inj.2346108.054 PMID:37280754

Kim, J. (2021). Advertising in the Metaverse: Research Agenda. *Journal of Interactive Advertising*, *21*(3), 141–144. doi:10.1080/15252019.2021.2001273

Kim, J., Hwang, L., Kwon, S., & Lee, S. (2022). Change in Blink Rate in the Metaverse VR HMD and AR Glasses Environment. *International Journal of Environmental Research and Public Health*, *19*(14), 8551. https://www.mdpi.com/1660-4601/19/14/8551. doi:10.3390/ijerph19148551 PMID:35886402

Kim, M., Oh, J., Son, S., Park, Y., Kim, J., & Park, Y. (2023). Secure and Privacy-Preserving Authentication Scheme Using Decentralized Identifier in Metaverse Environment. *Electronics (Basel)*, *12*(19), 4073. doi:10.3390/electronics12194073

Kim, Y. B., Lee, J., Park, N., Choo, J., Kim, J. H., & Kim, C. H. (2017). When Bitcoin encounters information in an online forum: Using text mining to analyse user opinions and predict value fluctuation. *PLoS One*, *12*(5), e0177630. doi:10.1371/journal.pone.0177630 PMID:28498843

Kim, Y., Park, J., & Sohn, D. (2022). Understanding user acceptance of the metaverse: Integrating the technology acceptance model and the flow theory. *Journal of Information Technology Management*, *13*(2), 357–377.

Klein, T., Thu, H. P., & Walther, T. (2018). Bitcoin is not the New Gold–A comparison of volatility, correlation, and portfolio performance. *International Review of Financial Analysis*, *59*, 105–116. doi:10.1016/j.irfa.2018.07.010

Kock, N. (2015). Common method bias in PLS-SEM: A full collinearity assessment approach. [ijec]. *International Journal of e-Collaboration, 11*(4), 1–10. doi:10.4018/ijec.2015100101

Koohang, A., Nord, J. H., Ooi, K. B., Tan, G. W. H., Al-Emran, M., Aw, E. C. X., Baabdullah, A. M., Buhalis, D., Cham, T. H., Dennis, C., Dutot, V., Dwivedi, Y. K., Hughes, L., Mogaji, E., Pandey, N., Phau, I., Raman, R., Sharma, A., Sigala, M., & Wong, L. W. (2023). Shaping the Metaverse into Reality: A Holistic Multidisciplinary Understanding of Opportunities, Challenges, and Avenues for Future Investigation. *Journal of Computer Information Systems, 63*(3), 735–765. doi:10.1080/08874417.2023.2165197

Kraus, S., Kanbach, D. K., Krysta, P. M., Steinhoff, M. M., & Tomini, N. (2022). Facebook and the creation of the metaverse: Radical business model innovation or incremental transformation? *International Journal of Entrepreneurial Behaviour & Research, 28*(9), 52–77. doi:10.1108/IJEBR-12-2021-0984

Kroner, K. F., & Sultan, J. (1993). Time-varying distributions and dynamic hedging with foreign currency futures. *Journal of Financial and Quantitative Analysis, 28*(4), 535–551. doi:10.2307/2331164

Kuen, T. Y., & Hoong, T. S. (1992). Forecasting volatility in the Singapore stock market. *Asia Pacific Journal of Management, 9*(1), 1–13. doi:10.1007/BF01732034

Kumar, M. (2024). Virtual Reality in Education: Analyzing the Literature and Bibliometric State of Knowledge. In Transforming Education with Virtual Reality (pp. 379-402). Wiley Online Library.

Kumawat, V., Dhaked, R., Sharma, L., & Jain, S. (2020). Evolution of Immersive Technology. *Journey of Computational Reality.*

Kuo, C. M., Chen, L. C., & Tseng, C. Y. (2017). Investigating an innovative service with hospitality robots. *International Journal of Contemporary Hospitality Management, 29*(5), 1305–1321. doi:10.1108/IJCHM-08-2015-0414

Lada, S., Chekima, B., Karim, M. R. A., Fabeil, N. F., Ayub, M. S., Amirul, S. M., Ansar, R., Bouteraa, M., Fook, L. M., & Zaki, H. O. (2023). Determining factors related to artificial intelligence (AI) adoption among Malaysia's small and medium-sized businesses. *Journal of Open Innovation, 9*(4), 100144. doi:10.1016/j.joitmc.2023.100144

Lai, Y. S., & Sheu, H. J. (2011). On the importance of asymmetries for dynamic hedging during the subprime crisis. *Applied Financial Economics, 21*(11), 801–813. doi:10.1080/09603107.2010.539535

Lan, Y. J. (2024). 3D immersive scaffolding game for enhancing Mandarin learning in children with ADHD. *Journal of Educational Technology & Society.*

Lau, M. C. K., Vigne, S. A., Wang, S., & Yarovaya, L. (2017). Return spillovers between white precious metal ETFs: The role of oil, gold, and global equity. *International Review of Financial Analysis, 52*, 316–332. doi:10.1016/j.irfa.2017.04.001

Laura, P. (2023). *A water smart city: Learning from Singapore.* https://www.beesmart.city/en/solutions/a-water-smart-city-learning-from-singapore

Law, R., Buhalis, D., & Cobanoglu, C. (2014). Progress on information and communication technologies in hospitality and tourism. *International Journal of Contemporary Hospitality Management, 26*(5), 727–750. doi:10.1108/IJCHM-08-2013-0367

Lazaroiu, G., Androniceanu, A., Grecu, I., Grecu, G., & Neguriță, O. (2022). Artificial intelligence-based decision-making algorithms, Internet of Things sensing networks, and sustainable cyber-physical management systems in big data-driven cognitive manufacturing. *Oeconomia Copernicana, 13*(4), https://doi.org/. doi:1047-1080

Lee, H., & Leonas, K. (2018). Consumer experiences, the key to survive in an omni-channel environment: Use of virtual technology. *Journal of Textile and Apparel, Technology and Management, 10*(3).

Lee, C. T., Ho, T. Y., & Xie, H. H. (2023). Building brand engagement in metaverse commerce: The role of branded non-fungible toekns (BNFTs). *Electronic Commerce Research and Applications*, *58*, 101248. Advance online publication. doi:10.1016/j.elerap.2023.101248

Lee, C. T., Li, Z., & Shen, Y. C. (2024). Building bonds: An examination of relational bonding in continuous content contribution behaviors on metaverse-based non-fungible token platforms. *Internet Research*. Advance online publication. doi:10.1108/INTR-11-2022-0883

Lee, C. W. (2022). Application of metaverse service to healthcare industry: A strategic perspective. *International Journal of Environmental Research and Public Health*, *19*(20), 13038. doi:10.3390/ijerph192013038 PMID:36293609

Lee, J., & Kwon, K. H. (2022). The significant transformation of life into health and beauty in metaverse era. *Journal of Cosmetic Dermatology*, *21*(12), 6575–6583. doi:10.1111/jocd.15151 PMID:35686389

Lee, J., Park, H., & Song, J. (2023). Safety assessment of augmented reality and virtual reality in the metaverse: A review. *International Journal of Occupational Safety and Health*, ●●●, 1–10.

Lee, J.-W. (2023). The Future of Online Barrier-Free Open Space Cultural Experiences for People with Disabilities in the Post-COVID-19 Era. *Land (Basel)*, *13*(1), 33. doi:10.3390/land13010033

Lee, K. L., Teong, C. X., Alzoubi, H. M., Alshurideh, M. T., Khatib, M. E., & Al-Gharaibeh, S. M. (2024). Digital supply chain transformation: The role of smart technologies on operational performance in manufacturing industry. *International Journal of Engineering Business Management*, *16*, 18479790241234986. doi:10.1177/18479790241234986

Lee, K. L., Wong, S. Y., Alzoubi, H. M., Al Kurdi, B., Alshurideh, M. T., & El Khatib, M. (2023). Adopting smart supply chain and smart technologies to improve operational performance in manufacturing industry. *International Journal of Engineering Business Management*, *15*, 18479790231200614. doi:10.1177/18479790231200614

Lee, M., Min, K. Z. L., & Kim, S.-H. (2024). Does the Experience of Using Metaverse Affect the Relationship between Social Identity, Psychological Ownership, and Engagement? *Proceedings of the 57th Hawaii International Conference on System Sciences*. University of Hawai.

Lee, S., Lee, Y., & Park, E. (2023). Sustainable Vocational Preparation for Adults with Disabilities: A Metaverse-Based Approach. *Sustainability (Basel)*, *15*(15), 12000. doi:10.3390/su151512000

Lee, Y., Kim, J., & Lee, Y. (2012). The role of perceived realism and trust in the continued usage of virtual worlds. *Computers in Human Behavior*, *28*(2), 346–352.

Lemos, L., Ainse, D., & Faras, A. (2022). DAO meets the Estonian e-residency program: a stance from Synergy's blockchain-based open-source toolkit. Conference Proceedings of the STS Conference Graz 2022, Lloyd Owen, D. (2021). *Defining 'Smart Water'*. Wily Online Library. https://doi.org/10.1002/9781119531241.ch4

Leonidou, L. C., Leonidou, C. N., Fotiadis, T. A., & Zeriti, A. (2013). Resources and capabilities as drivers of hotel environmental marketing strategy: Implications for competitive advantage and performance. *Tourism Management*, *35*, 94–110. doi:10.1016/j.tourman.2012.06.003

Letafati, M., & Otoum, S. (2023). Digital Healthcare in The Metaverse: Insights into Privacy and Security. *arXiv preprint arXiv:2308.04438*.

Liberatore, M. J., & Wagner, W. P. (2021). Virtual, mixed, and augmented reality: A systematic review for immersive systems research. *Virtual Reality (Waltham Cross)*, *25*(3), 773–799. doi:10.1007/s10055-020-00492-0

Lien, D., & Yang, L. (2006). Spot-futures spread, time-varying correlation, and hedging with currency futures. *Journal of Futures Markets*, *26*(10), 1019–1038. doi:10.1002/fut.20225

Li, F., Xing, W., Su, M., & Xu, J. (2021). The evolution of China's marine economic policy and the labor productivity growth momentum of the marine economy and its three economic industries. *Marine Policy*, *134*, 104777. doi:10.1016/j.marpol.2021.104777

Li, H., Li, Z., & Zhang, X. (2021). Understanding users' acceptance of the metaverse: An extended UTAUT model and empirical test. *International Journal of Information Management*, *59*, 102495.

Li, H., & Zhang, Y. (2021). Data integration challenges and technologies in the metaverse. *IEEE Access : Practical Innovations, Open Solutions*, *9*, 149696–149709.

Li, J. (2022). Impact of Metaverse cultural communication on the mental health of international students in China: Highlighting effects of healthcare anxiety and cyberchondria. *American Journal of Health Behavior*, *46*(6), 809–820. doi:10.5993/AJHB.46.6.21 PMID:36721290

Li, J. J. (2024). Virtual Currency and Smart Financial Management in Immersive Online Games in the Metaverse Environment. *Computer-Aided Design and Applications*.

Lin, C. C., & Huang, Y. (2022). The impact of metaverse technology on human resource development: A review of the literature. *Journal of Human Resources Development*, *41*(4), 599–618.

Lindstrom, M. (2009). *Buy.ology: A ciência do Neuromarketing*. Gestão Plus.

Lin, H. (2019). The acceptance of virtual worlds: A meta-analysis. *Computers in Human Behavior*, *93*, 113–122.

Li, T., Yang, C., Yang, Q., Lan, S., Zhou, S., Luo, X., Huang, H., & Zheng, Z. (2023). Metaopera: A Cross-Metaverse Interoperability Protocol. *IEEE Wireless Communications*, *30*(5), 136–143. doi:10.1109/MWC.011.2300042

Liu, Y., & Tsyvinski, A. (2021). Risks and returns of cryptocurrency. *Review of Financial Studies*, *34*(6), 2689–2727. doi:10.1093/rfs/hhaa113

Ljungholm, D. P. (2022). Metaverse-based 3D visual modeling, virtual reality training experiences, and wearable biological measuring devices in immersive workplaces. *Psychosociological Issues in Human Resource Management*, *10*(1), 64–77. doi:10.22381/pihrm10120225

Lodha, S. (2017). A Cointegration and Causation Study of Gold Prices, Crude Oil Prices and Exchange Rates. *IUP Journal of Financial Risk Management*, *14*(3), 55–66.

Lombart, C., Millan, E., Normand, J. M., Verhulst, A., Labbé-Pinlon, B., & Moreau, G. (2020). Effects of physical, non-immersive virtual, and immersive virtual store environments on consumers' perceptions and purchase behavior. *Computers in Human Behavior*, *110*, 106374. doi:10.1016/j.chb.2020.106374

Louzis, D. P. (2015). Measuring spillover effects in Euro area financial markets: A disaggregate approach. *Empirical Economics*, *49*(4), 1367–1400. doi:10.1007/s00181-014-0911-x

Lowood, H. E. (2022). *virtual reality*. Encyclopedia Britannica. https://www.britannica.com/technology/virtual-reality

Lv, Z., Qiao, L., Li, Y., Yuan, Y., & Wang, F. Y. (2022). BlockNet: Beyond reliable spatial Digital Twins to Parallel Metaverse. *Patterns (New York, N.Y.)*, *3*(5), 100468. doi:10.1016/j.patter.2022.100468 PMID:35607617

Macedo, C. R., Miro, D. A., & Hart, T. (2022). *The Metaverse: From Science Fiction to Commercial Reality—Protecting Intellectual Property in the Virtual Landscape*. *31*(1).

Maden, A., & Yücenur, G. N. (2024). Evaluation of sustainable metaverse characteristics using scenario-based fuzzy cognitive map. *Computers in Human Behavior*, *152*, 108090. doi:10.1016/j.chb.2023.108090

Madhavan, A. (2000). Market microstructure: A survey. *Journal of Financial Markets*, *3*(3), 205–258. doi:10.1016/S1386-4181(00)00007-0

Maier, D., Maier, A., Aşchilean, I., Anastasiu, L., & Gavriş, O. (2020). The relationship between innovation and sustainability: A bibliometric review of the literature. *Sustainability (Basel)*, *12*(10), 4083. doi:10.3390/su12104083

Mainardes, E. W., & Freitas, N. P. D. (2023). The effects of perceived value dimensions on customer satisfaction and loyalty: A comparison between traditional banks and fintechs. *International Journal of Bank Marketing*, *41*(3), 641–662. doi:10.1108/IJBM-10-2022-0437

Majerová, J., & Pera, A. (2022). Haptic and biometric sensor technologies, spatio-temporal fusion algorithms, and virtual navigation tools in the decentralized and interconnected metaverse. *Review of Contemporary Philosophy*, *21*(0), 105–121. doi:10.22381/RCP2120227

Makarigakis, A., Partey, S., Nagabhatla, N., De Lombaerde, P., Libert, B., Trombitcaia, I., Zerrath, E., Guerrier, D., Faloutsos, D., & Krol, D. (2023). *Regional Perspectives*. https://cris.unu.edu/sites/cris.unu.edu

Malerba, S. (2023). *Exploring the Potential of the Metaverse for Value Creation: An Analysis of Opportunities, Challenges, and Societal Impact, with a Focus on the Chinese Context* Ca' Foscari University of Venice. http://dspace.unive.it/bitstream/handle/10579/24277/890613-1281454

Mammadova, A. (2023). *Digital big-bang Metaverse: opportunities and threats* [Master's thesis, Università Ca' Foscari Venezia]. http://dspace.unive.it/handle/10579/25766

Mancuso, I., Petruzzelli, A. M., & Panniello, U. (2023). Digital business model innovation in metaverse: How to approach virtual economy opportunities. *Information Processing & Management*, *60*(5), 103457. doi:10.1016/j.ipm.2023.103457

Manera, M., McAleer, M., & Grasso, M. (2006). Modelling time-varying conditional correlations in the volatility of Tapis oil spot and forward returns. *Applied Financial Economics*, *16*(07), 525–533. doi:10.1080/09603100500426465

Mantelli, A. (2021). Learning Japanese through VR technology. The case of altspace VR. *Annali di Ca'Foscari. Serie Orientale*, *57*, 663–684. 10278/3742133/1/art-10.30687

Marinescu, I. A., & Iordache, D.-D. (2023). Exploring relevant technologies for simulating user interaction in Metaverse virtual spaces. *Romanian Journal of Information Technology & Automatic Control*, *33*(3), 129–142. doi:10.33436/v33i3y202310

Martinez-Millana, A., Bayo-Monton, J. L., Lizondo, A., Fernandez-Llatas, C., & Traver, V. (2016). Evaluation of Google Glass technical limitations on their integration in medical systems. *Sensors (Basel)*, *16*(12), 2142. doi:10.3390/s16122142 PMID:27983691

Marzaleh, M. A., Peyravi, M., & Shaygani, F. (2022). A revolution in health: Opportunities and challenges of the Metaverse. *EXCLI Journal*, *21*, 791. PMID:35949490

Massaro, M. (2023). Digital transformation in the healthcare sector through blockchain technology. Insights from academic research and business developments. *Technovation*, *120*, 102386. doi:10.1016/j.technovation.2021.102386

Maurizio Unali, G. C. (2024). Towards a Virtual Museum of Ephemeral Architecture: Methods, Techniques and Semantic Models for a Post-digital Metaverse. In M. R. Andrea Giordano, Beyond Digital Representation. Springer Nature Switzerland.

McCall, R., Shell, J., Kacperski, C., Greenstein, S., Whitton, N., & Summers, J. (2022, October). Workshop on Social and Ethical Issues in Entertainment Computing. In *International Conference on Entertainment Computing* (pp. 429-435). Cham: Springer International Publishing.

Mclean, G., Al-Nabhani, K., & Wilson, A. (2018). Developing a mobile applications customer experience model (MACE)-implications for retailers. *Journal of Business Research*, *85*, 325–336. doi:10.1016/j.jbusres.2018.01.018

Meichler, M. (2023, June 19). *The Future of NFTs: Is Gaming the Solution?* NFT Evening. https://nftevening.com/the-future-of-nfts-is-gaming-the-solution/

Mejia, J. M. R., & Rawat, D. B. (2022, July). recent advances in a medical domain metaverse: Status, challenges, and perspective. In *2022 Thirteenth International Conference on Ubiquitous and Future Networks (ICUFN)* (pp. 357-362). IEEE. 10.1109/ICUFN55119.2022.9829645

Mensi, W., Hammoudeh, S., Nguyen, D. K., & Yoon, S. M. (2014). Dynamic spillovers among major energy and cereal commodity prices. *Energy Economics*, *43*, 225–243. doi:10.1016/j.eneco.2014.03.004

Messinger, P. R., Stroulia, E., Lyons, K., Bone, M., Niu, R. H., Smirnov, K., & Perelgut, S. (2009). Virtual worlds—past, present, and future: New directions in social computing. *Decision Support Systems*, *47*(3), 204–228. doi:10.1016/j.dss.2009.02.014

Metaverse Live Entertainment—Global | Market Forecast. (n.d.). Statista. https://www.statista.com/outlook/amo/metaverse/metaverse-live-entertainment/worldwide

Metaverse: The Revolution of the Sports World & Entire Life. (n.d.). ISPO. https://www.ispo.com/en/news-trends/metaverse-revolution-sports-world

Metavertainment: A Vision Into The World of The Metaverse and Entertainment. (n.d.). HackerNoon. https://hackernoon.com/metavertainment-a-vision-into-the-world-of-the-metaverse-and-entertainment

Miao, F., Kozlenkova, I. V., Wang, H., Xie, T., & Palmatier, R. W. (2022). An emerging theory of avatar marketing. *Journal of Marketing*, *86*(1), 67–90. doi:10.1177/0022242921996646

Mirza-Babaei, P., Robinson, R., Mandryk, R., Pirker, J., Kang, C., & Fletcher, A. (2022, November). Games and the Metaverse. In *Extended abstracts of the 2022 annual symposium on computer-human interaction in play*. ACM. 10.1145/3505270.3558355

Mishra, P., & Singh, G. (2023). Energy management systems in sustainable smart cities based on the internet of energy: A technical review. *Energies*, *16*(19), 6903. doi:10.3390/en16196903

Mittal, G., & Bansal, R. (2023). Driving Force Behind Consumer Brand Engagement: The Metaverse. In Cultural Marketing and Metaverse for Consumer Engagement (pp. 164-181). IGI Global. doi:10.4018/978-1-6684-8312-1.ch012

Mogaji, E. (2023). Metaverse influence on transportation: A mission impossible? *Transportation Research Interdisciplinary Perspectives*, *22*, 100954. doi:10.1016/j.trip.2023.100954

Mogaji, E., Dwivedi, Y. K., & Raman, R. (2024). Fashion marketing in the metaverse. *Journal of Global Fashion Marketing*, *15*(1), 115–130. doi:10.1080/20932685.2023.2249483

Mohamed, E. S., & Naqishbandi, T. A. (2023). Metaverse! Possible Potential Opportunities and Trends in E-Healthcare and Education. *International Journal of E-Adoption*, *15*(2), 1–21. doi:10.4018/IJEA.316537

Moher, D., Liberati, A., Tetzlaff, J., & Altman, D. G. (2009). Preferred reporting items for systematic reviews and meta-analyses: The PRISMA statement. *Annals of Internal Medicine*, *151*(4), 264–269. doi:10.7326/0003-4819-151-4-200908180-00135 PMID:19622511

Momtaz, P. P. (2021). The pricing and performance of cryptocurrency. *European Journal of Finance*, *27*(4-5), 367–380. doi:10.1080/1351847X.2019.1647259

Morales-Fernández, B. (2024). New Linguistic Spaces in Cyberculture: The Influence of the Metaverse on the Minification of Social Networks. In The Future of Digital Communication (pp. 27-38). CRC Press.

Moro-Visconti, R. (2022). Metaverse: A Digital Network Valuation. In *The Valuation of Digital Intangibles: Technology, Marketing, and the Metaverse* (pp. 515–559). Springer International Publishing. doi:10.1007/978-3-031-09237-4_18

Mourtzis, D. (2023). The Metaverse in Industry 5.0: A Human-Centric Approach towards Personalized Value Creation. *Encyclopedia*, *3*(3), 1105–1120. doi:10.3390/encyclopedia3030080

Moztarzadeh, O., Jamshidi, M., Sargolzaei, S., Jamshidi, A., Baghalipour, N., Malekzadeh Moghani, M., & Hauer, L. (2023). Metaverse and Healthcare: Machine Learning-Enabled Digital Twins of Cancer. *Bioengineering (Basel, Switzerland)*, *10*(4), 455. doi:10.3390/bioengineering10040455 PMID:37106642

Mozumder, M. A. I., Sheeraz, M. M., Athar, A., Aich, S., & Kim, H. C. (2022, February). Overview: Technology roadmap of the future trend of metaverse based on IoT, blockchain, AI technique, and medical domain metaverse activity. In *2022 24th International Conference on Advanced Communication Technology (ICACT)* (pp. 256-261). IEEE.

Mozumder, M. A. I., Armand, T. P. T., Imtiyaj Uddin, S. M., Athar, A., Sumon, R. I., Hussain, A., & Kim, H. C. (2023). Metaverse for Digital Anti-Aging Healthcare: An Overview of Potential Use Cases Based on Artificial Intelligence, Blockchain, IoT Technologies, Its Challenges, and Future Directions. *Applied Sciences (Basel, Switzerland)*, *13*(8), 5127. doi:10.3390/app13085127

Mughal, A. A. (2018). Artificial Intelligence in Information Security: Exploring the Advantages, Challenges, and Future Directions. *Journal of Artificial Intelligence and Machine Learning in Management*, *2*(1), 22–34.

Muhuri, P. K., Shukla, A. K., & Abraham, A. (2019). Industry 4.0: A bibliometric analysis and detailed overview. *Engineering Applications of Artificial Intelligence*, *78*, 218–235. doi:10.1016/j.engappai.2018.11.007

Munn, N., & Weijers, D. (2023). The real ethical problem with metaverses. *Frontiers in Human Dynamics*, *5*, 1226848. doi:10.3389/fhumd.2023.1226848

Mystakidis, S. (2022). *Metaverse. Encyclopedia, 2*(1).

Mystakidis, S. (2022). Metaverse. [Key Characteristics of the metaverse]. *Encyclopedia*, *2*(1), 486–497. doi:10.3390/encyclopedia2010031

Nabukalu, R., & Wanjohi, A. (2023). *Impact of Metaverse on Marketing Communication: A case study of the fashion industry*. Lulea University of Technology.

Naderi, H., & Shojaei, A. (2023). Digital twinning of civil infrastructures: Current state of model architectures, interoperability solutions, and future prospects. *Automation in Construction*, *149*, 104785. doi:10.1016/j.autcon.2023.104785

Nakamoto, S. (2008). Bitcoin: A peer-to-peer electronic cash system. *Decentralized business review*, 21260.

Narula, H. (2022). *Virtual Society: The Metaverse and the New Frontiers of Human Experience*. Crown Currency.

NathK. (2022). Evolution of the Internet from Web 1.0 to Metaverse: The Good, The Bad and The Ugly. TechRxiv. doi:10.36227/techrxiv.19743676

Nayak, D. K., Mishra, P., Das, P., Jamader, A. R., & Acharya, B. (2022). Application of Deep Learning in Biomedical Informatics and Healthcare. In *Smart Healthcare Analytics: State of the Art* (pp. 113–132). Springer. doi:10.1007/978-981-16-5304-9_9

Nazma, R. B., & Devi, R. (2023). Sustainable Development Using Green Finance and Triple Bottom Line: A Bibliometric Review. *Management*, *1*, 22. doi:10.1177/ijim.231184138

Needleman, S. E. (2021). The Amazing Things You'll Do in the 'Metaverse' and What It Will Take to Get There. *The Wall Street Journal*.

Netemeyer, R. G., Bearden, W. O., & Sharma, S. (2003). *Scaling procedures: Issues and applications*. sage publications.

Netemeyer, R. G., Bearden, W. O., & Sharma, S. (2003). *Scaling procedures: Issues and applications*. Sage publications.

Nevelsteen, K. J. L. (2018). Virtual world, defined from a technological perspective and applied to video games, mixed reality, and the Metaverse. *Computer Animation and Virtual Worlds, 29*(1), 22, Article e1752. doi:10.1002/cav.1752

Neves, J., Bacalhau, L. M., & Santos, V. (2024). *A Systematic Review on the Customer Journey Between Two Worlds: Reality and Immersive World*. Marketing and Smart Technologies.

Ng, D. T. K. (2022). What is the metaverse? Definitions, technologies and the community of inquiry. *Australasian Journal of Educational Technology, 38*(4), 190–205. doi:10.14742/ajet.7945

Nica, E. (2022). Virtual healthcare technologies and consultation systems, smart operating rooms, and remote sensing data fusion algorithms in the medical metaverse. *American Journal of Medical Research (New York, N.Y.), 9*(2), 105–120. doi:10.22381/ajmr9220227

Novak, K. (2022). Introducing the Metaverse, Again! *TechTrends, 66*(5), 737–739. doi:10.1007/s11528-022-00767-0

Nunes, C. C. (2023). *The Importance on Self-Expression Through Clothing and Fashion: A view on Digital Identity and Digital Fashion* Universidade Da Beira Interior. https://ubibliorum.ubi.pt/handle/10400.6/13583

Nunes, G. S., & Filho, E. J. M. A. (2018b). Consumer behavior regarding wearable technologies: Google Glass. *Innovation & Management Review, 15*(3), 230–246. doi:10.1108/INMR-06-2018-0034

Nuñez, J., Krynski, L., & Otero, P. (2024). The metaverse in the world of health: The present future. Challenges and opportunities. *Archivos Argentinos de Pediatria, 122*(1). doi:10.5546/aap.2022-02942.eng PMID:37171469

Oh, H. J., Kim, J., Chang, J. J., Park, N., & Lee, S. (2023). Social benefits of living in the metaverse: The relationships among social presence, supportive interaction, social self-efficacy, and feelings of loneliness. *Computers in Human Behavior, 139*, 107498. doi:10.1016/j.chb.2022.107498

Olaleye, S. (2023). The Bibliometric Commingling of Metaverse and Non-fungible Tokens in Marketing. In J. R. Reis, Marketing and Smart Technologies. Springer Nature Singapore.

Oliveira, A., & Cruz, M. (2023). Virtually Connected in a Multiverse of Madness?—Perceptions of Gaming, Animation, and Metaverse. *Applied Sciences (Basel, Switzerland), 13*(15), 15. doi:10.3390/app13158573

Oliveira, C. M. (2023). *Humantech Marketing: o marketing molecular e humano*. Conjuntura Actual Editora.

Ooi, K. B., Tan, G. W. H., Al-Emran, M., Al-Sharafi, M. A., Arpaci, I., Zaidan, A. A., ... Iranmanesh, M. (2023). The metaverse in engineering management: Overview, opportunities, challenges, and future research agenda. *IEEE Transactions on Engineering Management*.

Ooi, K., Tan, G. W., Aw, E. C., Cham, T., Dwivedi, Y. K., Dwivedi, R., Hughes, L., Kar, A. K., Loh, X., Mogaji, E., Phau, I., & Sharma, A. (2023). Banking in the metaverse: A new frontier for financial institutions. *International Journal of Bank Marketing, 41*(7), 1829–1846. doi:10.1108/IJBM-03-2023-0168

Orr, E. (2022). The Metaverse Can Create A Boundless Healthcare Experience. *Forbes*. https://www.forbes.com/sites/forbestechcouncil/2022/01/26/the-metaverse-can-create-a-boundless-healthcare-experience/?sh=1b21c0ab2340

Othman, A., Chemnad, K., Hassanien, A. E., Tlili, A., Zhang, C. Y., Al-Thani, D., ... Altınay, Z. (2024). Accessible Metaverse: A Theoretical Framework for Accessibility and Inclusion in the Metaverse. *Multimodal Technologies and Interaction, 8*(3), 21. doi:10.3390/mti8030021

Ozdemir, H., & Ozdemir, Z. A. (2021). *A Survey of Hedge and Safe Havens Assets against G-7 Stock Markets before and during the COVID-19 Pandemic* (No. 14888). IZA Discussion Papers.

Özdemir, O. (2022). Cue the volatility spillover in the cryptocurrency markets during the COVID-19 pandemic: Evidence from DCC-GARCH and wavelet analysis. *Financial Innovation, 8*(1), 1–38. doi:10.1186/s40854-021-00319-0 PMID:35132369

Özkurt, M. (2023). *A Jungian Archetypal analysis of Earnest Cline's Ready Player One: quest for the Axis mMundi* Pamukkale University]. https://hdl.handle.net/11499/56004

Öztürk, B., & Hersono, R. (2023). *Playing to Win: How Gamification Can Boost Customer Engagement and Turn Non-Fans into Brand Advocates.*

Pachouri, V., Singh, R., Gehlot, A., Pandey, S., Akram, S. V., & Abbas, M. I. (2024). Empowering sustainability in the built environment: A technological Lens on industry 4.0 Enablers. *Technology in Society, 76*, 102427. doi:10.1016/j.techsoc.2023.102427

Panda, T. K. (2022). In the world of Metaverse. *NMIMS Management Review, 30*(03), 03-05. doi:10.53908/NMMR.300210

Papagiannidis, S., Pantano, E., See-To, E. W., Dennis, C., & Bourlakis, M. (2017). To immerse or not? Experimenting with two virtual retail environments. *Information Technology & People, 30*(1), 163–188. doi:10.1108/ITP-03-2015-0069

Pappas, N. (2015). Marketing hospitality industry in an era of crisis. *Tourism Planning & Development, 12*(3), 333–349. doi:10.1080/21568316.2014.979226

Pareliussen, J., & Purwin, A. (2023). Climate policies and Sweden's green industrial revolution. *OECD Economics Department Working Papers*(1778), 1-48. https://doi.org/ doi:10.1787/18151973

Park, S., & Kim, S. (2022). Identifying world types to deliver gameful experiences for sustainable learning in the Metaverse. *Sustainability, 14*(3), 14. doi:10.3390/su14031361

Park, A., Wilson, M., Robson, K., Demetis, D., & Kietzmann, J. (2023). Interoperability: Our exciting and terrifying Web3 future. *Business Horizons, 66*(4), 529–541. doi:10.1016/j.bushor.2022.10.005

Park, H., Ahn, D., & Lee, J. (2023). Towards a Metaverse Workspace: Opportunities, Challenges, and Design Implications. In *Proceedings of the 2023 CHI Conference on Human Factors in Computing Systems* (pp. 1-20). ACM. 10.1145/3544548.3581306

Park, J., & Kim, N. (2024). Examining self-congruence between user and avatar in purchasing behavior from the metaverse to the real world. *Journal of Global Fashion Marketing, 15*(1), 23–38. doi:10.1080/20932685.2023.2180768

Park, S. M., & Kim, Y.-G. (2022). A Metaverse: Taxonomy, Components, Applications, and Open Challenges. *IEEE Access : Practical Innovations, Open Solutions, 10*, 4209–4251. doi:10.1109/ACCESS.2021.3140175

Pearce, M., Zeadally, S., & Hunt, R. (2013). Virtualization: Issues, security threats, and solutions. *ACM Computing Surveys, 45*(2), 1–39. doi:10.1145/2431211.2431216

Pellas, N., Mystakidis, S., & Kazanidis, I. (2021). Immersive Virtual Reality in K-12 and Higher Education: A systematic review of the last decade scientific literature. *Virtual Reality (Waltham Cross), 25*(3), 835–861. doi:10.1007/s10055-020-00489-9

Peltonen, T. (2019). Case Study 4: The Collapse of Nokia's Mobile Phone Business, Springer Books. In *Towards Wise Management* (pp. 163–188). Springer. doi:10.1007/978-3-319-91719-1_6

Pérez, J., Castro, M., & López, G. (2023). Serious Games and AI: Challenges and Opportunities for Computational Social Science. *IEEE Access : Practical Innovations, Open Solutions, 11*, 62051–62061. doi:10.1109/ACCESS.2023.3286695

Periyasami, S., & Periyasamy, A. P. (2022). Metaverse as future promising platform business model: Case study on fashion value chain. *Businesses, 2*(4), 527–545. doi:10.3390/businesses2040033

Petrigna, L., & Musumeci, G. (2022). The metaverse: A new challenge for the healthcare system: A scoping review. *Journal of Functional Morphology and Kinesiology, 7*(3), 63. doi:10.3390/jfmk7030063 PMID:36135421

Pirnar, I., Icoz, O., & Icoz, O. (2010). The new tourist: Impacts on the hospitality marketing strategies. *EuroCHRIE Amsterdam*, 25-28.

Pizzi, G., Scarpi, D., Pichierri, M., & Vannucci, V. (2019). Virtual reality, real reactions?: Comparing consumers' perceptions and shopping orientation across physical and virtual-reality retail stores. *Computers in Human Behavior, 96*, 1–12. doi:10.1016/j.chb.2019.02.008

Podmurnyi, S. (2022). Business Insights On The Opportunity For The Educational Metaverse. *Forbes*. https://www.forbes.com/sites/forbestechcouncil/2022/08/05/business-insights-on-the-opportunity-for-the-educational-metaverse/?sh=240d59874a3f

Polas, M. R. H., Jahanshahi, A. A., Kabir, A. I., Sohel-Uz-Zaman, A. S. M., Osman, A. R., & Karim, R. (2022). Artificial intelligence, blockchain technology, and risk-taking behavior in the 4.0 IR Metaverse Era: Evidence from Bangladesh-based SMEs. *Journal of Open Innovation, 8*(3), 168. doi:10.3390/joitmc8030168

Popescu, G. H., Ciurlău, C. F., Stan, C. I., Băcănoiu, C., & Tănase, A. (2022). Virtual workplaces in the metaverse: Immersive remote collaboration tools, behavioral predictive analytics, and extended reality technologies. *Psychosociological Issues in Human Resource Management, 10*(1), 21–34. doi:10.22381/pihrm10120222

Popescu, G. H., Valaskova, K., & Horak, J. (2022). Augmented reality shopping experiences, retail business analytics, and machine vision algorithms in the virtual economy of the metaverse. *Journal of Self-Governance and Management Economics, 10*(2), 67–81.

Popp, J., & Cuțitoi, A. C. (2022). Immersive Visualization Systems, Spatial Simulation and Environment Mapping Algorithms, and Decision Intelligence and Modeling Tools in the Web3-powered Metaverse World. *Journal of Self-Governance and Management Economics, 10*(3), 56–72.

Prasetyo, J. (2022). The Future of Post-Covid-19 Health Services using Metaverse Technology. *The Journal for Nurse Practitioners, 6*(1), 93–99. doi:10.30994/jnp.v6i1.295

Proelss, J., Sévigny, S., & Schweizer, D. (2023). GameFi: The perfect symbiosis of blockchain, tokens, DeFi, and NFTs? *International Review of Financial Analysis, 90*, 102916. doi:10.1016/j.irfa.2023.102916

Profumo, G., Testa, G., Viassone, M., & Ben Youssef, K. (2024). Metaverse and the fashion industry: A systematic literature review. *Journal of Global Fashion Marketing, 15*(1), 131–154. doi:10.1080/20932685.2023.2270587

Qarni, M. O., & Gulzar, S. (2021). Portfolio diversification benefits of alternative currency investment in Bitcoin and foreign exchange markets. *Financial Innovation, 7*(1), 1–37. doi:10.1186/s40854-021-00233-5

Qiu, C. S., Majeed, A., Khan, S., & Watson, M. (2022). Transforming health through the metaverse. *Journal of the Royal Society of Medicine, 115*(12), 484–486. doi:10.1177/01410768221144763 PMID:36480946

Qi, W. (2022). The Investment Value of Metaverse in the Media and Entertainment Industry. *BCP Business &amp. Management*, *34*, 279–283. doi:10.54691/bcpbm.v34i.3026

Queiroz, M. M., Wamba, S. F., Pereira, S. C. F., & Jabbour, C. J. C. (2023). The metaverse as a breakthrough for operations and supply chain management: Implications and call for action. *International Journal of Operations & Production Management*, *43*(10), 1539–1553. doi:10.1108/IJOPM-01-2023-0006

Raad, H., & Rashid, F. K. M. (2023). The Metaverse: Applications, Concerns, Technical Challenges, Future Directions and Recommendations. *IEEE Access : Practical Innovations, Open Solutions*, *11*, 110850–110861. doi:10.1109/ACCESS.2023.3321650

Rad, A. I., & Far, S. B. (2023). SocialFi transforms social media: An overview of key technologies, challenges, and opportunities of the future generation of social media. *Social Network Analysis and Mining*, *13*(1), 42. doi:10.1007/s13278-023-01050-7

Rahaman, T. (2022). Into the metaverse–perspectives on a new reality. *Medical Reference Services Quarterly*, *41*(3), 330–337. doi:10.1080/02763869.2022.2096341 PMID:35980623

Rahi, P., Sood, S. P., Dandotiya, M., Kalhotra, S. K., & Khan, I. R. (2023). Artificial Intelligence of Things (AIoT) and Metaverse Technology for Brain Health, Mental Health, and Wellbeing. In Contemporary Applications of Data Fusion for Advanced Healthcare Informatics (pp. 429-445). IGI Global. https://doi.org/ doi:10.4018/978-1-6684-8913-0.ch019

Rahman, K. R., Shitol, S. K., Islam, M. S., Iftekhar, K. T., & Pranto, S. A. H. A. (2023). Use of Metaverse Technology in Education Domain. *Journal of Metaverse*, *3*(1), 79–86. doi:10.57019/jmv.1223704

Rajan, A., Nassiri, N., Akre, V., Ravikumar, R., Nabeel, A., Buti, M., et al. (2018). *Virtual Reality Gaming Addiction.* Fifth HCT Information Technology Trends (ITT).

Rana, J., Gaur, L., Singh, G., Awan, U., & Rasheed, M. I. (2022). Reinforcing customer journey through artificial intelligence: A review and research agenda. *International Journal of Emerging Markets*, *17*(7), 1738–1758. doi:10.1108/IJOEM-08-2021-1214

Rane, N., Choudhary, S., & Rane, J. (2023). *Metaverse for Enhancing Customer Loyalty: Effective Strategies to Improve Customer Relationship, Service, Engagement, Satisfaction, and Experience* (SSRN Scholarly Paper 4624197). doi:10.2139/ssrn.4624197

Rane, N., Choudhary, S., & Rane, J. (2023). Metaverse for Enhancing Customer Loyalty: Effective Strategies to Improve Customer Relationship, Service, Engagement, Satisfaction, and Experience. *Service, Engagement, Satisfaction, and Experience.*

Rathore, S., & Arora, M. (2024). Sustainability Reporting in the Metaverse: A Multi-Sectoral Analysis. In Exploring the Use of Metaverse in Business and Education (pp. 147-165). IGI Global. doi:10.4018/979-8-3693-5868-9.ch009

Rathore, B. (2017). Virtual consumerism: An exploration of e-commerce in the metaverse. *International Journal of New Media Studies*, *4*(2), 61–69. doi:10.58972/eiprmj.v4i2y17.109

Rauschnabel, P. A., Babin, B. J., tom Dieck, M. C., Krey, N., & Jung, T. (2022). What is augmented reality marketing? Its definition, complexity, and future. *Journal of Business Research*, *142*, 1140–1150. doi:10.1016/j.jbusres.2021.12.084

Rejeb, A., Rejeb, K., & Treiblmaier, H. (2023). Mapping metaverse research: Identifying future research areas based on bibliometric and topic modeling techniques. *Information (Basel)*, *14*(7), 356. doi:10.3390/info14070356

Richter, S., & Richter, A. (2023). What is novel about the Metaverse? *International Journal of Information Management*, *73*, 102684. doi:10.1016/j.ijinfomgt.2023.102684

Rogers, E. M. (2003). *Diffusion of innovations*. Simon and Schuster.

Romano, B., Sands, S., & Pallant, J. I. (2021). Augmented reality and the customer journey: An exploratory study. *Australasian Marketing Journal*, *29*(4), 354–363. doi:10.1016/j.ausmj.2020.06.010

Rosenblum, L., & Cross, R. (1997). Challenges in Virtual Reality. In *In Visualization and Modelling*. Academic Press.

Rubio-Tamayo, J. L., Gertrudix Barrio, M., & García García, F. (2017). Immersive environments and virtual reality: Systematic review and advances in communication, interaction and simulation. *Multimodal Technologies and Interaction*, *1*(4), 21. doi:10.3390/mti1040021

Ryu, S. (2024). Zepeto: Developing a Business Model for the Metaverse World.

Sagayam, K. M., Das, P., Jamader, A. R., Acharya, B. R., Bonyah, E., & Elngar, A. A. (2022). DeepCOVIDNet [Detection of Chest Image Using Deep Learning Model.]. *COVID*, 19.

Saka, E. (2023). Metaverse and Diversity. In *The Future of Digital Communication* (pp. 73–89). CRC Press., doi:10.1201/9781003379119-6

Sandal, M. M., Taner, T., Firat, B. B., Ünal, H. T., Ulucan, S., & Mendi, A. F. Ö, Ö., & Nacar, M. A. (2023, 8-10 June 2023). *WEB 3.0 Applications and Projections. 2023 5th International Congress on Human-Computer Interaction, Optimization and Robotic Applications (HORA)*. IEEE. 10.1109/HORA58378.2023.10156728

Schauman, S., Greene, S. K., & Korkman, O. (2023). Sufficiency and the dematerialization of fashion: How digital substitutes are creating new market opportunities. *Business Horizons*, *66*(6), 741–751. doi:10.1016/j.bushor.2023.03.003

Scheiding, R. (2023). Designing the Future? The Metaverse, NFTs, & the Future as Defined by Unity Users. *Games and Culture*, *18*(6), 804–820. doi:10.1177/15554120221139218

Schlemmer, E., & Backes, L. (2015). The metaverse: 3D digital virtual worlds. In *Learning in Metaverses: Co-Existing in Real Virtuality* (pp. 48–81). IGI Global., doi:10.4018/978-1-4666-6351-0.ch003

Schnack, A., Wright, M. J., & Elms, J. (2021). Investigating the impact of shopper personality on behaviour in immersive Virtual Reality store environments. *Journal of Retailing and Consumer Services*, *61*, 102581. doi:10.1016/j.jretconser.2021.102581

Scholz, J., & Smith, A. N. (2016). Augmented reality: Designing immersive experiences that maximize consumer engagement. *Business Horizons*, *59*(2), 149–161. doi:10.1016/j.bushor.2015.10.003

Schumacher, P. (2022). The metaverse as opportunity for architecture and society: Design drivers, core competencies. *Architectural Intelligence*, *1*(1), 11. doi:10.1007/s44223-022-00010-z PMID:35993030

Sebastian, S. R., & Babu, B. P. (2022). Impact of metaverse in health care: A study from the care giver's perspective. *International Journal of Community Medicine and Public Health*, *9*(12), 4613. doi:10.18203/2394-6040.ijcmph20223221

Seo, J., Kim, K., Park, M., Park, M., & Lee, K. (2018). An Analysis of Economic Impact on IOT Industry under GDPR. *Mobile Information Systems*, *2018*, 1–6. doi:10.1155/2018/6792028

Seong, S., Hoefer, R., & McLaughlin, S. (2021). NFT revolution [in Korean]. *The Quest*.

Sestino, A., & D'Angelo, A. (2023). My doctor is an avatar! The effect of anthropomorphism and emotional receptivity on individuals' intention to use digital-based healthcare services. *Technological Forecasting and Social Change*, *191*, 122505. doi:10.1016/j.techfore.2023.122505

Shah, D., & Shay, E. (2019). How and why artificial intelligence, mixed reality and blockchain technologies will change marketing we know today. Handbook of advances in marketing in an era of disruptions: Essays in honour of Jagdish N. Sheth. Sage. doi:10.4135/9789353287733.n32

Shahbaz Badr, A., & De Amicis, R. (2023). An empirical evaluation of enhanced teleportation for navigating large urban immersive virtual environments. *Frontiers in Virtual Reality*, *3*, 1075811. https://www.frontiersin.org/articles/10.3389/frvir.2022.1075811. doi:10.3389/frvir.2022.1075811

Shah, D., & Murthi, B. P. S. (2021). Marketing in a data-driven digital world: Implications for the role and scope of marketing. *Journal of Business Research*, *125*, 772–779. doi:10.1016/j.jbusres.2020.06.062

Sharma, R., Fantin, A. R., Prabhu, N., Guan, C., & Dattakumar, A. (2016). Digital literacy and knowledge societies: A grounded theory investigation of sustainable development. *Telecommunications Policy*, *40*(7), 628–643. doi:10.1016/j.telpol.2016.05.003

Sharma, R., Jabbour, C. J. C., & Lopes de Sousa Jabbour, A. B. (2021). Sustainable manufacturing and industry 4.0: What we know and what we don't. *Journal of Enterprise Information Management*, *34*(1), 230–266. doi:10.1108/JEIM-01-2020-0024

Shen, B., Tan, W., Guo, J., Zhao, L., & Qin, P. (2021). How to promote user purchase in metaverse? A systematic literature review on consumer behavior research and virtual commerce application design. *Applied Sciences (Basel, Switzerland)*, *11*(23), 11087. doi:10.3390/app112311087

Shen, X., Zhang, Y., Tang, Y., Qin, Y., Liu, N., & Yi, Z. (2021). A study on the impact of digital tobacco logistics on tobacco supply chain performance: Taking the tobacco industry in Guangxi as an example. *Industrial Management & Data Systems*, *122*(6), 1416–1452. doi:10.1108/IMDS-05-2021-0270

Sheth, J. (2020). Business of business is more than business: Managing during the Covid crisis. *Industrial Marketing Management*, *88*, 261–264. doi:10.1016/j.indmarman.2020.05.028

Shi, J., Mo, X., & Sun, Z. (2012). Content validity index in scale development. *Zhong nan da xue xue bao. Yi xue ban= Journal of Central South University. Medical Science*, *37*(2), 152–155.

Shin, D. (2022). The actualization of meta affordances: Conceptualizing affordance actualization in the metaverse games. *Computers in Human Behavior*, *133*, 107292. doi:10.1016/j.chb.2022.107292

Sigala, M. (2003). Developing and benchmarking internet marketing strategies in the hotel sector in Greece. *Journal of Hospitality & Tourism Research (Washington, D.C.)*, *27*(4), 375–401. doi:10.1177/10963480030274001

Silitonga, D., Rohmayanti, S. A. A., Aripin, Z., Kuswandi, D., Sulistyo, A. B., & Juhari. (2024). Edge Computing in E-commerce Business: Economic Impacts and Advantages of Scalable Information Systems. *EAI Endorsed Transactions on Scalable Information Systems*, *11*(1). Advance online publication. doi:10.4108/eetsis.4375

Šimáková, J. (2011). Analysis of the relationship between oil and gold prices. *The Journal of Finance*, *51*(1), 651–662.

Siponen, M., & Vance, A. (2010). User trust in information systems: A critical review of the literature. *Management Information Systems Quarterly*, *34*(2), 339–368.

Situmorang, D. D. B. (2022). "Rapid tele-psychotherapy" with single-session music therapy in the metaverse: An alternative solution for mental health services in the future. *Palliative & Supportive Care*, 1–2. PMID:36218066

Situmorang, D. D. B. (2023). Metaverse as a new place for online mental health services in the post-COVID-19 era: Is it a challenge or an opportunity? *Journal of Public Health (Oxford, England)*, *45*(2), e379–e380. doi:10.1093/pubmed/fdac159 PMID:36542106

Slater, M., & Sanchez-Vives, M. V. (2016). Enhancing our lives with immersive virtual reality. *Frontiers in Robotics and AI, 3*, 74. doi:10.3389/frobt.2016.00074

Smith, A. H., & Shakeri, M. (2022). The future's not what It used to be: Urban wormholes, simulation, participation, and planning in the Metaverse. *Urban Planning, 7*(2), 214–217. doi:10.17645/up.v7i2.5893

Smith, J., & Jones, A. (2023). The metaverse: A potential game-changer for industries. *Journal of Emerging Technologies, 12*(3), 45–62.

Solomon, P. R. (2018). Neuromarketing: Applications, Challenges and Promises. *Biomedical Journal of Scientific & Technical Research, 12*(2). doi:10.26717/BJSTR.2018.12.002230

Song, Y. T., & Qin, J. (2022). Metaverse and personal healthcare. *Procedia Computer Science, 210*, 189–197. doi:10.1016/j.procs.2022.10.136

Sowmya, G., Chakraborty, D., Polisetty, A., Khorana, S., & Buhalis, D. (2023). Use of metaverse in socializing: Application of the big five personality traits framework. *Psychology and Marketing, 40*(10), 2132–2150. doi:10.1002/mar.21863

Spence, C. (2021). Scenting Entertainment: Virtual Reality Storytelling, Theme Park Rides, Gambling, and Video-Gaming. *IPerception, 12*(4), 20416695211034538. doi:10.1177/20416695211034538 PMID:34457231

Stefanic, D. (2023, December 7). Hosting Concerts and Shows in the Metaverse. *Hyperspace^mv - the Metaverse for Business Platform.* https://hyperspace.mv/metaverse-concerts-and-shows/

Stephenson, N. (1992). Snow Crash (Spectra, Ed.). Bantam Books.

Stephenson, N. (1992). *Snow Crash.* Bantam Books.

Stephenson, N. (1992). Snow crash. *Futures, 26*(7), 798–800. doi:10.1016/0016-3287(94)90052-3

Stephenson, N. (1992). *Snow Crash: A Novel.* Bantam Books.

Stoklasová, R. (2018). Short-term and Long-term relationships between Gold Prices and Oil Prices. *Scientific papers of the University of Pardubice. Series D. Faculty of Economics and Administration., 43*, 221–231.

Sudhakar, M. (2023). Artificial Intelligence Applications in Water Treatment and Water Resource Assessment: Challenges, Innovations, and Future Directions. In Intelligent Engineering Applications and Applied Sciences for Sustainability (pp. 248-269). IGI Global.

Suh, I., McKinney, T., & Siu, K. C. (2023, April). Current Perspective of Metaverse Application in Medical Education, Research and Patient Care. In Virtual Worlds, 2(2). MDPI.

Sullivan, C., & Tyson, S. (2023). A global digital identity for all: The next evolution. *Policy Design and Practice, 6*(4), 433–445. doi:10.1080/25741292.2023.2267867

Sung, E., Kwon, O., & Sohn, K. (2023). NFT luxury brand marketing in the metaverse: Leveraging blockchain-certified NFTs to drive consumer behavior. *Psychology and Marketing, 40*(11), 2306–2325. doi:10.1002/mar.21854

Sutherland, K. E., & Barker, R. (2023). The Future of Transmedia Brand Storytelling and a Model for Practice. In Transmedia Brand Storytelling: Immersive Experiences from Theory to Practice (pp. 247-271). Singapore: Springer Nature Singapore. doi:10.1007/978-981-99-4001-1_12

Swan, M. (2023). Metaverse Marketing: A Review and Research Agenda. *Journal of Marketing Management, 39*(3-4), 291–318.

Sweeney, J. C., & Soutar, G. N. (2001). Consumer perceived value: The development of a multiple item scale. *Journal of Retailing*, 77(2), 203–220. doi:10.1016/S0022-4359(01)00041-0

Taçgın, Z., & Dalgarno, B. (2021). Building an Instructional Design Model for Immersive Virtual Reality Learning Environments. In *Designing* (pp. 20–47). Deploying, and Evaluating Virtual and Augmented Reality in Education. doi:10.4018/978-1-7998-5043-4.ch002

TanA. (2021). Metaverse Realities: A Journey Through Governance, Legal Complexities, and the Promise of Virtual Worlds. SSRN. https://doi.org/ doi:10.2139/ssrn.4393422

TansuchatR.ChangC. L.McAleerM. (2010). Crude oil hedging strategies using dynamic multivariate GARCH. *Available at* SSRN 1531187. doi:10.2139/ssrn.1531187

Tan, T. F., Li, Y., Lim, J. S., Gunasekeran, D. V., Teo, Z. L., Ng, W. Y., & Ting, D. S. (2022). Metaverse and virtual health care in ophthalmology: Opportunities and challenges. *Asia-Pacific Journal of Ophthalmology*, 11(3), 237–246. doi:10.1097/APO.0000000000000537 PMID:35772084

Taylor, S. E., & Todd, P. A. (1995). Understanding information technology use as a process: A conceptual model of user acceptance and use. *Management Information Systems Quarterly*, 19(4), 197–217.

Teo, K. S., & Wong, Y. W. (2023). *The determinants of Augmented Reality (AR) marketing affect purchase intention in the beauty and makeup industry among gen z in Malaysia* [Doctoral dissertation, UTAR].

Thomas, N. J., Baral, R., Crocco, O. S., & Mohanan, S. (2023). A framework for gamification in the metaverse era: How designers envision gameful experience. *Technological Forecasting and Social Change*, 193, 122544. Advance online publication. doi:10.1016/j.techfore.2023.122544

Thomason, J. (2021). Metahealth-how will the metaverse change health care? *Journal of Metaverse*, 1(1), 13–16.

Tlili, A., Huang, R., & Kinshuk, K. (2023). Metaverse for climbing the ladder toward 'Industry 5.0' and 'Society 5.0'? *Service Industries Journal*, 43(3–4), 260–287. doi:10.1080/02642069.2023.2178644

Toraman, C., Basarir, C., & Bayramoglu, M. F. (2011). Effects of crude oil price changes on sector indices of Istanbul stock exchange. *European Journal of Economic and Political Studies*, 4(2), 109–124.

Toraman, Y., & Geçit, B. B. (2023). User acceptance of metaverse: An analysis for e-commerce in the framework of technology acceptance model (TAM). *Sosyoekonomi*, 31(55), 85–104. doi:10.17233/sosyoekonomi.2023.01.05

Tornatzky, L. G., & Fleischer, M. (1990). *The process of technological innovation*. Lexington Books.

Torous, J., Bucci, S., Bell, I. H., Kessing, L. V., Faurholt-Jepsen, M., Whelan, P., Carvalho, A. F., Keshavan, M., Linardon, J., & Firth, J. (2021). The growing field of digital psychiatry: Current evidence and the future of apps, social media, chatbots, and virtual reality. *World Psychiatry; Official Journal of the World Psychiatric Association (WPA)*, 20(3), 318–335. doi:10.1002/wps.20883 PMID:34505369

Toyoshima, Y., Nakajima, T., & Hamori, S. (2013). Crude oil hedging strategy: New evidence from the data of the financial crisis. *Applied Financial Economics*, 23(12), 1033–1041. doi:10.1080/09603107.2013.788779

Trevor, A. (2022). *Metaverso 360 - La guida più completa su Metaverse e investimenti, web 3.0, NFT, DeFi, augemented reality (AR), cryptoassets, digital real estate e future networking*. Independently published.

Tse, Y. K., & Tsui, A. K. C. (2002). A multivariate generalized autoregressive conditional heteroscedasticity model with time-varying correlations. *Journal of Business & Economic Statistics*, 20(3), 351–362. doi:10.1198/073500102288618496

Tuomi, A., Tussyadiah, I. P., & Stienmetz, J. (2021). Applications and implications of service robots in hospitality. *Cornell Hospitality Quarterly*, *62*(2), 232–247. doi:10.1177/1938965520923961

Turab, M., & Jamil, S. (2023). A Comprehensive Survey of Digital Twins in Healthcare in the Era of Metaverse. *BioMedInformatics*, *3*(3), 563–584. doi:10.3390/biomedinformatics3030039

Ud Din, I., & Almogren, A. (2023). Exploring the psychological effects of Metaverse on mental health and well-being. *Information Technology & Tourism*, *25*(3), 367–389. doi:10.1007/s40558-023-00259-8

Ud Din, I., Awan, K. A., Almogren, A., & Rodrigues, J. J. (2023). Integration of IoT and blockchain for decentralized management and ownership in the metaverse. *International Journal of Communication Systems*, *36*(18), e5612. doi:10.1002/dac.5612

Uddin, M. R. (2024). The role of the digital economy in Bangladesh's economic development. *Sustainable Technology and Entrepreneurship*, *3*(1), 100054. doi:10.1016/j.stae.2023.100054

Ullah, H., Manickam, S., Obaidat, M., Laghari, S. U. A., & Uddin, M. (2023). Exploring the Potential of Metaverse Technology in Healthcare: Applications, Challenges, and Future Directions. *IEEE Access : Practical Innovations, Open Solutions*, *11*, 69686–69707. doi:10.1109/ACCESS.2023.3286696

Um, T., Kim, H., Kim, H., Lee, J., Koo, C., & Chung, N. (2022, January). Travel Incheon as a metaverse: smart tourism cities development case in Korea. In *ENTER22 e-Tourism Conference* (pp. 226–231). Springer International Publishing. doi:10.1007/978-3-030-94751-4_20

Upadhyay, U., Kumar, A., Sharma, G., Saini, A. K., Arya, V., Gaurav, A., & Chui, K. T. (2024). Mitigating Risks in the Cloud-Based Metaverse Access Control Strategies and Techniques. [IJCAC]. *International Journal of Cloud Applications and Computing*, *14*(1), 1–30. doi:10.4018/IJCAC.334364

Upadhyay, Y., Paul, J., & Baber, R. (2022). Effect of online social media marketing efforts on customer response. *Journal of Consumer Behaviour*, *21*(3), 554–571. doi:10.1002/cb.2031

Urquhart, A., & Zhang, H. (2019). Is Bitcoin a hedge or safe haven for currencies? An intraday analysis. *International Review of Financial Analysis*, *63*, 49–57. doi:10.1016/j.irfa.2019.02.009

Usmani, S. S., Sharath, M., & Mehendale, M. (2022). Future of mental health in the metaverse. *General Psychiatry*, *35*(4), e100825. doi:10.1136/gpsych-2022-100825 PMID:36189180

Van Beers, D., Bossilkov, A., Corder, G., & Van Berkel, R. (2007). Industrial symbiosis in the Australian minerals industry: the cases of Kwinana and Gladstone.

Van Eck, N. J., & Waltman, L. (2011). Text mining and visualization using VOSviewer. arXiv preprint arXiv:1109.2058.

Van Eck, N., & Waltman, L. (2010). Software survey: VOSviewer, a computer program for bibliometric mapping. *Scientometrics*, *84*(2), 523–538. doi:10.1007/s11192-009-0146-3 PMID:20585380

Van Huynh, D., Khosravirad, S. R., Masaracchia, A., Dobre, O. A., & Duong, T. Q. (2022). Edge intelligence-based ultra-reliable and low-latency communications for digital twin-enabled metaverse. *IEEE Wireless Communications Letters*, *11*(8), 1733–1737. doi:10.1109/LWC.2022.3179207

Vemula, S. (2020). Leveraging VR/AR/MR and AI as Innovative Educational Practices for "iGeneration" Students. In Handbook of Research on Equity in Computer Science in P-16 Education (pp. 265-277). doi:10.4018/978-1-7998-4739-7.ch015

Venkatesh, V., Brown, S. A., & Bala, H. (2013). Bridging the qualitative-quantitative divide: Guidelines for conducting mixed methods research in information systems. *Management Information Systems Quarterly, 37*(1), 21–54. doi:10.25300/MISQ/2013/37.1.02

Venkatesh, V., & Davis, F. D. (2000). A theoretical extension of the technology acceptance model: Four longitudinal field studies. *Management Science, 46*(2), 186–204. doi:10.1287/mnsc.46.2.186.11926

Venkatesh, V., Morris, M. G., Davis, G. B., & Davis, F. D. (2003). User acceptance of information technology: Toward a unified view. *Management Information Systems Quarterly, 27*(3), 425–478. doi:10.2307/30036540

Verhoef, P C., Broekhuizen, T., Bart, Y., Bhattacharya, A., Dong, J Q., Fabian, N E., & Haenlein, M. (2021, January 1). Digital transformation: A multidisciplinary reflection and research agenda. doi:10.1016/j.jbusres.2019.09.022

Viana-Lora, A., & Nel-lo-Andreu, M. G. (2022). Bibliometric analysis of trends in COVID- 19 and tourism. *Humanities & Social Sciences Communications, 9*(1), 173. doi:10.1057/s41599-022-01194-5

Vidal-Tomás, D. (2022). The new crypto niche: NFTs, play-to-earn, and metaverse tokens. *Finance Research Letters, 47*, 102742. doi:10.1016/j.frl.2022.102742

Vidal-Tomás, D. (2023). The illusion of the metaverse and meta-economy. *International Review of Financial Analysis, 86*, 102560. doi:10.1016/j.irfa.2023.102560

Vig, S. (2023). Preparing for the New Paradigm of Business: The Metaverse. *Foresight and STI Governance (Foresight-Russia till No. 3/2015), 17*(3), 6-18. doi:10.17323/2500-2597.2023.3.6.18

Villalonga-Gómez, C., Ortega-Fernández, E., & Borau-Boira, E. (2023). Fifteen years of metaverse in Higher Education: A systematic literature review. *IEEE Transactions on Learning Technologies, 16*(6), 1057–1070. doi:10.1109/TLT.2023.3302382

Violante, M. G., Vezzetti, E., & Piazzolla, P. (2019). How to design a virtual reality experience that impacts the consumer engagement: The case of the virtual supermarket. [IJIDeM]. *International Journal on Interactive Design and Manufacturing, 13*(1), 243–262. doi:10.1007/s12008-018-00528-5

Vlăduțescu, Ș., & Stănescu, G. C. (2023). Environmental Sustainability of Metaverse: Perspectives from Romanian Developers. *Sustainability (Basel), 15*(15), 11704. doi:10.3390/su151511704

Voinea, G. D., Gîrbacia, F., Postelnicu, C. C., Duguleana, M., Antonya, C., Soica, A., & Stănescu, R.-C. (2022). Study of Social Presence While Interacting in Metaverse with an Augmented Avatar during Autonomous Driving. *Applied Sciences (Basel, Switzerland), 12*(22), 22. Advance online publication. doi:10.3390/app122211804

Volchek, K., & Brysch, A. (2023, January). Metaverse and tourism: From a new niche to a transformation. In *ENTER22 e-Tourism Conference* (pp. 300–311). Springer Nature Switzerland. doi:10.1007/978-3-031-25752-0_32

Volvo. (2022). *The Volvoverse: Volvo Cars launches first car in the metaverse.* Volvo. https://www.volvocars.com/au/news/technology/The-Volvoverse/

Vosmeer, M., & Schouten, B. (2014). Interactive Cinema: Engagement and Interaction. In A. Mitchell, C. Fernández-Vara, & D. Thue (Eds.), *Interactive Storytelling* (Vol. 8832, pp. 140–147). Springer International Publishing., doi:10.1007/978-3-319-12337-0_14

Wallace, R. S. O., & Cooke, T. E. (1990). The diagnosis and resolution of emerging issues in corporate disclosure practices. *Accounting and Business Research, 20*(78), 143–151. doi:10.1080/00014788.1990.9728872

Wallin, J. A. (2005). Bibliometric methods: Pitfalls and possibilities. *Basic & Clinical Pharmacology & Toxicology*, *97*(5), 261–275. doi:10.1111/j.1742-7843.2005.pto_139.x PMID:16236137

Wang, G., Badal, A., Jia, X., Maltz, J. S., Mueller, K., Myers, K. J., Niu, C., Vannier, M., Yan, P., Yu, Z., & Zeng, R. (2022). Development of metaverse for intelligent healthcare. *Nature Machine Intelligence*, *4*(11), 922–929. doi:10.1038/s42256-022-00549-6 PMID:36935774

Wang, I. (2022). *The Digital Mind of Tomorrow: Rethink, transform, and thrive in today's fast-changing and brutal digital world*. Digital Thinker.

Wang, M. H., Yu, T. C., & Ho, Y. S. (2010). A bibliometric analysis of the performance of Water Research. *Scientometrics*, *84*(3), 813–820. doi:10.1007/s11192-009-0112-0

Wang, M., Yu, H., Bell, Z., & Chu, X. (2022). Constructing an edu-metaverse ecosystem: A new and innovative framework. *IEEE Transactions on Learning Technologies*, *15*(6), 685–696. doi:10.1109/TLT.2022.3210828

Wang, Y., & Qualls, W. (2007). Towards a theoretical model of technology adoption in hospitality organizations. *International Journal of Hospitality Management*, *26*(3), 560–573. doi:10.1016/j.ijhm.2006.03.008

Wanick, V., & Stallwood, J. (2022). *Brand storytelling, gamification, and social media marketing in the "Metaverse": a case study of The Ralph Lauren winter escape*.

Wan, X., Zhang, G., Yuan, Y., & Chai, S. (2023). How to drive the participation willingness of supply chain members in metaverse technology adoption? *Applied Soft Computing*, *145*, 110611. doi:10.1016/j.asoc.2023.110611

Wedel, M., Bigné, E., & Zhang, J. (2020). Virtual and augmented reality: Advancing research in consumer marketing. *International Journal of Research in Marketing*, *37*(3), 443–465. doi:10.1016/j.ijresmar.2020.04.004

Weinberg, B. H. (1974). Bibliographic coupling: A review. *Information Storage and Retrieval*, *10*(5–6), 189–196. doi:10.1016/0020-0271(74)90058-8

Weinberger, M. (2022). What Is Metaverse?—A Definition Based on Qualitative Meta-Synthesis. *Future Internet*, *14*(11), 310. doi:10.3390/fi14110310

Wiangkham, A., & Vongvit, R. (2023). Exploring the Drivers for the Adoption of Metaverse Technology in Engineering Education using PLS-SEM and ANFIS. *Education and Information Technologies*, 1–28.

Wider, W., Jiang, L., Lin, J., Fauzi, M. A., Li, J., & Chan, C. K. (2023). Metaverse chronicles: A bibliometric analysis of its evolving landscape. *International Journal of Human-Computer Interaction*, 1–14. doi:10.1080/10447318.2023.2227825

Wiederhold, B. K. (2022). Metaverse games: Game changer for healthcare? *Cyberpsychology, Behavior, and Social Networking*, *25*(5), 267–269. doi:10.1089/cyber.2022.29246.editorial PMID:35549346

Wiederhold, B. K. (2023). (Mental) Healthcare Consumerism in the Metaverse: Is There a Benefit? *Cyberpsychology, Behavior, and Social Networking*, *26*(3), 145–146. doi:10.1089/cyber.2023.29269.editorial PMID:36880891

Wiederhold, B. K., & Riva, G. (2022). Metaverse creates new opportunities in healthcare. *Ann. Rev. Cyber. Telemed*, *20*, 3–7.

Williams, A. (2006). Tourism and hospitality marketing: Fantasy, feeling and fun. *International Journal of Contemporary Hospitality Management*, *18*(6), 482–495. doi:10.1108/09596110610681520

Wongkitrungrueng, A., & Suprawan, L. (2023). Metaverse meets branding: Examining consumer responses to immersive brand experiences. *International Journal of Human-Computer Interaction*, 1–20. doi:10.1080/10447318.2023.2175162

Wong, L. W., Tan, G. W. H., Ooi, K. B., & Dwivedi, Y. K. (2023). Metaverse in hospitality and tourism: A critical reflection. *International Journal of Contemporary Hospitality Management*. doi:10.1108/IJCHM-05-2023-0586

World Commission on Environment and Development (WCED). (1987). *Our Common Future (Brundtland Report)*. United Nations. https://sustainabledevelopment.un.org

Wu, C. H., & Liu, C. Y. (2023). Educational Applications of Non-Fungible Token (NFT). *Sustainability (Basel)*, *15*(1), 7. Advance online publication. doi:10.3390/su15010007

Wu, D., Yang, Z., Zhang, P., Wang, R., Yang, B., & Ma, X. (2023). Virtual-Reality Inter-Promotion Technology for Metaverse: A Survey. *IEEE Internet of Things Journal*, *10*(18), 1–15. doi:10.1109/JIOT.2023.3265848

Wynn, M., & Jones, P. (2023). New technology deployment and corporate responsibilities in the metaverse. *Knowledge (Beverly Hills, Calif.)*, *3*(4), 543–556.

Xiang, H., Zhang, X., & Bilal, M. (2023). A cloud-edge service offloading method for the metaverse in smart manufacturing. *Software, Practice & Experience*, spe.3301. doi:10.1002/spe.3301

Xi, N., & Hamari, J. (2021). Shopping in virtual reality: A literature review and future agenda. *Journal of Business Research*, *134*, 37–58. doi:10.1016/j.jbusres.2021.04.075

Xu, M., Ng, W. C., Lim, W. Y. B., Kang, J., Xiong, Z., Niyato, D., Yang, Q., Shen, X. S., & Miao, C. (2022). A Full Dive into Realizing the Edge-enabled Metaverse: Visions, Enabling Technologies, and Challenges. *IEEE Communications Surveys and Tutorials*, *1*. doi:10.1109/COMST.2022.3221119

Yakura, H., & Goto, M. (2020). Enhancing Participation Experience in VR Live Concerts by Improving Motions of Virtual Audience Avatars. *2020 IEEE International Symposium on Mixed and Augmented Reality (ISMAR)*, (pp. 555–565). IEEE. 10.1109/ISMAR50242.2020.00083

Yang, L., Ni, S. T., Wang, Y., Yu, A., Lee, J. A., & Hui, P. (2024). Interoperability of the Metaverse: A Digital Ecosystem Perspective Review. *arXiv preprint arXiv:2403.05205*.

Yang, F. X., & Wang, Y. (2023). Rethinking Metaverse Tourism: A Taxonomy and an Agenda for Future Research. *Journal of Hospitality & Tourism Research (Washington, D.C.)*. doi:10.1177/10963480231163509

Yang, L. (2023). Recommendations for metaverse governance based on technical standards. *Humanities & Social Sciences Communications*, *10*(1), 1–10. doi:10.1057/s41599-023-01750-7

Yang, Q., Al Mamun, A., Hayat, N., Salleh, M. F. M., Jingzu, G., & Zainol, N. R. (2022). Modelling the mass adoption potential of wearable medical devices. *PLoS One*, *17*(6), e0269256. doi:10.1371/journal.pone.0269256 PMID:35675373

Yang, S. (2023, April). Storytelling and user experience in the cultural metaverse. *Heliyon*, *9*(4), e14759. doi:10.1016/j.heliyon.2023.e14759 PMID:37035365

Yang, Y., Siau, K., Xie, W., & Sun, Y. (2022). Smart health: Intelligent healthcare systems in the metaverse, artificial intelligence, and data science era. [JOEUC]. *Journal of Organizational and End User Computing*, *34*(1), 1–14. doi:10.4018/JOEUC.308814

Yao, X., Ma, N., Zhang, J., Wang, K., Yang, E., & Faccio, M. (2024). Enhancing wisdom manufacturing as industrial metaverse for industry and society 5.0. *Journal of Intelligent Manufacturing*, *35*(1), 235–255. doi:10.1007/s10845-022-02027-7

Yaqoob, I., Salah, K., Jayaraman, R., & Omar, M. (2023). Metaverse applications in smart cities: Enabling technologies, opportunities, challenges, and future directions. *Internet of Things : Engineering Cyber Physical Human Systems, 23,* 100884. doi:10.1016/j.iot.2023.100884

Yemenici, A. D. (2022). Entrepreneurship in the world of metaverse: Virtual or real? *Journal of Metaverse, 2*(2), 71–82. doi:10.57019/jmv.1126135

Yilmaz, M., O'Farrell, E. & Clarke, P. (2023). Examining the training and education potential of the metaverse: results from an empirical study of next generation SAFe training. *Journal of Software: Evolution and Process.* doi:10.1002/smr.2531

Yoo, M., Lee, S., & Bai, B. (2011). Hospitality marketing research from 2000 to 2009: topics, methods, and trends. *International Journal of Contemporary Hospitality Management.*

Yu, X., & Fang, B. (2020). *Cybersecurity challenges and opportunities in the metaverse.* Research Gate.

Yu, F., Jian, S., Shen, C., Xue, W., & Fu, Y. (2022). On the Issue of "Digital Human" in the context of digital transformation. In *2022 International Conference on Culture-Oriented Science and Technology (CoST)* (pp. 258-262). IEEE. 10.1109/CoST57098.2022.00060

Zainurin, M. Z. L., Masri, M. H., Besar, M. H. A., & Anshari, M. (2023). Towards an understanding of metaverse banking: A conceptual paper. *Journal of Financial Reporting and Accounting, 21*(1), 178–190. doi:10.1108/JFRA-12-2021-0487

Zakarneh, B., Annamalai, N., Alquqa, E. K., Mohamed, K. M., & Al Salhi, N. R. (2024). Virtual Reality and Alternate Realities in Neal Stephenson's—Snow Crash‖. *World Journal of English Language, 14*(2), 244. doi:10.5430/wjel.v14n2p244

Zallio, M., & Clarkson, P. J. (2022). Designing the metaverse: A study on inclusion, diversity, equity, accessibility and safety for digital immersive environments. *Telematics and Informatics, 75,* 101909. doi:10.1016/j.tele.2022.101909

Zamanifard, S., & Freeman, G. (2023). A Surprise Birthday Party in VR: Leveraging Social Virtual Reality to Maintain Existing Close Ties over Distance. International Conference on Information, Zhang, W., Zhao, S., Wan, X., & Yao, Y. (2021). Study on the effect of digital economy on high-quality economic development in China. *PLoS One, 16*(9), e0257365. doi:10.1371/journal.pone.0257365

Zaman, U., Koo, I., Abbasi, S., Raza, S. H., & Qureshi, M. G. (2022). Meet your digital twin in space? Profiling international expat's readiness for metaverse space travel, Tech-Savviness, COVID-19 travel anxiety, and travel fear of missing out. *Sustainability (Basel), 14*(11), 6441. doi:10.3390/su14116441

Zawish, M., Dharejo, F. A., Khowaja, S. A., Raza, S., Davy, S., Dev, K., & Bellavista, P. (2024). AI and 6G into the metaverse: Fundamentals, challenges and future research trends. *IEEE Open Journal of the Communications Society, 5,* 730–778. doi:10.1109/OJCOMS.2024.3349465

Zhai, X., Chu, X., Wang, M., Zhang, Z., & Dong, Y. (2022). Education metaverse: Innovations and challenges of the new generation of Internet education formats. *Metaverse, 3*(1), 13. doi:10.54517/met.v3i1.1804

Zhang, C., & Tu, X. (2016). The effect of global oil price shocks on China's metal markets. *Energy Policy, 90,* 131–139. doi:10.1016/j.enpol.2015.12.012

Zhang, D., Lei, L., Ji, Q., & Kutan, A. M. (2019). Economic policy uncertainty in the US and China and their impact on the global markets. *Economic Modelling, 79,* 47–56. doi:10.1016/j.econmod.2018.09.028

Zhang, Q. (2023). Secure Preschool Education Using Machine Learning and Metaverse Technologies. *Applied Artificial Intelligence, 37*(1), 2222496. doi:10.1080/08839514.2023.2222496

Zhang, T., Shen, J., Lai, C. F., Ji, S., & Ren, Y. (2023). Multi-server assisted data sharing supporting secure deduplication for metaverse healthcare systems. *Future Generation Computer Systems*, *140*, 299–310. doi:10.1016/j.future.2022.10.031

Zhang, X., Yu, L., Wang, S., & Lai, K. K. (2009). Estimating the impact of extreme events on crude oil price: An EMD-based event analysis method. *Energy Economics*, *31*(5), 768–778. doi:10.1016/j.eneco.2009.04.003

Zhang, Y. J., Bouri,.E., Gupta, R., & Ma, S. J. (2021). Risk spillover between Bitcoin and conventional financial markets: An expectile-based approach. *The North American Journal of Economics and Finance*, *55*, 101296. doi:10.1016/j.najef.2020.101296

Zhang, Z., & Wen, X. (2023). Physical or virtual showroom? The decision for omni-channel retailers in the context of cross-channel free-riding. *Electronic Commerce Research*, 1–27. doi:10.1007/s10660-022-09616-x

Zhao, Y., Jiang, J., Chen, Y., Liu, R., Yang, Y., Xue, X., & Chen, S. (2022). Metaverse: Perspectives from graphics, interactions and visualization. *Visual Informatics*, *6*(1), 56–67. doi:10.1016/j.visinf.2022.03.002

Zheng, Z., Li, T., Li, B., Chai, X., Song, W., Chen, N., & Li, R. (2022, December). Industrial metaverse: connotation, features, technologies, applications and challenges. In *Asian Simulation Conference* (pp. 239-263). Singapore: Springer Nature Singapore. 10.1007/978-981-19-9198-1_19

Zhou, Z. (2023). Will the Metaverse Revolutionize the Narrative? *Critical Arts*, 1–15. doi:10.1080/02560046.2023.2282489

Zhu, H. Y., Hieu, N. Q., Hoang, D. T., Nguyen, D. N., & Lin, C. T. (2023). A human-centric metaverse enabled by brain-computer interface: A survey. *arXiv preprint arXiv:2309.01848*.

Zonaphan, L., Northus, K., Wijaya, J., Achmad, S., & Sutoyo, R. (2022, November). Metaverse as a future of education: A systematic review. In *2022 8th International HCI and UX Conference in Indonesia (CHIuXiD)*, 1, 77-81). 10.1109/CHIuXiD57244.2022.10009854

Zupic, I., & Čater, T. (2015). Bibliometric methods in management and organization. *Organizational Research Methods*, *18*(3), 429–472. doi:10.1177/1094428114562629

Zyda, M. (2022). Let's rename everything "the Metaverse!". *Computer*, *55*(3), 124–129. doi:10.1109/MC.2021.3130480

About the Contributors

Jeetesh Kumar is Head (a) of Research at the Faculty of Social Sciences and Leisure Management, Senior Lecturer at the School of Hospitality, Tourism and Events, Associate Director for Information Management & Documentation at the Centre for Research and Innovation in Tourism (CRiT), and Hub Leader of the "Responsible Tourism for Inclusive Economic Growth" Sustainable Tourism Impact Lab at Taylor's University, Malaysia.

Manpreet Arora, a Senior Assistant Professor of Management at the Central University of Himachal Pradesh, Dharamshala, India, brings over twenty-two years of rich teaching experience. She holds academic accolades including a Ph.D. in International Trade, an M.Phil, a gold medalist and several other academic distinctions from Himachal Pradesh University, Shimla. Dr. Arora's diverse research interests encompass Accounting, Finance, Strategic Management, Entrepreneurship, Qualitative Research and Microfinance. She works on Mixed methods research. Noteworthy for guiding doctoral research and delving into Microfinance, Entrepreneurship, Behavioral Finance and Corporate Reporting, she has presented at numerous seminars, delivering talks on various academic subjects across multiple universities and colleges. An accomplished academic, she has an impressive publication record, having authored over 30 papers in esteemed national and international journals listed in Scopus, WOS and Category journals, alongside contributing to fifty-five book chapters in publications by reputed publishers like Emerald, Routledge, CABI, Springer Nature, AAP, Wiley and more. Her commitment to management research is evident through the editing of six books. She is presently working in the area of Metaverse. Her impactful contributions showcase a multifaceted professional excelling in academia, research, and social advocacy.

Erkol Bayram is currently an Associate Professor in the School of tourism and hotel management, department of tour guiding, University of Sinop, Sinop, Turkey. Dr. Erkol Bayram has worked as an internal trainer and teacher in the tour guiding arena. Her doctorate is in Tourism Management from the Sakarya University, Turkey, and she completed her dissertation research on Tour Guiding in Turkey. Her core subjects are Tourism, tour guiding, tourism policy and Planning, women studies. Erkol Bayram has also worked as a professional tour guide in the tourism sector. The editor has many book chapters in the international arena and published her books as an editor in the national arena. She also has many book chapters under IGI GLOBAL related women, tourism and management studies. She has been invited for many talks/lectures/ panel discussions by different Universities.

Kausar Alam is working as an Assistant Professor of Accounting at BRAC Business School, BRAC University. He completed PhD from Universiti Putra Malaysia (UPM). His research interests are accounting, Shariah governance, institutional theory, Islamic banking, legitimacy theory, corporate governance, integrated reporting, working capital management, and qualitative research. His research works were published in APE, MDE, JAAR, ARA, Pacific Accounting Review, JIABR, AJAR, JPA, and QROM.

Lara Sofia Mendes Bacalhau holds a Ph.D. in Management - Specialization in Marketing and Strategy from the Faculty of Economics of the University of Porto (FEP-UP), where she also completed a Master's degree in Data Analysis and Decision Support Systems. This master's degree allowed her to combine her previous degrees, a Bachelor's degree in Mathematics - Teaching Branch of the Faculty of Science and Technology of the University of Coimbra and a Bachelor's degree in Business Management and a degree in Accounting and Auditing - via Business Management at the Coimbra Higher Institute of Accounting and Administration of the Polytechnic Institute of Coimbra (ISCAC | Coimbra Business School - IPC). She has other complementary training, including an MBA in Digital Marketing, a Postgraduate Diploma in Information Technology and Multimedia Communication, and a Training Course for Trainers to Obtain Specialization in Gender Equality. Lecturer at ISCAC since 2003, she has always been teaching in Marketing, Business Management, Accounting, and Taxation areas. In addition, she is also a lecturer/trainer at the Viseu School of Technology and Management of the Polytechnic Institute of Viseu (ESTGV-IPV), Coimbra Business School Executive, Institute for Employment and Vocational Training (IEFP), and ISLA Santarém. This teaching experience has led her to teach various undergraduate, master's, postgraduate and short courses. In addition to teaching, she was a member of the Direction of the Marketing and International Business Bachelor Degree (2013-April 2021) and is currently the director of this course. She is also a member of the Direction of the corresponding Master's Degree (2020-present). She was co-coordinator of the Preparation Workshops for the Certified Accountants Bar Exam (2016-2022). She is a researcher in the areas of Marketing (Branding, Digital Marketing, Social Media Marketing, E-commerce, and Relationship Marketing) and Business Management. She participates in national and international research projects. She is a peer reviewer and co-author of scientific publications in conference proceedings, book chapters, and journals. She is also a Certified Accountant.

Himani Gupta is an Associate Professor at JIMS, New Delhi, India. She has numerous research paper published in ABDC, SCOPUS and WOS listed journals. She has authored various books on accounts, finance and tax. She has completed projects from NHRC and ICSSR. She has won various research awards in conferences. She has uploaded various research and subject related videos on her YouTube channel. She has also taken many webinars/FDPs on econometrics (time series), finance, accounting and indirect taxes.

Manisha Gupta is working as an Associate Professor in Sharda University. She has various research paper published in ABDC, SCOPUS and WOS listed Journals.

Nusrat Hafiz, serving as the Assistant Professor of Entrepreneurship and International Business at BRAC Business School, is committed to driving impactful change. Armed with a Ph.D. from Putra Business School (AACSB Accredited), her outstanding research contribution has garnered her "quality journal publication awards" in multiple categories, recognizing her as one of the top contributors to Q1 journals. She possesses a decade's worth of experience in academia and half a decade of corporate exposure, complemented by her deep-rooted family values and unwavering work ethics. Dr. Hafiz's teaching philosophy prioritizes pragmatic approaches, while her research interests span strategic management, organizational sustainability, women's empowerment, digitalization and innovation, dynamic capabilities and social entrepreneurship. Her personal slogan, "Empowering Students, Every Step of the Way," embodies her commitment to student-centricity.

Mohammad Imtiaz Hossain is a PhD Fellow and Graduate research assistant (GRA) at Multimedia University, Malaysia. He pursued MSc in Business Economics from the School of Business and Economics, Universiti Putra Malaysia (UPM), Malaysia [AACSB & EQUIS accredited]. He has completed Bachelor in Business Management from Binary University, Malaysia and Diploma in Business from Mahsa Prima International College, Malaysia. His research interests include sustainability, SME, entrepreneurship, ambidexterity, leadership, technology adoption, tourism, service quality, human resource management, innovation, and many other interdisciplinary areas. Mr. Imtiaz has published numerous scholarly articles in Web of science, ABDC, Scopus, ERA, Google scholar and other indexed journals. Additionally, he is also serving as a reviewer for some prominent journals.

Tariqul Islam, a Ph.D. student in Hospitality and Tourism at Taylor's University, Malaysia. He holds a Master of Science (by research) in Tourism from Universiti Putra Malaysia, Malaysia. He graduated with distinction in Airlines, Tourism, and Hospitality from Lovely Professional University, India. Tariqul has published several research articles in ABDC- listed and Scopus-indexed journals and presented the findings of his research at various national and international conferences. His area of research includes consumer behaviour and technology adoption.

Yasmin Jamadar is currently serving as an Assistant Professor (Finance) at the BRAC Business School (BBS), BRAC University (BRACU). She is involved actively in teaching, supervision, research, development of new curricula and courses at the undergraduate and postgraduate levels. Before joining BRACU, she worked as a lecturer (Accounting & Finance) at Alfa University College, Malaysia. Dr. Yasmin obtained her Doctor of Philosophy (PhD) in Finance from the School of Business and Economics, Universiti Putra Malaysia (UPM) [AACSB & EQUIS accredited] and she graduated on time (GOT). She also served as an academic mentor at SBE, UPM. Moreover, as an invited member, she participated and contributed to the peer review process for EQUIS accreditation and AACSB re-accreditation of SBE, UPM. She achieved several merit and full bright scholarships throughout her academic career. Her research areas include corporate finance, corporate governance, accounting, sustainability, Insider trading, and earnings management. Her publications have appeared in various international refereed journals indexed in the Chartered Association of Business Schools (ABS), Web of Science (WoS), Australian Business Deans Council (ABDC) and Scopus. Additionally, Dr. Yasmin is also serving as a reviewer for some prominent journals including the Journal of Islamic Accounting and Business Research; Investment analyst; and Managerial and Decision Economics to name a few. She is a certified expert on STATA, Eviews, and SPSS software. She presented papers at several international conferences in UK, Malaysia, UAE, and Bahrain. Her corporate experience includes working as a business development executive in Nascenia IT, Bangladesh. She has also engaged in different social and professional development activities.

Asik Rahaman Jamader is working as an Assistant Professor in the department of Hospitality & Hotel Administration at Pailan College of Management & Technology, Kolkata, India, also he is the Corporate Advisory Board Member of the Smart Journal of Business Management Studies indexed by Emerging Sources Citation Index (ESCI) - Web of Science (Clarivate Analytics) with 5.748 Impact factor. His research interest is in Hospitality and innovative Technique implemented in Hospitality Industry. He is a scientist by having 23 numbers of International granted patents & 12 numbers of registered and published national & International patents also have a good number of authored Book/Book Chapters publications, including some SCOPUS/SCIE/ESCI/WOS publications. Recently he joined as an Ad Hoc reviewer of the International Journal of Business Intelligence Research (IJBIR), IGI Global publishing indexed by WOS and Scopus.

Rupinder Katoch is working as a Professor in Lovely Professional University. She has various research paper published in ABDC, SCOPUS and WOS listed Journals.

Nrnnesa Begum Momo is an undergraduate student at BRAC Business School, BRAC University, Bangladesh.

Jana Neves has a master's degree in marketing and international business at Coimbra Business School, specializing in Marketing strategies, international business dynamics, and consumer behavior. Prior academic achievements include a Bachelor's degree in Applied Communication from Lusofona University - Porto Center, focusing on communication theories, Marketing, and media studies. Practical expertise was gained as a Cisco Certified Network Associate through the Cisco Networking Academy, where skills in networking principles and system security were developed. Complementing the academic background, a three-year Informatic Internship at Lusofona University - Porto provided opportunities to offer technical support and perform system maintenance. Currently engaged in research in marketing and technology, with a focus on Digital Marketing strategies, E-commerce, and the integration of technology in Marketing campaigns. Furthermore, continuous knowledge enhancement is pursued through online courses, particularly in Data Analysis, Digital Marketing, and emerging technologies.

Harleen Pabla is a researcher in the field of marketing, whose expertise spans various areas including brand experience, consumer behavior, the metaverse, artificial intelligence, sustainability and the aviation sector. Her work has been published in prestigious international journals recognized by respected bodies like the Web of Science (WoS), Australian Business Deans Council (ABDC) and Scopus.

Sbyasachi Pramanik is a professional IEEE member. He obtained a PhD in Computer Science and Engineering from Sri Satya Sai University of Technology and Medical Sciences, Bhopal, India. Presently, he is an Associate Professor, Department of Computer Science and Engineering, Haldia Institute of Technology, India. He has many publications in various reputed international conferences, journals, and book chapters (Indexed by SCIE, Scopus, ESCI, etc). He is doing research in the fields of Artificial Intelligence, Data Privacy, Cybersecurity, Network Security, and Machine Learning. He also serves on the editorial boards of several international journals. He is a reviewer of journal articles from IEEE, Springer, Elsevier, Inderscience, IET and IGI Global. He has reviewed many conference papers, has been a keynote speaker, session chair, and technical program committee member at many international conferences. He has authored a book on Wireless Sensor Network. He has edited 8 books from IGI Global, CRC Press, Springer and Wiley Publications.

Rfaida Nurain Saiba is an undergraduate student at BRAC Business School, BRAC University, Bangladesh.

Aiesh Kumar Sharma is a Research Scholar at Mittal School of Business, Lovely Professional University, Phagwara, Punjab, India. His research interests are digital marketing, social media marketing, search engine marketing, remarketing, data analytics, artificial intelligence, machine learning, and the applications of technology in business.

Rhul Sharma is a highly accomplished professor of marketing with over 14 years of experience in academia. He has a PhD in marketing and has published over 15 articles in high-quality journals in the field. Dr Sharma's research interests include consumer behaviour, business analytics and digital marketing. In addition to his research, Dr Sharma is also a highly sought-after resource person in various faculty development programmes.

Menu Sharma is currently working as an Associate Professor and Head of the Department of Public Administration at the Assam Royal Global University, Guwahati, Assam. She has 19 years of teaching experience. She has supervised the research work of 10 doctoral scholars and 16 M.Phil Scholars. She has presented 60 research papers at international and national conferences/seminars in India. She has attended and completed 20 faculty development programs/refresher programs/orientation programs/workshops. Her 46 research papers have been published in national and international journals. Her 17 chapters in edited books have been published. She is a life member of the Indian Institute of Public Administration, New Public Administration Society of India, Indian Political Science Association, Indian Political Economy Association, Indian Public Administration Association, Agricultural Economics and Social Science Research Association (AESSRA), Indian Association for Women's Studies. She has supervised 10 doctoral research work and 16 M.Phil research work, She is supervising 5 doctoral research work.

Hreen Soch is a Professor of Marketing at the Department of Management and Hospitality, I.K. Gujral Punjab Technical University, Kapurthala, India. Her research interests focus on customer relationship management, adoption of mobile technologies, scale development and validation, customer loyalty, service recovery and brand experience. She has published articles in various national and international journals like Journal of Asia Business Studies, Journal of Indian Business Research, Journal of Services Research, Global Business Review, Journal of Global Marketing and Journal of Air Transport Management.

Bana Taneja has a doctorate in Management and an MBA specializing in marketing and finance. She has over 18 years of teaching experience In premium institutes like Xiss, Xaviers College Ranchi, Birsa Agricultural University, etc. Presently she is associated with Amity University Jharkhand. She has several publications to her name. Dr. Taneja is an active Rotarian and is presently on the board of directors of the Rotary Club of Ranchi. She is a Pranic healer.

Rajesh Verma is Sr. Dean & Professor of Strategy at Mittal School of Business (NIRF, Government of India Ranking #32; ACBSP, USA Accredited), Lovely Professional University, Punjab, India. His research & teaching interests entail areas like Business Models, Strategic Management & Political Marketing.

Index

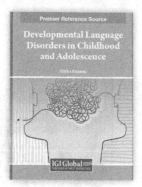

   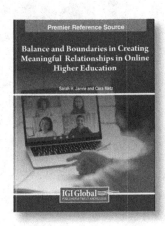

www.igi-global.com

Publishing Tomorrow's Research Today
IGI Global's Open Access Journal Program

Including Nearly 200 Peer-Reviewed, Gold (Full) Open Access Journals across IGI Global's Three Academic Subject Areas:
Business & Management; Scientific, Technical, and Medical (STM); and Education

Consider Submitting Your Manuscript to One of These Nearly 200 Open Access Journals for to Increase Their Discoverability & Citation Impact

| Web of Science Impact Factor | 6.5 | Web of Science Impact Factor | 4.7 | Web of Science Impact Factor | 3.2 | Web of Science Impact Factor | 2.6 |

JOURNAL OF
Organizational and End User Computing

JOURNAL OF
Global Information Management

INTERNATIONAL JOURNAL ON
Semantic Web and Information Systems

JOURNAL OF
Database Management

Choosing IGI Global's Open Access Journal Program Can Greatly Increase the Reach of Your Research

Higher Usage
Open access papers are 2-3 times more likely to be read than non-open access papers.

Higher Download Rates
Open access papers benefit from 89% higher download rates than non-open access papers.

Higher Citation Rates
Open access papers are 47% more likely to be cited than non-open access papers.

Submitting an article to a journal offers an invaluable opportunity for you to share your work with the broader academic community, fostering knowledge dissemination and constructive feedback.

Submit an Article and Browse the IGI Global Call for Papers Pages

We can work with you to find the journal most well-suited for your next research manuscript.
For open access publishing support, contact: journaleditor@igi-global.com

Multidisciplinary Applications of AI Robotics and Autonomous Systems

Tanupriya Choudhury
Graphic Era University, India

Anitha Mary X.
Karunya Institute of Technology and Sciences, India

Subrata Chowdhury
Sreenivasa Institute of Technology and Management Studies, India

C. Karthik
Jyothi Engineering College, India

C. Suganthi Evangeline
Sri Eshwar College of Engineering, India

A volume in the Advances in Computational
Intelligence and Robotics (ACIR) Book Series

Published in the United States of America by
IGI Global
Engineering Science Reference (an imprint of IGI Global)
701 E. Chocolate Avenue
Hershey PA, USA 17033
Tel: 717-533-8845
Fax: 717-533-8661
E-mail: cust@igi-global.com
Web site: http://www.igi-global.com

Library of Congress Cataloging-in-Publication Data

CIP Pending
ISBN: 979-8-3693-5767-5
EISBN: 979-8-3693-5769-9

This book is published in the IGI Global book series Advances in Computational Intelligence and Robotics (ACIR) (ISSN: 2327-0411; eISSN: 2327-042X).

British Cataloguing in Publication Data
A Cataloguing in Publication record for this book is available from the British Library.

All work contributed to this book is new, previously-unpublished material. The views expressed in this book are those of the authors, but not necessarily of the publisher.

For electronic access to this publication, please contact: eresources@igi-global.com.

Advances in Computational Intelligence and Robotics (ACIR) Book Series

Ivan Giannoccaro
University of Salento, Italy

ISSN:2327-0411
EISSN:2327-042X

MISSION

While intelligence is traditionally a term applied to humans and human cognition, technology has progressed in such a way to allow for the development of intelligent systems able to simulate many human traits. With this new era of simulated and artificial intelligence, much research is needed in order to continue to advance the field and also to evaluate the ethical and societal concerns of the existence of artificial life and machine learning.

The **Advances in Computational Intelligence and Robotics (ACIR) Book Series** encourages scholarly discourse on all topics pertaining to evolutionary computing, artificial life, computational intelligence, machine learning, and robotics. ACIR presents the latest research being conducted on diverse topics in intelligence technologies with the goal of advancing knowledge and applications in this rapidly evolving field.

COVERAGE

- Algorithmic Learning
- Synthetic Emotions
- Neural Networks
- Cognitive Informatics
- Computational Logic
- Evolutionary Computing
- Artificial Life
- Computational Intelligence
- Automated Reasoning
- Intelligent Control

IGI Global is currently accepting manuscripts for publication within this series. To submit a proposal for a volume in this series, please contact our Acquisition Editors at Acquisitions@igi-global.com or visit: http://www.igi-global.com/publish/.

Titles in this Series

AI Algorithms and ChatGPT for Student Engagement in Online Learning
Rohit Bansal (Vaish College of Engineering, India) Aziza Chakir (Faculty of Law, Economics, and Social Sciences, Hassan II University, Casablanca, Morocco) Abdul Hafaz Ngah (Faculty of Business Economics and Social Development, Universiti Malaysia, Terengganu, Malaysia) Fazla Rabby (Stanford Institute of Management and Technology, Australia) and Ajay Jain (Shri Cloth Market Kanya Vanijya Mahavidyalaya, Indore, ndia)
Information Science Reference • © 2024 • 292pp • H/C (ISBN: 9798369342688) • US $265.00

Applications, Challenges, and the Future of ChatGPT
Priyanka Sharma (Swami Keshvanand Institute of Technology, Management, and Gramothan, Jaipur, India) Monika Jyotiyana (Manipal University Jaipur, India) and A. V. Senthil Kumar (Hindusthan College of Arts and Sciences, ndia)
Engineering Science Reference • © 2024 • 309pp • H/C (ISBN: 9798369368244) • US $365.00

Modeling, Simulation, and Control of AI Robotics and Autonomous Systems
Tanupriya Choudhury (Graphic Era University, India) Anitha Mary X. (Karunya Institute of Technology and Sciences, India) Subrata Chowdhury (Sreenivasa Institute of Technology and Management Studies, India) C. Karthik (Jyothi Engineering College, India) and C. Suganthi Evangeline (Sri Eshwar College of Engineering, India)
Engineering Science Reference • © 2024 • 295pp • H/C (ISBN: 9798369319628) • US $300.00

Explainable AI Applications for Human Behavior Analysis
P. Paramasivan (Dhaanish Ahmed College of Engineering, India) S. Suman Rajest (Dhaanish Ahmed College of Engineering, India) Karthikeyan Chinnusamy (Veritas, USA) R. Regin (SRM Institute of Science and Technology, India) and Ferdin Joe John Joseph (Thai-Nichi Institute of Technology, Thailand)
Engineering Science Reference • © 2024 • 369pp • H/C (ISBN: 9798369313558) • US $300.00

Bio-Inspired Intelligence for Smart Decision-Making
Ramkumar Jaganathan (Sri Krishna Arts and Science College, India) Shilpa Mehta (Auckland University of Technology, New Zealand) and Ram Krishan (Mata Sundri University Girls College, Mansa, India)
Information Science Reference • © 2024 • 334pp • H/C (ISBN: 9798369352762) • US $385.00

AI and IoT for Proactive Disaster Management
Mariyam Ouaissa (Chouaib Doukkali University, Morocco) Mariya Ouaissa (Cadi Ayyad University, Morocco) Zakaria Boulouard (Hassan II University, Casablanca, Morocco) Celestine Iwendi (University of Bolton, UK) and Moez Krichen (Al-Baha University, Saudi Arabia)
Engineering Science Reference • © 2024 • 299pp • H/C (ISBN: 9798369338964) • US $355.00

701 East Chocolate Avenue, Hershey, PA 17033, USA
Tel: 717-533-8845 x100 • Fax: 717-533-8661
E-Mail: cust@igi-global.com • www.igi-global.com

Table of Contents

Detailed Table of Contents

Chapter 1

N. Dheerthi, Sri Ramakrishna Engineering College, India
A. Kishore Kumar, Sri Ramakrishna Engineering College, India
S. Sarveswaran, Sri Ramakrishna Engineering College, India
A. Murugarajan, Sri Ramakrishna Engineering College, India

In recent years, there has been a growing interest in the development of soft robotic technologies inspired by biological systems for various applications, particularly in healthcare. The study encompasses a multidisciplinary approach, integrating principles from biomechanics, robotics, and materials science to design and characterize the soft robotic arm. By examining the mechanical structure, actuation mechanisms, and control strategies, this research aims to elucidate the advantages and challenges associated with deploying bio-inspired soft robotic arms in healthcare settings. Furthermore, the investigation delves into the materials selection process, considering factors such as biocompatibility, durability, and flexibility to ensure safe and effective interaction with biological tissues. Overall, this comprehensive analysis contributes to advancing the understanding of bio-inspired soft robotics and highlights its potential transformative impact on healthcare by offering innovative solutions for improving patient care, surgical outcomes, and quality of life.

Chapter 2

S. Sarveswaran, Sri Ramakrishna Engineering College, India
Kishore Kumar Arjunsingh, Sri Ramakrishna Engineering College, India
N. Dheerthi, Sri Ramakrishna Engineering College, India
A. Murugarajan, Sri Ramakrishna Engineering College, India

Delta robots, known for their unique design featuring parallel linkages and a stationary base, have emerged as transformative tools in various industries, including healthcare. In surgery, delta robots enable minimally invasive procedures with enhanced precision and shorter recovery times. They facilitate targeted therapies in rehabilitation, promoting better outcomes for patients with neurological and musculoskeletal conditions. Delta robots also improve medication dispensing accuracy in pharmacies and automate repetitive tasks in laboratories, increasing efficiency and reducing errors. Additionally, the chapter explores the potential of delta robots in specialized fields such as orthopedic, neuro, and cardiac surgery, as well as their role in enhancing medical imaging accuracy and guiding interventional procedures in real-time. It also discusses the future of AI-powered diagnostics and personalized medicine, envisioning a healthcare landscape where delta robots play a central role in improving patient outcomes and shaping the future of healthcare delivery.

Chapter 3

    A. Madhesh, Karpagam Academy of Higher Education, India
    Clara Barathi Priyadharshini, Karpagam Academy of Higher Education, India

Earlier methods focused on reducing the forecast uncertainty for individual agents and avoiding this unduly cautious behavior by either employing more experienced models or heuristically restricting the predictive covariance. Findings indicate neither the individual prediction nor the forecast uncertainty have a major impact on the frozen robot problem. The result is that dynamic agents can solve the frozen robot problem by employing joint collision avoidance and clear the way for each other to build feasible pathways. Potential paths for safety evaluation are ranked according to the likelihood of collisions with known objects and those that happen outside the planning horizon. The whole collision probability is examined. Monte Carlo sampling is utilized to approximate the collision probabilities. Designing and selecting routes to reach the intended location, this approach aims to provide a navigation framework that reduces the likelihood of collisions.

Chapter 4

    K. Yogesh, Karpagam Academy of Higher Education, India
    R. Gunasudari, Karpagam Academy of Higher Education, India

Machine vision systems have emerged as a viable non-invasive approach for investigating the connection between fruit visual traits and physicochemical qualities at varying ripening degrees, and have been used in recent research efforts to identify the stages. The current study aims to develop an intelligent algorithm that can estimate various physical properties, such as firmness and soluble solid content, as well as three chemical properties, namely starch, acidity, and titratable acidity. A hybrid approach was used to further optimise the physicochemical estimation method of PSO with CNN. This method was applied to the evaluation parameters in order to describe their classification behaviour. The sample accuracy was 95.84% when using the different parameters to characterise them. A second set of apples was utilised for validation after the first set was used as trial samples in PSO+CNN.

Chapter 5

    Johnwesily Chappidi, VIT-AP University, India
    Divya Meena Sundaram, VIT-AP University, India

In the field of conserving wildlife, the utilization of autonomous systems equipped with computer vision holds tremendous promise. This research explores the potential of integrating YOLO v7, a cutting-edge object recognition model, with stochastic gradient descent (SGD) optimization techniques to bolster wild animal conservation efforts. The primary objective is to enhance the precision, accuracy, and scalability of autonomous systems in detecting and monitoring wild animals across diverse habitats. The experimental results showcase substantial advancements, demonstrating the efficacy of the YOLOv7-SGD amalgamation in autonomous systems. The model exhibits superior detection accuracy and robustness in identifying a multitude of wild animal species across diverse landscapes.

Chapter 6

Aruna Kasinathan, Karunya Institute of Technology and Science, India
Shrilatha Sampath, Christian Medical College, India
Hemalatha Sampath, University of Maryland, USA

The study aims to assess customer satisfaction and trust in autonomous artificial intelligence (AAI) systems within the banking sector. Its primary objectives include exploring factors contributing to customer trust in AAI, investigating preferences for AI-driven features in banking, and determining the impact of AAI on perceived service quality. The research, adopting a descriptive design, employs both qualitative and quantitative methods. A survey, distributed to customers of leading banks in India, particularly in Tamil Nadu, with a sample size of 213, utilizes simple random and convenient sampling. Results highlight customer preferences for customized services, financial advice, and automation in banking. The implementation of AAI is perceived positively, especially in terms of transparency in processes like loans, account management, and more. Practical implications include helping banks understand customer expectations, identify weaknesses in AAI features, and enhance service quality in Tamil Nadu.

Chapter 7

Xavier Arockiaraj Santhappan, Adhiyamaan College of Engineering, India
Ronica Bis, Sathyabama Institute of Science and Technology, India

Ultrasound is a conventional diagnostic instrument employed in prenatal care to track the progression and advancement of the fetus. In routine clinical obstetric assessments, the standard planes of fetal ultrasound hold considerable importance in evaluating fetal growth metrics and identifying abnormalities. In this work, a method to detect FFSP using deep convolutional neural network (DCNN) architecture to improve detection efficiency is presented. Squeeze net, 16 convolutional layers with small 3x3 large kernel, and all three layers form the proposed DCNN. The final pooling layer uses global average pooling (GAP) to reduce inconsistency in the network. This helps reduce the problem of overfitting and improves the performance from different training data. To improve cognitive performance, data augmentation methods developed specifically for FFSP are used in conjunction with adaptive learning strategies. Extensive testing shows that the proposed method gives accuracy of 96% which outperforms traditional methods, and DCNN is an important tool to identify FFSP in clinical diagnosis.

Chapter 8

Abhishek Choubey, Sreenidhi Institute of Science and Technology, Hyderabad, India
Shruti Bhargava Choubey, Sreenidhi Institute of Science and Technology, Hyderabad, India

Biorobotics and nanobots represent a cutting-edge area of biotechnology with tremendous promise to transform scientific research, environmental monitoring, and healthcare delivery. In this chapter, the authors explore their cutting-edge ideas, applications, and advances, showing their ability to radically change future industries like industry medicine. This chapter's primary objective is to explore both existing and emerging applications of bio-robots and nanobots in healthcare, environmental monitoring, environmental inspection, and materials science research. These technological advancements offer real-time diagnostics, minimally invasive surgery, and targeted drug delivery as well as environmental quality evaluation through bio-robot water quality evaluation and nanobot pollution detection at unprecedented scales. Furthermore, bio-robots and nanobots have proven invaluable for scientific study fields like neuroscience, synthetic biology, and materials science.

Chapter 9

V. Saran, Karpagam Academy of Higher Education, India
R. Chennappan, Karpagam Academy of Higher Education, India

Machine learning (ML), deep learning, fuzzy logic, and traditional neural networks are just a few of the subsets that make up artificial intelligence (AI). These subgroups possesses unique qualities and skills that could improve the effectiveness of modern medical sciences. Human intervention in clinical diagnostics, medical imaging, and decision-making is facilitated by these clever solutions. The development of information technology, the concept of intelligent healthcare has become more and more popular. Intelligent healthcare is a revolutionary approach to healthcare that leverages state-of-the-art technology such as AI and the internet of things (loT) to improve overall efficacy, convenience, and personalisation of the medical system.

Chapter 10

R. Gokulakrishnan, Karpagam Academy of Higher Education, India
C. Balakumar, Karpagam Academy of Higher Education, India

This research provides a method for gesture recognition that integrates two separate recognizers. These two recognizers use the CAR equation to ascertain the hands sign. The robot's two main parts are its sending and receiving ends. Within the process of developing the same, three domains were specifically combined: biomedicine, which involved registering biosignals using analog channels composed of instrumental amplifiers; software development, involving microcontrollers, core processing (DSP), and the resulting control of the robot hand; PC software for tracking the registered biosignals; and mechatronics, involving the design and mechanical construction of the robot hand. The hand can control how much pressure is given to things because of the force sensor (FSR) in each finger. While developing a hand and wrist prototype that can rotate in response to EMG signal pulses, this was discovered.

Chapter 11

N. Nissi Angel, Department of ECE, Velagapudi Ramakrishna Siddhartha Engineering
College, Vijayawada, India
Gunnam Suryanarayana, Department of ECE, Velagapudi Ramakrishna Siddhartha
Engineering College, Vijayawada, India
Siva Ramakrishna Pillutla, School of Electronics Engineering, VIT-AP University,
Amaravati, India
Kathik Chandran, Jyothi Engineering College, India

Image steganography methods use manual features for hiding payload data in cover images. These manual features allow less payload capacity and also cause image distortion. In this chapter, the authors detail a CNN-based network image steganography. The major contributions are twofold. First, they presented a CNN-based encoder-decoder architecture for hiding image. Secondly, they introduce a loss function, which checks joint end-to-end encoder-decoder networks. They evaluate this architecture on publicly available datasets CIFAR10. The results indicate an increase in payload capacity with high peak signal-to-noise ratio and structural similarity index values.

Chapter 12

    Nalla Bhanu Teja, Department of Mechanical Engineering, Aditya College of Engineering, Surampalem, India

    V. Kannagi, Department of Electronics and Communication Engineering, R.M.K. College of Engineering and Technology, Puduvoyal, India

    A. Chandrashekhar, Department of Mechanical Engineering, Faculty of Science and Technology, ICFAI Foundation for Higher Education, Hyderabad, India

    T. Senthilnathan, Department of Applied Physics, Sri Venkateswara College of Engineering, Sriperumbudur, India

    Tarun Kanti Pal, Department of Mechanical Engineering, College of Engineering and Management, Kolaghat, India

    Sampath Boopathi, Department of Mechanical Engineering, Muthayammal Engineering College, Namakkal, India

The integration of nanotechnology into robotics has revolutionized the design, manufacturing, and performance of robotic systems. Nano-materials, with their unique properties at the nanoscale, enhance strength, flexibility, and functionality, revolutionizing the construction and operation of robots. Nano fluids, with their superior heat transfer properties, address overheating issues, improving performance, extended operational lifespans, and increased adaptability in diverse environmental conditions. The chapter also explores the environmental impact of robotics, highlighting the integration of nano-materials and nano fluids in eco-friendly solutions. The chapter delves into the challenges and future directions of the synergy between nanotechnology and robotics, discussing potential breakthroughs, ethical considerations, and the need for ongoing research. It provides a comprehensive analysis of the impacts of nano-materials and nano fluids on the robot industry and their environments.

Chapter 13

    Ahamed Thaiyub, KPR Institute of Engineering and Technology, India

    Akshay Bhuvaneswari Ramakrishnan, SASTRA University, India

    Shriram Kris Vasudevan, Intel Corporation, India

    T. S. Murugesh, Government College of Engineering, Srirangam, India

    Sini Raj Pulari, Bahrain Polytechnic, Bahrain

Organizations face enormous issues when it comes to employee turnover, which is why they need to develop accurate predictive models for retention. The purpose of this chapter is to present a three-tiered machine learning approach for predicting employee turnover that makes use of resume parsing, performance analysis, and advanced algorithms. In addition, the authors make use of Intel oneAPI, which is a unified programming model that is increasingly becoming the industry standard, in order to improve the scalability and performance of the solution. The system that is offered delivers full HR (human resource) analytics, which enables firms to make educated decisions regarding recruiting and retention tactics. The results of the experimental evaluation show that the solution is effective in providing an accurate forecast of attrition, which paves the way for proactive retention measures. The approach enhances system performance by utilizing oneAPI, which in turn ensures that it is scalable over a variety of different hardware architectures.

Chapter 14

D. Faridha Banu, Sri Eshwar College of Engineering, Coimbatore, India
P. T. Kousalya, Sri Eshwar College of Engineering, Coimbatore, India
Kavin Varsha, Sri Eshwar College of Engineering, Coimbatore, India
C. Keerthi Prashanth, Sri Eshwar College of Engineering, Coimbatore, India
P. Madhumohan, Sri Eshwar College of Engineering, Coimbatore, India
S. Meivel, M. Kumarasamy College of Engineering, Karur, India

Any attempt to explain the relevance of data by putting it in a visual context is referred to as data visualization. With the aid of data visualization software, patterns, trends, and correlations that could go unnoticed in text-based data can be exposed and identified more easily. The graphical presentation of quantitative information is known as data visualization. In other words, data visualizations convert big and small data sets into pictures that the human brain can comprehend and digest more readily. In our daily lives, data visualizations are surprisingly prevalent, yet they frequently take the shape of recognizable charts and graphs. It can be applied to find unknown trends and facts. When communication, data science, and design come together, good data visualizations are produced. When done well, data visualizations provide important insights into complex data sets in clear, understandable ways. The authors talk about data visualization, its significance, tools for data visualization, etc. in this chapter.

Chapter 15

A. Kishore Kumar, Sri Ramakrishna Engineering College, India
S. Sarveswaran, Sri Ramakrishna Engineering College, India
N. Dheerthi, Sri Ramakrishna Engineering College, India
A. Murugarajan, Sri Ramakrishna Engineering College, India

In the rapidly evolving landscape of Healthcare 4.0/5.0, the integration of artificial intelligence (AI) and robotics has shown immense potential in transforming patient care. However, the deployment of these technologies in human-robot interactions (HRI) demands a delicate balance between efficiency and transparency. This chapter explores the research directions and challenges associated with the implementation of Explainable AI (XAI) in the context of HRI for the advancement of healthcare services. The authors delve into the critical aspects of ensuring transparency and interpretability in AI-driven robotic systems, emphasizing the need for explainability to foster trust and collaboration between healthcare professionals, patients, and intelligent robotic entities. The chapter highlights key challenges, proposes potential research directions, and suggests methodologies to address the complexities in deploying XAI within the healthcare ecosystem.

The chapter intends to create a system that alerts the victim of theft in real time. The current system does not distinguish between people and objects; instead, it uses a methodology to identify the burglar after the theft has taken place. The internet of things and advancements in wireless sensor networks make it possible to create a smart, safe home that can detect burglars in real time and notify the homeowner while the theft is occurring. The suggested approach is better than the current ones that use CCTV cameras for surveillance.

Nano robotics is a rapidly developing technology that operates at microscopic scales, revolutionizing fields like medicine and manufacturing. However, it faces numerous challenges, including technical, ethical, and practical issues. These include precision engineering, control mechanisms, and power sources, as well as ethical concerns about autonomy, safety, and societal impact. The chapter explores the future of nano robotics, highlighting its potential in various fields such as medicine and manufacturing. It highlights the potential of nano robots in enhancing durability and functionality, offering targeted drug delivery, minimally invasive surgeries, and precise diagnostics. The chapter also addresses technical challenges, ethical considerations, and potential developments, aiming to make the seemingly impossible achievable at the tiniest scales, emphasizing the need for further advancements.

Preface

Welcome to the realm of Intelligent Robotics and Autonomous Systems (IRAS), a captivating intersection of robotics, artificial intelligence (AI), and control systems. As editors, it is our pleasure to present to you this edited reference book, *Multidisciplinary Applications of AI Robotics and Autonomous Systems*, curated by Tanupriya Choudhury, Anitha Mary X, Subrata Chowdhury, C. Karthik, and C. Suganthi Evangeline.

Intelligent Robotics and Autonomous Systems (IRAS) is a dynamic field where innovation knows no bounds. Within its realm, system modeling, simulation, and control with Artificial Intelligence (AI) are indispensable pillars. These facets empower engineers and researchers to craft intelligent machines capable of navigating complex tasks autonomously, thus reshaping industries and redefining possibilities.

System modeling entails the creation of mathematical representations that capture the essence of robotic systems, encompassing their dynamics, kinematics, sensors, actuators, and interrelations. Simulation, on the other hand, provides a virtual playground for testing these models rigorously, fostering insights and foresight without the constraints of the physical realm. Complementing these, control algorithms infused with AI breathe life into robotic systems, endowing them with the autonomy to make informed decisions based on sensory input.

The applications of these methodologies are boundless. From autonomous driving systems revolutionizing transportation to industrial automation streamlining production processes, the impact of IRAS reverberates across various domains. Through meticulous system modeling, rigorous simulation, and intelligent control, engineers navigate the challenges of designing machines that not only perform tasks but do so with finesse and efficiency.

The landscape of autonomous systems is ever-evolving, propelled by advancements in AI, control theory, and distributed intelligence. As we stand on the precipice of a new era, where autonomous systems permeate everyday life, this book serves as a beacon, illuminating the path towards further exploration and innovation.

We invite you to embark on this journey through the pages of *Multidisciplinary Applications of AI Robotics and Autonomous Systems*. Within these chapters lie insights, breakthroughs, and a glimpse into the future of robotics and autonomy. May this compilation inspire curiosity, spark ideas, and pave the way for new frontiers in the realm of intelligent machines.

ORGANIZATION OF THE BOOK

Chapter 1: A Comprehensive Analysis of Bio-inspired Soft Robotic Arm for Healthcare Applications

In this chapter, the authors explore the burgeoning field of soft robotics, particularly in healthcare applications. By amalgamating principles from biomechanics, robotics, and materials science, they delve into the design and characterization of bio-inspired soft robotic arms. The research scrutinizes mechanical structures, actuation mechanisms, and control strategies, shedding light on the advantages and challenges of deploying such systems in healthcare settings. Moreover, the chapter delves into materials selection criteria, emphasizing biocompatibility, durability, and flexibility to ensure safe interaction with biological tissues. Overall, this thorough analysis offers insights into the transformative potential of bio-inspired soft robotics in healthcare, promising innovative solutions for enhancing patient care and surgical outcomes.

Chapter 2: A Comprehensive Insights and Research Focus on Delta Robots in the Healthcare Industry

The second chapter delves into the multifaceted applications of delta robots in healthcare, showcasing their unique design and transformative impact. From enabling minimally invasive surgeries to enhancing medication dispensing accuracy, delta robots have found versatile utility in various healthcare domains. The authors explore their potential in specialized fields such as orthopedics and neurosurgery, alongside their role in medical imaging and interventional procedures. Additionally, they envision a future where AI-powered diagnostics and personalized medicine converge with delta robots, revolutionizing patient outcomes and healthcare delivery.

Chapter 3: A Data-Driven Model for Predicting Fault-Tolerant Safe Navigation in Multi-Robot Systems

This chapter navigates through the intricate realm of multi-robot systems, focusing on predictive modeling for fault-tolerant safe navigation. The authors propose a dynamic approach that prioritizes joint collision avoidance, facilitating the smooth traversal of dynamic environments. By leveraging Monte Carlo sampling and data-driven techniques, they develop a robust navigation framework that minimizes collision probabilities. The chapter underscores the significance of proactive safety measures in multi-robot systems, offering insights into enhancing navigation efficiency while mitigating potential risks.

Chapter 4: A Novel Method to Detect Ripeness Level of Apples Using Machine Vision (PSOCNN) Approach

Machine vision takes center stage in this chapter as the authors present a novel method for detecting the ripeness level of apples. By integrating Particle Swarm Optimization (PSO) with Convolutional Neural Networks (CNN), they develop an intelligent algorithm capable of estimating various physical and chemical properties of apples. Through meticulous image processing and AI-driven analysis, the proposed approach achieves high accuracy in ripeness detection, promising advancements in quality control and agricultural practices.

Chapter 5: Advancing Wild Animal Conservation through Autonomous Systems Leveraging YOLOV7 With SGD Optimization Technique

Wildlife conservation receives a technological boost in this chapter, where autonomous systems equipped with computer vision take the spotlight. The authors explore the integration of YOLOv7 with Stochastic Gradient Descent (SGD) optimization techniques to bolster wild animal conservation efforts. Through experimental validation, they demonstrate the superior detection accuracy and scalability of the YOLOv7-SGD amalgamation, envisioning a future where autonomous systems play a pivotal role in safeguarding biodiversity across diverse habitats.

Chapter 6: Evaluating Customer Satisfaction and Trust in Autonomous AI Banking Systems

The sixth chapter delves into the realm of autonomous Artificial Intelligence (AAI) systems within the banking sector, aiming to assess customer satisfaction and trust. Employing both qualitative and quantitative methods, the authors investigate customer preferences and perceptions regarding AI-driven features in banking. Their findings highlight the positive reception of AAI, particularly in terms of service quality and transparency. This research offers valuable insights for banks seeking to enhance customer experience and adapt to evolving technological landscapes.

Chapter 7: Foetal Activity Detection Using Deep Convolution Neural Networks

In prenatal care, fetal ultrasound plays a crucial role, and this chapter introduces a method for enhancing fetal face and spine plane (FFSP) detection using Deep Convolutional Neural Networks (DCNN). Through innovative architecture design and data augmentation techniques, the authors achieve remarkable accuracy in FFSP detection, promising advancements in clinical obstetric assessments and fetal monitoring. Their research underscores the transformative potential of DCNNs in improving diagnostic efficiency and maternal-fetal health outcomes.

Chapter 8: Future Nano- and Biorobots Miniaturized Machines for Biotechnology and Beyond

Nano- and biorobots take center stage in this chapter, offering a glimpse into the future of biotechnology and scientific research. The authors explore the myriad applications of these miniature marvels, ranging from targeted drug delivery to environmental monitoring. Their analysis delves into the integration of nanotechnology with robotics, highlighting the transformative potential in healthcare, materials science, and beyond. This chapter serves as a roadmap for harnessing the power of nano- and biorobots to address pressing societal challenges and unlock new frontiers in scientific exploration.

Chapter 9: HRI in ITs Using ML Techniques

Machine Learning (ML) techniques intersect with Human-Robot Interactions (HRI) in this chapter, offering insights into the burgeoning field of intelligent healthcare. The authors explore the convergence of AI, IoT, and healthcare, highlighting the transformative potential in clinical diagnostics and decision-making. Through a hybrid approach combining Convolutional Neural Networks (CNN) and Ant Colony Optimization (ACO), they present innovative methodologies for disease detection and medical technology advancement. This research lays the groundwork for intelligent healthcare systems that prioritize efficacy, convenience, and personalization.

Chapter 10: Human-Robot Safety Guarantees Using Confidence-Aware-Game-Theoretic Human Models With EMG Signal

Gesture recognition and human-robot interactions converge in this chapter, presenting a method for enhancing safety guarantees in robotics. The authors propose a confidence-aware-game-theoretic model integrated with Electromyography (EMG) signals, offering a novel approach to gesture-based robot control. Through meticulous design and integration of multiple domains, they develop a robust system that prioritizes user safety and intuitive control. Their research paves the way for seamless human-robot collaboration, promising advancements in robotics applications across diverse domains.

Chapter 11: Image Steganography-Embedding Secret Data in Images Using Convolutional Neural Networks: CNN-Based Image Steganography

Image steganography takes center stage in this chapter, where the authors present a novel approach leveraging Convolutional Neural Networks (CNNs). Their methodology focuses on concealing secret data within images, offering a secure and efficient communication channel. By introducing a CNN-based encoder-decoder architecture and novel loss function, they achieve increased payload capacity and improved signal-to-noise ratio. This research promises advancements in secure communication and data privacy, addressing contemporary challenges in information security.

Chapter 12: Impacts of Nano-Materials and Nano Fluids on the Robot Industry and Environments

Nanotechnology's integration with robotics is explored in this chapter, highlighting its transformative impact on robot design and performance. The authors delve into the applications of nano-materials and nano fluids, emphasizing their role in enhancing robot durability, functionality, and adaptability to environmental conditions. Through a comprehensive analysis, they address technical challenges, ethical considerations, and potential developments, envisioning a future where nano-enhanced robots revolutionize industries and environmental monitoring. This chapter serves as a roadmap for harnessing the synergies between nanotechnology and robotics to address societal challenges and unlock new possibilities.

Chapter 13: Predictive Modelling for Employee Retention: A Three-Tier Machine Learning Approach With oneAPI

Employee retention receives a technological overhaul in this chapter, where the authors propose a three-tiered machine learning approach for predictive modeling. By leveraging resume parsing, performance analysis, and advanced algorithms, they develop a robust system capable of accurately forecasting attrition. Moreover, the integration of Intel oneAPI enhances scalability and performance across diverse hardware architectures, paving the way for proactive retention measures in organizations. This research offers practical insights for HR analytics, empowering firms to make informed decisions regarding recruitment and retention strategies.

Chapter 14: Research Analysis of Data Exploration and Visualization Dashboard Using Data Science

Data visualization emerges as a powerful tool in this chapter, where the authors analyze its significance and application in diverse domains. By elucidating the relevance of data visualization and exploring visualization tools and techniques, they showcase its potential in uncovering hidden insights and trends. This research underscores the importance of effective communication between data science, design, and decision-making, offering practical insights for leveraging data visualization to gain actionable insights from complex datasets.

Chapter 15: Research Directions and Challenges in the Deployment of Explainable AI in Human Robot Interactions for Healthcare 4.0/5.0

Explainable AI (XAI) takes the spotlight in this chapter, focusing on its deployment in Human-Robot Interactions (HRI) within the healthcare domain. The authors explore research directions and challenges associated with ensuring transparency and interpretability in AI-driven robotic systems. By fostering trust and collaboration between healthcare professionals, patients, and intelligent robotic entities, they envision a future where XAI enhances healthcare services and patient outcomes. This research offers insights into addressing the complexities of deploying XAI within the healthcare ecosystem, emphasizing the need for transparency and ethical considerations.

Chapter 16: Security System for Smart Homes to Prevent Theft

Smart home security receives a technological boost in this chapter, where the authors propose a real-time theft detection system. By leveraging IoT and wireless sensor networks, they develop a smart home security system capable of identifying burglars during theft events. This innovative approach offers advantages over traditional surveillance methods, promising enhanced security and peace of mind for homeowners. The chapter highlights the potential of IoT-driven solutions in preventing theft and ensuring residential safety.

Chapter 17: Study on Nano Robotic Systems for Industry 4.0: Overcoming Challenges and Shaping Future Developments

Nano robotics takes center stage in this chapter, offering insights into its applications and challenges in Industry 4.0. The authors explore the transformative potential of nano robots in various sectors, ranging from medicine to manufacturing. By addressing technical challenges and ethical considerations, they envision a future where nano robots revolutionize industrial processes and environmental monitoring. This research lays the groundwork for harnessing the synergy between nanotechnology and robotics, paving the way for future advancements in diverse industries.

CONCLUSION

In concluding this edited reference book on global practices in talent acquisition and retention, we reflect on the journey we've embarked upon—a journey marked by exploration, discovery, and collaboration. Each chapter within this volume represents a unique contribution to the collective understanding of talent management in the contemporary world.

As editors, we have been privileged to witness the depth and breadth of expertise showcased by our esteemed contributors. From the intricacies of artificial intelligence in recruitment to the nuances of fostering diversity and inclusion, from the challenges of employee well-being to the strategies for retaining top talent, this book encapsulates a wealth of knowledge and insights.

Through empirical research, theoretical frameworks, and practical applications, the chapters offer actionable strategies and thought-provoking perspectives for scholars, practitioners, and policymakers alike. They underscore the evolving nature of talent management and the imperative for organizations to adapt to an ever-changing landscape.

As we bid farewell to this volume, we extend our heartfelt appreciation to all who have contributed to its creation. The dedication, passion, and intellectual rigor of our authors have been the driving force behind this endeavor. We also express our gratitude to our readers, whose engagement and curiosity fuel the advancement of knowledge in this field.

As we turn the final page, we envision this book not as an endpoint, but as a catalyst for continued dialogue, innovation, and progress in talent acquisition and retention. May the insights shared within these pages inspire transformative action and contribute to the cultivation of thriving, inclusive workplaces around the globe.

Tanupriya Choudhury
Graphic Era University, India

X. Anitha Mary
Karunya Institute of Technology and Sciences, India

Subrata Chowdhury
Sreenivasa Institute of Technology and Management Studies, India

C. Karthik
Jyothi Engineering College, India

C. Suganthi Evangeline
Sri Eshwar College of Engineering, India

Chapter 1
A Comprehensive Analysis of Bio–Inspired Soft Robotic Arm for Healthcare Applications

N. Dheerthi
Sri Ramakrishna Engineering College, India

A. Kishore Kumar
(iD) https://orcid.org/0000-0003-4876-319X
Sri Ramakrishna Engineering College, India

S. Sarveswaran
Sri Ramakrishna Engineering College, India

A. Murugarajan
Sri Ramakrishna Engineering College, India

ABSTRACT

In recent years, there has been a growing interest in the development of soft robotic technologies inspired by biological systems for various applications, particularly in healthcare. The study encompasses a multidisciplinary approach, integrating principles from biomechanics, robotics, and materials science to design and characterize the soft robotic arm. By examining the mechanical structure, actuation mechanisms, and control strategies, this research aims to elucidate the advantages and challenges associated with deploying bio-inspired soft robotic arms in healthcare settings. Furthermore, the investigation delves into the materials selection process, considering factors such as biocompatibility, durability, and flexibility to ensure safe and effective interaction with biological tissues. Overall, this comprehensive analysis contributes to advancing the understanding of bio-inspired soft robotics and highlights its potential transformative impact on healthcare by offering innovative solutions for improving patient care, surgical outcomes, and quality of life.

DOI: 10.4018/979-8-3693-5767-5.ch001

1. INTRODUCTION TO BIO-INSPIRED SOFT ROBOTICS

1.1 Definition and Principles of Bio-Inspired Soft Robotics

Bio-inspired soft robotics is a branch of robotics that creates soft, flexible robot bodies by modelling them after biological structures and species. These robots are designed to resemble live things in terms of their robustness, flexibility, and other traits. Bio-inspired soft robotics frequently combines concepts from biology, materials science, and biomechanics to build robots that can securely interact with people, navigate challenging settings, and carry out activities that are beyond the capabilities of conventional rigid robots (Li et al., 2022). Soft actuators inspired by muscle architecture, soft-bodied grippers modelled after octopus tentacles, and crawling robots modelled after caterpillar or snake locomotion are a few examples of bio-inspired soft robotics. There has been a broad shift in recent years toward robots that are service-oriented, meaning they must be able to handle a variety of uncertainty and adapt to complicated dynamic situations (Rus & Tolley, 2015). Owing to the advantageous characteristics of living things, like resilience, flexibility, adaptability, and agility, scientists have been attempting to integrate biological elements into robots. intelligence that will allow autonomous robots to navigate safely and collaborate effectively in changing contexts (Bekey, 2005). Biologically inspired intelligence refers to the methods that have been influenced by biological intelligence and has been investigated and studied for many years in robotics research (Li, Yang, and Xu, 2019). Numerous biological phenomena involving agonist and antagonist interaction have been satisfactorily explained by the gated dipole paradigm (Oh et al., 2017).

The idea behind bio-inspired robotics is to build robots with similar capabilities by imitating different parts of biological organisms. Several fundamental principles are:

Soft and Flexible Structures: Soft, flexible bodies are a common feature of bio-inspired robots, which emulate the pliable properties of biological tissues.

Biomechanics: Understanding the biomechanics of biological organisms helps in designing robots that can mimic natural movements and behaviours.

Sensory Systems: Bio-inspired robots often incorporate sensory systems inspired by those found in nature, such as vision, touch, and proprioception.

Integration of Multi-disciplinary Approaches: Bio-inspired robotics often involves collaboration across multiple disciplines, including biology, engineering, computer science, and materials science.

1.2 Overview of the Motivation Behind Developing Soft Robotic Arms for Healthcare

The motivation behind developing soft robotic arms for healthcare stems from the need to address specific challenges and requirements within medical contexts. Here's an overview of the key motivations:

Safe Human Interaction: Traditional rigid robotic arms used in medical settings may pose a risk of injury to patients or medical staff due to their hard and heavy structures (Rus & Tolley, 2015). Soft robotic arms, with their compliant and flexible nature, offer a safer alternative for close interaction with humans. They can perform tasks such as patient care, rehabilitation, or surgical assistance with reduced risk of accidental collisions or harm.

Gentle Manipulation: Soft robotic arms can exert gentle forces and adapt their shape to conform to the contours of biological tissues, making them suitable for delicate procedures such as surgery or patient assistance. Their soft and compliant nature reduces the likelihood of tissue damage or trauma during manipulation, enhancing patient comfort and safety.

Accessibility and Affordability: Soft robotic arms can be designed using lightweight and cost-effective materials, making them more accessible and affordable compared to traditional rigid robotic systems. This accessibility can benefit healthcare facilities with limited resources or in remote areas, enabling them to incorporate robotic technology into their practice.

Versatility and Adaptability: Soft robotic arms offer versatility in performing a wide range of tasks, from assisting with daily activities for elderly or disabled individuals to assisting surgeons in minimally invasive procedures. Their flexible and adaptable nature allows them to navigate complex anatomical structures and perform intricate motions with precision.

Minimally Invasive Surgery: Soft robotic arms are particularly well-suited for minimally invasive surgical procedures, where access to the surgical site is restricted and precision is paramount. Their flexibility and dexterity enable them to navigate through narrow or confined spaces within the body, performing complex maneuvers with minimal trauma to surrounding tissues.

The development of soft robotic arms for healthcare is driven by the goal of improving patient outcomes, enhancing the efficiency and safety of medical procedures, and expanding the accessibility of robotic technology in healthcare settings. These versatile and adaptable robotic systems have the potential to revolutionize various aspects of healthcare delivery, from patient care to surgical interventions and rehabilitation therapy.

2. BIOLOGICAL INSPIRATIONS

2.1 Exploration of Natural Organisms and Structures Inspiring Soft Robotic Arm Design (e.g., Octopus Arms, Elephant Trunks)

Biological inspirations for soft robotic arms in healthcare can come from a variety of organisms and systems. Here are some examples:

Muscle Structure: Mimicking the structure and function of biological muscles can inspire the design of soft actuators for robotic arms. Biological muscles contract and expand in response to electrical signals, providing the necessary force and motion for movement. Soft robotic actuators, such as pneumatic artificial muscles or electroactive polymers, can replicate this functionality to generate motion and manipulate objects gently.

Octopus Tentacles: The dexterous and flexible tentacles of octopuses inspire the design of soft robotic arms with versatile manipulation capabilities. Octopus tentacles are composed of muscular hydrostats, allowing them to bend and stretch in various directions without a rigid skeleton. Soft robotic arms can emulate this flexibility using compliant materials and distributed actuators, enabling them to navigate complex environments and interact delicately with objects.

Elephant Trunks: The trunk of an elephant serves as another biological inspiration for soft robotic arms, particularly in terms of its strength, dexterity, and sensitivity. Elephant trunks are capable of grasping and manipulating objects with precision, while also being sensitive to touch and pressure. Soft robotic arms can replicate these characteristics using flexible materials, tactile sensors, and multi-modal feedback systems, making them suitable for tasks requiring both strength and sensitivity, such as surgical procedures or rehabilitation therapy.

Human Anatomy: The structure and biomechanics of the human arm and hand provide valuable insights for designing soft robotic arms for healthcare applications. By studying the musculoskeletal system and neural control mechanisms of human limbs, researchers can develop soft robotic arms that emulate natural movements and gestures. This bio-inspired approach enables the creation of assistive devices and prosthetic limbs that closely mimic the functionality of biological appendages, enhancing mobility and independence for individuals with disabilities.

2.2 Comparison of Biological Features With Engineered Soft Robotics

By drawing inspiration from these biological sources, researchers can develop soft robotic arms that combine the advantages of flexibility, dexterity, and sensitivity, making them well-suited for a wide range of healthcare applications, including surgical assistance, rehabilitation therapy, and assistive devices for individuals with mobility impairments. The various comparisons of biological features with soft Robotics is discussed in the Table 1.

3. DESIGN AND MATERIALS

3.1 Structural Design Considerations for Bio-Inspired Soft Robotic Arms

Designing bio-inspired soft robotic arms involves careful consideration of various structural factors to ensure functionality, flexibility, and reliability. Here are some key structural design considerations:

Soft and Compliant Materials: Selecting appropriate soft and compliant materials is crucial for achieving the desired flexibility and adaptability in soft robotic arms. Elastomers, hydrogels, silicone, and flexible polymers are commonly used materials that mimic the softness and flexibility of biological tissues.

Table 1. Comparisons of biological features with soft robotics

Parameters	Biological	Soft Robotics
Flexibility and Compliance	Many organisms exhibit soft, compliant structures that allow for flexibility and adaptability to different environments and tasks. Muscles, tendons, and ligaments provide compliant movement in animals.	Engineered soft robotics aim to replicate this flexibility and compliance using materials such as elastomers and hydrogels.
Sensory Systems	Organisms possess sophisticated sensory systems that allow them to perceive and interact with their environment. These include vision, touch, proprioception, and other sensory modalities.	Soft robotic systems integrate sensors inspired by biological counterparts to perceive their surroundings and respond accordingly.
Biological	Animals have evolved complex biomechanical systems that enable efficient movement, manipulation, and force generation. Examples include the musculoskeletal system and hydrostatic skeletons found in soft-bodied organisms.	Soft robotics draws inspiration from biological biomechanics to design robotic systems with similar capabilities.
Integration and Multi-functionality	Biological organisms often exhibit integrated functionality, with multiple systems working together seamlessly to achieve diverse tasks. For example, the human hand can perform gripping, manipulation, and tactile sensing simultaneously	Soft robotic systems aim to integrate multiple functions into a single platform, mimicking the multi-functionality observed in biological organisms. By combining sensors, actuators, and control systems, soft robotics enables versatile and adaptive behaviour for various applications

Distributed Actuation and Control: Distributing actuators and control mechanisms throughout the robotic arm enables smoother and more natural movements, resembling biological motion patterns. By decentralizing actuation and control, soft robotic arms can achieve greater flexibility, dexterity, and adaptability in various tasks.

Biologically-inspired Kinematics: Emulating the kinematics and motion patterns observed in biological limbs can enhance the functionality and efficiency of soft robotic arms. Bio-inspired design principles, such as the use of parallel mechanisms or compliant joints, can improve motion range, agility, and energy efficiency.

Embedded Sensing and Feedback: Integrating sensors for proprioception, force sensing, and tactile feedback enables soft robotic arms to perceive and respond to their environment. Embedded sensors provide crucial feedback for control algorithms, enhancing precision, safety, and adaptability in various tasks.

By carefully considering these structural design considerations, engineers and researchers can develop bio-inspired soft robotic arms that exhibit enhanced flexibility, adaptability, and performance in healthcare applications, such as surgical assistance, rehabilitation therapy, and assistive devices for individuals with mobility impairments.

3.2 Materials Selection, Including Soft and Flexible Materials for Enhanced Compliance

Selecting appropriate materials is crucial for the structural design of bio-inspired soft robotic arms, particularly when aiming for enhanced compliance and flexibility. Here are some materials commonly used for soft and flexible components in such robotic systems

Silicone Elastomers: Silicone elastomers are widely used in soft robotics due to their excellent flexibility, durability, and biocompatibility. They can be easily moulded into complex shapes and have tuneable mechanical properties, allowing for customization based on the specific requirements of the robotic arm.

Polyurethane Elastomers: Polyurethane elastomers offer similar properties to silicone elastomers and are often used as alternatives or in combination with silicone for soft robotic applications. They provide good resilience, tear resistance, and chemical stability, making them suitable for dynamic and long-term use.

Hydrogels: Hydrogels are water-swollen polymer networks that exhibit high flexibility and biocompatibility, resembling the mechanical properties of biological tissues. They are suitable for soft robotic applications requiring interactions with biological systems, such as biomedical devices or wearable sensors.

Soft Pneumatic Actuators (SPAs): Soft pneumatic actuators are made from flexible materials, such as silicone or elastomers, and actuated by pneumatic pressure. These actuators exhibit compliant behaviour and can generate bending, twisting, or elongation motions, making them suitable for soft robotic arm applications requiring gentle manipulation and interaction with the environment.

4. ACTUATION MECHANISMS

4.1 Overview of Actuation Methods for Soft Robotic Arms

Actuation methods for soft robotic arms enable these devices to achieve motion, manipulation, and interaction with the environment (Li et al., 2020)/ Here's an overview of various actuation methods commonly used in soft robotics, tabulated in Table 2.

4.2 Pneumatic, Hydraulic, and Soft Artificial Muscles

Pneumatic, hydraulic, and soft artificial muscles are actuation mechanisms commonly used in soft robotics, each offering unique advantages and characteristics. Here's an overview of each type shown in the following Table 3.

5. SENSORY FEEDBACK AND CONTROL

5.1 Integrating Sensors for Feedback and Environmental Awareness

It is essential for enabling soft robotic arms to perceive and respond to their surroundings effectively. Here's how sensors can be integrated into soft robotic systems:

Tactile Sensors

Detect contact or pressure on the arm's surface, often using arrays of pressure-sensitive elements like piezoresistive or capacitive sensors.

Force Sensors

Measure applied forces directly at joints, actuators, or end-effectors using load cells, strain gauges, or force-sensitive resistors.

Table 2. Various actuating methods

Type of Actuation	Principle	Advantages	Disadvantages
Pneumatic Actuation	Uses compressed air or gas to deform and move soft structures	Lightweight, compliant, safe, and capable of complex motions	Requires a pneumatic system for control, potentially limiting portability
Hydraulic Actuation	Utilizes pressurized liquid (like oil or water) to actuate soft structures.	Offers higher force and power density, ideal for strong and dynamic movements.	Needs hydraulic fluid supply and control systems, increasing complexity and maintenance.
Shape Memory Alloys (SMAs):	Undergo reversible shape changes with temperature, enabling shape memory effect and super elasticity.	Fast response times, high energy efficiency, and compact form factor.	Limited actuation range, relatively low force output, requires precise temperature control
Soft Fluidic Actuation	Generates motion in soft structures using fluid flow (air or liquid) through inflation and deflation.	Simple, lightweight, compliant, capable of a wide range of motions and shapes.	Requires external fluid supply and control systems, potentially slower response times.

Table 3. Types of artificial muscles

Types of Artificial Muscles	Principle	Advantages	Disadvantages
Pneumatic Artificial Muscles	Flexible tubes or bladders expand or contract with changes in air pressure. Air pressure control dictates muscle length and shape for desired motions.	Lightweight, compliant, high force-to-weight ratio, simple control via pneumatic systems.	Limited lifespan due to wear, nonlinear responses requiring careful calibration.
Hydraulic Artificial Muscles	Similar to PAMs but use pressurized fluid instead of air. Fluid pressure controls muscle expansion for various motions.	High force output, smooth control, resistance to compression.	Complexity due to hydraulic systems, potential for leakage requiring maintenance.
Soft Artificial Muscles	Emulate biological muscle contraction using soft materials like EAPs, SMAs, or dielectric elastomers. Deform in response to electrical, thermal, or mechanical stimuli.	Versatility in design, biomimetic motion, low-profile and lightweight	Limited force output compared to pneumatic or hydraulic actuators, complexity of control with some mechanisms.

Position and Velocity Sensors

Principle & Integration: Provide feedback on arm components' position, orientation, and velocity using encoders, potentiometers, or magnetic sensors integrated into joints or actuators.

Proximity Sensors

Detect nearby objects using sensors like infrared (IR), ultrasonic, or time-of-flight (ToF) mounted on the arm or deployed separately for obstacle detection.

Environmental Sensors

Measure environmental parameters like temperature, humidity, or gas concentration using sensors integrated into the arm or attached externally.

Integrating these sensors enables soft robotic arms to perceive their environment, interact effectively, and adapt behaviour, facilitating applications in healthcare, manufacturing, exploration, and human-robot interaction.

5.2 Control Mechanisms for Precise and Adaptable Movements

Achieving precise and adaptable movements in soft robotic arms requires sophisticated control mechanisms that can accurately regulate actuation, respond to sensory feedback, and adapt to changing conditions. Here are several control mechanisms commonly used for this purpose:

Proportional-Integral-Derivative (PID) Control

Adjusts system output based on present, past, and predicted future errors using proportional, integral, and derivative terms. Widely used in soft robotics for stable and responsive control of actuator position, velocity, or force, enabling precise motion and manipulation.

Model Predictive Control (MPC)

Utilizes a dynamic model to predict future states and optimize control actions over a finite time horizon. Suitable for predictive control of complex movements or interactions in soft robotic arms, optimizing motion trajectories, improving tracking performance, and handling system non-linearities.

Adaptive Control

Adjusts control parameters in real-time based on changes in system dynamics or operating conditions to maintain performance. Useful for soft robotic arms operating in dynamic environments or with varying payloads/frictional forces, compensating for uncertainties or disturbances.

Reinforcement Learning (RL)

Agent learns optimal control policies through trial-and-error interactions with the environment, receiving rewards or penalties (Ji et al., 2022). Applied to soft robotic arms for learning complex motion behaviours or manipulation strategies without explicit models, enabling autonomous and adaptive behaviour over time.

6. APPLICATIONS IN MINIMALLY INVASIVE SURGERY

6.1 Use of Bio-Inspired Soft Robotic Arms in Minimally Invasive Surgical Procedures

The use of bio-inspired soft robotic arms in minimally invasive surgical procedures offers several advantages, including enhanced dexterity, safety, and patient outcomes. Here's how bio-inspired soft robotic arms are being applied in this context:

Flexible and Compliant Manipulation

Soft robotic arms can mimic the flexibility and compliance of biological tissues, allowing them to navigate through narrow and complex anatomical structures with minimal trauma. This flexibility reduces the risk of tissue damage and improves patient safety during minimally invasive surgeries.

Dexterous Instrumentation

Bio-inspired soft robotic arms can incorporate multi-degree-of-freedom manipulators and end-effectors inspired by natural appendages, such as tentacles or elephant trunks. These dexterous instruments enable precise and versatile manipulation of surgical tools within confined spaces, enhancing the surgeon's capabilities and surgical outcomes.

Adaptive Control and Feedback

Soft robotic arms can integrate sensors for real-time feedback on tissue properties, forces, and tool interactions during surgery. This feedback enables adaptive control algorithms to adjust the robotic arm's motion and force application, ensuring accurate and safe tissue manipulation while minimizing the risk of complications.

Precise Targeting and Localization

Soft robotic arms equipped with imaging modalities, such as cameras or ultrasound probes, can provide enhanced visualization and localization of surgical targets. This enables precise targeting of lesions or diseased tissues, facilitating more accurate surgical interventions and reducing the risk of inadvertent damage to surrounding structures.

6.2 Advantages Over Traditional Rigid Robotic Arms in Surgical Applications

Bio-inspired soft robotic arms offer several advantages over traditional rigid robotic arms in surgical applications, particularly in minimally invasive procedures. Here are some key advantages:

Flexibility and Compliance: Soft robotic arms mimic the compliant and flexible nature of biological tissues, allowing them to navigate through complex anatomical structures with greater ease and safety.

Gentle Tissue Interaction: Soft robotic arms exert gentle forces on tissues and organs, minimizing the risk of trauma or injury during surgery.

Adaptability to Anatomical Variability: Soft robotic arms can adapt to patient-specific anatomies and variations in tissue properties, enabling personalized and tailored surgical interventions.

Reduced Risk of Instrument Clashes: Soft robotic arms, with their compliant and deformable structures, are less likely to cause instrument clashes or collisions during surgery compared to rigid robotic arms.

Improved Ergonomics and Surgeon Comfort: Soft robotic arms can be designed with ergonomic considerations in mind, providing surgeons with greater comfort and ease of use during prolonged surgical procedures. Their lightweight and flexible construction reduce operator fatigue and strain, allowing for more precise and controlled movements over extended periods.

Cost-Effectiveness and Accessibility: Soft robotic arms can be fabricated using cost-effective and readily available materials, making them more affordable and accessible compared to traditional rigid robotic systems. This affordability enables wider adoption of robotic-assisted surgery in healthcare facilities with limited resources or in remote areas, expanding access to advanced surgical technologies.

The advantages of bio-inspired soft robotic arms over traditional rigid robotic arms in surgical applications lie in their flexibility, compliance, adaptability, and enhanced dexterity, which contribute to improved surgical outcomes, reduced complications, and enhanced patient care.

7. REHABILITATION AND ASSISTIVE DEVICES

7.1 Applications in Physical Therapy and Rehabilitation

Bio-inspired soft robotic arms hold significant potential for applications in physical therapy and rehabilitation, offering innovative solutions to assist individuals with mobility impairments, facilitate recovery from injuries, and enhance rehabilitation outcomes. Here are several key applications in this field:

Assistive Devices for Activities of Daily Living (ADLs): Soft robotic arms can be integrated into assistive devices to help individuals with mobility impairments perform activities of daily living, such as eating, dressing, and personal hygiene. These devices can provide assistance with grasping, reaching, and manipulating objects, enabling greater independence and autonomy for users.

Rehabilitation Robotics: Soft robotic arms can be used in rehabilitation robotics to provide targeted assistance and resistance during therapeutic exercises and functional training. By guiding and supporting the movements of the affected limbs, soft robotic arms can help individuals regain strength, range of motion, and motor control following injuries or surgeries.

Home-Based Rehabilitation: Soft robotic devices designed for home use can enable individuals to continue their rehabilitation exercises and therapies outside of clinical settings. These devices can provide personalized and interactive rehabilitation programs, allowing individuals to participate in their recovery process and maintain adherence to treatment regimens.

7.2 Development of Assistive Devices for Individuals With Mobility Challenges

The development of assistive devices for individuals with mobility challenges is a crucial area where bio-inspired soft robotic arms can make a significant impact. These devices aim to enhance mobility, independence, and quality of life for individuals with disabilities or mobility impairments. Here's how bio-inspired soft robotic arms can contribute to the development of assistive devices:

Enhanced Flexibility and Adaptability: Bio-inspired soft robotic arms offer greater flexibility and adaptability compared to traditional rigid assistive devices. Their compliant and deformable structures allow for better accommodation of individual anatomies and movements, improving comfort and usability for users with varying mobility needs.

Natural and Intuitive Interaction: Soft robotic arms can mimic the natural flexibility and compliance of biological limbs, providing more natural and intuitive interaction with the environment. This allows users to perform daily activities with greater ease and confidence, enhancing their independence and autonomy.

Customized Assistive Solutions: Soft robotic arms can be customized to meet the specific needs and preferences of individual users. Their modular design and customizable features allow for tailored solutions that address unique mobility challenges, such as limited range of motion, muscle weakness, or coordination difficulties.

Assistance with Activities of Daily Living (ADLs): Soft robotic arms can assist individuals with mobility challenges in performing activities of daily living, such as eating, dressing, grooming, and household chores. These devices can provide support and assistance with grasping, reaching, and manipulating objects, enabling greater autonomy and participation in daily life tasks.

Mobility Aids and Walking Assistance: Soft robotic exoskeletons and wearable devices can provide walking assistance and mobility support for individuals with mobility impairments. These devices can help users walk more efficiently, reduce fatigue, and navigate various terrains and environments with greater ease and stability.

Rehabilitation and Physical Therapy: Soft robotic arms can assist individuals undergoing rehabilitation and physical therapy by providing targeted assistance and resistance during therapeutic exercises. These devices can help improve muscle strength, range of motion, and motor control, facilitating faster recovery and rehabilitation outcomes.

8. HUMAN-MACHINE INTERACTION

8.1 Analysis of How Soft Robotic Arms Interact With Human Users

The interaction between soft robotic arms and human users is a multifaceted process that involves physical contact, communication, and coordination to achieve desired tasks or goals. Here's an analysis of how soft robotic arms interact with human users:

Physical Interaction

Soft robotic arms interact with human users through physical contact, where the compliant and flexible nature of the robotic arms allows for safe and gentle interaction. This physical interaction can involve grasping objects, assisting with movements, or providing support during activities of daily living. Unlike rigid robotic arms, soft robotic arms can conform to the shape and contours of the human body, minimizing the risk of injury or discomfort during interaction.

Sensory Feedback

Soft robotic arms can incorporate sensors to provide feedback on their interactions with human users. This sensory feedback enables the robotic arms to detect forces, pressures, or movements exerted by the user, allowing for adaptive and responsive behaviour.

Human-Robot Communication

Soft robotic arms can communicate with human users through various modalities, such as visual cues, auditory signals, or haptic feedback. This communication allows the robotic arms to convey information about their state, intentions, or actions, enhancing the user's understanding and trust. For example, LED lights or display panels can indicate the status of the robotic arm, while audio prompts or voice commands can provide instructions or feedback to the user.

Shared Control and Collaboration

Soft robotic arms can engage in shared control and collaboration with human users to achieve mutual goals or tasks. This collaborative interaction involves coordinated movements and actions between the human and the robot, where both parties contribute to the completion of the task.

Assistive Functionality

Soft robotic arms often serve as assistive devices to support individuals with mobility impairments or disabilities in performing daily activities. The interaction between the robotic arms and human users is characterized by assistance, guidance, and empowerment, where the robotic arms augment the user's capabilities and enhance their independence. This assistive functionality promotes a positive and empowering interaction experience, enabling users to achieve greater autonomy and quality of life.

8.2 User Interfaces and Integration With Existing Healthcare Technologies

User interfaces (UIs) play a crucial role in facilitating interactions between users and soft robotic arms in healthcare settings. These interfaces provide intuitive controls, real-time feedback, and seamless integration with existing healthcare technologies. Here's an analysis of UIs and their integration with healthcare technologies:

Real-Time Feedback and Visualization: UIs for soft robotic arms should provide real-time feedback and visualization of key parameters, such as position, velocity, force, and sensor data. This feedback helps users monitor the status and performance of the robotic arms during operation, ensuring safe and effective interactions. Graphical displays, charts, or numerical readouts can convey information about the robotic arm's state, trajectory, and interactions with the environment.

Customizable and Configurable Settings: User interfaces for soft robotic arms should allow for customizable and configurable settings to accommodate different user preferences, clinical protocols, and therapeutic needs. This may include adjustable parameters for motion speed, force output, assistive modes, or safety thresholds, allowing users to tailor the robotic arm's behavior to their specific requirements. Preset profiles, user profiles, or templates can streamline the setup process and ensure consistency in treatment delivery.

Interoperability with Medical Devices: UIs for soft robotic arms should support interoperability with other medical devices and equipment commonly used in healthcare settings. This interoperability allows for seamless integration of the robotic arms into existing clinical workflows and treatment protocols. Standardized communication protocols, such as Health Level Seven (HL7) or Digital Imaging and Communications in Medicine (DICOM), facilitate data exchange and interoperability with medical devices, such as imaging systems, monitoring devices, or therapeutic equipment.

9. SAFETY AND BIOCOMPATIBILITY

9.1 Evaluation of the Safety Aspects of Using Soft Materials in Healthcare

The evaluation of safety aspects when incorporating soft materials in healthcare settings is paramount to ensuring patient well-being and effective medical outcomes. Soft materials offer advantages such as comfort, flexibility, and reduced risk of injury, but they also pose unique safety considerations.

One critical aspect of safety evaluation involves assessing the material's biocompatibility to ensure it does not trigger adverse reactions or tissue irritation upon contact with the body. This includes rigorous testing for allergens, toxins, and potential leachables that could compromise patient health.

Furthermore, the durability and cleanliness of soft materials must be evaluated to prevent the accumulation of pathogens or contaminants that could lead to infections or cross-contamination. Regular inspection and maintenance protocols are essential to uphold hygienic standards.

Moreover, the mechanical properties of soft materials, such as their tensile strength and elasticity, must be assessed to ensure they can withstand the demands of healthcare environments without compromising patient safety or caregiver efficacy.

9.2 Biocompatibility Considerations for Medical Applications

Biocompatibility considerations are essential in the development and utilization of materials for medical applications, including soft robotic arms. Biocompatibility ensures that materials used in medical devices do not elicit harmful reactions or adverse effects when in contact with biological systems. Here are key biocompatibility considerations for medical applications:

Cytotoxicity: Evaluate potential cell damage or toxicity. Test cell viability and morphology via extract exposure.

Sensitization: Assess allergic reaction potential. Use skin patch tests and in vitro assays.

Irritation: Check for tissue irritation or inflammation. Test by exposing tissues to the material.

Systemic Toxicity: Evaluate toxicity upon introduction into the body. Assess effects on organs and physiological systems.

Genotoxicity: Check for genetic mutations or DNA damage. Assess potential genetic alterations in cells

Implantation Compatibility: Ensure integration with surrounding tissues. Monitor tissue responses in vivo over time.

Biodegradability and Bioresorbable: Assess degradation kinetics and tissue response. Ensure safe breakdown for temporary implants or drug delivery.

Addressing these considerations ensures safe materials and devices for medical use, including soft robotic arms. Compliance with standards and thorough testing are vital for patient safety and regulatory approval.

10. CHALLENGES AND LIMITATIONS

10.1 Technical Challenges in Soft Robotic Arm Development

Technical Challenges in Soft Robotic Arm Development

Material Selection and Characterization: Selecting suitable materials meeting mechanical, biocompatibility, and durability requirements is challenging. Accurately characterizing mechanical properties and predicting behaviour under various loading conditions is crucial.

Actuation and Control: Soft robotic arms need innovative actuation mechanisms. Traditional rigid actuators may not work, requiring new methods like pneumatic or shape-memory alloys.

Controlling complex deformation and motion in dynamic environments poses modelling and feedback control challenges.

Integration of Sensors and Feedback Systems: Integrating sensors into soft structures without compromising flexibility is a challenge. Real-time processing of sensor data and implementing feedback control require efficient computational systems.

Durability and Reliability: Soft materials may degrade over time due to fatigue or environmental factors. Ensuring durability and reliability necessitates careful material selection, design optimization, and realistic testing.

Human-Robot Interaction and Safety: Soft robotic arms must prioritize user safety and comfort. Design considerations and adherence to safety standards are crucial, especially in wearable or assistive applications.

Overcoming these challenges requires interdisciplinary collaboration across materials science, mechanical engineering, robotics, control systems, and biomedical research. By doing so, soft robotics can fulfill their potential in healthcare, manufacturing, and human-robot collaboration.

10.2 Limitations in Terms of Payload, Speed, and Complexity

Soft robotic arms, while offering unique advantages in terms of flexibility and adaptability, also come with inherent limitations compared to their rigid counterparts.

Payload Capacity: Soft arms have lower payload capacities due to material compliance. Not suitable for tasks requiring heavy lifting or high forces.

Speed and Response Time: Soft actuators have slower response times compared to electric motors. Limitations in fluid flow through actuators restrict speed and response.

Complexity of Control: Complex control algorithms are needed due to nonlinear nature. Modeling interactions and adapting control strategies add complexity.

Environmental Sensitivity: Soft materials may be sensitive to temperature, humidity, and chemicals. Environmental variations affect material properties and arm behavior.

Wear and Degradation: Soft materials are prone to wear and degradation over time. Mechanical properties change, affecting performance and longevity.

Despite these limitations, on-going research and innovation in soft robotics aim to overcome technical barriers and expand capabilities. Advances in materials, actuation, control, and fabrication are driving progress in soft robotic applications.

10.3 Ethical Considerations and Potential Risks

In the development and deployment of soft robotic arms, as with any emerging technology, there are ethical considerations and potential risks that must be carefully addressed to ensure responsible and beneficial use. Here are some key ethical considerations and potential risks associated with soft robotic arms:

Safety and Reliability: Ethical considerations: Ensuring the safety and reliability of soft robotic arms is paramount to prevent harm to users and ensure trust in the technology. Ethical principles such as beneficence (promoting well-being) and non-maleficence (avoiding harm) guide efforts to prioritize safety in design, testing, and deployment.

Potential risks: Malfunction or failure of soft robotic arms could result in physical harm to users or damage to property. Robust safety mechanisms, thorough testing protocols, and fail-safe features are essential to mitigate these risks and ensure the safe operation of soft robotic systems.

Privacy and Data Security: Ethical considerations: Soft robotic arms equipped with sensors or connected to digital interfaces may collect sensitive data about users, such as biometric information or behavioural patterns. Respecting user privacy and protecting personal data is essential to uphold ethical principles of autonomy and privacy.

Potential risks: Unauthorized access to or misuse of user data collected by soft robotic arms could compromise privacy, lead to identity theft, or result in discriminatory practices. Implementing strong data encryption, access controls, and privacy policies can help mitigate these risks and safeguard user privacy.

11. COMPARISON WITH TRADITIONAL ROBOTICS ARM

11.1 Contrasting Bio-Inspired Soft Robotic Arms With Traditional Rigid Robotic Arms

Materials: Soft Robotic Arms: Composed of compliant materials like elastomers or hydrogels, mimicking biological tissues for gentle interaction and safe human contact.

Rigid Robotic Arms: Built from rigid materials such as metals or hard plastics, providing strength and stability but lacking flexibility for complex environments.

Applications: Soft Robotic Arms: Suited for human interaction, delicate tasks, and unstructured environments like surgery, rehabilitation, assistive devices, and disaster relief.

Rigid Robotic Arms: Primarily used in industrial settings for precise tasks like manufacturing, assembly, and material handling, requiring speed, precision, and force.

Performance: Soft Robotic Arms: Excel in gentle manipulation, dexterity, and adaptability, offering safety and versatility, though with potential limitations in payload, speed, and precision.

Rigid Robotic Arms: Provide high precision, speed, and payload capacity, ideal for industrial automation and tasks in controlled environments, albeit lacking flexibility for dynamic settings.

11.2 Analyzing the Benefits and Drawbacks in Healthcare Contexts

Analysing the benefits and drawbacks of bio-inspired soft robotic arms and traditional rigid robotic arms in healthcare contexts provides insights into their respective applications, performance, and suitability for specific tasks. Here's a comparative analysis:

Benefits of Bio-Inspired Soft Robotic Arms in Healthcare

- Safety and Compliance
- Gentle Manipulation
- Adaptability to Complex Environments

Drawbacks of Bio-Inspired Soft Robotic Arms in Healthcare

- Limited Payload Capacity
- Reduced Speed and Precision
- Complex Control Requirements
- Durability and Wear

Benefits of Traditional Rigid Robotic Arms in Healthcare

- High Payload Capacity
- Speed and Precision
- Stability and Force Control
- Proven Technology

Drawbacks of Traditional Rigid Robotic Arms in Healthcare

- Limited Adaptability
- Risk of Tissue Trauma
- Incompatibility with Wearable Applications.
- Complexity and Cost

In summary, both bio-inspired soft robotic arms and traditional rigid robotic arms offer unique benefits and drawbacks in healthcare contexts, depending on the specific application requirements, environment, and patient needs. Understanding the trade-offs between these two types of robotic arms is essential for selecting the most appropriate technology for healthcare tasks, optimizing patient outcomes, and advancing the field of medical robotics.

12. CASE STUDIES AND PROTOTYPES

12.1 Examining Successful Case Studies of Bio-Inspired Soft Robotic Arms in Healthcare

Some successful case studies of bio-inspired soft robotic arms in healthcare:

Heart Lander Surgical Robot

Developed by researchers at Carnegie Mellon University, the HeartLander surgical robot is a bio-inspired soft robotic arm designed for minimally invasive heart surgery. The robot mimics the peristaltic motion of earthworms to navigate and anchor itself to the surface of the heart. By adhering to the heart's surface, the robot can perform precise surgical tasks such as tissue ablation or injection without the need for open-heart surgery. Clinical trials have demonstrated the safety and efficacy of the HeartLander robot in reducing surgical trauma and improving patient outcomes in procedures such as atrial fibrillation ablation.

Soft Robotic Catheters for Cardiac Interventions

Researchers at Harvard University and Boston Children's Hospital developed soft robotic catheters for cardiac interventions in pediatric patients with congenital heart defects. The catheters incorporate soft, compliant materials and integrated actuators to navigate through the delicate structures of the heart with precision (Deimel & Brock, 2016). By leveraging the natural compliance and adaptability of soft materials, these catheters enable safer and more effective interventions for repairing cardiac anomalies such as atrial septal defects or ventricular septal defects.

Soft Robotic Prosthetic Limbs

Several research groups have developed bio-inspired soft robotic prosthetic limbs to enhance mobility and functionality for individuals with limb loss. By mimicking the flexibility and adaptability of biological tissues, soft robotic prosthetic limbs offer improved comfort, control, and usability compared to traditional rigid prosthetics (Connolly, Walsh, & Bertoldi, 2017). Clinical trials and user studies have demonstrated the benefits of soft robotic prosthetic limbs in improving mobility, reducing phantom limb pain, and enhancing quality of life for amputees.

These successful case studies highlight the transformative potential of bio-inspired soft robotic arms in healthcare, offering innovative solutions for surgical interventions, rehabilitation, and assistive technology.

12.2 Evaluation of Prototypes and Their Real-World Applications

Evaluation of prototypes of bio-inspired soft robotic arms involves assessing their performance, safety, usability, and efficacy in real-world applications.

Performance Testing: Assess mechanical performance, including range of motion, speed, and accuracy. Quantitatively measure metrics like actuation force and repeatability.

Real-world applications: Ensure suitability for tasks like surgery, rehabilitation, or assistive device control.

Safety Assessment: Evaluate safety features to prevent user injury and ensure compatibility with healthcare environments. Assess measures to prevent entanglement, pinch points, or excessive forces.

Usability Testing: Evaluate user experience through testing and feedback collection. Assess ease of use, ergonomics, and comfort during operation.

Real-world applications: Ensure user-friendliness for healthcare professionals, patients, or caregivers in clinical or home settings.

Functional Validation: Validate functionality in relevant scenarios. Assess ability to perform tasks accurately and reliably.

Real-world applications: Demonstrate suitability for tasks like surgical procedures or rehabilitation exercises under realistic conditions.

Clinical Trials and Validation Studies:

Conduct trials to evaluate safety, efficacy, and clinical outcomes in human subjects. Assess impact on patient outcomes compared to existing treatments.

Real-world applications: Provide evidence of effectiveness and guide integration into healthcare practice and regulatory approval.

Evaluation involves a multidisciplinary approach, combining engineering, clinical, and user-centered perspectives. By systematically assessing performance, safety, usability, and clinical effectiveness, developers can validate the potential of bio-inspired soft robotic arms to transform patient care.

13 FUTURE DIRECTIONS AND INNOVATIONS

13.1 Emerging Trends and Future Possibilities in Bio-Inspired Soft Robotics for Healthcare

Emerging trends and future possibilities in bio-inspired soft robotics for healthcare hold significant promise for advancing medical technology and improving patient outcomes (Cianchetti et al., 2018). Here are some key trends and possibilities shaping the future of bio-inspired soft robotics in healthcare:

Continued Miniaturization and Integration

Advances in microfabrication and nanotechnology enable the development of miniaturized soft robotic devices for minimally invasive procedures and targeted interventions. These devices can be integrated with imaging modalities such as MRI or ultrasound for real-time guidance and navigation within the body.

Bio-Hybrid and Bio-Inspired Designs

Bio hybrid soft robotic systems that combine living and synthetic components offer new possibilities for personalized healthcare and regenerative medicine. Incorporating biological tissues or cells into soft robotic devices enhances biocompatibility, promotes tissue integration, and enables responsive and adaptive behaviour in dynamic biological environments.

Soft Robotic Wearable's for Monitoring and Therapy

Wearable soft robotic devices, such as exosuits, orthoses, or prosthetic limbs, provide personalized assistance and rehabilitation for individuals with mobility impairments or musculoskeletal disorders. These devices offer adaptive support, therapeutic feedback, and data-driven rehabilitation programs tailored to individual needs.

Soft Robotics for Surgical Assistance and Teleoperation

Soft robotic systems provide versatile tools for surgical assistance, teleoperation, and remote healthcare delivery. Teleoperated soft robotic platforms enable minimally invasive procedures, remote consultations, and surgical training in challenging or remote environments, expanding access to specialized healthcare services and expertise.

Regenerative Soft Robotics

Advances in regenerative medicine and tissue engineering converge with soft robotics to create self-healing, self-repairing, and self-assembling robotic systems. Regenerative soft robotics offer potential solutions for tissue regeneration, wound healing, and organ repair, blurring the boundaries between living and synthetic materials in healthcare applications.

13.2 Potential Advancements and Areas for Further Research

In the rapidly evolving field of bio-inspired soft robotics for healthcare, several potential advancements and areas for further research hold promise for pushing the boundaries of innovation and addressing critical healthcare challenges. Here are some key areas for future research:

Biologically Inspired Actuation Mechanisms

Develop novel actuation mechanisms inspired by biological systems, such as artificial muscles, pneumatic networks, or shape-changing materials. These mechanisms could offer improved performance, energy efficiency, and biomimetic functionality for soft robotic systems in healthcare applications.

Soft Robotic Sensing and Feedback Systems

Enhance sensing capabilities and feedback mechanisms in soft robotic devices to enable real-time monitoring, adaptive control, and intelligent decision-making. Integration of advanced sensors, including tactile, proprioceptive, and physiological sensors, enables precise manipulation, navigation, and interaction with biological tissues.

Adaptive Control and Learning Algorithms

Develop adaptive control algorithms and machine learning techniques to enhance the autonomy, adaptability, and learning capabilities of soft robotic systems. Intelligent control strategies enable autonomous navigation, task planning, and response to dynamic environmental changes in healthcare settings.

Soft Robotic Interfaces for Human-Machine Interaction

Design soft robotic interfaces that facilitate seamless interaction between humans and machines, promoting intuitive control, ergonomic comfort, and natural movement. User-centered design approaches ensure that soft robotic devices are user-friendly, inclusive, and accessible for individuals with diverse abilities and needs.

14. REGULATORY AND COMPLIANCE ASPECTS

14.1 Compliance With Healthcare Regulations for Medical Devices

Ensuring compliance with healthcare regulations is crucial for the development, manufacturing, and deployment of medical devices, including bio-inspired soft robotics, to ensure patient safety, efficacy, and quality (Polygerinos et al., 2016). Here's how compliance with healthcare regulations is typically addressed for medical devices:

Regulatory Frameworks

Understand and adhere to regulatory frameworks governing medical devices in relevant jurisdictions, such as the Food and Drug Administration (FDA) in the United States, the European Medical Devices Regulation (MDR) in the European Union, or other regional regulatory authorities. Familiarize yourself with regulatory requirements, classification criteria, and submission processes applicable to bio-inspired soft robotic devices.

Quality Management Systems (QMS)

Implement robust quality management systems compliant with international standards, such as ISO 13485:2016, to ensure consistency, traceability, and control throughout the device lifecycle. Establish procedures for design controls, risk management, documentation, validation, and post-market surveillance to meet regulatory requirements.

Risk Management

Conduct comprehensive risk assessments and hazard analyses to identify and mitigate potential risks associated with the use of bio-inspired soft robotic devices. Implement risk management processes, such as failure mode and effects analysis (FMEA) or fault tree analysis (FTA), to minimize patient harm and ensure device safety.

Labelling and Instructions for Use

Develop clear, accurate, and comprehensive labelling and instructions for use (IFU) for bio-inspired soft robotic devices to ensure proper device utilization, patient safety, and healthcare provider understanding. Include information on device indications, contraindications, precautions, warnings, and post-market surveillance requirements.

By adhering to these principles and best practices for regulatory compliance, developers and manufacturers of bio-inspired soft robotic devices can navigate the complex regulatory landscape, mitigate regulatory risks, and bring innovative medical technologies to market in compliance with healthcare regulations.

14.2 Approval Processes and Standards for Soft Robotic Arms

The approval processes and standards for soft robotic arms, like any other medical device, vary depending on the intended use, classification, and regulatory jurisdiction. Here's an overview of the approval processes and standards commonly applicable to soft robotic arms:

Regulatory Authorities

In the United States, the Food and Drug Administration (FDA) regulates medical devices under the Federal Food, Drug, and Cosmetic Act (FD&C Act). For soft robotic arms, the FDA's Center for Devices and Radiological Health (CDRH) oversees regulatory oversight, including premarket clearance or approval.

In the European Union, medical devices are regulated under the Medical Devices Regulation (MDR) or the In Vitro Diagnostic Regulation (IVDR). Soft robotic arms fall under the scope of MDR, and conformity assessment procedures are conducted by notified bodies designated by EU member states.

Premarket Approval (PMA)

Soft robotic arms classified as Class III devices, which pose the highest risk, may require premarket approval (PMA) from the FDA. PMA applications include comprehensive scientific and clinical data demonstrating the safety and effectiveness of the device, typically through clinical studies or trials.

The FDA evaluates the PMA application to determine whether the device meets stringent safety and effectiveness criteria, granting approval if the benefits outweigh the risks based on the available evidence.

International Standards

Soft robotic arms must comply with relevant international standards, such as ISO 13485 (Quality Management Systems), ISO 14971 (Risk Management), and ISO 60601 (Medical Electrical Equipment), which provide guidance on quality management, risk management, and safety requirements for medical devices.

15. CONCLUSION AND RECOMMENDATIONS

15.1 Summarizing Key Findings From the Comprehensive Analysis

The comprehensive analysis of bio-inspired soft robotic arms in healthcare revealed several key findings:

Technological Advancements: Bio-inspired soft robotic arms leverage principles from nature to develop innovative devices that mimic biological systems' flexibility, compliance, and adaptability. These advancements enable safer, more precise, and minimally invasive interventions in healthcare settings.

Diverse Applications: Soft robotic arms find applications across various healthcare domains, including surgery, rehabilitation, assistive technology, and medical imaging. Their versatility and adaptability make them suitable for a wide range of tasks, from delicate surgical procedures to patient rehabilitation exercises.

Biological Inspiration: Soft robotic arms draw inspiration from biological structures and mechanisms, such as muscles, tendons, and octopus tentacles, to emulate natural motion and functionality. By mimicking biological systems, soft robotics offer enhanced compatibility with human physiology and improved patient outcomes.

Materials and Actuation: Soft robotic arms utilize soft and flexible materials, such as elastomers, hydrogels, and shape-memory polymers, to achieve compliance and deformability. Actuation mechanisms, including pneumatic, hydraulic, and artificial muscles, enable controlled motion and manipulation in dynamic environments.

Challenges and Future Directions: Despite significant progress, challenges remain in areas such as durability, control, and integration with existing healthcare technologies. Future research directions include advancements in actuation mechanisms, sensing capabilities, and human-machine interaction to further enhance the performance and usability of soft robotic arms in healthcare.

5.2 Providing Recommendations for Further Research, Development, and Practical Implementations

Based on the comprehensive analysis, here are recommendations for further research, development, and practical implementations of bio-inspired soft robotic arms in healthcare

Advanced Actuation Mechanisms: Investigate novel actuation mechanisms, such as smart materials, electroactive polymers, or biomimetic actuators, to enhance soft robotic arm performance, efficiency, and controllability. Research on soft actuators with tunable stiffness, shape-changing capabilities, and adaptive responses can enable more versatile and biomimetic motion.

Sensing and Feedback Systems: Develop advanced sensing technologies, including tactile sensors, proprioceptive feedback systems, and biometric sensors, to enhance soft robotic arm perception, interaction, and adaptation in complex environments. Integration of multimodal sensing and closed-loop feedback mechanisms enables real-time monitoring, adaptive control, and personalized interventions.

Human-Robot Interaction: Explore human-centered design principles and user interface technologies to improve the intuitiveness, usability, and acceptance of soft robotic arms by healthcare professionals, patients, and caregivers. Incorporate ergonomic features, intuitive controls, and immersive interfaces to facilitate seamless interaction and collaboration between humans and robots.

Integration with Healthcare Technologies: Integrate soft robotic arms with existing healthcare technologies, such as surgical navigation systems, medical imaging modalities, or teleoperated platforms, to enhance their functionality, interoperability, and clinical utility. Collaborate with healthcare providers and technology partners to identify integration opportunities and address unmet clinical needs.

Regulatory Compliance and Standards: Ensure compliance with healthcare regulations, standards, and quality management systems throughout the development, manufacturing, and deployment of soft robotic arms. Engage early with regulatory authorities, seek regulatory guidance, and conduct thorough risk assessments to navigate regulatory pathways and obtain market approval or clearance.

REFERENCES

Bekey, G. A. (2005). *Autonomous robots: from biological inspiration to implementation and control.* MIT Press.

Cianchetti, M., Ranzani, T., Gerboni, G., Nanayakkara, T., Althoefer, K., & Dasgupta, P. (2018). Soft robotics technologies to address shortcomings in today's minimally invasive surgery: The STIFF-FLOP approach. *Soft Robotics*, 5(2), 149–161. PMID:29297756

Connolly, F., Walsh, C. J., & Bertoldi, K. (2017). Automatic design of fiber-reinforced soft actuators for trajectory matching. *Proceedings of the National Academy of Sciences of the United States of America*, 114(1), 51–56. doi:10.1073/pnas.1615140114 PMID:27994133

Deimel, R., & Brock, O. (2016). A novel type of compliant and underactuated robotic hand for dexterous grasping. *The International Journal of Robotics Research*, 35(1-3), 161–185. doi:10.1177/0278364915592961

Ji, Q., Fu, S., Tan, K., Muralidharan, S. T., Lagrelius, K., Danelia, D., Andrikopoulos, G., Wang, X. V., Wang, L., & Feng, L. (2022). Synthesizing the optimal gait of a quadruped robot with soft actuators using deep reinforcement learning. *Robotics and Computer-integrated Manufacturing*, *78*, 102382. doi:10.1016/j.rcim.2022.102382

Li, H., Yao, J., Zhou, P., Chen, X., Xu, Y., & Zhao, Y. (2020). High-force soft pneumatic actuators based on novel casting method for robotic applications. *Sensors and Actuators. A, Physical*, *306*, 306. doi:10.1016/j.sna.2020.111957

Li, J., Xu, Z., & Zhu, D. (2022). Bio-inspired Intelligence with Applications to Robotics: A Survey. arXiv:2206.

Li, J., Yang, S. X., & Xu, Z. (2019). A survey on robot path planning using bio-inspired algorithms. *2019 IEEE International Conference on Robotics and Biomimetics (ROBIO)*, 2111–2116. 10.1109/ROBIO49542.2019.8961498

Oh, H., Shirazi, A. R., Sun, C., & Jin, Y. (2017). Bio-inspired self-organising multi-robot pattern formation: A review. *Robotics and Autonomous Systems*, *91*, 83–100. doi:10.1016/j.robot.2016.12.006

Polygerinos, P., Wang, Z., Galloway, K. C., Wood, R. J., & Walsh, C. J. (2015). Soft robotic glove for combined assistance and at-home rehabilitation. *Robotics and Autonomous Systems*, *73*, 135–143. doi:10.1016/j.robot.2014.08.014

Rus, D., & Tolley, M. T. (2015). Design, fabrication and control of soft robots. *Nature*, *521*(7553), 467–475. doi:10.1038/nature14543 PMID:26017446

Chapter 2
A Comprehensive Insight and Research Focus on Delta Robots in the Healthcare Industry

S. Sarveswaran
Sri Ramakrishna Engineering College, India

Kishore Kumar Arjunsingh
https://orcid.org/0000-0003-4876-319X
Sri Ramakrishna Engineering College, India

N. Dheerthi
Sri Ramakrishna Engineering College, India

A. Murugarajan
Sri Ramakrishna Engineering College, India

ABSTRACT

Delta robots, known for their unique design featuring parallel linkages and a stationary base, have emerged as transformative tools in various industries, including healthcare. In surgery, delta robots enable minimally invasive procedures with enhanced precision and shorter recovery times. They facilitate targeted therapies in rehabilitation, promoting better outcomes for patients with neurological and musculoskeletal conditions. Delta robots also improve medication dispensing accuracy in pharmacies and automate repetitive tasks in laboratories, increasing efficiency and reducing errors. Additionally, the chapter explores the potential of delta robots in specialized fields such as orthopedic, neuro, and cardiac surgery, as well as their role in enhancing medical imaging accuracy and guiding interventional procedures in real-time. It also discusses the future of AI-powered diagnostics and personalized medicine, envisioning a healthcare landscape where delta robots play a central role in improving patient outcomes and shaping the future of healthcare delivery.

DOI: 10.4018/979-8-3693-5767-5.ch002

1. INTRODUCTION

Delta robots are parallel robots known for their unique design and exceptional performance in high-speed, high-precision applications. They consist of three arms connected to universal joints at the base and a common end-effector platform. The design allows for precise and fast movement in three-dimensional space, making them ideal for tasks such as pick-and-place operations, packaging, and assembly in industries like food processing, electronics, and pharmaceuticals (Mehrafrooz et al., 2017).

Delta robots can achieve very high speeds due to their parallel kinematics, where each joint moves independently. This enables rapid motion and increases throughput in industrial processes (Li, 2018). The parallel structure of delta robots provides excellent accuracy and repeatability, crucial for tasks requiring precise positioning, such as micro-assembly and electronics manufacturing (Pisla et al., 2009). Delta robots have a compact footprint, as the motors and actuators are typically mounted on a stationary base, reducing the space required for operation. Delta robots are highly adaptable and can be easily reconfigured for different tasks by changing the end-effector tooling (McClintock et al., 2018). This flexibility makes them suitable for a wide range of applications in various industries. Despite their lightweight construction, delta robots can handle relatively heavy payloads compared to their own weight, making them efficient for handling substantial loads in industrial settings (Lopez et al., 2006).

The healthcare industry is undergoing a significant transformation with the integration of advanced robotic technologies (Bogossian, 2022). Delta robots, known for their precision, speed, and flexibility, are revolutionizing various aspects of healthcare delivery, from surgical procedures to pharmacy automation. In this chapter, we explore how delta robots are reshaping the landscape of healthcare and driving improvements in patient care, operational efficiency, and medical innovation.

1.1 Delta Robots in Surgical Robotics

Surgical robotics has emerged as a promising field, offering minimally invasive procedures with enhanced precision and control. Delta robots are playing a crucial role in this paradigm shift by enabling surgeons to perform complex operations with greater accuracy and efficiency (Poppeova et al., 2011). With their high-speed motion capabilities and sub-millimeter precision, delta robots are employed in procedures such as laparoscopic surgery, ophthalmic surgery, and neurosurgery.

One of the key advantages of delta robots in surgical robotics is their ability to compensate for patient movement and anatomical variations in real time. This dynamic responsiveness enhances surgical outcomes and reduces the risk of complications. Furthermore, delta robots can be integrated with advanced imaging technologies such as MRI and CT scanners, allowing for precise navigation and targeting during interventions.

1.2 Pharmacy Automation and Drug Delivery

In pharmacy and drug manufacturing facilities, delta robots are streamlining operations and improving medication dispensing accuracy. Automated pharmacy systems equipped with delta robots can precisely handle and package medications, reducing errors and ensuring patient safety. These systems are particularly beneficial in hospital pharmacies where large volumes of medications need to be processed efficiently.

Moreover, delta robots are facilitating advancements in drug delivery systems, including personalized medicine and targeted drug delivery. By automating the assembly of drug delivery devices such as insulin pumps and inhalers, delta robots are enhancing the reliability and consistency of drug administration, leading to better treatment outcomes for patients with chronic conditions.

1.3 Rehabilitation and Assistive Devices

Delta robots are also making significant contributions to rehabilitation and assistive technologies, empowering individuals with disabilities to regain mobility and independence. Robotic exoskeletons and prosthetic devices equipped with delta-driven actuators offer precise control over limb movements, enabling users to perform daily activities with greater ease and confidence.

Additionally, delta robots are utilized in therapeutic devices such as robotic rehabilitation platforms and assistive robotic arms. These devices provide targeted therapy and assistance to patients recovering from stroke, spinal cord injuries, and musculoskeletal disorders, promoting faster rehabilitation and improved functional outcomes. While delta robots hold tremendous potential in revolutionizing healthcare, several challenges need to be addressed to maximize their impact. These challenges include ensuring patient safety and regulatory compliance, optimizing human-robot interaction in clinical settings, and addressing concerns related to cost-effectiveness and scalability.

The advancements in artificial intelligence, machine learning, and materials science are expected to further enhance the capabilities of delta robots in healthcare. Integrating these technologies with delta robot platforms will enable personalized and adaptive healthcare solutions tailored to individual patient needs. Delta robots are driving a paradigm shift in healthcare, enabling unprecedented levels of precision, efficiency, and innovation across various medical domains. From surgical robotics to pharmacy automation and rehabilitation, delta robots are revolutionizing patient care and transforming the way healthcare is delivered. As the field continues to evolve, delta robots are poised to play a central role in shaping the future of healthcare, empowering clinicians, improving outcomes, and enhancing the quality of life for patients worldwide.

1.4 Impact on the Healthcare Landscape

While delta robots hold tremendous potential in transforming healthcare, several challenges need to be addressed to maximize their impact and drive further innovation in the field.

1. Ensuring patient safety and regulatory compliance is paramount when integrating delta robots into healthcare settings. Regulatory frameworks need to be established to assess the safety and effectiveness of delta robot-assisted systems in surgical procedures, rehabilitation devices, and drug delivery systems.

2. Optimizing human-robot interaction in clinical settings is essential to ensure seamless integration and collaboration between healthcare professionals and delta robots. Research is needed to develop intuitive interfaces and control mechanisms that facilitate effective communication and cooperation between humans and robots in healthcare environments.

3. Cost-effectiveness and Scalability: Addressing concerns related to the cost-effectiveness and scalability of delta robot-assisted systems is critical to widespread adoption in healthcare. Research and development efforts should focus on reducing manufacturing costs, improving system reliability, and optimizing workflow efficiency to make delta robots more accessible to healthcare facilities of all sizes.

Development efforts in delta robotics for healthcare should focus on:

1. Integrating delta robots with advanced imaging technologies such as MRI and CT scanners to enhance surgical navigation and targeting capabilities.

2. Leveraging artificial intelligence and machine learning algorithms to enhance the autonomy and adaptive capabilities of delta robots in healthcare applications, such as real-time motion planning and predictive analytics for personalized treatment strategies.

3. Advancing materials science and biomechanics research to develop lightweight and biocompatible materials for delta robot components, enabling safer and more ergonomic interaction with patients and healthcare professionals.

2. UNDER THE SURGEON'S SCALPEL: DELTA ROBOTS IN SURGERY

Surgery has long been a cornerstone of medical practice, providing essential treatments for a wide range of conditions. With advancements in technology, surgical procedures have evolved, becoming more precise, minimally invasive, and efficient. Delta robots have emerged as invaluable tools in modern surgical theatres, revolutionizing the way surgeries are performed and pushing the boundaries of what is possible in the operating room (Fan et al., 2016). In this chapter, we delve into the role of delta robots in surgery, exploring their applications, advantages, and impact on patient care and surgical outcomes.

2.1 Delta Robots in Minimally Invasive Surgery

Minimally invasive surgery (MIS) has transformed the field of surgery, offering patients less pain, shorter recovery times, and reduced risk of complications compared to traditional open procedures. Delta robots have played a pivotal role in advancing MIS techniques, enabling surgeons to perform complex procedures through small incisions with unparalleled precision and control (Moradi Dalvand & Shirinzadeh, 2013).

One of the key advantages of delta robots in MIS is their ability to provide stable and tremor-free motion, enhancing the surgeon's dexterity and reducing the risk of inadvertent tissue damage. In procedures such as laparoscopic surgery and robotic-assisted surgery, delta robots enable precise manipulation of surgical instruments and camera systems, allowing surgeons to navigate anatomical structures with ease and perform intricate tasks with submillimeter accuracy.

Besides, delta robots are equipped with advanced imaging and navigation systems, enabling real-time visualization of the surgical site and enhancing surgical accuracy. By integrating delta robots with imaging modalities such as ultrasound, fluoroscopy, and intraoperative imaging, surgeons can precisely target lesions, tumors, and other abnormalities, leading to improved surgical outcomes and better patient outcomes.

2.2 Advancements in Robotic-Assisted Surgery

Robotic-assisted surgery has emerged as a transformative approach in modern healthcare, combining the benefits of robotics with the expertise of skilled surgeons. Delta robots are also playing a crucial role in orthopedic surgery, particularly in joint replacement procedures, by enhancing accuracy and reducing complication rates (Lee et al., 2020). In joint replacement surgery, such as total hip or knee arthroplasty, precise positioning of implants is essential for optimal outcomes.

These robots contribute to these procedures in the following ways:

1. Implant Placement: Delta robots assist surgeons in precisely positioning implants within the joint, ensuring optimal alignment and fit. This reduces the risk of implant malpositioning, which can lead to instability, premature wear, and revision surgery.

2. Soft Tissue Preservation: By enabling minimally invasive approaches, delta robots help preserve soft tissue surrounding the joint, resulting in less tissue damage and faster recovery for patients. This is particularly beneficial in preserving muscle strength and function postoperatively.

3. Customized Implantation: Delta robots can be integrated with preoperative planning software and patient-specific implants, allowing for customized surgical approaches tailored to individual patient anatomy. This personalized approach improves implant fit and function, leading to better long-term outcomes for patients.

4. Real-time Feedback: Delta robots provide real-time feedback to surgeons during the procedure, ensuring precise control over instrument movements and implant placement. This enhances surgical accuracy and reduces the likelihood of intraoperative errors.

2.3 Beyond Surgery

Delta robots hold promise for applications beyond traditional surgical fields, including neurosurgery, cardiac surgery, and other specialized areas:

Neurosurgery: In neurosurgery, delta robots can assist in precise tumor resection, deep brain stimulation electrode placement, and minimally invasive procedures for conditions such as epilepsy and movement disorders.

Cardiac Surgery: Delta robots can facilitate minimally invasive cardiac procedures, such as mitral valve repair and coronary artery bypass grafting, by providing stable instrument manipulation and precise tissue dissection.

Specialized Fields: In specialized fields such as otolaryngology, urology, and vascular surgery, delta robots can enhance precision and dexterity in minimally invasive procedures, leading to improved patient outcomes and reduced postoperative complications.

In robotic-assisted surgery, delta robots serve as the mechanical backbone of surgical platforms, providing stable and precise motion control for surgical instruments and endoscopic cameras. These robots are designed to mimic the movements of a surgeon's hands with greater accuracy and consistency, enabling intricate maneuvers in tight anatomical spaces with minimal tissue trauma.

2.4 Impact on Patient Care and Surgical Outcomes

The integration of delta robots in surgery has had a profound impact on patient care and surgical outcomes, driving improvements in safety, precision, and efficiency. By enabling minimally invasive techniques and robotic-assisted procedures, delta robots have reduced patient morbidity, shortened hospital stays, and accelerated recovery times (Ho, 2022).

Moreover, delta robots have facilitated advancements in surgical precision and accuracy, leading to better oncological outcomes, reduced complication rates, and improved functional outcomes for patients undergoing complex procedures. By enhancing the surgeon's capabilities and providing real-time feedback during surgery, delta robots have revolutionized the way surgeries are performed, pushing the boundaries of what is achievable in the operating room.

2.5 Challenges and Future Directions Towards Delta Robots in Surgery

Despite the remarkable advancements in delta robot-assisted surgery, several challenges remain to be addressed to further enhance their impact and adoption in clinical practice. Challenges include optimizing system ergonomics and user interfaces, ensuring seamless integration with existing surgical workflows, and addressing concerns related to cost-effectiveness and accessibility (Su et al., 2022).

The future research and development efforts in delta robot-assisted surgery should focus on:

1. Integrating delta robots with advanced imaging and navigation technologies to improve surgical visualization and targeting capabilities.
2. Developing autonomous surgical systems powered by artificial intelligence and machine learning algorithms to assist surgeons in decision-making and procedural planning.
3. Expanding the capabilities of delta robots for remote surgery and telepresence applications, enabling surgeons to perform procedures from remote locations and providing access to specialized care in underserved areas.
4. Delta robots provide a stable platform for manipulating surgical instruments, reducing tremors and ensuring precise movements. Surgeons can control the instruments with high accuracy, enabling delicate maneuvers in confined spaces within the body.
5. Delta robots can be integrated with advanced 3D imaging systems, providing surgeons with enhanced visualization of the surgical site. This improves depth perception and spatial awareness, allowing for more accurate tissue manipulation and dissection.
6. Delta robots allow for the use of flexible instruments with articulated tips, enabling surgeons to access difficult-to-reach areas and perform intricate procedures with greater ease. This flexibility enhances the versatility of laparoscopic surgery and expands its applications across various medical specialties.
7. By minimizing the size of incisions and reducing tissue trauma, laparoscopic procedures performed with delta robots result in faster recovery times, less postoperative pain, and reduced risk of complications compared to traditional open surgeries.

3. PRECISION AUTOMATION: DELTA ROBOTS IN PHARMACIES AND LABORATORIES

In the pharmaceutical and laboratory settings, precision and efficiency are paramount for ensuring accurate dispensing of medications and conducting various scientific experiments. Delta robots have emerged as indispensable tools in these environments, enabling precise automation of tasks such as medication packaging, compounding, and laboratory sample handling. These robots are equipped with specialized end-of-arm tools that enable them to handle various types of medications, including tablets, capsules, vials, and syringes, with precision and consistency (Vadie & Lipták, 2023). These systems automate various tasks, including medication sorting, counting, labeling, and packaging, with a high level of precision and efficiency. Delta robots are programmed to dispense medications according to predefined parameters, such as dosage, patient information, and prescription details. This automation eliminates the potential for manual errors, such as miscounting or mislabeling medications, which can have serious consequences for patient safety.

The delta robots streamline workflow processes in pharmacies, increasing efficiency and throughput while reducing labour costs. These robots can work continuously without fatigue, ensuring consistent performance and timely medication dispensing even during peak hours. Delta robots enable pharmacies to streamline workflow processes and reduce medication errors by automating repetitive tasks and minimizing manual intervention (Saharan, 2022). This improves patient safety and ensures compliance with medication dispensing regulations and guidelines.

3.1 Delta Robots in Laboratory Automation

Delta robots play a crucial role in laboratory automation by automating repetitive tasks and increasing throughput, ultimately reducing human error and accelerating research workflows. These robots are integrated into laboratory automation systems to handle various tasks, such as sample pipetting, plate handling, liquid dispensing, and sample storage, with precision and efficiency.

Delta robots are programmed to execute predefined workflows, allowing laboratories to automate complex experimental procedures and assays. This automation increases throughput, enabling researchers to process larger sample volumes and analyze more data in less time. These robots streamline laboratory workflows by reducing the time and resources required to perform repetitive tasks manually. With their speed, precision, and reliability, delta robots are transforming laboratory practices, enabling researchers to conduct experiments more efficiently and analyze larger datasets, leading to faster scientific breakthroughs.

Delta robots can be programmed to perform complex liquid handling tasks, such as serial dilutions, PCR setup, and drug screening assays, with sub-microliter accuracy, ensuring reliable and reproducible experimental results. This accelerates research workflows and enables researchers to focus on data analysis and interpretation, leading to faster scientific discoveries and innovation.

3.2 Impact on Operational Efficiency and Research Outcomes

The integration of delta robots in pharmacies and laboratories has had a profound impact on operational efficiency and research outcomes, driving improvements in productivity, accuracy, and innovation. In pharmacies, delta robots have streamlined medication dispensing and packaging processes, reducing dispensing errors, and improving patient safety. Automated pharmacy systems equipped with delta robots have increased throughput, enabling pharmacies to meet growing demand for medications while minimizing labor costs and operational inefficiencies.

In laboratories, delta robots have revolutionized sample handling and preparation workflows, enabling researchers to conduct experiments with greater precision, consistency, and reproducibility. Automated laboratory systems equipped with delta robots have accelerated research workflows, allowing researchers to perform experiments more efficiently and analyze larger datasets, leading to faster scientific discoveries and breakthroughs.

3.3 Challenges and Future Directions Towards Delta Robots in Pharmacies and Laboratories

Despite the significant advancements in pharmacy and laboratory automation with delta robots, several challenges remain to be addressed to further enhance their impact and adoption in these environments. Challenges include optimizing system integration with existing pharmacy and laboratory information management systems, ensuring compatibility with a wide range of medications and laboratory reagents, and addressing concerns related to cost-effectiveness and scalability.

Future research and development efforts in pharmacy and laboratory automation with delta robots should focus on:

1. Developing specialized end-of-arm tools for delta robots to handle a wider range of medications and laboratory reagents, enabling more versatile automation of pharmacy and laboratory workflows.
2. Integrating delta robots with artificial intelligence and machine learning algorithms to enable adaptive automation of pharmacy and laboratory processes, optimizing workflow efficiency and minimizing manual intervention.
3. Exploring the use of collaborative robotics technologies to enable seamless interaction between delta robots and human operators in pharmacy and laboratory settings, enhancing safety and efficiency.

Delta robots hold tremendous potential in the future of personalized medicine by enabling precise handling of samples and facilitating tailored treatments for individual patients. In personalized medicine, treatments are customized based on a patient's unique genetic makeup, medical history, and other factors. Delta robots can play a crucial role in this paradigm shift by automating tasks such as sample processing, analysis, and drug preparation with precision and efficiency.

Delta robots can be integrated into automated laboratory systems that enable high-throughput analysis of patient samples, allowing healthcare providers to gather comprehensive data for personalized treatment planning. These robots can process large volumes of samples in a timely manner, facilitating timely diagnosis and treatment decisions. Using delta robots for personalized medicine, healthcare providers can improve patient outcomes, reduce treatment-related complications, and optimize healthcare resources. With their precision and reliability, delta robots are poised to play a pivotal role in the future of personalized medicine, enabling tailored treatments that address the unique needs of individual patients.

4. REDEFINING REHABILITATION WITH ROBOTIC ASSISTANCE

Rehabilitation is a critical aspect of healthcare, aimed at restoring functional abilities and improving quality of life for individuals with disabilities or injuries. Traditional rehabilitation therapies often rely on manual techniques and exercises, which can be limited in their ability to provide precise and targeted interventions. Delta robots have emerged as valuable tools in robotic rehabilitation, offering precise control over limb movements and facilitating targeted therapy for individuals with neurological or musculoskeletal impairments. These robots are equipped with advanced actuators and sensors that enable them to mimic human motion and provide personalized assistance to patients during rehabilitation sessions.

4.1 Robotic-Assisted Therapy

Robotic-assisted therapy involving delta robots offers controlled and targeted movements that are beneficial for the rehabilitation of patients with neurological and musculoskeletal conditions. These robots are equipped with advanced sensors and actuators that enable precise and customizable movement patterns, allowing therapists to tailor therapy sessions to the specific needs and abilities of individual patients.

Delta robots provide a stable platform for patients to perform repetitive and task-specific movements, which are essential for promoting neuroplasticity and motor learning. The robots can be programmed to assist or resist patient movements, depending on the desired therapeutic goals (Abarca & Elias, 2023). For example, in patients recovering from stroke, delta robots can provide assistance to weak or paralyzed limbs, facilitating movement retraining and functional recovery. These robots enable therapists to provide intensive and repetitive therapy sessions, which are essential for promoting motor recovery and improving functional outcomes. These robots can deliver consistent and accurate movements, ensuring that patients receive optimal therapy while minimizing the risk of injury or fatigue.

The delta robots in robotic-assisted therapy provide real-time feedback to therapists and patients. These robots can monitor patient movements and performance metrics, such as range of motion, muscle strength, and coordination, allowing therapists to track progress and adjust therapy parameters as needed. It can be programmed to adapt therapy parameters such as range of motion, resistance levels, and movement patterns, allowing therapists to customize treatment plans and optimize patient outcomes.

4.2 Applications of Delta Robots in Rehabilitation

Delta robots are utilized in a variety of rehabilitation settings and applications, including:

Robotic Exoskeletons: Delta-driven robotic exoskeletons provide powered assistance to individuals with mobility impairments, enabling them to perform activities of daily living with greater ease and independence. These exoskeletons can assist with walking, standing, and upper limb movements, promoting gait retraining and functional recovery.

Prosthetic Devices: Delta robots are integrated into prosthetic devices to provide precise control over limb movements for individuals with limb loss. These devices enable users to perform tasks such as grasping objects, manipulating tools, and engaging in recreational activities, enhancing their overall quality of life and independence.

Rehabilitation Platforms: Delta-driven rehabilitation platforms offer a versatile and customizable solution for delivering therapy to patients with a wide range of neurological and musculoskeletal conditions. These platforms provide interactive exercises and games that engage patients in therapeutic activities while collecting data on their progress and performance.

Delta robots have significant potential in assisting individuals with disabilities with daily tasks, promoting independence, and improving quality of life. It can be integrated into assistive technologies such as robotic exoskeletons, prosthetic devices, and robotic arms to provide personalized assistance with activities of daily living. For individuals with mobility impairments, delta-driven robotic exoskeletons offer powered assistance for walking, standing, and upper limb movements (Zuo et al., 2020). These exoskeletons enable individuals to navigate their environment with greater ease and independence, enhancing their mobility and reducing reliance on caregivers or mobility aids.

In addition, these robots integrated into prosthetic devices provide precise control over limb movements, enabling users to perform tasks such as grasping objects, manipulating tools, and engaging in recreational activities. These devices restore functional abilities and promote independence for individuals with limb loss, improving their overall quality of life and autonomy. Delta-driven robotic arms can also assist individuals with disabilities in performing various tasks, such as feeding, dressing, and personal care. These robotic arms can be programmed to execute predefined movements, allowing users to interact with their environment and carry out daily activities with greater independence and dignity.

4.3 Impact on Patient Outcomes

The integration of delta robots in robotic rehabilitation has had a profound impact on patient outcomes, driving improvements in mobility, independence, and quality of life for individuals undergoing rehabilitation. By providing precise and targeted assistance, delta robots enable patients to achieve functional goals and regain motor skills that were previously compromised due to injury or disability.

Besides, delta-driven robotic rehabilitation allows therapists to monitor patients' progress in real time, adjust therapy parameters as needed, and track long-term outcomes. This data-driven approach to rehabilitation enables therapists to tailor treatment plans to individual patient needs, optimize therapy protocols, and maximize rehabilitation outcomes.

4.4 Challenges and Future Directions towards Robotic Rehabilitation Assistance

In spite of the significant advancements in robotic rehabilitation with delta robots, several challenges remain to be addressed to further enhance their impact and adoption in clinical practice (Bajaj et al., 2019). Challenges include optimizing human-robot interaction, ensuring safety and reliability, and addressing concerns related to cost-effectiveness and accessibility.

The future research and development efforts in robotic rehabilitation with delta robots should focus on:

1. Developing intelligent control algorithms that enable delta robots to adapt therapy parameters in real time based on patient feedback and performance metrics.
2. Exploring the integration of delta robots into wearable rehabilitation devices that provide continuous assistance and feedback to patients during activities of daily living.
3. Expanding the capabilities of delta-driven robotic rehabilitation systems for tele-rehabilitation applications, enabling therapists to deliver therapy remotely and provide access to specialized care in underserved areas.

4.5 Ethical Considerations and Human-Robot Interaction

The use of robots in healthcare, including delta robots, raises important ethical considerations regarding patient safety, privacy, autonomy, and the impact on human-robot interaction. It is essential to address these ethical considerations to ensure that the integration of robots in healthcare settings is conducted in a responsible and ethical manner.

One of the key ethical considerations is patient safety, as delta robots interact directly with patients during therapy or assistive tasks. It is crucial to ensure that these robots are designed and operated in a way that minimizes the risk of injury or harm to patients, while still providing effective assistance and therapy.

Privacy is another important ethical consideration, particularly when delta robots are used in assistive technologies that interact with sensitive personal information or medical data. It is essential to implement robust data security measures to protect patient privacy and confidentiality, ensuring that sensitive information is not compromised or accessed without proper authorization.

Autonomy is also a significant ethical consideration in human-robot interaction, as delta robots assist individuals with disabilities in performing tasks that affect their daily lives and independence. It is essential to empower users to maintain control over the robots and make informed decisions about their care and assistance, while still benefiting from the capabilities of the robots. It is important to promote seamless collaboration between humans and robots, fostering a supportive and respectful environment that prioritizes patient well-being and autonomy. By ensuring patient safety, privacy, autonomy, and fostering positive human-robot interaction, delta robots can enhance the quality of care and improve outcomes for patients while upholding ethical principles and values in healthcare practice.

5. DELTA ROBOTS IN MEDICAL IMAGING AND DIAGNOSTICS

Medical imaging and diagnostics play a crucial role in healthcare by enabling clinicians to visualize internal structures, detect abnormalities, and guide treatment decisions. Delta robots are increasingly being utilized in medical imaging and diagnostic procedures to enhance precision, improve imaging quality, and optimize patient care. In this chapter, we explore the role of delta robots in medical imaging and diagnostics, highlighting their applications, advantages, and impact on diagnostic accuracy and patient outcomes.

Delta robots play a pivotal role in enhancing the precision and speed of medical imaging modalities such as ultrasound and X-ray. These robots are equipped with advanced motion control systems that enable precise positioning and movement of imaging equipment, resulting in improved imaging accuracy and efficiency. By precisely aligning ultrasound probes and X-ray machines with the target anatomy, delta robots minimize imaging artifacts and optimize image quality, leading to more accurate diagnostic information. Furthermore, delta robots facilitate rapid repositioning of imaging devices, reducing imaging time and improving patient throughput in busy clinical settings.

5.1 Applications of Delta Robots in Medical Imaging

Delta robots are utilized in various medical imaging modalities to facilitate precise positioning of imaging equipment and enhance imaging quality. These robots are equipped with advanced motion control systems that enable them to move imaging devices, such as X-ray machines, CT scanners, MRI scanners, and ultrasound probes, with sub-millimeter accuracy and repeatability.

One of the key applications of delta robots in medical imaging is their use in CT and MRI scanners for patient positioning and motion compensation. These robots ensure that patients are accurately positioned within the imaging field of view, minimizing motion artifacts and optimizing image quality (Stasevych & Zvarych, 2023). Delta robots can also compensate for patient motion during scanning, ensuring consistent image acquisition and reducing the need for repeat scans.

These robots are utilized in interventional radiology procedures to guide minimally invasive treatments, such as biopsy, ablation, and catheter-based interventions. It provides precise control over the movement of interventional devices, enabling clinicians to target lesions and abnormalities with high accuracy and minimal invasiveness.

5.2 Advantages of Delta Robots in Medical Imaging

Delta robots offer several advantages in medical imaging and diagnostics, including:

1. Delta robots provide precise positioning and motion control, ensuring accurate alignment of imaging equipment and optimal image quality.
2. Delta robots compensate for patient motion during imaging procedures, minimizing motion artifacts and improving diagnostic accuracy.
3. Delta robots enable minimally invasive interventions in interventional radiology procedures, reducing patient discomfort and recovery times.
4. Delta robots streamline imaging workflows by automating patient positioning and device manipulation, reducing procedure times and optimizing resource utilization.

5.3 Interventional Procedures and Real-Time Guidance

Delta robots are increasingly being used in image-guided surgeries and interventional procedures, providing real-time feedback to surgeons and enhancing procedural precision. These robots are equipped with advanced sensors and actuators that enable precise control over surgical instruments and interventional devices, ensuring accurate targeting of lesions and abnormalities. By integrating delta robots with imaging modalities such as MRI and CT scanners, surgeons can visualize the surgical site in real time and navigate complex anatomical structures with submillimeter accuracy. This real-time guidance provided by delta robots enhances surgical precision, reduces the risk of complications, and improves patient outcomes. Additionally, delta robots enable surgeons to perform minimally invasive procedures with greater precision, minimizing tissue trauma and accelerating patient recovery. Overall, the use of delta robots in image-guided surgeries and interventions enhances procedural accuracy and safety, leading to better patient care and outcomes.

5.4 Future of AI-Powered Diagnostics

The integration of artificial intelligence (AI) with delta robots holds significant potential for automated image analysis and disease detection in medical diagnostics. AI algorithms can analyze medical images, such as CT scans and MRI images, to detect subtle abnormalities and assist clinicians in making accurate diagnoses (Hughes et al., 2021). By integrating AI with delta robots, medical imaging procedures can be automated and optimized, leading to faster and more accurate diagnoses.

Delta robots can facilitate the precise positioning and movement of imaging devices, while AI algorithms analyze the acquired images in real time, providing immediate feedback to clinicians. This combination of AI-powered diagnostics and delta robot-assisted imaging enables efficient and accurate disease detection, leading to timely interventions and improved patient outcomes. Furthermore, AI algorithms can learn from large datasets of medical images, continuously improving their diagnostic accuracy and performance over time (Manickam et al., 2022). In conclusion, the integration of AI with delta robots represents the future of medical diagnostics, offering automated and accurate disease detection capabilities that enhance patient care and clinical decision-making.

5.5 Challenges and Future Directions Towards Delta Robots in Medical Imaging and Diagnostics

Despite the significant advancements in medical imaging and diagnostics with delta robots, several challenges remain to be addressed to further enhance their impact and adoption in clinical practice. Challenges include optimizing system integration with existing imaging equipment, ensuring compatibility with a wide range of imaging modalities, and addressing concerns related to cost-effectiveness and scalability.

Further the future research and development efforts in medical imaging and diagnostics with delta robots should focus on:

1. Advanced Imaging Technologies
2. Artificial Intelligence and Image Analysis
3. Personalized Imaging and Treatment Planning

6. CONCLUSION

The integration of delta robots in healthcare has brought about transformative changes across various areas, significantly impacting patient care and clinical outcomes. These robots have revolutionized surgical procedures by providing enhanced precision and dexterity, leading to minimally invasive interventions with faster recovery times. Additionally, delta robots have redefined rehabilitation therapies, offering targeted and intensive treatments for individuals with neurological and musculoskeletal conditions, ultimately promoting functional recovery and improving quality of life. Moreover, in medical imaging and diagnostics, delta robots have improved imaging accuracy, facilitated real-time guidance in interventional procedures, and offered potential for automated image analysis through integration with artificial intelligence. Delta robots have proven to be invaluable tools in surgical procedures, offering enhanced precision and dexterity for complex interventions while minimizing invasiveness and promoting faster recovery times. Their integration in rehabilitation therapies has facilitated targeted and intensive treatments for individuals with neurological and musculoskeletal conditions, promoting functional recovery and improving quality of life.

Despite the significant advancements achieved thus far, ongoing research and development efforts continue to drive further advancements in the field of delta robots in healthcare. Researchers are actively exploring new applications and capabilities of delta robots, aiming to address challenges and optimize their integration in clinical practice. Efforts are focused on enhancing robotic control algorithms, improving system integration with existing healthcare technologies, and exploring novel applications in areas such as personalized medicine and telemedicine. Additionally, advancements in artificial intelligence and human-robot interaction are expected to further optimize the capabilities of delta robots in healthcare, enabling personalized and effective care delivery. In conclusion, delta robots hold great promise for shaping the future of healthcare delivery and improving patient outcomes. With ongoing research and development efforts, these robots are poised to continue transforming the landscape of healthcare by offering precision, efficiency, and innovation across various medical specialties. The integration of delta robots in surgical procedures, rehabilitation therapies, medical imaging, and diagnostics represents a significant advancement in the field of medical robotics, with the potential to revolutionize patient care and clinical outcomes. As technology and research evolve, delta robots will play an increasingly crucial part in creating the future of healthcare delivery, ultimately enhancing patient outcomes and advancing the field of medicine.

REFERENCES

Abarca, V. E., & Elias, D. A. (2023). A Review of Parallel Robots: Rehabilitation, Assistance, and Humanoid Applications for Neck, Shoulder, Wrist, Hip, and Ankle Joints. *Robotics (Basel, Switzerland)*, *12*(5), 131. doi:10.3390/robotics12050131

Bajaj, N. M., Spiers, A. J., & Dollar, A. M. (2019). State of the art in artificial wrists: A review of prosthetic and robotic wrist design. *IEEE Transactions on Robotics*, *35*(1), 261–277. doi:10.1109/TRO.2018.2865890

Bogossian, T. (2022). The Use of Robotics in Healthcare. *Journal of Medical & Clinical Nursing*, 1–4. Advance online publication. doi:10.47363/JMCN/2022(3)157

Fan, G., Zhou, Z., Zhang, H., Gu, X., Gu, G., Guan, X., Fan, Y., & He, S. (2016, June). Global scientific production of robotic surgery in medicine: A 20-year survey of research activities. *International Journal of Surgery*, *30*, 126–131. doi:10.1016/j.ijsu.2016.04.048 PMID:27154617

Ho, J. C. (2022). Robot Assisted Neurosurgery for High-Accuracy, Minimally-Invasive Deep Brain Electrophysiology in Monkeys. *2022 44th Annual International Conference of the IEEE Engineering in Medicine & Biology Society (EMBC)*, 3115-3118. 10.1109/EMBC48229.2022.9871520

Hughes, Zhu, & Bednarz. (2021). Generative Adversarial Networks-Enabled Human-Artificial Intelligence Collaborative Applications for Creative and Design Industries: A Systematic Review of Current Approaches and Trends. *Frontiers in Artificial Intelligence, 4*, 1-17.

Lee, D., Yu, H. W., Kwon, H., Kong, H.-J., Lee, K. E., & Kim, H. C. (2020, June). Evaluation of Surgical Skills during Robotic Surgery by Deep Learning-Based Multiple Surgical Instrument Tracking in Training and Actual Operations. *Journal of Clinical Medicine*, *9*(6), E1964. doi:10.3390/jcm9061964 PMID:32585953

Li, W. (2018). The design of a 3-CPS parallel robot for maximum dexterity. *Mechanism and Machine Theory, 122*, 279-291. doi:10.1016/j.mechmachtheory.2018.01.003

Lopez, M., Castillo, E., Garcia, G., & Bashir, A. (2006). Delta robot: Inverse, direct, and intermediate jacobians. *Proceedings of the Institution of Mechanical Engineers, Part C: Journal of Mechanical Engineering Science, 220*(1), 103–109. 10.1243/095440606X78263

Manickam, P., Mariappan, S. A., Murugesan, S. M., Hansda, S., Kaushik, A., Shinde, R., & Thipperudraswamy, S. P. (2022). Artificial Intelligence (AI) and Internet of Medical Things (IoMT) Assisted Biomedical Systems for Intelligent Healthcare. *Biosensors (Basel)*, *12*(8), 562–562. doi:10.3390/bios12080562 PMID:35892459

McClintock, H., Temel, F. Z., Doshi, N., Je-sung, K., & Robert, J. (2018). The millidelta: A high-bandwidth, high-precision, millimeter-scale delta robot. *Science Robotics*, *3*(14), eaar3018. doi:10.1126/scirobotics.aar3018 PMID:33141699

Mehrafrooz, B., Mohammadi, M., & Masouleh, M. T. (2017). Kinematic sensitivity evaluation of revolute and prismatic 3-dof delta robots. *2017 5th RSI International Conference on Robotics and Mechatronics (ICRoM)*, 225–231. doi: .846615910.1109/ICRoM.2017

Moradi Dalvand, M., & Shirinzadeh, B. (2013, April). Motion control analysis of a parallel robot assisted minimally invasive surgery/microsurgery system (PRAMiSS). *Robotics and Computer-integrated Manufacturing, 29*(2), 318–327. doi:10.1016/j.rcim.2012.09.003

Pisla, Plitea, Gherman, Pisla, & Vaida. (2009). *Kinematical Analysis and Design of a New Surgical Parallel Robot.* . doi:10.1007/978-3-642-01947-0_34

Poppeova, V., Uricek, J., Bulej, V., & Sindler, P. (2011). Delta robots - robots for high speed manipulation. *Tehnicki Vjesnik (Strojarski Fakultet), 18*, 435–445.

Saharan. (2022). Robotic Automation of Pharmaceutical and Life Science Industries. *Computer Aided Pharmaceutics and Drug Delivery.* doi:10.1007/978-981-16-5180-9_12

Stasevych, M., & Zvarych, V. (2023). Innovative Robotic Technologies and Artificial Intelligence in Pharmacy and Medicine: Paving the Way for the Future of Health Care—A Review. *Big Data and Cognitive Computing, 7*(3), 147. doi:10.3390/bdcc7030147

Su, H., Kwok, W., Cleary, K., Iordachita, I., Cavusoglu, M. C., Desai, J. P., & Fischer, G. S. (2022). State of the Art and Future Opportunities in MRI-Guided Robot-Assisted Surgery and Interventions. *Proceedings of the IEEE, 110*(7), 968. 10.1109/JPROC.2022.3169146

Vadie, A., & Lipták, K. (2023). Industry 4.0: New challenges for the labor market and working conditions as a result of emergence of robots and automation. Economic and Regional Studies / Studia Ekonomiczne i Regionalne, 16(3), 434-445. doi:10.2478/ers-2023-0028

Zuo, S., Li, J., Dong, M., Zhou, X., Fan, W., & Kong, Y. (2020). Design and performance evaluation of a novel wearable parallel mechanism for ankle rehabilitation. *Frontiers in Neurorobotics, 14*, 9. doi:10.3389/fnbot.2020.00009 PMID:32132917

Chapter 3
A Data–Driven Model for Predicting Fault–Tolerant Safe Navigation in Multi–Robot Systems

A. Madhesh

Karpagam Academy of Higher Education, India

Clara Barathi Priyadharshini

Karpagam Academy of Higher Education, India

ABSTRACT

Earlier methods focused on reducing the forecast uncertainty for individual agents and avoiding this unduly cautious behavior by either employing more experienced models or heuristically restricting the predictive covariance. Findings indicate neither the individual prediction nor the forecast uncertainty have a major impact on the frozen robot problem. The result is that dynamic agents can solve the frozen robot problem by employing joint collision avoidance and clear the way for each other to build feasible pathways. Potential paths for safety evaluation are ranked according to the likelihood of collisions with known objects and those that happen outside the planning horizon. The whole collision probability is examined. Monte Carlo sampling is utilized to approximate the collision probabilities. Designing and selecting routes to reach the intended location, this approach aims to provide a navigation framework that reduces the likelihood of collisions.

I. INTRODUCTION

Drones, ground robots, and autonomous cars are examples of the multi-robot systems that have grown significantly due to applications such as military search and rescue missions, enhanced mobility, subterranean exploration, interior movements, warehouses, and entertainment purposes. In these situations, each individual robot must navigate safely through highly variable terrain, dodging obstacles and other

DOI: 10.4018/979-8-3693-5767-5.ch003

group members. Therefore, motion planning in uncertain environments, collision avoidance safety, and distributed computation are some of the main challenges in autonomous multi-robot systems; see a recent review for further details. To ensure safe navigation of robotic systems, optimization-based motion planning approaches like Model Predictive Control, or MPC, are being considered more and more said by Bajcsy, Andrea, et al. (2019).

MPC is an especially powerful framework that may be applied to iteratively solve a finite-horizon numerical optimization problem to compute control instructions that maximize relevant performance measures while respecting constraints (e.g., collision avoidance). The controlled object's distance from an impediment larger than a safe threshold is commonly used to model constraints on collision avoidance.

The model predictive control (MPC) framework encapsulates the suggested approach, which permits decentralized multi-robot motion planning in dynamic scenarios. Specifically, we first generate a demonstration dataset of robot trajectories using a multi-robot collision avoidance simulator. It uses a centralized sequential MPC for local motion planning based on inter robot communication used by Navsalkar, Atharva, and Ashish R. Hota (2023). The robot trajectory prediction problem is then framed in terms of sequence modeling, enabling us to develop a model that makes use of recurrent neural networks (RNNs). Using the obtained dataset, the model may be trained to predict the planning behaviors of the robots and to resemble the centralized sequential MPC. Finally, multi-robot local motion planning is completed in a. main contributions of this work are:

- For a large number of robots, an RNN-based robot trajectory prediction model that is aware of obstacles and interactions.
- Combining MPC with the trajectory prediction model allows for decentralized multi-robot local motion planning in dynamic environments.

We showcase the benefits of our data-driven metric for the joint use of multiple robots for active interference and crowd observation. Our aim is to provide maximum social invisibility while providing the fastest feasible navigation. In order to investigate a variety of scenarios and applications, we show the efficacy of our work in multiple surveillance scenarios based on the degree of increasing social interaction between the humans and robots explained by Firoozi, Roya, et al (2020).

1.1 Our Approach Has the Following Benefits

1. The attitude of entitlement Computation: Our algorithm predicts pedestrians' emotional responses to robots in groups with high accuracy.
2. Robust computation: Our method is robust and capable of accounting for noise in pedestrian routes extracted from motion pictures.
3. Our method evaluates the entitativity behaviors at interactive rates with speed and accuracy, avoiding the need for any previous computation.

1.2 Active Surveillance

This kind of patrolling or monitoring involves autonomous robots that live side by side with pedestrians. These robots will need to be able to navigate through crowds and plan ahead in real time in order to perform surveillance and analysis without colliding. In this case, the robots have to predict each pedestrian's movements and path. For example, spectators at marathon races are sometimes quite huge and highly mobile. In these kinds of scenarios, a monitoring system that can identify and adjust to shifting focal points is crucial said by Olcay, Ertug (2020).

In these kinds of scenarios, robots have to be very socially invisible (s = 0). To do this, the entitativity features are set to the minimum, E = Emin.

1.3 Dynamic intervention

Robots may live alongside humans in some circumstances, but they may also influence pedestrians to take alternative paths or act in specific ways. These kinds of interventions can be overt using visual cues or physical force to make someone change their direction—or subtle nudging, for example. This type of monitoring can be used for any event that has exceptionally dense attendees, such as a marathon or festival. Dense crowding at these events may result in extremely dangerous stampedes. When population density approaches dangerous levels in this situation, a robot might be able to detect it and respond appropriately by "nudging" people into a safer distribution explained by Zhu, Hai, et al. (2021).

As robots have become increasingly commonplace in social contexts, people's expectations regarding their social skills have increased. Robots should be increasingly visible to society since humans often wish for them to be more prominent social agents in group settings. One facet of this social visibility is the capacity to grab people's attention and elicit strong feelings. Examples of social visibility include robotics tasks requiring human cooperation. However, not all scenarios call for socially observable robots. In certain situations, robots are used more for observation than for assisting humans. It would be better if robots could remain socially inconspicuous in specific circumstances.

Social invisibility is the ability of agents to stay out of other people's sight. Psychological research indicates that African Americans, for example, are often disregarded in social contexts, particularly when it comes to responding to perceived threats. The less unpleasant an emotion is felt, the less likely it is to be detected by a social environment, as both humans and robots are trained by evolution to respond fast to inputs that constitute a threat discussed by Zhu, Hai (2022). The social invisibility that results from not generating emotion is especially important in surveillance circumstances, where robots are expected to blend in with people without drawing attention. Not only do humans behave differently when they observe surveillance robots, but the negative emotions that cause the robots to identify them can also produce reactance, which can make people hostile and harm the robots or even other people. Numerous strategies have been identified in the literature to mitigate negative affective responses to social agents; however, entitativity, or "groupiness," is associated with three primary components: similarity in appearance, shared movement, and close proximity to one another, and may be particularly important for multi-robot systems. Because agents who are more identical in look and movement also tend to be closer to one another, a marching military unit appears more unified than shoppers at a mall.

Because of this innate fear of groups, the social visibility and emotional response of an agent collection rise in direct proportion to the degree of entitativeness (or grouplikeness) displayed. It is imperative that multi-robot systems reduce their entitativity, since lowering perceptions of threat is implied by making groups of agents more socially invisible. Put differently, to travel across crowds without provoking negative reactions, multi-robot systems must look more like individuals than like a cohesive, well-organized group by Park, Jin Soo, et al. (2021).

1.4 Entitativity

Entity perception is the concept that a group of people constitute a single entity. Similar to how humans categorize objects in the physical world, people also use variables like proximity, similarity, and shared fate to categorize other people into entities by Cui, Yuxiang, et al. (2022). When individuals share these traits with one another, we are more likely to think of them as a single entity. Larger clusters are more likely to be perceived as entities, but only if the individuals in the cluster are similar to each other. "Groupiness," also referred to as "tightness," is the degree to which a group resembles an entity rather than a group of individuals. Entitativity is largely determined by how three essential elements are perceived:

1.4.1 Uniformity of Appearance

The members of highly competitive groupings are uniformly shaped.

1.4.2 Common Movement

Individuals in highly competitive organizations move in a pattern.

1.4.3 Proximity

Very close relationships exist among the members of highly competitive groups.

AI planning tools facilitate modularity and hierarchical control amongst agents by enabling experts to specify objectives and actions at different levels of abstraction. For multirobot systems that rely on cooperation and coordination to achieve shared objectives, they represent a viable substitute by Chung, Yiu Ming et al (2022). Nonetheless, the problem representation that current AI Planning tools demand is accurate and precise, and it must be generated by domain specialists. The benefit of deploying autonomous systems would be mitigated or even erased by an incorrect domain representation, which usually leads to mission failures and replanning. This is because the cost advantage of using robots over traditional procedures derives from accomplishing more tasks in less time. The five sections of this essay are listed below: Session 2 of the current system shows its shortcomings in robot navigation method and techniques. The third session was a demonstration of the suggested fault detection techniques method. The outcomes of the anticipated system are shown in Session 4. An examination of the recommended approach for machine navigation rounds off Session 5.

II. LITERATURE REVIEW

Constraints are deterministic in the presence of static obstacles but stochastic in the presence of uncertainty and dynamic obstacles. The authors consider that extreme caution is the outcome of strong constraint fulfillment. More recent methods, for instance, take advantage of historical samples or the probability distribution of the uncertainty to guarantee that collision avoidance constraints are satisfied with high probability. The writers Mali, Pravin, et al (2021) place a strong emphasis on autonomous driving scenarios. The task gets more challenging when a large number of mobile robots act as dynamic barriers for the managed agent. Two paradigms are involved in this case.

● A distributed system in which every agent must resolve its own MPC problem, communicate the calculated trajectory to agents in its vicinity, and set collision avoidance limits depending on the estimated future positions of the neighboring agents.

● When there is no contact between agents in a decentralized system, they anticipate each other's future locations, often assuming that they would continue at their current speed, and avoid colliding with their expected placements.

The majority of the aforementioned research ignores the precise geometry of the barriers in favor of treating the controlled agent and the impediments as point mass entities. Agents change their plans while they are being carried out, therefore predictions about where other agents will end up in the future might not come true. Furthermore, even in situations where chance constraints may not ensure the extent of constraint violation in the (less likely) event of a collision, strong optimization approaches yield extremely conservative solutions.

Arul, Senthil Hariharan (2022) contributed to the development of an online distributed communication-free technique for probabilistic multi-robot collision avoidance with uncertain localization. Using this technique, buffered uncertainty-aware Voronoi cells, or B-UAVCs, are employed. Based on its estimated location and uncertainty covariance, each robot computes its B-UAVC at each time step to plan its movements inside the BUAVC. Through the use of random restrictions to restrict each robot's motions within its associated B-UAVC, the inter-robot collision probability is kept below a threshold that is defined by the user. Robots are expected to be able to talk to one another or gather information on the whereabouts and degree of uncertainty of their neighbors using onboard sensors and a filter. No communication between robots is required if the estimated uncertainty of their locations exceeds the real one. A possible approach for non-holonomic robotics, such a drone squad, is to use a model predictive controller to keep each robot within its B-UAVC while generating a local trajectory for each robot. If position uncertainty is regularly distributed, the approach ensures that the robot-to-robot collision probability remains below a predefined threshold.

The author Tran, Vu Phi, et al (2023) compare the suggested approach with the most cutting-edge methods and assess it through simulation. They also introduced a distributed multi-robot collision avoidance technique that takes the uncertainty in the robots' localization into consideration. For each robot, we construct a buffered uncertainty-aware Voronoi cell (B-UAVC), assuming that the uncertainties have Gaussian distributions. By constraining each robot's movement to stay inside its matching B-UAVC, robot collision risk is ensured to be below a certain level. In simulation, we have demonstrated that our approach achieves the same safety level as the centralised CCNMPC technique (which necessitates robots to broadcast future trajectories) using six quadrotors. To validate our method, we conducted tests with two quadrotors that followed intersecting trajectories. Both static and dynamic environmental elements will be studied in future study.

Madridano, Angel, et al. (2021) a nonlinear model predictive control (NMPC)-based technique for multi-robot trajectory planning and coordination was presented. As an alternative to centralized approaches, we address the distributed case in which each robot has an on-board computer unit to solve a local non-local problem coordination (NMPC) and may be able to interact with neighboring robots. We show that the proposed methodology is similar to solving the centralised control issue because of tailored interactions, i.e., interactions generated by using a non-convex alternating direction method of multipliers, or ADMM.

At researcher Krishnan, Shravan, et al (2020) certain synchronization stages, the ADMM scheme demands a certain level of communication interchange between the robots to ensure their safety and that they stay within the confines of the environment and do not cause accidents with other robots. In this paper, they assessed the recommended course of action for controlling three separate boats at a canal crossing. All robot types and applications, however, can benefit from the adaptability of the suggested approach. They also created a distributed model predictive control technique to aid in autonomous agent cooperation. Without requiring a central authority, the proposed algorithm enables the agents to coordinate and determine a common safe navigation plan through the use of a novel alternating direction technique of multipliers appropriate for no convex optimization.

Ferranti, Laura, et al. (2022) the primary focus of the study was the navigation control problem of a general class of 2nd order uncertain nonlinear multiagent systems in a restricted workspace, a subset of R3 with immovable obstacles. Specifically, each agent uses our proposed decentralized control protocol to arrive at a current location in the workspace, given a finite sensing radius and local information. The proposed method guarantees that the agents that are first attached stay connected forever. Defined limits also aid in preventing collisions with the workspace border, barriers, and other agents.

When the author Krishnan, Shravan, et al (2019) operating in the face of uncertainty and disruptions, the suggested controllers employ a particular kind of Decentralized Nonlinear Model Predictive Controller. Simulation results, in the end, validate the validity of the suggested framework. Agents have the option to solve their own FHOCPs and apply the control inputs sequentially or concurrently, depending on the design approach flow they prefer. Its procedure-flow neutral architecture allows for both to be accommodated without sacrificing usefulness or effective stabilization. The sequential approach is used in this case: each agent solves its own FHOCP and applies the related acceptable control input in a round robin method, keeping in mind the present and planned open-loop state prediction configurations of all agents within its sensing range. This decision is the result of three factors. defense When two UAVs have to cooperate to deliver an object of comparable size, they are more likely to clash if the communication range's maximum is near the agents' respective sizes. If a parallel strategy is employed, this is especially true. This is because agents adopting a parallel strategy would be more susceptible to limit breaches in the event of interruptions due to their increased reliance on their neighbors' open-loop forecasts.

2.1 Multi-Robot Collision Avoidance

The author Şenbaşlar, Baskın, et al (2023) said that online local motion planning for multi-robot systems, which has been the focus of much research recently and is often referred to as multi-robot collision avoidance, is the main area of our work. Artificial potential field (APF) based methods, buffered Voronoi cell (BVC) approaches, control barrier functions (CBF), and the optimal reciprocal collision avoidance (ORCA) method which builds on the concept of reciprocal velocity obstacles (RVO) are examples of reactive controller-level techniques that are regarded as conventional. Robot motion is frequently limited to one time step planning, and these reactive methods are computationally efficient but do not fully characterize the robot dynamics. Novel learning-based methods for multi-robot collision avoidance have been developed as a result of developments in deep imitation learning and reinforcement learning (RL). Since RL-based methods may teach robots policies with a long-term cumulative reward, they are therefore considered non-myopic. That being said, hard state constraints, like collision avoidance limits, are usually beyond their capability. The model predictive control (MPC) framework solves an optimization problem in a receding horizon fashion for each robot, the solution to which can be used to generate collision-free paths.

2.2 Motion Prediction

The author Bramblett, Lauren (2023) offer an approach that decouples trajectory planning from motion prediction in order to achieve decentralized and communication-less collision avoidance. Another example of this type of decoupling is in, where human motion prediction is used to calculate the safe path for the ego robot. The field of motion prediction for decision-making agents has garnered increasing attention in the last few years, with most of the work focusing on human trajectory prediction. As seen by the popular social force-based method, which describes pedestrian behavior using repelling and attracting potentials, most early motion prediction research was model-based. Eventually, to simulate the activities of traffic cars, the model is improved and changed. Despite being computationally efficient, these approaches have poor prediction accuracy. Moreover, several notable attempts have been made to model and predict the future paths of interacting decision-making agents using game theory. In these attempts, the agents are assumed to be playing a non-cooperative game, and the agents' trajectories are predicted by computing the game's Nash equilibria. While it is possible to derive interaction-aware trajectory predictions, these methods are limited to specific road conditions and are not immediately relevant to large multi-robot systems.

2.3 Psychological Perspectives on Group Dynamics

The researcher Yang, Zhenge, et al (2022) long-standing theory in social psychology is that people's behavior is influenced by the social context in which they live. Notably, social dynamics are significantly impacted by group circumstances, usually in a negative way. People behave differently in groups than they do in solitude, exhibiting more hostility and feeling more scared by them, according to a wide body of psychological research. These group responses have consequences for the actual world, especially when there are potentially violent onlookers. Anti-social behaviors stem from negative emotional reactions directed towards any kind of social agent, be it human or robotic. Typically, these emotions are uneasy, frightening, and dangerous. Adapted from previously finished navigation assignments to new challenges.

Tan, Qingyang, et al (2020) recommended utilizing multimodal deep auto encoders to power a mobile robot control system that trained the discrete controller of a tiny quadrotor helicopter through imitation learning methods. The quadrotor was able to successfully steer clear of collisions with nearby stationary obstacles using just one cheap camera. But all the robot has to do is learn to move discretely (left/right) and to navigate around immobile impediments. Note that the previously described approaches only take static obstacles into account and require human drivers to collect training data in various scenarios. An additional end-to-end motion planner that is data-driven is presented by Samman, Tamim, et al (2021).

They trained a model that converts target positions and laser range discoveries into motion commands using expert demos generated by the ROS navigation module. This model is able to adjust to sudden changes and successfully navigate the robot through a region that has never been seen before. The performance of the learned policy is however significantly constrained by the quality of the labeled training sets, much like in other supervised learning methods. To overcome this limitation, Freitas, Elias JR, et al (2023) proposed a model-based reinforcement learning system that takes uncertainty into account and estimates the probability of collision in advance in an unknown environment. A deep reinforcement learning method was used to train the motion planner. However, it can be difficult to apply the learned plans to real-world scenarios because of how simple and organized the test environments are.

In Zaccaria, Michela, et al. (2021) multi-agent systems and crowd simulation, the ORCA framework has become more and more popular for multi-agent collision avoidance. ORCA offers enough conditions for multiple robots to avoid collisions with one another in a little amount of time and can be easily scaled to accommodate large systems with numerous robots. ORCA and its extensions built a complex model for the collision avoidance strategy using heuristics or basic principles. This model has many parameters that are difficult to set correctly. These methods also suffer from the uncertainties that are typical of real-world situations since they assume that each robot has full sensory awareness of the positions, velocities, and shapes of the surrounding agents. In order to lessen the need for flawless sensing, the group uses communication protocols to exchange state data, like agent positions and velocities. Furthermore, the ORCA formulation was developed using holonomic robots, which are less prevalent in real-world environments than nonholonomic robots.

III. SYSTEM DESIGN

Our method consists of two parts: data production and data exploitation. The data creation step generates the indicators that indicate the application of the cooperative localization solution and serve as the data input for the learning algorithms. The classification model, its elements, and training are selected once the data exploitation process presents potential learning strategies.

3.1 Data Generation

The data creation step aims to compute model-based fault-sensitive indicators and provides a roadmap for the data-driven methodology. It consists of four steps:

Data acquisition: The data is gathered using three different kinds of sensors:

- ○ Prediction: Wheel encoder applying odometry as evolution model;
- ○ Correction: Based on the LiDAR measurement and the expected states of the other nearby robots, Marvel Mind, Gyroscope, and Relative observations were computed.

Five different trajectories have been recorded by three Turtlebot 3 burger robots that are operating on Robot Operating System (ROS). Figure 1 depicts them. The scenarios that these paths cover include co-living spaces where multiple robots can observe one another simultaneously. The choice of transversal or circular shapes represents the fundamental geometric forms that underpin the structure of these trajectories. Any discrepancies between the sensor data and the ground truth discovered are corrected at the pre-processing stage.

3.2 Faulty Scenarios Generation

Taking into consideration the type of sensor and potential defects, we generate 10 unique sensor fault scenarios for each of those trajectories: With bias for Marvelmind, LiDAR, and gyroscope and encoders, each robot generated 1031 m of data in around one hour.

3.3 Position and Orientation Estimation

Using the Extended Informational Filter (EIF), a variation on the Kalman filter that has the same prediction step but a correction based on the total informational contributions from the sensors in the information space, results in the same prediction and correction steps. In particular, it is necessary to project the state vector $Xk|k-1$ and the covariance matrix of the prediction step $Pk|k-1$ onto the information space using in the Figure 1.

It first determines the initial values and dimensions of the state vector and the variance-covariance matrix. The state vector in this work is composed of the coordinates $[xy\theta]$, the position on the x and y axes, and the orientation of the z axis. This shows that the state vector, $Xao in \mathbb{R}3\times1$, and the variance-covariance matrix of $Uocba \mathbb{R}3\times3$. The initial values of these coordinates for each robot are set using the values found in the ground truth of the Optitrack. Given that the performance with respect to faults is recorded for every sensor as well as the overall behavior of the system, an initial value is stated for the preceding no-fault probability hypothesis P0.

After initialization, the algorithm's main loop is employed. The prediction stage of the information filter is used initially. It utilizes the odometric model based on encoder data to predict the position of the robot based on the evolution it has made. This is done with the aid of the input vector $ua=[\Delta a\omega a]$, the rotation performed during the iteration when it is computed, and the elementary displacement.

Preparing for the corrective stage involves projecting the forecast into the information space. If the adjustment is made using the sensor that is monitoring the robot itself, the informational contribution vector and matrix are computed with consideration for the embedded sensor's properties, including the observation matrix and the uncertainty. Should the adjustment be obtained from the LiDAR and there are no more robots in the system, the portable landmarks take effect. The robots can communicate their position and variance-covariance matrix to one another via a shared network. The robot learns where this is by observing other robots. After that, it calculates this observation's informational contribution and adds a LiDAR observation to determine the robot's relative location. When all accessible informational contributions have been computed, the correction model is applied as demonstrated in, summing these values with the information vector and matrix appropriately, and projecting back to the Kalman space.

After receiving the correction, the robot begins diagnosing the position. The initial step in the detection method is to ascertain whether the system as a whole has a fault, which is accomplished by applying information theory and determining the Jensen-Shannon divergence between the prediction and correction. To ascertain the functional hypothesis, the trained detection model is employed. If this model indicates that a fault exists, the isolation step is applied. As mentioned before, the generalized observer scheme (GOS) is employed in the computation of failure indicators. These indications are input into each isolation model that is specific to a given sensor, and the functioning hypothesis of each is output together with the value of the prior no-fault hypothesis of sensors. The location and covariance are updated using the output of these models after the designated problematic sensors are eliminated

Figure 1. Algorithm 1 fault tolerant cooperative localization algorithm

Require: Initialization of state with Xao and its covariance Pao obtained from Optitrack for each robot.

Require: Set initial values of $P0$ and $Pobsa0$

.while $k{\neq}Nbiterations$

do

* Apply prediction step:

Read data from encoders: $ua{\leftarrow}[\Delta a,\omega a]T$

Compute $\{Xak|k{-}1,|k{-}1\}$ using the previous state and the evolution model.

Compute the information vector and matrix $\{yak|k{-}1,|k{-}1\}$

by using (1).

* Apply correction step:

Compute the informational contribution $\{iobskk, Iobskk\}$ for $obsa{\in}\{ma,ga\}$, by using (2).

if $Robotb$ or $Robotc$ in sight **then**

      Get their position and covariance $\{Xb,|k{-}1,Pb,ck|k{-}1\}$

      Get the relative observation $\{ZLa{\rightarrow}b,,La{\rightarrow}b,ck\}$ toward them.

      Compute the correction $\{Xobskk, Pobskk\}$ for $obsa{\in}\{La{\rightarrow}b,La{\rightarrow}c\}$

end if

Compute $\{Xak|k, Pak|k\}$ using the Extended Information filter in (2).

* Apply Diagnosis step:

Compute $gDaJS$ using (3).

if $\{gDaJS,P0\}$ tested on the detection model implies the presence of a fault **then**

Compute $JSobsaGOS$ using (3)

Get the faulty sensors using the isolation models

Exclude the faulty sensors

Update the position and covariance $\{Xak|k, Pak|k$

$\}$

end if

Update $P0$

Update $Pobsa0$

$k = k + 1$

end while

from the fusion process. Finally, the values of the preceding no-fault hypothesis are changed in light of the current iteration's findings.

3.4 Data Exploitation

Two distinct model types are utilized to detect and remove errors: several models for isolation and a unique identification model. These models are trained using both centralized and federated methods: With federated training, the central unit only receives the models' averages from the local training data, which remains on the computer.

3.5 Data Organization

A system where several individuals produce the data required to train a model can be organized in a variety of ways. The primary subjects of this book are federated and centralized learning.

All of the network members' data is collected and arranged using the centralized data organization technique at this single location. The learning model that was trained on this centralized dataset is then distributed to each participant. This method has multiple benefits because it is easy to use and employs a range of training algorithms. Furthermore, it allows for the comprehensive processing and analysis of the entire dataset and, should the consolidated dataset be representative and diverse, could result in better performance. It does, however, restrict the system's usefulness to the central unit's responsiveness and availability and requires the transfer of user data to a central location, which raises privacy and security concerns. Moreover, it is considered that the combined dataset represents.

A decentralized architecture is the outcome of federated learning. This approach makes it possible to train a model on distributed data right away, as opposed to moving the raw data to a central place. In federated learning, local training is carried out on each network member's unique data after the model has been loaded on them all. Afterwards, the model's parameters are routinely averaged or aggregated throughout the network to create a global model that protects data privacy and makes use of existing collective knowledge.

Instead of providing raw data, this method preserves data privacy and secrecy by training the model locally using each member's data. More broadly, it allows learning from a large number of distributed devices or nodes, enabling greater involvement, and lowers transmission costs since only model changes or gradients, not raw data, are exchanged. However, this requires combining and coordinating model changes, which could increase the intricacy. Moreover, it may run into issues with the network's participants' heterogeneous data distribution, which could lead to variations in the performing model. When systems have different operating histories, they are more likely to exhibit behavior that is somewhat different from the other systems' and not tailored to the system as a whole. Furthermore, how well this approach works.

3.6 Model Optimization and Training

Machine learning can use a range of models to meet this demand for discriminative learning, which is necessary to solve the classification problem. For federated learning aggregation, we select the logistic regression model so that we can evaluate the effectiveness of decentralized and centralized techniques. Because the input for all models is the same, federated learning, in contrast to other models, uses a minimal number of parameters that are shared by all subsystems.

For binary and multi-class classification tasks, the logit or logistic regression model is a particular application of the Generalized Linear Model (GLM). It provides a probabilistic framework for estimating class membership likelihood with input. The lack of processing capacity, the availability of other algorithms, and the gradual awareness of this tool's advantages delayed its usage, even though it was first proposed in the middle of the 20th century.

Logistic regression provides an alternative approach to applying linear regression methods to classification problems by changing the space in which these values are calculated. It employs a linear regression model of the type

$$z = \beta 0 + \beta 1 x 1 + \ldots + \beta n x n$$

In this instance, weights or intercepts are represented by $\beta 0$ to βn, while n characteristics, or input variables, are represented by $x1$ to xn. The legit function is used to map this model onto the interval [0, 1]. It has the following definition:

$$(c0|x1,2,\ldots,xn) = 11 + e - z$$

The logarithm of the odds, or logit, is impacted by β. In logistic regression, the terms odds and odds ratios are called parameters. To obtain the best-fitting curve for classification, the log-likelihood ratio for continuous input variables needs to be maximized.

Logistic regression is used to predict a categorical variable, as opposed to continuous regression. It can also be applied to assess the relationship between one or more independent factors and a dependent variable. The best logistic regression model fit is obtained with the following fitting parameters:

3.6.1 Penalty

Identifies the type of regularization applied to the logistic regression model. Regularization minimizes over-fitting by including a penalty term in the loss function. There are the L1 and L2 approaches.

Adding a regularization component to the cost function and using the $l1$ norm of the weight vector, L1 Regularization (also called Lasso Regularization, Least Absolute Shrinkage, and Selection Operator Regression) operates. The cost function is enhanced by a regularization factor of $\alpha \sum i = 1 n \theta 2 i$ in L2 Regularization, sometimes referred to as Ridge Regularization. This means that in addition to fitting the data, the learning method must minimize the model weights.

3.6.2 Solver

Explains the optimization algorithm used during the model's training. Various factors are considered by different solvers: the size of the dataset, the rate of convergence, the support for regularization, and the linearity of the data, memory efficiency, constraints, parallelization capability, Hessian approximation, and batch vs. stochastic update utilization.

3.6.3 Weight Class

Should the model be trained on the unbalanced data, it will be skewed toward the abundant class. In order to prevent this, cost-sensitive learning is used. In a multi-class classification task, the cost of wrongly identifying different classes is taken into consideration. Due to this, a certain weight must be assigned to each label. In order to preserve all parameters, the L2 Regularization is employed. We set C to 0.01 to make use of the memory that we have. Broyden-Fletcher-Goldfarb-Shanno (lbfgs) is the standard solution for logistic regression. Although there are several ways to aggregate data, Federeated Averaging (FedAvg) is the most fundamental approach. This method uses the following equation to aggregate the data over the hyper-parameters ω of the models for K customers, each of which has a subset Dk of length nk:

$$\omega t + 1 = \sum k K n k \sum K k n k \times \omega k t + 1$$

In our example, the detection model is based on two variables: $P0$, which is the prior probability of the no-fault hypothesis; and $gDJS$, which is the detection residual after Jensen–Shannon divergence. Accordingly, the single output, the existence of a fault, the slopes $\beta1$ and $\beta2$, and the intercept $\beta0$ make up the equation's three parameters. In terms of isolation, the intercept, the $P0$ of every sensor, and the isolation residuals $JSobsaCS$ are the 10 variables for which we have slopes βi. This indicates that the number of parameters that require optimization is $10 + 4 + 1 = 15$.

In a system with four sensors, faults could occur simultaneously and result in six separate output classes. Individual faults for each sensor (4 classes), no fault (0), and a distinct class for simultaneous faults are all included. Its unique properties prevent this model from being reduced to a single model since it is not a "one against all" classifier. Because the residuals are constructed using the Generalized Observer Scheme, it should be emphasized that not every model may make use of every input. These inputs are supplied with the $P0$ of the encoder, marvelmind, gyroscope, and LiDAR attached to it, respectively, in the same order as the *obsaGOS*.

IV. RESULT AND DISCUSSION

To evaluate and confirm the proposed framework's feasibility, we put it into practice and conducted tests on our mobile robot platform. We tested our robot in an environment akin to an office to make sure it could maneuver safely and socially in a real-world situation.

4.1 Experiment Setup

A Microsoft Kinect sensor and a laser range finder were installed on our Eddie mobile robot platform. The typical Kinect sensor, which consists of an RGB camera, depth sensor, infrared light projector, and multiarray microphone, was mounted 1.35 meters above the ground. The depth sensor's viewing angles are 43 degrees vertically and 57 degrees horizontally, with a range of 0.8 to 6.0 meters. With a maximum frame rate of 30 frames per second, this low-cost equipment can produce RGB-D data at a resolution of 640 480 pixels. The 240 angular field of vision of the laser range finder UGR- 04LX-UG01 allows it to measure distances up to 6.0 m at a height of 0.4 m.

4.2 Navigation Performance

In order to illustrate how our system functions in comparison to pedestrians and PCLRHC, we begin this section with some anecdotal data. Interestingly, this behavior held true for all ten of our experiments: IGP outperformed the pedestrian and PCLRHC acted evasively, usually going outside to avoid the crowd. Figure 2 displays the main experimental result reported in this study. Figure 2 displays our program's output throughout the course of ten experiments. For each of the ten tests, the boxes surrounding the colorful dots reflect the standard error bars. The IGP green dot's average safety was approximately 22 pixels, with a standard error of more than 2 pixels, and the Columns with the label "s" indicate safety (in pixels), and columns with the label "}" show path length (in pixels). Both path length and safety are significantly greater for IGP than for pedestrians. Additionally, as theoretically demonstrated earlier, PCLRHC is not appropriate for densely populated locations. Large path length evasive maneuvers are nearly always used by PCLRHC to avoid the crowds.

Figure 2. The experimental result

Building on social psychology research, we develop a novel algorithm to minimize entitativity and maximize the social invisibility of multi-robot systems in pedestrian crowds. Unique entitativity profiles—characterized by appearance, trajectory, and spatial distance—are linked to different emotional reactions, with people in high entitativity groups reporting negative emotions. This is evident from a user research. Then, we use the trajectory information from low-entitative groups to develop a real-time navigation algorithm that should increase the social invisibility of multi-robot systems.

Our approach has some shortcomings. We find that, albeit generalizing across several environmental contexts, judgments such as social salience depend on factors other than motion-based entitativity. When forming opinions and reacting emotionally to social agents, people employ a wide range of indicators, including impressions of gender, race, class, and religion. Since our method just employs mobility trajectories, not all relevant social features are properly recorded. Since robots may lack these higher-level social characteristics, the low-level entitativity component that matters most to them is motion trajectories.

This method of mimicking robot looks in multi-robot systems ought to be investigated further in subsequent research. Robots can have their appearance customized even though many social characteristics, such as race, may not apply to them. Because of their increased entitativity, marching robots are expected to become more visible in society. Businesses that produce surveillance robots may find this problematic since mass production typically yields similar looks. Further study is needed to determine how a perceiver's personality affects the features of multi-robot systems, as some individuals may be less likely to react negatively to entitative groups of robots because of things like having more experience with robots or being less sensitive to general threat cues.

V. CONCLUSION

Visibility information was considered in this work to give a fast and safe navigation approach. The environmental risks were estimated statistically to address contact with occluded dynamic obstacles. Course planning and speed control both made use of the quantitatively derived and structurally employed collision risk. Simulations and presented experimental results show that the proposed indoor mobile robot navigation system is a safe and efficient method. Thinking about the safety and future of the trajectory is made possible by the proposed definition. Simulations show that in addition to the robot itself, it is crucial to consider the likelihood of any object in the workplace colliding with the robot. The robot's navigation might run afoul of workplace objects in the absence of such protection. Working with the navigation algorithm, the robot's job is to make results verification possible.

REFERENCES

Arul, S. H., Bedi, A. S., & Manocha, D. (2022). Multi Robot Collision Avoidance by Learning Whom to Communicate. arXiv preprint arXiv:2209.06415.

Bajcsy, A., Herbert, S. L., Fridovich-Keil, D., Fisac, J. F., Deglurkar, S., Dragan, A. D., & Tomlin, C. J. (2019, May). A scalable framework for real-time multi-robot, multi-human collision avoidance. In 2019 international conference on robotics and automation (ICRA) (pp. 936-943). IEEE. doi:10.1109/ICRA.2019.8794457

Bramblett, L., Gao, S., & Bezzo, N. (2023). Epistemic Prediction and Planning with Implicit Coordination for Multi-Robot Teams in Communication Restricted Environments. arXiv preprint arXiv:2302.10393. doi:10.1109/ICRA48891.2023.10161553

Chung, Y. M., Youssef, H., & Roidl, M. (2022, May). Distributed Timed Elastic Band (DTEB) Planner: Trajectory Sharing and Collision Prediction for Multi-Robot Systems. In 2022 International Conference on Robotics and Automation (ICRA) (pp. 10702-10708). IEEE. 10.1109/ICRA46639.2022.9811762

Cui, Y., Lin, L., Huang, X., Zhang, D., Wang, Y., Jing, W., ... Wang, Y. (2022, May). Learning Observation-Based Certifiable Safe Policy for Decentralized Multi-Robot Navigation. In 2022 International Conference on Robotics and Automation (ICRA) (pp. 5518-5524). IEEE. 10.1109/ICRA46639.2022.9811950

Ferranti, L., Lyons, L., Negenborn, R. R., Keviczky, T., & Alonso-Mora, J. (2022). Distributed nonlinear trajectory optimization for multi-robot motion planning. IEEE Transactions on Control Systems Technology, 31(2), 809–824. doi:10.1109/TCST.2022.3211130

Firoozi, R., Ferranti, L., Zhang, X., Nejadnik, S., & Borrelli, F. (2020). A distributed multi-robot coordination algorithm for navigation in tight environments. arXiv preprint arXiv:2006.11492.

Freitas, E. J., Vangasse, A. D. C., Raffo, G. V., & Pimenta, L. C. (2023, October). Decentralized Multi-robot Collision-free Path Following Based on Time-varying Artificial Vector Fields and MPC-ORCA. In 2023 Latin American Robotics Symposium (LARS), 2023 Brazilian Symposium on Robotics (SBR), and 2023 Workshop on Robotics in Education (WRE) (pp. 212-217). IEEE. 10.1109/LARS/SBR/WRE59448.2023.10333004

Krishnan, S., Rajagopalan, G. A., Kandhasamy, S., & Shanmugavel, M. (2019). Towards scalable continuous-time trajectory optimization for multi-robot navigation. arXiv preprint arXiv:1910.13463.

Krishnan, S., Rajagopalan, G. A., Kandhasamy, S., & Shanmugavel, M. (2020). Continuous-time trajectory optimization for decentralized multi-robot navigation. IFAC-PapersOnLine, 53(1), 494–499. doi:10.1016/j.ifacol.2020.06.083

Madridano, A., Al-Kaff, A., Martín, D., & De La Escalera, A. (2021). Trajectory planning for multi-robot systems: Methods and applications. Expert Systems with *Applications, 173, 114660. doi:10.1016/j.* eswa.2021.114660

Mali, P., Harikumar, K., Singh, A. K., Krishna, K. M., & Sujit, P. B. (2021, June). Incorporating prediction in control barrier function based distributive multi-robot collision avoidance. In 2021 European *Control Conference (ECC) (pp. 2394-2399)*. IEEE. 10.23919/ECC54610.2021.9655081

Navsalkar, A., & Hota, A. R. (2023, May). Data-driven risk-sensitive model predictive control for safe navigation in multi-robot systems. In 2023 IEEE Inte*rnational Conference on Robotics and Automation (ICRA) (pp. 1442-144*8). IEEE. 10.1109/ICRA48891.2023.10161002

Olcay, E., Schuhmann, F., & Lohmann, B. (2020). Collective navigation of a multi-robot system in an unknown environment. Robotics and *Autonomous Systems, 132, 103*604. doi:10.1016/j.robot.2020.103604

Park, J. S., Tsang, B., Yedidsion, H., Warnell, G., Kyoung, D., & Stone, P. (2021, October). Learning to improve multi-robot hallway navigation. In Conferen*ce on Robot Learning (pp. 1*883-1895). PMLR.

Samman, T., Spearman, J., Dutta, A., Kreidl, O. P., Roy, S., & Bölöni, L. (2021, October). Secure multi-robot adaptive information sampling. In 2021 *IEEE International Symposium on Safety, Security, and Rescue Robotics (SSRR) (pp.* 125-131). IEEE. 10.1109/SSRR53300.2021.9597867

Şenbaşlar, B., Luiz, P., Hönig, W., & Sukhatme, G. S. (2023). Mrnav: Multi-robot aware planning and control stack for collision and deadlock-free navigation in cluttered environments. ar*Xiv preprint arXiv:2308.13499.*

Tan, Q., Fan, T., Pan, J., & Manocha, D. (2020, October). Deepmnavigate: Deep reinforced multi-robot navigation unifying local & global collision avoidance. In *2020 IEEE/RSJ International Conference on Intelligent Robots and Systems (IROS) (pp. 6952-6959)*. IEEE. 10.1109/IROS45743.2020.9341805

. Tran, V. P., Garratt, M. A., Kasmarik, K., & Anavatti, S. G. (2023). Dynamic frontier-led swarming: Multi-robot repeated coverage in dynamic environments. *IEEE/CAA Journal of Automatica Sinica, 10*(3), 646-661.

Yang, Z., Bi, L., Chi, W., Shi, H., & Guan, C. (2022). Brain-Controlled Multi-Robot at Servo-Control Level Based on Nonlinear Model Predictive Control. *Complex System Modeling and Simulation, 2*(4), 307–321. doi:10.23919/CSMS.2022.0019

Zaccaria, M., Giorgini, M., Monica, R., & Aleotti, J. (2021, July). Multi-robot multiple camera people detection and tracking in automated warehouses. In *2021 IEEE 19th International Conference on Industrial Informatics (INDIN)* (pp. 1-6). IEEE. 10.1109/INDIN45523.2021.9557363

Zhu, H. (2022). *Probabilistic Motion Planning for Multi-Robot Systems*. Academic Press.

Zhu, H., Claramunt, F. M., Brito, B., & Alonso-Mora, J. (2021). Learning interaction-aware trajectory predictions for decentralized multi-robot motion planning in dynamic environments. *IEEE Robotics and Automation Letters*, 6(2), 2256–2263. doi:10.1109/LRA.2021.3061073

Chapter 4
A Novel Method to Detect Ripeness Level of Apples Using Machine Vision PSOCNN Approach

K. Yogesh
Karpagam Academy of Higher Education, India

R. Gunasudari
Karpagam Academy of Higher Education, India

ABSTRACT

Machine vision systems have emerged as a viable non-invasive approach for investigating the connection between fruit visual traits and physicochemical qualities at varying ripening degrees, and have been used in recent research efforts to identify the stages. The current study aims to develop an intelligent algorithm that can estimate various physical properties, such as firmness and soluble solid content, as well as three chemical properties, namely starch, acidity, and titratable acidity. A hybrid approach was used to further optimise the physicochemical estimation method of PSO with CNN. This method was applied to the evaluation parameters in order to describe their classification behaviour. The sample accuracy was 95.84% when using the different parameters to characterise them. A second set of apples was utilised for validation after the first set was used as trial samples in PSO+CNN.

I. INTRODUCTION

The most commonly grown pome fruit in the world is the Apple (Maluscommunis L.). Global output amounts to around 133 million tons per year. China stands as leading producer and India took its position as fifth. In the fiscal year 2022, a total of 2.4 million metric tons of apples were produced in India. Comparing this to the prior fiscal year, there was an increase. For that fiscal year, the bulk of the nation's apple output came from the northern state of Jammu & Kashmir.

DOI: 10.4018/979-8-3693-5767-5.ch004

1.1 Contribution of India in Agriculture and Automation of Agriculture

The Ministry of Statistics and Programme Implementation provided that India's GDP is 15.4% derived from agriculture. Gathering, processing, and storing are the three primary categories into which agriculture activities are often divided.

After China, India is the world's second-largest fruit grower. 30% to 35% of the harvested fruits are wasted because there are not enough skilled labourers. Once more, fruit identification, classification, and grading are not done precisely due to the subjectivity of human perception. Therefore, the fruit business must implement the automated system. Automated fruit sorting systems based on fruit type, variety, maturity, and intactness can be designed with high intelligence thanks to machine learning approaches that incorporate sufficient image processing concepts.

In agriculture, automated systems are required for the precise, quick, and high-quality determination of fruits since they are essential to the nation's economic growth and increased production. Researchers have developed numerous algorithms to classify and rank fruit according to its quality. Colour is the most obvious factor in identifying fruit illness and ripeness.

We refer to the uniform distribution of a single color—the primary color—on the skin surface of some fruits. A good way to determine the quality of these fruits is to look at their average surface colour. Nevertheless, certain fruits (including certain types of peaches, apples, and tomatoes) possess a secondary hue that serves as a reliable gauge of their maturity. Only using the global colour as a quality parameter is not an option in this situation.

1.2 Machine Learning in Agriculture

To overcome difficulties progressing in the field of machine learning has contributed to enhanced agricultural yields. By offering insightful advice and detailed knowledge about the crops, machine learning is a modern technology that helps farmers reduces farming losses.

Recent years have seen the evaluation of numerous agriculture-related issues through the integration of remote sensing and AI tools. More specifically, a number of recent research have been developed employing DL approaches applied to photos taken at different acquisition levels in fruit recognition challenges.

Apples present one of the greatest challenges when it comes to fruit detection in photos, mostly due to the presence of target occlusion issues. The establishment of high-density apple tree orchards further complicates the identification of individual fruits.

As per IBM definition ML, a branch of AI, is the study of building computer systems with data-learning capabilities. Algorithms for machine learning and machine vision are among the many approaches that machine learning (ML) uses to improve software applications' performance over time are critical components to solve major issues regarding fruits post harvesting period.

1.3 Machine Vision

For applications including process control, robot guiding, and autonomous inspection, machine vision (MV) technology enabled imaging-based autonomous inspection and analysis.

The necessity for a sufficient level of food production with fewer agricultural areas has arisen due to the swift expansion of the global population. Machine vision would ensure an increase in agricultural productivity by efficent way. Significant progress has been made in a number of agricultural fields in recent years. These developments combine machine learning methods with machine vision approaches to handle colour from object images by Penumuru, D. P., et al (2020).

1.4 Machine Vision System

Numerous evaluations have been conducted with an emphasis on this topic because of the current developments in machine vision applications in agriculture. CV techniques have been used in the development of fruit categorization and identification systems within the past 10 years, including by Pereira, C.S., et al (2017). The general machine vision system is depicted in the below Figure 1.

To facilitate objective and non-destructive food examination, an MVS consists of two basic components: 1) Gathering information; and 2) analyzing it.

- The process of acquiring photographs determines their information and quality. It serves as the cornerstone for the success of any further image processing.
- Machine vision systems are able to multitask because image processing directs the operation.

1.5 Advantages of Machine Vision System

The most important thing of using machine vision technology is, for its merits. These are listed in below:

- Conserve time
- lower the cost of production
- streamline the logistical procedure
- Reduce equipment downtime
- Boost output and caliber of output
- Lessen the personnel's and the test's labor intensity
- Cut back on things that aren't qualified
- Increase the rate of machine use and so on.

Figure 1. Machine vision system

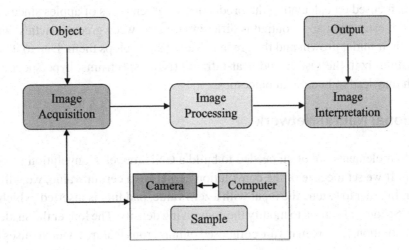

1.6 Applications of Machine Vision

1. While the uses of machine vision are expanding in tandem with technological advancements, there are a few key areas where machine vision has shown to be quite beneficial.
2. OCR stands for "optical character recognition". Through OCR, printed or handwritten text can be extracted from photographs by a computer.

1.6.1 Recognition of Signatures and Handwriting: These characteristics enable a computer to identify patterns in pictures of signatures and handwriting.

1.6.2 Identification of Objects: Self-driving automobiles in the automotive industry recognize objects in camera-captured photos to identify roadblocks. Additionally, machine vision systems are used to locate objects, such as figuring out where a label should go on a pill bottle.

1.6.3 Identifying Patterns: Pattern recognition is used in medical imaging analysis to diagnose patients using technologies including brain, blood, and magnetic resonance imaging scans.

1.6.4 Examination of Materials: The use of machine vision in materials inspection systems guarantees quality control. Machine vision examines various objects for imperfections, impurities.

1.6.5 Robot Guidance: One quickly expanding field in machine vision is the use of cameras for robot guidance. In order to teach robots how to handle individual or bulk components efficiently, 2D and 3D cameras are both crucial. Because they need less physical effort, these applications offer a high return on investment.

In the future, large-scale dataset-based computer vision intelligence technology will be extensively employed in all facets of agricultural production management, and it will be further deployed to address present-day agricultural issues. Agricultural automation systems will function better economically, generally, cooperatively, and robustly as artificial intelligence algorithms and computer vision technologies are integrated.

1.7 Machine Vision in Apple Storage

Numerous academics have been drawn to the novel idea of automatically evaluating ripeness using computer vision systems because they offer a cost-effective and speedy alternative to the labor-intensive and time-consuming manual assessment process.

This inquiry is focused on calculating the production of green types of apples since one of the most challenging parts of estimating apple output is differentiating between green varieties that is, types that are green during their initial growth and the green foliage that envelops them. Due to its ability to yield a multitude of data in both the visible and near-infrared (NIR) spectrums, hyperspectral imaging was employed, which may lead to beneficial outcomes.

1.8 Convolutional Neural Network

More precisely, four elements are often needed to build a CNN model. Convolution is a crucial step in feature extraction. If we set the size of the convolution kernels to a certain value, we will lose information in the border. In order to extend the input with a zero value, padding is inserted, which inadvertently modifies the size. Stride is also used to modify the convolving density. The longer the stride, the lower the density. After convolution, feature maps are composed of numerous features, which raises the possibility of an overfitting problem. Sivanantham, K. (2022) is advised to remove maximum and average pooling, as well as redundancy. Loss functions and optimizers were created in order to teach the CNN system as a whole to understand what we meant. CNN has extensive knowledge artificial neural networks in general.

This paper work is divided into five components. The section of the introduction to the work that was discussed in Section I. Section II looks at the limitations and flaws in the current systems. An explanation of our recently suggested system design work for apple ripeness level detection using machine vision method was provided in Section III. Section IV contains the justification and comprehensive output result for our newly constructed system. Section V deals with the conclusion of this work.

II. LITERATURE REVIEW

This section on literature studies discusses the shortcomings and restrictions of the numerous current approaches used in the detection and classification of apple ripeness level using different methods.

Xiao, B., Nguyen, M., & Yan, W. Q., (2021) have examined theripeness of apples in digital images and categorised with the use of deep learning's CNN, also known as ConvNets. Apple identification, ripeness classification, resulting evaluations, and image pre-processing are the four components of this experiment, which aims to validate the potential of DL models for fruit classification in order to reduce the amount of human labour required.

2.1 Image Processing Technology

Wan, P., et al (2018) have described The BPNN classification algorithm is used with the feature colour value to identify the three maturation levels (green, orange, and red) of fresh market tomatoes. With the express purpose of gathering the tomato photos in the lab, a computer vision-based maturity detection device was created. Following the processing of the tomato photos and the acquisition of the tomato targets using image processing technology, the average accuracy of this method for identifying the three tomato maturity levels in samples of tomatoes was 99.31%, with a 1.2% standard deviation.

2.2 Apple Ripeness Determination via Artificial Neural Network Technologies

Hamza, R., & Chtourou, M. (2018), have approached Artificial Neural Network (ANN) classification and estimated the color-based indicator of apple fruit maturity. In order to achieve optimal performance, this work has addressed a number of issues, including colour feature vectors, pedagogy, and ANN classifier structure. The simulation results showed how well the ripeness categorization system performed.

Çetin, N., et al (2022) have analysed the three harvest phases' worth of hyperspectral photos of pink lady apples were used to forecast certain interior traits (firmness and SSC). For every harvest phase, a total of 100 samples were subjected to the hyperspectral camera to get reflectance data in 300 spectral bands ranging from 386 to 1028 nm. Furthermore, the prediction capabilities of DT, ANN, KNN, PLSR, and MLR were assessed.

2.3 Machine Learning in Agriculture

Patil, K., et al (2021) have examined thorough examination of the most recent applications of Pre-harvest, harvesting, and post-harvest problems in agriculture can be resolved with ML. With less effort required and higher-quality results, machine learning in agriculture allows for more precise and effective farming.

Zhu, L., et al (2021) have provided a summary of the deep learning and traditional methods of machine learning in addition to machine vision techniques that are useful in the food processing sector. They described the methods and challenges of the past as well as projected patterns and logical future directions.

Tian, H., et al (2020) have summarized and analyzed systematically the difficulties and technologies of the previous three years, as well as potential future developments, to create the most recent resource for scholars. According to the assessments, small field farmers can benefit from low costs, high efficiency, and high precision by developing agricultural automation with the use of current technology.

Firouz, M. S., et al (2019) have reported about the Within the field of food science and technology, the fruit, juice, and dairy industries the uses of ultrasound in high- and low-power modes for processing, instrumentation, and industrial operation control are investigated. The focus is on the fundamentals of these methods and how they affect the physicochemical properties of the final products. The benefits and limitations of each ultrasound-assisted technique are also discussed, along with a thorough study of these approaches and key variables affecting their effectiveness. This technique's productivity issues would be addressed, and the technology's future trends would be described.

Biffi, L. J., et al (2021) have detected apple fruits efficiently and presented a solution for close-range and inexpensive terrestrial RGB image analysis based on the ATSS deep learning technique. Precise identification helps with apple production projections and provides local growers with more insight into future management strategies. ATSS method's primary benefit was that it just labelled the object's centre point, in fruit orchards with high population density; this is significantly more practical and realistic than bounding-box annotations.

Behera, S. K., Rath, A. K., & Sethy, P. K. (2021) have reviewed the novel non- Classifying papaya fruits according to their damaging ripeness status. The paper suggested two strategies based on transfer learning and machine learning for grading the maturity state of papayas. Additionally, a comparison analysis using various Research was done using transfer learning and machine learning approaches. VGG19, utilising a transfer learning strategy, achieved 100% accuracy, a 6% improvement over the present approach.

2.4 Evaluation of Current Advancements in Traditional and Innovative Methods for Measuring Lycopene Content of Fruit

Hussain, A., Pu, H., & Sun, D. W. (2019) have reviewed the efforts to demonstrate the worth of using both traditional and cutting-edge methods to assess the lycopene content in fruit. Along with spectrum imaging techniques like multispectral, hyperspectral, and Raman imaging, the revolutionary techniques also include spectroscopic techniques like near infrared spectroscopy and Raman spectroscopy. Future trends are also offered, along with a summary of the techniques' guiding principles and a discussion of their specific applications. Lycopene concentration and distribution in different fruits can be evaluated using both conventional and innovative methods described in this paper.

Bhargava, A., & Bansal, A. (2020) presented a system that distinguishes between four different fruit varieties and evaluates each fruit's ranking according to its quality. The split-and-merge procedure was used to separate the photos' backgrounds after the programme had first extracted the different images. Subsequently, the thirty distinct features color, statistical, textural, and geometric are retrieved. Only geometrical features are utilised to distinguish between different types of fruit; other features are used to evaluate the fruit's quality. In addition, the quality is classified using four distinct classifiers: artificial neural network (ANN), SVM, sparse representative classifier (SRC), and k-nearest neighbour (k-NN).

Mavridou, E., et al (2019), have reviewed the most current research on using machine vision in agriculture, primarily for agricultural production. When it came to using cognitive technology in agriculture, this study acted as a research guide for both practitioners and researchers. Studies of various agricultural practices, such as fruit grading, fruit counting, and yield estimation, that assist crop harvesting are reviewed. Furthermore discussed are methods for monitoring plant health, such as weed, insect, and disease detection. Last but not least, new studies have taken agricultural harvesting robots and vehicle navigation systems into consideration.

Rehman, T. U., (2019) have outlined the statistical machine learning technologies that are used in agriculture using machine vision systems, given the wide range of machine learning applications. Agriculture has made use of both supervised and unsupervised learning, two categories of statistical ML approaches. This study provides a thorough examination of the current use of statistical ML algorithms in machine vision systems, assesses the prospective applications of each methodology, and provides an overview of instructive case studies in various agricultural domains. This paper also formulates and discusses future trends in statistical ML technology applications.

2.5 Use of Machine Vision Technology for Food Identification

Xiao, Z., et al (2022) have examined the use regarding the hardware and software of machine vision systems in the context of food detection, presented the state of research on machine vision as it stands today, and offered a forecast for the difficulties that machine vision systems encounter.

Wang, W., et al (2023) have estimated The method used to determine the freshness state of apples involved using Back Propagation (BP) as a neural network predictive model and an enhanced SSA based on chaotic sequence (Tent) for optimisation. Utilising an array of gas sensors and a wireless gearbox module, an electronic nose system was created. To finish predicting the freshness of apples, odour data is analysed from apples.

III. SYSTEM DESIGN

The following portion demonstrates the several stages of the suggested hybrid PSO with CNN machine vision algorithm to evaluate the apple ripeness levels in different situations.

3.1 Particle Swarm Optimization (PSO)

The initial translations xi_0 inside bounds to the challenge the user has to set the population size (p_s) beforehand. $P_{Besti,g}$ is the result of evaluating and storing values of the particle starting points for the objective function. The generation counter, represented by g in this instance, starts at 0the following equation:

$$v^d_{i,g+1}=w_g \cdot v^d_{i,g}+c_1 \cdot rand1^d_{i,g}(0,1)\cdot\left(pBest^d_{i,g}-x^d_{i,g}\right)+C_2 rand2^d_{i,g}(0,1)\cdot\left(gBest^d_g-x^d_{i,g}\right)$$

$$x^d_{i,g+1}=x^d_{i,g}+v^d_{i,g+1}$$

The user-specified acceleration coefficients c1 and c2 are the inertia weight, and all other particles in the swarm are represented by d = 1,...,D (where D is the problem dimensionality). For every i^{th} particle and d^{th} dimension, two random numbers, $rand1_{di,g}(0,1)$ and $rand2_{di,g}(0,1)$, are generated independently using the [0,1] interval.In addition to the matching each particle in the run is associated with three vectors: the particle's $x_{i,g}$, v_{i}g, and the best position ($P_{Besti,g}$) it has visited since the search was started. The procedure keeps on until the predefined maximum number of function calls is completed.

3.1.1 PSO Structure Algorithm

From the one iteration to the next, particle swarms modify their relative positions, which allow the PSO algorithm to efficiently conduct the search. To find the best feasible solution, each particle in the swarm moves toward its prior Pbest and gbest. Assume, f is objective function to minimized or optimized, There are t iterations in total, and i is the particle index.

A swarm a group of people in the PSO algorithm, whereas an individual represents a possible solution. The PSO algorithm is a widely used population-based evolutionary computing method. A vector represents the ith particle's velocity in an N-dimensional optimisation problem, vi = (vi1, vi2,...,viN). Similarly, xi = (x_{i1}, x_{i2}, ...,x_{iN}) represents the position vector of the ith particle. The equations for updating the position and velocity of particle I are given below:

$v_i(k+1)= w\times v_i(k)+c_1\times r_1\times(p_i(k)-x_i(k))+c_2\times r_2\times(p_g(k)-x_i(k))x_i(k+1)= x_i(k)+v_i(k+1)$

The pseudocode of the PSO is given in the figure 2. Members of interval [0, 1] are the two unique random integers, r1 and r2. The range of m, the domain of the optimization problem, is where the particle's position can only be. The following represents the updated equation for at the kth repetition, the inertia weight w: w= $(w_1-(w_1-w_2)\times k)$ /maxiter. While w1 and w2 show the maximum and minimum inertia weights, respectively; maxiter is the number of iterations that can be made.

3.2 Convolutional Neural Network (CNN)

Convolutional layers, max-pooling, and sparse connectivity are the three basic facets of CNN architecture. The local connection of neurons on neighbouring layers takes advantage of the spatial dependency of the image's pixels.

The convolution kernel, from which the term "convolution neural network" derives, is the most crucial component of the CNN. An n-column two-dimensional matrix makes up the convolution kernel and matching weights for each point. Convolution kernels resemble neurons, and their size is referred to as the receptive field of a neuron. The receptive field of the CNN is filled with the addition of the values of the pixels and the convolution kernel's weights at the pertinent locations in the image. The system's k convolution kernels do this. Once all of the pixels in the image have been counted, to the following

Figure 2. Pseudocode of the particle swarm optimization

```
Initialization
Give the definition of the number of dimensions D and the swarm size S.
for each particle i ∈ [1..S]
Produce at random Xi and Vi, and assess the health of Xi indicating it as f(Xi)
SetPbesti = Xiand f(Pbesti) = f(Xi)
end for
Set Gbest = Pbest1 and f(Gbest) = f(Pbest1)
for each particle i ∈ [1..S]
           if f(Pbesti) < f(Gbest) then
                    f(Gbest) = f(Pbesti)
        end if
end for
while t < maximum quantity of repetitions
for each particle i ∈ [1..S]
Analyse its speed vid (t + 1)
Update the position xid (t + 1) of the particle
if f (xi (t + 1)) < f (Pbesti) then
Pbesti = xi (t + 1)
          f(Pbesti) = f(xi(t + 1)
end if
if f(Pbesti) < f(Gbest) then
        Gbest = Pbesti
        f(Gbest) = f(Pbesti)
end if
end for
t = t + 1
end while
go back to Gbest
```

point in the image in accordance with the step size. The original image's feature map is now the output pixel matrix.

$$O_w = [\frac{i_w - n + 2_p}{s}] + 1 \tag{1}$$

$$Oh = [\frac{i_h - n + 2_p}{s}] + 1 \tag{2}$$

The most common pooling techniques are maximal combining, averaging, etc. Here, we select the highest pooling approach and the associated calculation. The area of the image the highest value per pixel in the range of 2 is chosen using a filter of size 2 2, and it is then kept as the distinctive feature of this area. A feature map is created once the filter repeats this process for the subsequent range. The convolution network's performance has increased with end-to-end training, not just in terms of overall data classification but also in terms of the local task's progress toward producing structured output. As a result, it has seen extensive use in the fields of data detection and categorization.

CNNs will quickly run into problems when using a typical multi-layer perceptron, meaning all layers are completely connected, because the data dimensions are too big. There is no available space information on CNN. The final efficiency may be quite low if we use the pooling layer. CNNs suffer a significant of information in the pooling layer, which lowers the spatial resolution, because only the most active neurons can be communicated between each layer during the transfer of neurons.

The above Figure 3 shows the pseudocode for convolutional Neural Network. CNNs won't be able to discern between variations in postures and other features as a result. Overtraining from every viewpoint is one technique to overcome this issue, but it typically takes more time and computer power.

Figure 3. Pseudocode for CNN

CNN Algorithm Pseudocode:

Input:

d: dataset,

1: real labels in the dataset

W: Word-to-Vec matrix

Output:

Test dataset score for the CNN-trained model

Assume that f is the 3D matrix of features.

For i in dataset **do**

Allow f to represent the sample i's feature set matrix.

For jin i **do**

Vj - vectorize(j, w)

Append vj to f

Append fi to f

ftrain, ftest, Itrain, Itest Create a train and test subsets from the feature set and labels

M-CNN (ftrain, Itrain)

Score-analysis (i, Itest, M)

Return score

When dealing with extremely complicated field-of-view data that has a lot of overlap, mutual masking, and diverse backgrounds, traditional CNN cannot be identified properly. We will go over the rationale behind removing the fully connected layers, the parameters for the skip and pooling layers in the suggested approach, and the use of two convolutional layers as a skip layer. More specifically, the tail of CNN is frequently added with several fully-connected layers.

IV. RESULT AND DISCUSSION

The evaluation of the experiment proved to be successful, yielding several results for different parameters. The proposed hybrid PSOCNN and conventional methods underwent successful experimental study, yielding several results for various parameters. MATLAB 2013A is used to find the performance evaluation with hybrid of PSOCNN for the detection of ripeness level of apples.

4.1 Confusion Matrix

It is frequently employed in evaluating effectiveness categorization models, which strive to assign a categorical label to each instance of input. The quantity of TP, TN, FP, and FN generated by the model with the test data set is displayed in Figure 4 below.

4.2 Accuracy

The model's correctness is a critical performance parameter that determines if our assumptions about the positive and negative classes are accurate.

$$\text{Accuracy} = \frac{TP + TN}{TP + TN + FN + FP}$$

The output graph of accuracy from the above table 1 for existing and proposed system is clearly shown in the Figure 5. From this graph, our proposed PSO+CNN system outperforms the better accuracy of 95.84% comparing with the other systems.

Figure 4. Confusion matrix

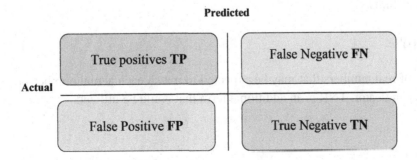

Table 1. Accuracy result of existing and proposed algorithm

Algorithm	Accuracy (%)
SVM	79.12
KNN	86.34
ANN	89.28
PSO+CNN	95.84

Figure 5. Accuracy graph

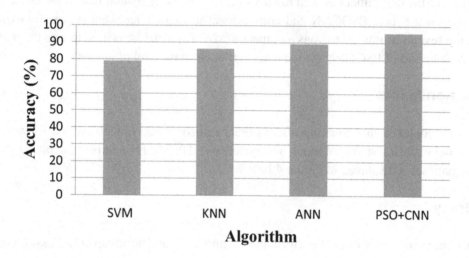

4.3 Sensitivity

The sensitivity (SN) can be calculated simply calculating the ratio of all the positives to all the correct positive forecasts.

$$Sensitivity = \frac{TP}{TP + FN}$$

The sensitivity output graph of existing and proposed system from the above table 2 is shown in the figure 6. The newly proposed PSO+CNN algorithm gives the better sensitivity result of 93.24% among the all other algorithms.

4.4 Specificity

The percentage of real numbers that may be expected to match each actual number precisely is known as the specificity indicator. TNR is an additional term that could be utilized.

Table 2. Sensitivity result of existing and proposed algorithm

Algorithm	Sensitivity (%)
SVM	77.72
KNN	79.53
ANN	85.43
PSO+CNN	93.24

Figure 6. Sensitivity graph

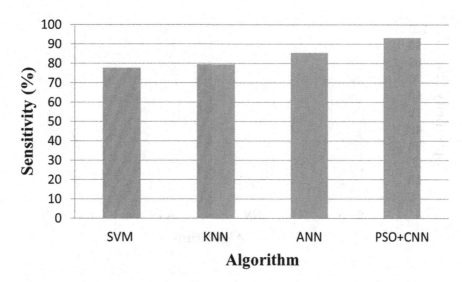

$$\text{Specificity} = \frac{TN}{TN + FP}$$

The specificity output graph from the above table 3 for existing and proposed system is shown in the Figure 7. The new approach of our proposed PSO+CNN algorithm works and gives the better specificity result of 92.74% comparing with the other existing algorithms.

4.5 Time Duration

Choosing the best Using a machine learning model to address an issue can be time-consuming if done carelessly.

The time duration output graph from the above table 4 for existing and proposed system is shown in the Figure 8. The new approach of our proposed PSO+CNN algorithm works and consumes the less time duration of 8.58 milliseconds comparing with the other existing algorithms.

Table 3. Specificity result of existing and proposed algorithm

Algorithm	Specificity (%)
SVM	78.84
KNN	76.42
ANN	83.67
PSO+CNN	92.74

Figure 7. Specificity graph

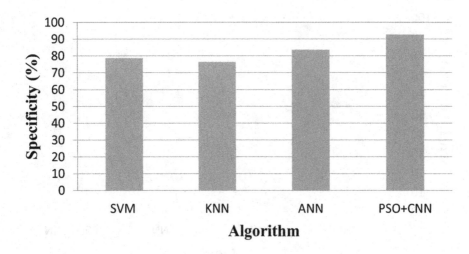

Table 4. Time duration result of existing and proposed algorithm

Algorithm	Time Duration (ms)
SVM	18.86
KNN	16.93
ANN	12.68
PSO+CNN	8.58

V. CONCLUSION

An innovative method was created to use artificial intelligence and an image processing algorithm to determine the physicochemical characteristics and ripeness levels of apples in different situations. A collection of ripeness-varying apple images was obtained. Using a CNN-based algorithm to process image frames allowed for the identification of the best colour and texture features, which allowed for the reliable prediction of the observed physicochemical values. Apples' ripening stages were then fore-casted using the anticipated physicochemical characteristics. To determine when apples were ready, the most advanced machine vision system was put to the test. A CCR of 95.84% was attained, indicating a dependable performance of the generated models, in a shorter time of 8.58 milliseconds. Nonetheless,

Figure 8. Time duration graph

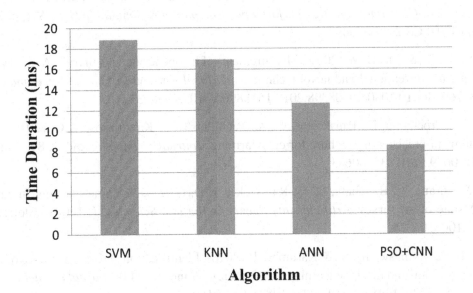

more investigation is needed to develop a field-scale prototype and train the algorithm using several apple cultivars. In order to provide effective these models can be integrated into harvesting robots and/or drones for real-time resource management in the field.

REFERENCES

Behera, S. K., Rath, A. K., & Sethy, P. K. (2021). Maturity status classification of papaya fruits based on machine learning and transfer learning approach. *Information Processing in Agriculture*, *8*(2), 244–250. doi:10.1016/j.inpa.2020.05.003

Bhargava, A., & Bansal, A. (2020). Automatic detection and grading of multiple fruits by machine learning. *Food Analytical Methods*, *13*(3), 751–761. doi:10.1007/s12161-019-01690-6

Biffi, L. J., Mitishita, E., Liesenberg, V., Santos, A. A. D., Goncalves, D. N., Estrabis, N. V., Silva, J. A., Osco, L. P., Ramos, A. P. M., Centeno, J. A. S., Schimalski, M. B., Rufato, L., Neto, S. L. R., Marcato Junior, J., & Goncalves, W. N. (2021). ATSS deep learning-based approach to detect apple fruits. *Remote Sensing (Basel)*, *13*(1), 54. doi:10.3390/rs13010054

Çetin, N., Karaman, K., Kavuncuoğlu, E., Yıldırım, B., & Jahanbakhshi, A. (2022). Using hyperspectral imaging technology and machine learning algorithms for assessing internal quality parameters of apple fruits. *Chemometrics and Intelligent Laboratory Systems*, *230*, 104650. doi:10.1016/j.chemolab.2022.104650

Firouz, M. S., Farahmandi, A., & Hosseinpour, S. (2019). Recent advances in ultrasound application as a novel technique in analysis, processing and quality control of fruits, juices and dairy products industries: A review. *Ultrasonics Sonochemistry*, *57*, 73–88. doi:10.1016/j.ultsonch.2019.05.014 PMID:31208621

Hamza, R., & Chtourou, M. (2018, July). Apple ripeness estimation using artificial neural network. In *2018 International Conference on High Performance Computing & Simulation (HPCS)* (pp. 229-234). IEEE. 10.1109/HPCS.2018.00049

Hussain, A., Pu, H., & Sun, D. W. (2019). Measurements of lycopene contents in fruit: A review of recent developments in conventional and novel techniques. *Critical Reviews in Food Science and Nutrition*, *59*(5), 758–769. doi:10.1080/10408398.2018.1518896 PMID:30582342

Mavridou, E., Vrochidou, E., Papakostas, G. A., Pachidis, T., & Kaburlasos, V. G. (2019). Machine vision systems in precision agriculture for crop farming. *Journal of Imaging*, *5*(12), 89. doi:10.3390/jimaging5120089 PMID:34460603

Patil, K., Meshram, V., Hanchate, D., & Ramkteke, S. D. (2021). Machine learning in agriculture domain: A state-of-art survey. *Artificial Intelligence in the Life Sciences*, *1*, 100010. doi:10.1016/j.ailsci.2021.100010

Penumuru, D. P., Muthuswamy, S., & Karumbu, P. (2020). Identification and classification of materials using machine vision and machine learning in the context of industry 4.0. *Journal of Intelligent Manufacturing*, *31*(5), 1229–1241. doi:10.1007/s10845-019-01508-6

Pereira, C. S., Morais, R., & Reis, M. J. C. S. (2017). Recent advances in image processing techniques for automated harvesting purposes: A review. *Proceedings of the 2017 Intelligent Systems Conference (IntelliSys)*, 566-575. 10.1109/IntelliSys.2017.8324352

Rehman, T. U., Mahmud, M. S., Chang, Y. K., Jin, J., & Shin, J. (2019). Current and future applications of statistical machine learning algorithms for agricultural machine vision systems. *Computers and Electronics in Agriculture*, *156*, 585–605. doi:10.1016/j.compag.2018.12.006

Sivanantham, K. (2022). Deep learning-based convolutional neural network with cuckoo search optimization for MRI brain tumour segmentation. In *Computational Intelligence Techniques for Green Smart Cities* (pp. 149–168). Springer International Publishing. doi:10.1007/978-3-030-96429-0_7

Tian, H., Wang, T., Liu, Y., Qiao, X., & Li, Y. (2020). Computer vision technology in agricultural automation—A review. *Information Processing in Agriculture*, *7*(1), 1–19. doi:10.1016/j.inpa.2019.09.006

Wan, P., Toudeshki, A., Tan, H., & Ehsani, R. (2018). A methodology for fresh tomato maturity detection using computer vision. *Computers and Electronics in Agriculture*, *146*, 43–50. doi:10.1016/j.compag.2018.01.011

Wang, W., Yang, W., Li, M., Zhang, Z., & Du, W. (2023). A Novel Approach for Apple Freshness Prediction Based on Gas Sensor Array and Optimized Neural Network. *Sensors (Basel)*, *23*(14), 6476. doi:10.3390/s23146476 PMID:37514770

Xiao, B., Nguyen, M., & Yan, W. Q. (2021). Apple ripeness identification using deep learning. In *Geometry and Vision: First International Symposium, ISGV 2021, Auckland, New Zealand, January 28-29, 2021, Revised Selected Papers 1* (pp. 53-67). Springer International Publishing.

Xiao, Z., Wang, J., Han, L., Guo, S., & Cui, Q. (2022). Application of machine vision system in food detection. *Frontiers in Nutrition*, *9*, 888245. doi:10.3389/fnut.2022.888245 PMID:35634395

Zhu, L., Spachos, P., Pensini, E., & Plataniotis, K. N. (2021). Deep learning and machine vision for food processing: A survey. *Current Research in Food Science*, *4*, 233–249. doi:10.1016/j.crfs.2021.03.009 PMID:33937871

Chapter 5
Advancing Wild Animal Conservation Through Autonomous Systems Leveraging YOLOV7 With SGD Optimization Technique

Johnwesily Chappidi

(iD) https://orcid.org/0009-0005-2000-2462

VIT-AP University, India

Divya Meena Sundaram

VIT-AP University, India

ABSTRACT

In the field of conserving wildlife, the utilization of autonomous systems equipped with computer vision holds tremendous promise. This research explores the potential of integrating YOLO v7, a cutting-edge object recognition model, with stochastic gradient descent (SGD) optimization techniques to bolster wild animal conservation efforts. The primary objective is to enhance the precision, accuracy, and scalability of autonomous systems in detecting and monitoring wild animals across diverse habitats. The experimental results showcase substantial advancements, demonstrating the efficacy of the YOLOv7-SGD amalgamation in autonomous systems. The model exhibits superior detection accuracy and robustness in identifying a multitude of wild animal species across diverse landscapes.

I. INTRODUCTION

The delicate balance between human development and wildlife conservation has become increasingly strained in recent decades, with ecological sustainability and biodiversity facing unprecedented threats. Habitat loss, climate change, and burgeoning human populations have given rise to complex conserva-

DOI: 10.4018/979-8-3693-5767-5.ch005

tion challenges, underscoring the pressing need for innovative solutions that reconcile human activities with the protection of our planet's diverse fauna. In light of this, the integration of autonomous systems has become an issue of concern in the discipline of wildlife conservation, providing a range of tools that could fundamentally alter the methods by which we protect ecosystems and animal species.

The 21st century has witnessed the rapid expansion of urban areas, encroaching on once-wild territories, often leading to Animal-Human Conflict (AHC) and the degradation of natural habitats (Kundu et al., 2023). These conflicts, such as those involving large carnivores and agriculture, elephants and crop damage, or primates and urban infrastructure, pose risks to both animal populations and human livelihoods. Concurrently, The severity of animal-vehicle collisions (AVCs) has risen as a result of developing modes of transportation, killing humans as well as animals. (Mammeri et al., 2016). Additionally, the poaching and trafficking of endangered species remain persistent threats to conservation efforts, threatening to erase irreplaceable links in the web of life.

The research topic's importance arises from its ability to tackle these complex problems of conservation. Autonomous systems encompass a spectrum of technologies, including artificial intelligence, sensors, robotics, and data analytics, that empower researchers, conservationists, and policymakers with a new set of tools to protect and preserve wildlife and their habitats. These technologies not only facilitate real-time monitoring and data collection but also enable proactive measures to mitigate conflicts, enhance animal well-being, and improve overall conservation strategies. In the face of an accelerating environmental crisis, the role of autonomous systems in animal conservation is pivotal, as they offer a ray of hope for redefining humanity's relationship with the natural world.

This paper aims to comprehensively examine the various applications of autonomous systems in the realm of animal conservation, spanning a wide spectrum of endeavours. This research endeavours to offer a comprehensive view of how autonomous systems can shape the future of animal conservation by providing innovative solutions to mitigate conflict, prevent harm, and promote coexistence between humans and the animal kingdom. Despite remarkable advancements in computer vision, the precise detection and monitoring of wild animals in varying environmental conditions remain a significant challenge. This challenge becomes particularly pronounced in expansive and often remote habitats, where manual surveillance is limited in feasibility and efficiency. The demand for accurate and real-time identification of species, especially endangered ones, prompts the exploration of advanced technologies to address this critical conservation need.

The objective of this research study is to investigate the potential applications of YOLO v7., an emerging animal detection architecture popular for its precision and rapidity, in the field of wild animal conservation (Li et al., 2023). Complementing this exploration, the study aims to harness the advantages offered by Stochastic Gradient Descent (SGD) optimisation techniques to fine-tune the YOLOv7 model for heightened performance in wildlife detection. By amalgamating the robustness of YOLOv7 with the strategic optimisation capabilities of SGD, this research endeavours to revolutionise the landscape of autonomous systems deployed in wildlife conservation. Through a comprehensive investigation into the adaptation and optimisation of YOLOv7 with SGD for wild animal detection, this study seeks to usher in a new era of efficient and precise monitoring methods. The subsequent sections delve deeper into the methodologies employed, the experimental results attained, and the implications of this research on wildlife conservation practices. Proceeding from this section in the rest of the sections contain as follows. Section 2 contains the literature review, which includes an extensive examination of existing research, methods, advances, and findings. Section 3 is about methodology; that part includes a discussion of the Model Architecture of YOLOv7 and the performance of SGD. Results and Performance Analysis will be seen in Section 4. There will be a discussion of Quantitative Evaluation Metrics, Comparison with Baselines and Previous Models

II. LITERATURE REVIEW

The literature surrounding object detection in wildlife conservation and ecological studies showcases a spectrum of methodologies and their efficacy in addressing the challenges of monitoring wildlife populations. Numerous research works have investigated the use of computer vision techniques such as convolutional neural networks (CNNs), for population estimation, behavioural evaluation, and identifying different species. Notably, You Only Look Once (YOLO) has evolved. Models, such as YOLO's V4 and v5, has significantly improved object detection accuracy and speed, demonstrating promise in diverse domains, including wildlife monitoring.

The utilisation of Deep Neural Networks (DNN) for object recognition was first introduced in the Pascal Visual Object Classes (VOC) challenge (Sermanet et al., 2014). Later, the ImageNet Large Scale Visual Recognition Challenge (ILSVRC) emerged as the primary standard for evaluating object detection using Convolutional Neural Networks (CNNs) (LeCun et al., 2015). (Krizhevsky et al., 2012) devised a Convolutional Neural Network (CNN) to generate a bounding box around an object. However, its performance is suboptimal when dealing with photos containing many objects. (Girshick et al., 2014) integrated masks at the pixel level for individual object instances alongside a bounding box. The method is referred to as Mask R-CNN (He et al., 2017). These enhancements are substantial and can be implemented for the detection of animal species. The authors utilised convolutional neural networks (CNNs) to generate region recommendations and named their approach the R-CNN detector, specifically referring to regions containing CNN properties. Fast R-CNN (Girshick et al., 2015) was offered as a solution to decrease the computational complexity of CNN and enhance both the speed and precision of object detection, building upon the achievements of region proposal approaches. (Ren et al., 2016) combined the region proposal network (RPN) and Fast R-CNN into a single network known as Faster R-CNN.

However, within the scope of wildlife conservation, challenges persist in achieving high-precision object detection across varying environmental conditions and species diversity. The adaptability of object detection models to complex habitats, varying lighting conditions, and the identification of multiple species within a single frame remains a research focal point. Additionally, the optimization of training strategies and the integration of advanced optimization techniques tailored explicitly for object detection in wildlife conservation contexts are areas demanding further exploration.

A deep learning model which is YOLO known for its accuracy, and speed in detecting wild animals. YOLO is based on a neural network design designed for accurate real-time object detection. and image segmentation (Redmon et al., 2016) YOLOv1, which is unified and real-time object detection, has been proposed and released.; (Redmon et al., 2017) released YOLOv2, or YOLO9000, which is stronger, faster, and better; and (Redmon et al., 2018) released YOLOv3 (an incremental improvement). PyTorch was used to implement YOLOv3. However, in the shortest possible amount of duration, YOLOv4, which has optimal accuracy in detecting objects and speed (Bochkovskiy et al., 2020) and YOLO's v5 (Jocher et al., 2022) were released, respectively. YOLOv4 obtained 65 FPS on the Tesla V100 and 43.5% average precision on the COCO data set after being deployed on the Darknet. YOLOv5 comes with a CSP as the backbone and PA-NET as the neck, working like version YOLOv4. YOLOv5 brings two main advancements: automatic learning of bounding box anchors and augmentation of mosaic data. (Li et al., 2022) developed and published YOLO v6, a framework for one-stage detection of objects intended for applications in industry, in 2022. The authors claim that YOLOv6 achieves the best accuracy and speed trade-off. YOLOv7 (Wang et al., 2023) In terms of both speed and precision, version E6 results are better than transformer-based detectors like SWINL Cascade Mask R-CNN. Furthermore, YOLO v7 outperformed Scaled-YOLO v4, YOLO v5, Vit-Adapter-B, PP-YOLO, YOLO X, YOLO R, DETR, Deformable DETR, and DINO-5 scale-R50. YOLO algorithms have been applied to agricultural tasks in several works, including (Hatton-Jones et al., 2021) (Schütz et al., 2021) (Jintasuttisak et al., 2022) (Siriani et al., 2022).

This review emphasises the need for new strategies that combine sophisticated detection models—like YOLO v7—with efficient training techniques to increase detection precision, resilience, and generalizability. By leveraging the strengths of YOLOv7 and incorporating advanced optimisation techniques using detector methods, this research aims to close the disparity between present techniques and the need for successful wildlife conservation.

III. PROPOSED METHODOLOGY

The choice of YOLOv7 as the base architecture stems from its inherent efficiency in object detection and its ability to balance speed and accuracy. The YOLOv7 is renowned for its exceptional performance in a range of tasks related to object detection. Extensive comprehension of YOLOv7's architecture, comprising its backbone network, feature extraction mechanisms, and detection head structures, serves as the foundation for adaptation.

Modifications are strategically introduced to the YOLOv7 architecture to optimise it specifically for wildlife detection scenarios. Attention mechanisms, such as spatial and channel-wise attention modules, are integrated within the backbone network to enhance the model's focus on crucial wildlife features while reducing noise from the background. Feature fusion techniques, including feature pyramid networks (FPN) (Li et al., 2019) or spatial pyramid pooling (SPP) (Huang et al., 2020), are implemented to capture multi-scale information vital for detecting wildlife in various sizes and poses across diverse environments.

The anchor box configurations within YOLOv7, responsible for predicting bounding boxes, are adapted to align with the diverse aspect ratios and scales of wildlife species. Fine-tuning anchor box priors ensures better localisation and recognition of animals with varying shapes and proportions. Furthermore, output layers are tailored to accommodate the detection of a comprehensive range of wildlife species, augmenting the model's capacity to discern multiple classes of animals. The YOLOv7 adaptation process involves the integration of domain-specific knowledge and features relevant to wildlife detection. For better results, the model's capacity to distinguish between similar-looking wildlife and precisely recognise particular wildlife categories involves adding texture patterns, colour gradients, and distinctive features inherent to different wildlife.

Figure 1. Wild animal detection using YOLOv7 and SGD optimizer

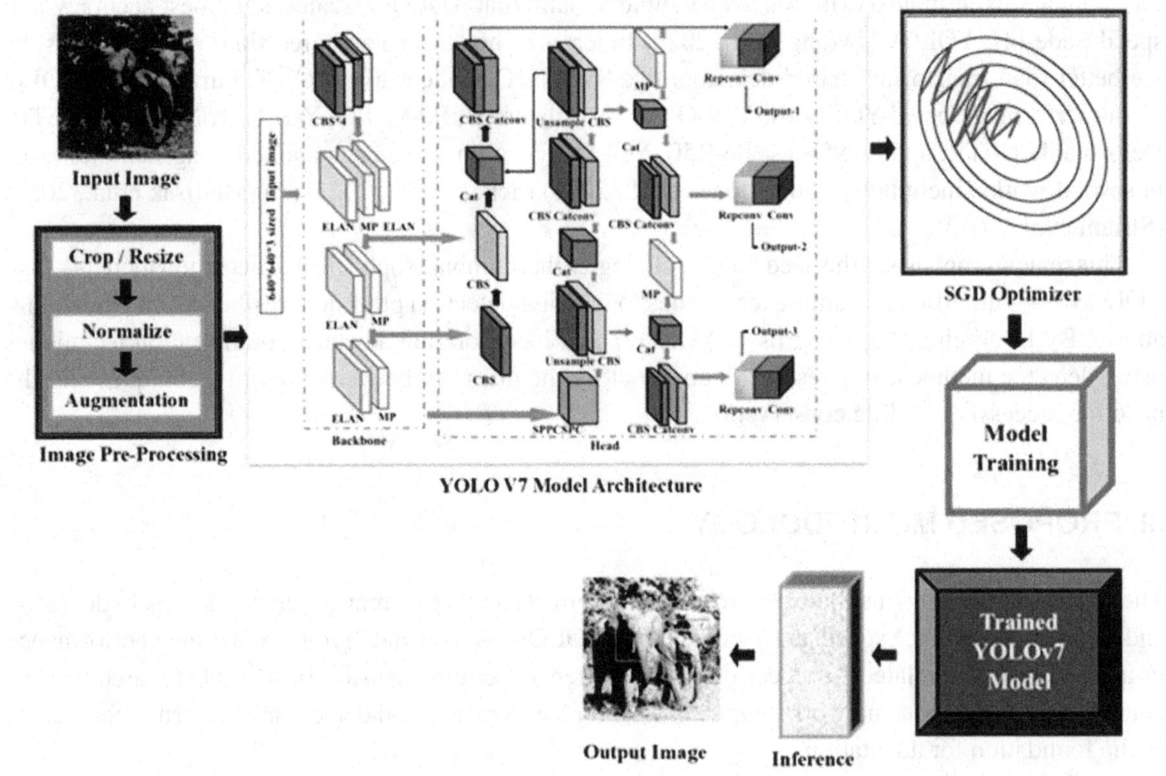

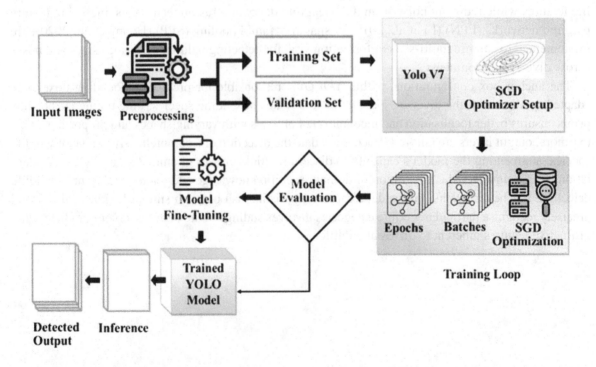

Figure 2. Flow diagram YOLO v7 with SGD

3.1

3.1.1 Utilisation of Stochastic Gradient Descent (SGD) With Momentum

Stochastic Gradient Descent (SGD) serves as the cornerstone optimisation algorithm for training the adapted YOLOv7 model. The utilisation of SGD with momentum introduces an adaptive learning approach, enabling the model to navigate the high-dimensional parameter space efficiently. This technique helps alleviate the issues of local minima by integrating momentum to accelerate convergence and smoothen the optimisation trajectory, facilitating quicker convergence towards optimal solutions.

3.1.2 Learning Rate Schedules and Adaptive Strategies

Sophisticated learning rate schedules, such as step decay, exponential decay, or cyclic learning rates, are employed to dynamically adjust the learning rates during training. These schedules facilitate adaptive learning by modulating the learning rates based on the model's performance or the number of training iterations. Specifically, warm-up techniques involving gradual learning rate increments at the initial training stages aid in stabilising the optimisation process, preventing abrupt changes that might hinder convergence.

3.1.3 Regularization Techniques for Model Generalization

To mitigate overfitting and enhance the model's generalisation capabilities, regularisation techniques are integrated into the optimisation process. Weight decay, a form of L2 regularisation, is applied to impose penalty terms on the model's weights during optimisation, preventing excessively large weight magnitudes and promoting simpler model solutions. Additionally, dropout layers are strategically introduced to randomly deactivate certain neurons during training, encouraging the network to learn more robust and generalised features.

3.1.4 Hyperparameter Tuning and Optimization Strategies

Fine-tuning of hyperparameters, including batch sizes, momentum coefficients, weight decay rates, and dropout probabilities, is conducted through systematic experimentation and grid search methodologies. Optimisation strategies are refined based on empirical observations from validation metrics, ensuring optimal convergence behaviour and preventing underfitting or overfitting tendencies.

3.2 Training Procedure

3.2.1 Initialisation and Pretrained Weights

The training procedure commences with initialising the adapted YOLOv7 model's weights, either randomly or through transfer learning from pre-trained weights on a large-scale dataset. Transfer learning leverages the knowledge acquired from training on general object recognition tasks, aiding the model in learning domain-specific features for wildlife detection.

3.2.2 Mini-Batch Stochastic Optimization

The training process employs mini-batch stochastic optimisation, where batches of annotated wildlife images are fed into the model iteratively. This stochastic approach helps in achieving faster convergence and facilitates efficient utilisation of computational resources. Each mini batch undergoes forward propagation to generate predictions and subsequent backward propagation to compute gradients for updating the model's weights.

3.2.3 Backpropagation and Weight Updates

Backpropagation, augmented by the chain rule of calculus, computes the gradients of the loss function with respect to the model's parameters. These gradients are then utilised to update the model's weights iteratively through optimisation algorithms, such as SGD with momentum. Adaptive learning rates and regularisation techniques guide the weight updates, ensuring gradual convergence towards an optimal solution while preventing overfitting.

3.2.4 Epoch-Based Training

The training process is organised into multiple epochs, where each epoch represents a complete iteration over the entire training dataset. At the end of each epoch, the model's performance metrics on the validation set are evaluated to monitor convergence and prevent overfitting. The training continues until convergence criteria are met or until the model exhibits stable performance on the validation set.

3.2.5 Fine-Tuning and Iterative Refinement

Fine-tuning iterations are conducted based on observed performance on the validation set. Adjustments in hyperparameters, optimisation strategies, or architectural modifications are implemented iteratively to further refine the model's performance. This iterative process aims to enhance the model's accuracy, robustness, and generalisation abilities.

IV. EXPERIMENTAL FRAMEWORK

4.1 System Setup

4.1.1 Hardware and Software Configuration

The experiments are conducted using a high-performance computing infrastructure equipped with GPU accelerators to expedite model training. GPU specifications, including type, memory, and compute capability, are documented. The training environment comprises deep learning frameworks such as TensorFlow or PyTorch, along with associated libraries and dependencies for efficient model development and training.

4.1.2 Hyperparameter Tuning

Systematic experimentation is conducted to fine-tune hyperparameters critical for the model's performance. Parameters such as batch sizes, learning rates, momentum coefficients, weight decay rates, dropout probabilities, and optimisation configurations are adjusted through grid search or random search methodologies. Cross-validation techniques may be employed on the validation set to identify optimal hyperparameter combinations that yield superior model performance.

4.1.3 Training Duration and Computational Resources

The duration of model training and the computational resources utilised are documented. Training duration per epoch, total training epochs, and computational resources, including GPU utilisation and memory consumption, are recorded. This information facilitates the reproducibility and scalability of the experimental setup.

4.2 Training and Fine-Tuning

4.2.1 Model Initialization and Pretraining

The training process commences with initialising the YOLOv7 model's weights, leveraging either random initialisation or transfer learning from pre-trained weights on a large-scale dataset. Transfer learning allows the model to leverage previously learned features from general object recognition tasks, aiding in the extraction of domain-specific features crucial for wildlife detection.

4.2.2 Iterative Mini-Batch Stochastic Optimization

The adapted YOLOv7 model undergoes iterative mini-batch stochastic optimisation, where batches of annotated wildlife images are fed into the model for training. During each iteration, the model computes predictions, computes gradients through backpropagation, and updates its weights using optimisation algorithms like SGD with momentum. This stochastic optimisation facilitates faster convergence and efficient utilisation of computational resources.

4.2.3 Validation-Based Fine-Tuning

The training process incorporates periodic evaluations of the validation set to monitor the model's convergence and prevent overfitting. Based on the observed performance metrics on the validation set, fine-tuning iterations are conducted. Adjustments in hyperparameters, optimisation strategies, or architectural modifications are iteratively implemented to further enhance the model's accuracy and generalisation ability.

4.2.4 Regularisation and Optimization Strategies

To prevent overfitting and enhance generalisation, regularisation techniques such as weight decay and dropout layers are employed. Weight decay imposes penalty terms on the model's weights during optimisation, preventing excessively large weight magnitudes. Dropout layers randomly deactivate certain neurons during training, encouraging the network to learn more robust features.

4.2.5 Model Complexity and Convergence Analysis

The model's complexity and convergence behaviour is monitored throughout the training process. Analysis of training curves, including loss plots and accuracy trends, provides insights into the model's learning dynamics. Additionally, convergence criteria, such as stability in validation metrics or convergence of loss functions, guide the termination of training to prevent overfitting.

4.3 Dataset Description

The presented study utilises two open-access datasets: the Wild Animals Computer Vision Project and the Animal Image Dataset. The Wild Animals Computer Vision Project dataset is a carefully selected set of images intended for the aim of training and evaluating wild animal detection and classification algorithms. The dataset comprises a wide variety of wildlife species that were captured in their natural environments. Every individual image in the dataset has been extensively annotated with metadata, which comprises species labels, geographic coordinates, and supplementary contextual details. Bear, Cheetah, Elephant, Fox, Giraffe, Jaguar, Leopard, Lion, Tiger, Zebra, and many others are among its many classes. The Animal Image Dataset, the second dataset, comprises 5400 images of animals organised into 90 classes of distinct classifications.

4.4 Performance Metrics

4.4.1 Quantitative Evaluation Metrics

The performance of the trained YOLOv7 model is quantitatively assessed using a suite of evaluation metrics, including Mean Average Precision (mAP), precision, recall, Intersection over Union (IoU), accuracy, and F1 score. These metrics provide a comprehensive evaluation of the model's accuracy, localisation precision, and generalisation across diverse wildlife species and environmental conditions.

4.4.2 Comparison With Baselines and Previous Models

The performance of the adapted YOLOv7 model is benchmarked against baseline models and previous iterations of YOLO architectures, such as YOLOv4 or YOLOv5, on the same dataset. Comparative analyses highlight the advancements achieved in wildlife detection accuracy and robustness, emphasising the superiority of the adapted YOLOv7 model.

4.4.3 Qualitative Visualizations and Error Analysis

Visualisations of detection outputs, including bounding boxes overlaying predicted wildlife instances on test images, provide qualitative insights into the model's performance. Error analysis elucidates the model's strengths and weaknesses, identifying common failure cases, misclassifications, or localisation errors. This qualitative assessment aids in understanding the model's behaviour and guiding potential improvements.

4.4.3 Statistical Significance and Confidence Intervals

Statistical analyses, such as significance testing or confidence interval estimation, may be performed to validate the observed performance improvements. This ensures the robustness of the obtained results and confirms the statistical significance of performance differences between the adapted YOLOv7 model and baseline methods.

V. RESULTS AND DISCUSSION

A range of evaluation metrics, such as precision, recall, mAP, F1 score, IoU, and accuracy, are used to measure the effectiveness of the trained YOLOv7 model. These metrics offer a thorough assessment of the model's accuracy, precise localisation, and generalisation across different kinds of wildlife and conditions in the environment.

The enhanced YOLOv7 model's performance is compared to the baseline models and earlier YOLO architecture iterations. such as YOLOv4 or YOLOv5, on the same dataset. Comparative analyses highlight the advancements achieved in wildlife detection accuracy and robustness, emphasizing the superiority of the adapted YOLOv7 model. Bounding boxes superimposed over estimated wildlife cases on testing images have an instance of visualizations of detection outputs that offer qualitative perspectives into the performance of the model. Error analysis elucidates the model's strengths and weaknesses, identifying common failure cases, misclassifications, or localization errors. This qualitative assessment aids in understanding the model's behaviour and guiding potential improvements.

To validate the observed performance improvements, statistical analyses such as significance testing or confidence interval estimation may be performed. This ensures the robustness of the obtained results and confirms the statistical significance of performance differences between the adapted YOLOv7 model and baseline methods. The results are critically analysed, highlighting the strengths, limitations, and implications of the developed YOLOv7-based wildlife detection model.

The model's adaptability, accuracy, scalability to different environments, and possibilities for use in practical applications conservation situations are all thoroughly discussed. The obtained results are comprehensively analysed, highlighting the model's strengths in accurately detecting wildlife across diverse habitats. The model's robustness in handling varying lighting conditions, occlusions, and species diversity is discussed based on the achieved performance metrics and visual analyses of detection outputs. A comparative analysis is conducted, juxtaposing the developed YOLOv7-based model's performance with existing methodologies and previous versions of YOLO models in wildlife conservation. Insights are drawn regarding the significance of integrating YOLOv7 with SGD optimization techniques in advancing object detection capabilities for conservation purpose.

The practical implications of the research findings in real-world wildlife conservation scenarios are discussed. Potential applications of the developed object detection system in monitoring endangered species, preserving ecosystems, and informing conservation strategies are outlined. Moreover, avenues for future research, including model refinement, dataset expansion, and exploration of additional op-

Figure 3. Input images along with detected images

Table 1. Quantitative metrics

S.No	Metrics	Animal Classes (AC)					
		AC 1	AC 2	AC 3	AC 4	AC 5	AC 6
1.	mAP	0.87	0.81	0.92	0.89	0.84	0.90
2.	Precision	0.80	0.85	0.89	0.91	0.88	0.86
3.	Recall	0.84	0.78	0.91	0.87	0.83	0.92
4.	IoU	0.79	0.83	0.88	0.92	0.86	0.90
5.	F1 Score	0.82	0.80	0.90	0.88	0.85	0.91

timisation techniques, are proposed to further enhance object detection accuracy and applicability in wildlife conservation efforts.

Figure 4. (a) mAP comparison among models, (b) IoU comparison among models, (c) Precision comparison among models, (d) F1 Score comparison among models

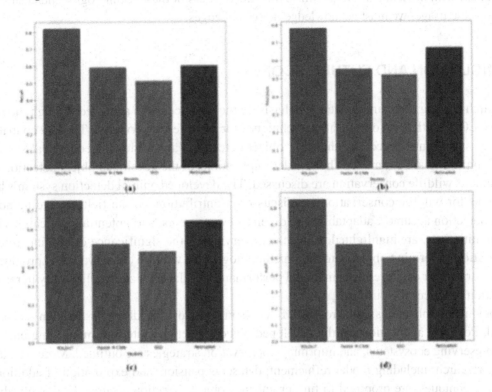

Table 2. Result analysis of the wild animals computer vision project dataset

S.NO	Algorithm	Precision (%)	Recall (%)	F1 Score (%)	mAP (%)	Inference Speed (fps)
1	YOLOv7 (SGD)	94.1	91.5	92.8	90.3	30
2	YOLOv7	90.5	87.2	88.8	86.5	25
3	YOLOv5	91.8	88.7	90.2	87.9	20
4	Faster R-CNN	86.5	84.7	86.4	83.9	12
5	SSD	86.7	82.5	84.5	82.0	18
6	R-CNN	85.9	81.6	83.7	81.2	10

Table 3. Comparing the proposed method with others using the animal image dataset

S.NO	Algorithm	Precision (%)	Recall (%)	F1 Score (%)	mAP (%)	Inference Speed (fps)
1	YOLOv7 (SGD	92.1	89.5	90.8	88.3	30
2	YOLOv7	90.5	87.2	88.8	86.5	25
3	YOLOv5	91.8	88.7	90.2	87.9	20
4	Faster R-CNN	88.2	85.3	87.4	83.9	12
5	SSD	86.7	82.5	84.5	82.0	18
6	R-CNN	85.9	81.6	83.7	81.2	10

While the use of autonomous systems in animal conservation holds great promise, their implementation is fraught with difficulties. To maximise the effectiveness of these technologies and ensure ethical and responsible usage, we must acknowledge these challenges.

VI. CONCLUSION AND FUTURE SCOPE

The research findings are summarised, emphasising the advancements achieved through the integration of YOLOv7 with SGD optimisation techniques for wildlife conservation. The key contributions and novel aspects introduced in enhancing object detection capabilities for ecological studies and wildlife monitoring are reiterated. The broader implications of the developed object detection system in the realm of wildlife conservation are discussed. The developed animal detection system's broader implications for wildlife conservation are discussed. Contributions to the field, including advancements in detection accuracy, adaptability to diverse environments, and potential applications in conservation initiatives, are highlighted. A succinct overview of the significance of continued research and innovation in refining object detection methodologies for wildlife conservation is provided. The prospects for further enhancements in model performance, scalability, and applicability in real-world conservation practices are outlined.

The practical implications of the research findings in real-world wildlife conservation scenarios are discussed. Potential applications of the developed object detection system in monitoring endangered species, preserving ecosystems, and informing conservation strategies are outlined. Moreover, avenues for future research, including model refinement, dataset expansion, and exploration of additional optimization techniques, are proposed to further enhance object detection accuracy and applicability in wildlife conservation efforts.

REFERENCES

Girshick, R. (2015). Fast r-cnn. In *Proceedings of the IEEE international conference on computer vision* (pp. 1440-1448). Academic Press.

Girshick, R., Donahue, J., Darrell, T., & Malik, J. (2014). Rich feature hierarchies for accurate object detection and semantic segmentation. In *Proceedings of the IEEE conference on computer vision and pattern recognition* (pp. 580-587). 10.1109/CVPR.2014.81

Hatton-Jones, K. M., Christie, C., Griffith, T. A., Smith, A. G., Naghipour, S., Robertson, K., Russell, J. S., Peart, J. N., Headrick, J. P., Cox, A. J., & du Toit, E. F. (2021). A YOLO based software for automated detection and analysis of rodent behaviour in the open field arena. *Computers in Biology and Medicine*, *134*, 104474. doi:10.1016/j.compbiomed.2021.104474 PMID:34058512

He, K., Gkioxari, G., Dollár, P., & Girshick, R. (2017). Mask r-cnn. In *Proceedings of the IEEE international conference on computer vision* (pp. 2961-2969). Academic Press.

Huang, Z., Wang, J., Fu, X., Yu, T., Guo, Y., & Wang, R. (2020). DC-SPP-YOLO: Dense connection and spatial pyramid pooling based YOLO for object detection. *Information Sciences*, *522*, 241–258. doi:10.1016/j.ins.2020.02.067

Jintasuttisak, T., Leonce, A., Sher Shah, M., Khafaga, T., Simkins, G., & Edirisinghe, E. (2022, March). Deep learning based animal detection and tracking in drone video footage. In *Proceedings of the 8th International Conference on Computing and Artificial Intelligence* (pp. 425-431). 10.1145/3532213.3532280

Krizhevsky, A., Sutskever, I., & Hinton, G. E. (2012). Imagenet classification with deep convolutional neural networks. *Advances in Neural Information Processing Systems*, 25.

Kundu, K., Vishwakarma, V., Rai, A., Srivastava, M., & Mishra, A. (2023, April). Design and Deployment of Wild Animal Intrusion Detection & Repellent System Employing IOT. In *2023 International Conference on Computational Intelligence and Sustainable Engineering Solutions (CISES)* (pp. 763-767). IEEE. 10.1109/CISES58720.2023.10183532

LeCun, Y., Bengio, Y., & Hinton, G. (2015). Deep learning. *Nature, 521*(7553), 436-444.

Li, S., Zhang, H., & Xu, F. (2023). Intelligent Detection Method for Wildlife Based on Deep Learning. *Sensors (Basel), 23*(24), 9669. doi:10.3390/s23249669 PMID:38139515

Li, X., Lai, T., Wang, S., Chen, Q., Yang, C., Chen, R., ... Zheng, F. (2019, December). Weighted feature pyramid networks for object detection. In *2019 IEEE Intl Conf on Parallel & Distributed Processing with Applications, Big Data & Cloud Computing, Sustainable Computing & Communications, Social Computing & Networking (ISPA/BDCloud/SocialCom/SustainCom)* (pp. 1500-1504). IEEE.

Mammeri, A., Zhou, D., & Boukerche, A. (2016). Animal-vehicle collision mitigation system for automated vehicles. *IEEE Transactions on Systems, Man, and Cybernetics. Systems, 46*(9), 1287–1299. doi:10.1109/TSMC.2015.2497235

Redmon, J., Divvala, S., Girshick, R., & Farhadi, A. (2016). You only look once: Unified, real-time object detection. In *Proceedings of the IEEE conference on computer vision and pattern recognition* (pp. 779-788). 10.1109/CVPR.2016.91

Redmon, J., & Farhadi, A. (2017). YOLO9000: better, faster, stronger. In *Proceedings of the IEEE conference on computer vision and pattern recognition* (pp. 7263-7271).

Redmon, J., & Farhadi, A. (2018). Yolov3: An incremental improvement. *arXiv preprint arXiv:1804.02767*.

Ren, S., He, K., Girshick, R., & Sun, J. (2016). Faster R-CNN: Towards real-time object detection with region proposal networks. *IEEE Transactions on Pattern Analysis and Machine Intelligence, 39*(6), 1137–1149. doi:10.1109/TPAMI.2016.2577031 PMID:27295650

Schütz, A. K., Schöler, V., Krause, E. T., Fischer, M., Müller, T., Freuling, C. M., Conraths, F. J., Stanke, M., Homeier-Bachmann, T., & Lentz, H. H. (2021). Application of YOLOv4 for detection and Motion monitoring of red Foxes. *Animals (Basel), 11*(6), 1723. doi:10.3390/ani11061723 PMID:34207726

Sermanet, P., Eigen, D., Zhang, X., Mathieu, M., Fergus, R., & LeCun, Y. (2013). Overfeat: Integrated recognition, localization and detection using convolutional networks. arXiv preprint arXiv:1312.6229.

Siriani, A. L. R., Kodaira, V., Mehdizadeh, S. A., de Alencar Nääs, I., de Moura, D. J., & Pereira, D. F. (2022). Detection and tracking of chickens in low-light images using YOLO network and Kalman filter. *Neural Computing & Applications, 34*(24), 21987–21997. doi:10.1007/s00521-022-07664-w

Wang, C. Y., Bochkovskiy, A., & Liao, H. Y. M. (2023). YOLOv7: Trainable bag-of-freebies sets new state-of-the-art for real-time object detectors. In *Proceedings of the IEEE/CVF Conference on Computer Vision and Pattern Recognition* (pp. 7464-7475). 10.1109/CVPR52729.2023.00721

Chapter 6
Evaluating Customer Satisfaction and Trust in Autonomous AI Banking Systems

Aruna Kasinathan

 https://orcid.org/0000-0002-5800-0340

Karunya Institute of Technology and Science, India

Shrilatha Sampath

 https://orcid.org/0000-0002-5951-4175

Christian Medical College, India

Hemalatha Sampath

University of Maryland, USA

ABSTRACT

The study aims to assess customer satisfaction and trust in autonomous artificial intelligence (AAI) systems within the banking sector. Its primary objectives include exploring factors contributing to customer trust in AAI, investigating preferences for AI-driven features in banking, and determining the impact of AAI on perceived service quality. The research, adopting a descriptive design, employs both qualitative and quantitative methods. A survey, distributed to customers of leading banks in India, particularly in Tamil Nadu, with a sample size of 213, utilizes simple random and convenient sampling. Results highlight customer preferences for customized services, financial advice, and automation in banking. The implementation of AAI is perceived positively, especially in terms of transparency in processes like loans, account management, and more. Practical implications include helping banks understand customer expectations, identify weaknesses in AAI features, and enhance service quality in Tamil Nadu.

DOI: 10.4018/979-8-3693-5767-5.ch006

INTRODUCTION

In the context of the aforementioned key players in the Indian banking sector, the research article establishes a direct connection between the adoption of artificial intelligence (AI) and the stated objectives. Suparna Biswas, Brant Carson, Violet Chung, Shwaitang Singh, and Renny Thomas (2023). Firstly, the implementation of AI applications, such as smart chat assistants, chatbots, and robotics, by banks like the SBI, HDFC, ICICI, Axis, Bank of Baroda, Andhra Bank, and Kotak Mahindra Bank, is intricately linked to the objective of building customer trust in autonomous AI systems. The study delves into how these technologies enhance customer experiences, thereby fostering trust through efficient and personalized services. Additionally, the research investigates customer preferences concerning AI-driven features, aligning with the objective of understanding what elements contribute to customer trust and satisfaction in the context of autonomous AI systems in banking. . Larson (2021) and Baesens et al. (2005) Furthermore, the article analyzes the impact of autonomous AI on the perceived quality of banking services, shedding light on how these technological advancements contribute to efficiency gains, cost reduction, and improved customer service, thereby influencing the overall service quality perception. In exploring the implications on the workforce, the study emphasizes the pivotal roles of new professional categorics, such as AI specialists, data scientists, and machine learning engineers, who are instrumental in designing and maintaining these AI-driven systems. The research also addresses the evolving roles of traditional banking professionals, like customer service representatives and risk analysts, showcasing how they collaborate with AI tools to enhance efficiency and personalization. This detailed exploration provides a comprehensive understanding of the interplay between AI technology adoption, workforce dynamics, and the overarching objectives of building customer trust, understanding preferences, and assessing service quality in the Indian banking sector.

Objectives

1. Explore the factors that contribute to building customer trust in autonomous AI systems.
   2. Investigate customer preferences regarding AI-driven features in banking.
   3. Determine the impact of autonomous AI on the perceived quality of banking services.

RESEARCH METHODOLOGY

This research aims to assess customer satisfaction and trust in Autonomous AI Banking Systems across India through an online survey questionnaire, encompassing a sample population of 213 respondents through Simple Random sampling Technique. The research begins with an introduction highlighting the growing significance of Autonomous AI Banking Systems and articulating specific research objectives and questions. The literature review and theoretical framework provide a comprehensive background, grounding the study in relevant theories and existing knowledge. The research design details the sampling strategy, sample size justification, and the use of the online survey instrument, while also emphasizing variable measurement. Data analysis techniques, including ANOVA, T-test, and frequency distribution, are outlined to provide a robust statistical approach. The questionnaire design section covers the structure, types of questions, and pilot testing process. Ethical considerations address privacy, confidentiality, and informed consent. The data processing and validation section outlines steps to ensure accuracy. A realistic timeline is provided, and potential limitations are discussed. The conclusion summarizes the methodology's appropriateness for achieving the research objectives, and references are cited for all sources utilized.

LITERATURE REVIEW

Arif et al. (2023) employed a neural network methodology to examine the obstacles hindering customer adoption of internet banking. Their study aimed to identify and understand the barriers associated with this adoption, leveraging neural network techniques for a comprehensive analysis. Suparna Biswas, Brant Carson, Violet Chung, Shwaitang Singh, and Renny Thomas (2023) The statement emphasizes that the deployment of AI technologies, when carefully managed to mitigate risks, can result in increased automation and improvements in decision-making compared to human processes, particularly in terms of speed and accuracy. The assertion of AI's potential to unlock significant incremental value, estimated at $1 trillion annually for banks, underscores the transformative impact and value creation potential across industries through the integration of artificial intelligence. Belanche et al. (2022) conducted a study focusing on factors influencing the adoption of AI-driven technology within the banking sector. Their research aimed to identify and analyze the key determinants shaping the integration of artificial intelligence in banking operations.

Payne et al. (2020) explored the factors influencing the adoption of AI-enabled mobile banking services, while also highlighting the opportunity for bank marketers to leverage AI in enhancing customer segmentation, targeting, and overall positioning of banking products and services. Within the sub-theme of AI and marketing, the authors identified nine papers that collectively addressed various aspects of utilizing AI for marketing activities, such as customer segmentation, model development, and the execution of more impactful marketing campaigns. Smeureanu et al. (2013) introduced a machine learning technique for the segmentation of banking customers, employing algorithms designed to categorize customers based on relevant features. Their approach aimed to enhance the understanding of diverse customer profiles in the banking sector through the application of machine learning methodologies. Schwartz et al. (2017) employed an AI-based approach to scrutinize resource allocation in targeted advertisements, likely using artificial intelligence algorithms to optimize advertising strategies. Their research reflects a growing trend in exploring the impact of AI on shaping customer experiences, highlighting the evolving landscape of how artificial intelligence technologies are influencing and enhancing interactions between businesses and customers.

Soltani et al. (2019) and Trivedi (2019) contributed to the sub-theme of AI and customer experience, focusing on the utilization of artificial intelligence to improve banking services and overall customer experience. This theme likely encompasses research exploring how AI technologies are applied to enhance various aspects of the customer journey within the banking sector. Trivedi (2019) conducted an investigation into the use of chatbots in the banking sector and assessed their influence on customer experience. The motivation for this study may have stemmed from the suggested application of AI in predicting stock market movements and stock selection, indicating a broader exploration of AI's impact on financial services and customer interactions within the banking domain. Kim and Lee (2004) and Tseng (2003) likely contributed to the literature on artificial intelligence (AI) in the banking sector during a period when the focus was primarily on its application in credit and loan analysis. The mentioned studies suggest that, at that time, researchers were exploring how AI technologies could be employed to enhance the analysis and decision-making processes associated with credit and loans within the banking industry.

Baesens et al. (2005), Ince and Aktan (2009), Kao et al. (2012), and Khandani et al. (2010) likely contributed to the early stages of AI implementation, emphasizing the importance of developing fast and reliable AI infrastructure. This suggests that, during that period, researchers were recognizing the foundational need for robust AI frameworks to support the effective deployment of artificial intelligence in various applications, possibly including those within the banking sector. Larson (2021) and Baesens et al. (2005) likely contributed to the field of predicting loan defaults and early repayments, with Baesens et al. utilizing a neural network approach for improved accuracy in such predictions. This indicates a continued interest and application of advanced techniques, such as neural networks, in the domain of credit risk assessment within the banking sector. Ince and Aktan (2009) employed a data mining technique to analyze credit scores and concluded that the AI-driven data mining approach was more effective than traditional methods. This suggests that their research highlighted the advantages of utilizing artificial intelligence in data mining for enhanced accuracy and efficiency in assessing credit scores within the banking sector. Khandani et al. (2010) discovered that machine-learning-driven models were effective in analyzing consumer credit risk. This indicates that their research demonstrated the utility of machine learning in improving the accuracy and efficiency of credit risk analysis in the context of consumer credit within the banking sector.

Alborzi and Khanbabaei (2016) investigated the application of data mining neural network techniques for the development of a customer credit scoring model. Their research likely delved into the effectiveness and accuracy of using neural networks within the context of data mining to assess and predict customer credit scores in the banking sector. Trivedi (2019) conducted a study on chatbot satisfaction, identifying information, system, and service quality as factors with a significant positive association with overall satisfaction. This suggests that the effectiveness of chatbots in delivering satisfactory user experiences is influenced by the quality of information provided, the functionality of the system, and the overall service quality. Ekinci et al. (2014) proposed a customer lifetime value (CLV) model in the banking sector, leveraging a deep learning approach. Their research likely aimed to use advanced techniques from deep learning to identify and emphasize key indicators relevant to customer lifetime value, providing insights for more effective customer relationship management in the banking industry. Xu et al. (2020) investigated the effects of AI versus human customer service and discovered that customers are more inclined to use AI for low-complexity tasks, while a human agent is preferred for high-complexity tasks. This suggests that customer preferences vary based on the complexity of the tasks involved, with AI being favored for simpler tasks and human assistance preferred for more complex and nuanced interactions.

Khandani et al. (2010) employed machine learning techniques to construct a model aimed at predicting customers' credit risk. This indicates that their research involved leveraging advanced computational methods within the realm of machine learning to enhance the accuracy and efficiency of credit risk prediction in the banking sector. Koutanaei et al. (2015) proposed a data mining model with the goal of enhancing confidence in credit scoring systems. From an organizational risk standpoint, their research likely focused on improving the reliability and accuracy of credit scoring models through advanced data mining techniques, ultimately contributing to more robust risk management practices within the financial domain. Mall (2018) employed a neural network approach to analyze the behavior of defaulting customers, aiming to minimize credit risk and enhance profitability for credit-providing institutions. This suggests that the study focused on leveraging neural network techniques to better understand and predict customer behavior related to credit default, thereby aiding financial institutions in risk mitigation and financial decision-making.

PILOT STUDY REPORT

All the (55) variables and statements in the questionnaire for 213 sample size is validated through the Cronbach's Alpha of 0.888 represents of 88% existence of reliability and validity.

RESPONDENT PREFERENCES

The respondent preferences in this study were gender, age, qualification, annual income, and nature of the employment. All these are mere representation used to describe the sample size of the population.

A total of 213 samples were collected from all over Tamil Nadu Bank customers through Google Forms. Among the above sample 54% are male respondents and 46% are female respondents. Nearly 35.2% of the respondents falls under the age group of 18 to 25 years old. This represents that the respondents of this study possess very basic level of understanding and experience towards the autonomous artificial intelligence system of banking.

Moreover, 33.8% of the respondents have a Post Graduate Degree in various domain. About 37.6% of them were Professional in this survey such as Doctors, Engineers, Lawyers, Chartered Accountants and so on. They were also earning with an annual income of less than Rs.2,50,000. The annual income base was taken on the basis of income tax slab rates. These demographic profile of the banking customers helps to understand their satisfaction level towards autonomous artificial intelligence.

Out of 213 samples 37.6% of respondents (80) holds account in the HDFC bank, 23.5% (50) holds in ICICI bank, 19.7% (42) respondents hold account in SBI, 6.1% (13) respondents hold account in Punjab National Bank and finally 9.4% (20) of the respondents holds in other banks like IDFC, Tamil Nadu

Table 1. Case processing summary

		N	%
Cases	Valid	212	99.5
	Excluded[a]	1	.5
	Total	213	100.0

Source: Computed Value
a. Listwise deletion based on all variables in the procedure.

Table 2. Reliability statistics

Cronbach's Alpha	N of Items
.888	55

Source: Computed Value

Table 3. Respondent preferences

Demographics	Categories	Frequency	Percent
Gender	Male	115	54.0
	Female	98	46.0
Age	18 – 25 years	75	35.2
	26 - 35 years	53	24.9
	36 - 45 years	53	24.9
	Above 46 years	32	15.0
Qualification	10 & 12th Std	37	17.4
	Under Graduate	52	24.4
	Post Graduate	72	33.8
	Professional Degree	41	19.2
	Others	11	5.2
Occupation	Students	43	20.2
	Employee	50	23.5
	Professionals	80	37.6
	Business	15	7.0
	Housewife/ Retired and Others	25	11.7
Annual Income	Below 2.5 lakhs	88	41.3
	2.5 to 3 lakhs	43	20.2
	3 to 5 lakhs	38	17.8
	5 to 7.5 lakhs	44	20.7

Table 4. Bank names

Banks	Frequency	Percent
HDFC	80	37.6
ICICI	50	23.5
SBI	42	19.7
Kotak Mahindra	13	6.1
PNB	8	3.8
Other Category	20	9.4
Total	213	100.0

Mercantile Bank, Axis Bank, Indian Overseas Bank, Indian Bank, and so on. The above banks were taken according to the existing market share held in India. According to the survey conducted by Forbes India on October 16th, 2023- HDFC tops with 11.61%; ICICI as second with 6.65%; SBI as third with 5.13%; Kotak Mahindra as fourth with 3.47% and PNB as eighth with score of 0.828%.

FACTORS AND PREFERENCE OF CUSTOMERS TOWARDS AUTONOMOUS ARTIFICIAL INTELLIGENCE (AAI)

The below factors such as customized service, financial advice, risk management, cyber security and detecting the fraud, integrates chatbots, credit rating information, customer experience, market trends, moves towards automations and voice recognition are contributing to build customers trust in autonomous AI in banking sector.

CUSTOMER-RELATED FACTORS

Table 5 presents the variables related to the AAI providing to the customers focused service as an individual/ company. Bank serves according to their requirements and needs through the AAI applications without the dependency.

Table 5. Factors and preference of customers towards Autonomous Artificial Intelligence (AAI)

S. No	Customized Service (CS)	Financial Advice (FA)	Risk Management (RM)	Cyber Security and Detect the Fraud (CFD)	Integrates ChatBot with banking apps (IC)
1	Personalized Product Recommendations	Personalized Financial Analysis	Alerts the customers regarding currency fluctuations	AI-Powered Threat Detection	24/7 Availability through ChatBot Integration
2	Customized Financial Advice	Timely and Informed Recommendations	Detailed evaluation of loan application of the customers	Behavioral Analytics for Fraud Prevention	Personalized Financial Product Suggestions
3	Targeted Offers and Promotions	Dynamic Adaptation to Changing Circumstances	Regulatory Compliance and Monitoring	Real-time Transaction Monitoring	Enhanced Convenience and Customer Support
4	Individualized Credit Scoring	Strengthening Customer Loyalty	Predictive Risk Assessment (in investments)	Identity Verification & Authentication	Real-time Card Security Updates
5	Tailored Customer Experiences	Optimizing Financial Well-Being	Continuous Portfolio Monitoring	Advanced Cybersecurity Measures	

Table 6. Factors and preference of customers towards Autonomous Artificial Intelligence (AAI)

S. No	Credit Rating Information (CR)	Customer Experience (CE)	Market Trends (MT)	Moves towards Automation (AI)	Voice Recognition (VR)
1	AI-Powered Credit Scoring	More creativity and innovation (ATM/ Chatbot)	Indicates the sale opportunities	Reduce the time of loan application process	Protected from unauthorized access
2	Real-time credit Assessment of individual/ clients	Elimination of manual transactions	Gives warning towards the risk in investment	Reducing the workload of the Bank employees	Transactions are done in more secured way
3	Improved Loan Decision-making	Enhances accuracy and transparency in the transactions	Evaluate the sentiments of market	Processing time of transactions are fast	Increased customer satisfaction
4		Offers and products are informed on time		Documentation are reduced	Authentication for customers through their voice
5		Errors are reduced and increases customer experience		Reduce the time of loan application process	Future of banking service

Table 7. Customers related factors

Factors	One-Sample Test					
	Test Value = 0					
	T	Df	Sig. (2-tailed)	Mean Difference	95% Confidence Interval of the Difference	
					Lower	Upper
CS1	68.042	212	.000	3.9859	3.870	4.101
CS2	59.645	212	.000	4.1925	4.054	4.331
CS3	53.776	212	.000	3.8779	3.736	4.020
CS4	64.015	212	.000	3.9718	3.850	4.094
CS5	66.148	212	.000	4.3850	4.254	4.516
FA1	34.903	212	.000	3.4648	3.269	3.660
FA2	55.679	212	.000	4.0939	3.949	4.239
FA3	56.551	212	.000	4.0704	3.929	4.212
FA4	56.573	212	.000	4.2958	4.146	4.445
FA5	34.144	212	.000	3.4648	3.265	3.665
CE1	41.837	212	.000	3.8169	3.637	3.997
CE2	45.963	212	.000	3.9061	3.739	4.074
CE3	42.762	212	.000	3.8592	3.681	4.037
CE4	41.604	212	.000	3.7793	3.600	3.958
CE5	55.801	212	.000	3.8028	3.668	3.937

The variables related to customized service, financial advice and customer service are statistically significant at 5 percent level. It is indicated that in the first category of customized services provided by the banks through AAI to the customers tops with personalised product recommendations variable has scored highest of 68.04. Personalised product indicates the needs transaction history, mini statement, balance enquiry and so on. Second category is financial advice, strengthening the customer loyalty has secured first with highest score of 56.573 as strongly agreed by the customers. Banks assist the customers regarding the loan and credit facilities at right in their hands (apps) by means of AAI which in turn increase the customer loyalty and satisfaction. The third category of customer experience, the highest score of 55.801 has been given to the variable errors are reduced and increase the customer experience. The operational as well as informational errors could be reduced on behalf of the bank by implementing AI applications. In this case when errors are reduced by solving through the customer queries then they start trusting more the Banks quality of service and experience will enhance. State Bank of India is the country's largest supplier of financial services to the public sector (SBI). The bank offers effective financial services by utilizing artificial intelligence. The artificial intelligence (AI)-driven SBI Intelligent Assistant (SIA) is a chatbot that helps users with everyday banking tasks and promptly responds to inquiries. According to insiders, this clever chatbot—developed by AI banking platform Payjo—can handle up to 10,000 requests per second, or 864 million queries every day, or over 25% of all queries that Google processes on a daily basis (analyticsinsight.net).

RISK-RELATED FACTORS

The below factors are related towards the risk management (RM) and credit rating (CR) information offered through AI by the banks. The customers can seek the information about the credit assessment and assessing the risk in investing the banks by means of AI.

The above variables of risk management (RM) and credit rating of AI (CR) preferred by the customers possess significant value at 5 percent level. It specifies that the customers strongly agree towards Predictive Risk Assessment (in investments) in risk management factor with the high score of 72.00. Hence, customers prefer risk management in AI applications offered by banks where it gives the clear analysis of expected future risk involved in the operations and investments through smartphone by banking apps. Followed by improved loan decision making as secured with 42.500 in credit rating factor of AI by the customers. This ensures that the AI application of the banks helps sanction and approve the loan within few minutes by verifying the clients/ customers credit status.

PERFORMANCE-RELATED FACTORS

The below factors denote the variables of cyber security and detection of frauds (CDF) and integrating the chatbot with banking apps (IC). These two factors are much related with performing the banking operations efficiently and securely. With help of AI into detection of fraud and chatbot customers can perform the transactions as well as guidance will be provided through the apps.

All the above variables are representing the cyber security and detecting the frauds (CDF) and integrating the chatbot with banking apps (IC) are statistically significant at 5 percent. The highest preference and agreed by the customers was real-time transactions monitoring (37.647) through the AI implementation in the banks. In case of any frauds the history of transactions enables AI to detect the fraud easily and take necessary actions immediately. Followed by enhanced convenience and customer support (55.462) scores first in integrating the chatbot with banking apps. Chatbot will solve the custom-

Table 8. Risk related factors

Factors	One-Sample Test					
	Test Value = 0					
	T	Df	Sig. (2-tailed)	Mean Difference	95% Confidence Interval of the Difference	
					Lower	Upper
RM1	36.174	212	.000	3.7183	3.516	3.921
RM2	36.961	212	.000	3.7418	3.542	3.941
RM3	37.761	212	.000	3.8075	3.609	4.006
RM4	72.000	212	.000	4.1925	4.078	4.307
RM5	37.567	212	.000	3.7324	3.537	3.928
CR1	37.804	212	.000	3.3052	3.133	3.478
CR2	42.238	212	.000	3.8263	3.648	4.005
CR3	42.500	212	.000	3.5869	3.420	3.753

Table 9. Performance related factors

Factors	One-Sample Test					
	Test Value = 0					
	T	Df	Sig. (2-tailed)	Mean Difference	95% Confidence Interval of the Difference	
					Lower	Upper
CDF1	37.494	212	.000	3.9014	3.696	4.107
CDF2	37.085	212	.000	3.6197	3.427	3.812
CDF3	37.647	212	.000	3.9061	3.702	4.111
CDF4	37.038	212	.000	3.7183	3.520	3.916
CDF5	35.917	212	.000	3.8216	3.612	4.031
IC1	36.160	212	.000	3.5915	3.396	3.787
IC2	41.445	212	.000	3.8075	3.626	3.989
IC3	55.462	212	.000	4.0094	3.867	4.152
IC4	53.573	212	.000	4.1408	3.988	4.293

ers' queries and provide guidance faster as it is strongly agreed by the customers. Hence, it increases the customer service and support. HDFC Bank has introduced Chatbot system in the banking service as an initial attempt for AI applications. Another Indian company that uses AI is HDFC, a banking and financial services corporation headquartered in Mumbai. The bank's intelligent chatbot, called "Eva," answers consumer inquiries and improves services by utilizing Google Assistant on millions of Android smartphones. Eva was created by Senseforth AI Research, a Bengaluru-based company that claims it can answer over five million client queries with over 85% accuracy. Furthermore, HDFC offers OnChat, an AI-powered chatbot that first appeared on Facebook Messenger in 2016.

In addition to HDFC, Bank of Baroda has also introduced Chatbot system as an AI application in the Banking Service. AI is being used by Bank of Baroda, another public sector lender, to enhance customer service, increase banking services, and reduce account management expenses. The bank uses cutting edge technology, like the AI robot Baroda Brainy and the free Wi-Fi offered by Digital Lab. Its chatbot is sometimes called ADI (Assisted Digital Interaction). Bank of Baroda collaborated with IBM and Accenture in 2018 to create a state-of-the-art IT Center of Excellence and Analytics Center of Excellence (analyticsinsight.net).

TECHNOLOGICAL-RELATED FACTORS

The below variables are related to the market trends (MT), moves towards automation (A) and voice recognition (VR). These factors are indicating the latest and updated technology implemented through AI in the banks. Thus, customers can analyse the trends of the market to invest in the various ventures without much time and money. Through the automation of AI the banking system moves towards digitalisation of banking operations and voice recognition ensures that respective customer alone avail the services appropriately.

Table 10. Technological related factors

Factors	\multicolumn{6}{c}{One-Sample Test}

Factors	T	Df	Sig. (2-tailed)	Mean Difference	95% Confidence Interval of the Difference Lower	Upper
MT1	45.050	212	.000	4.0000	3.825	4.175
MT2	52.110	212	.000	4.0282	3.876	4.181
MT3	37.494	212	.000	3.9014	3.696	4.107
A1	101.014	211	.000	4.4198	4.334	4.506
A2	111.245	212	.000	4.3146	4.238	4.391
A3	111.067	212	.000	4.3192	4.243	4.396
A4	62.184	212	.000	4.1972	4.064	4.330
VR1	28.477	212	.000	2.8169	2.622	3.012
VR2	98.909	212	.000	4.3146	4.229	4.401
VR3	45.141	212	.000	3.8826	3.713	4.052
VR4	98.317	212	.000	4.3474	4.260	4.435
VR5	33.400	212	.000	3.2394	3.048	3.431

The variables of Market Trends, moves towards automation and Voice recognition values are significant at 5 percent. In market trends (MT) the variable that has secured highest scoring of 52.110 is give warning towards the risk involved in the investment. The customers strongly agreed that AI application guides them when and where to invest like shares/ stocks/ mutual funds and the amount of risk involved. Thus, AAI warns to the customers through their apps. In case of moving towards automation (A) the variable that has secured 111. 245 is reduction in workload of the bank staff. Hence, customers strongly agree that implementing AI will reduce the work pressure of bank employees by moving towards digitalisation (e-kyc through Aadhaar number and loan process through online). Finally, voice recognition (VR) is the latest technology to recognise and confirm the customers' identity while contacting the customer care or support. Customers strongly agreed by preferring the variable of transactions are done in more secured way with a score of 98. 909. The process of transactions are done only when the voice is properly recognised. In Voice Recognition (VR) Kotak Mahindra has announced its new VR. The multilingual chatbot, called Keya, will supplement the present Interactive Voice Response (IVR) technology and is linked to Kotak's phone-banking hotline. In 2019, the bank released Keya 2.0, an enhanced voicebot. India boasts a highly developed and efficiently run financial sector. As per the study, public sector banks concluded the 2020 fiscal year with assets of US$1.52 trillion. Furthermore, between FY16 and FY20, bank loans increased at a CAGR of 3.57%. The total credit amount extended at the end of FY2020 was $1,698.97 billion.

Axis Bank has also announced its new VR in July 2020. Axis Bank customers can use an AI-powered chatbot to discuss their banking concerns anytime and wherever they desire. Interactive Voice Response (IVR) technology that is conversational in nature, called AXAA, was introduced by India's third-largest private sector bank. AXAA is a multilingual voice bot of the future that helps users navigate the IVR and responds to their questions, often without requiring human assistance. Also, the private lender operates an innovation center named "Though Factory" to hasten the creation of cutting-edge AI technology solutions for the banking industry (analyticsinsight.net).

DISCUSSION OF THE FINDINGS

The above analysis were done on the basis of various factors relating to AI enabled Banking operations. The factors were related to customer, risk, performance, and technological of AI services provided by the Banks. After the detailed analysis it was found out that among these four factors, the dominant factor preferred and trusted by the customers' were technology factor. As among these factors AI moves towards the Automation like Processing time of transactions are fast, Reducing the workload of the Bank employees, and Reduce the time of loan application process were strongly agreed by the customers. They trust that AI can help the Bankers in reducing the processing time and workload respectively. It also further completes the banking operations and transaction time more quickly. Voice Recognition is also preferred and agreed by the customers as the transactions are done in more secured as well as protected way. Customers also think that they are more secured that fingerprint identification in voice recognition. Moreover, Voice Recognition is implemented by the Kotak Mahindra and Axis Bank successfully. AI's important and essential factor is technology as it involves the Automation involves more of digitalisation and Voice Recognition for identification and clarifying customer queries. Apart from Voice Recognition, HDFC and Bank of Baroda has successfully implemented chatbot towards implementation of AI in their Banks. Chatbot were helpful in sorting out customer issues and increasing their service. According to our analysis Integrating Chatbot has attracted by the customers towards increasing the convenience and support of the customers. Hence, from the analysis the preference of customers were Automation and Voice recognition leads towards the technological advancement of AI enabled Banking Service through more customer service and centre. The implementation of AI in different Banks proved that digitalisation is most prominent service.

IMPACT OF AAI TOWARDS QUALITY OF BANKING SERVICE

The table below clearly indicates the impact towards service quality of AAI to the customers in the Banks with three-point rating scale of High to Low. It measures the impact in terms of transparency, accuracy, safety, authentication and reduction. Among 213 sample size more than 150 respondents has high impact towards all the above five aspects of AAI features provided in the Banks. This denotes that customers are highly (172) effected towards the authenticated information provided by AAI services as per their requirements and followed by ensuring safe as well as security (169) towards their personal database in their Banks without being hacked or breached. On the other hand, customer feels that they possess low effectiveness of AAI featured services in the Bank were towards the transparency (23) of all the process like loan, investments, insurance and etc. It is also found that AAI helps in employees' workload in the Banks are completed and reported (15) among 213 respondents as least impact.

   The greatest impact of AAI enabled Banking Service is providing proper and authenticated information. Followed by providing safe and secured customer details by protecting them from unwanted access. Bank staff also agree that through AI service they can deliver transparency in the banking operations to the customers (Shetty et all, 2022).

Figure 1. Impact of AAI towards quality of banking service

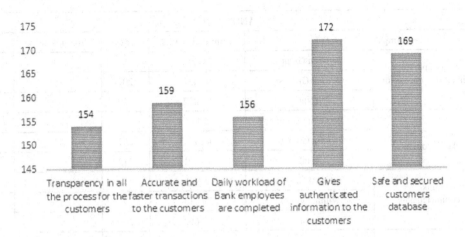

INFLUENCE OF HOLDING BANK ACCOUNT IN DIFFERENT BANKS OVER AN IMPACT OF AAI FEATURES

It compares between the different banks where the customers maintain their account and impact of AAI features in terms of transparent services, accuracy and fastest transactions, workload of the employees are completed, providing proper information and finally by safeguarding the customers' personal data through One Time Password (OTP).

The above table reveals that there is no influence between the different Banks and Impact of AAI featured services provides transparency in all the process (F=0.431; Sig = .826); workload of the employees is completed and reported daily (F=0.431; Sig = .074); ensures AAI gives authenticated information to the customers (F=1.688; Sig = .139) as it is not significantly acceptable range at 5 percent level.

There is an influence between different bank accounts maintained by the customers on more accurate and faster transactions (F=3.102; Sig = .010); and increases the safe and security for the customers database (F=2.380; Sig = .040); as the values are significantly accepted at 5 percent level. It is also observed that the HDFC, SBI and other category of banks has got different level of influence towards the impact of AAI featured services provided by the Banks.

ASSOCIATION BETWEEN WORKLOAD OF THE BANK EMPLOYEES AND AUTHENTICATED INFORMATION TO THE CUSTOMERS

The table below explains the association between the factor of AAI and Impact of AAI in the banks. It compares between the most influencing factor of reducing the work burden of the Bank employees and the highest impact towards the customers was ensuring the authentic information according to their requirements.

The table proves that $\chi2 = 4.023$; Sig = .112 are significantly not accepted at 95 percent confidence level. Thus, it is evident that there is no association between the reduction of workload among the Bank staff through AAI applications and effectiveness of authenticated information provided to the customers. It is also evident that customers agree towards reduction of work burden (digitalisation like reduction to

Table 11. Impact of AAI towards quality of banking service

ANOVA						
Impact		**Sum of Squares**	**df**	**Mean Square**	**F**	**Sig.**
AAI featured services provides transparency in all the process for the customers	Between Groups	.994	5	.199	.431	.826
	Within Groups	95.437	207	.461		
	Total	96.432	212			
It has more accurate and faster transactions to the customers	Between Groups	5.178	5	1.036	3.102	.010
	Within Groups	69.113	207	.334		
	Total	74.291	212			
Daily workload of Bank employees are completed and reported	Between Groups	3.649	5	.730	2.041	.074
	Within Groups	74.013	207	.358		
	Total	77.662	212			
Gives authenticated information to the customers	Between Groups	2.104	5	.421	1.688	.139
	Within Groups	51.623	207	.249		
	Total	53.728	212			
Enhances safe and security for the customers database	Between Groups	3.143	5	.629	2.380	.040
	Within Groups	54.669	207	.264		
	Total	57.812	212			

Table 12. Association between workload of the bank employees and authenticated information to the customers

Factors/ Impact		Gives authenticated information to the customers			Total	
		High	**Moderate**	**Least**		
Reducing the workload of the Bank employees	Strongly Disagree	1	0	0	1	$\chi2 = 4.023$ Sig = .112
	Disagree	1	0	0	1	
	Neutral	2	0	0	2	
	Agree	113	17	5	135	
	Strongly Agree	55	16	3	74	
Total		172	33	8	213	

paperless work and online process) to the Bank employees by performance of AAI features has a high impact on providing validated and true information to the customers through Autonomous Artificial Intelligence feature services in the Banks.

WEAKNESS OF THE STUDY

The major weakness of this study were its time duration and sample size. As time is major drawback for limiting sample size to 213. Another weakness of this study identified were the technical aspect of machine learning in AI and theories of AI perspectives not included in this study.

SUGGESTIONS

The following suggestions are based on the data analysis:

1. *Transparency:* AI enabled Banking services must provide transparency in its operations for the customers. Transparency of the operations indicates clear procedure of account opening, loan process, etc. Further, customer can identify their status of operations without visiting or approaching the Bankers/ Bank through AI application in the Mobile Apps or Internet Banking.

2. *Awareness on Voice Recognition:* Create an awareness among the customers that the Voice Recognition helps to protect from unauthorized access. Unauthorised access implies that anyone other than the recognised customer through their voice cannot access the Bank accounts. Hence, they are protected from hacking their personal details. Only when recognised voice of the customer is heard then the Banking operations and queries are also can be carried out. It also confirms the identification of customers through voice (eg: fingerprint identification). In future fingerprint could be replaced by voice or face recognition.

3. *Financial Wealth:* AI can increase the financial wealth of the customers by accessing and managing the report as well as guiding efficiently. As and when customers are browsing the details or banking products, AI can suggest suitable products for the customers according to their earning capacity and interest. Apart from this AI will guide them relating to the risk of selling or investing according to market trends of increasing/ decreasing price.

4. *Chatbots:* Chatbot as an AI feature plays a major role in banking operations and customer service. Many banks have implemented Chatbot as AI service and customers have reported its successful rate. But in our study customers are not aware of the features of Chatbot. As chatbot can reply to the customer queries as well as guide them within few seconds or minutes.

SCOPE FOR FUTURE RESEARCH

Banks have already implemented AI in different aspects like chatbot, IVR. A separate study can be conducted on its effectiveness. Future study from customers and Banker's point of view which aspect of implementing AI in the Banks is essential could be done. A study on major issues and challenges of AAI regarding privacy and security can be done.

CONCLUSION

This study is conducted to analyse the various aspects of Customer Satisfaction and Trust in Autonomous AI Banking Systems. AI has been already existing in the front office, middle office and back office. Front office in the banks is dealing with the customers queries like interactions relating to their required information on websites/ apps and identifying the customers through biometric, advising the customers relating to managing the finance. Customer queries are handled through the Chatbot in AI by leading Banks in India. Financial advice are also provided by the AI to the customers through their behaviour. Middle office operations are dealing with the detection of frauds and crime in the Banking

Sector, Know Your Customer (KYC), and credit rating scores to the customers on the basis of their loan repayment, decisions regarding loan. AI helps in detecting the frauds earlier, loan process are done in digital mode (online process represents paperless) and credit rating scores are revealed in few minutes as the customers repay or settle their credit. Back office mainly dealing with managing and settling the customer transactions and records. They also regularly adjust and ensure banking records are complying with regulatory acts and IT services. AI has enabled many programs to reconcile and settle the accounting system of customers as earliest. The records can be maintained in the Bank/ Cloud data without any hacking through AI.

The above operations of the Bank were categorised into customer related factors, risk related factors, technology related factors and performance related factors. As digital transactions are expanding AI features are also expanding in the Banking sector. Thus, customers strongly agree that AI can reduce the workload of employees in the Bank like replacing the role of staff in front, middle and backend office work relating to the latest technology. Customers agree that AI provides personalised services according to the customer needs of loans, insurance, deposits and withdrawal. Risk related factors were agreed by the customers is that helps to detect risk involved in investment earlier by AI applications in Apps itself. In performance related factors customers agreed that AI improves their support and convenience by Chatbot technology as well as 24*7 service. The major impact of AAI towards service quality of Banks is giving valuable information to the customers relating to the interest rates, loans, deposits and etc. It is also concluding that there is no relationship between factors of AAI features and its impact.

REFERENCES

Alborzi, M., & Khanbabaei, M. (2016). Using data mining and neural networks techniques to propose a new hybrid customer behavior analysis and credit scoring model in banking services based on a developed RFM analysis method. *International Journal of Business Information Systems*, 23(1), 1–22. doi:10.1504/IJBIS.2016.078020

Arif, I., Aslam, W., & Hwang, Y. (2023). Barriers in adoption of internet banking: A structural equation modeling-neural network approach. *Technology in Society*, 61, 101231. doi:10.1016/j.techsoc.2020.101231

Baesens, B., Van Gestel, T., Stepanova, M., Van den Poel, D., & Vanthienen, J. (2005). Neural network survival analysis for personal loan data. *The Journal of the Operational Research Society*, 56(9), 1089–1098. doi:10.1057/palgrave.jors.2601990

Belanche, D., Casaló, L. V., & Flavián, C. (2020). Artificial intelligence in FinTech: Understanding robo-advisors adoption among customers. *Industrial Management & Data Systems*, 119(7), 1411–1430. doi:10.1108/IMDS-08-2018-0368

Biswas, S., Carson, B., Chung, V., Singh, S., & Thomas, R. (2023). Artificial intelligence technologies are increasingly integral to the world we live in, and banks need to deploy these technologies at scale to remain relevant. Success requires a holistic transformation spanning multiple layers of the organization. Larson, E.J. 2021. The myth of artificial intelligence. In *The Myth of Artificial Intelligence*. Harvard University Press.

Ekinci, Y., Uray, N., & Ülengin, F. (2014). A customer lifetime value model for the banking industry: A guide to marketing actions. *European Journal of Marketing, 48*(3–4), 761–784. doi:10.1108/EJM-12-2011-0714

Ince, H., & Aktan, B. (2009). A comparison of data mining techniques for credit scoring in banking: A managerial perspective. *Journal of Business Economics and Management, 10*(3), 233–240. doi:10.3846/1611-1699.2009.10.233-240

Khan, K. S., Kunz, R., Kleijnen, J., & Antes, G. (2010). Five steps to conducting a systematic review. *Journal of the Royal Society of Medicine, 96*(3), 118–121. doi:10.1177/014107680309600304 PMID:12612111

Khandani, A. E., Kim, A. J., & Lo, A. W. (2010). Consumer credit-risk models via machine-learning algorithms. *Journal of Banking & Finance, 34*(11), 2767–27. doi:10.1016/j.jbankfin.2010.06.001

Kim, K. J., & Lee, W. B. (2004). Stock market prediction using artificial neural networks with optimal feature transformation. *Neural Computing & Applications, 13*(3), 255–260. doi:10.1007/s00521-004-0428-x

Koutanaei, F. N., Sajedi, H., & Khanbabaei, M. (2015). A hybrid data mining model of feature selection algorithms and ensemble learning classifiers for credit scoring. *Journal of Retailing and Consumer Services, 27*, 11–23. doi:10.1016/j.jretconser.2015.07.003

Mall, S. (2018). An empirical study on credit risk management: The case of nonbanking financial companies. *The Journal of Credit Risk, 14*(3), 49–66. doi:10.21314/JCR.2017.239

Payne, E. M., Peltier, J. W., & Barger, V. A. (2018). Mobile banking and AI-enabled mobile banking: The differential effects of technological and non-technological factors on digital natives' perceptions and behavior. *Journal of Research in Interactive Marketing, 12*(3), 328–346. doi:10.1108/JRIM-07-2018-0087

Schwartz, E. M., Bradlow, E. T., & Fader, P. S. (2017). Customer acquisition via display advertising using multi-armed bandit experiments. *Marketing Science, 36*(4), 500–522. doi:10.1287/mksc.2016.1023

Shetty. (2022). Impact of Artificial Intelligence in Banking Sector with Reference to Private Banks in India. *Annals of the University of Craiova, Physics, 32*, 59-75.

Smeureanu, I., Ruxanda, G., & Badea, L. M. (2013). Customer segmentation in private banking sector using machine learning techniques. *Journal of Business Economics and Management, 14*(5), 923–939. doi:10.3846/16111699.2012.749807

Soltani, M., Samorani, M., & Kolfal, B. (2019). Appointment scheduling with multiple providers and stochastic service times. *European Journal of Operational Research, 277*(2), 667–683. doi:10.1016/j.ejor.2019.02.051

Trivedi, J. (2019). Examining the customer experience of using banking Chatbots and its impact on brand love: The moderating role of perceived risk. *Journal of Internet Commerce, 18*(1), 91–111. doi:10.1080/15332861.2019.1567188

Xu, Y., Shieh, C. H., van Esch, P., & Ling, I. L. (2020). AI customer service: Task complexity, problem-solving ability, and usage intention. *Australasian Marketing Journal, 28*(4), 189–199. doi:10.1016/j.ausmj.2020.03.005

Chapter 7
Foetal Activity Detection Using Deep Convolution Neural Networks

Xavier Arockiaraj Santhappan
ⓘ https://orcid.org/0000-0002-6420-7364
Adhiyamaan College of Engineering, India

Ronica Bis
Sathyabama Institute of Science and Technology, India

ABSTRACT

Ultrasound is a conventional diagnostic instrument employed in prenatal care to track the progression and advancement of the fetus. In routine clinical obstetric assessments, the standard planes of fetal ultrasound hold considerable importance in evaluating fetal growth metrics and identifying abnormalities. In this work, a method to detect FFSP using deep convolutional neural network (DCNN) architecture to improve detection efficiency is presented. Squeeze net, 16 convolutional layers with small 3x3 large kernel, and all three layers form the proposed DCNN. The final pooling layer uses global average pooling (GAP) to reduce inconsistency in the network. This helps reduce the problem of overfitting and improves the performance from different training data. To improve cognitive performance, data augmentation methods developed specifically for FFSP are used in conjunction with adaptive learning strategies. Extensive testing shows that the proposed method gives accuracy of 96% which outperforms traditional methods, and DCNN is an important tool to identify FFSP in clinical diagnosis.

1. INTRODUCTION

Ultrasound (US) screening is a widely used, cost-effective, and radiation-free method for pregnancy diagnosis in routine clinical examinations (Lei et al., 2015a; Lei et al., 2015b; Rahmatullah et al., 2011; Chen et al., 2015a; Chen et al., 2015b; Lei et al., 2014; Zhang et al., 2012; Rahmatullah & Noble, 2013). Typically performed between 18 and 24 weeks of gestation, antenatal US screening involves acquiring

DOI: 10.4018/979-8-3693-5767-5.ch007

serial standard images of fetal structures following a standardized protocol for biometric measurement and malformation detection (Dudley & Chapman, 2002). One crucial aspect is obtaining standard planes, such as the fetal facial standard plane (FFSP), for accurate fetal diagnosis and subsequent measurements (Lei et al., 2015a; Rahmatullah et al., 2011; Chen et al., 2015a; Lei et al., 2014; Zhang et al., 2012). However, manual identification and evaluation of FFSP by clinicians are time-consuming, subjective, and prone to variations among different practitioners, particularly in underprivileged regions lacking experienced clinicians. Hence, there is a significant need for an automatic FFSP recognition method.

Recognizing FFSP presents challenges due to high intra-class and low inter-class variations caused by fetal postures, scanning orientations, and artifacts like speckle noise and shadow (Lei et al., 2015a). Distinguishing FFSP from non-FFSP is particularly challenging. To address this, various methods have been proposed, typically employing a two-step pipeline: feature extraction and classification (Chatfield et al., 2011; Shi et al., 2015a; Shi et al., 2016a; Shi et al., 2016b). Traditional approaches rely on low-level hand-crafted features (Lei et al., 2015a; Zhang et al., 2012; Dudley & Chapman, 2002; Ni et al., 2014; Lei et al., 2015c), such as scale-invariant feature transform (SIFT), Dense-SIFT (DSIFT), Haar, and histogram-of-gradient (HOG), encoded by algorithms like bag of visual words (BoVW), vector of locally aggregated descriptor (VLAD), Fisher vector (FV), and multi-layer Fisher vector (MFV), followed by classification using support vector machines (SVM). However, these hand-crafted features often fall short for accurate FFSP recognition.

In recent years, deep convolutional neural networks (DCNNs) have demonstrated remarkable success in image recognition tasks, benefiting from large annotated datasets like ImageNet and their ability to automatically learn feature representations from raw data without manual design (Deng, 2009; Krizhevsky et al., 2012; Lin et al., 2013; He et al., 2016). DCNNs, with alternating convolutional and pooling layers, outperform shallow networks, producing robust and sophisticated representations (He et al., 2015). While various studies have applied deep models like VGG Net, batch normalization (BN) Net, and ResNet in challenging benchmark datasets, their application in medical US image datasets remains limited due to data scarcity and convergence issues (Ioffe & Szegedy, 2015; Simonyan & Zisserman, 2014; Szegedy et al., 2015). Despite the significant achievements of DCNNs in medical image recognition, their application in US images is underexplored, and systematic investigations into their performance are lacking.

Inspired by the success of DCNNs, we propose a DCNN squeeze net model (19 layers) with small-sized kernels (3×3) for FFSP recognition. Additionally, a global average pooling (GAP) in the last pooling layer is incorporated to enhance performance and efficiency.

2. LITERATURE REVIEW

Traditional hand-crafted feature-based classification models typically involve three main steps: (i) feature extraction (Lei et al., 2014; Zhu et al., 2017), (ii) feature encoding (Chatfield et al., 2011; Maji et al., 2008; Zhu et al., 2016; Zhu et al., 2014), and (iii) feature classification (Grauman & Darrell, 2005). Spatial pyramid matching (SPM) (Lazebnik et al., 2006; Grauman & Darrell, 2005) can be employed to integrate spatial information of image features for enhanced feature representation. In conventional models, carefully designed data-specific features play a crucial role. Over the past few years, considerable effort has been dedicated to devising suitable features for image representation (Ronneberger et al., 2015; Lowe, 2004). Commonly used feature representations include SIFT, DSIFT, Haar, HoG, and combinations of these features with intensity, shape, motion, and edges (Ronneberger et al., 2015; Zhu et al., 2017). Feature encoding techniques like BoVW, VLAD, FV, and MFV (Perronnin et al., 2010; Csurka et al., 2004; Sánchez et al., 2013; Sánchez et al., 2010) have been introduced to improve classification performance, generating more robust and stable information. For instance, Lei et al. (2015a) proposed a hand-crafted DSIFT feature representation method based on an MFV feature encoding approach for FFSP recognition.

DCNNs possess remarkable representation capabilities for recognition or detection tasks based on the provided training dataset (LeCun et al., 2015). These models comprise multiple processing layers to learn features at different levels, and combining these hierarchical features preserves highly discriminative and effective deep representations (Glorot & Bengio, 2010). Consequently, state-of-the-art performance has been achieved in various applications (Krizhevsky et al., 2012; Girshick et al., 2014; Long et al., 2015; Ronneberger et al., 2015; Chen et al., 2016).

The deep hierarchical architecture of DCNN models is crucial due to their potent representation learning capabilities. Recent years have seen the proposal of well-designed initialization strategies, activation functions (He et al., 2015; He et al., 2015), and efficient intermediate regularization strategies (Srivastava et al., 2014; Goodfellow et al., 2013), significantly improving the optimization of deep models (Bengio, 2012). With remarkable performance in natural image processing and natural language processing, DCNNs have asserted their dominance in the machine learning domain and found extensive applications in medical image analysis (Anthimopoulos et al., 2016; Gao et al., 2016; Yan et al., 2016; Song et al., 2015; Yu et al., 2016). Numerous studies have reported promising results across various applications, including object recognition (Anthimopoulos et al., 2016; Gao et al., 2016; Yan et al., 2016; Song et al., 2015), detection (Dou et al., 2016), and segmentation (Chen et al., 2018; Ronneberger et al., 2015; Chen et al., 2017).

3. METHODOLOGY

The proposed model mainly consists of two steps and the framework is illustrated in Figure 1. The deep CNNs are trained using the fetal US images training dataset, and the most informative features are extracted. After that, MLP is used to classify fetal ultrasound images into three classes.

3.1 Feature Extraction

Extracting relevant deep features is a crucial step in any classification process. This study aims to improve classification performance by extracting deep features extracted from deep CNN, Squeeze net-GAP. Figure 1 illustrates the block diagram of this proposed feature extraction approach. Typically, deep CNN designs consist of multiple hidden layers. It is possible to increase classification performance by using these hidden layers, which are helpful in determining which aspects of the input image data are the most informative. The Squeeze net architecture is given as

3.2 Multi-Layer Perceptron

An MLP is a class of fully connected feedforward artificial neural networks (LeCun et al., 2015). Generally, MLP consists of an input layer, one or more hidden layers, and an output layer. The proposed MLP consists input layer, three fully connected layers, and an output SoftMax layer. Every node or

Figure 1. Squeeze net architecture

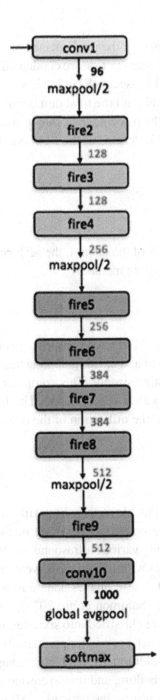

neuron of the hidden layers except the input layer uses a nonlinear activation function. The deep feature integrated descriptor is treated as input to the input layer of MLP. Firstly, the input layer output is input to the hidden layer. In the same way, the output of the last hidden layer is fed into the output layer. The first and second hidden layers of MLP are designed with 1024 neurons each, while the last hidden layer is designed with 512 neurons.

3.3 Evaluation

A quantitative evaluation and comparison of the performance of the proposed automatic classification of fetal US images using MLP and feature extraction are conducted based on four major metrics, namely accuracy, precision (P), recall (R), and F1-score (F1). A measure of accuracy is the ratio between the number of correctly predicted class labels and the total number of ground truth class labels. Generally, precision (recall) can be described as the percentage or rate of true positives (true negatives). The harmonic mean of the precision and recall is defined as the F1-score. Furthermore, confusion matrices are also evaluated.

4. EXPERIMENTAL RESULTS

This section describes the characteristics of the dataset, the performance of the proposed approach, and a comparison of the results with the existing methods.

4.1 Experimental Set-Up

The suggested model was applied on the MATLAB platform, specifically in version R2023a. All computations pertaining to both the proposed and existing approaches were conducted on a computer running the 64-bit Windows 10 Pro operating system. This computer is powered by an Intel(R) Xeon(R) E-2104G CPU running at 3.20 GHz, with 8 GB of RAM. The implementation of the proposed and existing methods in MATLAB involved the utilization of the deep learning toolbox, image processing toolbox, and machine learning toolbox.

4.2 Dataset Details

The proposed study utilizes the largest available maternal-fetal ultrasound image dataset (Burgos-Artizzu et al., 2020) to train and evaluate both proposed and existing methods. This dataset comprises images gathered from two distinct hospitals using various ultrasound machines and operators (Burgos-Artizzu et al., 2020). The fetal ultrasound images within the dataset were captured during routine clinical practices from October 2018 to April 2019. These images adhere to standard clinical screening protocols established by the scientific committee (Salomon et al., 2022), and a skilled maternal-fetal clinician manually annotated them. The images are classified into six categories, encompassing four fetal planes (abdomen, brain, femur, thorax), the mother's cervix for prematurity screening, and less commonly used planes like kidney, leg, foot, spine, etc. Additionally, fetal brain images are further categorized into three major planes: trans-thalamic, trans-cerebellum, and trans-ventricular. The dataset is randomly divided, allocating 75% for training and 25% for testing the networks. All images in the dataset are in portable network graphic (PNG) format and grayscale, with varying sizes. During the training of deep Convolutional Neural Networks (CNNs), the sizes of the training image dataset B and testing image dataset S are optimized to match the corresponding input size of the deep CNN. All images are resized to $227 \times 227 \times 3$ for the SqueezeNet model.

4.3 Performance of the Proposed Method

This section highlights the significance of integrating deep features and assesses the performance of the proposed approach based on class-wise precision, recall, F1-score, and overall accuracy. The classification effectiveness of the SqueezeNet is evaluated in the context of the proposed work. In this study, two classification techniques—MLP and softmax classifiers—are employed to classify common maternal-fetal ultrasound images by incorporating deep features. Tables 1 present the class-wise precision, recall, F1-score, and overall accuracy of the proposed method using both the softmax classifier and MLP. The proposed method, specifically the Deep Feature Integration (DFI) with SqueezeNet's deep feature representations using MLP, attains an accuracy of 96%, as depicted in Table 1 and the corresponding confusion matrix is shown in Figure 2.

4.4 Comparison of the Proposed Method With the Existing Methods

Figure 2. Confusion matrix

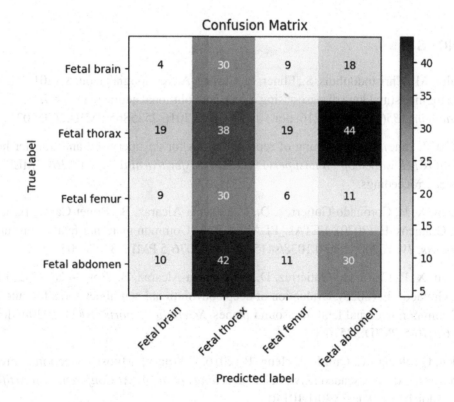

5. CONCLUSION

This study presents a method for automatically classifying fetal ultrasound (US) images using Multilayer Perceptron (MLP) with feature extraction to enhance detection and diagnostic efficiency. The training and testing of deep Convolutional Neural Networks (CNNs) utilized a publicly available extensive dataset

Table 1. Comparison of existing vs proposed work

Method	Fetal abdomen (%)			Fetal brain (%)			Fetal femur (%)			Fetal thorax (%)			Maternal cervix (%)			Other (%)			Accuracy (%)
	P	R	F1	P	R	F1	P	R	F1	P	R	F1	P	R	F1	P	R	F1	
ResNet-50 [66]	85.7	91	88.3	98.9	99.6	99.2	84	90.8	87.3	92.9	93.9	93.2	98.8	99.5	99.1	94.2	90.1	92.1	94.3
Inception-v3 [67]	85.6	90.4	87.9	98.9	99.7	99.3	82.5	87.3	84.8	92.6	93.2	92.9	99.0	99.8	99.4	93.1	89.8	91.4	93.8
Proposed work	91.1	92.3	93.3	98.9	99.5	99.9	90	91	91	95	93.7	94.1	98.6	98.3	99.1	95.1	92.1	93.5	95.9

known as common fetal US images. To enhance the classification process, a combination of various deep features extracted from the SqueezeNet-GAP has been employed. These extracted deep features from the SqueezeNet-GAP descriptor are input to the MLP to categorize fetal US images into three classes: Benign, Malignant, and Normal. The proposed method achieves an impressive accuracy of 96%, surpassing the performance of other state-of-the-art methods presented in (He et al., 2016; Szegedy et al., 2016). As a result, the proposed framework can be considered reliable to assist doctors in accurate fetal US image detection during screening, contributing to early detection (Burgos-Artizzu et al., 2020).

REFERENCES

Anthimopoulos, M., Christodoulidis, S., Ebner, L., Christe, A., & Mougiakakou, S. (2016). Lung pattern classification for interstitial lung diseases using a deep convolutional neural network. *IEEE Transactions on Medical Imaging*, *35*(5), 1207–1216. doi:10.1109/TMI.2016.2535865 PMID:26955021

Bengio, Y. (2012, June). Deep learning of representations for unsupervised and transfer learning. In *Proceedings of ICML workshop on unsupervised and transfer learning* (pp. 17-36). JMLR Workshop and Conference Proceedings.

Burgos-Artizzu, X. P., Coronado-Gutierrez, D., Valenzuela-Alcaraz, B., Bonet-Carne, E., Eixarch, E., Crispi, F., & Gratacós, E. (2020). FETAL_PLANES_DB: Common maternal-fetal ultrasound images. *Scientific Reports*, *19*, 10200. doi:10.1038/s41598-020-67076-5 PMID:32576905

Burgos-Artizzu, X. P., Coronado-Gutiérrez, D., Valenzuela-Alcaraz, B., Bonet-Carne, E., Eixarch, E., Crispi, F., & Gratacós, E. (2020). Evaluation of deep convolutional neural networks for automatic classification of common maternal fetal ultrasound planes. *Scientific Reports*, *10*(1), 10200. doi:10.1038/s41598-020-67076-5 PMID:32576905

Chen, H., Dou, Q., Wang, X., Qin, J., & Heng, P. (2016, February). Mitosis detection in breast cancer histology images via deep cascaded networks. *Proceedings of the AAAI Conference on Artificial Intelligence*, *30*(1). doi:10.1609/aaai.v30i1.10140

Chen, H., Dou, Q., Yu, L., Qin, J., & Heng, P. A. (2018). VoxResNet: Deep voxelwise residual networks for brain segmentation from 3D MR images. *NeuroImage*, *170*, 446–455. doi:10.1016/j.neuroimage.2017.04.041 PMID:28445774

Chen, H., Ni, D., Qin, J., Li, S., Yang, X., Wang, T., & Heng, P. A. (2015). Standard plane localization in fetal ultrasound via domain transferred deep neural networks. *IEEE Journal of Biomedical and Health Informatics*, *19*(5), 1627–1636. doi:10.1109/JBHI.2015.2425041 PMID:25910262

Chen, H., Qi, X., Yu, L., Dou, Q., Qin, J., & Heng, P. A. (2017). DCAN: Deep contour-aware networks for object instance segmentation from histology images. *Medical Image Analysis*, *36*, 135–146. doi:10.1016/j. media.2016.11.004 PMID:27898306

Csurka, G., Dance, C., Fan, L., Willamowski, J., & Bray, C. (2004, May). Visual categorization with bags of keypoints. In *Workshop on statistical learning in computer vision, ECCV* (Vol. 1, No. 1-22, pp. 1-2).

Dalal, N., & Triggs, B. (2005, June). Histograms of oriented gradients for human detection. In *2005 IEEE computer society conference on computer vision and pattern recognition (CVPR'05)* (Vol. 1, pp. 886-893). IEEE. doi:10.1109/CVPR.2005.177

Deng, J. (2009). A large-scale hierarchical image database. *Proc. of IEEE Computer Vision and Pattern Recognition*.

Donahue, J., Jia, Y., Vinyals, O., Hoffman, J., Zhang, N., Tzeng, E., & Darrell, T. (2014, January). Decaf: A deep convolutional activation feature for generic visual recognition. In *International conference on machine learning* (pp. 647-655). PMLR.

Dou, Q., Chen, H., Yu, L., Zhao, L., Qin, J., Wang, D., Mok, V. C. T., Shi, L., & Heng, P. A. (2016). Automatic detection of cerebral microbleeds from MR images via 3D convolutional neural networks. *IEEE Transactions on Medical Imaging*, *35*(5), 1182–1195. doi:10.1109/TMI.2016.2528129 PMID:26886975

Dudley, N. J., & Chapman, E. (2002). The importance of quality management in fetal measurement. *Ultrasound in Obstetrics & Gynecology*, *19*(2), 190–196. doi:10.1046/j.0960-7692.2001.00549.x PMID:11876814

Gao, Z., Wang, L., Zhou, L., & Zhang, J. (2016). HEp-2 cell image classification with deep convolutional neural networks. *IEEE Journal of Biomedical and Health Informatics*, *21*(2), 416–428. doi:10.1109/ JBHI.2016.2526603 PMID:26887016

Girshick, R., Donahue, J., Darrell, T., & Malik, J. (2014). Rich feature hierarchies for accurate object detection and semantic segmentation. In *Proceedings of the IEEE conference on computer vision and pattern recognition* (pp. 580-587). 10.1109/CVPR.2014.81

Glorot, X., & Bengio, Y. (2010, March). Understanding the difficulty of training deep feedforward neural networks. In *Proceedings of the thirteenth international conference on artificial intelligence and statistics* (pp. 249-256). JMLR Workshop and Conference Proceedings.

Goodfellow, I., Warde-Farley, D., Mirza, M., Courville, A., & Bengio, Y. (2013, May). Maxout networks. In *International conference on machine learning* (pp. 1319-1327). PMLR.

Grauman, K., & Darrell, T. (2005, October). The pyramid match kernel: Discriminative classification with sets of image features. In *Tenth IEEE International Conference on Computer Vision (ICCV'05) Volume 1* (Vol. 2, pp. 1458-1465). IEEE. 10.1109/ICCV.2005.239

Greenspan, H., Van Ginneken, B., & Summers, R. M. (2016). Guest editorial deep learning in medical imaging: Overview and future promise of an exciting new technique. *IEEE Transactions on Medical Imaging*, *35*(5), 1153–1159. doi:10.1109/TMI.2016.2553401

He, K., Zhang, X., Ren, S., & Sun, J. (2015). Delving deep into rectifiers: Surpassing human-level performance on imagenet classification. In *Proceedings of the IEEE international conference on computer vision* (pp. 1026-1034). 10.1109/ICCV.2015.123

He, K., Zhang, X., Ren, S., & Sun, J. (2016). Deep residual learning for image recognition. In *Proceedings of the IEEE conference on computer vision and pattern recognition* (pp. 770-778). Academic Press.

He, K., Zhang, X., Ren, S., & Sun, J. (2016). Deep residual learning for image recognition. In *Proceedings of the IEEE Conference on Computer Vision and Pattern Recognition* (pp. 770–778). IEEE.

Ioffe, S., & Szegedy, C. (2015, June). Batch normalization: Accelerating deep network training by reducing internal covariate shift. In *International conference on machine learning* (pp. 448-456). PMLR.

Jégou, H., Perronnin, F., Douze, M., Sánchez, J., Pérez, P., & Schmid, C. (2011). Aggregating local image descriptors into compact codes. *IEEE Transactions on Pattern Analysis and Machine Intelligence*, *34*(9), 1704–1716. doi:10.1109/TPAMI.2011.235 PMID:22156101

Krizhevsky, A., Sutskever, I., & Hinton, G. E. (2012). Imagenet classification with deep convolutional neural networks. *Advances in Neural Information Processing Systems*, 25.

Lazebnik, S., Schmid, C., & Ponce, J. (2006, June). Beyond bags of features: Spatial pyramid matching for recognizing natural scene categories. In *2006 IEEE computer society conference on computer vision and pattern recognition (CVPR'06)* (Vol. 2, pp. 2169-2178). IEEE.

LeCun, Y., Bengio, Y., & Hinton, G. (2015). Deep learning. *Nature*, *521*(7553), 436-444.

Lei, B., Tan, E. L., Chen, S., Ni, D., & Wang, T. (2015). Saliency-driven image classification method based on histogram mining and image score. *Pattern Recognition*, *48*(8), 2567–2580. doi:10.1016/j.patcog.2015.02.004

Lei, B., Tan, E. L., Chen, S., Zhuo, L., Li, S., Ni, D., & Wang, T. (2015). Automatic recognition of fetal facial standard plane in ultrasound image via fisher vector. *PLoS One*, *10*(5), e0121838. doi:10.1371/journal.pone.0121838 PMID:25933215

Lei, B., Yao, Y., Chen, S., Li, S., Li, W., Ni, D., & Wang, T. (2015). Discriminative learning for automatic staging of placental maturity via multi-layer fisher vector. *Scientific Reports*, *5*(1), 12818. doi:10.1038/srep12818 PMID:26228175

Lei, B., Zhuo, L., Chen, S., Li, S., Ni, D., & Wang, T. (2014, April). Automatic recognition of fetal standard plane in ultrasound image. In *2014 IEEE 11th International Symposium on Biomedical Imaging (ISBI)* (pp. 85-88). IEEE. 10.1109/ISBI.2014.6867815

Li, Q., Cai, W., Wang, X., Zhou, Y., Feng, D. D., & Chen, M. (2014, December). Medical image classification with convolutional neural network. In *2014 13th international conference on control automation robotics & vision (ICARCV)* (pp. 844-848). IEEE. 10.1109/ICARCV.2014.7064414

Lin, M., Chen, Q., & Yan, S. (2013). Network in network. *arXiv preprint arXiv:1312.4400*.

Liu, C., Yuen, J., & Torralba, A. (2010). Sift flow: Dense correspondence across scenes and its applications. *IEEE Transactions on Pattern Analysis and Machine Intelligence, 33*(5), 978–994. doi:10.1109/TPAMI.2010.147 PMID:20714019

Long, J., Shelhamer, E., & Darrell, T. (2015). Fully convolutional networks for semantic segmentation. In *Proceedings of the IEEE conference on computer vision and pattern recognition* (pp. 3431-3440). IEEE.

Lowe, D. G. (2004). Distinctive image features from scale-invariant keypoints. *International Journal of Computer Vision, 60*(2), 91–110. doi:10.1023/B:VISI.0000029664.99615.94

Maji, S., Berg, A. C., & Malik, J. (2008, June). *Classification using intersection kernel support vector machines is efficient. In 2008 IEEE conference on computer vision and pattern recognition*. IEEE.

Ni, D., Yang, X., Chen, X., Chin, C. T., Chen, S., Heng, P. A., Li, S., Qin, J., & Wang, T. (2014). Standard plane localization in ultrasound by radial component model and selective search. *Ultrasound in Medicine & Biology, 40*(11), 2728–2742. doi:10.1016/j.ultrasmedbio.2014.06.006 PMID:25220278

Perronnin, F., Sánchez, J., & Mensink, T. (2010). Improving the fisher kernel for large-scale image classification. *Computer Vision–ECCV 2010: 11th European Conference on Computer Vision, Heraklion, Crete, Greece, September 5-11, 2010 Proceedings, 11*(Part IV), 143–156.

Rahmatullah, B., & Noble, J. A. (2013, September). Anatomical object detection in fetal ultrasound: computer-expert agreements. In *International Conference on Biomedical Informatics and Technology* (pp. 207-218). Springer Berlin Heidelberg.

Rahmatullah, B., Papageorghiou, A., & Noble, J. A. (2011). Automated selection of standardized planes from ultrasound volume. In *Machine Learning in Medical Imaging: Second International Workshop, MLMI 2011, Held in Conjunction with MICCAI 2011, Toronto, Canada, September 18, 2011. Proceedings 2* (pp. 35-42). Springer Berlin Heidelberg. 10.1007/978-3-642-24319-6_5

Ronneberger, O., Fischer, P., & Brox, T. (2015). U-net: Convolutional networks for biomedical image segmentation. In *Medical image computing and computer-assisted intervention–MICCAI 2015: 18th international conference, Munich, Germany, October 5-9, 2015, proceedings, part III 18* (pp. 234-241). Springer International Publishing.

Salomon, L., Alfirevic, Z., Berghella, V., Bilardo, C., Chalouhi, G., Costa, F. D. S., ... Paladini, D. (2022). ISUOG practice guidelines (updated): Performance of the routine mid-trimester fetal ultrasound scan. *Ultrasound in Obstetrics & Gynecology, 59*(6), 840–856. doi:10.1002/uog.24888 PMID:35592929

Sánchez, J., Perronnin, F., Mensink, T., & Verbeek, J. (2013). Image classification with the fisher vector: Theory and practice. *International Journal of Computer Vision, 105*(3), 222–245. doi:10.1007/s11263-013-0636-x

Shi, J., Jiang, Q., Mao, R., Lu, M., & Wang, T. (2015). FR-KECA: Fuzzy robust kernel entropy component analysis. *Neurocomputing, 149*, 1415–1423. doi:10.1016/j.neucom.2014.08.054

Shi, J., Wu, J., Li, Y., Zhang, Q., & Ying, S. (2016). Histopathological image classification with color pattern random binary hashing-based PCANet and matrix-form classifier. *IEEE Journal of Biomedical and Health Informatics, 21*(5), 1327–1337. doi:10.1109/JBHI.2016.2602823 PMID:27576270

Shi, J., Zhou, S., Liu, X., Zhang, Q., Lu, M., & Wang, T. (2016). Stacked deep polynomial network based representation learning for tumor classification with small ultrasound image dataset. *Neurocomputing, 194*, 87–94. doi:10.1016/j.neucom.2016.01.074

Simonyan, K., & Zisserman, A. (2014). Very deep convolutional networks for large-scale image recognition. *arXiv preprint arXiv:1409.1556.*

Song, Y., He, L., Zhou, F., Chen, S., Ni, D., Lei, B., & Wang, T. (2016). Segmentation, splitting, and classification of overlapping bacteria in microscope images for automatic bacterial vaginosis diagnosis. *IEEE Journal of Biomedical and Health Informatics, 21*(4), 1095–1104. doi:10.1109/JBHI.2016.2594239 PMID:27479982

Song, Y., Zhang, L., Chen, S., Ni, D., Lei, B., & Wang, T. (2015). Accurate segmentation of cervical cytoplasm and nuclei based on multiscale convolutional network and graph partitioning. *IEEE Transactions on Biomedical Engineering, 62*(10), 2421–2433. doi:10.1109/TBME.2015.2430895 PMID:25966470

Srivastava, N., Hinton, G., Krizhevsky, A., Sutskever, I., & Salakhutdinov, R. (2014). Dropout: A simple way to prevent neural networks from overfitting. *Journal of Machine Learning Research, 15*(1), 1929–1958.

Szegedy, C., Liu, W., Jia, Y., Sermanet, P., Reed, S., Anguelov, D., ... Rabinovich, A. (2015). Going deeper with convolutions. In *Proceedings of the IEEE conference on computer vision and pattern recognition* (pp. 1-9). IEEE.

Szegedy, C., Vanhoucke, V., Ioffe, S., Shlens, J., & Wojna, Z. (2016). Rethinking the inception architecture for computer vision. In *Proceedings of the IEEE Conference on Computer Vision and Pattern Recognition* (pp. 2818–2826). 10.1109/CVPR.2016.308

Van der Maaten, L., & Hinton, G. (2008). Visualizing data using t-SNE. *Journal of Machine Learning Research, 9*(11).

Yan, Z., Zhan, Y., Peng, Z., Liao, S., Shinagawa, Y., Zhang, S., Metaxas, D. N., & Zhou, X. S. (2016). Multi-instance deep learning: Discover discriminative local anatomies for bodypart recognition. *IEEE Transactions on Medical Imaging, 35*(5), 1332–1343. doi:10.1109/TMI.2016.2524985 PMID:26863652

Yaqub, M., Kelly, B., Papageorghiou, A. T., & Noble, J. A. (2015). Guided random forests for identification of key fetal anatomy and image categorization in ultrasound scans. In *Medical Image Computing and Computer-Assisted Intervention–MICCAI 2015: 18th International Conference, Munich, Germany, October 5-9, 2015, Proceedings, Part III 18* (pp. 687-694). Springer International Publishing. 10.1007/978-3-319-24574-4_82

Yosinski, J., Clune, J., Bengio, Y., & Lipson, H. (2014). How transferable are features in deep neural networks? *Advances in Neural Information Processing Systems, 27*.

Yu, Z., Ni, D., Chen, S., Li, S., Wang, T., & Lei, B. (2016, August). Fetal facial standard plane recognition via very deep convolutional networks. In *2016 38th annual international conference of the IEEE Engineering in Medicine and Biology Society (EMBC)* (pp. 627-630). IEEE. 10.1109/EMBC.2016.7590780

Zhang, L., Chen, S., Chin, C. T., Wang, T., & Li, S. (2012). Intelligent scanning: Automated standard plane selection and biometric measurement of early gestational sac in routine ultrasound examination. *Medical Physics*, 39(8), 5015–5027. doi:10.1118/1.4736415 PMID:22894427

Zhu, X., Li, X., & Zhang, S. (2015). Block-row sparse multiview multilabel learning for image classification. *IEEE Transactions on Cybernetics*, 46(2), 450–461. doi:10.1109/TCYB.2015.2403356 PMID:25730838

Zhu, X., Li, X., Zhang, S., Ju, C., & Wu, X. (2016). Robust joint graph sparse coding for unsupervised spectral feature selection. *IEEE Transactions on Neural Networks and Learning Systems*, 28(6), 1263–1275. doi:10.1109/TNNLS.2016.2521602 PMID:26955053

Zhu, X., Suk, H. I., Wang, L., Lee, S. W., & Shen, D. (2017). A novel relational regularization feature selection method for joint regression and classification in AD diagnosis. *Medical Image Analysis*, 38, 205–214. doi:10.1016/j.media.2015.10.008 PMID:26674971

Zhu, X., Zhang, L., & Huang, Z. (2014). A sparse embedding and least variance encoding approach to hashing. *IEEE Transactions on Image Processing*, 23(9), 3737–3750. doi:10.1109/TIP.2014.2332764 PMID:24968174

Chapter 8
Future Nano and Biorobots Miniaturized Machines for Biotechnology and Beyond

Abhishek Choubey

iD https://orcid.org/0000-0002-6789-8199

Sreenidhi Institute of Science and Technology, Hyderabad, India

Shruti Bhargava Choubey

Sreenidhi Institute of Science and Technology, Hyderabad, India

ABSTRACT

Biorobotics and nanobots represent a cutting-edge area of biotechnology with tremendous promise to transform scientific research, environmental monitoring, and healthcare delivery. In this chapter, the authors explore their cutting-edge ideas, applications, and advances, showing their ability to radically change future industries like industry medicine. This chapter's primary objective is to explore both existing and emerging applications of bio-robots and nanobots in healthcare, environmental monitoring, environmental inspection, and materials science research. These technological advancements offer real-time diagnostics, minimally invasive surgery, and targeted drug delivery as well as environmental quality evaluation through bio-robot water quality evaluation and nanobot pollution detection at unprecedented scales. Furthermore, bio-robots and nanobots have proven invaluable for scientific study fields like neuroscience, synthetic biology, and materials science.

1. INTRODUCTION

Nanotechnology and biotechnology have come together to open up a new era in robotics, leading to the invention of future nano- and biorobots. Nanorobots represent an exciting frontier of nanotechnology and biotechnology research, showing great promise across various fields from medicine and healthcare to environmental monitoring and industrial applications.

DOI: 10.4018/979-8-3693-5767-5.ch008

Nanorobots serve as an intermediary between these fields of study that have experienced tremendous development over time. Nanotechnology involves changing matter at the molecular and atomic levels while biotechnology employs biological principles for developing technologies and devices. Nanorobots and biorobots differ by being relatively smaller devices ranging in size between nanometres to micrometers. These characteristics allow them to operate within the tight confines of microscopic environments typically found within living organisms or complex structures. Modern robots boast sophisticated sensing, actuation, and communication features that enable them to explore their environment effectively, interact, when necessary, with those nearby, and perform duties more efficiently than humanly possible. Researchers are devoting considerable time and attention to nanorobotics and bio robotics - two emerging disciplines with vast scientific and industrial potential. Specialized field specializations of micro-robotic technology specialize in designing micro-robot systems capable of performing specific nanoscale tasks precisely while using organic components and synthetic materials to bolster robot capabilities and features. Furthermore, their devices come equipped with sensing capabilities as well as actuator and communication protocols to interact effectively with their surroundings and accomplish specified tasks effectively (Guo et al., 2023).

Nanorobotics and biorobots are two new disciplines of research that have a great deal of potential for a wide variety of scientific and technical undertakings. In these domains, the development of nanoscale robotic systems that are capable of carrying out exact tasks is the focus of concentrated expertise. Additional issues that fall under this category include the incorporation of organic components with synthetic materials to improve the functionality and attributes of robots.

The development of hybrid intelligent nanorobotics, which is a cutting-edge technology for the design of intelligent biomedical systems, would not have been conceivable. Within the realm of biomedical research, this implies that nanorobots have the potential to be utilized in a wide variety of applications that are of significant importance. There is a wide range of medical applications that make use of nanorobots. Some of these applications include the delivery of medications, the diagnosis of diseases, imaging, tissue engineering, microsurgery, and target therapy. The applications that have been shown here illustrate the revolutionary potential of nanorobots to improve the outcomes of efforts to improve patient care and biomedical research. "Biohybrid robot" is a word that describes robot systems that blend biological components and synthetic parts to achieve higher levels of performance (Peng et al., 2023).

The biohybrid when biological components, like as cells, tissues, or enzymes, are mixed with synthetic materials, and the result is the creation of something called a robot. Several sizes are offered for hybrid robots. In the case of smaller systems, enzymes are used to propel minuscule particles, whereas in the case of higher systems, millions of cells are utilized. These hybrid systems maximize the performance of robotics by making use of the abilities that are specific to each component (Li & Yu, 2023). The purpose of this area is to take advantage of the distinctive features of biological entities to achieve the highest possible levels of efficiency and performance in robotic systems.

Biohybrid robotics may provide advantages in robotics that are hard to obtain with traditional materials, including improved performance and features that would otherwise be difficult to achieve. By combining biological entities with artificial materials, biohybrid robots can exploit the unique capabilities of biological systems at both nanoscale and macroscale levels; such as drug delivery systems, self-propelling capabilities, biomimetic movements, and functions.

2. OVERVIEW OF NANOROBOT AND BIO ROBOTICS

Nanotechnology is a scientific and Engineering discipline focused on the manipulation and utilization of atoms and molecules at the nanoscale typically measuring 100 nanometers or less. it encompasses the design fabrication and application of structures devices and systems with precise control over their properties and functionalities nanotechnology works by manipulating and controlling matter at the nanoscale which involves working with individual atoms and molecules. it utilizes various techniques and approaches to engineer materials structures and devices with specific properties and functionalities working on such a small-scale nanotechnology offers unique opportunities to explore and exploit the extraordinary properties of materials.

Scientists and Engineers employ various techniques such as bottom-up and top-down approaches to manipulate and assemble nanoscale components this enables the creation of new materials with tailored characteristics and behaviors that differ from their bulk counterparts. A nanorobot also known as a nanobot is a tiny machine or device that operates on the nanoscale typically measuring in the range of nanometres (Gotovtsev, 2023). These minuscule robots are designed to perform specific tasks at the molecular or cellular level they are constructed using nanotechnology which involves manipulating and controlling matter at the atomic and molecular levels nanorobotics is an interdisciplinary field that combines the principles of Robotics nanotechnology and Material Science to develop robots at the nanoscale nanorobotics is an emerging field of science and technology that deals with the design development and control of robots at the Nanoscale. There are various applications of nanorobots.

2.1 Disease Detection and Diagnosis

Detection and diagnosis are critical aspects of healthcare and nanorobots are equipped with advanced sensing capabilities. The potential to revolutionize these areas with their ability to operate at the molecular level Nano robots offer a powerful tool for early and accurate detection of diseases including cancer nanorobots can detect specific biomarkers or abnormalities associated with various diseases. These sensors can recognize molecular signatures indicative of disease presence or progression even before symptoms manifest by analyzing samples at the molecular level. Nanorobots can provide highly sensitive and specific diagnostic information enabling early intervention and treatment for example in the case of cancer nanorobots can be programmed to detect specific tumor markers or genetic mutations that are associated with different types of cancer. They can be introduced into the body to search for these biomarkers and provide real-time information on their presence location and concentration. This information can aid in early cancer detection allowing for timely and targeted treatment interventions.

Medical Treatment nanorobots hold immense promise for revolutionizing patient care. These tiny machines have the potential to perform medical procedures with unparalleled accuracy and precision. The capabilities of human hands by leveraging their small size and maneuverability. Nanorobots can navigate through the intricate pathways of the human body reaching targeted sites with remarkable precision. This precision opens up possibilities for minimally invasive surgeries where nanorobots can access hard-to-reach areas with minimal disruption to surrounding tissues. One of the key advantages of nanorobots is their ability to deliver therapeutics directly to the site of action with their controlled and targeted drug delivery mechanisms. Nanorobots can transport medications with pinpoint accuracy to specific cells or tissues (Popescu & Ungureanu, 2023). This targeted approach allows for higher drug concentrations at the desired location resulting in more effective treatment while minimizing systemic side effects. Furthermore, nanorobots can be engineered to carry out a range of therapeutic functions for example they can be designed to selectively destroy cancer cells precisely delivering anti-cancer agents to tumors while sparing healthy tissues. This targeted approach has the potential to enhance the efficacy of cancer treatments while minimizing the debilitating side effects often associated with traditional chemotherapy while nanorobots are still in the early stages of development and face numerous challenges.

Nanorobots and biorobots are small machines engineered to perform specific tasks at the nanoscale. Nano-robots typically consist of synthetic materials while biobots consist of living cells or tissues - both types have the potential for revolutionizing disease detection by providing more precise, efficient, minimally invasive ways of diagnosing diseases and monitoring their progress.

2.1.1 Disease Detection

Nano- and biorobots offer some promising applications in disease detection, with specific biomarkers such as cancer cells or bacteria being detected by these robots and relaying this information directly to doctors or healthcare providers. To identify diseases, nanorobots can be deployed in a variety of methods, including the following:

Targeted drug delivery: Nano-robots can be equipped with pharmaceuticals and directed toward specific cells or tissues to optimize efficacy while minimizing adverse effects.

Imaging: Nanorobots, equipped with imaging sensors, can capture images of damaged cells or tissues, enabling doctors to make more precise diagnoses and monitor the effectiveness of treatment programs. This technology has the potential to enable them to deliver regular updates on the progress of treatment over some time.

Sensing: Nanorobots, which are equipped with sensors capable of detecting certain indicators of disease, can aid clinicians in the early and more precise diagnosis of diseases.

2.1.2 Disease Diagnosis

Nanorobots and biobots have the potential to be employed for illness diagnosis as well. These robots are capable of extracting cellular or tissue samples, which can subsequently be examined for indications of illness. Nanorobots can be employed in diverse manners for disease diagnosis, including:

Nano-robots have the potential to perform biopsies on tumors or other diseased tissues, aiding physicians in more precise illness diagnosis and assessment of the disease's stage.

Blood testing: Nano-robots can extract blood samples and examine them for indications of illness. This enables physicians to promptly diagnose medical issues while simultaneously monitoring the course of treatment.

Tissue analysis: Nano-robots can aid in the identification of disease indicators in tissues, facilitating clinicians in making more precise illness diagnoses and formulating an optimal treatment plan.

2.2 Manufacturing Assembly

The production and assembling of Nanorobots have a significant potential impact on manufacturing and assembly processes. These tiny machines offer unparalleled precision and control at the Nanoscale opening up new avenues for creating intricate structures and devices with enhanced properties. Nano robots can manipulate and assemble materials at the atomic and molecular levels allowing for the precise positioning and arrangement of individual building blocks. This level of control enables the fabrication of complex structures and devices that were previously unattainable using conventional manufacturing methods by harnessing the capabilities of Nano robots manufacturers can achieve higher levels of efficiency and quality in their production processes. These robots can perform tasks with exceptional Precision reducing errors and variations in product specifications. This leads to improved product consistency enhanced quality control and increased customer satisfaction. Moreover, the use of Nano robots in manufacturing can contribute to waste reduction their ability to handle and position materials at the nanoscale minimizes material waste and optimizes resource utilization by precisely depositing materials and assembling components. Nanorobots can reduce the need for excess materials and decrease production waste worker safety can also be improved through the integration of nanorobots in manufacturing processes. Energy Production holds tremendous potential for revolutionizing energy production and addressing critical challenges in this field. Nano robots can improve the efficiency and performance of solar cells by enhancing light absorption reducing reflection and optimizing charge separation and transport processes.

Nano robots can enhance the thermoelectric properties of materials boosting energy conversion efficiencies. The Environmental Cleanup application of Nanorobots and environmental cleanup presents a promising solution to the pressing challenges of pollution and contamination. These tiny machines have the potential to contribute significantly to the removal of pollutants from water soil and air. Nanorobots can facilitate the process of water purification by enhancing filtration mechanisms and improving the efficiency of water treatment systems for soil remediation. Nanorobots can assist in the removal of toxic substances such as industrial pollutants pesticides and chemical residues they can be designed to break down or encapsulate contaminants facilitating their removal from the soil in air pollution mitigation. Nano-robots can play a vital role in capturing and neutralizing airborne pollutants they can be deployed to target specific pollutants such as particulate matter and volatile organic compounds (Bhandari et al., 2023).

2.3 Material Science

Nanorobots offer exciting possibilities in the field of material science. The development of advanced materials with unique properties and functionalities and their integration can pave the way for the creation of self-healing materials smart coatings and responsive surfaces that adapt to environmental conditions or stimuli. One key application of nanorobots in material science is the development of self-healing materials nanorobots can be designed to detect and repair damage in materials at the nanoscale. They can autonomously navigate through the material matrix identify cracks or defects and initiate healing mechanisms by releasing healing agents or catalyzing chemical reactions. This self-healing capability extends the lifespan of materials reduces maintenance requirements and enhances their overall durability and reliability smart coatings enabled by Nanorobots can revolutionize surface properties and functionalities. Nanorobots can be programmed to respond to specific stimuli such as temperature light or chemical changes by incorporating them into coatings surfaces and can exhibit adaptive properties such as self-cleaning anti-fouling anti-corrosion or anti-icing functionalities. These smart coatings can have broad applications in various Industries including Automotive Aerospace and architecture (Kučuk, Primožič, Knez, & Leitgeb, 2023).

2.4 Exploration and Sensing

Exploration and sensing nanorobots have the potential to revolutionize exploration and sensing by offering into challenging and inaccessible environments. It is providing valuable data and insights that were previously unattainable whether it's deep-sea exploration or space missions. Nanorobots offer a compact and versatile solution for gathering information and navigating through extreme conditions in deep-sea exploration. Nanorobots can be deployed to explore the depths of the ocean where human access is limited and equipped with sensors and imaging capabilities. These tiny machines can delve into uncharted territory mapping. The ocean floor studying marine life and collecting data on geological formations their small size allows them to access narrow crevices and fragile ecosystems without causing significant disturbance similarly in space missions nanorobots can play a crucial role in exploring celestial bodies and conducting research in outer space. They can be utilized to navigate through challenging terrains collect samples and perform experiments in environments with extreme temperatures radiation or low gravity conditions. Nanorobots can contribute to the study of planetary bodies such as Mars or the moon aiding in the search for signs of life or resources.

3. OVERVIEW BIO ROBOTICS

Bio robotics is a multidisciplinary field that integrates biomedical engineering, cybernetics, and robotics to create innovative technologies that blend biology with mechanical systems. Its aims include enhancing communication efficiency, affecting genetic information, and developing machines that resemble biological systems.

Cybernetics is defined as the science of communications and automatic control systems in both machines and living things however while robotic and biological systems are both cybernetic systems they're separate fields of study their communication control systems and locomotion function differently at least they did traditionally the future of robotics is unfolding quickly increasingly in the field of robotics and biology (Li, Dekanovsky, Khezri, Wu, Zhou, & Sofer, 2022). There were different levels of revolution in biorobotics years ago.

3.1 Biomimicry

Biomimicry is the practice of learning and copying solutions to problems that nature has already managed to solve. it is used to develop modern technologies from aircraft wings. The nanostructure of butterfly wings to superhydrophobic coatings. The lotus leaf building mobile and adaptive autonomous is a challenge but the natural world has been doing something similar for billions of years. It's no surprise that few fields have embraced biomimicry. The way robotics has been and it remains a potent driving force for its continued innovation for mobile autonomous. It's easy to identify how robots have been directly inspired by the unique locomotion of animals such as spiders birds and fish. Biomimicry in robots goes beyond general appearance and applies to cybernetic systems. They used to operate for example applications of point control are modeled.

3.2 Soft Robotics

Soft robotics is a subfield of robotics that deals with the design, control, and fabrication of soft robots made out of compliant materials like silicone rubber or fabric instead of rigid links. Soft robots can be filled with air or fluid for shape modification or movement purposes. Soft robots offer several advantages over their traditional counterparts. They're lighter, more flexible, and safer to interact with humans - not to mention easier to customize for specific applications. Soft robots offer great promise in healthcare settings. Soft robots can be utilized for minimally invasive surgery, rehabilitation, and prosthetics; surgeons even employ soft robots for delicate procedures on both brain and heart surgeries (Jahromi et al., 2021).

3.3 Swarm Robotics

Swarm robotics is an exciting field of robotics inspired by nature. This field involves designing and controlling large groups of robots that work collectively towards one common goal; typically, these simple and cheap robots communicate and collaborate locally with one another to achieve their purpose. Swarm robotics offers numerous advantages over traditional approaches to robotics, including being more robust and adaptable to changing environments as well as being more efficient at covering large areas or manipulating complex objects. Autonomous Swarms Autonomous swarms rely on simple onboard intelligence that creates a much greater degree of emergent intelligence and functioning. This is similar to how individual unintelligent ants follow basic procedures and communicate through pheromones to build vast and complex cities.

Swarm robots typically feature basic sensors and actuators, communicating wirelessly among themselves. Their basic rules of behavior may include following a leader, avoiding obstacles, and sharing information - however, as the robots interact with one another and their environment they develop complex collective behavior patterns that emerge over time (Hu, 2021).

3.4 Nano Robotics

Nanorobotics is an emerging technological domain focused on the creation and advancement of robots operating at the nanoscale. The nanoscale refers to a range of measurements between 1 and 100 nanometers, which is approximately 100,000 times smaller than the breadth of a human hair (Primožič et al., 2021). Nanorobots are commonly energized utilizing light, electricity, or chemical interactions. They exhibit movement through diverse means, including microscopic flagella, and cilia, or by altering their body morphology. Nanorobots can establish communication among themselves and with external controllers through several means, including electromagnetic waves, chemical signals, and even quantum entanglement. The advancement in nanotechnology is shown in table 1. Nanorobots are miniature machines on the scale of billionths of meters that can be programmed to perform specific tasks, such as those related to surgery. Such tasks could include:

- Minimally Invasive Surgery (MIS): Nanorobots offer minimally invasive surgical solutions with their ability to be introduced through small incisions or even natural orifices, thus eliminating large and open wounds while speeding recovery times.
- Targeted drug delivery: Nanorobots can be loaded with drugs and programmed to deliver them directly to diseased cells, limiting damage to healthy tissues.

- Intracellular surgery: Nanorobots can be miniaturized sufficiently to operate within individual cells, potentially enabling us to repair damage caused by cell damage or modify genetic material at its source.

4. BIO-NANOTECHNOLOGY

Bionanotechnology is found across bacterial archaeal and eukaryotic cells. it generates locomotion similar to a propeller through a rotary motor an arm just 20 nanometres thick and built from proteins capabilities like the nanoscale mobility of the flagellum has spawned a new field of robotics not as inspiration or biomimicry but for directly building electromechanical components. Bio nano technologies utilize existing biological components like proteins lipids and DNA to manufacture new molecules or inorganic nanoscale components that are used in the assembly of nanorobots. This is biology directly interacting with robotics and it can work both ways since nanorobots can also be used to build biological components. This may be in its early stages but it's part of the broader field of biofactoring where living organisms like bacteria fungi and algae build inorganic materials and components used in many industrial applications including robotics. This varies from macroscopic materials such as hard or soft plastics, and earlier robots down to metallic nanoparticles (Shen et al., 2021).

Applications of Bio-Nanotechnology:

Medicine: Targeted drug delivery, regenerative medicine, tissue engineering, personalized medicine, and biosensors for diagnostics. Healthcare: Early disease detection, gene therapy treatments, and nanorobots designed for surgery provide biocompatible implants as solutions.

Environment: Bioremediation of polluted sites, water purification, environmental monitoring, biosensors to detect environmental contaminants;

Energy: biofuel production, solar energy conversion, and monitoring with biosensors.

Nanoparticles for drug delivery: Nanoparticles can be loaded with drugs and targeted towards specific cells or tissues for improved efficiency and reduced side effects of medication delivery. Examples of bio-nanotechnologies:

Table 1. The advancement in nanotechnology

S.No	Areas	Description
1	DNA origami nanorobots	Researchers have created nanorobots made of folded DNA strands - also known as DNA origami - which can be programmed with specific shapes and functions, such as carrying drugs or manipulating cells.
2	Light-powered nanorobots	Scientists have developed nanorobots powered solely by light. This eliminates the need for batteries or onboard power sources, simplifying design, reducing risks, and potentially cutting costs.
3	Magnetically controlled nanorobots	Nanorobots can be controlled using external magnetic fields, giving surgeons greater control and accuracy during surgery
4	AI-powered nanorobots:	Researchers are creating nanorobots equipped with artificial intelligence capable of learning and adapting in real-time, which could allow them to make autonomous decisions during surgery, such as detecting diseased tissue.
5	Nanorobotic swarms:	Scientists are investigating swarms of nanorobots as possible collaborators to perform complex surgical tasks that might exceed individual robot capabilities

Nanoparticles for drug delivery: Nanoparticles can be loaded with drugs and targeted to specific cells or tissues, improving drug delivery efficiency and reducing side effects.

Biosensors for diagnostics: Bio-nanotechnologies can develop biosensors that detect specific biomarkers or pathogens with high sensitivity, enabling early diagnosis and treatment of diseases.

Biocompatible implants: Bio-nanotechnologies offer biocompatible implants that integrate seamlessly with the body, decreasing rejection rates and improving patient outcomes.

4.1 Biohybrids

Biohybrids are the interaction between biological and mechanical cybernetics. In 2017 researchers used a laser to locate a buried landline 20 meters away but the laser wasn't designed to detect landmines instead the laser was programmed to detect a special type of bacteria engineered to grow fluorescent green in the presence of a nearby explosive compound. This is a biosensor a new type of cybernetic system that's part mechanical and part biological. They use organic components like enzymes and organelles as part of a sensing and transducing circuit that can be integrated directly into a robotic system. Biohybrids aren't just about integrating biology into robotics it works both ways this is perhaps most apparent in the field of bionic prosthesis where robotics are used to substitute or augment living components from arms and legs to hearts and lungs even eyes and the brain itself. In 2015 at a medical facility in Tokyo a dog with late-stage terminal bone cancer was treated with drugs encapsulated in a basic nanocarrier and an ultrasonic activator on a robotic arm was used to trigger the release of drugs at the tumor site. This was intended to only be an initial safety test for the procedure but to the researcher's surprise the tumor shrunk by 15. The dog-to-walk-again follow-up procedures extended the dog's life by over a year if this procedure were applied to humans' researchers estimate the increase in life expectancy would be 10 years with the emergence of nanoscale robotics. These techniques can go further nanoscale robots are small enough to flow through blood vessels and can be used to deliver drugs in much lower doses to specific target sites clear dangerous plaques from arteries and perhaps even perform microsurgeries while this technology is still in the research phase with many human trials planned for the next few years. It's becoming increasingly likely that robots at the smallest scales may become a part of us and this is just the medical application of nanobots robotics at this scale may be a key step towards enabling atomically precise manufacture of the assembly of large structures atom by atom the capabilities (Li, Dekanovsky, Khezri, Wu, Zhou, & Sofer, 2022). The Overview of biohybrid nano- and microrobots is shown in Figure 1.

There is an ever-increasing variety of biohybrids being developed, each one with its specific focus.

Figure 1. Overview of biohybrid nano- and microrobots

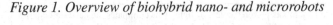

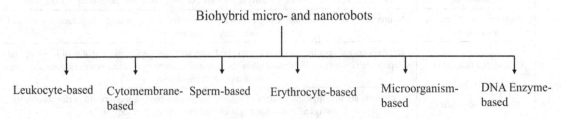

Biohybrid materials: These advanced materials combine living cells (such as stem cells or bacteria) with synthetic materials (such as polymers or hydrogels) to produce materials with enhanced properties, like wound dressings that release growth factors or biocompatible sensors that detect environmental changes.

Biohybrid robots: Biohybrid robots refer to machines that combine biological components like muscle cells or tissues for more natural and efficient movement, such as robotic prostheses that mimic human muscle function powered by sperm cells to deliver targeted drugs.

Biohybrid sensors: These sensors combine biological receptors (such as enzymes or antibodies) with synthetic materials for high-sensitivity detection of certain chemicals or biological signals, making them useful in environmental monitoring, disease diagnosis, or personalized medicine applications.

4.2 Xenobots

Imagine a world where little entities composed of living cells can autonomously form, move by swimming or rolling, and even reproduce. The xenobots represent a groundbreaking organism that is challenging the distinction between biology and technology.

These minuscule wonders are neither animals nor machines. These are autonomous robots, created using frog stem cells and carefully engineered by computers to carry out precise functions. Xenobots emerge through an innovative mechanism known as evolutionary design. Scientists apply algorithms to model numerous possible shapes and motions, ultimately choosing the most successful ones for actual implementation. It represents accelerated evolution, enabling scientists to investigate a wide range of designs and identify valuable functional features (Akolpoglu et al., 2020; Kučuk, Primožič, Knez, & Leitgeb, 2023). The fabrication of Xenobots

Computational Design: Utilizing evolutionary AI, scientists perform simulations on thousands of body shapes and swimming motions using evolutionary AI software. An algorithm then selects those designs that most effectively meet desired functional goals as "breeding stock."

Cell Harvesting: Stem cells derived from frog embryos are harvested and cultured in the lab, before being meticulously arranged into their desired shapes by microscopic needles as predicted by AI simulations. Eventually, Patterning occurs: Once all stem cells have been assembled into their desired patterns predicted by AI simulations.

Cell Fusion and Development: Over several days, stem cells fuse into functioning Xenobots and grow.

5. LITERATURE REVIEW

Recent developments in the area of nano- and biorobots have shown promising applications in numerous areas. In 2023, Yuan developed nanorobots that move by magnets. These nanorobots are designed to quickly remove reactive α-dicarbonyl species and prevent the formation of advanced glycation end products.

In Zhang's (2023) study, twin-engine self-adaptive micro/nanorobots were utilized for gastrointestinal inflammation therapy. The study showed that these robots were able to accumulate drugs more effectively at locations of inflammation. Guo (2023) conducted a comprehensive analysis of the development of intelligent moving micro/nanomotors and their use in biosensing and disease therapy. The study emphasized the need to resolve material and biocompatibility challenges. In Liu's (2023) study, the focus was on the development of responsive magnetic nanocomposites for shape-morphing microrobots. The study highlighted the potential of magnetic fields in enabling control without the need for tethers and emphasized the significance of future fabrication approaches. This research collectively emphasizes the promise of nano- and biorobots in addressing diverse biomedical concerns. (Li 2022, Refaai 2022) has focused on drug delivery and the neutralization of pathogenic bacteria and toxins. Sun 2022 has developed combinedly biological and artificial components that have been shown to enhance drug retention, precise operation of minimally invasive surgery, and medical sensing.

(Wang 2021) The possible applications of magnetic actuation-based micro/nanorobots include targeted delivery, minimally invasive surgery, cellular and intracellular monitoring, intelligent sensing, and detoxification. Despite these progressions, obstacles such as biosafety and clinical translation still need to be resolved. Research has investigated the production and possible uses of nanobots, namely in the field of biomedicine. The emphasis has been on their ability to be programmed and their potential for delivering drugs and treating diseases. The detailed literature review of existing work is shown in Table 2.

Table 2. Literature review of existing work

S.No.		Main findings
1	Guo *et al.(2023)*	The article discusses the utilization of micro/nanomotors in biosensing, cancer treatment, gynecological illness treatment, and assisted fertilization.
2	Peng *et al.(2023)*	An independent nanorobot with the ability to actively deliver drugs to mitochondria, inducing mitochondrial-mediated apoptosis and dysregulation to enhance the anticancer effect in vitro and inhibit cancer cell metastasis.
3	Li *et al.(2023)*	The biodegradability of microrobots is essential to prevent the accumulation of hazardous residue within the human body during therapeutic applications.
4	Gotovtsev (2023)	The review focused mostly on evaluating the system utilizing microbial cells. This technique hinges on harnessing microbes as the core element of a robot, responsible for tasks such as locomotion, conveyance of products, and, in some cases, the production of advantageous substances. The inclusion of living cells in these microrobots brings both advantages and disadvantages.
5	Popescu (2023)	Nanoparticles manufactured by environmentally friendly methods and combined with biopolymers offer a possible solution to the issue of chemical waste resulting from biosensor fabrication.
6	Bhandari *et.al* (2023)	Nanomaterials have the potential to serve as nanosensors, nanocides, nanofertilizers, nanobarcodes, and nano-remediators in contemporary agricultural methods.
7	Kučuk *et.al* (2023)	Biopolymeric nanoparticles have great potential as delivery vehicles for a wide range of medicinal medicines.
8	Li, *et.al* (2022)	Biohybrid micro- and nanorobots can do several medical activities, including targeted medication administration, single-cell manipulation, and cell microsurgery. They are equipped with onboard actuation, sensing, and control, and may execute numerous functions.
9	Jahromi, *et.al* (2021)	Various therapeutic approaches including living immune cells, immune cells modified at the surface, cell membranes of immunocytes, extracellular vesicles or exosomes produced from leukocytes, and artificial immune cells have been studied, and a small number of these have been commercially released.
10	Hu *et.al* (2021)	DNA nanorobots are very suitable as biomedical robots for the field of precision medicine.
11	Primožič, *et.al* (2021)	The utilization of nanoparticles and nanocomposites in food packaging enhances the mechanical durability and characteristics of the water and oxygen resistance of the packaging, while potentially offering additional advantages such as antibacterial qualities and light obstruction. There are uncertainties regarding the migration of nanoparticles from packaging to food, as migration assays and risk assessment procedures are not well-defined. The use of nanomaterials in the food packaging sector is limited due to the assumed toxicity, insufficient data from clinical trials, and the absence of risk assessment studies.
12	Shen *et.al* (2021)	DNA nanostructures can interact with various entities such as tiny molecules, nucleic acids, proteins, viruses, and cancer cells.

6. FABRICATION OF ROBOT AND BIOROBOTS

Fabrication methods for nano- and biorobots are constantly evolving as new materials and techniques are developed. Some of the most common methods include:

(i) Top-down approaches

Top-down approaches involve physically removing or sculpting material to create the desired nanorobotic structure. Some common top-down fabrication approaches include:

- Electron beam lithography (EBL) employs a concentrated stream of electrons to selectively expose a substrate coated with resist, thereby transferring the intended pattern onto the substrate.
- Focused Ion Beam (FIB) milling uses a concentrated ion beam to physically eliminate material from a substrate, enabling the fabrication of intricate and extremely accurate structures.
- Nanoimprint lithography (NIL) uses a mold with the desired nanostructure to imprint the pattern onto a substrate.

    (ii) Bottom-up approaches

Bottom-up approaches comprise assembling atoms or molecules into the anticipated nanorobotic structure. Some common bottom-up fabrication methods include:

- Self-assembly: Self-assembly relies on the natural interactions between molecules to drive the formation of the desired nanostructure.
- Directed assembly: Directed assembly involves using external forces, such as electric fields or magnetic fields, to guide the assembly of molecules into the desired nanostructure.
- Chemical synthesis: Chemical synthesis involves using chemical reactions to create the desired nanorobotic structure.

    (iii) Hybrid approaches

Hybrid approaches combine top-down and bottom-up methods or biofabrication techniques with top-down/ bottom-up approaches to create complex nanorobotic structures with multifunctional capabilities. The choice of fabrication method depends on the specific design and functionality of a nanorobot being created. Top-down approaches tend to be more established and provide higher precision; bottom-up methods may allow for creating more complex or multipurpose nanobots; bio-fabrication techniques still have yet to mature fully but have great potential in terms of producing biocompatible and biodegradable devices. As nanorobotics manufacturing advances rapidly, new methods are constantly being devised. Over time, we can expect increasingly sophisticated nanorobots with multiple functions (Chelliah et al., 2021; Naghdi et al., 2023; Rodrigues et al., 2021).

6.1 Biofabrication

Biofabrication involves using living cells or biological materials to create the desired nanorobotic structure. Some common bio-fabrication methods include:

- Tissue engineering: Tissue engineering involves using scaffolds or cell culture techniques to create three-dimensional tissue structures.

- ○ Genetic engineering: Genetic engineering involves modifying the genetic makeup of cells to give them new or enhanced functions.
- ○ Synthetic biology: Synthetic biology involves designing and engineering new biological systems from scratch.

Fabrication processes involve precise manufacturing techniques at the nanoscale, using techniques such as nanolithography, self-assembly, or merging biological entities with artificial materials. Further research and exploration in nanofabrication technology are necessary to fully comprehend these fabrication methods used in creating nanorobots. The classification of nanomaterials according to their physical dimensions is shown in Figure 2.

6.2 Fabrication of Biorobots

The process of biorobot fabrication includes the integration of synthetic materials and biological entities to produce hybrid systems that possess improved functionality and attributes. The fabrication techniques and approaches described in the provided documents will be elaborated upon in this section. The authors discuss the utilization of enzymes as power sources for self-propelled nanoparticles at the nanoscale. Enzymes of this nature facilitate biocompatible reactions and can be integrated into nanoparticles exhibiting diverse geometries and compositions. This facilitates the development of active matter systems, which find applicability in biomedical contexts including drug delivery systems.

Moving to the microscale, the article mentions the use of single cells, such as bacteria or spermatozoa, as substitutes for enzymes. These self-propelling cells can transport cargo, serve as drug delivery systems, aid in in vitro fertilization practices, or remove biofilms. At the macro level, the integration of millions of cells forming tissues is discussed. Muscle cells, for example, can be combined to power biorobotic devices or actuators. The article mentions untethered biorobots that can crawl or swim due to the contractions of the tissue. The authors also mention ongoing developments in integrating different types of tissue to create more realistic biomimetic devices (Kim et al., 2022; Sun et al., 2020). Hu *et.*

Figure 2. The classification of nanomaterials according to their physical dimensions

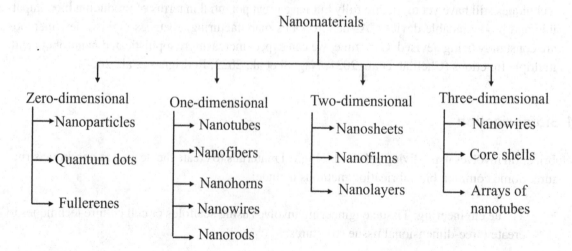

all highlights the use of advanced manufacturing technologies such as 3D bioprinting and microfluidic manufacturing for fabricating cell-laden hydrogel structures.

These technologies enable precise and customizable fabrication of biohybrid constructs. Furthermore, the article describes the development of engineered functional materials by combining living cells with hydrogels; such materials can then transport drugs, peptides, or artificial substances, making them suitable for transplantation, tissue engineering, or controllable biomedicine applications. Lin *et. all* describes biohybrid micro-robots powered by living cells. These authors outline its many advantages over rigid drives - including microscale self-assembly, high-energy efficiency, flexibility, self-repair capabilities, and multiple degrees of freedom (Koleoso et al., 2020; Zheng et al., 2021). The review article discusses challenges related to biohybrid micro-robot development, such as ethical considerations surrounding primary cell extraction from mammals or muscle tissues. Furthermore, the authors highlight the need for intelligent perception and control functions within biohybrid robots as well as highlighting current systems' limited lifespan and functionality. Overall, biorobot fabrication involves the combination of biological entities with artificial materials using various techniques and approaches. These may include using enzymes and cells at various scales - nanoparticles, self-propelling cells, and tissue constructs - while advanced manufacturing technologies like 3D bioprinting and microfluidic manufacturing play a key role in fabricating complex hybrid structures. Yet ethical considerations, intelligent control issues, lifespan issues, and functionality issues still need to be resolved before designing biorobots (Markande et al., 2021; Zhou et al., 2021).

7. CONCLUSION

In summary, the literature review regarding biohybrid robotics and nanofabrication technology advancements underscores the significant achievements and the future uses of these technologies across diverse domains, including but not limited to biomedical research, wearable electronics, human-machine interfaces, personal health monitoring systems, space exploration, and biomanufacturing. The literature on nanofabrication technology encompasses an examination of the evolution of hybrid intelligent nanorobotics, a paradigm shift in biomedical research concerning the design of intelligent systems. Drug delivery, disease diagnosis, imaging, surgery, tissue engineering, monitoring, and sensing, targeted therapy, and microsurgery are all potential applications of nanorobots in this field. The aforementioned applications exemplify the capacity of nanorobots to radically transform biomedical research and substantially enhance patient outcomes.

In contrast, biohybrid robotics integrates synthetic materials with biological entities to augment the functionality and characteristics of robotic systems. Biological entities and synthetic materials are integrated at various scales, including the nanoscale, microscale, and macroscale. The benefits of biohybrid robotics include enhanced functionality and biomimicry within the field of robotics. Biomimicry in robotics, enhanced performance, and improved functionality are all potential advantages of biohybrid robotics.

Soft electronics find diverse utility in human-machine interfaces, wearable electronics, and personal health-care monitoring systems. These technologies facilitate the creation of conformable and comfortable wearable devices, wearable sensors capable of acquiring physiological signals, and interfaces capable of seamless integration with the human body. Ultra-thin electronics, encompassing devices and components that are exceptionally thin, provide enhanced surface conformability for purposes such as personal health-care monitoring systems, wearable electronics, and human-machine interfaces.

In general, the literature review offers significant contributions by examining the development, utilization, and prospects of biohybrid robotics, soft electronics, ultra-thin electronics, hydrogels containing living cells, responsive biohybrid systems, biohybrid microrobots, and magneto/catalytic nanostructured BioBots. These technologies are capable of bringing about significant changes across multiple sectors, enhancing interactions between humans and machines, and potentially reshaping the course of human history on an international scale. Nevertheless, additional investigation and progress are required to rectify constraints, enhance functionality, and surmount obstacles linked to these technologies.

REFERENCES

Akolpoglu, M. B., Dogan, N. O., Bozuyuk, U., Ceylan, H., Kizilel, S., & Sitti, M. (2020). High-yield production of biohybrid microalgae for on-demand cargo delivery. *Advancement of Science*, 7(16), 2001256. doi:10.1002/advs.202001256 PMID:32832367

Bhandari, G., Dhasmana, A., Chaudhary, P., Gupta, S., Gangola, S., Gupta, A., Rustagi, S., Shende, S. S., Rajput, V. D., Minkina, T. M., Malik, S., & Sláma, P. (2023). A Perspective Review on Green Nanotechnology in Agro-Ecosystems: Opportunities for Sustainable Agricultural Practices & Environmental Remediation. *Agriculture*, 13(3), 668. doi:10.3390/agriculture13030668

Chelliah, R., Wei, S., Daliri, E. B. M., Rubab, M., Elahi, F., Yeon, S. J., Jo, K. H., Yan, P., Liu, S., & Oh, D. H. (2021). Development of Nanosensors Based Intelligent Packaging Systems: Food Quality and Medicine. *Nanomaterials (Basel, Switzerland)*, 11(6), 1515. doi:10.3390/nano11061515 PMID:34201071

Gotovtsev, P. M. (2023). Microbial Cells as a Microrobots: From Drug Delivery to Advanced Biosensors. *Biomimetics*, 8(1), 8. doi:10.3390/biomimetics8010109 PMID:36975339

Guo, Y., Jing, D., Liu, S., & Yuan, Q. (2023). Construction of intelligent moving micro/nanomotors and their applications in biosensing and disease treatment. *Theranostics*, 13(9), 2993–3020. doi:10.7150/thno.81845 PMID:37284438

Hu, Y. (2021). Self-Assembly of DNA Molecules: Towards DNA Nanorobots for Biomedical Applications. *Cyborg and Bionic Systems (Washington, D.C.)*, 2021, 2021. doi:10.34133/2021/9807520 PMID:36285141

Jahromi, L. P., Shahbazi, M., Maleki, A., Azadi, A., & Santos, H. A. (2021). Chemically Engineered Immune Cell-Derived Microrobots and Biomimetic Nanoparticles: Emerging Biodiagnostic and Therapeutic Tools. *Advancement of Science*, 8(8), 8. doi:10.1002/advs.202002499 PMID:33898169

Kim, D. S., Yang, X., Lee, J. H., Yoo, H. Y., Park, C., Kim, S. W., & Lee, J. (2022). Development of GO/Co/Chitosan-Based Nano-Biosensor for Real-Time Detection of D-Glucose. *Biosensors (Basel)*, 12(7), 464. doi:10.3390/bios12070464 PMID:35884266

Koleoso, M., Feng, X., & Xue, Y. (2020). *Materials Today Bio Micro/nanoscale magnetic robots for biomedical applications*. https://doi.org/ doi:10.1016/j.mtbio.2020.100085

Kučuk, N., Primožič, M., Knez, Ž., & Leitgeb, M. (2023). Sustainable Biodegradable Biopolymer-Based Nanoparticles for Healthcare Applications. *International Journal of Molecular Sciences*, 24. PMID:36834596

Li, J., Dekanovsky, L., Khezri, B., Wu, B., Zhou, H., & Sofer, Z. (2022). Biohybrid Micro- and Nano-robots for Intelligent Drug Delivery. *Cyborg and Bionic Systems (Washington, D.C.)*, *2022*, 2022. doi:10.34133/2022/9824057 PMID:36285309

Li, J., & Yu, J. (2023). Biodegradable Microrobots and Their Biomedical Applications: A Review. *Nanomaterials (Basel, Switzerland)*, *13*(10), 13. doi:10.3390/nano13101590 PMID:37242005

Markande, A., Mistry Kruti, U., & Shraddha, J. A. (2021) magnetic nanoparticles from bacteria. In Biobased Nanotechnology for Green Applications. SpringerNature Switzerland AG.

Naghdi, T., Ardalan, S., Asghari Adib, Z., Sharifi, A. R., & Golmohammadi, H. (2023). Moving toward Smart Biomedical Sensing. *Biosensors & Bioelectronics*, *223*, 115009. doi:10.1016/j.bios.2022.115009 PMID:36565545

Peng, X., Tang, S., Tang, D., Zhou, D., Li, Y., Chen, Q., Wan, F., Lukas, H., Han, H., Zhang, X., Gao, W., & Wu, S. (2023). Autonomous metal-organic framework nanorobots for active mitochondria-targeted cancer therapy. *Science Advances*, *9*(23), 9. doi:10.1126/sciadv.adh1736 PMID:37294758

Popescu, M., & Ungureanu, C. (2023). Biosensors in Food and Healthcare Industries: Bio-Coatings Based on Biogenic Nanoparticles and Biopolymers. *Coatings*, *13*(3), 486. doi:10.3390/coatings13030486

Primožič, M., Knez, Ž., & Leitgeb, M. (2021). (Bio)Nanotechnology in Food Science—Food Packaging. *Nanomaterials (Basel, Switzerland)*, 11. PMID:33499415

Rodrigues, C., Souza, V. G. L., Coelhoso, I., & Fernando, A. L. (2021). Bio-Based Sensors for Smart Food Packaging—Current Applications and Future Trends. *Sensors (Basel)*, *21*(6), 2148. doi:10.3390/s21062148 PMID:33803914

Shen, L., Wang, P., & Ke, Y. (2021). DNA Nanotechnology-Based Biosensors and Therapeutics. *Advanced Healthcare Materials*, 10. PMID:34085411

Sun, M., Liu, Q., Fan, X., Wang, Y., Chen, W., Tian, C., Sun, L., & Xie, H. (2020). Autonomous biohybrid urchin-like microperforator for intracellular payload delivery. *Small*, *16*(23), 1906701. doi:10.1002/smll.201906701 PMID:32378351

Zheng, S., Wang, Y., Pan, S., Ma, E., Jin, S., Jiao, M., Wang, W., Li, J., Xu, K., & Wang, H. (2021). Biocompatible nanomotors as active diagnostic imaging agents for enhanced magnetic resonance imaging of tumor tissues in vivo. *Advanced Functional Materials*, *31*(24), 2100936. doi:10.1002/adfm.202100936

Zhou, H., Mayorga-Martinez, C. C., Pané, S., Zhang, L., & Pumera, M. (2021). Magnetically Driven Micro and Nanorobots. *Chemical Reviews*, *121*(8), 4999–5041. doi:10.1021/acs.chemrev.0c01234 PMID:33787235

Chapter 9
HRI in ITs Using ML Techniques

V. Saran

Karpagam Academy of Higher Education, India

R. Chennappan

iD https://orcid.org/0000-0002-6252-4614

Karpagam Academy of Higher Education, India

ABSTRACT

Machine learning (ML), deep learning, fuzzy logic, and traditional neural networks are just a few of the subsets that make up artificial intelligence (AI). These subgroups possesses unique qualities and skills that could improve the effectiveness of modern medical sciences. Human intervention in clinical diagnostics, medical imaging, and decision-making is facilitated by these clever solutions. The development of information technology, the concept of intelligent healthcare has become more and more popular. Intelligent healthcare is a revolutionary approach to healthcare that leverages state-of-the-art technology such as AI and the internet of things (loT) to improve overall efficacy, convenience, and personalisation of the medical system.

I. INTRODUCTION

Artificial intelligence (AI) and medical technology have brought in a new age in healthcare in the twenty-first century. Diagnostics, patient care, and medical practices are changing as a result of the integration of intelligent systems and the unrelenting search of innovation. Known as Intelligent Healthcare, this paradigm shift offers opportunities for proactive and personalised health management in addition to increased efficiency and accuracy. Moerenhout, T., et al (2018). This introduction explores the innovative advancements that are reshaping healthcare and takes the reader on a voyage into the centre of this revolutionary convergence.

Modern healthcare has significantly advanced thanks to the collaboration of artificial intelligence and medical technology. AI has become a potent tool for data analysis, pattern recognition, and decision-making, whereas medical technology has historically fueled advances in diagnosis and treatment. A

DOI: 10.4018/979-8-3693-5767-5.ch009

revolutionary force that could completely reshape the healthcare system is unleashed by the union of these two domains.

Precision medicine, which considers individual variations in patients' genetics, environments, and lifestyles, is the primary idea behind this groundbreaking advancement. Healthcare professionals can now more precisely personalise therapies thanks to AI-driven technologies that enable the extraction of relevant insights from large datasets. This promises increased effectiveness as well as a move towards preventative treatment, which identifies and treats possible health problems before they materialise details from Dongari, S., et al (2023).

The field of diagnostics and medical imaging is one of the most innovative uses of AI in healthcare. Medical image analysis may now be done more accurately and efficiently than ever before because to machine learning algorithms that have been trained on large datasets. Artificial Intelligence is quickly turning into a vital tool for medical practitioners, helping them with everything from seeing minute irregularities in X-rays to assisting with cancer early detection through advanced imaging methods.

1.1 Realtime Usage of Intelligent Healthcare

Intelligent healthcare is no longer limited to conventional hospital settings. Healthcare professionals may remotely monitor patients thanks to AI-powered remote patient monitoring devices that track vital signs in real time. This improves the standard of care for long-term illnesses while simultaneously promoting the growth of telehealth, which allows for virtual consultations and diagnosis.

Barbosa, H. C., et al (2021), to find patterns and trends in patient data, artificial intelligence (AI) uses its predictive skills. AI is capable of forecasting possible health problems and suggesting preventive actions by evaluating past medical records and merging them with current data. By focusing on preventive measures to delay the start of diseases, this movement in healthcare towards proactive approaches encourages people to take responsibility for their health.

Intelligent healthcare encompasses all aspect of the healthcare system, not just programmes that interact with patients. Artificial intelligence (AI)-powered systems improve resource allocation, expedite appointment scheduling, and optimise administrative duties. In addition to lessening the workload for medical personnel, this efficiency improves resource efficiency and cost-effectiveness.

1.2 AI in Healthcare

Ethical issues grow more pressing when AI is incorporated more fully into healthcare. Critical issues that require close consideration include the ethical use of patient data, maintaining security and privacy, and resolving any biases in algorithms. It is essential for the long-term development of intelligent healthcare technology to strike a balance between innovation and ethical issues.

Intelligent healthcare holds great potential for change, but there are also impending difficulties. Important obstacles include the requirement for regulatory frameworks, data format standardisation, and system interoperability. Furthermore, it's critical to guarantee that these technologies are available to people from a variety of socioeconomic backgrounds in order to avoid making healthcare inequities worse. The research that is now being conducted to improve AI algorithms, increase datasets, and remove the obstacles in the way of developing a more inclusive and fair healthcare system bodes well for the future.

Figure 1 depicts AI employed in medical technology and intelligent healthcare. Here, we examine the potentially revolutionary nature of this synergy as we examine the innovative development of AI and medical technology for Intelligent Healthcare. Intelligent Healthcare is a promising new field that is expected to transcend science fiction and bring about a time when healthcare is not just personalised, but also proactive, available to all. From the microcosm of AI-powered diagnostics to the macrocosm of a redesigned healthcare ecosystem, the upcoming chapters of this story will elucidate the nuances of every aspect of this paradigm shift, Dzobo, K., et al (2020).

A new era of intelligent healthcare has begun with the merging of medical technology and artificial intelligence (AI), driven by the unwavering goal of improving healthcare outcomes. The medical field is undergoing a transformation thanks to the symbiotic link between cutting-edge technology and sophisticated algorithms, which promises previously unheard-of levels of precision, efficiency, and individualised care. This article explores the innovative advancements that have occurred at the nexus of AI and medical technology, and how they are transforming patient care, treatment modalities, diagnostics, and the larger healthcare ecosystem.

1.3 Technical Innovations

With technological advancements pushing the limits of medical knowledge, the healthcare sector is at a turning point in its history. An increasingly data-driven, networked, and intelligent healthcare system is replacing traditional methods of patient care. The proliferation of wearable technology, the exponential expansion of medical data, and the growing processing capacity of AI systems are all driving forces behind this change.

Healthcare data is growing at an exponential rate; this phenomenon is commonly known as "big data," and it has created opportunities for previously unheard-of insights and well-informed decisions.

Figure 1. Intelligent healthcare using artificial intelligence

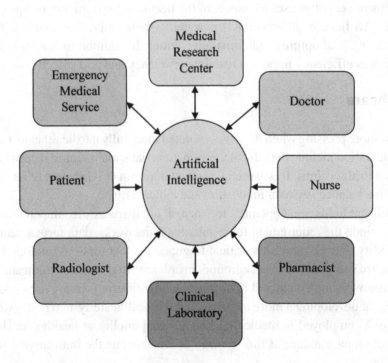

A thorough picture of both individual and public health can be obtained by successfully using the massive amounts of data generated by genomic sequencing, medical imaging, electronic health records (EHRs), and real-time patient monitoring. Healthcare workers are able to make data-driven decisions and anticipate future health hazards with the use of AI algorithms and big data analytics, which enable the extraction of significant patterns.

The emergence of precision medicine is one of the main characteristics of the union of AI and medical technology. Precision medicine develops treatment regimens that are specific to each patient, as opposed to using a one-size-fits-all strategy. In order to develop individualised treatment plans that maximise therapeutic success and minimise side effects, AI algorithms examine genetic, clinical, and lifestyle data. A paradigm change in illness prevention and management is brought about by this move towards personalised healthcare, which also improves patient outcomes.

With the introduction of AI-based diagnostic technologies, medical imaging has seen a revolutionary revolution. After being trained on enormous medical picture datasets, machine learning algorithms show amazing precision in identifying abnormalities and deciphering intricate diagnostic images. These AI-enhanced diagnostic technologies provide healthcare practitioners with faster and more accurate insights, enabling them to forecast cardiovascular risks and spot cancer early. This leads to increased diagnostic precision as well as better prognosis and early intervention possibilities.

Technological developments in healthcare have made it easier to create AI-powered remote patient monitoring systems that track health in real-time and continuously. Wearable technology with sensors can track vital signs, exercise levels, and other health parameters, according to Shaik, T., et al. (2023). With the use of AI algorithms, this data is analysed to find minute variations or abnormalities that enable early intervention and individualised treatment plan revisions. Enhancing patient engagement and increasing access to healthcare services, telehealth solutions with AI-driven diagnostics allow for remote consultations. Though there is much promise in the combination of AI and medical technology, there are drawbacks. Careful consideration is needed for correcting biases in AI models, handling sensitive patient data, and maintaining algorithmic transparency. Additionally, there are serious cybersecurity risks, which highlight the necessity of taking strong precautions to protect patient privacy and the integrity of healthcare systems. Maintaining the responsible implementation of intelligent healthcare technology requires striking a balance between innovation and ethical considerations.

The nexus between AI and medical technology marks a turning point in the development of healthcare. The healthcare environment is changing as a result of the convergence of big data analytics, AI-driven diagnostics, precision medicine, and remote patient monitoring. This convergence promises more precise diagnosis, individualised treatment plans, and better patient outcomes. Ensuring that the advantages of intelligent healthcare are accessible, equitable, and responsibly implemented requires us to give ethical issues top priority as we traverse this revolutionary journey. In order to provide a thorough examination of the rapidly developing field of intelligent healthcare, the ensuing chapters will focus on particular applications, case studies, and potential future developments of this dynamic interaction between medical technology and AI.

This paper consists of five parts. The section I discussed about the introduction of the work. The drawbacks and limitations of present systems are discussed in the section II. The section III explained about our new suggested system design work for medical technology and AI healthcare system. Section IV contains our newly constructed system's overall output result and discussion. Section V covers this paper's conclusion.

II. LITERATURE REVIEW

This literature review part discusses the shortcomings and restrictions of the current AI-based healthcare and medical technology solutions. Distinguished contributions from a broad spectrum of scholars in this field are included in the discussion of the literature review.

Wang .G & et al., (2022), enables people to interact with their avatars in a world facilitated by technologies like digital twins, blockchain, augmented reality, mixed reality, virtual reality, and high-speed internet. The metaverse offers the integration of physical and virtual realities, all enhanced by virtually limitless data. Recently, social media and entertainment platforms have evolved from the metaverse; however, if this concept is extended to the healthcare industry, patient outcomes and clinical practice may be significantly impacted. We as a team of academics from academia, industry, medicine, and regulation see special prospects for metaverse methods in the healthcare sector. The creation, testing, assessment, control, translation, and improvement of AI-based medicine, particularly imaging-guided diagnosis and treatment, can be aided by a metaverse of "medical technology and AI" (MeTAI).

Tian .S & et al., (2019) focuses on how information technology is developing, the idea of smart healthcare has progressively gained prominence. With the use of cutting-edge information technologies like big data, cloud computing, artificial intelligence, and the internet of things (IoT), smart healthcare transforms the conventional medical system from the inside out and offers more individualised, convenient, and effective care. In an attempt to present the notion of smart healthcare, we first enumerate the essential technologies that facilitate smart healthcare and outline the state of smart healthcare as of right now in a number of significant domains. Next, we outline the current issues with smart healthcare and make an attempt to provide fixes. Lastly, we consider the future and assess the potential for smart healthcare.

Ahmed.Z & et al, (2020), discusses the One of the most recent and significant advances in healthcare is precision medicine, which holds promise for enhancing the conventional symptom-driven practice of medicine by enabling early interventions through enhanced diagnostics and customising more effective and cost-effective treatments. The power of electronic health records must be harnessed to integrate disparate data sources, identify patient-specific patterns of disease progression, and enable real-time decision support in order to improve the networking and interoperability of clinical, laboratory, and public health systems as well as to effectively balance ethical and social concerns regarding the privacy and protection of healthcare data, useful analytical tools, technologies, databases, and methodologies are needed. By effectively classifying subjects to comprehend certain scenarios and enhance decision-making, the development of multifunctional machine learning systems for clinical data extraction, aggregation, management, and analysis can assist physicians. The goal of offering real-time, more personalised, and affordable population medicine at a reduced cost may be significantly improved by implementing artificial intelligence in healthcare, which is an appealing idea.

Manickam.P & et al, (2022), Addresses the A contemporary method founded in computer science, artificial intelligence (AI) creates algorithms and programmes to provide machines intelligence and efficiency for carrying out jobs that often call for highly trained human intellect. Artificial intelligence (AI) encompasses a number of subsets, each with special powers and functions that might enhance the performance of contemporary medical sciences. These subsets include machine learning (ML), deep learning (DL), conventional neural networks, fuzzy logic, and speech recognition. Medical imaging, clinical diagnosis, and decision-making are all made easier for humans by such intelligent systems. A software programme and network-linked biomedical gadget are combined to create the Internet of Medical Things (IoMT), a next-generation bio-analytical tool that advances human health in the same period. They go over the value of AI in enhancing IoMT and point-of-care (POC) device capabilities in cutting-edge healthcare domains like diabetes management, cancer diagnosis, and cardiac monitoring in this review.

Talukder.A & et al, (2021), told that, For sustainable societies and economies, providing high-quality healthcare to all communities is a key objective. Physicians are facing increased workloads and time constraints, despite working in highly developed healthcare facilities. Artificial Intelligence (AI), Big Data, Web technologies, and telemedicine can all be powerful tools for improving diagnosis accuracy and care delivery. Because of the COVID-19 pandemic, telemedicine via the internet is growing in popularity. We describe a unique smartphone-based care solution in this work that collects patient data using progressive web applications (PWA), combines it with a variety of medical knowledge sources, and uses artificial intelligence (AI) to facilitate patient stratification and differential diagnosis. The programme has been developed with special attention to cyber security and can recommend courses of action and therapy. A smart hospital may easily incorporate the smart care system, which is built on next-generation web technologies including PWA, WebBluetooth, Web Speech API, WebUSB, and WebRTC.

Banerjee.A & et al, (2020) deals with The biomedical and healthcare technologies have opened up exciting opportunities due to the recent revolutions in Internet of Things (IoT) and big data analytics. The subjects covered in this chapter's interesting examples include theoretical, methodological, empirical, and validated concepts. First, a brief explanation of how IoT and big data are used to analyse a large image database that is created daily from a variety of sources using big data along with machine learning and other artificial intelligence techniques to create structured information for use in remote diagnostics is given. Examples are provided. The use of artificial intelligence in robotic health care to further emergent trends in telemedicine has been explored. Moreover, information on wearable technology that is now on the market focuses on biomedical and healthcare applications that can gather data, analyse it using standard procedures, and use machine intelligence to forecast health-related problems.

Rani.S & et al (2023), discusses about nowadays, Observing and monitoring the numerous clinical parameters of patients in their daily lives through the use of various technologies is the industry's primary goal. As these apps enable more affordable healthcare services, distant patient observation apps are growing in popularity. Equal consideration must also be given to the data management procedure used with these apps. Healthcare apps that are enabled by cloud computing offer a range of ways to store patient records and provide the necessary data to meet the needs of all parties involved; nevertheless, these solutions are hampered by security risks, slower reaction times, and issues that impair the system's availability. This chapter suggests an intelligent distributed framework for IoT-based remote healthcare service deployment in order to address these issues. Distributed Database Management Systems (DDBMS) are employed in the suggested model to provide patients and healthcare professionals with quick and secure access to data. The system's many entities are connected through the Internet of Things. To guarantee the security of the patient's medical records, the blockchain idea is employed. In the suggested model, clinical records obtained via DDBMS and encrypted using blockchain would be intelligently analysed.

Tripathy.S,S & et al, (2023) deals with The healthcare industry has not been immune to the widespread usage of internet-enabled gadgets. Regardless of a person's medical concerns, their overall health is being observed. The introduction of these medical gadgets helps patients as well as doctors, hospitals, and insurance companies. It facilitates hassle-free, dependable, and quick healthcare. Individuals are able to monitor their own blood pressure, pulse rate, and other health parameters and take proactive steps. Hospitals are also utilising the Internet of Things (IoT) for a number of purposes, including electrocardiograms (ECGs), blood sugar and oxygen monitoring, and more. IoT in healthcare also lowers the cost of many diseases by quickly and thoroughly analysing data. Machine learning methods based on symptom analysis have emerged as a potential notion for disease prediction. In certain circumstances, real-time analysis can also be necessary. Fog computing becomes indispensable in such a latency-sensitive scenario. Fog reduces latency by eliminating the need to establish contact with the cloud on a per-occassion basis. Applications in the healthcare industry must respond quickly. Therefore, it is crucial that fog computing be implemented in this field. Our efforts are concentrated on enhancing the system's effectiveness in providing accurate heart disease diagnosis and recommendations. Using a machine-learning module, it assesses the system.

Ganji.K & Parimi.S (2022) deals with Undoubtedly, the COVID-19 pandemic transformed the world's lifestyle, particularly in the realm of health care. The future holds a significant transformation for the delivery of healthcare services. In particular, during pandemics, the goal is to examine the growing use of digital and IoT technologies in conjunction with health care systems. To categorise users' perceptions of using IoT-based smart health-care monitoring wearables according to their knowledge and experience, an efficient artificial neural network (ANN)-based predictive model is implemented.

Bohr, A., & Memarzadeh, K. (2020) said that, From entertainment to commerce to healthcare, big data and machine learning are influencing most facets of contemporary life. Search terms and symptoms are known to Google, Amazon and Netflix, respectively, and Netflix is aware of the films and TV shows that its users enjoy watching and when they want to buy certain products. In addition to being useful for behavioural targeting and understanding, all of this data may be utilised for extremely detailed personal profiling, which may also be useful for forecasting trends in healthcare. The potential for significant advancements in artificial intelligence (AI) to enhance healthcare in every facet, from diagnosis to treatment, is highly encouraging. AI technologies are often seen as enhancing and supporting human labour rather than taking the place of doctors and other healthcare professionals. When it comes to a range of duties, including clinical documentation, patient outreach, administrative workflow, and specialised support like image analysis, medical device automation, and patient monitoring, AI is prepared to assist healthcare professionals. Several significant uses of artificial intelligence (AI) in healthcare will be covered in this chapter, including those that are directly related to the field as well as those that are part of the healthcare value chain, such medication development and ambient assisted living.

Gilbert, S., & et al (2021) discussed about The ability to continuously enhance performance based on updates from automated learning from data is one of the main advantages of artificial intelligence (AI) and machine learning (ML) technologies in the healthcare industry. Nonetheless, the regulations that currently govern health care machine learning models were created for a bygone period of slowly evolving medical equipment, necessitating significant documentation updates, reshaping, and revalidation for each major model update produced by the ML algorithm. For models that are meant to be retrained and updated infrequently, this poses modest issues; but, for models that are meant to learn from data in real-time or almost real-time, it poses significant challenges. The announcement of action plans by regulators reflects a significant shift in their regulatory strategies. We analyse the laws and advancements in this field from this point of view. After reviewing the current state of affairs and recent advancements, we contend that these creative approaches to healthcare demand creative methods to regulation, and that patients will profit from these approaches.

Yaeger, K. A., & et al (2019) explores The way medical devices are regulated in the US has changed as technology has advanced. The FDA in the United States has further defined risk categories and intended uses for software applications and computer-based devices that are being incorporated into routine clinical practice. This is done to promote innovation in medical technology while also better ensuring patient safety. Yet, regulatory agencies will need to act quickly when new software technologies like artificial intelligence (AI) are created, improved, and applied in the healthcare industry. Within this analysis, we go over how the US FDA has regulated medical devices over time first with hardware and then with software and how they currently stand on artificial intelligence-enhanced devices.

Minopoulos, G. M., & et al (2022) discussed The medical techniques used today still face many obstacles and restrictions in their efforts to identify and treat diseases. It is projected that the use of new technology in the healthcare sector would make it possible to implement cutting-edge medical procedures for a smart healthcare system that is both successful and efficient. The rapid diagnosis of illnesses, diseases, infections, or abnormalities can be greatly aided by the IoT, WSN, Big Data Analytics (BDA), and Cloud Computing (CC). The discovery of new drugs and antibiotics may be accelerated by complex methods like AI, ML, and DL. In addition, medical professionals can use the integration of visualisation techniques like Virtual Reality (VR), Augmented Reality (AR), and Mixed Reality (MR) with Tactile Internet (TI) to give patients the most accurate diagnosis and treatment possible. This study suggests a new system architecture that integrates multiple next-generation technologies. In order to create a smart healthcare system that may be installed in hospitals or medical centres, the goal is to explain how a variety of cutting-edge technologies are integrated with support from innovative networks. A system like this will be able to offer medical personnel with fast, precise data so they can target patients and administer treatment with accuracy.

Amann, J., et al (2020), deals with Regarding artificial intelligence (AI) and its application to healthcare, one of the most hotly contested subjects is explainability. Its failure to explain itself continues to draw criticism, despite evidence that AI-driven systems can do better than humans in some analytical tasks. Explainable technology, however, raises a number of social, legal, ethical, and medical issues that need careful consideration rather than being limited to a technological one.

Nasar, M & et al, (2021), deals with a new paradigm for healthcare systems is desperately needed, as seen by the sharp rise in the number of people with chronic illnesses, including the aged and disabled. With decreased reliance on conventional physical healthcare facilities like hospitals, assisted living facilities, and long-term care facilities, the developed model will be more individualised. Major advancements in contemporary technology, particularly in the areas of artificial intelligence (AI) and machine learning (ML), have led to a growing interest in and necessity for the smart healthcare system.

III. SYSTEM DESIGN

The proposed study describes an experiment utilising deep learning techniques for the medical technology and healthcare industry, with Ant Colony Optimisation (ACO) handling the optimisation process and employing artificial intelligence (AI) in the form of convolution neural networks (CNNs) for detection and classification. With the help of this study, an artificial intelligence-based intelligent healthcare system with lifetime aid for patients will be built.

3.1 AI for Intelligent Healthcare

The latest technical advances in AI have stunned people all around the world, and medical experts are trying to embrace it. With the help of AI's new indications, doctors can discover new uses for current drugs and leverage biological information to develop new ones. By evaluating drugs on cells, AI also

Figure 2. CNN employs patient data to determine appropriate treatment

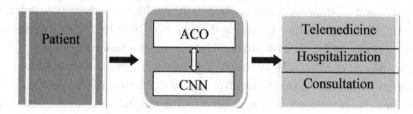

plays a critical role in identifying which chemicals need more investigation and work. We used the CNN method with ACO from the AI technique in this proposed work, which is shown in the Figure 2.

3.2 Ant Colony Optimization (ACO)

A metaheuristic called Ant Colony Optimisation (ACO) was developed after observing how some ant species leave and follow pheromone trails. Making use of tailored (false) pheromone data Based on the ant's search history and any potentially accessible heuristic data provided. Artificial ants in ACO are stochastic techniques for generating solutions that propose potential fixes for the issue instance in question.

To locate the area in the input text data that is affected, the ACO method is employed. Where different iterations of the ACO algorithm are present and it clearly explained in below figure 3. In each iterations, a number of ants construct comprehensive answers based on heuristic input and the knowledge collected by prior populations of ants. A component of a solution leaves a pheromone trail that is a representation of these collected experiences. This initial stage involves setting up all settings and pheromone variables. A group of ants builds a solution to the problem at hand after initiating it by using pheromone values and extra information. In this optional stage, the ants refine the created solution. At this step, pheromone variables are modified depending on observations from search behaviour in ants.

Now that we are aware of how the ants acted in the example above, we can construct an algorithm. For simplicity's sake, one food source, one ant colony, and two potential travel routes have been examined. The complete scenario may be simulated using weighted graphs: the paths are the edges, the ant colony and food source are the vertices (or nodes), and the weights associated with the pathways are the pheromone levels.

Take into account the graph as $G = (V, E)$, where V, E are the graph's vertices and edges, respectively. Assuming that we take it into mind, the vertices are (Vs - Source vertex, an ant colony, and Vd - Destination vertex, a food source). The lengths of the two edges, E1 and E2, are L1 and L2, respectively. Now, it may be hypothesised that, depending on their strength, Vertices E1 and E2 have related pheromone values of R1 and R2, respectively. As a result, the probability that each ant will first select a path (between E1 and E2) is as follows:

$$Pi = \frac{Ri}{R1 + R2}; i = 1, 2$$

Apparently, if R1>R2 and vice versa, there is a larger possibility of choosing E1. As you return along that path, say along, the pheromone value for that route now changes, Ei.

Figure 3. ACO algorithm pseudocode

Ant Colony Optimization:

Initialise the pheromone experiments and relevant parameters;

Do not terminate, but instead

Create an ant colony;

Determine the fitness ratings for each ant;

Using selection techniques, determine the optimal option;

Pheromone trial updates;

Stop while

Process over

---

1. Considering the length of the path

$$Ri \leftarrow Ri + \frac{K}{Li}$$

In the aforementioned update, "K" and "i=1, 2" serve as model parameters.

2. Dependent on the pheromone's rate of evaporation

$$Ri \leftarrow (1-v)*Ri$$

"V," a parameter with a range of [0, 1], controls the evaporation of pheromones. Similarly, "i" is equal to 1 plus 2 plus 3.

The optimized values are fed to the classification based Artificial Neural Network techniques.

3.3 Convolutional Neural Network (CNN)

Convolutional layers, max-pooling, and sparse connectivity are the three basic facets of CNN architecture. The local connection of neurons on neighbouring layers takes advantage of the spatial dependency of the image's pixels.

The convolution kernel, from which the term "convolution neural network" derives, is the most crucial component of the CNN. An n-column two-dimensional matrix makes up the convolution kernel and matching weights for each point. Convolution kernels resemble neurons, and their size is referred to as the receptive field of a neuron. The receptive field of the CNN is filled with the addition of the weight values of the convolution kernel and the pixel values at the pertinent locations in the image. The system's k convolution kernels do this. Once all of the pixels in the image have been counted, to the following point in the image in accordance with the step size. The original image's feature map is now the output pixel matrix.

$$Ow = [\frac{i_w - n + 2_p}{s}] + 1 \qquad (1)$$

$$Oh = [\frac{i_h - n + 2_p}{s}] + 1 \qquad (2)$$

The most common pooling techniques are maximal combining, averaging, etc. Here, we select the highest pooling approach and the associated calculation. The area of the image the highest value per pixel in the range of 2 is chosen using a filter of size 2 2, and it is then kept as the distinctive feature of this area. A feature map is created once the filter repeats this process for the subsequent range. The convolution network's performance has increased with end-to-end training, not just in terms of overall data classification but also in terms of the local task's progress toward producing structured output. As a result, it has seen extensive use in the fields of data detection and categorization. CNNs will quickly run into problems when using a typical multi-layer perceptron, meaning all layers are completely connected, because the data dimensions are too big. There is no available space information on CNN. The final efficiency may be quite low if we use the pooling layer. CNNs suffer a significant of information in the pooling layer, which lowers the spatial resolution, because only the most active neurons can be communicated between each layer during the transfer of neurons.

The above Figure 4 shows the pseudocode for convolutional Neural Network. CNNs won't be able to discern between variations in postures and other features as a result. Overtraining from every viewpoint is one technique to overcome this issue, but it typically takes more time and computer power. When dealing with extremely complicated field-of-view data that has a lot of overlap, mutual masking, and diverse backgrounds, traditional CNN cannot be identified properly. We will go over the rationale behind removing the fully connected layers, the parameters for the skip and pooling layers in the suggested approach, and the use of two convolutional layers as a skip layer. More specifically, the tail of CNN is frequently added with several fully-connected layers.

IV. RESULT AND DISCUSSION

The suggested model's recognition performance is calculated using the accuracy, sensitivity, specificity, and execution time parameters. To assess how well the process of existing classifiers like ANN, BPNN, and CNN. The proposed system of Ant Colony Optimization (ACO) with Convolution Neural Network (CNN) achieves the highest accuracy.

Figure 4. Pseudocode for CNN

CNN Algorithm Pseudocode:

Input:

d: dataset,

1: real labels in the dataset

W: Word-to-Vec matrix

Output:

Test dataset score for the CNN-trained model

Assume that f is the 3D matrix of features.

For i in dataset **do**

Allow f to represent the sample i's feature set matrix.

For j in i **do**

Vj - vectorize(j, w)

Append vj to f

Append fi to f

ftrain, ftest, Itrain, Itest Create a train and test subsets from the feature set and labels

M-CNN (ftrain, Itrain)

Score-analysis (i, Itest, M)

Return score

4.1 Performance Evaluation Matrix

The effectiveness of the trained machine learning models may be evaluated by using performance evaluation metrics. In order to determine how well the machine learning model will work, it will be able to do this by using an unknown dataset. A confusion matrix is utilised to illustrate and provide a summary of the efficacy of a categorization strategy. This matrix of perplexity is seen in Figure 5.

True Positive (TP): Effective detection of the bounding box on the ground.

False Positive (FP): Incorrectly detecting an object that is present or incorrectly detecting one that is not.

False Negative (FN): A bounding box for ground truth that is hidden.

True Negative (TN): Because there are numerous bounding boxes in every image that shouldn't be recognised, a true negative (TN) outcome is irrelevant while discussing object detection.

Accuracy: By deviating from 100% in the error rate, the accuracy formula represents accuracy. Before we can assess accuracy, we must first assess error rate. Next, we divide the observed value by the actual value to get a percentage that represents the mistake rate.

Figure 5. Confusion matrix

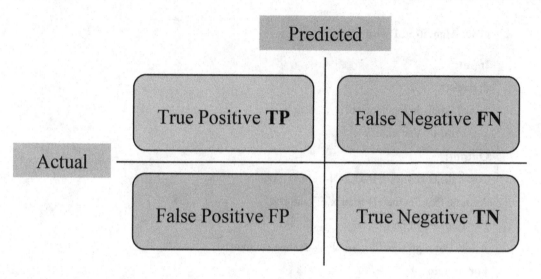

$$Accuracy = \frac{TP + TN}{TP + TN + FN + FP}$$

The output graph of accuracy from table 1 for existing and proposed system is clearly shown in the Figure 6. From this graph, our proposed ACO+CNN system outperforms the better accuracy of 96.23% comparing with the other current systems.

Sensitivity: Sensitivity is defined as the sum of positives divided by the number of accurate positive forecasts.

$$Sensitivity = \frac{TP}{TP + FN}$$

The results for sensitivity with the proposed and existing systems are shown in the aforementioned Figure 7 and are taken from Table 2. It shows the ACO+CNN gives higher sensitivity result of 94.52%, it is comparatively better than the current approaches.

Specificity: Calculating specificity involves dividing the entire number of accurate negative predictions by the total number of negatives. The specificity is calculated using the formula shown below.

Table 1. Accuracy

Algorithm	Accuracy (%)
ANN	84.64
BPNN	86.47
CNN	88.28
ACO+CNN	96.23

Figure 6. Accuracy graph

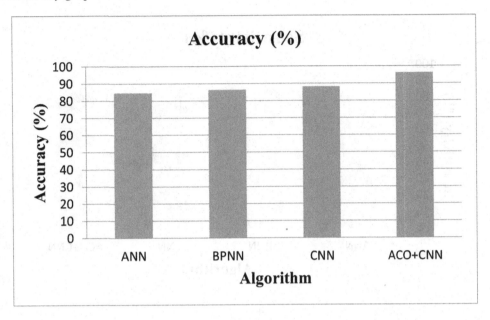

Table 2. Sensitivity

Algorithm	Sensitivity (%)
ANN	83.72
BPNN	86.25
CNN	87.61
ACO+CNN	94.52

$$\text{Specificity} = \frac{TN}{\left(TN + FP\right)}$$

The results for specificity with the proposed and existing systems are shown in the aforementioned Figure 8 and are taken from Table 3. It shows the ACO+CNN gives higher specificity result of 92.46%, it is comparatively better than the current approaches.

Time of Execution: The total time duration is how long the something lasts, from the beginning to the end.

The Table 4 explains the execution time of proposed system comparison with existing systems; the indicated results are plotted in the Figure 9. The proposed ACO+CNN take 12.75 milliseconds time duration. The results show that suggested system consumes minimum time duration comparing with the other existing systems.

The overall performances of a novel proposed hybrid ACOCNN system was well and good for the diseases diagnosis in medical technology using the Artificial Intelligence in intelligent healthcare sector.

Figure 7. Sensitivity graph

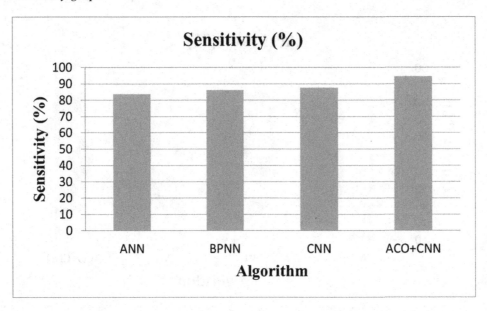

Table 3. Specificity

Algorithm	Specificity (%)
ANN	84.34
BPNN	82.69
CNN	89.18
ACO+CNN	92.46

Figure 8. Specificity graph

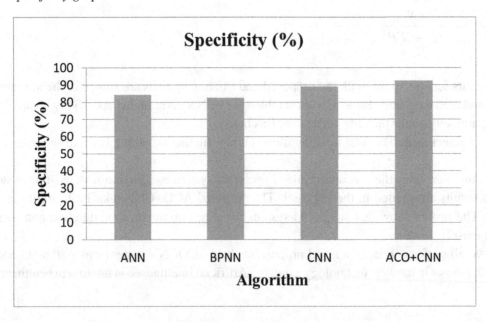

Table 4. Execution time

Algorithm	Execution Time (ms)
ANN	24.53
BPNN	18.58
CNN	20.43
ACO+CNN	12.75

Figure 9. Execution time graph

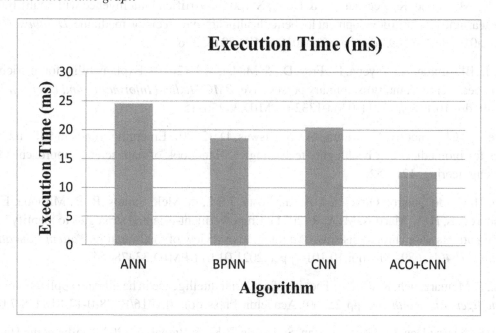

V. CONCLUSION

All things considered, smart healthcare has a bright future. People can take better care of their health on their own by using smart healthcare. When needed, quick, appropriate medical care can be obtained; the type of care provided will be more customised. Smart healthcare could result in reduced costs for healthcare institutions, lighter workloads for employees, unified material and information management, and improved patient outcomes. Research institutions may perform studies more quickly, more cheaply, and more effectively overall with the use of smart healthcare. Smart healthcare can help with macro decision-making by promoting preventative care uptake, lowering social medical costs, and improving the current condition of medical resource disparity. AI-based findings verify earlier hypotheses and evaluate risk in the diagnosis process. Many physicians use machine learning algorithms for prediction since they generate accurate data. As with any innovation, there are challenges along the way. In the case of artificial intelligence, these include heterogeneity, connectivity, and intricate data management issues. The answers to these problems have been discussed in this investigation. AI doesn't appear to be multitasking, and it hasn't advanced to the point where a physician can be fully replaced by it. Despite this disadvantage, further developments in the medical field have shown AI's supremacy. In addition to being a cutting-edge method, AI subsets like ACO with CNN are also frequently employed in the healthcare field. In comparison to the current methods, it attains a high accuracy of 96.23% while requiring only 12.75 milliseconds to diagnose a condition. The review's conclusions inspire young scientists to investigate and develop combinational strategies that integrate IoMT, AI, and nano-enabled sensing for efficient biosensing a crucial component of tailored illness control and treatment.

REFERENCES

Ahmed, Z., Mohamed, K., Zeeshan, S., & Dong, X. (2020). Artificial intelligence with multi-functional machine learning platform development for better healthcare and precision medicine. *Database (Oxford)*, *2020*, baaa010. doi:10.1093/database/baaa010 PMID:32185396

Amann, J., Blasimme, A., Vayena, E., Frey, D., & Madai, V. I. (2020). Explainability for artificial intelligence in healthcare: A multidisciplinary perspective. *BMC Medical Informatics and Decision Making*, *20*(1), 1–9. doi:10.1186/s12911-020-01332-6 PMID:33256715

Banerjee, A., Chakraborty, C., Kumar, A., & Biswas, D. (2020). Emerging trends in IoT and big data analytics for biomedical and health care technologies. Handbook of data science approaches for biomedical engineering, 121-152.

Barbosa, H. C., de Queiroz Oliveira, J. A., da Costa, J. M., de Melo Santos, R. P., Miranda, L. G., de Carvalho Torres, H., ... Martins, M. A. P. (2021). Empowerment-oriented strategies to identify behavior change in patients with chronic diseases: An integrative review of the literature. *Patient Education and Counseling*, *104*(4), 689–702. doi:10.1016/j.pec.2021.01.011 PMID:33478854

Bohr, A., & Memarzadeh, K. (2020). The rise of artificial intelligence in healthcare applications. In *Artificial Intelligence in healthcare* (pp. 25–60). Academic Press. doi:10.1016/B978-0-12-818438-7.00002-2

Dongari, S., Nisarudeen, M., Devi, J., Irfan, S., Parida, P. K., & Bajpai, A. (2023). Advancing Healthcare through Artificial Intelligence: Innovations at the Intersection of AI and Medicine. *Tuijin Jishu/Journal of Propulsion Technology, 44*(2).

Dzobo, K., Adotey, S., Thomford, N. E., & Dzobo, W. (2020). Integrating artificial and human intelligence: A partnership for responsible innovation in biomedical engineering and medicine. *OMICS: A Journal of Integrative Biology*, *24*(5), 247–263. doi:10.1089/omi.2019.0038 PMID:31313972

Ganji, K., & Parimi, S. (2022). ANN model for users' perception on IOT based smart healthcare monitoring devices and its impact with the effect of COVID 19. *Journal of Science and Technology Policy Management*, *13*(1), 6–21. doi:10.1108/JSTPM-09-2020-0128

Gilbert, S., Fenech, M., Hirsch, M., Upadhyay, S., Biasiucci, A., & Starlinger, J. (2021). Algorithm change protocols in the regulation of adaptive machine learning–based medical devices. *Journal of Medical Internet Research*, *23*(10), e30545. doi:10.2196/30545 PMID:34697010

Manickam, P., Mariappan, S. A., Murugesan, S. M., Hansda, S., Kaushik, A., Shinde, R., & Thippe-rudraswamy, S. P. (2022). Artificial intelligence (AI) and internet of medical things (IoMT) assisted biomedical systems for intelligent healthcare. *Biosensors (Basel)*, *12*(8), 562. doi:10.3390/bios12080562 PMID:35892459

Minopoulos, G. M., Memos, V. A., Stergiou, C. L., Stergiou, K. D., Plageras, A. P., Koidou, M. P., & Psannis, K. E. (2022). Exploitation of Emerging Technologies and Advanced Networks for a Smart Healthcare System. *Applied Sciences (Basel, Switzerland)*, *12*(12), 5859. doi:10.3390/app12125859

Moerenhout, T., Devisch, I., & Cornelis, G. C. (2018). E-health beyond technology: Analyzing the paradigm shift that lies beneath. *Medicine, Health Care, and Philosophy*, *21*(1), 31–41. doi:10.1007/s11019-017-9780-3 PMID:28551772

Nasr, M., Islam, M. M., Shehata, S., Karray, F., & Quintana, Y. (2021). Smart healthcare in the age of AI: Recent advances, challenges, and future prospects. *IEEE Access : Practical Innovations, Open Solutions*, *9*, 145248–145270. doi:10.1109/ACCESS.2021.3118960

Rani, S., Chauhan, M., Kataria, A., & Khang, A. (2023). IoT equipped intelligent distributed framework for smart healthcare systems. In *Towards the Integration of IoT, Cloud and Big Data: Services, Applications and Standards* (pp. 97–114). Springer Nature Singapore. doi:10.1007/978-981-99-6034-7_6

Shaik, T., Tao, X., Higgins, N., Li, L., Gururajan, R., Zhou, X., & Acharya, U. R. (2023). Remote patient monitoring using artificial intelligence: Current state, applications, and challenges. *Wiley Interdisciplinary Reviews. Data Mining and Knowledge Discovery*, *13*(2), e1485. doi:10.1002/widm.1485

Talukder, A., & Haas, R. (2021, June). AIoT: AI meets IoT and web in smart healthcare. In *Companion Publication of the 13th ACM Web Science Conference 2021* (pp. 92-98). Academic Press.

Tian, S., Yang, W., Le Grange, J. M., Wang, P., Huang, W., & Ye, Z. (2019). Smart healthcare: Making medical care more intelligent. *Global Health Journal (Amsterdam, Netherlands)*, *3*(3), 62–65. doi:10.1016/j.glohj.2019.07.001

Tripathy, S. S., Imoize, A. L., Rath, M., Tripathy, N., Bebortta, S., Lee, C. C., & Pani, S. K. (2023). A novel edge-computing-based framework for an intelligent smart healthcare system in smart cities. *Sustainability (Basel)*, *15*(1), 735. doi:10.3390/su15010735

Wang, G., Badal, A., Jia, X., Maltz, J. S., Mueller, K., Myers, K. J., & Zeng, R. (2022). Development of metaverse for intelligent healthcare. *Nature Machine Intelligence*, *4*(11), 922–929. doi:10.1038/s42256-022-00549-6 PMID:36935774

Yaeger, K. A., Martini, M., Yaniv, G., Oermann, E. K., & Costa, A. B. (2019). United States regulatory approval of medical devices and software applications enhanced by artificial intelligence. *Health Policy and Technology*, *8*(2), 192–197. doi:10.1016/j.hlpt.2019.05.006

Chapter 10
Human–Robot Safety Guarantees Using Confidence-Aware–Game–Theoretic Human Models With EMG Signal

R. Gokulakrishnan

Karpagam Academy of Higher Education, India

C. Balakumar

 https://orcid.org/0009-0002-4655-2786

Karpagam Academy of Higher Education, India

ABSTRACT

This research provides a method for gesture recognition that integrates two separate recognizers. These two recognizers use the CAR equation to ascertain the hands sign. The robot's two main parts are its sending and receiving ends. Within the process of developing the same, three domains were specifically combined: biomedicine, which involved registering biosignals using analog channels composed of instrumental amplifiers; software development, involving microcontrollers, core processing (DSP), and the resulting control of the robot hand; PC software for tracking the registered biosignals; and mechatronics, involving the design and mechanical construction of the robot hand. The hand can control how much pressure is given to things because of the force sensor (FSR) in each finger. While developing a hand and wrist prototype that can rotate in response to EMG signal pulses, this was discovered.

I. INTRODUCTION

We investigate safety considerations for people in highly dynamic interactions with robots, such as autonomous vehicles merging approaching. Safety monitors are becoming a desired additional layer of safety, even though there are numerous ways that planning strategies incorporate safety constraints. With the use of these strategies, the planner may not only operate the robot but also anticipate when

DOI: 10.4018/979-8-3693-5767-5.ch010

a collision is likely to ability to detect approaching collisions is one of their key features. Thus, we attempt to determine ways to reduce the conservativeness of safety monitors without compromising their capacity to carry out their primary responsibility of guaranteeing safety explained by Lees, Michael J., and Monique C. Johnstone (2021). We suggest two methods to settle this dispute: Initially, we employ providing with limit protect by excluding to be extremely. The functionality of the model in Figure 1 can be viewed online.

We are interested in guaranteeing vehicles merging different methods different are now considered an extra safety precaution that is wanted. With these methods, the planner can still operate the robot while keeping an eye out for potential collisions and taking over in case of one. A key component of predicting approaching usually, the worst-case scenario is used to determine this approach that is widely used to analyze interactions that protects from human directives is called reverse reachability analysis. Hao, Jianli, et al (2020) said about Safety monitors, in their overzealous interference, wind up preventing progress while simultaneously ensuring safety. Hence, we search for methods to make safety monitors less cautious so that they can continue to successfully fulfill their primary responsibility of guaranteeing safety. The challenge here is that any human behavior model that is substituted for the zero-sum game assumption runs the risk of being inaccurate and causing a loss of safety. We suggest using two distinct approaches to mediate this conflict:

- Maintain the limit collection we protect against by removing those that the human behavior model determines to be highly unlikely;
- Examine the model's efficacy on the internet. The robot automobile (white) and a nearby human-driven car (orange) merge into a roundabout. To the left Humans adapt to the robot despite its extraordinary caution and protection against the complete backwards reaching tube (BRT).

By assuming the effects of the robot on the human, our Bayesian BRT minimizes the set of hazardous states. The robot quickly returns to the full BRT when it detects a deviation in human behavior from the model. Suits the human, and uses this data to adjust the limitation in the worst case, return when the model is completely erroneous.

Figure 1. Basic of human robot interaction

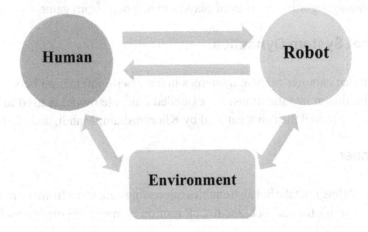

1.1 HRI Can Be Divided Roughly Into Four Areas of Application

1. These include handling items production obtaining and delivering, parts, prescriptions, hospitals, warehouses. These referred to as telerobots, can environment own locations. Telerobots are computer programs that enable them to carry out a restricted range of tasks automatically.
2. Remote of spacecraft, aircraft, land vehicles, and underwater vehicles for unreachable areas. When carry out manipulation mobility activities sync with Teleoperators are people who continuously control movements from a distance by using human intervention. If a computer is routinely reprogrammed by a human supervisor to perform certain duties within the greater objective, the computer is referred to as a telerobot.
3. Automated automobiles human occupants, such as automated commercial airplanes and railroads.
4. Human-robot social interaction, such as when robots are used to amuse, instruct, comfort, and assist the elderly, the disabled, and kids with autism said by Onnasch, Linda, and Eileen Roesler (2021).

1.2 Human Supervisory Control of Robots for Routine Industrial Tasks

There are undoubtedly fully automated vehicle and other product production lines that readers are aware of. Insofar as supervisory control functions such as planning, training, monitoring automated control, problem-solving, and experience-gathering require human operators, these machines are referred to as telerobots. The Boston-based company Rethink Robotics this meant work to humans the visible eyes of instead permitting, this enables its present focused on. Baxter can also be programmed to move its hands manually in order to teach it tasks involving manipulation or humans.

The questions of which recognize inaccurate remain unsolved. Despite the fact that these "human-in-isolation" models are popular and models would step to prevent the planner from merging in front of the human humans and robots, consider robot as well as human influence by Kumar, Shitij (2020). To further spectrum against which can defend itself, we propose extending these kinds of models to safety monitoring as well. Because human models are not perfect, relying only on them could result in the elimination of constraints that humans ultimately carry out. Nevertheless, this would mean less conservatism. Our methodology assesses adjusts constraint using determine whether prediction accuracy is decreasing and, if so, to step up conservatism. Expanding on earlier work in safe planning, our method for automated adaptation cognitive abilities of players in a general-sum game.

1.3 Human-Robot System Dynamics

A dynamical system that captures relative dynamics in a pairwise interaction between the robot cars is considered in our simulation investigations. An extended unicycle model is used to simulate a fidelity bicycle model is used to model the robot car said by Khoramshahi, Mahdi, and Aude Billard (2019).

1.3.1 Robot Planner

This leads to some modeling mistake but also enables interesting behaviors from the robot and emphasizes how important it is to verify the real because not all motion planners are made equal. The present uses method dangerous regardless of how complicated the upstream robot planner is. Stated differently, when the human-driven vehicle gets close to the BRT boundary, the safety controller takes over the planner controls by Sanchez-Ibanez, Jose Ricardo (2021).

1.3.2 Simulated Humans

We model three different human types: unmodeled non-Stackelberg human driving with constant controls, a (noisy) suboptimal Stackelberg human, and a rational Stackelberg human. Metrics we assess the robot's mobility plan's safety performance, conservatism, and total reward when depending on different safety monitors explained by Vianello, Alvise, et al (2019).

1.3.3 Reward Improvement Percent

The robots performed trajectory's % reward increase when it uses our Bayesian BRT instead of a baseline BRT technique (the appropriate baseline is chosen based on our case study). In terms of math, given any baseline safety technique discussed by Putra, Maha, and Nurevi Damayanti (2020), This study describes a method for assessing danger awareness. More precisely, we are shown to be able to model how this concept affects people's decisions using a binary variable known as the danger awareness coefficient. This work also proposes a method by which the robot constantly learns the value of this coefficient by making on-the-spot observations. It should be noted that a probabilistically safe strategy is one in which the likelihood of a human-robot collision is less than a certain value.

The five portions of this essay are summarized below: Session 2 illustrates the shortcomings of the current system in terms of artificial intelligence, machine learning, and human-robot interaction. In the third session, the suggested Human Robot Interaction analysis method was presented. The anticipated system's output is shown in Session 4. A summary of the recommended methodology for human-robot interaction wraps up Session 5.

II. LITERATURE REVIEW

In this paper, we present an overview summarizing in order to identify the scientific and technological advances that have enabled HRI to develop into a separate field. Rather than just restating and reformulating previous research, we argue that HRI with important structure the assessment from the standpoint of the designer, the topic entails considerable interdisciplinary mixing from multiple scientific and engineering fields.

An author Połap, Dawid (2022) focus components mold after a study of important elements in the development of HRI as a field. The application domains that underpin a large portion of contemporary HRI are then described. Many of these issues have significant societal ramifications and are quite difficult. We classify application domains into the two broad categories of remote and proximate interactions that were previously discussed, and we highlight significant, thought-provoking, or influential work that falls into each of these two categories. We then proceed to describe barrier challenges and common solution concepts that cut across application areas and types of interactions. The review is then summarized and we quickly point out relevant work from other domains involving the interaction of humans and technology.

2.1 Safety for Robots Operating Around Humans

According to Zacharaki, Angeliki, et al (2020) the robot uses algorithms future might, and prepares its movements despite being cautious actions by the robot, especially when interaction is close at hand. In previous studies, "human-in-isolation" and empirical models were used to limit the forward accessible set of human controls and, eventually, them. Since naturally adapt its settings, more is added on the other hand, reverse based on follow regulations. This method, complete frequently suffers from misclassifying safe states as dangerous due to the full control power. Lessening this conservatism, subsequent work has attempted to use data-driven human trajectory forecasts to constrain the range however, this approach depends too much on the data-driven forecasts and is not able to spot hence, deteriorates does so endangering.

2.2 Structured Human Decision-Making Models

The researcher Shrestha, Yash Ra et al (2019) field of navigation has witnessed a great deal of study and implementation of "human-in-isolation wherein agent thought to behave to that describe individuals make decisions about what to do by considering the behavior of others. Research published recently value generic provide modeling in study, leveraging these game theoretic human models. Ancient Greek and Chinese texts mention human-like that employed as workers and attendants, illustrating human obsession with creating a mechanical. In the past century, robots have captured the attention of both imagination and research and development funds more than any other type of automaton. Some contemporary models are even beginning to resemble the romanticized fictions from ages before showcased in these publications, which lay the groundwork for neurocognitive perspectives on human-robot interactions.

When the author Eckstein, Maria K., and Anne GE Collins (2020) humans and an industrial robot arm perform identical tasks connected the action observation (AON) exhibit different reactions. This was discovered in an early study on the adaptability of this network. Supporting these results was human and robotic individuals the AON is actually action independent produced according to (fMRI) investigations published by researchers. These results expanded on earlier discoveries about duplicated them increased more has been explained as a result of the unfamiliarity of robotic motion, along with other first surprising findings. It is unknown to what extent human observers imbue inanimate objects with emotions and goals, even if witnessing robotic movements stimulates brain regions associated with action. Conditions in which brain reactions linked with empathy could arise while comparing humans and robots experiencing simulated misery, or when trying to understand the intentions of, are still being explorer participants in an MRI only metalizing-related actions they someone else was in charge.

2.3 Task Dynamic Analysis

A key toolset used by Chen, Ruifeng, et al (2020) relatively separate field study in the division labor machines popular hierarchy of "man" and "machine" talents is outdated and hasn't been updated in a long time. Try creating a robot that can gently assist the elderly and crippled with getting in and out of bed or using the restroom if ergonomics is merely a fancy word for outdated human factors. Many human caretakers today fill this task, often at the expense of back pain. Planning and simulating tasks in terms of force, energy, time, space, and money has never been more challenging, even with the use of virtual reality visualization technologies. Furthermore, experience shows that the most effective method for determining a robot's physical form is task context. An additional query is whether it makes sense to construct humanoid-looking general-purpose robots. Analyzing HRI tasks to identify the ideal physical form presents another difficulty.

2.4 Teaching a Robot and Avoiding Unintended Consequences

The author O'Brolcháin, Fiachra (2019) robot hand can be controlled by a human using geometric commands, but it requires symbolic language to tell it when and how to move as well as what to avoid. The rapid progress in speech interpretation promises the ease of operating robots. Unexpected results are, nevertheless, highly likely. Before signaling that the robot is ready to move forward, human supervisors could see what the robot does in response to spoken instructions via a real-time virtual reality simulation. This technique, which updates its models of the regulated process continuously, would essentially be a continuation of predictor displays through the use of model extrapolation.

2.5 Interfacing Mutual "Mental" Models to Avoid Working at Cross-Purposes

There has long been a theory that humans and robots are just internal (mental) replicas of one another. Modern computer vision techniques enable data to be stored as conduct and monitor human behaviour explained by Lai, Hsueh-Yi (2023). Human-robot interaction (HRI) challenges involve deriving human mental models according to AI experience visual pattern recognition, language translation.

2.6 Role of Robots in Education

The researcher Alam, Ashraf (2022) tells about adults with cognitive disabilities or young children who are non-readers cannot even choose to study this way. When students interact with a real teacher or cleaner, learning is nearly always improved. Since Paper experiments, in which children were taught to educate a mechanical "turtle," the robot has been taken into consideration in conversations concerning the future of education. In addition to adding amusement, it can serve as a talking or teaching avatar, depict react replies by offering advice or criticism. Robots that can learn from humans and other common workshop topic. One significant difficulty is figuring out all ages and abilities learn from robots.

2.7 Lifestyle, Fears, and Human Values

The Constant, Aymery, et al (2020) explain about his science fiction/horror performance first caused entertainment, it appeared ridiculous. He being to introduce robot these days, we watch new horror movies where robots invade people's personal space and take over jobs. Due both its advantages and disadvantages for society, robots have gained a lot of attention in the media. Naturally, there are trade-offs that merit careful consideration. These include the following: robots enhancing human security versus turning into spies, killers, and tiny UAVs; robots improving human security versus taking jobs away from humans; and robots acting as helpful assistants that increase it. I think the average less realities human factors scientists are thus, human have a duty to take part making about matters awareness campaigns.

III. SYSTEM DESIGN

Consider an interaction between a human and a robot when both are heading to two different ongoing destinations. We will use driving following formulation of problem for a general interaction to illustrate the use of the proposed method. In Figure 2, the HRI is shown.

3.1 Experimental Setup

A roundabout, an intersection, and a highway. We modelled the driving environment and sensitive participants drove in person. After a predetermined period of time, each interaction ended. After watching an animated video, online participants choose their course of action from a list of options. Points were given to who, both physically and digitally, avoided collisions, stayed on the road, and moved up in their lane. We presented the subject's current score at each stage of the trial.

3.2 Danger Signalling System

Even if the majority of studies in the literature suggests otherwise, we assume that people can be influenced by the actions of robots. More specifically, we believe it is ludicrous to presume that humans behave irrationally in human-robot scenarios and deliberately disregard the robots, which greatly diminishes the efficacy of robots.

The principal aim of utilizing danger signalling is to enhance the robot's capacity to gauge the human's level of danger awareness and to ensure that the robot continues to operate efficiently towards the goal state, unaffected by the potentially hazardous behaviors of the human. We suppose that the robot has a suitable pre-collision that signals or indicators to warn the human of the impending collision in order to resolve this problem. The binary variable dR indicates the on/off status of the warning signals.

Figure 2. Human robot interaction structure

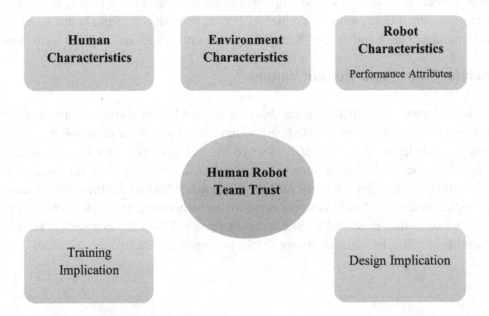

Where dR = 0 if the signal is off and dR = 1 if it is on.

3.3 Human Action Prediction

Our presumption is that the robot is familiar with QH g (•) and QH s (•), as was previously mentioned. Assuming this, the robot is able to forecast the human's behavior as actions dependent on subjective Operating As an Assuming that the pedestrian wishes to go from one sidewalk to the other, the goal objective function QH g (•) is easily formulated. For pedestrians1, the safety objective function QH s (•) can be learned based on their behavioral pattern.

The robot uses a game-theoretic predictive model of human behavior to plan utilizing model-predictive control. The robot determines an open-loop control trajectory u∗ R at each time step by solving:

maxuR EuH [RR(x0, uR, uH) | P(uH | x0, uR)]

The conditional expectation in this case replaces game-theoretic human paths with fixed rationality. In figure 3, the algorithm planning scheme is explained. Re-planning in a receding-horizon method, original the next time Remember that, consistent with earlier always engage in the interaction as a fixed follower.

3.4 Dual Control Effect

Therefore, the human's future uncertainty, as determined by their belief states, may be influenced by optimal policy uR,∗ t:= πR 0 (^xt, ^bt). Therefore, the optimal policy uR,∗ t, as stated explicitly in Definition 1, possesses the dual control characteristic. The concept of optimality, which the policy delivers,

Figure 3. Algorithm planning scheme

1. Observe the human's state $x_H[t]$ and the state of the robot $x_R[t]$.

2. Compute the mixture distribution $P(u_H|x_H[t],x_R[t];\beta)$ for every $u_H \in U_H$ and β via.

3. Compute the probability distribution of human's states $P(x_H[k])$ for $k \in \{t+1,t+T_R\}$ via.

4. Compute the probability of collision $P_{Coll}[k]$ for $k \in \{t+1,t+T_R\}$ via.

5. Determine the action of the robot $u*_R[t]$ and the on/off status of the danger signal d_R via.

6. Observe the human's action $u_H[t]$.

7. Update the belief about the danger awareness coefficient via, i.e.,

allows the robot to optimize its predicted performance target while simultaneously actively learning the uncertainty of the human. To emphasize, the optimal strategy is to automatically communicate with human agents in order degree of improves efficiency.

By choosing its own actions, the self-driving automobile was able to solve the Stackelberg game. The robot was awarded for preventing crashes and slowing down.

We chose:

$r_R(s, U_R, U_H) = -S_H - 10 \cdot 1\{\text{collision in } s\}$

$r_H(s, U_R, U_H) = S_H - 10 \cdot 1\{\text{on road in } s\} - 100 \cdot 1\{\text{collision in } s\}$

The robot combines and attempts to encourage others to give way in order to slow down their progress in their lane.

3.5 Human Decides

The hazard awareness coefficient β and the objective QH g (•) and QH s (•) serve as the foundation for human decision-making. We consider the robot to be conversant with QH g (•) and QH s (•). This supposition is reasonable given that the robot can either directly acquire these functionalities from the system designers or acquire them through prior interactions with humans. However, in practice, any supposition about the value of the coefficient β will often be wrong; humans can perceive safety in a different way or pay less attention than normal when they are among robots because they think the robot should remain a safe distance from them therefore, reliable human in future, the robot must have quick reasoning over the value of β.

3.6 Agent Dynamics

Our dynamical system model of each agent has the notations xR ∈ Rn for the robot state and xH ∈ Rm for the human state.

xi = f (xi, ui) i ∈ [R, H]

Furthermore, we permit ξ(τ ; xi, ui(•), t) to represent the agent state at time τ. Control ui(•) is implemented over the time horizon [t, τ], starting at time t at the state xi. The thought a task objective, desired for which It is imperative that, in the course of doing its duties, the robot never breaches any safety laws. C denotes a group of states that the robot should stay out of in order to preserve safety. These conditions could indicate actual collisions with people. The objective of this work is to the accessible here, xr and xh stand for respectively T(), the track reward, pays the agent for the distance both ahead of the human player and down the track.

Using centerline points evenly distributed along the course, the nearest point is returned as the distance between the person and the robot at that precise moment. The safety cost is repaid based on the level of risk, projected speeds, current player conditions, and anticipated future opponent behavior. Furthermore, the safety cost for the separation between agents and the distance to the racecourse borders is simulated using a sigmoid curve, where agents who are closer together pay a higher cost than those that are farther apart.

Additionally, this final step is to take and scale the difference between the opponent's expected position, xo, and the agent's position. First, we will suggest a probabilistic Boltzmann model to forecast human behavior in the sections that follow. Next, a mechanism for updating the belief on the danger awareness coefficient's value will be suggested. Lastly, how the robot can forecast the likelihood of a collision in the future will be covered.

IV. RESULT AND DISCUSSION

The proof that complexity exists the degree to which a traffic signal's transient adjustments to traffic circumstances are intricate can significantly affect how the signal flows within a lane. It is possible to move the traffic signal as well as the two road segments' locations. Furthermore, a single city has the power to alter the traffic light control system. In the urban environment, there are several traffic patterns the road. Compared to a typical transportation system, the spatial linkages between these two sectors are more intricate.

4.1 Initial Human

Trials and Encounters to establish baseline methodologies for policy benchmarking and initial assessments for curriculum training, fifty distinct human opponent runs with full state information were recorded. Through the study of human runs from two player opponents, closely related races showed indications of similar risk levels and differences in danger. The normal course of races was to level off at a constant danger threshold. Risk was always changing since it was frequent for novice players to face opponents who had aggressive driving and control skills. This shows that risk can be used as a useful metric to encourage a range of behaviors and may also be useful in enhancing the accuracy of future agent.

4.2 Initial Training

So far, a rudimentary policy that was educated through simulation has been put into place for both and human participants. Constant initiatives include developing curricula, improving incentives, and optimizing safety and risk awareness. The neural network's initial training yielded error rates of 12% for calculated risk, 43% for adaptability, and 24% for future state. In order to acquire more accurate adaption parameters and collect more human trials to produce a more plausible future state in figure 4, these are the topics of ongoing study.

The primary innovations we offer in this study are efficient, probabilistically-safe motion planning while maintaining tractable methods for joint planning and prediction. Our real-time robust motion planning is done using the reachability-based FaSTrack framework. Robots employ a basic model that disregards potential interaction effects in order to forecast human movements and ensure real-time feasibility. Since the presumed model will be a simplification of actual human motion, we employ confidence-aware predictions that are more cautious more humans diverge from the model. Lastly, groups of robots consecutively plan using a priority ordering that has been previously set.

We will compare and contrast our innovative predictor with throughout the study. That being said, all prediction techniques eventually yield a collection can employ detection $t + \tau$, which represents the probable human situations at a future time, is defined as follows: $\mathscr{K} t (\tau), \forall \tau \in [0, N]$.

Hardware demonstration by Figure 5 preserving against purposeful humans, external disruptions, and internal dynamics. Each quad copter's projected trajectory is displayed, and a box containing the tracking error bound is displayed around it. Before each human is displayed in pink the probability distribution

Figure 4. Fine tuning for risk awareness and safety parameters

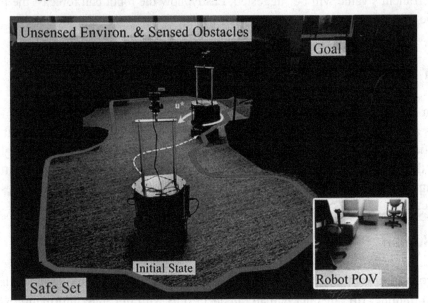

Figure 5. Hardware demonstration of real-time multi-agent

over their future mobility. Robots plan dangerous motions with confidence described (top) our method (bottom), robot plans are safer even with a stated model since we only trust eliminate utterly implausible order for the robot to escape the anticipated human state when utilizing the worst-case prediction, it must completely exit the surroundings.

The robot's objective $u\mathrm{R}(t)$, $t \in [0, \cdot T]$, so attains its goal $g\mathrm{R}$ by $\cdot T$ while avoiding collisions with the person and any known static impediments. Recessing horizon planning will be the method used to

Figure 6. Bridges robust control and intent-driven

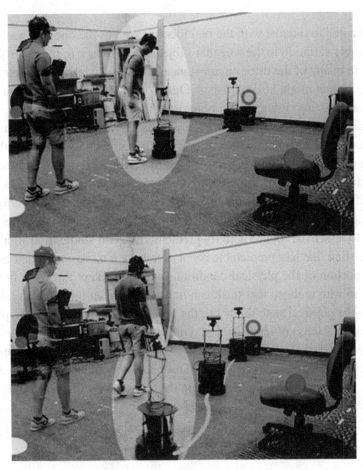

overcome this problem in this work. Unfortunately, the robot cannot plan collision-free routes because the human's future states are unknown in advance. Instead, it must anticipate human movements.

Our goal in this work is to find a method that combines intent-driven predictors in Figure 6 with robust control to create a predictor that is safer to reduce conservatism while still being more resilient to given models and priors. Our main notion is to trust inform the extremely, and so calculate a constrained forward reachable set. We will not, however, base our predictions on the precise likelihood of every action in our model, in contrast to intent-driven predictors. Instead, we split the collection of human behaviors into two distinct sets of likely and unlikely acts using similarly whole forward reachable we then use this approach to forecast human motion we treat plausible prediction problem that arises from using this limited control set is easily formulated and solved using current robust control techniques and tools. In order to ensure safety for continuous-time, nonlinear dynamical systems, we apply Hamilton Jacobi (HJ) reachability analysis.

V. CONCLUSION

The subjects were excited to interact with the real robot as well as the one that was displayed on video. There was no noticeable variation in the way that subjects waved back to the real robot and the one that was shown on camera in any of the three circumstances. If the easy job is completed, the book-moving paradigm of the experiment might be established. Our proposal was to integrate game theoretic models with confidence-awareness into robot safety monitors. Limiting the set of possible human controls according to the degree to which autonomously dangerous the whole investigations demonstrate on derivative actual and our control constraint architecture. Even though they were first unable to decide which pile of books to move, the majority of participants in the virtual group (90%) moved a pile of books after getting instruction. Progress toward ongoing human-robot communication can be made with our research. For powerful robots, we first demonstrated that a shared basis can function effectively in the short term, but eventually, people grow acclimated to these strong behaviors. Afterward, we proposed three modifications to lessen the robot's activity predictability. Our studies and simulations corroborate these changes, suggesting that less predictable robots can have a more significant long-term influence. However, a sizable portion of the physical condition individuals kept throwing books in the garbage. Even when only those who realized that trash can move were taken into consideration, a much higher number of people in the physical state threw out the books. This suggests that the physical presence of oneself increased people's sense of legitimacy and motivated them to fulfill a request that was unusual. As demonstrated by centered fast updating of the human's forward accessible tube allows for safer human-robot interactions. Our paradigm's potential uses in autonomous navigation and assisted including human-robot interaction should be fascinating in the future. We will also explore large-scale human population work and closed-loop human-robot interactions.

REFERENCES

Alam, A. (2022). Social robots in education for long-term human-robot interaction: Socially supportive behaviour of robotic tutor for creating robo-tangible learning environment in a guided discovery learning interaction. EC*S Transactions, 107(1)*, 12389–12403. doi:10.1149/10701.12389ecst

Chen, R., Xu, C., Dong, Z., Liu, Y., & Du, X. (2020). DeepCQ: Deep multi-task conditional quantification network for estimation of left ventricle parameters. *Computer Methods and Programs in Biomedicine, 184*, 105288. doi:10.1016/j.cmpb.2019.105288 PMID:31901611

Constant, A., Conserve, D. F., Gallopel-Morvan, K., & Raude, J. (2020). Socio-cognitive factors associated with lifestyle changes in response to the COVID-19 epidemic in the general population: Results from a cross-sectional study in France. *Frontiers in Psychology, 11*, 579460. doi:10.3389/fpsyg.2020.579460 PMID:33132989

Eckstein, M. K., & Collins, A. G. (2020). Computational evidence for hierarchically structured reinforcement learning in humans. *Proceedings of the National Academy of Sciences of the United States of America, 117*(47), 29381–29389. doi:10.1073/pnas.1912330117 PMID:33229518

Hao, J., Li, M., Chen, W., Yu, L., & Ye, L. (2022). Experimental research on space distribution of reverse flow U-tubes in steam generator primary side. *Nuclear Engineering and Design*, *388*, 111650. doi:10.1016/j.nucengdes.2022.111650

Khoramshahi, M., & Billard, A. (2019). A dynamical system approach to task-adaptation in physical human–robot interaction. *Autonomous Robots*, *43*(4), 927–946. doi:10.1007/s10514-018-9764-z

Kumar, S., Savur, C., & Sahin, F. (2020). Survey of human–robot collaboration in industrial settings: Awareness, intelligence, and compliance. *IEEE Transactions on Systems, Man, and Cybernetics. Systems*, *51*(1), 280–297. doi:10.1109/TSMC.2020.3041231

Lai, H. Y. (2023). Breakdowns in team resilience during aircraft landing due to mental model disconnects as identified through machine learning. *Reliability Engineering & System Safety*, *237*, 109356. doi:10.1016/j.ress.2023.109356

Lees, M. J., & Johnstone, M. C. (2021). Implementing safety features of Industry 4.0 without compromising safety culture. *IFAC-PapersOnLine*, *54*(13), 680–685. doi:10.1016/j.ifacol.2021.10.530

O'Brolcháin, F. (2019). Robots and people with dementia: Unintended consequences and moral hazard. *Nursing Ethics*, *26*(4), 962–972. doi:10.1177/0969733017742960 PMID:29262739

Onnasch, L., & Roesler, E. (2021). A taxonomy to structure and analyze human–robot interaction. *International Journal of Social Robotics*, *13*(4), 833–849. doi:10.1007/s12369-020-00666-5

Połap, D., Włodarczyk-Sielicka, M., & Wawrzyniak, N. (2022). Automatic ship classification for a riverside monitoring system using a cascade of artificial intelligence techniques including penalties and rewards. *ISA Transactions*, *121*, 232–239. doi:10.1016/j.isatra.2021.04.003 PMID:33888294

Putra, M., & Damayanti, N. (2020). The Effect of Reward and Punishment to Performance of Driver Grabcar in Depok. *International Journal of Research and Review*, *7*(1), 312–319.

Sanchez-Ibanez, J. R., Perez-del-Pulgar, C. J., & García-Cerezo, A. (2021). Path planning for autonomous mobile robots: A review. *Sensors (Basel)*, *21*(23), 7898. doi:10.3390/s21237898 PMID:34883899

Shrestha, Y. R., Ben-Menahem, S. M., & Von Krogh, G. (2019). Organizational decision-making structures in the age of artificial intelligence. *California Management Review*, *61*(4), 66–83. doi:10.1177/0008125619862257

Vianello, A., Jensen, R. L., Liu, L., & Vollertsen, J. (2019). Simulating human exposure to indoor airborne microplastics using a Breathing Thermal Manikin. *Scientific Reports*, *9*(1), 8670. doi:10.1038/s41598-019-45054-w PMID:31209244

Zacharaki, A., Kostavelis, I., Gasteratos, A., & Dokas, I. (2020). Safety bounds in human robot interaction: A survey. *Safety Science*, *127*, 104667. doi:10.1016/j.ssci.2020.104667

Chapter 11
Image Steganography– Embedding Secret Data in Images Using Convolutional Neural Networks

N. Nissi Angel

Department of ECE, Velagapudi Ramakrishna Siddhartha Engineering College, Vijayawada, India

Gunnam Suryanarayana

Department of ECE, Velagapudi Ramakrishna Siddhartha Engineering College, Vijayawada, India

Siva Ramakrishna Pillutla

School of Electronics Engineering, VIT-AP University, Amaravati, India

Kathik Chandran

Jyothi Engineering College, India

ABSTRACT

Image steganography methods use manual features for hiding payload data in cover images. These manual features allow less payload capacity and also cause image distortion. In this chapter, the authors detail a CNN-based network image steganography. The major contributions are twofold. First, they presented a CNN-based encoder-decoder architecture for hiding image. Secondly, they introduce a loss function, which checks joint end-to-end encoder-decoder networks. They evaluate this architecture on publicly available datasets CIFAR10. The results indicate an increase in payload capacity with high peak signal-to-noise ratio and structural similarity index values.

DOI: 10.4018/979-8-3693-5767-5.ch011

1. INTRODUCTION

Massive amounts of data have been flowing over the internet in the modern world as its accessibility has improved, making the internet more appealing to individuals. In addition to the aforementioned critics, the emergence of wireless communication technology has resulted in the devices connecting to the internet. Individuals fear as a result of data risks and securities. Because of the sensitive nature of private information, this flexibility raises a slew of issues in terms of data privacy and security. Consider the following example: personal data in a medical report reflect the entire state of the patient as well as the necessary diagnosis. In this context, intruders may generate incorrect data during transmission, resulting in incorrect patient diagnosis.

To overcome these challenges, one project that has sparked concern is data protection. Data hiding or embedding is the process of embedding any digital data within another digital data without causing any distortion for identification or copyright. As a result, images, texts, audios, and videos are used as a medium for secret communication.

Watermarking and steganography are two major perspectives that would be considered when studying data shielding or hiding in general. Watermarking's main applications/objectives are ownership assertion, content authentication, fingerprinting, and the message inserted is related to the cover (Kumar & Kumar, n.d.). Whereas the steganography process conceals unrelated/irrelevant data. The goals of steganalysis involve identifying potentially concealed content within data packets, determining the presence of encoded payloads, and subsequently extracting these payloads. Consequently, the primary hurdles in achieving effective steganography can be outlined as follows: Numerous researchers have dedicated their efforts to developing steganography algorithms aimed at impeding the detection and extraction of concealed information through steganalysis. They also strive to make it challenging for the Human Visual System (HVS) to discern any subtle alterations that may occur in the original data, whether it be in the form of audio, images, or videos, after the concealment process. Furthermore, there has been a noticeable uptick in the utilization of multi-level steganography techniques in recent times (Alanzy et al., 2023). However, steganography is preferred over watermarking due to its inherent properties such as hiding capacity or payload, imperceptibility and robustness. Furthermore, cryptography can be used in this context, but it has its own drawbacks. The study of secure communication methods, such as encryption, that only the message's sender and intended recipient can access, is known as cryptography. In the realm of cryptography, two key texts come into play: plaintext and ciphertext. Plaintext refers to data that has not undergone encryption, remaining in its original, unencrypted form. Ciphertext, on the other hand, represents the encrypted counterpart of plaintext, created through the application of encryption techniques (Simmons, 2019).

Steganography is the process/practice of concealing a secret message behind other data, so the only data types used in this procedure are secret and covered data. In this case, the primary goal is to hide a secret object it may be text/image in a cover object without modifying its characteristics. The two major factors affecting change are the cover object and the amount of data to be concealed. There are many traditional methods to implement steganography. LSB (Least Significant Bit method) is a simple method of hiding images. This method allows the secret image to hide in the least significant bits of the cover image (Chan & Cheng, 2004; Kavitha et al., 2012). Though it is easy to hide, it's pretty simple to spot the secret image. PVD (pixel value differencing) is a method which divides the image into blocks of two consecutive pixels, and then calculates the difference value for each block. PVD (Liu et al., 2020; Sahu & Swain, 2016) has great data hiding capacity but it degrades the image quality. Another method is DTC which is a frequency domain technique in which the image is transformed into frequency domain from spatial domain. This method is more complicated than the spatial domain (Patel & Dave, 2012). The DFT-based technique is similar to the DCT-based technique (Hemachandran, 2016), but it is less resistant to severe geometric distortions because it employs the Fourier transform instead of the cosine.

The primary benefit of the Discrete Fourier Transform (DFT) lies in its substantial improvement in computational precision without requiring additional computation time. It offers significantly enhanced efficiency and swiftness.

For image steganography, discrete wavelet transforms can be employed. A higher quality photograph uses quite a lot of disc space. DWT is used to shrink an image's size without sacrificing quality, increasing resolution (Chen & Lin, 2006; Narasimmalou & Allen Joseph, 2012). Spread spectrum image steganography (SSIS) disguises a message within an image as Gaussian noise (Marvel et al., 1999). The degradation of the image is invisible to the human eye at low noise power levels, but becomes visible at higher levels as "snow" or speckles. There are many other methods such as Image steganography based on canny edge detection, dilation operator and hybrid coding (Gaurav & Ghanekar, 2018) and a genetic algorithm based steganography using discrete cosine transformation (Khamrui & Mandal, 2013). Instead of plain regions, the best steganography involves hiding data in high frequency filled and noisy portions of an image while causing less perturbation. We present an efficient, automated steganography method in this paper that causes the least amount of distortion to the cover image while concealing a secret image. To accomplish this, a convolution neural network is created that merges data and extracts the best attributes from both cover and secret images (Rahim & Nadeem, 2018; Subramanian et al., 2021). The main advantage of our method is that it is not specific and can be applied to a wide range of images.

2. METHODOLOGY

Figure 1 depicts the overall workflow of the proposed method, which is comprised of three modules: preparation, hiding, and extraction networks. The preparation network extracts secret image features, and the hiding network combines cover image and secret image features. The extraction network, on the other hand, extracts the secret image hidden in the stego image, which is the output of the hiding network.

2.1 Preparation Network

The preparation network extract features from the cover and secret images rather than processing them in their raw form. High resolution images have many noisy regions and also redundant data, we can extract the important features from those regions. The input size should be in x*x*y format, which represents the width, height, depth dimensions. The width and height both are represented by x because they should be in same size.

The size of the secret image can be any size but should be equal to or less than cover image. The preparation network extracts the useful features. This network consists of convolutional layers, each composed of filters. As we move up the layers, the filter sizes grow larger. Smaller filters primarily capture basic image features like edges, while larger filters, when employed, allow for the extraction of a broader range of features.

Figure 1. Network architecture of image steganography using convolution layers

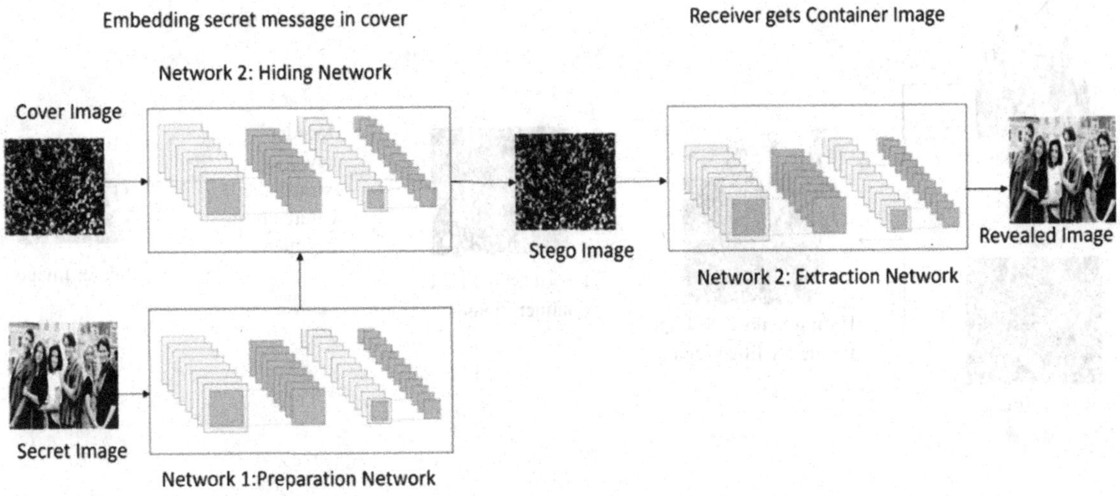

2.2 Hiding Network

The hiding network is also functions as the encoder component of the architecture. This network mainly extracts the important features of the cover image. This hiding network also combines the features of the cover image with those of the secret image. The features extracted from cover image are noisy regions. Based on the size of the filter used the features are extracted. In the hiding network, first the filter is increased and then it is decreased. Later ReLu activation is introduced to attain maximum linearity. Finally, a 3-unit filter is employed to transform the feature vector image into a stego image.

2.3 Extraction Network

The work of extraction network is to find the hidden image and to extract it from the cover image. This CNN network gives the best results. The filters and filter size that are used in the network are fine tuned.

Within the extraction network, the encoder phase comprises five convolutional layers where the filter sizes progressively increase. This is followed by a decoding phase consisting of five convolutional layers, with filter sizes decreasing. Additionally, three filters are applied to eliminate the perfectly concealed image from the cover image. The following equation reduces error and trains the system accordingly, (c and s represent the cover and secret images, respectively).

$$L(c, c0, s, s0) = \|c - c0\| + \beta\|s - s0\| \tag{1}$$

In Figure 2, the dimensions of the secret image are denoted as N*N, while the dimensions of the cover image are specified as M*M. The hidden image can be of any size that is equal to or smaller than the header image(cover). After the extraction of features, the secret image is hidden in the noisy regions of cover image. The result obtained after this encoding process is referred to as the embedded or hybrid image. Subsequently, this hybrid image is then subjected to this network that is designed to eliminate the hidden secret image. The output is measured in a metric PSNR (Setiadi, 2021) and payload capacity.

Figure 2. Encoding and decoding of secret image

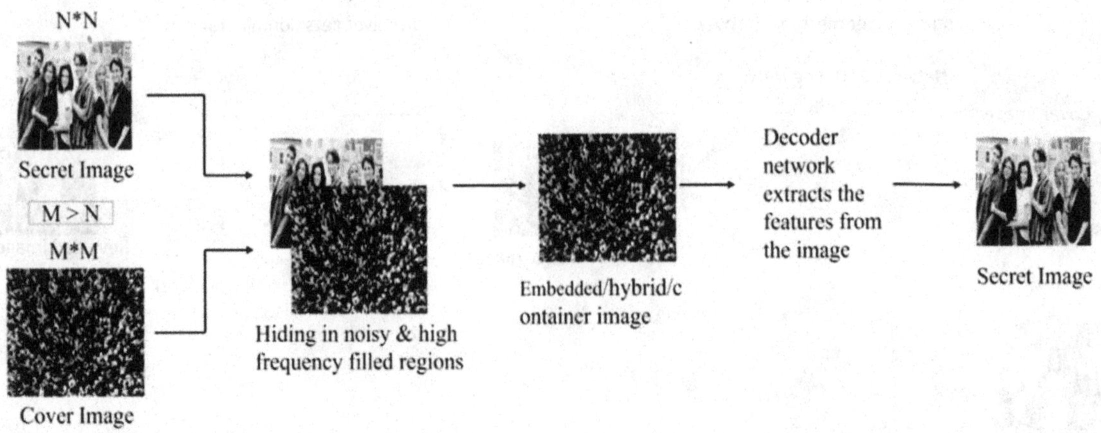

3. RESULTS

In this section, we outline the criteria that guided our design choices. We also present the qualitative and statistical outcomes of our approach on a range of publicly available datasets, which include ImageNet.

The considered dataset has been divided into three distinct sets: the training set, the testing set, and the validation set. All adjustments and alterations were exclusively applied using the validation set, and the outcomes of the simulation are reported based on the test set. From the corresponding dataset, we choose two RGB images at random; one serves as the cover image, while the other is converted to grayscale for the payload. 6000 images from the ImageNet database were chosen at random to serve as the training set, and 2000 additional images were chosen at random to act as the test set. The network learning rate is held at 0.001 and $\alpha = 0.75$, lr is adapted utilizing Adam optimization. s. From the results we can observe that our method is able to hide the image with less humanly detectable perturbations with better results. Table 1 shows the comparison of the proposed method's PSNR and payload capacity with those of other traditional methods.

Table 1. Comparison of our method's PSNR and payload capacity with those of other traditional methods

Technique	Capacity	PSNR
DCT	20.71	28.30
LSB	33	30.99
LSB and MSB modification	22.52	32
PVD	5.56	31.99
k-LSB	21.33	32.45
Proposed method	24	38.83

Figure 3. Sample results of our output in ImageNet

4. CONCLUSION

According to the research presented above, image steganography is a widely used technology for securing any type of data, including text, digital, audio, and video. Steganography is accomplished using a variety of techniques. Many techniques have been developed in various domains. The method we proposed outperforms all other traditional techniques in terms of payload capacity and PSNR. Hence the algorithm we proposed produces high imperceptibility, data embedding, and good data reconstruction without distortion and provides better security and quality.

REFERENCES

Alanzy, M., Alomrani, R., Alqarni, B., & Almutairi, S. (2023). Image Steganography Using LSB and Hybrid Encryption Algorithms. *Applied Sciences (Basel, Switzerland)*, *13*(21), 11771. doi:10.3390/app132111771

Chan, C.-K., & Cheng, L.-M. (2004). Hiding data in images by simple LSB substitution. *Pattern Recognition*, *37*(3), 469–474. doi:10.1016/j.patcog.2003.08.007

Chen, P.-Y., & Lin, H.-J. (2006). A DWT based approach for image steganography. *International Journal of Applied Science and Engineering*, *4*(3), 275–290.

Gaurav, K., & Ghanekar, U. (2018). Image steganography based on Canny edge detection, dilation operator and hybrid coding. *Journal of Information Security and Applications*, *41*, 41–51. doi:10.1016/j.jisa.2018.05.001

Hemachandran, K. (2016). Study of Image Steganography using LSB, DFT and DWT. *International Journal of Computers and Technology*, *11*, 2618–2627.

Kavitha, K.K., Koshti, A., & Dunghav, P. (2012). Steganography using least significant bit algorithm. *International Journal of Engineering Research and Applications*.

Khamrui, A., & Mandal, J. K. (2013). A genetic algorithm-based steganography using discrete cosine transformation (GASDCT). *Procedia Technology*, *10*, 105–111. doi:10.1016/j.protcy.2013.12.342

Kumar & Kumar. (n.d.). *Techniques of Digital Watermarking*. Academic Press.

Liu, H. H., Su, P. C., & Hsu, M. H. (2020). An improved steganography method based on least-significant-bit substitution and pixel-value differencing. *KSII Transactions on Internet and Information Systems*, *14*(11), 4537–4556.

Marvel, L. M., Boncelet, C. G., & Retter, C. T. (1999). Spread spectrum image steganography. *IEEE Transactions on Image Processing*, *8*(8), 1075–1083. doi:10.1109/83.777088 PMID:18267522

Narasimmalou, T., & Allen Joseph, R. (2012). Discrete wavelet transform based steganography for transmitting images. In *IEEE-International Conference on Advances In Engineering, Science And Management (ICAESM2012)* (pp. 370-375). IEEE.

Patel, H., & Dave, P. (2012). Steganography technique based on DCT coefficients. *International Journal of Engineering Research and Applications*, *2*(1), 713–717.

Rahim, R., & Nadeem, S. (2018). End-to-end trained CNN encoder-decoder networks for image steganography. *Proceedings of the European Conference on Computer Vision (ECCV) Workshops*.

Sahu, A. K., & Swain, G. (2016). A review on LSB substitution and PVD based image steganography techniques. *Indonesian Journal of Electrical Engineering and Computer Science*, *2*(3), 712–719. doi:10.11591/ijeecs.v2.i3.pp712-719

Setiadi, D. R. I. M. (2021). PSNR vs SSIM: Imperceptibility quality assessment for image steganography. *Multimedia Tools and Applications*, *80*(6), 8423–8444. doi:10.1007/s11042-020-10035-z

Simmons, G. (2019). *Secure communications and asymmetric cryptosystems*. Routledge. doi:10.4324/9780429305634

Subramanian, N., Cheheb, I., Elharrouss, O., Al-Maadeed, S., & Bouridane, A. (2021). End-to-end image steganography using deep convolutional autoencoders. *IEEE Access : Practical Innovations, Open Solutions*, *9*, 135585–135593. doi:10.1109/ACCESS.2021.3113953

Chapter 12
Impacts of Nano–Materials and Nano Fluids on the Robot Industry and Environments

Nalla Bhanu Teja

Department of Mechanical Engineering, Aditya College of Engineering, Surampalem, India

V. Kannagi

Department of Electronics and Communication Engineering, R.M.K. College of Engineering and Technology, Puduvoyal, India

A. Chandrashekhar

Department of Mechanical Engineering, Faculty of Science and Technology, ICFAI Foundation for Higher Education, Hyderabad, India

T. Senthilnathan

Department of Applied Physics, Sri Venkateswara College of Engineering, Sriperumbudur, India

Tarun Kanti Pal

Department of Mechanical Engineering, College of Engineering and Management, Kolaghat, India

Sampath Boopathi

iD https://orcid.org/0000-0002-2065-6539

Department of Mechanical Engineering, Muthayammal Engineering College, Namakkal, India

ABSTRACT

The integration of nanotechnology into robotics has revolutionized the design, manufacturing, and performance of robotic systems. Nano-materials, with their unique properties at the nanoscale, enhance strength, flexibility, and functionality, revolutionizing the construction and operation of robots. Nano fluids, with their superior heat transfer properties, address overheating issues, improving performance, extended operational lifespans, and increased adaptability in diverse environmental conditions. The chapter also explores the environmental impact of robotics, highlighting the integration of nano-materials and nano fluids in eco-friendly solutions. The chapter delves into the challenges and future directions of the synergy between nanotechnology and robotics, discussing potential breakthroughs, ethical considerations, and the need for ongoing research. It provides a comprehensive analysis of the impacts of nano-materials and nano fluids on the robot industry and their environments.

DOI: 10.4018/979-8-3693-5767-5.ch012

INTRODUCTION

The integration of nanotechnology and robotics has led to significant innovation across various industries. The use of nanomaterials and nanofluids in robotics can enhance mechanical performance and promote environmental sustainability. This chapter examines the profound impacts of these materials on the robot industry, highlighting their impact on technological advancements and ecological considerations (Jakkula & Sethuramalingam, 2023).

The integration of nanotechnology and robotics is revolutionizing the field, enhancing the mechanical, electrical, and thermal capabilities of robots. Nanomaterials, with dimensions at the nanoscale, offer unique properties that can significantly improve the performance of these systems. By integrating these materials into the design and manufacturing processes, engineers and researchers are pushing the boundaries of what was once thought possible. This convergence leads to more efficient and versatile robots, with nanocomposites offering superior strength, durability, and lightweight properties. This results in robots with enhanced agility, increased load-bearing capacities, and prolonged operational lifespans. The integration of nanomaterials enhances robot performance in various industries (He et al., 2018).

Nano-fluids, colloidal suspensions of nanoparticles in conventional fluids, have emerged as a game-changer in thermal management for robotic systems. The exceptional thermal conductivity and heat transfer capabilities of nano-fluids enable more efficient cooling of robotic components, preventing overheating and optimizing energy consumption. As robots become more sophisticated and undertake tasks with higher energy demands, the implementation of nano-fluids becomes crucial in ensuring the reliability and longevity of these systems. This chapter will delve into specific case studies and applications where nano-fluids have proven instrumental in revolutionizing the thermal dynamics of robots (Hassani et al., 2020).

While the integration of nanomaterials and nano-fluids brings about remarkable advancements in robotic technology, it is imperative to assess their environmental impact. As robots become ubiquitous across industries, understanding the ecological footprint of these nanotechnology-infused systems is crucial. This chapter will explore the sustainability aspects of using nano-materials, considering factors such as recyclability, resource consumption, and end-of-life disposal. By addressing environmental concerns, the robotics industry can steer towards eco-friendly practices and contribute to a more sustainable future (Malik et al., 2023).

This chapter explores the impact of nano-materials and nano-fluids on the robot industry and its environment. It delves into their applications in various robotic domains, including manufacturing, healthcare, and agriculture. The chapter also examines the challenges and future prospects of integrating nanotechnology into robotics. Nanotechnology is a pioneering force in the robotics industry, with the potential to redefine its capabilities. The chapter focuses on the environmental impact of this symbiotic relationship, as nanomaterials are widely used in robot design, manufacturing, and operation. The chapter aims to provide an in-depth exploration of how nanotechnology is shaping the robot industry while raising questions about its environmental footprint (Ramesh et al., 2020).

Nanotechnology, operating at the scale of one billionth of a meter, has catalyzed a paradigm shift in the development of robotic systems. The integration of nanomaterials into the fabric of robotics introduces a new era of possibilities, ranging from improved structural integrity to enhanced functionality. Robots are no longer bound by the constraints of traditional materials; instead, they are endowed with unprecedented strength, durability, and versatility. This chapter aims to dissect the manifold ways in which nanotechnology is propelling the robot industry forward, with a particular emphasis on the transformative potential that nanomaterials bring to the design and performance of robotic systems (Sethuramalingam et al., 2023).

As the robot industry expands its horizons, driven by technological advancements, the integration of nanomaterials becomes a central theme. Nanotechnology is not merely a tool for incremental improvement; it is a catalyst for disruptive innovation. From autonomous manufacturing robots to sophisticated medical nanobots, the applications span across diverse sectors, each bringing its unique set of challenges and opportunities. This chapter will navigate through the varied landscapes of the robot industry, highlighting important nanotechnological contributions that are reshaping the way robots operate, communicate, and interact with their environment (Kiran & Prabhu, 2020).

While the marriage of nanotechnology and robotics ushers in a wave of transformative possibilities, it is crucial to pause and assess the environmental implications of this revolution. The production, utilization, and disposal of nanomaterials raise questions about their long-term impact on ecosystems. This chapter will delve into the life cycle assessment of nanotechnology in the robot industry, considering factors such as resource extraction, energy consumption, and waste management. By critically evaluating the environmental footprint, we aim to provide insights into how the robot industry can navigate toward sustainable practices without compromising technological advancements (Singh et al., 2021).

The inherent tension between technological innovation and environmental stewardship becomes apparent in the context of nanotechnology in the robot industry. Striking a balance between pushing the boundaries of what is achievable and adopting eco-conscious practices is a challenge that demands careful consideration. This chapter will explore case studies, best practices, and emerging frameworks that showcase how the robot industry can embrace nanotechnology responsibly, mitigating adverse environmental effects while fostering groundbreaking advancements (Sonika, 2023).

The chapters will explore the application of nanotechnology in the robot industry, focusing on technological advancements and environmental implications. They will explore nanomaterial-enhanced components and eco-friendly manufacturing processes, providing a comprehensive understanding of the relationship between nanotechnology, the robot industry, and environmental impact. The aim is to provide a nuanced perspective for future developments.

Objectives of the Chapter

- The study explores the integration of nanomaterials in robot design and manufacturing, evaluating their impact on structural integrity, durability, and performance, and highlighting case studies and advancements in nanotechnology.
- The study aims to analyze the environmental impact of nanomaterials in the robot industry, focusing on resource extraction, energy consumption, and waste management, to determine the sustainability of these innovations.
- Explore nanotechnology's applications in manufacturing, healthcare, agriculture, and beyond, highlighting its contributions to advancements and examining the challenges and opportunities of their integration into diverse robotic applications.
- The study explores the environmental challenges of integrating nanotechnology into the robot industry, focusing on resource consumption, recyclability, and responsible waste management, offering insights for sustainable practices in nanorobotics.
- The study aims to develop guidelines and recommendations for responsible and sustainable nanorobotics development, guiding the robot industry to balance technological innovation with envi-

ronmental stewardship, ensuring nanotechnology advancements positively impact both industries and the environment.

NANOTECHNOLOGY IN ROBOTICS

This chapter explores the fundamentals of nanotechnology and its integration into robotics. It delves into the core principles and concepts of nanotechnology, aiming to provide readers with a comprehensive understanding of how nanoscale phenomena are harnessed to enhance the capabilities of robotic systems (Sharmin, 2020; Sheikh et al., 2020).

- *Nanotechnology Primer:* Nanotechnology involves the manipulation and utilization of materials and devices at the nanoscale, typically ranging from 1 to 100 nanometers. At this scale, the properties of materials undergo significant changes, enabling scientists and engineers to exploit novel phenomena not observed at larger scales. This section will provide a primer on nanotechnology, introducing concepts such as quantum effects, surface area dominance, and unique mechanical, thermal, and optical properties that become pronounced at the nanoscale (Boopathi, Umareddy, et al., 2023; Boopathi & Davim, 2023b).
- *Building Blocks of Nanomaterials:* The fundamental building blocks of nanotechnology are nanomaterials, which serve as the cornerstone for advancements in robotics. Nanomaterials, such as nanoparticles, nanotubes, and nanocomposites, exhibit exceptional mechanical, electrical, and thermal properties. This chapter will explore the diverse nature of nanomaterials and elucidate their role in augmenting the structural and functional aspects of robotic systems. Readers will gain insights into the synthesis, manipulation, and application of nanomaterials in the context of robotics (Fowziya et al., 2023; Vijayakumar et al., 2024).
- *Tools and Techniques in Nanofabrication:* Nanofabrication techniques play a pivotal role in shaping the landscape of nanotechnology. This section will introduce readers to state-of-the-art tools and techniques employed in the creation of nanoscale structures. From top-down approaches like photolithography to bottom-up methods such as self-assembly, we will examine how these techniques contribute to the precision and reproducibility required in nanorobotics. Understanding these techniques is essential for grasping the practical aspects of implementing nanotechnology in robotic systems (Boopathi & Davim, 2023b, 2023a).
- *Quantum Mechanics at the Nanoscale:* Quantum mechanics governs the behavior of matter at the nanoscale and is instrumental in shaping the properties of nanomaterials. This chapter will provide an overview of main quantum mechanical principles relevant to nanotechnology, including quantum tunneling, confinement effects, and quantum dots. Understanding these principles is crucial for appreciating the unique characteristics and potential applications of nanomaterials in robotics (Paul et al., 2024).
- *Integration of Nanotechnology in Robotics:* Building on the fundamentals established, this section will explore how nanotechnology is seamlessly integrated into robotics. From nanoscale sensors and actuators to the development of nanobots for medical applications, we will examine the diverse applications and contributions of nanotechnology to the field of robotics. By elucidating these connections, readers will gain a holistic understanding of how nanotechnology shapes the future of robotic systems (Mohanty et al., 2023).

In subsequent chapters, we will delve into specific applications of nanotechnology in robotics, showcasing real-world examples and emerging trends that exemplify the transformative power of the fusion between these two cutting-edge fields.

Applications of Nanomaterials in Robotics: Harnessing Unique Properties

This chapter explores the diverse applications of nanomaterials in robotics, highlighting their unique properties that enhance the capabilities of robotic systems. It highlights the impact of nanomaterials on the design, performance, and functionality of robots, highlighting the wide range of applications they offer (Joe et al., 2023).

- *The Versatility of Nanomaterials:* Nanomaterials encompass a wide array of substances, including nanoparticles, nanocomposites, and nanotubes, each with its unique set of properties. This section will provide an overview of the versatility of nanomaterials, emphasizing their adaptability and applicability across various robotic applications. From enhancing structural strength to enabling precise sensing, nanomaterials serve as the fundamental building blocks that drive innovation in modern robotics.
- *Improved Structural Integrity and Durability:* One of the primary applications of nanomaterials in robotics lies in improving the structural integrity and durability of robotic components. Nanocomposites, for instance, exhibit remarkable strength and lightweight characteristics. This chapter will delve into how the integration of nanomaterials in the fabrication of robotic exoskeletons, frames, and limbs enhances mechanical properties, making robots more resilient and capable of withstanding challenging environments (Boopathi, Thillaivanan, et al., 2022).
- *Sensing and Actuation at the Nanoscale:* Nanomaterials play a crucial role in the development of sensors and actuators that operate at the nanoscale. Quantum dots and nanosensors, for instance, enable robots to perceive their surroundings with unprecedented precision. This section will explore how nanomaterials contribute to advancements in sensing technologies, allowing robots to detect and respond to stimuli with enhanced sensitivity and efficiency (S. Karthik et al., 2023).
- *Nanomaterials in Biomedical Robotics:* In the realm of biomedical robotics, nanomaterials hold immense promise for transformative applications. Nanoparticles can be engineered for targeted drug delivery, and nanobots can navigate through the human body to perform intricate medical procedures. This chapter will delve into specific examples of how nanomaterials are revolutionizing biomedical robotics, highlighting their potential in diagnostics, therapy, and minimally invasive surgeries (Sengeni et al., 2023).
- *Energy Efficiency and Environmental Sustainability:* Nanomaterials contribute to the pursuit of energy-efficient and environmentally sustainable robotic systems. With enhanced thermal conductivity and lightweight properties, nanomaterials facilitate better heat dissipation, leading to energy savings in robotic operations. Moreover, the recyclability of certain nanomaterials aligns with the growing emphasis on sustainable practices in robotics. This section will explore how nanomaterials contribute to eco-friendly advancements in the robot industry (Boopathi, 2022a, 2022b).

It explores the transformative impact of nanomaterials in robotics through case studies and real-world examples, aiming to provide readers with a nuanced understanding of their role in shaping the future of robotic systems.

IMPACT OF NANO-MATERIALS ON ROBOTIC SYSTEMS

Figure 1 depicts the significant impact of nano-materials on various aspects of robotic systems.

Figure 1. Impact of nano-materials on robotic systems in various aspects

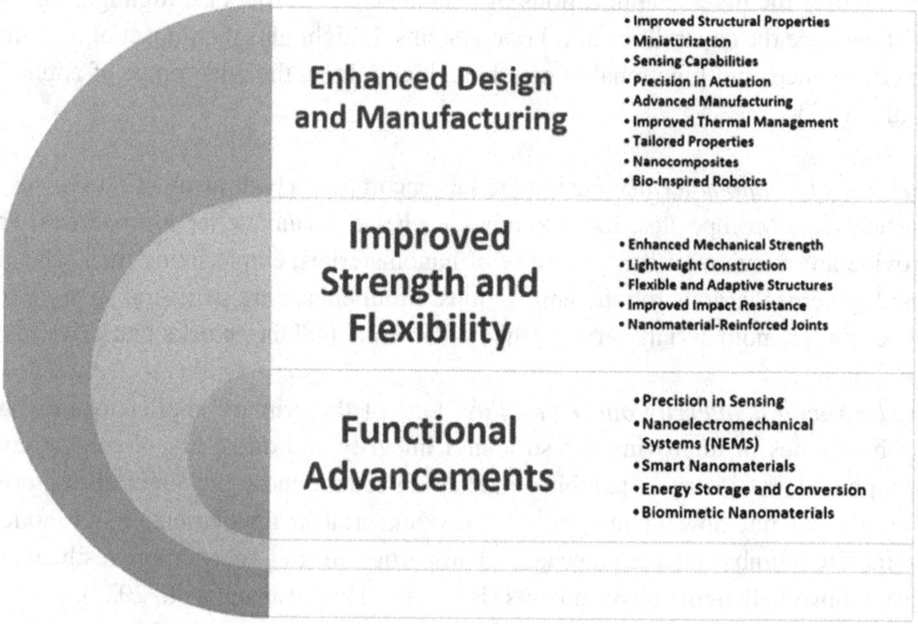

Enhanced Design and Manufacturing
- Improved Structural Properties
- Miniaturization
- Sensing Capabilities
- Precision in Actuation
- Advanced Manufacturing
- Improved Thermal Management
- Tailored Properties
- Nanocomposites
- Bio-Inspired Robotics

Improved Strength and Flexibility
- Enhanced Mechanical Strength
- Lightweight Construction
- Flexible and Adaptive Structures
- Improved Impact Resistance
- Nanomaterial-Reinforced Joints

Functional Advancements
- Precision in Sensing
- Nanoelectromechanical Systems (NEMS)
- Smart Nanomaterials
- Energy Storage and Conversion
- Biomimetic Nanomaterials

Enhanced Design and Manufacturing

Improved Structural Properties: Nano-materials, such as carbon nanotubes and graphene, offer exceptional strength-to-weight ratios and structural integrity. Integration of these materials in robotic frames and components results in lighter yet more robust structures, enhancing overall durability (Chakraborty et al., 2021; Mouchou et al., 2021).

Miniaturization and Increased Efficiency: Nanomaterials enable the development of smaller and more efficient robotic components, allowing for the miniaturization of robots. This facilitates the creation of compact, agile robots capable of navigating confined spaces and executing precise tasks with higher efficiency.

Enhanced Sensing Capabilities: Quantum dots and nanosensors made from nanomaterials provide robots with improved sensing capabilities at the nanoscale. The heightened sensitivity of these sensors allows robots to perceive and respond to their environment more accurately, enhancing their adaptability.

Precision in Actuation: Nanomaterials contribute to the development of high-precision actuators, enabling robots to perform intricate movements and tasks. This precision is particularly crucial in applications such as surgical robotics, where nanomaterial-based actuators can enhance the accuracy of procedures.

Advanced Manufacturing Processes: Nanomaterials are integrated into manufacturing processes, such as 3D printing and nanoscale assembly techniques, allowing for the creation of intricate robotic components. These advanced manufacturing methods enable the production of complex structures that were previously unattainable, pushing the boundaries of design possibilities (Revathi et al., 2024; Senthil et al., 2023).

Improved Thermal Management: Nano-materials exhibit superior thermal conductivity, addressing challenges related to heat dissipation in robotic systems. Efficient thermal management ensures that robots can operate for extended periods without overheating, contributing to enhanced reliability and longevity (Boopathi, Jeyakumar, et al., 2022).

Customization and Tailored Properties: The ability to engineer nanomaterials with specific properties allows for the customization of robotic components based on application requirements. Tailored properties, such as electrical conductivity or magnetism, enable the creation of specialized robotic systems for diverse tasks.

Nanocomposites for Multifunctionality: Nanocomposites, combining nanomaterials with traditional materials, result in multifunctional robotic components. This integration allows for the simultaneous improvement of mechanical, thermal, and electrical properties, contributing to the overall efficiency of robotic systems (Gowri et al., 2023; K. Karthik et al., 2023; Murali et al., 2023).

Facilitation of Bio-Inspired Robotics: Nanomaterials play a crucial role in the development of bio-inspired robotic systems by mimicking biological structures at the nanoscale. This bio-mimicry enhances the performance of robots in tasks inspired by nature, such as agile locomotion or adaptive responses to environmental stimuli (Koshariya, Khatoon, et al., 2023; Maheswari et al., 2023).

Streamlined Production Processes: The integration of nanomaterials often simplifies and streamlines the production processes for robotic components. Reduced material complexity and improved manufacturing efficiency contribute to cost-effectiveness in the production of advanced robotic systems.

Nanomaterials significantly impact robotic systems in design and manufacturing, offering enhanced structural properties, improved efficiency, advanced sensing capabilities, and innovative manufacturing processes. These advancements contribute to the development of more capable, efficient, and versatile robotic systems across various applications.

Improved Strength and Flexibility

- **Enhanced Mechanical Strength:** Nano-materials, such as carbon nanotubes and nanocomposites, contribute to significant improvements in the mechanical strength of robotic components. The incorporation of these materials in structural elements enhances the overall robustness of robots, allowing them to withstand higher loads and impacts (Oluwasanu et al., 2019).
- **Lightweight Construction:** Nano-materials offer high strength-to-weight ratios, enabling the creation of lightweight yet durable robotic structures. This lightweight construction enhances the mobility and agility of robots, making them more versatile in various applications, including exploration and search-and-rescue missions (Boopathi, 2023a).
- **Flexible and Adaptive Structures:** Nanomaterials, particularly those with flexible properties, allow for the development of robotic components that can bend, stretch, and adapt to varying conditions. This flexibility is advantageous in applications where robots need to navigate complex environments or perform tasks that require adaptive movements.

- **Improved Impact Resistance:** Nanomaterials enhance the impact resistance of robotic systems, reducing the risk of damage in scenarios where robots may encounter collisions or harsh conditions. This impact resistance is particularly crucial in applications like industrial automation and field robotics, where robots operate in dynamic and unpredictable environments.
- **Nanomaterial-Reinforced Joints and Connectors:** Nano-materials are employed to reinforce joints and connectors in robotic systems, ensuring greater durability and longevity. This reinforcement enhances the structural integrity of robotic limbs and joints, reducing wear and tear during repetitive movements.

Functional Advancements

- **Precision in Sensing:** Nanomaterial-based sensors enable robots to achieve high precision in sensing various stimuli, such as temperature, pressure, and chemical changes. This precision enhances the ability of robots to gather accurate data from their environment, contributing to improved decision-making and adaptability (Kumar et al., 2023).
- **Nanoelectromechanical Systems (NEMS):** NEMS, built using nanomaterials, enable the integration of electromechanical functionalities at the nanoscale. This advancement allows for the creation of ultra-sensitive sensors, actuators, and transducers, enhancing the overall performance of robotic systems.
- **Smart Nanomaterials for Adaptive Behavior:** Smart nanomaterials with responsive properties, such as shape memory alloys and piezoelectric materials, enable robots to exhibit adaptive behaviors. These materials can change their physical properties in response to external stimuli, allowing for dynamic adjustments in the robot's form and function (Maguluri et al., 2023; Maheswari et al., 2023).
- **Improved Energy Storage and Conversion:** Nanomaterials contribute to the development of advanced energy storage and conversion systems for robotic applications. Nanostructured materials in batteries and energy storage devices enhance the energy density, leading to longer operational periods for robots between charging cycles (Satav et al., 2023; Syamala et al., 2023).
- **Biomimetic Nanomaterials for Soft Robotics:** Nanomaterials with biomimetic properties are utilized in soft robotics, enabling robots to mimic the flexibility and dexterity of natural organisms. Soft robotic structures built with nanomaterials find applications in fields like medical robotics and human-machine interaction.

The integration of nanomaterials into robotic systems enhances their strength, flexibility, and functional advancements, enhancing the robustness and adaptability of robots and paving the way for the development of more sophisticated and capable robotic systems across various applications.

NANO FLUIDS IN ROBOTIC THERMAL MANAGEMENT

Importance of Thermal Management in Robotics

Effective thermal management is a critical aspect of ensuring the optimal performance, reliability, and longevity of robotic systems. As robots become more sophisticated and engage in tasks with higher energy demands, managing heat dissipation becomes imperative. This section will underscore the importance of thermal management in robotics, exploring the impact of excessive heat on components and the overarching significance of maintaining optimal operating temperatures for enhanced efficiency and functionality (Du et al., 2021; Ramalingam & Rasool Mohideen, 2021).

Characteristics of Nano Fluids

Nano fluids, colloidal suspensions of nanoparticles in conventional fluids, present a cutting-edge solution to the thermal management challenges faced by robotic systems. This segment will delve into the unique characteristics of nano fluids that set them apart in heat transfer applications. Attributes such as enhanced thermal conductivity, stability, and the ability to disperse uniformly will be discussed, highlighting how these properties make nano fluids well-suited for cooling and thermal regulation in robotics (Sevinchan et al., 2018).

Applications in Cooling Systems

Nano fluids have found widespread applications in robotic cooling systems, contributing to superior heat dissipation and overall thermal control. This section will explore specific use cases of nano fluids in cooling robotic components, ranging from microprocessors and motors to entire robotic frames. Real-world examples and case studies will be presented to showcase the efficacy of nano fluids in optimizing thermal performance, thus ensuring the reliability and sustained operation of robotic systems (Harris et al., 2022).

Overcoming Thermal Challenges

Robotic systems often face formidable thermal challenges, from heat concentration in compact spaces to the need for continuous operation under varying environmental conditions. Nano fluids offer innovative solutions to these challenges. This part of the chapter will elucidate how nano fluids overcome thermal obstacles in robotics. Topics such as the role of nano fluids in preventing overheating, reducing thermal resistance, and facilitating efficient heat dissipation will be explored, providing insights into how these advanced fluids address important thermal management concerns.

USE OF NANO-FLUID IN ROBOT THERMAL MANAGEMENTS

Nano fluids, colloidal suspensions of nanoparticles in a base fluid, are known for their unique thermal properties. They are utilized in robotic systems for thermal management, addressing challenges in heat dissipation, cooling, and temperature control (Harris et al., 2022; Sevinchan et al., 2018). Figure 2 depicts the various roles of nano fluids in the thermal management of robots.

Enhanced Heat Transfer: Nano fluids exhibit significantly higher thermal conductivity compared to traditional fluids. By incorporating nano fluids in the cooling systems of robotic components, heat transfer is greatly enhanced. This ensures more efficient dissipation of heat generated during the operation of motors, processors, and other heat-emitting components.

Figure 2. Roles of nano fluids in the robot thermal managements

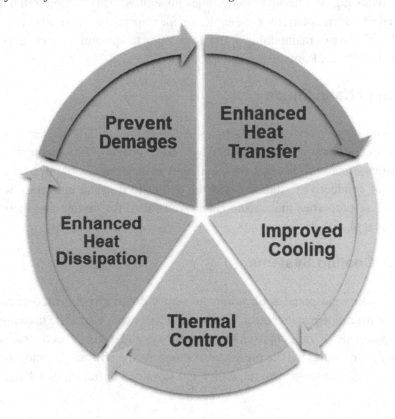

Improved Cooling of Electronics: Robotics often involve the use of electronic components that generate heat during operation. Nano fluids are employed in cooling systems to extract and carry away heat from electronic circuits more effectively than conventional coolants. This prevents overheating and ensures optimal performance and longevity of electronic components (Myilsamy & Sampath, 2021; Sampath & Myilsamy, 2021).

Thermal Control in Motors and Actuators: Motors and actuators in robotic systems can experience temperature fluctuations during operation. Nano fluids help maintain consistent temperatures by efficiently absorbing and dissipating heat. This is particularly crucial in precision applications where thermal stability is essential for accurate movements.

Miniaturization of Cooling Systems: The high thermal conductivity of nano fluids allows for the miniaturization of cooling systems. In small-scale robotic applications or devices with limited space, nano fluids enable the design of compact and efficient cooling solutions, ensuring that size constraints do not compromise thermal management.

Heat Dissipation in 3D Printing: In the field of robotics, especially in the manufacturing of robotic components using 3D printing, controlling heat is critical. Nano fluids can be utilized in the cooling systems of 3D printers to manage the heat generated during the printing process. This contributes to the production of high-quality, precisely manufactured robotic parts (Boopathi, Khare, et al., 2023; Boopathi & Kumar, 2024; Mohanty et al., 2023).

Thermal Management in Exoskeletons: Exoskeletons, worn by humans to augment strength and endurance, can generate heat due to the motors and actuators involved. Nano fluids play a role in the thermal management of these exoskeletons, ensuring that the temperature remains within a comfortable and safe range for the user.

Efficient Cooling in Harsh Environments: In robotic applications deployed in harsh environments, such as space exploration or industrial settings with high temperatures, nano fluids provide efficient cooling. Their superior thermal properties enable robots to operate reliably in extreme conditions without succumbing to heat-related issues.

Medical robotics, particularly in surgeries and diagnostic procedures, benefit from precise thermal management using nano fluids. These fluids regulate the temperature of components, ensuring optimal operation without discomfort or tissue damage. They also prevent hot spots, which can cause uneven temperature distribution and overheating. By integrating nano fluids with advanced materials, these fluids enhance the thermal performance of the components, leading to more heat-resistant and thermally efficient robotic systems.

Nano fluids play a significant role in robotic thermal management, enhancing heat transfer, cooling electronic components, and enabling miniaturization of cooling systems. They optimize thermal performance in robotic systems across various applications. This section explores the application of nano fluids in robotics, their impact on thermal dynamics, and their role in overcoming thermal challenges. It discusses the importance of thermal management, unique characteristics of nano fluids, their use in cooling systems, and their transformative role in enhancing thermal efficiency.

ENVIRONMENTAL CONSIDERATIONS IN ROBOTICS

Ecological Impact of Robotics

Resource Consumption: Robotics often involves the use of materials and energy-intensive manufacturing processes, contributing to resource depletion. Exploration of the ecological impact includes assessing the extraction and utilization of raw materials in robot production (Cui et al., 2021).

Electronic Waste (E-Waste): The disposal of obsolete or malfunctioning robotic components contributes to the growing problem of electronic waste. Examining the life cycle of robots involves considering strategies for minimizing e-waste and promoting responsible recycling (Harikaran et al., 2023; Selvakumar, Adithe, et al., 2023; Selvakumar, Shankar, et al., 2023; Sengeni et al., 2023).

Energy Consumption: The energy demands of robotic systems, particularly in industries like manufacturing and transportation, have implications for carbon footprints. Evaluating the environmental impact includes analyzing the energy sources powering robots and exploring avenues for energy efficiency (Naveeenkumar et al., 2024).

Sustainable Technology in Robotics

Renewable Energy Integration: Adopting sustainable practices involves exploring the integration of renewable energy sources, such as solar or wind power, to reduce reliance on conventional energy grids.

Life Cycle Assessment: Conducting a life cycle assessment of robotic systems helps identify and mitigate environmental impacts at every stage, from design and manufacturing to operation and disposal.

Efficient Materials Usage: Sustainable technology in robotics emphasizes the use of eco-friendly and recyclable materials to reduce the environmental footprint of manufacturing processes and end-of-life disposal.

Role of Nanotechnology in Eco-Friendly Robotics

Figure 3 depicts the significant role of nanotechnology in the development of eco-friendly robotics.

Nanomaterials for Light weighting: Nanotechnology contributes to eco-friendly robotics by providing lightweight nanomaterials that enhance structural integrity without excessive resource consumption (Gellers, 2020).

Energy-Efficient Nanodevices: The development of energy-efficient nanodevices, facilitated by nanotechnology, plays a crucial role in minimizing the energy consumption of robotic systems.

Recyclable Nanomaterials: Nanomaterials engineered for recyclability contribute to sustainable practices in robotics, ensuring that materials used in robots can be efficiently repurposed at the end of their life cycle.

Nanofluids for Thermal Efficiency: The use of nanofluids in robotics, enabled by nanotechnology, enhances thermal efficiency, reducing the need for excessive cooling mechanisms and contributing to energy savings.

Figure 3. Role of nanotechnology in eco-friendly robotics

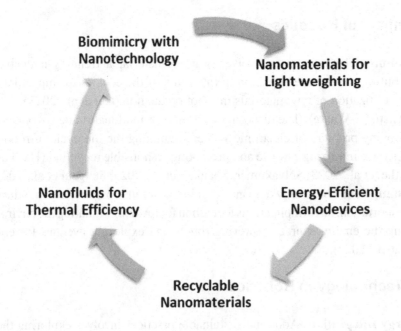

Biomimicry with Nanotechnology: Nanotechnology facilitates biomimicry in robotic design, allowing robots to emulate natural structures and processes, leading to more energy-efficient and environmentally friendly robotic systems.

Nanotechnology improves eco-friendly robotics by providing lightweight, energy-efficient nanomaterials that maintain structural integrity without excessive resource consumption. It also facilitates the development of energy-efficient nanodevices and contributes to sustainable robotic practices by ensuring efficient material repurposing.

OPERATIONAL EFFICIENCY AND ADAPTABILITY

This chapter emphasizes the importance of operational efficiency and adaptability in robotics, focusing on energy-efficient manufacturing processes, improved operational lifespan, and adaptability to diverse environmental conditions. These aspects are crucial for the sustainability of robotic systems and their applicability across various industries (Bragança et al., 2019; Marinoudi et al., 2019).

Energy-Efficient Manufacturing Processes

Nanotechnology in Materials and Manufacturing: The integration of nanotechnology into robotic manufacturing processes has revolutionized the energy efficiency of creating robotic components. Nanomaterials, such as carbon nanotubes and graphene, exhibit extraordinary strength and conductivity, enabling the production of lightweight yet robust components with minimal material usage. Nanotechnology has also facilitated precision engineering at the nanoscale, allowing for the creation of intricate robotic parts with reduced waste.

Additive Manufacturing (3D Printing): Additive manufacturing, commonly known as 3D printing, plays a pivotal role in energy-efficient robotic manufacturing. This process allows for the layer-by-layer construction of complex structures, minimizing material wastage and energy consumption. Additionally, 3D printing enables the customization of robotic components, tailoring designs to specific applications and optimizing their overall energy efficiency.

Sustainable Materials and Recycling Practices: The pursuit of energy efficiency extends to the choice of materials used in robotic manufacturing. Sustainable materials, such as bioplastics and recycled metals, contribute to reducing the environmental impact of the production process. Moreover, implementing recycling practices for robotic components at the end of their operational lifespan aligns with a circular economy, minimizing waste and conserving resources.

Integration of Renewable Energy Sources: Energy-efficient manufacturing extends beyond material usage to the power sources driving production facilities. Integration of renewable energy sources, such as solar or wind power, not only reduces the carbon footprint of robotic manufacturing but also aligns with sustainable practices. Implementing energy-efficient technologies, such as regenerative braking systems in manufacturing equipment, further contributes to the overall efficiency of the production process.

Improved Operational Lifespan

Robust Materials and Design: Enhancing the operational lifespan of robotic systems involves the use of robust materials and thoughtful design. Nanomaterials, with their exceptional strength and durability, contribute to the creation of components that can withstand the rigors of continuous operation. Additionally, adopting modular design principles facilitates the replacement of specific components, prolonging the overall lifespan of the robotic system (Javaid et al., 2021).

Predictive Maintenance and Monitoring: Implementing predictive maintenance strategies is crucial for optimizing operational lifespan. Advanced sensors and monitoring systems, often utilizing nano-technology, enable real-time data collection on the health and performance of robotic components. This data-driven approach allows for proactive maintenance, addressing potential issues before they escalate and ensuring the longevity of the robotic system (Boopathi, 2021, 2023b).

Upgradability and Adaptation; Designing robotic systems with upgradability in mind is another strategy to extend operational lifespan. This involves creating platforms that can accommodate hardware and software upgrades, allowing robots to evolve with technological advancements. The ability to adapt to new requirements and integrate the latest technologies enhances the relevance and longevity of robotic systems in dynamic operational environments.

Adaptability to Diverse Environmental Conditions

Sensory Systems and Environmental Perception: Achieving adaptability to diverse environmental conditions requires sophisticated sensory systems that enable robots to perceive and respond to their surroundings. Advanced sensors, often leveraging nanotechnology, provide robots with enhanced environmental perception capabilities. These sensors can detect changes in temperature, humidity, terrain, and other variables, allowing robots to adapt their behavior in real-time (Atilano et al., 2019).

Machine Learning and AI Algorithms: Machine learning and artificial intelligence (AI) algorithms empower robots to adapt and learn from their experiences in different environments. These technologies enable robots to analyze data, make informed decisions, and optimize their performance based on the specific conditions they encounter. Adaptive learning algorithms enhance the versatility of robotic systems across various applications (Maheswari et al., 2023; Ramudu et al., 2023; Syamala et al., 2023).

Soft Robotics for Flexible Environments: Soft robotics, a field that integrates flexible and deformable materials, enables robots to navigate and operate in complex and dynamic environments. Soft robotic components, often inspired by natural organisms, enhance adaptability by allowing robots to squeeze through tight spaces, conform to uneven surfaces, and interact safely with humans. This adaptability is particularly advantageous in applications like search-and-rescue missions or healthcare settings.

Robotic Swarms and Collaborative Adaptation: The concept of robotic swarms involves multiple robots working collaboratively to achieve a common goal. In diverse environmental conditions, robotic swarms can adapt and coordinate their actions based on the collective intelligence of the group. This collaborative approach enhances adaptability, allowing the swarm to accomplish tasks more efficiently and effectively than individual robots operating in isolation.

The robotics field is undergoing significant transformation due to its emphasis on operational efficiency and adaptability, encompassing energy-efficient manufacturing, sustainable materials, predictive maintenance, and adaptability to diverse environments, thereby maximizing the potential of robotic systems across various industries.

CHALLENGES IN THE INTEGRATION OF NANOTECHNOLOGY AND ROBOTICS

The integration of nanotechnology and robotics holds great potential for transformative advancements in various industries. However, it also presents challenges like ethical considerations, safety concerns, and regulatory hurdles. Researchers and engineers must navigate these issues to ensure responsible development and deployment of these cutting-edge technologies (Jakkula & Sethuramalingam, 2023; Ness et al., 2023; Sevinchan et al., 2018).

Ethical Considerations

Privacy Concerns in Nanorobotics: The miniaturization afforded by nanotechnology raises concerns about privacy, especially in the context of nanorobotics used for surveillance or medical applications. Ethical dilemmas arise when considering the potential intrusion into personal spaces and the collection of sensitive information through nanoscale devices.

Autonomous Decision-Making: As robots equipped with nanotechnology become more autonomous, ethical questions arise about their decision-making capabilities. Determining the ethical framework for robots making decisions in dynamic and unpredictable environments poses challenges, especially when human lives or critical tasks are at stake.

Dual-Use Dilemma: The dual-use nature of nanotechnology and robotics, where the same technology can have both beneficial and harmful applications, raises ethical concerns. Striking a balance between promoting innovation and preventing misuse requires thoughtful consideration and robust ethical guidelines.

Equity and Access: Ensuring equitable access to nanotechnology-enhanced robotics is an ethical challenge, as disparities in technology adoption can exacerbate existing societal inequalities. Addressing issues related to accessibility, affordability, and the potential exacerbation of socio-economic divides is crucial in the ethical integration of nanotechnology and robotics.

Safety Concerns

Nanomaterial Toxicity: The safety of nanomaterials used in robotic systems is a significant concern, as the potential toxicity of certain nanoparticles raises health and environmental risks. Understanding the long-term effects of exposure to nanomaterials and implementing safety measures in their production and use are essential for responsible integration.

Human-Robot Interaction Safety: As nanotechnology enhances the capabilities of robots, ensuring the safety of human-robot interactions becomes more complex. Safety measures must be implemented to prevent accidents or harm during close collaborations between humans and nanotechnology-enhanced robotic systems (Puranik et al., 2024).

Cybersecurity Risks: With increased connectivity and the incorporation of nanoscale sensors and communication devices, cybersecurity risks become a critical safety concern. Safeguarding robotic systems from cyber threats, such as unauthorized access or manipulation of nanotechnology-driven functionalities, requires robust cybersecurity measures (Maguluri et al., 2023; Rahamathunnisa et al., 2023; Srinivas et al., 2023).

Unintended Consequences of Autonomy: As robots gain autonomy through advanced nanotechnology, the potential for unintended consequences and malfunctions increases. Establishing fail-safe mechanisms and comprehensive testing procedures is crucial to mitigate safety risks associated with the autonomous behavior of nanotechnology-driven robotic systems.

Regulatory Challenges

Lack of Standardization: The fast-paced nature of technological advancements in nanotechnology and robotics poses challenges for regulatory bodies to establish standardized guidelines. The lack of universally accepted standards hinders regulatory efforts, making it challenging to ensure consistency and safety across different applications and industries.

Ethical and Legal Frameworks: Developing ethical and legal frameworks that keep pace with the evolving capabilities of nanotechnology-driven robotics is a regulatory challenge. Establishing guidelines for responsible research, development, and deployment of these technologies is essential to prevent misuse and ethical violations (Boopathi & Khang, 2023).

Cross-Disciplinary Regulations: Nanotechnology and robotics span multiple disciplines, and existing regulatory frameworks may not adequately address the convergence of these fields. Regulatory bodies face the challenge of fostering collaboration across disciplines to create comprehensive regulations that account for the unique aspects of nanotechnology-enhanced robotics.

International Coordination: The global nature of technological innovation requires international coordination in regulatory efforts. Coordinating regulatory frameworks across borders is challenging, given differing cultural, ethical, and legal perspectives, and establishing effective international collaboration is essential for responsible integration.

The integration of nanotechnology and robotics holds immense potential for enhancing industries, healthcare, and daily life. However, ethical concerns, safety concerns, and regulatory hurdles must be addressed for responsible technology development, necessitating a collaborative approach between researchers, policymakers, and industry stakeholders.

FUTURE DIRECTIONS AND BREAKTHROUGHS

This chapter delves into the ongoing research and development efforts, potential breakthroughs, and ethical and social implications of nanotechnology-enhanced robotics, highlighting its potential to revolutionize industries and redefine human-machine interactions (Bragança et al., 2019; Cui et al., 2021; Malik et al., 2023; Ramesh et al., 2020).

Ongoing Research and Development

Nanorobotics in Medicine: Ongoing research focuses on the development of nanorobots for targeted drug delivery, cancer treatment, and minimally invasive surgeries. Nano-scale robots could navigate the human body, delivering drugs precisely to targeted cells or assisting in intricate medical procedures with unprecedented precision.

Swarm Robotics: Research in swarm robotics, utilizing nanoscale components, explores the collective intelligence of robotic swarms for tasks such as environmental monitoring, disaster response, and exploration. Swarm robotics holds potential breakthroughs in collaborative problem-solving, adaptability, and scalability.

Soft Robotics with Nanomaterials: Ongoing efforts investigate the integration of nanomaterials in soft robotics, enabling robots with flexible and deformable structures. This research aims to create robots that can navigate complex environments, interact safely with humans, and perform delicate tasks in fields like healthcare and manufacturing.

Energy Harvesting at the Nanoscale: Research focuses on nanotechnology-enabled energy harvesting mechanisms for robotic systems. Nanoscale devices could harness ambient energy sources, such as vibrations or thermal gradients, to power robotic components, reducing dependence on traditional energy sources.

Potential Breakthroughs

Nanoscale Energy Storage: Breakthroughs in nanotechnology may lead to advancements in energy storage, allowing for high-capacity and lightweight nanobatteries. This breakthrough could significantly extend the operational lifespan and efficiency of nanotechnology-enhanced robotic systems.

Nano sensors for Enhanced Perception: Advancements in nanosensors could revolutionize the perception capabilities of robots, enabling them to detect and respond to stimuli with unparalleled sensitivity. This breakthrough could enhance robotic applications in areas like environmental monitoring, healthcare, and industrial automation.

Quantum Computing in Robotics: Integration of quantum computing with nanotechnology could unlock unprecedented computational power for robotic systems. Quantum-enhanced robotics may lead to breakthroughs in optimization, machine learning, and complex decision-making processes.

Self-Healing Nanomaterials: Breakthroughs in self-healing nanomaterials could enhance the durability and longevity of robotic components. This advancement may lead to robotic systems capable of autonomously repairing minor damages, reducing maintenance requirements.

Ethical and Social Implications

Privacy Concerns with Nanorobotics: As nanorobots advance in medical applications, concerns about privacy arise regarding the collection and transmission of sensitive health data. Striking a balance between the potential benefits of nanorobotics in healthcare and ensuring patient privacy will be a critical ethical consideration.

Autonomy and Decision-Making: The increasing autonomy of robots, fueled by nanotechnology, raises ethical questions about the responsibility and accountability for robotic decisions. Establishing ethical guidelines for autonomous systems to ensure alignment with human values and legal frameworks becomes paramount.

Socio-Economic Impact: The widespread adoption of nanotechnology-enhanced robotics may lead to shifts in the job market and socio-economic structures. Ethical considerations include addressing potential job displacement, ensuring access to new technologies, and mitigating inequalities in technology adoption.

Ethical Use of AI in Nanorobotics: Integrating artificial intelligence (AI) with nanorobotics requires ethical considerations to prevent unintended consequences and misuse. Developing frameworks for responsible AI use in nanotechnology-enhanced robotics involves addressing biases, ensuring transparency, and preventing malicious applications (Boopathi & Khang, 2023; Koshariya, Kalaiyarasi, et al., 2023; Zekrifa et al., 2023).

The future of nanotechnology-enhanced robotics is promising, with advancements in medical nanorobotics and energy storage. However, ethical and social implications must be considered, and stakeholders must collaborate across disciplines for responsible development, deployment, and societal integration.

CONCLUSION

The integration of nanotechnology into robotics has revolutionized the design, manufacturing, and performance of robotic systems. The use of nano-materials at the nanoscale has improved the fundamental attributes of robots, enhancing strength, flexibility, and functionality. This paradigm shift has not only revolutionized the construction of robots but also elevated their operational capabilities. The unique properties of nano-materials have opened new horizons for the robotic industry, enabling robots to navigate complex environments, perform intricate tasks, and adapt dynamically to changing conditions. The marriage of nano-materials with robotic frameworks has redefined possibilities and allowed for unprecedented innovations.

The integration of nano fluids into robotic systems has improved performance and extended operational lifespans, ensuring sustained functionality in diverse environmental conditions. This breakthrough has set the stage for energy-efficient and adaptable solutions, contributing to the eco-friendliness of advanced systems. Nano-materials and nano fluids offer eco-friendly solutions, mitigating resource consumption, minimizing electronic waste, and promoting energy efficiency in robotic systems. This chapter emphasizes the role of nanotechnology in addressing the environmental impact of robotics and promoting sustainability.

The integration of nanotechnology and robotics presents challenges such as ethical considerations, safety concerns, and the need for robust regulatory frameworks. However, potential breakthroughs like nanoscale energy storage and self-healing nanomaterials are promising. It's essential to focus on ongoing research and collaboration between researchers, engineers, and policymakers to navigate the complexities of nanotechnology-enhanced robotics. Ethical considerations must guide the trajectory, ensuring the integration benefits humanity positively and inclusively.

This chapter explores the significant impact of nano-materials and nano fluids on the robot industry and their environments, highlighting the revolutionary changes brought by nanotechnology. It highlights the strengths, flexibility, and adaptability of nanotechnology in robotics. As we approach a future characterized by nanotechnology and robotics convergence, it urges responsibility, innovation, and commitment to harnessing this transformative synergy's full potential.

ABBREVIATIONS

3D- Three Dimensional
   AI - Artificial intelligence
   E-Waste - Electronic Waste
   NEMS - Nanoelectromechanical Systems

REFERENCES

Atilano, L., Martinho, A., Silva, M., & Baptista, A. (2019). Lean Design-for-X: Case study of a new design framework applied to an adaptive robot gripper development process. *Procedia CIRP, 84*, 667–672. doi:10.1016/j.procir.2019.04.190

Boopathi, S. (2021). *Pollution monitoring and notification: Water pollution monitoring and notification using intelligent RC boat.* Academic Press.

Boopathi, S. (2022a). An investigation on gas emission concentration and relative emission rate of the near-dry wire-cut electrical discharge machining process. *Environmental Science and Pollution Research International, 29*(57), 86237–86246. doi:10.1007/s11356-021-17658-1 PMID:34837614

Boopathi, S. (2022b). Cryogenically treated and untreated stainless steel grade 317 in sustainable wire electrical discharge machining process: A comparative study. *Springer :Environmental Science and Pollution Research,* 1–10.

Boopathi, S. (2023a). An Investigation on Friction Stir Processing of Aluminum Alloy-Boron Carbide Surface Composite. In *Springer:Advances in Processing of Lightweight Metal Alloys and Composites* (pp. 249–257). Springer. doi:10.1007/978-981-19-7146-4_14

Boopathi, S. (2023b). Internet of Things-Integrated Remote Patient Monitoring System: Healthcare Application. In *Dynamics of Swarm Intelligence Health Analysis for the Next Generation* (pp. 137–161). IGI Global. doi:10.4018/978-1-6684-6894-4.ch008

Boopathi, S., & Davim, J. P. (2023a). Applications of Nanoparticles in Various Manufacturing Processes. In *Sustainable Utilization of Nanoparticles and Nanofluids in Engineering Applications* (pp. 1–31). IGI Global. doi:10.4018/978-1-6684-9135-5.ch001

Boopathi, S., & Davim, J. P. (2023b). *Sustainable Utilization of Nanoparticles and Nanofluids in Engineering Applications.* IGI Global. doi:10.4018/978-1-6684-9135-5

Boopathi, S., Jeyakumar, M., Singh, G. R., King, F. L., Pandian, M., Subbiah, R., & Haribalaji, V. (2022). An experimental study on friction stir processing of aluminium alloy (AA-2024) and boron nitride (BNp) surface composite. *Materials Today: Proceedings, 59*(1), 1094–1099. doi:10.1016/j.matpr.2022.02.435

Boopathi, S., & Khang, A. (2023). AI-Integrated Technology for a Secure and Ethical Healthcare Ecosystem. In *AI and IoT-Based Technologies for Precision Medicine* (pp. 36–59). IGI Global. doi:10.4018/979-8-3693-0876-9.ch003

Boopathi, S., Khare, R., KG, J. C., Muni, T. V., & Khare, S. (2023). Additive Manufacturing Developments in the Medical Engineering Field. In Development, Properties, and Industrial Applications of 3D Printed Polymer Composites (pp. 86–106). IGI Global.

Boopathi, S., & Kumar, P. (2024). Advanced bioprinting processes using additive manufacturing technologies: Revolutionizing tissue engineering. *3D Printing Technologies: Digital Manufacturing, Artificial Intelligence, Industry 4.0,* 95.

Boopathi, S., Thillaivanan, A., Mohammed, A. A., Shanmugam, P., & VR, P. (2022). Experimental investigation on Abrasive Water Jet Machining of Neem Wood Plastic Composite. *IOP: Functional Composites and Structures, 4,* 025001.

Boopathi, S., Umareddy, M., & Elangovan, M. (2023). Applications of Nano-Cutting Fluids in Advanced Machining Processes. In *Sustainable Utilization of Nanoparticles and Nanofluids in Engineering Applications* (pp. 211–234). IGI Global. doi:10.4018/978-1-6684-9135-5.ch009

Bragança, S., Costa, E., Castellucci, I., & Arezes, P. M. (2019). A brief overview of the use of collaborative robots in industry 4.0: Human role and safety. *Occupational and Environmental Safety and Health*, 641–650.

Chakraborty, A., Ravi, S. P., Shamiya, Y., Cui, C., & Paul, A. (2021). Harnessing the physicochemical properties of DNA as a multifunctional biomaterial for biomedical and other applications. *Chemical Society Reviews*, *50*(13), 7779–7819. doi:10.1039/D0CS01387K PMID:34036968

Cui, Y., Qin, Z., Wu, H., Li, M., & Hu, Y. (2021). Flexible thermal interface based on self-assembled boron arsenide for high-performance thermal management. *Nature Communications*, *12*(1), 1284. doi:10.1038/s41467-021-21531-7 PMID:33627644

Du, C., Ren, Y., Qu, Z., Gao, L., Zhai, Y., Han, S.-T., & Zhou, Y. (2021). Synaptic transistors and neuromorphic systems based on carbon nano-materials. *Nanoscale*, *13*(16), 7498–7522. doi:10.1039/D1NR00148E PMID:33928966

Fowziya, S., Sivaranjani, S., Devi, N. L., Boopathi, S., Thakur, S., & Sailaja, J. M. (2023). Influences of nano-green lubricants in the friction-stir process of TiAlN coated alloys. *Materials Today: Proceedings*. Advance online publication. doi:10.1016/j.matpr.2023.06.446

Gellers, J. C. (2020). *Rights for robots: Artificial intelligence, animal and environmental law* (1st ed.). Routledge. doi:10.4324/9780429288159

Gowri, N. V., Dwivedi, J. N., Krishnaveni, K., Boopathi, S., Palaniappan, M., & Medikondu, N. R. (2023). Experimental investigation and multi-objective optimization of eco-friendly near-dry electrical discharge machining of shape memory alloy using Cu/SiC/Gr composite electrode. *Environmental Science and Pollution Research International*, *30*(49), 1–19. doi:10.1007/s11356-023-26983-6 PMID:37126160

Harikaran, M., Boopathi, S., Gokulakannan, S., & Poonguzhali, M. (2023). Study on the Source of E-Waste Management and Disposal Methods. In *Sustainable Approaches and Strategies for E-Waste Management and Utilization* (pp. 39–60). IGI Global. doi:10.4018/978-1-6684-7573-7.ch003

Harris, M., Wu, H., Zhang, W., & Angelopoulou, A. (2022). Overview of recent trends in microchannels for heat transfer and thermal management applications. *Chemical Engineering and Processing*, *181*, 109155. doi:10.1016/j.cep.2022.109155

Hassani, S. S., Daraee, M., & Sobat, Z. (2020). Advanced development in upstream of petroleum industry using nanotechnology. *Chinese Journal of Chemical Engineering*, *28*(6), 1483–1491. doi:10.1016/j.cjche.2020.02.030

He, L., Xu, J., Dekai, Z., Qinghai, Y., & Longqiu, L. (2018). Potential application of functional micro-nano structures in petroleum. *Petroleum Exploration and Development*, *45*(4), 745–753. doi:10.1016/S1876-3804(18)30077-6

Jakkula, R. V. S. K., & Sethuramalingam, P. (2023). Analysis of coatings based on carbon-based nanomaterials for paint industries-A review. *Australian Journal of Mechanical Engineering*, *21*(3), 1008–1036. doi:10.1080/14484846.2021.1938953

Javaid, M., Haleem, A., Singh, R. P., & Suman, R. (2021). Substantial capabilities of robotics in enhancing industry 4.0 implementation. *Cognitive Robotics*, *1*, 58–75. doi:10.1016/j.cogr.2021.06.001

Joe, S., Bliah, O., Magdassi, S., & Beccai, L. (2023). Jointless Bioinspired Soft Robotics by Harnessing Micro and Macroporosity. *Advancement of Science*, *10*(23), 2302080. doi:10.1002/advs.202302080 PMID:37323121

Karthik, K., Teferi, A. B., Sathish, R., Gandhi, A. M., Padhi, S., Boopathi, S., & Sasikala, G. (2023). Analysis of delamination and its effect on polymer matrix composites. *Materials Today: Proceedings*. Advance online publication. doi:10.1016/j.matpr.2023.07.199

Karthik, S., Hemalatha, R., Aruna, R., Deivakani, M., Reddy, R. V. K., & Boopathi, S. (2023). Study on Healthcare Security System-Integrated Internet of Things (IoT). In Perspectives and Considerations on the Evolution of Smart Systems (pp. 342–362). IGI Global.

Kiran, J. S., & Prabhu, S. (2020). Robot nano spray painting-A review. *IOP Conference Series. Materials Science and Engineering*, *912*(3), 032044. doi:10.1088/1757-899X/912/3/032044

Koshariya, A. K., Kalaiyarasi, D., Jovith, A. A., Sivakami, T., Hasan, D. S., & Boopathi, S. (2023). AI-Enabled IoT and WSN-Integrated Smart Agriculture System. In *Artificial Intelligence Tools and Technologies for Smart Farming and Agriculture Practices* (pp. 200–218). IGI Global. doi:10.4018/978-1-6684-8516-3.ch011

Koshariya, A. K., Khatoon, S., Marathe, A. M., Suba, G. M., Baral, D., & Boopathi, S. (2023). Agricultural Waste Management Systems Using Artificial Intelligence Techniques. In *AI-Enabled Social Robotics in Human Care Services* (pp. 236–258). IGI Global. doi:10.4018/978-1-6684-8171-4.ch009

Kumar, M. R., Reddy, V. P., Meheta, A., Dhiyani, V., Al-Saady, F. A., & Jain, A. (2023). Investigating the Effects of Process Parameters on the Size and Properties of Nano Materials. *E3S Web of Conferences*, *430*, 01125.

Maguluri, L. P., Arularasan, A., & Boopathi, S. (2023). Assessing Security Concerns for AI-Based Drones in Smart Cities. In Effective AI, Blockchain, and E-Governance Applications for Knowledge Discovery and Management (pp. 27–47). IGI Global. doi:10.4018/978-1-6684-9151-5.ch002

Maheswari, B. U., Imambi, S. S., Hasan, D., Meenakshi, S., Pratheep, V., & Boopathi, S. (2023). Internet of things and machine learning-integrated smart robotics. In Global Perspectives on Robotics and Autonomous Systems: Development and Applications (pp. 240–258). IGI Global. doi:10.4018/978-1-6684-7791-5.ch010

Malik, S., Muhammad, K., & Waheed, Y. (2023). Nanotechnology: A revolution in modern industry. *Molecules (Basel, Switzerland)*, *28*(2), 661. doi:10.3390/molecules28020661 PMID:36677717

Marinoudi, V., Sørensen, C. G., Pearson, S., & Bochtis, D. (2019). Robotics and labour in agriculture. A context consideration. *Biosystems Engineering*, *184*, 111–121. doi:10.1016/j.biosystemseng.2019.06.013

Mohanty, A., Jothi, B., Jeyasudha, J., Ranjit, P., Isaac, J. S., & Boopathi, S. (2023). Additive Manufacturing Using Robotic Programming. In *AI-Enabled Social Robotics in Human Care Services* (pp. 259–282). IGI Global. doi:10.4018/978-1-6684-8171-4.ch010

Mouchou, R., Laseinde, T., Jen, T.-C., & Ukoba, K. (2021). Developments in the Application of Nano Materials for Photovoltaic Solar Cell Design, Based on Industry 4.0 Integration Scheme. *Advances in Artificial Intelligence, Software and Systems Engineering: Proceedings of the AHFE 2021 Virtual Conferences on Human Factors in Software and Systems Engineering, Artificial Intelligence and Social Computing, and Energy,* July 25-29, 2021, USA, 510–521.

Murali, B., Padhi, S., Patil, C. K., Kumar, P. S., Santhanakrishnan, M., & Boopathi, S. (2023). Investigation on hardness and tensile strength of friction stir processing of Al6061/TiN surface composite. *Materials Today: Proceedings*.

Myilsamy, S., & Sampath, B. (2021). Experimental comparison of near-dry and cryogenically cooled near-dry machining in wire-cut electrical discharge machining processes. *Surface Topography : Metrology and Properties*, 9(3), 035015. doi:10.1088/2051-672X/ac15e0

Naveeenkumar, N., Rallapalli, S., Sasikala, K., Priya, P. V., Husain, J., & Boopathi, S. (2024). Enhancing Consumer Behavior and Experience Through AI-Driven Insights Optimization. In *AI Impacts in Digital Consumer Behavior* (pp. 1–35). IGI Global. doi:10.4018/979-8-3693-1918-5.ch001

Ness, S., Shepherd, N. J., & Xuan, T. R. (2023). Synergy Between AI and Robotics: A Comprehensive Integration. *Asian Journal of Research in Computer Science*, 16(4), 80–94. doi:10.9734/ajrcos/2023/v16i4372

Oluwasanu, A. A., Oluwaseun, F., Teslim, J. A., Isaiah, T. T., Olalekan, I. A., & Chris, O. A. (2019). Scientific applications and prospects of nanomaterials: A multidisciplinary review. *African Journal of Biotechnology*, 18(30), 946–961. doi:10.5897/AJB2019.16812

Paul, A., Thilagham, K., KG, J.-, Reddy, P. R., Sathyamurthy, R., & Boopathi, S. (2024). Multi-criteria Optimization on Friction Stir Welding of Aluminum Composite (AA5052-H32/B4C) using Titanium Nitride Coated Tool. Engineering Research Express.

Puranik, T. A., Shaik, N., Vankudoth, R., Kolhe, M. R., Yadav, N., & Boopathi, S. (2024). Study on Harmonizing Human-Robot (Drone) Collaboration: Navigating Seamless Interactions in Collaborative Environments. In Cybersecurity Issues and Challenges in the Drone Industry (pp. 1–26). IGI Global.

Rahamathunnisa, U., Subhashini, P., Aancy, H. M., Meenakshi, S., Boopathi, S., & ... (2023). Solutions for Software Requirement Risks Using Artificial Intelligence Techniques. In *Handbook of Research on Data Science and Cybersecurity Innovations in Industry 4.0 Technologies* (pp. 45–64). IGI Global.

Ramalingam, S., & Rasool Mohideen, S. (2021). Composite materials for advanced flexible link robotic manipulators: An investigation. *International Journal of Ambient Energy*, 42(14), 1670–1675. doi:10.1080/01430750.2019.1613263

Ramesh, R. D., Santhosh, A., & Syamala, S. R. N. A. (2020). Implementation of Nanotechnology in the Aerospace and Aviation Industry. In *Smart Nanotechnology with Applications* (pp. 51–69). CRC Press. doi:10.1201/9781003097532-4

Ramudu, K., Mohan, V. M., Jyothirmai, D., Prasad, D., Agrawal, R., & Boopathi, S. (2023). Machine Learning and Artificial Intelligence in Disease Prediction: Applications, Challenges, Limitations, Case Studies, and Future Directions. In Contemporary Applications of Data Fusion for Advanced Healthcare Informatics (pp. 297–318). IGI Global.

Revathi, S., Babu, M., Rajkumar, N., Meti, V. K. V., Kandavalli, S. R., & Boopathi, S. (2024). Unleashing the Future Potential of 4D Printing: Exploring Applications in Wearable Technology, Robotics, Energy, Transportation, and Fashion. In Human-Centered Approaches in Industry 5.0: Human-Machine Interaction, Virtual Reality Training, and Customer Sentiment Analysis (pp. 131–153). IGI Global.

Sampath, B., & Myilsamy, S. (2021). Experimental investigation of a cryogenically cooled oxygen-mist near-dry wire-cut electrical discharge machining process. *Stroj. Vestn. Jixie Gongcheng Xuebao*, *67*(6), 322–330.

Satav, S. D., Lamani, D., Harsha, K., Kumar, N., Manikandan, S., & Sampath, B. (2023). Energy and Battery Management in the Era of Cloud Computing: Sustainable Wireless Systems and Networks. In Sustainable Science and Intelligent Technologies for Societal Development (pp. 141–166). IGI Global.

Selvakumar, S., Adithe, S., Isaac, J. S., Pradhan, R., Venkatesh, V., & Sampath, B. (2023). A Study of the Printed Circuit Board (PCB) E-Waste Recycling Process. In Sustainable Approaches and Strategies for E-Waste Management and Utilization (pp. 159–184). IGI Global.

Selvakumar, S., Shankar, R., Ranjit, P., Bhattacharya, S., Gupta, A. S. G., & Boopathi, S. (2023). E-Waste Recovery and Utilization Processes for Mobile Phone Waste. In *Handbook of Research on Safe Disposal Methods of Municipal Solid Wastes for a Sustainable Environment* (pp. 222–240). IGI Global. doi:10.4018/978-1-6684-8117-2.ch016

Sengeni, D., Padmapriya, G., Imambi, S. S., Suganthi, D., Suri, A., & Boopathi, S. (2023). Biomedical waste handling method using artificial intelligence techniques. In *Handbook of Research on Safe Disposal Methods of Municipal Solid Wastes for a Sustainable Environment* (pp. 306–323). IGI Global. doi:10.4018/978-1-6684-8117-2.ch022

Senthil, T., Puviyarasan, M., Babu, S. R., Surakasi, R., Sampath, B., & ... (2023). Industrial Robot-Integrated Fused Deposition Modelling for the 3D Printing Process. In *Development, Properties, and Industrial Applications of 3D Printed Polymer Composites* (pp. 188–210). IGI Global.

Sevinchan, E., Dincer, I., & Lang, H. (2018). A review on thermal management methods for robots. *Applied Thermal Engineering*, *140*, 799–813. doi:10.1016/j.applthermaleng.2018.04.132

Sharmin, I. (2020). *Preparation and evaluation of carbon nano tube based nanofluid in milling alloy steel*. Academic Press.

Sheikh, J. A., Waheed, M. F., Khalid, A. M., & Qureshi, I. A. (2020). Use of 3D printing and nano materials in fashion: From revolution to evolution. *Advances in Design for Inclusion: Proceedings of the AHFE 2019 International Conference on Design for Inclusion and the AHFE 2019 International Conference on Human Factors for Apparel and Textile Engineering*, July 24-28, 2019, Washington DC, USA *10*, 422–429.

Singh, K., Sharma, S., Shriwastava, S., Singla, P., Gupta, M., & Tripathi, C. (2021). Significance of nano-materials, designs consideration and fabrication techniques on performances of strain sensors-A review. *Materials Science in Semiconductor Processing*, *123*, 105581. doi:10.1016/j.mssp.2020.105581

Srinivas, B., Maguluri, L. P., Naidu, K. V., Reddy, L. C. S., Deivakani, M., & Boopathi, S. (2023). Architecture and Framework for Interfacing Cloud-Enabled Robots. In *Handbook of Research on Data Science and Cybersecurity Innovations in Industry 4.0 Technologies* (pp. 542–560). IGI Global. doi:10.4018/978-1-6684-8145-5.ch027

Syamala, M., Komala, C., Pramila, P., Dash, S., Meenakshi, S., & Boopathi, S. (2023). Machine Learning-Integrated IoT-Based Smart Home Energy Management System. In *Handbook of Research on Deep Learning Techniques for Cloud-Based Industrial IoT* (pp. 219–235). IGI Global. doi:10.4018/978-1-6684-8098-4.ch013

Vijayakumar, G. N. S., Domakonda, V. K., Farooq, S., Kumar, B. S., Pradeep, N., & Boopathi, S. (2024). Sustainable Developments in Nano-Fluid Synthesis for Various Industrial Applications. In Adoption and Use of Technology Tools and Services by Economically Disadvantaged Communities: Implications for Growth and Sustainability (pp. 48–81). IGI Global.

Zekrifa, D. M. S., Kulkarni, M., Bhagyalakshmi, A., Devireddy, N., Gupta, S., & Boopathi, S. (2023). Integrating Machine Learning and AI for Improved Hydrological Modeling and Water Resource Management. In *Artificial Intelligence Applications in Water Treatment and Water Resource Management* (pp. 46–70). IGI Global. doi:10.4018/978-1-6684-6791-6.ch003

Chapter 13
Predictive Modelling for Employee Retention:
A Three-Tier Machine Learning Approach With oneAPI

Ahamed Thaiyub
KPR Institute of Engineering and Technology, India

Shriram Kris Vasudevan
Intel Corporation, India

Akshay Bhuvaneswari Ramakrishnan
https://orcid.org/0009-0000-1578-0984
SASTRA University, India

T. S. Murugesh
Government College of Engineering, Srirangam, India

Sini Raj Pulari
Bahrain Polytechnic, Bahrain

ABSTRACT

Organizations face enormous issues when it comes to employee turnover, which is why they need to develop accurate predictive models for retention. The purpose of this chapter is to present a three-tiered machine learning approach for predicting employee turnover that makes use of resume parsing, performance analysis, and advanced algorithms. In addition, the authors make use of Intel oneAPI, which is a unified programming model that is increasingly becoming the industry standard, in order to improve the scalability and performance of the solution. The system that is offered delivers full HR (human resource) analytics, which enables firms to make educated decisions regarding recruiting and retention tactics. The results of the experimental evaluation show that the solution is effective in providing an accurate forecast of attrition, which paves the way for proactive retention measures. The approach enhances system performance by utilizing oneAPI, which in turn ensures that it is scalable over a variety of different hardware architectures.

DOI: 10.4018/979-8-3693-5767-5.ch013

1. INTRODUCTION

The loss of employees results in significant financial expenses and impedes the smooth running of business operations, making it a significant worry for businesses all over the world. It is of the utmost importance for businesses that are interested in retaining key personnel and lowering the costs associated with turnover to have the ability to both predict and manage employee turnover (Jarrahi, 2018; Vardarlier & Zafer, 2020). This study provides a three-tier machine learning (ML) method to handle this difficulty. The solution makes use of advanced algorithms and predictive analytics to accurately forecast staff turnover. The three-tiered solution includes resume parsing, a review of employee performance, and a prediction of future attrition. In the initial level of the selection process, procedures for "resume parsing" are utilized in order to extract pertinent information from candidate resumes. This information includes skills, experience, and education. The second level does an analysis of past employee performance data, taking into consideration a variety of indicators and characteristics such as attendance records. The third layer makes use of advanced machine learning techniques to make predictions about future attrition based on the data that has been acquired. These algorithms include Gradient Boosting, Logit, KNN, Sequential, and XGBoost. The integration of these three tiers enables firms to make educated decisions regarding staff recruitment and retention. A full HR analytics platform is provided by the system, which helps in proactively detecting attrition concerns and putting targeted retention initiatives into action. This strategy ultimately assists companies in cutting the costs associated with employee turnover, keeping valuable people as staff, and preserving a stable and productive workforce. In this article, we go further into the specifics of the three-tiered machine learning solution, examining the methodology, data collecting, and pre-processing processes along the way. We discuss the outcomes of the experiment as well as the analysis conducted to demonstrate how accurate the proposed solution is in forecasting employee turnover. In addition, we address the benefits and implications of deploying such a solution in the real-world organizational settings, which will provide HR professionals and decision-makers with information that can help them improve their employee retention efforts.

2. LITERATURE REVIEW

Fallucchi et al. (2020) have recognized the primary contributors to the turnover rate of employees and proposed a real classification based on the statistical examination of the data collected. The Gaussian Nave Bayes classifier was seen as the algorithm that generated the best results for the specific dataset used. It suggested the best recall rate, a metric measuring a classifier's ability to find all of the positive events, and it attained an overall false negative rate that was equivalent to 4.5% of the total measurements. These are the two metrics which assessed a classifier's ability to find all of the positive instances. Researchers in Raza et al. (2022) have attempted to forecast employee turnover by employing ETC (Extra Trees Classifier), SVM (Support Vector Machine), LR (Logistic Regression), and DTC (Decision Tree Classifier), which are the four sophisticated machine learning algorithms. Using dataset 10folds, the applied machine learning methods have achieved an accuracy score of 88% in SVM, 74% in the LR technique, 84% in the DTC method and 93% with the proposed method. In the work Najafi-Zangeneh et al. (2021), a thorough comparison of the outcomes with the existing approaches was carried out. The comparison demonstrates that the proposed feature selection improves the predictor's overall performance. This study proposed a three-stage, pre-processing, processing, and post-processing framework for creating an accurate employee attrition prediction model and for corroborating the validity of the model's parameters. The binary and continuous feature sets were selected using the max-out feature selection approach. This method was applied to the set of feature sets. The objective of the researchers in Pratt et al. (2021) was to provide a comparison of several machine learning approaches in order to make an estimate of employees who are likely to leave their firm. In this paper, a total of six different ML algorithms were utilized. According to the findings of the work, the Random Forest method displayed the best ability to estimate the attrition rate of employees. The most accurate prediction was made with a score of 85.12, which was considered to be a good accuracy.

3. METHODOLOGY

The methodology that we propose contains three stages: the first one is "resume parsing" the second one "employee performance analysis," and the third is "future attrition prediction." We make use of a total of five distinct machine learning models. This section offers a comprehensive explanation of each tier, including the methods involved in data collection and pre-processing as well as the models that are implemented is as shown in Figure 1.

3.1 The Three-Tier Architecture

In this study, a three-tier machine learning approach is provided as depicted in Fig 2, which includes resume parsing, employee performance analysis, and attrition prediction in the future. In the overall architecture, each tier is essential to the correct prediction of staff attrition and the facilitation of well-informed decisions for retention tactics.

Tier 1: Parsing Resumes

The first tier is on employing sophisticated parsing techniques to obtain pertinent data from candidate resumes. The textual content of resumes is analyzed using Natural Language Processing (NLP) algorithms, allowing the extraction of crucial details that includes abilities, experience, education, and certifications. These extracted qualities offer a thorough overview of candidate qualifications and potential, serving as useful inputs for the following tiers.

Tier 2: Employee Performance Analysis

In the second stage, historical employee performance data are analyzed to find the trends and warning signs of attrition risks. Numerous criteria are taken into account, including attendance records, productivity levels, performance evaluations, and more pertinent elements unique to the firm. The performance data is analyzed and modelled using statistical and machine learning approaches, which reveals correlations and trends that might help forecast attrition.

Figure 1. Methodology flow

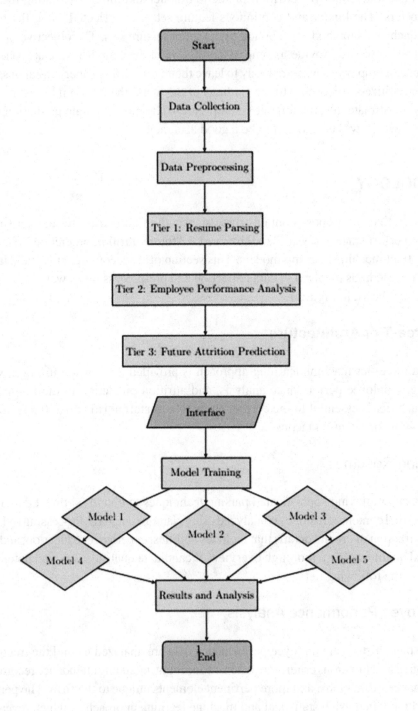

Tier 3: Prediction of Future Attrition

Based on the data obtained from the previous layers, the third and final tier aims to forecast future attrition. Predictive models are created using cutting-edge machine learning techniques including Gradient

Boosting, Logit (logistic regression), KNN (K-Nearest Neighbor), Sequential, and XGBoost. These models take into account the insights obtained from employee performance analysis as well as the features acquired from resume parsing. The solution forecasts the probability that a worker would leave the company in the future using historical data and sophisticated algorithms.

Figure 2. The three-tier architecture

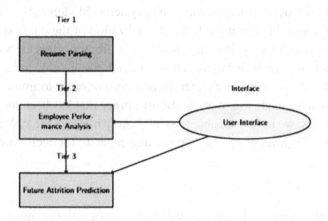

3.2 Data Collection

During the phase of data gathering, we extract essential information from GitHub repositories in order to construct a complete dataset for the prediction of employee turnover. GitHub is an outstanding platform that provides access to a wealth of useful information, such as code repositories, commit histories, issue tracking, and activities involving collaborative efforts.

3.3 Data Pre-Processing

Data pre-processing is a key part of our method because it changes the collected data and gets it ready for analysis and model building. It requires cleaning the data to deal with missing numbers, outliers, and duplicates, making sure that the data is correct. Techniques for selecting the most important traits are used to reduce the number of dimensions. To improve the performance of a model, feature engineering includes changing and making new features, like encoding categorical variables and scaling numerical features. Before information is taken from the resumes, a number of steps are taken to make sure the data is in a format that can be used for analysis. First, the necessary tools are brought in. These include NLTK (Natural Language Toolkit), spaCy, pyresparser, and pandas. Then, the Resume Parser class from pyresparser is used to read and pull out the data from the resume. The important information from the resumes is extracted from the parsed data, which is then saved to a file called "resume.txt" using the open() function. This step makes it possible to do more work and research. Also, skills are taken from the resume info that has been parsed. A CSV file called "skills.csv" stores a list of skills that has already been set up. The list of skills is read from the CSV file by the code. The application data that has been parsed is then looked over, and any skills that are found are added to a skill_list. These steps make sure that the data from the resumes is well organized and ready to be analyzed and modelled.

3.4 Optimization With oneAPI

In order to optimize and increase the performance of our staff retention system, we have taken benefit of the capabilities offered by oneAPI (Intel, n.d.). Intel's oneAPI is a unified programming model which allows efficient execution across a variety of computing systems. Models such as logit, KNN, and gradient boosting are among those that benefited from our utilization of the oneDAL library, which is part of the oneAPI Data Analytics Library. Because the oneDAL library offers algorithms and methods for data analytics activities that have been extensively optimized, we are able to handle and analyze massive amounts of data in a more efficient manner. In addition, in order to improve the functionality of the XGBoost model, we have made use of an XGBoost library that has been tuned for the oneAPI. By utilizing these technologies, we have been able to significantly improve the system that we use to retain our employees in terms of its level of efficacy, speed, and capacity for decision-making.

3.5 Models

In the Models component of our three-tier design, we make use of a variety of machine learning techniques to forecast employee attrition. We use a total of five distinct models, namely Gradient Boosting, Logit, K-Nearest Neighbors, Sequential, and XGBoost. Each of these models is distinguished by a distinct set of qualities and advantages.

3.5.1 Gradient Boosting

The concept of boosting is rethought by gradient boosting, which recasts it as a numerical optimization problem with the goal of reducing the loss value of the model through the addition of base learners through the use of gradient descent (Bentéjac et al., 2021; Johnson et al., 2017). The process of obtaining a local estimate of a variational function using an incremental optimization procedure of the first degree is called gradient descent. The idea behind the gradient boosting approach is to use the pattern in the residuals to strengthen a poor forecasting model as much as possible until the residuals are arbitrarily (or possibly random normally) distributed. This is the goal of the algorithm. It consists mostly of the following three stages:

1. A measure of loss that needs to be optimised.
2. An unreliable learner when it comes to making predictions.
3. An incremental model in which weaker learners are added in order to reduce the magnitude of the error function.

3.5.2 Logistic Regression

Logistic regression is a popular technique that can be utilised to predict the chance that a given occurrence corresponds to a specific class. If the predicted probability of an occurrence is higher than fifty percent, then the model suggests that the instance is a member of category 1, and if it is less than fifty percent, then it suggests that the occurrence is not a member of class 1 (Marvin et al., 2021; Midi et al., 2010). This transforms it into a two-way classifier. Analysts devised the logistic function, which is also known as the sigmoid function, in order to characterise the qualities of demographic increase in ecology. These properties include rising swiftly and reaching their maximum at the carrying capacity of the ecosystem. It is an S-shaped arc which can translate any real-valued integer into a value ranging from 0 to 1, but just not directly at those boundaries. It might take any integer and map it to one of those values. Natural logarithms use e as their base, and the quantity X that you want to modify using the logistic function is what you pass into the function.

3.5.3 K-Nearest Neighbors

The K-Nearest Neighbors approach is considered to be a supervised kind of machine learning because the goal variable for the task at hand is already known. A non-parametric method is one that would not establish any assumptions about the input distribution structure that lies under the surface. K is a number that is used to determine neighbouring data points that are comparable to the new information point. It does a head count of how many data items fall under each category across the k surrounding neighbours. The newly added data item will be assigned to the class which contains the most neighbouring points. The Euclidean distance between two clusters is determined by taking the square root of the total of the squared distances between those two points. This determines the length among two neighbours (Chowdhury et al., 2022; Madeti & Singh, 2018). The L2 norm is another name for this concept.

3.5.4 Sequential

The sequential model allows for the input of a list that specifies the different layers that make up the neural network's architecture as illustrated in Fig 3. The data moves in a linear fashion from one layer to the next until it reaches the output layer at the very end. When building a neural network, the input layer is the very first layer to be added. It is not difficult at all when using keras (Gulli & Pal, 2017; Hutter et al., 2011). We begin by generating a layer consisting of 256 neurons, activated by ReLU, with an input size of 4. When compared to the other layers, the output layer depicted in equation (1) is distinguished by the requirement that it accurately reflect the quantity of values that are desired to be produced by the neural network.

$$X = f\_n(f\_{n-1}(...f\_2(f\_1(Input))...)) \tag{1}$$

3.5.5 XGBoost

Extreme Gradient Boosting, often known as XGBoost, is a technique that can assist tree-boosting algorithms in making the most of the available memory and hardware resources. It has the advantages of improving algorithms and fine-tuning models, and it can also be implemented in computing environments (Lee et al., 2021; Li et al., 2020). Gradient boosting, regularized boosting, and stochastic boosting are the three primary types of gradient boosting, and XGBoost is capable of implementing all of them. In addition to that, it enables the inclusion of regularization parameters as well as the adjustment of those parameters, setting it apart from other libraries. During development of XGBoost, both extensive considerations in terms of system optimization and fundamentals of machine learning are taken into account.

Figure 3. Sequential model architecture

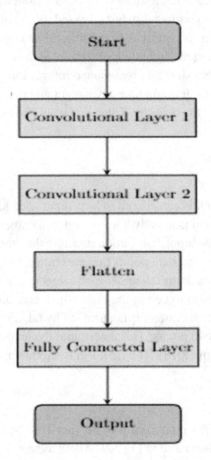

4. RESULTS AND DISCUSSION

The accuracy of the logistic regression model is obtained as 82.45%, which is considered to be a reasonable level of prediction performance. The KNN model is seen to achieve an accuracy of 76.87%, which, despite being significantly lower than the accuracy achieved by logistic regression, is still indicative of satisfactory outcomes. The gradient boosting model attains an accuracy of 72.45%, which indicates that there is room for improvement or that hyper parameters need fine-tuning. On the other hand, the sequential model displays an accuracy that is substantially higher than 95%. This hints that the sequential design, with its layered structure and capability of capturing hierarchical representations, is a good choice for the task of retaining employees. Because of its higher performance, the sequential model demonstrates its capacity to learn intricate patterns and relationships in the data, which ultimately leads to more accurate predictions. In addition, the XGBoost model produces the results with the best accuracy, which is 96.06%. We are able to improve the performance of the XGBoost model by applying the optimized XGBoost library, which results in the XGBoost model being an outstanding option for the employee retention system as indicated in Table. 1. The outstanding predictive capability of the XGBoost algorithm is contributed to by the fact that it could handle complicated relationships and make use of approaches involving boosting. To conclude, in terms of accuracy, the sequential and XGBoost models perform better than the KNN model, the logistic regression model, and the gradient boosting model. Fig 4 shows a comparison between all the models used. These findings highlight how important it is to select the suitable model and make use of optimized libraries in order to attain excellent performance in employee retention systems. The whole system is also hosted as an interface as seen in Fig 5.

Table 1. Accuracy of different models

S:No	Models	Validation Accuracy
1	XGBoost	96.06%
2	Sequential	95.00%
3	Gradient Boosting	72.45%
4	KNN	76.87%
5	Logistic Regression	82.45%

Figure 4. Accuracy comparison of the models used

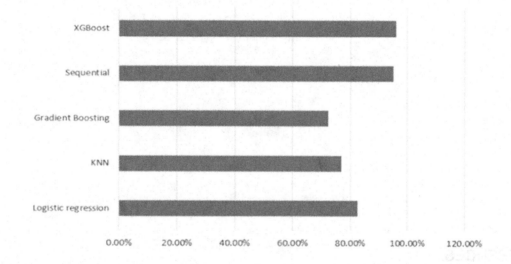

4.1 Directions for Future Works

Our approach for retaining employees has room for improvement in the future, and those improvements can partake a few different forms. To begin, we have the option of investigating additional features or data sources to enhance the strength of prediction. These can include things like employee satisfaction surveys or external economic indicators. Second, there is a possibility of implementing model ensemble techniques, which involve pooling the predictions of numerous models in order to improve the overall performance. Thirdly, improving the results of already-existing models by fine-tuning the hyper parameters of those models using methods such as grid search or Bayesian optimization can produce superior results. In addition, utilizing time-series analysis techniques can allow for the identification of temporal patterns as well as the relationships in the data pertaining to employee retention. By concentrating on these aspects, we can possibly continue to enhance the accuracy, interpretability, and efficiency of our employee retention system, which will be of use to enterprises in reducing the risks associated with employee turnover.

Figure 5. System interface

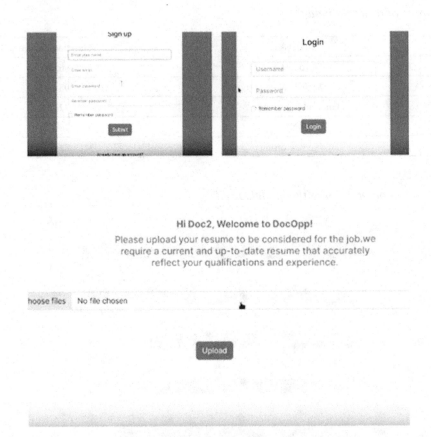

REFERENCES

Bentéjac, C., Csörgő, A., & Martínez-Muñoz, G. (2021). A comparative analysis of gradient boosting algorithms. *Artificial Intelligence Review*, *54*(3), 1937–1967. doi:10.1007/s10462-020-09896-5

Chowdhury, A. H., Malakar, S., Seal, D. B., & Goswami, S. (2022). Understanding employee attrition using machine learning techniques. In *Data Management, Analytics and Innovation: Proceedings of ICDMAI 2021,* Volume 2 (pp. 101-109). Springer Singapore. 10.1007/978-981-16-2937-2_8

Fallucchi, F., Coladangelo, M., Giuliano, R., & William De Luca, E. (2020). Predicting employee attrition using machine learning techniques. *Computers*, *9*(4), 86. doi:10.3390/computers9040086

Gulli, A., & Pal, S. (2017). *Deep learning with Keras*. Packt Publishing Ltd.

Hutter, F., Hoos, H. H., & Leyton-Brown, K. (2011). Sequential model-based optimization for general algorithm configuration. In *Learning and Intelligent Optimization: 5th International Conference, LION 5, Rome, Italy, January 17-21, 2011. Selected Papers 5* (pp. 507-523). Springer Berlin Heidelberg. 10.1007/978-3-642-25566-3_40

Intel. (n.d.). https://www.intel.com/content/www/us/en/developer/tools/oneapi/overview.html

Jarrahi, M. H. (2018). Artificial intelligence and the future of work: Human-AI symbiosis in organizational decision making. *Business Horizons*, *61*(4), 577–586. doi:10.1016/j.bushor.2018.03.007

Johnson, N. E., Ianiuk, O., Cazap, D., Liu, L., Starobin, D., Dobler, G., & Ghandehari, M. (2017). Patterns of waste generation: A gradient boosting model for short-term waste prediction in New York City. *Waste Management (New York, N.Y.)*, *62*, 3–11. doi:10.1016/j.wasman.2017.01.037 PMID:28216080

Lee, J. J., Lee, Y. R., Lim, D. H., & Ahn, H. C. (2021). A Study on the Employee Turnover Prediction using XGBoost and SHAP. *Journal of Information Systems*, *30*(4), 21–42.

Li, H., Cao, Y., Li, S., Zhao, J., & Sun, Y. (2020). XGBoost model and its application to personal credit evaluation. *IEEE Intelligent Systems*, *35*(3), 52–61. doi:10.1109/MIS.2020.2972533

Madeti, S. R., & Singh, S. N. (2018). Modeling of PV system based on experimental data for fault detection using kNN method. *Solar Energy*, *173*, 139–151. doi:10.1016/j.solener.2018.07.038

Marvin, G., Jackson, M., & Alam, M. G. R. (2021, August). A machine learning approach for employee retention prediction. In *2021 IEEE Region 10 Symposium (TENSYMP)* (pp. 1-8). IEEE. 10.1109/TENSYMP52854.2021.9550921

Midi, H., Sarkar, S. K., & Rana, S. (2010). Collinearity diagnostics of binary logistic regression model. *Journal of Interdisciplinary Mathematics*, *13*(3), 253–267. doi:10.1080/09720502.2010.10700699

Najafi-Zangeneh, S., Shams-Gharneh, N., Arjomandi-Nezhad, A., & Hashemkhani Zolfani, S. (2021). An Improved Machine Learning-Based Employees Attrition Prediction Framework with Emphasis on Feature Selection. *Mathematics*, *9*(11), 1226. doi:10.3390/math9111226

Pratt, M., Boudhane, M., & Cakula, S. (2021). Employee attrition estimation using random forest algorithm. *Baltic Journal of Modern Computing*, *9*(1), 49–66. doi:10.22364/bjmc.2021.9.1.04

Raza, A., Munir, K., Almutairi, M., Younas, F., & Fareed, M. M. S. (2022). Predicting Employee Attrition Using Machine Learning Approaches. *Applied Sciences (Basel, Switzerland)*, *12*(13), 6424. doi:10.3390/app12136424

Vardarlier, P., & Zafer, C. (2020). Use of artificial intelligence as business strategy in recruitment process and social perspective. *Digital Business Strategies in Blockchain Ecosystems: Transformational Design and Future of Global Business*, 355-373.

Chapter 14
Research Analysis of Data Exploration and Visualization Dashboard Using Data Science

D. Faridha Banu

Sri Eshwar College of Engineering, Coimbatore, India

C. Keerthi Prashanth

Sri Eshwar College of Engineering, Coimbatore, India

P. T. Kousalya

Sri Eshwar College of Engineering, Coimbatore, India

P. Madhumohan

Sri Eshwar College of Engineering, Coimbatore, India

Kavin Varsha

Sri Eshwar College of Engineering, Coimbatore, India

S. Meivel

(iD) https://orcid.org/0000-0002-8717-3881

M. Kumarasamy College of Engineering, Karur, India

ABSTRACT

Any attempt to explain the relevance of data by putting it in a visual context is referred to as data visualization. With the aid of data visualization software, patterns, trends, and correlations that could go unnoticed in text-based data can be exposed and identified more easily. The graphical presentation of quantitative information is known as data visualization. In other words, data visualizations convert big and small data sets into pictures that the human brain can comprehend and digest more readily. In our daily lives, data visualizations are surprisingly prevalent, yet they frequently take the shape of recognizable charts and graphs. It can be applied to find unknown trends and facts. When communication, data science, and design come together, good data visualizations are produced. When done well, data visualizations provide important insights into complex data sets in clear, understandable ways. The authors talk about data visualization, its significance, tools for data visualization, etc. in this chapter.

DOI: 10.4018/979-8-3693-5767-5.ch014

I. INTRODUCTION

Organizations are adopting data visualizations and data technologies to improve their queries and decisions more than ever before. Making better data-driven business decisions has never been easier thanks to developing computer technologies and new, user-friendly software programs (Aparicio & Costa, 2014). Compared to pictures, complicated data is far more difficult for human brains to comprehend when it is stored in numbers and text. Utilizing dataviz approaches, one can convey vast volumes of information in the most effective, visual way possible (Friedman, 2008) (Tukey, 1977). In reality, data that is presented visually is simpler to interpret and evaluate, allowing decision-makers to uncover patterns including new and hidden ones and comprehend even complex ideas more quickly. Data visualization tools like as charts, graphs, maps, and dashboards can be useful in a variety of ways, including identifying problems and inadequacies, selecting the best approach for a product or business operation, predicting sales volume and stock prices, optimizing project management and resource allocation, and many other things. No matter how much data you have, using sophisticated analysis and clear visualizations is one of the greatest ways to identify significant links. The capacity to explore, analyze, and visualize data efficiently is crucial in the age of data-driven decision-making. The Data Exploration and Visualization Dashboard project is an innovative approach created to give users the means to extract useful information from their datasets. Due to the constantly increasing volume of data, this dashboard acts as a portal for both inexperienced and seasoned data aficionados to easily upload, explore, and alter data before turning it into useful visual representations. This project offers users an interactive environment that streamlines data exploration, promotes informed decision-making, and enables a deeper understanding of underlying trends by integrating powerful Python libraries like Pandas, NumPy, Matplotlib, Plotly, Seaborn, and Streamlit. This study examines how the Data Exploration and Visualization Dashboard was developed, its features, and its results, demonstrating how its user-friendly interface closes the gap between data and insights.

II. DATA VISUALIZATION WORKING METHOD

The majority of data visualization tools available today have connectors to widely used data sources, such as Hadoop, the most popular relational databases, and a number of cloud storage platforms. These sources' data are retrieved by the visualization program, which then applies a graphic style to the data. A designer's job is greatly facilitated by automating the process of constructing a visualization, at least in part, when working with data sets that contain hundreds of thousands or millions of data points (Friendly, 2017). Though increasingly technologies automates this process, data visualization software still lets the user choose the best manner to present the data. Some technologies automatically analyze the data's form, find correlations between particular variables, and then insert these findings into the appropriate chart type, as determined by the software (DATA VISUALIZATION FOR HUMAN PERCEPTION). The dashboard feature of data visualization software typically enables users to combine many analysis' visuals into a single interface, which is typically a web portal. A graphical and visual representation of information is a dashboard. Initially, a dashboard was intended to help technology managers of organizations plan, build, execute, and direct applications in real-time while also keeping track of the information that is working. Dashboards are a popular tool for monitoring and analyzing corporate operations nowadays. Your "span of control" over a large amount of business data is improved by cognitive tools

207

like dashboards and visualization. These instruments aid in the visual identification of trends, patterns, and anomalies. They assist people in making sense of what they perceive and direct them toward wise choices. Therefore, these tools must take advantage of users' visual talents. The importance of visual information design has increased due to the prominence of dashboards and the ease with which business users can now review their data .

III. DATA VISUALIZATION LIBRARIES: MATPLOTLIB, PLOTLY, AND SEABORN

The selection of data visualization libraries is essential for a project's success in producing smart and useful representations. The Matplotlib, Plotly, and Seaborn packages are three that are frequently used for data visualization in Python. These libraries are useful resources for various areas of data visualization because each one has particular advantages and use cases. Matplotlib, Plotly, and Seaborn together gave the project the power to produce a wide variety of interactive visualizations. Matplotlib's versatility made it possible to create conventional plots, and Plotly's interactive graphs improved the user experience. The stylistic improvements made by Seaborn improved the outputs of the dashboard. One of the most popular and functional data visualization libraries in Python is Matplotlib. It offers a complete set of tools for producing static charts and figures of publication-caliber. Matplotlib may be used to create a broad variety of visualizations, from straightforward line charts and scatter plots to intricate heatmaps and three-dimensional graphs. It is frequently used for static data visualizations and exploratory data analysis (EDA). Because Matplotlib provides fine-grained control over plot components, users can alter every piece of the visualization. It has a wide range of customization options and is compatible with other libraries.

A strong library for building web-based and interactive data visualizations is Plotly. Building interactive dashboards and web apps is where it shines the most. Plotly excels at producing interactive charts, maps, and dashboards that are dynamic and dynamic. It can be used to create interactive web applications that let users examine data. Plotly creates interactive visuals that are simple to include in online programs. There are many other chart kinds and customization choices available. Python and JavaScript are only two of the many programming languages for which Plotly supports APIs. A high-level data visualization library based on Matplotlib is called Seaborn. It is intended to make it simpler to create visually appealing statistics visuals. For making statistical visualizations like distribution plots, pair plots, and heatmaps, Seaborn is extremely helpful. It is frequently used in data analysis and statistical modeling because it is excellent at displaying relationships between variables. Seaborn offers a high-level interface for writing little to no code while producing complex visuals. It has pre-installed color schemes and themes for visually appealing visualizations. Seaborn works well with Pandas DataFrames as well.

IV. STREAMLIT FRAMEWORK

An open-source Python framework called Streamlit makes it easier to build web applications for data science and visualization projects. Data professionals may quickly and easily convert data scripts into interactive web apps because to its straightforward architecture. The dashboard's user interface was developed with the primary help of Streamlit. Its ease of use and ability to convert data scripts into shareable web applications sped up the dashboard deployment process. User engagement was enabled using Streamlit, enabling for fluid exploration of data and visuals.

V. PANDAS AND NUMPY LIBRARIES

For data handling and mathematical computations, Pandas and NumPy have become essential tools. I successfully organized and worked with the data by utilizing the features of Pandas' DataFrame. Advanced numerical operations were made easier by NumPy, which also provided the structural support for data conversions and statistical calculations. Each of these tools helped students gain a more comprehensive understanding of data manipulation, analysis, and visualization approaches. Additionally, their integration demonstrated how well they worked together, creating a thorough and user-focused Data Exploration and Visualization Dashboard.

VI. ANALYSIS

1. Product Definition

The Data Exploration and Visualization Dashboard project's core objective is to meet the urgent demand for an interactive platform that makes effective data exploration and visualization possible. The project's goal is to develop a user-friendly web application that will enable users to easily upload datasets, receive insights from a variety of visualizations, apply filters, and even alter data without having to have a deep understanding of coding. The key goal is to create a link between data and insights so that decision-makers, analysts, and domain experts may interact with data in a way that promotes quick decision-making and better understanding.

2. Feasibility Analysis

The availability of sophisticated Python modules, which allow for smooth data handling, manipulation, and display, supports the viability of the Data Exploration and display Dashboard project. Pandas, NumPy, Matplotlib, Plotly, Seaborn, and Streamlit integration creates a solid basis for the project's growth. These reputable libraries provide thorough functionality for data analysis and visualization, guaranteeing that the project may successfully achieve its goals. The project's breadth also fits with Streamlit's capabilities, an approachable framework that turns data scripts into web apps. The popularity of data-driven decision-making across numerous industries, which emphasizes the need for easily available data exploration tools, further supports the project's viability.

VII. SOFTWARE REQUIREMENTS

The successful implementation of the Data Exploration and Visualization Dashboard project relies on a comprehensive understanding of the software requirements. This analysis outlines the key components and specifications that the project must adhere to:

1. User Interface

Users should be able to upload datasets in a number of different formats, including CSV and Excel, using the dashboard's straightforward and user-friendly interface. To access data summaries, fundamental statistics, visualizations, data filtering, and modification features, the interface should provide simple 10 navigation. The user interface (UI) should prominently display an easy-to-use data upload button that enables users to pick and upload datasets. In order to provide a smooth import procedure, it should also feature built-in techniques to handle popular data formats like CSV and Excel. Users should be guided through numerous data exploration and visualization tools via the dashboard's clear and organized navigation menu. Users should be able to create and alter several chart kinds, such as bar charts, scatter plots, and histograms, in the dashboard's visualization area. Users should be able to interactively add filters to the dataset using the interface to promote data exploration. By concentrating on particular data subsets, users can improve their analysis and visualization.

2. Data Handling and Manipulation

The project must effectively utilize the Pandas and NumPy libraries for data manipulation. It should provide functionalities to filter data based on numerical ranges and categorical values, as well as the option to add and remove columns seamlessly. The project utilizes the extensive data manipulation and numerical computation capabilities of the Pandas and NumPy libraries through seamless integration. Users can work with datasets effectively thanks to this integration, which makes use of NumPy arrays and Pandas DataFrames. Data may be readily filtered by numerical ranges for users. Users should be able to enter minimum and maximum values for particular numerical columns via input forms on the interface. The data is then appropriately filtered by the system, which only shows the records that satisfy the given requirements. Users should have the option to filter data for categorical data based on particular categorical values or categories. By using user-defined criteria, this functionality streamlines the process of segmenting and evaluating data subsets. The project gives users the ability to clean, modify, and prepare their data for insightful analysis and visualization, ultimately boosting their data exploration experience. This is accomplished by successfully utilizing Pandas and NumPy for data handling and manipulation.

A) Visualization Capabilities

Multiple visualization formats, such as histograms, line charts, scatter plots, bar charts, and pie charts, should be supported by the dashboard. Users should have the ability to examine data patterns dynamically thanks to the seamless integration of the Matplotlib, Plotly, and Seaborn libraries. In order to provide both static and interactive visualizations, the project incorporates Matplotlib, a flexible and well-liked Python charting package. Users can access interactive, web-based visualizations thanks to Plotly. It makes it possible to zoom, pan, hover, and do other things. The quality and selection of accessible plots are improved thanks to Seaborn, which is renowned for its beautiful and instructive statistical visualizations. To see how the distribution of numerical data is distributed, users can generate histograms. The dashboard ought to support customizing the histogram's properties, including bin sizes. The visualization of trends and patterns in time series or sequential data is best accomplished with line charts. Multiple lines can be plotted by users for comparison. Comparing categorical data is effectively done with bar charts. In addition to choosing between vertical and horizontal bars, users can change the labels' colors.

Pie charts are great for showing how something is put together as a whole. Users should have access to interactive zoom and pan features for large datasets so they may concentrate on particular data subsets. To filter the dataset or get more information, users can choose data points in scatter plots or bar charts. For greater context and interpretation, users of the dashboard can add axis labels, titles, and legends to their visualizations. For greater context and interpretation, users of the dashboard can add axis labels, titles, and legends to their visualizations.

B) Real-Time Interactivity

The Streamlit framework should be used for the project to provide real-time interactivity. Without requiring page reloads, users should be able to interact with visualizations, use filters, and see immediate updates. The project is based on the Streamlit framework, a Python toolkit made for quickly and easily building interactive web applications. Data exploration and visualization are made very responsive and dynamic thanks to Streamlit's integration, making it suitable for both technical and non-technical users. The project's generated visualizations are by nature dynamic and interactive. To get more information, users can zoom, pan, and hover over data points. Users can quickly switch between various chart kinds or setups thanks to real-time interactivity. With the help of the Streamlit framework, users can easily interact with the data and visualizations thanks to a number of widgets including sliders, buttons, text inputs, and choose boxes. Changes are made instantly as users engage with the dashboard, whether by applying filters, changing the data, or choosing data points. Users can now view the results of their activities in real time. For instance, changing the filter range on a histogram immediately changes the plot, enabling users to explore various elements of the data in real-time. The lack of page reloads in Streamlit is a key benefit of real-time engagement. Users can continuously examine data and visualize trends, improving workflow effectiveness and user experience.

C) Data Export and Saving

The capability to save processed data in CSV format must be offered by the dashboard. Users should also be able to download the raw data for additional research and save visualizations as image files. The processed and changed data can be readily exported in CSV format by users. For users who want to save their cleaned and modified datasets for use in outside programs or for sharing with coworkers, this functionality is essential. A clear button or option to start the CSV export should be provided in the export procedure. The export and save options are user-configurable. For stored visualizations, they can select the resolution, file type, and file name. Users can choose several CSV file delimiter options to match the specifications of their analysis tools when exporting data. Users can keep a record of their data changes and analyses by using the versioning or timestamping options the dashboard may implement for data exports.

D) Compatibility and Deployment

The project ought to work with a variety of browsers and operating systems. Users should be able to access it using web browsers as an independent web application that may be deployed. The project's platform independence ensures interoperability with well-known operating systems including Windows, macOS, and Linux. Regardless of the OS they want, users can access the dashboard. The user interface and capabilities have undergone extensive testing and optimization for cross-browser compatibility. This includes, but is not limited to, Safari, Opera, Microsoft Edge, Mozilla Firefox, and Google Chrome. Different browser versions should be taken into consideration during compatibility testing to guarantee a consistent user experience. The project can be used to deploy a standalone web application that is hosted on a web server and reachable by a URL. Users are not required to locally install any dependencies or software. The program hosting on a web server should be done according to simple deployment instructions.

E) Security and Privacy

Data security and privacy must be given top priority in the dashboard, ensuring that uploaded datasets are handled securely. Additionally, it must to provide options for erasing user inputs and private data after use. The Data Exploration and Visualization Dashboard project can be created to effectively satisfy the expectations and needs of its consumers by considering these software requirements. User data and uploaded datasets are safely saved on the server. Access control and encryption at rest are just two examples of appropriate safeguards that are used to protect data privacy and integrity. The dashboard's user access is restricted via procedures for authentication and authorisation. Role-based access control ensures that users can only access information and functionality that are pertinent to their responsibilities. Users must log in using secure credentials. Sensitive data in datasets is if necessary anonymised or hidden to preserve user privacy. This stops personally identifiable information (PII) from being displayed in visualizations or exported.

VIII. DESIGN

Table 1. Design

Upload Dataset	Allows users to upload CSV or Excel datasets for analysis.
Display Data Summary	Presents a preview of the uploaded dataset's initial rows.
Display Basic Statistics	Provides basic statistical measures (mean, median, etc.) for numerical columns.
Visualize Numerical Columns	Enables users to select a numerical column and visualize it using various chart types (Histogram, Line Chart, Scatter Plot).
Visualize Categorical Columns	Allows users to select a categorical column and visualize it using chart types (Bar Chart, Pie Chart).
Data Filtering by Numerical	Provides the option to filter data based on a numerical column by specifying a numerical range.
Data Filtering by Categorical	Enables data filtering based on a categorical column by selecting specific categorical values.
Add Column	Allows users to add a new column to the dataset with a user-defined name and default value.
Remove Column	Permits users to remove a selected column from the dataset.
Save Processed Data	Enables users to save the processed dataset after filtering and manipulation in CSV format.
Save Visualization	Allows users to save visualizations generated from selected columns as image files (e.g., PNG).

IX. OUTPUT

The dashboard gives a succinct overview of the uploaded dataset along with important facts and details. Users can rapidly understand the most important details of their data.

The robust data filtering tool of our Data Exploration and Visualization Dashboard is one of its core components, enabling you to precisely segment and examine your collection. You can concentrate on particular subsets of data that are important to your research or analytical goals by filtering the data. By defining a range of values, you can filter data based on columns with numerical values. You can specify minimum and maximum values in the filtering tool to make sure the data provided satisfies your unique requirements. A key technique for honing your data analysis and obtaining accurate insights is filtering. Our dashboard's filtering features provide you control over your data exploration trip whether you're performing exploratory data analysis, market segmentation, or any other data-driven work.

Figure 1. Dashboard

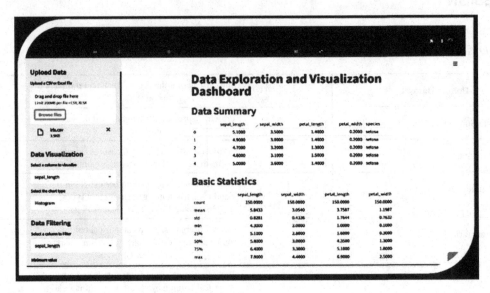

Figure 2. Filtering data

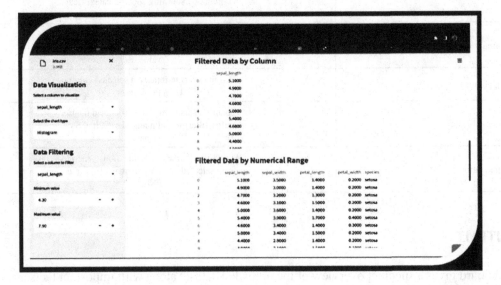

By converting raw data into visual representations, data visualization is a potent tool that makes it simpler to comprehend patterns, trends, and insights using a range of graphs and charts.

Data grouping based on particular attributes or columns is one of the basic data analysis operations. By combining data points with similar qualities, we can acquire insights into the patterns and relationships present in our collection. We include a strong grouping tool in this dashboard that enables you to dynamically group your data. By grouping your data, you can find patterns or trends that might not be visible when viewing the collection as a whole. You may produce insightful summaries by aggregating data within groups, which helps you make complex datasets easier to grasp.

Figure 3. Data visualization

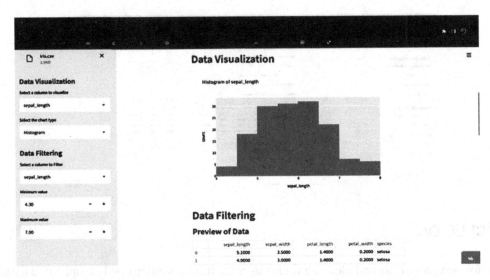

Figure 4. Grouping

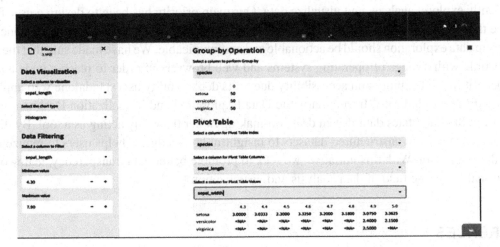

With the organized and dynamic perspective of your dataset that the Pivot Table analysis offers, you can quickly extract insightful information and investigate data correlations. This tool is essential for flexible and interactive data summarization, aggregation, and visualization. You can select the columns for the rows and columns in the pivot table as well as the aggregated data. The summary statistics and calculations performed on your data are completely under your control. By pivoting and displaying data in real time, it is simple to discover links and patterns in the data. Produce individualized reports and visualizations for presentations or additional research. Gaining a deeper grasp of your data will help you make decisions that are more based on data.

Figure 5. Pivot table

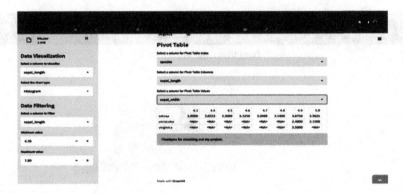

X. CONCLUSION

Making informed judgments and gleaning useful insights from enormous and complicated datasets is a crucial problem in the age of big data. In order to help users overcome this obstacle, the Data Exploration and Visualization Dashboard project was designed and created. It gives users a strong and simple tool to efficiently explore, analyze, and visualize data. Our main priority has been to design a user-friendly interface that is both technical and non-technical people can utilize. We are aware that the conclusions drawn from data exploration should be actionable and communicable. We have made sure that the project is compatible with a range of operating systems and web browsers in order to reach a wide audience. Users benefit from flexibility and accessibility due to its deployability as a standalone web application hosted on different platforms. In summary, the Data Exploration and Visualization Dashboard project is a platform that facilitates data-driven decision-making rather than only acting as a tool. By directing users on a journey from unstructured datasets to insightful knowledge, it helps users to realize the full potential of their data. With this initiative, we seek to promote better data transparency, teamwork, and decision-making in the field of data analysis and visualization.

REFERENCES

Ahmed, L. J., Anish Fathima, B., Mahaboob, M., & Gokulavasan, B. (2021). Biomedical Image Processing with Improved SPIHT Algorithm and optimized Curvelet Transform Technique. *2021 7th International Conference on Advanced Computing and Communication Systems, ICACCS 2021*. 10.1109/ICACCS51430.2021.9441832

Ahmed, L. J., Bruntha, P. M., Dhanasekar, S., Chitra, V., Balaji, D., & Senathipathi, N. (2022). An Improvised Image Registration Technique for Brain Tumor Identification and Segmentation Using ANN Approach. *ICDCS 2022 - 2022 6th International Conference on Devices, Circuits and Systems*, 80-84. 10.1109/ICDCS54290.2022.9780846

Dency Flora, G., Sekar, G., Nivetha, R., Thirukkumaran, R., Silambarasan, D., & Jeevanantham, V. (2022). An Optimized Neural Network for Content Based Image Retrieval in Medical Applications. *8th International Conference on Advanced Computing and Communication Systems, ICACCS 2022*, 1560-1563. 10.1109/ICACCS54159.2022.9785151

Faridha Banu, D., Sindhwani, N. S., G, K. R. A, & M, S. (2022). Fuzzy acceptance Analysis of Impact of Glaucoma and Diabetic Retinopathy using Confusion Matrix. *2022 10th International Conference on Reliability, Infocom Technologies and Optimization (Trends and Future Directions) (ICRITO),* 1-5. 10.1109/ICRITO56286.2022.9964858

Friedman, V. (2008). Data visualization and infographics. Graphics, Monday Inspiration.

Friendly, M. (2017). *A brief history of data visualization.* Springer-Verlag.

Manuela & Costa. (2014, November). Data Visualization. *Communication Design Quarterly Review.*

Meivel, S., Maheswari, S., & Faridha Banu, D. (2023). Design and Method of an Agricultural Drone System Using Biomass Vegetation Indices and Multispectral Images. In *Proceedings of UASG 2021: Wings 4 Sustainability. UASG 2021. Lecture Notes in Civil Engineering* (vol. 304). Springer. 10.1007/978-3-031-19309-5_25

Mercy, J., Lawanya, R., Nandhini, S., & Saravanan, M. (2022). Effective Image Deblurring Based on Improved Image Edge Information and Blur Kernel Estimation. *8th International Conference on Advanced Computing and Communication Systems, ICACCS 2022*, 855-859.

Tukey, J. (1977). *Exploratory Data Analysis.* Addison-Wesley.

Chapter 15
Research Directions and Challenges in the Deployment of Explainable AI in Human-Robot Interactions for Healthcare 4.0/5.0

A. Kishore Kumar

(iD) https://orcid.org/0000-0003-4876-319X

Sri Ramakrishna Engineering College, India

S. Sarveswaran

Sri Ramakrishna Engineering College, India

N. Dheerthi

Sri Ramakrishna Engineering College, India

A. Murugarajan

Sri Ramakrishna Engineering College, India

ABSTRACT

In the rapidly evolving landscape of Healthcare 4.0/5.0, the integration of artificial intelligence (AI) and robotics has shown immense potential in transforming patient care. However, the deployment of these technologies in human-robot interactions (HRI) demands a delicate balance between efficiency and transparency. This chapter explores the research directions and challenges associated with the implementation of Explainable AI (XAI) in the context of HRI for the advancement of healthcare services. The authors delve into the critical aspects of ensuring transparency and interpretability in AI-driven robotic systems, emphasizing the need for explainability to foster trust and collaboration between healthcare professionals, patients, and intelligent robotic entities. The chapter highlights key challenges, proposes potential research directions, and suggests methodologies to address the complexities in deploying XAI within the healthcare ecosystem.

DOI: 10.4018/979-8-3693-5767-5.ch015

INTRODUCTION

Central to Healthcare 4.0/5.0 is the reliance on data analytics and artificial intelligence for informed decision-making. The integration of big data, machine learning, and predictive analytics empowers healthcare professionals with actionable insights, optimizing treatment plans and resource allocation. There is a notable shift towards personalized and patient-centric care in Healthcare 4.0/5.0. AI-driven technologies enable the tailoring of treatments based on individual patient data, preferences, and real-time health monitoring, fostering a more holistic and effective approach to healthcare. Robotics, powered by AI, plays a pivotal role in automating routine tasks, such as diagnostics, surgeries, and medication dispensing. This not only enhances efficiency but also minimizes errors, thereby improving overall patient safety (Vale et al., 2022).

The Transformative Role of AI and Robotics

AI algorithms analyze vast datasets, including genetic information, to identify patterns and predict patient responses to specific treatments. This enables the customization of medical interventions, moving towards a precision medicine approach. AI and robotics facilitate remote monitoring of patients, enabling healthcare professionals to track vital signs and disease progression in real-time. This not only enhances patient comfort but also allows for early intervention and prevention. Robotics in surgery, guided by AI, enhances precision and minimizes invasiveness. Surgeons can now perform complex procedures with greater accuracy, reducing recovery times and improving overall patient outcomes. AI's ability to analyze historical data aids in predicting potential health risks and complications. This proactive approach enables healthcare providers to implement preventive measures, ultimately reducing the burden on healthcare systems (Gupta et al., 2022).

The integration of AI and robotics in modern healthcare systems has revolutionized the way medical services are delivered, enhancing efficiency, accuracy, and patient outcomes.

AI-driven robotic systems, such as the da Vinci Surgical System, assist surgeons in performing minimally invasive procedures with greater precision and control. These robots can execute complex maneuvers with high dexterity, leading to reduced recovery times, less scarring, and improved patient safety. AI algorithms analyze medical images such as X-rays, MRIs, and CT scans to detect abnormalities and assist radiologists in diagnosis. Deep learning algorithms can identify patterns and anomalies in medical images more accurately and efficiently than human experts, leading to earlier detection of diseases like cancer and faster treatment decisions. AI-powered devices and wearable sensors enable continuous monitoring of patients' vital signs and health metrics outside of traditional clinical settings. These systems can alert healthcare providers to potential issues in real-time, allowing for timely interventions and proactive management of chronic conditions. AI algorithms analyze vast amounts of patient data, including genetic information, medical history, and treatment outcomes, to tailor treatment plans to individual patients. This personalized approach improves treatment efficacy and reduces the risk of adverse reactions by considering each patient's unique characteristics and needs. AI accelerates the drug discovery process by predicting the efficacy and safety of potential drug candidates and identifying new therapeutic targets. Machine learning algorithms analyze large datasets to identify patterns in biological data, leading to the development of novel treatments for various diseases (Mbunge et al., 2021).

Robotic exoskeletons and rehabilitation devices aid patients in recovering from injuries or surgeries by providing targeted physical therapy and assistance with mobility. These devices can adapt their assistance levels based on patients' progress and feedback, facilitating faster recovery and improved functional outcomes. AI-powered chatbots and virtual assistants help patients schedule appointments, access medical information, and receive personalized health recommendations.

These virtual agents can triage patients, provide basic medical advice, and offer support for managing chronic conditions, relieving the burden on healthcare providers and improving patient access to care. AI algorithms analyze healthcare data to predict disease outbreaks, optimize resource allocation, and improve operational efficiency within healthcare systems. By identifying trends and patterns in data, these predictive models enable proactive decision-making and resource planning to better meet patient needs. Overall, the integration of AI and robotics in modern healthcare systems holds immense promise for improving patient outcomes, enhancing operational efficiency, and advancing medical research and innovation. However, it also raises important ethical and regulatory considerations related to data privacy, algorithm transparency, and the equitable distribution of healthcare resources (Mohanta et al., 2019). Healthcare 4.0/5.0 represents a transformative era where AI and robotics synergistically contribute to the advancement of healthcare delivery. As we navigate this new frontier, it is essential to explore the challenges and opportunities posed by these technologies, ensuring that the benefits of innovation are harnessed responsibly for the betterment of global healthcare.

EXPLAINABILITY IN HUMAN-ROBOT INTERACTIONS

Explainability in human-robot interactions refers to the ability of an AI-driven system to transparently communicate its reasoning and decision-making processes to humans in a way that is understandable and interpretable. Human users are more likely to trust and accept the decisions made by AI-driven robots if they understand the rationale behind those decisions. When robots can explain their actions in a clear and transparent manner, users are more likely to feel comfortable interacting with them and relying on their assistance. In safety-critical applications such as healthcare, manufacturing, and autonomous vehicles, it's essential for humans to understand why a robot made a particular decision or took a specific action.

Explainable AI enables users to identify potential errors or biases in the system's reasoning and intervene if necessary to prevent accidents or malfunctions (Pawar et al., 2020).

By providing explanations for their actions, robots can help humans identify and correct errors in the system's behaviour more effectively. If a robot makes a mistake or encounters a situation it doesn't understand, an explanation of its decision-making process can facilitate troubleshooting and problem-solving. Explainable AI can serve as a valuable educational tool by helping users, particularly students and novice users, understand complex concepts and processes. By explaining how they reach decisions or solve problems, AI-driven systems can enhance users' understanding of the underlying principles and encourage learning and skill development. In regulated industries such as finance and healthcare, there may be legal and ethical requirements mandating transparency and accountability in AI-driven decision-making. Explainable AI enables organizations to demonstrate compliance with these regulations by providing clear explanations for their actions and decisions. Explainable AI can enhance the overall user experience by making interactions with robots more intuitive and meaningful. When users understand why a robot behaves in a certain way or makes a particular recommendation, they are more likely to engage with the system in a positive and productive manner. Transparent explanations can help users identify and mitigate biases in AI-driven systems, thereby promoting fairness and equity in decision-making processes. By revealing the factors influencing their decisions, robots can enable users to assess whether those decisions are fair and unbiased across different demographic groups. Thus, explainability is essential for fostering trust, ensuring safety, promoting learning, and enhancing the overall user experience in human-robot interactions (Shaban Nejad et al., 2020). By providing transparent explanations for their actions and decisions, AI-driven robots can empower users to understand, trust, and effectively collaborate with intelligent systems in various domains.

Explainable AI facilitates communication between humans and robots by enabling robots to provide clear and interpretable explanations for their actions. This communication is essential for effective collaboration, as it allows humans to understand the intentions and goals of robots and coordinate their efforts accordingly. Transparent explanations create a feedback loop between humans and robots, enabling mutual learning and adaptation. When robots explain their decisions, humans can provide feedback and guidance to improve the performance and behaviour of the system, leading to more productive collaboration over time. Overall, explainability plays a crucial role in shaping the dynamics of trust, acceptance, and collaboration in HRI. By providing transparent explanations for their actions and decisions, robots can establish trust with users, increase acceptance of their presence and role, and facilitate effective collaboration in various domains ranging from healthcare and manufacturing to education and entertainment.

Overview of Explainable AI Techniques

Explainable AI (XAI) techniques aim to provide insights into the decision-making processes of AI models, making their outputs understandable to humans. Here's an overview of some common XAI techniques:

Feature Importance Methods:
- Feature Attribution: Techniques such as LIME (Local Interpretable Model-agnostic Explanations) and SHAP (SHapley Additive exPlanations) attribute importance to input features by analysing how changes in those features affect the model's output.
- Saliency Maps: Saliency methods visualize the regions of input data that are most influential in the model's decision, providing insights into which features the model is focusing on.

Model-Specific Interpretation:
- Decision Trees: Decision trees provide a transparent representation of the decision-making process by partitioning the input space based on features and assigning decision rules to each partition.
- Rule-based Models: Rule-based models directly express decision rules in the form of human-interpretable if-then statements, making them easy to understand and interpret.

Local Explanations:
- Local Models: Techniques such as surrogate models and interpretable neural networks learn simpler models to approximate the behavior of complex black-box models locally around specific instances, providing explanations at the individual prediction level.
- Counterfactual Explanations: Counterfactual explanations generate alternative scenarios that could have led to a different prediction, helping users understand why a particular outcome was predicted.

Global Explanations:
- Model Summarization: Methods like global surrogate models and prototype-based explanations summarize the behavior of complex models across the entire dataset, providing insights into general trends and patterns.

  ◦ Partial Dependence Plots: Partial dependence plots visualize the relationship between a specific feature and the model's output while marginalizing over the effects of other features, allowing users to understand how the model's predictions change with variations in individual features.

Natural Language Explanations:

  ◦ Text Explanations: Techniques generate natural language explanations to describe the rationale behind model predictions in a human-readable format, making them more accessible to users who may not have technical expertise.

  ◦ Interactive Explanations: Interactive interfaces allow users to explore and interact with explanations, enabling a more intuitive understanding of the model's behaviour.

Certainty and Uncertainty Estimation:

  ◦ Confidence Intervals: Estimating uncertainty provides users with information about the model's confidence in its predictions, helping users gauge the reliability of the model's outputs.

  ◦ Probabilistic Models: Probabilistic models quantify uncertainty by providing probability distributions over predictions, allowing users to assess the likelihood of different outcomes.

These XAI techniques offer various approaches to elucidate the inner workings of AI models, promoting transparency, trust, and interpretability in AI-driven decision-making processes across different application domains (Islam et al., 2022).

Real-Time Explainability

Real-time explanations play a critical role in enhancing the transparency, trustworthiness, and utility of AI-driven healthcare systems, ultimately improving patient care, safety, and outcomes. By integrating real-time explanation capabilities into AI-driven clinical decision support systems and patient-facing applications, healthcare organizations can leverage the full potential of AI technologies while ensuring ethical, safe, and patient-centered care. Real-time explanations provide healthcare professionals and patients with transparency into the decision-making process of AI-driven systems. Understanding why a particular diagnosis, treatment recommendation, or decision was made is essential for building trust and confidence in AI technologies. Real-time explanations help build trust between healthcare professionals and AI systems by enabling them to understand the rationale behind AI-generated recommendations or decisions. When healthcare professionals and patients trust AI systems, they are more likely to accept and adopt them as valuable tools in clinical practice (Han and Liu, 2022).

  Real-time explanations enhance the utility of AI-driven clinical decision support systems by enabling healthcare professionals to interpret and contextualize AI-generated recommendations in the context of individual patient cases. Real-time explanations help healthcare professionals make informed decisions by providing additional insights and justifications for AI recommendations. Real-time explanations serve as valuable educational tools for healthcare professionals, enabling them to learn from AI-driven systems and improve their understanding of complex medical concepts and decision-making processes. By providing real-time insights into AI algorithms' reasoning, healthcare professionals can enhance their clinical knowledge and skills. Thus real-time explanations play a critical role in enhancing the transparency, trustworthiness, and utility of AI-driven healthcare systems, ultimately improving patient care, safety, and outcomes. By integrating real-time explanation capabilities into AI-driven clinical decision support systems and patient-facing applications, healthcare organizations can leverage the full potential of AI technologies while ensuring ethical, safe, and patient-centered care.

CHALLENGES IN HUMAN-ROBOT INTERACTIONS

Human-robot interactions (HRI) present a range of challenges, stemming from technical, social, ethical, and psychological factors. Here are some of the key challenges in HRI:

- Ensuring the safety of humans when interacting with robots is paramount. Robots need to be designed with robust collision detection and avoidance mechanisms to prevent accidents and injuries. Additionally, as robots become more autonomous, ensuring that they adhere to safety standards and regulations is essential.
- Building trust between humans and robots is crucial for effective collaboration. However, trust can be challenging to establish, particularly if humans perceive robots as unpredictable or unreliable. Designing robots that are transparent, consistent, and capable of explaining their actions can help foster trust and acceptance.
- Achieving natural and intuitive communication between humans and robots remains a significant challenge. Robots need to understand and interpret human gestures, facial expressions, speech, and other non-verbal cues accurately. Developing natural language processing algorithms and multimodal interfaces can improve communication effectiveness.
- Balancing autonomy and human control in HRI is complex. While autonomous robots can improve efficiency and productivity, humans may feel uncomfortable relinquishing control, particularly in safety-critical environments. Designing interfaces that allow humans to intervene and override autonomous behaviours when necessary is essential.
- As robots collect and process sensitive information about humans, ensuring privacy and data security is paramount. Robots must adhere to data protection regulations and employ robust encryption and authentication mechanisms to safeguard sensitive data from unauthorized access or misuse.
- Ethical dilemmas arise in HRI, particularly concerning the impact of robots on human employment, autonomy, and dignity. Ensuring that robots adhere to ethical principles such as beneficence, non-maleficence, and respect for human rights is essential. Additionally, addressing issues of robot bias, discrimination, and fairness is critical to promoting ethical HRI.
- Cultural differences and social norms influence human perceptions and interactions with robots. Designing culturally sensitive robots that respect diverse values and customs is essential for promoting acceptance and adoption across different societies and demographics.
- Maintaining user engagement and satisfaction over extended periods is challenging. Users may become bored or disinterested in interacting with robots if they perceive them as repetitive or unresponsive. Incorporating personalized experiences, adaptive behaviors, and emotional intelligence into robots can enhance long-term user engagement.
- Designing robots that accommodate the physical and cognitive abilities of humans is crucial for ensuring usability and accessibility. Considering factors such as anthropometry, reachability, visibility, and cognitive load can improve the user experience and prevent user fatigue or discomfort.

Addressing these challenges requires interdisciplinary collaboration between robotics engineers, human-computer interaction specialists, ethicists, psychologists, and other stakeholders. By considering the technical, social, ethical, and psychological dimensions of HRI, researchers and practitioners can develop robots that are safe, trustworthy, and socially acceptable in diverse human environments (Folke et al., 2021).

Addressing Biases in AI Algorithms in the Healthcare Domain

Addressing biases in AI algorithms in the healthcare domain is crucial to ensure fairness, equity, and accuracy in medical decision-making. Here are several strategies to mitigate biases in AI algorithms used in healthcare:

- Ensuring that AI algorithms are trained on diverse and representative datasets is essential to mitigate biases. This involves collecting data from diverse populations, including individuals of different races, genders, ages, socioeconomic backgrounds, and geographic locations. By incorporating a wide range of data sources, AI algorithms can learn more comprehensive and unbiased representations of the underlying phenomena.
- Implementing rigorous methods to detect and evaluate biases in AI algorithms is essential. This involves analyzing the data used to train the algorithms and identifying any patterns or disparities that may indicate bias. Techniques such as fairness metrics, disparity analysis, and sensitivity analysis can help quantify and assess the presence of biases in AI models.
- Interpretability and Transparency: Enhancing the interpretability and transparency of AI algorithms can help identify and address biases more effectively. By providing explanations for their predictions or decisions, AI models enable users to understand the underlying factors influencing the outcomes and detect potential biases more easily.
- Human Oversight and Validation: Incorporating human oversight and validation into the AI decision-making process can help mitigate biases and ensure accountability. Human experts can review AI predictions, evaluate their fairness and accuracy, and intervene when biases are detected to ensure equitable outcomes.
- Continuous Monitoring and Evaluation: Implementing mechanisms for continuous monitoring and evaluation of AI algorithms in real-world settings is essential to identify and address biases over time. By regularly assessing the performance of AI models and their impact on different population groups, healthcare organizations can proactively mitigate biases and improve algorithmic fairness.

BIAS MITIGATION TECHNIQUES

Bias mitigation techniques aim to reduce or eliminate biases present in AI algorithms, ensuring fair and equitable outcomes. Here are several commonly employed techniques:

- Data Preprocessing:
  Data Cleaning: Identify and correct errors, inconsistencies, and outliers in the training data to ensure its quality and integrity.

Data Augmentation: Increase the diversity of the training dataset by synthesizing new data samples or perturbing existing ones, helping to mitigate biases caused by underrepresentation or imbalances.
Data Balancing: Adjust the class distribution in the training data to mitigate biases caused by skewed or unbalanced datasets, ensuring that all classes are represented equally.

- Algorithmic Fairness:

Fairness Constraints: Incorporate fairness constraints into the learning process to ensure that the model's predictions or decisions satisfy predefined fairness criteria, such as demographic parity or equalized odds.

Fair Loss Functions: Design loss functions that penalize discriminatory behavior and encourage fairness in model predictions, helping to mitigate biases against certain demographic groups.

Fairness Regularization: Add regularization terms to the model's objective function to penalize discriminatory patterns and encourage fairness in the learned representations.

- Bias Detection and Mitigation:

Fairness Metrics: Define and compute fairness metrics to quantify biases in model predictions across different demographic groups, enabling the identification of discriminatory patterns.

Bias Correction: Develop post-processing techniques to adjust model predictions or decisions to mitigate biases identified during model evaluation, ensuring fair outcomes for all individuals.

Counterfactual Analysis: Generate counterfactual explanations to identify alternative scenarios that could mitigate biases in model predictions, enabling targeted interventions to address discriminatory behavior.

- Model Interpretability:

Interpretable Models: Use transparent and interpretable machine learning models, such as decision trees or linear models, to facilitate the inspection and understanding of model predictions, helping to identify and mitigate biases.

Feature Importance Analysis: Analyze the importance of input features in model predictions to identify potential sources of bias and assess their impact on model outputs.

- Human Oversight and Intervention:

Human-in-the-Loop Systems: Incorporate human oversight and intervention mechanisms into AI systems to review and validate model predictions, enabling human experts to detect and mitigate biases as necessary.

Ethical Review Boards: Establish ethical review boards or committees to evaluate the potential societal impact of AI systems and ensure that they adhere to ethical principles, including fairness and non-discrimination.

- Regular Monitoring and Evaluation:

Continuous Evaluation: Continuously monitor and evaluate the performance of AI systems in real-world settings to detect and address biases as they emerge, ensuring that models remain fair and equitable over time.

Feedback Mechanisms: Collect feedback from users and stakeholders to identify potential biases or discriminatory behaviors in AI systems and take corrective actions to mitigate them.

By implementing these strategies and adopting a multi-faceted approach to addressing biases in AI algorithms, healthcare organizations can improve the fairness, accuracy, and equity of AI-driven decision-making processes, ultimately enhancing patient outcomes and healthcare delivery.

EMERGING TRENDS AND FUTURE DIRECTIONS IN THE DEPLOYMENT OF EXPLAINABLE AI IN HRI FOR HEALTHCARE

Emerging trends and future directions in the deployment of explainable AI (XAI) in Human-Robot Interaction (HRI) for healthcare are shaping the development of more transparent, trustworthy, and effective AI-driven healthcare systems. Here are some key trends and directions:

- Interpretability in Robotic Assistance: As robots play increasingly active roles in healthcare settings, there is a growing need for interpretable AI models that can explain their decisions and actions to healthcare professionals and patients. Future research may focus on developing robot-assisted systems that provide real-time explanations for their behavior during medical procedures, rehabilitation exercises, or patient care tasks.

- Patient-Centric Explainability: Future deployments of XAI in HRI for healthcare will prioritize patient-centric explanations, tailoring the level and format of explanations to individual patient preferences, health literacy levels, and cultural backgrounds. Personalized explanations will enhance patient understanding, engagement, and trust in AI-driven healthcare systems.

- Collaborative Decision-Making: XAI techniques will enable collaborative decision-making between healthcare professionals, patients, and AI-driven systems in real-time clinical settings. Future research may explore interactive interfaces that facilitate dialogue and negotiation between human users and AI models, allowing for shared decision-making processes that incorporate both clinical expertise and patient preferences.

- Human-Robot Trust and Acceptance: Addressing trust and acceptance issues will be a key focus of future research on XAI in HRI for healthcare. Future deployments may incorporate explainability features into healthcare robots to enhance human-robot trust through transparent communication, reliable decision-making, and accountability for actions taken in clinical settings.

- Adaptive Explainability: Future XAI systems deployed in HRI for healthcare will be adaptive and context-aware, providing explanations that are tailored to specific interaction contexts, user preferences, and task requirements. Adaptive explainability will enhance the relevance, clarity, and effectiveness of explanations provided by healthcare robots in diverse clinical scenarios.

- Integration with Clinical Workflows: XAI techniques will be integrated seamlessly into clinical workflows, supporting healthcare professionals in decision-making processes without disrupting existing practices or workflows. Future deployments may involve embedding XAI capabilities into electronic health record systems, medical devices, and robotic platforms to provide transparent decision support and enhance clinical decision-making.

Overall, the deployment of XAI in HRI for healthcare is poised to transform the way AI-driven systems interact with healthcare professionals and patients, promoting transparency, trust, and collaboration in clinical settings. By addressing emerging trends and future directions, researchers and practitioners can harness the full potential of XAI to improve patient care, safety, and outcomes in healthcare environments (Guo, 2020).

Training Healthcare Professionals

Training healthcare professionals and end-users on understanding AI decisions is crucial for fostering trust, promoting acceptance, and facilitating effective collaboration between humans and AI-driven systems in healthcare settings. Here are some recommendations for training programs:

Foundational Knowledge: Provide healthcare professionals and end-users with foundational knowledge about AI technologies, including machine learning algorithms, deep learning architectures, and explainable AI techniques. Ensure that participants understand the basic principles and concepts underlying AI-driven decision-making processes.

Clinical Relevance: Emphasize the clinical relevance of AI-driven decision-making in healthcare by illustrating real-world examples and case studies. Demonstrate how AI algorithms are used to analyze medical data, diagnose diseases, recommend treatments, and optimize patient care pathways (Kwong et al., 2022).

Explainability Techniques: Educate participants about various explainability techniques used in AI, such as feature importance analysis, local interpretations, model-agnostic explanations, and natural language explanations. Teach participants how to interpret and understand the explanations provided by AI-driven systems in healthcare contexts.

Interpretation Skills: Develop participants' interpretation skills to enable them to assess the reliability, validity, and relevance of AI-generated predictions or recommendations. Teach participants how to critically evaluate AI outputs, identify potential biases or errors, and make informed decisions based on AI insights.

Transparency and Trust: Highlight the importance of transparency and trust in AI-driven decision-making by discussing ethical principles, regulatory requirements, and best practices for responsible AI deployment in healthcare. Foster a culture of transparency and openness to encourage dialogue and collaboration between healthcare professionals and AI systems.

Interactive Learning: Incorporate interactive learning activities, such as case studies, role-playing exercises, and hands-on demonstrations, to engage participants and reinforce learning objectives. Encourage active participation and discussion to facilitate knowledge sharing and peer learning among participants.

Continuing Education: Offer continuing education and professional development opportunities to healthcare professionals to keep them updated on advances in AI technologies and best practices for AI-driven decision-making in healthcare. Provide access to online courses, workshops, webinars, and conferences focused on AI in healthcare.

Multidisciplinary Collaboration: Facilitate multidisciplinary collaboration and knowledge exchange between healthcare professionals, data scientists, AI engineers, ethicists, and other stakeholders involved in AI-driven healthcare initiatives. Foster interdisciplinary teamwork to leverage diverse expertise and perspectives in addressing complex challenges related to AI decision-making.

By implementing comprehensive training programs that cover foundational knowledge, explainability techniques, interpretation skills, and ethical considerations, healthcare organizations can empower healthcare professionals and end-users to understand AI decisions effectively and leverage AI technologies to improve patient care and outcomes.

Identifying Best Practices for Deploying and Maintaining XAI Systems

Deploying and maintaining Explainable AI (XAI) systems effectively involves a combination of technical considerations, organizational strategies, and ethical principles (Amann et al., 2020). Here are some best practices for deploying and maintaining XAI systems:

Understand the Context: Before deploying an XAI system, it's crucial to understand the specific context in which it will be used. Consider the stakeholders involved, the domain of application, regulatory requirements, and potential ethical implications.

Select Appropriate XAI Techniques: Choose XAI techniques that are suitable for the specific needs of the application and align with the level of transparency required. Techniques such as LIME (Local Interpretable Model-agnostic Explanations), SHAP (SHapley Additive exPlanations), and decision trees are commonly used for providing explanations in machine learning models. The importance of XAI in healthcare applications in trainable attention refers to a set of methodologies aimed at directing focus towards significant content within digital multimedia data, including images, videos, audio, and text. One illustrative application involves integrating text and image data within a hidden layer, enabling clinicians to concentrate on pertinent information relating to regions of interest (ROIs) in images alongside electronic health records. This technique facilitates the alignment of relevant textual and visual cues, enhancing the ability of healthcare professionals to discern critical information in medical data (Chaddad et al., 2023). Integrate XAI into Development Pipeline: Integrate XAI considerations into the entire development pipeline, from data collection and model training to deployment and monitoring. Ensure that XAI techniques are incorporated early in the process to facilitate transparency and interpretability throughout the system's lifecycle.

Provide Transparent Explanations: Ensure that the explanations provided by the XAI system are clear, understandable, and relevant to the end-users. Use visualizations, natural language explanations, or interactive interfaces to convey the reasoning behind AI decisions effectively.

Validate and Evaluate XAI Systems: Conduct rigorous validation and evaluation of XAI systems to assess their effectiveness, reliability, and impact on decision-making processes. Use appropriate metrics and methodologies to measure the quality of explanations and user satisfaction.

Address Bias and Fairness: Pay attention to potential biases in the data and algorithms used by the XAI system. Implement techniques to mitigate bias and ensure fairness, such as fairness-aware machine learning algorithms, bias detection methods, and fairness constraints.

Ensure Robustness and Stability: XAI systems should be robust and stable across different datasets, environments, and user interactions. Perform robustness testing and sensitivity analysis to evaluate the system's performance under various conditions and edge cases.

Provide Continuous Monitoring and Feedback: Establish mechanisms for monitoring the performance of XAI systems in real-world settings and collecting feedback from users. Use this feedback to iteratively improve the system's transparency, accuracy, and usability over time.

Educate Users and Stakeholders: Educate users, stakeholders, and decision-makers about the capabilities and limitations of XAI systems. Provide training and resources to help them understand how to interpret and trust the explanations provided by the system.

Adhere to Ethical Guidelines: Ensure that the deployment and maintenance of XAI systems adhere to relevant ethical guidelines, privacy regulations, and industry standards. Consider the potential societal impact of the system and prioritize ethical considerations in decision-making processes. By following these best practices, organizations can deploy and maintain XAI systems effectively, fostering trust, transparency, and accountability in AI-powered decision-making processes (Tjoa & Guan, 2021).

CONCLUSION

Collaborative efforts play a crucial role in addressing challenges and advancing research in the deployment of Explainable AI (XAI) in Human-Robot Interactions (HRI) for Healthcare 4.0/5.0. Collaborative efforts often involve interdisciplinary research teams comprising experts from fields such as artificial intelligence, robotics, human-computer interaction, healthcare, and ethics. These teams bring diverse perspectives and expertise to tackle the multifaceted challenges of deploying XAI in HRI for healthcare. Collaborations between academia and industry facilitate the translation of research findings into practical solutions. Academic researchers contribute theoretical insights and experimental validation, while industry partners provide real-world data, resources, and implementation expertise. These partnerships accelerate the development and deployment of XAI-enabled healthcare robots. Collaborating with healthcare professionals, clinicians, and medical institutions is essential for understanding the specific requirements, workflows, and challenges in clinical settings. Clinical collaborations enable researchers to design XAI systems that are aligned with the needs of healthcare practitioners and patients, ensuring usability, safety, and effectiveness. Involving end-users, including healthcare professionals, patients, and caregivers, in the design and evaluation of XAI-enabled healthcare robots ensures that the technology meets their needs and preferences. User-centered design approaches, such as participatory design workshops, usability studies, and co-creation sessions, facilitate collaboration between researchers and stakeholders to iteratively refine the system. Collaboration with ethicists, policymakers, and stakeholders in the broader society is essential for addressing ethical and societal implications associated with the deployment of XAI in HRI for healthcare (Taimoor & Rehman, 2022). Collaborative efforts focus on developing ethical guidelines, regulatory frameworks, and governance mechanisms to ensure transparency, fairness, accountability, and privacy in AI-powered healthcare systems. Collaborative efforts often extend beyond national boundaries through international partnerships and collaborations. International collaboration enables knowledge sharing, cross-cultural understanding, and benchmarking of XAI technologies across different healthcare systems and cultural contexts. By fostering collaborative efforts among researchers, industry partners, healthcare professionals, policymakers, and stakeholders, the deployment of Explainable AI in Human-Robot Interactions for Healthcare 4.0/5.0 can be accelerated, leading to transformative advancements in patient care, clinical decision-making, and healthcare delivery.

REFERENCES

Amann, J., Blasimme, A., Vayena, E., Frey, D., & Madai, V. I. (2020). Explainability for artificial intelligence in healthcare: A multidisciplinary perspective. *BMC Medical Informatics and Decision Making*, *20*(no. 1), 310. doi:10.1186/s12911-020-01332-6 PMID:33256715

Chaddad, A., Peng, J., Xu, J., & Bouridane, A. (2023). Survey of Explainable AI Techniques in Healthcare. *Sensors (Basel)*, *23*(2), 1–19. doi:10.3390/s23020634 PMID:36679430

Folke, T., Yang, S. C., Anderson, S., & Shafto, P. (2021). Explainable AI for medical imaging: Explaining pneumothorax diagnoses with Bayesian teaching. *CoRR*, vol. abs/2106.04684.

Guo, W. (2020). Explainable artificial intelligence for 6G: Improving trust between human and machine. *IEEE Communications Magazine*, *58*(6), 39–45. doi:10.1109/MCOM.001.2000050

Gupta, R., Shukla, A., & Tanwar, S. (2020). Aayush: A smart contract-based telesurgery system for healthcare 4.0. *2020 IEEE International Conference on Communications Workshops (ICC Workshops)*, 1–6. 10.1109/ICCWorkshops49005.2020.9145044

Han, H., & Liu, X. (2022, January). The challenges of explainable ai in biomedical data science. *BMC Bioinformatics*, *22*(12), 443. PMID:35057748

Islam, A. M. R., Ahmed, M. U., Barua, S., & Begum, S. (2022). A systematic review of explainable artificial intelligence in terms of different application domains and tasks. *Applied Sciences (Basel, Switzerland)*, *12*(3), 1353. doi:10.3390/app12031353

Kwong, J. C., Khondker, A., Tran, C., Evans, E., Cozma, A. I., Javidan, A., Ali, A., Jamal, M., Short, T., Papanikolaou, F., Srigley, J. R., Fine, B., & Feifer, A. (2022). Explainable artificial intelligence to predict the risk of side-specific extraprostatic extension in pre-prostatectomy patients. *Canadian Urological Association Journal*, *16*(6). Advance online publication. doi:10.5489/cuaj.7473 PMID:35099382

Mbunge, E., Muchemwa, B., Jiyane, S., & Batani, J. (2021). Sensors and healthcare 5.0: Transformative shift in virtual care through emerging digital health technologies. *Global Health Journal (Amsterdam, Netherlands)*, *5*(4), 169–177. doi:10.1016/j.glohj.2021.11.008

Mohanta, B., Das, P., & Patnaik, S. (2019). Healthcare 5.0: A paradigm shift in digital healthcare system using artificial intelligence, IOT and 5G communication. *2019 International Conference on Applied Machine Learning (ICAML)*, 191–196. 10.1109/ICAML48257.2019.00044

Pawar, U., O'Shea, D., Rea, S., & O'Reilly, R. (2020). Incorporating explainable artificial intelligence (XAI) to aid the understanding of machine learning in the healthcare domain. *Irish Conference on Artificial Intelligence and Cognitive Science*.

Shaban Nejad, M. (2020). *Explainable AI in healthcare and medicine: building a culture of transparency and accountability* (Vol. 914). Springer Nature.

Taimoor, N., & Rehman, S. (2022). Reliable and resilient AI and IOT-based personalised healthcare services: A survey. *IEEE Access : Practical Innovations, Open Solutions*, *10*, 535–563. doi:10.1109/ACCESS.2021.3137364

Tjoa, E., & Guan, C. (2021). A survey on explainable artificial intelligence (XAI): Toward medical xai. *IEEE Transactions on Neural Networks and Learning Systems*, *32*(11), 4793–4813. doi:10.1109/TNNLS.2020.3027314 PMID:33079674

Vale, D., El-Sharif, A., & Ali, M. (2022, March). Explainable artificial intelligence (XAI) post-hoc explainability methods: Risks and limitations in non-discrimination law. *AI and Ethics*, *2*(4), 815–826. doi:10.1007/s43681-022-00142-y

Chapter 16
Security System for Smart Homes to Prevent Theft

Anitha Mary
Karunya University, India

P. Kingston Stanley
Karunya Institute of Technology and Sciences, India

V. Evelyn Brindha
Karunya Institute of Technology and Sciences, India

J. Jency Joseph
Krishna College of Technology, India

ABSTRACT

The chapter intends to create a system that alerts the victim of theft in real time. The current system does not distinguish between people and objects; instead, it uses a methodology to identify the burglar after the theft has taken place. The internet of things and advancements in wireless sensor networks make it possible to create a smart, safe home that can detect burglars in real time and notify the homeowner while the theft is occurring. The suggested approach is better than the current ones that use CCTV cameras for surveillance.

1. INTRODUCTION

Security is a significant concern for both homes and offices, especially in light of recent theft activities. There is a clear need for a security system capable of detecting intruders in real-time during theft incidents. The current approach relies on CCTVs and DTRs, but these systems cannot distinguish between humans and objects. Additionally, they can only analyze stored images after an incident has occurred, requiring human intervention. In contrast, the proposed system not only detects intruders live but also promptly alerts homeowners or office occupants via a GSM module, notifying them of the theft immediately. This

DOI: 10.4018/979-8-3693-5767-5.ch016

solution is both cost-effective and efficient, offering a reliable security measure for properties without the need for surveillance cameras.

2. RELATED WORKS

The absence of smart devices and sophisticated facial recognition software at home is contributing to an increase in theft tracking (Ahmed et.al. 2010). The inaccuracy of face detection techniques acquired by CCTV cameras arises from theft victims hiding their faces, either completely or partially, using materials made of leather or cloth. Numerous researchers have directed their efforts towards improving face recognition technology (Jian et.al.2018). For example, Zhiwei et al. (Zhang et.al.2012) introduced a regularization technique aimed at enhancing face identification across different spectrums. Additionally, many researchers have focused on refining face and eye detection using the Haar classifier algorithm. Xin et al. (Xin et.al 2018) proposed a system for person face recognition, claiming it offers superior security compared to unimodal biometric systems. Nguyen et al. Nguyen et.al. 2018 suggested employing deep learning techniques, while Cho et al. Cho et.al 2018 advocated for the use of convolutional neural networks to improve image features in face recognition systems, particularly those equipped with visible light camera sensors. Binary pattern techniques were used in the creation of the face detection system by Alobaidi et al.2018. Zhang et al.'s approach to face detection in a stable environment combines model-driven and data-driven methods. Using support vector machines, Omid et al. created a face recognition system that works in the presence of cosmetics like contact lenses and facial makeup (Sharifi et.al.2018). Door and window security is a major consideration when it comes to house security. These days, digital doors that don't require a physical key are employed because to advancements in IoT technology. Nevertheless, it is simple to damage digital doors, and the owners are only aware of theft once they get home. Huth et al. devised a wirelessly connected security system employing a physical key generation method, demonstrating its application in smart homes (Andreasa et.al.2019). To enhance energy efficiency, WiFi modules, temperature sensors, and door sensors are commonly employed.

Intruder detection systems often utilize laser and LDR sensors to detect movement, with alerts sent to homeowners via SMS (Cristian et.al.2016). However, this method may fail to transmit messages through a GSM module in areas lacking internet coverage. Anitha et al. proposed an artificial intelligence-based home system (Anitha 2016).

Patel et al. introduced a modern door lock system for homes, incorporating a Raspberry Pi system-on-chip (SoC), a camera, and an infrared sensor (Jay Patel et.al.2019). This system operates by granting access to individuals whose images are stored in the cloud. Nivo Suranth et al. implemented a home security system utilizing a PIR sensor, an Arduino microcontroller, and a Raspberry Pi 3 SoC (Nicosurantha 2018). The Raspberry Pi processes images captured by a webcam connected to the SoC, along with sensor data from the Arduino microcontroller. Additionally, intruders can be identified using a support vector algorithm, capable of detecting intruders within 2 seconds.

Beyond home security, several researchers have developed anti-theft systems for vehicles. Kiruthiga et al. devised a system employing a global system and a PIC microcontroller (Kiruthigara et.al 2015). This controller identifies unauthorized access and notifies the owner via SMS. Although GPS technology is utilized for vehicle tracking (win et.al.2011), it may encounter limitations at the receiver end, resulting in inaccurate location data due to limited sky view. Radio frequency identification (RFID) is another method used for theft tracking, allowing access to the card, which poses a risk of theft.

3. METHODOLOGY

Figure 1 illustrates the block diagram of the anti-theft detection system. The controller acts as the master and interfaces with sensors to detect intruders using a PIR sensor and a Reed Switch. These sensors can be affixed to doors or windows in homes and/or offices. When an intruder opens a door or window, the controller detects their presence and promptly sends a message to the owner via a GSM module.

3.1 Sensor Module

The sensor module comprises a Passive Infrared (PIR) sensor and a Piezo vibration sensor. The PIR sensor contains a pyroelectric sensor that produces an electrical signal when there is a change in temperature. This enables detection of human presence within a range of 14 meters. The piezo-vibration sensor generates an electric signal output in response to vibrations, aiding in the identification of intruders, such as when they bore holes in walls.

3.2 Controller

The controller utilized in the system is the Atmel 2560 microcontroller, an 8-bit microcontroller offering several advantages over an Arduino UNO board, including a higher number of analog and digital pins. It operates at a voltage of 3.3V and a frequency of 16MHz, supporting various types of digital and analog sensors.

3.3 SIM 808 Global System for Mobile communication (GSM)

For GSM communication, the system employs the SIM808 GSM Module, which integrates both GPRS and GPS modules. This combination ensures cost-effectiveness and quick response times. Operating at voltages ranging from 3.3V to 4.4V, the GSM module communicates with the controller via UART (Universal Asynchronous Receiver Transmitter), facilitating the transmission of theft-related SMS alerts to the owner.

3.4 Real Time Clock (RTC) Module

The Real-Time Clock (RTC) Module is responsible for maintaining accurate timekeeping, including seconds, minutes, and hours. Additionally, it offers provisions for adjusting the date, month, and year, including corrections for leap years. The module features a square wave output pin (SQW) providing frequencies of 1, 4, 8, or 32 KHz, which can be modified through programming. These features serve as interrupts during theft detection. To mitigate the effects of temperature variations on the circuit, the RTC Module includes an inbuilt temperature-compensated crystal oscillator.

3.5 Radio Frequency (RF) Module (Transmitter and Receiver)

The RF Module uses simplex communication to create a 433MHz frequency. The transmitter and receiver are two separate devices; the transmitter sends information from one end (such as one microcontroller board), while the receiver receives it from another controller board. Amplitude shift keying and an

HT12E encoder are needed for controller interface. Long-distance communication typically uses these kinds of modules.

Figure 1. Methodology-block diagram

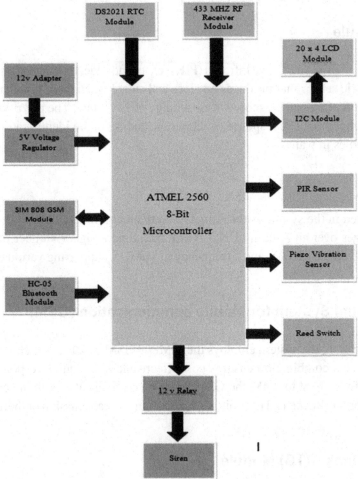

3.6 Li-Ion Battery

With a capacity of providing power up to 1000 mA, the 4300 mAh Li-ion battery sustains the proposed system for nearly 1 hour. Charging occurs in two stages: the constant current stage, where a steady current is applied until reaching the voltage threshold, and the constant voltage stage, where a stable voltage is applied as the current decreases to the threshold limit.

3.7 LCD (Liquid Crystal Display)

The 20x4 LCD, featuring 20 columns and 4 rows, is designed to display large amounts of text with a resolution of 5x8 pixels. Communication with the microcontroller is facilitated through the 2-wire communication I2C protocol.

3.8 Buzzer

The buzzer emits a continuous beep sound upon activation and comes in two types: the simple buzzer emits a continuous sound when supplied with voltage, while the readymade buzzer produces a beeping sound through an oscillating circuit. Commonly used in automobile electronics and portable equipment, it operates on a +5V power supply.

3.9 Siren

A siren serves as a noise-making system typically mounted on rooftops or posts, used to warn of natural disasters or attacks.

3.10 Relay Module

The relay module acts as an electromagnetic switch, toggling ON/OFF when current flows through the circuit. It includes three terminals—normally open (NO), common (COM), and normally closed (NC)—with the NO connecting to the COM and the NC disconnected. When current flows, the NC connects with the COM, returning to its initial position when the current is cut off.

3.11 Bluetooth Module (HC-05)

The HC-05 Bluetooth module utilizes the Serial Port Protocol (SPP) and features Tx and Rx terminals for communication with the microcontroller. Powered by a +5V battery, it enters command mode during power-up and switches to data mode when idle.

3.12 Android Studio

Android Studio, based on Google's Android OS, is the Integrated Development Environment (IDE) utilized for this project. It supports languages such as C, C++, and JAVA, along with their extensions, facilitating software development.

4. WORKFLOW

This suggested work is a self-diagnostic anti-theft system that, without the need for a service technician, examines the state of interfaced sensor modules and notifies the owner appropriately. It is a full security system made for residences and retail spaces. The PIR and vibration sensors are part of the sensor module. PIR sensors are employed to detect theft based on variations in temperature. If a dacoit creates a hole in the wall, vibration sensors are utilised to detect the vibration. The microcontroller is interfaced with these sensors. The microcontroller notifies the owner in real time when the security system is activated, based on the data that the sensor has received.

4.1 Operating Modes

As seen in Figure 2, this system has five modes of operation, each of which has a distinct functional operation. A standard security feature that assists elderly individuals living alone at night is called "stay mode." A siren that uses a PIR sensor and reed switch is activated if an unknown person enters the house.Using the GSM module, an outing mode sends a real-time message to the owner alerting them to the theft. Using the emergency mode makes it easier for the user to message the local police station or ask for assistance from neighbours.

Figure 2. Modes of operation

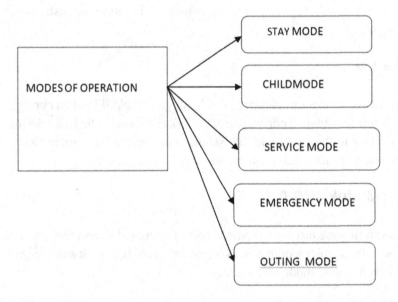

The 500-meter radius around the child is protected when in child mode (Figure 3). This option uses the child's GPS position to follow their whereabouts, updating the parents via a mobile app every ten minutes. The system has a safety button that the child can press if they are in distress. The CPU calls the preprogrammed list of phone numbers when the safety button is pressed. It will call the subsequent number till it reaches the last one if no one answers. This option assists children who are missing, abducted, or involved in accidents.

In addition to the five operating modes listed above, there is one more mode known as service mode. Service mode guarantees that the device is operating properly by allowing it to self-check the system once a month.

Figure 3. Self-protection system for children

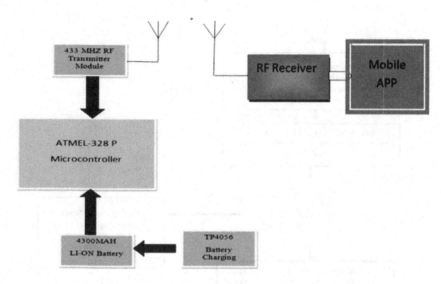

5. RESULTS AND DISCUSSION

A feature of the suggested anti-theft system (Figure 4) allows for voice, GPS, and SMS permissions. Bluetooth is enabled to pair the device with the mobile app after authorization is granted. There are five modes to choose from on the programme (Figure 6), which include stay, outing, emergency, and child mode. Any mode can be used by the user. The owner's phone number and GPS location are forwarded to the local police station when the system is in emergency mode and there are intruders inside the home. The youngster can be viewed up to 500 metres away while the system is in child mode and the RF tag is active. The flowchart for the suggested anti-theft system is displayed in Figure 5. Figure 3: Self Protection system for children

Figure 4. Experimental set-up

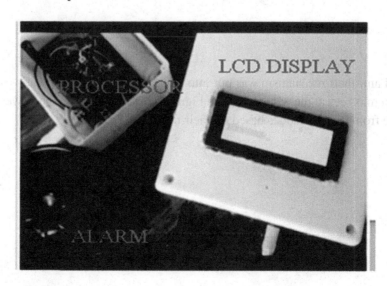

Figure 5. Flowchart for the proposed system

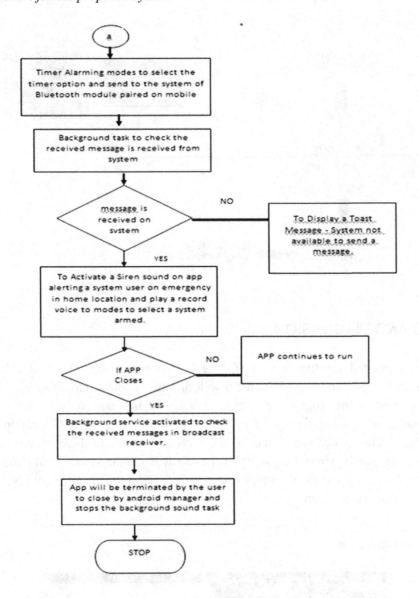

The suggested anti-theft mechanism was put into place. With all of its operating modes displayed, the suggested system is seen at the window side in Figure 7. The red LED on the power on button allows the user to choose from various modes based on their needs.

Figure 6. Mobile app for selecting modes

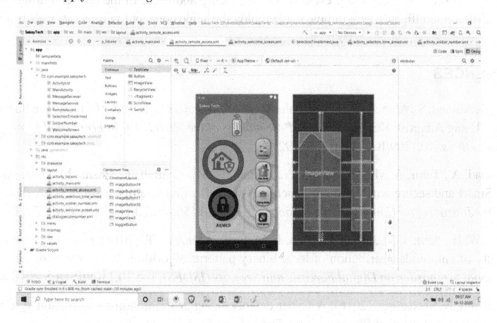

Figure 7. Implementation of proposed system

6. CONCLUSION

The suggested system offers superior protection for not only houses but also workplaces, cars, and other spaces. It may be operated by an Android smartphone user through an application. Through a GSM phone and Bluetooth, the user can get the status update. Using kid mode configuration, it is possible to keep an eye on the youngster and prevent them from being abducted. In the future, a drone equipped with an artificial intelligence programme may employ the same concept to protect its user from theft.

REFERENCES

Ahmed, T., Ahmed, S., Ahmed, S., & Motiwala, M. (2010). Real-Time Intruder Detection in Surveillance Networks Using Adaptive Kernel Methods. *Proceedings of the 2010 IEEE International Conference on Communications.* 10.1109/ICC.2010.5502592

Almohamad, A., Tahir, A. M., Al-Kababji, A., Furqan, H. M., Khattab, T., Hasna, M. O., & Arslan, H. (2020). Smart and secure wireless communications via reflecting intelligent surfaces: A short survey. *IEEE Open Journal of the Communications Society, 1,* 1442–1456. doi:10.1109/OJCOMS.2020.3023731

Alobaidi, W. H., Aziz, I. T., Jawad, T., Flaih, F. M. F., & Azeez, A. T. (2018). Face detection based on probability of amplitude distribution of local binary patterns algorithm. *Proceedings of the 2018 6th International Symposium on Digital Forensic and Security (ISDFS),* 1–5 10.1109/ISDFS.2018.8355319

Anitha, Kalra, & Shrivastav. (2016). A Cyber defence using artificial home automation system using IoT. *International Journal of Pharmacy and Technology, 8,* 25358-64.

Cristian, Ursache, Popa, & Pop. (2016). *Energy efficiency and robustness for IoT: Building a smart home security system.* Faculty of Automatic Control and Computers University Politehnica of Bucharest.

Enoch Sam, M., Misra, S. K., Anitha Mary, X., Karthik, C., & Chowdhury, S. (2023, November). Review of different types of spatial positioning platforms. In AIP Conference Proceedings (Vol. 2878, No. 1). AIP Publishing. doi:10.1063/5.0171256

Evangeline, C. S., Sarah, M., Lenin, A., Reddy, J. H. V., Mary, X. A., & Karthiga, M. (2023, May). Design of On-Board Unit for Vehicular Applications. In *2023 2nd International Conference on Vision Towards Emerging Trends in Communication and Networking Technologies (ViTECoN)* (pp. 1-6). IEEE. 10.1109/ViTECoN58111.2023.10157654

Evelyn Brindha, V., & Anitha Mary, X. (2023). Analysing Control Algorithms for Controlling the Speed of BLDC Motors Using Green IoT. *Power Converters, Drives and Controls for Sustainable Operations,* 779-788.

Huth, C. (2015). Securing systems on the Internet of Things via physical properties of devices and communications. In Systems Conference (SysCon), 9th Annual IEEE International. IEEE.

Jian, Z., Chao, Z., Shunli, Z., Tingting, L., Weiwen, S., & Jian, J. (2018). Pre-detection and dual-dictionary sparse representation based face recognition algorithm in non-sufficient training samples. *Journal of Systems Engineering and Electronics*, 29(1), 196–202. doi:10.21629/JSEE.2018.01.20

Makarfi, A. U., Rabie, K. M., Kaiwartya, O., Li, X., & Kharel, R. (2020, May). Physical layer security in vehicular networks with reconfigurable intelligent surfaces. In *2020 IEEE 91st Vehicular Technology Conference (VTC2020-Spring)* (pp. 1-6). IEEE. 10.1109/VTC2020-Spring48590.2020.9128438

Ramadan, M. N., Al-Khedher, M. A., & Al-Kheder, S. A. (2012). Intelligent anti-theft and tracking system for automobiles. *International Journal of Machine Learning and Computing*, *2*(1), 83–88. doi:10.7763/IJMLC.2012.V2.94

Ritharson, P. I., Raimond, K., Mary, X. A., Robert, J. E., & Andrew, J. (2024). DeepRice: A deep learning and deep feature based classification of Rice leaf disease subtypes. *Artificial Intelligence in Agriculture*, *11*, 34–49. doi:10.1016/j.aiia.2023.11.001

Sadagopan, V. K., Rajendran, U., & Francis, A. J. (2011, July). Anti theft control system design using embedded system. In *Proceedings of 2011 IEEE International Conference on Vehicular Electronics and Safety* (pp. 1-5). IEEE. 10.1109/ICVES.2011.5983776

Sharifi, O., & Eskandari, M. (2018). Cosmetic Detection Framework for Face and Iris Biometrics. *Sensors (Basel)*, *10*, 122.

Win, Z. M., & Sein, M. M. (2011). *Fingerprint recognition system for low quality images*. Presented at the SICE Annual Conference, Waseda University, Tokyo, Japan.

Xin, Y., Kong, L., Liu, Z., Wang, C., Zhu, H., Gao, M., Zhao, C., & Xu, X. (2018). Multimodal Feature-Level Fusion for Biometrics Identification System on IoMT Platform. *IEEE Access, 6*, 21418–21426.

Zhang, H., Li, Q., Sun, Z., & Liu, Y. (2018). Combining Data-Driven and Model-Driven Methods for Robust Facial Landmark Detection. *IEEE Transactions on Information Forensics and Security*, *13*(10), 2409–2422. doi:10.1109/TIFS.2018.2800901

Zhang, Z., Yi, D., Lei, Z., & Li, S.Z. (2012). Regularized Transfer Boosting for Face Detection Across Spectrum. *IEEE Signal Process. Lett., 19*, 131–134.

Chapter 17
Study on Nano Robotic Systems for Industry 4.0:
Overcoming Challenges and Shaping Future Developments

G. V. Krishna Pradeep

Department of Mechanical Engineering, Aditya Engineering College, Surampalem, India

M. Balaji

Department of Mechanical Engineering, V.R. Siddhartha Engineering College, Vijayawada, India

Vivek Narula

Department of Management, Shri Venkateshwara University, India

V. Nirmala

Department of Mathematics, R.M.K. Engineering College, Chennai, India

I. John Solomon

Department of Mechanical Engineering, Panimalar Engineering College, Chennai, India

M. Sudhakar

Department of Mechanical Engineering, Sri Sai Ram Engineering College, Chennai, India

ABSTRACT

Nano robotics is a rapidly developing technology that operates at microscopic scales, revolutionizing fields like medicine and manufacturing. However, it faces numerous challenges, including technical, ethical, and practical issues. These include precision engineering, control mechanisms, and power sources, as well as ethical concerns about autonomy, safety, and societal impact. The chapter explores the future of nano robotics, highlighting its potential in various fields such as medicine and manufacturing. It highlights the potential of nano robots in enhancing durability and functionality, offering targeted drug delivery, minimally invasive surgeries, and precise diagnostics. The chapter also addresses technical challenges, ethical considerations, and potential developments, aiming to make the seemingly impossible achievable at the tiniest scales, emphasizing the need for further advancements.

DOI: 10.4018/979-8-3693-5767-5.ch017

INTRODUCTION

Nano robotics is a groundbreaking field that combines robotics, nanotechnology, and engineering at an unprecedented scale. These tiny mechanical marvels, operating in the nanometer range, can navigate realms imperceptible to the human eye, offering potential breakthroughs in medicine, manufacturing, and beyond. Originating from the visionary concepts of manipulating matter at molecular scales, pioneers like Richard Feynman have made significant progress in developing nano robots capable of traversing and interacting within the nanoworld's infinitesimally small dimensions (Daudi, 2015).

Nano robotics faces a challenge in precision engineering due to the need for devices at minuscule scales. This requires innovations in materials science, manufacturing techniques, and control mechanisms. Inspired by biological systems, these robots mimic the agility of nature's smallest organisms but require unparalleled complexity. However, their potential applications in medicine are boundless. These machines can revolutionize diagnostics, drug delivery, and surgical procedures with unprecedented precision. Their ability to navigate the human body at cellular or molecular levels offers new avenues for targeted therapies and treatments (Gheorghe et al., 2014).

This chapter delves into the intricacies, challenges, and transformative potential of nano robotics, a cutting-edge field that has the potential to revolutionize manufacturing processes by creating materials and products with unprecedented precision, durability, and functionality. It explores the intricacies and challenges of this cutting-edge field. Understanding operations at the nanoscale is fundamental to grasp the intricacies and challenges of nano robotics. At this minute level, physical laws and behaviors diverge from those in the macroscopic world, demanding a nuanced comprehension of how matter interacts, moves, and functions (Halder & Sun, 2019).

The nanoscale, characterized by dimensions typically between 1 and 100 nanometers, introduces a realm where quantum effects dominate and classical mechanics often lose their relevance. Quantum phenomena such as tunneling, where particles traverse barriers they theoretically shouldn't overcome, become significant at this scale. Moreover, surface forces such as Van der Waals and electrostatic forces become remarkably influential, even overpowering gravitational or inertial forces. Manipulating matter at this scale involves harnessing these unique properties and overcoming the challenges they pose. Precision becomes paramount; slight disturbances or fluctuations that might be inconsequential at larger scales can significantly impact nanoscale operations. Additionally, materials behave differently at the nanoscale, with altered mechanical, electrical, and optical properties, necessitating specialized approaches for design and manipulation (Chen et al., 2022a).

Nano robotics capitalizes on these principles by developing mechanisms and machines tailored to exploit nanoscale phenomena. For instance, nanorobots may leverage molecular motors inspired by biological structures or use specialized materials exhibiting unique properties at the nanoscale to achieve desired functionalities. However, navigating this domain is rife with challenges. Fabricating nanoscale components with precision, ensuring their reliability, and developing control mechanisms that operate effectively in this realm are formidable tasks. Moreover, environmental factors, such as temperature fluctuations or surface interactions, can significantly influence the behavior and stability of nanorobots, necessitating robust solutions (Ghanbarzadeh-Dagheyan et al., 2021).

A comprehensive understanding of nanoscale operations serves as the bedrock for advancements in nano robotics. By delving into the nuances of this scale, researchers and engineers aim to harness its peculiarities to design and create innovative nano robots capable of operating seamlessly in these unique environments, unlocking a world of possibilities across various disciplines. The 1980s saw significant advancements in nano-scale structures, thanks to the development of scanning tunneling and atomic force microscopes. These tools allowed scientists to visualize and manipulate individual atoms and molecules, paving the way for nanotechnology and nano robotics (Sivasankar & Durairaj, 2012).

Advancements in technology led to the development of nano robots capable of performing basic tasks at the nanoscale. These robots often drew inspiration from biological systems, mirroring the functionality of cellular machinery or molecular motors. Advancements in nanomaterials and fabrication techniques, such as self-assembly and DNA origami, expanded the range of nano robotic systems. The convergence of disciplines, including robotics, materials science, biology, and engineering, has led to the development of advanced nano robots. These tiny machines have potential applications in medicine, manufacturing, and environmental remediation. The evolution of nano robotic systems is driven by ongoing research and innovation, with the future promising further advancements and potential industry revolution (Ghanbarzadeh-Dagheyan et al., 2021).

Nano robotics is poised to revolutionize various industries, including healthcare, manufacturing, environmental remediation, and information technology, with its potential impact being far-reaching and promising, marking a transformative era in the field. Nano robotics holds great potential in medicine and healthcare, as they can navigate the human body with precision, enabling targeted drug delivery to specific cells or tissues. These nano-scale instruments can perform minimally invasive surgeries, minimizing trauma and recovery times (Pedram & Nejat Pishkenari, 2017).

They can also facilitate accurate diagnostics at the cellular or molecular level, potentially revolutionizing disease detection and treatment. Beyond healthcare, nano robotics holds promise in manufacturing and materials science, as they can assemble materials with unparalleled precision, creating novel materials with enhanced properties. This could lead to the development of innovative products across various industries. Nano robotics can be used in environmental remediation by precisely targeting pollutants at their source, offering potential solutions for water purification and soil remediation (Daudi, 2015; Pedram & Nejat Pishkenari, 2017).

They can also revolutionize data storage, computing, and communication by packing more information into smaller spaces. This paradigm shift in various industries presents new possibilities and challenges. However, achieving these applications requires technical hurdles, ethical considerations, and ensuring the safety and reliability of nano robotic systems. Despite these challenges, the transformative potential of nano robotics in shaping the future landscape of various industries is undeniable.

The following provides an overview of the background and scope of nano robotics (Puranik et al., 2024a; Srinivas et al., 2023).

- Nano robotics is a rapidly growing field that combines nanotechnology and robotics, focusing on designing and controlling robots at the nanoscale. Initially a futuristic concept, it has become a practical reality due to advancements in materials science, nanofabrication techniques, and control systems.

- Nano robotics has a wide range of applications across various industries, including medicine, manufacturing, electronics, and environmental remediation. In medicine, they could revolutionize diagnostics, drug delivery, and surgical procedures. In manufacturing, they could improve assembly and quality control. Additionally, nanorobots could help tackle environmental pollution at the molecular level.

- Nano robotics faces technical challenges such as precision engineering, robust control mechanisms, and identifying suitable power sources for operation. To overcome these, interdisciplinary collaboration and innovative approaches from fields like materials science, computer science, and bioengineering are needed, leveraging advances in these fields.

- The ethical implications of nano robotics are significant, as they could impact human health, privacy, and societal dynamics. These concerns include autonomy, safety, equitable access, and potential misuse. Balancing technological advancements with ethical responsibilities requires stakeholder engagement, robust regulatory frameworks, and ongoing scientific deliberation.
- Nano robotics holds immense promise despite challenges, with ongoing research aiming to overcome technical hurdles, expand applications, and address ethical concerns. Future developments include nanomaterial advancements for durability and functionality, control algorithm breakthroughs for precise manipulation, and power generation innovations for sustained operation. Interdisciplinary collaboration, ethical foresight, and societal dialogue are crucial for navigating complexities and maximizing benefits.

CHALLENGES IN NANO ROBOTICS

Technical Constraints at Nanoscale

Nano robot manufacturing presents significant technical challenges due to the unique constraints of the nanoscale environment. The principles of physics differ from larger scales, necessitating innovative design, fabrication, and assembly approaches. Precision engineering is required at an unprecedented level, and conventional manufacturing techniques struggle to maintain accuracy and consistency. Novel manufacturing processes, like DNA origami or molecular self-assembly, are crucial for constructing nano robots with precision (Dash & Maiti, 2023; Patwardhan, 2006).

Materials selection at the nanoscale is crucial due to their unique properties like surface area, conductivity, and strength, which differ significantly from bulk materials. Identifying and using these materials is essential for creating robust and functional nano robots. The assembly and manipulation of nano-scale components pose challenges due to the limitations of traditional tools, necessitating the development of specialized nanomanipulation techniques using atomic force microscopes, electron beams, or biological processes for accurate positioning and assembly (Mohanty et al., 2023; Pramila et al., 2023).

Nano robots face challenges in reliability and stability due to environmental factors like temperature fluctuations and surface interactions. Robust design methodologies are crucial for their functionality and longevity. Interdisciplinary collaboration between robotics, materials science, nanotechnology, and engineering is needed to overcome these technical constraints. Advancements in nanofabrication techniques, innovative materials, and precision assembly methods are essential for developing functional and reliable nano robotic systems for real-world applications (Pramila et al., 2023; Rahamathunnisa, Sudhakar, et al., 2023).

Control Mechanisms and Precision Engineering

Nano robotics relies on precise control mechanisms and precision engineering to ensure their functionality and efficacy. Conventional control methods are often insufficient due to the limitations of physics at nanoscale. Innovative control strategies, such as feedback loops, stochastic algorithms, and biological principles, are being explored to enable precise manipulation and navigation of nano robots. Reliability and predictability are crucial for nano robots to perform tasks accurately and consistently, despite inherent uncertainties and fluctuations. This requires robust control systems that can adapt to environmental changes and variations, maintaining stability and reliability in operation (Karimov et al., 2022).

Nano robotics relies on precision engineering to design and fabricate nano-scale components with accuracy and repeatability. Nanorobotics, created using advanced nanofabrication techniques like electron beam lithography and molecular self-assembly, require intricate structures and intricate engineering to integrate various functionalities. These robots require diverse components like sensors, actuators, and power sources, all scaled down to nanometers while maintaining functionality. Interdisciplinary collaboration between robotics, control systems, materials science, and nanotechnology is crucial for developing robust, reliable nano robotic systems (Rahamathunnisa, Sudhakar, et al., 2023; Srinivas et al., 2023).

MATERIALS INNOVATIONS IN NANO ROBOTICS

Advanced Nanomaterials for Construction

Advanced nanomaterials are crucial in the development of nano robotic systems due to their unique properties and functionalities. These materials, engineered and manipulated at atomic or molecular levels, offer exceptional mechanical, electrical, or optical properties. Carbon-based nanomaterials like carbon nanotubes or graphene are ideal for constructing structural elements or providing electrical pathways within nano robots due to their exceptional strength, flexibility, and electrical conductivity (Walsh & Strano, 2018).

Nanoparticles of metals, semiconductors, or magnetic materials offer functionalities like catalytic activity, sensing, and magnetic manipulation, expanding the capabilities of nano robotic systems. These nanoparticles can be integrated into specific components for tasks like targeted drug delivery or precise object manipulation. Biomimetic nanomaterials, inspired by natural structures, offer promising possibilities in nano robotics, such as self-healing polymers and nanoscale structures mimicking biological systems, enabling resilient and adaptable nano robots in dynamic environments (Puranik et al., 2024b; Revathi et al., 2024).

Advanced nanomaterials are produced using techniques like molecular self-assembly, nanolithography, and chemical vapor deposition, allowing precise manipulation of atoms or molecules. However, challenges remain in ensuring scalability, reproducibility, and stability. Quality control and standardization are crucial for nano robotics production to ensure consistent performance and reliability. Advancements in materials science, nanotechnology, and engineering drive the development of novel nanomaterials, offering new possibilities for nano robotic systems with enhanced capabilities and performance at the nanoscale (Pramila et al., 2023; Rahamathunnisa, Sudhakar, et al., 2023).

Functionalities and Durability Enhancements

Nano robotic systems, with their enhanced functionality and durability, can perform complex tasks with precision, adapt to dynamic environments, and offer extended operational capabilities, extending their potential in various fields (Maheswari et al., 2023; Mohanty et al., 2023; Rahamathunnisa, Sudhakar, et al., 2023).

- **Enhanced Sensing Abilities:** Nano robots can be equipped with advanced sensors capable of detecting various physical and chemical parameters at the nanoscale. These sensors enable precise measurements, facilitating tasks such as environmental monitoring, medical diagnostics, or quality control in manufacturing processes (Chen et al., 2022b; Walsh & Strano, 2018).

- **Targeted Drug Delivery:** Nano robots with specialized functionalities can transport drugs or therapeutic agents to specific cells or tissues in the body, minimizing side effects and maximizing treatment efficiency. Functional modifications allow for controlled release mechanisms triggered by specific stimuli.

- **Adaptive and Responsive Behavior:** Incorporating responsive materials and mechanisms enables nano robots to adapt to changing environments. Responsive functionalities can be designed to react to stimuli like pH changes, temperature variations, or specific biomarkers, enhancing their versatility in diverse applications.

- **Self-Healing and Self-Repair:** Integration of self-healing materials or mechanisms within nano robots enhances their durability. These capabilities enable the robots to autonomously repair damage or wear, prolonging their operational lifespan in challenging conditions.

- **Multimodal Capabilities:** Nano robots can possess multiple functionalities, combining tasks such as manipulation, sensing, and drug delivery within a single system. This multimodal approach enhances their utility and efficiency in performing complex tasks.

- **Improved Energy Efficiency:** Enhancements in power sources and energy harvesting technologies lead to more energy-efficient nano robots. Utilizing nanoscale power generation or energy harvesting mechanisms can prolong operational periods and reduce the need for frequent recharging or maintenance.

- **Durability in Harsh Environments:** Nano robots engineered with materials resistant to extreme conditions, such as high temperatures, corrosive environments, or radiation exposure, ensure their functionality and reliability in challenging operational environments.

- **Bio-Inspired Design:** Drawing inspiration from biological systems allows for the development of nano robots with biomimetic functionalities. Mimicking natural structures and processes enhances adaptability, efficiency, and durability in various applications.

Integration of Nanoscale Components

The integration of nanoscale components into nano robotic systems necessitates meticulous engineering and innovative approaches due to the inherent challenges of working at such tiny scales (Indiveri et al., 2013). The figure 1 depicts the integration of nanoscale components into nano robotic systems. The integration of nanoscale components into nano robotic systems requires a comprehensive approach considering functionality, compatibility, interaction, and collective performance within the nano robot's confined space (Boopathi, 2023; Malathi et al., 2024).

- **Miniaturization and Compact Design:** Nano robots demand compact designs that accommodate various functionalities within a limited space. Integrating diverse nanoscale components—sensors, actuators, power sources—requires meticulous design to optimize space and functionality without compromising performance.

- **Nanoscale Assembly Techniques:** Specialized assembly techniques like DNA origami, self-assembly, or bottom-up fabrication methods are employed to precisely position and integrate nanoscale components. These methods enable the construction of intricate structures with nanometer precision.

- **Multifunctional Platforms:** Designing platforms that can host multiple functionalities is crucial. Nanoscale components with different purposes—such as drug delivery, sensing, or manipulation—need to seamlessly integrate and work in tandem within the confined space of a nano robot.

Figure 1. Integration of nanoscale components into nano robotic systems

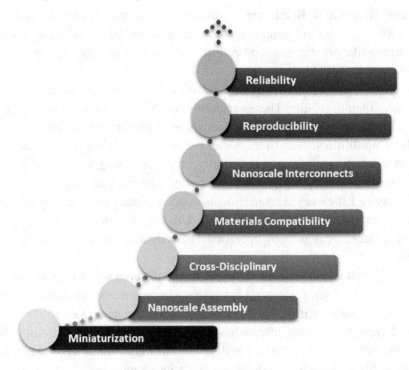

- **Cross-Disciplinary Collaboration:** Integrating nanoscale components necessitates collaboration across various disciplines, including materials science, nanotechnology, robotics, and biology. Experts from these fields collaborate to design and integrate components effectively.
- **Materials Compatibility and Interface Engineering:** Ensuring compatibility between different nanoscale components is crucial. Materials used in different components should exhibit compatibility to avoid adverse reactions or functionality issues. Interface engineering is essential to promote interaction between components while maintaining stability.
- **Nanoscale Interconnects and Communication:** Establishing communication and interconnectivity between nanoscale components is vital for their coordinated operation. Developing nanoscale communication protocols or methods for transmitting signals within nano robots is essential for seamless functionality.
- **Scalability and Reproducibility:** Methods for integrating nanoscale components should be scalable and reproducible. Consistent fabrication processes enable the mass production of reliable nano robots, critical for practical applications.

- **Reliability and Robustness Testing:** Stress tests and simulations are crucial for rigorous testing and validation of integrated nanoscale components, identifying potential weaknesses and optimizing design for enhanced performance and durability.

ADVANCEMENTS IN AI AND MACHINE LEARNING

Empowering Nano Robots With AI Capabilities

AI and machine learning advancements are revolutionizing nano robotics, providing autonomy, adaptability, and enhanced functionality. Important factors include AI integration into nano robots (Pugliese & Regondi, 2022). The integration of AI and machine learning in nano robots enhances their adaptability, intelligence, and versatility, enabling autonomous operation in complex environments, paving the way for applications in medicine, manufacturing, and environmental monitoring.

- **Autonomous Decision-Making:** AI algorithms enable nano robots to make decisions autonomously in dynamic environments. These algorithms process sensory data, analyze patterns, and make real-time decisions, allowing nano robots to adapt their actions without human intervention.
- **Adaptive Behavior:** Machine learning algorithms equipped within nano robots enable adaptive behavior. They learn from experience, adjusting their actions based on feedback, optimizing performance, and enhancing efficiency in completing tasks.
- **Sensory Processing and Analysis:** AI enhances the processing and analysis of sensory information gathered by nano robots. Machine learning algorithms can interpret complex data gathered at the nanoscale, enabling precise and efficient decision-making based on environmental cues.
- **Navigation and Control:** AI algorithms aid in navigation and control at the nanoscale. They assist in precise maneuvering within intricate environments, ensuring accurate positioning and manipulation of nano-scale objects or within biological systems.
- **Fault Detection and Self-Repair:** AI facilitates fault detection and self-repair mechanisms in nano robots. Machine learning algorithms can identify anomalies or malfunctions, triggering corrective actions or self-repair processes to maintain functionality.
- **Task Optimization and Learning:** Nano robots equipped with AI continuously optimize their tasks and operations. They learn from previous experiences, refining strategies and techniques to improve performance and achieve better outcomes.
- **Energy Efficiency and Resource Management:** AI enables efficient resource utilization and energy management within nano robots. Algorithms optimize power consumption, ensuring prolonged operational periods or the ability to harvest energy from the environment.
- **Security and Redundancy:** AI-driven security protocols enhance the robustness of nano robots against external threats or potential malfunctions. Redundancy and fail-safe mechanisms guided by AI algorithms ensure continued operation even in challenging scenarios.

Autonomous Decision-Making at Microscopic Levels

Advancements in AI and machine learning have enabled microscopic autonomous decision-making, a transformative capability in nano robotics (Vigelius et al., 2014). Nano robots with autonomous decision-making capabilities are revolutionizing applications in precision medicine, targeted therapies, environmental monitoring, and nanoscale manufacturing. These advancements revolutionize the operation, navigation, and interaction of these miniature machines, offering unprecedented possibilities for innovation and impact (Sampath et al., 2022).

- **Sensory Perception:** Nano robots equipped with sophisticated sensors capture and interpret data at the microscopic scale. These sensors detect environmental cues, molecular interactions, or cellular responses, providing essential input for decision-making.
- **AI Algorithms for Nanoscale Environments:** AI algorithms process vast amounts of sensory data collected by nano robots. These algorithms are designed to interpret and make decisions based on nanoscale phenomena, leveraging pattern recognition and analysis techniques specific to this level.
- **Real-time Adaptation:** Autonomous decision-making in nano robots involves real-time adaptation to dynamic environments. AI algorithms continuously assess and respond to changes at the microscopic level, enabling swift adjustments in operations or tasks.
- **Environmental Sensing and Response:** Nano robots autonomously sense and respond to variations in their environment. They detect factors like temperature shifts, chemical gradients, or cellular behaviors, altering their actions accordingly for specific tasks or interventions.
- **Decision Trees and Predictive Modeling:** AI-driven decision-making involves the creation of decision trees and predictive models at the nanoscale. These models enable nano robots to anticipate outcomes or responses based on various sensory inputs, optimizing their actions.
- **Learning from Interactions:** Machine learning capabilities within nano robots allow them to learn from their interactions. They adapt their decision-making processes based on past experiences, refining strategies for improved outcomes.
- **Adaptive Control Systems:** Autonomous decision-making is complemented by adaptive control systems within nano robots. These systems modulate actions, movements, or functions in response to the information processed by AI algorithms.
- **Safety Protocols and Redundancy:** Autonomous decision-making in nano robots incorporates safety protocols and redundancy measures. AI algorithms ensure that decisions prioritize safety and reliability, while redundant systems act as fail-safes in case of unexpected circumstances.

Applications in Complex Environments

Nano robots, equipped with advanced capabilities, find diverse applications in complex environments, navigating unique challenges in these intricate settings (Balaguer et al., 2000). The figure 2 depicts the applications of nano robots in complex environments. Nano robots' adaptability, precision, and versatility in complex environments reveal their potential in various fields, addressing challenges that traditional technology cannot overcome due to their ability to navigate and perform tasks at the smallest scales.

- **Biomedical Applications:** Nano robots excel in navigating complex biological environments. They can perform precise tasks such as targeted drug delivery within the human body, maneuvering through intricate networks of cells and tissues to reach specific targets.

Figure 2. Nano robots applications in complex environments

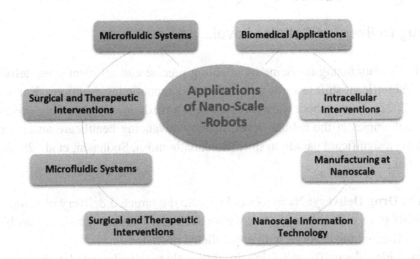

- **Intracellular Interventions:** These tiny machines have the potential to operate within cells, performing interventions or carrying out repairs at the molecular level. They navigate within cellular structures, aiding in diagnostics or therapeutic interventions.

- **Environmental Sensing and Remediation:** Nano robots are deployed in complex environmental settings for tasks like pollution monitoring or remediation. They navigate diverse and challenging terrains, detecting and neutralizing pollutants or assisting in environmental cleanup.

- **Manufacturing at Nanoscale:** In complex manufacturing processes, nano robots facilitate precision assembly and manipulation of materials at the atomic or molecular level. They operate in intricate setups, enabling the creation of advanced materials or devices.

- **Nanoscale Information Technology:** Nano robots contribute to advancements in information technology by enabling data storage at the molecular level or facilitating nanoscale computing. They navigate and manipulate information-bearing structures at this minuscule scale.

- **Surgical and Therapeutic Interventions:** Within the medical field, nano robots perform minimally invasive surgeries, offering precise interventions with minimal disruption. They navigate complex anatomical structures, enabling highly targeted treatments.

- **Exploration in Extreme Environments:** Nano robots navigate and explore extreme environments, such as deep-sea or outer space, where conventional technology faces challenges. They collect data, perform tasks, or assist in scientific exploration in these harsh settings.

- **Microfluidic Systems:** Nano robots contribute to the development of microfluidic systems by navigating and manipulating fluids at the microscale. They assist in tasks like controlled mixing, sorting, or analysis within microfluidic devices.

NANO ROBOTICS IN MEDICINE

Targeted Drug Delivery at Cellular Levels

Nano robotics is revolutionizing medicine by enabling precise and efficient drug delivery at cellular levels, offering a significant shift towards personalized therapeutic interventions (Karan & Majumder, 2011; Xu et al., 2022). Nano robotics are revolutionizing medicine by providing precision, efficacy, and personalized therapies at the cellular level, thereby advancing healthcare and improving patient outcomes, marking a significant paradigm shift (Rahamathunnisa, Sudhakar, et al., 2023; Senthil et al., 2023; Srinivas et al., 2023).

- **Precision in Drug Delivery:** Nano robots facilitate the targeted delivery of drugs or therapeutic agents directly to specific cells or tissues within the body. They navigate complex biological environments, delivering medications with unparalleled precision.
- **Minimizing Side Effects:** By delivering drugs directly to the affected cells or tissues, nano robots minimize systemic exposure and reduce side effects commonly associated with conventional drug delivery methods.
- **Enhanced Efficacy:** Targeted drug delivery at the cellular level enhances the efficacy of treatments. Nano robots ensure that therapeutic agents reach their intended targets, improving the effectiveness of medications in treating diseases.
- **Navigating Biological Barriers:** Nano robots are designed to navigate through biological barriers such as the blood-brain barrier or cellular membranes. They can transport drugs across these barriers, accessing areas that were previously challenging to reach.
- **Site-Specific Treatments:** Nano robots enable site-specific treatments, addressing diseases at their origin. They can target cancerous cells, infectious agents, or specific diseased tissues, offering tailored and precise interventions.
- **Controlled Release Mechanisms:** Nano robots can be engineered to carry payloads of drugs or therapeutic compounds and release them in a controlled manner. This controlled release ensures a sustained therapeutic effect at the cellular level.
- **Real-time Monitoring:** Some nano robots are equipped with sensors for real-time monitoring of cellular responses or drug efficacy. They gather feedback on treatment effectiveness, enabling adjustments or modifications in drug delivery strategies.
- **Potential for Personalized Medicine:** Nano robotics in targeted drug delivery holds promise for personalized medicine. These technologies can be tailored to individual patient needs, offering customized treatments based on specific cellular characteristics or conditions.

Minimally Invasive Surgeries and Nano Surgical Tools

Nano robotics has brought forth a new era in minimally invasive surgeries by introducing advanced nano surgical tools that enable precise interventions with minimal tissue disruption (Xu et al., 2022). Nano robotics and nano surgical tools are revolutionizing minimally invasive surgeries, providing precision, reduced risks, and faster recovery times. These advancements enhance patient outcomes and pave the way for future surgical interventions.

- **Microscale Precision:** Nano surgical tools operate at the micro and nanoscale, allowing surgeons to perform extremely precise interventions. These tools navigate intricate anatomical structures with high precision.
- **Reduced Tissue Trauma:** Minimally invasive surgeries utilizing nano surgical tools result in minimal tissue damage compared to traditional surgical procedures. Nano robots perform delicate procedures with minimal disruption to surrounding tissues.
- **Enhanced Dexterity:** Nano surgical tools offer enhanced dexterity, enabling surgeons to manipulate tissues or perform intricate tasks with precision that surpasses the capabilities of human hands or conventional surgical instruments.
- **Access to Challenging Areas:** Nano robots provide access to anatomical areas that are hard to reach using traditional surgical methods. They can navigate within confined spaces or delicate structures within the body.
- **Remote Surgical Procedures:** Some nano surgical tools enable remote surgical procedures. Surgeons can control these tools from a distance, offering the potential for remote surgeries, especially in scenarios where physical access is limited (Boopathi, 2023; Rahamathunnisa, Subhashini, et al., 2023).
- **Intraoperative Imaging and Sensing:** Nano robots equipped with imaging or sensing capabilities provide real-time information to surgeons during procedures. This aids in navigation, decision-making, and ensuring precision during surgery.
- **Faster Recovery and Reduced Risks:** Minimally invasive surgeries using nano surgical tools result in faster recovery times for patients due to reduced trauma. Additionally, there is a lower risk of complications and infections associated with these procedures.
- **Future Integration with AI:** Integration with AI and machine learning could further enhance the capabilities of nano surgical tools. AI algorithms could aid in real-time decision-making, optimizing surgical techniques, and providing additional guidance to surgeons.

Diagnostic Innovations With Nano Robots

Nano robots provide precise and efficient methods for disease detection and diagnostic imaging at the cellular or molecular level (S. Kumar et al., 2018). The figure 3 depicts nano robots being utilized for precise and efficient disease detection. Nano robots offer precise, accurate, and minimally invasive diagnostic techniques, enhancing patient outcomes and facilitating more effective treatments through early detection and precise imaging, thus advancing healthcare.

- **Early Disease Detection:** Nano robots equipped with sensors can detect biomarkers or abnormalities at early stages of diseases. They enable early detection of conditions such as cancer, infections, or other illnesses before symptoms manifest.
- **High Precision Imaging:** Nano robots facilitate high-resolution imaging at the cellular or molecular level. They can provide detailed images of tissues, organs, or cellular structures, aiding in accurate diagnosis and treatment planning.
- **Targeted Biopsy and Sampling:** Nano robots enable targeted biopsies or sampling of specific cells or tissues. They extract samples precisely, minimizing invasiveness and reducing the need for extensive tissue sampling.

- **In Vivo Imaging and Monitoring:** Some nano robots operate within the body, providing real-time in vivo imaging and monitoring of physiological processes. They offer continuous observation of cellular activities or responses during treatments.
- **Nanoscale Sensors for Diagnostics:** Nano robots carry nanoscale sensors capable of detecting minute changes or biomarkers indicative of diseases. These sensors provide sensitive and specific diagnostic information, improving accuracy.
- **Multiplexed Diagnostics:** Nano robots with multiplexed diagnostic capabilities can simultaneously detect multiple biomarkers or indicators within a single sample. This capability enhances efficiency and accuracy in diagnostics.
- **Point-of-Care Diagnostics:** Nano robots contribute to the development of point-of-care diagnostic tools. They enable rapid and accurate diagnostics at the patient's bedside or in resource-limited settings, improving access to healthcare.
- **Customized and Personalized Diagnostics:** Nano robotics allows for personalized diagnostics based on individual patient profiles. The ability to tailor diagnostic tests to specific cellular or molecular characteristics offers personalized and precise treatment strategies.

Figure 3. Nano robots provide precise and efficient methods for disease detection

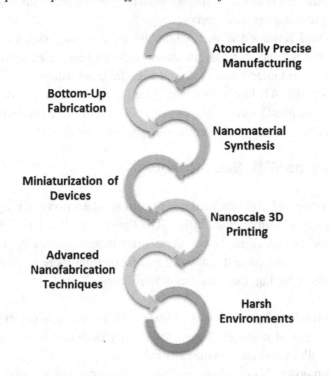

NANO ROBOTICS IN MANUFACTURING

Precision Assembly and Manipulation at Nanoscale

Nano robotics in manufacturing is revolutionizing processes by enabling precision assembly and manipulation at the nanoscale, paving the way for innovative material creation and device fabrication (Dash & Maiti, 2023). Nano robotics in manufacturing offers precision-driven creation of advanced materials, devices, and structures, transforming industries by enabling the development of novel products with enhanced functionalities and tailored properties.

- **Atomically Precise Manufacturing:** Nano robots facilitate manufacturing processes with atomic precision, allowing the assembly of materials at the molecular or atomic level. This precision leads to the creation of materials with specific properties and functionalities.
- **Bottom-Up Fabrication:** Nano robotics enables bottom-up fabrication techniques, where materials are built atom by atom or molecule by molecule. This approach allows for precise control over material structure and properties.
- **Nanomaterial Synthesis:** Nano robots contribute to the synthesis of advanced nanomaterials. They manipulate nanoparticles or nanostructures, assembling them into desired configurations, leading to the development of novel materials with unique properties.
- **Miniaturization of Devices:** Nano robots aid in the miniaturization of devices by assembling components at the nanoscale. They contribute to the production of smaller, more efficient devices with enhanced functionalities.
- **Nanoscale 3D Printing:** Nano robotics enables 3D printing at the nanoscale, allowing the creation of intricate structures with precise dimensions. This capability opens avenues for the production of nanoscale devices or components (Boopathi, Khare, et al., 2023; Palaniappan et al., 2023; Senthil et al., 2023).
- **Advanced Nanofabrication Techniques:** Nano robots employ advanced nanofabrication techniques such as molecular self-assembly, nanolithography, or nanoimprinting. These techniques enable precise manipulation of materials and structures.
- **Precision Manipulation in Harsh Environments:** Nano robots can operate in challenging environments such as extreme temperatures or pressures, facilitating precision manipulation of materials under conditions unsuitable for traditional manufacturing methods (Boopathi, 2022; Gowri et al., 2023).
- **Tailored Material Properties:** Manufacturing with nano robots allows for tailoring material properties at the nanoscale. By controlling material composition and structure, unique mechanical, electrical, or optical properties can be achieved.

Impact on Production Processes

Nano robotics is revolutionizing various industries by enhancing efficiency, precision, and novel capabilities, with significant impacts on production processes highlighted in important factors (Dash & Maiti, 2023). The integration of nano robotics into production processes redefines manufacturing paradigms, offering unprecedented precision, efficiency, and the ability to create materials and devices with unique properties. This transformative impact extends across industries, driving innovation and shaping the future of production.

- **Increased Precision and Accuracy:** Nano robotics elevates precision in production processes to the atomic or molecular level. This precision ensures unparalleled accuracy in manufacturing components or structures, reducing errors and enhancing quality.
- **Miniaturization and Efficiency:** Nano robots contribute to the miniaturization of components and devices, improving efficiency by reducing material wastage and optimizing resource utilization.
- **Novel Material Development:** Nano robotics enables the creation of novel materials with unique properties and functionalities. These materials find applications in diverse industries, offering innovative solutions and improved performance.
- **Customization and Personalization:** The precision afforded by nano robotics allows for customization and personalization of products. Tailored components or devices can be manufactured to meet specific customer requirements.
- **Advanced Manufacturing Techniques:** Nano robots drive the development of advanced manufacturing techniques such as nanolithography, molecular self-assembly, or nanoscale 3D printing. These techniques revolutionize how materials are manipulated and structured (Revathi et al., 2024).
- **Speed and Efficiency in Prototyping:** Nano robotics accelerates prototyping processes by enabling rapid and precise fabrication of prototypes at the nanoscale. This speed expedites innovation and product development.
- **Resource Conservation:** Nano robotics minimizes material wastage and energy consumption in manufacturing processes. The precision and efficiency of these technologies reduce resource utilization, contributing to sustainable production practices.
- **Cross-Industry Applications:** Nano robotics transcends industry boundaries, impacting sectors ranging from electronics and healthcare to materials science and environmental remediation. Its versatility opens doors to diverse applications.
- **Emergence of New Industries:** The capabilities unlocked by nano robotics pave the way for the emergence of entirely new industries and markets. Novel materials, devices, and production methods spur innovation and economic growth (Ravisankar et al., 2024; Vijayakumar et al., 2024).

Future of Nanoscale Manufacturing

The future of nanoscale manufacturing holds immense potential for industry transformation, groundbreaking advancements, and the creation of novel materials, devices, and applications (S. Kumar et al., 2018).

- **Nanoscale Additive Manufacturing:** Advancements in nanoscale 3D printing technologies will enable the precise fabrication of intricate structures at the molecular or atomic level. This will revolutionize manufacturing by allowing the creation of custom-designed nanoscale components and devices.
- **Nanomaterials with Tailored Properties:** Future nanoscale manufacturing techniques will focus on engineering materials with precisely tailored properties. This includes materials with superior strength, conductivity, flexibility, or other desired characteristics for various applications.

- **On-Demand Nanofabrication:** The future of nanoscale manufacturing envisions on-demand and decentralized fabrication capabilities. This may involve the development of portable or desktop-scale nanofabrication devices, enabling rapid prototyping and customization.
- **Nanorobot Swarms for Manufacturing:** The use of swarms of autonomous nanorobots working collaboratively is anticipated. These nanorobot swarms will perform complex tasks, such as assembly, manufacturing, or environmental remediation, in a coordinated manner.
- **AI-Driven Nanoscale Production:** Integration of AI and machine learning into nanoscale manufacturing will optimize processes, predict material behaviors, and enhance decision-making in real time. AI algorithms will enable autonomous control and optimization of nanoscale manufacturing systems (Boopathi & Khang, 2023; Koshariya, Kalaiyarasi, et al., 2023; Koshariya, Khatoon, et al., 2023; Maguluri et al., 2023).
- **Nanoscale Biomanufacturing:** Future developments might explore nanoscale biomanufacturing, leveraging biological systems or biomimetic approaches to produce functional nanomaterials or devices inspired by natural structures.
- **Nanomedicine and Therapeutics:** Nanoscale manufacturing will continue to advance in the medical field, facilitating the creation of targeted drug delivery systems, nanoscale implants, or diagnostic devices for personalized medicine.
- **Nanotechnology Integration in Everyday Products:** Nanoscale manufacturing will lead to the integration of nanotechnology in everyday products, enhancing their functionalities, durability, and performance (Boopathi, Umareddy, et al., 2023; Fowziya et al., 2023; Vijayakumar et al., 2024).
- **Sustainable Nanomanufacturing:** There will be a focus on developing sustainable and environmentally friendly nanomanufacturing techniques. Innovations will aim to reduce energy consumption, minimize waste, and employ eco-friendly materials.

Nanoscale manufacturing holds immense potential for innovation across industries, shaping technological progress and addressing global challenges as advancements continue.

ENVISIONING THE FUTURE OF NANO ROBOTICS

Overcoming Current Limitations

The future of nano robotics is predicted to be significantly enhanced through innovative methods and technological advancements. The following strategies can be employed to tackle obstacles (Pandya & Auner, 2004):

- **Enhanced Control and Manipulation:** Developing more precise and adaptable control mechanisms at the nanoscale is critical. Advancements in nanomanipulation techniques, such as improved nano grippers or nanomanipulators, will enable more accurate manipulation of nano-scale objects.
- **Improved Energy Sources:** Overcoming limitations in power sources for nano robots is crucial. Research into nanoscale power generation or energy harvesting methods could provide sustainable and efficient energy sources for these miniature machines.

- **Reliability and Durability:** Enhancing the reliability and durability of nano robots remains a challenge. Future advancements in materials science may yield more robust materials suitable for nanoscale applications, ensuring longevity and stability in various environments.
- **Miniaturization of Components:** Shrinking components without sacrificing functionality is essential. Advances in nanofabrication techniques and the development of nanoscale components, sensors, and actuators will further miniaturize nano robots, improving their capabilities.
- **Biocompatibility and Safety:** Ensuring the biocompatibility and safety of nano robots used in medical applications is critical. Continued research into materials that are safe for biological systems and the development of biodegradable nanomaterials will address these concerns.
- **Scalability and Mass Production:** Scaling up nanoscale manufacturing processes for mass production is challenging. Innovations in scalable nanofabrication techniques and automated assembly methods will enable the large-scale production of nano robotic systems.
- **Interdisciplinary Collaboration:** Collaborations between various scientific disciplines are vital for overcoming limitations. Continued cooperation between robotics, nanotechnology, materials science, and biomedicine will drive innovation in nano robotics.
- **Integration with AI and Machine Learning:** Further integration of AI and machine learning will enhance the capabilities of nano robots. AI algorithms can optimize decision-making, improve autonomous functionalities, and enable adaptive behavior in these miniature systems (Hussain et al., 2023; M. Kumar et al., 2023).

Nano robotics advancements will revolutionize fields like medicine, manufacturing, and environmental remediation, necessitating collaboration among researchers, engineers, policymakers, and ethicists. The advancement and widespread adoption of nano robotics are poised to bring about substantial societal and economic impacts across various domains. Here are potential impacts in both societal and economic spheres:

Societal Impacts

- **Healthcare Transformation:** Nano robotics in medicine could revolutionize healthcare by offering personalized treatments, precise diagnostics, and targeted drug delivery. This could lead to improved patient outcomes, reduced treatment costs, and better overall health for individuals (Kushwah et al., 2024; Ramudu et al., 2023; Satav et al., 2023).
- **Enhanced Quality of Life:** Nano robotics might lead to the development of assistive devices or technologies that enhance the quality of life for individuals with disabilities or age-related limitations, enabling greater independence.
- **Environmental Remediation:** Nano robots could be utilized for environmental cleanup, pollution monitoring, or remediation, contributing to cleaner ecosystems and sustainable environmental practices (Boopathi, Alqahtani, et al., 2023; Gowri et al., 2023; Hanumanthakari et al., 2023).
- **Access to Advanced Technologies:** Advancements in nano robotics might offer access to advanced technologies in developing regions, bridging technological gaps and providing innovative solutions in healthcare, agriculture, and infrastructure.
- **Ethical Considerations:** Societal impacts also involve addressing ethical concerns related to the use of nano robotics, including privacy, autonomy, and equitable access to these technologies across different socio-economic groups.

Economic Impacts

Understanding and harnessing the potential societal and economic impacts of nano robotics will require collaboration among policymakers, researchers, industries, and communities to ensure responsible and inclusive development, maximizing the benefits for society while addressing any associated challenges or risks (Babu et al., 2022; Dhanya et al., 2023; Hussain et al., 2023; Ravisankar et al., 2023).

- **Innovation and New Industries:** Nano robotics will spur innovation, leading to the emergence of new industries and markets. Companies investing in nano robotics could drive economic growth and create job opportunities in research, development, and manufacturing sectors.
- **Increased Productivity:** Adoption of nano robotic technologies in manufacturing processes could enhance productivity and efficiency. Precise manufacturing capabilities may lead to cost savings, reduced waste, and higher-quality products.
- **Healthcare Expenditure Reduction:** Improved healthcare through nano robotics may lower healthcare costs by providing targeted treatments and early disease detection, potentially reducing long-term healthcare expenditures.
- **Global Competitiveness:** Nations investing in nano robotics research and development may enhance their global competitiveness. Leading the way in advanced technologies could strengthen a country's position in the global economy.
- **Resource Optimization:** Nano robotics may lead to better utilization of resources, whether in manufacturing, energy production, or environmental management, contributing to sustainable economic practices.

FUTURE POSSIBILITIES AND TRANSFORMATIONS

Nano robotics holds immense potential for transformative changes in industries, healthcare, sustainability, and technology interaction. However, careful consideration of ethical, societal, and environmental implications is crucial for harnessing these advancements for the greater good (Mbunge et al., 2021; Pokrajac et al., 2021). The figure 4 depicts the potential for future possibilities and transformations.

Figure 4. Future possibilities and transformations

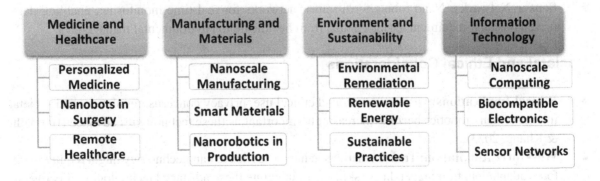

Medicine and Healthcare

- **Personalized Medicine:** Nano robots enable precise targeted therapies, personalized drug delivery, and diagnostics tailored to individual genetic profiles, revolutionizing healthcare.
- **Nanobots in Surgery:** Surgical procedures become minimally invasive, with nanobots performing precise interventions within the body, reducing risks and improving recovery times.
- **Remote Healthcare:** Nanobots equipped with sensors could provide remote monitoring and treatments, extending healthcare access to remote or underserved areas (Malathi et al., 2024).

Manufacturing and Materials

- **Nanoscale Manufacturing:** Advanced nanofabrication techniques enable the production of novel materials, leading to the development of highly efficient devices and structures.
- **Smart Materials:** Nano robotics contribute to the creation of smart materials with adaptive functionalities, finding applications in electronics, construction, and energy.
- **Nanorobotics in Production:** Nanobots aid in advanced manufacturing processes, optimizing production efficiency, reducing waste, and enabling rapid prototyping.

Environment and Sustainability

- **Environmental Remediation:** Nano robots assist in cleaning pollutants, monitoring ecosystems, and remediating environmental damage in a targeted and efficient manner.
- **Renewable Energy:** Nanotechnology contributes to the development of advanced materials for energy harvesting, storage, and more efficient renewable energy devices.
- **Sustainable Practices:** Nanoscale technologies promote sustainability by optimizing resource utilization, reducing energy consumption, and fostering eco-friendly manufacturing processes (Boopathi, Umareddy, et al., 2023; Boopathi & Davim, 2023b, 2023a).

Information Technology

- **Nanoscale Computing:** Advances in nanoscale computing and data storage could revolutionize information technology, leading to faster and more efficient devices.
- **Biocompatible Electronics:** Nanoscale electronics enable the development of biocompatible devices, potentially integrating technology with biology for various applications.
- **Sensor Networks:** Nano robots form sensor networks for real-time monitoring, enabling data-driven decision-making in various fields, from healthcare to environmental management.

Societal and Ethical Considerations

- **Ethical Implications:** Discussions around ethical use, privacy concerns, regulation, and societal impact of nano robotics become increasingly important as these technologies advance (Boopathi & Khang, 2023).
- **Workforce Adaptation:** Transformations in industries due to nanotechnology might require workforce adaptation, training, and new skillsets to integrate these advanced technologies effectively.

- • **Global Collaboration:** International collaboration and ethical frameworks become crucial in ensuring responsible development and equitable access to nano robotics across regions.

CONCLUSION

The advancement of nano robotics is a significant technological advancement, poised to revolutionize various fields with its precision, adaptability, and transformative capabilities, marking a new era of advancements and possibilities in various fields. Nanotechnology and robotics are combining to create precision at atomic and molecular levels, enabling improved treatments and outcomes in medicine and manufacturing. Nano robots offer targeted drug delivery, minimally invasive surgeries, and personalized healthcare, while manufacturing machines enable the creation of novel materials and efficient production processes.

Nano robotics have significant societal and economic impacts, including healthcare transformation, environmental remediation, and increased accessibility to advanced technologies. However, ethical considerations and regulatory frameworks are crucial for responsible development and equitable access to these technologies. Nano robotics holds immense potential for personalized medicine, smart materials, and renewable energy. However, navigating this transformative landscape requires collaboration, ethical discourse, and a proactive approach to societal and environmental implications to harness its potential for humanity's betterment.

Nano robotics is a cutting-edge technology that is poised to revolutionize industries, redefine possibilities, and positively impact our lives, presenting a promising future.

Abbreviations

AI: Artificial Intelligence
  3D: Three-Dimensional

REFERENCES

Babu, B. S., Kamalakannan, J., Meenatchi, N., Karthik, S., & Boopathi, S. (2022). Economic impacts and reliability evaluation of battery by adopting Electric Vehicle. *IEEE Explore*, 1–6.

Balaguer, C., Giménez, A., Pastor, J. M., Padron, V., & Abderrahim, M. (2000). A climbing autonomous robot for inspection applications in 3d complex environments. *Robotica, 18*(3), 287–297. doi:10.1017/S0263574799002258

Boopathi, S. (2022). Performance Improvement of Eco-Friendly Near-Dry wire-Cut Electrical Discharge Machining Process Using Coconut Oil-Mist Dielectric Fluid. *World Scientific: Journal of Advanced Manufacturing Systems*.

Boopathi, S. (2023). Internet of Things-Integrated Remote Patient Monitoring System: Healthcare Application. In *Dynamics of Swarm Intelligence Health Analysis for the Next Generation* (pp. 137–161). IGI Global. doi:10.4018/978-1-6684-6894-4.ch008

Boopathi, S., Alqahtani, A. S., Mubarakali, A., & Panchatcharam, P. (2023). Sustainable developments in near-dry electrical discharge machining process using sunflower oil-mist dielectric fluid. *Environmental Science and Pollution Research International*, 1–20. doi:10.1007/s11356-023-27494-0 PMID:37199846

Boopathi, S., & Davim, J. P. (2023a). Applications of Nanoparticles in Various Manufacturing Processes. In *Sustainable Utilization of Nanoparticles and Nanofluids in Engineering Applications* (pp. 1–31). IGI Global. doi:10.4018/978-1-6684-9135-5.ch001

Boopathi, S., & Davim, J. P. (2023b). *Sustainable Utilization of Nanoparticles and Nanofluids in Engineering Applications*. IGI Global. doi:10.4018/978-1-6684-9135-5

Boopathi, S., & Khang, A. (2023). AI-Integrated Technology for a Secure and Ethical Healthcare Ecosystem. In *AI and IoT-Based Technologies for Precision Medicine* (pp. 36–59). IGI Global. doi:10.4018/979-8-3693-0876-9.ch003

Boopathi, S., Khare, R., KG, J. C., Muni, T. V., & Khare, S. (2023). Additive Manufacturing Developments in the Medical Engineering Field. In Development, Properties, and Industrial Applications of 3D Printed Polymer Composites (pp. 86–106). IGI Global.

Boopathi, S., Umareddy, M., & Elangovan, M. (2023). Applications of Nano-Cutting Fluids in Advanced Machining Processes. In *Sustainable Utilization of Nanoparticles and Nanofluids in Engineering Applications* (pp. 211–234). IGI Global. doi:10.4018/978-1-6684-9135-5.ch009

Chen, Y., Chen, D., Liang, S., Dai, Y., Bai, X., Song, B., Zhang, D., Chen, H., & Feng, L. (2022). Recent Advances in Field-Controlled Micro–Nano Manipulations and Micro–Nano Robots. *Advanced Intelligent Systems*, 4(3), 2100116. doi:10.1002/aisy.202100116

Dash, T., & Maiti, C. K. (2023). An overview of nanoscale device fabrication technology—Part I. *Nanoelectronics: Physics, Materials and Devices*, 193–214.

Daudi, J. (2015). An overview of application of artificial immune system in swarm robotic systems. *Advances in Robotics & Automation, 4*(1).

Dhanya, D., Kumar, S. S., Thilagavathy, A., Prasad, D., & Boopathi, S. (2023). Data Analytics and Artificial Intelligence in the Circular Economy: Case Studies. In Intelligent Engineering Applications and Applied Sciences for Sustainability (pp. 40–58). IGI Global.

Fowziya, S., Sivaranjani, S., Devi, N. L., Boopathi, S., Thakur, S., & Sailaja, J. M. (2023). Influences of nano-green lubricants in the friction-stir process of TiAlN coated alloys. *Materials Today: Proceedings*. Advance online publication. doi:10.1016/j.matpr.2023.06.446

Ghanbarzadeh-Dagheyan, A., Jalili, N., & Ahmadian, M. T. (2021). A holistic survey on mechatronic Systems in Micro/Nano scale with challenges and applications. *Journal of Micro-Bio Robotics*, 17(1), 1–22. doi:10.1007/s12213-021-00145-8

Gheorghe, P. E. E. G. I., Ilie, P. S. I., Istriteanu, P. E. S., & Bajenaru, P. E. V. (2014). Research in micro-nano-robotics. *The Romanian Review Precision Mechanics*, *46*, 83.

Gowri, N. V., Dwivedi, J. N., Krishnaveni, K., Boopathi, S., Palaniappan, M., & Medikondu, N. R. (2023). Experimental investigation and multi-objective optimization of eco-friendly near-dry electrical discharge machining of shape memory alloy using Cu/SiC/Gr composite electrode. *Environmental Science and Pollution Research International*, *30*(49), 1–19. doi:10.1007/s11356-023-26983-6 PMID:37126160

Halder, A., & Sun, Y. (2019). Biocompatible propulsion for biomedical micro/nano robotics. *Biosensors & Bioelectronics*, *139*, 111334. doi:10.1016/j.bios.2019.111334 PMID:31128479

Hanumanthakari, S., Gift, M. M., Kanimozhi, K., Bhavani, M. D., Bamane, K. D., & Boopathi, S. (2023). Biomining Method to Extract Metal Components Using Computer-Printed Circuit Board E-Waste. In *Handbook of Research on Safe Disposal Methods of Municipal Solid Wastes for a Sustainable Environment* (pp. 123–141). IGI Global. doi:10.4018/978-1-6684-8117-2.ch010

Hussain, Z., Babe, M., Saravanan, S., Srimathy, G., Roopa, H., & Boopathi, S. (2023). Optimizing Biomass-to-Biofuel Conversion: IoT and AI Integration for Enhanced Efficiency and Sustainability. In Circular Economy Implementation for Sustainability in the Built Environment (pp. 191–214). IGI Global.

Indiveri, G., Linares-Barranco, B., Legenstein, R., Deligeorgis, G., & Prodromakis, T. (2013). Integration of nanoscale memristor synapses in neuromorphic computing architectures. *Nanotechnology*, *24*(38), 384010. doi:10.1088/0957-4484/24/38/384010 PMID:23999381

Karan, S., & Majumder, D. D. (2011). Molecular machinery-a nanorobotics control system design for cancer drug delivery. *2011 International Conference on Recent Trends in Information Systems*, 197–202. 10.1109/ReTIS.2011.6146867

Karimov, K., Akhmedov, A., & Adilova, S. (2022). Theoretical and engineering solutions of the controlled vibration mechanisms for precision engineering. *AIP Conference Proceedings*, *2637*(1), 060001. doi:10.1063/5.0118863

Koshariya, A. K., Kalaiyarasi, D., Jovith, A. A., Sivakami, T., Hasan, D. S., & Boopathi, S. (2023). AI-Enabled IoT and WSN-Integrated Smart Agriculture System. In *Artificial Intelligence Tools and Technologies for Smart Farming and Agriculture Practices* (pp. 200–218). IGI Global. doi:10.4018/978-1-6684-8516-3.ch011

Koshariya, A. K., Khatoon, S., Marathe, A. M., Suba, G. M., Baral, D., & Boopathi, S. (2023). Agricultural Waste Management Systems Using Artificial Intelligence Techniques. In *AI-Enabled Social Robotics in Human Care Services* (pp. 236–258). IGI Global. doi:10.4018/978-1-6684-8171-4.ch009

Kumar, M., Kumar, K., Sasikala, P., Sampath, B., Gopi, B., & Sundaram, S. (2023). Sustainable Green Energy Generation From Waste Water: IoT and ML Integration. In Sustainable Science and Intelligent Technologies for Societal Development (pp. 440–463). IGI Global.

Kumar, S., Nasim, B., & Abraham, E. (2018). Nanorobots a future device for diagnosis and treatment. *Journal of Pharmacy and Pharmaceutics*, *5*(1), 44–49. doi:10.15436/2377-1313.18.1815

Kushwah, J. S., Gupta, M., Shrivastava, S., Saxena, N., Saini, R., & Boopathi, S. (2024). Psychological Impacts, Prevention Strategies, and Intervention Approaches Across Age Groups: Unmasking Cyberbullying. In Change Dynamics in Healthcare, Technological Innovations, and Complex Scenarios (pp. 89–109). IGI Global.

Maguluri, L. P., Arularasan, A., & Boopathi, S. (2023). Assessing Security Concerns for AI-Based Drones in Smart Cities. In Effective AI, Blockchain, and E-Governance Applications for Knowledge Discovery and Management (pp. 27–47). IGI Global. doi:10.4018/978-1-6684-9151-5.ch002

Maheswari, B. U., Imambi, S. S., Hasan, D., Meenakshi, S., Pratheep, V., & Boopathi, S. (2023). Internet of things and machine learning-integrated smart robotics. In Global Perspectives on Robotics and Autonomous Systems: Development and Applications (pp. 240–258). IGI Global. doi:10.4018/978-1-6684-7791-5.ch010

Malathi, J., Kusha, K., Isaac, S., Ramesh, A., Rajendiran, M., & Boopathi, S. (2024). IoT-Enabled Remote Patient Monitoring for Chronic Disease Management and Cost Savings: Transforming Healthcare. In Advances in Explainable AI Applications for Smart Cities (pp. 371–388). IGI Global.

Mbunge, E., Muchemwa, B., Batani, J., & ... (2021). Sensors and healthcare 5.0: Transformative shift in virtual care through emerging digital health technologies. *Global Health Journal (Amsterdam, Netherlands)*, 5(4), 169–177. doi:10.1016/j.glohj.2021.11.008

Mohanty, A., Jothi, B., Jeyasudha, J., Ranjit, P., Isaac, J. S., & Boopathi, S. (2023). Additive Manufacturing Using Robotic Programming. In *AI-Enabled Social Robotics in Human Care Services* (pp. 259–282). IGI Global. doi:10.4018/978-1-6684-8171-4.ch010

Palaniappan, M., Tirlangi, S., Mohamed, M. J. S., Moorthy, R. S., Valeti, S. V., & Boopathi, S. (2023). Fused Deposition Modelling of Polylactic Acid (PLA)-Based Polymer Composites: A Case Study. In Development, Properties, and Industrial Applications of 3D Printed Polymer Composites (pp. 66–85). IGI Global.

Pandya, A., & Auner, G. (2004). Robotics technology: A journey into the future. *The Urologic Clinics of North America*, 31(4), 793–800. doi:10.1016/j.ucl.2004.06.013 PMID:15474607

Patwardhan, J. (2006). *Architectures for nanoscale devices* (Vol. 68). Academic Press.

Pedram, A., & Nejat Pishkenari, H. (2017). Smart micro/nano-robotic systems for gene delivery. *Current Gene Therapy*, 17(2), 73–79. doi:10.2174/1566523217666170511111000 PMID:28494736

Pokrajac, L., Abbas, A., Chrzanowski, W., Dias, G. M., Eggleton, B. J., Maguire, S., Maine, E., Malloy, T., Nathwani, J., Nazar, L., & ... (2021). *Nanotechnology for a sustainable future: Addressing global challenges with the international network4sustainable nanotechnology*. ACS Publications.

Pramila, P., Amudha, S., Saravanan, T., Sankar, S. R., Poongothai, E., & Boopathi, S. (2023). Design and Development of Robots for Medical Assistance: An Architectural Approach. In Contemporary Applications of Data Fusion for Advanced Healthcare Informatics (pp. 260–282). IGI Global.

Pugliese, R., & Regondi, S. (2022). Artificial intelligence-empowered 3D and 4D printing technologies toward smarter biomedical materials and approaches. *Polymers, 14*(14), 2794. doi:10.3390/polym14142794 PMID:35890571

Puranik, T. A., Shaik, N., Vankudoth, R., Kolhe, M. R., Yadav, N., & Boopathi, S. (2024). Study on Harmonizing Human-Robot (Drone) Collaboration: Navigating Seamless Interactions in Collaborative Environments. In Cybersecurity Issues and Challenges in the Drone Industry (pp. 1–26). IGI Global.

Rahamathunnisa, U., Subhashini, P., Aancy, H. M., Meenakshi, S., Boopathi, S., & ... (2023). Solutions for Software Requirement Risks Using Artificial Intelligence Techniques. In *Handbook of Research on Data Science and Cybersecurity Innovations in Industry 4.0 Technologies* (pp. 45–64). IGI Global.

Rahamathunnisa, U., Sudhakar, K., Murugan, T. K., Thivaharan, S., Rajkumar, M., & Boopathi, S. (2023). Cloud Computing Principles for Optimizing Robot Task Offloading Processes. In *AI-Enabled Social Robotics in Human Care Services* (pp. 188–211). IGI Global. doi:10.4018/978-1-6684-8171-4.ch007

Ramudu, K., Mohan, V. M., Jyothirmai, D., Prasad, D., Agrawal, R., & Boopathi, S. (2023). Machine Learning and Artificial Intelligence in Disease Prediction: Applications, Challenges, Limitations, Case Studies, and Future Directions. In Contemporary Applications of Data Fusion for Advanced Healthcare Informatics (pp. 297–318). IGI Global.

Ravisankar, A., Sampath, B., & Asif, M. M. (2023). Economic Studies on Automobile Management: Working Capital and Investment Analysis. In Multidisciplinary Approaches to Organizational Governance During Health Crises (pp. 169–198). IGI Global.

Ravisankar, A., Shanthi, A., Lavanya, S., Ramaratnam, M., Krishnamoorthy, V., & Boopathi, S. (2024). Harnessing 6G for Consumer-Centric Business Strategies Across Electronic Industries. In AI Impacts in Digital Consumer Behavior (pp. 241–270). IGI Global.

Revathi, S., Babu, M., Rajkumar, N., Meti, V. K. V., Kandavalli, S. R., & Boopathi, S. (2024). Unleashing the Future Potential of 4D Printing: Exploring Applications in Wearable Technology, Robotics, Energy, Transportation, and Fashion. In Human-Centered Approaches in Industry 5.0: Human-Machine Interaction, Virtual Reality Training, and Customer Sentiment Analysis (pp. 131–153). IGI Global.

Sampath, B., Naveenkumar, N., Sampathkumar, P., Silambarasan, P., Venkadesh, A., & Sakthivel, M. (2022). Experimental comparative study of banana fiber composite with glass fiber composite material using Taguchi method. *Materials Today: Proceedings, 49*, 1475–1480. doi:10.1016/j.matpr.2021.07.232

Satav, S. D., Hasan, D. S., Pitchai, R., Mohanaprakash, T., Sultanuddin, S., & Boopathi, S. (2023). Next generation of internet of things (ngiot) in healthcare systems. In *Sustainable Science and Intelligent Technologies for Societal Development* (pp. 307–330). IGI Global.

Senthil, T., Puviyarasan, M., Babu, S. R., Surakasi, R., Sampath, B., & Associates. (2023). Industrial Robot-Integrated Fused Deposition Modelling for the 3D Printing Process. In Development, Properties, and Industrial Applications of 3D Printed Polymer Composites (pp. 188–210). IGI Global.

Sivasankar, M., & Durairaj, R. (2012). Brief review on nano robots in bio medical applications. *Adv Robot Autom, 1*(101), 2. doi:10.4172/2168-9695.1000101

Srinivas, B., Maguluri, L. P., Naidu, K. V., Reddy, L. C. S., Deivakani, M., & Boopathi, S. (2023). Architecture and Framework for Interfacing Cloud-Enabled Robots. In *Handbook of Research on Data Science and Cybersecurity Innovations in Industry 4.0 Technologies* (pp. 542–560). IGI Global. doi:10.4018/978-1-6684-8145-5.ch027

Vigelius, M., Meyer, B., & Pascoe, G. (2014). Multiscale modelling and analysis of collective decision making in swarm robotics. *PLoS One*, *9*(11), e111542. doi:10.1371/journal.pone.0111542 PMID:25369026

Vijayakumar, G. N. S., Domakonda, V. K., Farooq, S., Kumar, B. S., Pradeep, N., & Boopathi, S. (2024). Sustainable Developments in Nano-Fluid Synthesis for Various Industrial Applications. In Adoption and Use of Technology Tools and Services by Economically Disadvantaged Communities: Implications for Growth and Sustainability (pp. 48–81). IGI Global.

Walsh, S. M., & Strano, M. S. (2018). *Robotic systems and autonomous platforms: Advances in materials and manufacturing*. Woodhead Publishing.

Xu, Y., Bian, Q., Wang, R., & Gao, J. (2022). Micro/nanorobots for precise drug delivery via targeted transport and triggered release: A review. *International Journal of Pharmaceutics*, *616*, 121551. doi:10.1016/j.ijpharm.2022.121551 PMID:35131352

Compilation of References

Abarca, V. E., & Elias, D. A. (2023). A Review of Parallel Robots: Rehabilitation, Assistance, and Humanoid Applications for Neck, Shoulder, Wrist, Hip, and Ankle Joints. *Robotics (Basel, Switzerland), 12*(5), 131. doi:10.3390/robotics12050131

Ahmed, L. J., Anish Fathima, B., Mahaboob, M., & Gokulavasan, B. (2021). Biomedical Image Processing with Improved SPIHT Algorithm and optimized Curvelet Transform Technique. *2021 7th International Conference on Advanced Computing and Communication Systems, ICACCS 2021.* 10.1109/ICACCS51430.2021.9441832

Ahmed, L. J., Bruntha, P. M., Dhanasekar, S., Chitra, V., Balaji, D., & Senathipathi, N. (2022). An Improvised Image Registration Technique for Brain Tumor Identification and Segmentation Using ANN Approach. *ICDCS 2022 - 2022 6th International Conference on Devices, Circuits and Systems,* 80-84. 10.1109/ICDCS54290.2022.9780846

Ahmed, T., Ahmed, S., Ahmed, S., & Motiwala, M. (2010). Real-Time Intruder Detection in Surveillance Networks Using Adaptive Kernel Methods. *Proceedings of the 2010 IEEE International Conference on Communications.* 10.1109/ICC.2010.5502592

Ahmed, Z., Mohamed, K., Zeeshan, S., & Dong, X. (2020). Artificial intelligence with multi-functional machine learning platform development for better healthcare and precision medicine. *Database (Oxford), 2020,* baaa010. doi:10.1093/database/baaa010 PMID:32185396

Akolpoglu, M. B., Dogan, N. O., Bozuyuk, U., Ceylan, H., Kizilel, S., & Sitti, M. (2020). High-yield production of biohybrid microalgae for on-demand cargo delivery. *Advancement of Science, 7*(16), 2001256. doi:10.1002/advs.202001256 PMID:32832367

Alam, A. (2022). Social robots in education for long-term human-robot interaction: Socially supportive behaviour of robotic tutor for creating robo-tangible learning environment in a guided discovery learning interaction. *ECS Transactions, 107*(1), 12389–12403. doi:10.1149/10701.12389ecst

Alanzy, M., Alomrani, R., Alqarni, B., & Almutairi, S. (2023). Image Steganography Using LSB and Hybrid Encryption Algorithms. *Applied Sciences (Basel, Switzerland), 13*(21), 11771. doi:10.3390/app132111771

Alborzi, M., & Khanbabaei, M. (2016). Using data mining and neural networks techniques to propose a new hybrid customer behavior analysis and credit scoring model in banking services based on a developed RFM analysis method. *International Journal of Business Information Systems, 23*(1), 1–22. doi:10.1504/IJBIS.2016.078020

Almohamad, A., Tahir, A. M., Al-Kababji, A., Furqan, H. M., Khattab, T., Hasna, M. O., & Arslan, H. (2020). Smart and secure wireless communications via reflecting intelligent surfaces: A short survey. *IEEE Open Journal of the Communications Society, 1,* 1442–1456. doi:10.1109/OJCOMS.2020.3023731

Alobaidi, W. H., Aziz, I. T., Jawad, T., Flaih, F. M. F., & Azeez, A. T. (2018). Face detection based on probability of amplitude distribution of local binary patterns algorithm. *Proceedings of the 2018 6th International Symposium on Digital Forensic and Security (ISDFS),* 1–5 10.1109/ISDFS.2018.8355319

Amann, J., Blasimme, A., Vayena, E., Frey, D., & Madai, V. I. (2020). Explainability for artificial intelligence in healthcare: A multidisciplinary perspective. *BMC Medical Informatics and Decision Making, 20*(1), 1–9. doi:10.1186/s12911-020-01332-6 PMID:33256715

Anitha, Kalra, & Shrivastav. (2016). A Cyber defence using artificial home automation system using IoT. *International Journal of Pharmacy and Technology, 8,* 25358-64.

Anthimopoulos, M., Christodoulidis, S., Ebner, L., Christe, A., & Mougiakakou, S. (2016). Lung pattern classification for interstitial lung diseases using a deep convolutional neural network. *IEEE Transactions on Medical Imaging, 35*(5), 1207–1216. doi:10.1109/TMI.2016.2535865 PMID:26955021

Arif, I., Aslam, W., & Hwang, Y. (2023). Barriers in adoption of internet banking: A structural equation modeling-neural network approach. *Technology in Society, 61,* 101231. doi:10.1016/j.techsoc.2020.101231

Arul, S. H., Bedi, A. S., & Manocha, D. (2022). Multi Robot Collision Avoidance by Learning Whom to Communicate. *arXiv preprint arXiv:2209.06415.*

Atilano, L., Martinho, A., Silva, M., & Baptista, A. (2019). Lean Design-for-X: Case study of a new design framework applied to an adaptive robot gripper development process. *Procedia CIRP, 84,* 667–672. doi:10.1016/j.procir.2019.04.190

Babu, B. S., Kamalakannan, J., Meenatchi, N., Karthik, S., & Boopathi, S. (2022). Economic impacts and reliability evaluation of battery by adopting Electric Vehicle. *IEEE Explore,* 1–6.

Baesens, B., Van Gestel, T., Stepanova, M., Van den Poel, D., & Vanthienen, J. (2005). Neural network survival analysis for personal loan data. *The Journal of the Operational Research Society, 56*(9), 1089–1098. doi:10.1057/palgrave.jors.2601990

Bajaj, N. M., Spiers, A. J., & Dollar, A. M. (2019). State of the art in artificial wrists: A review of prosthetic and robotic wrist design. *IEEE Transactions on Robotics, 35*(1), 261–277. doi:10.1109/TRO.2018.2865890

Bajcsy, A., Herbert, S. L., Fridovich-Keil, D., Fisac, J. F., Deglurkar, S., Dragan, A. D., & Tomlin, C. J. (2019, May). A scalable framework for real-time multi-robot, multi-human collision avoidance. In 2019 international conference on robotics and automation (ICRA) (pp. 936-943). IEEE. doi:10.1109/ICRA.2019.8794457

Balaguer, C., Giménez, A., Pastor, J. M., Padron, V., & Abderrahim, M. (2000). A climbing autonomous robot for inspection applications in 3d complex environments. *Robotica, 18*(3), 287–297. doi:10.1017/S0263574799002258

Banerjee, A., Chakraborty, C., Kumar, A., & Biswas, D. (2020). Emerging trends in IoT and big data analytics for biomedical and health care technologies. Handbook of data science approaches for biomedical engineering, 121-152.

Barbosa, H. C., de Queiroz Oliveira, J. A., da Costa, J. M., de Melo Santos, R. P., Miranda, L. G., de Carvalho Torres, H., ... Martins, M. A. P. (2021). Empowerment-oriented strategies to identify behavior change in patients with chronic diseases: An integrative review of the literature. *Patient Education and Counseling, 104*(4), 689–702. doi:10.1016/j.pec.2021.01.011 PMID:33478854

Behera, S. K., Rath, A. K., & Sethy, P. K. (2021). Maturity status classification of papaya fruits based on machine learning and transfer learning approach. *Information Processing in Agriculture, 8*(2), 244–250. doi:10.1016/j.inpa.2020.05.003

Bekey, G. A. (2005). *Autonomous robots: from biological inspiration to implementation and control.* MIT Press.

Belanche, D., Casaló, L. V., & Flavián, C. (2020). Artificial intelligence in FinTech: Understanding robo-advisors adoption among customers. *Industrial Management & Data Systems, 119*(7), 1411–1430. doi:10.1108/IMDS-08-2018-0368

Bengio, Y. (2012, June). Deep learning of representations for unsupervised and transfer learning. In *Proceedings of ICML workshop on unsupervised and transfer learning* (pp. 17-36). JMLR Workshop and Conference Proceedings.

Bentéjac, C., Csörgő, A., & Martínez-Muñoz, G. (2021). A comparative analysis of gradient boosting algorithms. *Artificial Intelligence Review, 54*(3), 1937–1967. doi:10.1007/s10462-020-09896-5

Bhandari, G., Dhasmana, A., Chaudhary, P., Gupta, S., Gangola, S., Gupta, A., Rustagi, S., Shende, S. S., Rajput, V. D., Minkina, T. M., Malik, S., & Sláma, P. (2023). A Perspective Review on Green Nanotechnology in Agro-Ecosystems: Opportunities for Sustainable Agricultural Practices & Environmental Remediation. *Agriculture, 13*(3), 668. doi:10.3390/agriculture13030668

Bhargava, A., & Bansal, A. (2020). Automatic detection and grading of multiple fruits by machine learning. *Food Analytical Methods, 13*(3), 751–761. doi:10.1007/s12161-019-01690-6

Biffi, L. J., Mitishita, E., Liesenberg, V., Santos, A. A. D., Goncalves, D. N., Estrabis, N. V., Silva, J. A., Osco, L. P., Ramos, A. P. M., Centeno, J. A. S., Schimalski, M. B., Rufato, L., Neto, S. L. R., Marcato Junior, J., & Goncalves, W. N. (2021). ATSS deep learning-based approach to detect apple fruits. *Remote Sensing (Basel), 13*(1), 54. doi:10.3390/rs13010054

Biswas, S., Carson, B., Chung, V., Singh, S., & Thomas, R. (2023). Artificial intelligence technologies are increasingly integral to the world we live in, and banks need to deploy these technologies at scale to remain relevant. Success requires a holistic transformation spanning multiple layers of the organization.Larson, E.J. 2021. The myth of artificial intelligence. In *The Myth of Artificial Intelligence*. Harvard University Press.

Bogossian, T. (2022). The Use of Robotics in Healthcare. *Journal of Medical & Clinical Nursing*, 1–4. Advance online publication. doi:10.47363/JMCN/2022(3)157

Bohr, A., & Memarzadeh, K. (2020). The rise of artificial intelligence in healthcare applications. In *Artificial Intelligence in healthcare* (pp. 25–60). Academic Press. doi:10.1016/B978-0-12-818438-7.00002-2

Boopathi, S. (2021). *Pollution monitoring and notification: Water pollution monitoring and notification using intelligent RC boat*. Academic Press.

Boopathi, S. (2022). Performance Improvement of Eco-Friendly Near-Dry wire-Cut Electrical Discharge Machining Process Using Coconut Oil-Mist Dielectric Fluid. *World Scientific: Journal of Advanced Manufacturing Systems*.

Boopathi, S. (2022b). Cryogenically treated and untreated stainless steel grade 317 in sustainable wire electrical discharge machining process: A comparative study. *Springer :Environmental Science and Pollution Research*, 1–10.

Boopathi, S., & Kumar, P. (2024). Advanced bioprinting processes using additive manufacturing technologies: Revolutionizing tissue engineering. *3D Printing Technologies: Digital Manufacturing, Artificial Intelligence, Industry 4.0*, 95.

Boopathi, S., Khare, R., KG, J. C., Muni, T. V., & Khare, S. (2023). Additive Manufacturing Developments in the Medical Engineering Field. In Development, Properties, and Industrial Applications of 3D Printed Polymer Composites (pp. 86–106). IGI Global.

Boopathi, S., Thillaivanan, A., Mohammed, A. A., Shanmugam, P., & VR, P. (2022). Experimental investigation on Abrasive Water Jet Machining of Neem Wood Plastic Composite. *IOP: Functional Composites and Structures, 4*, 025001.

Boopathi, S. (2022a). An investigation on gas emission concentration and relative emission rate of the near-dry wire-cut electrical discharge machining process. *Environmental Science and Pollution Research International, 29*(57), 86237–86246. doi:10.1007/s11356-021-17658-1 PMID:34837614

Boopathi, S. (2023a). An Investigation on Friction Stir Processing of Aluminum Alloy-Boron Carbide Surface Composite. In *Springer:Advances in Processing of Lightweight Metal Alloys and Composites* (pp. 249–257). Springer. doi:10.1007/978-981-19-7146-4_14

Boopathi, S. (2023b). Internet of Things-Integrated Remote Patient Monitoring System: Healthcare Application. In *Dynamics of Swarm Intelligence Health Analysis for the Next Generation* (pp. 137–161). IGI Global. doi:10.4018/978-1-6684-6894-4.ch008

Boopathi, S., Alqahtani, A. S., Mubarakali, A., & Panchatcharam, P. (2023). Sustainable developments in near-dry electrical discharge machining process using sunflower oil-mist dielectric fluid. *Environmental Science and Pollution Research International*, 1–20. doi:10.1007/s11356-023-27494-0 PMID:37199846

Boopathi, S., & Davim, J. P. (2023a). Applications of Nanoparticles in Various Manufacturing Processes. In *Sustainable Utilization of Nanoparticles and Nanofluids in Engineering Applications* (pp. 1–31). IGI Global. doi:10.4018/978-1-6684-9135-5.ch001

Boopathi, S., & Davim, J. P. (2023b). *Sustainable Utilization of Nanoparticles and Nanofluids in Engineering Applications*. IGI Global. doi:10.4018/978-1-6684-9135-5

Boopathi, S., Jeyakumar, M., Singh, G. R., King, F. L., Pandian, M., Subbiah, R., & Haribalaji, V. (2022). An experimental study on friction stir processing of aluminium alloy (AA-2024) and boron nitride (BNp) surface composite. *Materials Today: Proceedings, 59*(1), 1094–1099. doi:10.1016/j.matpr.2022.02.435

Boopathi, S., & Khang, A. (2023). AI-Integrated Technology for a Secure and Ethical Healthcare Ecosystem. In *AI and IoT-Based Technologies for Precision Medicine* (pp. 36–59). IGI Global. doi:10.4018/979-8-3693-0876-9.ch003

Boopathi, S., Umareddy, M., & Elangovan, M. (2023). Applications of Nano-Cutting Fluids in Advanced Machining Processes. In *Sustainable Utilization of Nanoparticles and Nanofluids in Engineering Applications* (pp. 211–234). IGI Global. doi:10.4018/978-1-6684-9135-5.ch009

Bragança, S., Costa, E., Castellucci, I., & Arezes, P. M. (2019). A brief overview of the use of collaborative robots in industry 4.0: Human role and safety. *Occupational and Environmental Safety and Health*, 641–650.

Bramblett, L., Gao, S., & Bezzo, N. (2023). Epistemic Prediction and Planning with Implicit Coordination for Multi-Robot Teams in Communication Restricted Environments. *arXiv preprint arXiv:2302.10393*. doi:10.1109/ICRA48891.2023.10161553

Burgos-Artizzu, X. P., Coronado-Gutierrez, D., Valenzuela-Alcaraz, B., Bonet-Carne, E., Eixarch, E., Crispi, F., & Gratacós, E. (2020). FETAL_PLANES_DB: Common maternal-fetal ultrasound images. *Scientific Reports, 19*, 10200. doi:10.1038/s41598-020-67076-5 PMID:32576905

Çetin, N., Karaman, K., Kavuncuoğlu, E., Yıldırım, B., & Jahanbakhshi, A. (2022). Using hyperspectral imaging technology and machine learning algorithms for assessing internal quality parameters of apple fruits. *Chemometrics and Intelligent Laboratory Systems, 230*, 104650. doi:10.1016/j.chemolab.2022.104650

Chaddad, A., Peng, J., Xu, J., & Bouridane, A. (2023). Survey of Explainable AI Techniques in Healthcare. *Sensors (Basel), 23*(2), 1–19. doi:10.3390/s23020634 PMID:36679430

Chakraborty, A., Ravi, S. P., Shamiya, Y., Cui, C., & Paul, A. (2021). Harnessing the physicochemical properties of DNA as a multifunctional biomaterial for biomedical and other applications. *Chemical Society Reviews*, *50*(13), 7779–7819. doi:10.1039/D0CS01387K PMID:34036968

Chan, C.-K., & Cheng, L.-M. (2004). Hiding data in images by simple LSB substitution. *Pattern Recognition*, *37*(3), 469–474. doi:10.1016/j.patcog.2003.08.007

Chelliah, R., Wei, S., Daliri, E. B. M., Rubab, M., Elahi, F., Yeon, S. J., Jo, K. H., Yan, P., Liu, S., & Oh, D. H. (2021). Development of Nanosensors Based Intelligent Packaging Systems: Food Quality and Medicine. *Nanomaterials (Basel, Switzerland)*, *11*(6), 1515. doi:10.3390/nano11061515 PMID:34201071

Chen, H., Dou, Q., Wang, X., Qin, J., & Heng, P. (2016, February). Mitosis detection in breast cancer histology images via deep cascaded networks. *Proceedings of the AAAI Conference on Artificial Intelligence*, *30*(1). doi:10.1609/aaai. v30i1.10140

Chen, H., Dou, Q., Yu, L., Qin, J., & Heng, P. A. (2018). VoxResNet: Deep voxelwise residual networks for brain segmentation from 3D MR images. *NeuroImage*, *170*, 446–455. doi:10.1016/j.neuroimage.2017.04.041 PMID:28445774

Chen, H., Ni, D., Qin, J., Li, S., Yang, X., Wang, T., & Heng, P. A. (2015). Standard plane localization in fetal ultrasound via domain transferred deep neural networks. *IEEE Journal of Biomedical and Health Informatics*, *19*(5), 1627–1636. doi:10.1109/JBHI.2015.2425041 PMID:25910262

Chen, H., Qi, X., Yu, L., Dou, Q., Qin, J., & Heng, P. A. (2017). DCAN: Deep contour-aware networks for object instance segmentation from histology images. *Medical Image Analysis*, *36*, 135–146. doi:10.1016/j.media.2016.11.004 PMID:27898306

Chen, P.-Y., & Lin, H.-J. (2006). A DWT based approach for image steganography. *International Journal of Applied Science and Engineering*, *4*(3), 275–290.

Chen, R., Xu, C., Dong, Z., Liu, Y., & Du, X. (2020). DeepCQ: Deep multi-task conditional quantification network for estimation of left ventricle parameters. *Computer Methods and Programs in Biomedicine*, *184*, 105288. doi:10.1016/j. cmpb.2019.105288 PMID:31901611

Chen, Y., Chen, D., Liang, S., Dai, Y., Bai, X., Song, B., Zhang, D., Chen, H., & Feng, L. (2022). Recent Advances in Field-Controlled Micro–Nano Manipulations and Micro–Nano Robots. *Advanced Intelligent Systems*, *4*(3), 2100116. doi:10.1002/aisy.202100116

Chowdhury, A. H., Malakar, S., Seal, D. B., & Goswami, S. (2022). Understanding employee attrition using machine learning techniques. In *Data Management, Analytics and Innovation: Proceedings of ICDMAI 2021,* Volume 2 (pp. 101-109). Springer Singapore. 10.1007/978-981-16-2937-2_8

Chung, Y. M., Youssef, H., & Roidl, M. (2022, May). Distributed Timed Elastic Band (DTEB) Planner: Trajectory Sharing and Collision Prediction for Multi-Robot Systems. In *2022 International Conference on Robotics and Automation (ICRA)* (pp. 10702-10708). IEEE. 10.1109/ICRA46639.2022.9811762

Cianchetti, M., Ranzani, T., Gerboni, G., Nanayakkara, T., Althoefer, K., & Dasgupta, P. (2018). Soft robotics technologies to address shortcomings in today's minimally invasive surgery: The STIFF-FLOP approach. *Soft Robotics*, *5*(2), 149–161. PMID:29297756

Connolly, F., Walsh, C. J., & Bertoldi, K. (2017). Automatic design of fiber-reinforced soft actuators for trajectory matching. *Proceedings of the National Academy of Sciences of the United States of America*, *114*(1), 51–56. doi:10.1073/ pnas.1615140114 PMID:27994133

Constant, A., Conserve, D. F., Gallopel-Morvan, K., & Raude, J. (2020). Socio-cognitive factors associated with lifestyle changes in response to the COVID-19 epidemic in the general population: Results from a cross-sectional study in France. *Frontiers in Psychology*, *11*, 579460. doi:10.3389/fpsyg.2020.579460 PMID:33132989

Cristian, Ursache, Popa, & Pop. (2016). *Energy efficiency and robustness for IoT: Building a smart home security system*. Faculty of Automatic Control and Computers University Politehnica of Bucharest.

Csurka, G., Dance, C., Fan, L., Willamowski, J., & Bray, C. (2004, May). Visual categorization with bags of keypoints. In *Workshop on statistical learning in computer vision, ECCV* (Vol. 1, No. 1-22, pp. 1-2).

Cui, Y., Lin, L., Huang, X., Zhang, D., Wang, Y., Jing, W., ... Wang, Y. (2022, May). Learning Observation-Based Certifiable Safe Policy for Decentralized Multi-Robot Navigation. In *2022 International Conference on Robotics and Automation (ICRA)* (pp. 5518-5524). IEEE. 10.1109/ICRA46639.2022.9811950

Cui, Y., Qin, Z., Wu, H., Li, M., & Hu, Y. (2021). Flexible thermal interface based on self-assembled boron arsenide for high-performance thermal management. *Nature Communications*, *12*(1), 1284. doi:10.1038/s41467-021-21531-7 PMID:33627644

Dalal, N., & Triggs, B. (2005, June). Histograms of oriented gradients for human detection. In 2005 IEEE computer society conference on computer vision and pattern recognition (CVPR'05) (Vol. 1, pp. 886-893). IEEE. doi:10.1109/CVPR.2005.177

Dash, T., & Maiti, C. K. (2023). An overview of nanoscale device fabrication technology—Part I. *Nanoelectronics: Physics, Materials and Devices*, 193–214.

Daudi, J. (2015). An overview of application of artificial immune system in swarm robotic systems. *Advances in Robotics & Automation, 4*(1).

Deimel, R., & Brock, O. (2016). A novel type of compliant and underactuated robotic hand for dexterous grasping. *The International Journal of Robotics Research*, *35*(1-3), 161–185. doi:10.1177/0278364915592961

Dency Flora, G., Sekar, G., Nivetha, R., Thirukkumaran, R., Silambarasan, D., & Jeevanantham, V. (2022). An Optimized Neural Network for Content Based Image Retrieval in Medical Applications. *8th International Conference on Advanced Computing and Communication Systems, ICACCS 2022*, 1560-1563. 10.1109/ICACCS54159.2022.9785151

Deng, J. (2009). A large-scale hierarchical image database. *Proc. of IEEE Computer Vision and Pattern Recognition*.

Dhanya, D., Kumar, S. S., Thilagavathy, A., Prasad, D., & Boopathi, S. (2023). Data Analytics and Artificial Intelligence in the Circular Economy: Case Studies. In Intelligent Engineering Applications and Applied Sciences for Sustainability (pp. 40–58). IGI Global.

Donahue, J., Jia, Y., Vinyals, O., Hoffman, J., Zhang, N., Tzeng, E., & Darrell, T. (2014, January). Decaf: A deep convolutional activation feature for generic visual recognition. In *International conference on machine learning* (pp. 647-655). PMLR.

Dongari, S., Nisarudeen, M., Devi, J., Irfan, S., Parida, P. K., & Bajpai, A. (2023). Advancing Healthcare through Artificial Intelligence: Innovations at the Intersection of AI and Medicine. *Tuijin Jishu/Journal of Propulsion Technology, 44*(2).

Dou, Q., Chen, H., Yu, L., Zhao, L., Qin, J., Wang, D., Mok, V. C. T., Shi, L., & Heng, P. A. (2016). Automatic detection of cerebral microbleeds from MR images via 3D convolutional neural networks. *IEEE Transactions on Medical Imaging*, *35*(5), 1182–1195. doi:10.1109/TMI.2016.2528129 PMID:26886975

Du, C., Ren, Y., Qu, Z., Gao, L., Zhai, Y., Han, S.-T., & Zhou, Y. (2021). Synaptic transistors and neuromorphic systems based on carbon nano-materials. *Nanoscale*, *13*(16), 7498–7522. doi:10.1039/D1NR00148E PMID:33928966

Dudley, N. J., & Chapman, E. (2002). The importance of quality management in fetal measurement. *Ultrasound in Obstetrics & Gynecology, 19*(2), 190–196. doi:10.1046/j.0960-7692.2001.00549.x PMID:11876814

Dzobo, K., Adotey, S., Thomford, N. E., & Dzobo, W. (2020). Integrating artificial and human intelligence: A partnership for responsible innovation in biomedical engineering and medicine. *OMICS: A Journal of Integrative Biology, 24*(5), 247–263. doi:10.1089/omi.2019.0038 PMID:31313972

Eckstein, M. K., & Collins, A. G. (2020). Computational evidence for hierarchically structured reinforcement learning in humans. *Proceedings of the National Academy of Sciences of the United States of America, 117*(47), 29381–29389. doi:10.1073/pnas.1912330117 PMID:33229518

Ekinci, Y., Uray, N., & Ülengin, F. (2014). A customer lifetime value model for the banking industry: A guide to marketing actions. *European Journal of Marketing, 48*(3–4), 761–784. doi:10.1108/EJM-12-2011-0714

Enoch Sam, M., Misra, S. K., Anitha Mary, X., Karthik, C., & Chowdhury, S. (2023, November). Review of different types of spatial positioning platforms. In AIP Conference Proceedings (Vol. 2878, No. 1). AIP Publishing. doi:10.1063/5.0171256

Evangeline, C. S., Sarah, M., Lenin, A., Reddy, J. H. V., Mary, X. A., & Karthiga, M. (2023, May). Design of On-Board Unit for Vehicular Applications. In *2023 2nd International Conference on Vision Towards Emerging Trends in Communication and Networking Technologies (ViTECoN)* (pp. 1-6). IEEE. 10.1109/ViTECoN58111.2023.10157654

Evelyn Brindha, V., & Anitha Mary, X. (2023). Analysing Control Algorithms for Controlling the Speed of BLDC Motors Using Green IoT. *Power Converters, Drives and Controls for Sustainable Operations*, 779-788.

Fallucchi, F., Coladangelo, M., Giuliano, R., & William De Luca, E. (2020). Predicting employee attrition using machine learning techniques. *Computers, 9*(4), 86. doi:10.3390/computers9040086

Fan, G., Zhou, Z., Zhang, H., Gu, X., Gu, G., Guan, X., Fan, Y., & He, S. (2016, June). Global scientific production of robotic surgery in medicine: A 20-year survey of research activities. *International Journal of Surgery, 30*, 126–131. doi:10.1016/j.ijsu.2016.04.048 PMID:27154617

Faridha Banu, D., Sindhwani, N. S., G, K. R. A, & M, S. (2022). Fuzzy acceptance Analysis of Impact of Glaucoma and Diabetic Retinopathy using Confusion Matrix. *2022 10th International Conference on Reliability, Infocom Technologies and Optimization (Trends and Future Directions) (ICRITO)*, 1-5. 10.1109/ICRITO56286.2022.9964858

Ferranti, L., Lyons, L., Negenborn, R. R., Keviczky, T., & Alonso-Mora, J. (2022). Distributed nonlinear trajectory optimization for multi-robot motion planning. *IEEE Transactions on Control Systems Technology, 31*(2), 809–824. doi:10.1109/TCST.2022.3211130

Firoozi, R., Ferranti, L., Zhang, X., Nejadnik, S., & Borrelli, F. (2020). A distributed multi-robot coordination algorithm for navigation in tight environments. *arXiv preprint arXiv:2006.11492*.

Firouz, M. S., Farahmandi, A., & Hosseinpour, S. (2019). Recent advances in ultrasound application as a novel technique in analysis, processing and quality control of fruits, juices and dairy products industries: A review. *Ultrasonics Sonochemistry, 57*, 73–88. doi:10.1016/j.ultsonch.2019.05.014 PMID:31208621

Folke, T., Yang, S. C., Anderson, S., & Shafto, P. (2021). Explainable AI for medical imaging: Explaining pneumothorax diagnoses with Bayesian teaching. CoRR, vol. abs/2106.04684.

Fowziya, S., Sivaranjani, S., Devi, N. L., Boopathi, S., Thakur, S., & Sailaja, J. M. (2023). Influences of nano-green lubricants in the friction-stir process of TiAlN coated alloys. *Materials Today: Proceedings*. Advance online publication. doi:10.1016/j.matpr.2023.06.446

Freitas, E. J., Vangasse, A. D. C., Raffo, G. V., & Pimenta, L. C. (2023, October). Decentralized Multi-robot Collision-free Path Following Based on Time-varying Artificial Vector Fields and MPC-ORCA. In *2023 Latin American Robotics Symposium (LARS), 2023 Brazilian Symposium on Robotics (SBR), and 2023 Workshop on Robotics in Education (WRE)* (pp. 212-217). IEEE. 10.1109/LARS/SBR/WRE59448.2023.10333004

Friedman, V. (2008). Data visualization and infographics. Graphics, Monday Inspiration.

Friendly, M. (2017). *A brief history of data visualization.* Springer-Verlag.

Ganji, K., & Parimi, S. (2022). ANN model for users' perception on IOT based smart healthcare monitoring devices and its impact with the effect of COVID 19. *Journal of Science and Technology Policy Management, 13*(1), 6–21. doi:10.1108/JSTPM-09-2020-0128

Gao, Z., Wang, L., Zhou, L., & Zhang, J. (2016). HEp-2 cell image classification with deep convolutional neural networks. *IEEE Journal of Biomedical and Health Informatics, 21*(2), 416–428. doi:10.1109/JBHI.2016.2526603 PMID:26887016

Gaurav, K., & Ghanekar, U. (2018). Image steganography based on Canny edge detection, dilation operator and hybrid coding. *Journal of Information Security and Applications, 41*, 41–51. doi:10.1016/j.jisa.2018.05.001

Gellers, J. C. (2020). *Rights for robots: Artificial intelligence, animal and environmental law* (1st ed.). Routledge. doi:10.4324/9780429288159

Ghanbarzadeh-Dagheyan, A., Jalili, N., & Ahmadian, M. T. (2021). A holistic survey on mechatronic Systems in Micro/Nano scale with challenges and applications. *Journal of Micro-Bio Robotics, 17*(1), 1–22. doi:10.1007/s12213-021-00145-8

Gheorghe, P. E. E. G. I., Ilie, P. S. I., Istriteanu, P. E. S., & Bajenaru, P. E. V. (2014). Research in micro-nano-robotics. *The Romanian Review Precision Mechanics, 46*, 83.

Gilbert, S., Fenech, M., Hirsch, M., Upadhyay, S., Biasiucci, A., & Starlinger, J. (2021). Algorithm change protocols in the regulation of adaptive machine learning–based medical devices. *Journal of Medical Internet Research, 23*(10), e30545. doi:10.2196/30545 PMID:34697010

Girshick, R. (2015). Fast r-cnn. In *Proceedings of the IEEE international conference on computer vision* (pp. 1440-1448). Academic Press.

Girshick, R., Donahue, J., Darrell, T., & Malik, J. (2014). Rich feature hierarchies for accurate object detection and semantic segmentation. In *Proceedings of the IEEE conference on computer vision and pattern recognition* (pp. 580-587). 10.1109/CVPR.2014.81

Glorot, X., & Bengio, Y. (2010, March). Understanding the difficulty of training deep feedforward neural networks. In *Proceedings of the thirteenth international conference on artificial intelligence and statistics* (pp. 249-256). JMLR Workshop and Conference Proceedings.

Goodfellow, I., Warde-Farley, D., Mirza, M., Courville, A., & Bengio, Y. (2013, May). Maxout networks. In *International conference on machine learning* (pp. 1319-1327). PMLR.

Gotovtsev, P. M. (2023). Microbial Cells as a Microrobots: From Drug Delivery to Advanced Biosensors. *Biomimetics, 8*(1), 8. doi:10.3390/biomimetics8010109 PMID:36975339

Gowri, N. V., Dwivedi, J. N., Krishnaveni, K., Boopathi, S., Palaniappan, M., & Medikondu, N. R. (2023). Experimental investigation and multi-objective optimization of eco-friendly near-dry electrical discharge machining of shape memory alloy using Cu/SiC/Gr composite electrode. *Environmental Science and Pollution Research International, 30*(49), 1–19. doi:10.1007/s11356-023-26983-6 PMID:37126160

Grauman, K., & Darrell, T. (2005, October). The pyramid match kernel: Discriminative classification with sets of image features. In *Tenth IEEE International Conference on Computer Vision (ICCV'05)* Volume 1 (Vol. 2, pp. 1458-1465). IEEE. 10.1109/ICCV.2005.239

Greenspan, H., Van Ginneken, B., & Summers, R. M. (2016). Guest editorial deep learning in medical imaging: Overview and future promise of an exciting new technique. *IEEE Transactions on Medical Imaging, 35*(5), 1153–1159. doi:10.1109/TMI.2016.2553401

Gulli, A., & Pal, S. (2017). *Deep learning with Keras.* Packt Publishing Ltd.

Guo, W. (2020). Explainable artificial intelligence for 6G: Improving trust between human and machine. *IEEE Communications Magazine, 58*(6), 39–45. doi:10.1109/MCOM.001.2000050

Guo, Y., Jing, D., Liu, S., & Yuan, Q. (2023). Construction of intelligent moving micro/nanomotors and their applications in biosensing and disease treatment. *Theranostics, 13*(9), 2993–3020. doi:10.7150/thno.81845 PMID:37284438

Gupta, R., Shukla, A., & Tanwar, S. (2020). Aayush: A smart contract-based telesurgery system for healthcare 4.0. *2020 IEEE International Conference on Communications Workshops (ICC Workshops),* 1–6. 10.1109/ICCWorkshops49005.2020.9145044

Halder, A., & Sun, Y. (2019). Biocompatible propulsion for biomedical micro/nano robotics. *Biosensors & Bioelectronics, 139,* 111334. doi:10.1016/j.bios.2019.111334 PMID:31128479

Hamza, R., & Chtourou, M. (2018, July). Apple ripeness estimation using artificial neural network. In *2018 International Conference on High Performance Computing & Simulation (HPCS)* (pp. 229-234). IEEE. 10.1109/HPCS.2018.00049

Han, H., & Liu, X. (2022, January). The challenges of explainable ai in biomedical data science. *BMC Bioinformatics, 22*(12), 443. PMID:35057748

Hanumanthakari, S., Gift, M. M., Kanimozhi, K., Bhavani, M. D., Bamane, K. D., & Boopathi, S. (2023). Biomining Method to Extract Metal Components Using Computer-Printed Circuit Board E-Waste. In *Handbook of Research on Safe Disposal Methods of Municipal Solid Wastes for a Sustainable Environment* (pp. 123–141). IGI Global. doi:10.4018/978-1-6684-8117-2.ch010

Hao, J., Li, M., Chen, W., Yu, L., & Ye, L. (2022). Experimental research on space distribution of reverse flow U-tubes in steam generator primary side. *Nuclear Engineering and Design, 388,* 111650. doi:10.1016/j.nucengdes.2022.111650

Harikaran, M., Boopathi, S., Gokulakannan, S., & Poonguzhali, M. (2023). Study on the Source of E-Waste Management and Disposal Methods. In *Sustainable Approaches and Strategies for E-Waste Management and Utilization* (pp. 39–60). IGI Global. doi:10.4018/978-1-6684-7573-7.ch003

Harris, M., Wu, H., Zhang, W., & Angelopoulou, A. (2022). Overview of recent trends in microchannels for heat transfer and thermal management applications. *Chemical Engineering and Processing, 181,* 109155. doi:10.1016/j.cep.2022.109155

Hassani, S. S., Daraee, M., & Sobat, Z. (2020). Advanced development in upstream of petroleum industry using nanotechnology. *Chinese Journal of Chemical Engineering, 28*(6), 1483–1491. doi:10.1016/j.cjche.2020.02.030

Hatton-Jones, K. M., Christie, C., Griffith, T. A., Smith, A. G., Naghipour, S., Robertson, K., Russell, J. S., Peart, J. N., Headrick, J. P., Cox, A. J., & du Toit, E. F. (2021). A YOLO based software for automated detection and analysis of rodent behaviour in the open field arena. *Computers in Biology and Medicine, 134,* 104474. doi:10.1016/j.compbiomed.2021.104474 PMID:34058512

He, K., Gkioxari, G., Dollár, P., & Girshick, R. (2017). Mask r-cnn. In *Proceedings of the IEEE international conference on computer vision* (pp. 2961-2969). Academic Press.

He, K., Zhang, X., Ren, S., & Sun, J. (2016). Deep residual learning for image recognition. In *Proceedings of the IEEE conference on computer vision and pattern recognition* (pp. 770-778). Academic Press.

He, K., Zhang, X., Ren, S., & Sun, J. (2015). Delving deep into rectifiers: Surpassing human-level performance on imagenet classification. In *Proceedings of the IEEE international conference on computer vision* (pp. 1026-1034). 10.1109/ICCV.2015.123

He, K., Zhang, X., Ren, S., & Sun, J. (2016). Deep residual learning for image recognition. In *Proceedings of the IEEE Conference on Computer Vision and Pattern Recognition* (pp. 770–778). IEEE.

He, L., Xu, J., Dekai, Z., Qinghai, Y., & Longqiu, L. (2018). Potential application of functional micro-nano structures in petroleum. *Petroleum Exploration and Development*, 45(4), 745–753. doi:10.1016/S1876-3804(18)30077-6

Hemachandran, K. (2016). Study of Image Steganography using LSB, DFT and DWT. *International Journal of Computers and Technology*, 11, 2618–2627.

Ho, J. C. (2022). Robot Assisted Neurosurgery for High-Accuracy, Minimally-Invasive Deep Brain Electrophysiology in Monkeys. *2022 44th Annual International Conference of the IEEE Engineering in Medicine & Biology Society (EMBC)*, 3115-3118. 10.1109/EMBC48229.2022.9871520

Huang, Z., Wang, J., Fu, X., Yu, T., Guo, Y., & Wang, R. (2020). DC-SPP-YOLO: Dense connection and spatial pyramid pooling based YOLO for object detection. *Information Sciences*, 522, 241–258. doi:10.1016/j.ins.2020.02.067

Hughes, Zhu, & Bednarz. (2021). Generative Adversarial Networks-Enabled Human-Artificial Intelligence Collaborative Applications for Creative and Design Industries: A Systematic Review of Current Approaches and Trends. *Frontiers in Artificial Intelligence, 4*, 1-17.

Hussain, Z., Babe, M., Saravanan, S., Srimathy, G., Roopa, H., & Boopathi, S. (2023). Optimizing Biomass-to-Biofuel Conversion: IoT and AI Integration for Enhanced Efficiency and Sustainability. In Circular Economy Implementation for Sustainability in the Built Environment (pp. 191–214). IGI Global.

Hussain, A., Pu, H., & Sun, D. W. (2019). Measurements of lycopene contents in fruit: A review of recent developments in conventional and novel techniques. *Critical Reviews in Food Science and Nutrition*, 59(5), 758–769. doi:10.1080/10408398.2018.1518896 PMID:30582342

Huth, C. (2015). Securing systems on the Internet of Things via physical properties of devices and communications. In Systems Conference (SysCon), 9th Annual IEEE International. IEEE.

Hutter, F., Hoos, H. H., & Leyton-Brown, K. (2011). Sequential model-based optimization for general algorithm configuration. In *Learning and Intelligent Optimization: 5th International Conference, LION 5, Rome, Italy, January 17-21, 2011. Selected Papers 5* (pp. 507-523). Springer Berlin Heidelberg. 10.1007/978-3-642-25566-3_40

Hu, Y. (2021). Self-Assembly of DNA Molecules: Towards DNA Nanorobots for Biomedical Applications. *Cyborg and Bionic Systems (Washington, D.C.)*, 2021, 2021. doi:10.34133/2021/9807520 PMID:36285141

Ince, H., & Aktan, B. (2009). A comparison of data mining techniques for credit scoring in banking: A managerial perspective. *Journal of Business Economics and Management*, 10(3), 233–240. doi:10.3846/1611-1699.2009.10.233-240

Indiveri, G., Linares-Barranco, B., Legenstein, R., Deligeorgis, G., & Prodromakis, T. (2013). Integration of nanoscale memristor synapses in neuromorphic computing architectures. *Nanotechnology*, 24(38), 384010. doi:10.1088/0957-4484/24/38/384010 PMID:23999381

Intel. (n.d.). https://www.intel.com/content/www/us/en/developer/tools/oneapi/overview.html

Ioffe, S., & Szegedy, C. (2015, June). Batch normalization: Accelerating deep network training by reducing internal covariate shift. In *International conference on machine learning* (pp. 448-456). PMLR.

Islam, A. M. R., Ahmed, M. U., Barua, S., & Begum, S. (2022). A systematic review of explainable artificial intelligence in terms of different application domains and tasks. *Applied Sciences (Basel, Switzerland), 12*(3), 1353. doi:10.3390/app12031353

Jahromi, L. P., Shahbazi, M., Maleki, A., Azadi, A., & Santos, H. A. (2021). Chemically Engineered Immune Cell-Derived Microrobots and Biomimetic Nanoparticles: Emerging Biodiagnostic and Therapeutic Tools. *Advancement of Science, 8*(8), 8. doi:10.1002/advs.202002499 PMID:33898169

Jakkula, R. V. S. K., & Sethuramalingam, P. (2023). Analysis of coatings based on carbon-based nanomaterials for paint industries-A review. *Australian Journal of Mechanical Engineering, 21*(3), 1008–1036. doi:10.1080/14484846.2021.1938953

Jarrahi, M. H. (2018). Artificial intelligence and the future of work: Human-AI symbiosis in organizational decision making. *Business Horizons, 61*(4), 577–586. doi:10.1016/j.bushor.2018.03.007

Javaid, M., Haleem, A., Singh, R. P., & Suman, R. (2021). Substantial capabilities of robotics in enhancing industry 4.0 implementation. *Cognitive Robotics, 1*, 58–75. doi:10.1016/j.cogr.2021.06.001

Jégou, H., Perronnin, F., Douze, M., Sánchez, J., Pérez, P., & Schmid, C. (2011). Aggregating local image descriptors into compact codes. *IEEE Transactions on Pattern Analysis and Machine Intelligence, 34*(9), 1704–1716. doi:10.1109/TPAMI.2011.235 PMID:22156101

Jian, Z., Chao, Z., Shunli, Z., Tingting, L., Weiwen, S., & Jian, J. (2018). Pre-detection and dual-dictionary sparse representation based face recognition algorithm in non-sufficient training samples. *Journal of Systems Engineering and Electronics, 29*(1), 196–202. doi:10.21629/JSEE.2018.01.20

Jintasuttisak, T., Leonce, A., Sher Shah, M., Khafaga, T., Simkins, G., & Edirisinghe, E. (2022, March). Deep learning based animal detection and tracking in drone video footage. In *Proceedings of the 8th International Conference on Computing and Artificial Intelligence* (pp. 425-431). 10.1145/3532213.3532280

Ji, Q., Fu, S., Tan, K., Muralidharan, S. T., Lagrelius, K., Danelia, D., Andrikopoulos, G., Wang, X. V., Wang, L., & Feng, L. (2022). Synthesizing the optimal gait of a quadruped robot with soft actuators using deep reinforcement learning. *Robotics and Computer-integrated Manufacturing, 78*, 102382. doi:10.1016/j.rcim.2022.102382

Joe, S., Bliah, O., Magdassi, S., & Beccai, L. (2023). Jointless Bioinspired Soft Robotics by Harnessing Micro and Macroporosity. *Advancement of Science, 10*(23), 2302080. doi:10.1002/advs.202302080 PMID:37323121

Johnson, N. E., Ianiuk, O., Cazap, D., Liu, L., Starobin, D., Dobler, G., & Ghandehari, M. (2017). Patterns of waste generation: A gradient boosting model for short-term waste prediction in New York City. *Waste Management (New York, N.Y.), 62*, 3–11. doi:10.1016/j.wasman.2017.01.037 PMID:28216080

Karan, S., & Majumder, D. D. (2011). Molecular machinery-a nanorobotics control system design for cancer drug delivery. *2011 International Conference on Recent Trends in Information Systems*, 197–202. 10.1109/ReTIS.2011.6146867

Karimov, K., Akhmedov, A., & Adilova, S. (2022). Theoretical and engineering solutions of the controlled vibration mechanisms for precision engineering. *AIP Conference Proceedings, 2637*(1), 060001. doi:10.1063/5.0118863

Karthik, S., Hemalatha, R., Aruna, R., Deivakani, M., Reddy, R. V. K., & Boopathi, S. (2023). Study on Healthcare Security System-Integrated Internet of Things (IoT). In Perspectives and Considerations on the Evolution of Smart Systems (pp. 342–362). IGI Global.

Karthik, K., Teferi, A. B., Sathish, R., Gandhi, A. M., Padhi, S., Boopathi, S., & Sasikala, G. (2023). Analysis of delamination and its effect on polymer matrix composites. *Materials Today: Proceedings*. Advance online publication. doi:10.1016/j.matpr.2023.07.199

Kavitha, K.K., Koshti, A., & Dunghav, P. (2012). Steganography using least significant bit algorithm. *International Journal of Engineering Research and Applications*.

Khamrui, A., & Mandal, J. K. (2013). A genetic algorithm-based steganography using discrete cosine transformation (GASDCT). *Procedia Technology*, *10*, 105–111. doi:10.1016/j.protcy.2013.12.342

Khandani, A. E., Kim, A. J., & Lo, A. W. (2010). Consumer credit-risk models via machine-learning algorithms. *Journal of Banking & Finance*, *34*(11), 2767–27. doi:10.1016/j.jbankfin.2010.06.001

Khan, K. S., Kunz, R., Kleijnen, J., & Antes, G. (2010). Five steps to conducting a systematic review. *Journal of the Royal Society of Medicine*, *96*(3), 118–121. doi:10.1177/014107680309600304 PMID:12612111

Khoramshahi, M., & Billard, A. (2019). A dynamical system approach to task-adaptation in physical human–robot interaction. *Autonomous Robots*, *43*(4), 927–946. doi:10.1007/s10514-018-9764-z

Kim, D. S., Yang, X., Lee, J. H., Yoo, H. Y., Park, C., Kim, S. W., & Lee, J. (2022). Development of GO/Co/Chitosan-Based Nano-Biosensor for Real-Time Detection of D-Glucose. *Biosensors (Basel)*, *12*(7), 464. doi:10.3390/bios12070464 PMID:35884266

Kim, K. J., & Lee, W. B. (2004). Stock market prediction using artificial neural networks with optimal feature transformation. *Neural Computing & Applications*, *13*(3), 255–260. doi:10.1007/s00521-004-0428-x

Kiran, J. S., & Prabhu, S. (2020). Robot nano spray painting-A review. *IOP Conference Series. Materials Science and Engineering*, *912*(3), 032044. doi:10.1088/1757-899X/912/3/032044

Koleoso, M., Feng, X., & Xue, Y. (2020). *Materials Today Bio Micro/nanoscale magnetic robots for biomedical applications*. https://doi.org/ doi:10.1016/j.mtbio.2020.100085

Koshariya, A. K., Kalaiyarasi, D., Jovith, A. A., Sivakami, T., Hasan, D. S., & Boopathi, S. (2023). AI-Enabled IoT and WSN-Integrated Smart Agriculture System. In *Artificial Intelligence Tools and Technologies for Smart Farming and Agriculture Practices* (pp. 200–218). IGI Global. doi:10.4018/978-1-6684-8516-3.ch011

Koshariya, A. K., Khatoon, S., Marathe, A. M., Suba, G. M., Baral, D., & Boopathi, S. (2023). Agricultural Waste Management Systems Using Artificial Intelligence Techniques. In *AI-Enabled Social Robotics in Human Care Services* (pp. 236–258). IGI Global. doi:10.4018/978-1-6684-8171-4.ch009

Koutanaei, F. N., Sajedi, H., & Khanbabaei, M. (2015). A hybrid data mining model of feature selection algorithms and ensemble learning classifiers for credit scoring. *Journal of Retailing and Consumer Services*, *27*, 11–23. doi:10.1016/j.jretconser.2015.07.003

Krishnan, S., Rajagopalan, G. A., Kandhasamy, S., & Shanmugavel, M. (2019). Towards scalable continuous-time trajectory optimization for multi-robot navigation. *arXiv preprint arXiv:1910.13463*.

Krishnan, S., Rajagopalan, G. A., Kandhasamy, S., & Shanmugavel, M. (2020). Continuous-time trajectory optimization for decentralized multi-robot navigation. *IFAC-PapersOnLine*, *53*(1), 494–499. doi:10.1016/j.ifacol.2020.06.083

Krizhevsky, A., Sutskever, I., & Hinton, G. E. (2012). Imagenet classification with deep convolutional neural networks. *Advances in Neural Information Processing Systems*, *25*.

Kučuk, N., Primožič, M., Knez, Ž., & Leitgeb, M. (2023). Sustainable Biodegradable Biopolymer-Based Nanoparticles for Healthcare Applications. *International Journal of Molecular Sciences*, 24. PMID:36834596

Kumar & Kumar. (n.d.). *Techniques of Digital Watermarking*. Academic Press.

Kumar, M. R., Reddy, V. P., Meheta, A., Dhiyani, V., Al-Saady, F. A., & Jain, A. (2023). Investigating the Effects of Process Parameters on the Size and Properties of Nano Materials. *E3S Web of Conferences, 430*, 01125.

Kumar, M., Kumar, K., Sasikala, P., Sampath, B., Gopi, B., & Sundaram, S. (2023). Sustainable Green Energy Generation From Waste Water: IoT and ML Integration. In Sustainable Science and Intelligent Technologies for Societal Development (pp. 440–463). IGI Global.

Kumar, S., Nasim, B., & Abraham, E. (2018). Nanorobots a future device for diagnosis and treatment. *Journal of Pharmacy and Pharmaceutics*, *5*(1), 44–49. doi:10.15436/2377-1313.18.1815

Kumar, S., Savur, C., & Sahin, F. (2020). Survey of human–robot collaboration in industrial settings: Awareness, intelligence, and compliance. *IEEE Transactions on Systems, Man, and Cybernetics. Systems, 51*(1), 280–297. doi:10.1109/TSMC.2020.3041231

Kundu, K., Vishwakarma, V., Rai, A., Srivastava, M., & Mishra, A. (2023, April). Design and Deployment of Wild Animal Intrusion Detection & Repellent System Employing IOT. In *2023 International Conference on Computational Intelligence and Sustainable Engineering Solutions (CISES)* (pp. 763-767). IEEE. 10.1109/CISES58720.2023.10183532

Kushwah, J. S., Gupta, M., Shrivastava, S., Saxena, N., Saini, R., & Boopathi, S. (2024). Psychological Impacts, Prevention Strategies, and Intervention Approaches Across Age Groups: Unmasking Cyberbullying. In Change Dynamics in Healthcare, Technological Innovations, and Complex Scenarios (pp. 89–109). IGI Global.

Kwong, J. C., Khondker, A., Tran, C., Evans, E., Cozma, A. I., Javidan, A., Ali, A., Jamal, M., Short, T., Papanikolaou, F., Srigley, J. R., Fine, B., & Feifer, A. (2022). Explainable artificial intelligence to predict the risk of side-specific extraprostatic extension in pre-prostatectomy patients. *Canadian Urological Association Journal, 16*(6). Advance online publication. doi:10.5489/cuaj.7473 PMID:35099382

Lai, H. Y. (2023). Breakdowns in team resilience during aircraft landing due to mental model disconnects as identified through machine learning. *Reliability Engineering & System Safety, 237*, 109356. doi:10.1016/j.ress.2023.109356

Lazebnik, S., Schmid, C., & Ponce, J. (2006, June). Beyond bags of features: Spatial pyramid matching for recognizing natural scene categories. In 2006 IEEE computer society conference on computer vision and pattern recognition (CVPR'06) (Vol. 2, pp. 2169-2178). IEEE.

LeCun, Y., Bengio, Y., & Hinton, G. (2015). Deep learning. *Nature, 521*(7553), 436-444.

Lee, D., Yu, H. W., Kwon, H., Kong, H.-J., Lee, K. E., & Kim, H. C. (2020, June). Evaluation of Surgical Skills during Robotic Surgery by Deep Learning-Based Multiple Surgical Instrument Tracking in Training and Actual Operations. *Journal of Clinical Medicine, 9*(6), E1964. doi:10.3390/jcm9061964 PMID:32585953

Lee, J. J., Lee, Y. R., Lim, D. H., & Ahn, H. C. (2021). A Study on the Employee Turnover Prediction using XGBoost and SHAP. *Journal of Information Systems, 30*(4), 21–42.

Lees, M. J., & Johnstone, M. C. (2021). Implementing safety features of Industry 4.0 without compromising safety culture. *IFAC-PapersOnLine, 54*(13), 680–685. doi:10.1016/j.ifacol.2021.10.530

Lei, B., Zhuo, L., Chen, S., Li, S., Ni, D., & Wang, T. (2014, April). Automatic recognition of fetal standard plane in ultrasound image. In *2014 IEEE 11th International Symposium on Biomedical Imaging (ISBI)* (pp. 85 88). IEEE. 10.1109/ISBI.2014.6867815

Lei, B., Tan, E. L., Chen, S., Ni, D., & Wang, T. (2015). Saliency-driven image classification method based on histogram mining and image score. *Pattern Recognition*, *48*(8), 2567–2580. doi:10.1016/j.patcog.2015.02.004

Lei, B., Tan, E. L., Chen, S., Zhuo, L., Li, S., Ni, D., & Wang, T. (2015). Automatic recognition of fetal facial standard plane in ultrasound image via fisher vector. *PLoS One*, *10*(5), e0121838. doi:10.1371/journal.pone.0121838 PMID:25933215

Lei, B., Yao, Y., Chen, S., Li, S., Li, W., Ni, D., & Wang, T. (2015). Discriminative learning for automatic staging of placental maturity via multi-layer fisher vector. *Scientific Reports*, *5*(1), 12818. doi:10.1038/srep12818 PMID:26228175

Li, J., Xu, Z., & Zhu, D. (2022). Bio-inspired Intelligence with Applications to Robotics: A Survey. arXiv:2206.

Li, Q., Cai, W., Wang, X., Zhou, Y., Feng, D. D., & Chen, M. (2014, December). Medical image classification with convolutional neural network. In *2014 13th international conference on control automation robotics & vision (ICARCV)* (pp. 844-848). IEEE. 10.1109/ICARCV.2014.7064414

Li, W. (2018). The design of a 3-CPS parallel robot for maximum dexterity. *Mechanism and Machine Theory, 122*, 279-291. doi:10.1016/j.mechmachtheory.2018.01.003

Li, X., Lai, T., Wang, S., Chen, Q., Yang, C., Chen, R., ... Zheng, F. (2019, December). Weighted feature pyramid networks for object detection. In *2019 IEEE Intl Conf on Parallel & Distributed Processing with Applications, Big Data & Cloud Computing, Sustainable Computing & Communications, Social Computing & Networking (ISPA/BDCloud/SocialCom/SustainCom)* (pp. 1500-1504). IEEE.

Li, H., Cao, Y., Li, S., Zhao, J., & Sun, Y. (2020). XGBoost model and its application to personal credit evaluation. *IEEE Intelligent Systems*, *35*(3), 52–61. doi:10.1109/MIS.2020.2972533

Li, H., Yao, J., Zhou, P., Chen, X., Xu, Y., & Zhao, Y. (2020). High-force soft pneumatic actuators based on novel casting method for robotic applications. *Sensors and Actuators. A, Physical*, *306*, 306. doi:10.1016/j.sna.2020.111957

Li, J., Dekanovsky, L., Khezri, B., Wu, B., Zhou, H., & Sofer, Z. (2022). Biohybrid Micro- and Nanorobots for Intelligent Drug Delivery. *Cyborg and Bionic Systems (Washington, D.C.)*, *2022*, 2022. doi:10.34133/2022/9824057 PMID:36285309

Li, J., Yang, S. X., & Xu, Z. (2019). A survey on robot path planning using bio-inspired algorithms. *2019 IEEE International Conference on Robotics and Biomimetics (ROBIO)*, 2111–2116. 10.1109/ROBIO49542.2019.8961498

Li, J., & Yu, J. (2023). Biodegradable Microrobots and Their Biomedical Applications: A Review. *Nanomaterials (Basel, Switzerland)*, *13*(10), 13. doi:10.3390/nano13101590 PMID:37242005

Lin, M., Chen, Q., & Yan, S. (2013). Network in network. *arXiv preprint arXiv:1312.4400*.

Li, S., Zhang, H., & Xu, F. (2023). Intelligent Detection Method for Wildlife Based on Deep Learning. *Sensors (Basel)*, *23*(24), 9669. doi:10.3390/s23249669 PMID:38139515

Liu, C., Yuen, J., & Torralba, A. (2010). Sift flow: Dense correspondence across scenes and its applications. *IEEE Transactions on Pattern Analysis and Machine Intelligence*, *33*(5), 978–994. doi:10.1109/TPAMI.2010.147 PMID:20714019

Liu, H. H., Su, P. C., & Hsu, M. H. (2020). An improved steganography method based on least-significant-bit substitution and pixel-value differencing. *KSII Transactions on Internet and Information Systems*, *14*(11), 4537–4556.

Long, J., Shelhamer, E., & Darrell, T. (2015). Fully convolutional networks for semantic segmentation. In *Proceedings of the IEEE conference on computer vision and pattern recognition* (pp. 3431-3440). IEEE.

Lopez, M., Castillo, E., Garcia, G., & Bashir, A. (2006). Delta robot: Inverse, direct, and intermediate jacobians. *Proceedings of the Institution of Mechanical Engineers, Part C: Journal of Mechanical Engineering Science*, *220*(1), 103–109. 10.1243/095440606X78263

Lowe, D. G. (2004). Distinctive image features from scale-invariant keypoints. *International Journal of Computer Vision, 60*(2), 91–110. doi:10.1023/B:VISI.0000029664.99615.94

Madeti, S. R., & Singh, S. N. (2018). Modeling of PV system based on experimental data for fault detection using kNN method. *Solar Energy, 173*, 139–151. doi:10.1016/j.solener.2018.07.038

Madridano, A., Al-Kaff, A., Martín, D., & De La Escalera, A. (2021). Trajectory planning for multi-robot systems: Methods and applications. *Expert Systems with Applications, 173*, 114660. doi:10.1016/j.eswa.2021.114660

Maguluri, L. P., Arularasan, A., & Boopathi, S. (2023). Assessing Security Concerns for AI-Based Drones in Smart Cities. In Effective AI, Blockchain, and E-Governance Applications for Knowledge Discovery and Management (pp. 27–47). IGI Global. doi:10.4018/978-1-6684-9151-5.ch002

Maheswari, B. U., Imambi, S. S., Hasan, D., Meenakshi, S., Pratheep, V., & Boopathi, S. (2023). Internet of things and machine learning-integrated smart robotics. In Global Perspectives on Robotics and Autonomous Systems: Development and Applications (pp. 240–258). IGI Global. doi:10.4018/978-1-6684-7791-5.ch010

Maji, S., Berg, A. C., & Malik, J. (2008, June). *Classification using intersection kernel support vector machines is efficient. In 2008 IEEE conference on computer vision and pattern recognition.* IEEE.

Makarfi, A. U., Rabie, K. M., Kaiwartya, O., Li, X., & Kharel, R. (2020, May). Physical layer security in vehicular networks with reconfigurable intelligent surfaces. In *2020 IEEE 91st Vehicular Technology Conference (VTC2020-Spring)* (pp. 1-6). IEEE. 10.1109/VTC2020-Spring48590.2020.9128438

Malathi, J., Kusha, K., Isaac, S., Ramesh, A., Rajendiran, M., & Boopathi, S. (2024). IoT-Enabled Remote Patient Monitoring for Chronic Disease Management and Cost Savings: Transforming Healthcare. In Advances in Explainable AI Applications for Smart Cities (pp. 371–388). IGI Global.

Malik, S., Muhammad, K., & Waheed, Y. (2023). Nanotechnology: A revolution in modern industry. *Molecules (Basel, Switzerland), 28*(2), 661. doi:10.3390/molecules28020661 PMID:36677717

Mali, P., Harikumar, K., Singh, A. K., Krishna, K. M., & Sujit, P. B. (2021, June). Incorporating prediction in control barrier function based distributive multi-robot collision avoidance. In *2021 European Control Conference (ECC)* (pp. 2394-2399). IEEE. 10.23919/ECC54610.2021.9655081

Mall, S. (2018). An empirical study on credit risk management: The case of nonbanking financial companies. *The Journal of Credit Risk, 14*(3), 49–66. doi:10.21314/JCR.2017.239

Mammeri, A., Zhou, D., & Boukerche, A. (2016). Animal-vehicle collision mitigation system for automated vehicles. *IEEE Transactions on Systems, Man, and Cybernetics. Systems, 46*(9), 1287–1299. doi:10.1109/TSMC.2015.2497235

Manickam, P., Mariappan, S. A., Murugesan, S. M., Hansda, S., Kaushik, A., Shinde, R., & Thipperudraswamy, S. P. (2022). Artificial Intelligence (AI) and Internet of Medical Things (IoMT) Assisted Biomedical Systems for Intelligent Healthcare. *Biosensors (Basel), 12*(8), 562–562. doi:10.3390/bios12080562 PMID:35892459

Manuela & Costa. (2014, November). Data Visualization. *Communication Design Quarterly Review*.

Marinoudi, V., Sørensen, C. G., Pearson, S., & Bochtis, D. (2019). Robotics and labour in agriculture. A context consideration. *Biosystems Engineering, 184*, 111–121. doi:10.1016/j.biosystemseng.2019.06.013

Markande, A., Mistry Kruti, U., & Shraddha, J. A. (2021) magnetic nanoparticles from bacteria. In Biobased Nanotechnology for Green Applications. SpringerNature Switzerland AG.

Marvel, L. M., Boncelet, C. G., & Retter, C. T. (1999). Spread spectrum image steganography. *IEEE Transactions on Image Processing, 8*(8), 1075–1083. doi:10.1109/83.777088 PMID:18267522

Marvin, G., Jackson, M., & Alam, M. G. R. (2021, August). A machine learning approach for employee retention prediction. In *2021 IEEE Region 10 Symposium (TENSYMP)* (pp. 1-8). IEEE. 10.1109/TENSYMP52854.2021.9550921

Mavridou, E., Vrochidou, E., Papakostas, G. A., Pachidis, T., & Kaburlasos, V. G. (2019). Machine vision systems in precision agriculture for crop farming. *Journal of Imaging, 5*(12), 89. doi:10.3390/jimaging5120089 PMID:34460603

Mbunge, E., Muchemwa, B., Jiyane, S., & Batani, J. (2021). Sensors and healthcare 5.0: Transformative shift in virtual care through emerging digital health technologies. *Global Health Journal (Amsterdam, Netherlands), 5*(4), 169–177. doi:10.1016/j.glohj.2021.11.008

McClintock, H., Temel, F. Z., Doshi, N., Je-sung, K., & Robert, J. (2018). The millidelta: A high-bandwidth, high-precision, millimeter-scale delta robot. *Science Robotics, 3*(14), eaar3018. doi:10.1126/scirobotics.aar3018 PMID:33141699

Mehrafrooz, B., Mohammadi, M., & Masouleh, M. T. (2017). Kinematic sensitivity evaluation of revolute and prismatic 3-dof delta robots. *2017 5th RSI International Conference on Robotics and Mechatronics (ICRoM),* 225–231. doi:.846615910.1109/ICRoM.2017

Meivel, S., Maheswari, S., & Faridha Banu, D. (2023). Design and Method of an Agricultural Drone System Using Biomass Vegetation Indices and Multispectral Images. In *Proceedings of UASG 2021: Wings 4 Sustainability. UASG 2021. Lecture Notes in Civil Engineering* (vol. 304). Springer. 10.1007/978-3-031-19309-5_25

Mercy, J., Lawanya, R., Nandhini, S., & Saravanan, M. (2022). Effective Image Deblurring Based on Improved Image Edge Information and Blur Kernel Estimation. *8th International Conference on Advanced Computing and Communication Systems, ICACCS 2022,* 855-859.

Midi, H., Sarkar, S. K., & Rana, S. (2010). Collinearity diagnostics of binary logistic regression model. *Journal of Interdisciplinary Mathematics, 13*(3), 253–267. doi:10.1080/09720502.2010.10700699

Minopoulos, G. M., Memos, V. A., Stergiou, C. L., Stergiou, K. D., Plageras, A. P., Koidou, M. P., & Psannis, K. E. (2022). Exploitation of Emerging Technologies and Advanced Networks for a Smart Healthcare System. *Applied Sciences (Basel, Switzerland), 12*(12), 5859. doi:10.3390/app12125859

Moerenhout, T., Devisch, I., & Cornelis, G. C. (2018). E-health beyond technology: Analyzing the paradigm shift that lies beneath. *Medicine, Health Care, and Philosophy, 21*(1), 31–41. doi:10.1007/s11019-017-9780-3 PMID:28551772

Mohanta, B., Das, P., & Patnaik, S. (2019). Healthcare 5.0: A paradigm shift in digital healthcare system using artificial intelligence, IOT and 5G communication. *2019 International Conference on Applied Machine Learning (ICAML),* 191–196. 10.1109/ICAML48257.2019.00044

Mohanty, A., Jothi, B., Jeyasudha, J., Ranjit, P., Isaac, J. S., & Boopathi, S. (2023). Additive Manufacturing Using Robotic Programming. In *AI-Enabled Social Robotics in Human Care Services* (pp. 259–282). IGI Global. doi:10.4018/978-1-6684-8171-4.ch010

Moradi Dalvand, M., & Shirinzadeh, B. (2013, April). Motion control analysis of a parallel robot assisted minimally invasive surgery/microsurgery system (PRAMiSS). *Robotics and Computer-integrated Manufacturing, 29*(2), 318–327. doi:10.1016/j.rcim.2012.09.003

Mouchou, R., Laseinde, T., Jen, T.-C., & Ukoba, K. (2021). Developments in the Application of Nano Materials for Photovoltaic Solar Cell Design, Based on Industry 4.0 Integration Scheme. *Advances in Artificial Intelligence, Software and Systems Engineering: Proceedings of the AHFE 2021 Virtual Conferences on Human Factors in Software and Systems Engineering, Artificial Intelligence and Social Computing, and Energy,* July 25-29, 2021, USA, 510–521.

Murali, B., Padhi, S., Patil, C. K., Kumar, P. S., Santhanakrishnan, M., & Boopathi, S. (2023). Investigation on hardness and tensile strength of friction stir processing of Al6061/TiN surface composite. *Materials Today: Proceedings.*

Myilsamy, S., & Sampath, B. (2021). Experimental comparison of near-dry and cryogenically cooled near-dry machining in wire-cut electrical discharge machining processes. *Surface Topography : Metrology and Properties, 9*(3), 035015. doi:10.1088/2051-672X/ac15e0

Naghdi, T., Ardalan, S., Asghari Adib, Z., Sharifi, A. R., & Golmohammadi, H. (2023). Moving toward Smart Biomedical Sensing. *Biosensors & Bioelectronics, 223,* 115009. doi:10.1016/j.bios.2022.115009 PMID:36565545

Najafi-Zangeneh, S., Shams-Gharneh, N., Arjomandi-Nezhad, A., & Hashemkhani Zolfani, S. (2021). An Improved Machine Learning-Based Employees Attrition Prediction Framework with Emphasis on Feature Selection. *Mathematics, 9*(11), 1226. doi:10.3390/math9111226

Narasimmalou, T., & Allen Joseph, R. (2012). Discrete wavelet transform based steganography for transmitting images. In *IEEE-International Conference on Advances In Engineering, Science And Management (ICAESM2012)* (pp. 370-375). IEEE.

Nasr, M., Islam, M. M., Shehata, S., Karray, F., & Quintana, Y. (2021). Smart healthcare in the age of AI: Recent advances, challenges, and future prospects. *IEEE Access : Practical Innovations, Open Solutions, 9,* 145248–145270. doi:10.1109/ACCESS.2021.3118960

Naveeenkumar, N., Rallapalli, S., Sasikala, K., Priya, P. V., Husain, J., & Boopathi, S. (2024). Enhancing Consumer Behavior and Experience Through AI-Driven Insights Optimization. In *AI Impacts in Digital Consumer Behavior* (pp. 1–35). IGI Global. doi:10.4018/979-8-3693-1918-5.ch001

Navsalkar, A., & Hota, A. R. (2023, May). Data-driven risk-sensitive model predictive control for safe navigation in multi-robot systems. In *2023 IEEE International Conference on Robotics and Automation (ICRA)* (pp. 1442-1448). IEEE. 10.1109/ICRA48891.2023.10161002

Ness, S., Shepherd, N. J., & Xuan, T. R. (2023). Synergy Between AI and Robotics: A Comprehensive Integration. *Asian Journal of Research in Computer Science, 16*(4), 80–94. doi:10.9734/ajrcos/2023/v16i4372

Ni, D., Yang, X., Chen, X., Chin, C. T., Chen, S., Heng, P. A., Li, S., Qin, J., & Wang, T. (2014). Standard plane localization in ultrasound by radial component model and selective search. *Ultrasound in Medicine & Biology, 40*(11), 2728–2742. doi:10.1016/j.ultrasmedbio.2014.06.006 PMID:25220278

O'Brolcháin, F. (2019). Robots and people with dementia: Unintended consequences and moral hazard. *Nursing Ethics, 26*(4), 962–972. doi:10.1177/0969733017742960 PMID:29262739

Oh, H., Shirazi, A. R., Sun, C., & Jin, Y. (2017). Bio-inspired self-organising multi-robot pattern formation: A review. *Robotics and Autonomous Systems, 91,* 83–100. doi:10.1016/j.robot.2016.12.006

Olcay, E., Schuhmann, F., & Lohmann, B. (2020). Collective navigation of a multi-robot system in an unknown environment. *Robotics and Autonomous Systems, 132,* 103604. doi:10.1016/j.robot.2020.103604

Oluwasanu, A. A., Oluwaseun, F., Teslim, J. A., Isaiah, T. T., Olalekan, I. A., & Chris, O. A. (2019). Scientific applications and prospects of nanomaterials: A multidisciplinary review. *African Journal of Biotechnology*, *18*(30), 946–961. doi:10.5897/AJB2019.16812

Onnasch, L., & Roesler, E. (2021). A taxonomy to structure and analyze human–robot interaction. *International Journal of Social Robotics*, *13*(4), 833–849. doi:10.1007/s12369-020-00666-5

Palaniappan, M., Tirlangi, S., Mohamed, M. J. S., Moorthy, R. S., Valeti, S. V., & Boopathi, S. (2023). Fused Deposition Modelling of Polylactic Acid (PLA)-Based Polymer Composites: A Case Study. In Development, Properties, and Industrial Applications of 3D Printed Polymer Composites (pp. 66–85). IGI Global.

Pandya, A., & Auner, G. (2004). Robotics technology: A journey into the future. *The Urologic Clinics of North America*, *31*(4), 793–800. doi:10.1016/j.ucl.2004.06.013 PMID:15474607

Park, J. S., Tsang, B., Yedidsion, H., Warnell, G., Kyoung, D., & Stone, P. (2021, October). Learning to improve multi-robot hallway navigation. In *Conference on Robot Learning* (pp. 1883-1895). PMLR.

Patel, H., & Dave, P. (2012). Steganography technique based on DCT coefficients. *International Journal of Engineering Research and Applications*, *2*(1), 713–717.

Patil, K., Meshram, V., Hanchate, D., & Ramkteke, S. D. (2021). Machine learning in agriculture domain: A state-of-art survey. *Artificial Intelligence in the Life Sciences*, *1*, 100010. doi:10.1016/j.ailsci.2021.100010

Patwardhan, J. (2006). *Architectures for nanoscale devices* (Vol. 68). Academic Press.

Paul, A., Thilagham, K., KG, J.-, Reddy, P. R., Sathyamurthy, R., & Boopathi, S. (2024). Multi-criteria Optimization on Friction Stir Welding of Aluminum Composite (AA5052-H32/B4C) using Titanium Nitride Coated Tool. Engineering Research Express.

Pawar, U., O'Shea, D., Rea, S., & O'Reilly, R. (2020). Incorporating explainable artificial intelligence (XAI) to aid the understanding of machine learning in the healthcare domain. *Irish Conference on Artificial Intelligence and Cognitive Science*.

Payne, E. M., Peltier, J. W., & Barger, V. A. (2018). Mobile banking and AI-enabled mobile banking: The differential effects of technological and non-technological factors on digital natives' perceptions and behavior. *Journal of Research in Interactive Marketing*, *12*(3), 328–346. doi:10.1108/JRIM-07-2018-0087

Pedram, A., & Nejat Pishkenari, H. (2017). Smart micro/nano-robotic systems for gene delivery. *Current Gene Therapy*, *17*(2), 73–79. doi:10.2174/1566523217666170511111000 PMID:28494736

Peng, X., Tang, S., Tang, D., Zhou, D., Li, Y., Chen, Q., Wan, F., Lukas, H., Han, H., Zhang, X., Gao, W., & Wu, S. (2023). Autonomous metal-organic framework nanorobots for active mitochondria-targeted cancer therapy. *Science Advances*, *9*(23), 9. doi:10.1126/sciadv.adh1736 PMID:37294758

Penumuru, D. P., Muthuswamy, S., & Karumbu, P. (2020). Identification and classification of materials using machine vision and machine learning in the context of industry 4.0. *Journal of Intelligent Manufacturing*, *31*(5), 1229–1241. doi:10.1007/s10845-019-01508-6

Pereira, C. S., Morais, R., & Reis, M. J. C. S. (2017). Recent advances in image processing techniques for automated harvesting purposes: A review. *Proceedings of the 2017 Intelligent Systems Conference (IntelliSys)*, 566-575. 10.1109/IntelliSys.2017.8324352

Perronnin, F., Sánchez, J., & Mensink, T. (2010). Improving the fisher kernel for large-scale image classification. *Computer Vision–ECCV 2010: 11th European Conference on Computer Vision, Heraklion, Crete, Greece, September 5-11, 2010 Proceedings, 11*(Part IV), 143–156.

Pisla, Plitea, Gherman, Pisla, & Vaida. (2009). *Kinematical Analysis and Design of a New Surgical Parallel Robot.* . doi:10.1007/978-3-642-01947-0_34

Pokrajac, L., Abbas, A., Chrzanowski, W., Dias, G. M., Eggleton, B. J., Maguire, S., Maine, E., Malloy, T., Nathwani, J., Nazar, L., & ... (2021). *Nanotechnology for a sustainable future: Addressing global challenges with the international network4sustainable nanotechnology.* ACS Publications.

Połap, D., Włodarczyk-Sielicka, M., & Wawrzyniak, N. (2022). Automatic ship classification for a riverside monitoring system using a cascade of artificial intelligence techniques including penalties and rewards. *ISA Transactions, 121,* 232–239. doi:10.1016/j.isatra.2021.04.003 PMID:33888294

Polygerinos, P., Wang, Z., Galloway, K. C., Wood, R. J., & Walsh, C. J. (2015). Soft robotic glove for combined assistance and at-home rehabilitation. *Robotics and Autonomous Systems, 73,* 135–143. doi:10.1016/j.robot.2014.08.014

Popescu, M., & Ungureanu, C. (2023). Biosensors in Food and Healthcare Industries: Bio-Coatings Based on Biogenic Nanoparticles and Biopolymers. *Coatings, 13*(3), 486. doi:10.3390/coatings13030486

Poppeova, V., Uricek, J., Bulej, V., & Sindler, P. (2011). Delta robots - robots for high speed manipulation. *Tehnicki Vjesnik (Strojarski Fakultet), 18,* 435–445.

Pramila, P., Amudha, S., Saravanan, T., Sankar, S. R., Poongothai, E., & Boopathi, S. (2023). Design and Development of Robots for Medical Assistance: An Architectural Approach. In Contemporary Applications of Data Fusion for Advanced Healthcare Informatics (pp. 260–282). IGI Global.

Pratt, M., Boudhane, M., & Cakula, S. (2021). Employee attrition estimation using random forest algorithm. *Baltic Journal of Modern Computing, 9*(1), 49–66. doi:10.22364/bjmc.2021.9.1.04

Primožič, M., Knez, Ž., & Leitgeb, M. (2021). (Bio)Nanotechnology in Food Science—Food Packaging. *Nanomaterials (Basel, Switzerland),* 11. PMID:33499415

Pugliese, R., & Regondi, S. (2022). Artificial intelligence-empowered 3D and 4D printing technologies toward smarter biomedical materials and approaches. *Polymers, 14*(14), 2794. doi:10.3390/polym14142794 PMID:35890571

Puranik, T. A., Shaik, N., Vankudoth, R., Kolhe, M. R., Yadav, N., & Boopathi, S. (2024). Study on Harmonizing Human-Robot (Drone) Collaboration: Navigating Seamless Interactions in Collaborative Environments. In Cybersecurity Issues and Challenges in the Drone Industry (pp. 1–26). IGI Global.

Putra, M., & Damayanti, N. (2020). The Effect of Reward and Punishment to Performance of Driver Grabcar in Depok. *International Journal of Research and Review, 7*(1), 312–319.

Rahamathunnisa, U., Subhashini, P., Aancy, H. M., Meenakshi, S., Boopathi, S., & ... (2023). Solutions for Software Requirement Risks Using Artificial Intelligence Techniques. In *Handbook of Research on Data Science and Cybersecurity Innovations in Industry 4.0 Technologies* (pp. 45–64). IGI Global.

Rahamathunnisa, U., Sudhakar, K., Murugan, T. K., Thivaharan, S., Rajkumar, M., & Boopathi, S. (2023). Cloud Computing Principles for Optimizing Robot Task Offloading Processes. In *AI-Enabled Social Robotics in Human Care Services* (pp. 188–211). IGI Global. doi:10.4018/978-1-6684-8171-4.ch007

Rahim, R., & Nadeem, S. (2018). End-to-end trained CNN encoder-decoder networks for image steganography. *Proceedings of the European Conference on Computer Vision (ECCV) Workshops.*

Rahmatullah, B., & Noble, J. A. (2013, September). Anatomical object detection in fetal ultrasound: computer-expert agreements. In *International Conference on Biomedical Informatics and Technology* (pp. 207-218). Springer Berlin Heidelberg.

Rahmatullah, B., Papageorghiou, A., & Noble, J. A. (2011). Automated selection of standardized planes from ultrasound volume. In *Machine Learning in Medical Imaging: Second International Workshop, MLMI 2011, Held in Conjunction with MICCAI 2011, Toronto, Canada, September 18, 2011. Proceedings 2* (pp. 35-42). Springer Berlin Heidelberg. 10.1007/978-3-642-24319-6_5

Ramadan, M. N., Al-Khedher, M. A., & Al-Kheder, S. A. (2012). Intelligent anti-theft and tracking system for automobiles. *International Journal of Machine Learning and Computing*, 2(1), 83–88. doi:10.7763/IJMLC.2012.V2.94

Ramalingam, S., & Rasool Mohideen, S. (2021). Composite materials for advanced flexible link robotic manipulators: An investigation. *International Journal of Ambient Energy*, 42(14), 1670–1675. doi:10.1080/01430750.2019.1613263

Ramesh, R. D., Santhosh, A., & Syamala, S. R. N. A. (2020). Implementation of Nanotechnology in the Aerospace and Aviation Industry. In *Smart Nanotechnology with Applications* (pp. 51–69). CRC Press. doi:10.1201/9781003097532-4

Ramudu, K., Mohan, V. M., Jyothirmai, D., Prasad, D., Agrawal, R., & Boopathi, S. (2023). Machine Learning and Artificial Intelligence in Disease Prediction: Applications, Challenges, Limitations, Case Studies, and Future Directions. In Contemporary Applications of Data Fusion for Advanced Healthcare Informatics (pp. 297–318). IGI Global.

Rani, S., Chauhan, M., Kataria, A., & Khang, A. (2023). IoT equipped intelligent distributed framework for smart healthcare systems. In *Towards the Integration of IoT, Cloud and Big Data: Services, Applications and Standards* (pp. 97–114). Springer Nature Singapore. doi:10.1007/978-981-99-6034-7_6

Ravisankar, A., Sampath, B., & Asif, M. M. (2023). Economic Studies on Automobile Management: Working Capital and Investment Analysis. In Multidisciplinary Approaches to Organizational Governance During Health Crises (pp. 169–198). IGI Global.

Ravisankar, A., Shanthi, A., Lavanya, S., Ramaratnam, M., Krishnamoorthy, V., & Boopathi, S. (2024). Harnessing 6G for Consumer-Centric Business Strategies Across Electronic Industries. In AI Impacts in Digital Consumer Behavior (pp. 241–270). IGI Global.

Raza, A., Munir, K., Almutairi, M., Younas, F., & Fareed, M. M. S. (2022). Predicting Employee Attrition Using Machine Learning Approaches. *Applied Sciences (Basel, Switzerland)*, 12(13), 6424. doi:10.3390/app12136424

Redmon, J., & Farhadi, A. (2018). Yolov3: An incremental improvement. *arXiv preprint arXiv:1804.02767*.

Redmon, J., Divvala, S., Girshick, R., & Farhadi, A. (2016). You only look once: Unified, real-time object detection. In *Proceedings of the IEEE conference on computer vision and pattern recognition* (pp. 779-788). 10.1109/CVPR.2016.91

Redmon, J., & Farhadi, A. (2017). YOLO9000: better, faster, stronger. In *Proceedings of the IEEE conference on computer vision and pattern recognition* (pp. 7263-7271).

Rehman, T. U., Mahmud, M. S., Chang, Y. K., Jin, J., & Shin, J. (2019). Current and future applications of statistical machine learning algorithms for agricultural machine vision systems. *Computers and Electronics in Agriculture*, 156, 585–605. doi:10.1016/j.compag.2018.12.006

Ren, S., He, K., Girshick, R., & Sun, J. (2016). Faster R-CNN: Towards real-time object detection with region proposal networks. *IEEE Transactions on Pattern Analysis and Machine Intelligence*, 39(6), 1137–1149. doi:10.1109/TPAMI.2016.2577031 PMID:27295650

Revathi, S., Babu, M., Rajkumar, N., Meti, V. K. V., Kandavalli, S. R., & Boopathi, S. (2024). Unleashing the Future Potential of 4D Printing: Exploring Applications in Wearable Technology, Robotics, Energy, Transportation, and Fashion. In Human-Centered Approaches in Industry 5.0: Human-Machine Interaction, Virtual Reality Training, and Customer Sentiment Analysis (pp. 131–153). IGI Global.

Ritharson, P. I., Raimond, K., Mary, X. A., Robert, J. E., & Andrew, J. (2024). DeepRice: A deep learning and deep feature based classification of Rice leaf disease subtypes. *Artificial Intelligence in Agriculture*, *11*, 34–49. doi:10.1016/j.aiia.2023.11.001

Rodrigues, C., Souza, V. G. L., Coelhoso, I., & Fernando, A. L. (2021). Bio-Based Sensors for Smart Food Packaging—Current Applications and Future Trends. *Sensors (Basel)*, *21*(6), 2148. doi:10.3390/s21062148 PMID:33803914

Ronneberger, O., Fischer, P., & Brox, T. (2015). U-net: Convolutional networks for biomedical image segmentation. In *Medical image computing and computer-assisted intervention–MICCAI 2015: 18th international conference, Munich, Germany, October 5-9, 2015, proceedings, part III 18* (pp. 234-241). Springer International Publishing.

Rus, D., & Tolley, M. T. (2015). Design, fabrication and control of soft robots. *Nature*, *521*(7553), 467–475. doi:10.1038/nature14543 PMID:26017446

Sadagopan, V. K., Rajendran, U., & Francis, A. J. (2011, July). Anti theft control system design using embedded system. In *Proceedings of 2011 IEEE International Conference on Vehicular Electronics and Safety* (pp. 1-5). IEEE. 10.1109/ICVES.2011.5983776

Saharan. (2022). Robotic Automation of Pharmaceutical and Life Science Industries. *Computer Aided Pharmaceutics and Drug Delivery*. doi:10.1007/978-981-16-5180-9_12

Sahu, A. K., & Swain, G. (2016). A review on LSB substitution and PVD based image steganography techniques. *Indonesian Journal of Electrical Engineering and Computer Science*, *2*(3), 712–719. doi:10.11591/ijeecs.v2.i3.pp712-719

Salomon, L., Alfirevic, Z., Berghella, V., Bilardo, C., Chalouhi, G., Costa, F. D. S., ... Paladini, D. (2022). ISUOG practice guidelines (updated): Performance of the routine mid-trimester fetal ultrasound scan. *Ultrasound in Obstetrics & Gynecology*, *59*(6), 840–856. doi:10.1002/uog.24888 PMID:35592929

Samman, T., Spearman, J., Dutta, A., Kreidl, O. P., Roy, S., & Bölöni, L. (2021, October). Secure multi-robot adaptive information sampling. In *2021 IEEE International Symposium on Safety, Security, and Rescue Robotics (SSRR)* (pp. 125-131). IEEE. 10.1109/SSRR53300.2021.9597867

Sampath, B., & Myilsamy, S. (2021). Experimental investigation of a cryogenically cooled oxygen-mist near-dry wire-cut electrical discharge machining process. *Stroj. Vestn. Jixie Gongcheng Xuebao*, *67*(6), 322–330.

Sampath, B., Naveenkumar, N., Sampathkumar, P., Silambarasan, P., Venkadesh, A., & Sakthivel, M. (2022). Experimental comparative study of banana fiber composite with glass fiber composite material using Taguchi method. *Materials Today: Proceedings*, *49*, 1475–1480. doi:10.1016/j.matpr.2021.07.232

Sanchez-Ibanez, J. R., Perez-del-Pulgar, C. J., & García-Cerezo, A. (2021). Path planning for autonomous mobile robots: A review. *Sensors (Basel)*, *21*(23), 7898. doi:10.3390/s21237898 PMID:34883899

Sánchez, J., Perronnin, F., Mensink, T., & Verbeek, J. (2013). Image classification with the fisher vector: Theory and practice. *International Journal of Computer Vision*, *105*(3), 222–245. doi:10.1007/s11263-013-0636-x

Satav, S. D., Lamani, D., Harsha, K., Kumar, N., Manikandan, S., & Sampath, B. (2023). Energy and Battery Management in the Era of Cloud Computing: Sustainable Wireless Systems and Networks. In Sustainable Science and Intelligent Technologies for Societal Development (pp. 141–166). IGI Global.

Satav, S. D., Hasan, D. S., Pitchai, R., Mohanaprakash, T., Sultanuddin, S., & Boopathi, S. (2023). Next generation of internet of things (ngiot) in healthcare systems. In *Sustainable Science and Intelligent Technologies for Societal Development* (pp. 307–330). IGI Global.

Schütz, A. K., Schöler, V., Krause, E. T., Fischer, M., Müller, T., Freuling, C. M., Conraths, F. J., Stanke, M., Homeier-Bachmann, T., & Lentz, H. H. (2021). Application of YOLOv4 for detection and Motion monitoring of red Foxes. *Animals (Basel), 11*(6), 1723. doi:10.3390/ani11061723 PMID:34207726

Schwartz, E. M., Bradlow, E. T., & Fader, P. S. (2017). Customer acquisition via display advertising using multi-armed bandit experiments. *Marketing Science, 36*(4), 500–522. doi:10.1287/mksc.2016.1023

Selvakumar, S., Adithe, S., Isaac, J. S., Pradhan, R., Venkatesh, V., & Sampath, B. (2023). A Study of the Printed Circuit Board (PCB) E-Waste Recycling Process. In Sustainable Approaches and Strategies for E-Waste Management and Utilization (pp. 159–184). IGI Global.

Selvakumar, S., Shankar, R., Ranjit, P., Bhattacharya, S., Gupta, A. S. G., & Boopathi, S. (2023). E-Waste Recovery and Utilization Processes for Mobile Phone Waste. In *Handbook of Research on Safe Disposal Methods of Municipal Solid Wastes for a Sustainable Environment* (pp. 222–240). IGI Global. doi:10.4018/978-1-6684-8117-2.ch016

Şenbaşlar, B., Luiz, P., Hönig, W., & Sukhatme, G. S. (2023). Mrnav: Multi-robot aware planning and control stack for collision and deadlock-free navigation in cluttered environments. *arXiv preprint arXiv:2308.13499.*

Sengeni, D., Padmapriya, G., Imambi, S. S., Suganthi, D., Suri, A., & Boopathi, S. (2023). Biomedical waste handling method using artificial intelligence techniques. In *Handbook of Research on Safe Disposal Methods of Municipal Solid Wastes for a Sustainable Environment* (pp. 306–323). IGI Global. doi:10.4018/978-1-6684-8117-2.ch022

Senthil, T., Puviyarasan, M., Babu, S. R., Surakasi, R., Sampath, B., & Associates. (2023). Industrial Robot-Integrated Fused Deposition Modelling for the 3D Printing Process. In Development, Properties, and Industrial Applications of 3D Printed Polymer Composites (pp. 188–210). IGI Global.

Senthil, T., Puviyarasan, M., Babu, S. R., Surakasi, R., Sampath, B., & ... (2023). Industrial Robot-Integrated Fused Deposition Modelling for the 3D Printing Process. In *Development, Properties, and Industrial Applications of 3D Printed Polymer Composites* (pp. 188–210). IGI Global.

Sermanet, P., Eigen, D., Zhang, X., Mathieu, M., Fergus, R., & LeCun, Y. (2013). Overfeat: Integrated recognition, localization and detection using convolutional networks. arXiv preprint arXiv:1312.6229.

Setiadi, D. R. I. M. (2021). PSNR vs SSIM: Imperceptibility quality assessment for image steganography. *Multimedia Tools and Applications, 80*(6), 8423–8444. doi:10.1007/s11042-020-10035-z

Sevinchan, E., Dincer, I., & Lang, H. (2018). A review on thermal management methods for robots. *Applied Thermal Engineering, 140*, 799–813. doi:10.1016/j.applthermaleng.2018.04.132

Shaban Nejad, M. (2020). *Explainable AI in healthcare and medicine: building a culture of transparency and accountability* (Vol. 914). Springer Nature.

Shaik, T., Tao, X., Higgins, N., Li, L., Gururajan, R., Zhou, X., & Acharya, U. R. (2023). Remote patient monitoring using artificial intelligence: Current state, applications, and challenges. *Wiley Interdisciplinary Reviews. Data Mining and Knowledge Discovery, 13*(2), e1485. doi:10.1002/widm.1485

Sharifi, O., & Eskandari, M. (2018). Cosmetic Detection Framework for Face and Iris Biometrics. *Sensors (Basel), 10*, 122.

Sharmin, I. (2020). *Preparation and evaluation of carbon nano tube based nanofluid in milling alloy steel*. Academic Press.

Sheikh, J. A., Waheed, M. F., Khalid, A. M., & Qureshi, I. A. (2020). Use of 3D printing and nano materials in fashion: From revolution to evolution. *Advances in Design for Inclusion: Proceedings of the AHFE 2019 International Conference on Design for Inclusion and the AHFE 2019 International Conference on Human Factors for Apparel and Textile Engineering,* July 24-28, 2019, Washington DC, USA *10,* 422–429.

Shen, L., Wang, P., & Ke, Y. (2021). DNA Nanotechnology-Based Biosensors and Therapeutics. *Advanced Healthcare Materials,* 10. PMID:34085411

Shetty. (2022). Impact of Artificial Intelligence in Banking Sector with Reference to Private Banks in India. *Annals of the University of Craiova, Physics, 32,* 59-75.

Shi, J., Jiang, Q., Mao, R., Lu, M., & Wang, T. (2015). FR-KECA: Fuzzy robust kernel entropy component analysis. *Neurocomputing, 149,* 1415–1423. doi:10.1016/j.neucom.2014.08.054

Shi, J., Wu, J., Li, Y., Zhang, Q., & Ying, S. (2016). Histopathological image classification with color pattern random binary hashing-based PCANet and matrix-form classifier. *IEEE Journal of Biomedical and Health Informatics, 21*(5), 1327–1337. doi:10.1109/JBHI.2016.2602823 PMID:27576270

Shi, J., Zhou, S., Liu, X., Zhang, Q., Lu, M., & Wang, T. (2016). Stacked deep polynomial network based representation learning for tumor classification with small ultrasound image dataset. *Neurocomputing, 194,* 87–94. doi:10.1016/j.neucom.2016.01.074

Shrestha, Y. R., Ben-Menahem, S. M., & Von Krogh, G. (2019). Organizational decision-making structures in the age of artificial intelligence. *California Management Review, 61*(4), 66–83. doi:10.1177/0008125619862257

Simmons, G. (2019). *Secure communications and asymmetric cryptosystems.* Routledge. doi:10.4324/9780429305634

Simonyan, K., & Zisserman, A. (2014). Very deep convolutional networks for large-scale image recognition. *arXiv preprint arXiv:1409.1556.*

Singh, K., Sharma, S., Shriwastava, S., Singla, P., Gupta, M., & Tripathi, C. (2021). Significance of nano-materials, designs consideration and fabrication techniques on performances of strain sensors-A review. *Materials Science in Semiconductor Processing, 123,* 105581. doi:10.1016/j.mssp.2020.105581

Siriani, A. L. R., Kodaira, V., Mehdizadeh, S. A., de Alencar Nääs, I., de Moura, D. J., & Pereira, D. F. (2022). Detection and tracking of chickens in low-light images using YOLO network and Kalman filter. *Neural Computing & Applications, 34*(24), 21987–21997. doi:10.1007/s00521-022-07664-w

Sivanantham, K. (2022). Deep learning-based convolutional neural network with cuckoo search optimization for MRI brain tumour segmentation. In *Computational Intelligence Techniques for Green Smart Cities* (pp. 149–168). Springer International Publishing. doi:10.1007/978-3-030-96429-0_7

Sivasankar, M., & Durairaj, R. (2012). Brief review on nano robots in bio medical applications. *Adv Robot Autom, 1*(101), 2. doi:10.4172/2168-9695.1000101

Smeureanu, I., Ruxanda, G., & Badea, L. M. (2013). Customer segmentation in private banking sector using machine learning techniques. *Journal of Business Economics and Management, 14*(5), 923–939. doi:10.3846/16111699.2012.749807

Soltani, M., Samorani, M., & Kolfal, B. (2019). Appointment scheduling with multiple providers and stochastic service times. *European Journal of Operational Research, 277*(2), 667–683. doi:10.1016/j.ejor.2019.02.051

Song, Y., He, L., Zhou, F., Chen, S., Ni, D., Lei, B., & Wang, T. (2016). Segmentation, splitting, and classification of overlapping bacteria in microscope images for automatic bacterial vaginosis diagnosis. *IEEE Journal of Biomedical and Health Informatics, 21*(4), 1095–1104. doi:10.1109/JBHI.2016.2594239 PMID:27479982

Song, Y., Zhang, L., Chen, S., Ni, D., Lei, B., & Wang, T. (2015). Accurate segmentation of cervical cytoplasm and nuclei based on multiscale convolutional network and graph partitioning. *IEEE Transactions on Biomedical Engineering*, 62(10), 2421–2433. doi:10.1109/TBME.2015.2430895 PMID:25966470

Srinivas, B., Maguluri, L. P., Naidu, K. V., Reddy, L. C. S., Deivakani, M., & Boopathi, S. (2023). Architecture and Framework for Interfacing Cloud-Enabled Robots. In *Handbook of Research on Data Science and Cybersecurity Innovations in Industry 4.0 Technologies* (pp. 542–560). IGI Global. doi:10.4018/978-1-6684-8145-5.ch027

Srivastava, N., Hinton, G., Krizhevsky, A., Sutskever, I., & Salakhutdinov, R. (2014). Dropout: A simple way to prevent neural networks from overfitting. *Journal of Machine Learning Research*, 15(1), 1929–1958.

Stasevych, M., & Zvarych, V. (2023). Innovative Robotic Technologies and Artificial Intelligence in Pharmacy and Medicine: Paving the Way for the Future of Health Care—A Review. *Big Data and Cognitive Computing*, 7(3), 147. doi:10.3390/bdcc7030147

Su, H., Kwok, W., Cleary, K., Iordachita, I., Cavusoglu, M. C., Desai, J. P., & Fischer, G. S. (2022). State of the Art and Future Opportunities in MRI-Guided Robot-Assisted Surgery and Interventions. *Proceedings of the IEEE, 110*(7), 968. 10.1109/JPROC.2022.3169146

Subramanian, N., Cheheb, I., Elharrouss, O., Al-Maadeed, S., & Bouridane, A. (2021). End-to-end image steganography using deep convolutional autoencoders. *IEEE Access : Practical Innovations, Open Solutions*, 9, 135585–135593. doi:10.1109/ACCESS.2021.3113953

Sun, M., Liu, Q., Fan, X., Wang, Y., Chen, W., Tian, C., Sun, L., & Xie, H. (2020). Autonomous biohybrid urchin-like microperforator for intracellular payload delivery. *Small*, 16(23), 1906701. doi:10.1002/smll.201906701 PMID:32378351

Syamala, M., Komala, C., Pramila, P., Dash, S., Meenakshi, S., & Boopathi, S. (2023). Machine Learning-Integrated IoT-Based Smart Home Energy Management System. In *Handbook of Research on Deep Learning Techniques for Cloud-Based Industrial IoT* (pp. 219–235). IGI Global. doi:10.4018/978-1-6684-8098-4.ch013

Szegedy, C., Liu, W., Jia, Y., Sermanet, P., Reed, S., Anguelov, D., ... Rabinovich, A. (2015). Going deeper with convolutions. In *Proceedings of the IEEE conference on computer vision and pattern recognition* (pp. 1-9). IEEE.

Szegedy, C., Vanhoucke, V., Ioffe, S., Shlens, J., & Wojna, Z. (2016). Rethinking the inception architecture for computer vision. In *Proceedings of the IEEE Conference on Computer Vision and Pattern Recognition* (pp. 2818–2826). 10.1109/CVPR.2016.308

Taimoor, N., & Rehman, S. (2022). Reliable and resilient AI and IOT-based personalised healthcare services: A survey. *IEEE Access : Practical Innovations, Open Solutions*, 10, 535–563. doi:10.1109/ACCESS.2021.3137364

Talukder, A., & Haas, R. (2021, June). AIoT: AI meets IoT and web in smart healthcare. In *Companion Publication of the 13th ACM Web Science Conference 2021* (pp. 92-98). Academic Press.

Tan, Q., Fan, T., Pan, J., & Manocha, D. (2020, October). Deepmnavigate: Deep reinforced multi-robot navigation unifying local & global collision avoidance. In *2020 IEEE/RSJ International Conference on Intelligent Robots and Systems (IROS)* (pp. 6952-6959). IEEE. 10.1109/IROS45743.2020.9341805

Tian, H., Wang, T., Liu, Y., Qiao, X., & Li, Y. (2020). Computer vision technology in agricultural automation—A review. *Information Processing in Agriculture*, 7(1), 1–19. doi:10.1016/j.inpa.2019.09.006

Tian, S., Yang, W., Le Grange, J. M., Wang, P., Huang, W., & Ye, Z. (2019). Smart healthcare: Making medical care more intelligent. *Global Health Journal (Amsterdam, Netherlands)*, 3(3), 62–65. doi:10.1016/j.glohj.2019.07.001

Tjoa, E., & Guan, C. (2021). A survey on explainable artificial intelligence (XAI): Toward medical xai. *IEEE Transactions on Neural Networks and Learning Systems*, *32*(11), 4793–4813. doi:10.1109/TNNLS.2020.3027314 PMID:33079674

Tripathy, S. S., Imoize, A. L., Rath, M., Tripathy, N., Bebortta, S., Lee, C. C., & Pani, S. K. (2023). A novel edge-computing-based framework for an intelligent smart healthcare system in smart cities. *Sustainability (Basel)*, *15*(1), 735. doi:10.3390/su15010735

Trivedi, J. (2019). Examining the customer experience of using banking Chatbots and its impact on brand love: The moderating role of perceived risk. *Journal of Internet Commerce*, *18*(1), 91–111. doi:10.1080/15332861.2019.1567188

Tukey, J. (1977). *Exploratory Data Analysis*. Addison-Wesley.

Vadie, A., & Lipták, K. (2023). Industry 4.0: New challenges for the labor market and working conditions as a result of emergence of robots and automation. Economic and Regional Studies / Studia Ekonomiczne i Regionalne, 16(3), 434-445. doi:10.2478/ers-2023-0028

Vale, D., El-Sharif, A., & Ali, M. (2022, March). Explainable artificial intelligence (XAI) post-hoc explainability methods: Risks and limitations in non-discrimination law. *AI and Ethics*, *2*(4), 815–826. doi:10.1007/s43681-022-00142-y

Van der Maaten, L., & Hinton, G. (2008). Visualizing data using t-SNE. *Journal of Machine Learning Research*, *9*(11).

Vardarlier, P., & Zafer, C. (2020). Use of artificial intelligence as business strategy in recruitment process and social perspective. *Digital Business Strategies in Blockchain Ecosystems: Transformational Design and Future of Global Business*, 355-373.

Vianello, A., Jensen, R. L., Liu, L., & Vollertsen, J. (2019). Simulating human exposure to indoor airborne microplastics using a Breathing Thermal Manikin. *Scientific Reports*, *9*(1), 8670. doi:10.1038/s41598-019-45054-w PMID:31209244

Vigelius, M., Meyer, B., & Pascoe, G. (2014). Multiscale modelling and analysis of collective decision making in swarm robotics. *PLoS One*, *9*(11), e111542. doi:10.1371/journal.pone.0111542 PMID:25369026

Vijayakumar, G. N. S., Domakonda, V. K., Farooq, S., Kumar, B. S., Pradeep, N., & Boopathi, S. (2024). Sustainable Developments in Nano-Fluid Synthesis for Various Industrial Applications. In Adoption and Use of Technology Tools and Services by Economically Disadvantaged Communities: Implications for Growth and Sustainability (pp. 48–81). IGI Global.

Walsh, S. M., & Strano, M. S. (2018). *Robotic systems and autonomous platforms: Advances in materials and manufacturing*. Woodhead Publishing.

Wang, C. Y., Bochkovskiy, A., & Liao, H. Y. M. (2023). YOLOv7: Trainable bag-of-freebies sets new state-of-the-art for real-time object detectors. In *Proceedings of the IEEE/CVF Conference on Computer Vision and Pattern Recognition* (pp. 7464-7475). 10.1109/CVPR52729.2023.00721

Wang, G., Badal, A., Jia, X., Maltz, J. S., Mueller, K., Myers, K. J., & Zeng, R. (2022). Development of metaverse for intelligent healthcare. *Nature Machine Intelligence*, *4*(11), 922–929. doi:10.1038/s42256-022-00549-6 PMID:36935774

Wang, W., Yang, W., Li, M., Zhang, Z., & Du, W. (2023). A Novel Approach for Apple Freshness Prediction Based on Gas Sensor Array and Optimized Neural Network. *Sensors (Basel)*, *23*(14), 6476. doi:10.3390/s23146476 PMID:37514770

Wan, P., Toudeshki, A., Tan, H., & Ehsani, R. (2018). A methodology for fresh tomato maturity detection using computer vision. *Computers and Electronics in Agriculture*, *146*, 43–50. doi:10.1016/j.compag.2018.01.011

Win, Z. M., & Sein, M. M. (2011). *Fingerprint recognition system for low quality images*. Presented at the SICE Annual Conference, Waseda University, Tokyo, Japan.

291

Xiao, B., Nguyen, M., & Yan, W. Q. (2021). Apple ripeness identification using deep learning. In *Geometry and Vision: First International Symposium, ISGV 2021, Auckland, New Zealand, January 28-29, 2021, Revised Selected Papers 1* (pp. 53-67). Springer International Publishing.

Xiao, Z., Wang, J., Han, L., Guo, S., & Cui, Q. (2022). Application of machine vision system in food detection. *Frontiers in Nutrition*, 9, 888245. doi:10.3389/fnut.2022.888245 PMID:35634395

Xin, Y., Kong, L., Liu, Z., Wang, C., Zhu, H., Gao, M., Zhao, C., & Xu, X. (2018). Multimodal Feature-Level Fusion for Biometrics Identification System on IoMT Platform. *IEEE Access, 6*, 21418–21426.

Xu, Y., Bian, Q., Wang, R., & Gao, J. (2022). Micro/nanorobots for precise drug delivery via targeted transport and triggered release: A review. *International Journal of Pharmaceutics*, *616*, 121551. doi:10.1016/j.ijpharm.2022.121551 PMID:35131352

Xu, Y., Shieh, C. H., van Esch, P., & Ling, I. L. (2020). AI customer service: Task complexity, problem-solving ability, and usage intention. *Australasian Marketing Journal*, *28*(4), 189–199. doi:10.1016/j.ausmj.2020.03.005

Yaeger, K. A., Martini, M., Yaniv, G., Oermann, E. K., & Costa, A. B. (2019). United States regulatory approval of medical devices and software applications enhanced by artificial intelligence. *Health Policy and Technology, 8*(2), 192–197. doi:10.1016/j.hlpt.2019.05.006

Yang, Z., Bi, L., Chi, W., Shi, H., & Guan, C. (2022). Brain-Controlled Multi-Robot at Servo-Control Level Based on Nonlinear Model Predictive Control. *Complex System Modeling and Simulation*, *2*(4), 307–321. doi:10.23919/CSMS.2022.0019

Yan, Z., Zhan, Y., Peng, Z., Liao, S., Shinagawa, Y., Zhang, S., Metaxas, D. N., & Zhou, X. S. (2016). Multi-instance deep learning: Discover discriminative local anatomies for bodypart recognition. *IEEE Transactions on Medical Imaging*, *35*(5), 1332–1343. doi:10.1109/TMI.2016.2524985 PMID:26863652

Yaqub, M., Kelly, B., Papageorghiou, A. T., & Noble, J. A. (2015). Guided random forests for identification of key fetal anatomy and image categorization in ultrasound scans. In *Medical Image Computing and Computer-Assisted Intervention–MICCAI 2015: 18th International Conference, Munich, Germany, October 5-9, 2015, Proceedings, Part III 18* (pp. 687-694). Springer International Publishing. 10.1007/978-3-319-24574-4_82

Yosinski, J., Clune, J., Bengio, Y., & Lipson, H. (2014). How transferable are features in deep neural networks? *Advances in Neural Information Processing Systems*, 27.

Yu, Z., Ni, D., Chen, S., Li, S., Wang, T., & Lei, B. (2016, August). Fetal facial standard plane recognition via very deep convolutional networks. In *2016 38th annual international conference of the IEEE Engineering in Medicine and Biology Society (EMBC)* (pp. 627-630). IEEE. 10.1109/EMBC.2016.7590780

Zaccaria, M., Giorgini, M., Monica, R., & Aleotti, J. (2021, July). Multi-robot multiple camera people detection and tracking in automated warehouses. In *2021 IEEE 19th International Conference on Industrial Informatics (INDIN)* (pp. 1-6). IEEE. 10.1109/INDIN45523.2021.9557363

Zacharaki, A., Kostavelis, I., Gasteratos, A., & Dokas, I. (2020). Safety bounds in human robot interaction: A survey. *Safety Science*, *127*, 104667. doi:10.1016/j.ssci.2020.104667

Zekrifa, D. M. S., Kulkarni, M., Bhagyalakshmi, A., Devireddy, N., Gupta, S., & Boopathi, S. (2023). Integrating Machine Learning and AI for Improved Hydrological Modeling and Water Resource Management. In *Artificial Intelligence Applications in Water Treatment and Water Resource Management* (pp. 46–70). IGI Global. doi:10.4018/978-1-6684-6791-6.ch003

Zhang, Z., Yi, D., Lei, Z., & Li, S.Z. (2012). Regularized Transfer Boosting for Face Detection Across Spectrum. *IEEE Signal Process. Lett., 19*, 131–134.

Zhang, H., Li, Q., Sun, Z., & Liu, Y. (2018). Combining Data-Driven and Model-Driven Methods for Robust Facial Landmark Detection. *IEEE Transactions on Information Forensics and Security, 13*(10), 2409–2422. doi:10.1109/TIFS.2018.2800901

Zhang, L., Chen, S., Chin, C. T., Wang, T., & Li, S. (2012). Intelligent scanning: Automated standard plane selection and biometric measurement of early gestational sac in routine ultrasound examination. *Medical Physics, 39*(8), 5015–5027. doi:10.1118/1.4736415 PMID:22894427

Zheng, S., Wang, Y., Pan, S., Ma, E., Jin, S., Jiao, M., Wang, W., Li, J., Xu, K., & Wang, H. (2021). Biocompatible nanomotors as active diagnostic imaging agents for enhanced magnetic resonance imaging of tumor tissues in vivo. *Advanced Functional Materials, 31*(24), 2100936. doi:10.1002/adfm.202100936

Zhou, H., Mayorga-Martinez, C. C., Pané, S., Zhang, L., & Pumera, M. (2021). Magnetically Driven Micro and Nano-robots. *Chemical Reviews, 121*(8), 4999–5041. doi:10.1021/acs.chemrev.0c01234 PMID:33787235

Zhu, H. (2022). *Probabilistic Motion Planning for Multi-Robot Systems.* Academic Press.

Zhu, H., Claramunt, F. M., Brito, B., & Alonso-Mora, J. (2021). Learning interaction-aware trajectory predictions for decentralized multi-robot motion planning in dynamic environments. *IEEE Robotics and Automation Letters, 6*(2), 2256–2263. doi:10.1109/LRA.2021.3061073

Zhu, L., Spachos, P., Pensini, E., & Plataniotis, K. N. (2021). Deep learning and machine vision for food processing: A survey. *Current Research in Food Science, 4*, 233–249. doi:10.1016/j.crfs.2021.03.009 PMID:33937871

Zhu, X., Li, X., & Zhang, S. (2015). Block-row sparse multiview multilabel learning for image classification. *IEEE Transactions on Cybernetics, 46*(2), 450–461. doi:10.1109/TCYB.2015.2403356 PMID:25730838

Zhu, X., Li, X., Zhang, S., Ju, C., & Wu, X. (2016). Robust joint graph sparse coding for unsupervised spectral feature selection. *IEEE Transactions on Neural Networks and Learning Systems, 28*(6), 1263–1275. doi:10.1109/TNNLS.2016.2521602 PMID:26955053

Zhu, X., Suk, H. I., Wang, L., Lee, S. W., & Shen, D. (2017). A novel relational regularization feature selection method for joint regression and classification in AD diagnosis. *Medical Image Analysis, 38*, 205–214. doi:10.1016/j.media.2015.10.008 PMID:26674971

Zhu, X., Zhang, L., & Huang, Z. (2014). A sparse embedding and least variance encoding approach to hashing. *IEEE Transactions on Image Processing, 23*(9), 3737–3750. doi:10.1109/TIP.2014.2332764 PMID:24968174

Zuo, S., Li, J., Dong, M., Zhou, X., Fan, W., & Kong, Y. (2020). Design and performance evaluation of a novel wearable parallel mechanism for ankle rehabilitation. *Frontiers in Neurorobotics, 14*, 9. doi:10.3389/fnbot.2020.00009 PMID:32132917

About the Contributors

Tanupriya Choudhury completed his undergraduate studies in Computer Science and Engineering at the West Bengal University of Technology in Kolkata (2004-2008), India, followed by a Master's Degree in the same field from Dr. M.G.R University in Chennai, India (2008-2010). In 2016, he successfully obtained his PhD degree from Jagannath University Jaipur. With a total of 14 years of experience in both teaching and research, Dr. Choudhury holds the position of Professor at CSE Department, Symbiosis Institute of Technology, Symbiosis International University, Pune, Maharashtra, 412115, India and also he is holding Visiting Professor at Daffodil International University Bangladesh and Director Research (Honorary) at AI University, Montana US. Prior to this role, he served Graphic Era Hill University Dehradun (Research Professor), UPES Dehradun (Professor), Amity University Noida (Assistant Professor), and other prestigious academic institutions (Dronacharya College of Engineering Gurgaon, Lingaya's University Faridabad, Babu Banarsi Das Institute of Technology Ghaziabad, Syscon Solutions Pvt. Ltd. Kolkata etc.).Recently recognized for his outstanding contributions to education with the Global Outreach Education Award for Excellence in Best Young Researcher Award at GOECA 2018. His areas of expertise encompass Human Computing, Soft Computing, Cloud Computing, Data Mining among others. Notably accomplished within his field thus far is filing 25 patents and securing copyrights for 16 software programs from MHRD (Ministry of Human Resource Development). He has actively participated as an attendee or speaker at numerous National and International conferences across India and abroad. With over hundred plus quality research papers (Scopus) authored to date on record; Dr. Choudhury has also been invited as a guest lecturer or keynote speaker at esteemed institutions such as Jamia Millia Islamia University India, Maharaja Agersen College (Delhi University), Duy Tan University Vietnam, etc. He has also contributed significantly to various National/ International conferences throughout India and abroad serving roles like TPC chair/ member and session chairperson. As an active professional within the technical community; Dr.Choudhury holds lifetime membership with IETA (International Engineering & Technology Association) along with being affiliated with IEEE (Institute of Electrical and Electronics Engineers), IET(UK) (Institution of Engineering & Technology UK),and other reputable technical societies. Additionally, he is associated with corporate entities and serves as a Technical Adviser for Deetya Soft Pvt. Ltd., Noida, IVRGURU, and Mydigital360.He is also serving a Editor's in reputed Journals. He currently serves as the Honorary Secretary in IETA (Indian Engineering Teacher's Association-India), alongside his role as the Senior Advisor Position in INDO-UK Confederation of Science, Technology and Research Ltd., London, UK and International Association of Professional and Fellow Engineers-Delaware-USA.

Anitha Mary X. completed her B.E Electronics and Instrumentation Engineering from Karunya University, Coimbatore in the year 2001 and M.E in VLSI Design from ANNA University, Coimbatore in the year 2009. She has completed Ph.D in control system from Karunya University. she has published several journals.

Subrata Chowdhury, Associate Professor, Department Dr. Subrata Chowdhury (Associate Professor) is working in the Department of the Computer Science of Engineering of Sreenivasa Institute of Technology And Management as a Associate Professor. He is been working in the IT Industry for more than 5 years in the R&D developments, he has handled many projects in the industry with much dedications and perfect time limits. He has been handling projects related to AI, Blockchains and the Cloud Computing for the companies from various National and Internationals Clients. He had published (4) books from 2014 - 2019 at the domestic market and Internationally Publishers CRC, River . And he been the editor for the 2 books for the CRC& River publisher. He has participated in the Organizing committee, Technical Programmed Committee and Guest Speaker for more than 10 conference and the webinars. He also Reviewed and evaluated more than 50 papers from the conferences.

C. Karthik (Member, ACM, Senior Member, IEEE) was born in Madurai, Tamil Nadu, India in 1986. He received the Bachelor of Engineering in Electronics and Instrumentation Engineering at Kamaraj College of Engineering and Technology, India in 2007, the Master's Degree and Ph.D. Degree in Control and Instrumentation Engineering from Kalasalingam Academy of Research and Education (KARE), in 2011 and 2017. In 2011, he joined the Department of Instrumentation and Control Engineering of KARE, India as Assistant Professor. After that, He served as a Lecturer in the Department of Electrical and Computer Engineering, University of Woldia, Ethiopia from 2016–2018. Presently, He was served as a Postdoctoral Researcher at Shanghai Jiaotong University, China. He is serving as Associate Professor in Mechatronics Engineering, at Jyothi Engineering College, Kerala. He is currently involved in research related to Time delay Control problems, Nonlinear system identification, Cascade Control system, and Unmanned vehicle.

C. Suganthi Evangeline is currently working as Assistant Professor in the department of Electronics and Communication Engineering at Sri Eshwar College of Engineering, Coimbatore. She received her B.E degree in Electronics and Communication Engineering (ECE) from Anna University in 2010, M.E degree in Communication Systems from Coimbatore Institute of Technology in 2012, and Ph.D. from Vellore Institute of Technology in 2022. She is serving as an Academic Editor in PLOS ONE Journal (IF: 3.752, SCIE). Her research areas include Wireless ad-hoc networks, Blockchain Technology, vehicular communication, resource allocation, wireless network security, and the Internet of Vehicles. She is the author of the book "A Beginners Guide for Machine Learning Models with Python Environment" published by LAP LAMBERT Academic Publishing. Apart from her research experiences, she has served as a faculty for 11 years in the Department of ECE at Deemed University. She instructed courses for undergraduate and graduate students in the field of Embedded Systems, Internet of Things, Computer Networks, Electronics Devices and Circuits, Linear Integrated Circuits, and Wireless Communication. Furthermore, she also contributed as a reviewer in many reputed journals, delivered guest lectures in workshops and conferences. Apart from her research experiences, she has served as a faculty for 11 years in the Department of ECE at Karunya Institute of Technology and Sciences and instructed courses for undergraduate and graduate students in the field of Embedded Systems, Internet of Things, Computer

Networks, Electronics Devices and Circuits, Linear Integrated Circuits, and Wireless Communication. Furthermore, she also contributed as a reviewer in many reputed journals, delivered guest lectures in workshops and conferences.

* * *

Kishore Kumar A. received his PhD in Information & Communication Engineering (2014) from Anna University, Chennai. He earned his M.E. Communication Systems (2008) from Anna University, Chennai and his B.E. Electronics and Instrumentation Engineering (2002) from Bharthiar University, Coimbatore. He also holds an MBA in Human Resource Management from IGNOU-New Delhi. He has 15 years of teaching experience and 2 years of R&D experience in the industry. He is currently employed at Sri Ramakrishna Engineering College, Coimbatore as an Assistant Professor (Sel.Gr) in the Department of Robotics and Automation. He has over 60 research papers published in the various international conferences and reputed journals. His research interest includes Sensors Technology, Communication Systems, and Computer Networking & Industrial Automation. He is a Life member of ISTE, IETE and The Robotics Society, India.

Murugarajan A. is currently Professor and Head of the Department of Robotics and Automation at Sri Ramakrishna Engineering College, Coimbatore. He received his Ph.D. in Mechanical Engineering from the Indian Institute of Technology Madras, Chennai. He has obtained his Masters' Degree in Industrial Engineering (University Gold Medalist) and Bachelor's degree in Mechanical Engineering (with distinction) from Bharathiar University, Coimbatore. Also, he has completed MBA in Operations Management at IGNOU, New Delhi. He has 19 years of academic and 5 years of research experience. His major fields of interest are in the area of Mechanical Measurements and Metrology, Optimization techniques in Engineering and Operations Management, Predictive data analytics, Machine Tool Metrology using sensors, and natural fiber composites manufacturing. He has published twenty-four research papers in reputed International Journals and Conferences. He has been associated with industrial consultancy projects by the SREC innovation center. He is a technical member and reviewer of two International Journals. He is currently guiding five research scholars and one Ph.D. thesis awarded under him. He has been invited as chairperson and resource person in various institutions' Conferences/Symposiums and Workshops.

Ronica B. I. S. obtained B.E. degree from PRIST university and M.E. from SASTRA University. She is pursuing his PhD in Electronics and Communication Engineering from the Sathyabama University, Chennai, India. Currently, she is working as Assistant Professor in Electronics and Communication Engineering from the Sathyabama University, Chennai, India. Her areas of interest in research include Signal Processing, Image processing. She has published several papers in International Conferences and journals.

Sampath Boopathi is an accomplished individual with a strong academic background and extensive research experience. He completed his undergraduate studies in Mechanical Engineering and pursued his postgraduate studies in the field of Computer-Aided Design. Dr. Boopathi obtained his Ph.D. from Anna University, focusing his research on Manufacturing and optimization. Throughout his career, Dr. Boopathi has made significant contributions to the field of engineering. He has authored and published over 200 research articles in internationally peer-reviewed journals, highlighting his expertise and dedication to advancing knowledge in his area of specialization. His research output demonstrates his commitment to conducting rigorous and impactful research. In addition to his research publications, Dr. Boopathi has also been granted one patent and has three published patents to his name. This indicates his innovative thinking and ability to develop practical solutions to real-world engineering challenges. With 17 years of academic and research experience, Dr. Boopathi has enriched the engineering community through his teaching and mentorship roles.

V. Evelyn Brindha is currently working as Professor in the Department of EEE, Karunya Institute of Technology and Sciences.

Balakumar C. received his MCA from Kongu Engineering College, in 2013, M. E(CSE) from Anna University, Chennai in 2015. He published more then 10 articles in PG level.His research interests include Vechicular Adhoc Networks, Network Security, Wireless Sensor Networks.

Johnwesily Chappidi is currently affiliated with VIT-AP University, Amaravati as Research Scholar in the School of Computer Science and Engineering (SCOPE). he received the B.Tech. degree in Computer Science and engineering from the JNTU-Kakinada, India, in 2013, and the M.Tech. degree in Computer Science and Engineering from Acharya Nagarjuna University, Guntur, in 2015. After briefly working for a year as Assistant Professor at Paladugu Parvathi Devi College of Engineering & Technology, Vijayawada, after joined as Assistant Professor in Sasi Institute of Technology and Engineering, Tadepalli Gudem, India. he started his Ph.D. from VIT University in 2021.

Abhishek Choubey received a Ph.D. degree in the field of VLSI for digital signal processing from Jayppe University and technology Guna MP, in 2017. He is currently associated with Sreenidhi institute of science and technology, Hyderabad, as an Associate Professor. He has published nearly 70 technical articles. His research interest includes reconfigurable architectures, approximate-computation, algorithm design, and implementation of high- performance VLSI systems for signal processing applications. He was a recipient of the Sydney R. Parker and M. N. S. Swamy Best Paper Award for Circuits, Systems, and Signal Processing in 2018.

Shruti Bhargava Choubey received BE with honors from RGPV Bhopal and M. Tech. degree in Digital Communication Engineering from RGPV Bhopal subsequently she carried out her research from Dr.K.N. Modi University Banasthali Rajasthan and was awarded Ph.D. in 2015. Presently she is working as an Associate Professor & Dean of Innovation & Research in the Department of Electronics and Communication at Sreenidhi Institute of Science and Technology, Hyderabad. She is a Senior member of IEEE, member of IETE, New Delhi, and the International Association of Engineers (IAENG). She worked in different positions like Dean Academic & HOD in numerous capacities. She was awarded the MP Young Scientist fellowship in 2015 & Received the MP Council fellowship in 2014 for her contribution to Research.

R. Gunasundari received the Ph.D. Degree in Computer Science from Karpagam Academy of Higher Education, Coimbatore in 2014. She is working as Professor and Head in the Department of Computer Applications, Karpagam Academy of Higher Education, Coimbatore. She has produced 12 PhD candidates and guiding 8 candidates. She has organized various National and International conferences, workshops, Seminars and Guest Lectures. She has published 43 National and 25 International papers in various journals. Her broad field of research is in Data mining.

Divya Meena Sundaram is currently affiliated with VIT-AP University, Amaravati as Assistant Professor Sr. Grade 1 in the School of Computer Science and Engineering (SCOPE). She received the B.Tech. degree in Information Technology from the Vellore Institute of Technology (VIT), Vellore, India, in 2014, and the M.E. degree in Computer Science and Engineering from Anna University, Chennai, in 2016. After briefly working for a year as Assistant Professor at Jansons Institute of Technology, she started her Ph.D. from VIT University in 2017 and completed in 2020. She had worked as Assistant professor at Jain University, Bangalore before moving to VIT-AP University, Amaravati in 2021. In a span of 3 years' experience, she has published more than 45 research articles in SCOPUS and SCI. She has around 11 patents and 1 seed grant of 3.5 lakh to her credit. Currently, she is guiding 4 Ph.D scholars, of which 2 are International students. Her areas of interests include Artificial intelligence, image processing, deep learning, thermal imaging, cloud computing and remote sensing. She has got the Best Researcher Award since 2017 to 2023.

Dheerthi N. received her Bachelor's Degree in Electrical and Electronics Engineering from K.S.R College of Engineering, Thiruchengode in 2011. She received her Master's degree in Embedded System Technologies from Sri Ramakrishna Engineering College, Coimbatore in 2015. She has 5 years of experience in teaching various subjects like Microprocessors and Microcontrollers, Controller-based System Design, and Embedded systems and 2 years of experience in the Software industry as a Net developer and Quality Analyst. She has published 2 papers in SCOPUS index International Journals in the area of Embedded Systems. She has completed an internship program in Embedded System Technologies and mentored Under Graduate students in their projects. Her area of interest is Embedded Protocols, Real-Time Operating Systems, and Controllers.

Meivel S. completed a Ph.D. in remote sensing of agricultural drones. He is working as an Assistant Professor at the M. Kumarasamy College of Engineering, Karur. He had 15 years of teaching experience and 5 years of industrial experience. He is Coordinating the Texas Instruments Innovation Centre Lab, MKCE, and Karur for the business and entrepreneurship development of students. He has 5 SCI papers with 24 Scopus indexed journals. He presented at 20 international conferences in his career. He had granted Two Australian patents and 6 Indian patents and published 10 Indian patents that are based on the drone agricultural system. He completed 6 R&D-funded projects in industry and one MNC consultancy project at Root View Technologies, Coimbatore. He has researched the technical problems of IoT and drone hardware and tested innovative programmes in the funded projects. He has guided UG and PG students in handling drone surveys and has conducted research on remote sensing analysis, multispectral image processing, IoT controllers, and drone programming.

Sarveswaran S. completed his M.E. Degree in Engineering Design at P.S.G. College of Technology, Coimbatore in 2013, his B.E. in Mechatronics Engineering at Kongu Engineering College in 2009. He has 3 years of teaching experience and 3 Years of Industrial Experience. His research interests include Robotics,FEA, Computational Fluid Dynamics, and Programmable Logic Controllers. His Software skills include ANSYS Workbench, ANSA, FLUENT, SIMULINK, and LabVIEW. Apart from their Mechanical domain interest, his works included coding skills in Web Automation through Java Eclipse.

Hemalatha Sampath, a Research Analyst, completed her B.E.(ECE), and M.S.(EEE) at the United States in West Virginia University.

Shrilatha Sampath holds a Ph.D. in commerce and boasts a decade of experience as an Assistant Professor. During this time, she actively contributed in various administrative and academic roles such as Coordinator for the Examination Committee, Research Cell Member, Dean of student welfare, and Head In-Charge. With a versatile teaching background encompassing finance, marketing, business communication, auditing, human resources, and management for B.Com., B.B.A., B.C.A., M.Com., and M.Phil. students, she has showcased expertise in diverse subjects. Passionate about writing books, Dr. S. Shrilatha has published three books in commerce and banking, along with 17 articles in peer-reviewed journals. Her research interests span accounting, marketing, human resources, business communication, and digital banking. She has actively contributed to both national and international conferences, presenting research papers and participating in workshops, Faculty Development, and Knowledge Programmes. Dr. Shrilatha has earned Guide Ship for M.Phil. & Ph.D. and has successfully guided three M.Phil. research scholars. As an Editorial Member of the International Journal of Economics, Finance, and Social Sciences, she continues to contribute to scholarly publications. Additionally, she has reviewed numerous articles for e-transportation journals. Driven by a commitment to continuous learning, she has completed online courses in Human Resources Management and a refresher course. Currently, she serves as an External Examiner for Project viva-voce for higher secondary students, further demonstrating her dedication to both academia and research.

Xavier Santhappan obtained B.E degree from K.S.R College of Technology in 2010, M.E degree from Sri Krishna College of Engineering and Technology in 2012. Later, in 2020 he obtained Ph.D. degree from Indian Institute of Information Technology Design and Manufacturing, Kancheepuram (IIITDM), Govt. of India. Currently, he is working as Associate Professor in Adhiyamaan College of Engineering, Hosur. His research interests includes Signal Processing, Image processing, Machine Learning and Deep Learning.

Index

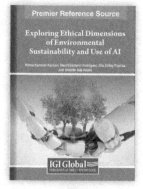

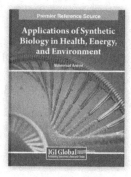

Ensure Quality Research is Introduced to the Academic Community

Become a Reviewer for IGI Global Authored Book Projects

Premier Reference Source

The Use of Artificial Intelligence in Digital Marketing
Competitive Strategies and Tactics

Sandrine Taleote and Jorge Remondes

IGI Global

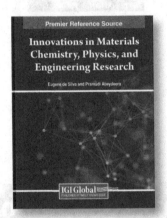

Premier Reference Source

Innovations in Materials Chemistry, Physics, and Engineering Research

Eugene de Silva and Pramudi Abeydeera

IGI Global

Premier Reference Source

Experimental and Clinical Evidence of the Neuropathology of Parkinson's Disease

Ahmed Draoui, Omar El Hiba, and Arumugam R. Jayakumar

IGI Global

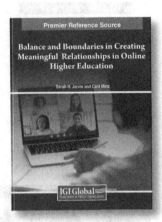

Premier Reference Source

Balance and Boundaries in Creating Meaningful Relationships in Online Higher Education

Sarah H. Jarvie and Cara Metz

IGI Global

The overall success of an authored book project is dependent on quality and timely manuscript evaluations.

Applications and Inquiries may be sent to:
development@igi-global.com

Applicants must have a doctorate (or equivalent degree) as well as publishing, research, and reviewing experience. Authored Book Evaluators are appointed for one-year terms and are expected to complete at least three evaluations per term. Upon successful completion of this term, evaluators can be considered for an additional term.

If you have a colleague that may be interested in this opportunity, we encourage you to share this information with them.

Printed in the United States
by Baker & Taylor Publisher Services

Printed in the United States
by Baker & Taylor Publisher Services